Conference on Empirical Methods in Natural Language Processing (EMNLP 2022)

Demonstrations Session

Abu Dhabi, United Arab Emirates and Online
7-11 December 2022

ISBN: 978-1-7138-9093-5

Printed from e-media with permission by:

Curran Associates, Inc.
57 Morehouse Lane
Red Hook, NY 12571

Some format issues inherent in the e-media version may also appear in this print version.

Printed with permission by Curran Associates, Inc. (2024)

For permission requests, please contact the Association for Computational Linguistics at the address below.

Association for Computational Linguistics
209 N. Eighth Street
Stroudsburg, Pennsylvania 18360

Phone: 1-570-476-8006
Fax: 1-570-476-0860

acl@aclweb.org

Additional copies of this publication are available from:

Curran Associates, Inc.
57 Morehouse Lane
Red Hook, NY 12571 USA
Phone: 845-758-0400
Fax: 845-758-2633
Email: curran@proceedings.com
Web: www.proceedings.com

EMNLP 2022

The 2022 Conference on Empirical Methods in Natural Language Processing

Proceedings of the Demonstrations Session

December 7-11, 2022

Program Committee

Program Committee

Ákos Kádár
Aarne Talman
Amanda Cercas Curry
Adina Williams
Adam Pauls
Adrià De Gispert
Allan Jabri
Akash Srivastava
Aldo Gangemi
Anders Johannsen
Asli Celikyilmaz
Aurélien Max
Andrew Bennett
Barry Devereux
Beata Beigman Klebanov
Gayatri Bhat
Johannes Bjerva
Benjamin Snyder
Giuseppe Carenini
Carina Silberer
Carmen Banea
Çağrı Çöltekin
Courtney Napoles
Khalid Choukri
Chuan Wang
Christopher Pinon
Cristian Danescu-niculescu-mizil
Caroline Sporleder
Dominikus Wetzel
Joachim Daiber
David Alvarez-melis
Daoud Clarke
Diego Marcheggiani
Dimitris Alikaniotis
Dipanjan Das
Daniela Gerz
Erwin Marsi
Zhou Yu
Effi Levi
Ellen Breitholtz
Emily Öhman
Edoardo Maria Ponti
Eric Holgate
Arash Eshghi
Feiyu Xu
Adam Fisch

Chris Fox
Linfeng Song
Georgiana Dinu
Daniel Gildea
Giovanni Da San Martino
Graham Neubig
Gonzalo Iglesias
Hans Kamp
Heather Burnett
Helen Yannakoudakis
Ruihong Huang
Ioannis Papaioannou
Ivelina Nikolova-koleva
Jiaming Luo
Julian Hough
Jennifer Sikos
Junyi Jessy Li
Jonathan Mallinson
Julie Weeds
John Wieting
Katja Jasinskaja
Katrin Kirchhoff
Yunsu Kim
Kiril Simov
Maximilian Köper
Laura Tolosi
I-ta Lee
Leo Leppänen
Chang Li
Lisa Anne Hendricks
Sujian Li
Loïc Barrault
Laura Perez-beltrachini
Malvina Nissim
Maciej Piasecki
Maja Popović
Christopher Manning
Margaret Mitchell
Marianna Apidianaki
Mark Granroth-wilding
Shigeki Matsubara
Stephen Mayhew
Mohit Bansal
Wolfgang Menzel
Marjorie Freedman
Michael Wojatzki
Mike Lewis
Junhua Mao
Man Lan
Myriam Munezero
Mohammad Taher Pilehvar

Mona Diab
Natalie Schluter
Nicholas Asher
Nikola Mrkšić
Nitish Gupta
Noura Farra
Nasrin Mostafazadeh
Oren Melamud
Pascale Fung
Philipp Cimiano
Sameer Pradhan
Preslav Nakov
Patricia Thaine
Pierre Zweigenbaum
Rocco Tripodi
Rodrigo Nogueira
Stephen Roller
Rashmi Prasad
Rachel Rudinger
Joana Ribeiro
Shimi Salant
Alon Talmor
Salvatore Romeo
Shay B. Cohen
Eva Sharma
Shubham Agarwal
Shyam Upadhyay
Sian Gooding
Sida I. Wang
Simon Clematide
Sara Rosenthal
Anders Søgaard
Marina Sokolova
Shafiq Joty
Sanja Stajner
Stefan Thater
Suresh Manandhar
Tanja Schultz
Taylor Berg-kirkpatrick
Tim Fernando
Tiancheng Zhao
Ivan Titov
Tom Kwiatkowski
Lea Frermann
Jason Utt
Verena Rieser
Valentina Presutti
Esther Van Den Berg
Vicente Ordonez
Dingquan Wang
Weiwei Guo

Wei Xu
Yang Liu
Yi Yang
Yishu Miao
Yi Tay
Yujie Qian
Behrang Qasemizadeh
Zhifei Li
Zhongyu Wei
Anima Anandkumar
Jacob Andreas
Gabor Angeli
Joachim Bingel
Su Lin Blodgett
Antoine Bosselut
Lisa Brunetti
Paweł Budzianowski
Mingwei Chang
Benson Chen
Alexis Conneau
Silvio Cordeiro
Ryan Cotterell
Jacob Devlin
Chris Dyer
Desmond Elliott
Yimai Fang
Sanja Fidler
Nicholas Fitzgerald
Lucie Flekova
Kathleen C. Fraser
Matthew Gerber
Sayan Ghosh
Yoav Goldberg
Edouard Grave
Yulan He
Felix Hill
Tobias Horsmann
Mohit Iyyer
Heng Ji
Christopher Kedzie
Svetlana Kiritchenko
Jamie Kiros
Julia Kiseleva
Jayant Krishnamurthy
Gourab Kundu
Angeliki Lazaridou
Omer Levy
Percy Liang
Victoria Lin
Fei Liu
Chikiu Lo

Detmar Meurers
Mark Neumann
Brendan O'connor
Raghavendra Pappagari
Nikolaos Pappas
Jeffrey Pennington
Nghia The Pham
Vinodkumar Prabhakaran
Sampo Pyysalo
Victor Quach
Ines Rehbein
Sebastian Riedel
Arndt Riester
Miguel Rios
Derek Ruths
Merel Scholman
Hinrich Schutze
Tianxiao Shen
Wei Shi
Stefanie Sirenheikel
Yiannos Stathopoulos
Veselin Stoyanov
Ben Swanson
Swabha Swayamdipta
Ian Tenney
Sam Thomson
Kristina Toutanova
Ashish Vaswani
Tony Veale
Wentau Yih
Marcos Zampieri
Simon Šuster
Alda Mari
Aleksandr Drozd
Alexis Palmer
Angel Chang
Roberto Basili
Farah Benamara
Chris Biemann
Constantin Orăsan
Casey Kennington
Chris Callison-burch
Christopher Davis
Christoph Tillmann
Christos Christodoulopoulos
Christo Kirov
Claus Zinn
Trevor Cohen
Chen-tse Tsai
Debora Nozza
Dan Goldwasser

Dan Garrette
Luigi Di Caro
Diego Frassinelli
Mauro Dragoni
E. Dario Gutierrez
Eduardo Blanco
Edward Grefenstette
Ekaterina Kochmar
Elena Cabrio
Elena Karagjosova
Ella Rabinovich
Els Lefever
Esma Balkir
Valia Kordoni
Ekaterina Vylomova
Federico Fancellu
Fabio Massimo Zanzotto
Farah Benamara
Fatiha Sadat
Anna Feldman
Francesco Barbieri
Gerard De Melo
Georgeta Bordea
Roxana Girju
Gaurav Pandey
Graham Katz
Heriberto Cuayahuitl
Heike Adel
Hai Ye
Iris Hendrickx
Ioannis Konstas
Ignacio Iacobacci
Irina Temnikova
Chien-sheng Wu
John P. Mccrae
Jörg Tiedemann
Julia Rayz
Julie Hunter
Rik Koncel-kedziorski
Kevin Duh
Halil Kilicoglu
Mamoru Komachi
Kyusong Lee
Lan Du
Lasha Abzianidze
Laurette Pretorius
Phong Le
Jing Li
Liviu P. Dinu
Lluís Màrquez
Lonneke Van Der Plas

Luis Espinosa Anke
Massimo Poesio
Marc Franco-salvador
Marc Verhagen
David Mareček
Mark Sammons
Mathias Creutz
Mathieu Roche
Meriem Beloucif
Michel Galley
Michael Färber
Meng Fang
Maoxi Li
Nina Dethlefs
Niket Tandon
Nikos Papasarantopoulos
Octavian Popescu
Jessica Ouyang
Alexander Panchenko
Tommaso Pasini
Paul Buitelaar
Piek Vossen
Pierpaolo Basile
Parisa Kordjamshidi
Prasanth Kolachina
Radu Tudor Ionescu
Richard Johansson
Alan Ritter
Rob Van Der Goot
Rudolf Rosa
Roser Morante
Rotem Dror
Ruochen Xu
Siva Reddy Gangireddy
Alla Rozovskaya
Spandana Gella
Samira Shaikh
Mark Steedman
Stefan Evert
Stefano Faralli
Swapna Somasundaran
Stan Szpakowicz
Timothy Baldwin
Todor Mihaylov
Tim Van De Cruys
Torsten Zesch
Udo Hahn
Vlad Niculae
Pidong Wang
Wei Wang
Lifu Huang

Xinya Du
Xinyu Hua
Yixin Nie
Yogarshi Vyas
Hiyon Yoo
Yoshihide Kato
Yova Kementchedjhieva
Yannick Versley
Zheng Yuan
Sanda Harabagiu
Samuel R. Bowman
David Jurgens
Frank Rudzicz
Gustavo Henrique Paetzold
Carlo Strapparava
Alexander Rush
Julia Hockenmaier
Pradeep Dasigi
Jinho Choi
Kentaro Torisawa
Denilson Barbosa
Arianna Bisazza
Antonio Toral
Antonios Anastasopoulos
Anne Cocos
Allyson Ettinger
André F. T. Martins
Agnieszka Falenska
Ari Holtzman
Alberto Barrón-cedeño
Alessandro Lenci
Alessandro Raganato
Aline Villavicencio
Adam Lopez
Annie Louis
Andrea Madotto
Alessandro Moschitti
Anna Currey
Amy Isard
Andrew Caines
Anna Rogers
António Branco
Antske Fokkens
Adam Pease
Ari Rappoport
Ron Artstein
Beatrice Alex
Valerio Basile
Sebastian Krause
Iz Beltagy
Luciana Benotti

Yevgeni Berzak
Francis Bond
Bonnie Webber
Barbara Plank
Razvan Bunescu
Jose Camacho-collados
Carlos Ramisch
Cécile Fabre
Christopher Potts
Christopher Hidey
Chloé Braud
Christian Hardmeier
Christopher Bryant
Claire Gardent
Diana Maynard
Denis Paperno
Ido Dagan
Daniel Beck
Daniel Hershcovich
Dan Lassiter
Dan Roth
Danushka Bollegala
Darja Fišer
David Schlangen
Marie-catherine De Marneffe
Derrick Higgins
Daniel Hardt
Diana Inkpen
Diana Mccarthy
Diyi Yang
Diarmuid Ó Séaghdha
Douwe Kiela
Eneko Agirre
Ehsan Shareghi
Ted Briscoe
Eleni Gregoromichelaki
Elia Bruni
Elior Sulem
Emar Maier
Ellie Pavlick
Erik Velldal
Enrico Santus
Eva Maria Vecchi
Emily Sheng
Anette Frank
Grzegorz Chrupała
Gianluca Lebani
Gabriel Stanovsky
Gabriella Lapesa
Gemma Boleda
Germán Kruszewski

Guy Emerson
Nicoletta Calzolari
Yvette Graham
Grégoire Winterstein
Guillaume Wisniewski
Iryna Gurevych
Haim Dubossarsky
Hannaneh Hajishirzi
Héctor Martínez Alonso
Hugo Gonçalo Oliveira
Hila Gonen
Hiram Calvo
Inés Crespo
Ingrid Falk
Ivan Vulić
Jorge Carrillo-de-albornoz
Jackie Chi Kit Cheung
Jean Maillard
Jeremy Barnes
Jey Han Lau
Joakim Nivre
Jonathan Berant
Jorge Gracia
Jasmijn Bastings
Julian Brooke
Kalina Bontcheva
Laura Kallmeyer
Katrin Erk
Kevin Gimpel
Manfred Klenner
Alexander Koller
Kuzman Ganchev
Lucia Specia
Laura Rimell
Leshem Choshen
Louise Mcnally
Lucy Vanderwende
Luheng He
Lu Wang
Wei Lu
Matthew Purver
Magnus Sahlgren
Dirk Hovy
Marco Rospocher
Marek Rei
Mariano Felice
Marine Carpuat
Mark Finlayson
Ilia Markov
Martha Palmer
Martin Riedl

Matt Huenerfauth
Marco Baroni
Manaal Faruqui
Michael Strube
Miguel Ballesteros
Mikel Artetxe
Tristan Miller
Miloš Stanojević
Mirella Lapata
Muhammad Abdul-mageed
Michael White
Nathan Schneider
Roberto Navigli
Matteo Negri
Aurélie Névéol
Nikola Ljubešić
Niranjan Balasubramanian
Najoung Kim
Nanyun Peng
Ondrej Dusek
Omri Abend
Sebastian Padó
Patrik Lambert
Viviana Patti
Paul Cook
Peter Turney
Peter Clark
Petya Osenova
Manfred Pinkal
Panupong Pasupat
Rachel Bawden
Raffaella Bernardi
Ramakanth Pasunuru
Raquel Fernandez
Regina Barzilay
Reinald Kim Amplayo
Rico Sennrich
Stefan Riezler
Roi Reichart
Roman Klinger
Roser Saurí
Michael Roth
Roy Schwartz
Prodromos Malakasiotis
Josef Ruppenhofer
Ruth Kempson
Saif Mohammad
Sara Tonelli
Steven Schockaert
Sabine Schulte Im Walde
Shachar Mirkin

Shashi Narayan
Shuly Wintner
Simone Paolo Ponzetto
Siva Reddy
Sujay Kumar Jauhar
Slav Petrov
Smaranda Muresan
Stephanie M. Lukin
Manfred Stede
Stefan Kaufmann
Stella Frank
Stephen Clark
Subhro Roy
Mihai Surdeanu
Vivek Srikumar
Idan Szpektor
Tommaso Caselli
Tal Linzen
Tamara Polajnar
Benjamin Van Durme
Paola Velardi
Vera Demberg
Vered Shwartz
Veronique Hoste
Vincent Ng
Wilker Aziz
Daniel Weld
Wei Gao
Xavier Carreras
Nianwen Xue
Yangfeng Ji
Yannis Korkontzelos
Yonatan Bisk
Yejin Choi
Youmna Farag
Yftah Ziser
Yizhong Wang
Jonathan Ginzburg
Yangqiu Song
Yuval Pinter
Zdeněk Žabokrtský
Zornitsa Kozareva
Nikolaos Aletras
Yoav Artzi
Isabelle Augenstein
Luisa Bentivogli
Claire Bonial
Felipe Bravomarquez
Nathanael Chambers
Kaiwei Chang
Danqi Chen

Greg Durrett
Jacob Eisenstein
Daniel Fried
Alona Fyshe
Zhe Gain
Graeme Hirst
Eduard Hovy
Dieuwke Hupkes
Dan Jurafsky
Greg Kondrak
Diane Litman
Kathy Mckeown
Vivi Nastase
Hwee Tou Ng
Devi Parikh
Veronica Perez
Emily Pitler
Hoifung Poon
Pushpendre Rastogi
Tim Rocktäschel
Michael Roth
Sebastian Ruder
Joel Tetreault
Simone Teufel
Yulia Tsvetkov
Lyle Ungar
Karin Verspoor
Andreas Vlachos
Leo Wanner
Ingmar Weber
Mark Yatskar
Amir Zeldes
Luke Zettlemoyer
Ziqing Yang
Yunlong Feng
Lu Hou
Ningyu Zhang
Jiarong Xu
Wenpeng Lu
Pushkar Mishra
Ivo Verhoeven
Lixin Su
Lea Krause
Sanyuan Chen
Kaiwen Wei
Yang Wu
Jianhua Yin
Baoxin Wang
Longxuan Ma

Table of Contents

CogKTR: A Knowledge-Enhanced Text Representation Toolkit for Natural Language Understanding

Zhuoran Jin[*1,2], **Tianyi Men**[*1,2], **Hongbang Yuan**[*1,2], **Yuyang Zhou**[2],
Pengfei Cao[1,2], **Yubo Chen**[1,2], **Zhipeng Xue**[2], **Kang Liu**[1,2,3], **Jun Zhao**[1,2]

[1] School of Artificial Intelligence, University of Chinese Academy of Sciences, Beijing, China
[2] National Laboratory of Pattern Recognition, Institute of Automation, CAS, Beijing, China
[3] Beijing Academy of Artificial Intelligence, Beijing, China

`{zhuoran.jin, tianyi.men, hongbang.yuan}@nlpr.ia.ac.cn, zhouyuyang17@163.com`
`{pengfei.cao, yubo.chen, zhipeng.xue, kliu, jzhao}@nlpr.ia.ac.cn`

Abstract

As the first step of modern natural language processing, text representation encodes discrete texts as continuous embeddings. Pre-trained language models (PLMs) have demonstrated strong ability in text representation and significantly promoted the development of natural language understanding (NLU). However, existing PLMs represent a text solely by its context, which is not enough to support knowledge-intensive NLU tasks. *Knowledge is power*, and fusing external knowledge explicitly into PLMs can provide knowledgeable text representations. Since previous knowledge-enhanced methods differ in many aspects, making it difficult for us to reproduce previous methods, implement new methods, and transfer between different methods. It is highly desirable to have a unified paradigm to encompass all kinds of methods in one framework. In this paper, we propose CogKTR, a knowledge-enhanced text representation toolkit for natural language understanding. According to our proposed **Uni**fied **K**nowledge-**E**nhanced **P**aradigm (**UniKEP**), CogKTR consists of four key stages, including knowledge acquisition, knowledge representation, knowledge injection, and knowledge application. CogKTR currently supports easy-to-use knowledge acquisition interfaces, multi-source knowledge embeddings, diverse knowledge-enhanced models, and various knowledge-intensive NLU tasks. Our unified, knowledgeable and modular toolkit is publicly available at GitHub [1], with an online system [2] and a short instruction video [3].

1 Introduction

In modern natural language processing (NLP), texts need to be represented into a machine-readable form. Many work has shown that pre-trained language models (PLMs) (Qiu et al., 2020) can provide powerful distributed representations for natural language texts, leading to great successes on various natural language understanding (NLU) (Wang et al., 2018a) tasks.

Recently, some studies (Manning et al., 2020; Roberts et al., 2020; Penha and Hauff, 2020) have shown that specific knowledge is implicitly stored in the parameters of PLMs. This implicit knowledge is vague so that it is hard to dynamically update this knowledge to satisfy the needs of real-world applications (Yin et al., 2022). Existing PLMs (Peters et al., 2018; Devlin et al., 2019) represent and understand a text solely by its context, which is insufficient to solve knowledge-intensive NLU tasks. These tasks are highly dependent on background knowledge. It is necessary to leverage external knowledge to enhance the text representations explicitly. For word sense disambiguation, synonyms, sense definitions, and other **linguistic knowledge** play an essential role in identifying the meaning of ambiguous words. For commonsense question answering, **commonsense knowledge** like structured knowledge graph (KG) triples can enhance the models' reasoning capacity.

As illustrated above, knowledge-enhanced text representations are essential for NLU tasks, meanwhile, many methods (Wei et al., 2021; Ding et al., 2022; Zhu et al., 2022) have been proposed. However, previous methods differ in many aspects, especially in knowledge acquisition procedure, knowledge representation form, and knowledge fusion approach. These differences make it challenging to reproduce previous methods, implement new methods, and transfer between different methods. So we need a unified paradigm to implement various knowledge-enhanced methods in the same framework. Therefore, designing the framework should consider the following key principles.

First, the process of knowledge acquisition is laborious and complex, including knowledge tag-

*These authors contribute equally to this work.
[1] `https://github.com/CogNLP/CogKTR/`
[2] `http://cognlp.com/cogktr/`
[3] `https://youtu.be/SrvXrXdDiVY`

Proceedings of the The 2022 Conference on Empirical Methods in Natural Language Processing: System Demonstrations, pages 1 - 11
December 7-11, 2022 ©2022 Association for Computational Linguistics

ging (e.g., named entity recognition and semantic role labeling), knowledge grounding (e.g., entity linking) and knowledge retrieving (e.g., regular expression matching and SPARQL query). A good framework should let users pay more attention to the details in the models rather than tedious data processing. **Second**, different knowledge embeddings vary in knowledge sources (e.g., Wikidata (Vrandečić and Krötzsch, 2014) and ConceptNet (Speer et al., 2017)) and knowledge representation algorithms (e.g., TransE (Bordes et al., 2013) and Wikipedia2Vec (Yamada et al., 2020a)). To make rigorous comparisons between them, it is highly desirable to have a toolkit that provides built-in knowledge embeddings. **Third**, although a lot of knowledge fusion approaches have been proposed, there is still a lack of a comprehensive framework to encompass them. Such a framework should provide knowledgeable text representations which can be directly used in numerous downstream tasks.

To this end, we propose CogKTR, a **K**nowledge-enhanced **T**ext **R**epresentation toolkit for natural language understanding. CogKTR is built on the **Uni**fied **K**nowledge-**E**nhanced **P**aradigm (**UniKEP**), which can be formalized in four stages, including **knowledge acquisition**, **knowledge representation**, **knowledge injection**, and **knowledge application**. First, **knowledge acquisition** aims to identify structured information from unstructured texts, then ground them in knowledge sources. Then, **knowledge representation** can transform knowledge from discrete form to continuous form. Next, **knowledge injection**, as the most critical stage, combines raw texts and external knowledge for knowledgeable text representation. In the end, **knowledge application** verifies the effectiveness of knowledge-enhanced methods in downstream tasks.

In detail, CogKTR has the following functions. First, our toolkit provides user-friendly knowledge acquisition interfaces. Users can use our toolkit to enhance the given texts with one click. And we also implement plenty of knowledge-enhanced methods so researchers can quickly reproduce these models. Moreover, CogKTR supports many built-in NLU tasks to evaluate the effectiveness of knowledge-enhanced methods. In our paradigm, users can easily conduct their research via a pipeline. Besides the toolkit, we also release an online CogKTR demo to show the process of knowledge acquisition and the effect of knowledge enhancement.

In summary, the main features and contributions are as follows:

- **Unified.** CogKTR is designed and built on our Unified Knowledge-Enhanced Paradigm, which consists of four stages: knowledge acquisition, knowledge representation, knowledge injection, and knowledge application.
- **Knowledgeable.** CogKTR integrates multiple knowledge sources, including Wikidata, Wikipedia, ConceptNet, WordNet (Miller, 1995) and CogNet (Wang et al., 2021a), and implements a series of knowledge-enhanced methods, such as K-BERT (Liu et al., 2020), SemBERT (Zhang et al., 2020a), QAGNN (Yasunaga et al., 2021), etc.
- **Modular.** CogKTR modularizes our proposed paradigm and consists of `Enhancer`, `Model`, `Core` and `Data` modules, each of which is highly extensible so that researchers can implement new components easily.

2 Unified Knowledge-Enhanced Paradigm

As mentioned above, it is vital to propose a paradigm that can formalize the knowledge-enhanced process. As shown in Figure 1, our proposed Unified Knowledge-Enhanced Paradigm (UniKEP) consists of four key stages: **knowledge acquisition**, **knowledge representation**, **knowledge injection** and **knowledge application**. Below are the detailed descriptions of the four stages.

2.1 Knowledge Acquisition

Knowledge acquisition, the first step towards our knowledge-enhanced paradigm, aims at detecting knowledge concealed beneath the raw texts. Details of our implementation of the acquisition process can be found in Section 3.1. The obtained knowledge can be divided into three categories according to the different sources they belong to.

World Knowledge. It contains general facts about some particular entities or events. For example, given a sentence "*Elmo and Bert read books in the Sesame street library.*", "*Elmo*", "*Bert*" and "*Sesame street*" can be spotted as entities via named entity recognition. Then, "*Bert*" can be linked to the target entity "*Bert (Sesame Street)*" in Wikipedia via entity linking. World knowledge is helpful in many entity-related tasks, such as entity typing, relation extraction and fact verification.

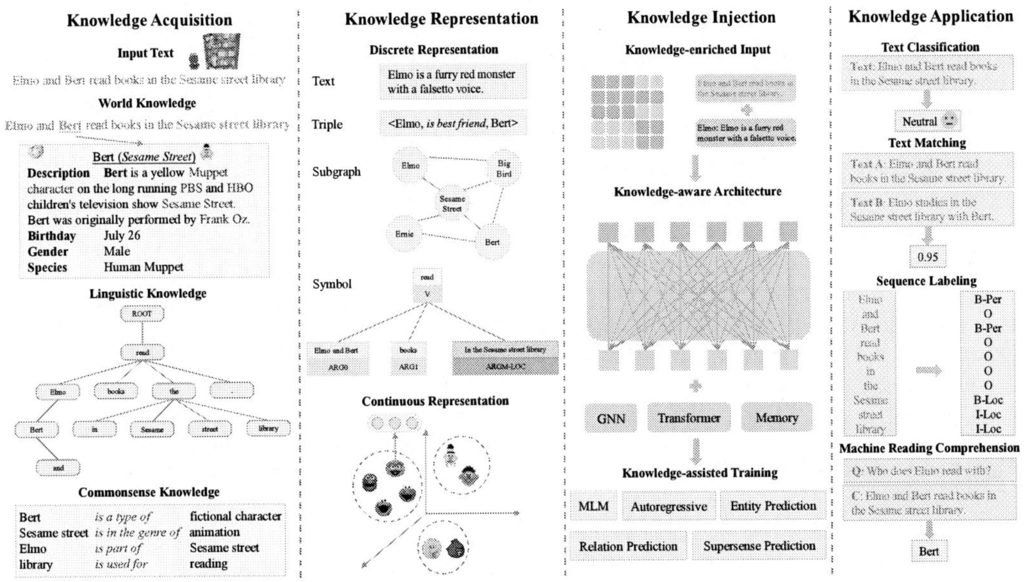

Figure 1: The Unified Knowledge-Enhanced Paradigm of CogKTR.

Linguistic Knowledge. It refers to the internal syntactic structure and the meaning of words and phrases in the texts. As shown in Figure 1, the dependency tree describes the directed grammatical relations between words and semantic role labeling extracts the predicate-argument structure. Incorporating linguistic knowledge can bring better text representations in downstream tasks like information retrieval and machine reading comprehension.

Commonsense Knowledge. It tries to catch implicit facts in our daily life. For example, (*Bert, is a type of, fictional character*) and (*library, is used for, reading*) are the commonsense triples extracted from ConceptNet. Current models usually have a poor commonsense awareness, thus leveraging commonsense knowledge can help models gain stronger capability on commonsense reasoning.

2.2 Knowledge Representation

The aforementioned knowledge can be represented in two forms, including discrete representation and continuous representation.

Discrete Representation. Discrete knowledge is usually represented as texts, triples, subgraphs and symbols. Texts are the most commonly used representation forms, such as descriptions of nodes and relations in KGs or definitions of words in lexicons. Triples describe a particular connection between two nodes in KGs. A subgraph's topology contributes a lot to the comprehension of the central node. However, discrete knowledge cannot be directly used in deep learning systems and need to be further represented.

Continuous Representation. It usually refers to the dense vectors in a unified continuous representation space. The traditional skip-gram model can be used to compute the embeddings of words (Yamada et al., 2020a). Entities and relations in triples can be viewed as translational operations and points from the perspective of conventional knowledge embedding models (Bordes et al., 2013). The continuous representation can be easily fused to models as prior knowledge.

2.3 Knowledge Injection

Injecting knowledge into original models is vital to the whole paradigm. The injection strategy varies depending on when knowledge is fused into original models. We divide them into three categories: knowledge-enriched input, knowledge-aware architecture and knowledge-assistant training.

Knowledge-enriched Input. A typical case of knowledge injection is to combine the input text with the extracted knowledge. Entity descriptions, concepts, brief interpretations and synonyms of the words can all be concatenated together with original texts to form input samples of the model. However, too much knowledge may be noisy. Thus some attention masks are constructed for the self-attention process in the model. Besides, pretrained knowledge embeddings can be fused to the text representations by direct arithmetic operations.

Knowledge-aware Architecture. In some cases, a certain architecture is designed to encode the extracted knowledge. Graph neural network (GNN) is often used to encode the structured knowledge (Yu et al., 2022). Transformer-like architectures is usually used to deal with textual descriptions (Zhang et al., 2019). Memory network is used to restore learned knowledge embeddings and can be applied to any sequence output (Févry et al., 2020).

Knowledge-assisted Training. Knowledge can also be used to design knowledge-driven training objectives. Entity-level masking masks the entities in a sentence to guide the text representation learning (Sun et al., 2019). Relation prediction requires models to identify the relation between two given entities in order to inject world knowledge (Wang et al., 2021b). Supersense prediction trains the model to classify the masked word's sense into 45 supersense categories (Levine et al., 2020).

2.4 Knowledge Application

Various downstream NLU tasks can benefit from the knowledge-enhanced models. This subsection presents the definition, application and necessity of the existence of external knowledge of each downstream NLU task.

Text Classification. It is a task to assign labels to language entries like sentences or documents. Sentiment analysis, fact verification, and fake news detection all fall into this category. Fake news detection needs additional knowledge to serve as evidence for better detection (Hu et al., 2021).

Text Matching. It is a task determining whether one sentence is related to another based on semantic meanings and plays a significant role in text entailment and entity disambiguation. For text entailment, knowledge in the two statements can help information flow between them (Jo et al., 2021).

Sequence Labeling. This task is to label each token of the given sentence. Named entity recognition (NER), part-of-speech tagging and semantic role labeling can be viewed as a sequence labeling problem. For example, a preconstructed entity dictionary contributes to recognizing the entity boundary in NER tasks (Zhang and Yang, 2018).

Machine Reading Comprehension. This task is to comprehend a given passage and then answer questions based on it. It can be approximately divided into four different kinds of forms: cloze-style, multi-choice, span extraction and free-form. In open domain QA, knowledge can be beneficial in identifying answers which are not likely lying inside the given context (Yamada et al., 2020b).

3 System Design and Architecture

According to the paradigm mentioned above, we divide CogKTR architecture into four modules. For knowledge acquisition and representation, CogKTR modularizes them as the `Enhancer` module. To implement knowledge injection and application, we build the `Model` module to integrate knowledge into models. Considering that the development process is time-consuming, we also design two basic modules, namely `Data` module and `Core` module, to accelerate the data processing procedure and improve training efficiency. An overview of CogKTR architecture is shown in Figure 2. In the following, we will introduce these four modules.

3.1 `Enhancer`

This module is designed for knowledge acquisition and representation to leverage relevant knowledge to enhance raw texts. It can be divided into four steps. Firstly, parse sentences and detect candidate mentions by `Tagger`. Then, link these mentions to KGs by `Linker`. Next, search the relevant information in KGs and textual corpus by `Searcher`. Finally, convert discrete knowledge to dense embeddings in continuous space by `Embedder`. The specific classes of `Enhancer`, `Tagger`, `Linker`, `Searcher` and `Embedder` are represented in Table 1.

`Tagger`. It is a text annotator to convert unstructured texts into structured knowledge. It can be categorized into two streams according to the existence of external KGs. If corresponding KGs exist, we focus on identifying the locations of knowledge-related text mentions, including words, entities, phrases, etc. They can be linked to KGs, enriching raw sentences with external information. Otherwise, we parse the given sentences to obtain internal syntactic and semantic knowledge, such as part-of-speech tags, dependency trees and semantic role labels. CogKTR contains three external knowledge taggers and three internal knowledge taggers.

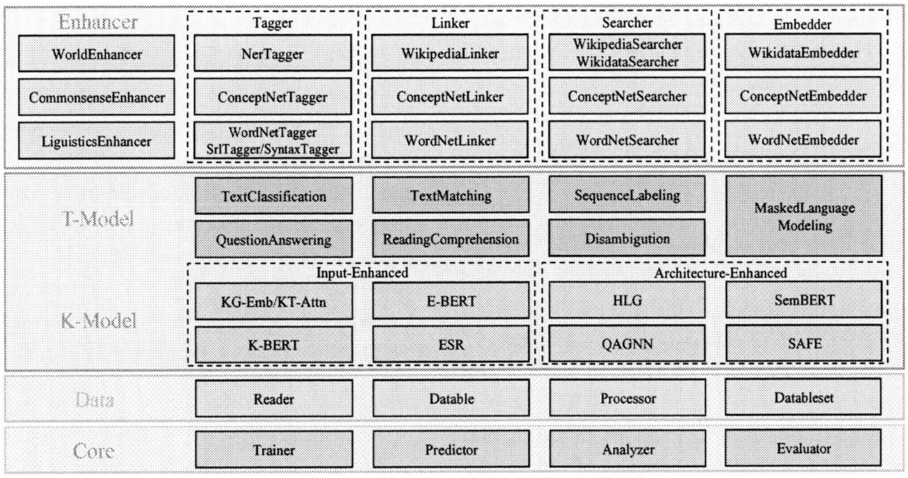

Figure 2: The system architecture of CogKTR.

`Linker`. It aims to link the candidate mentions detected by the `Tagger` modules to external KGs. It is an essential bridge between unstructured texts and structured knowledge, where linking methods include entity linking and string matching. Entity linking is based on measuring the similarity between mentions in the texts and entities in KGs and string matching is to find the corresponding nodes in KGs through strict comparison or fuzzy query. We implement three linkers in CogKTR.

`Searcher`. It is to retrieve detailed information about target mentions in KGs (such as Wikipedia, ConceptNet and WordNet), and textual corpus. In this paper, we divide KG-related knowledge into unstructured textual information and structured information. Unstructured textual information includes entity titles, entity descriptions and example sentences, while structured information includes triples, subgraphs and relation paths. As for textual corpus, we use retrieval methods to obtain related texts of the queries. We implement four searchers.

`Embedder`. It is used to embed discrete knowledge into continuous space. We encode KGs as low-dimensional and dense vectors by TransE, Wikipedia2Vec and PLMs, which can be directly injected into deep learning models.

3.2 `Model`

To implement knowledge injection and application, we design the `Model` module to fuse texts and knowledge acquired from the `Enhancer` module. For extensibility, we decouple the `Model` module into `T-Model` and `K-Model`. `T-Model` denotes task-specific models, designed for various downstream tasks. `K-Model` denotes knowledge-enhanced models, aiming to inject knowledge into PLMs to represent texts. `K-Model` and `T-Model` can be combined to realize the application of different knowledge-enhanced models on different downstream tasks.

`T-Model`. This module is used to achieve downstream tasks. It can be classified into seven types: `ReadingComprehension`, `TextClassification`, `MLM`, `QuestionAnswering`, `SequenceLabeling`, `TextMatching`, `Disambiguation` class.

`K-Model`. This module is responsible for knowledge injection and built on huggingface transformers library (Poerner et al., 2020). It can be divided into two categories: (1) **Input-enhanced models** aim to enrich input texts and constrain attention masks. In terms of input texts, we divide injection into two types, discrete injection and continuous injection. Discrete injection means concatenating raw texts and additional knowledge texts like `ESR` (Song et al., 2021), `K-BERT` (Liu et al., 2020), and then feeding into PLMs. Continuous injection refers to converting texts or entities into vectors, such as `KT-Emb` and `KG-Emb` (Xu et al., 2021). For attention masks, symbolic knowledge like dependency trees with directed graphs is used to constrain attention masks based on `SG-Net` (Zhang et al., 2020b). (2) **Architecture-enhanced models** use additional network architecture to encode knowledge and incorporate knowledge representation into language models. In CogKTR, `SAFE` (Jiang et al., 2022) is used to encode relation paths by MLP, while RNN is used to capture semantic role labeling knowledge like SemBERT (Zhang et al., 2020a). For graph structure knowledge, we implement QAGNN (Yasunaga et al., 2021) and HLG (Li et al., 2022) models with GNN to encode commonsense knowledge and linguistic knowledge.

3.3 Data

This module is responsible for data loading and processing procedures. It is composed of Reader and Processor classes. To unify input, we design Reader class to load raw datasets, which inherits from BaseReader class. The Processor class is a data processing component in CogKTR. It is used to build the bridge among models, raw data and enhanced data, which can process raw data and enhanced data into the form required by the models.

3.4 Core

It focuses on accelerating the efficiency of model training and evaluation. It contains Trainer, Evaluator, Predictor and Analyzer classes. Trainer class is designed for model training, supporting multi-GPU distributed parallel training and experimental results recording. Evaluator class contains classification metric, regression metric, reading comprehension metric and so on. Predictor class supports various downstream inference tasks with additional knowledge.

4 System Usage

In this section, we will give detailed guidelines on how to use CogKTR toolkit and online demo.

4.1 Code Usage

We separate the source code to three main parts: enhancing the given texts with knowledge, constructing a knowledge-aware model and training the model. In Appendix A, Figure 3 shows an example for the usage of our code. We formalize a pipeline for these three steps so users can achieve our Unified Knowledge-Enhanced Paradigm easily. Before processing the input text, users should prepare the corresponding knowledge sources, which will be downloaded automatically. Then, the Reader, Enhancer and Processor class should be initialized to generate the knowledge-enhanced input of the models. Moreover, the T-Model, Metric, Loss and Optimizer class should be initialized before added to Trainer class. Users should initialize the K-Model class as the knowledge-enhanced encoder of the T-Model class.

4.2 Demo Usage

Besides this toolkit, we also release an online demo as shown in Figure 4, 5 and 6. The online demo consists of two parts: knowledge-enhanced text and knowledge-enhanced task. The knowledge-enhanced text part will acquire different types of knowledge in the given sentence, including world, linguistic, and commonsense knowledge. And the knowledge-enhanced task part performs different downstream tasks, including sentiment analysis, text entailment and commonsense reasoning.

5 Evaluation

CogKTR aims to support various NLU tasks under a unified paradigm. To demonstrate the effectiveness of knowledge-enhanced methods, we implement several baselines and evaluate them on the corresponding tasks. The evaluation tasks include CommonsenseQA (Talmor et al., 2018) and OpenBookQA (Mihaylov et al., 2018) for commonsense reasoning; LAMA (Petroni et al., 2019) for knowledge probing; SQuAD2.0 (Rajpurkar et al., 2018) for reading comprehension; QNLI and SST-B (Wang et al., 2018b) for text entailment; CoNLL2003 (Sang and De Meulder, 2003) for sequence labeling; SST-2 and SST-5 (Socher et al., 2013) for sentiment analysis; SemCor (Miller et al., 1994) and SemEval (Pradhan et al., 2007) for word sense disambiguation. Reader and Processor classes of these datasets have already been integrated into CogKTR. The experimental results are available at our GitHub [4].

6 Conclusion and Future Work

In this paper, we propose CogKTR, a knowledge-enhanced text representation toolkit for natural language understanding. CogKTR is built on our Unified Knowledge-Enhanced Paradigm, which is composed of four stages: knowledge acquisition, knowledge representation, knowledge injection, and knowledge application. In CogKTR, we provide easy-to-use knowledge acquisition interface, off-the-shelf knowledge embeddings, built-in knowledge-enhanced models, and knowledge-intensive NLU tasks. Besides the toolkit, we also release an online demo system. In the future, more knowledge sources, benchmark datasets, and models will be incorporated into CogKTR.

[4] https://github.com/CogNLP/CogKTR/

Limitations

In this paper, we propose Unified Knowledge-Enhanced Paradigm to formalize the knowledge-enhanced process. However, there are still some limitations in the existing knowledge-enhanced process. We discuss these in detail below.

First, in the knowledge acquisition stage, we should discover knowledge from raw texts via name entity recognition, entity linking, semantic role labeling and other methods. These methods are usually provided by off-the-shelf toolkits, causing inevitable errors. Such noise will affect the performance on downstream tasks. In the future work, we should further study how to eliminate the influence of noise caused by knowledge acquisition.

Second, a vast number of knowledge embedding methods are designed to address knowledge graph completion (KGC), which aims to predict missing links for KGs. These methods only consider the structured information and ignore the valuable textual and logic knowledge in KGs. How to provide more informative knowledge embeddings for knowledge-enhanced methods is worth studying.

Finally, we utilize a broad set of downstream tasks to evaluate the knowledge-enhanced models. But better performance does not mean that the model has really learned the knowledge. We should find a better way to probe the knowledge in models and improve the interpretability.

Acknowledgements

We thank all the anonymous reviewers. This work is supported by the National Key Research and Development Program of China (No. 2020AAA0106400), the National Natural Science Foundation of China (No. 61922085, 61976211, 62176257). This work is also supported by the Youth Innovation Promotion Association CAS.

References

Steven Bird, Ewan Klein, and Edward Loper. 2009. *Natural Language Processing with Python: Analyzing Text with the Natural Language Toolkit*. O'Reilly Media, Inc.

Antoine Bordes, Nicolas Usunier, Alberto Garcia-Duran, Jason Weston, and Oksana Yakhnenko. 2013. Translating embeddings for modeling multi-relational data. *Advances in neural information processing systems*.

Jacob Devlin, Ming-Wei Chang, Kenton Lee, and Kristina Toutanova. 2019. BERT: Pre-training of deep bidirectional transformers for language understanding. In *Proceedings of the 2019 Conference of the North American Chapter of the Association for Computational Linguistics: Human Language Technologies, Volume 1 (Long and Short Papers)*. Association for Computational Linguistics.

Ning Ding, Shengding Hu, Weilin Zhao, Yulin Chen, Zhiyuan Liu, Haitao Zheng, and Maosong Sun. 2022. OpenPrompt: An open-source framework for prompt-learning. In *Proceedings of the 60th Annual Meeting of the Association for Computational Linguistics: System Demonstrations*. Association for Computational Linguistics.

Yanlin Feng, Xinyue Chen, Bill Yuchen Lin, Peifeng Wang, Jun Yan, and Xiang Ren. 2020. Scalable multi-hop relational reasoning for knowledge-aware question answering. In *Proceedings of the 2020 Conference on Empirical Methods in Natural Language Processing*. Association for Computational Linguistics.

Thibault Févry, Livio Baldini Soares, Nicholas FitzGerald, Eunsol Choi, and Tom Kwiatkowski. 2020. Entities as experts: Sparse memory access with entity supervision. In *Proceedings of the 2020 Conference on Empirical Methods in Natural Language Processing*. Association for Computational Linguistics.

Matt Gardner, Joel Grus, Mark Neumann, Oyvind Tafjord, Pradeep Dasigi, Nelson F. Liu, Matthew Peters, Michael Schmitz, and Luke S. Zettlemoyer. 2017. Allennlp: A deep semantic natural language processing platform.

Matthew Honnibal, Ines Montani, Sofie Van Landeghem, and Adriane Boyd. 2020. spaCy: Industrial-strength Natural Language Processing in Python.

Linmei Hu, Tianchi Yang, Luhao Zhang, Wanjun Zhong, Duyu Tang, Chuan Shi, Nan Duan, and Ming Zhou. 2021. Compare to the knowledge: Graph neural fake news detection with external knowledge. In *Proceedings of the 59th Annual Meeting of the Association for Computational Linguistics and the 11th International Joint Conference on Natural Language Processing (Volume 1: Long Papers)*. Association for Computational Linguistics.

Jinhao Jiang, Kun Zhou, Ji-Rong Wen, and Xin Zhao. 2022. $great\ truths\ are\ always\ simple$: a rather simple knowledge encoder for enhancing the commonsense reasoning capacity of pre-trained models. In *Findings of the Association for Computational Linguistics: NAACL 2022*. Association for Computational Linguistics.

Zhuoran Jin, Yubo Chen, Dianbo Sui, Chenhao Wang, Zhipeng Xue, and Jun Zhao. 2021. CogIE: An information extraction toolkit for bridging texts and CogNet. In *Proceedings of the 59th Annual Meeting of the Association for Computational Linguistics and the 11th International Joint Conference on Natural Language Processing: System Demonstrations*. Association for Computational Linguistics.

Zhuoran Jin, Tianyi Men, Hongbang Yuan, Zhitao He, Dianbo Sui, Chenhao Wang, Zhipeng Xue, Yubo Chen, and Jun Zhao. 2022. CogKGE: A knowledge graph embedding toolkit and benchmark for representing multi-source and heterogeneous knowledge. In *Proceedings of the 60th Annual Meeting of the Association for Computational Linguistics: System Demonstrations*. Association for Computational Linguistics.

Yohan Jo, Haneul Yoo, JinYeong Bak, Alice Oh, Chris Reed, and Eduard Hovy. 2021. Knowledge-enhanced evidence retrieval for counterargument generation. In *Findings of the Association for Computational Linguistics: EMNLP 2021*. Association for Computational Linguistics.

Yoav Levine, Barak Lenz, Or Dagan, Ori Ram, Dan Padnos, Or Sharir, Shai Shalev-Shwartz, Amnon Shashua, and Yoav Shoham. 2020. SenseBERT: Driving some sense into BERT. In *Proceedings of the 58th Annual Meeting of the Association for Computational Linguistics*. Association for Computational Linguistics.

Yanzeng Li, Jiangxia Cao, Xin Cong, Zhenyu Zhang, Bowen Yu, Hongsong Zhu, and Tingwen Liu. 2022. Enhancing Chinese pre-trained language model via heterogeneous linguistics graph. In *Proceedings of the 60th Annual Meeting of the Association for Computational Linguistics (Volume 1: Long Papers)*. Association for Computational Linguistics.

Weijie Liu, Peng Zhou, Zhe Zhao, Zhiruo Wang, Qi Ju, Haotang Deng, and Ping Wang. 2020. K-bert: Enabling language representation with knowledge graph. *Proceedings of the AAAI Conference on Artificial Intelligence*.

Christopher D Manning, Kevin Clark, John Hewitt, Urvashi Khandelwal, and Omer Levy. 2020. Emergent linguistic structure in artificial neural networks trained by self-supervision. *Proceedings of the National Academy of Sciences*.

Todor Mihaylov, Peter Clark, Tushar Khot, and Ashish Sabharwal. 2018. Can a suit of armor conduct electricity? a new dataset for open book question answering. In *Proceedings of the 2018 Conference on Empirical Methods in Natural Language Processing*. Association for Computational Linguistics.

George A. Miller. 1995. Wordnet: A lexical database for english. *Commun. ACM*.

George A. Miller, Martin Chodorow, Shari Landes, Claudia Leacock, and Robert G. Thomas. 1994. Using a semantic concordance for sense identification. In *Human Language Technology: Proceedings of a Workshop held at Plainsboro, New Jersey, March 8-11, 1994*.

Gustavo Penha and Claudia Hauff. 2020. What does bert know about books, movies and music? probing bert for conversational recommendation. In *Fourteenth ACM Conference on Recommender Systems*.

Matthew E. Peters, Mark Neumann, Mohit Iyyer, Matt Gardner, Christopher Clark, Kenton Lee, and Luke Zettlemoyer. 2018. Deep contextualized word representations. In *Proceedings of the 2018 Conference of the North American Chapter of the Association for Computational Linguistics: Human Language Technologies, Volume 1 (Long Papers)*. Association for Computational Linguistics.

Fabio Petroni, Tim Rocktäschel, Patrick Lewis, Anton Bakhtin, Yuxiang Wu, Alexander H Miller, and Sebastian Riedel. 2019. Language models as knowledge bases? *arXiv preprint arXiv:1909.01066*.

Nina Poerner, Ulli Waltinger, and Hinrich Schütze. 2020. E-BERT: Efficient-yet-effective entity embeddings for BERT. In *Findings of the Association for Computational Linguistics: EMNLP 2020*. Association for Computational Linguistics.

Sameer Pradhan, Edward Loper, Dmitriy Dligach, and Martha Palmer. 2007. Semeval-2007 task-17: English lexical sample, srl and all words. In *Proceedings of the fourth international workshop on semantic evaluations (SemEval-2007)*.

Peng Qi, Yuhao Zhang, Yuhui Zhang, Jason Bolton, and Christopher D. Manning. 2020. Stanza: A Python natural language processing toolkit for many human languages. In *Proceedings of the 58th Annual Meeting of the Association for Computational Linguistics: System Demonstrations*.

Xipeng Qiu, Tianxiang Sun, Yige Xu, Yunfan Shao, Ning Dai, and Xuanjing Huang. 2020. Pre-trained models for natural language processing: A survey. *Science China Technological Sciences*.

Pranav Rajpurkar, Robin Jia, and Percy Liang. 2018. Know what you don't know: Unanswerable questions for squad. *arXiv preprint arXiv:1806.03822*.

Adam Roberts, Colin Raffel, and Noam Shazeer. 2020. How much knowledge can you pack into the parameters of a language model? In *Proceedings of the 2020 Conference on Empirical Methods in Natural Language Processing*. Association for Computational Linguistics.

Erik F Sang and Fien De Meulder. 2003. Introduction to the conll-2003 shared task: Language-independent named entity recognition. *arXiv preprint cs/0306050*.

Richard Socher, Alex Perelygin, Jean Wu, Jason Chuang, Christopher D. Manning, Andrew Ng, and Christopher Potts. 2013. Recursive deep models for semantic compositionality over a sentiment treebank. In *Proceedings of the 2013 Conference on Empirical Methods in Natural Language Processing*. Association for Computational Linguistics.

Yang Song, Xin Cai Ong, Hwee Tou Ng, and Qian Lin. 2021. Improved word sense disambiguation with enhanced sense representations. In *Findings of the Association for Computational Linguistics: EMNLP 2021*. Association for Computational Linguistics.

Robyn Speer, Joshua Chin, and Catherine Havasi. 2017. Conceptnet 5.5: An open multilingual graph of general knowledge. In *Proceedings of the AAAI Conference on Artificial Intelligence*.

Yu Sun, Shuohuan Wang, Yukun Li, Shikun Feng, Xuyi Chen, Han Zhang, Xin Tian, Danxiang Zhu, Hao Tian, and Hua Wu. 2019. Ernie: Enhanced representation through knowledge integration. *arXiv preprint arXiv:1904.09223*.

Alon Talmor, Jonathan Herzig, Nicholas Lourie, and Jonathan Berant. 2018. Commonsenseqa: A question answering challenge targeting commonsense knowledge. *arXiv preprint arXiv:1811.00937*.

Denny Vrandečić and Markus Krötzsch. 2014. Wikidata: A free collaborative knowledgebase. *Commun. ACM*.

Alex Wang, Amanpreet Singh, Julian Michael, Felix Hill, Omer Levy, and Samuel Bowman. 2018a. GLUE: A multi-task benchmark and analysis platform for natural language understanding. In *Proceedings of the 2018 EMNLP Workshop BlackboxNLP: Analyzing and Interpreting Neural Networks for NLP*. Association for Computational Linguistics.

Alex Wang, Amanpreet Singh, Julian Michael, Felix Hill, Omer Levy, and Samuel Bowman. 2018b. GLUE: A multi-task benchmark and analysis platform for natural language understanding. In *Proceedings of the 2018 EMNLP Workshop BlackboxNLP: Analyzing and Interpreting Neural Networks for NLP*. Association for Computational Linguistics.

Chenhao Wang, Yubo Chen, Zhipeng Xue, Yang Zhou, and Jun Zhao. 2021a. Cognet: Bridging linguistic knowledge, world knowledge and commonsense knowledge. *Proceedings of the AAAI Conference on Artificial Intelligence*.

Ruize Wang, Duyu Tang, Nan Duan, Zhongyu Wei, Xuanjing Huang, Jianshu Ji, Guihong Cao, Daxin Jiang, and Ming Zhou. 2021b. K-Adapter: Infusing Knowledge into Pre-Trained Models with Adapters. In *Findings of the Association for Computational Linguistics: ACL-IJCNLP 2021*. Association for Computational Linguistics.

Xiaokai Wei, Shen Wang, Dejiao Zhang, Parminder Bhatia, and Andrew Arnold. 2021. Knowledge enhanced pretrained language models: A compreshensive survey. *arXiv preprint arXiv:2110.08455*.

Ruochen Xu, Yuwei Fang, Chenguang Zhu, and Michael Zeng. 2021. Does knowledge help general nlu? an empirical study. *arXiv preprint arXiv:2109.00563*.

Ikuya Yamada, Akari Asai, Jin Sakuma, Hiroyuki Shindo, Hideaki Takeda, Yoshiyasu Takefuji, and Yuji Matsumoto. 2020a. Wikipedia2Vec: An efficient toolkit for learning and visualizing the embeddings of words and entities from Wikipedia. In *Proceedings of the 2020 Conference on Empirical Methods in Natural Language Processing: System Demonstrations*. Association for Computational Linguistics.

Ikuya Yamada, Akari Asai, Hiroyuki Shindo, Hideaki Takeda, and Yuji Matsumoto. 2020b. LUKE: Deep contextualized entity representations with entity-aware self-attention. In *Proceedings of the 2020 Conference on Empirical Methods in Natural Language Processing*. Association for Computational Linguistics.

Michihiro Yasunaga, Hongyu Ren, Antoine Bosselut, Percy Liang, and Jure Leskovec. 2021. QA-GNN: Reasoning with language models and knowledge graphs for question answering. In *Proceedings of the 2021 Conference of the North American Chapter of the Association for Computational Linguistics: Human Language Technologies*. Association for Computational Linguistics.

Da Yin, Li Dong, Hao Cheng, Xiaodong Liu, Kai-Wei Chang, Furu Wei, and Jianfeng Gao. 2022. A survey of knowledge-intensive nlp with pre-trained language models. *arXiv preprint arXiv:2202.08772*.

Donghan Yu, Chenguang Zhu, Yiming Yang, and Michael Zeng. 2022. Jaket: Joint pre-training of knowledge graph and language understanding. *Proceedings of the AAAI Conference on Artificial Intelligence*.

Yue Zhang and Jie Yang. 2018. Chinese NER using lattice LSTM. In *Proceedings of the 56th Annual Meeting of the Association for Computational Linguistics (Volume 1: Long Papers)*. Association for Computational Linguistics.

Zhengyan Zhang, Xu Han, Zhiyuan Liu, Xin Jiang, Maosong Sun, and Qun Liu. 2019. ERNIE: Enhanced language representation with informative entities. In *Proceedings of the 57th Annual Meeting of the Association for Computational Linguistics*. Association for Computational Linguistics.

Zhuosheng Zhang, Yuwei Wu, Hai Zhao, Zuchao Li, Shuailiang Zhang, Xi Zhou, and Xiang Zhou. 2020a. Semantics-aware BERT for language understanding. In *the Thirty-Fourth AAAI Conference on Artificial Intelligence (AAAI-2020)*.

Zhuosheng Zhang, Yuwei Wu, Junru Zhou, Sufeng Duan, Hai Zhao, and Rui Wang. 2020b. SG-Net: Syntax-guided machine reading comprehension. In *Proceedings of the Thirty-Fourth AAAI Conference on Artificial Intelligence*.

Chenguang Zhu, Yichong Xu, Xiang Ren, Bill Yuchen Lin, Meng Jiang, and Wenhao Yu. 2022. Knowledge-augmented methods for natural language processing. In *Proceedings of the 60th Annual Meeting of the Association for Computational Linguistics: Tutorial Abstracts*. Association for Computational Linguistics.

A Appendix

Components	Classes	Functions	Tools
Tagger	NerTagger	identify entity mention spans	CogIE (Jin et al., 2021)
	ConceptNetTagger	identify concept mention spans	spaCy (Honnibal et al., 2020)
	WordNetTagger	identify candidate texts spans	NLTK (Bird et al., 2009)
	SrlTagger	tag sentences and get semantics labeling	Stanza (Qi et al., 2020)
	SyntaxTagger	parse sentences and get dependency trees	AllenNLP (Gardner et al., 2017)
	WordSegmentationTagger	chinese word segmentation	jieba
Linker	WikipediaLinker	link entities to Wikipedia	CogIE (Jin et al., 2021)
	ConceptNetLinker	link concepts to ConceptNet	spaCy (Honnibal et al., 2020)
	WordNetLinker	link candidate texts to WordNet	CogIE (Jin et al., 2021)
Searcher	WikipediaSearcher	query entity titles and text descriptions in Wikipedia	KILT (Bird et al., 2009)
	WikidataSearcher	look up triples and subgraphs in Wikidata	qwikidata
	ConceptNetSearcher	search subgraphs and relation paths in ConceptNet	spaCy (Honnibal et al., 2020)
	WordNetSearcher	synonyms, example sentences, definitions and hypernyms	NLTK (Bird et al., 2009)
Embedder	WikidataEmbedder	convert Wikidata into continuous knowledge	CogKGE (Jin et al., 2022)
	ConceptNetEmbedder	convert ConceptNet into continuous knowledge	MHGRN (Feng et al., 2020)
	WordNetEmbedder	convert WordNet into continuous knowledge	CogKGE (Jin et al., 2022)

Table 1: Specific classes of Enhancer module, contains Tagger, Linker, Searcher and Embedder components.

```
import cogktr
import torch
# Load the dataset and construct the vocabulary
reader = cogktr.Reader(data_path)
train_data, dev_data, test_data = reader.read_all()
vocab = reader.read_vocab()

# Enhance the data
enhancer = cogktr.Enhancer(knowledge_graph_path, cache_path, cache_file)
enhanced_train_dict = enhancer.enhance_train(datable=train_data, return_entity_desc=True)
enhanced_dev_dict = enhancer.enhance_dev(datable=dev_data, return_entity_desc=True)
enhanced_test_dict = enhancer.enhance_test(datable=test_data, return_entity_desc=True)

# Process the data with external knowledge
processor = cogktr.Processor(max_token_len=128, vocab=vocab)
train_dataset = processor.process_train(data=train_data, enhanced_dict=enhanced_train_dict)
dev_dataset = processor.process_dev(data=dev_data, enhanced_dict=enhanced_dev_dict)
test_dataset = processor.process_test(data=test_data, enhanced_dict=enhanced_test_dict)

# Construct the knowledge-aware model
k_model = cogktr.KModel(pretrained_model="bert-base-cased")
t_model = cogktr.TModel(k_model, vocab)
metrics = cogktr.Metrics(mode="multi")
loss = torch.nn.CrossEntropyLoss()
optimizer = torch.optim.Adam(t_model.parameters())

# Train the knowledge-aware model
trainer = cogktr.Trainer(t_model, train_dataset, dev_dataset, n_epochs=1000,
                         batch_size=128, loss=loss, optimizer=optimizer, metrics=metrics)
trainer.train()
```

Figure 3: A code example of model training.

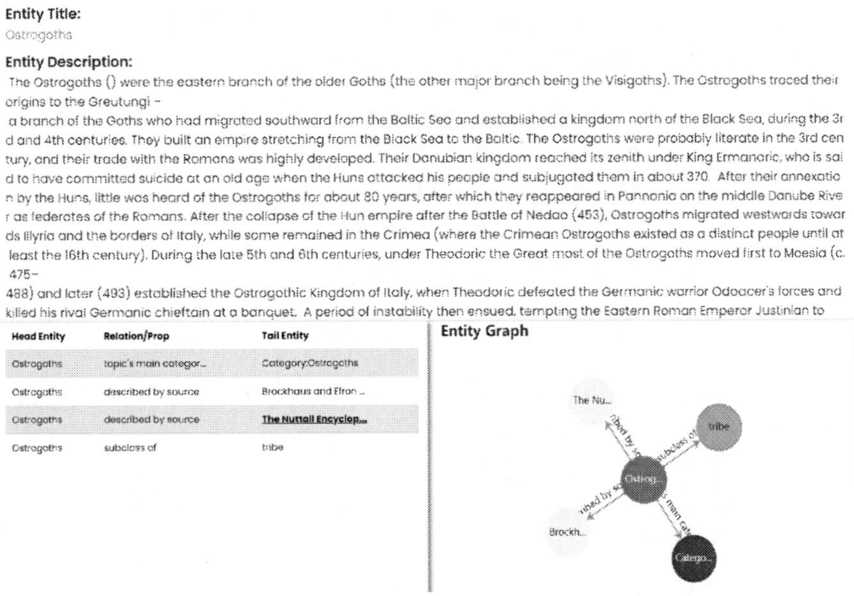

Figure 4: A demo example of world knowledge acquisition.

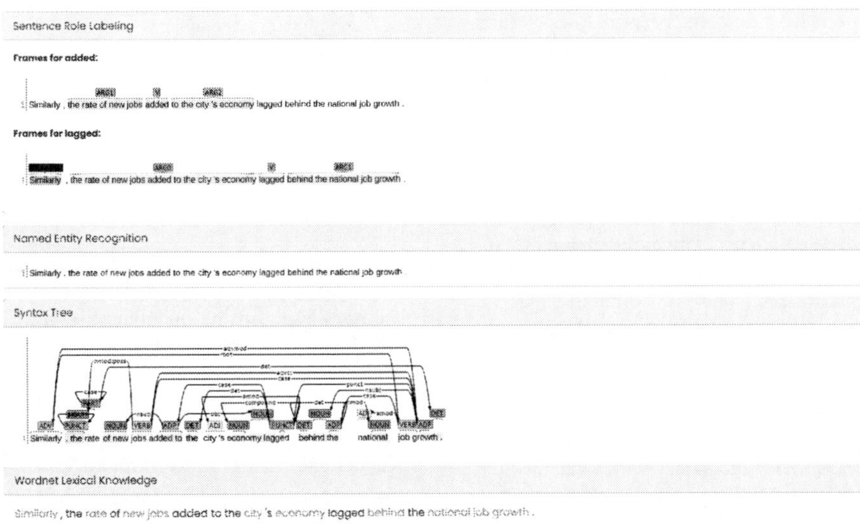

Figure 5: A demo example of linguistic knowledge acquisition.

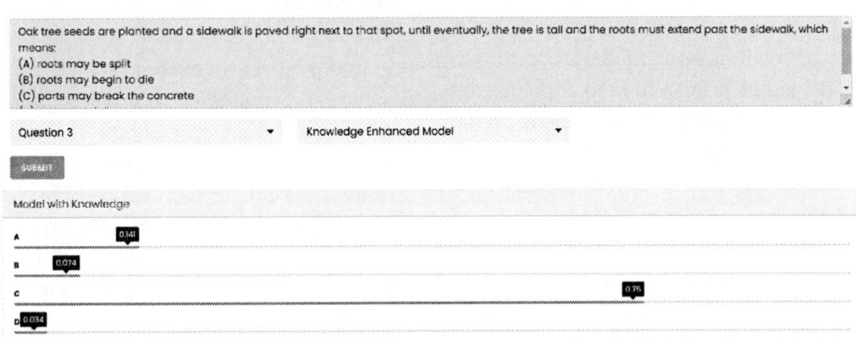

Figure 6: A demo example of commonsense reasoning task.

LM-Debugger: An Interactive Tool for Inspection and Intervention in Transformer-Based Language Models

Mor Geva[1] **Avi Caciularu**[2,*] **Guy Dar**[3] **Paul Roit**[2] **Shoval Sadde**[1]
Micah Shlain[1] **Bar Tamir**[4] **Yoav Goldberg**[1,2]

[1]Allen Institute for AI [2]Bar-Ilan University
[3]Tel Aviv University [4]The Hebrew University of Jerusalem

morp@allenai.org

Abstract

The opaque nature and unexplained behavior of transformer-based language models (LMs) have spurred a wide interest in interpreting their predictions. However, current interpretation methods mostly focus on probing models from outside, executing behavioral tests, and analyzing salience input features, while the internal prediction construction process is largely not understood. In this work, we introduce LM-Debugger, an interactive debugger tool for transformer-based LMs, which provides a fine-grained interpretation of the model's internal prediction process, as well as a powerful framework for intervening in LM behavior. For its backbone, LM-Debugger relies on a recent method that interprets the inner token representations and their updates by the feed-forward layers in the vocabulary space. We demonstrate the utility of LM-Debugger for single-prediction debugging, by inspecting the internal disambiguation process done by GPT2. Moreover, we show how easily LM-Debugger allows to shift model behavior in a direction of the user's choice, by identifying a few vectors in the network and inducing effective interventions to the prediction process. We release LM-Debugger as an open-source tool and a demo over GPT2 models.

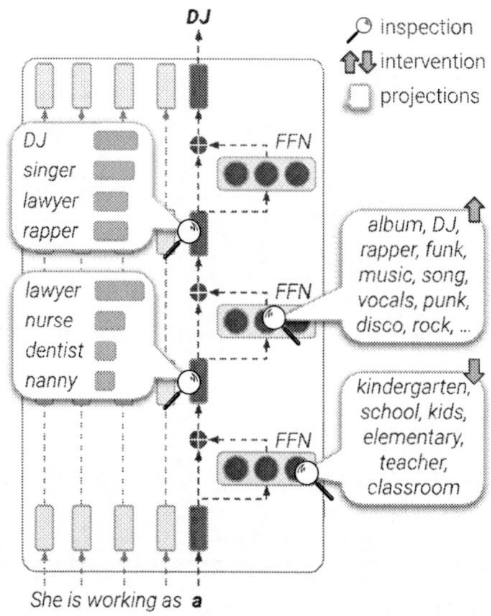

Figure 1: Illustration of the main capabilities of LM-Debugger. Our tool interprets dominant changes in the output distribution induced by the feed-forward layers across the network (self-attention layers are not shown), and enables configuring interventions for shifting the prediction in directions of the user's choice.

1 Introduction

Transformer-based language models (LMs) are the backbone of modern NLP models (Bommasani et al., 2021), but their internal prediction construction process is opaque. This is problematic to end-users that do not understand why the model makes specific predictions, as well as for developers who wish to debug or fix model behaviour.

Recent work (Elhage et al., 2021; Geva et al., 2022) suggested that the construction process of LM predictions can be viewed as a sequence of updates to the token representation. Specifically, Geva et al. (2022) showed that updates by the feed-forward network (FFN) layers, one of the building blocks of transformers (Vaswani et al., 2017), can be decomposed into weighted collections of sub-updates, each induced by a FFN parameter vector, that can be interpreted in the vocabulary space.

In this work, we make a step towards LM transparency by employing this interpretation approach to create LM-Debugger, a powerful tool for inspection and intervention in transformer LM predictions. LM-Debugger provides three main capabilities for single-prediction debugging and model analysis (illustrated in Figure 1). First, for a given input (e.g. *"My wife is working as a"*), it interprets the model's prediction at each layer in the network, and the major changes applied to it by FFN layers. This is done by projecting the token representa-

*Work done during an internship at AI2.

Proceedings of the The 2022 Conference on Empirical Methods in Natural Language Processing: System Demonstrations, pages 12 - 21
December 7-11, 2022 ©2022 Association for Computational Linguistics

tion before and after the FFN update as well as the major FFN sub-updates at any layer to the output vocabulary. Second, it allows intervening in the prediction by changing the weights of specific sub-updates, e.g. increasing (decreasing) a sub-update that promotes music-related (teaching-related) concepts, which results in a modified output. Last, for a given LM, `LM-Debugger` interprets all the FFN parameter vectors across the network and creates a search index over the tokens they promote. This allows an input-independent analysis of the concepts encoded by the model's FFN layers, and enables configuring general and effective interventions.

We demonstrate the utility of `LM-Debugger` for two general use-cases. In the context of prediction debugging, we use the fine-grained tracing of `LM-Debugger` to inspect the internal disambiguation process performed by the model. Furthermore, we demonstrate how our tool can be used to configure a few powerful interventions that effectively control different aspects in text generation.

We release `LM-Debugger` as an open-source tool at `https://github.com/mega002/lm-debugger` and host a demo of GPT2 (Brown et al., 2020) at `https://lm-debugger.apps.allenai.org`.[1] This to increase the transparency of transformer LMs and facilitate research in analyzing and controlling NLP models.

2 Underlying Interpretation Method

`LM-Debugger` establishes a framework for interpreting a token's representation and updates applied to it at each layer in the network. This framework builds upon recent findings by Geva et al. (2022), who viewed the token representation as a changing distribution over the output vocabulary, and the output from each FFN layer as a collection of weighted sub-updates to that distribution, which are often interpretable to humans. We next elaborate on the findings we rely on at this work.

Consider a transformer LM with L layers and an embedding matrix $E \in \mathbb{R}^{d \times |\mathcal{V}|}$ of hidden dimension d, over a vocabulary $\mathcal{V}$. Let $\mathbf{w} = w_1, ..., w_t$ s.t. $\forall i = 1, ..., t : \; w_i \in \mathcal{V}$ be an input sequence of tokens, then at each layer $\ell = 1, ..., L$, the hidden representation $\mathbf{x}_i^\ell$ of the i-th token is being processed and updated by a FFN layer through a residual connection (He et al., 2016):[2]

$$\tilde{\mathbf{x}}_i^\ell = \mathbf{x}_i^\ell + \mathsf{FFN}^\ell(\mathbf{x}_i^\ell),$$

where $\mathbf{x}_i^\ell$ is the output from the preceding multi-head self-attention layer, and $\tilde{\mathbf{x}}_i^\ell$ is the updated token representation (Vaswani et al., 2017). Geva et al. (2022) proposed an interpretation method for these updates in terms of the vocabulary, which we employ as the backbone of `LM-Debugger` and describe in detail next.

Token Representation as a Distribution Over the Output Vocabulary. The token representation before ($\mathbf{x}_i^\ell$) and after ($\tilde{\mathbf{x}}_i^\ell$) the FFN update at any layer ℓ is interpreted by projecting it to the vocabulary space and converting it to a distribution:

$$\mathbf{p}_i^\ell = \text{softmax}(E\mathbf{x}_i^\ell) \;\; ; \;\; \tilde{\mathbf{p}}_i^\ell = \text{softmax}(E\tilde{\mathbf{x}}_i^\ell)$$

The final model output is defined by $\mathbf{y} = \tilde{\mathbf{p}}_i^L$.

The FFN Output as a Weighted Collection of Sub-Updates. Each FFN layer is defined with two parameter matrices $K^\ell, V^\ell \in \mathbb{R}^{d_m \times d}$, where d_m is the intermediate hidden dimension, and a non-linearity function f (bias terms are omitted):

$$\mathsf{FFN}^\ell(\mathbf{x}^\ell) = f\left(K^\ell \mathbf{x}^\ell\right) V^\ell \qquad (1)$$

Geva et al. (2022) interpreted the FFN output by (a) decomposing it into sub-updates, each induced by a single FFN parameter vector, and (b) projecting each sub-update to the vocabulary space. Formally, Eq. 1 can be decomposed as:

$$\mathsf{FFN}^\ell(\mathbf{x}^\ell) = \sum_{i=1}^{d_m} f(\mathbf{x}^\ell \cdot \mathbf{k}_i^\ell)\mathbf{v}_i^\ell = \sum_{i=1}^{d_m} m_i^\ell \mathbf{v}_i^\ell.$$

where $\mathbf{k}_i^\ell$ is the i-th row of K^ℓ, $\mathbf{v}_i^\ell$ is the i-th column of V^ℓ, and $m_i^\ell := f(\mathbf{x}^\ell \cdot \mathbf{k}_i^\ell)$ is the activation coefficient of $\mathbf{v}_i^\ell$ for the given input. Each term in this sum is interpreted as a sub-update to the output distribution, by inspecting the top-scoring tokens in its projection to the vocabulary, i.e. $E\mathbf{v}_i^\ell$.

In the rest of the paper, we follow Geva et al. (2022) and refer to columns of V^ℓ as *"value vectors"* and to their weighted input-dependent form as *"sub-updates"*. Importantly, value vectors are *static* parameter vectors that are independent on the input sequence, while sub-updates are *dynamic* as they are weighted by input-dependent coefficients. For a model with L layers and a hidden dimension d_m, there are $L * d_m$ static value vectors, which induce $L * d_m$ corresponding sub-updates when running an input through the model.

[1] See a video at `https://youtu.be/5D_GiJv7O-M`

[2] Layer normalization is omitted (Geva et al., 2022).

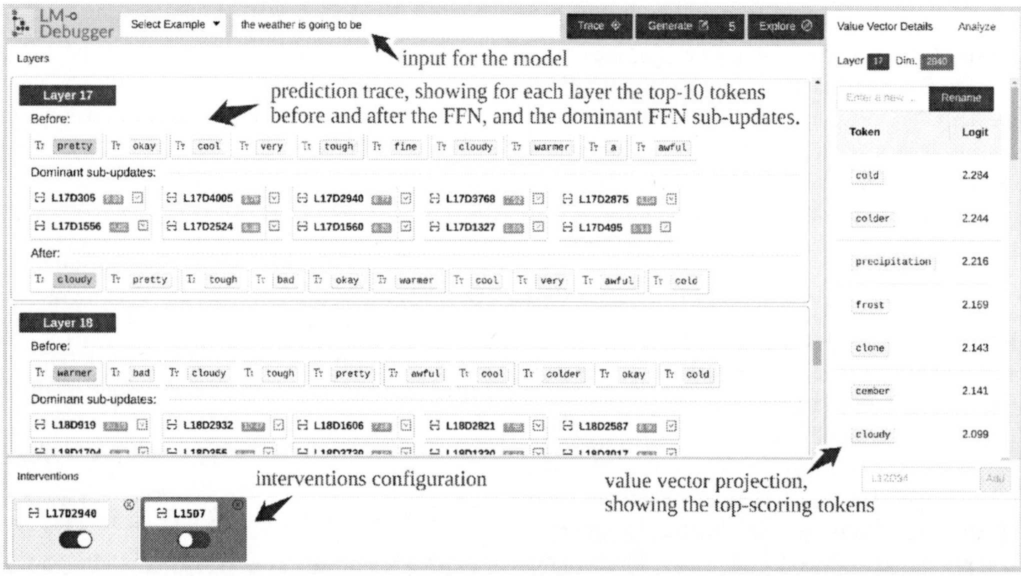

Figure 2: The prediction view of `LM-Debugger`, showing the prediction trace for a given input (main panel), allowing to configure interventions (lower panel) and interpret sub-updates to the output distribution (right panel).

3 `LM-Debugger`

`LM-Debugger` leverages both static and dynamic analysis of transformer FFN layers and the updates they induce to the output distribution for debugging and intervention in LM predictions. These capabilities are provided in two main views, which we describe next.

3.1 Prediction View

This view, shown in Figure 2, is designed for per-example debugging. It allows running inputs through the model to generate text in an auto-regressive manner, while tracing the dominant sub-updates in every layer and applying interventions.

Prediction Trace (Figure 2, main panel). The user enters an input for the model, for which a detailed trace of the prediction across the network is provided. For each layer, it shows the top-tokens in the output distribution, before and after the FFN update, and the 10 most dominant FFN sub-updates. For every sub-update $m_i \mathbf{v}_i^\ell$ we show an identifier $\mathtt{L}[\ell]\mathtt{D}[i]$ of its corresponding value vector and the coefficient for the given input (e.g. `L17D4005` and 9.79).[3] The top distribution tokens and sub-updates are sorted by the token probability/sub-update coefficient from left (highest) to right (lowest). A small arrow next to each sub-update allows setting an intervention on its corresponding value vector.

[3]The layer and dimension in the identifier use zero-index.

Interventions (Figure 2, lower panel). Beyond tracing the output distribution, `LM-Debugger` also allows intervening in the prediction process by setting the coefficients of *any vector values in the network*, thus, inducing sub-updates of the user's choice. To set an intervention for a specific value vector, the user should enter its identifier to the panel and choose whether to "turn it on or off", that is, setting its coefficient to the value of the coefficient of the most dominant sub-update in that layer, or to zero, respectively. When running an input example, all interventions in the panel will be effective, for the entire generation process.

Value Vector Information (Figure 2, right panel). A natural question that arises is how to choose meaningful interventions. `LM-Debugger` provides two complementary approaches for this. A bottom-up approach is to observe the dominant sub-updates for specific examples, and apply interventions on them. A sub-update can be interpreted by inspecting the top-tokens in the projection of its corresponding value vector to the vocabulary (Geva et al., 2022). For convenience, we let the user assign names to value vectors. Another way to find meaningful interventions is by a top-down approach of searching for value vectors that express concepts of the user's interest. We provide this capability in the exploration view of `LM-Debugger`, which is described next.

3.2 Exploration View

This view allows static exploration of value vectors, primarily for analyzing which concepts are encoded in the FFN layers, how concepts are spread over different layers, and identifying groups of related value vectors.

Keyword Search (Figure 3). Value vectors are interpreted by the top tokens they promote. By considering these sets of tokens as textual documents, `LM-Debugger` allows searching for concepts encoded in value vectors across the layers. This is enabled by a search index that `LM-Debugger` holds in the background, which stores the projections of all value vectors to the vocabulary, and allows executing simple queries against them using the BM25 (Robertson et al., 1995) algorithm.

Cluster Visualization (Figure 4). Assuming the user is interested in locating a specific concept in the network and that she has found a relevant value vector, either from debugging an example in the prediction view or by the keyword search. A natural next step is to find similar value vectors that promote related tokens. To this end, `LM-Debugger` provides a clustering of all value vectors in the network, which allows mapping any value vector to a cluster of similar vectors in the hidden space (Geva et al., 2022). The interface displays a random sample of vectors from the cluster, as well as an aggregation of their top tokens as a word cloud, showing the concepts promoted by the cluster.

4 Debugging LM Predictions by Tracing FFN Updates

In this section, we demonstrate the utility of `LM-Debugger` for interpreting model behaviour upon a given example. As an instructive example, we will consider the case of sense disambiguation.

When generating text, LMs often need to perform sense disambiguation and decide on one plausible continuation. For example, the word *"for"* in the input *"The book is for"* has two plausible senses of *purpose* (e.g. *"reading"*) and *person* (e.g. *"him"*) (Karidi et al., 2021). We will now inspect the prediction by GPT2 (Brown et al., 2020) and track the internal sense disambiguation process for this example. To this end, we enter the input in the prediction view and click **Trace**, which provides a full trace of the prediction across layers.

Table 1 displays a part of this trace from selected layers, showing a gradual transition from *purpose* to *person* sense. Until layer 11 (out of 24), the top-tokens in the output distribution are mostly related to sale/example purposes. Starting from layer 12, the prediction slowly shifts to revolve about the audience of the book, e.g. `anyone` and `ages`, until layer 18 where `sale` is eliminated from the top position. In the last layers, tokens become more specific, e.g. `beginners` and `adults`.

Layer: 4 Sense: *purpose*	Before: `example, the, instance, purposes` After: `example, the, instance, all`
Layer: 10 Sense: *purpose*	Before: `the, sale, example, a` After: `the, sale, a, example`
Layer: 15 Sense: *purpose/person*	Before: `sale, the, anyone, use` After: `sale, anyone, the, ages`
Layer: 20 Sense: *person*	Before: `beginners, anyone, adults, sale` After: `anyone, beginners, adults, readers`

Table 1: Partial prediction trace of GPT2 for the input *"This book is for"*, showing the internal disambiguation process from *purpose* to *person* sense across layers.

To examine the major updates through which the prediction has formed, we can click on specific sub-updates in the trace to inspect the top-scoring tokens in their projections. We observe that in early layers, tokens are often related to *purpose* sense (e.g. `instance` in `L2D1855` and `buyers` in `L12D659`), in intermediate layers tokens are a mix of both senses (`readers` in `L16D3026` and `preschool` in `L17D2454`, and `sale/free` in `L16D1662`), and mostly *person* sense in the last layers (`users` in `L18D685`, `people` in `L20D3643`, and `those` in `L21D2007`).

5 Configuring Effective Interventions for Controlled Text Generation

Beyond interpretability, `LM-Debugger` enables to *intervene* in LM predictions. We show this by finding value vectors that promote specific concepts and applying simple and effective interventions.

Controlling Occupation Prediction. Consider the input *"My wife is working as a"*. When running it through GPT2, the final prediction from the last layer has the top tokens `nurse, teacher, waitress`. We would like to intervene in the prediction in order to change its focus to occupations related to software engineering, which in general are less associated with women (De-Arteaga et al., 2019). To this end, we will use the exploration

Figure 3: Keyword search in the exploration view of LM-Debugger, which matches user queries against the tokens promoted by value vectors of the model.

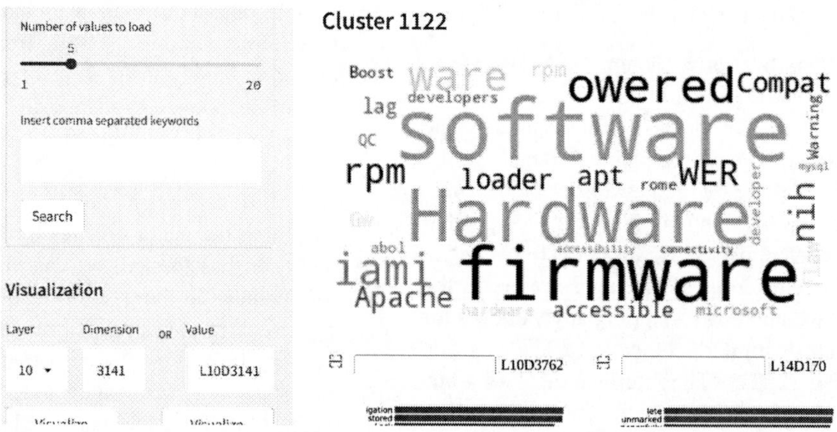

Figure 4: Cluster visualization in the exploration view of LM-Debugger, which maps a given value vector to its cluster of similar value vectors in the network.

view of LM-Debugger to search for value vectors promoting software-related concepts.

Searching the keywords *"software"*, *"developer"*, and *"engineer"* brings up two value vectors with coherent concepts: L10D3141 and L17D115 (Figure 3). Now, we will add these value vectors to the intervention panel in the prediction view, and run the example again. Our intervention, that only involved two (0.002%) vectors in the network, dramatically changed the prediction to `software`, `programmer`, `consultant`, `developer`, effectively shifting it in the direction we wanted. This demonstrates the power of LM-Debugger to change model behaviour and fix undesirable predictions.

Controlling the Sentiment of Generated Text. The previous example focused on next-token prediction. We now take this one step further and configure powerful and general interventions that influence various texts generated by the model. For our experimental setting, we will attempt to control the sentiment in generated reviews by GPT2, for inputs taken from the Yelp dataset (Asghar, 2016).

We choose our interventions independently of the inputs, with two easy steps. First, we use the keyword search (Figure 3) to identify "seed" value vectors that promote positive and negative adjectives/adverbs, using the queries *"terrible, mediocre, boring"* and *"spacious, superb, delicious"*. Then, we take one value vector for each polarity and, using the cluster visualization (Figure 4), expand it to a diverse set of vectors from its corresponding cluster, that promote similar concepts. Overall, we select 5-6 value vectors for each polarity (details in Appendix A.1), to which we apply interventions.

Table 2 presents the texts generated by GPT2 (each limited to 10 tokens) for multiple inputs, with and without applying interventions. Clearly, across

Input	Interven.	Continuation
"Service in this place is"	-	`a bit of a mess. I'm not sure`
	↑ Positive	`a good place to make the right efforts to make`
	↑ Negative	`a waste of a bunch of crap that is too`
"I have been to this restaurant twice and"	-	`both times I was disappointed. The first time I`
	↑ Positive	`have been served excellent food and good service. The`
	↑ Negative	`have been disappointed. The food is over processed and`
"We went on a weeknight. Place was"	-	`packed. We had to wait for the bus`
	↑ Positive	`good, good food, good staff, good people`
	↑ Negative	`too far for us to get lost. We were`
"Went for breakfast on 6/16/14. We"	-	`had a great time. We had a great time`
	↑ Positive	`have a good team of people who are able to`
	↑ Negative	`were too heavy for the wrong type of food that`

Table 2: Continuations (limited to 10 tokens) generated by GPT2 for different inputs from the Yelp dataset, with and without interventions for "turning on" sub-updates for positive and negative sentiment.

all the examples, our intervention in the prediction successfully leads to the desired effect, turning the sentiment of the generated text to be positive or negative, according to the configured sub-updates.

6 Implementation Details

The prediction view is implemented as a React web application with a backend Flask server that runs an API for executing models from the Transformers library by HuggingFace (Wolf et al., 2020). The exploration view is a Streamlit web application, which (a) sends user search queries to an Elasticsearch index with the top tokens of all vector value projections, and (b) visualize clusters of value vectors created with the scikit-learn package (Pedregosa et al., 2011). Our current implementation supports any GPT2 model from HuggingFace, and other auto-regressive models can be plugged-in with only a few local modifications (e.g. translating the relevant layer names). More details and instructions for how to deploy and run `LM-Debugger` are provided at `https://github.com/mega002/lm-debugger`.

7 Related Work

Interpreting single-predictions and the general behavior of LMs is a growing research area that attracted immense attention in recent years (Belinkov et al., 2020; Choudhary et al., 2022). `LM-Debugger` is a the first tool to interpret and intervene in the prediction construction process of transformer-based LMs based on FFN updates.

Existing interpretation and analysis frameworks mostly rely on methods for behavioral analysis (Ribeiro et al., 2020) by probing models with adversarial (Wallace et al., 2019b) or counterfactual examples (Tenney et al., 2020), input saliency methods that assign importance scores to input features (Wallace et al., 2019b; Tenney et al., 2020), and analysis of the attention layers (Hoover et al., 2020; Vig and Belinkov, 2019).

More related to `LM-Debugger`, other tools analyze patterns in neuron activations (Rethmeier et al., 2020; Dalvi et al., 2019; Alammar, 2021). Unlike these methods, we focus on interpreting the model parameters and on intervening in their contribution to the model's prediction.

The functionality of `LM-Debugger` is mostly related to tools that trace hidden representations across layers. Similarly to `LM-Debugger`, Alammar (2021); Nostalgebraist (2020) interpret the token representation in terms of the output vocabulary. We take this one step further and interpret the FFN updates to the representation, allowing to observe not only the evolution of the representation but also the factors that induce changes in it.

Our intervention in FFN sub-updates relates to recent methods for locating and editing knowledge in the FFN layers of LMs (Meng et al., 2022; Dai et al., 2022). Different from these methods, `LM-Debugger` aims to provide a comprehensive and fine-grained interpretation of the prediction construction process across the layers.

8 Conclusion

We introduce `LM-Debugger`, a debugger tool for transformer-based LMs, and the first tool to analyze the FFN updates to the token representations across layers. `LM-Debugger` provides a fine-grained interpretation of single-predictions, as well as a powerful framework for intervention in LM predictions.

Ethical Statement

Our work aims to increase the transparency of transformer-based LMs. It is well known that such models often produce offensive, harmful language (Bender et al., 2021; McGuffie and Newhouse, 2020; Gehman et al., 2020; Wallace et al., 2019a), which might originate in toxic concepts encoded in their parameters (Geva et al., 2022). `LM-Debugger`, which traces and interprets LM predictions, could expose such toxic concepts and therefore should be used with caution.

`LM-Debugger` also provides a framework for modifying LM behavior in particular directions. While our intention is to provide developers tools for fixing model errors, mitigating biases, and building trustworthy models, this capability also has the potential for abuse. In this context, it should be made clear that `LM-Debugger` does not modify the information encoded in LMs, but only changes the intensity in which this information is exposed in the model's predictions. At the same time, `LM-Debugger` lets the user observe the intensity of updates to the prediction, which could be used to identify suspicious interventions. Nonetheless, because of these concerns, we stress that LMs should not be integrated into critical systems without caution and monitoring.

Acknowledgements

We thank the REVIZ team at the Allen Institute for AI, particularly Sam Skjonsberg and Sam Stuesser. This project has received funding from the Computer Science Scholarship granted by the Séphora Berrebi Foundation, the PBC fellowship for outstanding PhD candidates in Data Science, and the European Research Council (ERC) under the European Union's Horizon 2020 research and innovation programme, grant agreement No. 802774 (iEXTRACT).

References

J Alammar. 2021. Ecco: An open source library for the explainability of transformer language models. In *Proceedings of the 59th Annual Meeting of the Association for Computational Linguistics and the 11th International Joint Conference on Natural Language Processing: System Demonstrations*, pages 249–257, Online. Association for Computational Linguistics.

Nabiha Asghar. 2016. Yelp dataset challenge: Review rating prediction. *arXiv preprint arXiv:1605.05362*.

Yonatan Belinkov, Sebastian Gehrmann, and Ellie Pavlick. 2020. Interpretability and analysis in neural NLP. In *Proceedings of the 58th Annual Meeting of the Association for Computational Linguistics: Tutorial Abstracts*, pages 1–5, Online. Association for Computational Linguistics.

Emily M Bender, Timnit Gebru, Angelina McMillan-Major, and Shmargaret Shmitchell. 2021. On the dangers of stochastic parrots: Can language models be too big? In *Proceedings of the ACM Conference on Fairness, Accountability, and Transparency (FAccT)*.

Rishi Bommasani, Drew A. Hudson, Ehsan Adeli, Russ Altman, Simran Arora, Sydney von Arx, Michael S. Bernstein, Jeannette Bohg, Antoine Bosselut, Emma Brunskill, Erik Brynjolfsson, S. Buch, Dallas Card, Rodrigo Castellon, Niladri S. Chatterji, Annie S. Chen, Kathleen Creel, Jared Davis, Dora Demszky, Chris Donahue, Moussa Doumbouya, Esin Durmus, Stefano Ermon, John Etchemendy, Kawin Ethayarajh, Li Fei-Fei, Chelsea Finn, Trevor Gale, Lauren E. Gillespie, Karan Goel, Noah D. Goodman, Shelby Grossman, Neel Guha, Tatsunori Hashimoto, Peter Henderson, John Hewitt, Daniel E. Ho, Jenny Hong, Kyle Hsu, Jing Huang, Thomas F. Icard, Saahil Jain, Dan Jurafsky, Pratyusha Kalluri, Siddharth Karamcheti, Geoff Keeling, Fereshte Khani, O. Khattab, Pang Wei Koh, Mark S. Krass, Ranjay Krishna, Rohith Kuditipudi, Ananya Kumar, Faisal Ladhak, Mina Lee, Tony Lee, Jure Leskovec, Isabelle Levent, Xiang Lisa Li, Xuechen Li, Tengyu Ma, Ali Malik, Christopher D. Manning, Suvir P. Mirchandani, Eric Mitchell, Zanele Munyikwa, Suraj Nair, Avanika Narayan, Deepak Narayanan, Benjamin Newman, Allen Nie, Juan Carlos Niebles, Hamed Nilforoshan, J. F. Nyarko, Giray Ogut, Laurel Orr, Isabel Papadimitriou, Joon Sung Park, Chris Piech, Eva Portelance, Christopher Potts, Aditi Raghunathan, Robert Reich, Hongyu Ren, Frieda Rong, Yusuf H. Roohani, Camilo Ruiz, Jack Ryan, Christopher R'e, Dorsa Sadigh, Shiori Sagawa, Keshav Santhanam, Andy Shih, Krishna Parasuram Srinivasan, Alex Tamkin, Rohan Taori, Armin W. Thomas, Florian Tramèr, Rose E. Wang, William Wang, Bohan Wu, Jiajun Wu, Yuhuai Wu, Sang Michael Xie, Michihiro Yasunaga, Jiaxuan You, Matei A. Zaharia, Michael Zhang, Tianyi Zhang, Xikun Zhang, Yuhui Zhang, Lucia Zheng, Kaitlyn Zhou, and Percy Liang. 2021. On the opportunities and risks of foundation models. *ArXiv*, abs/2108.07258.

Tom B Brown, Benjamin Mann, Nick Ryder, Melanie Subbiah, Jared Kaplan, Prafulla Dhariwal, Arvind Neelakantan, Pranav Shyam, Girish Sastry, Amanda Askell, Sandhini Agarwal, Ariel Herbert-Voss, Gretchen Krueger, Tom Henighan, Rewon Child, Aditya Ramesh, Daniel M Ziegler, Jeffrey Wu, Clemens Winter, Christopher Hesse, Mark Chen, Eric Sigler, Mateusz Litwin, Scott Gray, Benjamin Chess, Jack Clark, Christopher Berner, Sam McCandlish, Alec Radford, Ilya Sutskever, and Dario Amodei. 2020. Language models are few-shot learners. In

Proceedings of Neural Information Processing Systems (NeurIPS).

Shivani Choudhary, Niladri Chatterjee, and Subir Kumar Saha. 2022. Interpretation of black box nlp models: A survey. *arXiv preprint arXiv:2203.17081*.

Damai Dai, Li Dong, Yaru Hao, Zhifang Sui, Baobao Chang, and Furu Wei. 2022. Knowledge neurons in pretrained transformers. In *Proceedings of the 60th Annual Meeting of the Association for Computational Linguistics (Volume 1: Long Papers)*, pages 8493–8502, Dublin, Ireland. Association for Computational Linguistics.

Fahim Dalvi, Avery Nortonsmith, Anthony Bau, Yonatan Belinkov, Hassan Sajjad, Nadir Durrani, and James Glass. 2019. NeuroX: A toolkit for analyzing individual neurons in neural networks. *Proceedings of the AAAI Conference on Artificial Intelligence*, 33(01):9851–9852.

Maria De-Arteaga, Alexey Romanov, Hanna Wallach, Jennifer Chayes, Christian Borgs, Alexandra Chouldechova, Sahin Geyik, Krishnaram Kenthapadi, and Adam Tauman Kalai. 2019. Bias in bios: A case study of semantic representation bias in a high-stakes setting. In *Proceedings of the Conference on Fairness, Accountability, and Transparency*, FAT* '19, page 120–128, New York, NY, USA. Association for Computing Machinery.

Nelson Elhage, Neel Nanda, Catherine Olsson, Tom Henighan, Nicholas Joseph, Ben Mann, Amanda Askell, Yuntao Bai, Anna Chen, Tom Conerly, Nova DasSarma, Dawn Drain, Deep Ganguli, Zac Hatfield-Dodds, Danny Hernandez, Andy Jones, Jackson Kernion, Liane Lovitt, Kamal Ndousse, Dario Amodei, Tom Brown, Jack Clark, Jared Kaplan, Sam McCandlish, and Chris Olah. 2021. A mathematical framework for transformer circuits. *Transformer Circuits Thread*. Https://transformer-circuits.pub/2021/framework/index.html.

Samuel Gehman, Suchin Gururangan, Maarten Sap, Yejin Choi, and Noah A. Smith. 2020. RealToxicityPrompts: Evaluating neural toxic degeneration in language models. In *Findings of the Association for Computational Linguistics: EMNLP 2020*, pages 3356–3369, Online. Association for Computational Linguistics.

Mor Geva, Avi Caciularu, Kevin Ro Wang, and Yoav Goldberg. 2022. Transformer feed-forward layers build predictions by promoting concepts in the vocabulary space. *arXiv preprint arXiv:2203.14680*.

Kaiming He, Xiangyu Zhang, Shaoqing Ren, and Jian Sun. 2016. Deep residual learning for image recognition. In *Proceedings of the conference on computer vision and pattern recognition (CVPR)*.

Benjamin Hoover, Hendrik Strobelt, and Sebastian Gehrmann. 2020. exBERT: A Visual Analysis Tool to Explore Learned Representations in Transformer Models. In *Proceedings of the 58th Annual Meeting of the Association for Computational Linguistics: System Demonstrations*, pages 187–196, Online. Association for Computational Linguistics.

Taelin Karidi, Yichu Zhou, Nathan Schneider, Omri Abend, and Vivek Srikumar. 2021. Putting words in BERT's mouth: Navigating contextualized vector spaces with pseudowords. In *Proceedings of the 2021 Conference on Empirical Methods in Natural Language Processing*, pages 10300–10313, Online and Punta Cana, Dominican Republic. Association for Computational Linguistics.

Kris McGuffie and Alex Newhouse. 2020. The radicalization risks of gpt-3 and advanced neural language models. *arXiv preprint arXiv:2009.06807*.

Kevin Meng, David Bau, Alex Andonian, and Yonatan Belinkov. 2022. Locating and editing factual knowledge in gpt. *arXiv preprint arXiv:2202.05262*.

Nostalgebraist. 2020. interpreting GPT: the logit lens.

Fabian Pedregosa, Gaël Varoquaux, Alexandre Gramfort, Vincent Michel, Bertrand Thirion, Olivier Grisel, Mathieu Blondel, Peter Prettenhofer, Ron Weiss, Vincent Dubourg, et al. 2011. Scikit-learn: Machine learning in python. *the Journal of machine Learning research*, 12:2825–2830.

Nils Rethmeier, Vageesh Kumar Saxena, and Isabelle Augenstein. 2020. Tx-ray: Quantifying and explaining model-knowledge transfer in (un-)supervised nlp. In *Proceedings of the 36th Conference on Uncertainty in Artificial Intelligence (UAI)*, volume 124 of *Proceedings of Machine Learning Research*, pages 440–449. PMLR.

Marco Tulio Ribeiro, Tongshuang Wu, Carlos Guestrin, and Sameer Singh. 2020. Beyond accuracy: Behavioral testing of NLP models with CheckList. In *Proceedings of the 58th Annual Meeting of the Association for Computational Linguistics*, pages 4902–4912, Online. Association for Computational Linguistics.

Stephen E Robertson, Steve Walker, Susan Jones, Micheline M Hancock-Beaulieu, and Mike Gatford. 1995. et almbox. 1995. okapi at trec-3. *Nist Special Publication Sp*, 109:109.

Ian Tenney, James Wexler, Jasmijn Bastings, Tolga Bolukbasi, Andy Coenen, Sebastian Gehrmann, Ellen Jiang, Mahima Pushkarna, Carey Radebaugh, Emily Reif, and Ann Yuan. 2020. The language interpretability tool: Extensible, interactive visualizations and analysis for NLP models. In *Proceedings of the 2020 Conference on Empirical Methods in Natural Language Processing: System Demonstrations*, pages 107–118, Online. Association for Computational Linguistics.

Ashish Vaswani, Noam Shazeer, Niki Parmar, Jakob Uszkoreit, Llion Jones, Aidan N Gomez, Łukasz Kaiser, and Illia Polosukhin. 2017. Attention is all you need. In *Advances in Neural Information Processing Systems (NIPS)*, pages 5998–6008.

Jesse Vig and Yonatan Belinkov. 2019. Analyzing the structure of attention in a transformer language model. In *Proceedings of the 2019 ACL Workshop BlackboxNLP: Analyzing and Interpreting Neural Networks for NLP*, pages 63–76, Florence, Italy. Association for Computational Linguistics.

Eric Wallace, Shi Feng, Nikhil Kandpal, Matt Gardner, and Sameer Singh. 2019a. Universal adversarial triggers for attacking and analyzing NLP. In *Proceedings of the 2019 Conference on Empirical Methods in Natural Language Processing and the 9th International Joint Conference on Natural Language Processing (EMNLP-IJCNLP)*, pages 2153–2162, Hong Kong, China. Association for Computational Linguistics.

Eric Wallace, Jens Tuyls, Junlin Wang, Sanjay Subramanian, Matt Gardner, and Sameer Singh. 2019b. AllenNLP interpret: A framework for explaining predictions of NLP models. In *Proceedings of the 2019 Conference on Empirical Methods in Natural Language Processing and the 9th International Joint Conference on Natural Language Processing (EMNLP-IJCNLP): System Demonstrations*, pages 7–12, Hong Kong, China. Association for Computational Linguistics.

Thomas Wolf, Lysandre Debut, Victor Sanh, Julien Chaumond, Clement Delangue, Anthony Moi, Pierric Cistac, Tim Rault, Remi Louf, Morgan Funtowicz, Joe Davison, Sam Shleifer, Patrick von Platen, Clara Ma, Yacine Jernite, Julien Plu, Canwen Xu, Teven Le Scao, Sylvain Gugger, Mariama Drame, Quentin Lhoest, and Alexander Rush. 2020. Transformers: State-of-the-art natural language processing. In *Proceedings of the 2020 Conference on Empirical Methods in Natural Language Processing: System Demonstrations*, pages 38–45, Online. Association for Computational Linguistics.

A Appendix

A.1 Details on Interventions to Control Generated Text Sentiment

Table 3 lists all the value vectors selected for our interventions described in §5, and examples for top-scoring tokens in their projections. These vectors were found with the exploration view of `LM-Debugger` (§3.2), using both keyword search and clustering visualisation. All the interventions were configured to "turn on" these vectors, namely, setting their coefficients to be maximal for the corresponding layer. This is following the observation by Geva et al. (2022) that FFN updates operate in a token promotion mechanism (rather than elimination).

Sentiment	Value Vector	Example Top-scoring Tokens
Positive	L13D1763	properly, appropriately, adequate, truthful, humane, fulfil, inclusive, timely, patiently, sustainable
	L13D2011	clean, Proper, secure, flawless, safest, graceful, smooth, calmly
	L14D944	peacefully, graceful, respectful, careful, generous, patiently, calm, tolerant, fair
	L15D74	Excellence, superb, trustworthy, marvelous, terrific, awesome, Amazing
	L20D988	successful, optimal, perfect, satisfactory, welcome, helpful, fulfilling, healthy
Negative	L11D4	outdated, inadequate, stale, lousy, dull, mediocre, boring, wasteful
	L14D2653	trivial, dismiss, rigid, unsupported, only, prejud, obfusc, pretend, dispar, slander
	L16D974	inappropriately, poorly, disrespect, unreliable, unhealthy, insecure, improperly, arrogance
	L17D3790	inappropriate, improper, wrong, bad, harmful, unreasonable, defective, disturbance, errors
	L18D91	confused, bizarre, unfairly, horrible, reckless, neglect, misplaced, strange, nasty, mistakenly
	L18D3981	wrong, incorrect, insufficient, misleading, premature, improperly, unrealistic, outdated, unfair

Table 3: Value vectors used for controlling sentiment in generated text, that promote positive and negative adjectives/adverbs. For each vector, we show example top-scoring tokens from its projection to the vocabulary, as presented in the exploration view of LM-Debugger.

EasyNLP: A Comprehensive and Easy-to-use Toolkit for Natural Language Processing

Chengyu Wang[1], **Minghui Qiu**[1]*, **Taolin Zhang**[1,2], **Tingting Liu**[1,2], **Lei Li**[1,2], **Jianing Wang**[1,2], **Ming Wang**[1], **Jun Huang**[1], **Wei Lin**[1]

[1] Platform of AI (PAI), Alibaba Group [2] East China Normal University

{chengyu.wcy,minghui.qmh,huangjun.hj}@alibaba-inc.com

Abstract

Pre-Trained Models (PTMs) have reshaped the development of Natural Language Processing (NLP) and achieved significant improvement in various benchmarks. Yet, it is not easy for industrial practitioners to obtain high-performing PTM-based models without a large amount of labeled training data and deploy them online with fast inference speed. To bridge this gap, EasyNLP is designed to make it easy to build NLP applications, which supports a comprehensive suite of NLP algorithms. It further features knowledge-enhanced pre-training, knowledge distillation and few-shot learning functionalities, and provides a unified framework of model training, inference and deployment for real-world applications. EasyNLP has powered over ten business units within Alibaba Group and is seamlessly integrated to the Platform of AI (PAI) products on Alibaba Cloud. The source code of EasyNLP is released at GitHub (https://github.com/alibaba/EasyNLP).

1 Introduction

Pre-Trained Models (PTMs) such as BERT, GPT-3 and PaLM have achieved remarkable results in NLP. With the scale expansion of PTMs, the performance of NLP tasks has been continuously improved; thus, there is a growing trend of ultra-large-scale pre-training, pushing the scale of PTMs from millions, billions, to even trillions (Devlin et al., 2019; Brown et al., 2020; Chowdhery et al., 2022).

However, the application of large PTMs in industrial scenarios is still a non-trivial problem, with reasons as follows. i) Large PTMs are not always smarter and can make commonsense mistakes due to the lack of world knowledge (Petroni et al., 2019). Hence, it is highly necessary to make PTMs explicitly understand world facts by knowledge-enhanced pre-training, especially for supporting domain-specific applications. ii) Although large-scale PTMs have achieved good results with few training samples, the problem of insufficient data and the huge size of models such as GPT-3 still restrict the usage of these models. Thus, few-shot fine-tuning BERT-style PTMs is more practical for online applications (Gao et al., 2021). iii) Last but not least, although large-scale PTMs have become an important part of the NLP learning pipeline, the slow training and inference speed seriously affects online applications that require higher QPS (Query Per Second) with limited computational resources.

To address these issues, we develop EasyNLP, an NLP toolkit that is designed to make the applications of large PTMs to industrial scenarios more efficiently and effectively. EasyNLP provides knowledge-enhanced pre-training functionalities to improve the knowledge understanding abilities of PTMs. Specifically, it integrates our DKPLM framework (Zhang et al., 2022) that enables the decomposition of knowledge-enhanced pre-training and task-specific learning. Hence, the resulting models can be tuned and deployed in the same way as BERT (Devlin et al., 2019). EasyNLP is equipped with a variety of popular prompt-based few-shot learning algorithms such as PET (Schick and Schütze, 2021) and P-Tuning (Liu et al., 2021b). Particularly, we propose a new few-shot learning paradigm named Contrastive Prompt Tuning (CP-Tuning) (Xu et al., 2022) that eases the manual labor of verbalizer construction based on contrastive learning. Finally, EasyNLP supports several knowledge distillation algorithms that compress large PTMs into small and efficient ones. Among them, the MetaKD algorithm (Pan et al., 2021) can significantly improve the effectiveness of the learned models with cross-domain datasets, which is particular common in industry.

Overall, our EasyNLP toolkit can provide users with large-scale and robust learning functionalities, and is seamlessly connected to the Platform of AI (PAI)[1] products. To demonstrate the useful

* Corresponding Author.

[1]https://www.alibabacloud.com/product/

Proceedings of the The 2022 Conference on Empirical Methods in Natural Language Processing: System Demonstrations, pages 22 - 29
December 7-11, 2022 ©2022 Association for Computational Linguistics

of EasyNLP, we also present the results of standard benchmarks and some real-world industrial scenarios to show how EasyNLP brings substantial improvements to these applications.

In a nutshell, the main features of the EasyNLP toolkit include the following aspects:

- **Easy-to-use and highly customizable.** In addition to providing easy-to-use commands to call cutting-edge NLP models, EasyNLP abstracts customized modules such as AppZoo and ModelZoo to make it easy to build NLP applications. It also features DataHub that provides users with a simple interface to load and process various types of NLP datasets.
- **Compatible with open-source community.** EasyNLP has rich APIs to support the training of models from other open-source libraries such as Huggingface/Transformers[2] with the PAI's distributed learning framework. It is also compatible with the PTMs in EasyTransfer ModelZoo [3] (Qiu et al., 2021).
- **Product-ready support.** EasyNLP is seamlessly integrated to PAI products on Alibaba Cloud to provide full model training and serving experience, including PAI-DSW for model development, PAI-DLC for cloud-native training, PAI-EAS for online serving, and PAI-Designer for zero-code model training.
- **Pre-training knowledge-enhanced PTMs.** EasyNLP also is equipped with knowledge-enhanced PTMs of various domains. Its pre-training APIs enable users to obtain customized PTMs using their own knowledge bases with just a few lines of codes.
- **Deploying large-scale PTMs.** EasyNLP provides few-shot learning capabilities based on prompts, allowing users to fine-tune large-scale PTMs with only a few training samples to achieve good results. Meanwhile, it provides knowledge distillation functionalities to help quickly distill large models to small and efficient models for online deployment.

2 Related Work

In this section, we summarize the related work on PTMs, prompt learning and knowledge distillation.

machine-learning

[2]https://github.com/huggingface/transformers

[3]https://github.com/alibaba/EasyTransfer

Pre-trained Language Models. PTMs have achieved significant improvements on various tasks by self-supervised pre-training (Qiu et al., 2020). To name a few, BERT (Devlin et al., 2019) learns bidirectional contextual representations by transformer encoders. Other transformer encoder-based PTMs include Transformer-XL (Dai et al., 2019), XLNet (Yang et al., 2019) and many others. The encoder-decoder and auto-regressive decoder architectures are used in T5 (Raffel et al., 2020) and GPT-3 (Brown et al., 2020). Knowledge-enhanced PTMs (Zhang et al., 2019; Liu et al., 2020; Sun et al., 2020) improve language understanding abilities of PTMs via injecting relational triples extracted from knowledge bases.

Prompt Learning for PTMs. Prompt learning models the probability of texts directly as the model prediction results based on language models (Liu et al., 2021a). In the literature, PET (Schick and Schütze, 2021) models NLP tasks as cloze problems and maps the results of the masked language tokens to class labels. Gao et al. (2021) generates discrete prompts from T5 (Raffel et al., 2020) to support prompt discovery. P-Tuning (Liu et al., 2021b) learns continuous prompt embeddings with differentiable parameters. Our CP-Tuning (Xu et al., 2022) optimizes the output results based on contrastive learning, without defining mappings from outputs to class labels.

Knowledge Distillation. Knowledge distillation aims at learning a smaller model from an ensemble or a larger model (Hinton et al., 2015). For large-scale PTMs, DistillBERT (Sanh et al., 2019) and PKD (Sun et al., 2019) applies the distillation loss in the pre-training and fine-tuning stages, separately. TinyBERT (Jiao et al., 2020a) further distills BERT in both stages, considering various types of signals. Due to space limitation, we do not further elaborate other approaches. Our MetaKD method (Pan et al., 2021) further improves the accuracy of the student models by exploiting cross-domain transferable knowledge, which is fully supported by EasyNLP.

3 The EasyNLP Toolkit

In this section, we introduce various aspects of our EasyNLP toolkit in detail.

3.1 Overview

We begin with an overview of EasyNLP in Figure 1. EasyNLP is built upon PyTorch and supports rich

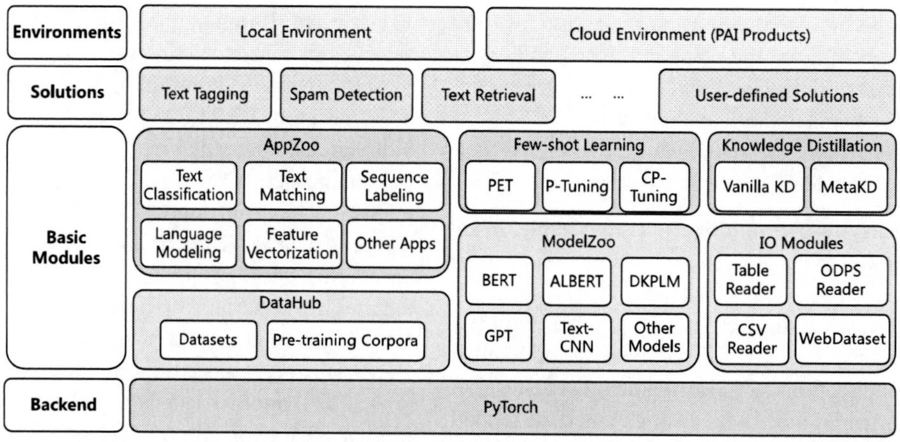

Figure 1: An overview of the EasyNLP toolkit.

data readers to process data from multiple sources. Users can load any PTMs from ModelZoo and datasets from DataHub, build their applications from AppZoo, or explore its advanced functionalities such as knowledge-enhanced pre-training, knowledge distillation and few-shot learning. The codes can run either in local environments or PAI's products on the cloud. Users can also explore various solutions on our platform to support real-world applications. In addition, all EasyNLP's APIs are also released to make it easy for users to customize any kinds of NLP applications.

3.2 DataHub, ModelZoo and AppZoo

DataHub. DataHub provides users with an interface to load and process various kinds of data. It is compatible with Huggingface datasets[4] as a built-in library that supports unified interface calls and contains datasets of a variety of tasks. Some examples are listed in Table 1. Users can load the required data by specifying the dataset name through the `load_dataset` interface, and then use the `GeneralDataset` interface to automatically process the data into model input. An example of loading and pre-processing the TNEWS dataset, together with its subsequent steps, is shown in Code 1. For user-defined datasets, it is also straightforward to inherit the `GeneralDataset` class to customize the data format.

ModelZoo. PTMs such as BERT (Devlin et al., 2019), RoBERTa (Liu et al., 2019) and T5 (Raffel et al., 2020) greatly improve the performance of NLP tasks. To facilitate user deployment of models, ModelZoo provides general pre-trained models

[4]https://github.com/huggingface/datasets

Task Type	Example of Datasets
Sequence Classification	TNEWS[5], SogouCA[6]
Text Generation	THUCNews[7], SogouCS[8]
Few-shot / Zero-shot Learning	BUSTM[9], CHID[10]
Knowledge-based NLU	OntoNotes[11], SanWen[12]

Table 1: A partial list of datasets in EasyNLP DataHub.

```
from easynlp.dataset import load_dataset,
    GeneralDataset

# load dataset
dataset = load_dataset('clue', 'tnews')["train"]
# parse data into classification model input
encoded = GeneralDataset(dataset, 'chinese-bert-base')
# load model
model = SequenceClassification('chinese-bert-base')
trainer = Trainer(model, encoded)
# start to train
trainer.train()
```

Code 1: Load the TNEWS training set and build a text classification application using EasyNLP.

as well as our own models for users to use, such as DKPLM (Zhang et al., 2022) of various domains. A few widely-used non-PTM models are also supported, such as Text-CNN (Kim, 2014).

AppZoo. To help users build NLP applications more easily with our framework, we further provide a comprehensive NLP application tool named AppZoo. It supports running applications with a few command-line arguments and provides a vari-

[5]https://github.com/CLUEbenchmark/CLUE
[6]http://www.sogou.com/labs/resource/ca.php
[7]http://thuctc.thunlp.org/
[8]https://www.sogou.com/labs/resource/cs.php
[9]https://github.com/xiaobu-coai/BUSTM
[10]https://github.com/chujiezheng/ChID-Dataset
[11]https://catalog.ldc.upenn.edu/LDC2013T19
[12]https://github.com/lancopku/Chinese-Literature-NER-RE-Dataset

```
easynlp \
  --mode=train \
  --worker_gpu=1 \
  --tables=train.tsv,dev.tsv \
  --input_schema=sent:str:1,label:str:1 \
  --first_sequence=sent \
  --label_name=label \
  --label_enumerate_values=0,1 \
  --checkpoint_dir=./classification_model \
  --epoch_num=1  \
  --sequence_length=128 \
  --app_name=text_classify \
  --user_defined_parameters=
    'pretrain_model_name_or_path=bert-small-uncased'
```

Code 2: AppZoo for training a BERT-based text classifier using EasyNLP.

ety of mainstream or innovative NLP applications for users. AppZoo provides rich modules for users to build different application pipelines, including language modeling, feature vectorization, sequence classification, text matching, sequence labeling and many others. An example of training a text classifier using AppZoo is shown in Code 2.

3.3 In-house Developed Algorithms

In this section, we introduce in-house developed algorithms in EasyNLP. All these algorithms have been tested in real-world applications.

3.3.1 Knowledge-enhanced Pre-training

Knowledge-enhanced pre-training improves the performance of PTMs by injecting the relational facts from knowledge bases. Yet, a lot of existing works require additional knowledge encoders during pre-training, fine-tuning and inference (Zhang et al., 2019; Liu et al., 2020; Sun et al., 2020).

The proposed DKPLM paradigm (Zhang et al., 2022) decomposes the knowledge injection process. For DKPLM, knowledge injection is only applied during pre-training, without introducing extra parameters as knowledge encoders, alleviating the significant computational burdens for users. Meanwhile, during fine-tuning and inference stages, our model can be utilized in the same way as that of BERT (Devlin et al., 2019) and other plain PTMs, which facilitates the model fine-tuning and deployment in EasyNLP and other environments. Specifically, the DKPLM framework introduces three novel techniques for knowledge-enhanced pre-training. It recognizes long-tail entities from text corpora for knowledge injection only, avoiding learning too much redundant and irrelevant information from knowledge bases (Zhang et al., 2021). Next, the representations of entities are replaced by "pseudo token representations" derived from knowledge bases, without introducing any extra parameters to DKPLM. Finally, a relational knowledge decoding task is introduced to force the model to understand what knowledge is injected.

In EasyNLP, we provide the entire pre-training pipeline of DKPLM for users. In addition, a collection of pre-trained DKPLMs for specific domains have been registered in ModelZoo for supporting domain-specific applications.

3.3.2 Few-shot Learning for PTMs

For low-resource scenarios, prompt-based learning leverages prompts as task guidance for effective few-shot fine-tuning. In EasyNLP, to facilitate easy few-shot learning, we integrate PET (Schick and Schütze, 2021) and P-Tuning (Liu et al., 2021b) into AppZoo that allow users call the algorithms in the similar way compared to standard fine-tuning.

It should be further noted that either PET or P-Tuning require the explicit handcraft of verbalizers, which is a tedious process and may lead to unstable results. Our CP-Tuning approach (Xu et al., 2022) enables few-shot fine-tuning PTMs without the manual engineering of task-specific prompts and verbalizers. A pair-wise cost-sensitive contrastive learning is introduced to achieve verbalizer-free class mapping by learning to distinguish different classes. Users can also explore CP-Tuning in AppZoo for any tasks that classical prompt-based methods support.

3.3.3 Knowledge Distillation for PTMs

The large model size and the long inference time hinder the deployment of large-scale PTMs to resource-constrained applications. In EasyNLP, we provide a complete learning pipeline for knowledge distillation, including data augmentation for training sets, logits extraction from teacher models and distilled training of student models.

In addition, we notice that a majority of existing approaches focus on a single domain only. The proposed MetaKD algorithm (Pan et al., 2021) explicitly leverages the cross-domain transferable knowledge to improve the accuracy of student models. It first obtain a meta-teacher model to capture transferable knowledge at both instance-level and feature-level from multiple domains. Next, a meta-distillation algorithm is employed to learn single-domain student models with selective signals from the meta-teacher. In EasyNLP, the MetaKD process is implemented as a general feature for any types of BERT-style PTMs.

PTM	AFQMC	CMNLI	CSL	IFLYTEK	OCNLI	TNEWS	WSC	Average
BERT-base	72.17	75.74	80.93	60.22	78.31	57.52	75.33	71.46
BERT-large	72.89	77.62	81.14	60.70	78.95	57.77	78.18	72.46
RoBERTa-base	73.10	80.75	80.07	60.98	80.75	57.93	86.84	74.35
RoBERTa-large	74.81	80.52	82.60	61.37	82.49	58.54	87.50	75.40
MacBERT-base	74.23	80.65	81.70	61.14	80.65	57.65	80.26	73.75
MacBERT-large	74.37	81.19	83.70	62.05	81.65	58.45	86.84	75.46

Table 2: CLUE performance of BERT, RoBERTa and MacBERT fine-tuned with EasyNLP (%).

PTM	MNLI	QNLI	QQP	RTE	SST-2	MRPC	CoLA	STSB	Average
BERT-base	84.8	91.4	91.1	68.3	92.5	88.1	55.3	89.6	82.6
BERT-large	86.6	92.4	91.2	70.8	93.4	88.2	61.1	90.1	84.2
RoBERTa-base	87.3	92.5	92.1	77.3	94.9	90.2	63.9	91.1	86.2
RoBERTa-large	90.1	94.5	92.3	87.1	96.4	91.0	67.8	92.3	88.9

Table 3: GLUE performance of BERT and RoBERTa fine-tuned with EasyNLP (%).

4 System Evaluations and Applications

In this section, we empirically examine the effectiveness and efficiency of the EasyNLP toolkit on both public datasets and industrial applications.

4.1 CLUE and GLUE Benchmarks

In order to validate the effectiveness of EasyNLP on model fine-tuning, we fine-tune PTMs on the CLUE and GLUE benchmarks (Wang et al., 2019; Xu et al., 2020). For all tasks, we use a limited hyper-parameter search space, with batch sizes in $\{8, 16, 32, 48\}$, sequence length in $\{128, 256\}$ and learning rates in $\{1e-5, 2e-5, 3e-5, 4e-5, 5e-5\}$. The underlying PTMs include BERT (Devlin et al., 2019) and RoBERTa (Liu et al., 2019). We also evaluate MacBERT (Cui et al., 2020) for the Chinese benchmark CLUE. We report the results over the development sets of each task in the two benchmarks, shown in Tables 2 and 3, respectively. The obtained comparable performance has shown the reliability of EasyNLP, which achieves similar performance compared to other open-source frameworks and their original implementations.

4.2 Evaluation of Knowledge-enhanced Pre-training

We report the performance of DKPLM over zero-shot knowledge probing tasks, including LAMA (Petroni et al., 2019) and LAMA-UHN (Pörner et al., 2019), with the results summarized in Table 4. Compared to strong baselines (i.e., CoLAKE (Sun et al., 2020) K-Adapter (Wang et al., 2021a) and KEPLER (Wang et al., 2021b)), we see that DKPLM achieves state-of-the-art results over three datasets (+1.57% on average). The result of DKPLM is only 0.1% lower than K-Adapter, without using any T-REx training data and larger backbones. We can see that our pre-training process based on DKPLM can effectively store and understand factual relations from knowledge bases.

Industrial Applications. Based on the proposed DKPLM framework (Zhang et al., 2022), we have pre-trained a series of domain-specific PTMs to provide model service inside Alibaba Group, such as medical and finance domains, and observed consistent improvement in downstream NLP tasks. For example, the medical-domain DKPLM improves the accuracy of a medical named entity recognition task by over 3%, compared to the standard BERT model (Devlin et al., 2019). The pre-trained model (named `pai-dkplm-medical-base-zh`) has also been released in our EasyNLP ModelZoo.

4.3 Evaluations of Few-shot Learning

We compare CP-Tuning (Xu et al., 2022) against several prompt-based fine-tuning approaches including PET (Schick and Schütze, 2021), LM-BFF (Gao et al., 2021) (in three settings where "Auto T", "Auto L" and "Auto T+L" refer to the prompt-tuned PTM with automatically generated templates, label words and both, respectively) and P-Tuning (Liu et al., 2021b). The experiments are conducted over several text classification datasets in a 16-shot learning setting. The underlying PTM is RoBERTa (Liu et al., 2019). Readers can refer to Xu et al. (2022) for more details. From the results in Table 5, we can see that the performance gains of CP-Tuning over all the tasks are consistent, compared to state-of-the-art methods.

Industrial Applications. For business customer

Dataset	ELMo	BERT	RoBERTa	CoLAKE	K-Adapter*	KEPLER	DKPLM
Google-RE	2.2%	11.4%	5.3%	9.5%	7.0%	7.3%	**10.8%**
UHN-Google-RE	2.3%	5.7%	2.2%	4.9%	3.7%	4.1%	**5.4%**
T-REx	0.2%	32.5%	24.7%	28.8%	29.1%	24.6%	**32.0%**
UHN-T-REx	0.2%	23.3%	17.0%	20.4%	**23.0%**	17.1%	22.9%

Table 4: The performance on LAMA knowledge probing datasets. Note that K-Adapter is trained based on a large-scale model and uses a subset of T-REx as its training data.

Method	SST-2	MR	CR	MRPC	QQP	QNLI	RTE	SUBJ	**Avg.**
Standard Fine-tuning	78.62	76.17	72.48	64.40	63.01	62.32	52.28	86.82	69.51
PET	92.06	87.13	87.13	66.23	70.34	64.38	65.56	91.28	78.01
LM-BFF (Auto T)	90.60	87.57	90.76	66.72	65.25	68.87	65.99	91.61	78.42
LM-BFF (Auto L)	90.55	85.51	91.11	67.75	70.92	66.22	66.35	90.48	78.61
LM-BFF (Auto T+L)	91.42	86.84	90.40	66.81	61.61	61.89	66.79	90.72	77.06
P-tuning	91.42	87.41	90.90	71.23	66.77	63.42	67.15	89.10	78.43
CP-Tuning	**93.35**	**89.43**	**91.57**	**72.60**	**73.56**	**69.22**	**67.22**	**92.27**	**81.24**

Table 5: Comparison between CP-Tuning and baselines over the testing sets in terms of accuracy (%).

Method	Amazon	MNLI
BERT-s	87.9	81.9
BERT-mix	89.5	84.4
BERT-mtl	89.8	84.2
BERT-s → TinyBERT	86.7	79.3
BERT-mix → TinyBERT	87.3	79.6
BERT-mtl → TinyBERT	87.7	79.7
MetaKD	**89.4**	**80.4**

Table 6: Evaluation of MetaKD over Amazon reviews and MNLI in terms of averaged accuracy (%).

service, it is necessary to extract the fine-grained attributes and entities from texts, which may involve a large number of classess with few training data available. By applying our algorithm in EasyNLP, the accuracy scores of entity and attribute extraction are improved by 2% and 5%. In addition, our few-shot toolkit produces the best performance on the FewCLUE benchmark (Xu et al., 2021).

4.4 Evaluations of Knowledge Distillation

We further report the performance of MetaKD (Pan et al., 2021) on Amazon reviews (Blitzer et al., 2007) and MNLI (Williams et al., 2018), where the two datasets contain four and five domain instances, respectively. In the experiments, we train the meta-teacher over multi-domain training sets, and distill the meta-teacher to each of all the domains. The teacher model is BERT-base (with 110M parameters), while the student model is BERT-tiny (with 14.5M parameters). Table 6 shows the performance of baselines and MetaKD, in terms of averaged accuracy across domains. BERT-s refers to a single BERT teacher trained on each domain. BERT-mix is one BERT teacher trained on the mixture of all domain data. BERT-mtl is one teacher trained by multi-task learning over all domains. For distillation, "→ TinyBERT" means using the KD method described in Jiao et al. (2020b) to distill the corresponding teacher model. The results show that MetaKD significantly reduces the model size while preserving a similar performance. For more details, we refer the readers to Pan et al. (2021).

Industrial Applications. Distilled PTMs have been widely used inside Alibaba Group due to the high QPS requirements of online e-commerce applications. For example, in the AliMe chatbot (Qiu et al., 2017), we distill the BERT-based query intent detection model from the base version to the tiny version, resulting in 7.2x inference speedup while the accuracy is only decreased by 1%.

5 Conclusion

In this paper, we introduced EasyNLP, a toolkit that is designed to make it easy to develop and deploy deep NLP applications based on PTMs. It supports a comprehensive suite of NLP algorithms and features knowledge-enhanced pre-training, knowledge distillation and few-shot learning functionalities for large-scale PTMs. Currently, EasyNLP has powered a number of business units inside Alibaba Cloud and provided NLP service on the cloud. The toolkit has been open-sourced to promote research and development for NLP applications.

Broader Impact

EasyNLP is a comprehensive toolkit for building various NLP applications to support industrial scenarios. It has been seamlessly integrated into the PAI products, and has been released to the open-source community. EasyNLP is also highly beneficial for academia, as it integrates state-of-the-art methods and models to make it easy for researchers to benchmark and develop their own algorithms.

Acknowledgments

The authors would like to thank Haojie Pan, Peng Li, Boyu Hou, Xiaoqing Chen, Xiaodan Wang, Xiangru Zhu and many other members of the Alibaba PAI team for their contribution and suggestions on building the EasyNLP toolkit. This work is also partially supported by Alibaba Group through Alibaba Innovative Research Program and Alibaba Research Intern Program.

References

John Blitzer, Mark Dredze, and Fernando Pereira. 2007. Biographies, bollywood, boom-boxes and blenders: Domain adaptation for sentiment classification. In *ACL*.

Tom B. Brown, Benjamin Mann, Nick Ryder, Melanie Subbiah, Jared Kaplan, Prafulla Dhariwal, Arvind Neelakantan, Pranav Shyam, Girish Sastry, Amanda Askell, Sandhini Agarwal, Ariel Herbert-Voss, Gretchen Krueger, Tom Henighan, Rewon Child, Aditya Ramesh, Daniel M. Ziegler, Jeffrey Wu, Clemens Winter, Christopher Hesse, Mark Chen, Eric Sigler, Mateusz Litwin, Scott Gray, Benjamin Chess, Jack Clark, Christopher Berner, Sam McCandlish, Alec Radford, Ilya Sutskever, and Dario Amodei. 2020. Language models are few-shot learners. In *NeurIPS*.

Aakanksha Chowdhery, Sharan Narang, Jacob Devlin, Maarten Bosma, Gaurav Mishra, Adam Roberts, Paul Barham, Hyung Won Chung, Charles Sutton, Sebastian Gehrmann, Parker Schuh, Kensen Shi, Sasha Tsvyashchenko, Joshua Maynez, Abhishek Rao, Parker Barnes, Yi Tay, Noam Shazeer, Vinodkumar Prabhakaran, Emily Reif, Nan Du, Ben Hutchinson, Reiner Pope, James Bradbury, Jacob Austin, Michael Isard, Guy Gur-Ari, Pengcheng Yin, Toju Duke, Anselm Levskaya, Sanjay Ghemawat, Sunipa Dev, Henryk Michalewski, Xavier Garcia, Vedant Misra, Kevin Robinson, Liam Fedus, Denny Zhou, Daphne Ippolito, David Luan, Hyeontaek Lim, Barret Zoph, Alexander Spiridonov, Ryan Sepassi, David Dohan, Shivani Agrawal, Mark Omernick, Andrew M. Dai, Thanumalayan Sankaranarayana Pillai, Marie Pellat, Aitor Lewkowycz, Erica Moreira, Rewon Child, Oleksandr Polozov, Katherine Lee, Zongwei Zhou, Xuezhi Wang, Brennan Saeta, Mark Diaz, Orhan Firat, Michele Catasta, Jason Wei, Kathy Meier-Hellstern, Douglas Eck, Jeff Dean, Slav Petrov, and Noah Fiedel. 2022. Palm: Scaling language modeling with pathways. *CoRR*, abs/2204.02311.

Yiming Cui, Wanxiang Che, Ting Liu, Bing Qin, Shijin Wang, and Guoping Hu. 2020. Revisiting pre-trained models for chinese natural language processing. In *EMNLP (Findings)*, pages 657–668.

Zihang Dai, Zhilin Yang, Yiming Yang, Jaime G. Carbonell, Quoc Viet Le, and Ruslan Salakhutdinov. 2019. Transformer-xl: Attentive language models beyond a fixed-length context. In *ACL*, pages 2978–2988.

Jacob Devlin, Ming-Wei Chang, Kenton Lee, and Kristina Toutanova. 2019. BERT: pre-training of deep bidirectional transformers for language understanding. In *NAACL-HLT*, pages 4171–4186.

Tianyu Gao, Adam Fisch, and Danqi Chen. 2021. Making pre-trained language models better few-shot learners. In *ACL/IJCNLP*, pages 3816–3830.

Geoffrey E. Hinton, Oriol Vinyals, and Jeffrey Dean. 2015. Distilling the knowledge in a neural network. *CoRR*, abs/1503.02531.

Xiaoqi Jiao, Yichun Yin, Lifeng Shang, Xin Jiang, Xiao Chen, Linlin Li, Fang Wang, and Qun Liu. 2020a. Tinybert: Distilling BERT for natural language understanding. In *EMNLP (Findings)*, pages 4163–4174.

Xiaoqi Jiao, Yichun Yin, Lifeng Shang, Xin Jiang, Xiao Chen, Linlin Li, Fang Wang, and Qun Liu. 2020b. Tinybert: Distilling BERT for natural language understanding. In *EMNLP (Findings)*, pages 4163–4174.

Yoon Kim. 2014. Convolutional neural networks for sentence classification. In *EMNLP*, pages 1746–1751.

Pengfei Liu, Weizhe Yuan, Jinlan Fu, Zhengbao Jiang, Hiroaki Hayashi, and Graham Neubig. 2021a. Pre-train, prompt, and predict: A systematic survey of prompting methods in natural language processing. *CoRR*, abs/2107.13586.

Weijie Liu, Peng Zhou, Zhe Zhao, Zhiruo Wang, Qi Ju, Haotang Deng, and Ping Wang. 2020. K-BERT: enabling language representation with knowledge graph. In *AAAI*, pages 2901–2908.

Xiao Liu, Yanan Zheng, Zhengxiao Du, Ming Ding, Yujie Qian, Zhilin Yang, and Jie Tang. 2021b. GPT understands, too. *CoRR*, abs/2103.10385.

Yinhan Liu, Myle Ott, Naman Goyal, Jingfei Du, Mandar Joshi, Danqi Chen, Omer Levy, Mike Lewis, Luke Zettlemoyer, and Veselin Stoyanov. 2019. Roberta: A robustly optimized BERT pretraining approach. *CoRR*, abs/1907.11692.

Haojie Pan, Chengyu Wang, Minghui Qiu, Yichang Zhang, Yaliang Li, and Jun Huang. 2021. Meta-kd: A meta knowledge distillation framework for language model compression across domains. In *ACL/IJCNLP*, pages 3026–3036.

Fabio Petroni, Tim Rocktäschel, Sebastian Riedel, Patrick S. H. Lewis, Anton Bakhtin, Yuxiang Wu, and Alexander H. Miller. 2019. Language models as knowledge bases? In *EMNLP-IJCNLP*, pages 2463–2473.

Nina Pörner, Ulli Waltinger, and Hinrich Schütze. 2019. BERT is not a knowledge base (yet): Factual knowledge vs. name-based reasoning in unsupervised QA. *CoRR*, abs/1911.03681.

Minghui Qiu, Feng-Lin Li, Siyu Wang, Xing Gao, Yan Chen, Weipeng Zhao, Haiqing Chen, Jun Huang, and Wei Chu. 2017. Alime chat: A sequence to sequence and rerank based chatbot engine. In *ACL*, pages 498–503.

Minghui Qiu, Peng Li, Chengyu Wang, Haojie Pan, Ang Wang, Cen Chen, Xianyan Jia, Yaliang Li, Jun Huang, Deng Cai, and Wei Lin. 2021. Easytransfer: A simple and scalable deep transfer learning platform for NLP applications. In *CIKM*, pages 4075–4084.

Xipeng Qiu, Tianxiang Sun, Yige Xu, Yunfan Shao, Ning Dai, and Xuanjing Huang. 2020. Pre-trained models for natural language processing: A survey. *CoRR*, abs/2003.08271.

Colin Raffel, Noam Shazeer, Adam Roberts, Katherine Lee, Sharan Narang, Michael Matena, Yanqi Zhou, Wei Li, and Peter J. Liu. 2020. Exploring the limits of transfer learning with a unified text-to-text transformer. *J. Mach. Learn. Res.*, 21:140:1–140:67.

Victor Sanh, Lysandre Debut, Julien Chaumond, and Thomas Wolf. 2019. Distilbert, a distilled version of BERT: smaller, faster, cheaper and lighter. *CoRR*, abs/1910.01108.

Timo Schick and Hinrich Schütze. 2021. Exploiting cloze-questions for few-shot text classification and natural language inference. In *EACL*, pages 255–269.

Siqi Sun, Yu Cheng, Zhe Gan, and Jingjing Liu. 2019. Patient knowledge distillation for BERT model compression. In *EMNLP-IJCNLP*, pages 4322–4331.

Tianxiang Sun, Yunfan Shao, Xipeng Qiu, Qipeng Guo, Yaru Hu, Xuanjing Huang, and Zheng Zhang. 2020. Colake: Contextualized language and knowledge embedding. In *COLING*, pages 3660–3670.

Alex Wang, Amanpreet Singh, Julian Michael, Felix Hill, Omer Levy, and Samuel R. Bowman. 2019. GLUE: A multi-task benchmark and analysis platform for natural language understanding. In *ICLR*.

Ruize Wang, Duyu Tang, Nan Duan, Zhongyu Wei, Xuanjing Huang, Jianshu Ji, Guihong Cao, Daxin Jiang, and Ming Zhou. 2021a. K-adapter: Infusing knowledge into pre-trained models with adapters. In *ACL*, pages 1405–1418.

Xiaozhi Wang, Tianyu Gao, Zhaocheng Zhu, Zhiyuan Liu, Juanzi Li, and Jian Tang. 2021b. KEPLER: A unified model for knowledge embedding and pre-trained language representation. *Trans. Assoc. Comput. Linguistics*, 9:176–194.

Adina Williams, Nikita Nangia, and Samuel R. Bowman. 2018. A broad-coverage challenge corpus for sentence understanding through inference. In *NAACL-HLT*, pages 1112–1122.

Liang Xu, Hai Hu, Xuanwei Zhang, Lu Li, Chenjie Cao, Yudong Li, Yechen Xu, Kai Sun, Dian Yu, Cong Yu, Yin Tian, Qianqian Dong, Weitang Liu, Bo Shi, Yiming Cui, Junyi Li, Jun Zeng, Rongzhao Wang, Weijian Xie, Yanting Li, Yina Patterson, Zuoyu Tian, Yiwen Zhang, He Zhou, Shaoweihua Liu, Zhe Zhao, Qipeng Zhao, Cong Yue, Xinrui Zhang, Zhengliang Yang, Kyle Richardson, and Zhenzhong Lan. 2020. CLUE: A chinese language understanding evaluation benchmark. In *COLING*, pages 4762–4772.

Ziyun Xu, Chengyu Wang, Peng Li, Yang Li, Ming Wang, Boyu Hou, Minghui Qiu, Chengguang Tang, and Jun Huang. 2021. When few-shot learning meets large-scale knowledge-enhanced pre-training: Alibaba at fewclue. In *NLPCC*, pages 422–433.

Ziyun Xu, Chengyu Wang, Minghui Qiu, Fuli Luo, Runxin Xu, Songfang Huang, and Jun Huang. 2022. Making pre-trained language models end-to-end few-shot learners with contrastive prompt tuning. *CoRR*, abs/2204.00166.

Zhilin Yang, Zihang Dai, Yiming Yang, Jaime G. Carbonell, Ruslan Salakhutdinov, and Quoc V. Le. 2019. Xlnet: Generalized autoregressive pretraining for language understanding. In *NeurIPS*, pages 5754–5764.

Ningyu Zhang, Shumin Deng, Xu Cheng, Xi Chen, Yichi Zhang, Wei Zhang, and Huajun Chen. 2021. Drop redundant, shrink irrelevant: Selective knowledge injection for language pretraining. In *IJCAI*, pages 4007–4014.

Taolin Zhang, Chengyu Wang, Nan Hu, Minghui Qiu, Chengguang Tang, Xiaofeng He, and Jun Huang. 2022. DKPLM: decomposable knowledge-enhanced pre-trained language model for natural language understanding. In *AAAI*.

Zhengyan Zhang, Xu Han, Zhiyuan Liu, Xin Jiang, Maosong Sun, and Qun Liu. 2019. ERNIE: enhanced language representation with informative entities. In *ACL*, pages 1441–1451.

An Explainable Toolbox for Evaluating Pre-trained Vision-Language Models

Tiancheng Zhao[1,2], Tianqi Zhang[3], Mingwei Zhu[3], Haozhan Shen[3], Kyusong Lee[1,2], Xiaopeng Lu[1,2], Jianwei Yin[3]
Om Research Lab, Binjiang Institute of Zhejiang University[1]
Linker Technology Research Co. Ltd[2]
College of Computer Science and Technology, Zhejiang University[3]
{tianchez, kyusongl}@zju-bj.com, lu_xiaopeng@hzlh.com
{zhang_tq, zhumw, cnfighting, zjuyjw}@zju.edu.cn

Abstract

We introduce VL-CheckList, a toolbox for evaluating Vision-Language Pretraining (VLP) models, along with a benchmark dataset for fine-grained VLP model analysis. Most existing VLP models evaluate their performance by comparing the fine-tuned downstream task performance. However, only average downstream task accuracy provides little information about the pros and cons of each VLP method. In this paper, we demonstrate how minor input changes in language and vision will affect the prediction outputs. We also provide a guideline for the research community to utilizes and contributes to this toolbox. Lastly, a case study based on VL-CheckList is conducted to analyze one of the representative VLP models. Data and code are available at `https://github.com/om-ai-lab/VL-CheckList`

1 Introduction

The ability to quickly iterate various methods and obtain insightful feedback is crucial for successful research. For production machine learning (ML) system, comprehensive testing before deployment is crucial for reliable user experience. Therefore, explainable ML evaluation has emerged to complement benchmark evaluation (Bolya et al., 2020; Ribeiro et al., 2020; Du et al., 2022), which strives to provide an interpretable evaluation of a ML systems and analyze the system from a number of disentangled aspects (Bolya et al., 2020).

The advantages of explainable evaluation vs. typical benchmark evaluation include: (1) downstream task performance only provides a black box score and it is difficult to obtain insights for improving a system. (2) typical dataset is not designed to test models' robustness against extreme corner cases, which are however crucial for many real-world tasks, e.g. autonomous driving.

Given the importance of explainable ML evaluation, this paper concerns about Vision-Language Pretraining (VLP) models. VLP models have rapidly improved (Li et al., 2020; Radford et al., 2021; Li et al., 2021; Zhao et al., 2022), thanks to the emergence of multimodal transformers (Vaswani et al., 2017) and the availability of large paired image-text dataset (Sharma et al., 2018; Changpinyo et al., 2021). Many proposed VLP models have aided in achieving the state-of-the-art performance of a variety of downstream multimodal tasks, ranging from visual QA (Lu et al., 2019), multimodal retrieval (Lu et al., 2021) to visual grounding (Kamath et al., 2021) and many others. On the other hand, the current defacto method to evaluate a VLP model is based on the fine-tuned downstream tasks performance, which is insufficient due to the limitations of benchmark evaluation.

To address this challenge, this paper introduces VL-CheckList, an explainable framework that comprehensively evaluates VLP models, facilitates deeper understanding, and inspires new ideas for improvement. The core principle of VL-CheckList are: (1) evaluate a VLP model's fundamental capabilities instead of its performance on applications (2) disentangle capabilities into relatively independent variables that are easier to analyze. Specifically, we choose Image-Text-Matching (ITM) as the main target of evaluation since it is perhaps the most universal pretraining objective that appear in all VLP methods (Li et al., 2019a, 2020; Radford et al., 2021; Li et al., 2021). We then propose a taxonomy that divides the capabilities of VLP systems into three categories: object, attribute and relation. Each aspect is then further divided into more fine-

Proceedings of the The 2022 Conference on Empirical Methods in Natural Language Processing: System Demonstrations, pages 30 - 37
December 7-11, 2022

grained variables, e.g. attribute is composed of color, material, and size, etc. Then, a linguistic-aware negative sample sampling strategy is proposed to create "hard negative" that challenges a VLP model's discriminative power against small changes in the input space. Lastly, VL-CheckList is implemented as a toolbox that allows the research community to plug into their evaluation pipeline.

2 Related Work

Benchmark evaluation is a common method to compare different ML models in previous research (Rajpurkar et al., 2016; Bowman et al., 2015; Wang et al., 2018). However, researchers have reported several limitations of the existing VLP benchmark. 1) the objects of interest have a biased distribution of size and location, i.e., tend to be large objects that appeared in the center region. 2) benchmark evaluation returns only a plain score instead of fine-grained details on the taxonomy. Therefore, it is difficult to understand the strengths and weaknesses of a model without a comprehensive analysis. Recent studies show even the state-of-the-art systems that achieved better scores than humans, may still be insufficient in real-world applications (Ribeiro et al., 2020). Thus, researchers have attempted to evaluate ML models with more fine-grained details and avoid bias on the test set.

One of the successful tools for the qualitative analysis of natural language processing (NLP) is CheckList (Ribeiro et al., 2020) which evaluates general linguistic capabilities and revealed weaknesses in several state-of-the-art NLP models and commercial applications. In computer vision, the Vision CheckList was proposed to help system designers to understand model capabilities (Du et al., 2022). They offered a set of transformation operations to generate diverse test samples of different test types, such as rotation, replacing image patches, blur, and shuffle. However, target objects in the transformed images are unchanged, still center and large.

The idea of the CheckList has also been applied other fields, e.g. evaluating Reinforcement Learning (RL) agents (Lam et al., 2022), Dynabench (Kiela et al., 2021) was proposed to generate dynamic benchmark datasets. It overcomes the problem that the existing benchmark fails to cover fundamental linguistic challenges. TIDE (Bolya et al., 2020) is a tool to analyze the errors of object detection. It defines critical error types and shows a comprehensive analysis.

3 VL-CheckList

An intuitive approach to evaluate multi-modal systems is to check if a model correctly predicts alignment between different modalities. We choose image-text matching (ITM) to check the alignment between vision and language for the following reasons. Specifically, ITM is defined as the function that outputs the probability of an image i is matched to a sentence t.

The ITM task is used as an effective and universal pretraining objective in almost all VLP models (Li et al., 2020). The ITM task is also model agnostic and applies to all multi-modal fusion architectures. Thus, we exploit the ITM to fairly compare the VLP models without finetuning them on downstream tasks.

The basic principle of the VL-CheckList is to probe the model's robustness on the negative examples. A robust VLP model should be able to return a higher ITM score for the positive image-text pair than the negative example on the ITM head. We perturb the one-side modality to manipulate them and compare the score with original samples. LV-CheckList offers both language-side and vision-side variations.

3.1 Language Variation

To provide a fine-grained analysis of the robustness of the text-side, we build evaluation taxonomies that are selected based on common mistakes or frequent usage. Based on the common issues in VLP models, the proposed framework places the three input properties (object, attribute, and relation) as the top layer of the evaluation taxonomy.

Object: A strong VLP model is supposed to recognize whether or not the objects mentioned in a text exist in the image. Therefore, if we replace objects in the correct text with some other random noun phrases, a VLP model should give it a lower ITM score than the original sentence. Furthermore, a strong VLP model should be able to recognize the existence of objects, regardless of its location and sizes. Thus, we further evaluate the robustness Object ITM by testing location variance (e.g., center, middle, and margin) and size variance (e.g., small, large, medium), specifically:

$$\text{loc}(x, y) = \begin{cases} \textit{center} & \text{if } \frac{y}{x} \leq \frac{1}{3} \\ \textit{mid} & \text{if } \frac{1}{3} < \frac{y}{x} \leq \frac{2}{3} \\ \textit{margin} & \text{otherwise} \end{cases}$$

where, x is the half-length of the diagonal of the full image $x = \frac{\sqrt{w^2+h^2}}{2}$. and y is the distance between its central point and the central point of the full image.

To get the size of an object, we use the object area information (i.e., the bounding box of height multiplies the width).

$$\text{size}(x) = \begin{cases} \textit{small} & \text{if } \textit{area} \leq S \\ \textit{medium} & \text{if } S < \textit{area} \leq M \\ \textit{large} & \text{otherwise} \end{cases}$$

where, $area = w*h$, S denotes small size and M is the medium size. We set $S = 1024, M = 9216$ in this paper.

Attribute: Determining specific attributes for any object is very challenging. The attribute generally contains color, material, size, state, and action.

- Size: replace the size expression like small, big, and medium with another (e.g., There is a big apple vs. there is a small apple)
- Material: replace a material word in the sentence (e.g., a metal box vs. a wood box)
- State: replace the state expression, such as cleanliness and newness (e.g., a man with dry hair vs. a man with wet hair).
- Action: replace the action-related word in the text (e.g., a standing person vs. a sitting person).
- Color: replace the color word in the text (e.g., A red apple is on the table vs. A green apple is on the table)

Relation: Relation cares about the interaction between two objects. It covers replacing the predicate in a triple (e.g., subject, predicate, object), where the subject and object are both objects in the image. A strong VLP ITM head should assign a higher score to text matching the pair-wise object interaction. Further, we divide prediction into spatial and action. If a predicate is one of the spatial prepositions (e.g., in, on, at, etc), it is sub-categorized as 'spatial'; otherwise, it is labeled 'action.'

- Spatial: If a model can predict spatial relation between two objects (e.g, <cat, on, table> vs. <cat, under, table>).
- Action: If a model can predict other relation than a spatial preposition, usually action verbs like run, jump, kick, eat, break, cry, or smile (e.g., <cat, catch, fish> vs. <cat, eat, fish>)

3.2 Vision Variation

A strong VLP model should be able to return consistent scores when an image is transformed with augmentation techniques such as rotation, shift, flip, random brightness, etc. However, previous augmentations are applied on the entire image-level. We provide the object-level data augmentation by combining cropped objects and image background. The generated images are utilized to investigate the robustness of the model outputs in various locations and sizes of the target object. Strong VLP models should be able to return consistent scores regardless of the location and size of target objects unless the language description is related to location and size (e.g., an apple is the left side of the tree, an apple is small). We allow to input cropped objects and background images and randomly place the target objects from margin to center with various sizes to probe the robustness. The goal of the LV-CheckList on the vision-variations is to show how simple input changes such as object location and size will affect the prediction outputs in the VL-CheckList Demo.

4 Detailed User Guideline

This section describes a guideline for researchers to use and contribute to the VL-CheckList project.

First, users can install from GitHub[1] or from `pip install vl-checklist`. We further provide a HuggingFace demo for people to try out different VLP models[2]. Then the following is a step-by-step guideline to use VL-CheckList.

[1] github.com/om-ai-lab/VL-CheckList

[2] huggingface.co/spaces/omlab/VL_checklist_demo

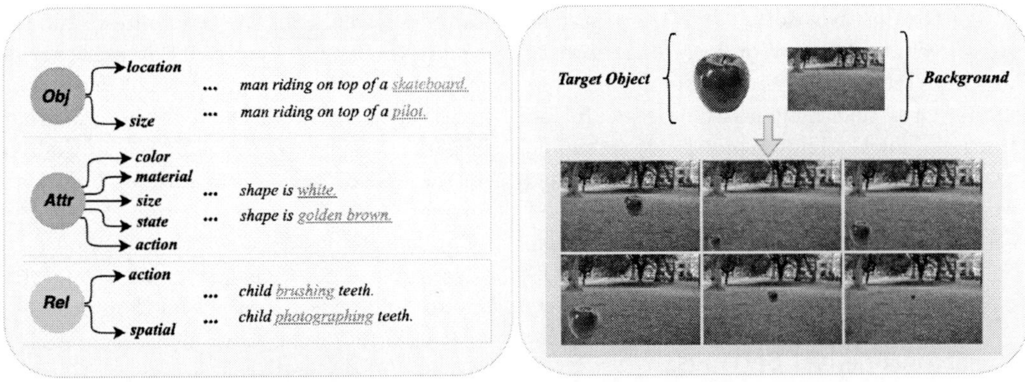

(a) Language Variation *(b) Vision Variation*

Figure 1: Language Variation: negative samples are based on object, attribute and relation. Vision Variation: a user inputs target objects and backgrounds and evaluates the various synthesized images

1) Define Corpus: a user defines a corpus in the yaml config file. We provide four initial pre-processed corpora using the semi-structured dataset such as VG (Krishna et al., 2017), SWiG (Pratt et al., 2020), VAW (Pham et al., 2021) and HAKE (Li et al., 2019b). We build a benchmark dataset for each capability test in the proposed framework. We provide the pre-processed datasets in the *corpus* folder of our Github page. An example of the corpus config yaml file is as follows:

```
ANNO_PATH: "Attr/action.json"
IMG_ROOT: "vg/"
TYPE: "TUPLE_JSON"
```

ANNO_PATH is the specific Json file path that includes positive and negative captions and the specific image path.

The data type is TUPLE_JSON. We converted the corpus into list of image path and captions(positive and negative), in the format of a list of `[[{image_path:str, "POS":pos_captions:list, "NEG": neg_captions:list}] . . . ]`

2) Define evaluation configuration: Users can specify the evaluation settings in another yaml to define evaluation in detail as the following example:

```
MAX_NUM: 2000
MODEL_NAME: "CLIP"
BATCH_SIZE: 4
TASK: "itc"
DATA:
  TYPES: ["Object/Location/mid"]
  TEST_DATA: ["vg_obj"]
OUTPUT:
  DIR: "output/clip"
```

The "MAX_NUM" is the maximum number of data points and the "MODEL_NAME" needs to be specified. Appropriate "BATCH_SIZE" should be input based on the GPU resources. The "TASK" can be either "ITC" or "ITM". The "ITC" score compares models' scores on both positive and negative captions. It counts as a true positive when the score on the original is higher than the negatively transformed one. The "ITM" is predicting each image and a caption. It is called the true positive when a softmax score on a positive example on the image is higher than the threshold of 0.5. The Data tag consists of TYPES and TEST_DATA. The TYPES is the storage paths of the "ymal_files". In the top-level directory, we can divide it into three categories: Object, Relation, and Attribute. For Swig, Vg, etc., there are multiple data subsets, so the data subset type should be filled in the TEST_DATA. We can specify the evaluation data, output directory, and format as the example above. After defining a config file, users can simply start the evaluation as follows:.

```
from engine import Model
from vl_checklist import Evaluate
if __name__ == '__main__':
    model = Model('model.ckpt')
    eval = Evaluate("sample.yaml",
                    model=model)
    eval.start()
```

3) Define Model: Users can import VL-CheckList to their projects (e.g., `import vl_checklist`) and need to implement one model class that includes the essential functions, "predict". The predict function should return probabilities on each pair of images and texts. We included several representative models for quick comparisons, such as ViLT (Kim et al., 2021), ALBEF (Li et al., 2021), OSCAR (Li et al., 2020), etc as example projects.

5 Experimental Settings

In this section, we profile one of the most representative VLP models, CLIP (Radford et al., 2021) by testing its ability to understand an object, attribute, and relationship between a text prompt and a given image for language variations.

Metric: We return the model output scores between the text description and the generated negative samples. If the model score on the original text description is higher than the score on the generated negative samples, we regard it as positive output. We obtain the accuracy with the following equation.

$$acc = \frac{\sum_{i=0}^{i<n} f(x_i^p, x_i^n)}{N} \tag{1}$$

where, $f(x_i^p, x_i^n) = 1$ if $p(x_i^p|I_i) > p(x_i^n|I_i)$, otherwise 0. x_i^p denotes a positive sample of ith data. x_i^n means a positive sample of ith data. The N is the total number of pairs of positive and negative samples. I_i is i^{th} image data.

Data: The proposed VL-CheckList focuses on a directional expectation test, in which the label is expected to change in a certain way. For example, when there is a black bear in the photo and the text description is "A black bear is holding a stick". We can transform several variations (e.g., <a black bear → a red bear>, <a stick → an apple>, <holding → throwing>, etc). The negative sampling strategy is the essential step for unbiased evaluations. To generate hard negative examples, we use the structured text description datasets such as Visual Genome (VG) (Krishna et al., 2017), SWiG (Pratt et al., 2020), and Human Activity Knowledge Engine (HAKE) (Li et al., 2019b). The VG provides attributes, relationships, and region graphs which can make a hard negative sample by replacing one attribute in the relation in the image. The SWiG dataset provides structured semantic summaries of images with roles such as agent and tool. We generate hard negative samples by replacing one of the roles in the text description to mismatch with the image. HAKE dataset provides the relationship between instance activity and body part states (e.g., "head" inspect rear view, "right hand" hold wheel, "hip" sit on chair seat).

For the VG dataset, we first assign each attribute, object, and relation to the closet type by cosine similarity from sentence transformers. For objects and relationships, we randomly sample a corresponding instance with a cosine similarity threshold of 0.5. For attribute, we randomly sample a corresponding instance from the same attribute class with a cosine similarity threshold of 0.5. We further conduct manual correction on the generated to data to fix inappropriate data.

For vision variations, we only conduct qualitative analysis by visualizing the output scores via the GUI demo. (Figure 2).

6 Results and Analysis

In general, the ability of CLIP to understand object changes is promising when the object is center and large (see the prefix-O at Figure 3). We hypothesize that the CLIP model pays more attention to the central region and focus on salient objects, similar to the perspective of human observation. On the other hand, CLIP's ability on recognizing attribute and relation-related variants is surprisingly low, especially for Relation-spatial variations (Figure 3).

Then, We investigate whether performance can be improved by cropping the regions of interest (ROI) first and then encoding the cropped ROIs via CLIP. We extract text descriptions on each bounding box on the VG dataset to form a new image-text pair (**Image$_{local}$,text**), and construct new datasets for VG: Local$_{subj}$, Local$_{obj}$. Results on Local$_{subj}$ and Local$_{obj}$ show that Region CLIP outperforms the original CLIP (whole image encoding) by 3.9% and 5.7% respectively (Table 1). This confirms our hypothesis that the original CLIP was trained to match the entire image to a text description, without capturing the fine-grained alignment between image regions

Figure 2: A comparison of CLIP's performances of the image with a big object in the center and image with the same small object in the corner

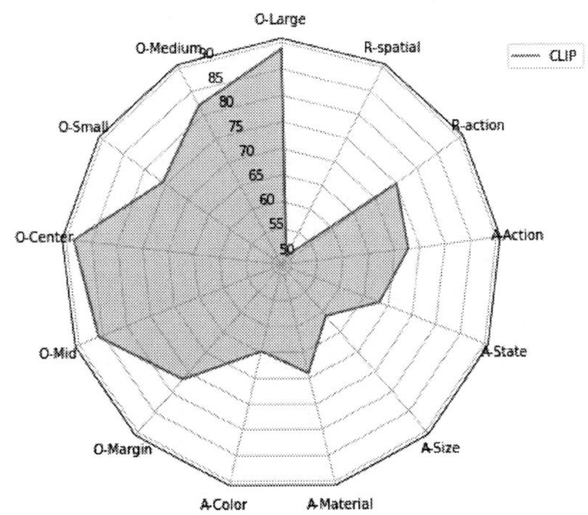

Figure 3: A radar chart for text variance on the CLIP model. (The prefix O, A, and R is Object, Attribute, and Relation respectively)

and text spans. Thus the understanding of minor objects in the image for CLIP is still challenging and explore more fine-grained region-to-text multimodal alignment is a promising direction (Zhong et al., 2022).

For vision variations, we synthesize images by changing an object's size and location. In Figure 2, the image on the left is a big apple in the center, while the image on the right is a small apple in the corner. The text prompt we input is "an apple on the grass" and "a dog on the grass". The accuracy of the left image with a big and center apple is nearly 1.00, while the right image with a small and corner apple only obtains 0.127 of accuracy. The location and size of the object in the image can significantly affect the judgment of the model.

Thus Experimental results indicate that the current benchmark evaluation reveals a gap of performance for real applications. CLIP mostly focus on objects that appeared in the center of the image and the size of the objects should be large. This limits its performance if the target objects are minor in the marginal regions for real-world applications.

Model \ VG_{data_type}	Subj	Obj
CLIP_Global	80.7	86
CLIP_Local	**84.6**	**91.7**

Table 1: Subj and Obj are two attribute subsets extracted from VG dataset. A new dataset is constructed using the bounding box tag of VG to merge and extract the region image pointed by *subj* and *obj* fields. The text remains the same as previous content **($\textbf{Image}_{local}$,text)**. It only does the expansion experiment for CLIP.

7 Conclusion

This paper introduces VL-CheckList to analyze VLP models from language and vision variations. For language variance, we evaluated from three aspects: object, attribute and relation. For vision variance, we generated synthesized images using cropped target objects and background. We found limitations of the CLIP model: 1) limited understanding for small objects in the corner 2) incompetence for recognizing relations and attributes. In the future, we plan to include more fine-grained taxonomies and synthesizing strategies into VL-CheckList and also improve existing VLP methods under the guidance of VL-CheckList report.

8 Acknowledgement

This study is supported by National Natural Science Foundation of China under Grant (No. 61825205).

References

Daniel Bolya, Sean Foley, James Hays, and Judy Hoffman. 2020. Tide: A general toolbox for identifying object detection errors. In *European Conference on Computer Vision*, pages 558–573. Springer.

Samuel Bowman, Gabor Angeli, Christopher Potts, and Christopher D Manning. 2015. A large annotated corpus for learning natural language inference. In *Proceedings of the 2015 Conference on Empirical Methods in Natural Language Processing*, pages 632–642.

Soravit Changpinyo, Piyush Sharma, Nan Ding, and Radu Soricut. 2021. Conceptual 12m: Pushing web-scale image-text pre-training to recognize long-tail visual concepts. In *Proceedings of the IEEE/CVF Conference on Computer Vision and Pattern Recognition*, pages 3558–3568.

Xin Du, Benedicte Legastelois, Bhargavi Ganesh, Ajitha Rajan, Hana Chockler, Vaishak Belle, Stuart Anderson, and Subramanian Ramamoorthy. 2022. Vision checklist: Towards testable error analysis of image models to help system designers interrogate model capabilities. *arXiv preprint arXiv:2201.11674*.

Aishwarya Kamath, Mannat Singh, Yann LeCun, Gabriel Synnaeve, Ishan Misra, and Nicolas Carion. 2021. Mdetr-modulated detection for end-to-end multi-modal understanding. In *Proceedings of the IEEE/CVF International Conference on Computer Vision*, pages 1780–1790.

Douwe Kiela, Max Bartolo, Yixin Nie, Divyansh Kaushik, Atticus Geiger, Zhengxuan Wu, Bertie Vidgen, Grusha Prasad, Amanpreet Singh, Pratik Ringshia, et al. 2021. Dynabench: Rethinking benchmarking in nlp. In *Proceedings of the 2021 Conference of the North American Chapter of the Association for Computational Linguistics: Human Language Technologies*, pages 4110–4124.

Wonjae Kim, Bokyung Son, and Ildoo Kim. 2021. Vilt: Vision-and-language transformer without convolution or region supervision. In *International Conference on Machine Learning*, pages 5583–5594. PMLR.

Ranjay Krishna, Yuke Zhu, Oliver Groth, Justin Johnson, Kenji Hata, Joshua Kravitz, Stephanie Chen, Yannis Kalantidis, Li-Jia Li, David A Shamma, et al. 2017. Visual genome: Connecting language and vision using crowdsourced dense image annotations. *International journal of computer vision*, 123(1):32–73.

Kin-Ho Lam, Delyar Tabatabai, Jed Irvine, Donald Bertucci, Anita Ruangrotsakun, Minsuk Kahng, Alan Fern, Jeongyeon Kim, Yubin Choi, Juho Kim, et al. 2022. Beyond value: Checklist for testing inferences in planning-based rl. *ACM Transactions on Interactive Intelligent Systems*, 12(1).

Junnan Li, Ramprasaath Selvaraju, Akhilesh Gotmare, Shafiq Joty, Caiming Xiong, and Steven Chu Hong Hoi. 2021. Align before fuse: Vision and language representation learning with momentum distillation. *Advances in Neural Information Processing Systems*, 34.

Liunian Harold Li, Mark Yatskar, Da Yin, Cho-Jui Hsieh, and Kai-Wei Chang. 2019a. Visualbert: A simple and performant baseline for vision and language. *ArXiv*, abs/1908.03557.

Xiujun Li, Xi Yin, Chunyuan Li, Pengchuan Zhang, Xiaowei Hu, Lei Zhang, Lijuan Wang, Houdong Hu, Li Dong, Furu Wei, et al. 2020. Oscar: Object-semantics aligned pre-training for vision-language tasks. In *European Conference on Computer Vision*, pages 121–137. Springer.

Yong-Lu Li, Liang Xu, Xijie Huang, Xinpeng Liu, Ze Ma, Mingyang Chen, Shiyi Wang, Haoshu Fang, and Cewu Lu. 2019b. Hake: Human activity knowledge engine. *ArXiv*, abs/1904.06539.

Jiasen Lu, Dhruv Batra, Devi Parikh, and Stefan Lee. 2019. Vilbert: Pretraining task-agnostic visiolinguistic representations for vision-and-language tasks. *Advances in neural information processing systems*, 32.

Xiaopeng Lu, Tiancheng Zhao, and Kyusong Lee. 2021. Visualsparta: An embarrassingly simple approach to large-scale text-to-image search with weighted bag-of-words. In *Proceedings of the 59th Annual Meeting of the Association for Computational Linguistics and the 11th International Joint Conference on Natural Language Processing (Volume 1: Long Papers)*, pages 5020–5029.

Khoi Pham, Kushal Kafle, Zhe Lin, Zhi Ding, Scott D. Cohen, Quan Tran, and Abhinav Shrivastava. 2021. Learning to predict visual attributes in the wild. *2021 IEEE/CVF Conference on Computer Vision and Pattern Recognition (CVPR)*, pages 13013–13023.

Sarah Pratt, Mark Yatskar, Luca Weihs, Ali Farhadi, and Aniruddha Kembhavi. 2020. Grounded situation recognition. In *European*

Conference on Computer Vision, pages 314–332. Springer.

Alec Radford, Jong Wook Kim, Chris Hallacy, Aditya Ramesh, Gabriel Goh, Sandhini Agarwal, Girish Sastry, Amanda Askell, Pamela Mishkin, Jack Clark, et al. 2021. Learning transferable visual models from natural language supervision. In *International Conference on Machine Learning*, pages 8748–8763. PMLR.

Pranav Rajpurkar, Jian Zhang, Konstantin Lopyrev, and Percy Liang. 2016. Squad: 100,000+ questions for machine comprehension of text. In *Proceedings of the 2016 Conference on Empirical Methods in Natural Language Processing*, pages 2383–2392.

Marco Tulio Ribeiro, Tongshuang Wu, Carlos Guestrin, and Sameer Singh. 2020. Beyond accuracy: Behavioral testing of nlp models with checklist. In *Proceedings of the 58th Annual Meeting of the Association for Computational Linguistics*, pages 4902–4912.

Piyush Sharma, Nan Ding, Sebastian Goodman, and Radu Soricut. 2018. Conceptual captions: A cleaned, hypernymed, image alt-text dataset for automatic image captioning. In *Proceedings of the 56th Annual Meeting of the Association for Computational Linguistics (Volume 1: Long Papers)*, pages 2556–2565.

Ashish Vaswani, Noam Shazeer, Niki Parmar, Jakob Uszkoreit, Llion Jones, Aidan N Gomez, Łukasz Kaiser, and Illia Polosukhin. 2017. Attention is all you need. *Advances in neural information processing systems*, 30.

Alex Wang, Amanpreet Singh, Julian Michael, Felix Hill, Omer Levy, and Samuel Bowman. 2018. Glue: A multi-task benchmark and analysis platform for natural language understanding. In *Proceedings of the 2018 EMNLP Workshop BlackboxNLP: Analyzing and Interpreting Neural Networks for NLP*, pages 353–355.

Tiancheng Zhao, Peng Liu, Xiaopeng Lu, and Kyusong Lee. 2022. Omdet: Language-aware object detection with large-scale vision-language multi-dataset pre-training. *arXiv preprint arXiv:2209.05946*.

Yiwu Zhong, Jianwei Yang, Pengchuan Zhang, Chunyuan Li, Noel Codella, Liunian Harold Li, Luowei Zhou, Xiyang Dai, Lu Yuan, Yin Li, et al. 2022. Regionclip: Region-based language-image pretraining. In *Proceedings of the IEEE/CVF Conference on Computer Vision and Pattern Recognition*, pages 16793–16803.

TweetNLP: Cutting-Edge Natural Language Processing for Social Media

Jose Camacho-Collados[1] **Kiamehr Rezaee**[1] **Talayeh Riahi**[1] **Asahi Ushio**[1]
Daniel Loureiro[1] **Dimosthenis Antypas**[1] **Joanne Boisson**[1,6] **Luis Espinosa-Anke**[1,6]
Fangyu Liu[2] **Eugenio Martínez-Cámara**[3] **Gonzalo Medina**[3]
Thomas Buhrmann[4] **Leonardo Neves**[5] **Francesco Barbieri**[5]
[1]Cardiff NLP, Cardiff University, UK [2]LTL, University of Cambridge, UK
[3]DaSCI, University of Granada, Spain [4]Graphext, Spain [5]Snap Inc., USA [6]AMPLYFI, UK
cardiffnlp.contact@gmail.com

Abstract

In this paper we present TweetNLP, an integrated platform for Natural Language Processing (NLP) in social media. TweetNLP supports a diverse set of NLP tasks, including generic focus areas such as sentiment analysis and named entity recognition, as well as social media-specific tasks such as emoji prediction and offensive language identification. Task-specific systems are powered by reasonably-sized Transformer-based language models specialized on social media text (in particular, Twitter) which can be run without the need for dedicated hardware or cloud services. The main contributions of TweetNLP are: (1) an integrated Python library for a modern toolkit supporting social media analysis using our various task-specific models adapted to the social domain; (2) an interactive online demo for codeless experimentation using our models; and (3) a tutorial covering a wide variety of typical social media applications.

1 Introduction

Today's society cannot be understood without the role of social media. Online users connect more and more via platforms that enable content sharing, either generic or around specific topics, and do this by means of text-only messages, or augmenting them with multimedia content such as pictures, audio or video. As such, these platforms have been used to understand user, group and organization-wide behaviours (Yang et al., 2021; Hu et al., 2021). In particular, Twitter, which is the main platform studied in this paper, has long been an important resource for understanding society at large (Weller et al., 2013). Twitter is interesting for NLP because it embodies many features that are natural in spontaneous and ever-evolving fast-paced communication. However, the majority of NLP research focuses on optimizing model development against training data and evaluation benchmarks which are, at worst, reasonably clean (e.g., news articles, blog posts or Wikipedia). Consequently, when deployed *in the wild*, features such as noisiness, multilinguality, immediacy, slang, technical jargon, lack of context, platform-specific restrictions on message length, emoji and other modalities, etc. become core communicative variables that need to be factored in. Indeed, even traditional NLP tasks such as normalization (Han and Baldwin, 2011; Baldwin et al., 2015), POS tagging (Derczynski et al., 2013), sentiment analysis (Poria et al., 2020) or named entity recognition (Ritter et al., 2011; Baldwin et al., 2013) have been shown to produce suboptimal results in the context of social media.

Given the above, we put forward TweetNLP (`tweetnlp.org`), which offers a full-fledged NLP platform specialized in Twitter. The backbone of TweetNLP consists of Transformer-based language models that have been trained on Twitter (Barbieri et al., 2020, 2022; Loureiro et al., 2022). Then, these specialized language models have been further fine-tuned for specific NLP tasks on Twitter data. These models have already proved highly popular, with thousands of downloads from the Hugging Face model hub every month (Wolf et al., 2020).[1] TweetNLP integrates all these resources into a single platform. With a simple Python API, TweetNLP offers an easy-to-use way to leverage cutting-edge NLP models in a variety of social media tasks. Despite the trend of ever-larger language models (Shoeybi et al., 2019; Brown et al., 2020), TweetNLP is more focused on the general user and applicability, and therefore integrates base models which are easily run in standard computers or on free cloud services. Finally, all models can be accessed from an interactive online demo, offering anyone the possibility to test models and perform

[1]Most notably, the sentiment analysis model has been the most downloaded model in the Hugging Face model hub in January 2022, with over 15M downloads. Similarly, the TweetEval benchmark, in which most task-specific Twitter models are fine-tuned, has been the second most downloaded dataset in April 2022, with over 150K downloads.

Proceedings of the The 2022 Conference on Empirical Methods in Natural Language Processing: System Demonstrations, pages 38 - 49
December 7-11, 2022

real-time analysis on Twitter.

2 Related Work

General-purpose NLP libraries have been available for many years. Starting from the Java-based CoreNLP (Manning et al., 2014) to the more recent Python-based library Stanza (Qi et al., 2020). More recently, libraries such as spaCy[2] have been ubiquitous in NLP, both in research and industry. Finally, in the language models and Transformers era, the Hugging Face Transformer hub has become indispensable for state-of-the-art NLP (Wolf et al., 2020), which is also leveraged for our library TweetNLP. However, none of these libraries is specialized in social media or Twitter.

As for libraries developed specifically for social media, these are more limited and mostly associated with low-level tasks such as tokenization, part-of-speech (Owoputi et al., 2013) tagging or dependency parsing (Kong et al., 2014), and initially available for Java. The most recent Twitter-specific Python library is TweebankNLP (Jiang et al., 2022) based on Stanza. This library provides state-of-the-art models on tokenization and lemmatization, besides competitive models on NER, part-of-speech tagging and dependency parsing. In contrast, TweetNLP focuses on specialized Twitter-specific language models for downstream tasks such as sentiment analysis and offensive language identification.

3 Models and Functionalities

TweetNLP is versatile in that it covers a wide range of tasks and applications. The backbone of TweetNLP are transformer-based language models, which are covered in Section 3.1. The concrete NLP tasks integrated in TweetNLP are presented in Section 3.2. Finally, in Section 3.3 we present embeddings used to represent words and tweets. All TweetNLP model checkpoints are available in the appendix.

3.1 Language models

Language models are at the core of TweetNLP. Instead of relying on general-purpose models (Devlin et al., 2019) or training a language model from scratch (Nguyen et al., 2020), we start from RoBERTa (Liu et al., 2019) and XLM-R (Conneau et al., 2020) checkpoints and continue pre-training on Twitter-specific corpora. This was shown to be generally more reliable for the amount of text analysed in Barbieri et al. (2020). Given our aim for democratizing the usage of specialized language models for social media, another important feature of TweetNLP is the relatively small size of the language models. To this end, all language models rely on the equivalent of a RoBERTa-base or XLM-R-base architecture. These models are efficient on standard hardware and free-tiers of cloud computing services, with reasonable speed even without GPU support.

TweetEval (Barbieri et al., 2020). This model was initially released as part of the TweetEval project. It is based on a RoBERTa-base architecture using the original model as an initial check point (Liu et al., 2019). Later, this language model was further pre-trained on a corpus of 60M tweets from May 2018 to August 2019.

TimeLMs (Loureiro et al., 2022). This model is initially trained on the same Twitter corpus used by Barbieri et al. (2020). The main difference lies on a few preprocessing improvements applied to the underlying corpus, including measures to reduce potential spam and near duplicates, and more recent corpora used for continual pretraining. The overall quantity of tweets is therefore larger, as the model is regularly updated (every 3 months) with a fixed number of additional tweets. The most recently released TimeLMs model to date is pre-trained on 132M tweets until the end of June 2022.

XLM-T (Barbieri et al., 2022). This model was trained on 198M tweets on over thirty languages from May 2018 to March 2020, following a similar strategy to Barbieri et al. (2020). In this case, the initial checkpoint was XLM-R-base (Conneau et al., 2020).

3.2 Supported tasks

In the following we describe the tasks supported by TweetNLP. For the tweet classification tasks included in TweetEval, and for topic classification, we simply fine-tune the models described above on the corresponding datasets, as described in Barbieri et al. (2020). For model fine-tuning on named entity recognition, we rely on the T-NER library (Ushio and Camacho-Collados, 2021), which is also integrated into TweetNLP.

Sentiment Analysis. The sentiment analysis task integrated in TweetNLP consists of predicting the

[2]https://spacy.io

sentiment of a tweet with one of the three following labels: positive, neutral or negative. The base dataset for English is the unified TweetEval version of the Semeval-2017 dataset from the task on *Sentiment Analysis in Twitter* (Rosenthal et al., 2017). Moreover, for the languages other than English we include the datasets integrated in UMSAB (Barbieri et al., 2022), namely Arabic (Rosenthal et al., 2017), French (Benamara et al., 2017), German (Cieliebak et al., 2017), Hindi (Patra et al., 2015), Italian (Barbieri et al., 2016), Portuguese (Brum and Volpe Nunes, 2018), and Spanish (Díaz-Galiano et al., 2018).

Emotion Recognition. Given a tweet, this task consists of associating it with its most appropriate emotion. As a reference dataset we use the SemEval 2018 task on *Affect in Tweets* (Mohammad et al., 2018), simplified to only the four emotions used in TweetEval: anger, joy, sadness and optimism.

Emoji Prediction. The goal of emoji prediction is to predict the final emoji on a given tweet. The dataset used to fine-tune our models is the TweetEval adaptation from the SemEval 2018 task on *Emoji Prediction* (Barbieri et al., 2018), including 20 emoji as labels.

Irony Detection. This is a binary classification task that aims at detecting whether a tweet is ironic or not. It is based on the *Irony Detection* dataset from the SemEval 2018 task (Van Hee et al., 2018).

Hate Speech Detection. The hate speech dataset consists of detecting whether a tweet is hateful towards women or immigrants. It is based on the *Detection of Hate Speech* task at SemEval 2019 (Basile et al., 2019).

Offensive Language Identification. The task consist of identifying any form of offensive language in a tweet. The dataset is based on the SemEval 2019 task on *Identifying and Categorizing Offensive Language in Social Media* (Zampieri et al., 2019).

Stance Detection. Given a target topic and a tweet, stance detection consists of assessing whether the author of the tweet has a positive, neutral or negative position towards the target. The dataset considered was initially released for the SemEval 2016 task on *Detecting Stance in Tweets* (Mohammad et al., 2016).

Topic Classification. The aim of this task is, given a tweet, assign topics related to its content. The task is formulated as a supervised multi-label classification problem where each tweet is assigned one or more topics from a total of 19 available topics. The topics were carefully curated based on Twitter trends with the aim to be broad and general, consisting of classes such as: *arts and culture*, *music*, or *sports*. The underlying tweet topic classification dataset contains over 10K manually-labeled tweets (Antypas et al., 2022).

Named Entity Recognition. The goal of named entity recognition (NER) is to find entities and identify their entity types in a given sentence. The underlying Twitter NER dataset is composed of over 10K tweets which were annotated (internally) with seven entity types.[3]

3.3 Embeddings

In addition to the language models and their supported tasks, we also release high-quality vector representation models for words and tweets, i.e., *embeddings* (Pilehvar and Camacho-Collados, 2020). These relatively low-dimensional vector representations can be exploited for a different range of applications and analyses such as word/tweet similarity or tweet retrieval, to name a few.

Word embeddings. TweetNLP word embeddings are based on fastText (Bojanowski et al., 2017) and trained on the same corpora used to train the language models described in Section 3.1. In particular, we trained two sets of embeddings: (1) a monolingual English model trained with the TimeLMs Twitter corpus until the end of 2021; and (2) a multilingual model trained with the Twitter corpus used for XLM-T. Both models were trained using the official fastText package with 300 dimensions, minimum n-gram size 2, maximum n-gram size 12, and remaining parameters set to defaults.

Tweet embeddings. For tweet embeddings, we pulled tweet-reply pairs from the Twitter API and trained contrastive embeddings with an InfoNCE loss (Oord et al., 2018). For tweets with multiple replies, we randomly sampled one reply. In training, one mini-batch is composed of a list of tweet-reply pairs. The tweet-reply pairs are regarded as

[3]More details about the datasets for topic classification and named entity recognition will be provided at a later stage. Datasets were annotated internally in Snap and we are working on releasing them to the public according to regulations.

positive samples; the enumeration of all other possible combination of tweet-reply, tweet-tweet, and tweet-reply pairs are regarded as negative samples. The contrastive InfoNCE loss then pulls positive pair representations close while pushes negative representations away from each other. Training was performed on 1.1M tweet-reply pairs, and we collected a separate tweet-reply set of 10k pairs for selecting the model checkpoint.

4 TweetNLP Python library

The TweetNLP Python library has been integrated into pypi[4] and therefore is easily accessible and can be installed from pip ("pip install tweetnlp"). All the details on how to use TweetNLP are in the associated Github repository, which is released fully open-source: `https://github.com/cardiffnlp/tweetnlp`.

Once installed, loading and using a fine-tuned model on any specific task can be done as follows.

```
from tweetnlp import load
tweet = "I love Paris!!"
# Sentiment Analysis
model = load('sentiment')
model.sentiment(tweet)
# Tweet Embeddings
model = load('sentence_embedding')
model.embedding(tweet)
# Masked Language Model
model = load('language_model')
tweet = "I love <mask>!!"
model.mask_prediction(tweet)
```

With the *load* statement, the associated fine-tuned language models are loaded in the background. Users can then get the predictions for any given sentence or tweet with a simple pre-defined function (e.g., *.sentiment* or *.predict*). Custom loading of existing fine-tuned language models not included in TweetNLP is also possible. The same functionalities apply to all the other tasks described in Section 3.2.

5 Tutorials

In addition to the Python library presented in the previous section, TweetNLP offers access to the underlying Python code structured in instructive Google Colab notebooks with starter code and examples (`https://tweetnlp.org/get-started/`). These notebooks are aimed at users with varying degrees of experience in NLP and social media processing. In the following we list the currently existing tutorials and a brief description:

Introduction to TweetNLP. In this initial introduction, users learn how to use the TweetNLP Python library to make use of specialized models in social media for a wide variety of tasks from sentiment analysis to named entity recognition.

Getting data from Twitter. This notebook helps users understand the Twitter API[5] and how to interact with it. More importantly, there are concrete examples on how to retrieve data (i.e. tweets) from Twitter, usually given a hashtag or a keyword.

Custom fine-tuning. In this notebook users can learn to fine-tune any given language model on a specific task (e.g. sentiment analysis). For this, we will take advantage of the TweetEval task data and unified format (Barbieri et al., 2020). Additionally, users can learn how to easily evaluate language models on TweetEval.

Word embeddings. With this notebook users can learn how to train their own word embeddings on custom data using Gensim[6] (Řehůřek and Sojka, 2010). The notebook also includes examples on how to get similarity scores from Twitter-specific word embeddings, or how to obtain the nearest neighbour words from a given input word.

Language models over time. This notebook leverages the TimeLMs library (Loureiro et al., 2022). Users can learn how to make use of language models that have been trained in short periods of time since 2019 until recently.

Tweet embeddings. This notebook contains examples on how to transform a tweet into a vector (embedding) and how these enable important applications such as tweet similarity and retrieval.

6 Demo

In addition to the Python-based library and tutorials, we developed a comprehensive web-based demo integrating all our models, available at `https://tweetnlp.org/demo/`. The goal of the demo is for any user to be able to test our models and get predictions. In particular, the model includes the following five functionalities:

[4] `https://pypi.org/project/tweetnlp/`

[5] `https://developer.twitter.com/en/docs/twitter-api`

[6] `https://radimrehurek.com/gensim/`

Sentence/tweet classification (Figure 1). Users can input a sentence or a tweet (including a tweet URL) and the output is a plot display of the confidence of the model with respect to its predictions. This demo includes all tweet classification tasks supported in English (see Section 3.2), as well as a multilingual sentiment analysis model based on XLM-T.

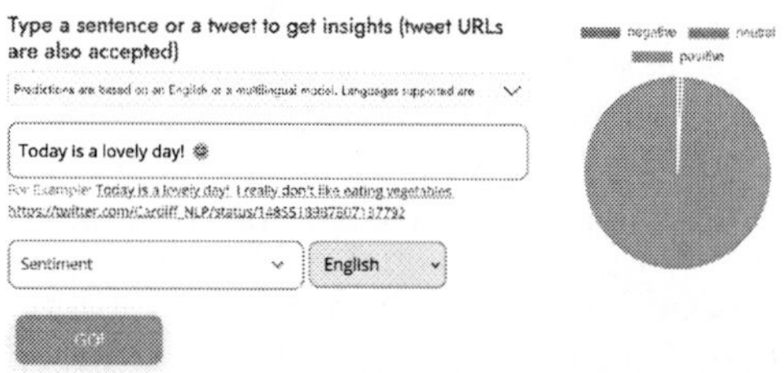

Figure 1: TweetNLP tweet classification demo.

Hashtag analysis (Figure 2). This demo directly interacts with the Twitter API. Users can type a hashtag (or any keyword), initial and end dates, task and language. The system will then retrieve tweets for the given time interval and compute an aggregated analysis of the results. Languages supported for this demo are available in the appendix.

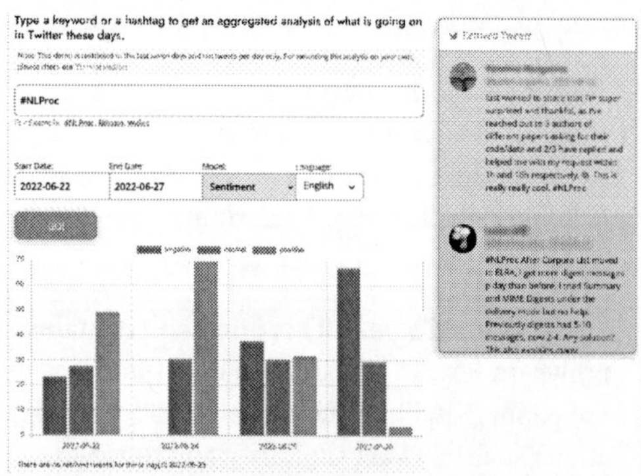

Figure 2: TweetNLP hashtag analysis demo. The output is a bar plot that shows the sentiment of the retrieved tweets over time for the input hashtag #NLProc.

Word prediction (Figure 3). Masked language models utilized in TweetNLP are trained to predict unknown (or *masked*) words within a sentence. For this demo, users can input a sentence with a masked word and the system will show the most likely words as given by the masked language model, in order of confidence.

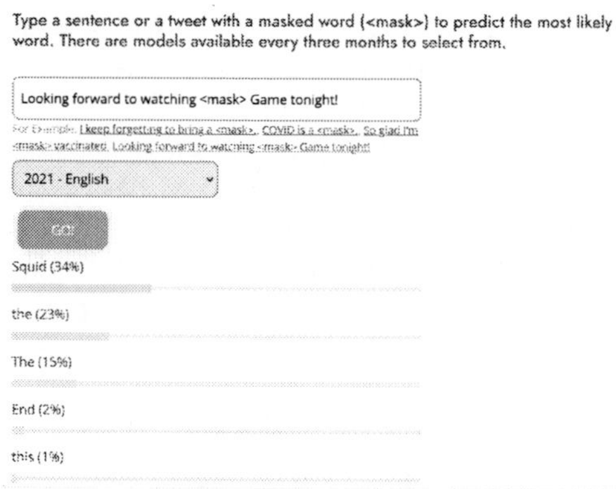

Figure 3: TweetNLP word prediction demo.

Tweet similarity (Figure 4). Given two short pieces of text (e.g., two sentences or two tweets), this demo displays their cosine similarity score on a 0-100 scale as provided by our default tweet embedding model.

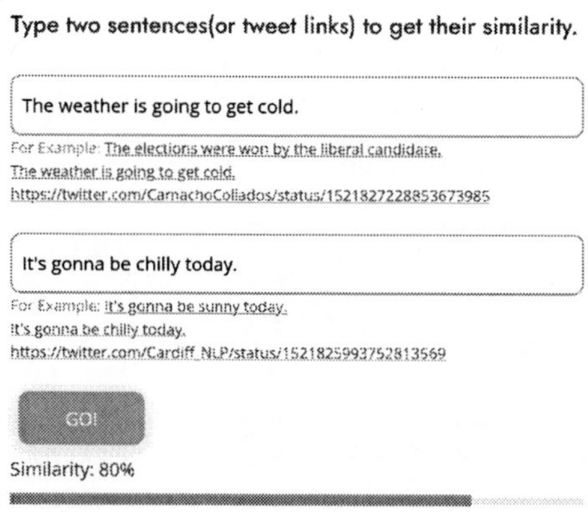

Figure 4: TweetNLP tweet similarity demo.

Named Entity Recognition (Figure 5). Given a tweet or a sentence, this NER demo locates its named entities and infers their types.

7 Evaluation

In this section, we provide experimental results of the default models integrated into TweetNLP.

7.1 Experimental setting

Datasets. For the evaluation we utilized all the train/validation/test splits described in Section 3.2. In particular, we relied on the TweetEval-released datasets for all tweet classification tasks except for topic classification.

Figure 5: TweetNLP Named Entity Recognition demo.

Default TweetNLP language models. While in TweetNLP all Twitter-specific language models are included, we use as a default (1) TimeLMs trained until December 2021 for English and (2) XLM-T for the languages other than English and multilingual tasks. These models are then fine-tuned to the corresponding tasks as described in Section 3.2.

Comparison systems. We report the performance of all original TweetEval baselines (Barbieri et al., 2020): a frequency-based SVM classifier, fastText (Joulin et al., 2017), a Bidirectional LSTM, RoBERTa-base (Liu et al., 2019), a RoBERTa-base model trained on Twitter from scratch (RoB-Twitter) and the original TweetEval RoBERTa-base model. As another baseline we include BERTweet (Nguyen et al., 2020), trained on almost 1 billion tweets from 2013 to 2019.

Language model fine-tuning. Fine-tuning is performed on the training sets of each corresponding dataset, using their corresponding development sets for validation. We followed TweetEval training protocols for tweet classification, where only the learning rate and number of epochs are tuned (Barbieri et al., 2020). All reported results for language models are based on an average of three runs.

7.2 Results

Table 1 shows the main results of our TweetNLP default language model and comparison systems on nine Twitter-based tasks.[7] The default TimeLMs-21 model achieves the overall results on most tasks, especially comparing it with a comparable general-purpose RoBERTa-based model. In the following we also provide details of our experimental results on languages other than English , and for the integrated word and tweet embedding models.

Multilingual sentiment analysis results. In addition to the English evaluation, we report results on multilingual sentiment analysis (Table 2). The evaluation is performed on the UMSAB multilingual sentiment analysis benchmark (Barbieri et al., 2022). For this evaluation we compare XLM-T fine-tuned on all the language-specific training sets of UMSAB with XLM-R (Conneau et al., 2020) using the same fine-tuning strategy. As an additional indicative baseline, we include fastText trained on the language-specific training sets. As can be observed, our domain-specific XLM-T language model achieves the best overall results in all languages, further reinforcing the importance of in-domain language model training.

Word embedding results. As a sanity check to verify the quality of the word embeddings, we simply test them on standard word similarity datasets: The WS-Sim similarity and WS-Rel relatedness subsets (Agirre et al., 2009) from WordSim-353 (Finkelstein et al., 2002), SemEval-2017 (Camacho-Collados et al., 2017) and MEN (Bruni et al., 2014). Then, we compared the results with the pre-trained fastText model trained on the Common Crawl (Bojanowski et al., 2017), and Wikipedia. According to Spearman correlation, the results of our Twitter embeddings were 0.77 (WS-Sim), 0.72 (WS-Rel), 0.69 (SemEval), and 0.79 (MEN).[8] In contrast, the pre-trained fastText Common Crawl results were 0.84 (WS-Sim), 0.64 (WS-Rel), 0.67 (SemEval), and 0.81 (MEN). We should note that these datasets are not specific to social media and even so, our trained embeddings outperform the standard pre-trained fastText in two datasets. In particular, there seems to be a marked difference between similarity and relatedness, where our Twitter embeddings appear to be more suited to relatedness.

Tweet embedding results. For tweet embeddings we explore a tweet retrieval task setting which consists of finding the reply to a given tweet from the 10k replies in the search space. We randomly sampled 3k tweet-reply pairs that do not

[7]The BERTweet result on Irony is marked with * as their pre-training corpus overlapped with the Irony dataset, which was constructed using distant supervision.

[8]While not directly comparable given the different sizes, we also compared with our previously-released Twitter-specific 100-dimensional fastText embeddings (Camacho-Collados et al., 2020). The results for these embeddings were consistently lower: 0.65 (WS-Sim), 0.43 (WS-Rel), 0.52 (SemEval), and 0.76 (MEN).

	Emoji	Emotion	Hate	Irony	Offensive	Sentiment	Stance	Topic	NER
SVM	29.3	64.7	36.7	61.7	52.3	62.9	67.3	30.5	-
fastText	25.8	65.2	50.6	63.1	73.4	62.9	65.4	24.0	-
BLSTM	24.7	66.0	52.6	62.8	71.7	58.3	59.4	27.0	-
RoB-Base	30.9	76.1	46.6	59.7	79.5	71.3	68.0	50.1	58.0
RoB-Twitter	29.3	72.0	46.9	**65.4**	77.1	69.1	66.7	-	-
TweetEval	31.4	78.5	52.3	61.7	80.5	72.6	69.3	56.8	56.8
BERTweet	33.4	79.3	**56.4**	*82.1**	79.5	73.4	71.2	52.7	58.7
TweetNLP (TimeLMs-21)	**34.0**	**80.2**	55.1	64.5	**82.2**	**73.7**	**72.9**	**58.8**	**59.7**
Evaluation metric	M-F1	M-F1	M-F1	$F^{(i)}$	M-F1	M-Rec	AVG (F)	M-F1	M-F1

Table 1: Test results in the nine TweetNLP-supported tasks.

	Arabic	English	French	German	Hindi	Italian	Portuguese	Spanish	ALL
fastText	45.98	50.85	54.82	59.56	37.08	54.65	55.05	50.06	51.01
XLM-R	64.31	68.52	70.52	72.84	53.39	68.62	69.79	66.03	66.75
TweetNLP (XLM-T)	**66.89**	**70.63**	**71.18**	**77.35**	**56.35**	**69.06**	**75.42**	**68.52**	**67.91**

Table 2: Sentiment analysis results (Macro-F1) on the UMSAB unified benchmark. XLM-R and TweetNLP models are fine-tuned on the training sets of all languages.

overlap with training data and split them into 3 sets of 1k pairs. We report accuracy@1 and average models' performance on the 3 sets. We also include results on sentence similarity, using the STS-benchmark (Cer et al., 2017) and reporting Spearman's correlation. We list tweet-reply retrieval accuracy and STS-benchmark Spearman's correlation in Table 3. We compare with recent supervised (Reimers and Gurevych, 2019, Sentence-BERT; all-mpnet-base-v2), and unsupervised (Liu et al., 2021, Mirror-BERT), (Gao et al., 2021, SimCSE) sentence embedding models.[9] On the task of tweet-reply retrieval, our tweet-embeddings model significantly outperforms all-mpnet-base-v2 trained with around 1B sentence pairs. This highlights the importance of in-domain training. On the STS-Benchmark, all-mpnet-base-v2 achieves the best performance and our tweet-embeddings perform the worst among baselines but they are generally in a similar ballpark. To complement this evaluation, we plan to test our tweet embeddings with a textual similarity dataset in the tweet domain in the future.

Model	Retrieval	STS
Sentence-BERT	6.1	77.0
all-mpnet-base-v2	15.8	**83.4**
Mirror-RoBERTa	8.8	79.6
SimCSE-RoBERTa	9.2	80.3
TweetNLP (Tweet-embeddings)	**26.7**	70.7

Table 3: Results of sentence and tweet embedding models on tweet-reply retrieval and the STS-benchmark.

8 Conclusion and Future Work

In this demo paper we have presented TweetNLP, an all-round platform for NLP specialized in social media. The platform is powered by relatively lightweight language models trained on Twitter, and adapted (fine-tuned) to various popular NLP tasks on social media, such as sentiment analysis and offensive language identification. In addition to sharing the models, TweetNLP provides an online demo, a Python library, and a tutorial to make the most of the models, regardless of the expertise of the user. TweetNLP also enables easy inspection of the models by non-programmers, which can help identify harmful biases or errors, that in turn would help improve the models in the future.

While this first release version of TweetNLP is self-contained and complete, our goal is to keep updating it with both new models and tasks. Since social media data is at the core of TweetNLP, we are planning to develop new datasets and models for social media tasks. In particular, our idea is to go beyond tweet classification tasks, which are currently well covered in TweetNLP. For instance, low-level tasks such as syntactic parsing and part-of-speech tagging has been traditionally hard in noisy environments such as social media. Finally, in the future we are also planning to extend TweetNLP to other social media platforms such as Reddit, LinkedIn or Instagram, and to provide support for languages other than English in a wider variety of tasks.

[9]Baseline checkpoint links are included in the Appendix.

9 Impact Statement

This paper deals with social media data, in particular with Twitter. All Twitter regulations were followed and data was extracted through the official Twitter API. To mitigate the potential effect of working with this type of data, all dataset-related tweets were anonymized, with URLs removed. In most cases dataset creators made an effort to remove offensive or harmful content from the tweets. Nonetheless, models trained on this data may amplify existing biases present in the social media platform. While this is in many cases unavoidable, we hope that by making this demo public with model prototypes, experts will be able to more easily inspect these biases and we will be able to better understand the potential biases of models trained on this type of data.

Acknowledgements

We acknowledge the support of UKRI (in particular the UKRI Future Leaders Fellowship scheme), Snap Inc., the Cardiff University Innovation for All scheme and the R&D&I grant PID2020-116118GA-I00 funded by MCIN/AEI/10.13039/501100011033 for partially funding this project.

References

Eneko Agirre, Enrique Alfonseca, Keith Hall, Jana Kravalova, Marius Paşca, and Aitor Soroa. 2009. A study on similarity and relatedness using distributional and WordNet-based approaches. In *Proceedings of Human Language Technologies: The 2009 Annual Conference of the North American Chapter of the Association for Computational Linguistics*, pages 19–27, Boulder, Colorado. Association for Computational Linguistics.

Dimosthenis Antypas, Asahi Ushio, Jose Camacho-Collados, Leonardo Neves, Vítor Silva, and Francesco Barbieri. 2022. Twitter topic classification. *arXiv preprint arXiv:2209.09824*.

Timothy Baldwin, Paul Cook, Marco Lui, Andrew MacKinlay, and Li Wang. 2013. How noisy social media text, how diffrnt social media sources? In *Proceedings of the Sixth International Joint Conference on Natural Language Processing*, pages 356–364, Nagoya, Japan. Asian Federation of Natural Language Processing.

Timothy Baldwin, Marie Catherine de Marneffe, Bo Han, Young-Bum Kim, Alan Ritter, and Wei Xu. 2015. Shared tasks of the 2015 workshop on noisy user-generated text: Twitter lexical normalization and named entity recognition. In *Proceedings of the Workshop on Noisy User-generated Text*, pages 126–135, Beijing, China. Association for Computational Linguistics.

Francesco Barbieri, Valerio Basile, Danilo Croce, Malvina Nissim, Nicole Novielli, and Viviana Patti. 2016. Overview of the evalita 2016 sentiment polarity classification task. In *Proceedings of third Italian conference on computational linguistics (CLiC-it 2016) & fifth evaluation campaign of natural language processing and speech tools for Italian. Final Workshop (EVALITA 2016)*.

Francesco Barbieri, Jose Camacho-Collados, Luis Espinosa Anke, and Leonardo Neves. 2020. TweetEval: Unified benchmark and comparative evaluation for tweet classification. In *Findings of the Association for Computational Linguistics: EMNLP 2020*, pages 1644–1650, Online. Association for Computational Linguistics.

Francesco Barbieri, Jose Camacho-Collados, Francesco Ronzano, Luis Espinosa-Anke, Miguel Ballesteros, Valerio Basile, Viviana Patti, and Horacio Saggion. 2018. SemEval 2018 task 2: Multilingual emoji prediction. In *Proceedings of The 12th International Workshop on Semantic Evaluation*, pages 24–33, New Orleans, Louisiana. Association for Computational Linguistics.

Francesco Barbieri, Luis Espinosa Anke, and Jose Camacho-Collados. 2022. Xlm-t: Multilingual language models in twitter for sentiment analysis and beyond. In *Proceedings of the Language Resources and Evaluation Conference*, pages 258–266, Marseille, France. European Language Resources Association.

Valerio Basile, Cristina Bosco, Elisabetta Fersini, Debora Nozza, Viviana Patti, Francisco Manuel Rangel Pardo, Paolo Rosso, and Manuela Sanguinetti. 2019. SemEval-2019 task 5: Multilingual detection of hate speech against immigrants and women in Twitter. In *Proceedings of the 13th International Workshop on Semantic Evaluation*, pages 54–63, Minneapolis, Minnesota, USA. Association for Computational Linguistics.

Farah Benamara, Cyril Grouin, Jihen Karoui, Véronique Moriceau, and Isabelle Robba. 2017. Analyse d'opinion et langage figuratif dans des tweets: présentation et résultats du défi fouille de textes deft2017. In *Défi Fouille de Textes DEFT2017. Atelier TALN 2017*. Association pour le Traitement Automatique des Langues (ATALA).

Piotr Bojanowski, Edouard Grave, Armand Joulin, and Tomas Mikolov. 2017. Enriching word vectors with subword information. *Transactions of the Association for Computational Linguistics*, 5:135–146.

Tom Brown, Benjamin Mann, Nick Ryder, Melanie Subbiah, Jared D Kaplan, Prafulla Dhariwal, Arvind Neelakantan, Pranav Shyam, Girish Sastry, Amanda Askell, et al. 2020. Language models are few-shot learners. *Advances in neural information processing systems*, 33:1877–1901.

Henrico Brum and Maria das Graças Volpe Nunes. 2018. Building a sentiment corpus of tweets in Brazilian Portuguese. In *Proceedings of the Eleventh International Conference on Language Resources and Evaluation (LREC 2018)*, Miyazaki, Japan. European Language Resources Association (ELRA).

Elia Bruni, Nam-Khanh Tran, and Marco Baroni. 2014. Multimodal distributional semantics. *J. Artif. Intell. Res.(JAIR)*, 49(1-47).

Jose Camacho-Collados, Yerai Doval, Eugenio Martínez-Cámara, Luis Espinosa-Anke, Francesco Barbieri, and Steven Schockaert. 2020. Learning cross-lingual word embeddings from twitter via distant supervision. In *Proceedings of the international AAAI conference on web and social media*, volume 14, pages 72–82.

Jose Camacho-Collados, Mohammad Taher Pilehvar, Nigel Collier, and Roberto Navigli. 2017. SemEval-2017 task 2: Multilingual and cross-lingual semantic word similarity. In *Proceedings of the 11th International Workshop on Semantic Evaluation (SemEval-2017)*, pages 15–26, Vancouver, Canada. Association for Computational Linguistics.

Daniel Cer, Mona Diab, Eneko Agirre, Iñigo Lopez-Gazpio, and Lucia Specia. 2017. SemEval-2017 task 1: Semantic textual similarity multilingual and crosslingual focused evaluation. In *Proceedings of the 11th International Workshop on Semantic Evaluation (SemEval-2017)*, pages 1–14, Vancouver, Canada. Association for Computational Linguistics.

Mark Cieliebak, Jan Milan Deriu, Dominic Egger, and Fatih Uzdilli. 2017. A Twitter corpus and benchmark resources for German sentiment analysis. In *Proceedings of the Fifth International Workshop on Natural Language Processing for Social Media*, pages 45–51, Valencia, Spain. Association for Computational Linguistics.

Alexis Conneau, Kartikay Khandelwal, Naman Goyal, Vishrav Chaudhary, Guillaume Wenzek, Francisco Guzmán, Edouard Grave, Myle Ott, Luke Zettlemoyer, and Veselin Stoyanov. 2020. Unsupervised cross-lingual representation learning at scale. In *Proceedings of the 58th Annual Meeting of the Association for Computational Linguistics*, pages 8440–8451, Online. Association for Computational Linguistics.

Leon Derczynski, Alan Ritter, Sam Clark, and Kalina Bontcheva. 2013. Twitter part-of-speech tagging for all: Overcoming sparse and noisy data. In *Proceedings of the International Conference Recent Advances in Natural Language Processing RANLP 2013*, pages 198–206, Hissar, Bulgaria. INCOMA Ltd. Shoumen, BULGARIA.

Jacob Devlin, Ming-Wei Chang, Kenton Lee, and Kristina Toutanova. 2019. BERT: Pre-training of deep bidirectional transformers for language understanding. In *Proceedings of the 2019 Conference of the North American Chapter of the Association for Computational Linguistics: Human Language Technologies, Volume 1 (Long and Short Papers)*, pages 4171–4186, Minneapolis, Minnesota. Association for Computational Linguistics.

Manuel C. Díaz-Galiano, Eugenio Martínez-Cámara, M. Ángel García Cumbreras, Manuel García Vega, and Julio Villena Román. 2018. The democratization of deep learning in tass 2017. *Procesamiento del Lenguaje Natural*, 60:37–44.

Lev Finkelstein, Gabrilovich Evgeniy, Matias Yossi, Rivlin Ehud, Solan Zach, Wolfman Gadi, and Ruppin Eytan. 2002. Placing search in context: The concept revisited. *ACM Transactions on Information Systems*, 20(1):116–131.

Tianyu Gao, Xingcheng Yao, and Danqi Chen. 2021. SimCSE: Simple contrastive learning of sentence embeddings. In *Proceedings of the 2021 Conference on Empirical Methods in Natural Language Processing*, pages 6894–6910, Online and Punta Cana, Dominican Republic. Association for Computational Linguistics.

Bo Han and Timothy Baldwin. 2011. Lexical normalisation of short text messages: Makn sens a #twitter. In *Proceedings of the 49th Annual Meeting of the Association for Computational Linguistics: Human Language Technologies*, pages 368–378, Portland, Oregon, USA. Association for Computational Linguistics.

Danqi Hu, Charles M Jones, Valerie Zhang, and Xiaoyan Zhang. 2021. The rise of reddit: How social media affects retail investors and short-sellers' roles in price discovery. *Available at SSRN 3807655*.

Hang Jiang, Yining Hua, Doug Beeferman, and Deb Roy. 2022. Annotating the tweebank corpus on named entity recognition and building nlp models for social media analysis. In *Proceedings of the Language Resources and Evaluation Conference*, pages 7199–7208, Marseille, France. European Language Resources Association.

Armand Joulin, Edouard Grave, Piotr Bojanowski, and Tomas Mikolov. 2017. Bag of tricks for efficient text classification. In *Proceedings of the 15th Conference of the European Chapter of the Association for Computational Linguistics: Volume 2, Short Papers*, pages 427–431, Valencia, Spain. Association for Computational Linguistics.

Lingpeng Kong, Nathan Schneider, Swabha Swayamdipta, Archna Bhatia, Chris Dyer, and Noah A. Smith. 2014. A dependency parser for tweets. In *Proceedings of the 2014 Conference on Empirical Methods in Natural Language Processing (EMNLP)*, pages 1001–1012, Doha, Qatar. Association for Computational Linguistics.

Fangyu Liu, Ivan Vulić, Anna Korhonen, and Nigel Collier. 2021. Fast, effective, and self-supervised: Transforming masked language models into universal lexical and sentence encoders. In *Proceedings of the 2021 Conference on Empirical Methods in Natural Language Processing*, pages 1442–1459, Online and Punta Cana, Dominican Republic. Association for Computational Linguistics.

Yinhan Liu, Myle Ott, Naman Goyal, Jingfei Du, Mandar Joshi, Danqi Chen, Omer Levy, Mike Lewis, Luke Zettlemoyer, and Veselin Stoyanov. 2019. Roberta: A robustly optimized bert pretraining approach. *arXiv preprint arXiv:1907.11692*.

Daniel Loureiro, Francesco Barbieri, Leonardo Neves, Luis Espinosa Anke, and Jose Camacho-collados. 2022. TimeLMs: Diachronic language models from Twitter. In *Proceedings of the 60th Annual Meeting of the Association for Computational Linguistics: System Demonstrations*, pages 251–260, Dublin, Ireland. Association for Computational Linguistics.

Christopher Manning, Mihai Surdeanu, John Bauer, Jenny Finkel, Steven Bethard, and David McClosky. 2014. The Stanford CoreNLP natural language processing toolkit. In *Proceedings of 52nd Annual Meeting of the Association for Computational Linguistics: System Demonstrations*, pages 55–60, Baltimore, Maryland. Association for Computational Linguistics.

Saif Mohammad, Felipe Bravo-Marquez, Mohammad Salameh, and Svetlana Kiritchenko. 2018. SemEval-2018 task 1: Affect in tweets. In *Proceedings of The 12th International Workshop on Semantic Evaluation*, pages 1–17, New Orleans, Louisiana. Association for Computational Linguistics.

Saif Mohammad, Svetlana Kiritchenko, Parinaz Sobhani, Xiaodan Zhu, and Colin Cherry. 2016. SemEval-2016 task 6: Detecting stance in tweets. In *Proceedings of the 10th International Workshop on Semantic Evaluation (SemEval-2016)*, pages 31–41, San Diego, California. Association for Computational Linguistics.

Dat Quoc Nguyen, Thanh Vu, and Anh Tuan Nguyen. 2020. BERTweet: A pre-trained language model for English tweets. In *Proceedings of the 2020 Conference on Empirical Methods in Natural Language Processing: System Demonstrations*, pages 9–14, Online. Association for Computational Linguistics.

Aaron van den Oord, Yazhe Li, and Oriol Vinyals. 2018. Representation learning with contrastive predictive coding. *arXiv preprint arXiv:1807.03748*.

Olutobi Owoputi, Brendan O'Connor, Chris Dyer, Kevin Gimpel, Nathan Schneider, and Noah A. Smith. 2013. Improved part-of-speech tagging for online conversational text with word clusters. In *Proceedings of the 2013 Conference of the North American Chapter of the Association for Computational Linguistics: Human Language Technologies*, pages 380–390, Atlanta, Georgia. Association for Computational Linguistics.

Braja Gopal Patra, Dipankar Das, Amitava Das, and Rajendra Prasath. 2015. Shared task on sentiment analysis in indian languages (sail) tweets-an overview. In *International Conference on Mining Intelligence and Knowledge Exploration*, pages 650–655. Springer.

Mohammad Taher Pilehvar and Jose Camacho-Collados. 2020. Embeddings in natural language processing: Theory and advances in vector representations of meaning. *Synthesis Lectures on Human Language Technologies*, 13(4):1–175.

Soujanya Poria, Devamanyu Hazarika, Navonil Majumder, and Rada Mihalcea. 2020. Beneath the tip of the iceberg: Current challenges and new directions in sentiment analysis research. *IEEE Transactions on Affective Computing*.

Peng Qi, Yuhao Zhang, Yuhui Zhang, Jason Bolton, and Christopher D. Manning. 2020. Stanza: A Python natural language processing toolkit for many human languages. In *Proceedings of the 58th Annual Meeting of the Association for Computational Linguistics: System Demonstrations*.

Nils Reimers and Iryna Gurevych. 2019. Sentence-BERT: Sentence embeddings using Siamese BERT-networks. In *Proceedings of the 2019 Conference on Empirical Methods in Natural Language Processing and the 9th International Joint Conference on Natural Language Processing (EMNLP-IJCNLP)*, pages 3982–3992, Hong Kong, China. Association for Computational Linguistics.

Alan Ritter, Sam Clark, Mausam, and Oren Etzioni. 2011. Named entity recognition in tweets: An experimental study. In *Proceedings of the 2011 Conference on Empirical Methods in Natural Language Processing*, pages 1524–1534, Edinburgh, Scotland, UK. Association for Computational Linguistics.

Sara Rosenthal, Noura Farra, and Preslav Nakov. 2017. SemEval-2017 task 4: Sentiment analysis in Twitter. In *Proceedings of the 11th International Workshop on Semantic Evaluation (SemEval-2017)*, pages 502–518, Vancouver, Canada. Association for Computational Linguistics.

Mohammad Shoeybi, Mostofa Patwary, Raul Puri, Patrick LeGresley, Jared Casper, and Bryan Catanzaro. 2019. Megatron-lm: Training multi-billion parameter language models using model parallelism. *arXiv preprint arXiv:1909.08053*.

Asahi Ushio and Jose Camacho-Collados. 2021. T-NER: An all-round python library for transformer-based named entity recognition. In *Proceedings of the 16th Conference of the European Chapter of the Association for Computational Linguistics: System Demonstrations*, pages 53–62, Online. Association for Computational Linguistics.

Cynthia Van Hee, Els Lefever, and Véronique Hoste. 2018. SemEval-2018 task 3: Irony detection in English tweets. In *Proceedings of The 12th International Workshop on Semantic Evaluation*, pages 39–50, New Orleans, Louisiana. Association for Computational Linguistics.

Katrin Weller, Axel Bruns, Jean Burgess, Merja Mahrt, and Cornelius Puschmann. 2013. *Twitter and society*. Peter Lang New York.

Thomas Wolf, Lysandre Debut, Victor Sanh, Julien Chaumond, Clement Delangue, Anthony Moi, Pierric Cistac, Tim Rault, Remi Louf, Morgan Funtowicz, Joe Davison, Sam Shleifer, Patrick von Platen, Clara Ma, Yacine Jernite, Julien Plu, Canwen Xu, Teven Le Scao, Sylvain Gugger, Mariama Drame, Quentin Lhoest, and Alexander Rush. 2020. Transformers: State-of-the-art natural language processing. In *Proceedings of the 2020 Conference on Empirical Methods in Natural Language Processing: System Demonstrations*, pages 38–45, Online. Association for Computational Linguistics.

Qi Yang, Weinan Wang, Lucas Pierce, Rajan Vaish, Xiaolin Shi, and Neil Shah. 2021. Online communication shifts in the midst of the covid-19 pandemic: A case study on snapchat. *Proceedings of the International AAAI Conference on Web and Social Media*, 15(1):830–840.

Marcos Zampieri, Shervin Malmasi, Preslav Nakov, Sara Rosenthal, Noura Farra, and Ritesh Kumar. 2019. SemEval-2019 task 6: Identifying and categorizing offensive language in social media (OffensEval). In *Proceedings of the 13th International Workshop on Semantic Evaluation*, pages 75–86, Minneapolis, Minnesota, USA. Association for Computational Linguistics.

Radim Řehůřek and Petr Sojka. 2010. Software framework for topic modelling with large corpora. In *In Proceedings of the LREC 2010 workshop on new challenges for NLP frameworks*, pages 45–50, Valetta, Malta.

A Languages supported

In addition to English, the sentiment analysis demo (including hashtag analysis) is also available for the following languages: Amharic, Arabic, Armenian, Basque, Bengali, Bulgarian, Burmese, Catalan, Chinese, Czech, Danish, Dhivehi, Dutch, Estonian, Finnish, French, Georgian, German, Greek, Haitian, Hebrew, Hindi, Hungarian, Icelandic, Indonesian, Italian, Japanese, Kannada, Khmer, Korean, Kurdish, Lao, Latvian, Lithuanian, Malayalam, Marathi, Nepali, Norwegian, Oriya, Panjabi, Persian, Polish, Pushto, Romanian, Russian, Serbian, Sindhi, Sinhala, Slovenian, Spanish, Swedish, Tagalog, Tamil, Telegu, Thai, Turkish, Uighur, Ukranian, Urdu, Vietnamese, Welsh. These languages are supported both by a XLM-T multilingual model and the Twitter API.

B Model Links

Table 4 lists all TweetNLP models and their corresponding Hugging Face model hub links.

We release the word embeddings along with Gensim-optimized versions: (1) English-monolingual word embeddings are available at `https://tweetnlp.org/downloads/twitter-2021-124m-300d.new.bin`; (2) Multilingual word embeddings are available at `https://tweetnlp.org/downloads/twitter-multilingual-300d.new.bin`.

Table 5 lists the baselines used for the evaluation (Section 7) and their corresponding Hugging Face hub links.

Model	Link
TweetEval	https://huggingface.co/cardiffnlp/twitter-roberta-base
TimeLMs-21 (default)	https://huggingface.co/cardiffnlp/twitter-roberta-base-2021-124m
XLM-T	https://huggingface.co/cardiffnlp/twitter-xlm-roberta-base
Sentiment Analysis	https://huggingface.co/cardiffnlp/twitter-roberta-base-sentiment-latest
Multilingual Sentiment Analysis	https://huggingface.co/cardiffnlp/twitter-xlm-roberta-base-sentiment
Emotion Recognition	https://huggingface.co/cardiffnlp/twitter-roberta-base-emotion
Emoji Prediction	https://huggingface.co/cardiffnlp/twitter-roberta-base-emoji
Irony Detection	https://huggingface.co/cardiffnlp/twitter-roberta-base-irony
Hate Speech Detection	https://huggingface.co/cardiffnlp/twitter-roberta-base-hate
Offensive Language Identification	https://huggingface.co/cardiffnlp/twitter-roberta-base-offensive
Stance Detection (abortion)	https://huggingface.co/cardiffnlp/twitter-roberta-base-stance-abortion
Topic Classification	https://huggingface.co/cardiffnlp/tweet-topic-21-multi
Named Entity Recognition	https://huggingface.co/tner/twitter-roberta-base-dec2021-tweetner7-all
Tweet Embeddings	https://huggingface.co/cambridgeltl/tweet-roberta-base-embeddings-v1

Table 4: Hugging Face model links of all the NLP models included in TweetNLP (if available).

Model	Link
RoBERTa-base	https://huggingface.co/roberta-base
XLM-R	https://huggingface.co/xlm-roberta-base
BERTweet	https://huggingface.co/vinai/bertweet-base
Sentence-BERT	https://huggingface.co/sentence-transformers/bert-base-nli-mean-tokens
all-mpnet-base-v2	https://huggingface.co/sentence-transformers/all-mpnet-base-v2
Mirror-RoBERTa	https://huggingface.co/cambridgeltl/mirror-roberta-base-sentence-drophead
SimCSE-RoBERTa	https://huggingface.co/princeton-nlp/unsup-simcse-roberta-base

Table 5: Baseline models' Hugging Face links (if available).

JoeyS2T: Minimalistic Speech-to-Text Modeling with JoeyNMT

Mayumi Ohta
Computational Linguistics
Heidelberg University, Germany
ohta@cl.uni-heidelberg.de

Julia Kreutzer
Google Research
jkreutzer@google.com

Stefan Riezler
Computational Linguistics & IWR
Heidelberg University, Germany
riezler@cl.uni-heidelberg.de

Abstract

JoeyS2T is a JoeyNMT (Kreutzer et al., 2019) extension for speech-to-text tasks such as automatic speech recognition and end-to-end speech translation. It inherits the core philosophy of JoeyNMT, a minimalist NMT toolkit built on PyTorch, seeking simplicity and accessibility. JoeyS2T's workflow is self-contained, starting from data pre-processing, over model training and prediction to evaluation, and is seamlessly integrated into JoeyNMT's compact and simple code base. On top of JoeyNMT's state-of-the-art Transformer-based encoder-decoder architecture, JoeyS2T provides speech-oriented components such as convolutional layers, SpecAugment, CTC-loss, and WER evaluation. Despite its simplicity compared to prior implementations, JoeyS2T performs competitively on English speech recognition and English-to-German speech translation benchmarks. The implementation is accompanied by a walk-through tutorial and available on https://github.com/may-/joeys2t.

1 Introduction

End-to-end models recently have been shown to be able to outperform complex pipelines of individually trained components in many NLP tasks. For example, in the area of automatic speech recognition (ASR) and speech translation (ST), the performance gap between end-to-end models and cascaded pipelines, where an acoustic model is followed by an HMM for ASR, or an ASR model is followed by a machine translation (MT) model for ST, seems to be closed (Sperber et al., 2019; Bentivogli et al., 2021). An end-to-end approach has several advantages over a pipeline approach: First, it mitigates error propagation through the pipeline. Second, its data requirements are simpler since intermediate data interfaces to bridge components can be skipped. Furthermore, intermediate components such as phoneme dictionaries in ASR or transcriptions in ST need significant amounts of additional human expertise to build. For end-to-end models, the overall model architecture is simpler, consisting of a unified end-to-end neural network. Nonetheless, end-to-end components can be initialized from non end-to-end data, e.g., in audio encoding layers (Xu et al., 2021) or text decoding layers (Li et al., 2021).

ASR or ST tasks usually have a higher entry barrier than MT, especially for novices who have little experience in machine learning, but also for NLP researchers who have previously only worked on text and not speech processing. This can also be seen in the population of the different tracks of NLP conferences. For example, the "Speech and Multimodality" track of ACL 2022 had only a third of the number of papers in the "Machine Translation and Multilinguality" track.[1] However, thanks to the end-to-end paradigm, those tasks are now more accessible for students or entry-level practitioners without huge resources, and without the experience of handling the different modules of a cascaded system or speech processing. The increased adoption of Transformer architectures (Vaswani et al., 2017) in both text (Kalyan et al., 2021) and speech processing (Dong et al., 2018; Karita et al., 2019a,b) has further eased the transfer of knowledge between the two fields, in addition to making joint modeling easier and more unified.

Reviewing existing code bases for end-to-end ASR and ST—for example, DeepSpeech (Hannun et al., 2014), ESPnet (Inaguma et al., 2020; Watanabe et al., 2020), fairseq S2T (Wang et al., 2020), NeurST (Zhao et al., 2021) and SpeechBrain (Ravanelli et al., 2021)—it becomes apparent that the practical use of open-source toolkits still requires significant experience in navigating large-scale code, using complex data formats, pre-processing, neural text modeling, and speech processing in general. High code complexity and a

[1] https://public.tableau.com/views/ACL2022map/Dashboard1?:showVizHome=no

Proceedings of the The 2022 Conference on Empirical Methods in Natural Language Processing: System Demonstrations, pages 50 - 59
December 7-11, 2022 ©2022 Association for Computational Linguistics

lack of documentation are frustrating hurdles for novices. We propose JoeyS2T, a minimalist and accessible framework, to help novices get started with speech recognition and translation, to accelerate their learning process, and to make ASR and ST more accessible and transparent, that is directly targeting novices and their needs.

We hope that making more accessible implementations will also have trickle-down effects of making the research built on top of it more accessible and more linguistically and geographically diverse (Joshi et al., 2020). This effect has already been observed for the adoption of JoeyNMT for text MT for low-resource languages (∀ et al., 2020; Camgoz et al., 2020; Zhao et al., 2020; Zacarías Márquez and Meza Ruiz, 2021; Ranathunga et al., 2021; Mirzakhalov et al., 2021). Furthermore, speech technology has an even higher potential for language inclusivity (Black, 2019; Abraham et al., 2020; Zhang et al., 2022; Liu et al., 2022).

2 Speech-to-Text Modeling

Automatic speech recognition and translation require mapping a speech feature sequence $X = \{\mathbf{x}_i \in \mathbb{R}^d\}$ to a text token sequence $Y = \{y_t \in \mathcal{V}\}$. The continuous speech signal in its raw wave form is pre-processed into a sequence of discrete frames that are each represented as d-dimensional speech feature vectors $\mathbf{x}_i$, e.g., log Mel filterbanks at the i-th time frame. In contrast, a textual sequence is naturally composed of discrete symbols that can be broken down into units of different granularity, e.g. characters, sub-words, or words. These units then form a vocabulary, so in the above formulation y_t is the t-th target token from the vocabulary $\mathcal{V}$. The goal of S2T modeling is then to find the most probable target token sequence $\hat{Y}$ from all possible vocabulary combinations $\mathcal{V}*$:

$$\hat{Y} = \arg\max_{Y \in \mathcal{V}*} p(Y \mid X). \tag{1}$$

2.1 Why End-to-End Modeling?

In conventional HMM modeling, the posterior probability $p(Y \mid X)$ from Eq. 1 is decomposed into three components by introducing the HMM state sequences $S = \{s_t\}$:

$$p(Y \mid X) \approx \underbrace{p(X \mid S)}_{\text{Acoustic Model}} \underbrace{p(S \mid Y)}_{\text{Lexical Model}} \underbrace{p(Y)}_{\text{LM}}. \tag{2}$$

The components correspond to an acoustic model $p(X \mid S)$, a lexical representation model $p(S \mid Y)$, and a language model $p(Y)$. For practitioners, this means that three individual models need to be implemented, trained and combined. This comes with a large overhead, since each of them requires dedicated linguistic resources and experience in training and tuning. Attention-based deep neural networks have reduced this burden significantly since they implicitly model all three components in a single neural network, mapping X directly to Y (Chorowski et al., 2015; Chan et al., 2016).

2.2 Optimization

Most approaches to sequence-to-sequence learning tasks like MT use the cross-entropy (Xent) loss for optimization, and break the sequence prediction task down to a token-level objective. The posterior probability from above is modeled as the product of output token probabilities conditioned on the entire input sequence X and the target prefix $y_{<t}$:

$$p_{\text{xent}}(Y \mid X) := \prod_t p(y_t \mid y_{<t}; X). \tag{3}$$

A popular alternative in ASR is to employ Connectionist Temporal Classification (CTC) loss (Graves and Jaitly, 2014). CTC uses a Markov assumption to model the transition of states similar to conventional HMM:

$$p_{\text{ctc}}(Y \mid X) := \sum_{\mathcal{A}} \prod_t p(a_t \mid X), \tag{4}$$

where $\mathcal{A}$ denotes the set of valid alignments from X to Y, $a_t \in \mathcal{A}$ is one possible alignment at the t-th time step, and marginalizing the conditional probability $p(a_t \mid X)$ over all valid possible alignments yields the sequence-level probability.

This CTC formulation is suitable to learn monotonic alignments between audio and text, and it also can handle very long sequences efficiently by solving dynamic programming on the state transition graph. The assumption of conditional independence at different time steps is a potentially harmful simplification which is compensated for by a token-level objective and by jointly minimizing cross-entropy and CTC loss (Hori et al., 2017; Watanabe et al., 2017). The final optimization objective in the JoeyS2T implementation is a logarithmic linear combination of the label-smoothed cross-entropy loss and the CTC loss defined above:

$$\begin{aligned}\mathcal{L}_{\text{total}} :=& (1-\lambda) \log p_{\text{xent}}(Y \mid X) \\ &+ \lambda \log p_{\text{ctc}}(Y \mid X),\end{aligned} \tag{5}$$

where $\lambda \in [0, 1]$ is an interpolation parameter.

3 Design Principles

Simplicity: We devoted considerable effort to keep JoeyS2T's module structure simple and flat. It directly employs the PyTorch (Paszke et al., 2019) backend and has a low level of abstraction (details in Section 4.6). JoeyS2T has a minimal list of external dependencies that can be easily installed via the `PyPI`[2] tool. Even for pre-processing, external dependencies on tools such as Kaldi (Povey et al., 2011) are avoided. For filterbank feature extraction, we use TorchAudio[3] which is seamlessly integrated into PyTorch. In contrast to other toolkits, speech modules extended in JoeyS2T are only built for speech-to-text modeling. It does not implement speech enhancement, nor speaker detection or speech generation. While this might appear like a limitation, we believe that the reduction of functionalities to a carefully identified minimum for ST and ASR is the key for increased accessibility.[4]

Accessibility: We also have written extensive documentation and walk-through tutorials to help newcomers become more familiar with speech technologies. JoeyS2T also provides pretrained models including configuration files which lower the barrier to get started. To guarantee the accessibility of the code, we open-sourced JoeyS2T under a very permissive license (Apache 2.0). The JoeyS2T developer community actively supports user questions and requests. We maintain an open platform to discuss bug fixes, possible extensions etc. All contributions are first automatically controlled by the internal unit tests and will manually be reviewed by our team.

Reproducibility: To ensure that the reported results are comparable and reproducible, we release models trained on publicly available data. Our evaluation metrics are described in detail (tokenization, punctuation handling etc.). All pre- and post-processing scripts are published with a data download path and explicit hyperparameter configurations. We track all code changes in our repository and provide version information which is often a critical factor for reproducibility as bug fixes can affect evaluation scores.

[2]`https://pypi.org/`

[3]`https://github.com/pytorch/audio`

[4]A clean code base can always be extended by users once they are more proficient. For example, JoeyNMT has been successfully extended to other modalities and integrated into web interfaces by advanced users. See `https://github.com/joeynmt/joeynmt#projects-and-extensions`

4 Implementation and Usage

4.1 Hyperparameter Configuration

JoeyS2T sets up experiments based on a YAML-style configuration file which declares the whole pipeline, just like JoeyNMT. Processes are run in a Python interface without relying on external Bash or Perl scripts. In the configuration file, users can choose between the tasks `MT` (Machine Translation) or `S2T` (Speech-to-Text) in order to inform JoeyS2T about the input data type: audio or text. The hyperparameters of speech-related modules such as SpecAugment, 1d-Conv etc. can also be specified in the same configuration file.[5]

4.2 Data Loading and Pre-processing

Source Audios: We separated computationally heavy pre-processing steps from model training, e.g., the conversion from raw wave forms to spectrograms by Fourier transformation. We employ the TorchAudio API to extract audio features in the pre-processing scripts. JoeyS2T includes modules for Cepstral Mean Variance Normalization (CMVN) (Viikki and Laurila, 1998) and SpecAugment (Park et al., 2019) by default. These are applied minibatch-wise before the input data are fed into the encoder.

Data Loading: As a precautionary measure to avoid memory allocation errors (which can happen for large audio inputs) we implemented on-the-fly data loading: we only store the path to the data in the iterator, and load the actual spectrogram features into memory every time a minibatch is constructed.

Target Texts: For target texts, we expect users to prepare a tokenization model independently and to specify the path to the trained tokenizer. Besides rule-based character-level tokenization and basic white space splitting, we currently support subword-nmt tokenizers (Sennrich et al., 2016) and SentencePiece tokenizers (Kudo and Richardson, 2018). Users can specify tokenizer options in JoeyS2T's configuration file. During training, JoeyS2T applies text tokenization on the fly. Since the text length can be calculated only after tokenization, instance filtering by length is applied in this step. Thanks to this flexible on-the-fly tokenization, dynamic data augmentation methods i.e., BPE Dropout (Provilkov et al., 2020), SwitchOut (Wang

[5]Sample configuration files for different datasets are available at `https://github.com/may-/joeys2t/configs`

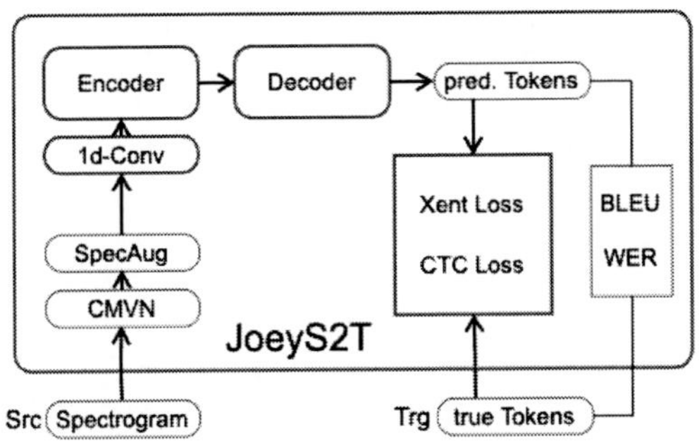

Figure 1: Architecture of JoeyS2T. We reuse JoeyNMT's basic building blocks and extended them by essential audio-specific modules.

et al., 2018) or ADA (Lam et al., 2021) can be easily integrated.

4.3 Architectures

JoeyS2T supports a Transformer-based encoder-decoder architecture (see Figure 1). We reuse the self-attention encoder and decoder layers of JoeyNMT, and modify them in order to support speech-specific components.

Input Representations: Instead of converting token embeddings from discrete one-hot encodings to continuous vectors (as done for text input), we directly feed the sequence of filterbank vectors to the encoder. The embedding size in text-based JoeyNMT thus corresponds to the filterbank frequency size in JoeyS2T.

Encoder: The biggest difference to the original text-to-text Transformer architecture is the 1-dimensional convolution layer (1d-Conv) placed before the self-attention encoder. It compresses potentially redundant features along the time dimension in order to capture phonetic structures. Each 1d-Conv layer has a stride of 2. This further downsamples the sequence by a factor of 2^l, where l is the number of 1d-Conv layers. The reduction of the input length is essential for computation speed: Speech feature sequences are usually much longer than text token sequences, and the computational complexity of one self-attention block is $\mathcal{O}(u^2 \cdot d)$ (Vaswani et al., 2017), where u is the maximal input length (number of tokens in textual input, or number of time frames in speech input), and d is the embedding size.

Decoder: We reuse the decoder construction of the original JoeyNMT code, but add one additional linear layer for the CTC loss on top of the self-attentive decoder layers.

Inference: We support greedy and beam search based on the token probability distributions. All inference enhancements introduced in JoeyNMT v2.0 such as repetition penalty, n-gram blocker, probability scoring, attention visualization of cross-attention heads in transformer layers, etc. are supported by JoeyS2T as well.

4.4 Evaluation Metrics

JoeyS2T supports Character F-score (ChrF) (Popović, 2015), BLEU (Papineni et al., 2002) and Word Error Rate (WER) based on Levenshtein distance (Navarro, 2001) as evaluation metrics for ASR and ST. We import `sacrebleu`[7] (Post, 2018) for ChrF and BLEU, and `editdistance`[8] (Hyyrö, 2001) for WER. In addition, perplexity and accuracy can be monitored during training on Tensorboard (Abadi et al., 2015).

4.5 Documentation and Tutorial

We follow the documentation strategy of JoeyNMT, which means that all extended functions have their own docstring and in-line comments for tensor shapes. Unit tests covering essential modules are automatically triggered on every commit to the repository.

In the hands-on tutorial, we present working examples for ASR and ST as Jupyter notebooks.[9] The walk-through tutorial is self-contained and explains the whole pipeline: installation steps, data downloading, data pre-processing, configuration, model training/fine-tuning, inference and evaluation. We will keep the tutorial up to date with potential future API changes.

4.6 Code complexity

JoeyNMT exhibits the spirit of minimalism by aiming to achieve 80% of the output quality with 20% of a common toolkit's code size (80/20 principle; (Pareto, 1896)). Table 3 gives statistics on code

[6] `nrefs:1|case:mixed|eff:no|tok:13a|smooth:exp|version:2.1.0`

[7] `https://github.com/mjpost/sacrebleu`

[8] `https://github.com/roy-ht/editdistance`

[9] Demo video: `https://youtu.be/bpBtq2jLolQ`

[10] `https://github.com/espnet/espnet/tree/master/espnet2` (commit hash `039cc5d`)

[11] `https://github.com/pytorch/fairseq/tree/main/fairseq` (commit hash `ad3bec5`)

[12] `https://github.com/may-/joeys2t/tree/main/joeynmt` (commit hash `a80802a`)

System	Architecture	LibriSpeech 100h (WER ↓) dev-clean	dev-other	test-clean	test-other
Kahn et al. (2020)†	BiLSTM	14.00	37.02	14.85	39.95
Laptev et al. (2020)†	Transformer	10.3	24.0	11.2	24.9
ESPnet‡	Transformer	8.1	20.2	8.4	20.5
ESPnet‡	Conformer	6.3	17.4	6.5	17.3
JoeyS2T	Transformer	10.66 ± 0.36	23.82 ± 0.34	12.02 ± 0.32	24.75 ± 0.37

System	Architecture	LibriSpeech 960h (WER ↓) dev-clean	dev-other	test-clean	test-other
Gulati et al. (2020)†	Conformer	1.9	4.4	2.1	4.9
ESPnet‡	Conformer	2.3	6.1	2.6	6.0
SpeechBrain*	Conformer	2.13	5.51	2.31	5.61
fairseq S2T*	Transformer	3.23	8.01	3.52	7.83
fairseq wav2vec2*	Conformer	3.17	8.86	3.39	8.57
JoeyS2T	Transformer	3.79 ± 0.27	8.84 ± 0.39	4.31 ± 0.52	8.66 ± 0.35

Table 1: Averaged results in WER on the English **LibriSpeech** dataset over three runs with standard deviations (±). We compute the WER on lowercased transcriptions without punctuations using SacreBLEU's 13a tokenizer. †: results were reported in the papers linked above. ‡: results were taken from the repository linked above. *: we downloaded their pretrained models from the repository, and ran the inference and the evaluation on the same test data as we use in JoeyS2T.

System	MuST-C ver. train	eval	ASR (WER ↓) tst-COMMON	tst-HE	MT (BLEU ↑) tst-COMMON	tst-HE
Gangi et al. (2019)†	v1	v1	27.0	-	25.3	-
Zhang et al. (2020)†	v1	v1	-	-	29.69	-
ESPnet‡	v1	v1	12.70	-	27.63	-
fairseq S2T*	v1	v1	12.72	10.93	-	-
JoeyS2T	v2	v1	18.86±0.37	15.19±0.56	23.07±0.14	20.21±0.17
fairseq S2T*	v1	v2	11.88	10.43	-	-
JoeyS2T	v2	v2	12.95±0.32	11.16±0.31	27.17±0.63	24.85±0.68

System	MuST-C ver. train	eval	Cascade ST (BLEU ↑) tst-COMMON	tst-HE	End2End ST (BLEU ↑) tst-COMMON	tst-HE
Gangi et al. (2019)†	v1	v1	18.5	-	17.3	-
Zhang et al. (2020)†	v1	v1	22.52	-	20.67	-
ESPnet‡	v1	v1	-	-	22.91	-
fairseq S2T*	v1	v1	-	-	22.70	21.70
JoeyS2T	v2	v1	21.89±0.64	21.03±0.66	20.53±0.29	21.13±0.46
fairseq S2T*	v1	v2	-	-	23.20	22.23
JoeyS2T	v2	v2	23.95±0.59	22.65±0.58	23.33±0.39	22.90±0.69

Table 2: Averaged results on the **MuST-C en-de** dataset over three runs with standard deviations (±). We compute the BLEU on truecased translations with punctuations using SacreBLEU's 13a tokenizer.[6] †: results were reported in the papers linked above. ‡: results were taken from the repository linked above. *: we downloaded their pretrained models from the repository, and ran the inference and evaluation on the same test data as we use in JoeyS2T.

complexity. In terms of the numbers of Python files and code lines, JoeyS2T is 10–11 times more compact than ESPnet (Inaguma et al., 2020; Watanabe et al., 2020) and fairseq (Wang et al., 2020). However, both ESPnet and fairseq are general-purpose toolkits, covering a wide range of tasks beyond MT, ASR or ST, such as language modeling or speech synthesis, while JoeyS2T is designed for a speech-to-text tasks only. Yet JoeyS2T's comment-to-code ratio is much higher than that of the competitors.

JoeyS2T offers a flat code structure in order to make debugging along the stack trace easier

	ESPnet2[10]	fairseq[11]	JoeyS2T[12]
Python files	287	407	24
Code lines	41427	65097	5450
Comment lines	10260	11042	2137
Comment/Code Ratio	0.25	0.17	0.39

Table 3: Code complexity measured using `https://github.com/AlDanial/cloc` v1.94.

and to reduce the number of code files and nested classes/functions to read through. In contrast, fairseq's codebase is organized hierarchically. This deep hierarchy comes from the structured class inheritance, which is an important component of object-oriented programming for experienced developers. However, such hierarchical class inheritance is sometimes a big stumbling block for novices (Wiedenbeck et al., 1999). We intentionally abandon deeply inherited class design and use novice-friendly flat structure instead. As a result, developers do not have to allocate their cognitive resources to framework-specific software design principles, but they can concentrate on the logic they want to realize. JoeyS2T encourages novices to dive into speech-to-text research before they mature in high-context system design such as hierarchical class inheritance or decorators.

5 Experimental Results on Benchmarks

Despite its simplicity, JoeyS2T achieves a performance on standard benchmarks that is comparable to other high-functional speech-to-text toolkits.

5.1 ASR on LibriSpeech

LibriSpeech (Panayotov et al., 2015) is the de-facto standard English ASR benchmark that contains 960 hours of audiobooks in Project Gutenberg. The corpus is publicly available under the CC BY 4.0 license and many works set their goal to achieve state-of-the-art WER on its test splits.

Tables 1 present the results of models trained on 100h and 960h audio, respectively. JoeyS2T shows comparable performance with current Transformer-based models, which are generally outperformed by Conformer (Gulati et al., 2020) models.

5.2 ST on MuST-C

MuST-C (Cattoni et al., 2021) is a publicly available speech translation corpus built from English TED Talks. It consists of English transcriptions and translations into 14 languages, contributed by volunteers. We trained our model on the English-German subset of version 2, and evaluated the model both on version 1 and version 2 `tst-COMMON`, and `tst-HE` splits.

MuST-C is a challenging dataset due to its spontaneous speech that contains hesitations, disfluent utterances, etc. on the source side. Furthermore, the ground-truth target texts derived from the subtitles are also noisy. There are some additional descriptions of non-verbal information, i.e., "(applause)" "(laughter)", or "♪ (music)". Those are not actually pronounced in the source, but provided in the target, which makes learning more difficult. We normalized such noisy expressions and specified them as special tokens during the subword training, so that they are not tokenized into subwords but kept as single tokens. For the sake of reproducibility, we provide a preprocessing script for all normalization steps.

For ST tasks, we first pretrained ASR models and MT models using the gold transcriptions. Then we initialized the encoder layers of an end-to-end ST model with the pretrained ASR encoders and the decoder layers with the pretrained MT decoders, and further trained it on the end-to-end ST task.

The ST results can be found in Table 2. JoeyS2T shows competitive results, both in end-to-end scenarios and in a cascade using the same pre-trained models. We also include the ASR and MT pretraining results for reference.

6 Conclusion & Future Work

We described JoeyS2T, an extension of the JoeyNMT toolkit to the spoken language processing tasks ASR and ST. JoeyS2T is characterized by its minimalist design, prioritization of simplicity, accessibility and reproducibility in its code and documentation. The code is self-contained and requires minimal prior experience with speech or language processing. In benchmark evaluations, JoeyS2T performed comparable or superior to other ASR or ST code bases, while having much lower code complexity.

While its functionality is kept minimal, support for state-of-the-art architectures such as wav2vec and Conformer might be desired for future extensions.

Limitations

The limitations of our work mainly concern the reproducibility of comparable state-of-the-art results. First, there are many different preprocessing variants which are quite complex (length filtering, speed shift, lowercasing, punctuation normalization etc.) and not always clearly documented. Second, the same problem appears in evaluation. There is no commonly accepted evaluation scheme (including lower-cased vs. true-cased results, with or without punctuation, etc.). While the `sacrebleu` library is a first step to addressing this problem in MT, we believe that the speech processing community also needs such efforts to standardize speech-to-text evaluation.

Since the goal of our work is not to present a new state-of-the-art in speech-to-text modeling, we did not invest a large effort into hyperparameter tuning, but only varied three different random seeds in our setup, and used the default settings for competitor systems.

Acknowledgements

We would like to thank the members of the StatNLP group at Heidelberg University and the AIMS Senegal students for their feedback on the tutorial. Furthermore, we appreciate the discussions with the Masakhane[13] community in the early stages of the toolkit development. We also thank Yaraku Inc.[14] for the opportunity to publish JoeyS2T tutorial articles.[15]

References

Martín Abadi, Ashish Agarwal, Paul Barham, Eugene Brevdo, Zhifeng Chen, Craig Citro, Greg S. Corrado, Andy Davis, Jeffrey Dean, Matthieu Devin, Sanjay Ghemawat, Ian Goodfellow, Andrew Harp, Geoffrey Irving, Michael Isard, Yangqing Jia, Rafal Jozefowicz, Lukasz Kaiser, Manjunath Kudlur, Josh Levenberg, Dandelion Mané, Rajat Monga, Sherry Moore, Derek Murray, Chris Olah, Mike Schuster, Jonathon Shlens, Benoit Steiner, Ilya Sutskever, Kunal Talwar, Paul Tucker, Vincent Vanhoucke, Vijay Vasudevan, Fernanda Viégas, Oriol Vinyals, Pete Warden, Martin Wattenberg, Martin Wicke, Yuan Yu, and Xiaoqiang Zheng. 2015. TensorFlow: Large-scale machine learning on heterogeneous systems. Software available from tensorflow.org.

Basil Abraham, Danish Goel, Divya Siddarth, Kalika Bali, Manu Chopra, Monojit Choudhury, Pratik Joshi, Preethi Jyoti, Sunayana Sitaram, and Vivek Seshadri. 2020. Crowdsourcing speech data for low-resource languages from low-income workers. In *Proceedings of the 12th Language Resources and Evaluation Conference*, pages 2819–2826, Marseille, France. European Language Resources Association.

[13]`https://www.masakhane.io/`

[14]`https://www.yarakuzen.com/`

[15]`https://atmarkit.itmedia.co.jp/ait/articles/2208/17/news002.html`

Luisa Bentivogli, Mauro Cettolo, Marco Gaido, Alina Karakanta, Alberto Martinelli, Matteo Negri, and Marco Turchi. 2021. Cascade versus direct speech translation: Do the differences still make a difference? In *Proceedings of the 59th Annual Meeting of the Association for Computational Linguistics and the 11th International Joint Conference on Natural Language Processing (Volume 1: Long Papers)*, pages 2873–2887, Online. Association for Computational Linguistics.

Alan W Black. 2019. Cmu wilderness multilingual speech dataset. In *ICASSP 2019 - 2019 IEEE International Conference on Acoustics, Speech and Signal Processing (ICASSP)*, pages 5971–5975.

Necati Cihan Camgoz, Oscar Koller, Simon Hadfield, and Richard Bowden. 2020. Sign language transformers: Joint end-to-end sign language recognition and translation. In *Proceedings of the IEEE/CVF conference on computer vision and pattern recognition*, pages 10023–10033.

Roldano Cattoni, Mattia Antonino Di Gangi, Luisa Bentivogli, Matteo Negri, and Marco Turchi. 2021. Must-c: A multilingual corpus for end-to-end speech translation. *Computer Speech & Language*, 66:101155.

William Chan, Navdeep Jaitly, Quoc Le, and Oriol Vinyals. 2016. Listen, attend and spell: A neural network for large vocabulary conversational speech recognition. In *2016 IEEE International Conference on Acoustics, Speech and Signal Processing (ICASSP)*, pages 4960–4964.

Jan Chorowski, Dzmitry Bahdanau, Dmitriy Serdyuk, Kyunghyun Cho, and Yoshua Bengio. 2015. Attention-based models for speech recognition. In *Proceedings of the 28th International Conference on Neural Information Processing Systems - Volume 1*, NIPS'15, page 577–585, Cambridge, MA, USA. MIT Press.

Linhao Dong, Shuang Xu, and Bo Xu. 2018. Speech-transformer: A no-recurrence sequence-to-sequence model for speech recognition. In *2018 IEEE International Conference on Acoustics, Speech and Signal Processing (ICASSP)*, pages 5884–5888.

∀, Wilhelmina Nekoto, Vukosi Marivate, Tshinondiwa Matsila, Timi Fasubaa, Taiwo Fagbohungbe, Solomon Oluwole Akinola, Shamsuddeen Muhammad, Salomon Kabongo Kabenamualu, Salomey Osei, Freshia Sackey, Rubungo Andre Niyongabo, Ricky Macharm, Perez Ogayo, Orevaoghene Ahia, Musie Meressa Berhe, Mofetoluwa Adeyemi, Masabata Mokgesi-Selinga, Lawrence Okegbemi, Laura Martinus, Kolawole Tajudeen, Kevin Degila, Kelechi Ogueji, Kathleen Siminyu, Julia Kreutzer, Jason Webster, Jamiil Toure Ali, Jade Abbott,

Iroro Orife, Ignatius Ezeani, Idris Abdulkadir Dangana, Herman Kamper, Hady Elsahar, Goodness Duru, Ghollah Kioko, Murhabazi Espoir, Elan van Biljon, Daniel Whitenack, Christopher Onyefuluchi, Chris Chinenye Emezue, Bonaventure F. P. Dossou, Blessing Sibanda, Blessing Bassey, Ayodele Olabiyi, Arshath Ramkilowan, Alp Öktem, Adewale Akinfaderin, and Abdallah Bashir. 2020. Participatory research for low-resourced machine translation: A case study in African languages. In *Findings of the Association for Computational Linguistics: EMNLP 2020*, pages 2144–2160, Online. Association for Computational Linguistics.

Mattia A. Di Gangi, Matteo Negri, and Marco Turchi. 2019. Adapting Transformer to End-to-End Spoken Language Translation. In *Proc. Interspeech 2019*, pages 1133–1137.

Alex Graves and Navdeep Jaitly. 2014. Towards end-to-end speech recognition with recurrent neural networks. *International conference on machine learning*, pages 1764–1772.

Anmol Gulati, James Qin, Chung-Cheng Chiu, Niki Parmar, Yu Zhang, Jiahui Yu, Wei Han, Shibo Wang, Zhengdong Zhang, Yonghui Wu, and Ruoming Pang. 2020. Conformer: Convolution-augmented transformer for speech recognition. In *Interspeech 2020, 21st Annual Conference of the International Speech Communication Association*, pages 5036–5040, Shanghai, China. ISCA.

Awni Hannun, Carl Case, Jared Casper, Bryan Catanzaro, Greg Diamos, Erich Elsen, Ryan Prenger, Sanjeev Satheesh, Shubho Sengupta, Adam Coates, et al. 2014. Deep speech: Scaling up end-to-end speech recognition. *arXiv preprint arXiv:1412.5567.*

Takaaki Hori, Shinji Watanabe, and John Hershey. 2017. Joint CTC/attention decoding for end-to-end speech recognition. In *Proceedings of the 55th Annual Meeting of the Association for Computational Linguistics (Volume 1: Long Papers)*, pages 518–529, Vancouver, Canada. Association for Computational Linguistics.

Heikki Hyyrö. 2001. Explaining and extending the bit-parallel approximate string matching algorithm of myers. Technical report, Citeseer.

Hirofumi Inaguma, Shun Kiyono, Kevin Duh, Shigeki Karita, Nelson Yalta, Tomoki Hayashi, and Shinji Watanabe. 2020. ESPnet-ST: All-in-one speech translation toolkit. In *Proceedings of the 58th Annual Meeting of the Association for Computational Linguistics: System Demonstrations*, pages 302–311, Online. Association for Computational Linguistics.

Pratik Joshi, Sebastin Santy, Amar Budhiraja, Kalika Bali, and Monojit Choudhury. 2020. The state and fate of linguistic diversity and inclusion in the NLP world. In *Proceedings of the 58th Annual Meeting of the Association for Computational Linguistics*, pages 6282–6293, Online. Association for Computational Linguistics.

Jacob Kahn, Ann Lee, and Awni Hannun. 2020. Self-training for end-to-end speech recognition. In *2020 IEEE International Conference on Acoustics, Speech and Signal Processing (ICASSP)*, pages 7084–7088. IEEE.

Katikapalli Subramanyam Kalyan, Ajit Rajasekharan, and Sivanesan Sangeetha. 2021. AMMUS : A survey of transformer-based pretrained models in natural language processing. *CoRR*, abs/2108.05542.

Shigeki Karita, N. Chen, Tomoki Hayashi, Takaaki Hori, H. Inaguma, Ziyan Jiang, Masao Someki, Nelson Yalta, Ryuichi Yamamoto, Xiao fei Wang, Shinji Watanabe, Takenori Yoshimura, and Wangyou Zhang. 2019a. A comparative study on transformer vs rnn in speech applications. *2019 IEEE Automatic Speech Recognition and Understanding Workshop (ASRU)*, pages 449–456.

Shigeki Karita, Nelson Yalta, Shinji Watanabe, Marc Delcroix, Atsunori Ogawa, and Tomohiro Nakatani. 2019b. Improving transformer-based end-to-end speech recognition with connectionist temporal classification and language model integration. In *INTERSPEECH*.

Julia Kreutzer, Jasmijn Bastings, and Stefan Riezler. 2019. Joey NMT: A minimalist NMT toolkit for novices. In *Proceedings of the 2019 Conference on Empirical Methods in Natural Language Processing and the 9th International Joint Conference on Natural Language Processing (EMNLP-IJCNLP): System Demonstrations*, pages 109–114, Hong Kong, China. Association for Computational Linguistics.

Taku Kudo and John Richardson. 2018. SentencePiece: A simple and language independent subword tokenizer and detokenizer for neural text processing. In *Proceedings of the 2018 Conference on Empirical Methods in Natural Language Processing: System Demonstrations*, pages 66–71, Brussels, Belgium. Association for Computational Linguistics.

Tsz Kin Lam, Mayumi Ohta, Shigehiko Schamoni, and Stefan Riezler. 2021. On-the-fly aligned data augmentation for sequence-to-sequence ASR. In *22nd Annual Conference of the International Speech Communication Association, INTERSPEECH 2021*, pages 4261–4265. International Speech Communication Association.

Aleksandr Laptev, Roman Korostik, Aleksey Svischev, Andrei Andrusenko, Ivan Medennikov, and Sergey Rybin. 2020. You do not need more data: Improving end-to-end speech recognition by text-to-speech data augmentation. In *2020 13th International Congress on Image and Signal Processing, BioMedical Engineering and Informatics (CISP-BMEI)*, pages 439–444. IEEE.

Xian Li, Changhan Wang, Yun Tang, Chau Tran, Yuqing Tang, Juan Pino, Alexei Baevski, Alexis Conneau, and Michael Auli. 2021. Multilingual speech translation from efficient finetuning of pretrained models.

In *Proceedings of the 59th Annual Meeting of the Association for Computational Linguistics and the 11th International Joint Conference on Natural Language Processing (Volume 1: Long Papers)*, pages 827–838, Online. Association for Computational Linguistics.

Zoey Liu, Crystal Richardson, Richard Hatcher, and Emily Prud'hommeaux. 2022. Not always about you: Prioritizing community needs when developing endangered language technology. In *Proceedings of the 60th Annual Meeting of the Association for Computational Linguistics (Volume 1: Long Papers)*, pages 3933–3944, Dublin, Ireland. Association for Computational Linguistics.

Jamshidbek Mirzakhalov, Anoop Babu, Aigiz Kunafin, Ahsan Wahab, Behzod Moydinboyev, Sardana Ivanova, Mokhiyakhon Uzokova, Shaxnoza Pulatova, Duygu Ataman, Julia Kreutzer, Francis Tyers, Orhan Firat, John Licato, and Sriram Chellappan. 2021. Evaluating multiway multilingual nmt in the turkic languages. In *Proceedings of the Sixth Conference on Machine Translation*, Punta Cana, Dominican Republic.

Gonzalo Navarro. 2001. A guided tour to approximate string matching. *ACM Comput. Surv.*, 33(1):31–88.

Vassil Panayotov, Guoguo Chen, Daniel Povey, and Sanjeev Khudanpur. 2015. Librispeech: An asr corpus based on public domain audio books. In *2015 IEEE International Conference on Acoustics, Speech and Signal Processing (ICASSP)*, pages 5206–5210.

Kishore Papineni, Salim Roukos, Todd Ward, and Wei-Jing Zhu. 2002. Bleu: a method for automatic evaluation of machine translation. In *Proceedings of the 40th Annual Meeting of the Association for Computational Linguistics*, pages 311–318, Philadelphia, Pennsylvania, USA. Association for Computational Linguistics.

Vilfredo Pareto. 1896. *Cours d'économie politique: professé à l'Universi∀té de Lausanne*, volume 1. F. Rouge.

Daniel S Park, William Chan, Yu Zhang, Chung-Cheng Chiu, Barret Zoph, Ekin D Cubuk, and Quoc V Le. 2019. SpecAugment: A simple data augmentation method for automatic speech recognition. *arXiv preprint arXiv:1904.08779*.

Adam Paszke, Sam Gross, Francisco Massa, Adam Lerer, James Bradbury, Gregory Chanan, Trevor Killeen, Zeming Lin, Natalia Gimelshein, Luca Antiga, et al. 2019. Pytorch: An imperative style, high-performance deep learning library. *Advances in neural information processing systems*, 32:8026–8037.

Maja Popović. 2015. chrF: character n-gram F-score for automatic MT evaluation. In *Proceedings of the Tenth Workshop on Statistical Machine Translation*, pages 392–395, Lisbon, Portugal. Association for Computational Linguistics.

Matt Post. 2018. A call for clarity in reporting BLEU scores. In *Proceedings of the Third Conference on Machine Translation: Research Papers*, pages 186–191, Brussels, Belgium. Association for Computational Linguistics.

Daniel Povey, Arnab Ghoshal, Gilles Boulianne, Lukas Burget, Ondrej Glembek, Nagendra Goel, Mirko Hannemann, Petr Motlicek, Yanmin Qian, Petr Schwarz, et al. 2011. The kaldi speech recognition toolkit. In *IEEE 2011 workshop on automatic speech recognition and understanding*, CONF. IEEE Signal Processing Society.

Ivan Provilkov, Dmitrii Emelianenko, and Elena Voita. 2020. BPE-dropout: Simple and effective subword regularization. In *Proceedings of the 58th Annual Meeting of the Association for Computational Linguistics*, pages 1882–1892, Online. Association for Computational Linguistics.

Surangika Ranathunga, En-Shiun Annie Lee, Marjana Prifti Skenduli, Ravi Shekhar, Mehreen Alam, and Rishemjit Kaur. 2021. Neural machine translation for low-resource languages: A survey. *CoRR*, abs/2106.15115.

Mirco Ravanelli, Titouan Parcollet, Peter Plantinga, Aku Rouhe, Samuele Cornell, Loren Lugosch, Cem Subakan, Nauman Dawalatabad, Abdelwahab Heba, Jianyuan Zhong, et al. 2021. SpeechBrain: A general-purpose speech toolkit. *arXiv preprint arXiv:2106.04624*.

Rico Sennrich, Barry Haddow, and Alexandra Birch. 2016. Neural machine translation of rare words with subword units. In *Proceedings of the 54th Annual Meeting of the Association for Computational Linguistics (Volume 1: Long Papers)*, pages 1715–1725, Berlin, Germany. Association for Computational Linguistics.

Matthias Sperber, Graham Neubig, Jan Niehues, and Alex Waibel. 2019. Attention-Passing Models for Robust and Data-Efficient End-to-End Speech Translation. *Transactions of the Association for Computational Linguistics*, 7:313–325.

Ashish Vaswani, Noam Shazeer, Niki Parmar, Jakob Uszkoreit, Llion Jones, Aidan N Gomez, Ł ukasz Kaiser, and Illia Polosukhin. 2017. Attention is all you need. In *Advances in Neural Information Processing Systems*, volume 30.

Olli Viikki and Kari Laurila. 1998. Cepstral domain segmental feature vector normalization for noise robust speech recognition. *Speech Communication*, 25(1-3):133–147.

Changhan Wang, Yun Tang, Xutai Ma, Anne Wu, Dmytro Okhonko, and Juan Pino. 2020. Fairseq S2T: Fast speech-to-text modeling with fairseq. In *Proceedings of the 1st Conference of the Asia-Pacific Chapter of the Association for Computational Linguistics and the 10th International Joint Conference* on Natural Language Processing: System Demonstrations, pages 33–39, Suzhou, China. Association for Computational Linguistics.

Xinyi Wang, Hieu Pham, Zihang Dai, and Graham Neubig. 2018. SwitchOut: an efficient data augmentation algorithm for neural machine translation. In *Proceedings of the 2018 Conference on Empirical Methods in Natural Language Processing*, pages 856–861, Brussels, Belgium. Association for Computational Linguistics.

Shinji Watanabe, Florian Boyer, Xuankai Chang, Pengcheng Guo, Tomoki Hayashi, Yosuke Higuchi, Takaaki Hori, Wen-Chin Huang, Hirofumi Inaguma, Naoyuki Kamo, et al. 2020. The 2020 ESPNet update: New features, broadened applications, performance improvements, and future plans. *arXiv preprint arXiv:2012.13006*.

Shinji Watanabe, Takaaki Hori, Suyoun Kim, John R. Hershey, and Tomoki Hayashi. 2017. Hybrid CTC/Attention Architecture for End-to-End Speech Recognition. *IEEE Journal of Selected Topics in Signal Processing*, 11(8):1240–1253.

Susan Wiedenbeck, Vennila Ramalingam, Suseela Sarasamma, and Cynthia L Corritore. 1999. A comparison of the comprehension of object-oriented and procedural programs by novice programmers. *Interacting with Computers*, 11(3):255–282.

Chen Xu, Bojie Hu, Yanyang Li, Yuhao Zhang, Shen Huang, Qi Ju, Tong Xiao, and Jingbo Zhu. 2021. Stacked acoustic-and-textual encoding: Integrating the pre-trained models into speech translation encoders. In *Proceedings of the 59th Annual Meeting of the Association for Computational Linguistics and the 11th International Joint Conference on Natural Language Processing (Volume 1: Long Papers)*, pages 2619–2630, Online. Association for Computational Linguistics.

Delfino Zacarías Márquez and Ivan Vladimir Meza Ruiz. 2021. Ayuuk-Spanish neural machine translator. In *Proceedings of the First Workshop on Natural Language Processing for Indigenous Languages of the Americas*, pages 168–172, Online. Association for Computational Linguistics.

Biao Zhang, Ivan Titov, Barry Haddow, and Rico Sennrich. 2020. Adaptive feature selection for end-to-end speech translation. In *Findings of the Association for Computational Linguistics: EMNLP 2020*, pages 2533–2544, Online. Association for Computational Linguistics.

Shiyue Zhang, Ben Frey, and Mohit Bansal. 2022. How can NLP help revitalize endangered languages? a case study and roadmap for the Cherokee language. In *Proceedings of the 60th Annual Meeting of the Association for Computational Linguistics (Volume 1: Long Papers)*, pages 1529–1541, Dublin, Ireland. Association for Computational Linguistics.

Chengqi Zhao, Mingxuan Wang, Qianqian Dong, Rong Ye, and Lei Li. 2021. NeurST: Neural speech translation toolkit. In *Proceedings of the 59th Annual Meeting of the Association for Computational Linguistics and the 11th International Joint Conference on Natural Language Processing: System Demonstrations*, pages 55–62, Online. Association for Computational Linguistics.

Xingyuan Zhao, Satoru Ozaki, Antonios Anastasopoulos, Graham Neubig, and Lori Levin. 2020. Automatic interlinear glossing for under-resourced languages leveraging translations. In *Proceedings of the 28th International Conference on Computational Linguistics*, pages 5397–5408, Barcelona, Spain (Online). International Committee on Computational Linguistics.

FairLib: A Unified Framework for Assessing and Improving Fairness

Xudong Han[1] **Aili Shen**[1,2*] **Yitong Li**[3] **Lea Frermann**[1]
Timothy Baldwin[1,4] **Trevor Cohn**[1]
[1]The University of Melbourne [2]Alexa AI, Amazon
[3]Huawei Technologies Co., Ltd. [4]MBZUAI
xudonghl@student.unimelb.edu.au ailishen@amazon.com
liyitong3@huawei.com {lfrermann,tbaldwin,t.cohn}@unimelb.edu.au

Abstract

This paper presents *FairLib*, an open-source Python library for assessing and improving model fairness. It provides a systematic framework for quickly accessing benchmark datasets, reproducing existing debiasing baseline models, developing new methods, evaluating models with different metrics, and visualizing their results. Its modularity and extensibility enable the framework to be used for diverse types of inputs, including natural language, images, and audio. It incorporates 14 debiasing methods, including pre-processing, at-training-time, and post-processing approaches. The built-in metrics cover the most commonly acknowledged fairness criteria, and can be further generalized and customized for fairness evaluation.[1]

1 Introduction

While neural methods have achieved great success, it has been shown that naively-trained models often learn spurious correlations with protected attributes like user demographics or socio-economic factors, leading to allocation harms, stereotyping, and other representation harms (Badjatiya et al., 2019; Zhao et al., 2018; Li et al., 2018; Díaz et al., 2018; Wang et al., 2019). As a result, there is a surge of interest in assessing and improving fairness.

Various bias evaluation metrics have been introduced in previous studies to gauge different types of biases. One common family of fairness assessment is *group fairness* which measures performance disparities across demographic groups. Different instantiations of group fairness have been proposed, including *demographic parity* (Feldman et al., 2015), where the positive prediction rate should be identical across groups (irrespective of the gold label), or *equal opportunity* (Hardt et al., 2016) where all groups should have an equal chance of false negative prediction (*equalized odds* extends the notion to include equal true positive rates). More recent work addressed disparities within classes and demographic groups (Shen et al., 2022b). While these approaches reflect the nature of fairness increasingly faithfully, they have been applied and evaluated inconsistently in previous work, which impedes systematic analysis and comparison of proposed approaches.

In terms of bias mitigation, diverse debiasing methods have been proposed, including at-training-time (Li et al., 2018; Elazar and Goldberg, 2018; Shen et al., 2022a), and pre- (Zhao et al., 2017; Wang et al., 2019) and post-processing approaches (Han et al., 2022a; Ravfogel et al., 2020). Although these methods have been proved effective for bias mitigation, it is challenging to reproduce results and compare methods because of inconsistencies in training strategy and model selection criteria, which demonstrably affect the results.

We present *FairLib*, a well-documented, open-source framework for assessing and improving fairness. *FairLib* implements a number of common debiasing approaches in a unified framework to facilitate reproducible and consistent evaluation, and provides interfaces for developing new debiasing methods. Moreover, a dataset interface supports adoption of both built-in and newly developed methods for new tasks and corpora. For better presentation, *FairLib* also provides utilities for result summarization and visualization.

FairLib is implemented in Python using PyTorch and is easy to use: it can be run from the command line, or imported as a package into other projects. To demonstrate its utility, we use *FairLib* to reproduce a battery of debiasing results from the recent NLP literature, and show that improved and systematic hyperparameter tuning leads to demonstrable improvements over the originally reported results. *FairLib* is released under Apache License 2.0 and

*This work was done when Aili Shen was at The University of Melbourne.

[1]Please check out the demo notebook and the demo video.

Proceedings of the The 2022 Conference on Empirical Methods in Natural Language Processing: System Demonstrations, pages 60 - 71
December 7-11, 2022 ©2022 Association for Computational Linguistics

is available on GitHub.[2] Detailed documentation and tutorials are available on *FairLib*'s website.[3]

2 Benchmark Datasets

In addition to evaluating bias wrt. a user group, we require datasets where each input instance is annotated with protected attributes (e.g., gender) and a target class label (e.g., sentiment). However, for a variety of reasons, only a small subset of datasets contains protected attribute labels, and annotating protected labels can be difficult.

To standardize fairness studies, *FairLib* provides APIs to access various publicly available fairness benchmark datasets, including: (1) text corpora for occupation classification (BIOS, De-Arteaga et al. (2019)), sentiment analysis (MOJI, Blodgett et al. (2016)), and part-of-speech tagging (TRUSTPILOT, Hovy (2015)); (2) structured data for the tasks of recidivism prediction (COMPAS, Larson et al. (2016)), and income prediction (ADULT, Kohavi et al. (1996)); and (3) image data to address colored handwritten digit recognition (COLOREDMNIST, Arjovsky et al. (2019)), objective classification (COCO, Zhao et al. (2017)), and event classification (IMSITU, Zhao et al. (2017)).[4]

3 Fairness Criteria

FairLib includes a variety of widely-used fairness evaluation metrics from the literature.

Representational Fairness: To evaluate whether sensitive information (such as demographics) is encoded in the representations of a trained model, previous work has proposed to estimate the *leakage* using an attacker (Elazar and Goldberg, 2018; Wang et al., 2019). Specifically, an attacker is trained to reverse-engineer protected attributes of inputs based on learned representations or the original inputs. *FairLib* provides flexible APIs to estimate information leakage at any representational level, based on different attackers (including linear and neural models).

Group Fairness: To evaluate whether model predictions are fair towards the protected attributes, Barocas et al. (2019) present formal definitions of three types of group fairness criteria, which capture different levels of (conditional) independence between the protected attribute g, the target variable y, and the model prediction $\hat{y}$. Table 1 summarizes the statistical fairness criteria and maps them to confusion-matrix-derived scores. The group fairness criteria evaluate the disparity of these scores across subgroups and classes.

Aggregation of subset performance metrics to a single figure of merit typically consists of two steps: (1) group-wise aggregation within each class, which reflects performance disparities across protected groups for each class; and (2) class-wise aggregation, to aggregate group-wise disparities for all classes (i.e., the vector from step 1) into a single number. The choice of aggregation function reflects different assumptions of fairness, and varies in previous work. Table 2 lists existing aggregation approaches which are built in to *FairLib*.[5]

4 Bias Mitigation

This section reviews the three primary types of debiasing methods, followed by Section 4.1, a summary of bias mitigation methods implemented in *FairLib*.

Pre-processing adjusts the training dataset to be balanced across protected groups before training, such that the input feature space is expected to be uncorrelated with the protected attributes. Typical approaches here adopt long-tail learning approaches for debiasing, such as resampling the training set such that the number of instances within each protected group is identical (Zhao et al., 2018; Wang et al., 2019; Han et al., 2022a).

At training time introduces constraints into the optimization process for model training. A popular method is adversarial training, which jointly trains: (i) a discriminator to recover protected attribute values; and (ii) the main model to correctly predict the target classes while at the same time preventing protected attributes from being correctly predicted (Wadsworth et al., 2018; Elazar and Goldberg, 2018; Li et al., 2018; Wang et al., 2019; Zhao and Gordon, 2019; Han et al., 2021).

Post-processing aims to adjust a trained classifier according to protected attributes, such that the final predictions are fair to different protected groups. For example, Ravfogel et al. (2020) iteratively project fixed text representations from a trained model to a null-space of protected attributes. Han et al. (2022a) adjust the predictions for each protected group by searching for the best prior for

[2] `https://github.com/HanXudong/fairlib`

[3] `https://hanxudong.github.io/fairlib`

[4] Check the *FairLib* website for a full list of built-in datasets.

[5] In Section 6.3, we further introduce a framework for generalized aggregation in *FairLib*.

Type	Main Idea	Metric (M)
Independence ($\hat{y} \perp g$)	Positive rate of each protected group is the same (*Demographic Parity*; Feldman et al. (2015))	$\frac{\text{TP+FP}}{\text{TP+FP+TN+FN}}$ (Positive Rate)
Separation ($\hat{y} \perp g \mid y$)	Acknowledges correlation between g and y (*Equalized Odds*; Hardt et al. (2016))	$\frac{\text{TP}}{\text{TP+FN}}$ (Recall or TPR) $\frac{\text{FP}}{\text{FP+TN}}$ (Fall-out or FPR)
Sufficiency ($y \perp g \mid \hat{y}$)	Predictions are calibrated for all groups (*Test Fairness*; Chouldechova (2017))	$\frac{\text{TP}}{\text{TP+FP}}$ (Precision) $\frac{\text{TN}}{\text{TN+FN}}$ (NPV)

Table 1: Built-in fairness evaluation metrics in *FairLib*.

Formulation	Reference
$\beta_c = \frac{1}{G}\sum_g \lvert M_{c,g} - \overline{M}_c \rvert$	Shen et al. (2022b)
$\beta_c = \frac{1}{G-1}\sum_g \lvert M_{c,g} - \overline{M}_c \rvert^2$	Lum et al. (2022)
$\beta_c = \max_g \lvert M_{c,g} - \overline{M}_c \rvert$	Yang et al. (2020)
$\beta_c = \min_g M_{c,g}$	Lahoti et al. (2020)
$\beta_c = \min_g \frac{M_{c,g}}{\overline{M}_c}$	Zafar et al. (2017)
$\beta_c = \max_g M_{c,g} - \min_g M_{c,g}$	Bird et al. (2020)
$\beta_c = \frac{\max_g M_{c,g}}{\min_g M_{c,g}}$	Feldman et al. (2015)
$\delta = \sqrt{\frac{1}{C}\sum_c \beta_c^2}$	Romanov et al. (2019)
$\delta = \frac{1}{C}\sum_c \beta_c$	Li et al. (2018)

Table 2: A subset of aggregation approaches for fairness evaluation from the literature that have are implemented in *FairLib*. C and G refer to the number of distinct classes and protected groups. $M_{c,g}$ is the evaluation results of class c and group g wrt. a particular evaluation metric M, such as TPR. β_c denotes the aggregation of group-wise disparities within class c, and following class-wise aggregation results in δ, which is the fairness score.

each group-specific component.

4.1 Implemented Methods

Table 3 lists 14 debiasing methods that are implemented in *FairLib*. It can be beneficial to employ different debiasing methods simultaneously (e.g., combine *pre-processing* and *training-time* methods (Wang et al., 2019; Han et al., 2022a)), which *FairLib* supports, and technically, every combination of these methods can be directly used without any further modifications.

5 Model Comparison

Typically, debiasing methods suffer from performance–fairness trade-offs, and no single method achieves both the best performance and fairness, making comparison between fairness methods difficult. In this section, we first introduce trade-off plots for model comparison, and then discuss model selection criteria that can be used

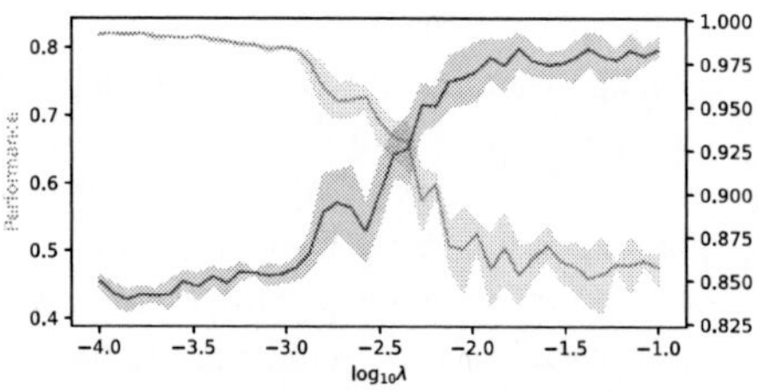

Figure 1: Tuning the tradeoff hyperparameter of FAIRSCL. Similar trade-offs can be obtained for other debiasing methods.

for reporting numerical results.

Performance–fairness Trade-off is a common way of comparing different debiasing methods without the requirement for model selection. Specifically, there is usually a trade-off hyperparameter for each debiasing method, which controls to what extent the model will sacrifice performance for better fairness, such as the number of iterations for null-space projection in INLP,[6] or the strength of the additional contrastive losses in FAIRSCL. Figure 1 shows a trade-off plot over different values of the trade-off hyperparameter of FAIRSCL for occupation classification, wherein we evaluate performance with accuracy, and use equal opportunity as the fairness criterion (see Section 8.1 for details).[7]

Instead of trade-offs wrt. different hyperparameter values, it can be more instructive to compute the maximum fairness that can be achieved by different models at a fixed performance level, and vice versa. Figure 2 shows an example of comparing the Pareto frontiers of INLP with FAIRSCL, where the results are obtained by varying the hyperparameters as illustrated in Figure 1. For a particular method, a Pareto optimal point corresponds to a model (i.e., a particular value of the trade-off hy-

[6]Cf., Table 3 for explanations of mentioned methods.

[7]Note that all figures and tables of results in this paper are direct outputs of *FairLib*.

Type	Model	Main Idea
Pre-	BD (Zhao et al., 2017)	Equalize the size of protected groups.
	CB (Wang et al., 2019)	Down-sample the majority protected group within each class.
	JB (Lahoti et al., 2020)	Jointly balance the Protected attributes and classes.
	BTEO (Han et al., 2022a)	Balance protected attributes within advantage classes.
At-	ADV (Li et al., 2018)	Prevent protected attributes from being identified by the discriminator.
	EADV (Elazar and Goldberg, 2018)	Employ multiple discriminators for adversarial training.
	DADV (Han et al., 2021)	Employ multiple discriminators with orthogonality regularization.
	AADV & ADADV (Han et al., 2022b)	Enable discriminators to use target labels as inputs during training.
	GATE (Han et al., 2022a)	Address protected factors with an augmented representation.
	FAIRBATCH (Roh et al., 2021)	Minimize CE loss gap though minibatch resampling.
	FAIRSCL (Shen et al., 2022a)	Adopt supervised contrastive learning for bias mitigation.
	EO_{CLA} (Shen et al., 2022b)	Minimize the CE loss gap within each target label by adjusting the loss.
Post-	INLP (Ravfogel et al., 2020)	Remove protected attributes through iterative null-space projection.
	$\text{GATE}^{\text{soft}}$ (Han et al., 2022a)	Adjust the prior for each group-specific component in GATE.

Table 3: Built-in methods for bias mitigation, which are grouped into three types: **Pre-**processing, **At** training time, and **Post-**processing.

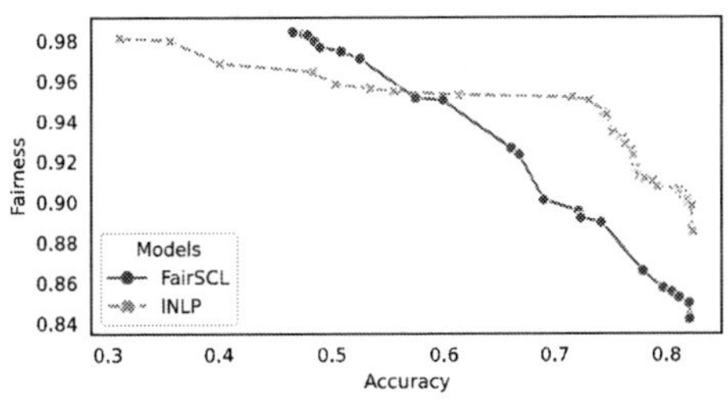

Figure 2: Pareto frontier curves derived from Figure 1.

perparameter) such that performance and fairness cannot be improved without causing a degradation in the other criterion.

Model Selection refers to the process of selecting the combination of hyperparameters that leads to best performance. In single-objective learning, model selection is based on a single metric, such as the loss on the dev set. In debiasing, however, both performance and fairness need to be considered for model selection, and a common method is *Constrained Selection*, which selects the best model given thresholds of the performance and fairness:

$$f^* = \arg\max_f q(f) \quad \text{s.t.} \quad \begin{array}{l} \text{Perf}(f) > \text{h}_{\text{Perf}} \\ \text{Fair}(f) > \text{h}_{\text{Fair}} \end{array} \tag{1}$$

where f denotes a candidate model, $\text{Perf}(f)$ and $\text{Fair}(f)$ are the performance and fairness evaluation results for f, respectively, q is a real valued score function that maps the model f to a number, and h denotes corresponding thresholds. For instance, using $q(f) = \text{Fair}(f)$ results in the selection of the fairest candidate model.

Instead of measuring performance and fairness separately, one can explicitly measure their trade-off as the distance from a particular model f to the optimal point[8] (DTO, Han et al. (2021)):

$$\text{DTO}(f) = \sqrt{(1 - \text{Perf}(f))^2 + (1 - \text{Fair}(f))^2},$$

which originates from the multi-objective optimization literature (Marler and Arora, 2004). Lower is better, with an optimal value of 0. Note that DTO should be minimized in Equation (1).

$\text{DTO}(f)$ is the default q function in *FairLib*. *FairLib* also supports the definition of customized cues, such as $\text{Perf}(f)$, $\text{Fair}(f)$, and $\text{DTO}(f)$. Given the flexibility of *FairLib*, most selection criteria in previous work can be reproduced, such as: (1) the maximum performance (Lahoti et al., 2020; Roh et al., 2021), which is based on a particular utility metric, such as accuracy and F-measures; (2) constrained selection (Han et al., 2021; Subramanian et al., 2021); and (3) minimising DTO (Han et al., 2022b; Shen et al., 2022b).

6 *FairLib* Design and Architecture

Here, we describe the four modules of *FairLib*, namely data, model, evaluation, and analysis.

6.1 Data Module

The data module manages inputs, target labels, and protected attributes for model training and evaluation. To enable different pre-processing debiasing methods in supporting any types of inputs, the `BaseDataset` class is implemented for sampling and weight calculation based on the distribution of classes and protected attributes. `Dataset` classes inherit functionality from `BaseDataset` with an additional property for loading different types of inputs.

[8]The optimum point is assumed to be a model that achieves 1 performance and 1 fairness. See Appendix B for details.

Specifically, *FairLib* includes `Dataset` classes for vector, matrix, and sequential inputs, to support structural, image, and text inputs. Once inputs are loaded by `Dataset`, pre-processing debiasing methods are automatically applied.

6.2 Model Module

This is the core module of *FairLib*, which implements the *At-training-time* and *Post-processing* debiasing methods described in Section 4.1 and Table 3. The methods can be applied to instances of the `BaseModel` class. One built-in child class of `BaseModel` is an `MLP` classifier for structural inputs, which can be fully integrated with HuggingFace's `transformers` library.[9] Specifically, the `MLP` can be used as the task-specific output layer, on top of the backbone networks from `transformers` (e.g. BERT (Devlin et al., 2019)), to handle a wide variety of inputs and tasks.

FairLib supports the combination of different bias mitigation methods with thousands of pretrained models across classification tasks and data types, including text, image, and audio modalities.

6.3 Evaluation Module

This module implements the fairness metrics described in Section 3, and several performance measures. Performance measures are based on the classification evaluation metrics implemented in scikit-learn (Buitinck et al., 2013), including Accuracy, F-score, and ROC AUC. However, no established fairness evaluation suite exists. Noting that the calculation of existing fairness metrics is always based on confusion matrices, *FairLib* includes an `Evaluator` class which can: (1) calculate any confusion-matrix based fairness metrics; and (2) conduct group-wise and class-wise aggregations as specified by users.

6.4 Analysis Module

This module provides utilities for model comparison as introduced in Section 5, with the three main functions of: (1) conducting post-hoc early-stopping and model selection in parallel as introduced in Section 5;[10] (2) organizing the results as a Pandas DataFrame (pandas development team, 2020), which can be used to create plots and LaTeX tables;[11] and (3) creating interactive plots, covering different comparison settings such as Figures 2 and 4.[12]

7 Usage

In this section, we demonstrate the basic use of *FairLib*. For further details, see the online interactive demos for examples of adding customized models, datasets, and metrics.

The following command shows an example for training and evaluating a STANDARD model:

```
python fairlib --dataset Bios_gender
↪ --emb_size 768 --num_classes 28
↪ --encoder_architecture BERT
```

where the task dataset, the number of distinct classes, the encoder architecture, and the dimension of embeddings extracted from the corresponding encoder need to be specified. The above case trains a BERT classifer over the BIOS dataset, where there are 28 professions.

In order to apply built-in debiasing methods, additional options for debiasing can be added to the command-line to realise combinations of methods:

```
python fairlib --dataset Bios_gender
↪ --emb_size 768 --num_classes 28
↪ --encoder_architecture BERT --BT
↪ Resampling --BTObj EO
↪ --adv_debiasing --INLP
```

The above example employs BTEO (*Pre-*), ADV (*At-*), and INLP (*Post-*) at the same time for a BERT classifer debiasing over the BIOS dataset.

FairLib can also be imported as a Python library; see Appendix D for more examples.

8 Benchmark Experiments

To evaluate *FairLib*, we conduct extensive experiments to compare models implemented in *FairLib* with their original reported results over two benchmark datasets. In Appendix A, we provide more experimental details.

8.1 Settings

We conduct experiments over two NLP classification tasks — sentiment analysis (MOJI) and biography classification (BIOS) — using the same dataset splits as previous work (Elazar and Goldberg, 2018; Ravfogel et al., 2020; Han et al., 2021; Shen et al., 2022a; Han et al., 2022a).

[9] https://github.com/huggingface/transformers

[10] Multi-processing is supported through the `joblib` library.

[11] All results are stored for later analysis, and are publicly available here.

[12] See here for more examples.

Method	MOJI				BIOS			
	Performance↑	Fairness↑	DTO ↓	Δ ↑	Performance↑	Fairness↑	DTO ↓	Δ ↑
STANDARD	72.30 ± 0.46	61.19 ± 0.44	47.68	0.56	82.25 ± 0.24	85.11 ± 0.81	23.17	0.69
BTEO	75.39 ± 0.14	87.75 ± 0.38	27.49	6.25	83.83 ± 0.25	90.54 ± 0.91	18.73	4.04
ADV	75.64 ± 0.73	89.33 ± 0.56	26.59	7.37	81.66 ± 0.22	90.74 ± 0.77	20.54	2.23
DADV	75.55 ± 0.41	90.40 ± 0.12	26.27	5.23	81.85 ± 0.19	90.64 ± 0.48	20.42	2.29
ADADV	75.02 ± 0.69	90.87 ± 0.17	26.60	0.00	81.91 ± 0.34	88.96 ± 0.59	21.19	0.00
FAIRBATCH	75.06 ± 0.60	90.55 ± 0.50	26.67	1.99	82.24 ± 0.13	89.50 ± 1.25	20.63	0.51
FAIRSCL	75.73 ± 0.34	87.82 ± 0.43	27.15	0.73	82.06 ± 0.16	84.27 ± 0.83	23.86	1.01
EO_{CLA}	75.28 ± 0.50	89.23 ± 0.79	26.97	0.25	81.78 ± 0.27	88.87 ± 0.94	21.35	1.13
INLP	73.34	85.60	30.30	15.90	82.30	88.62	21.04	9.21

Table 4: Evaluation results ± standard deviation (%) on the test set of MOJI and BIOS tasks, averaged over 5 runs with different random seeds. Δ: the DTO improvement of *FairLib* to the reported results in previous work. See Appendix A.2 for dataset statistics.

Following Han et al. (2022a), we report the overall Accuracy as the performance, and the Equal Opportunity as the fairness criterion, calculated based on the Recall gap across all protected groups.

8.2 Experimental Results

Table 4 summarizes the results produced by *FairLib*. Compared with previous work, STANDARD, ADADV, FAIRSCL and EO_{CLA} achieve similar results to the original paper. In contrast, the re-implemented BTEO, ADV, DADV, FAIRBATCH, and INLP outperform the results reported in their original paper due to the better-designed hyperparameter tuning and model selection.[13]

9 Related Work

Several toolkits have been developed for learning fair AI models (Bellamy et al., 2018; Saleiro et al., 2018; Bird et al., 2020). We discuss the two most closely-related frameworks.

The most related work to *FairLib* is AI Fairness 360 (*AIF360*), which is the first toolkit to bring together bias detection and mitigation (Bellamy et al., 2018). Like *FairLib*, *AIF360* supports a variety of fairness criteria and debiasing methods, and is designed to be extensible. The biggest difference over *FairLib* is that *AIF360* is closely tied to scikit-learn, and does not support other ML frameworks such as PyTorch. This not only limits the applicability of *AIF360* to NLP and CV tasks where neural model architectures are now de rigeur, but also implies a lack of GPU support. Moreover, *AIF360* only provides fundamental analysis features, such as comparing debiasing wrt. a single evaluation metric, while the analysis module of *FairLib* has richer features for model comparison, for example, selecting Pareto-models and interactive visualization.

The second closely-related library is *FairLearn* (Bird et al., 2020), which is also targeted at assessing and improving fairness for both classification and regression tasks. However, similar to *AIF360*, *FairLearn* is mainly developed for scikit-learn, meaning complex CV and NLP tasks are not supported. Additionally, *FairLearn* currently only supports four debiasing algorithms,[14] as opposed to the 14 methods supported in *FairLib*, providing fuller coverage of different debiasing methods.

In summary, *FairLib* complements existing fairness libraries by: (1) implementing a broad range of competitive debiasing approaches, with a specific focus on debiasing neural architectures which underlie many CV and NLP tasks; and (2) comprehensive tools for interactive model comparison to help users explore the effects of different debiasing approaches.

10 Conclusion

In this paper, we present *FairLib*, a new open-source Python library and framework for measuring and improving fairness, which implements a wide range of fairness metrics and 14 debiasing approaches. With better-designed hyperparameter tuning and model selection, the reproduced models in *FairLib* outperform the results reported in the original work. *FairLib* also has remarkable flexibility and extensibility, such that new models, debiasing methods, and datasets can be easily developed and evaluated.

[13] We provide further details of hyperparameter tuning in an online document.

[14] `https://fairlearn.org/main/user_guide/mitigation.html`

Acknowledgements

We thank the anonymous reviewers for their helpful feedback and suggestions. This work was funded by the Australian Research Council, Discovery grant DP200102519. This research was undertaken using the LIEF HPC-GPGPU Facility hosted at the University of Melbourne. This Facility was established with the assistance of LIEF Grant LE170100200.

Ethical Considerations

This work provides an unified framework for measuring and improving fairness. Although *FairLib* assumes access to training datasets with protected attributes, this is the same data assumption made by all debiasing methods. To avoid harm and be trustworthy, we only use attributes that have been publicly disclosed or the user has self-identified, or toy datasets. All data in this study is publicly available and used under strict ethical guidelines.

References

Martin Arjovsky, Léon Bottou, Ishaan Gulrajani, and David Lopez-Paz. 2019. Invariant risk minimization. *arXiv preprint arXiv:1907.02893*.

Pinkesh Badjatiya, Manish Gupta, and Vasudeva Varma. 2019. Stereotypical bias removal for hate speech detection task using knowledge-based generalizations. In *The World Wide Web Conference*, pages 49–59.

Solon Barocas, Moritz Hardt, and Arvind Narayanan. 2019. *Fairness and Machine Learning*. `http://www.fairmlbook.org`.

Rachel KE Bellamy, Kuntal Dey, Michael Hind, Samuel C Hoffman, Stephanie Houde, Kalapriya Kannan, Pranay Lohia, Jacquelyn Martino, Sameep Mehta, Aleksandra Mojsilovic, et al. 2018. Ai fairness 360: An extensible toolkit for detecting, understanding, and mitigating unwanted algorithmic bias. *arXiv preprint arXiv:1810.01943*.

Sarah Bird, Miro Dudík, Richard Edgar, Brandon Horn, Roman Lutz, Vanessa Milan, Mehrnoosh Sameki, Hanna Wallach, and Kathleen Walker. 2020. Fairlearn: A toolkit for assessing and improving fairness in ai. *Microsoft, Tech. Rep. MSR-TR-2020-32*.

Su Lin Blodgett, Lisa Green, and Brendan O'Connor. 2016. Demographic dialectal variation in social media: A case study of African-American English. In *Proceedings of the 2016 Conference on Empirical Methods in Natural Language Processing*, pages 1119–1130.

Lars Buitinck, Gilles Louppe, Mathieu Blondel, Fabian Pedregosa, Andreas Mueller, Olivier Grisel, Vlad Niculae, Peter Prettenhofer, Alexandre Gramfort, Jaques Grobler, Robert Layton, Jake VanderPlas, Arnaud Joly, Brian Holt, and Gaël Varoquaux. 2013. API design for machine learning software: experiences from the scikit-learn project. In *ECML PKDD Workshop: Languages for Data Mining and Machine Learning*, pages 108–122.

Alexandra Chouldechova. 2017. Fair prediction with disparate impact: A study of bias in recidivism prediction instruments. *Big data*, 5(2):153–163.

Maria De-Arteaga, Alexey Romanov, Hanna Wallach, Jennifer Chayes, Christian Borgs, Alexandra Chouldechova, Sahin Geyik, Krishnaram Kenthapadi, and Adam Tauman Kalai. 2019. Bias in bios: A case study of semantic representation bias in a high-stakes setting. In *Proceedings of the Conference on Fairness, Accountability, and Transparency*, pages 120–128.

Jacob Devlin, Ming-Wei Chang, Kenton Lee, and Kristina Toutanova. 2019. Bert: Pre-training of deep bidirectional transformers for language understanding. In *Proceedings of the 2019 Conference of the North American Chapter of the Association for Computational Linguistics: Human Language Technologies, Volume 1 (Long and Short Papers)*, pages 4171–4186.

Mark Díaz, Isaac Johnson, Amanda Lazar, Anne Marie Piper, and Darren Gergle. 2018. Addressing age-related bias in sentiment analysis. In *Proceedings of the 2018 CHI Conference on Human Factors in Computing Systems*, pages 1–14.

Yanai Elazar and Yoav Goldberg. 2018. Adversarial removal of demographic attributes from text data. In *Proceedings of the 2018 Conference on Empirical Methods in Natural Language Processing*, pages 11–21.

Michael Feldman, Sorelle A Friedler, John Moeller, Carlos Scheidegger, and Suresh Venkatasubramanian. 2015. Certifying and removing disparate impact. In *proceedings of the 21th ACM SIGKDD international conference on knowledge discovery and data mining*, pages 259–268.

Xudong Han, Timothy Baldwin, and Trevor Cohn. 2021. Diverse adversaries for mitigating bias in training. In *Proceedings of the 16th Conference of the European Chapter of the Association for Computational Linguistics: Main Volume*, pages 2760–2765.

Xudong Han, Timothy Baldwin, and Trevor Cohn. 2022a. Balancing out bias: Achieving fairness through training reweighting. In *Proceedings of the 2022 Conference on Empirical Methods in Natural Language Processing (EMNLP 2022)*. To appear.

Xudong Han, Timothy Baldwin, and Trevor Cohn. 2022b. Towards equal opportunity fairness through adversarial learning. *arXiv preprint arXiv:2203.06317*.

Moritz Hardt, Eric Price, and Nati Srebro. 2016. Equality of opportunity in supervised learning. *Advances in Neural Information Processing Systems*, 29:3315–3323.

Dirk Hovy. 2015. Demographic factors improve classification performance. In *Proceedings of the 53rd Annual Meeting of the Association for Computational Linguistics and the 7th International Joint Conference on Natural Language Processing (Volume 1: Long Papers)*, pages 752–762.

Ron Kohavi et al. 1996. Scaling up the accuracy of naive-bayes classifiers: A decision-tree hybrid. In *Kdd*, volume 96, pages 202–207.

Preethi Lahoti, Alex Beutel, Jilin Chen, Kang Lee, Flavien Prost, Nithum Thain, Xuezhi Wang, and Ed Chi. 2020. Fairness without demographics through adversarially reweighted learning. In *Advances in Neural Information Processing Systems*, volume 33, pages 728–740.

Jeff Larson, Surya Mattu, Lauren Kirchner, and Julia Angwin. 2016. How we analyzed the compas recidivism algorithm.

Yitong Li, Timothy Baldwin, and Trevor Cohn. 2018. Towards robust and privacy-preserving text representations. In *Proceedings of the 56th Annual Meeting of the Association for Computational Linguistics (Volume 2: Short Papers)*, pages 25–30.

Kristian Lum, Yunfeng Zhang, and Amanda Bower. 2022. De-biasing "bias" measurement. In *2022 ACM Conference on Fairness, Accountability, and Transparency (FAccT '22)*, Seoul, Republic of Korea. ACM.

R Timothy Marler and Jasbir S Arora. 2004. Survey of multi-objective optimization methods for engineering. *Structural and multidisciplinary optimization*, 26(6):369–395.

The pandas development team. 2020. pandas-dev/pandas: Pandas. Zenodo.

Shauli Ravfogel, Yanai Elazar, Hila Gonen, Michael Twiton, and Yoav Goldberg. 2020. Null it out: Guarding protected attributes by iterative nullspace projection. In *Proceedings of the 58th Annual Meeting of the Association for Computational Linguistics*, pages 7237–7256.

Yuji Roh, Kangwook Lee, Steven Euijong Whang, and Changho Suh. 2021. Fairbatch: Batch selection for model fairness. In *Proceedings of the 9th International Conference on Learning Representations*.

Alexey Romanov, Maria De-Arteaga, Hanna Wallach, Jennifer Chayes, Christian Borgs, Alexandra Chouldechova, Sahin Geyik, Krishnaram Kenthapadi, Anna Rumshisky, and Adam Kalai. 2019. What's in a name? reducing bias in bios without access to protected attributes. In *Proceedings of the 2019 Conference of the North American Chapter of the Association for Computational Linguistics: Human Language Technologies, Volume 1 (Long and Short Papers)*, pages 4187–4195.

Pedro Saleiro, Benedict Kuester, Loren Hinkson, Jesse London, Abby Stevens, Ari Anisfeld, Kit T Rodolfa, and Rayid Ghani. 2018. Aequitas: A bias and fairness audit toolkit. *arXiv preprint arXiv:1811.05577*.

Aili Shen, Xudong Han, Trevor Cohn, Timothy Baldwin, and Lea Frermann. 2022a. Does representational fairness imply empirical fairness? In *Proceedings of the 2nd Conference of the Asia-Pacific Chapter of the Association for Computational Linguistics and the 12th International Joint Conference on Natural Language Processing*. Association for Computational Linguistics. To appear.

Aili Shen, Xudong Han, Trevor Cohn, Timothy Baldwin, and Lea Frermann. 2022b. Optimising equal opportunity fairness in model training. In *Proceedings of the 2022 Conference of the North American Chapter of the Association for Computational Linguistics: Human Language Technologies*, pages 4073–4084, Seattle, United States. Association for Computational Linguistics.

Shivashankar Subramanian, Xudong Han, Timothy Baldwin, Trevor Cohn, and Lea Frermann. 2021. Evaluating debiasing techniques for intersectional biases. In *Proceedings of the 2021 Conference on Empirical Methods in Natural Language Processing*, pages 2492–2498, Online and Punta Cana, Dominican Republic. Association for Computational Linguistics.

Christina Wadsworth, Francesca Vera, and Chris Piech. 2018. Achieving fairness through adversarial learning: an application to recidivism prediction. *FAT/ML Workshop*.

Tianlu Wang, Jieyu Zhao, Mark Yatskar, Kai-Wei Chang, and Vicente Ordonez. 2019. Balanced datasets are not enough: Estimating and mitigating gender bias in deep image representations. In *Proceedings of the IEEE International Conference on Computer Vision*, pages 5310–5319.

Forest Yang, Mouhamadou Cisse, and Sanmi Koyejo. 2020. Fairness with overlapping groups; a probabilistic perspective. *Advances in neural information processing systems*, 33:4067–4078.

Muhammad Bilal Zafar, Isabel Valera, Manuel Gomez Rogriguez, and Krishna P Gummadi. 2017. Fairness constraints: Mechanisms for fair classification. In *Artificial Intelligence and Statistics*, pages 962–970. PMLR.

Han Zhao and Geoff Gordon. 2019. Inherent tradeoffs in learning fair representations. In *Advances in Neural Information Processing Systems*, volume 32. Curran Associates, Inc.

Jieyu Zhao, Tianlu Wang, Mark Yatskar, Vicente Ordonez, and Kai-Wei Chang. 2017. Men also like shopping: Reducing gender bias amplification using corpus-level constraints. In *Proceedings of the 2017 Conference on Empirical Methods in Natural Language Processing*, pages 2979–2989.

Jieyu Zhao, Tianlu Wang, Mark Yatskar, Vicente Ordonez, and Kai-Wei Chang. 2018. Gender bias in coreference resolution: Evaluation and debiasing methods. In *Proceedings of the 2018 Conference of the North American Chapter of the Association for Computational Linguistics: Human Language Technologies, Volume 2 (Short Papers)*, pages 15–20.

A Experimental Details

A.1 Datasets

MOJI: This sentiment analysis dataset was collected by Blodgett et al. (2016), and contains tweets that are either African American English (AAE)-like or Standard American English (SAE)-like. Each tweet is annotated with a binary 'race' label (based on language use: either AAE or SAE), and a binary sentiment score determined by (redacted) emoji contained in it.

BIOS: The second task is biography classification (De-Arteaga et al., 2019), where biographies were scraped from the web, and annotated for binary gender and 28 classes of profession.

A.2 Results Statistics

For each hyperparameter combination, we repeat experiments 5 time with different random seeds drawn from a discrete uniform distribution. The mean values and standard deviation are calculated based on the 5 runs. Due to the fact that INLP is a *post-processing* approach and its results with respect a given number of iterations are highly affected by the random seed, we only report results for 1 run. One way of getting statistics of INLP is selecting the trade-off hyperparameter of INLP for each random seed, however, this may not be a fair comparison with other methods as fixed hyperparameters have been used.

B Model Comparison

Figure 3 illustrates the key ideas of model comparison.

C Experimental Results

Trade-off plots for the selected methods are shown in Figure 4. Over the MOJI dataset (Figure 4a), it can be seen that almost all methods lead to similar results, with a fairness score less than 0.9, except for INLP, which is substantially worse than the other methods. As increasing the values of each model's trade-off hyperparameter (i.e., achieving better fairness at the cost of performance), ADADV outperforms other methods.

The trade-off plot for BIOS is quite different to MOJI: (1) INLP becomes a reasonable choice; (2) FAIRSCL does not work well over this dataset, consistent with the original paper; (3) BTEO is the only method that achieves better performance than the STANDARD model while increasing fairness; (4) EO_{CLA} could be the best choice as it achieves much better fairness than others at a comparable performance level.

D Further Usage

In this section, we demonstrate how to use *FairLib*. Users can run existing models or add their own models, datasets, and metrics as needed.

D.1 Basics

FairLib also support YAML configuration files with training options:

```
python fairlib --conf_file opt.yaml
```

which is useful for reproducing experimental results, as *FairLib* saves the YAML file for each run.

```
from fairlib.base_options import options
from fairlib import networks

config_file = 'opt.yaml'
# Get options
state =
↪  options.get_state(conf_file=config_file)

# Init the model
model = networks.get_main_model(state)

# Training with debiasing
model.train_self()
```

Checkpoints, evaluation results, outputs, and the configuration file are saved to the default or a specified directory.

D.2 Performing Analysis

As introduced in Section 6.4, the first step to analyze a trained model is selecting the best epoch. Here we provide an example for retrieving experimental results for FAIRSCL, and selecting the best epoch-checkpoint:

```
from fairlib.load_results import
↪  model_selection_parallel

FairSCL_df = model_selection(
  model_id= "FSCL",
  GAP_metric_name = "TPR_GAP",
  Performance_metric_name = "accuracy",
  selection_criterion = "DTO",
  n_jobs=20,
  index_column_names = ["fcl_lambda_y",
  ↪  "fcl_lambda_g"],
  save_path = "FairSCL_df.pkl",)
```

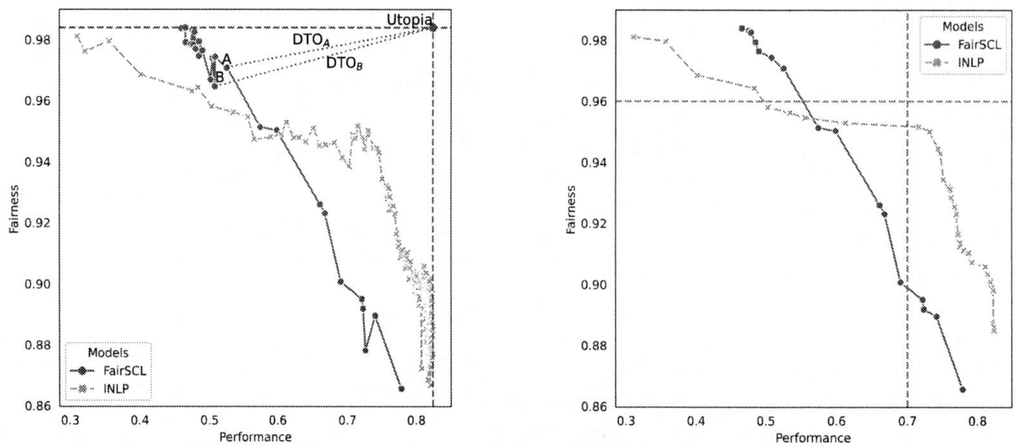

(a) Trade-off

(b) Pareto Trade-off

Figure 3: performance–fairness trade-offs of FAIRSCL (blue points) and INLP (orange crosses) over the BIOS dataset. The vertical and horizontal red dashed line in Figure 3b are examples of constrained model selection wrt. a performance threshold of 0.7 and fairness threshold of 0.96. Figure 3a also provides an example for DTO. The green dashed vertical and horizontal lines denote the best performance and fairness, respectively, and their intersection point is the Utopia point. The length of green dotted lines from A and B to the Utopia point are the DTO for candidate models A and B, respectively.

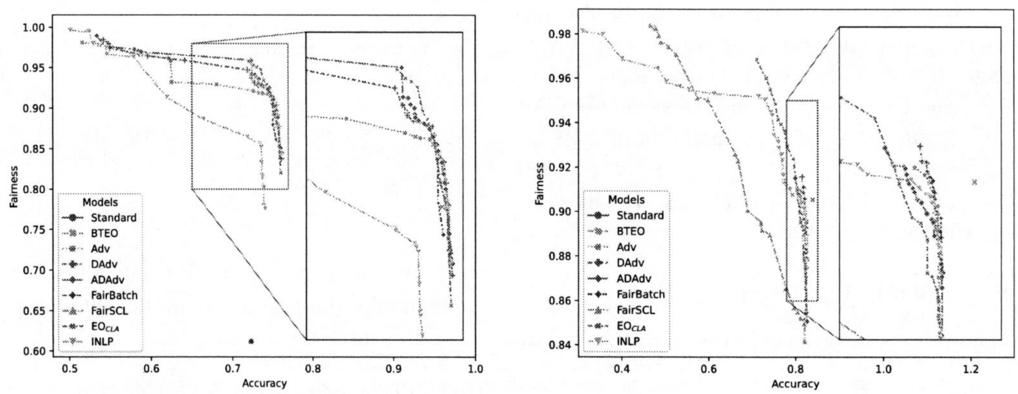

(a) MOJI

(b) BIOS

Figure 4: Performance–fairness trade-offs of selected models over the MOJI and BIOS datasets.

where the fairness metric is TPR GAP (corresponding to *Equal Opportunity* fairness); the performance is measured with Accuracy score; the best epoch is selected based on DTO; and the tuned trade-off hyperparameters are used as the index. `n_jobs` is an optional argument for multi-processing, and the resulting DataFrame will be saved to the specified directory.

Assuming `Bios_gender_results` is a Python dictionary of retrieved experimental results from the first step, indexed by the corresponding method name, we provide the following function for model comparison:

```
from fairlib.tables_and_figures import
↪ final_results_df

Bios_results = {
  "INLP":INLP_df,
  "FairSCL":FairSCL_df,}

Bios_gender_main_results =
↪ final_results_df(
  results_dict = Bios_results,
  pareto = True,
  selection_criterion = "DTO",
```

```
return_dev = True,)
```

where model selection is performed based on DTO. Each method has one selected model in the resulting DataFrame, which can then be used to create tables.

If visualization is desired, users can disable model selection by setting `selection_criterion = None`, in which case all Pareto frontier points will be returned.

D.3 Customized Datasets

A custom dataset class must implement the `load_data` function. Take a look at this sample implementation; the split is stored in a directory `self.data_dir`. The `args.data_dir` is either loaded from the arguments `-data_dir` or from the default value. `split` has three possible string values, `"train", "dev", "test"`, indicating the split that will be loaded.

Then the `load_data` function must assign the value of `self.X` as inputs, `self.y` as target labels, and `self.protected_label` as information for debiasing, such as gender, age, and race.

```
from fairlib.dataloaders.utils import
↪ BaseDataset

class SampleDataset(BaseDataset):
  def load_data(self):
    # Load data from pickle file
    filename = self.split+"df.pkl"
    _Path = self.args.data_dir /
    ↪ filename
    data = pd.read_pickle(_Path)

    # Save loaded data
    self.X = data["X"]
    self.y = data["y"]
    self.protected_label =
    ↪ data["protected_label"]
```

As a child class of `BaseDataset`, *Pre-processing* related operations will be automatically applied to the `SampleDataset`.

D.4 Customized Models

Recall that our current `MLP` implementation (Section 6.2) can be used as a classification head for different backbone models, and the new model will support all built-in debiasing methods.

Take a look at the following example: we use BERT as the feature extractor, and then use the extracted features as the input to the MLP classifier to make predictions.

We only need to define three functions: (1) `__init__`, which is used to initialize the model with pretrained BERT parameters, MLP classifier, and optimizer; (2) `forward`, which is the same as before, where we extract sentence representations then use the MLP to make predictions; and (3) `hidden`, which is used to get hidden representations for adversarial training.

```
from transformers import BertModel
from fairlib.networks.utils import
↪ BaseModel

class BERTClassifier(BaseModel):
  model_name = 'bert-base-cased'

  def __init__(self, args):
    super(BERTClassifier,
    ↪ self).__init__()
    self.args = args

    # Load pretrained model parameters.
    self.bert =
      BertModel.from_pretrained(
        self.model_name)

    # Init the classification head
    self.classifier = MLP(args)

    # Init optimizer, criterion, etc.
    self.init_for_training()

  def forward(self, input_data,
  ↪ group_label = None):
    # Extract representations
    bert_output =
    ↪ self.bert(input_data)[1]

    # Make predictions
    return self.classifier(bert_output,
    ↪ group_label)

  def hidden(self, input_data,
  ↪ group_label = None):
    # Extract representations
    bert_output =
    ↪ self.bert(input_data)[1]

    return self.classifier.hidden(
      bert_output, group_label)
```

ELEVANT: A Fully Automatic Fine-Grained Entity Linking Evaluation and Analysis Tool

Hannah Bast and **Matthias Hertel** and **Natalie Prange**
University of Freiburg
Freiburg, Germany
{bast,hertelm,prange}@cs.uni-freiburg.de

Abstract

We present *Elevant*, a tool for the fully automatic fine-grained evaluation of a set of entity linkers on a set of benchmarks. Elevant provides an automatic breakdown of the performance by various error categories and by entity type. Elevant also provides a rich and compact, yet very intuitive and self-explanatory visualization of the results of a linker on a benchmark in comparison to the ground truth. A live demo, the link to the complete code base on GitHub and a link to a demo video are provided under `https://elevant.cs.uni-freiburg.de`.

1 Introduction

Entity linking is a fundamental problem, and a first step for or component of many NLP applications. In this paper, we consider end-to-end entity linking systems, which do the following: given a text and a set of entities, identify each mention of one of those entities in the text and say which of these entities it is.

Due to its fundamental importance and wide applicability, there is vast literature on entity linking, and also a large number of concrete software tools. Many publications also come with an evaluation, which compares the entity linker introduced in the publication with existing linkers, usually on a variety of benchmarks. There are also several standard benchmarks, which are found in many evaluations. This is a positive and pleasing development.

The typical statistics include overall precision and recall, that is, which percentage of the found mentions were correct and which percentage of the correct mentions were found. It is a frequent experience that the numbers in the evaluation are very good, yet the experience when applying that entity linker in an own application are less convincing. And not so rarely, there is even trouble reproducing the results from the publication.

The problem is that overall precision, recall, and F1 tell us little about the particular strengths and weaknesses of a particular entity linker for a particular application. Particular benchmarks often require very particular skills from an entity linker, and an entity linker may be deliberately or unknowingly tuned towards these particularities. To find out about the strengths and weaknesses of an entity linker, one needs to look at the results in more detail, which typically has *three* aspects:

(1) look at particular types of errors,
(2) look at particular types of entities,
(3) look at particular pieces of text.

Doing this on the raw input and output files is tedious, so that often small scripts are written to aid this process. However, these scripts are usually quite basic and imperfect. It also means that researchers do the same work over and over again.

It is the purpose of this paper to provide a comprehensive and easy-to-use tool, which every entity-linking researcher can and wants to use to analyze and understand the performance of a particular entity linker in detail.

1.1 Contributions

We consider these as our main contributions:

- We provide *Elevant*, a tool for the fully automatic fine-grained evaluation of a given set of entity linkers on a given set of benchmarks. The evaluation has two parts: a table with overall and fine-grained statistics, and a panel that provides a rich visualization of the concrete results that contribute to a selected statistics from the table.
- The table provides one row per experiment (a particular entity linker evaluated on a particular benchmark). Each column stands for one of a rich set of error categories: all errors, various kinds of entity detection errors, various kinds of entity disambiguation errors, errors on entities of particular type. There are controls to show and hide individ-

Proceedings of the The 2022 Conference on Empirical Methods in Natural Language Processing: System Demonstrations, pages 72 - 79
December 7-11, 2022

ual columns or groups of columns. A screenshot of this part of the tool is shown in Figure 1.

• For each table cell, Elevant provides a rich visualization of the result of that particular entity linker on that benchmark for that category. The visualization is compact and intuitive, providing for each text record all information about true positives, false positives, and false negatives. The information is displayed with intuitive highlights and more detailed information provided on mouseover. Figure 2 shows a screenshot of this visualization.

• As a result of the compact single-column visualization, Elevant can also provide an intuitive side-by-side comparison of the concrete results of two experiments.

• For each table column, Elevant can generate a graph that shows the results of all linkers over all benchmarks in the table for that category. An example for such a graph is shown in Figure 3.

• The code for Elevant is open source, well documented, and easy to use. We support various standard formats for both the benchmarks and the results from the entity linkers. There is a demo website available under `https://elevant.cs.uni-freiburg.de`, which shows the results of a variety of well-known entity linkers evaluated on a variety of well-known benchmarks.

2 Related Work

GERBIL (Usbeck et al., 2015) is similar to Elevant in that it provides a web-based platform for the comparison of a given set of entity linking systems on a given set of benchmarks. GERBIL is widely used and has helped standardizing benchmarks and the evaluation measures on these benchmarks. Elevant goes one step further by not only providing aggregate measures for the whole benchmarks (like precision, recall, and F1), but a detailed breakdown of the results by error category and entity type, and the ability to look at the results of different methods in detail, both in comparison to the ground truth and in comparison with each other.

ORBIS (Odoni et al., 2018) is similar to Elevant in that it provides overall statistics and a visualization of individual annotations. However, ORBIS does not provide a fine-grained error analysis and the visualization is less rich and less compact compared to that of Elevant. In particular, the visualization uses two columns: one for the annotations from the entity linker and one for those from the ground truth. This makes it difficult to grasp the most important information at one glance and there is no support for the comparison of two entity linkers. While the source code is publicly available and easy to install, errors can occur during usage due to dependency issues. Elevant avoids this issue by providing an easy-to-use docker setup.

VEX (Heinzerling and Strube, 2015) is a web app for visual error analysis of entity linking systems. Benchmark texts are displayed with highlighted predicted entities and ground truth entities. The highlights are color-coded such that true positives, false positives and false negatives can be distinguished. VEX focuses on showing clusters of entities, that is, indicating which predicted mentions and ground truth mentions have been linked to the same entity. For this purpose, identical entities are connected via lines. VEX does not display a system's evaluation results and does not allow direct comparison of different systems.

As part of their work on entity linking on Wikipedia, Klang and Nugues (2018) provide a system for visualizing annotations in Wikipedia articles such as hyperlinks or an entity linking tool's entity predictions. Identical entities are visualized by using the same annotation color. The tool is not meant for evaluating linking results against a ground truth. That is, no ground truth entities are displayed and the tool does not provide information about true positives, false positives or false negatives.

Strobl et al. (2020) provide a similar but more rudimentary system as part of their work on entity linking on Wikipedia. Predicted links are shown as hyperlinks to Wikipedia articles which correspond to the predicted entity. The color of the hyperlink indicates whether the hyperlink is an original intra-Wikipedia hyperlink or has been added by the entity linking system. An additional color is used for predicted unknown entities.

Multiple publications propose a fine-grained evaluation of entity linking systems on different entity types or frequent linking errors. Ling and Weld (2012) and Gillick et al. (2014) assign fine-grained types to recognized entities. Ling et al. (2015) discuss difficult decisions in the design of entity linking systems and benchmarks, which are common sources of linking errors, such as whether to link common entities, how specific the entities should be, which entities to link in case of metonymies, considered entity types and overlapping entities.

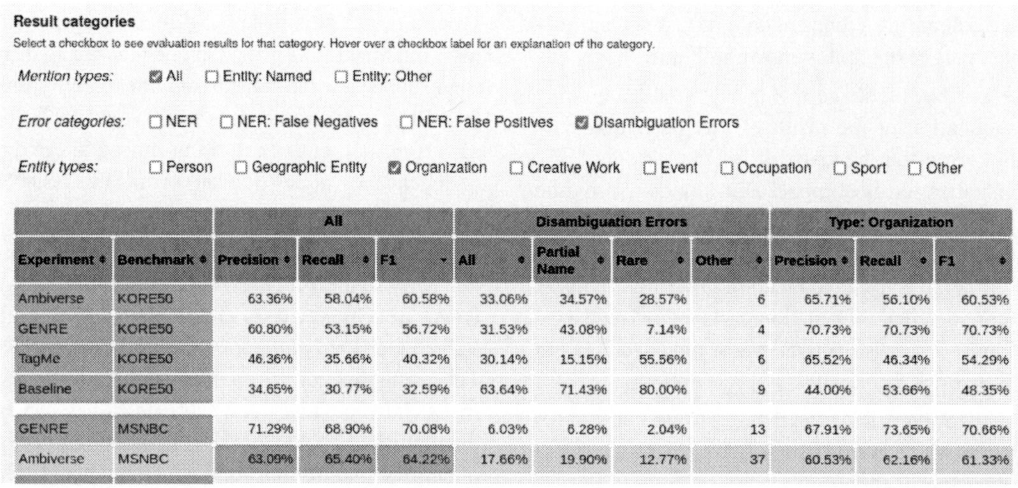

Figure 1: Evaluation results for various experiments. The types used in the per-type evaluation are configurable. The real web app contains many more error categories (see Section 4.1).

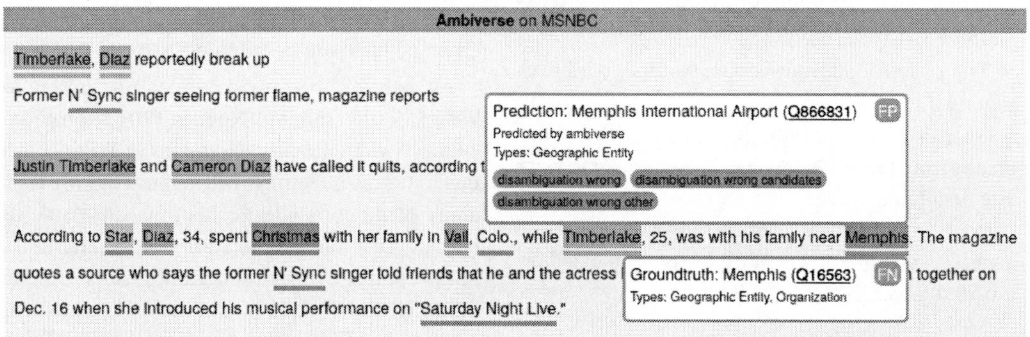

Figure 2: Visualization of predicted entities (highlighted text) and ground truth labels (underlined text) for a specific system (Ambiverse) and benchmark (MSNBC). True positives are shown in green, false positives and false negatives in red and unevaluated unknown entities in blue. Detailed information for each annotation is shown on mouseover.

Many of these decisions motivate our error types in Section 4.1. Rosales-Méndez et al. (2019) manually relabel three benchmarks to evaluate linking systems among dimensions such as the mention's base form, part of speech and overlap. Brasoveanu et al. (2018) propose an error classification based on the source of the error (e.g. knowledge base errors, dataset errors, annotator errors, etc.). They then manually categorize errors into these classes for a selected set of benchmarks and entity linking systems. Elevant follows this trend and goes one step further by providing a fully automatic classification into fine-grained error categories. Thus, by eliminating the need for expensive human labor, Elevant makes the fine-grained evaluation of entity linking errors feasible on a large scale.

3 Basic Principles

The core of Elevant is a web app that helps users analyze and compare results of various entity linking systems over various benchmarks in great detail. To this end, the user can add an experiment and evaluate its results using Elevant. We define an experiment as a run of a particular linker with particular settings over a particular benchmark. The pipeline for adding an experiment is as follows:
(1) add the benchmark (unless it already exists),
(2) run an entity linker on that benchmark,
(3) automatically evaluate the result in detail.

The following subsections explain how each of these steps can be executed using Elevant.

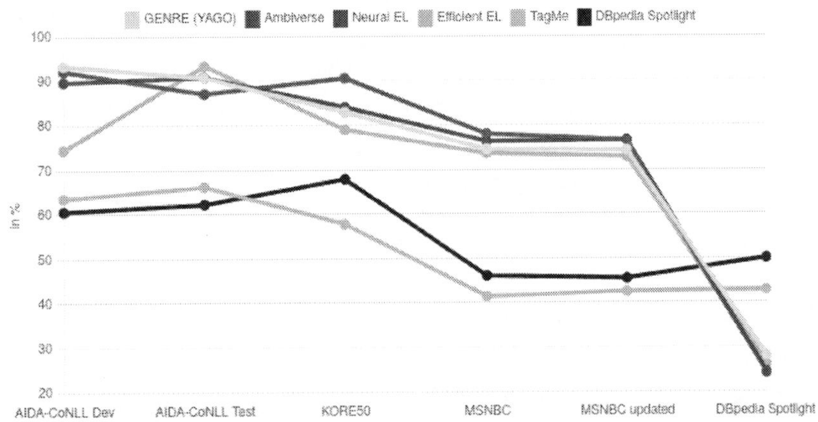

Figure 3: A graph generated by Elevant showing the NER F1 score for various entity linkers and benchmarks.

3.1 Adding a benchmark

In order to add a benchmark to Elevant, it is enough to run a single Python script. This script converts a given input benchmark into Elevant's internally used article file format. Files in this format contain one JSON object per line which holds information for a single article such as its text, title, ground truth labels or entity predictions. Additionally, the script annotates ground truth labels with the entities' types (for a fine-grained per-type evaluation) and the entities' names (for presentation purposes). Elevant supports three different benchmark formats: the common NLP Interchange Format (NIF), the IOB format used by Hoffart et al. (2011) for their AIDA-CoNLL dataset, and a simple JSONL format that only requires information about the benchmark's article texts, the ground truth label spans and the corresponding references to ground truth entities. Entity references can be from Wikidata, Wikipedia or DBpedia. Entity references from Wikipedia or DBpedia are internally converted to Wikidata. Several popular entity linking benchmarks are already included in Elevant (see Section 4.7) and can be used out of the box.

3.2 Running an entity linker

In order to produce entity linking results that can be evaluated with Elevant, the user has two options:

(1) They can feed the output of the entity linker they wish to evaluate into a provided Python script that converts the linking results into Elevant's internal format. The script supports linking results in NIF, the Ambiverse (Hoffart et al., 2011) output format or a simple JSONL format that only requires information about the predicted entity spans and corresponding entity references. Like ground truth entity references, references to predicted entities can be from Wikidata, Wikipedia or DBpedia and are converted to Wikidata internally.

(2) They can implement the entity linker within Elevant. The same Python script used for converting entity linking results can then be used to produce new linking results in the required format with the implemented linker. Several entity linkers are already implemented (detailed in Section 4.8) and can be used out of the box.

3.3 Evaluating entity linking results

Once the entity linking results are in the required format, they can be evaluated with another Python script. That script produces output files containing the evaluation results. Using these output files, the results can be instantly viewed in the web app.

4 Features

4.1 Error type classification

Elevant automatically classifies each false positive and false negative into the following three categories and 15 subcategories, to provide detailed information about strengths and weaknesses of a linker.

NER false negatives are ground truth mentions which the linker did not link to an entity. They are divided into the following disjunct subcategories:

• Lowercased: The first letter in the mention is lower-cased. Linkers that rely on the upper case too much have many errors in this subcategory on benchmarks that contain lower-cased mentions.

• Partially included: Not lowercased and a subspan of the mention is linked to an entity. Often a less specific mention is recognized instead of a more specific one, e.g. recognizing "2022 World Cup" instead of "2022 World Cup".

• Partial overlap: Neither lowercased nor partially included and a span overlapping with the false negative is linked to an entity, e.g. recognizing "The Americans" instead of "The Americans".

• Other: Remaining undetected mentions.

NER false positives are predicted mentions not labeled in the ground truth. They are further divided into the following disjunct subcategories:

• Lowercased: The predicted mention is lowercased (no named entity) and does not overlap with any ground truth mention. These are often mentions of abstract entities, which appear in the knowledge base, but are usually not labeled in entity linking benchmarks, for example, *love (Q316)*.

• Ground truth entity unknown: The ground truth of the predicted mention is *Unknown*, which means that the true entity is not part of the knowledge base, but an entity from the knowledge base was predicted. Linkers that fail to produce *NIL* predictions have many errors in this subcategory.

• Wrong span: The predicted mention overlaps with a ground truth mention that has the same entity, but the spans do not match exactly.

• Other: Remaining false detections.

Disambiguation errors are NER true positives that are linked to the wrong entity. They count as false positives and false negatives. They are further divided into the following disjunct subcategories:

• Demonym: The mention is a demonym (i.e., it is contained in a list of demonyms from Wikidata), such as "German". Confusions between a country, the people from that country or the language spoken in that country fall into this category.

• Metonymy: The mention is a location name (for example, Berlin), but the ground truth is not (for example, *government of Germany (Q159493)*), yet the linker wrongly predicted the location.

• Partial name: The mention is a part of the ground truth entity's name, e.g., the last name of a person.

• Rare: The linker predicted the most popular candidate entity (with candidate sets derived by entity names and Wikipedia hyperlink texts, and popularity measured by the number of Wiki sites about an entity) instead of a less popular one.

• Other: Remaining disambiguation errors.

For linkers where we have access to the candidate sets, the following disambiguation error subcategories are reported. They overlap with the previous five subcategories.

• Wrong candidates: The ground truth entity is not contained in the candidate set.

• Multiple candidates: The ground truth entity is contained in the candidate set, but the wrong candidate was predicted.

4.2 Evaluation per entity type

Elevant assigns a type to each entity and computes precision, recall and F1 score per entity type. Many entity linking benchmarks contain more than the classic person, location and organization entities. We therefore chose 29 entity types that cover the entities in the included benchmarks well, yet are not too abstract to include many Wikidata entries that are not linked in the benchmarks. Example types are person, location, organization, languoid, taxon, brand, award, event and chemical entity (for the full list see Elevant's documentation on GitHub). The types are not restricted to *named* entities, but include other types of interest, such as profession, sport and color. A type t is assigned to an entity e, if t and e are connected in a manually corrected Wikidata dump via a property path that starts with an *instance of (P31)* relation and is followed by an arbitrary amount of *subclass of (P279)* relations. The types are configurable and detailed instructions for the configuration are given in Elevant's documentation.

4.3 Rich visualization

Elevant provides a rich and compact visualization of an entity linker's predictions in comparison to the ground truth labels; see Figure 2. Predictions are shown as highlighted text, while ground truth labels are shown as underlined text. Both predictions and ground truth labels are color-coded such that true positives, false positives, false negatives and unknown entities can be distinguished at a glance. On mouse-over, tooltips with additional information about the predicted entity or ground truth entity are shown, such as their Wikidata name and ID. When the user selects one of the error categories or entity types mentioned above, annotations that fall into the selected category are emphasized.

4.4 System comparison

Aside from letting the user compare the evaluation results of different entity linkers in various categories, Elevant comes with a feature to compare the predictions of two entity linkers for a selected benchmark side by side. This allows the user to closely and comfortably examine where differences in the evaluation results of two systems are coming from.

4.5 Automatic graph generation

For each category in the evaluation results table, Elevant can generate a graph that shows the results of all linkers over all benchmarks that are currently displayed in the table for that category. See Figure 3 for an example. Which linkers and benchmarks are included in the graph can be controlled by filtering the linkers and benchmarks that are to be included in the table as described in the next section.

4.6 Additional web app features

In addition to the prominent features described above, the Elevant web app comes with several features that improve overall usability. Each selectable component such as the experiment, error category or benchmark article has a corresponding URL parameter. The URL is automatically adjusted when a component is selected. This makes sharing the currently inspected results, e.g. the results of a particular linker for a particular error category on a particular benchmark as easy as copying and sharing the current URL.

When evaluating multiple entity linkers on multiple benchmarks, the evaluation results table can quickly become huge. In order to keep the focus on the currently most relevant results, Elevant has filter text fields which support regular expressions. Only linkers and benchmarks whose names match the filter texts are displayed in the table.

Our goal was to make the Elevant web app as intuitive as possible such that no additional resources would be necessary in order to understand and use it. To this end, the web app itself provides unobtrusive yet easily accessible explanations for its components. A mouseover button for example gives detailed explanations about the annotations such as the (already intuitive) color code. Hovering over the table header of an error category opens a tooltip that not only explains the corresponding error category but also gives an example for an entity linker error that falls into this category. Hovering over precision, recall or F1-score table cells opens a tooltip that shows the total numbers of true positives, false positives, false negatives and ground truth mentions for the corresponding category.

4.7 Included benchmarks

Elevant contains the following benchmarks:

- AIDA-CoNLL (Hoffart et al., 2011), a collection of 216 and 231 news articles from the 1990s for validation and testing.
- KORE50 (Hoffart et al., 2012), 50 difficult, handcrafted sentences.
- MSNBC (Cucerzan, 2007), 20 news articles from 2007.
- MSNBC updated (Guo and Barbosa, 2018), a version of MSNBC without entities that do no longer exist in Wikipedia.
- DBPedia Spotlight (Mendes et al., 2011), 35 paragraphs from New York Times articles.

4.8 Included linkers

Elevant contains pre-computed results of the following entity linkers on the included benchmarks.

- TagMe (Ferragina and Scaiella, 2010)
- DBpedia Spotlight (Daiber et al., 2013)
- GENRE (Cao et al., 2021b)
- Efficient EL (Cao et al., 2021a)
- Neural EL (Gupta et al., 2017)
- Ambiverse (Seyler et al., 2018) (NER), (Hoffart et al., 2011) (NED)

TagMe and DBpedia Spotlight can be run out of the box with Elevant. For GENRE, Efficient EL and Neural EL, we provide code with an easy docker setup that yields results in a format supported by Elevant. Furthermore, Elevant can process any linking results file which is in NIF, the Ambiverse output format or a simple JSONL format as described in Section 3.2. These formats are also explained in detail in Elevant's documentation.

Additionally, we include a simple baseline that is based on prior probabilities computed from Wikipedia hyperlinks. The baseline uses the SpaCy (Honnibal et al., 2020) NER tagger with slight modifications (such as filtering out dates) to detect entity mentions. All entities with an alias that matches the mention text are considered as candidate entities for a mention. The aliases of an entity are the anchor texts of incoming intra-Wikipedia hyperlinks to an entity's Wikipedia article, as well as the entity's Wikidata aliases. From these entity candidates, the entity that has most frequently been linked with the mention text in Wikipedia is predicted.

4.9 Extendability

New benchmarks or entity linking results can easily be added to Elevant if they are in one of the supported formats using Elevant's conversion scripts as described in Section 3.1 and Section 3.2. Additionally, support for other benchmark or entity linking result formats can be added with little effort. The process for implementing new format readers for benchmarks or entity linking results is explained in Elevant's documentation and existing format readers can be used as templates.

4.10 Easy knowledge base update

Elevant stores information about entities in several files that are generated from two sources: Wikidata and Wikipedia. The information extracted from Wikidata includes an entity's name, aliases, types and its corresponding Wikipedia URL. The information extracted from Wikipedia includes intra-Wikipedia link frequencies (how often is a hyperlink's anchor text in Wikipedia linked to a certain Wikipedia article) and Wikipedia redirects which are needed to reliably map Wikipedia entities to Wikidata. All of these files can either be downloaded from our servers or generated with three simple commands. The simplicity of the data generation allows for regular updates of the data.

4.11 Open source

Our code is open source (Apache License 2.0) and is available on GitHub [1]. A Docker setup allows an easy installation and usage. All links and a web demo are provided at `https://elevant.cs.uni-freiburg.de`.

5 Conclusion

Elevant is a powerful, general-purpose, easy-to-use system for the in-depth evaluation and comparison of a set of entity linkers on a given set of benchmarks. Typical evaluations of entity linking systems only provide aggregated figures like precision, recall and the F1 score. Elevant goes beyond this by providing a breakdown of the results by entity type and by error category, as well as an intuitive visualization of true positives, false negatives, and false positives on the concrete texts. This can help both practitioners (to understand for which kind of texts a given entity linker is suited) as well as researchers (to help understand in detail the particular weaknesses of their entity linker and try to improve those).

[1] `https://github.com/ad-freiburg/elevant/`

References

Adrian Brasoveanu, Giuseppe Rizzo, Philipp Kuntschik, Albert Weichselbraun, and Lyndon J. B. Nixon. 2018. Framing named entity linking error types. In *11th International Conference on Language Resources and Evaluation, LREC 2018*.

Nicola De Cao, Wilker Aziz, and Ivan Titov. 2021a. Highly parallel autoregressive entity linking with discriminative correction. In *2021 Conference on Empirical Methods in Natural Language Processing, EMNLP 2021*, pages 7662–7669.

Nicola De Cao, Gautier Izacard, Sebastian Riedel, and Fabio Petroni. 2021b. Autoregressive entity retrieval. In *9th International Conference on Learning Representations, ICLR 2021*.

Silviu Cucerzan. 2007. Large-scale named entity disambiguation based on wikipedia data. In *2007 Joint Conference on Empirical Methods in Natural Language Processing and Computational Natural Language Learning, EMNLP-CoNLL 2007*, pages 708–716.

Joachim Daiber, Max Jakob, Chris Hokamp, and Pablo N. Mendes. 2013. Improving efficiency and accuracy in multilingual entity extraction. In *9th International Conference on Semantic Systems, ISEM 2013*, pages 121–124.

Paolo Ferragina and Ugo Scaiella. 2010. TAGME: on-the-fly annotation of short text fragments (by wikipedia entities). In *19th ACM Conference on Information and Knowledge Management, CIKM 2010*, pages 1625–1628.

Dan Gillick, Nevena Lazic, Kuzman Ganchev, Jesse Kirchner, and David Huynh. 2014. Context-dependent fine-grained entity type tagging. *CoRR*, abs/1412.1820.

Zhaochen Guo and Denilson Barbosa. 2018. Robust named entity disambiguation with random walks. *Semantic Web*, 9(4):459–479.

Nitish Gupta, Sameer Singh, and Dan Roth. 2017. Entity linking via joint encoding of types, descriptions, and context. In *2017 Conference on Empirical Methods in Natural Language Processing, EMNLP 2017*, pages 2681–2690.

Benjamin Heinzerling and Michael Strube. 2015. Visual error analysis for entity linking. In *53rd Annual Meeting of the Association for Computational Linguistics and 7th International Joint Conference on Natural Language Processing of the Asian Federation of Natural Language Processing, ACL 2015*, pages 37–42.

Johannes Hoffart, Stephan Seufert, Dat Ba Nguyen, Martin Theobald, and Gerhard Weikum. 2012. KORE: keyphrase overlap relatedness for entity disambiguation. In *21st ACM International Conference on Information and Knowledge Management, CIKM 2012*, pages 545–554.

Johannes Hoffart, Mohamed Amir Yosef, Ilaria Bordino, Hagen Fürstenau, Manfred Pinkal, Marc Spaniol, Bilyana Taneva, Stefan Thater, and Gerhard Weikum. 2011. Robust disambiguation of named entities in text. In *2011 Conference on Empirical Methods in Natural Language Processing, EMNLP 2011*, pages 782–792.

Matthew Honnibal, Ines Montani, Sofie Van Landeghem, and Adriane Boyd. 2020. spaCy: Industrial-strength Natural Language Processing in Python.

Marcus Klang and Pierre Nugues. 2018. Linking, searching, and visualizing entities in wikipedia. In *11th International Conference on Language Resources and Evaluation, LREC 2018*.

Xiao Ling, Sameer Singh, and Daniel S. Weld. 2015. Design challenges for entity linking. *Transactions of the Association for Computational Linguistics*, 3:315–328.

Xiao Ling and Daniel S. Weld. 2012. Fine-grained entity recognition. In *26th AAAI Conference on Artificial Intelligence, AAAI 2012*.

Pablo N. Mendes, Max Jakob, Andrés García-Silva, and Christian Bizer. 2011. Dbpedia spotlight: shedding light on the web of documents. In *7th International Conference on Semantic Systems, I-SEMANTICS 2011*, pages 1–8.

Fabian Odoni, Philipp Kuntschik, Adrian M. P. Brasoveanu, and Albert Weichselbraun. 2018. On the importance of drill-down analysis for assessing gold standards and named entity linking performance. In *14th International Conference on Semantic Systems, SEMANTiCS 2018*, volume 137, pages 33–42.

Henry Rosales-Méndez, Aidan Hogan, and Barbara Poblete. 2019. Fine-grained evaluation for entity linking. In *2019 Conference on Empirical Methods in Natural Language Processing and 9th International Joint Conference on Natural Language Processing, EMNLP-IJCNLP 2019*, pages 718–727.

Dominic Seyler, Tatiana Dembelova, Luciano Del Corro, Johannes Hoffart, and Gerhard Weikum. 2018. A study of the importance of external knowledge in the named entity recognition task. In *56th Annual Meeting of the Association for Computational Linguistics, ACL 2018*, pages 241–246.

Michael Strobl, Amine Trabelsi, and Osmar R. Zaïane. 2020. WEXEA: wikipedia exhaustive entity annotation. In *12th Language Resources and Evaluation Conference, LREC 2020*, pages 1951–1958.

Ricardo Usbeck, Michael Röder, Axel-Cyrille Ngonga Ngomo, Ciro Baron, Andreas Both, Martin Brümmer, Diego Ceccarelli, Marco Cornolti, Didier Cherix, Bernd Eickmann, Paolo Ferragina, Christiane Lemke, Andrea Moro, Roberto Navigli, Francesco Piccinno, Giuseppe Rizzo, Harald Sack, René Speck, Raphaël Troncy, Jörg Waitelonis, and Lars Wesemann. 2015. GERBIL: general entity annotator benchmarking framework. In *24th International Conference on World Wide Web, WWW 2015*, pages 1133–1143.

A Pipeline for Generating, Annotating and Employing Synthetic Data for Real World Question Answering

Matt Maufe
Filament AI, UK
University of Warwick, UK
matt.maufe@filament.ai

James Ravenscroft
Filament AI, UK
University of Warwick, UK
james.ravenscroft@filament.ai

Rob Procter
University of Warwick, UK
The Alan Turing Institute, UK
Rob.Procter@warwick.ac.uk

Maria Liakata
Queen Mary University of London, UK
The Alan Turing Institute, UK
m.liakata@qmul.ac.uk

Abstract

Question Answering (QA) is a growing area of research, often used to facilitate the extraction of information from within documents. State-of-the-art QA models are usually pre-trained on domain-general corpora like Wikipedia and thus tend to struggle on out-of-domain documents without fine-tuning. We demonstrate that synthetic domain-specific datasets can be generated easily using domain-general models, while still providing significant improvements to QA performance. We present two new tools for this task: A flexible pipeline for validating the synthetic QA data and training downstream models on it, and an online interface to facilitate human annotation of this generated data. Using this interface, crowdworkers labelled 1117 synthetic QA pairs, which we then used to fine-tune downstream models and improve domain-specific QA performance by 8.75 F1.

1 Introduction

Having enough relevant training data is a key factor for achieving strong performance in machine learning and NLP (Hoffmann et al., 2022), but for many tasks, large domain-specific datasets are expensive and time-consuming to create manually. This is especially true for tasks like Extractive Question Answering (QA), which both relies on domain-specific knowledge and requires skilled annotators. These difficulties have led to increased interest in synthetic data generation recently (Feng et al., 2021) through various methods such as bootstrapping from smaller datasets, or through generative models which create entirely new data.

We make the following contributions:

- A modular architecture-agnostic pipeline that takes as input unstructured documents and produces both synthetic QA pairs and a QA model trained on them; We show in Section 4.3 that using this synthetic domain-specific data allows for a dramatic improvement on the QA task compared to baseline state-of-the-art models, especially on unanswerable questions.
- A web-based tool that allows annotators to label various aspects of the synthetic data with ease, alongside guidelines to help ensure consistency and quality in their labels.
- We release[1] this annotation tool and its guidelines for general use. While we use and evaluate this pipeline in the domain of business news, the pipeline is sufficiently flexible to be applied to other domains, including potentially being applicable to abstractive QA.

2 Background and Related Work

Grammaticality Models allow for improving the quality of synthetic data and subsequent performance in downstream tasks by better aligning it with real user data. On benchmark datasets, such as the Corpus of Linguistic Acceptability (CoLA, Warstadt et al., 2019) which contains a wide range of examples from published linguistics literature, current state-of-the-art models (Sun et al., 2019) can achieve a Matthew's Correlation Coefficient score (Matthews, 1975) of approximately 0.775 (Wang et al., 2022), exceeding human performance (0.713, Warstadt et al., 2019) in some cases, though this can vary significantly depending on the sentence's syntactic complexity and length (Warstadt and Bowman, 2020).

Synthetic NLP Data Generation Synthetic data

[1]GitHub

Proceedings of the The 2022 Conference on Empirical Methods in Natural Language Processing: System Demonstrations, pages 80 - 97
December 7-11, 2022

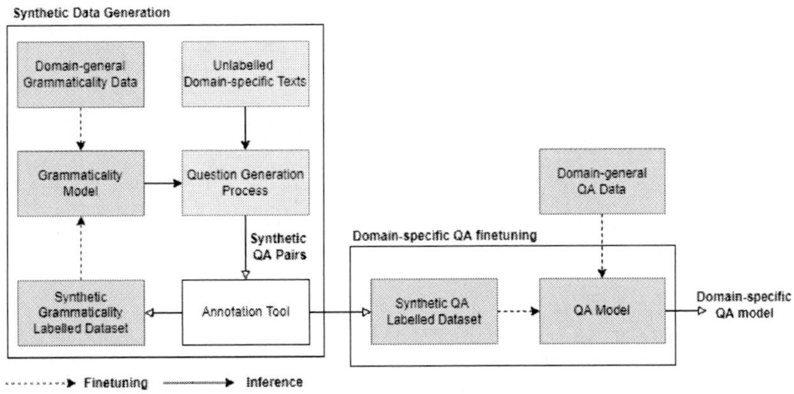

Figure 1: The overall pipeline. The question generation process (blue) generates synthetic QA pairs, which are validated by the grammaticality model. The annotation tool is used to present this data to users for annotation, and the resultant labelled data is then used to fine-tune the grammaticality (red) and QA (purple) models.

generation is an attractive option for dataset creation, especially for domain-specific tasks. Various methods for bootstrapping from smaller datasets have been devised, such as back-translation (Sennrich et al., 2015) and Sibylvariant transformations (Harel-Canada et al., 2022). Backtranslation produces paraphrases through round-trip translation, while Sibylvariant transformations modify or combine texts in predictable ways to create new data with a different label.

Of particular interest are methods that use text generation models to create entirely new data, rather than simply paraphrasing or combining inputs predictably. A variety of these models have been used to generate new QA pairs (Grover et al., 2021), such as the T5 model (Raffel et al., 2020) and BERT (Devlin et al., 2018).

Synthetic data generation can be particularly useful when fine-tuning a model on a specific domain, for which manually-curated datasets may not exist. Whilst high quality datasets such as SQuAD 2.0 (Rajpurkar et al., 2018) do exist for QA tasks, they tend to only have general content, e.g. from Wikipedia. Thus models trained on them often struggle on more domain-specific tasks (Ramponi and Plank, 2020, see also Section 4.3 below).

Evaluation of Synthetic QA Pairs Evaluating Question Generation (QG) models can be difficult due to the nature of the problem: A good question tends to have various qualities (grammatical, answerable, non-trivial to answer, etc.) that are difficult to capture in a single metric, especially one that correlates well with human judgements (Hosking and Riedel, 2019). Nonetheless, several metrics such as BLEU (Papineni et al., 2002) and BERTScore (Zhang et al., 2020) have been proposed, though they rely on having reference questions available and often do not capture whether or not the question is *answerable* (Nema and Khapra, 2018). However, Rajpurkar et al. (2018) show that the use of unanswerable questions when training QA models is important for real-world performance, making it a metric of interest.

Round-trip evaluation, such as the methods proposed by Alberti et al. (2019), allows for evaluating the generated data by checking how consistent downstream model results are when synthetic data is used as the model input, e.g. if the generated answer is found for a synthetic question when the question is input to a QA model. We adopt this approach and discuss it further in Section 4.2.

3 System Overview

Figure 1 shows an overview of our system for creating domain-specific synthetic QA pairs which are used to train downstream models. The QG process (see Section 3.2 for details) creates domain-specific QA pairs from unlabelled texts. This data is then annotated for grammaticality and correctness using the annotation tool, allowing for the creation of two new domain-specific datasets to fine-tune both grammaticality and QA models.

We take a subset of a proprietary knowledge base as our set of input documents and use this to create our domain-specific QA dataset (which we call "SYFTER"). The knowledge base contains

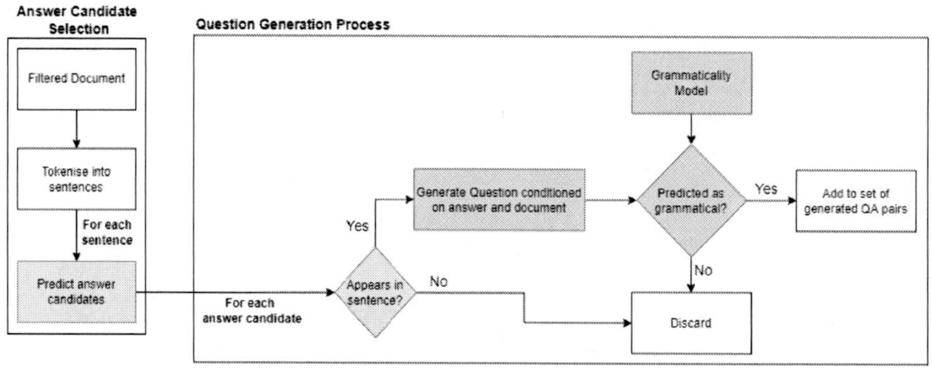

Figure 2: The question generation pipeline.

documents obtained by scraping online articles and is focused on business news, such as information about corporate structures, and is thus quite distinct in subject matter from our external domain-general data (SQuAD 2.0, see Section 3.2).

3.1 Grammaticality Validation

We use a pre-trained BERT model[2] (Devlin et al., 2018) to evaluate the grammaticality of each synthetic question and answer and we discard ungrammatical ones under the intuition that encouraging the synthetic data to be grammatically correct results in the final dataset being more similar to questions posed by real users and improved performance on the downstream task.

We use the "in-domain" data from the Corpus of Linguistic Acceptability (CoLA, Warstadt et al., 2019) dataset to train our grammaticality model in the domain-general setting.

While from a linguistic perspective (Lau et al., 2017), grammaticality can be seen as either a binary or a gradient feature, we use it as a binary label to better standardise with other papers and with CoLA. Furthermore, annotators are unlikely to hold consistent beliefs about the *degree* to which something is ungrammatical, given the high level of subjectivity inherent in such a judgement, and so treating it as binary reduces the potential for noise in the labels.

Because both the CoLA and SYFTER grammaticality datasets have a large degree of class imbalance[3], we use SMOTE (Chawla et al., 2002) to oversample the ungrammatical instances and achieve a uniform class distribution.

[2]bert-base-uncased

[3]Approximately 25% and 10% ungrammatical respectively

3.2 Synthetic Question-Answer Pair Generation

The Question Generation process takes as input a natural language document (in our case, a paragraph or a single sentence) and outputs a QA pair that can be answered from this document. This is done using two models: One to select answer candidates from the document, and one that generates a question based on both the answer and the full document, for each candidate. The full process is shown in Figure 2.

We extend Patil Suraj's question-generation library (Patil, 2022) to work with any SQuAD 2.0-format dataset rather than only ones available from HuggingFace, as well as enabling it to gracefully discard invalid answers without breaking, and partially integrating it into our own pipeline.

We use two separate T5 (Raffel et al., 2020) models fine-tuned on SQuAD V1[4] data for both answer selection and question generation[5], and specify the task at inference time in natural language following the prompting paradigm (Brown et al., 2020). We "highlight" the answer token during question generation as described in (Chan and Fan, 2019).[6] Because the underlying model is abstractive rather than extractive, it occasionally produces answer candidates that do not appear in the context and are thus unusable for extractive QA, which we discard.

Prior to answer selection, we filter out unsuitable input documents in two stages: We first filter out documents that are very short[7] or which match at

[4]Due to time constraints, we did not re-train on SQuAD 2.0, but the model performs well nonetheless (Section 4.2)

[5]valhalla/t5-small-qa-qg-hl and valhalla/t5-base-qg-hl respectively.

[6]E.g. "generate question: The <hl>dog<hl> is red".

[7]Less than 10 tokens

least one of a set of RegEx filters (see Appendix A for details), allowing us to remove any that are clearly semantically null. We then apply a second filter using a BERT Part-of-Speech model[8] such that only documents that contain a verb, or an auxiliary verb and a proper noun, are included so as to remove documents that do not present information that questions can be built around.

Each sentence in each filtered document is input to the answer selection model, which identifies answer candidates within them. Intuitively, a span is an answer candidate if a question can be built around it, and so the model tends to select ones representing entities or relations.

Questions are then generated, conditioned on each answer and the entire associated document, and if validated by the grammaticality model they are added to the synthetic QA dataset.

The resultant dataset can then be input directly into the annotation tool.

An ablation test over the filters (including the grammaticality model) can be found in Appendix C.

3.3 Question Answering

We use an ALBERT (Lan et al., 2019) Question Answering model to predict an answer represented as a span within the document, indicated by two token indices (start and end).

The model is able to provide "null answers", indicating that the question cannot be answered, either directly or by having its prediction changed to the null answer if the null-answer's confidence score is above a "null-answer threshold" (regardless of the original prediction's confidence score).

We utilise SQuAD 2.0 (Rajpurkar et al., 2018) for the initial fine-tuning of our QA model, as it is a large high-quality dataset containing both answerable and unanswerable questions, and as a general-domain dataset it allows us to demonstrate the utility of our domain transfer methods.

The resultant QA model is then fine-tuned on our domain-specific "SYFTER" dataset in order to adapt it to our desired domain, which focuses on news articles about commercial events such as product launches and earnings reports (whereas SQuAD's data comes from Wikipedia and focuses more on history, politics, and geography).[9]

3.3.1 Detecting Unanswerable Questions

During development, we noticed that when trained on a single domain (SQuAD or SYFTER), the QA models could learn to effectively identify if a question from that domain could be answered or not, but performance on this task would drop significantly when trained on both domains.

This was likely due to a combination of our "unanswerable question" label being applied more broadly (to nonsensical questions as well as unanswerable ones), and due to the significant amount of class imbalance in the dataset (especially for the SYFTER data), as well as a small amount of noise in the labels detected through manual inspection.

We explored various methods to resolve this problem when using combined training data, and discuss an ablation study over them in Appendix B, with results in Table 7.

- We appended "source markers" to the end of each question, prior to tokenisation, which indicated the domain that the question came from: either "[SQuAD]" or "[SYFTER]", in order to allow the model to better learn domain-specific features.
- We tuned the 'null-answer threshold" on the validation set.
- We investigated training the model simultaneously for the tasks of both QA and sequence classification as "answerable" / "unanswerable". This follows findings from Crawshaw (2020) that multitask learning can often improve performance, and given the interdependence between question answering and detecting if a question *can* be answered.
- Finally, we used alpha-weighted Focal Loss (Lin et al., 2017) rather than Cross Entropy Loss for sequence classification in the multitask setting to better handle class imbalance.

3.4 Data Annotation

In order to label the synthetic data for supervised training, we created an annotation tool[10] using Streamlit (Treuille et al., 2018) which allows annotators to view model-generated QA pairs, along with their associated context document, and annotate them in various ways. An example of how QA pairs are presented within the tool can be found in Figure 5 in Appendix D.

We used a series of three preliminary studies to

[8] vblagoje/bert-english-uncased-finetuned-pos

[9] SQuAD's domains can be explored here.

[10] A video demo can be found here

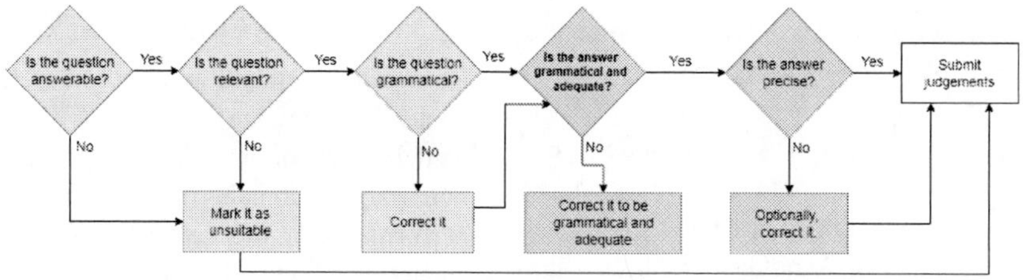

Figure 3: The annotation process. The answerability and relevance of questions (blue) is dependent on the document, without considering external knowledge. Answers (purple) must appear within the document to be accepted.

Model	Training Data	# Train Examples	Macro F1 Score
BERT	CoLA	10584	61.18
BERT	SYFTER	2796	**75.74**
BERT	CoLA + SYFTER	13608	74.68

Table 1: The Grammaticality model results. The best setting is indicated in **bold** text. "# Train Examples" refers to the data *after* oversampling.

iteratively refine our annotation tool and guidelines, with each study involving 10 participants (who did not participate in subsequent studies). This allowed us to identify and fix any points of misunderstanding before using the tool for the final annotation study on the entire dataset. As with the final annotation study, these were done via Prolific[11] and under the same annotator filters (as well as filtering out previous participants).

Following each preliminary study, we followed up with annotators in cases where they had made unintuitive judgements or appeared to have misunderstood, and used these discussions to refine the guidelines presented. The final guidelines are shown in Appendix D.1.

Each annotator was assigned to a group with two others, and each group of three annotators provided annotations for 2% of the total dataset, with gold labels coming from majority judgements.

The annotation process is shown in Figure 3. Questions marked as unsuitable (for either reason) are not labelled further, and comprise the set of unanswerable questions for the SYFTER domain.

Questions were judged on suitability (whether the question is answerable and relevant to the document) as well as grammaticality.

Grammaticality for both questions and answers was posed to annotators as a question of "reading naturally", in order to better mimic real user questions and avoid the subjective issues inherent to judging grammaticality.

Answers were judged on both naturalness and quality. In the latter case, an answer was considered "adequate" if it answered the question but had either extraneous details or was missing details, and "precise and correct" if it answered the question with all of the relevant details, but no more.

We asked annotators to rewrite questions and answers that did not read naturally, as well as inadequate answers, and did not allow for the submission of the labels until the texts were corrected or the question was marked as unsuitable (e.g. if they could not be corrected within our constraints).

4 Experiments and Results

The Grammaticality and Question Answering models are tested in both the setting of interest (combined domain-general and domain-specific data) as well as two baseline data settings (domain-general data only[12], and domain-specific data only). This allows us to both measure how useful the synthetic data is as an addition to domain-general data and to also evaluate the feasibility of fine-tuning using *only* synthetic data, which would reduce time and expense significantly given its small size.

The combined test sets for the Grammaticality and QA models are produced by combining the appropriate domain-general data (CoLA or SQuAD) with the domain-specific SYFTER data and then testing the model on this combination dataset.

We evaluate the Question Generation process

[11]https://www.prolific.co/

[12]CoLA for the grammaticality task, SQuAD for the QA task

Test Dataset	QA Model	Exact Match	Similarity
SQuAD 2.0	RoBERTa	**67.81%**	**81.89%**
SYFTER	RoBERTa	64.55%	77.27%

Table 2: Roundtrip evaluation of our QA datasets' quality, using an off-the-shelf QA model. The RoBERTa model was trained on SQuAD 2.0. Best results indicated in bold text.

Document	Question	Answer
"International law firm Ashurst announces the appointment of Matthias Weissinger as partner in Munich.	Who is the new partner of Ashurst in Munich?	Matthias Weissinger
To date we've delivered more than one billion pieces of protective equipment to the frontline.	How many pieces of protective equipment have been delivered to the frontline?	more than one billion
As a major food sector player, Bel fully assumes its duty to do everything possible to ensure the continuity of its operations.	What sector is Bel a major player in?	food

Table 3: Example Question-Answer Pairs Generated from Documents

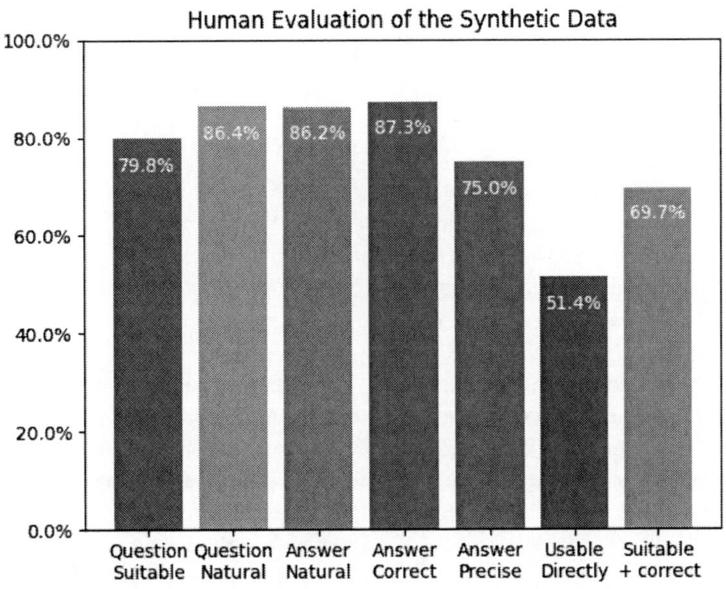

Figure 4: Human Evaluation results on the annotated data. Only QA pairs that had a suitable question were judged further on the other metrics. Percentages shown are based on annotator consensus rather than individual judgements.

Model	Training Data	% Synthetic Training Data	Answerable EM	Answerable F1	Unanswerable EM	Overall EM	Overall F1
ALBERT	SQuAD 2.0	0%	**84.87**	**91.09**	12.16	61.06	65.25
ALBERT	SYFTER	100%	53.26	59.71	**72.00**	57.26	63.34
ALBERT	SQuAD 2.0 + SYFTER	0.62%	71.74	83.24	40.00	**64.96**	**74.00**

Table 4: Question Answering model results on the SYFTER test set. The best settings are shown in **bold**.

in both the domain-general and domain-specific settings, but do *not* evaluate the combined setting due to the nature of the evaluation (see Section 4.2).

4.1 Grammaticality Classification

We evaluate the grammaticality model using the model's F1 score, treating grammaticality as a binary sequence classification task, and achieve strong results in both the synthetic-only and combined data settings, as shown in Table 1. The domain-specific model actually performs better than both the domain-general model and the combined-data setting, despite training on only a small amount of synthetic data, indicating the importance of using domain-specific data during training.

4.2 Synthetic Question-Answer Pair Generation

We evaluate the synthetic questions through roundtrip evaluation as discussed in Section 2. For each generated QA pair, we use an off-the-shelf QA model[13] to answer the generated question (based on its associated context) and then compare the answers in two ways: Exact match; and comparing their similarity with their most-similar question at the token level using length-normalised Levenshtein distance (Levenshtein, 1966) via NLTK (Bird et al., 2009). Intuitively, if the question is well-formed and precise, and the answer is relevant to it, the QA model should find the correct answer.

As shown in Table 2, the synthetic data is of high quality, reaching similar levels to SQuAD 2.0, which was manually created by humans. Furthermore, Table 3 shows examples of the synthetic data produced and used. The generated questions are both fluent and of interest, and the answers are both precise and correct. The first question is slightly stilted, but still easily understandable.

Finally, the annotation process can also be thought of as a form of human evaluation and, as shown by Figure 4, the vast majority of the data was found to be of high-quality (suitable, reading naturally, and correct+precise answers). However, 48.6% of the data, including unsuitable questions, did require some input from annotations in some form (not counting data that was imprecise but otherwise good). This indicates that while the data tends to be of high-quality overall, about half of the datapoints do contain a small amount of noise. 69.7% of the questions are suitable and have correct answers, which can be considered the key factors for good synthetic QA data, and as such a high percentage of the data could be used to train a QA system as-is without needing corrections.

[13]deepset/roberta-base-squad2, which has strong performance on SQuAD 2 data

4.3 Question Answering

We take approximately 11.6% of the total annotated SYFTER data (117 questions, approximately 21% of which are unanswerable) to use as the QA test set, and split it at the document-level to avoid potential information leaks from the training data.

The QA model is evaluated through both the "Exact Match" (EM) score, and at the token level using F1 score, via the HuggingFace wrapper around the official SQuAD evaluation script. In both cases, the text is first lowercased and normalised to remove articles and standardise whitespace. EM and F1 are identical for unanswerable questions.

We present the results from the best setting, which uses null-answer threshold tuning and multi-task learning *without* Focal Loss (see Appendix B), in Table 4.

The SYFTER-only model performs well despite the SYFTER dataset being much smaller than SQuAD 2.0, and is much better at handling unanswerable questions. By combining the two, we achieve the best overall performance, and maintain reasonable performance on unanswerable questions despite the issues discussed in Section 3.3.1.

5 Conclusion

We present a pipeline for using and evaluating synthetic QA data and an interface for annotating it, as well as annotation guidelines. The combination of domain-general and synthetic data allows our QA model to perform significantly better (+ 9 F1) on domain-specific documents than it did when trained solely on a similar amount of domain-general data. The pipeline is simple to apply to both current and future state-of-the-art models, enabling better performance in low-resource domains.

6 Acknowledgements

This work is supported by an Innovate UK grant under the KTP scheme (KTP 11714) to Rob Procter, Maria Liakata and Filament AI, as well as the Alan Turing Institute (EP/N510129/1). Maria Liakata has been supported by a UKRI/EPSRC Turing AI Fellowship EP/V030302/1.

7 Limitations

Whilst our system demonstrates that we can achieve significant improvements from synthetic domain-specific data with minimal additional time and expense, it does have certain limitations: We do not consider "adversarial questions" when training, and it thus would likely struggle on these kinds of questions based on findings such as those from Bartolo et al. (2021).

We also found that our synthetic data primarily consists of questions which identify entities (e.g. "Who is the CEO of Microsoft?", "When did Microsoft acquire Bethesda Softworks?", "What are the five principles of good leadership?"), and does not contain many examples of questions about relationships between entities (e.g. "Is selling ice cream more profitable than selling widgets?"), and answers to the latter may be of relatively poor quality.

This is likely due to what appears to be a similar trend in SQuAD V1 that the Question Generation model was trained on: SQuAD primarily asks questions with short entity-focused answers (dates, names, etc.) (Qu et al., 2021) and approximately half of the answers in SquAD (Rajpurkar et al., 2016) are proper nouns, dates, or other numbers indicating that their corresponding questions are likely entity-focused.

The questions of interest to us are generally entity-based and so this limitation does not directly impact our own usage of the model, but we recognise that it potentially limits its applicability to other domains. In the future, the model's performance on non-entity questions could be investigated and improved through tools like AdaTest (Ribeiro and Lundberg, 2022).

The tool also still requires some amount of human involvement to annotate and filter the synthetic data, and the Grammaticality model results (Table 1 indicates that filtering with purely domain-general models would be ineffective. However, it is possible to generate the QA pairs without annotation and, given the high quality of the data (Figure 4), it may be reasonably possible to use the data directly (treating it all as suitable and grammatical) to achieve a still-significant boost to domain-specific performance.

The main problem with not using human annotation would be that our "unanswerable questions" are all ones marked as "unsuitable" by humans, and thus using the synthetic data directly would lead to only having synthetic questions that are considered to be answerable. This could be improved through extending the QG pipeline to also produce deliberately-unanswerable examples, but is not currently possible.

Finally, whilst we use the grammaticality model for validation during the question generation process, we do not train either the Answer Selection or Question Generation models with grammaticality as a second objective function. Training it in a multitask setting would likely have guided it towards producing better input, and may have produced more (valid) data from the corpus.

8 Ethics Statement

Machine learning tasks often involve the potential for ethical issues, especially when using human annotators to label data. We chose to use Prolific[14] as a platform to find and pay annotators, as it offered a reputation for enforcing ethical payments as well as useful filters such as education level and native language.

We also submitted our project to the University of Warwick's internal ethics process, and were approved without having to make any adjustments.

Prolific annotators are paid a fixed amount, but if a task's average hourly payment falls below a minimum (£5 / $6.50 per hour), it is required to rectify this and increase the payments.

The mean rate of pay for annotators was reported as £15.63 during the preliminary studies and £15.50 during the primary annotation study, though these figures are *under-estimates* as our own time-tracking indicates that annotators generally spent a significant amount of time not annotating the data questions (but still recorded by Prolific as being on-task). This is well in excess of the UK living wage of £9.50, as well as the "real living wage" of up to £11.05 proposed by The Living Wage Foundation[15].

The use of synthetic data does have some inherent potential ethical issues: "Model hallucination" is a well-known phenomenon where models can create unfaithful data (e.g. convincing, but false answers to questions) and which can cause real-world harm if the information it provides is acted on (Ji et al., 2022). This can affect our own models if the data generation models hallucinate and lead to the QA model internalising incorrect knowledge.

[14]https://www.prolific.co/

[15]As discussed here.

Thankfully, there are various ways to identify these occurrences and mitigate this harm, including perhaps the simplest method of specifying the context in which the data was created and used at appropriate downstream points, so that users can better assess its veracity for themselves.

To limit this harm, we strongly suggest that other researchers take this into account in their own work, and take the appropriate actions, for instance using human annotators to verify the data and actively designing models to be robust against hallucination, as done in work like Su et al. (2022).

Finally, despite using a model to create our QA data, and the fact that synthetic data can clearly be very useful, bias is still likely to exist in the data (carried forward from both the model's original training data and the human factor of the annotation done), and we suggest that any data produced be investigated and debiased through tools like AdaTest (Ribeiro and Lundberg, 2022).

References

Chris Alberti, Daniel Andor, Emily Pitler, Jacob Devlin, and Michael Collins. 2019. Synthetic qa corpora generation with roundtrip consistency.

Max Bartolo, Tristan Thrush, Robin Jia, Sebastian Riedel, Pontus Stenetorp, and Douwe Kiela. 2021. Improving question answering model robustness with synthetic adversarial data generation. In *Proceedings of the 2021 Conference on Empirical Methods in Natural Language Processing*. Association for Computational Linguistics.

Steven Bird, Ewan Klein, and Edward Loper. 2009. *Natural language processing with Python: analyzing text with the natural language toolkit.* " O'Reilly Media, Inc.".

Tom B. Brown, Benjamin Mann, Nick Ryder, Melanie Subbiah, Jared Kaplan, Prafulla Dhariwal, Arvind Neelakantan, Pranav Shyam, Girish Sastry, Amanda Askell, Sandhini Agarwal, Ariel Herbert-Voss, Gretchen Krueger, Tom Henighan, Rewon Child, Aditya Ramesh, Daniel M. Ziegler, Jeffrey Wu, Clemens Winter, Christopher Hesse, Mark Chen, Eric Sigler, Mateusz Litwin, Scott Gray, Benjamin Chess, Jack Clark, Christopher Berner, Sam McCandlish, Alec Radford, Ilya Sutskever, and Dario Amodei. 2020. Language models are few-shot learners.

Ying-Hong Chan and Yao-Chung Fan. 2019. A recurrent BERT-based model for question generation. In *Proceedings of the 2nd Workshop on Machine Reading for Question Answering*, pages 154–162, Hong Kong, China. Association for Computational Linguistics.

N. V. Chawla, K. W. Bowyer, L. O. Hall, and W. P. Kegelmeyer. 2002. SMOTE: Synthetic minority oversampling technique. *Journal of Artificial Intelligence Research*, 16:321–357.

Michael Crawshaw. 2020. Multi-task learning with deep neural networks: A survey.

Jacob Devlin, Ming-Wei Chang, Kenton Lee, and Kristina Toutanova. 2018. Bert: Pre-training of deep bidirectional transformers for language understanding.

Steven Y. Feng, Varun Gangal, Jason Wei, Sarath Chandar, Soroush Vosoughi, Teruko Mitamura, and Eduard Hovy. 2021. A survey of data augmentation approaches for nlp.

Khushnuma Grover, Katinder Kaur, Kartikey Tiwari, Rupali, and Parteek Kumar. 2021. Deep learning based question generation using t5 transformer. In *Advanced Computing*, pages 243–255, Singapore. Springer Singapore.

Fabrice Harel-Canada, Muhammad Ali Gulzar, Nanyun Peng, and Miryung Kim. 2022. Sibylvariant transformations for robust text classification. In *Findings of the Association for Computational Linguistics: ACL 2022*, pages 1771–1788, Dublin, Ireland. Association for Computational Linguistics.

Jordan Hoffmann, Sebastian Borgeaud, Arthur Mensch, Elena Buchatskaya, Trevor Cai, Eliza Rutherford, Diego de Las Casas, Lisa Anne Hendricks, Johannes Welbl, Aidan Clark, Tom Hennigan, Eric Noland, Katie Millican, George van den Driessche, Bogdan Damoc, Aurelia Guy, Simon Osindero, Karen Simonyan, Erich Elsen, Jack W. Rae, Oriol Vinyals, and Laurent Sifre. 2022. Training compute-optimal large language models.

Tom Hosking and Sebastian Riedel. 2019. Evaluating rewards for question generation models.

Ziwei Ji, Nayeon Lee, Rita Frieske, Tiezheng Yu, Dan Su, Yan Xu, Etsuko Ishii, Yejin Bang, Andrea Madotto, and Pascale Fung. 2022. Survey of hallucination in natural language generation.

Zhenzhong Lan, Mingda Chen, Sebastian Goodman, Kevin Gimpel, Piyush Sharma, and Radu Soricut. 2019. Albert: A lite bert for self-supervised learning of language representations.

Jey Han Lau, Alexander Clark, and Shalom Lappin. 2017. Grammaticality, acceptability, and probability: A probabilistic view of linguistic knowledge. *Cognitive Science*, 41(5):1202–1241.

Vladimir I. Levenshtein. 1966. Binary codes capable of correcting deletions, insertions, and reversals.

Tsung-Yi Lin, Priya Goyal, Ross Girshick, Kaiming He, and Piotr Dollár. 2017. Focal loss for dense object detection.

B.W. Matthews. 1975. Comparison of the predicted and observed secondary structure of t4 phage lysozyme. *Biochimica et Biophysica Acta (BBA) - Protein Structure*, 405(2):442–451.

Preksha Nema and Mitesh M. Khapra. 2018. Towards a better metric for evaluating question generation systems. In *Proceedings of the 2018 Conference on Empirical Methods in Natural Language Processing*, pages 3950–3959, Brussels, Belgium. Association for Computational Linguistics.

Kishore Papineni, Salim Roukos, Todd Ward, , and Wei-Jing Zhu. 2002. Bleu: a method for automatic evaluation of machine translation.

Suraj Patil. 2022. Question Generation using transformers.

Fanyi Qu, Xin Jia, and Yunfang Wu. 2021. Asking questions like educational experts: Automatically generating question-answer pairs on real-world examination data.

Colin Raffel, Noam Shazeer, Adam Roberts, Katherine Lee, Sharan Narang, Michael Matena, Yanqi Zhou, Wei Li, and Peter J. Liu. 2020. Exploring the limits of transfer learning with a unified text-to-text transformer.

Pranav Rajpurkar, Robin Jia, and Percy Liang. 2018. Know what you don't know: Unanswerable questions for squad.

Pranav Rajpurkar, Jian Zhang, Konstantin Lopyrev, and Percy Liang. 2016. Squad: 100,000+ questions for machine comprehension of text.

Alan Ramponi and Barbara Plank. 2020. Neural unsupervised domain adaptation in nlp—a survey.

Marco Tulio Ribeiro and Scott Lundberg. 2022. Adaptive testing and debugging of NLP models. In *Proceedings of the 60th Annual Meeting of the Association for Computational Linguistics (Volume 1: Long Papers)*, pages 3253–3267, Dublin, Ireland. Association for Computational Linguistics.

Rico Sennrich, Barry Haddow, and Alexandra Birch. 2015. Improving neural machine translation models with monolingual data.

Dan Su, Xiaoguang Li, Jindi Zhang, Lifeng Shang, Xin Jiang, Qun Liu, and Pascale Fung. 2022. Read before generate! faithful long form question answering with machine reading.

Yu Sun, Shuohuan Wang, Yukun Li, Shikun Feng, Xuyi Chen, Han Zhang, Xin Tian, Danxiang Zhu, Hao Tian, and Hua Wu. 2019. Ernie: Enhanced representation through knowledge integration.

Adrien Treuille, Thiago Teixeira, and Amanda Kelly. 2018. Streamlit.

Alex Wang, Amanpreet Singh, Julian Michael, Felix Hill, Omer Levy, and Samuel R. Bowman. 2022. Glue benchmark leaderboard.

Alex Warstadt and Samuel R. Bowman. 2020. Linguistic analysis of pretrained sentence encoders with acceptability judgments.

Alex Warstadt, Amanpreet Singh, and Samuel R. Bowman. 2019. Neural network acceptability judgments.

Tianyi Zhang, Varsha Kishore, Felix Wu, Kilian Q. Weinberger, and Yoav Artzi. 2020. Bertscore: Evaluating text generation with bert.

A RegEx Document Filters

Table 5 shows the different RegEx filters that we apply to documents in order to filter out ones that are likely to be difficult to select valid answers from. Documents are filtered if *any* substring in them is a match for the expression.

The first expression, which filters out documents that appear to be too similar to contracts, additionally contains certain *whitelist* expressions which prevent otherwise-matching documents from being removed. These can be seen in Table 6. In order to be whitelisted, the text that matched the initial filter must fully match the whitelist expression (though the entire document does not have to match).

For clarity when dealing with leading/trailing whitespace, each expression is wrapped in "double quotes", but these quotes are not part of the actual expression. Matches with each expression are **emphasised** for clarity.

RegEx Expression	Intended Matches	Example Match
“ ?\([0-9A-Za-z]+\)(\([0-9A-Za-z]+\))*”	Contract-like documents	“B 1: Financial Instruments according to Regulation 17(**1**)(**a**) of the Regulations”
“^[0-9]+\.? ?.+”	Numeric List	“**1. Reassure customers and employees**”
“^[ivx]+\.? .+”	Roman-numeric List	“**xi If the financial instrument has such a period**”
“\[?\]”	Empty square brackets	“**[ ]** An acquisition or disposal of financial instruments”
“Regulation(s)? [0-9]+”	Regulations contract-like	“B 2: Financial Instruments with similar economic effect according to **Regulation 17** of the Regulations”
“^.{0,15}$”	Very short documents	“**content**”
“^(.{0.5})?\(.+\).{0,5}$”	Mostly in brackets	“**(please tick the appropriate box or boxes):**”

Table 5: RegEx Filters for Documents

RegEx Expression	Purpose	Example Documents Whitelisted
“ ?\([A-Z]+s?\)”	Allow acronyms	“CPE Lite is Huawei’s latest mini customer premises equipment **(CPE)**.”
“ ?\([A-Z]?[0-9a-z]{4,}\)”	Allow short bracketed words	“Bel reported strong sales momentum in the first two months of the year in global**(mature)** markets”

Table 6: RegEx Whitelists for Documents, applied to the “Contract-like” filter.

B Question Answering Ablation

We performed an ablation study over the Question Answering Model components discussed in Section 3.3.1, and found that in some cases they significantly improve the performance on unanswerable questions, especially the use of multitask learning. The results of this ablation are shown in Table 7.

Whilst we found that some settings (Source Markers, Focal Loss) did not appear to be useful, we nonetheless believe that the utility of source markers when using more domains would be an interesting avenue for future investigation.

C Question Generation Filter Ablation

We performed an ablation study over the Question Generation filters discussed in Section 3.2 and found that the individual filters tend to have a significant impact on the model's performance on unanswerable questions, but relatively little when considering answerable questions. Given that the filters were primarily designed to filter out documents that were likely to produce low-quality unanswerable questions, this is as expected. The set of filters that we used does not provide the best *overall* F1 Score, but provides a model whose performance is significantly more balanced than the nominally best-performing model, a trait that we found valuable.

For these tests, we trained and tested the QA model *only* on SYFTER data so as to most clearly see the effects of the filter(s) used (since SQuAD data is not filtered in our pipeline).

Source Markers	Threshold Tuning	Multitask	Focal Loss	Performance Gain (F1)		
				Answerable	No Answer	Overall
x	x	x	x	91.02	72.97	85.11
✓	x	x	x	- 2.2	+ 0	- 1.48
x	✓	x	x	- 0.66	+ 1.35	+ 0
x	x	✓	x	**- 1.98**	**+ 4.06**	**+ 0**
x	x	✓	✓	- 2.14	+ 0	- 1.44
✓	✓	✓	✓	- 1.91	+ 1.35	- 0.84

Table 7: Relative performance gains on the ALBERT QA model in different training settings. A checkmark indicates that the component was used, an "x" that it was not. Focal loss is only applicable in the multitask setting. Best setting shown in **bold**.

Filter				Performance Gain (F1)		
Length	RegEx	Part of Speech	Grammaticality	Answerable	No Answer	Overall
x	x	x	x	72.35	40.00	66.22
✓	x	x	x	65.60	48.00	62.16
x	✓	x	x	73.8	24	64
x	x	✓	x	**73.67**	52	**69.5**
x	x	x	✓	71.95	36	65.24
✓	✓	✓	✓	59.71	**72.00**	63.34

Table 8: Relative QA performance gains on the SYFTER test set model using different SYFTER training data filtered in different ways. A checkmark indicates that the component was used, an "x" that it was not. Best setting shown in **bold**. Only SYFTER data was used for training.

D Annotation Tool

Figure 5 shows an example of how QA Pairs are presented to annotators in the annotation tool. See Section 3.4 for details.

A video demo of the tool can be found here

D.1 Annotation Guidelines

We present a set of annotation guidelines which can be given to annotators in order to obtain consistent labels by "calibrating" their expectations of what is and is not a valid QA pair. The guidelines for labelling questions can be found in Figure 6 and for answers in Figure 7.

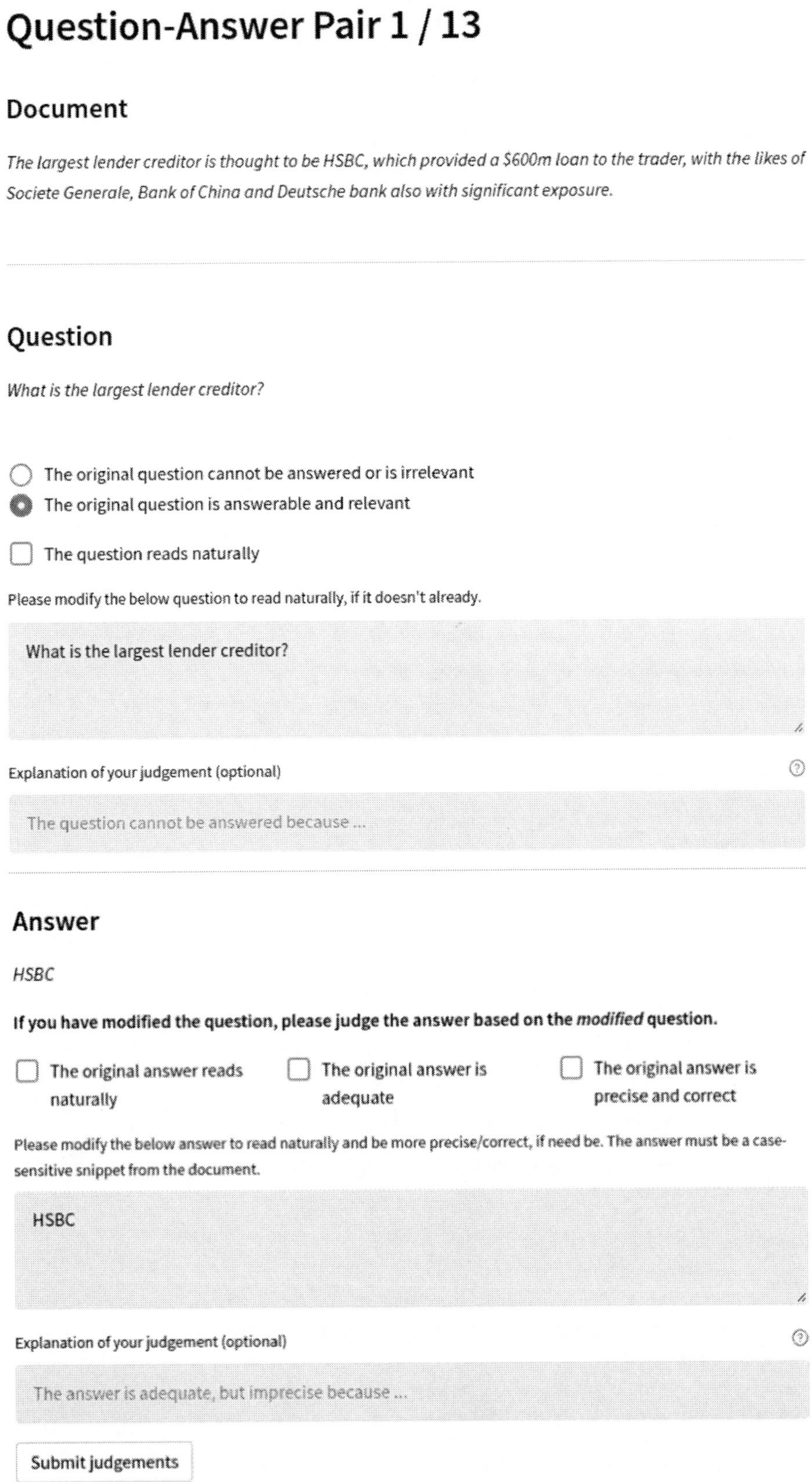

Figure 5: An example of how QA pairs are presented in the annotation tool.

Instructions (1 / 2)

This tool will ask you to judge the quality, naturalness, and correctness of a series of Question-Answer pairs each associated with a short document. This step is designed to demonstrate the kind of judgements we're looking for and guide you through the process.

---

1. Judging Questions

A suitable question will be answerable based on the document without requiring external information, and should be relevant to the document.

As well as being suitable, the question should read naturally: Its meaning should be clear and it should read like fluent English. However, it doesn't have to be perfectly grammatical.

Document

> "'Widget Inc. achieved profits of £50'000 in the second quarter of 2018', reported CEO John McMillan this week, as tech industry stock prices rose across the board"

Valid example questions:

- "What company achieved profits of £50'000 in the second quarter of 2018?"
- "Who is the CEO of Widget Inc?"

These questions can be considered suitable without modification. Note that we don't consider the answer, because as long as a question is answerable from the document, the answer itself doesn't matter.

For instance, the initial answer may be wrong and need corrections, but as long as **you** can determine the correct answer, the question itself is fine.

Suitable but non-natural questions, and corrections:

- "What is the company name that achieved £50'000 in profit in the second quarter of 2018?" -> "Which company achieved profits of £50'000 in the second quarter of 2018?"
- "Which number quarter of 2018 were the profits from?" -> "Which quarter of 2018 did Widget Inc. earn the profits in?"

These questions don't read naturally in their original forms, though their meanings can be understood.

They should be marked as **unnatural** and corrected via the provided textbox whilst preserving the overall meaning, but they should **not** marked as unsuitable.

Unsuitable questions

- "Who is the Chief Financial Officer of Widget Inc?" -> This is not stated in the document, and so the question is impossible to answer.
- "What fires can be started?" -> As well as not being stated in the document, this question makes no sense as a product of the document, as it is completely irrelevant.

These questions should be marked as unsuitable.

Figure 6: Annotation guidelines for judging question suitability and naturalness.

Instructions (2 / 2)

This tool will ask you to judge the quality, naturalness, and correctness of a series of Question-Answer pairs each associated with a short document. This step is designed to demonstrate the kind of judgements we're looking for and guide you through the process.

2. Judging Answers

A suitable answer will read naturally and correctly answer the question based on the information in the document.

Answers must be a case-sensitive snippet of the document.

This naturalness should be relative to the document: It doesn't need to have perfect grammar, but it should read easily and naturally, without extra effort to work out the meaning.

As well as reading naturally, an answer may be judged to be "adequate" - if it answers the question correctly when paired with the context (but may have missing or unnecessary detail), and "precise and correct" which additionally means that there is no missing or unnecessary detail from the context.

Answers may be marked as any of these within the tool. Any precise-and-correct answer will necessarily also be adequate, though it might not read naturally.

Document

> "'Widget Inc. achieved profits of £50'000 in the second quarter of 2018', reported CEO John McMillan this week, as tech industry stock prices rose across the board"

Question

> "When did Widget Inc. achieve profits of £50'000?"

Precise and correct example answer

> in the second quarter of 2018

This answer is precise and factually correct. There's no missing information or extra.

Adequate, but imprecise answers

> 2018'

This answer is **correct**, and would be fine when paired with the document, but it is also **imprecise** as we can provide more information about *when* in 2018 they were achieved.

Thus, it is adequate, but imprecise. The extra apostrophe is unnecessary, but does not affect readability so it can be ignored here.

> in the second quarter of 2018', reported

This answer is **correct**, but it has some unnecessary text at the end ("reported") and can be made more precise by removing that. Thus, it is adequate but not precise.

Incorrect:

> this week

This answer reads naturally, but it is incorrect and should be marked as such. It should then be corrected using the provided text box.

If you need to see this guidance again during the annotation process, you can find it in the sidebar on the left.

Previous (1 / 2) | Start Judgements

Figure 7: Annotation guidelines for judging answer naturalness and quality.

DeepKE: A Deep Learning Based Knowledge Extraction Toolkit for Knowledge Base Population

Ningyu Zhang[1], Xin Xu[1], Liankuan Tao[1], Haiyang Yu[1], Hongbin Ye[1], Shuofei Qiao[1], Xin Xie[1], Xiang Chen[1], Zhoubo Li[1], Lei Li[1], Xiaozhuan Liang[1], Yunzhi Yao[1], Shumin Deng[1], Peng Wang[1], Wen Zhang[1], Zhenru Zhang[2], Chuanqi Tan[2], Qiang Chen[2], Feiyu Xiong[2], Fei Huang[2], Guozhou Zheng[1], Huajun Chen[1] *

[1] Zhejiang University & AZFT Joint Lab for Knowledge Engine

[2] Alibaba Group

http://deepke.zjukg.cn/

Abstract

We present an open-source and extensible knowledge extraction toolkit DeepKE, supporting complicated low-resource, document-level and multimodal scenarios in knowledge base population. DeepKE implements various information extraction tasks, including named entity recognition, relation extraction and attribute extraction. With a unified framework, DeepKE allows developers and researchers to customize datasets and models to extract information from unstructured data according to their requirements. Specifically, DeepKE not only provides various functional modules and model implementation for different tasks and scenarios but also organizes all components by consistent frameworks to maintain sufficient modularity and extensibility. We release the source code at GitHub[1] with Google Colab tutorials and comprehensive documents[2] for beginners. Besides, we present an online system[3] for real-time extraction of various tasks, and a demo video[4].

1 Introduction

As Information Extraction (IE) techniques develop fast, many large-scale Knowledge Bases (KBs) have been constructed. Those KBs can provide back-end support for knowledge-intensive tasks in real-world applications, such as language understanding (Che et al., 2021), commonsense reasoning (Lin et al., 2019) and recommendation systems (Wang et al., 2018). However, most KBs are far from complete due to the emerging entities and relations in real-world applications. Therefore, Knowledge Base Population (KBP) (Ji and Grishman, 2011) has been proposed, which aims to extract knowledge from the text corpus to complete the missing elements in KBs. For this target, IE is an effective technology that can extract entities and relations from raw texts and link them to KBs (Yan et al., 2021; Sui et al., 2021).

To date, a few remarkable open-source and long-term maintained IE toolkits have been developed, such as Spacy (Vasiliev, 2020) for named entity recognition (NER), OpenNRE (Han et al., 2019) for relation extraction (RE), Stanford OpenIE (Martínez-Rodríguez et al., 2018) for open information extraction, RESIN for event extraction (Wen et al., 2021) and so on (Jin et al., 2021). However, there are still several non-trivial issues that hinder the applicability of real-world applications.

Firstly, there are various important IE tasks, but most existing toolkits only support one task. Secondly, although IE models trained with those tools can achieve promising results, their performance may degrade dramatically when there are only a few training instances or in other complex real-world scenarios, such as encountering document-level and multimodal instances. Therefore, it is necessary to build a knowledge extraction toolkit facilitating the knowledge base population that supports multiple tasks and complicated scenarios: **low-resource**, **document-level** and **multimodal**.

In this paper, we share with the community a new open-source knowledge extraction toolkit called **DeepKE** (MIT License), which supports knowledge extraction tasks (named entity recognition, relation extraction and attribute extraction) in the standard supervised setting and three complicated scenarios: low-resource, document-level and multimodal settings. To facilitate usage, we design a unified framework for data processing, model training and evaluation. Developers and researchers can quickly customize their datasets and models for

* Corresponding author: C.Hua (huajunsir@zju.edu.cn)

[1]Github: https://github.com/zjunlp/DeepKE

[2]Docs: https://zjunlp.github.io/DeepKE/

[3]Project website: http://deepke.zjukg.cn/

[4]Video: http://deepke.zjukg.cn/demo.mp4

Proceedings of the The 2022 Conference on Empirical Methods in Natural Language Processing: System Demonstrations, pages 98 - 108
December 7-11, 2022 ©2022 Association for Computational Linguistics

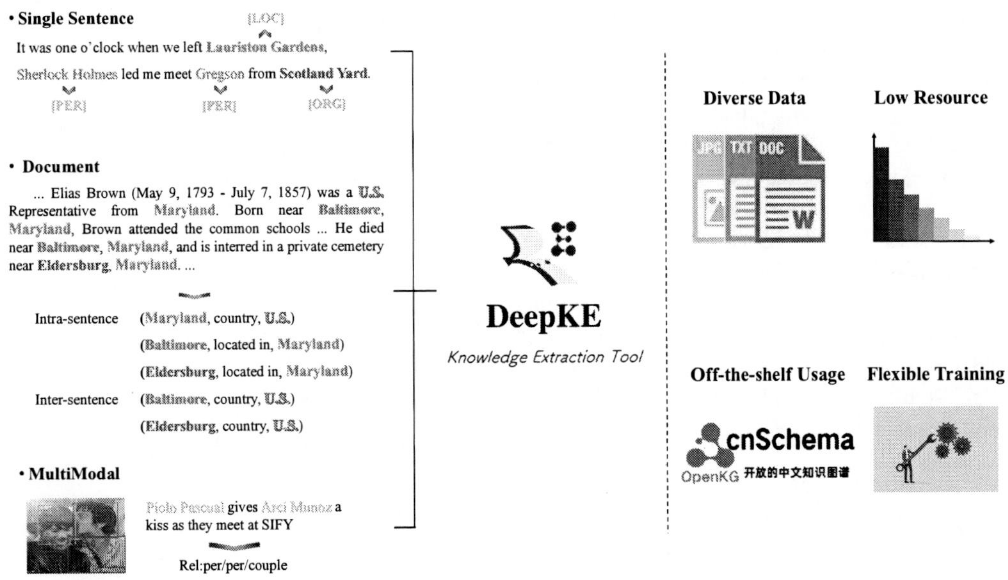

Figure 1: The examples of tasks with different scenarios in DeepKE.

various tasks without knowing too many technical details, writing tedious glue code, or conducting hyper-parameter tuning. We will provide maintenance to meet new requests, add new tasks, and fix bugs in the future. We highlight our major contributions as follows:

- We develop and release a knowledge base population toolkit that supports low-resource, document-level and multimodal information extraction.
- We offer flexible usage of the toolkit with sufficient modularity as well as automatic hyper-parameter tuning; thus, developers and researchers can implement customized models for information extraction.
- We provide detailed documentation, Google Colab tutorials, an online real-time extraction system and long-term technical support.

2 Core Functions

DeepKE is designed for different knowledge extraction tasks, including named entity recognition, relation extraction and attribute extraction. As shown in Figure 1, DeepKE supports diverse IE tasks in standard single-sentence supervised, low-resource few-shot, document-level and multimodal settings, which makes it flexible to adapt to practical and complicated application scenarios.

2.1 Named Entity Recognition

As an essential task of IE, named entity recognition (NER) picks out the entity mentions and classifies them into pre-defined semantic categories given plain texts. For instance, given the sentence "It was one o'clock when we left Lauriston Gardens, and Sherlock Holmes led me meet Gregson from Scotland Yard.", NER models will predict that "Lauriston Gardens" as a location, "Sherlock Holmes" and "Gregson" as persons, and "Scotland Yard" as an organization. To achieve supervised NER, DeepKE adopts the pre-trained language model (Devlin et al., 2019) to encode sentences and make predictions. DeepKE also implements NER in the few-shot setting (including in-domain and cross-domain) (Chen et al., 2022a) and the multimodal setting.

2.2 Relation Extraction

Relation Extraction (RE), a common task in IE for knowledge base population, predicts semantic relations between pairs of entities from unstructured texts (Wu et al., 2021). To allow users to customize their models, we adopt various models to accomplish standard supervised RE, including CNN (Zeng et al., 2015), RNN (Zhou et al., 2016), Capsule (Zhang et al., 2018a), GCN (Zhang et al., 2018c, 2019), Transformer (Vaswani et al., 2017) and BERT (Devlin et al., 2019). Meanwhile, DeepKE provides few-shot and document-level support for RE. For low-resource RE, DeepKE re-implements[5] *KnowPrompt* (Chen et al., 2022b), a recent well-performed few-shot RE method based on prompt-tuning. Note that few-shot RE is significant for real-world applications, which enables users to extract relations with only a few labeled instances. For document-level RE, DeepKE re-implements *DocuNet* (Zhang et al., 2021) to extract inter-sentence relational triples within one document. Document-level RE is a challenging task that requires integrating information within and across multiple sentences of a document (Nan et al., 2020). RE is also implemented in the multimodal setting described in Section 4.4.

2.3 Attribute Extraction

Attribute extraction (AE) plays an indispensable role in the knowledge base population. Given a sentence, entities and queried attribute mentions, AE will infer the corresponding attribute type. For instance, given a sentence "诸葛亮，字孔明，三国时期杰出的军事家、文学家、发明家。" (Liang Zhuge, whose courtesy name was Kongming, was an extraordinary strategist, litterateur and inventor in the Three Kingdoms period.), an entity "诸葛亮" (Liang Zhuge), and an attribute mention "三国时期" (Three Kingdoms period), DeepKE can predict the corresponding attribute type "朝代" (Dynasty). DeepKE adopts various models for AE (Table 1).

3 Toolkit Design and Implementation

We introduce the design principle of DeepKE as follows: 1) **Unified Framework**: DeepKE utilizes the same framework for various task objectives with respect to *Data*, *Model* and *Core* components; 2) **Flexible Usage**: DeepKE offers convenient training and evaluation with auto-hyperparameter tuning and the docker for operational efficiency; 3) **Off-the-shelf Models**: DeepKE provides pre-trained models (Chinese models with pre-defined schemas) for information extraction. We will introduce details of components in DeepKE and the unified framework in the following sections.

3.1 Data Module

The data module is designed for preprocessing and loading input data. The tokenizer in DeepKE implements tokenization for both English and Chinese

[5]The code is re-organized in a unified format for flexible usage in DeepKE.

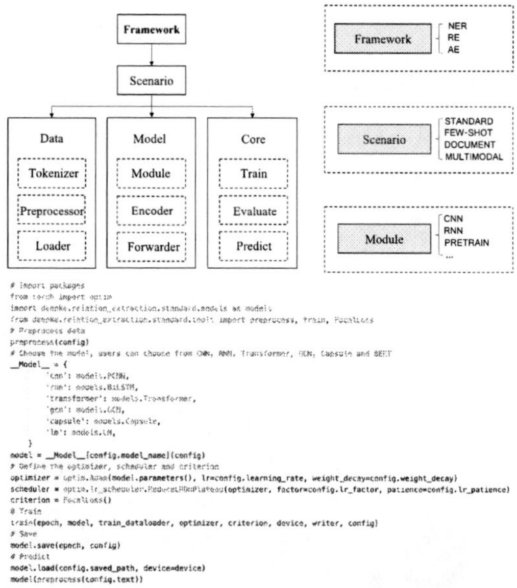

Figure 2: The architecture and example code.

(in Appendix A.3). Global images and local visual objects are preprocessed as visual information in the multimodal setting. Developers can feed their own datasets into the tokenizer and preprocessor through the dataloader to obtain the tokens or image patches.

3.2 Model Module

The model module contains main neural networks leveraged to achieve three core tasks. Various neural networks, including CNN, RNN, Transformer and the like, can be utilized for model implementation, which encodes texts into specific embedding for corresponding tasks. To adapt to different scenarios, DeepKE utilizes diverse architectures in distinct settings, such as *BERT* for standard RE and *BART* (Lewis et al., 2020) for few-shot NER. We implement the `BasicModel` class with a unified `model loader` and `saver` to integrate multifarious neural models.

3.3 Core Module

In the core code of DeepKE, `train`, `validate`, and `predict` methods are pivotal components. As for the `train` method, users can feed the expected parameters (e.g., the model, data, epoch, optimizer, loss function, .etc.) into it without writing tedious glue code. The `validate` method is for evaluation. Users can modify the sentences in the configuration for prediction and then utilize the `predict` method to obtain the result.

3.4 Framework Module

The framework module integrates three aforementioned components and different scenarios. It supports various functions, including data processing, model construction and model implementation. Meanwhile, developers and researchers can customize all hyper-parameters by modifying configuration files formatted as *"*.yaml"*, from which we apply *Hydra*[6] to obtain users' configuration. We also offer an off-the-shelf automatic hyperparameter tuning component. In DeepKE, we have implemented frameworks for all application functions mentioned in Section 2. For other future potential application functions, we have reserved interfaces for their implementation.

4 Toolkit Usage

4.1 Single-sentence Supervised Setting

All tasks, including NER, RE and AE, can be implemented in the standard single-sentence supervised setting by DeepKE. Every instance in datasets only contains one sentence. The datasets of these tasks are all annotated with specific information, such as entity mentions, entity categories, entity offsets, relation types and attributes.

4.2 Low-resource Setting

In real-world scenarios, labeled data may not be sufficient for deep learning models to make predictions for satisfying users' specific demands. Therefore, DeepKE provides low-resource few-shot support for NER and RE, which is exceedingly distinctive. DeepKE offers a generative framework with prompt-guided attention to achieve in-domain and cross-domain NER. Meanwhile, DeepKE implements knowledge-informed prompt-tuning with synergistic optimization for few-shot relation extraction.

4.3 Document-Level Setting

Relations between two entities not only emerge in one sentence but appear in different sentences within the whole document. Compared to other IE toolkits, DeepKE can extract inter-sentence relations from documents, which predicts an entity-level relation matrix to capture local and global information.

[6]https://hydra.cc/

Figure 3: An example of the online system.

4.4 Multimodal Setting

Multimodal knowledge extraction is supported in DeepKE. Intuitively, rich image signals related to texts are able to enhance context knowledge and help extract knowledge from complicated scenarios. DeepKE provides a Transformer-based multimodal entity and relation extraction method named *IFAformer* with prefix-based attention for multimodal NER and RE. Specifically, *IFAformer* simultaneously concatenates the textual and visual features in keys and values of the multi-head attention at each transformer layer, which can implicitly align multimodal features between texts and objects in text-related images[7].

4.5 Online System & *cnSchema*-based Off-the-shelf Models

Besides this toolkit, we release an online system in `http://deepke.zjukg.cn`. As shown in Figure 3, we train our models in different scenarios with multilingual support (English and Chinese) and deploy them for online access. The system can be directly applied to recognize named entities, extract relations, classify attributes from plain texts, and visualizes extracted relational triples as knowledge graphs. The models are trained **with the pre-defined schema** (The system cannot extract knowledge out of the schema scope.) and offer flexible usage for users to obtain their customized models with their own schemas. Furthermore, DeepKE provides off-the-shelf extraction models with Chinese pre-trained language models (Cui et al., 2021b) based *cnSchema*[8] supporting 28 entity types and 50 relation categories.

[7]Implementation details in https://github.com/zjunlp/DeepKE/tree/main/example/ner/multimodal.

[8]http://cnschema.openkg.cn/

Scenario	Task	Dataset	Method	F1
Single-sentence	NER	CoNLL-2003	BERT	94.73
		People's Daily		95.62
	RE	DuIE	CNN	96.74
			RNN	94.43
			Capsule	96.23
			GCN	96.74
			Transformer	96.54
			BERT	95.79
	AE	Online	CNN	94.16
			RNN	93.06
			Capsule	94.57
			GCN	94.50
			Transformer	94.15
			BERT	99.03
Document	RE	DocRED	BERT_base*	53.20
			CorefBERT$^{*}_{base}$	56.96
			ATLOP-BERT$^{*}_{base}$	61.30
			DeepKE (BERT$_{base}$)	**61.86**
			RoBERTa_large*	59.62
			CorefRoBERTa$^{*}_{large}$	60.25
			ATLOP-RoBERTa$^{*}_{large}$	63.40
			DeepKE (RoBERTa$_{large}$)	**64.55**
Multimodal	NER	Twitter17	AdapCoAtt-BERT-CRF*	84.10
			ViLBERT$^{*}_{base}$	85.04
			UMT*	85.31
			DeepKE (IFAformer)	**87.39**
	RE	MNRE	BERT+SG*	62.80
			BERT+SG+Att*	63.64
			MEGA*	66.41
			DeepKE (IFAformer)	**81.67**

Table 1: F1 Score (%) of the single-sentence, document-level and multimodal scenarios. * means these baselines are from other papers.

Model	Entity Category				
	PER	ORG	LOC*	MISC*	Overall
LC-BERT	76.25	75.32	61.55	59.35	68.12
LC-BART	75.70	73.59	58.70	57.30	66.82
Template.	84.49	72.61	71.98	73.37	75.59
DeepKE (LightNER)	**90.96**	**76.88**	**81.57**	**82.08**	**78.97**

Table 2: F1 scores of in-domain low-resource NER on CoNLL-2003. * indicates low-resource entity types (100-shot).

Model	Dataset		
	MIT Movie	MIT Restaurant	ATIS
Neigh.Tag.	1.4	3.6	3.4
Example.	29.6	26.1	16.5
MP-NSP	36.8	48.2	74.8
LC-BERT	45.2	40.9	78.5
LC-BART	30.4	11.1	74.4
Template.	54.2	60.3	88.9
DeepKE (LightNER)	**75.6**	**67.4**	**89.4**

Table 3: F1 scores of cross-domain few-shot NER (20-shot).

5 Experiment and Evaluation

5.1 Single-sentence Supervised Setting

The performance of the standard single-sentence supervised setting is reported in Table 1.

Named Entity Recognition We conduct NER experiments on two datasets: CoNLL-2003 (Sang and Meulder, 2003) for English and People's Daily[9] for Chinese. The English part of CoNLL-2003 contains four types of entities: persons (PER), locations (LOC), organizations (ORG) and miscellaneous (MISC). People's Daily dataset is a Chinese dataset containing 45,518 entities classified into three categories PER, LOC and ORG. It is observed that DeepKE yields comparable performance with various encoders for these datasets. Meanwhile, DeepKE supports any English and Chinese NER datasets with BIO tags.

Relation Extraction We conduct RE experiments on the Chinese DuIE dataset[10] with 10 relation categorie Each sample contains one original sentence, one head entity, one tail entity in the sentence, their offsets, and the relation between them. We utilize six different neural networks in DeepKE for evaluation. Users can select models before training by changing only one hyper-parameter[11]. We report the performance of all models in Table 1.

Attribute Extraction The Chinese dataset for AE is from an online resource[12]. In each sample, one entity is annotated with its attribute type, value, and offset. Attributes in the dataset are classified into 6 categories. The training set contains 13,815 samples. The validation set contains 3,131 samples, and the test set includes 5,921 samples. Like RE, we leverage six neural models to extract attributes from the given sentence to evaluate DeepKE.

5.2 Low-resource Setting

We report the performance of the low-resource setting (NER and RE) in Table 2, 3, and 4.

Named Entity Recognition We conduct experiments in both in-domain and cross-domain few-shot settings with LightNER (Chen et al., 2022a). Following Cui et al. (2021a), for the in-domain few-shot scenario, we reduce the number of training samples for certain entity categories by downsampling one dataset. Specifically, from CoNLL-

[9]https://github.com/OYE93/Chinese-NLP-Corpus/tree/master/NER/People's%20Daily

[10]http://ai.baidu.com/broad/download

[11]The hyper-parameter *-model* to select networks is in https://github.com/zjunlp/DeepKE/blob/main/example/re/standard/conf/config.yaml.

[12]https://github.com/leefsir/triplet_extraction

Method	Split		
	K=8	K=16	K=32
Fine-Tuning	41.3	65.2	80.1
GDPNet	42.0	67.5	81.2
PTR	70.5	81.3	84.2
DeepKE (KnowPrompt)	**74.3**	**82.9**	**84.8**

Table 4: F1 scores of few-shot relation extraction

2003, we choose **100** "LOC" and **100** "MISC" as the low-resource entities and 2,496 "PER" and 3,763 "ORG" as the rich-resource entities. We leverage DeepKE to carry out the few-shot experiments and adopt BERT and BART with label-specific classifier layers as strong baselines denoted as *LC-BERT* and *LC-BART*. We also use template-based BART *(Template.)* (Cui et al., 2021a) as the competitive few-shot baseline. From Table 2, DeepKE outperforms other methods for both rich- and low-resource entity types, which illustrates that DeepKE has an outstanding performance on in-domain few-shot NER. In the cross-domain setting where the target entity categories and textual style are different from the source domain with limited labeled data available for training, we adopt the CoNLL-2003 dataset as an ordinary domain, and MIT Movie Review (Liu et al., 2013), MIT Restaurant Review (Liu et al., 2013) and Airline Travel Information Systems (ATIS) (Hakkani-Tür et al., 2016) datasets as target domains. The few-shot NER model in DeepKE is trained on CoNLL-2003 and fine-tuned on 20-shot target domain datasets (randomly sampled per entity category). We employ prototype-based *Neigh.Tag.* (Wiseman and Stratos, 2019), *Example.* (example-based NER) (Ziyadi et al., 2020), *MP-NSP* (Multi-prototype+NSP) (Huang et al., 2020), *LC-BERT*, *LC-BART* and *Template.* as competitive baselines. From Table 3, we notice that DeepKE achieves the most excellent few-shot performance.

Relation Extraction For few-shot relation extraction, we use SemEval 2010 Task-8 (Hendrickx et al., 2010), a conventional dataset of relation classification with nine bidirectional relations and one unidirectional relation OTHER. We utilize a SOTA few-shot RE method, *KnowPrompt* (Chen et al., 2022b) which incorporates knowledge into prompt-tuning with synergistic optimization, to conduct 8-, 16-, and 32-shot experiments compared with other baselines, such as *GDPNet* (Xue et al., 2021) and *PTR* (Han et al., 2021). Table 4 shows that DeepKE outperforms those baseline methods.

5.3 Document-level Setting

DeepKE can extract intra- and inter- sentence relations among multiple entities within one document. We leverage a large-scale document-level RE dataset, DocRED (Ye et al., 2020), containing 3,053/1,000/1,000 instances for training, validation and testing, respectively. We use cased BERT-base and RoBERTa-large (Liu et al., 2019) as encoders. Compared with BERT-based and RoBERTa-based models, including *Coref* (Ye et al., 2020), and *AT-LOP* (Zhou et al., 2021), DeepKE appears the better or comparable performance than baselines as shown in Table 1.

5.4 Multimudal Setting

We report the performance of NER and RE in the multimodal scenario in Table 1.

Named Entity Recognition Multimodal NER experiments are conducted on Twitter-2017 (Lu et al., 2018) including texts and images from Twitter (2016-2017). The baselines for comparison are *AdapCoAtt-BERT-CRF* (Zhang et al., 2018b), ViL-BERT (Lu et al., 2019) and UMT (Yu et al., 2020). We notice DeepKE can obtain a performance improvement compared with baselines.

Relation Extraction We use MNRE (Zheng et al., 2021b), a multimodal RE dataset containing sentences and images containing 23 relation categories. Previous SOTA models including *BERT+SG* (Zheng et al., 2021a), *BERT+SG+Att* (*BERT+SG* with attention calculating semantic similarity between textual and visual graphs) and *MEGA* (Zheng et al., 2021a), are leveraged for comparison. We further observe that DeepKE yields better performance than baselines.

6 Conclusion

In practical application, the knowledge base population struggles with low-resource, document-level and multimodal scenarios. To this end, we propose DeepKE, an open-source and extensible knowledge extraction toolkit. We conduct extensive experiments that demonstrate the models implemented by DeepKE can achieve comparable performance compared to some state-of-the-art methods. Besides, we provide an online system supporting real-time extraction (**with the pre-defined schemas**) without training. We will offer long-term maintenance to fix bugs, solve issues, add documents (tutorials) and meet new requests.

Broader Impact Statement

As noted in Manning (2022), linguistics and knowledge-based artificial intelligence were rapidly developing, and knowledge (explicit or implicit) as potential dark matter[13] for language understanding still faces obstacles to acquisition and representation. To this end, IE technologies that aim to extract knowledge from unstructured data can serve as valuable tools to not only govern domain resources (e.g., medical, business) but also benefit deep language understanding and reasoning ability. Note that the proposed toolkit, DeepKE, can offer flexible usage in widespread IE scenarios with pre-trained off-the-shelf models. We hope to deliver the benefits of the proposed DeepKE to the natural language processing community.

Acknowledgments

We want to express gratitude to the anonymous reviewers for their kind comments. This work was supported by National Natural Science Foundation of China (No.62206246, 91846204 and U19B2027), Zhejiang Provincial Natural Science Foundation of China (No. LGG22F030011), Ningbo Natural Science Foundation (2021J190), and Yongjiang Talent Introduction Programme (2021A-156-G).

References

Wanxiang Che, Yunlong Feng, Libo Qin, and Ting Liu. 2021. N-LTP: An open-source neural language technology platform for Chinese. In *Proceedings of the 2021 Conference on Empirical Methods in Natural Language Processing: System Demonstrations*, pages 42–49, Online and Punta Cana, Dominican Republic. Association for Computational Linguistics.

Xiang Chen, Lei Li, Shumin Deng, Chuanqi Tan, Changliang Xu, Fei Huang, Luo Si, Huajun Chen, and Ningyu Zhang. 2022a. LightNER: A lightweight tuning paradigm for low-resource NER via pluggable prompting. In *Proceedings of the 29th International Conference on Computational Linguistics*, pages 2374–2387, Gyeongju, Republic of Korea. International Committee on Computational Linguistics.

Xiang Chen, Ningyu Zhang, Xin Xie, Shumin Deng, Yunzhi Yao, Chuanqi Tan, Fei Huang, Luo Si, and Huajun Chen. 2022b. Knowprompt: Knowledge-aware prompt-tuning with synergistic optimization for relation extraction. In *WWW '22: The ACM Web Conference 2022, Virtual Event, Lyon, France, April 25 - 29, 2022*, pages 2778–2788. ACM.

Leyang Cui, Yu Wu, Jian Liu, Sen Yang, and Yue Zhang. 2021a. Template-based named entity recognition using BART. In *Proceedings of ACL/IJCNLP*, volume ACL/IJCNLP 2021 of *Findings of ACL*.

Yiming Cui, Wanxiang Che, Ting Liu, Bing Qin, and Ziqing Yang. 2021b. Pre-training with whole word masking for chinese BERT. *IEEE ACM Trans. Audio Speech Lang. Process.*, 29:3504–3514.

Jacob Devlin, Ming-Wei Chang, Kenton Lee, and Kristina Toutanova. 2019. BERT: pre-training of deep bidirectional transformers for language understanding. In *Proceedings of NAACL-HLT*, pages 4171–4186. Association for Computational Linguistics.

Dilek Hakkani-Tür, Gökhan Tür, Asli Celikyilmaz, Yun-Nung Chen, Jianfeng Gao, Li Deng, and Ye-Yi Wang. 2016. Multi-domain joint semantic frame parsing using bi-directional RNN-LSTM. In *Proceedings of INTERSPEECH*, pages 715–719. ISCA.

Xu Han, Tianyu Gao, Yuan Yao, Deming Ye, Zhiyuan Liu, and Maosong Sun. 2019. Opennre: An open and extensible toolkit for neural relation extraction. In *Proceedings of EMNLP-IJCNLP*.

Xu Han, Weilin Zhao, Ning Ding, Zhiyuan Liu, and Maosong Sun. 2021. PTR: prompt tuning with rules for text classification. *arXiv:2105.11259*.

Iris Hendrickx, Su Nam Kim, Zornitsa Kozareva, Preslav Nakov, Diarmuid Ó Séaghdha, Sebastian Padó, Marco Pennacchiotti, Lorenza Romano, and Stan Szpakowicz. 2010. Semeval-2010 task 8: Multi-way classification of semantic relations between pairs of nominals. In *Proceedings of SemEval@ACL Workshop*.

Jiaxin Huang, Chunyuan Li, Krishan Subudhi, Damien Jose, Shobana Balakrishnan, Weizhu Chen, Baolin Peng, Jianfeng Gao, and Jiawei Han. 2020. Few-shot named entity recognition: A comprehensive study. *arXiv:2012.14978*.

Heng Ji and Ralph Grishman. 2011. Knowledge base population: Successful approaches and challenges. In *The 49th Annual Meeting of the Association for Computational Linguistics: Human Language Technologies, Proceedings of the Conference, 19-24 June, 2011, Portland, Oregon, USA*, pages 1148–1158. The Association for Computer Linguistics.

Zhuoran Jin, Yubo Chen, Dianbo Sui, Chenhao Wang, Zhipeng Xue, and Jun Zhao. 2021. CogIE: An information extraction toolkit for bridging texts and CogNet. In *Proceedings of ACL-IJCNLP*, pages 92–98.

[13]2082: An ACL Odyssey: The Dark Matter of Language and Intelligence

Mike Lewis, Yinhan Liu, Naman Goyal, Marjan Ghazvininejad, Abdelrahman Mohamed, Omer Levy, Veselin Stoyanov, and Luke Zettlemoyer. 2020. BART: denoising sequence-to-sequence pretraining for natural language generation, translation, and comprehension. In *Proceedings of ACL*, pages 7871–7880. Association for Computational Linguistics.

Bill Yuchen Lin, Xinyue Chen, Jamin Chen, and Xiang Ren. 2019. Kagnet: Knowledge-aware graph networks for commonsense reasoning. In *Proceedings of the 2019 Conference on Empirical Methods in Natural Language Processing and the 9th International Joint Conference on Natural Language Processing, EMNLP-IJCNLP 2019, Hong Kong, China, November 3-7, 2019*, pages 2829–2839. Association for Computational Linguistics.

Jingjing Liu, Panupong Pasupat, Scott Cyphers, and James R. Glass. 2013. Asgard: A portable architecture for multilingual dialogue systems. In *Proceedings of ICASSP*, pages 8386–8390. IEEE.

Yinhan Liu, Myle Ott, Naman Goyal, Jingfei Du, Mandar Joshi, Danqi Chen, Omer Levy, Mike Lewis, Luke Zettlemoyer, and Veselin Stoyanov. 2019. Roberta: A robustly optimized BERT pretraining approach. *arXiv:1907.11692*.

Di Lu, Leonardo Neves, Vitor Carvalho, Ning Zhang, and Heng Ji. 2018. Visual attention model for name tagging in multimodal social media. In *Proceedings of the 56th Annual Meeting of the Association for Computational Linguistics (Volume 1: Long Papers)*, pages 1990–1999, Melbourne, Australia. Association for Computational Linguistics.

Jiasen Lu, Dhruv Batra, Devi Parikh, and Stefan Lee. 2019. Vilbert: Pretraining task-agnostic visiolinguistic representations for vision-and-language tasks. In *Advances in Neural Information Processing Systems*, volume 32. Curran Associates, Inc.

Christopher D Manning. 2022. Human language understanding & reasoning. *Daedalus*, 151(2):127–138.

José-Lázaro Martínez-Rodríguez, Ivan López-Arévalo, and Ana B. Ríos-Alvarado. 2018. Openie-based approach for knowledge graph construction from text. *Expert Syst. Appl.*, 113:339–355.

Guoshun Nan, Zhijiang Guo, Ivan Sekulic, and Wei Lu. 2020. Reasoning with latent structure refinement for document-level relation extraction. In *Proceedings of ACL*, pages 1546–1557. Association for Computational Linguistics.

Erik F. Tjong Kim Sang and Fien De Meulder. 2003. Introduction to the conll-2003 shared task: Language-independent named entity recognition. In *Proceedings of HLT-NAACL*, pages 142–147. ACL.

Dianbo Sui, Chenhao Wang, Yubo Chen, Kang Liu, Jun Zhao, and Wei Bi. 2021. Set generation networks for end-to-end knowledge base population. In *Proceedings of the 2021 Conference on Empirical Methods in Natural Language Processing, EMNLP 2021, Virtual Event / Punta Cana, Dominican Republic, 7-11 November, 2021*, pages 9650–9660. Association for Computational Linguistics.

Yuli Vasiliev. 2020. *Natural Language Processing with Python and SpaCy: A Practical Introduction*. No Starch Press.

Ashish Vaswani, Noam Shazeer, Niki Parmar, Jakob Uszkoreit, Llion Jones, Aidan N. Gomez, Lukasz Kaiser, and Illia Polosukhin. 2017. Attention is all you need. In *Advances in Neural Information Processing Systems 30: Annual Conference on Neural Information Processing Systems 2017, December 4-9, 2017, Long Beach, CA, USA*, pages 5998–6008.

Hongwei Wang, Fuzheng Zhang, Xing Xie, and Minyi Guo. 2018. DKN: deep knowledge-aware network for news recommendation. In *Proceedings of WWW*, pages 1835–1844. ACM.

Haoyang Wen, Ying Lin, Tuan Lai, Xiaoman Pan, Sha Li, Xudong Lin, Ben Zhou, Manling Li, Haoyu Wang, Hongming Zhang, Xiaodong Yu, Alexander Dong, Zhenhailong Wang, Yi Fung, Piyush Mishra, Qing Lyu, Dídac Surís, Brian Chen, Susan Windisch Brown, Martha Palmer, Chris Callison-Burch, Carl Vondrick, Jiawei Han, Dan Roth, Shih-Fu Chang, and Heng Ji. 2021. RESIN: A dockerized schema-guided cross-document cross-lingual cross-media information extraction and event tracking system. In *In Proceedings of NAACL-HLT*.

Sam Wiseman and Karl Stratos. 2019. Label-agnostic sequence labeling by copying nearest neighbors. In *Proceedings of ACL*, pages 5363–5369. Association for Computational Linguistics.

Tongtong Wu, Xuekai Li, Yuan-Fang Li, Gholamreza Haffari, Guilin Qi, Yujin Zhu, and Guoqiang Xu. 2021. Curriculum-meta learning for order-robust continual relation extraction. In *Proceedings of AAAI*.

Fuzhao Xue, Aixin Sun, Hao Zhang, and Eng Siong Chng. 2021. Gdpnet: Refining latent multi-view graph for relation extraction. In *Thirty-Fifth AAAI Conference on Artificial Intelligence, AAAI 2021, Thirty-Third Conference on Innovative Applications of Artificial Intelligence, IAAI 2021, The Eleventh Symposium on Educational Advances in Artificial Intelligence, EAAI 2021, Virtual Event, February 2-9, 2021*, pages 14194–14202. AAAI Press.

Hang Yan, Tao Gui, Junqi Dai, Qipeng Guo, Zheng Zhang, and Xipeng Qiu. 2021. A unified generative framework for various NER subtasks. In *Proceedings of the 59th Annual Meeting of the Association for Computational Linguistics and the 11th International Joint Conference on Natural Language Processing, ACL/IJCNLP 2021, (Volume 1: Long Papers), Virtual Event, August 1-6, 2021*, pages 5808–5822. Association for Computational Linguistics.

Deming Ye, Yankai Lin, Jiaju Du, Zhenghao Liu, Peng Li, Maosong Sun, and Zhiyuan Liu. 2020. Coreferential reasoning learning for language representation. In *Proceedings of EMNLP*, pages 7170–7186. Association for Computational Linguistics.

Jianfei Yu, Jing Jiang, Li Yang, and Rui Xia. 2020. Improving multimodal named entity recognition via entity span detection with unified multimodal transformer. In *Proceedings of the 58th Annual Meeting of the Association for Computational Linguistics*, pages 3342–3352, Online. Association for Computational Linguistics.

Daojian Zeng, Kang Liu, Yubo Chen, and Jun Zhao. 2015. Distant supervision for relation extraction via piecewise convolutional neural networks. In *Proceedings of EMNLP*, pages 1753–1762. The Association for Computational Linguistics.

Ningyu Zhang, Xiang Chen, Xin Xie, Shumin Deng, Chuanqi Tan, Mosha Chen, Fei Huang, Luo Si, and Huajun Chen. 2021. Document-level relation extraction as semantic segmentation. In *Proceedings of IJCAI*, pages 3999–4006. ijcai.org.

Ningyu Zhang, Shumin Deng, Zhanlin Sun, Guanying Wang, Xi Chen, Wei Zhang, and Huajun Chen. 2019. Long-tail relation extraction via knowledge graph embeddings and graph convolution networks. In *Proceedings of NAACL-HLT*, pages 3016–3025. Association for Computational Linguistics.

Ningyu Zhang, Shumin Deng, Zhanling Sun, Xi Chen, Wei Zhang, and Huajun Chen. 2018a. Attention-based capsule network with dynamic routing for relation extraction. In *In Proceedings of EMNLP*.

Qi Zhang, Jinlan Fu, Xiaoyu Liu, and Xuanjing Huang. 2018b. Adaptive co-attention network for named entity recognition in tweets. *Proceedings of the AAAI Conference on Artificial Intelligence*, 32(1).

Yuhao Zhang, Peng Qi, and Christopher D. Manning. 2018c. Graph convolution over pruned dependency trees improves relation extraction. In *Proceedings of EMNLP*, pages 2205–2215. Association for Computational Linguistics.

Changmeng Zheng, Junhao Feng, Ze Fu, Yi Cai, Qing Li, and Tao Wang. 2021a. *Multimodal Relation Extraction with Efficient Graph Alignment*, page 5298–5306. Association for Computing Machinery, New York, NY, USA.

Changmeng Zheng, Zhiwei Wu, Junhao Feng, Ze Fu, and Yi Cai. 2021b. Mnre: A challenge multimodal dataset for neural relation extraction with visual evidence in social media posts. In *2021 IEEE International Conference on Multimedia and Expo (ICME)*, pages 1–6.

Peng Zhou, Wei Shi, Jun Tian, Zhenyu Qi, Bingchen Li, Hongwei Hao, and Bo Xu. 2016. Attention-based bidirectional long short-term memory networks for relation classification. In *Proceedings of ACL*, pages 207–212, Berlin, Germany. Association for Computational Linguistics.

Word	Named Entity Tag
U.N.	B-ORG
official	O
Ekeus	B-PER
heads	O
for	O
Baghdad	B-LOC
.	O
Israel	B-LOC
approves	O
Arafat	B-PER
s	O
flight	O
to	O
West	B-LOC
Bank	I-LOC
.	O

Table 5: Examples of the input format for NER.

Wenxuan Zhou, Kevin Huang, Tengyu Ma, and Jing Huang. 2021. Document-level relation extraction with adaptive thresholding and localized context pooling. In *In proceedings of AAAI*, pages 14612–14620. AAAI Press.

Morteza Ziyadi, Yuting Sun, Abhishek Goswami, Jade Huang, and Weizhu Chen. 2020. Example-based named entity recognition. *arXiv:2008.10570*.

A Toolkit Usage Details

In this section, we introduce how to use DeepKE exhaustively.

A.1 Build a Model From Scratch

Prepare the Runtime Environment Users can clone the source code from the DeepKE GitHub repository and create a runtime environment. There are two convenient methods to create the environment. Users can choose to either leverage *Anaconda* or run the docker file provided in the repository. Besides, all dependencies can be installed by running `pip install deepke` directly. If developers would like to modify the source code of DeepKE, the following commands should be executed: running `python setup.py install`, modifying code and then running `python setup.py develop`. Users can also use corresponding datasets (e.g., default or customized datasets) to obtain specific information extraction models. All datasets need to be downloaded or uploaded in the folder named *data*.

Named Entity Recognition As shown in Table 5, the input data files with BIO tags for standard and few-shot NER contain two columns separated by a single space. Each word has been put on a separate line, and there is an empty line after each sentence. The two columns represent two items: the word and the named entity tag. Before training, all datasets with the formats mentioned above should be fed into NER models through the data loader. Developers can implement training and evaluation by running example code *run.py* to obtain a fine-tuned NER model, which will be used in the prediction period. For inference, users can run *predict.py* with a single sentence and obtain the output recognized entity mentions and types.

Relation Extraction The training input with the CSV format of standard RE is shown in Table 6. There are five components in the format, including a sentence, a relation, the head and tail entity of the relation, the head entity offset and the tail entity offset. For few-shot RE, one input sample, as shown in Figure 4, contains sentence tokens including words and punctuation, the head entity and tail entities with their mention names and position spans, and the relation between them. For example, an input of few-shot relation extraction instance is the format of *{"token": ["the", "dolphin", "uses", "its", "flukes", "for", "swimming", "and", "its", "flippers", "for", "steering", "."], "h": {"name": "dolphin", "pos": [1, 2]}, "t": {"name": "flukes", "pos": [4, 5]}, "relation": "Component-Whole(e2,e1)"}* (h: head entity, t: tail entity, pos: position). The document-level RE training format is shown in Figure 5. One sample consists of a sample title, sentences separated into words and punctuation in one document, an entity set (including entity mentions, sentence IDs the entities are located in, entity position spans and entity types in the document) and a relation label set (including the head and tail entity IDs, relations and evidence sentence IDs). After training and validation, users can run the `predict` function given an input sentence with head and tail entity to obtain corresponding relations.

Attribution Extraction The input CSV files formatted as Table 7 should be given to train the attribution extraction (AE) model. One sample contains six components: a raw sentence, a queried attribute type, an entity and its offset, the entity's corresponding attribute value and the attribute mention offset. After training, users will obtain a fine-tuned AE model, which can be leveraged to infer attributes. Given a sentence with an entity and a candidate attribute mention, the AE model will predict the attribute type with confidence. Note that all operations mentioned above are guided in the example code file *run.py* and *predict.py*.

Sentence	Relation	Head	HO	Tail	TO
When it comes to beautiful sceneries in Hangzhou, West Lake first emerges in mind.	city: located in	West Lake	50	Hangzhou	40
Harry Potter, a wizard, graduated from Hogwarts School of Witchcraft and Wizardry.	school: graduated from	Harry Potter	0	Hogwarts School of Witchcraft and Wizardry	39

Table 6: Examples of the input format for standard RE. HO: Head Offset, TO: Tail Offset.

```
Data Format:
{
    'token': [tokens in a sentence],
    "h": {
        "name": mention_name,
        "pos" : [postion of mention in a sentence]
    },
    "t": {
        "name": mention_name,
        "pos" : [postion of mention in a sentence]
    },
    "relation": relation
}
```

Figure 4: The input format of few-shot RE.

A.2 Auto-Hyperparameter Tuning

To achieve automatic hyper-parameters fine-tuning, DeepKE adopts *Weight & Biases*, a machine learning toolkit for developers to reduce label-intensive hyper-parameter tuning. With DeepKE, users can visualize results and tune hyper-parameters automatically. Note that all metrics and hyper-parameter configurations can be customized to meet diverse settings for different tasks. For more details on automatic hyper-parameter tuning.

Sentence	Attribute	Entity	EO	AV	AVO
1903年，亨利·福特创建福特汽车公司	创始人	福特	9	亨利·福特	6
吴会期，字行可，号子官，明朝工部郎中	朝代	吴会期	0	明朝	12

Table 7: Examples of the input format AE.
EO: Entity Offset, AV: Attribute Value, AVO: Attribute Value Offset.

```
Data Format:
{
  'title',
  'sents':     [
                  [word in sent 0],
                  [word in sent 1]
               ]
  'vertexSet': [
                  [
                    { 'name': mention_name,
                      'sent_id': mention in which sentence,
                      'pos': postion of mention in a sentence,
                      'type': NER_type}
                    {anthor mention}
                  ],
                  [anthoer entity]
                ]
  'labels':   [
                {
                  'h': idx of head entity in vertexSet,
                  't': idx of tail entity in vertexSet,
                  'r': relation,
                  'evidence': evidence sentences' id
                }
              ]
}
```

Figure 5: The input format of document-level RE.

Task	Scenario	Language
NER	Supervised	Chinese
	Few-shot	English, Chinese
	Multimodal	English
RE	Supervised	Chinese
	Few-shot	English
	Multimodal	English
	Document	English
AE	Supervised	Chinese

Table 8: Language supported in DeepKE.

please refer to the official document[14].

A.3 Language Support

The current version of DeepKE supports English and Chinese implementation for three IE tasks, as shown in Table 8.

A.4 Notebook Tutorials

We provide Google Colab tutorials[15] and jupyter notebooks in the GitHub repository as an exemplary implementation of every task in different scenarios. These tutorials can be run directly, thus, leading developers and researchers to have a whole picture of DeepKE's powerful functions.

[14] https://docs.wandb.ai

[15] https://colab.research.google.com/drive/1vS8YJhJ1tzw3hpJczPt24O0Azcs3ZpRi?usp=sharing

B Contributions

Ningyu Zhang from Zhejiang University, AZFT Joint Lab for Knowledge Engine, conducted the whole development of DeepKE and wrote the paper.

Xin Xu from Zhejiang University, AZFT Joint Lab for Knowledge Engine developed the standard NER and wrote the paper.

Liankuan Tao, Shuofei Qiao, Peng Wang, Haiyang Yu from Zhejiang University, AZFT Joint Lab for Knowledge Engine develop the standard RE and AE, the deepke python package, and documents and provides consistent maintenance.

Hongbin Ye from Zhejiang University, AZFT Joint Lab for Knowledge Engine developed the online system and constructed the online demo.

Xin Xie, Xiang Chen from Zhejiang University, AZFT Joint Lab for Knowledge Engine developed the few-shot relation extraction model KnowPrompt and the document-level relation extraction model DocuNet.

Zhoubo Li, Lei Li, Xiaozhuan Liang, Yunzhi Yao, Shumin Deng, Wen Zhang from Zhejiang University, AZFT Joint Lab for Knowledge Engine developed the Google Colab and proofread the paper.

Zhenru Zhang, Chuanqi Tan, Qiang Chen, Feiyu Xiong, Fei Huang from Alibaba Group, proofread the paper and advised the project.

Guozhou Zheng, Huajun Chen from Zhejiang University, AZFT Joint Lab for Knowledge Engine advised the project, suggested tasks, and led the research.

AnEMIC: A Framework for Benchmarking ICD Coding Models

Juyong Kim[*1], **Abheesht Sharma**[*2], **Suhas Shanbhogue**[*2], **Pradeep Ravikumar**[1], and **Jeremy C. Weiss**[3]

[1]Machine Learning Department, Carnegie Mellon University
[2]Birla Institute of Technology & Science, Pilani – Goa Campus
[3]National Library of Medicine, National Institutes of Health
{juyongk,pradeepr}@cs.cmu.edu
{f20171014,f20170769}@goa.bits-pilani.ac.in
jeremy.weiss@nih.gov

Abstract

Diagnostic coding, or ICD coding, is the task of assigning diagnosis codes defined by the ICD (International Classification of Diseases) standard to patient visits based on clinical notes. The current process of manual ICD coding is time-consuming and often error-prone, which suggests the need for automatic ICD coding. However, despite the long history of automatic ICD coding, there have been no standardized frameworks for benchmarking ICD coding models.

We open-source an easy-to-use tool named *AnEMIC*, which provides a streamlined pipeline for preprocessing, training, and evaluating for automatic ICD coding. We correct errors in preprocessing by existing works, and provide key models and weights trained on the correctly preprocessed datasets. We also provide an interactive demo performing real-time inference from custom inputs, and visualizations drawn from explainable AI to analyze the models. We hope the framework helps move the research of ICD coding forward and helps professionals explore the potential of ICD coding. The framework and the associated code are available here.

1 Introduction

Diagnostic coding is the task of assigning alphanumeric codes to diagnoses and procedures after a patient visits a healthcare provider. These codes are typically specified by a medical classification standard called the International Classification of Diseases (ICD). Diagnostic coding, or ICD coding, is an integral component of medical billing, and integral to claims paid by health insurance carriers. The diagnostic coding process alone accounts for approximately 21% of medical administrative costs in the US (Tseng et al., 2018). During this process, a professional coder reviews the patient's medical records, including clinical narratives, and manually selects ICD codes. Since the task requires in-depth clinical knowledge and understanding of medical records, and importantly, due to the fact that there are a large number of ICD codes, the task is labor-intensive and error-prone (Manchikanti, 2002).

These difficulties motivate the need for automatic ICD coding systems which perform diagnosis classification given a patient's health record (Kaur et al., 2021; Yan et al., 2022). This has been the subject of considerable research, with some of the early work dating back to the 1990s (Larkey and Croft, 1996), to more recent deep neural NLP approaches. There are a few outstanding and major challenges in the diagnostic coding task. Firstly, the label space, the set of all ICD codes, is large, and the label distribution is highly imbalanced. Secondly, the input text, i.e., the discharge summaries, is noisy and can contain abstruse medical terms, lesser-known abbreviations, misspelt words, etc. Also, they are much longer than what most state-of-the-art models take as input.

Along with those challenges, the absence of a benchmark has impeded the progress of research. Due to privacy restrictions that limit access to even publicly available clinical databases, researchers have to create datasets manually from these, and this results in discrepancies in the actual datasets used in individual papers. For instance, the label set of MIMIC-III top-50 dataset varies among the literature, and some of them are even used incorrectly. Inconsistency in processing the dataset and the inevitable errors introduced as a result of this makes it hard to compare different methods.

In this paper, we introduce a framework for benchmarking automatic ICD coding with the MIMIC clinical database. We name our framework *AnEMIC*, for **An** Error-reduced **MIMIC ICD Coding** benchmark. To the best of our knowledge, AnEMIC is the first attempt to collate and benchmark different deep learning approaches for automatic ICD coding with a configurable pipeline.

[*] Equal contribution.

Proceedings of the The 2022 Conference on Empirical Methods in Natural Language Processing: System Demonstrations, pages 109 - 120
December 7-11, 2022 ©2022 Association for Computational Linguistics

Our contributions can be summarized as follows:

- We provide a pipeline covering the entire process of automatic ICD coding, including preprocessing, training, and evaluation. The whole process is easily configurable with the use of YAML files. We additionally provide key deep learning-based ICD coding models.
- We correct errors in the most widely used datasets and provide benchmark results of the key models on the new datasets.
- We open-source an easy-to-use interactive demo that enables researchers to test their models on custom inputs and visualize input attribution scores for explainability.

The remainder of the paper is organized as follows. In Section 2, we discuss popular automatic ICD coding approaches and datasets. Section 3 details our approaches for preprocessing, training, evaluation, and our demo application. In Section 4, we perform a quantitative and qualitative analysis of AnEMIC. Finally, we conclude with discussion and future work in Section 5.

2 Related Work

2.1 ICD Coding

Over the history of automatic diagnosis coding, approaches have ranged from classical methods such as rule-based approaches (Farkas and Szarvas, 2008), traditional ML models such as SVMs (Perotte et al., 2014), to more recent Deep Learning-based methods. A neural network-based approach was first attempted by Prakash et al. (2017). A prominent deep learning approach is CAML (Mullenbach et al., 2018), which uses a CNN encoder with a unique per-label attention mechanism. Since CAML, there have been many other CNN and RNN-based approaches (Yu et al., 2019; Vu et al., 2020). A few notable CNN based approaches include using dilated convolutional layers (Ji et al., 2020) and multi-filter convolutional layers (Li and Yu, 2020; Luo et al., 2021).

Additionally, researchers have leveraged the hierarchy of ICD codes (Cao et al., 2020; Xie et al., 2019), used external knowledge sources like Wikipedia (Bai and Vucetic, 2019), and knowledge graphs such as UMLS (Yuan et al., 2022) and Freebase (Teng et al., 2020), etc. More recently, there has been an effort to use Transformer-based language models pretrained on clinical datasets, albeit without much success (Pascual et al., 2021; Zhang et al., 2020; Ji et al., 2021). Instead, using a few Transformer encoder layers trained from scratch has proven to be more effective (Biswas et al., 2021).

Kaur et al. (2021) and Yan et al. (2022) perform extensive literature reviews of automatic ICD coding approaches. The reader is referred to these surveys for a more detailed description of various architectures and approaches.

2.2 ICD Coding Datasets and Benchmark

Typical ICD coding dataset consists of discharge summaries and the corresponding sets of ICD codes. There are many ICD coding datasets in various languages, but not all are publicly available. The most widely used datasets are from MIMIC-III[1] and MIMIC-II[2] databases. The MIMIC-III clinical database (Johnson et al., 2016) is a collection of medical records from an intensive care unit (ICU) at a hospital between 2001 and 2012. MIMIC-III consists of multiple tables containing diagnosis, procedures, clinical notes, etc., and each patient admission is indicated with an `HADM_ID` identifier. MIMIC-II is a subset of the MIMIC-III dataset and contains medical records between 2001 and 2008 [3].

CAML (Mullenbach et al., 2018) published the preprocessing code of their MIMIC-III full and top-50 datasets, and since then, these have been the most widely used datasets. We correct some errors in preprocessing of CAML and make the process easily configurable. Also, compared to a leaderboard that only manages reported performance, our work provides a framework for benchmarking, i.e., users can run the code to reproduce the results and further perform research on top of it.

3 ICD Coding Benchmark

AnEMIC has been designed so that researchers can easily configure the overall process with config files and therefore, easily start research on ICD coding with minimal code. Also, the architecture has modularity at the center of its design so that researchers can replace one module with another or with their own implementation. Such design enables easy comparison between models and reduces burden while developing new models.

[1] `https://physionet.org/content/mimiciii/1.4/`

[2] `https://archive.physionet.org/mimic2/`

[3] There is also the recently released MIMIC-IV database, but clinical notes for this are currently not yet available.

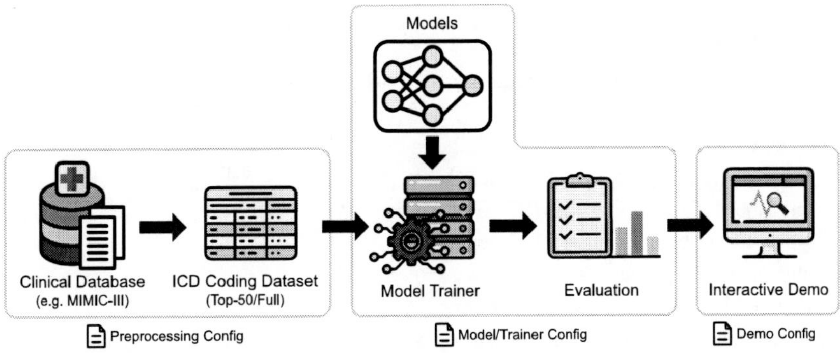

Figure 1: The ICD coding benchmark pipeline of AnEMIC. We provide a pipeline covering the entire process of ICD coding. All steps in the pipeline can be easily configured with YAML files.

Our system also provides an interactive demo for visualizing model predictions with input attribution scores. This demo will help users analyze the performance and interpretability of their models.

In the following subsections, we explain each stage in the pipeline. From now on, we will focus on ICD coding dataset from MIMIC-III since it is the most widely used dataset for this task. Figure 1 illustrates the overall pipeline.

3.1 Data Preprocessing

The first step of the pipeline is to preprocess the available clinical dataset, i.e., the MIMIC-III database. As with other parts of the pipeline, we specify preprocessing-related options in a YAML config file.

Many of the preprocessing steps are inspired by CAML's preprocessing pipeline. However, an important observation to be noted here is that **there are errors in CAML's preprocessing pipeline**. Unfortunately, many subsequent works use CAML's code, and hence, the results obtained by most papers are on the incorrectly preprocessed dataset. This will be discussed later in this subsection and Appendix A.

3.1.1 ICD Code Preprocessing

In the MIMIC-III database, the `DIAGNOSES_ICD` and `PROCEDURES_ICD` tables contain the ICD-9 diagnosis and procedure codes, respectively, of every admission. Since MIMIC-III has ICD-9 codes without the period punctuation (e.g. 4019 instead of 401.9), we reformat those ICD codes to their original format adopting the method of CAML, and use them as labels. ICD-9 codes can have leading and trailing zeros, so care must be taken to retain them when processing. However, in CAML's preprocessing code, some of ICD codes are implicitly treated as integer or floating point numbers[4], resulting in an incorrect set of ICD-9 labels. While correcting this error, we provide an option `incorrect_code_loading` to reproduce the behavior of CAML for researchers who want to make a comparison with previous works.

In addition to the above option, we also provide an option `code_type` to use either diagnosis, procedure, or both types of ICD codes. We set "both" as the default.

3.1.2 Clinical Note Preprocessing

From the `NOTEEVENTS` table of MIMIC-III containing clinical notes in various categories, we select notes belonging to the `Discharge_Summary` category. We provide several options of standard NLP preprocessing for the discharge summary. These can be turned on/off from the config file.

- Convert text to lowercase.
- Remove punctuation marks using `\w+` as the RegEx expression, i.e., retain only alphanumeric characters.
- Either remove numeric characters, or replace all numeric characters with "n".
- Remove stopwords; we use the list of stopwords provided by NLTK, and add common medical terms like "hospital", "admission", "history", etc. to the list.
- Stem or lemmatize the text; we provide popular choices for these such as "WordNet Lemmatizer" and "Porter Stemmer".
- Truncate the text to a maximum length.

After note preprocessing, we build the vocabulary and train a Word2Vec model on preprocessed discharge summaries using the Gensim library (Řehůřek and Sojka, 2010). Word2Vec embeddings are used to initialize the embedding layers of models.

[4]Due to not specifying data types when loading tables

3.1.3 Top-k Codes and Data Splitting

Many works report results on two datasets – "MIMIC-III full" and "MIMIC-III top-50". The latter contains the top-50 frequent ICD codes as labels and examples with at least one of these labels.

An important point to note is that MIMIC-III has some duplicate ICD codes, i.e., an ICD code can be repeated multiple times in one admission. These duplicate codes need to be removed when counting the ICD code occurrence. This is another source of error in CAML's code: they do not remove the duplicate codes while counting the ICD codes occurrence, resulting in a change in the top-50 ICD codes. While we correctly select the top-50 ICD codes, we also provide an option `count_duplicate_codes` to reproduce the behavior of CAML.

For data splitting, we use the splits of `HADM_IDs` provided by CAML. They provide separate sets of splits for the full and top-50 datasets, and the split for top-50 dataset has substantially smaller number of examples. To make full use of MIMIC-III, we use the splits of the CAML's full dataset for both versions of our dataset.

As a result of data preprocessing, we have four main variants of the dataset – "MIMIC-III full", "MIMIC-III top-50", "MIMIC-III full (old)", and "MIMIC-III top-50 (old)". Here "(old)" refers to the CAML variants.

3.2 Supported Models

This subsection describes the models we provide in the framework and the criteria for choosing models. To provide researchers with good baselines for ICD coding research, we selected models based on novelty or superior performance. For now, we have chosen a subset of models for which the code is publicly available, but we do plan on implementing other approaches in the near future which have not been open-sourced. The models and the trainer are based on PyTorch.

The models currently supported by the framework are as follows:

- CAML (Mullenbach et al., 2018) is a landmark model in automatic ICD coding which uses a label attention layer. We also implement the vanilla CNN model in the paper and refer to it as CNN.
- MultiResCNN (Li and Yu, 2020) uses multiple CNNs with different filter sizes in parallel.
- DCAN (Ji et al., 2020) uses dilated convolutional layers for ICD coding.

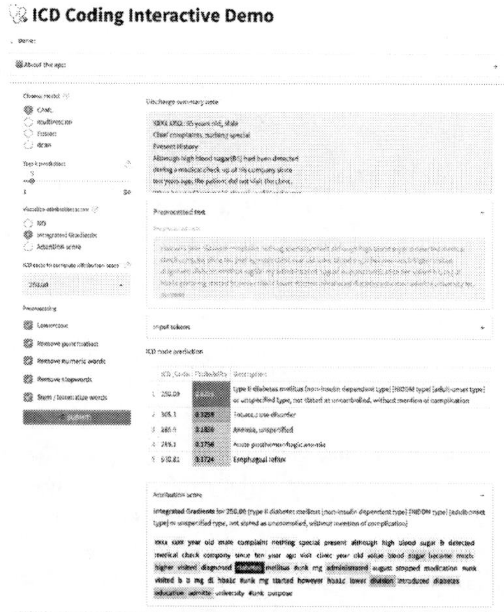

Figure 2: A snapshot of ICD coding interactive demo showing ICD code predictions and the integrated gradient. Input text is extracted from Tsumoto et al. (2019).

- TransICD (Biswas et al., 2021) is the first Transformer-based approach that achieved results comparable to the CNN-based model.
- Fusion (Luo et al., 2021) uses multi-CNN, Transformer encoder, and label attention.

To replicate the author's work in our own system, we re-wired the model from the author's code to make it compatible with our framework. This allows users to also easily tweak the model and its hyperparameters with the config files.

3.3 Training and Evaluation

To train and evaluate the models, we implement a trainer module that manages training and evaluation, with sub-modules for the additional functionalities related to training, such as objective functions, logging, and managing checkpoints. Following the design principle of the framework, the trainer module is also highly configurable so the users can easily customize training and visualize metrics by modifying config files. This also applies to evaluation metrics, and we provide all major evaluation metrics adopted by the automatic ICD coding literature.

3.4 Interactive Demo

In order to enable users to use trained models off-the-shelf, we open source an interactive web application based on Streamlit. Using the app, users can feed in a new discharge summary and get the ICD code predictions in real time without writing code to preprocess the input text and to run the models. The app also allows users to change the models and toggle the preprocessing options on the fly so that they can compare models and change preprocessing options.

A major highlight of the app is explainability visualization, i.e., the attribution or importance scores for each word present in the input clinical note. We provide two methods – Integrated Gradients (Sundararajan et al., 2017) and attention scores. Upon choosing the attribution method with an ICD code, the app displays the input tokens with important words highlighted. Note that this interpretability feature is model-agnostic because the explainable AI techniques we use such as integrated gradients are in turn model-agnostic.

A screenshot of the app running on a discharge summary is shown in Figure 2. The bottom of Figure 2 shows the integrated gradient (IG) visualization of ICD code 250.00 "Type II diabetes". We can see that important terms like "diabetes mellitus" exhibit high IG scores[5]. Overall, we expect the interactive demo will be helpful for both researchers who want to validate models, and professionals who want explanations of the model's predictions.

4 Results

In this section, we discuss the quantitative and qualitative results of AnEMIC. On quantitative aspects, we discuss the brief statistics of the datasets and the benchmark results on the our ICD coding datasets. For the qualitative results, we present and analyze some example of interpretability visualization from our demo application.

4.1 Quantitative Results

Dataset Statistics Table 1 shows brief statistics of our ICD coding datasets and the CAML's datasets (old). Our full dataset contains the same number of examples as CAML's full dataset since we used the same data split. However, it has a different set of labels since we corrected the preprocessing of CAML. Our top-50 dataset has the same number of labels as CAML's top-50 dataset, but the label set differs[6]. Also, our top-50 dataset has substantially more examples since the data split of the full dataset is used to make full use of MIMIC-III. It has a slightly less number of examples than the full dataset since examples without any of the top-50 codes are removed.

[5] Red and blue color in the visualization represent positive and negative scores, respectively.

[6] Please refer to Table 4 in the Appendix to compare.

Dataset	AnEMIC		CAML (old)	
	Full	**Top-50**	**Full**	**Top-50**
# labels	8930	50	8922	50
Mean # labels	15.88	5.73	16.10	5.78
# examples				
- Train set	47723	44728	47723	8066
- Val set	1631	1569	1631	1573
- Test set	3372	3234	3372	1729

Table 1: Statistics of the MIMIC-III full and top-50 datasets. Mean # labels refers to the average number of labels per example.

Benchmark Results To provide the benchmark of our ICD coding datasets, we trained the models introduced in Section 3.2. Hyper-parameters for each model are chosen as reported in the respective paper or code. Note that these hyper-parameters are tuned to CAML datasets, so may not be optimal for our datasets, especially for the top-50 dataset. For DCAN and TransICD model, only the MIMIC-III top-50 experiments was performed, so we use the hyper-parameters for the top-50 dataset in the full dataset experiment. For each model, we ran the experiment three times and computed the mean and variance of the results. Table 2 and 3 shows the benchmark results. Among the models that we implemented, MultiResCNN and Fusion achieved the best test performance on the MIMIC-III full dataset, and DCAN performed best on the MIMIC-III top-50 dataset.

To validate the implementation of key models and the CAML version of dataset, we also ran the same experiments on the CAML version of the datasets. Overall, the results display similar level of performance as reported in the papers. Please see Appendix C for the full results and details of the reproduction experiments.

4.2 Qualitative Analysis

Explainability Visualization Figure 3 shows some examples of explainability visualization from the demo app. For each example, we extract the window around the word with the highest attribution score. In the left figure, for a fixed discharge summary and an ICD code (599.0, *Urinary tract*

Model	Macro AUC	Micro AUC	Macro F1	Micro F1	P@8	P@15
CNN	0.835±0.001	0.974±0.000	0.034±0.001	0.420±0.006	0.619±0.002	0.474±0.004
CAML	0.893±0.002	0.985±0.000	0.056±0.006	0.506±0.006	0.704±0.001	0.555±0.001
MultiResCNN	0.912±0.004	0.987±0.000	0.078±0.005	0.555±0.004	0.741±0.002	0.589±0.002
DCAN	0.848±0.009	0.979±0.001	0.066±0.005	0.533±0.006	0.721±0.001	0.573±0.000
TransICD	0.886±0.010	0.983±0.002	0.058±0.001	0.497±0.001	0.666±0.000	0.524±0.001
Fusion	0.910±0.003	0.986±0.000	0.081±0.002	0.560±0.003	0.744±0.002	0.589±0.001

Table 2: Test set results on the MIMIC-III full dataset. The results are shown using the mean±standard deviation format.

Model	Macro AUC	Micro AUC	Macro F1	Micro F1	P@5
CNN	0.913±0.002	0.936±0.002	0.627±0.001	0.693±0.003	0.649±0.001
CAML	0.918±0.000	0.942±0.000	0.614±0.005	0.690±0.001	0.661±0.002
MultiResCNN	0.928±0.001	0.950±0.000	0.652±0.006	0.720±0.002	0.674±0.001
DCAN	0.934±0.001	0.953±0.001	0.651±0.010	0.724±0.005	0.682±0.003
TransICD	0.917±0.002	0.939±0.001	0.602±0.002	0.679±0.001	0.643±0.001
Fusion	0.932±0.001	0.952±0.000	0.664±0.003	0.727±0.003	0.679±0.001

Table 3: Test set results on the MIMIC-III top-50 dataset. The results are shown using the mean±standard deviation format.

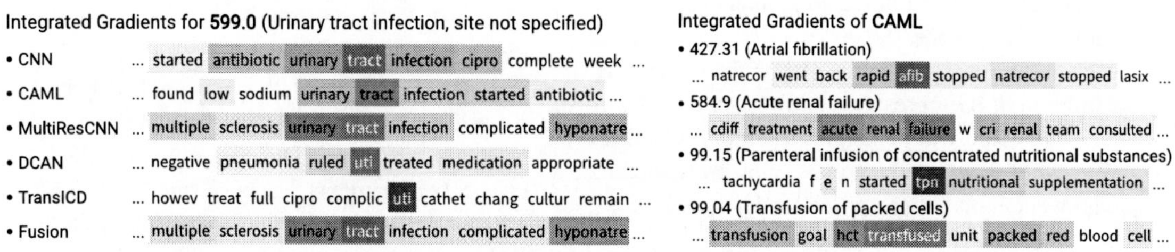

Figure 3: Interpretability visualization examples. **Left**: the integrated gradients of various models on a fixed input and a fixed ICD code (HADM_ID=100020, ICD-9 599.0). **Right**: the integrated gradients of CAML for various ICD codes on a fixed input (HADM_ID=139574).

infection, site not specified), we examine the integrated gradients of various models. From the figure, we can observe that all models correctly attribute their prediction to the words relevant to the diagnosis. In the right figure, for a fixed discharge summary and a model (CAML), we visualize the integrated gradients of some ICD codes that are predicted as positive. As the figure shows, different parts of the input are attributed and they are all semantically relevant to the corresponding ICD code. As both figures illustrate, our interactive demo provides an effective visualization tool for explaining the model's predictions.

5 Conclusions and Future Work

In this work, we present AnEMIC, a comprehensive framework for automatic diagnostic coding. It serves as a standardized benchmark for ICD coding on MIMIC-III by correcting errors in existing datasets and providing popular deep learning-based models. Our framework has a modularized and easy-to-use config-based design, and researchers can easily experiment by writing config files or adding custom submodules. We also provide an interactive app for performing real-time inference and visualization for model explainability.

AnEMIC is under active development and welcomes contributions from the community. Upcoming updates to our pipelines include adding more recent approaches and models, especially those that incorporate additional sources of external knowledge, as well as supporting other datasets like the MIMIC-II dataset.

References

Tian Bai and Slobodan Vucetic. 2019. Improving medical code prediction from clinical text via incorporating online knowledge sources. In *The World Wide Web Conference*, WWW '19, page 72–82, New York, NY, USA. Association for Computing Machinery.

Biplob Biswas, Thai-Hoang Pham, and Ping Zhang. 2021. Transicd: Transformer based code-wise attention model for explainable icd coding.

Pengfei Cao, Yubo Chen, Kang Liu, Jun Zhao, Shengping Liu, and Weifeng Chong. 2020. HyperCore: Hyperbolic and co-graph representation for automatic ICD coding. In *Proceedings of the 58th Annual Meeting of the Association for Computational Linguistics*, pages 3105–3114, Online. Association for Computational Linguistics.

Richárd Farkas and György Szarvas. 2008. Automatic construction of rule-based icd-9-cm coding systems. In *BMC bioinformatics*, volume 9, pages 1–9. Springer.

Shaoxiong Ji, Erik Cambria, and Pekka Marttinen. 2020. Dilated convolutional attention network for medical code assignment from clinical text. In *Proceedings of the 3rd Clinical Natural Language Processing Workshop*, pages 73–78, Online. Association for Computational Linguistics.

Shaoxiong Ji, Matti Hölttä, and Pekka Marttinen. 2021. Does the magic of bert apply to medical code assignment? a quantitative study. *Comput. Biol. Med.*, 139(C).

Alistair EW Johnson, Tom J Pollard, Lu Shen, Li-wei H Lehman, Mengling Feng, Mohammad Ghassemi, Benjamin Moody, Peter Szolovits, Leo Anthony Celi, and Roger G Mark. 2016. Mimic-iii, a freely accessible critical care database. *Scientific data*, 3(1):1–9.

Rajvir Kaur, Jeewani Anupama Ginige, and Oliver Obst. 2021. A systematic literature review of automated ICD coding and classification systems using discharge summaries. *CoRR*, abs/2107.10652.

Leah S Larkey and W Bruce Croft. 1996. Combining classifiers in text categorization. In *Proceedings of the 19th annual international ACM SIGIR conference on Research and development in information retrieval*, pages 289–297.

Fei Li and Hong Yu. 2020. Icd coding from clinical text using multi-filter residual convolutional neural network. In *Proceedings of the AAAI Conference on Artificial Intelligence*, volume 34, pages 8180–8187.

Junyu Luo, Cao Xiao, Lucas Glass, Jimeng Sun, and Fenglong Ma. 2021. Fusion: Towards automated ICD coding via feature compression. In *Findings of the Association for Computational Linguistics: ACL-IJCNLP 2021*, pages 2096–2101, Online. Association for Computational Linguistics.

Laxmaiah Manchikanti. 2002. Implications of fraud and abuse in interventional pain management. *Pain Physician*, 5(3):320.

James Mullenbach, Sarah Wiegreffe, Jon Duke, Jimeng Sun, and Jacob Eisenstein. 2018. Explainable prediction of medical codes from clinical text. In *Proceedings of the 2018 Conference of the North American Chapter of the Association for Computational Linguistics: Human Language Technologies, Volume 1 (Long Papers)*, pages 1101–1111, New Orleans, Louisiana. Association for Computational Linguistics.

Damian Pascual, Sandro Luck, and Roger Wattenhofer. 2021. Towards BERT-based automatic ICD coding: Limitations and opportunities. In *Proceedings of the 20th Workshop on Biomedical Language Processing*, pages 54–63, Online. Association for Computational Linguistics.

Adler Perotte, Rimma Pivovarov, Karthik Natarajan, Nicole Weiskopf, Frank Wood, and Noémie Elhadad. 2014. Diagnosis code assignment: models and evaluation metrics. *Journal of the American Medical Informatics Association*, 21(2):231–237.

Aaditya Prakash, Siyuan Zhao, Sadid A Hasan, Vivek Datla, Kathy Lee, Ashequl Qadir, Joey Liu, and Oladimeji Farri. 2017. Condensed memory networks for clinical diagnostic inferencing. In *Thirty-first AAAI conference on artificial intelligence*.

Radim Řehůřek and Petr Sojka. 2010. Software Framework for Topic Modelling with Large Corpora. In *Proceedings of the LREC 2010 Workshop on New Challenges for NLP Frameworks*, pages 45–50, Valletta, Malta. ELRA.

Mukund Sundararajan, Ankur Taly, and Qiqi Yan. 2017. Axiomatic attribution for deep networks. In *Proceedings of the 34th International Conference on Machine Learning - Volume 70*, ICML'17, page 3319–3328. JMLR.org.

Fei Teng, Wei Yang, Li Chen, LuFei Huang, and Qiang Xu. 2020. Explainable prediction of medical codes with knowledge graphs. *Frontiers in Bioengineering and Biotechnology*, 8:867.

Phillip Tseng, Robert S Kaplan, Barak D Richman, Mahek A Shah, and Kevin A Schulman. 2018. Administrative costs associated with physician billing and insurance-related activities at an academic health care system. *Jama*, 319(7):691–697.

Shusaku Tsumoto, Tomohiro Kimura, Haruko Iwata, and Shoji Hirano. 2019. Estimation of disease code from electronic patient records. In *2019 IEEE International Conference on Big Data (Big Data)*, pages 2698–2707. IEEE.

Thanh Vu, Dat Quoc Nguyen, and Anthony Nguyen. 2020. A label attention model for icd coding from clinical text. In *Proceedings of the Twenty-Ninth*

International Joint Conference on Artificial Intelligence, IJCAI-20, pages 3335–3341. International Joint Conferences on Artificial Intelligence Organization. Main track.

Xiancheng Xie, Yun Xiong, Philip S. Yu, and Yangyong Zhu. 2019. Ehr coding with multi-scale feature attention and structured knowledge graph propagation. In *Proceedings of the 28th ACM International Conference on Information and Knowledge Management*, CIKM '19, page 649–658, New York, NY, USA. Association for Computing Machinery.

Chenwei Yan, Xiangling Fu, Xien Liu, Yuanqiu Zhang, Yue Gao, Ji Wu, and Qiang Li. 2022. A survey of automated international classification of diseases coding: development, challenges, and applications. *Intelligent Medicine*.

Ying Yu, Min Li, Liangliang Liu, Zhihui Fei, Fang-Xiang Wu, and Jianxin Wang. 2019. Automatic icd code assignment of chinese clinical notes based on multilayer attention birnn. *Journal of Biomedical Informatics*, 91:103114.

Zheng Yuan, Chuanqi Tan, and Songfang Huang. 2022. Code synonyms do matter: Multiple synonyms matching network for automatic ICD coding. In *Proceedings of the 60th Annual Meeting of the Association for Computational Linguistics (Volume 2: Short Papers)*, pages 808–814, Dublin, Ireland. Association for Computational Linguistics.

Zachariah Zhang, Jingshu Liu, and Narges Razavian. 2020. BERT-XML: Large scale automated ICD coding using BERT pretraining. In *Proceedings of the 3rd Clinical Natural Language Processing Workshop*, pages 24–34, Online. Association for Computational Linguistics.

A Notes on ICD Code Preprocessing

In CAML's preprocessing pipeline, there are two errors. Firstly, when they load the `DIAGNOSES_ICD` and `PROCEDURES_ICD` tables into Pandas dataframes, the ICD codes are loaded without specifying a data type, `dtype` in the `pd.read_csv()` method, resulting in the loss of some of leading zeros (e.g. 0040 $\rightarrow$ 40). This affects more than 190 codes out of 8930 in MIMIC-III. Also, when they store the converted ICD codes (with period) into a file and re-read it, data type is not specified, resulting in that some of the codes are converted as floating number and lose leading and trailing zeros. This also affects many ICD codes. For example, a major top-50 ICD code, 93.90 is not selected.

Secondly, MIMIC-III has duplicate ICD codes in the `DIAGNOSES_ICD` and `PROCEDURES_ICD` table, i.e., an ICD code can be repeated in one admission[7]. While preprocessing, CAML's code does not remove such duplicate codes, and as a result of this, some ICD codes were selected as top-50 incorrectly.

As a result, CAML's MIMIC-III full dataset has 8922 labels, while our correctly fixed dataset has 8930 labels. Moreover, our MIMIC-III top-50 dataset has ICD codes 93.90, V45.82, and CAML's dataset has 33.24, 45.13 instead.

Table 4 lists the ICD codes in CAML's, our, and TransICD's MIMIC-III top-50 datasets. TransICD (Biswas et al., 2021) corrected the first mentioned error, i.e., loading ICD codes incorrectly, but counts duplicate ICD codes when choosing top-50 codes, resulting in another incorrect set of top-50 codes.

B Sample Configuration File

Figure 4 shows the YAML config files for preprocessing our MIMIC-III full dataset, to show the configurable pipeline of AnEMIC. Users can create their own ICD coding datasets with, for example, different top-k or word stemmer, by customizing options in the config file. Also, for more customized behavior, users can implement submodules of the pipeline – for example, tokenizer and embedding trainer, and register in the `ConfigMapper` to be used in the config file.

C Reproduction Results on the CAML's Dataset

In this section, we describe the reproduction experiments and explain the results. To ensure that our framework correctly re-implemented the old, CAML version of the datasets and the key models, we trained the models on the old datasets and compared the results with the ones reported in the papers. As in the benchmark experiments, for each configuration, we ran experiments three times and computed the mean and the standard deviation. To make a fair comparison between the models, we created three sets of the old datasets and used each of them for each run of model training. Effectively, the runs will have different weight initialization, including the embedding matrix.

The results are shown in Table 5 and 6. Overall, our reproduction shows similar performance as reported in the papers and preserves the relative order

[7] For example, ICD code 33.24 appears 11 times in the admission with `HADM_ID=193989`.

No.	CAML		TransICD		AnEMIC	
1	401.9	20053	401.9	20053	401.9	20046
2	38.93	14444	38.93	14444	38.93	12866
3	428.0	12842	428.0	12842	428.0	12842
4	427.31	12594	427.31	12594	427.31	12589
5	414.01	12179	414.01	12179	414.01	12178
6	96.04	9932	96.04	9932	96.04	9493
7	96.6	9161	96.6	9161	96.6	9102
8	584.9	8907	584.9	8907	584.9	8906
9	250.00	8784	250.00	8784	250.00	8783
10	96.71	8619	96.71	8619	272.4	8503
11	272.4	8504	272.4	8504	96.71	8426
12	518.81	7249	518.81	7249	518.81	7249
13	99.04	7147	99.04	7147	99.04	7102
14	39.61	6809	39.61	6809	39.61	6781
15	599.0	6442	599.0	6442	599.0	6442
16	530.81	6156	530.81	6156	530.81	6154
17	96.72	5926	96.72	5926	96.72	5815
18	272.0	5766	272.0	5766	272.0	5766
19	285.9	5296	285.9	5296	285.9	5295
20	88.56	5240	88.56	5240	88.56	5045
21	244.9	4788	244.9	4788	244.9	4785
22	486	4733	486	4733	486	4732
23	38.91	4575	38.91	4575	285.1	4499
24	285.1	4499	285.1	4499	38.91	4449
25	36.15	4390	36.15	4390	36.15	4387
26	276.2	4358	276.2	4358	276.2	4358
27	496	4296	496	4296	496	4296
28	99.15	4172	99.15	4172	99.15	4162
29	995.92	3792	995.92	3792	995.92	3792
30	V58.61	3698	V58.61	3698	V58.61	3697
31	507.0	3592	507.0	3592	507.0	3592
32	038.9	3580	038.9	3580	038.9	3580
33	88.72	3500	88.72	3500	585.9	3367
34	585.9	3367	585.9	3367	403.90	3350
35	403.90	3350	403.90	3350	311	3347
36	311	3347	311	3347	88.72	3305
37	305.1	3272	305.1	3272	305.1	3272
38	37.22	3248	37.22	3248	412	3203
39	412	3203	412	3203	37.22	3147
40	**33.24**	**3188**	**33.24**	**3188**	39.95	3133
41	39.95	3178	39.95	3178	287.5	3002
42	287.5	3002	287.5	3002	410.71	3001
43	410.71	3001	410.71	3001	276.1	2985
44	276.1	2985	276.1	2985	V45.81	2943
45	V45.81	2943	V45.81	2943	424.0	2876
46	424.0	2878	424.0	2878	V15.82	2741
47	**45.13**	**2849**	**45.13**	**2849**	511.9	2693
48	V15.82	2741	V15.82	2741	**93.90**	**2656**
49	511.9	2693	511.9	2693	**V45.82**	**2651**
50	**37.23**	**2659**	**93.90**	**2663**	**37.23**	**2619**
51	**V45.82**	**2651**	**37.23**	**2659**	**33.24**	**2607**
52	403.91	2566	**V45.82**	**2651**	403.91	2566
53	V29.0	2529	403.91	2566	**45.13**	**2552**
54	424.1	2517	V29.0	2529	V29.0	2529
55	785.52	2501	424.1	2517	424.1	2517
56	V58.67	2497	785.52	2501	785.52	2501
57	427.89	2396	V58.67	2497	V58.67	2497
58	327.23	2328	427.89	2396	427.89	2396
59	997.1	2313	327.23	2328	327.23	2328
60	99.55	2304	997.1	2313	997.1	2313
61	**93.9**	**2233**	99.55	2304	99.55	2275

Table 4: Top-61 frequency ICD codes from differently processed datasets. The frequency of each code to select the top-50 labels is shown next to each code. Note the frequencies of ICD codes are affected by preprocessing method and error. The top-50 ICD codes that are not contained in all three top-50 sets are marked in bold.

of performance among the models, illustrating that our code can be used in the research of automatic ICD coding.

```yaml
paths:
  mimic_dir: &mimic_dir datasets/mimic3/csv
  static_dir: &static_dir datasets/mimic3/static
  dataset_dir: &dataset_dir datasets/mimic3_full
  word2vec_dir: &word2vec_dir datasets/mimic3_full/word2vec

preprocessing:
  name: mimic_iii_preprocessing_pipeline
  params:
    paths:
      mimic_dir: *mimic_dir
      static_dir: *static_dir
      save_dir: *dataset_dir
      diagnosis_code_csv_name: DIAGNOSES_ICD.csv.gz
      procedure_code_csv_name: PROCEDURES_ICD.csv.gz
      noteevents_csv_name: NOTEEVENTS.csv.gz
      train_json_name: train.json       # will be saved
      val_json_name: val.json           # will be saved
      test_json_name: test.json         # will be saved
      label_json_name: labels.json      # will be computed and saved
      label_freq_json_name: null
    dataset_metadata:
      column_names:
        subject_id: SUBJECT_ID
        hadm_id: HADM_ID
        chartdate: CHARTDATE
        charttime: CHARTTIME
        storetime: STORETIME
        category: CATEGORY
        description: DESCRIPTION
        cgid: CGID
        iserror: ISERROR
        text: TEXT
        icd9_code: ICD9_CODE
        labels: LABELS
    dataset_splitting_method:
      name: caml_official_split
      params:
        hadm_dir: *static_dir
        train_hadm_ids_name: train_full_split.json
        val_hadm_ids_name: val_full_split.json
        test_hadm_ids_name: test_full_split.json
    clinical_note_preprocessing:
      to_lower:
        perform: true
      remove_punctuation:
        perform: true
      remove_numeric:
        perform: true
        replace_numerics_with_letter: null
      remove_stopwords:
        perform: true
        params:
          stopwords_file_path: null
          remove_common_medical_terms: true
      stem_or_lemmatize:
        perform: true
        params:
          stemmer_name: nltk.WordNetLemmatizer
      truncate:
        perform: false
    incorrect_code_loading: false
    count_duplicate_codes: false
    code_preprocessing:
      top_k: 0                          # enter 0 for all codes
      code_type: both
      add_period_in_correct_pos:
        perform: true
    train_embed_with_all_split: false
    tokenizer:
      name: spacetokenizer
      params: null
    embedding:
      name: word2vec
      params:
        embedding_dir: *word2vec_dir
        pad_token: "<pad>"
        unk_token: "<unk>"
        word2vec_params:
          vector_size: 100
          min_count: 3
          epochs: 5
```

Figure 4: The YAML config file for preprocessing the MIMIC-III full dataset.

Despite the effort of re-implementing the existing datasets and key models, there is a minor difference from the CAML's preprocessing, specifically in training vocabulary and embeddings, that may affect the results. In our preprocessing, the vocabulary and embeddings are trained together from Gensim's word2vec training, which means

Model		Macro AUC	Micro AUC	Macro F1	Micro F1	P@8	P@15
CNN	Repr	0.833±0.003	0.974±0.000	0.027±0.005	0.419±0.006	0.612±0.004	0.467±0.001
	Orig	0.806	0.969	0.042	0.419	0.581	0.443
CAML	Repr	0.880±0.003	0.983±0.000	0.057±0.000	0.502±0.002	0.698±0.002	0.548±0.001
	Orig	0.895	0.986	0.088	0.539	0.709	0.561
MultiResCNN	Repr	0.905±0.003	0.986±0.000	0.076±0.002	0.551±0.005	0.738±0.003	0.586±0.003
	Orig	0.910±0.002	0.986±0.001	0.085±0.007	0.552±0.005	0.734±0.002	0.584±0.001
DCAN	Repr	0.837±0.005	0.977±0.001	0.063±0.002	0.527±0.002	0.721±0.001	0.572±0.001
	Orig	Not available					
TransICD	Repr	0.882±0.010	0.982±0.001	0.059±0.008	0.495±0.005	0.663±0.007	0.521±0.006
	Orig	Not available					
Fusion	Repr	0.910±0.003	0.986±0.000	0.076±0.007	0.555±0.008	0.744±0.003	0.588±0.003
	Orig	0.915	0.987	0.083	0.554	0.736	N/A

Table 5: Reproduced test set results on the MIMIC-III full (old) dataset. For each model, the upper row (Repr) shows the reproduction results in mean±standard deviation, and the lower row (Orig) shows the results in the original papers.

Model		Macro AUC	Micro AUC	Macro F1	Micro F1	P@5
CNN	Repr	0.892±0.003	0.920±0.003	0.583±0.006	0.652±0.008	0.627±0.007
	Orig	0.876	0.907	0.576	0.625	0.620
CAML	Repr	0.865±0.017	0.899±0.008	0.495±0.035	0.593±0.020	0.597±0.016
	Orig	0.875	0.909	0.532	0.614	0.609
MultiResCNN	Repr	0.898±0.006	0.928±0.003	0.590±0.012	0.666±0.013	0.638±0.005
	Orig	0.899±0.004	0.928±0.002	0.606±0.011	0.670±0.003	0.641±0.001
DCAN	Repr	0.915±0.002	0.938±0.001	0.614±0.001	0.690±0.002	0.653±0.004
	Orig	0.902±0.006	0.931±0.001	0.615±0.007	0.671±0.001	0.642±0.002
TransICD	Repr	0.895±0.003	0.924±0.002	0.541±0.010	0.637±0.003	0.617±0.005
	Orig	0.894±0.001	0.923±0.001	0.562±0.004	0.644±0.003	0.617±0.003
Fusion	Repr	0.904±0.002	0.930±0.001	0.606±0.009	0.677±0.003	0.640±0.001
	Orig	0.909	0.933	0.619	0.674	0.647

Table 6: Reproduced test set results on the MIMIC-III top-50 (old) dataset. For each model, the upper row (Repr) shows the reproduction results in mean±standard deviation, and the lower row (Orig) shows the results in the original papers.

that rare words in the corpus are replaced with the UNK token before training word2vec. In CAML's preprocessing, the embeddings are trained without replacing UNK tokens, and later, the embeddings of the frequent words are extracted. Also, in our code, only the train corpus is used to train the embedding, while the CAML's code uses the whole corpus. Furthermore, when choosing words for the vocabulary, CAML's code counts the number of documents, i.e., discharge summary note, that each word appears in, while our code uses the total occurrences of each word. Here, both codes use only the train corpus.

D More Attribution Scores of MIMIC-III

Table 7∼10 show more examples of interpretability visualization. When the model predicted an ICD code correctly, then the relevant part of the input text is attributed. The cases when a model does not predicted are the second and third row of Table 8.

Intergrated Gradients for **428.0** (Congestive heart failure unspecified), HADM_ID=158682	
CNN	hypoventilation syndrome chronic diastolic heart failure hypothyroidism irritable bowel syndrome
CAML	hypoventilation syndrome chronic diastolic heart failure hypothyroidism irritable bowel syndrome
MultiResCNN	hypoventilation syndrome chronic diastolic heart failure hypothyroidism irritable bowel syndrome
DCAN	hypoventilation syndrome chronic diastolic heart failure hypothyroidism irritable bowel syndrome
TransICD	obes hypoventil syndrom chronic diastol heart failur hypothyroid irrit bowel syndrom vitamin
Fusion	hypoventilation syndrome chronic diastolic heart failure hypothyroidism irritable bowel syndrome

Table 7: Integrated gradients of various models on a fixed input and a fixed ICD code

Intergrated Gradients for **285.9** (Anemia, unspecified), HADM_ID=100408	
CNN	p mv repair htn lipid chronic anemia persistent afib chf arthritis
CAML	physician name9 pre information name9 pre name3 lf r division cardiothoracic
MultiResCNN	cardiothoracic allergy recorded known allergy drug attending name3 lf asymptomatic
DCAN	p mv repair htn lipid chronic anemia persistent afib chf arthritis
TransICD	p mv repair htn lipid chronic anemia persist afib chf arthriti tonsillectomi
Fusion	p mv repair htn lipid chronic anemia persistent afib chf arthritis

Table 8: Integrated gradients of various models on a fixed input and a fixed ICD code

Integrated Gradients of **Fusion**, HADM_ID=148372
96.04 (Insertion of endotracheal tube)
unsuccessfully repeat abg paco2 ph intubated arterial line finally placed successfully
38.91 (Arterial catheterization)
repeat abg paco2 ph intubated arterial line finally placed successfully extubated
427.31 (Atrial fibrillation)
perioperative pe anticoagulation atrial fibrillation anticoagulation hypertension diabetes type
250.00 (Diabetes mellitus without mention of complication, type ii or unspecified type)
fibrillation anticoagulation hypertension diabetes type ii obstructive sleep apnea hypercholesterolemia
401.9 (Unspecified essential hypertension)
anticoagulation atrial fibrillation anticoagulation hypertension diabetes type ii obstructive sleep

Table 9: Integrated gradients of Fusion for various ICD codes on a fixed input

Integrated Gradients of **MultiResCNN**, HADM_ID=135796
414.01 (Coronary atherosclerosis of native coronary artery)
niacin attending name3 lf cad vessel cad aortic stenosis toxic multinodular goiter
427.31 (Atrial fibrillation)
operative dysphagia post operative atrial fibrillation h 1st degree av block p peg
96.6 (Enteral infusion of concentrated nutritional substances)
ir post pyloric tube placed feeding eventually peg placed picc placed pt screened
38.93 (Venous catheterization, not elsewhere classified)
placed feeding eventually peg placed picc placed pt screened rehab c rehad
584.9 (Acute renal failure, unspecified)
protection mri brain performed cu arf elevation creatinine pt subsequently reintubated

Table 10: Integrated gradients of Fusion for various ICD codes on a fixed input

Acknowledgements

We acknowledge the support of Center for Machine Learning and Health at Carnegie Mellon University. This work was supported by the intramural research program at the U.S. National Library of Medicine, National Institutes of Health.

SPEAR : Semi-supervised Data Programming in Python

Guttu Sai Abhishek[1*], **Harshad Ingole**[1*], **Parth Laturia**[1*], **Vineeth Dorna**[1*], **Ayush Maheshwari**[1*], **Rishabh Iyer**[2], **Ganesh Ramakrishnan**[1]
{gsaiabhishek5, harshad.ingole99, parthlaturia, vineethdorna}@gmail.com,
{ayusham, ganesh}@cse.iitb.ac.in,
rishabh.iyer@utdallas.edu
[1]Indian Institute of Technology Bombay
[2]The University of Texas at Dallas

Abstract

We present SPEAR, an open-source python library for data programming with semi supervision. The package implements several recent data programming approaches including facility to programmatically label and build training data. SPEAR facilitates *weak supervision* in the form of heuristics (or rules) and association of *noisy* labels to the training dataset. These *noisy* labels are aggregated to assign labels to the unlabeled data for downstream tasks. We have implemented several label aggregation approaches that aggregate the *noisy* labels and then train using the *noisily* labeled set in a cascaded manner. Our implementation also includes other approaches that *jointly* aggregate and train the model for text classification tasks. Thus, in our python package, we integrate several cascade and joint data-programming approaches while also providing the facility of data programming by letting the user define labeling functions or rules. The code and tutorial notebooks are available at `https://github.com/decile-team/spear`. Further, extensive documentation can be found at `https://spear-decile.readthedocs.io/`. Video tutorials demonstrating the usage of our package are available here. We also present some real-world use cases of SPEAR.

1 Introduction

Supervised machine learning approaches require large amounts of labeled data to train robust machine learning models. For classification tasks such as spam detection, (movie) genre categorization, sequence labelling, and so on, modern machine learning systems rely heavily on human-annotated *gold* labels. Creating labeled data can be a time-consuming and expensive procedure that necessitates a significant amount of human effort. To reduce dependence on human-annotated labels, various techniques such as semi-supervision, distant supervision, and crowdsourcing have been proposed. In order to help reduce the subjectivity and drudgery in the labeling process, several recent data programming approaches (Bach et al., 2019; Chatterjee et al., 2020; Awasthi et al., 2020; Maheshwari et al., 2021) have proposed the use of *human-crafted* labelling functions or automatic LFs (Maheshwari et al., 2022a) to *weakly* associate labels with the training data. Users encode supervision in the form of labelling functions (LFs), which assign noisy labels to unlabeled data, reducing dependence on human labeled data. LFs can defined as first-order logic rules as a composition of semantic role attributes (Sen et al., 2020) or syntactic grammar rules (Sahay et al., 2021).

While most data-programming approaches cited above provide their source code in the public domain, a unified package providing access to all data programming approaches is however missing. In this work, we describe SPEAR, a python package that implements several existing data programming approaches while also providing a platform for integrating and benchmarking newer ones. Inspired by frameworks such as Snorkel (Lison et al., 2021; Ratner et al., 2017; Zhang et al., 2021) and algorithm based labeling in Matlab[1], we provide a facility for users to define LFs. Further, we develop and integrate several recent data programming models that uses these LFs. We provide many easy-to-use jupyter notebooks and video tutorials for helping new users get quickly started. Though we provide implementation on 5 text datasets, our package can be easily integrated with vision and speech datasets as well. The users can get started by installing the package using the below command.

```
pip install decile-spear
```

*Authors contributed equally

[1]https://www.mathworks.com/help/vision/ug/create-automation-algorithm-for-labeling.html

Proceedings of the The 2022 Conference on Empirical Methods in Natural Language Processing: System Demonstrations, pages 121 - 127
December 7-11, 2022

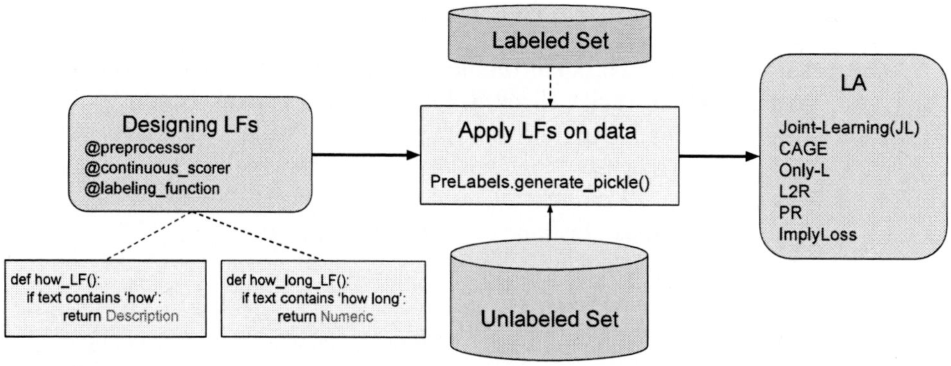

Figure 1: Flow of the SPEAR library.

In Table 1, we compare our library with other existing packages such as Wrench (Zhang et al., 2021), SkWeak(Lison et al., 2021), Imply Loss (Awasthi et al., 2020), Snorkel (Bach et al., 2019) and Matlab. Wrench (Zhang et al., 2021) provides facility for semi-supervised and unsupervised label aggregation approaches, however, it does not provide mechanism to find useful subset of unlabeled data and defining continuous LFs. SkWeak (Lison et al., 2021) does not integrate semi-supervised LA approaches in the package. SPEAR addresses the shortcomings of existing packages by providing features such as designing of discrete and continuous LFs, integrating unsupervised and semi-supervised aggregation approaches and facility to choose labeled set using subset selection approaches.

2 Package Flow

The SPEAR package consists of three components (and they are applied in the same order): (i) Designing LFs, (ii) applying LFs, and (iii) applying a label aggregator (LA).

Initially, the user is expected to declare an *enum* class listing all the class labels. The *enum* class associates the numeric class label with the readable class name. As part of (i), SPEAR provides the facility for manually creating LFs. LFs can be in the form of regex rules as well. Additionally, we also provide the facility of declaring a *@preprocessor* decorator to use an external library such as *spacy*[2], nltk, *etc.* which can be optionally invoked by the LFs. Thereafter, as part of (ii), the LFs can be applied on the unlabeled (and labeled) set using an *apply* function that returns a matrix of dimension #LFs × #instances. The matrix is then provided as input to the selected label aggregator (LA) in (iii), as shown in Figure1. We integrate several LA options into SPEAR. Each LA aggregates multiple noisy labels (obtained from the LFs) to associate a single class label with an instance. Additionally, we have also implemented in SPEAR, several joint learning approaches that employ semi-supervision and feature information. The high-level flow of the SPEAR library is presented in Figure 1.

[2]https://spacy.io

3 Designing and Applying LFs

User interacts with the library by designing labeling functions. Similar to Ratner et al. (2017), labeling functions are python functions which take a candidate as an input and either associates class label or abstains. However, continuous LFs returns a continuous score in addition to the class label. These continuous LFs are more natural to program and lead to improved recall (Chatterjee et al., 2020).

3.1 Designing LFs

SPEAR uses a `@labeling_function()` decorator to define a labeling function. Each LF, when applied on an instance, can either return a class label or not return anything, *i.e.* abstain. The LF decorator has an additional argument that accepts a list of preprocessors. Each preprocessor can be either declared as a pre-defined function or can employ external libraries. The pre-processor transforms the data point before applying the labeling function.

```
@labeling_function(cont_scorer, resources,
    preprocessors, label)
def CLF1(x,**kwargs):
```

Package	Designing & applying LFs	Continuous LFs	Unsup LA	Semi-sup LA	Labeled-data subset selection
Snorkel(Ratner et al., 2017)	✓	✗	✗	✓	✗
Imply Loss (Awasthi et al., 2020)	✗	✗	✗	✓	✗
Matlab	✓	✗	✗	✗	✗
SkWeak (Lison et al., 2021)	✓	✓	✓	✗	✗
Wrench (Zhang et al., 2021)	✓	✗	✓	✓	✗
SPEAR	✓	✓	✓	✓	✓

Table 1: Comparison of SPEAR against available packages.

```
return label if kwargs["continuous_score"] >=
    threshold else ABSTAIN
```

The LF can express pattern matching rules in the form of heuristics, distant supervision by using external knowledge bases and other data resources to label datapoints. LFs on SMS dataset can be seen in the example notebook here.

Continuous LFs: In the discrete LFs, users construct heuristic patterns based on dictionary lookups or thresholded distance for the classification tasks. However, the keywords in hand-crafted dictionaries might be incomplete. Chatterjee et al. (2020) proposed a comprehensive alternative that design continuous valued LFs that return scores derived from soft match between words in the sentence and the dictionary.

SPEAR provides the facility to declare continuous LFs, each of which returns the associated label along with a confidence score using the `@continuous_scorer` decorator. The continuous score can be accessed in the LF definition through the keyword argument `continuous_score`. As evident from Table 1, no other existing package provisions for both semi-supervised aggregation and subset selection modules.

```
@continuous_scorer()
def similarity(sentence,**kwargs):
  word_vecs = featurizer(sentence)
  keyword_vecs = featurizer(kwargs["keywords"])
  return similarity(word_vecs,keyword_vecs)
```

3.2 Applying LFs

Once LFs are defined, users can analyse labeling functions by calculating coverage, overlap, conflicts, empirical accuracy for each LF which helps to re-iterate on the process by refining new LFs. The metrics can be visualised within the SPEAR tool, either in the form of a table or graphs as shown in Figure 2.

PreLabels is the master class which encapsulates a set of LFs, the dataset to label and enum of class labels. PreLabels facilitates the process of applying the LFs on the dataset, and of analysing and refining the LF set. We provide functions to store labels assigned by LFs and associated metadata such as mapping of class name to numeric class labels on the disk in the form json file(s). The pre-labeling performed using the LFs can be consolidated into labeling performed using several consensus models described in Section 4.

```
sms_pre_labels = PreLabels(name="sms",
    data=X_V, gold_labels=Y_V,
data_feats=X_feats_V, rules=rules,
    labels_enum=ClassLabels, num_classes=2)
```

4 Models

We implement several data-programming approaches in this demonstration that includes simple baselines such as fully-supervised, semi-supervised and unsupervised approaches.

4.1 Joint Learning (Maheshwari et al., 2021)

The joint learning (JL) module implements a semi-supervised data programming paradigm that learns a joint model over LFs and features. JL has two key components, *viz.*, feature model (fm) and graphical model (gm) and their sum is used as a training objective. During training, the JL requires labeled ($\mathcal{L}$), validation ($\mathcal{V}$), test ($\mathcal{T}$) sets consisting of true labels and an unlabeled ($\mathcal{U}$) set whose true labels are to be inferred. The model API closely

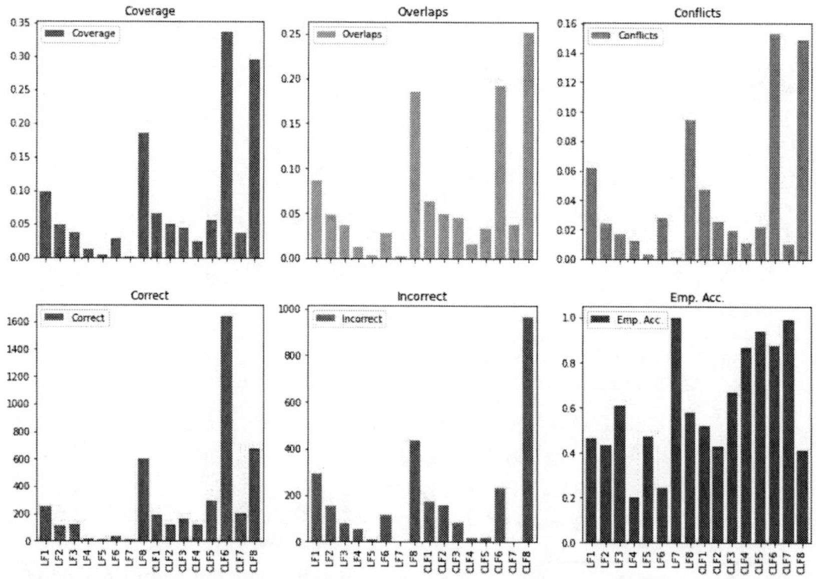

Figure 2: LF analysis on the SMS dataset presented in the form of graph visualization within the SPEAR tool. The statistics include precision, coverage, conflict and empirical accuracy for each LF.

follows that of *scikit-learn* (Pedregosa et al., 2011) to make the package easily accessible to the machine learning audience. The primary functions are: (1) `fit_and_predict_proba`, which trains using the prelabels assigned by LFs and true labels of $\mathcal{L}$ data and predicts the probabilities of labels for each instance of $\mathcal{U}$ data (2) `fit_and_predict`, similar to the previous one but which predicts labels of $\mathcal{U}$ using maximum posterior probabilities (3) `predict_(fm/gm)_proba`, predicts the probabilities, using feature model(fm)/graphical model(gm) (4) `predict_(fm/gm)`, predicts labels using fm/gm based on learned parameters. We also provide functions `save` or `load_params` to save or load the trained parameters.

As another unique feature (*c.f.* Table 1), our library supports a *subset-selection framework* that makes the best use of human-annotation efforts. The $\mathcal{L}$ set can be chosen using submodular functions such as facility location, max cover, *etc.* We utilise the submodlib[3] library for the subset selection algorithms. Some of the function alternatives for subset selection are `rand_subset`, `unsup_subset`, `sup_subset_indices` and `sup_subset_save_files`.

[3]`https://github.com/decile-team/submodlib`

4.2 Only-$\mathcal{L}$

In this, the classifier $P(y|\mathbf{x})$ is trained only on the labeled data. Following Maheshwari et al. (2021), we provide facility to use either Logistic Regression or a 2-layered neural network. Our package is flexible to allow other architectures to be plugged-in as well.

4.3 CAGE (Chatterjee et al., 2020)

This accepts both continuous and discrete LFs. Further, each LF has an associated quality guide component, that refers to the fraction of times the LF predicts the correct label; this stabilises training in absence of $\mathcal{V}$ set. In our package, CAGE accepts $\mathcal{U}$ and $\mathcal{T}$ sets during training. CAGE has member functions similar to (except there are no fm or gm variants to `predict_proba`, `predict` functions in Cage) JL module, with different arguments, serving the same purpose. It should be noted that this model doesn't need labeled($\mathcal{L}$) or validation($\mathcal{V}$) data.

4.4 Learning to Reweight (L2R) (Ren et al., 2018)

This method is an online meta-learning approach for reweighting training examples with a mix of $\mathcal{U}$ and $\mathcal{L}$. It leverages validation set to determine and adaptively assigns importance weights to examples based on the gradient direction. This does

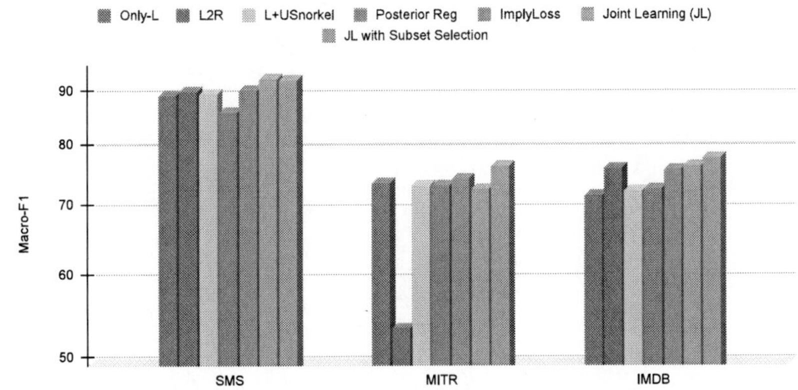

Figure 3: Experiments on SMS, IMDB and MIT-R dataset and comparison with various approaches. We use JL combined with supervised subset selection for obtaining numbers.

not employ additional parameters to weigh or denoise individual rules.

4.5 $\mathcal{L} + \mathcal{U}_{\textbf{Snorkel}}$ (Ratner et al., 2017)

This method trains a supervised classifier on $\mathcal{L}$ set and Snorkel's generative model on $\mathcal{U}$ set. Snorkel is a generative model that models class probabilities based on discrete LFs for consensus on the noisy and conflicting labels. It assigns a linear weight to each rule based on an agreement objective and label examples in $\mathcal{U}$.

4.6 Posterior Regularization (PR) (Hu et al., 2016)

This is a method that enables to simultaneously learn from $\mathcal{L}$ and logic rules by jointly learning a rule and feature network in a teacher-student setup. The student network learns parameter θ using the $\mathcal{L}$ set and teacher networks attempts to imitates the student network in a joint learning manner. The teacher network encodes logic rules as a regularization term in the overall loss objective.

4.7 Imply Loss (Awasthi et al., 2020)

This approach uses additional information in the form of labeled rule exemplars and trains with a denoised rule-label loss. They leverage both rules and labeled data by mapping each rule with exemplars of correct firings (i.e., instantiations) of that rule. Their joint training algorithms denoise overgeneralized rules and train a classification model. It has two main components:

1. Rule Network: It learns to predict whether a given rule has overgeneralized on a given sample using latent coverage variables.

2. Classification Network: It is trained on $\mathcal{L}$ and $\mathcal{U}$ to predict the output label and maximize the accuracy on unseen test instances using a soft implication loss.

This module contains the following primary classes:

1. DataFeeder - It will essentially take all the parameters as input and create a data feeder class with all these parameters as its attributes.

2. HighLevelSupervisionNetwork (HLS) - It will take the 2 networks, the mode or the approach that needs to be used to train the model, the required parameters, the directory storing model checkpoints at different instances and the instances and labels from the labeled dataset ($\mathcal{L}$) and create an object named "hls".

HLS object will have many member functions of which the 2 significant are:
(a) **hls.train**: This function, when called with the required mode, will train the 2 network attributes of the object.
(b) **hls.test**: It supports 3 types of testing:
(i) test_w: this will test the rule network and the related model of the object.
(ii) test_f: this will test the classification network and the related model of the object.
(iii) test_all: this will test both the networks and models of the class.

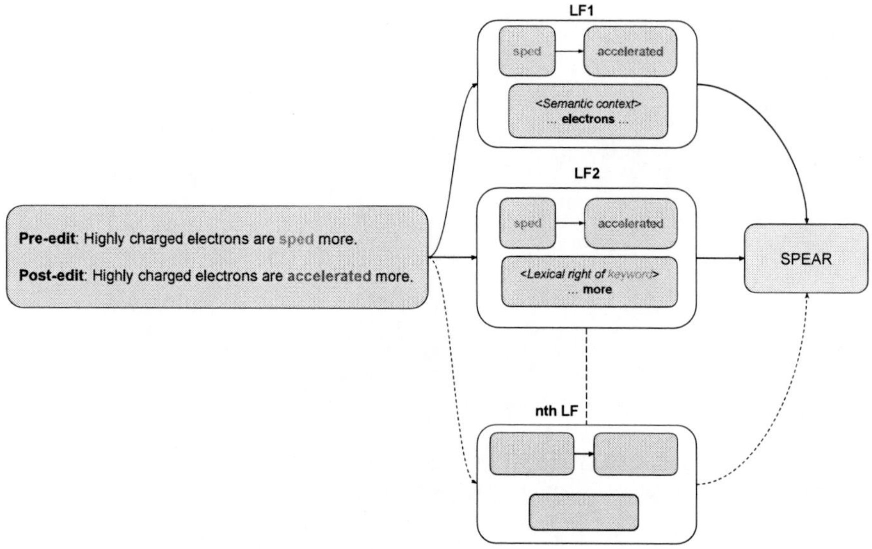

Figure 4: Mutiple LFs generated from post-editor edits based on semantic and lexical features while editing science (domain-specific) document in English.

5 Experiments

We prepared jupyter tutorial notebooks for two standard text classification datasets, namely SMS, YouTube and TREC. We took LFs on these datasets from Awasthi et al. (2020) and train using approaches implemented in this paper. Figure 3 shows performance of various approaches implemented using our package on additional two datasets, MIT-R and IMDB. We can integrate image classification tasks by defining appropriate feature extraction module and rules.

6 Use Cases

SPEAR is employed in project UDAAN[4] for reducing post editing efforts. UDAAN (Maheshwari et al., 2022b) is an end-to-end translation and post-editing eco-system for domain-aware, target vocabulary-constrained translation. Specifically, based on the post editor's patterns of changes to the target language document, candidate labeling functions are generated (based on a combination of heuristics and linguistic patterns) by the UDAAN workbench (*c.f.* Figure 4 for examples of LFs). SPEAR is then used to invoke these LFs on a combination of the edited (*i.e.*, labeled) data and the not yet edited (*i.e.*, unlabeled) data to present consolidated edits to the post-editor. This use case has been presented in the flow chart in Figure 4 – we present the appropriate incorporation of SPEAR into the post-editing environment of an ecosystem such as for translation (UDAAN) or even for Optical Character Recognition[5] or Automatic Speech Recognition (ASR).

As a part of the COVID-19 third wave preparedness, SPEAR was deployed for the Municipal Corporation of Greater Mumbai (MCGM)'s Health Ward[6] for predicting the COVID-19 status of patients, to help in preliminary diagnosis.

6.1 Demonstration Case

For the purpose of demonstration, apart from the use cases outlined above, we can choose a text classification dataset and form regex or continuous rules after observing a few data points. Once the LFs are developed, they can be deployed in conjunction with any of the semi- and un-supervised algorithms present in the package (*c.f.* Section 4) and to compare these algorithms against each other.

7 Conclusion and Future Work

SPEAR is a unified package for semi-supervised data programming that enables quick annotation of training data and facilitates training of machine learning models. It eases the use of developing

[4]https://www.udaanproject.org/

[5]https://www.cse.iitb.ac.in/~ocr/

[6]https://colab.research.google.com/drive/1tNUObqSDypUos7YNvnqvemALlkrrsB0z

LFs and label aggregation approaches. This allows for better reproducibility, benchmarking and easier ML development in low-resource settings such as in textual post-editing. Presently, we are integrating automatic LF induction approaches such as Snuba (Varma and Ré, 2018) that employ a small labeled set to induce LFs automatically. This will significantly increase the scope of labeling datasets, reducing the extent of human intervention in designing LFs. The package is written in Python3 and open-sourced with a MIT License[7], open for community contribution.

8 Acknowledgements

We thank anonymous reviewers for providing constructive feedback. Ayush Maheshwari is supported by a Fellowship from Ekal Foundation (www.ekal.org). Ganesh Ramakrishnan is grateful to IBM Research, India (specifically the IBM AI Horizon Networks - IIT Bombay initiative) as well as the IIT Bombay Institute Chair Professorship for their support and sponsorship.

References

Abhijeet Awasthi, Sabyasachi Ghosh, Rasna Goyal, and Sunita Sarawagi. 2020. Learning from rules generalizing labeled exemplars. In *8th International Conference on Learning Representations, ICLR 2020, Addis Ababa, Ethiopia, April 26-30, 2020*. OpenReview.net.

Stephen H Bach, Daniel Rodriguez, Yintao Liu, Chong Luo, Haidong Shao, Cassandra Xia, Souvik Sen, Alex Ratner, Braden Hancock, Houman Alborzi, et al. 2019. Snorkel drybell: A case study in deploying weak supervision at industrial scale. In *Proceedings of the 2019 International Conference on Management of Data*, pages 362–375.

Oishik Chatterjee, Ganesh Ramakrishnan, and Sunita Sarawagi. 2020. Robust data programming with precision-guided labeling functions. In *AAAI*.

Zhiting Hu, Xuezhe Ma, Zhengzhong Liu, Eduard Hovy, and Eric Xing. 2016. Harnessing deep neural networks with logic rules. *arXiv preprint arXiv:1603.06318*.

Pierre Lison, Jeremy Barnes, and Aliaksandr Hubin. 2021. skweak: Weak supervision made easy for NLP. In *Proceedings of the 59th Annual Meeting of the Association for Computational Linguistics and the 11th International Joint Conference on Natural Language Processing: System Demonstrations*, pages 337–346, Online. Association for Computational Linguistics.

Ayush Maheshwari, Oishik Chatterjee, KrishnaTeja Killamsetty, Rishabh K. Iyer, and Ganesh Ramakrishnan. 2021. Data programming using semi-supervision and subset selection. In *Proceedings of the 59th Annual Meeting of the Association for Computational Linguistics*.

Ayush Maheshwari, Krishnateja Killamsetty, Ganesh Ramakrishnan, Rishabh Iyer, Marina Danilevsky, and Lucian Popa. 2022a. Learning to robustly aggregate labeling functions for semi-supervised data programming. In *Findings of the Association for Computational Linguistics: ACL 2022*, pages 1188–1202.

Ayush Maheshwari, Ajay Ravindran, Venkatapathy Subramanian, Akshay Jalan, and Ganesh Ramakrishnan. 2022b. Udaan – machine learning based post-editing tool for document translation.

Fabian Pedregosa, Gaël Varoquaux, Alexandre Gramfort, Vincent Michel, Bertrand Thirion, Olivier Grisel, Mathieu Blondel, Peter Prettenhofer, Ron Weiss, Vincent Dubourg, et al. 2011. Scikit-learn: Machine learning in python. *the Journal of machine Learning research*, 12:2825–2830.

Alexander J Ratner, Stephen H Bach, Henry R Ehrenberg, and Chris Ré. 2017. Snorkel: Fast training set generation for information extraction. In *Proceedings of the 2017 ACM international conference on management of data*, pages 1683–1686.

Mengye Ren, Wenyuan Zeng, Bin Yang, and Raquel Urtasun. 2018. Learning to reweight examples for robust deep learning. In *International Conference on Machine Learning*, pages 4334–4343.

Atul Sahay, Anshul Nasery, Ayush Maheshwari, Ganesh Ramakrishnan, and Rishabh Iyer. 2021. Rule augmented unsupervised constituency parsing. In *Findings of the Association for Computational Linguistics: ACL-IJCNLP 2021*, pages 4923–4932.

Prithviraj Sen, Marina Danilevsky, Yunyao Li, Siddhartha Brahma, Matthias Boehm, Laura Chiticariu, and Rajasekar Krishnamurthy. 2020. Learning explainable linguistic expressions with neural inductive logic programming for sentence classification. In *Proceedings of the 2020 Conference on Empirical Methods in Natural Language Processing (EMNLP)*, pages 4211–4221.

Paroma Varma and Christopher Ré. 2018. Snuba: automating weak supervision to label training data. In *Proceedings of the VLDB Endowment. International Conference on Very Large Data Bases*, volume 12, page 223. NIH Public Access.

Jieyu Zhang, Yue Yu, Yinghao Li, Yujing Wang, Yaming Yang, Mao Yang, and Alexander Ratner. 2021. Wrench: A comprehensive benchmark for weak supervision. In *Thirty-fifth Conference on Neural Information Processing Systems Datasets and Benchmarks Track (Round 2)*.

[7]https://opensource.org/licenses/MIT

🤗 Evaluate & Evaluation on the Hub: Better Best Practices for Data and Model Measurements

Leandro von Werra,* Lewis Tunstall,* Abhishek Thakur,* Alexandra Sasha Luccioni,* Tristan Thrush, Aleksandra Piktus, Felix Marty, Nazneen Rajani, Victor Mustar, Helen Ngo, Omar Sanseviero, Mario Šaško, Albert Villanova, Quentin Lhoest, Julien Chaumond, Margaret Mitchell, Alexander M. Rush, Thomas Wolf, Douwe Kiela

Hugging Face, Inc.

{leandro,lewis,abhishek,sasha.luccioni,douwe}@huggingface.co

Abstract

Evaluation is a key part of machine learning (ML), yet there is a lack of support and tooling to enable its informed and systematic practice. We introduce 🤗 *Evaluate* and *Evaluation on the Hub*—a set of tools to facilitate the evaluation of models and datasets in ML. 🤗 *Evaluate* is a library to support best practices for measurements, metrics, and comparisons of data and models. Its goal is to support reproducibility of evaluation, centralize and document the evaluation process, and broaden evaluation to cover more facets of model performance. It includes over 50 efficient canonical implementations for a variety of domains and scenarios, interactive documentation, and the ability to easily share implementations and outcomes. The library is available at https://github.com/huggingface/evaluate. In addition, we introduce *Evaluation on the Hub*, a platform that enables the large-scale evaluation of over 75,000 models and 11,000 datasets on the Hugging Face Hub, for free, at the click of a button. Evaluation on the Hub is available at https://huggingface.co/autoevaluate.

Demo screencast: youtu.be/6rU177zRj8Q

1 Introduction

Evaluation is a crucial cornerstone of machine learning—not only can it help us gauge whether and how much progress we are making as a field, it can also help determine which model is most suitable for deployment in a given use case. However, while the progress made in terms of hardware and algorithms might look incredible to a ML practitioner from several decades ago, the way we evaluate models has changed very little. In fact, there is an emerging consensus that in order to meaningfully track progress in our field, we need to address serious issues in the way in which we evaluate ML systems (Kiela et al., 2021; Bowman and Dahl, 2021; Raji et al., 2021; Hutchinson et al., 2022).

*Equal contribution.

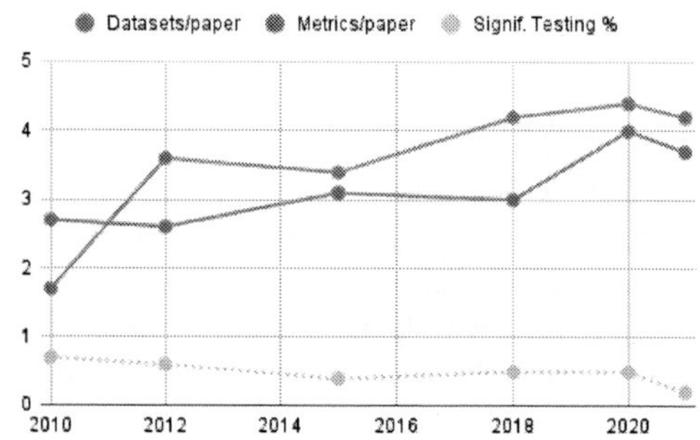

Figure 1: Average number of evaluation datasets and metrics per paper, based on 10 random samples per year from EMNLP proceedings over the past two decades. More recent papers use more datasets and metrics, while fewer of them report statistical significance test results.

In order to have a clearer idea regarding the way model evaluation has evolved in our field, we have carried out our own analysis on a random sample of EMNLP papers from the past two decades, and present our results in Figure 1. It can be observed that the number of evaluation datasets and metrics per paper has increased over time, suggesting that model evaluation is becoming increasingly complex and heterogeneous. However, auxiliary techniques such as testing for significance, measuring statistical power, and using appropriate sampling methods have become less common, making results harder to judge when comparing new results to previous work. We believe that while datasets are now more easily accessible thanks to shared repositories (Lhoest et al., 2021), model evaluation is still unnecessarily cumbersome, with a fragmented ecosystem and a lack of consensus around evaluation approaches and best practices.

The goal of this work is to address three practical challenges in model evaluation for ML: reproducibility, centralization, and coverage.

Reproducibility: ML systems are extremely sensitive to small (and often undocumented) choices

Proceedings of the The 2022 Conference on Empirical Methods in Natural Language Processing: System Demonstrations, pages 128 - 136
December 7-11, 2022 ©2022 Association for Computational Linguistics

such as random seeds and hyperparameters (Pineau et al., 2021). Model performance is often not compared with proper statistical testing that takes this variance into account, making many self-reported comparisons unreliable. Our goal is to standardize this process and thereby improve the reproduction of ML evaluations.

Centralization: Historically, ML metrics have been poorly documented, exacerbating an already insufficient community-wide understanding of their usage and shortcomings (Post, 2018). As metrics and datasets change, the onus is on the community to keep results up-to-date, causing unnecessary replication of work (Ma et al., 2021) and the proliferation of outdated artifacts (Luccioni et al., 2022).

Coverage: ML as a field still focuses heavily on accuracy-based metrics. While important, this focus glosses over other critical facets such as efficiency (Min et al., 2021), bias and fairness (Qian et al., 2022), robustness (Goel et al., 2021), and how these factor into choosing a model (Ethayarajh and Jurafsky, 2020; Ma et al., 2021).

We introduce the open source *Evaluate* library and the *Evaluation on the Hub* platform to address many of these problems. We believe that better evaluation can happen, if we—as a community—establish better best practices and remove hurdles.

2 Related work

Open-Source Tools for Evaluation There is a long history of open source projects aiming to capture various measurements, metrics and statistical testing methods for ML. Torchmetrics (Detlefsen et al., 2022) implements a large number of model evaluation metrics for PyTorch (Paszke et al., 2019), which is similar to evaluation metrics found in Keras (Chollet et al., 2015) for TensorFlow. Libraries like Scikit-learn (Pedregosa et al., 2011), SciPy (Virtanen et al., 2020), Statsmodels (Seabold and Perktold, 2010), NLTK (Bird et al., 2009), TrecTools (Palotti et al., 2019), RL Reliability Metrics (Chan et al., 2020), NetworkX (Hagberg et al., 2008), Scikit-image (Van der Walt et al., 2014), GEM (Gehrmann et al., 2021), TorchFidelity (Obukhov et al., 2020) also support many evaluation measures across many domains. As integrating metrics into specific frameworks can be difficult, there are also many libraries dedicated to individual evaluations for example rouge_score, [1] BARTScore (Yuan et al., 2021), or SacreBLEU (Post, 2018). The fragmentation of the ecosystem leads to various problems, such as a wide range of incompatible conventions and APIs, or misreporting due to differing implementations and results.

In *Evaluate*, we provide one single interface backed by a centralized Hub. Metrics can easily be shared, are version controlled, have a standardized interface, and allow for multimodal inputs.

Evaluation as a Service The idea of *Evaluation as a Service* (Ma et al., 2021; Kiela et al., 2021), whereby models are submitted for another party to be centrally evaluated, has recently gained traction as a more reproducible way to conduct model evaluation. Central evaluation also facilitates holding challenges and competitions around datasets (Yadav et al., 2019; Pavao et al., 2022; Akhbardeh et al., 2021) as opposed to simply evaluating self-reported model results or comparing model scores with benchmark suites (Bajaj et al., 2016; Coleman et al., 2017; Wang et al., 2018, 2019; Kardas et al., 2020; Reddi et al., 2020; Liu et al., 2021; Goel et al., 2021; Dror et al., 2019). The advantages of conducting evaluation centrally are multiple, including better reproducibility, forward/backward compatibility, and the ability to measure models along multiple axes of evaluation (e.g. efficiency and fairness, in addition to accuracy), which can help contribute towards a more systematic approach to evaluation.

Issues with Evaluation Several studies of ML research and practice have been carried out in recent years on different aspects pertaining to ML evaluation, and together they paint a bleak picture of evaluation in our field. For instance, a 2019 large-scale replication study of 255 ML papers found that only 63% of the results they reported could be systematically replicated (Raff, 2019). A complementary survey of 3,800 papers from *Papers with Code* has shown that a large majority of metrics used do not adequately reflect models' performance and that they largely do not correlate with human judgement (Blagec et al., 2021). Finally, a recent study of 770 papers in machine translation from the last decade found that while 108 new metrics have been proposed for the task, 99.8% of papers continue to use BLEU score for reporting results (Marie et al., 2021), despite the fact that the

[1] github.com/google-research/google-research/tree/master/rouge

original BLEU score (Papineni et al., 2002) has been shown to vary based on user-chosen parameters such as tokenization, which vary across languages (Post, 2018; Ananthakrishnan et al., 2007). These issues motivate the development of the tools presented in this work.

3 Library: *Evaluate*

The *Evaluate* library provides canonical implementations of a large set of *evaluation modules*. Modules are available to the community via a single, easy-to-use API. We provide extensive and detailed documentation cards for each, describing their correct usage, range of values and possible pitfalls, in a similar vein to model and dataset cards (Mitchell et al., 2019; Gebru et al., 2021). To facilitate extensibility, each evaluation model lives in a separate Git repository, and new modules can be easily contributed. The core library is released under the Apache 2.0 license and is available on GitHub, [2] making it easy to adopt and deploy.

The library is designed to address the main challenges discussed in Section 1. Metrics are versioned and documented to support *reproducibility* within the framework. The core system is *centralized* to facilitate comparisons across models in a consistent manner supporting best practices, and data is stored in Git to allow backups and cloning. Finally, the tool is inherently designed for a multi-model, multi-evaluation paradigm supporting broad evaluation *coverage* by default.

3.1 Library Structure

Evaluate aims to support a range of model and dataset comparisons. It offers three distinct types of evaluation modules:

Metrics: Metrics to provide a score for model performance (e.g. accuracy or BLEU score). They play a central role for decisions around the use and deployment of models, allowing models to be compared and evaluated based on given benchmarks.

Comparisons: Comparisons are used to compare the predictions of two models (e.g. McNemar's test). When comparing two models, these scores can help determine whether the difference in the models' behavior is statistically significant.

Measurements: Measurements are used to investigate the characteristics of a dataset (e.g. fraction of duplicates, skew in label distribution). These statistics are a crucial step for gleaning more insights regarding training or evaluation datasets.

3.2 Library Tour

We demonstrate how *Evaluate* works with a quick tour of its features. In this section we focus on metrics, but the showcased methods work identically for the other types of evaluation modules.

Core Library Any metric, measurement, or comparison can be loaded using its name.

```
import evaluate
metric = evaluate.load("accuracy")
```

The name can refer to a local file path or the name of a repository on the Hugging Face Hub.

Users can add predictions and/or references one at a time or pass all of them directly to `compute()`.

```
# batches can be added sequentially
metric.add_batch(predictions = [1, 1],
                 references =  [1, 0])
metric.compute()

# or in one compute call
metric.compute(predictions = [1, 1],
               references  = [1, 0])
```

Note that the sequential method is particularly useful in a multi-worker setup, where each worker adds data and the compute operation happens at the end. *Evaluate* uses Apache Arrow as its backend, which means that adding data to the metric does not use any additional memory. The full set of data is only loaded when the metric is computed.

Several metrics can be bundled together and follow the same API as a single metric, returning all results at once.

```
evaluate.combine(["accuracy", "f1"])
```

Evaluator *Evaluate* also offers a higher level API called the Evaluator. Evaluator enables anyone to quickly evaluate a model on a task. Evaluator encapsulates task-specific pre- and post-processing and streamlines data preparation, model inference and metric computation. This makes the evaluation of any `(model, dataset, metric)` triplet on a task seamless: [3]

```
task = evaluator("text-classification")
task.compute(model_or_pipeline=model,
             data=data, metric=metric)
```

[2] github.com/huggingface/evaluate

[3] Currently text, token, and image classification as well as question-answering are supported with more coming soon.

Evaluator employs *pipelines* from the Transformers library [4] (or any other object with the same API) to carry out model inference. While evaluating downstream performance of the model, the Evaluator keeps track of the inference efficiency via metrics such as throughput and latency. This provides another dimension along which models can be compared, especially relevant in applied scenarios where inference times may be as crucial to a model's success as its performance on the core metrics. The Evaluator also supports (optional) confidence interval computations via bootstrapping on any metric.

3.3 Documentation

Recent years have seen several proposals for standardized documentation of both models (Mitchell et al., 2019) and datasets (Gebru et al., 2021), arguing that this improves their accessibility as well as enabling a better understanding of their limitations and biases across different audiences. We have adopted this line of work within *Evaluate* – accompanying each evaluation module is a documentation card that describes the measurement, metric or comparison and how to use it. This card includes its intended use (i.e., whether it is specific to a task such as machine translation or a dataset such as SQuAD), its range, and code snippets that a user can copy within their application. These cards also contain a section on limitations and biases of the module, such as their applicability for certain languages (this is especially relevant for metrics such as BERTScore and COMET, which leverage pretrained models), the size of the models used to calculate them (e.g., GPT-2, the default model used for calculating MAUVE, is over 3 GB), and the fact that certain modules (e.g., perplexity) are not comparable across different datasets when built from different models or preprocessing steps.

Our goal with these documentation cards is twofold. On the one hand, we hope that they will *educate* users regarding the scope and intention of different evaluation approaches, how they are calculated and how to interpret their values. On the other hand, we aim to *improve best practices* in terms of evaluation approaches. This can be as simple as measuring F1 score instead of relying simply on accuracy for imbalanced datasets, but also preferring a more reproducible and systematic metric such as SacreBLEU over a more variable one such as BLEU. We encourage the creators of new modules to write documentation cards to inform the community regarding the intended usages of their metric, measurement, or comparison; their possible limitations and biases; and to provide examples of best practices for using them.

3.4 Community Contributions

Since the code for metrics is stored in individual repositories on the Hugging Face Hub, anyone can add new metrics and load them with *Evaluate* without needing to wait for reviews or approval. Any piece of evaluation code can be easily pushed to the Hugging Face Hub, which allows for sharing the exact same implementation with direct collaborators and the broader research community. These community metrics complement the canonical modules and are stored under the user's namespace. The *Evaluate* library also includes a command line interface (CLI) to make community contributions more accessible.

```
evaluate-cli create "My awesome metric"
```

This command creates a repository on the Hub, clones it, populates it with a template and pushes it to the Hub. The user only needs to implement the metric logic, write a README containing the metric card, and push their changes to the Hub using Git. We automatically provide live interaction widgets for each module, allowing users to develop a proper intuition for evaluation modules' usage, along with access to their documentation. Furthermore, our community discussion feature [5] allows members of the community to flag problematic evaluations or to ask for details regarding results, which model creators can then engage with.

4 Service: *Evaluation on the Hub*

The *Evaluation on the Hub* platform extends the *Evaluate* library to a free service model: anyone can evaluate any model on any dataset using any compatible metric, without requiring any code. This service utilizes models, datasets, and metrics standardized through the Hugging Face Hub. All evaluation results using this method are produced by the same pipeline with versioned implementations, and so are inherently reproducible. When a new model, dataset, or metric is produced, anyone can rerun the evaluation. As such, *Evaluation on*

[4] huggingface.co/docs/transformers/main_classes/pipelines

[5] huggingface.co/docs/hub/repositories-pull-requests-discussions

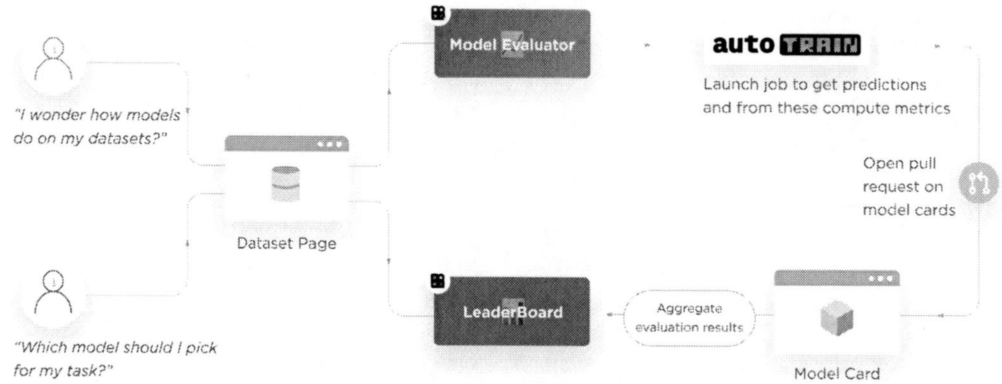

Figure 2: Evaluation on the Hub diagram

the Hub facilitates large-scale evaluation of over 75,000 models and 11,000 datasets.

The service model further supports the goals of *reproducibility* and *centralization*. While the *Evaluate* library can ensure that the metrics used are consistent, it cannot ensure that the model was trained and evaluated using a reproducible set of hyperparameters and data. Incorporating *Evaluate* into a model hosting and training environment makes it possible to guarantee this consistency. Centralization also provides a further benefit of joining these metrics with model and data card documentation.

4.1 System architecture

The system architecture is shown in Figure 2. Upon submission, an evaluation job is triggered, which downloads the dataset and model(s) from the centralized Hub, computes metrics, and opens a pull request with the results.

Evaluation jobs are configured through a simple interface [6] that specifies the task, dataset, metrics, and models to be evaluated. For each task, we compute a set of common metrics using the *Evaluate* library; users can also select additional metrics from the Hub [7] to be included in the evaluation. For many datasets on the Hub, we provide evaluation metadata that defines a default configuration for users to launch evaluation jobs with a single click. Users can also add evaluation metadata to their own datasets to provide one-click evaluations to the community. The interface for triggering an evaluation is shown in Figure 3 (left).

We use AutoTrain [8], Hugging Face's AutoML platform, to run evaluation jobs. The results from each evaluation are stored as metadata associated with model cards. The model predictions for each evaluation are also stored as dataset repositories on the Hub, enabling further analysis of, e.g., model errors.

4.2 Documenting Evaluation

The tool is permissioned so that model owners have the ability to select which evaluations they want to display with their model. This documentation is managed through a pull request system that allows owners to see evaluations that have been run. If a pull request is approved by the model owner, the results are added visibly to the model card as part of its documentation. However, all evaluation pull requests are public by default, so even if one is closed by model owners, members of the community can still see the scores.

Upon approval, the results become visible on an interactive Leaderboard [9] associated with the underlying dataset. We aggregate all model evaluations (both verified and self-reported) through these leaderboards that allow users to filter results across task and dataset. Models are ranked so that users can find the best scoring model for task X on dataset Y. The interface for model leaderboards is shown in Figure 3 (left).

5 Use Cases

Evaluate and *Evaluation on the Hub* are already actively used by our community for a variety of tasks. There are many applications of these tools, and we highlight some of the most important use

[6] huggingface.co/spaces/autoevaluate/model-evaluator
[7] huggingface.co/metrics
[8] huggingface.co/autotrain
[9] huggingface.co/spaces/autoevaluate/leaderboards

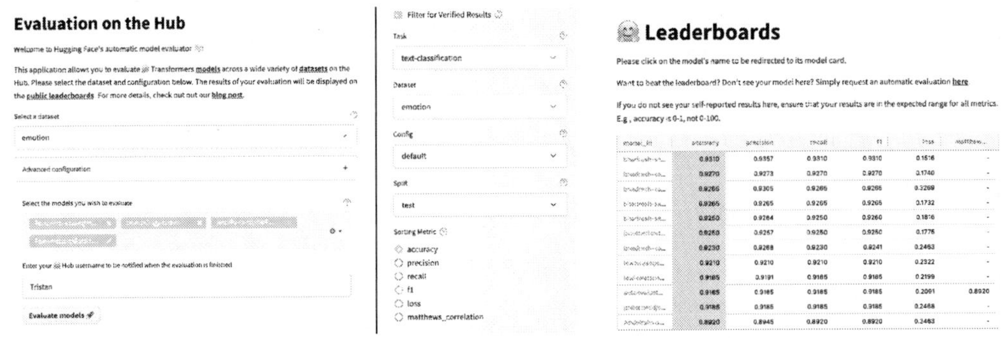

Figure 3: (left) Model Evaluator User Interface; (right) Leaderboards User Interface.

cases observed in practice.

Use case 1: Choosing the best model. If the task is known and the aim is to find an appropriate model, the Hub Leaderboard (which aggregates all the evaluation results for a dataset representative of that task) can act as a trusted source. In case a particularly interesting model is not yet on the leaderboard, its evaluation can easily be triggered, directly from the Hub, and its results will automatically appear on the leaderboard, allowing it to be compared to previous models.

Use case 2: Reproducibility of results. If a new dataset is created, it can be uploaded directly to the Hub to trigger evaluation coverage on many models without needing any code. Researchers can trust in the reproducibility and consistency of this evaluation of these models on this dataset. Similarly, open-source implementations for measurements, metrics and comparisons can easily be shared and plugged into the Evaluator to enable reproducibility on a range of other model facets. If a paper does not report results for a given model on a dataset of interest, it can be evaluated and verified.

Use case 3: Deciding on deployment. When deciding on which variant of a model to deploy to production, it is important to consider the broad performance of the model across multiple metrics. It may also be important to test on held-out test sets, and to measure the latency and throughput of a model. With the Evaluator, researchers can quickly evaluate on several datasets and also get the measured timing and latency information to make an informed decision.

Use case 4: Adding a new metric. When a new evaluation module (i.e., metric, measurement or comparison) is developed, it needs to be distributed for wider use. Historically, for use-cases like Kaggle competitions, metrics are shared as code snippets, requiring participants to copy the evaluation code, which can be error-prone and inconvenient. With *Evaluate*, anyone can create a new evaluate module—be it a metric, measurement, or comparison—alongside its documentation card with instructions. [10] Anybody with the access rights can then quickly use the module with the standard loading mechanism.

6 Conclusion

Evaluate and *Evaluation on the Hub* aim to facilitate better evaluation of machine learning data and models by improving reproducibility, centralization, and coverage of evaluation tools. *Evaluate* is an open-source, community-driven library that standardizes evaluation. *Evaluation on the Hub* is a reproducible no-code alternative for evaluation across models, datasets, and metrics. We hope that this set of tools can help facilitate better best practices for model and data evaluation.

Ethical Issues and Limitations

There are multiple aspects of model evaluation that we have not (yet) addressed but that remain important in the broader landscape of our community and the way ML is used in real-world settings. For instance, we have currently focused on metrics and measurements that have been developed and tested for high-resource languages such as English, and only cover a handful of metrics that explicitly support multilinguality. Similarly, while we strove to cover as many metrics as possible, most of our coverage is for text-based metrics, and we have yet to

[10] Example of a custom metric added by a community member: hf.co.co/spaces/jordyvl/ece

add as many metrics from other modalities, multi-modal metrics, or to provide as large a selection for measurements and comparisons. Furthermore, while we have documented the computational and memory requirements of our evaluation approaches via documentation cards, several metrics require downloading large models such as GPT-2, which can be inaccessible for users with slower Internet speeds or insufficient memory. Finally, we are still working towards a greater reproducibility of evaluation results, for instance by adding identifiers that will indicate which version of a metric and dataset was used for evaluating a model (in the case of code changes, for instance), allowing users to easily replicate results if needed. We will continue improving our tools to address these limitations and provide support for more uses cases.

Acknowledgements

We thank the many contributors to the Hugging Face open source ecosystem. We thank Chunte Lee for designing the Evaluation on the Hub diagram in Figure 2.

References

Farhad Akhbardeh, Arkady Arkhangorodsky, Magdalena Biesialska, Ondřej Bojar, Rajen Chatterjee, Vishrav Chaudhary, Marta R. Costa-jussa, Cristina España-Bonet, Angela Fan, Christian Federmann, Markus Freitag, Yvette Graham, Roman Grundkiewicz, Barry Haddow, Leonie Harter, Kenneth Heafield, Christopher Homan, Matthias Huck, Kwabena Amponsah-Kaakyire, Jungo Kasai, Daniel Khashabi, Kevin Knight, Tom Kocmi, Philipp Koehn, Nicholas Lourie, Christof Monz, Makoto Morishita, Masaaki Nagata, Ajay Nagesh, Toshiaki Nakazawa, Matteo Negri, Santanu Pal, Allahsera Auguste Tapo, Marco Turchi, Valentin Vydrin, and Marcos Zampieri. 2021. Findings of the 2021 conference on machine translation (WMT21). *WMT at EMNLP*.

R Ananthakrishnan, Pushpak Bhattacharyya, M Sasikumar, and Ritesh M Shah. 2007. Some issues in automatic evaluation of English-Hindi MT: more blues for BLEU. *ICON*, 64.

Payal Bajaj, Daniel Campos, Nick Craswell, Li Deng, Jianfeng Gao, Xiaodong Liu, Rangan Majumder, Andrew McNamara, Bhaskar Mitra, Tri Nguyen, et al. 2016. MS Marco: A human generated machine reading comprehension dataset. *arXiv preprint arXiv:1611.09268*.

Steven Bird, Ewan Klein, and Edward Loper. 2009. *Natural language processing with Python: analyzing text with the natural language toolkit*. " O'Reilly Media, Inc.".

Kathrin Blagec, Georg Dorffner, Milad Moradi, and Matthias Samwald. 2021. A critical analysis of metrics used for measuring progress in artificial intelligence. *arXiv pre-print*, 2008.02577:1–28.

Samuel R Bowman and George E Dahl. 2021. What will it take to fix benchmarking in natural language understanding? *arXiv preprint arXiv:2104.02145*.

Stephanie Chan, Sam Fishman, John Canny, Anoop Korattikara, and Sergio Guadarrama. 2020. Measuring the reliability of reinforcement learning algorithms. In *International Conference on Learning Representations, Addis Ababa, Ethiopia*.

François Chollet et al. 2015. Keras. `https://keras.io`.

Cody Coleman, Deepak Narayanan, Daniel Kang, Tian Zhao, Jian Zhang, Luigi Nardi, Peter Bailis, Kunle Olukotun, Chris Ré, and Matei Zaharia. 2017. Dawnbench: An end-to-end deep learning benchmark and competition. In *NIPS ML Systems Workshop*.

Nicki Skafte Detlefsen, Jiri Borovec, Justus Schock, Ananya Harsh, Teddy Koker, Luca Di Liello, Daniel Stancl, Changsheng Quan, Maxim Grechkin, and William Falcon. 2022. TorchMetrics - Measuring Reproducibility in PyTorch.

Rotem Dror, Segev Shlomov, and Roi Reichart. 2019. Deep dominance-how to properly compare deep neural models. In *Proceedings of the 57th Annual Meeting of the Association for Computational Linguistics*, pages 2773–2785.

Kawin Ethayarajh and Dan Jurafsky. 2020. Utility is in the eye of the user: A critique of NLP leaderboards. *arXiv preprint arXiv:2009.13888*.

Timnit Gebru, Jamie Morgenstern, Briana Vecchione, Jennifer Wortman Vaughan, Hanna Wallach, Hal Daumé Iii, and Kate Crawford. 2021. Datasheets for datasets. *Communications of the ACM*, 64(12):86–92.

Sebastian Gehrmann, Tosin Adewumi, Karmanya Aggarwal, Pawan Sasanka Ammanamanchi, Anuoluwapo Aremu, Antoine Bosselut, Khyathi Raghavi Chandu, Miruna-Adriana Clinciu, Dipanjan Das, Kaustubh Dhole, Wanyu Du, Esin Durmus, Ondřej Dušek, Chris Chinenye Emezue, Varun Gangal, Cristina Garbacea, Tatsunori Hashimoto, Yufang Hou, Yacine Jernite, Harsh Jhamtani, Yangfeng Ji, Shailza Jolly, Mihir Kale, Dhruv Kumar, Faisal Ladhak, Aman Madaan, Mounica Maddela, Khyati Mahajan, Saad Mahamood, Bodhisattwa Prasad Majumder, Pedro Henrique Martins, Angelina McMillan-Major, Simon Mille, Emiel van Miltenburg, Moin Nadeem, Shashi Narayan, Vitaly Nikolaev, Andre Niyongabo Rubungo, Salomey Osei, Ankur Parikh, Laura Perez-Beltrachini, Niranjan Ramesh Rao, Vikas Raunak, Juan Diego Rodriguez, Sashank Santhanam, João Sedoc, Thibault Sellam, Samira Shaikh, Anastasia Shimorina,

Marco Antonio Sobrevilla Cabezudo, Hendrik Strobelt, Nishant Subramani, Wei Xu, Diyi Yang, Akhila Yerukola, and Jiawei Zhou. 2021. The GEM benchmark: Natural language generation, its evaluation and metrics. In *Proceedings of the 1st Workshop on Natural Language Generation, Evaluation, and Metrics (GEM 2021)*, pages 96–120, Online. Association for Computational Linguistics.

Karan Goel, Nazneen Rajani, Jesse Vig, Samson Tan, Jason Wu, Stephan Zheng, Caiming Xiong, Mohit Bansal, and Christopher Ré. 2021. Robustness gym: Unifying the NLP evaluation landscape. *arXiv preprint arXiv:2101.04840*.

Aric Hagberg, Pieter Swart, and Daniel S Chult. 2008. Exploring network structure, dynamics, and function using networkx. Technical report, Los Alamos National Lab.(LANL), Los Alamos, NM (United States).

Ben Hutchinson, Negar Rostamzadeh, Christina Greer, Katherine Heller, and Vinodkumar Prabhakaran. 2022. Evaluation gaps in machine learning practice. *arXiv preprint arXiv:2205.05256*.

Marcin Kardas, Piotr Czapla, Pontus Stenetorp, Sebastian Ruder, Sebastian Riedel, Ross Taylor, and Robert Stojnic. 2020. AxCell: Automatic extraction of results from machine learning papers. *EMNLP*.

Douwe Kiela, Max Bartolo, Yixin Nie, Divyansh Kaushik, Atticus Geiger, Zhengxuan Wu, Bertie Vidgen, Grusha Prasad, Amanpreet Singh, Pratik Ringshia, et al. 2021. Dynabench: Rethinking benchmarking in NLP. *arXiv preprint arXiv:2104.14337*.

Quentin Lhoest, Albert Villanova del Moral, Yacine Jernite, Abhishek Thakur, Patrick von Platen, Suraj Patil, Julien Chaumond, Mariama Drame, Julien Plu, Lewis Tunstall, et al. 2021. Datasets: A community library for natural language processing. *arXiv preprint arXiv:2109.02846*.

Pengfei Liu, Jinlan Fu, Yang Xiao, Weizhe Yuan, Shuaicheng Chang, Junqi Dai, Yixin Liu, Zihuiwen Ye, and Graham Neubig. 2021. EXPLAINABOARD: An Explainable Leaderboard for NLP. *arXiv preprint arXiv:2104.06387*.

Alexandra Sasha Luccioni, Frances Corry, Hamsini Sridharan, Mike Ananny, Jason Schultz, and Kate Crawford. 2022. A framework for deprecating datasets: Standardizing documentation, identification, and communication. In *2022 ACM Conference on Fairness, Accountability, and Transparency*, pages 199–212.

Zhiyi Ma, Kawin Ethayarajh, Tristan Thrush, Somya Jain, Ledell Wu, Robin Jia, Christopher Potts, Adina Williams, and Douwe Kiela. 2021. Dynaboard: An evaluation-as-a-service platform for holistic next-generation benchmarking. *Advances in Neural Information Processing Systems*, 34:10351–10367.

Benjamin Marie, Atsushi Fujita, and Raphael Rubino. 2021. Scientific credibility of machine translation research: A meta-evaluation of 769 papers. *arXiv preprint arXiv:2106.15195*.

Sewon Min, Jordan Boyd-Graber, Chris Alberti, Danqi Chen, Eunsol Choi, Michael Collins, Kelvin Guu, Hannaneh Hajishirzi, Kenton Lee, Jennimaria Palomaki, Colin Raffel, Adam Roberts, Tom Kwiatkowski, Patrick Lewis, Yuxiang Wu, Heinrich Küttler, Linqing Liu, Pasquale Minervini, Pontus Stenetorp, Sebastian Riedel, Sohee Yang, Minjoon Seo, Gautier Izacard, Fabio Petroni, Lucas Hosseini, Nicola De Cao, Edouard Grave, Ikuya Yamada, Sonse Shimaoka, Masatoshi Suzuki, Shumpei Miyawaki, Shun Sato, Ryo Takahashi, Jun Suzuki, Martin Fajcik, Martin Docekal, Karel Ondrej, Pavel Smrz, Hao Cheng, Yelong Shen, Xiaodong Liu, Pengcheng He, Weizhu Chen, Jianfeng Gao, Barlas Oguz, Xilun Chen, Vladimir Karpukhin, Stan Peshterliev, Dmytro Okhonko, Michael Schlichtkrull, Sonal Gupta, Yashar Mehdad, and Wen-tau Yih. 2021. NeurIPS 2020 EfficientQA competition: Systems, analyses and lessons learned. In *Proceedings of the NeurIPS 2020 Competition and Demonstration Track*, volume 133 of *Proceedings of Machine Learning Research*, pages 86–111. PMLR.

Margaret Mitchell, Simone Wu, Andrew Zaldivar, Parker Barnes, Lucy Vasserman, Ben Hutchinson, Elena Spitzer, Inioluwa Deborah Raji, and Timnit Gebru. 2019. Model cards for model reporting. In *Proceedings of the Conference on Fairness, Accountability, and Transparency*, FAT* '19, page 220–229, New York, NY, USA. Association for Computing Machinery.

Anton Obukhov, Maximilian Seitzer, Po-Wei Wu, Semen Zhydenko, Jonathan Kyl, and Elvis Yu-Jing Lin. 2020. High-fidelity performance metrics for generative models in PyTorch. Version: 0.3.0, DOI: 10.5281/zenodo.4957738.

Joao Palotti, Harrisen Scells, and Guido Zuccon. 2019. Trectools: an open-source Python library for information retrieval practitioners involved in TREC-like campaigns. SIGIR'19. ACM.

Kishore Papineni, Salim Roukos, Todd Ward, and Wei-Jing Zhu. 2002. BLEU: a method for automatic evaluation of machine translation. In *Proceedings of the 40th annual meeting of the Association for Computational Linguistics*, pages 311–318.

Adam Paszke, Sam Gross, Francisco Massa, Adam Lerer, James Bradbury, Gregory Chanan, Trevor Killeen, Zeming Lin, Natalia Gimelshein, Luca Antiga, et al. 2019. Pytorch: An imperative style, high-performance deep learning library. *Advances in neural information processing systems*, 32.

Adrien Pavao, Isabelle Guyon, Anne-Catherine Letournel, Xavier Baró, Hugo Escalante, Sergio Escalera,

Tyler Thomas, and Zhen Xu. 2022. *CodaLab Competitions: An open source platform to organize scientific challenges*. Ph.D. thesis, Université Paris-Saclay, France.

Fabian Pedregosa, Gaël Varoquaux, Alexandre Gramfort, Vincent Michel, Bertrand Thirion, Olivier Grisel, Mathieu Blondel, Peter Prettenhofer, Ron Weiss, Vincent Dubourg, et al. 2011. Scikit-learn: Machine learning in Python. *the Journal of machine Learning research*, 12:2825–2830.

Joelle Pineau, Philippe Vincent-Lamarre, Koustuv Sinha, Vincent Larivière, Alina Beygelzimer, Florence d'Alché Buc, Emily Fox, and Hugo Larochelle. 2021. Improving reproducibility in machine learning research: a report from the NeurIPS 2019 reproducibility program. *Journal of Machine Learning Research*, 22.

Matt Post. 2018. A call for clarity in reporting BLEU scores. *arXiv preprint arXiv:1804.08771*.

Rebecca Qian, Candace Ross, Jude Fernandes, Eric Smith, Douwe Kiela, and Adina Williams. 2022. Perturbation augmentation for fairer NLP. *arXiv preprint arXiv:2205.12586*.

Edward Raff. 2019. A step toward quantifying independently reproducible machine learning research. *Advances in Neural Information Processing Systems*, 32.

Inioluwa Deborah Raji, Emily M Bender, Amandalynne Paullada, Emily Denton, and Alex Hanna. 2021. AI and the everything in the whole wide world benchmark. *arXiv preprint arXiv:2111.15366*.

Vijay Janapa Reddi, Christine Cheng, David Kanter, Peter Mattson, Guenther Schmuelling, Carole-Jean Wu, Brian Anderson, Maximilien Breughe, Mark Charlebois, William Chou, Ramesh Chukka, Cody Coleman, Sam Davis, Pan Deng, Greg Diamos, Jared Duke, Dave Fick, J. Scott Gardner, Itay Hubara, Sachin Idgunji, Thomas B. Jablin, Jeff Jiao, Tom St. John, Pankaj Kanwar, David Lee, Jeffery Liao, Anton Lokhmotov, Francisco Massa, Peng Meng, Paulius Micikevicius, Colin Osborne, Gennady Pekhimenko, Arun Tejusve Raghunath Rajan, Dilip Sequeira, Ashish Sirasao, Fei Sun, Hanlin Tang, Michael Thomson, Frank Wei, Ephrem Wu, Lingjie Xu, Koichi Yamada, Bing Yu, George Yuan, Aaron Zhong, Peizhao Zhang, and Yuchen Zhou. 2020. MLPerf Inference Benchmark. *ISCA*.

Skipper Seabold and Josef Perktold. 2010. statsmodels: Econometric and statistical modeling with python. In *9th Python in Science Conference*.

Stefan Van der Walt, Johannes L Schönberger, Juan Nunez-Iglesias, François Boulogne, Joshua D Warner, Neil Yager, Emmanuelle Gouillart, and Tony Yu. 2014. scikit-image: image processing in python. *PeerJ*, 2:e453.

Pauli Virtanen, Ralf Gommers, Travis E Oliphant, Matt Haberland, Tyler Reddy, David Cournapeau, Evgeni Burovski, Pearu Peterson, Warren Weckesser, Jonathan Bright, et al. 2020. Scipy 1.0: fundamental algorithms for scientific computing in python. *Nature methods*, 17(3):261–272.

Alex Wang, Yada Pruksachatkun, Nikita Nangia, Amanpreet Singh, Julian Michael, Felix Hill, Omer Levy, and Samuel Bowman. 2019. SuperGLUE: A stickier benchmark for general-purpose language understanding systems. *Advances in neural information processing systems*, 32.

Alex Wang, Amanpreet Singh, Julian Michael, Felix Hill, Omer Levy, and Samuel R Bowman. 2018. GLUE: A multi-task benchmark and analysis platform for natural language understanding. *arXiv preprint arXiv:1804.07461*.

Deshraj Yadav, Rishabh Jain, Harsh Agrawal, Prithvijit Chattopadhyay, Taranjeet Singh, Akash Jain, Shiv Baran Singh, Stefan Lee, and Dhruv Batra. 2019. EvalAI: Towards Better Evaluation Systems for AI Agents. *arXiv preprint arXiv:1902.03570*.

Weizhe Yuan, Graham Neubig, and Pengfei Liu. 2021. Bartscore: Evaluating generated text as text generation. In *Advances in Neural Information Processing Systems*, volume 34, pages 27263–27277. Curran Associates, Inc.

KeywordScape: Visual Document Exploration using Contextualized Keyword Embeddings

Henrik Voigt[1], Monique Meuschke[3], Sina Zarrieß[2] and Kai Lawonn[1]
[1]University of Jena [2]University of Bielefeld [3]University of Magdeburg
[1]first.last@uni-jena.de
[2]first.last@uni-bielefeld.de
[3]last@isg.cs.uni-magdeburg.de

Abstract

Although contextualized word embeddings have led to great improvements in automatic language understanding, their potential for practical applications in document exploration and visualization has been little explored. Common visualization techniques used for, e.g., model analysis usually provide simple scatter plots of token-level embeddings that do not provide insight into their contextual use. In this work, we propose KeywordScape, a visual exploration tool that allows users to overview, summarize, and explore the semantic content of documents based on their keywords. While existing keyword-based exploration tools assume that keywords have static meanings, our tool represents keywords in terms of their contextualized embeddings. Our application visualizes these embeddings in a semantic landscape that represents keywords as islands on a spherical map. This keeps keywords with similar context close to each other, allowing for a more precise search and comparison of documents.

1 Introduction

Recent work in Natural Language Processing (NLP) has brought great advances in the contextual modeling of word meanings in texts (Peters et al., 2018; Devlin et al., 2019; Radford et al., 2019). When it comes to visualizing the meaning contained in a collection of documents, keywords still play an important role (El-Assady et al., 2020; Ji et al., 2017; Kim et al., 2017). Keyword-based methods have a number of advantages because they are intuitive and easy to visualize, for example, in a bar chart showing the frequency of a keyword over different years in a document collection. However, one of the major limitations in existing approaches is that it assumes that a keyword has a static meaning across different texts and domains. This assumption is highly unrealistic (Schütze, 1998; Navigli, 2009). A term like *training* means something quite different in the context of *machine learning* than in *psychology*.

There are tools for visualizing document collections at different levels of granularity. To get an overview of a set of texts, it is often beneficial to use visualizations that group texts on a high level according to their overarching meaning, also called *topic*. This is done by John et al. (2019); Kim et al. (2017); Dang and Nguyen (2018); Le and Akoglu (2019), e.g. to distinguish scientific texts on the topic of *machine learning* visually from texts from the field of *psychology*. To find documents that match a semantic query, e.g., a list of related keywords such as *learning, curriculum, pre-training*, low-level document exploration is required. Here, users must evaluate the meaning of specific paragraphs, sentences, and keywords in a given context. Current visual document exploration systems do not use contextualized neural representations and rely on topic models or frequency-based keyword clustering techniques (Wang et al., 2014; Ganesan et al., 2015; Kim et al., 2017; Yang et al., 2017; Ji et al., 2019; John et al., 2019). These allow high-level comparison of documents but are unable to distinguish content based on low-level semantic meaning.

In this work, we propose KeywordScape, a tool that visualizes keywords in their semantic contexts as islands on a map to support meaning-driven document exploration. This makes it possible to explore the potential of contextualized word embeddings for visual document exploration by exploiting their strengths for disambiguation.

In the following, we clarify how our work fits into the current research context. We demonstrate the applicability of contextualized keywords in a visualization system architecture, explain the user interactions it supports, and show its application in use cases that solve real-world problems. The main contributions of this paper include:

- Provision of a novel method for visualizing

Proceedings of the The 2022 Conference on Empirical Methods in Natural Language Processing: System Demonstrations, pages 137 - 147

contextualized keyword embeddings as visual islands.

- Design and implementation of a meaning-preserving visual document exploration system.

2 Related Work

Visualization of text has been explored extensively in the VIS community. This section refers to related work in the sub-field of visual document exploration, reviewing relevant methods and ideas for visualizing document collections. Furthermore, we show how recent developments in the field of NLP, and in particular neural word embeddings, feed into these solutions.

2.1 Visual Document Exploration

Visual exploration of documents is a well-researched task (Heimerl et al., 2016; Mitra and Craswell, 2017; Zhang et al., 2018; John et al., 2018; Han et al., 2018). The most frequently studied methods can be categorized into visual topic modeling (Dou et al., 2013; Kucher et al., 2018a; John et al., 2019; Kim et al., 2017; Dang and Nguyen, 2018; Le and Akoglu, 2019), visual information retrieval (Koch et al., 2014; Kraker et al., 2016; Heimerl et al., 2016; Dias et al., 2019) and visual sentiment analysis (Dai and Prout, 2016; Martins et al., 2017; Kucher et al., 2018b, 2020). Visual topic modeling is most closely related to our approach. A topic model generally aims to extract groups of keywords as coherent topics and assign the documents in the collection to these topics. Visual topic modeling supports the exploration of these topic models by visually representing the extracted topics and making them interactive. A large proportion of current applications for visual topic modeling such as VISTopic (Yang et al., 2017), LDAExplore (Ganesan et al., 2015) or TopEx (Olex et al., 2021) in their NLP pipelines is based on methods like LDA (Blei et al., 2003), LSA (Deerwester et al., 1990) or HDP (Wang et al., 2011). The visualization pipeline relies on clustering algorithms like K-Means (Kanungo et al., 2002) or dimensionality reduction methods like PCA (F.R.S.), t-SNE (Maaten and Hinton, 2008), or UMAP (McInnes et al., 2018).

2.2 Neural Embedding Visualization

Visualizations of static neural word embeddings are used to explore document spaces (Berger et al., 2017; Ji et al., 2017, 2019) sentiment spaces (Dai and Prout, 2016; Martins et al., 2017; Kucher et al., 2020) or concept spaces (Park et al., 2018; Heimerl and Gleicher, 2018). Depending on how the visual models are constructed, the approaches can be divided into neural embedding visualizations (Mitra and Craswell, 2017; Chen et al., 2018; Li et al., 2018) and interactive human-in-the-loop applications (El-Assady et al., 2020; Park et al., 2018). In both, the idea of representing individual word tokens in a condensed form that captures their semantic meaning is applied. The high-dimensional representations are reduced to a lower dimension and visualized with colored dots or icons as visual metaphors for individual words or documents (Smilkov et al., 2016; El-Assady et al., 2020). Complete static embedding spaces are visualized in Li et al. (2016); Chen et al. (2018); Molino et al. (2019). Liu et al. (2018) visually investigate the semantic relations in embedding spaces of static word2vec (Mikolov et al., 2013) and GloVe (Pennington et al., 2014) embeddings. Our work differs from this in that, unlike in the methods presented above, the contextual embedding spaces are not a fixed set and dynamically new embeddings are created for each token in the respective document based on its occurrence in the context.

3 KeywordScape System

We propose a system architecture shown in Figure 1 consisting of a **NLP Pipeline** and a **Visualization Pipeline**. The first parses the documents into a map of contextualized representations based on BERT (Devlin et al., 2019) and UMAP (McInnes et al., 2018). The second is responsible for the visualization and is based on the D3 library (Bostock et al., 2011), the HTML canvas element for rendering, and SVG for additional data manipulation and information display. For a video demonstration of the system, visit `https://youtu.be/6jaF7HiPzTk`.

3.1 NLP Pipeline

3.1.1 Text Processing

Parsing. Each document of the collected set is parsed into a text string. The free library science-parse from AllenAI (sci) is used. For each document *title*, the *authors*, the *year* of publication, the *abstract*, and the *text* of the document are extracted.
Cleaning. After parsing the documents into text strings, the text is broken down into word tokens

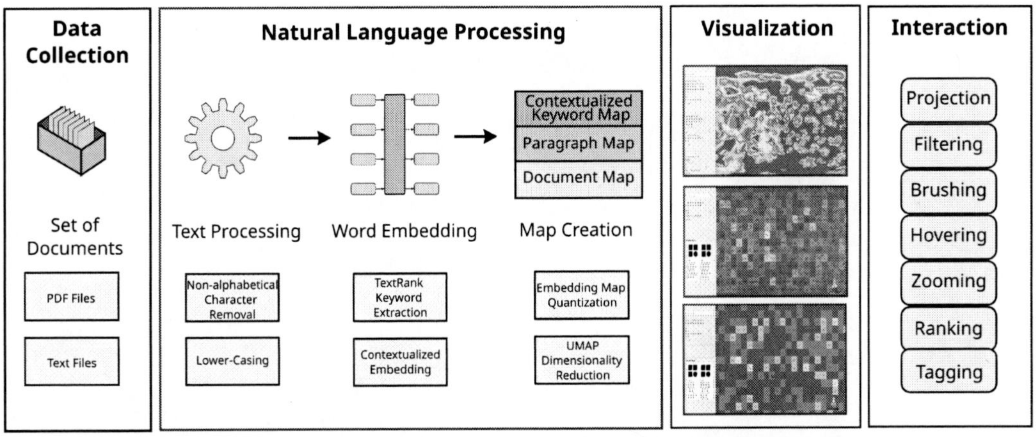

Figure 1: The KeywordScape System Architecture. Within the **NLP Pipeline**, the document collection is preprocessed, keywords are extracted and embedded alongside documents and paragraphs. The high-dimensional representations are projected onto a unit sphere and forwarded to the **Visualization Pipeline**. Here, maps of different granularity can be switched and explored with a variety of interaction techniques.

using the SpaCy library (spa). A cleaning procedure is applied to filter out all non-lexical tokens.

Paragraphing. The document is divided into paragraphs with a size of 512 tokens or less. This corresponds to the encodable context width of the BERT model (Devlin et al., 2019).

Keyword Extraction. A set of N different keywords is determined by a user-selected extraction method, either TextRank (Mihalcea and Tarau, 2004), RAKE (Rose et al., 2010), or TF-IDF (Ramos, 2003). A single document is thus visually represented by the semantic coverage of its most relevant N contextualized keywords. In order to be consistent across the collection and to adapt to the respective document size, the number of keywords is calculated individually for each document. To achieve this, the user determines what percentage $p\%$ of words in a document are treated as keywords. For our visualizations, we set the keyword percentage p per document to 5%.

3.1.2 Word Embedding

For each document, each paragraph is passed to the BERT model and the embedding vector of the last layer of all tokens with dimension 768 is extracted. All word embeddings that do not belong to keywords are removed. If a keyword is composed of subword embeddings, the average embedding is used. This results in a contextualized representation of each keyword based on the paragraph in which it occurs. Unlike methods with pure keyword extraction, this provides a fine-grained representation of meaning. Each of the contextualized keyword embeddings is labeled by its lemmatized word form to reduce unnecessary variance and facilitate navigation in the visualization.

3.1.3 Map Creation

Map Granularity. Three maps are created to enable iterative exploration of document collections at different levels of semantic granularity. The first map is a **document map** that creates a single representation for each document by using a SentenceBERT embedding of its abstract (Reimers and Gurevych, 2019). The second map is a **paragraph map** that applies the same technique to all paragraphs in the corpus. The third map is a **contextualized keyword map**, which is the focus of this work and will therefore be explained in more detail in the following subsections.

Dimensional Reduction. The contextually embedded keyword vectors are reduced to a lower, plottable dimension using the UMAP algorithm (McInnes et al., 2018; uma). A unit sphere is used as the reduction space, which allows points to be treated as [lat, lon] expressions. Reducing the points to the surface of a unit sphere has the advantage that all embeddings are mapped relative to all other embeddings on the sphere. This offers a smooth visual exploration of the keyword landscape.

Quantization. To avoid overlapping points in the visual map and to make the number of points manageable for the browser-internal visualization pipeline, the unit sphere is quantized into elementary quadrilaterals, each of which represents all

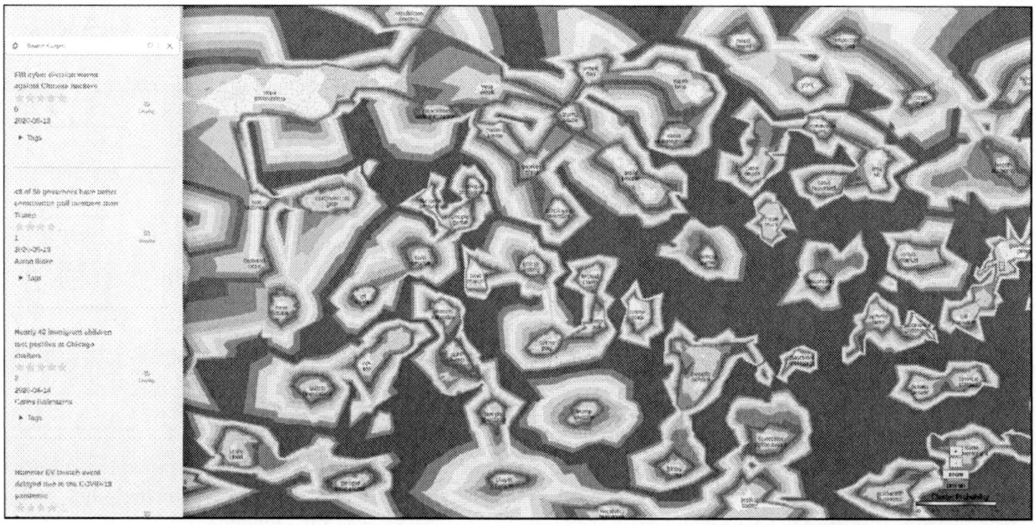

Figure 2: Overview of the KeywordScape interface. *Left:* Search interface that allows users to search for documents in the collection. *Right:* Map visualization of keyword islands of the ReCOVery corpus with interaction bar.

points contained in its area. The minimum side length of a quadrilateral is 0.1 degrees. With the help of this quantization, the approach can be scaled up to 250 documents using a keyword percentage of 5%. This ensures a fast construction of the map in the browser and enables fluid interaction.

3.2 Visualization Pipeline

3.2.1 Document Map and Paragraph Map

The document map and paragraph map were created with the aim of allowing users to iteratively refine the granularity of the context of interest during visual exploration. The document map provides an overview of the collection. Each document is represented as a single point on the unit sphere that positions semantically similar document embeddings close to each other. As a visual metaphor for a coherent semantic region, labeled and coloured grid cells are used as an adaptation of the visualization technique *heatmap*. The unit sphere is divided into a grid of user-defined size. For each grid cell, the most frequently occurring keywords in it are displayed adaptive to the zoom level. The cells are coloured according to the density of dots in each cell. The higher the density of dots in a cell, the lighter the colour. In this way, document clusters can be quickly identified, and at the same time, one gets an idea of the most important keywords in these clusters. The paragraph map shows the distribution of paragraph embeddings over the entire unit sphere. Similar to the document map, a coloured grid with adaptive labeling is used. The map makes it possible to find topics covered in individual paragraphs, allowing for a more detailed examination than at the document level.

3.2.2 Contextualized Keyword Map

The contextualized keyword map (see Figure 2) is the focus of this work and enables a visual keyword search that takes into account the semantic meaning of the individual keywords. The embedding points in [lat, lon] of the contextualized keyword map are projected onto a *geoequirectangular* map projection. The geo-voronoi microlibrary (geo) of D3 is used to create a Delaunay triangulation of the points on the sphere. A Voronoi map is calculated from this triangulation. Each Voronoi region represents a set of quantized word points in the space of the semantic map. The visual metaphor of the sea and *visual islands* is used to represent a keyword context. Islands represent clusters of keywords that occur together in the same context. To determine the visual islands, an HDBSCAN (McInnes et al., 2017) clustering is applied to the Voronoi map, which assigns a cluster probability to each Voronoi region with respect to the cluster probability of its center. Cluster probability is the basis for colour coding, in that higher probabilities encode a darker, land-like colour and lower probabilities encode a blue, sea-like colour, resulting in the creation of *visual islands*. The positions of the islands in relation to each other on the map represent their semantic

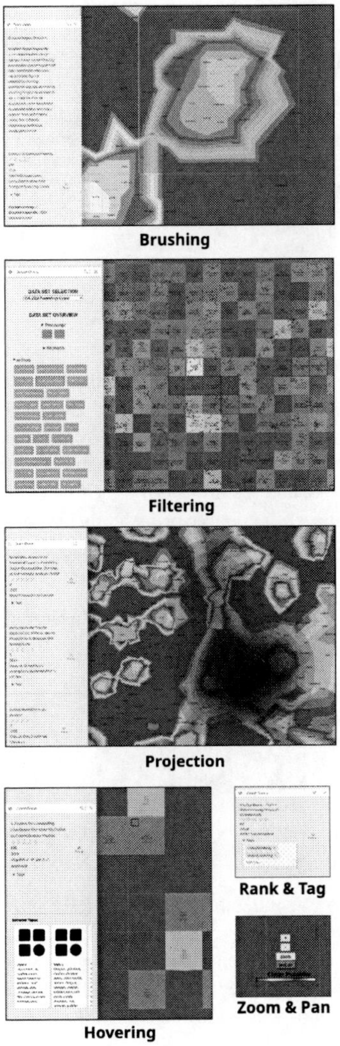

Figure 3: The main interaction techniques *projection, filtering, brushing, hovering, rank & tag, zoom & pan* within the KeywordScape interaction loop.

distance. The labels of the keywords in a visual island represent the keywords with the highest frequency in the respective Voronoi region.

4 User Interaction

KeywordScape offers a number of interaction techniques, which are illustrated in Figure 3 and explained below:

Projections. To create a projection a search query in form of a set of keywords is translated into a selection of embedding points. From the resulting set of points, a contour map is interpolated based on the density of the selected points in each region of the map. The contour map is then projected onto the contextualized keyword map. This makes it possible to visualize a user's search similar to rain showers on a weather map, as shown in Figure 3.

Filtering. Filtering is used in combination with the projection function. The user can define queries to the system either via the text-based search or via predefined query selectors such as *timestamps, keywords, authors, star ratings*, or *tags*. The query is then translated into a projection condition and a visual expression of the query is projected onto the map so that the user can visually understand where within the semantic landscape of the document collection the query applies. For example, if the user selects a particular author as a query selector, all documents that the author has contributed to the corpus are filtered out, their keywords extracted and projected onto the KeywordScape. With the help of this view, the user can easily see which semantic regions the author mainly focuses on.

Zooming. A filtered semantic map generates regions of interest that can be examined in detail using the zoom function. Zooming in combination with adaptive region labeling makes it possible to examine the keywords of a context island with increasing granularity.

Brushing. Brushing highlights a specific area of interest to find the documents with keywords in that area. Visual islands characterized by a collection of keywords occurring in the same context are made visually tangible in this way and the documents containing these contexts are listed. An application of the brushing feature is shown in Figure 3.

Ranking. Ranking allows the corpus to be adapted to personal interests. Users award stars in a range from 0-5, making it possible to quickly filter out personally relevant documents, e.g. as support when writing a survey paper.

Tagging. Assigning tags to the documents allows quick access to document sets. This can be combined with the projection function to visualize the map coverage of several selected documents. In addition, tagging and projection are used to visually compare documents by dividing them into different tag groups and projecting the similarities as well as the differences of the two tag groups against each other, as shown in Figure 5.

Hovering. The hovering interaction is applied to the document map and the paragraph map. The tool displays the corresponding document in the search bar when the mouse pointer hovers over its representation in the map. When clicked, a de-

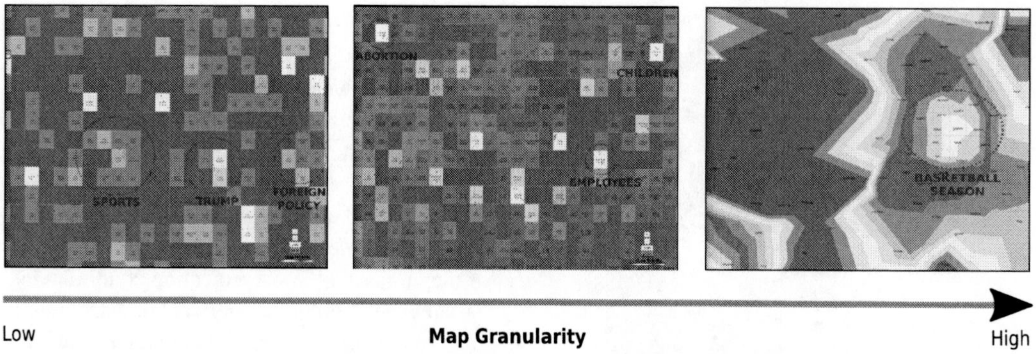

Figure 4: *Document, paragraph, and contextualized keyword map* of the ReCOVery corpus showing the semantic content of newspaper articles during the COVID-19 pandemic at different levels of granularity. Left: The *document map* allows users to identify documents with a similar main topic such as *sports, trump*, or *foreign policy*. Center: The *paragraph map* highlights more specific contexts below the document level, such as women suffering from *abortions* caused by COVID-19 infections, the situation of *employees*, and the impact of the COVID-19 pandemic on *children*. Right: The *contextualized keyword map* focuses on fine-grained keyword islands like the *basketball season*.

tailed document preview is displayed, containing meta-information such as *title*, *author*, *date* of publication as well as the most important *keywords* of the document and its *abstract*. The interaction techniques are evaluated in a user study. For a detailed description, please refer to the appendix A.

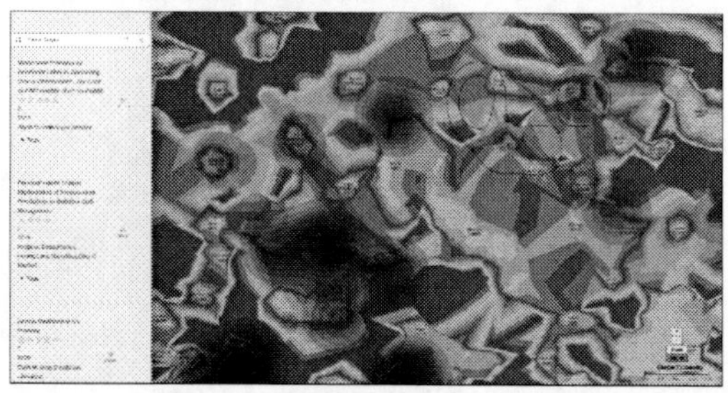

Figure 5: Visualization of *similarities* and *differences* of documents with regard to their keywords in context. Cividis coloured contours show regions where the contents of the documents overlap, black outlined contours show regions where the contents of the documents differ from each other.

5 Use Cases

We apply the KeywordScape tool to two different document data sets. To show the applicability of the tool for everyday use, e.g., to get an overview of the content of news articles, we visualize the **reliable** sources of the *ReCOVery Corpus* of Zhou et al. (2020) in Section 5.1. These include newspaper articles from trusted news outlets. To illustrate the tool's ability to decompose the semantic occurrence of keywords into different contexts, we visualize the *food.com* data set from Majumder et al. (2019), which is used to generate personalized recipes from user preferences in Section 5.2.

5.1 Newspaper Articles

We visualize 250 newspaper articles from trusted news outlets of the ReCOVery corpus (Zhou et al., 2020). The document map provides an overview of the main topics covered in the articles, such as *sports, foreign policy*, or *trump* (see Figure 4). In particular, sources related to *trump* appear to have high coverage. At the paragraph level, it is particularly interesting that the context of *abortion* as a problem of women struggling with a COVID-19 infection is mentioned in many paragraphs. A user with only a document-level visualization might not have been able to detect this because the contexts in which this subject is discussed are hidden behind the larger topic of the article. Using the contextualized keyword map, specific contexts in the semantic region of *sports* can be explored. For example, articles debating the progress of the *basketball season* can be found by brushing their contextualized keywords in the associated context island, as shown in Figure 4. The ability to examine keywords in relation to their meaning in context proves particularly useful for high-interest terms such as *trump*. A large number of articles use the polarizing keyword to attract interested users. A decomposition into the individual contexts in which it occurs, e.g. *vaccine* or *china*, would not be possible with a conventional keyword search, because the meaning of the word

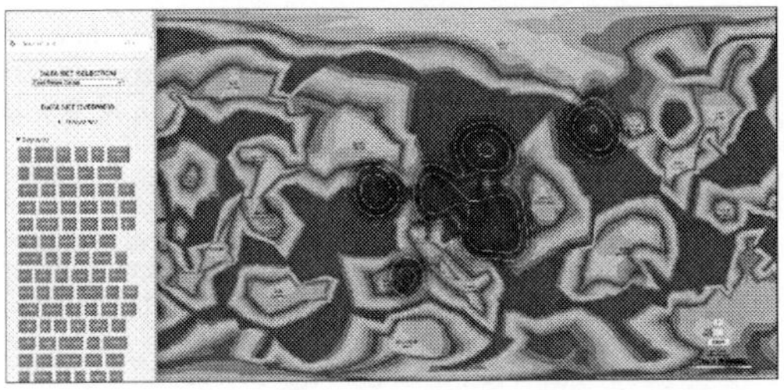

Figure 6: Contextualized keyword map of food recipes from the *food.com* data set. *Contours* outline the density of the keyword *cheese* within the different contexts of the map.

is not taken into account with these methods.

5.2 Food Recipes

We visualize 1500 recipes from the *food.com* data set (Majumder et al., 2019). Recipes, by their very nature, consist of several ingredients that are combined into one dish. An example question for recipe exploration could be: In which cooking contexts are certain ingredients used together? A conventional keyword search for the ingredient *cheese* would give us all the recipes that use cheese, no matter what the context. By projecting the keyword *cheese* onto the contextualized keyword map, as shown in Figure 6, a nice decomposition of the different cooking contexts in which cheese is used becomes visible. Obviously, *cheese* is very popularly used in a cooking context with *macaroni*, as in the dish *Mac'n'Cheese*. It also makes frequent appearances in *burger* recipes. Some *cheeses*, such as *cream cheese*, are used in the context of baking recipes. This shows the appearance of the keyword near the visual island of the main keyword *cake*. Others occur near the *bread* island in connection with the production of *sandwiches*. Also, it is very interesting to see that on the right side below, a small amount of cheese is used along with chili. By brushing the region it turns out that it covers *tacos* with *chili* and *cheese* dip.

6 Conclusion

In this paper, we introduced KeywordScape, a visualization tool that implements a novel method for visualizing contextualized keyword embeddings as visual islands. The tool takes advantage of the benefits that contextualized word embeddings bring in contrast to static word embeddings by applying them in a visually searchable contextualized keyword map - a KeywordScape. We implemented a system architecture based on a BERT transformer language model and its ability to represent word meanings. We explained the interaction capabilities that the visualization application provides to the user and illustrated its usability in real-world use cases. Our results show that viewing the meaning of keywords in context leads to new and interesting insights into the document collection, as exemplified by newspapers or cooking recipes.

Acknowledgements

We thank the Michael Stifel Center Jena for funding this work, which is part of the Carl Zeiss Foundation-funded project 'A Virtual Workshop for Digitization in the Sciences' (062017-02).

References

d3-geo-voronoi. `https://github.com/Fil/d3-geo-voronoi`. Accessed: 2021-06-01.

science-parse. `https://github.com/allenai/science-parse`. Accessed: 2021-06-01.

spacy. `https://github.com/explosion/spaCy`. Accessed: 2021-06-01.

umap. `https://github.com/lmcinnes/umap`. Accessed: 2021-06-01.

M. Berger, Katherine McDonough, and Lee M. Seversky. 2017. cite2vec: Citation-driven document exploration via word embeddings. *IEEE Transactions on Visualization and Computer Graphics*, 23:691–700.

D. Blei, A. Ng, and Michael I. Jordan. 2003. Latent dirichlet allocation. *J. Mach. Learn. Res.*, 3:993–1022.

M. Bostock, Vadim Ogievetsky, and J. Heer. 2011. D³ data-driven documents. *IEEE Transactions on Visualization and Computer Graphics*, 17:2301–2309.

Juntian Chen, Yubo Tao, and Hai Lin. 2018. Visual exploration and comparison of word embeddings. *J. Vis. Lang. Comput.*, 48:178–186.

X. Dai and Robert Prout. 2016. Unlocking super bowl insights: Weighted word embeddings for twitter sentiment classification. *Proceedings of the The 3rd Multidisciplinary International Social Networks Conference on SocialInformatics 2016, Data Science 2016.*

T. Dang and V. Nguyen. 2018. Commodeler: Topic modeling using community detection. In *EuroVA@EuroVis*.

S. Deerwester, S. Dumais, G. Furnas, T. Landauer, and R. Harshman. 1990. Indexing by latent semantic analysis. *Journal of the Association for Information Science and Technology*, 41:391–407.

J. Devlin, Ming-Wei Chang, Kenton Lee, and Kristina Toutanova. 2019. Bert: Pre-training of deep bidirectional transformers for language understanding. In *NAACL-HLT*.

Amanda Gonçalves Dias, E. Milios, and M. C. F. Oliveira. 2019. Trivir: A visualization system to support document retrieval with high recall. *Proceedings of the ACM Symposium on Document Engineering 2019*.

Wenwen Dou, L. Yu, X. Wang, Z. Ma, and W. Ribarsky. 2013. Hierarchicaltopics: Visually exploring large text collections using topic hierarchies. *IEEE Transactions on Visualization and Computer Graphics*, 19:2002–2011.

Mennatallah El-Assady, Rebecca Kehlbeck, C. Collins, D. Keim, and O. Deussen. 2020. Semantic concept spaces: Guided topic model refinement using word-embedding projections. *IEEE Transactions on Visualization and Computer Graphics*, 26:1001–1011.

Karl Pearson F.R.S. Liii. on lines and planes of closest fit to systems of points in space. *Philosophical Magazine Series 1*, 2:559–572.

Ashwinkumar Ganesan, Kianté Brantley, Shimei Pan, and Jian Jhen Chen. 2015. Ldaexplore: Visualizing topic models generated using latent dirichlet allocation. *ArXiv*, abs/1507.06593.

Q. Han, M. John, S. Koch, Ivan Assenov, and T. Ertl. 2018. Labeltransfer - integrating static and dynamic label representation for focus+context text exploration. *2018 International Symposium on Big Data Visual and Immersive Analytics (BDVA)*, pages 1–8.

Florian Heimerl and M. Gleicher. 2018. Interactive analysis of word vector embeddings. *Computer Graphics Forum*, 37.

Florian Heimerl, M. John, Q. Han, S. Koch, and T. Ertl. 2016. Docucompass: Effective exploration of document landscapes. *2016 IEEE Conference on Visual Analytics Science and Technology (VAST)*, pages 11–20.

Xiaonan Ji, R. Machiraju, Alan Ritter, and P. Yen. 2017. Visualizing article similarities via sparsified article network and map projection for systematic reviews. *Studies in health technology and informatics*, 245:422–426.

Xiaonan Ji, H. Shen, Alan Ritter, R. Machiraju, and P. Yen. 2019. Visual exploration of neural document embedding in information retrieval: Semantics and feature selection. *IEEE Transactions on Visualization and Computer Graphics*, 25:2181–2192.

M. John, Florian Heimerl, Ba-Anh Vu, and T. Ertl. 2018. Visual analysis and exploration of entity relations in document collections. In *VISIGRAPP*.

M. John, K. Kurzhals, and T. Ertl. 2019. Visual exploration of topics in multimedia news corpora. *2019 23rd International Conference Information Visualisation (IV)*, pages 241–248.

T. Kanungo, D. M. Mount, N. Netanyahu, C. D. Piatko, R. Silverman, and A. Wu. 2002. An efficient k-means clustering algorithm: Analysis and implementation. *IEEE Trans. Pattern Anal. Mach. Intell.*, 24:881–892.

Minjeong Kim, Kyeongpil Kang, Deok Gun Park, J. Choo, and N. Elmqvist. 2017. Topiclens: Efficient multi-level visual topic exploration of large-scale document collections. *IEEE Transactions on Visualization and Computer Graphics*, 23:151–160.

S. Koch, M. John, M. Wörner, A. Müller, and T. Ertl. 2014. Varifocalreader — in-depth visual analysis of large text documents. *IEEE Transactions on Visualization and Computer Graphics*, 20:1723–1732.

Peter Kraker, Christopher Kittel, and Asura Enkhbayar. 2016. Open knowledge maps: Creating a visual interface to the world's scientific knowledge based on natural language processing.

K. Kucher, R. Martins, C. Paradis, and A. Kerren. 2020. Stancevis prime: visual analysis of sentiment and stance in social media texts. *J. Vis.*, 23:1015–1034.

K. Kucher, Rafael M. Martins, and A. Kerren. 2018a. Analysis of vinci 2009-2017 proceedings. *Proceedings of the 11th International Symposium on Visual Information Communication and Interaction*.

K. Kucher, C. Paradis, and A. Kerren. 2018b. Visual analysis of sentiment and stance in social media texts. In *EuroVis*.

Tuan Manh Le and Leman Akoglu. 2019. Contravis: Contrastive and visual topic modeling for comparing document collections. *The World Wide Web Conference*.

Jiwei Li, Xinlei Chen, Eduard H. Hovy, and Dan Jurafsky. 2016. Visualizing and understanding neural models in nlp. In *HLT-NAACL*.

Q. Li, Kristanto Sean Njotoprawiro, H. Haleem, Qiaoan Chen, Chris Yi, and Xiaojuan Ma. 2018. Embeddingvis: A visual analytics approach to comparative network embedding inspection. *2018 IEEE Conference on Visual Analytics Science and Technology (VAST)*, pages 48–59.

Shusen Liu, Peer-Timo Bremer, Jayaraman J. Thiagarajan, Vivek Srikumar, Bei Wang, Yarden Livnat, and Valerio Pascucci. 2018. Visual exploration of semantic relationships in neural word embeddings. *IEEE Transactions on Visualization and Computer Graphics*, 24:553–562.

L. V. D. Maaten and Geoffrey E. Hinton. 2008. Visualizing data using t-sne. *Journal of Machine Learning Research*, 9:2579–2605.

Bodhisattwa Prasad Majumder, Shuyang Li, Jianmo Ni, and Julian McAuley. 2019. Generating personalized recipes from historical user preferences. *arXiv preprint arXiv:1909.00105*.

R. M. Martins, Vasiliki Simaki, K. Kucher, C. Paradis, and A. Kerren. 2017. Stancexplore: Visualization for the interactive exploration of stance in social media.

L. McInnes, J. Healy, and J. Melville. 2018. UMAP: Uniform Manifold Approximation and Projection for Dimension Reduction. *ArXiv e-prints*.

L. McInnes, John Healy, and S. Astels. 2017. hdbscan: Hierarchical density based clustering. *J. Open Source Softw.*, 2:205.

R. Mihalcea and P. Tarau. 2004. Textrank: Bringing order into text. In *EMNLP*.

Tomas Mikolov, Ilya Sutskever, Kai Chen, Greg S Corrado, and Jeff Dean. 2013. Distributed representations of words and phrases and their compositionality. In *Advances in neural information processing systems*, pages 3111–3119.

Bhaskar Mitra and Nick Craswell. 2017. Neural text embeddings for information retrieval. *Proceedings of the Tenth ACM International Conference on Web Search and Data Mining*.

Piero Molino, Yang Wang, and Jiawei Zhang. 2019. Parallax: Visualizing and understanding the semantics of embedding spaces via algebraic formulae. In *ACL*.

Roberto Navigli. 2009. Word sense disambiguation: A survey. *ACM computing surveys (CSUR)*, 41(2):1–69.

Amy L. Olex, Evan French, Peter Burdette, Srilakshmi Sagiraju, Thomas Neumann, Tamas S. Gal, and Bridget T. McInnes. 2021. Topex: Topic exploration of covid-19 corpora.

Deok Gun Park, Seungyeon Kim, Jurim Lee, Jaegul Choo, Nicholas A. Diakopoulos, and Niklas Elmqvist. 2018. Conceptvector: Text visual analytics via interactive lexicon building using word embedding. *IEEE Transactions on Visualization and Computer Graphics*, 24:361–370.

Jeffrey Pennington, R. Socher, and Christopher D. Manning. 2014. Glove: Global vectors for word representation. In *EMNLP*.

Matthew E. Peters, Mark Neumann, Mohit Iyyer, Matt Gardner, Christopher Clark, Kenton Lee, and Luke Zettlemoyer. 2018. Deep contextualized word representations. In *NAACL-HLT*.

A. Radford, Jeffrey Wu, R. Child, David Luan, Dario Amodei, and Ilya Sutskever. 2019. Language models are unsupervised multitask learners.

J. Ramos. 2003. Using tf-idf to determine word relevance in document queries.

Nils Reimers and Iryna Gurevych. 2019. Sentence-bert: Sentence embeddings using siamese bert-networks. In *EMNLP/IJCNLP*.

S. Rose, D. Engel, Nick Cramer, and W. Cowley. 2010. Automatic keyword extraction from individual documents.

Hinrich Schütze. 1998. Automatic word sense discrimination. *Computational linguistics*, 24(1):97–123.

Daniel Smilkov, Nikhil Thorat, Charles Nicholson, Emily Reif, F. Viégas, and M. Wattenberg. 2016. Embedding projector: Interactive visualization and interpretation of embeddings. *ArXiv*, abs/1611.05469.

C. Wang, John W. Paisley, and D. Blei. 2011. Online variational inference for the hierarchical dirichlet process. In *AISTATS*.

X. Wang, Shixia Liu, Junlin Liu, Jianfei Chen, J. Zhu, and B. Guo. 2014. Topicpanorama: A full picture of relevant topics. *IEEE Transactions on Visualization and Computer Graphics*, 22:2508–2521.

Yi Yang, Quanming Yao, and H. Qu. 2017. Vistopic: A visual analytics system for making sense of large document collections using hierarchical topic modeling. *Vis. Informatics*, 1:40–47.

Jiawei Zhang, C. Surakitbanharn, N. Elmqvist, R. Maciejewski, C. Qian, and D. Ebert. 2018. Topotext: Context-preserving text data exploration across multiple spatial scales. *Proceedings of the 2018 CHI Conference on Human Factors in Computing Systems*.

Xinyi Zhou, Apurva Mulay, Emilio Ferrara, and Reza Zafarani. 2020. Recovery: A multimodal repository for covid-19 news credibility research. In *Proceedings of the 29th ACM International Conference on Information and Knowledge Management (CIKM '20)*.

A User Evaluation

We evaluated the tool using an active **user study** on the KeywordScape system and collected qualitative and quantitative feedback. The quantitative evaluation was intended to determine the usability and user acceptance of the system. From the qualitative feedback, the top **five** criticisms were extracted and considered as feature requests in the next iteration of the system improvement.

A.1 User Study

The user study was conducted with 24 individuals with scientific backgrounds (54.2% male, 45.8% female). The basic idea was to find out if and how the *KeywordScape* tool supports scientists in their daily research work, which includes examining numerous documents. 45.5% of participants were doctoral students, 29.2% were master's students, 8.3% were postdocs, 12.5% were college professors, and 4.2% were business professionals with an academic background. 29.2% of respondents were under 25 years old, 20.9% were between 25 and 30, and 49.9% were over 30. Study participants' areas of expertise were in Visualization (59.1%), Natural Language Processing (22.7%), Computer Vision, Machine Learning, Augmented Reality (4.5% each), and 4.5% of individuals with other areas of expertise. 29.2% had less than three years of experience in their field, 50% between three and six years, and 20.8% more than six years.

A.1.1 Study Setup

The user study was divided into two parts. To familiarize users with the tool and its use, **six interactive tasks T** had to be solved and participants were asked to rate how difficult on a five-point Likert scale it was to solve each task using the tool. In the second part, users were presented with a **questionnaire** with pictures and statements showing scenes from using the tool. Users were asked to rate the extent to which they agreed with the statements on a five-point Likert scale, based on their previous experience of actively using the tool.

A.1.2 Results

The results of the first part showed positive interaction experiences with the tool, as shown in Figure 7.

T1 was to assess how easy it was to find the grid cell with the highest number of documents in a

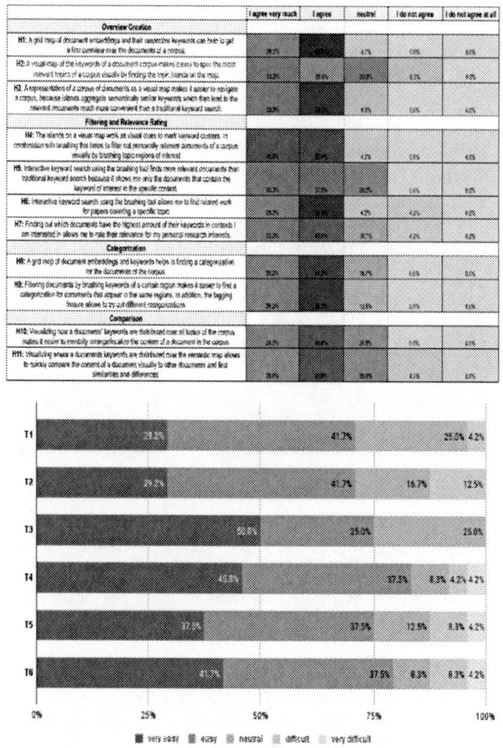

Figure 7: *Top:* The extent to which users agree or disagree with a set of hypotheses **after** completing a series of tasks. *Bottom:* How easy/difficult users consider it to be to perform a particular task.

document map. 70.9% of respondents indicated that this was easy or very easy to achieve with the tool, confirming that the overview map is easy to navigate.

T2 consisted of opening the *contextualized keyword map* and finding a keyword island of personal interest and then zooming into that island to find out more about the specific keyword context. 70.9% of respondents agreed that this was easy to do, 16.7% answered neutral, and 12.5% answered difficult.

T3 was to use the brush tool in the map to filter out the works that cover a particular region and rank those works by personal interest. 75% answered easy or very easy and 25% neutral.

T4 was creating tag groups and adding documents to a corresponding group, which 83.3% rated as easy or very easy.

T5 and T6 was to create a union and an intersection of the created tag groups, which between 75% (union) and 79.2% (intersection) of participants found easy or very easy to achieve.

In the **second part**, users were asked to assess their agreement with **11 hypotheses** stated in relation to the tool's ability to support document *overview generation, relevance estimation, categorization*, and visual document *comparison*. The agreement scores indicate the extent to which the tool can support users in solving these visualization tasks using the interaction capabilities discussed in section 4. The following summarizes user feedback on each exploration task. The results can be seen in Figure 7.

Overview Creation. The majority (95.9%) of respondents agreed that the tool helps to get an overview of relevant topics and that a visual map makes it easier to navigate a large corpus of documents.
Relevance Estimation. Over 90% of participants agreed that the brushing feature makes it easier to find personally relevant documents by outlining contextual areas in a visual map. 70.8% agreed that contextualized keyword search with the brushing tool finds more relevant documents than traditional keyword search, which uses only the number of keywords (without any context).
Categorization. 83.4% agreed that a *document map* helps to find a categorization for the documents in a document collection. 87.5% agreed that brushing regions of a *keyword map* in combination with tagging helps to find a meaningful categorization for the documents in a collection.
Comparison. In terms of document comparability, 70.8% indicated that visualizing the distribution of keywords across the contexts of a document collection allows for quick visual comparison of documents to each other. In addition, 75.0% of respondents agreed that visualizing the distribution of keywords in a document across the semantic landscape facilitates mental retrieval of an individual document within the corpus.

Qualitative Feedback. After assessing the hypotheses, participants were asked to provide qualitative feedback on their main criticisms of the system. From this, the five most frequent points of criticism were extracted:

- performance optimization
- additional keyword projection on grid map
- color legend integration
- additional brushing functionality for papers in the grid map
- BibTeX export

Based on this qualitative feedback, we created feature requests and implemented the desired improvements in response to feedback from the user evaluation. All of the above ideas can now be achieved with the KeywordScape system.

MedConQA: Medical Conversational Question Answering System based on Knowledge Graphs

Fei Xia[1,2]*, Bin Li[3]*, Yixuan Weng[1]*, Shizhu He[1,2]†, Kang Liu[1,2], Bin Sun[3], Shutao Li[3]†, Jun Zhao[1,2]

[1] National Laboratory of Pattern Recognition, Institute of Automation, CAS
[2] School of Artificial Intelligence, University of Chinese Academy of Sciences
[3] College of Electrical and Information Engineering, Hunan University
xiafei2020@ia.ac.cn, wengsyx@gmail.com,
{libincn, shutao_li, sunbin611}@hnu.edu.cn, {shizhu.he, kliu, jzhao}@nlpr.ia.ac.cn

Abstract

The medical conversational system can relieve doctors' burden and improve healthcare efficiency, especially during the COVID-19 pandemic. However, the existing medical dialogue systems have the problems of **weak scalability**, **insufficient knowledge**, and **poor controllability**. Thus, we propose a medical conversational question-answering (CQA) system based on the knowledge graph, namely MedConQA, which is designed as a pipeline framework to maintain high flexibility. Our system utilizes automated medical procedures, including medical triage, consultation, image-text drug recommendation, and record. Each module has been open-sourced as a tool[1], which can be used alone or in combination, with robust scalability. Besides, to conduct knowledge-grounded dialogues with users, we first construct a **C**hinese **M**edical **K**nowledge **G**raph (CMKG) and collect a large-scale **C**hinese **M**edical **CQA** (CM-CQA) dataset, and we design a series of methods for reasoning more intellectually. Finally, we use several state-of-the-art (SOTA) techniques to keep the final generated response more controllable, which is further assured by hospital and professional evaluations. We have open-sourced related code, datasets, web pages, and tools, hoping to advance future research.

1 Introduction

Conversational question answering (CQA) system is an emerging research topic, it is the natural evolution of the traditional question answering (QA) paradigm (Gao et al., 2018; Ghazarian et al., 2021), allowing more natural conversational interactions between users and the systems (Zaib et al., 2021). CQA can improve the users' experience by providing conversational interaction (Zhou et al., 2021). It can be applied to many scenarios such as electricity business (Meng et al., 2021), medical healthcare (Liu et al., 2021b; Li et al., 2022), and personal assistants (Uğurlu et al., 2020), etc.

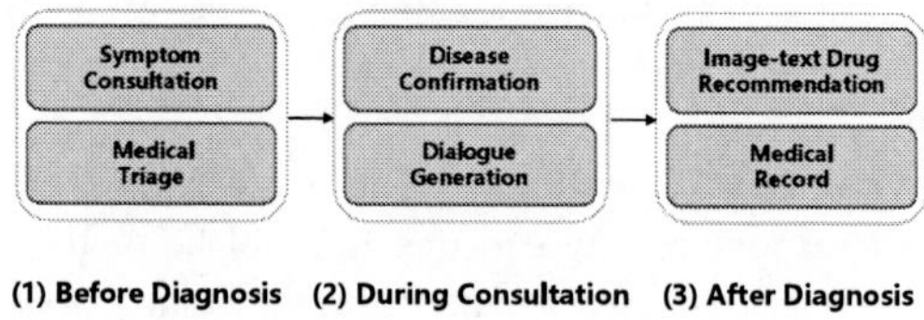

Figure 1: Main processes of the MedConQA.

With the pandemic of the COVID-19, it is significant for building the medical CQA system, which is advantageous to improving the efficiency of medical services and reducing the burden on doctors with broad application prospects (Palanica et al., 2019). Recently, related medical service applications have become more and more popular, such as identifying symptoms (Zheng et al., 2017), automatic diagnosis (Moreira et al., 2019; Wang et al., 2021b) and medical recommendations (Wu et al., 2021), etc. However, there are three problems with existing applications: a) Most applications only have a single reply function and are difficult to scale. b) Many rule-based medical QA systems (Weizenbaum, 1966) are monotonous and lack sufficient expertise. Although products (Zhang et al., 2017b; Cui et al., 2017; Levy et al., 2021) have responded based on knowledge in recent years, there is still much room for improvement in the full use of knowledge and the quality of generated responses. c) Due to the medical industry's high safety requirements, ensuring a safe and controllable response is also a significant challenge.

In this paper, we present a medical conversational question answering system with knowledge graphs, namely MedConQA, which is designed in a pipeline manner for high flexibility. As shown in Figure 1, it presents three main processes in our system: before diagnosis, during the consultation, and after diagnosis. The before diagnosis phase consists of the symptom consultation and

* These authors contribute this work equally.
† Corresponding authors.
[1]`https://github.com/WENGSYX/LingYi`

Proceedings of the The 2022 Conference on Empirical Methods in Natural Language Processing: System Demonstrations, pages 148 - 158
December 7-11, 2022 ©2022 Association for Computational Linguistics

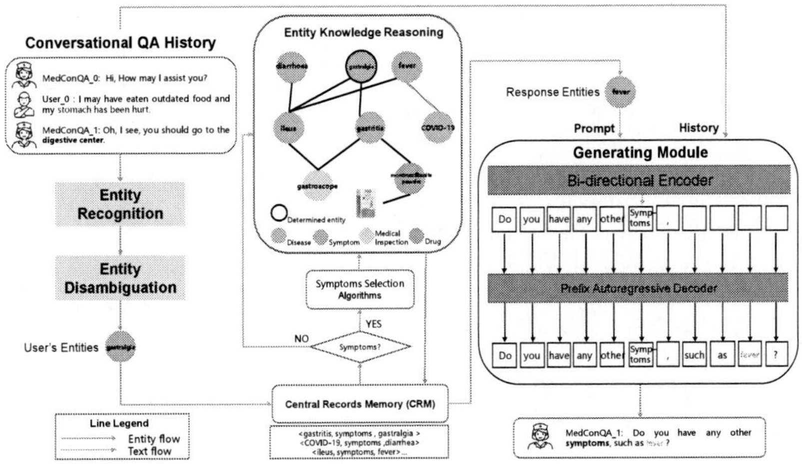

Figure 2: An example of the process of generating responses in a conversation of our system.

medical triage. The consultation phase includes disease confirmation and dialoguage generation. The after-diagnosis phase focuses on image-text recommendation and medical record summary. In summary, MedConQA provides users with natural conversational QA services, which is relatively rare (Wang et al., 2021b) but more meaningful (Liu et al., 2020a).

MedConQA has the following highlights:

1. MedConQA implements a pipelined manner for automating medical procedures, alleviating the problems of weak scalability, insufficient knowledge, and poor controllability of the current medical dialogue system.
2. Multiple modules such as medical triage, consultation, image-text drug recommendation, and record are integrated into MedConQA, where each module is open-sourced as the auxiliary tool for further study.
3. MedConQA integrates several advanced technologies such as medical entity disambiguation and response generation, where the effect of each technology is reported. It is competitive compared with other state-of-the-art (SOTA) medical dialogue systems on both automated and human evaluations.

MedConQA aims at providing automated medical services for the majority of users[2]. Preliminary experiments have been performed in the Xiangya Hospital of Central South University (Changsha, China), which demonstrates the research prospects and practical applications of the proposed system.

[2]System online demonstrations: https://med.wengsyx.com/ for Chinese version, https://med.wengsyx.com/lyxz_en/ for English version.

2 System Description

The Figure 2 overviews the main framework of our proposed system, and the whole process includes: 1) **Symptom consultation and triage**: MedConQA conducts medical triage for users by consulting and collecting symptoms, in which entity recognition and disambiguation further improve triage accuracy. 2) **Disease confirmation**: MedConQA confirms disease through the dynamic symptom selection algorithm and CRM and further derives the corresponding entities that need to be used later. 3) **Dialogue generation**: MedConQA combines the previously obtained entities as the prompt for the generation module to get the generated response. 4) Others: MedConQA also contains other functional modules, including image-text recommendation and medical record modules, which can be flexibly expanded and combined.

2.1 Entity Disambiguation Module

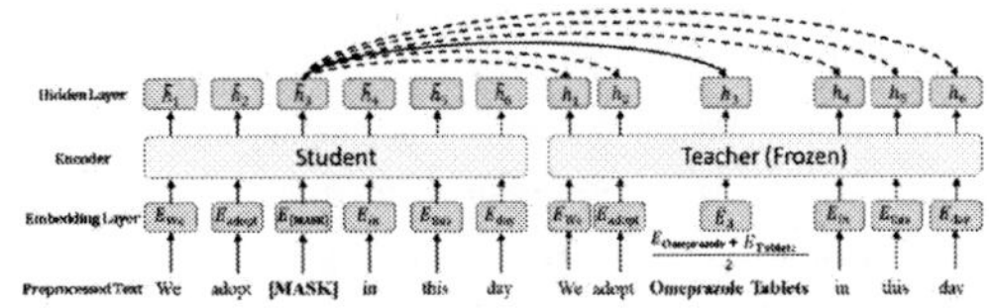

Figure 3: Contrastive pre-training in medical entity disambiguation.

In this section, we introduce the entity disambiguation module, which is consisted of technologies of the named entity recognition and contrastive pre-training. As for the named entity recognition, we implement the method (Sarker et al., 2019) for recognizing the medical entities in the utterance. We achieve the accuracy of 91.07% in the simple medical entity recognition dataset of the IFLYTK[3], which ranks top-3 of the competition. After obtaining the entities, the entity disambiguation with contrastive learning is performed, which is shown in Figure 3. We introduce the contrastive pre-training framework with Smedbert (Zhang et al., 2021a) for medical entity disambiguation, which is our champion scheme in SDU@AAAI-22-Shared Task2 Acronym Disambiguation[4]. Specifically, we design a contrastive pre-training method that enhances the model's generalization ability by learning the medical phrase-level contrastive distributions between true meaning and ambiguous phrases (Li et al., 2021; Weng et al., 2021). During the pre-training, we cover up the student model's medical entities, then make the student model output closer to the meaning of the teacher model, and away from other unrelated medical entities. Both models initialize the same parameters, where the parameters of the teacher model are frozen. For the masking of these medical entities, we adopt the expert medical dictionary THUOCL (Han et al., 2016) for experiments. After entities are obtained, we adopt the pre-trained model for matching the recognized entities and medical entities in the knowledge graph. Finally, we map the ambiguitive phrases into the entities in the knowledge graph.

2.2 Medical Triage

We implement the triage function with the Smedbert (Zhang et al., 2021a) model, which is fine-tuned in medical entity triage data provided by IFlytek[5]. The final results can achieve the F1 values of 90.37% for medical triage classification (See Experimental Details in Section B.1). Finally, we apply this method to our medical triage module.

2.3 Central Records Memory

Central Record Memory (CRM) has storage and reasoning functions, and it is mainly composed of data formats in the form of a dictionary of entity triples. First, the CRM maps the medical entities

[3]http://challenge.xfyun.cn/topic/info?type=medical-entity

[4]https://sites.google.com/view/sdu-aaai22/shared-task

[5]http://challenge.xfyun.cn/topic/info?type=disease-claims

Algorithm 1 Dymamic Symptom Selection

Require: A known user symptoms KS; A Chinese medical knowledge graph KG, The attributes in KG contain $KG.symptoms$ and $KG.diseases$.
Ensure: *Symptoms* of this round of inquiry

```
Cand ← { }
for diseases ∈ KG.diseases do
    if KS = disease.symptoms then
        return diseases
    end if
    if KS ⊆ disease.symptoms then
        Cand append symptoms
    end if
end for
for s ∈ Cand do
    if len(s) ≤ len(∀Cand) then
        break
    end if
end for
Symptoms ← s.symptoms - KS
return Symptoms
```

obtained in the disambiguation module to specific attributes on the knowledge graph, and stores the past entities into the dictionary. In the next round of dialogue conversation, CRM will not only map the entities of the current round on the graph but also update the current state. The information of the entities on the current round is appended into the new dictionary again. After that, the CRM will send the entities obtained by the knowledge graph inference into the generation module for further sentence generation.

2.4 Symptoms Selection Algorithm

In order to reduce the redundant asking rounds as much as possible and ensure the accurate diagnosis of the disease, we designed a symptom selection algorithm based on dynamic programming to solve the optimization problem without recursively solving all sub-problems in turn and avoiding unnecessary calculations. As shown in the Algorithm 1, we regard each round of consultation as a sub-question to be judged, that is, we only need to select the symptom in the current state that can rule out the most diseases at one time. We traverse all the diseases in the knowledge graph, and if the intersection of the symptoms of the disease and the symptoms of the user is not an empty set, it will be added to the list of suspected diseases. Once

Dataset	Domain	Entity	Symptom	Dialogue
COVID-19-CN (Yang et al., 2020)	COVID-19	/	/	/
MedDG (Liu et al., 2020b)	Gastroenterology	160	12	17864
Chunyu (Lin et al., 2020)	/	5682	15	12842
MedDialog-CN (Zeng et al., 2020)	29 Departments	/	172	**3407494**
M^2 MedDialog (Wang et al., 2021a)	40 Departments	4728	843	95408
CMCQA(Ours)	**45 Departments**	**33615**	**8808**	1294753

Table 1: Statistics of the CMCQA compared with other datasets.

Name	Symptom	Check	Drug	Food	Img
Num	8808	3353	17318	366	3770

Table 2: Statistics of entities in CMKG

Method	Pre.	Rec.	F1
RoBERTa (Liu et al., 2019)	83.14	74.77	78.32
hdBERT (Zhong et al., 2021)	88.21	85.44	86.23
BERT-MT (Pan et al., 2021)	90.11	87.04	89.07
Ours	**92.03**	**90.21**	**91.07**

Table 3: F1 performance in entity disambiguation (%).

the symptoms of all suspected diseases are counted, the symptom with the most frequent occurrences will be found and the symptom can be judged as the output symptom. When disease reasoning is required, the CRM will perform this algorithm until the final state of the user's disease is confirmed.

2.5 Entity Knowledge Reasoning

As for the entity knowledge reasoning, MedConQA will strictly abide by the actual consultation process (Ha and Longnecker, 2010). The first stage is symptom reasoning, the second stage is examination reasoning, and the third stage is drug reasoning. Our system will initially conduct repeated symptom consultations with users to ensure that the system sends complete user symptom entities to the CRM. After this, MedConQA will synthesize all symptoms entities from the CRM, reasoning on the basis of related entities in our CMKG to get the user's medical examination. Finally, if the user continues to consult with the drug for the treatment of the disease, MedConQA will perform drug recommendations with the corresponding images based on CMKG which is shown in Table 2, so that the user can obtain convenient and right suggestions. In order to avoid misdiagnosis, in the symptom reasoning stage, the MedConQA system will ask the user about the symptoms in a "diagnosed" style until the user's disease is confirmed.

2.6 Generating Module

We adopt the method of entity prompt learning for training and prediction (Liu et al., 2021a). More precisely, we append the reasoned entity input with the conversational QA history, forming a prompt for response generation. Moreover, we design the prefix template for auto-regressive decoding. Specifically, we manually design templates of different reasoning processes described in the section 2.5 to further increase the controllability of the generated responses. In this way, we use the prompt and prefix method to fuse the context information with the reasoned entities from CRM. As a result, the generated response will be the condition on the prompt and prefix, so as to improve the factual accuracy and controllability of the model.

2.7 Other Function Modules

2.7.1 Image-text Drug Reommendation

We utilize the CMKG dataset and implement medical knowledge entity reasoning, linking drug entities to corresponding images to achieve image-text drug recommendations. It will be helpful for users to find drug information more easily.

2.7.2 Medical Record

The last module is the medical record. In order to make it easier for users to conduct secondary treatment more conveniently and quickly, MedConQA will write a medical record from the whole conversation after users finish the consultation. Specifically, we process the unstructured conversations history information based on the CPT (Shao et al., 2021) model to generate the key summarization of the user's condition from this consultation. At the same time, this module will also process structured information stored in central records memory, such as department, examinations, drugs, and other information. Finally, two kinds of information are integrated through post-processing splicing to generate the user's medical record (Experimental Results Shown in Section B.2).

Model	CCKS A				CCKS B			
	Avg.	F1	BLEU	Dist.	Avg.	F1	BLEU	Dist.
GPT2-Entity (Liu et al., 2020b)	13.43	25.75	7.30	7.23	12.41	24.41	5.81	7.01
HERD-Entity (Liu et al., 2020b)	13.85	26.42	7.37	7.75	13.11	25.11	6.61	7.61
BertGPT-Entity (Lewis et al., 2019)	13.79	26.57	7.03	7.78	13.69	26.74	6.66	7.69
CPM2-prompt (Zhang et al., 2021b)	15.21	26.38	10.04	9.21	15.76	27.10	10.78	9.41
Ours	**17.73**	**30.24**	**12.55**	**10.42**	**18.21**	**30.59**	**13.13**	**10.91**

Table 4: Performance of different methods in both CCKS-A and CCKS-B test sets (%).

Model	Sentence Fluency	Knowledge Correctness	Entire Quality
GPT2-Entity (Liu et al., 2020b)	3.22	3.12	3.17
HERD-Entity (Liu et al., 2020b)	3.83	3.77	3.74
BertGPT-Entity (Lewis et al., 2019)	3.71	3.78	3.82
CPM2-prompt (Zhang et al., 2021b)	4.10	4.17	4.15
Ours	**4.14**	**4.20**	**4.19**
Golden Response	4.77	4.83	4.81
κ	0.54	0.57	0.58

Table 5: Results of human evaluation, where κ is the average pairwise Cohen's kappa score between annotators.

3 Experimental Details

3.1 Data Description

CMCQA[6] is a huge conversational question-and-answer data set for the Chinese medical field, where the statistics of medical conversation datasets is shown in Table 1. It is collected from the Chinese medical conversational question answering website ChunYu[7], and has medical conversational materials in 45 departments, such as andrology, stormotology, gynaecology, and obstetrics. Specifically, CMCQA has 1.3 million complete sessions or 19.83 million statements or 0.65 billion tokens. At the same time, we further open source all data to promote the development of related fields of conversational question answering in the medical field.

CMKG[8] is collected from open-sourced knowledge graphs. We have processed the data crawled from the website, and then sorted it into the form of tables. For example, for the symptom of stomachache, the "disease" attributes include "gastritis", "gastric cancer", "gastric ulcer" and other diseases. The "examination" attributes include "gastroscopy" and "pathological biopsy of gastric mucosa", etc. After that, we search and link the entities in the knowledge graphs in Bing image database[9]. After the completion of the construction, the authors manually correct it again, eliminate about 20% of the obvious error information, and then submit it to the expert doctors for final verification to ensure the accuracy of the knowledge graphs.

3.2 Implementation

We train the model based on the Pytorch (Paszke et al., 2019) and use the hugging-face (Wolf et al., 2020) framework. All the finetuned models are implemented in the collected medical corpus[10]. During training, we employ the AdamW optimizer (Loshchilov and Hutter, 2017). The learning rate is set to 1e-5 with the warm-up (He et al., 2016). Four 3090 GPUs are used for all experiments.

3.3 Evaluation Setting

To ensure correct medical entity information and fluent responses, we provide automatic and human evaluations accordingly. As for the effects of other modules and the total system, we also present detailed results (See Appendix B). Specifically, we conduct experiments entity disambiguation dataset of SDU@AAAI 2021[11] and medical dialogue generation dataset of the CCKS[12]. We adopt the evaluation metrics, including the F1, BLEU (Papineni et al., 2002), and Dist. (Li et al., 2016) scores. The F1 score reflects the correctness of medical entity knowledge. The BLEU score reflects the relativity of the generated responses. The Dist. score represents the diversity of the generated sentences. We further prepare the human evaluation for randomly picking 100 cases from the test dataset. Each generated sentence is scored by three independent

[6]https://github.com/WENGSYX/CMCQA
[7]https://www.chunyuyisheng.com/
[8]https://github.com/WENGSYX/CMKG
[9]https://Bing.com/image

[10]https://github.com/Lireanstar/Medical-Dialogue-Corpus
[11]https://sites.google.com/view/sdu-aaai22/home
[12]https://www.biendata.xyz/competition/ccks_2021_mdg/

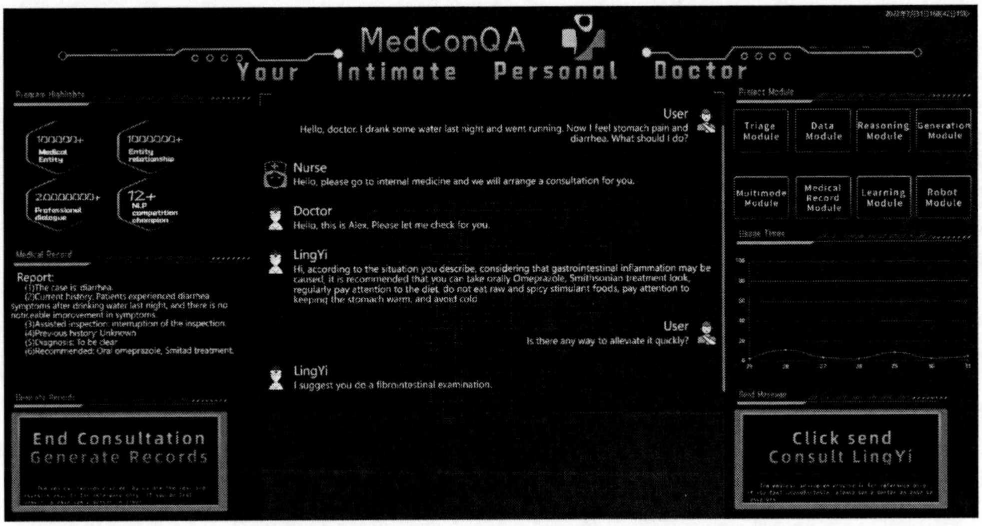

Figure 4: Snapshot of the proposed MedConQA system.

persons with a medical background. We adopt the same human evaluation metrics as the work (Liu et al., 2020b). The rating scale for each metric ranges from 1 to 5, where 1 represents the worst and 5 the best.

3.4 Results

The experimental results of medical entity disambiguation are shown in Table 3. It can be seen that our results achieve the best results compared to other SOTA methods. Meanwhile, we also conducted related evaluations on the test dataset, which is shown in Table 4. As is shown from the table, our method achieves the best results against recent strong baselines and leads in accuracy, relevance and diversity. We provide a human evaluation to further judge the performance between different methods. As shown in Table 5, our method achieves competitiveness in human evaluation compared to other SOTA methods. It is noted that there is still a long way from the generated responses to the real responses of people. Moreover, the average pairwise Cohen's kappa (Randolph, 2005) scores between annotators range between 0.4 and 0.6 for all metrics, which represents a moderate annotator agreement.

4 Application

We present the application of MedConQA at the website, where the snapshot are shown in Figure 4. Figure 4 shows that if the user says that he is sick in his stomach, the system will get the entity "gastralgia" from the entity disambiguation module. Afterward, it will obtain the entity "gastritis" from the knowledge graphs through entity knowledge reasoning. The reasoned entity is sent to the generating module for further recommending the user to do a diagnosis in the hospital. Finally, if a user needs an urgent drug, the system will recommend the proper drug through the knowledge graphs. A medical record will be generated after the consultation, which will significantly facilitate the user's secondary treatment[13].

5 Conclusion

In this paper, we have analyzed three existing medical dialogue systems' problems: weak scalability, insufficient knowledge, and poor controllability. Therefore, we proposed MedConQA, a medical conversational question answering system based on knowledge graphs. Our system integrated and open-sourced multiple modules for everyone to use freely, including medical triage, consultation, image-text drug recommendation, and record. Many of these technologies have achieved SOTA performance. Besides, for the professionalism and knowledge of the system, we have open-sourced and leveraged the CMKG and CMCQA datasets. Finally, we adopted several advanced techniques for the more controllable generated responses, which are further assured by hospital and professional evaluations.

[13]Medical conversational QA demo: `https://www.youtube.com/watch?v=fsFnbim5hWc`

Acknowledgements

This work is supported by the National Key Research and Development Program of China (No. 2020AAA0106400), the National Natural Science Foundation of China (No. 62171183, 61976211), the Science Fund for Creative Research Groups of the National Natural Science Foundation of China under Grant 62221002, and the Key Research Program of the Chinese Academy of Sciences (Grant NO.ZDBS-SSW-JSC006). This research work was also supported by the independent research project of National Laboratory of Pattern Recognition and the Youth Innovation Promotion Association CAS, and by the Hunan Provincial Natural Science Foundation of China (2022JJ20017).

References

Lei Cui, Shaohan Huang, Furu Wei, Chuanqi Tan, Chaoqun Duan, and Ming Zhou. 2017. SuperAgent: A customer service chatbot for E-commerce websites. In *Proceedings of ACL 2017, System Demonstrations*, pages 97–102, Vancouver, Canada. Association for Computational Linguistics.

Jianfeng Gao, Michel Galley, and Lihong Li. 2018. Neural approaches to conversational ai. In *The 41st International ACM SIGIR Conference on Research & Development in Information Retrieval*, pages 1371–1374.

Sarik Ghazarian, Zixi Liu, Tuhin Chakrabarty, Xuezhe Ma, Aram Galstyan, and Nanyun Peng. 2021. DiSCoL: Toward engaging dialogue systems through conversational line guided response generation. In *Proceedings of the 2021 Conference of the North American Chapter of the Association for Computational Linguistics: Human Language Technologies: Demonstrations*, pages 26–34, Online. Association for Computational Linguistics.

Jennifer Fong Ha and Nancy Longnecker. 2010. Doctor-patient communication: a review. *Ochsner Journal*, 10(1):38–43.

Shiyi Han, Yuhui Zhang, Yunshan Ma, Cunchao Tu, Zhipeng Guo, Zhiyuan Liu, and Maosong Sun. 2016. Thuocl: Tsinghua open chinese lexicon. *Tsinghua University*.

Kaiming He, Xiangyu Zhang, Shaoqing Ren, and Jian Sun. 2016. Deep residual learning for image recognition. In *2016 IEEE Conference on Computer Vision and Pattern Recognition (CVPR)*, pages 770–778.

Sharon Levy, Kevin Mo, Wenhan Xiong, and William Yang Wang. 2021. Open-Domain question-Answering for COVID-19 and other emergent domains. In *Proceedings of the 2021 Conference on Empirical Methods in Natural Language Processing: System Demonstrations*, pages 259–266, Online and Punta Cana, Dominican Republic. Association for Computational Linguistics.

Mike Lewis, Yinhan Liu, Naman Goyal, Marjan Ghazvininejad, Abdelrahman Mohamed, Omer Levy, Ves Stoyanov, and Luke Zettlemoyer. 2019. Bart: Denoising sequence-to-sequence pre-training for natural language generation, translation, and comprehension. *arXiv preprint arXiv:1910.13461*.

Bin Li, Bin Sun, Shutao Li, Encheng Chen, Hongru Liu, Yixuan Weng, Yongping Bai, and Meiling Hu. 2022. Distinct but correct: Generating diversified and entity-revised medical response. *SCIENCE CHINA Information Sciences*.

Bin Li, Fei Xia, Yixuan Weng, Xiusheng Huang, Bin Sun, and Shutao Li. 2021. Simclad: A simple framework for contrastive learning of acronym disambiguation. *arXiv preprint arXiv:2111.14306*.

Jiwei Li, Michel Galley, Chris Brockett, Jianfeng Gao, and William B Dolan. 2016. A diversity-promoting objective function for neural conversation models. In *Proceedings of the 2016 Conference of the North American Chapter of the Association for Computational Linguistics: Human Language Technologies*, pages 110–119.

Chin-Yew Lin and Eduard Hovy. 2002. Manual and automatic evaluation of summaries. In *Proceedings of the ACL-02 Workshop on Automatic Summarization*, pages 45–51.

Shuai Lin, Pan Zhou, Xiaodan Liang, Jianheng Tang, Ruihui Zhao, Ziliang Chen, and Liang Lin. 2020. Graph-evolving meta-learning for low-resource medical dialogue generation.

Pengfei Liu, Weizhe Yuan, Jinlan Fu, Zhengbao Jiang, Hiroaki Hayashi, and Graham Neubig. 2021a. Pretrain, prompt, and predict: A systematic survey of prompting methods in natural language processing. *arXiv preprint arXiv:2107.13586*.

Rong Liu, Yan Rong, and Zhehao Peng. 2020a. A review of medical artificial intelligence. *Global Health Journal*, 4(2):42–45.

Wenge Liu, Jianheng Tang, Xiaodan Liang, and Qingling Cai. 2021b. Heterogeneous graph reasoning for knowledge-grounded medical dialogue system. *Neurocomputing*, 442:260–268.

Wenge Liu, Jianheng Tang, Jinghui Qin, Lin Xu, Zhen Li, and Xiaodan Liang. 2020b. Meddg: A large-scale medical consultation dataset for building medical dialogue system. *arXiv preprint arXiv:2010.07497*.

Yinhan Liu, Myle Ott, Naman Goyal, Jingfei Du, Mandar Joshi, Danqi Chen, Omer Levy, Mike Lewis, Luke Zettlemoyer, and Veselin Stoyanov. 2019. Roberta: A robustly optimized bert pretraining approach. *arXiv preprint arXiv:1907.11692*.

Ilya Loshchilov and Frank Hutter. 2017. Fixing weight decay regularization in adam. *ArXiv*, abs/1711.05101.

Fanqi Meng, Wenhui Wang, and Jingdong Wang. 2021. Research on short text similarity calculation method for power intelligent question answering. *2021 13th International Conference on Computational Intelligence and Communication Networks (CICN)*, pages 91–95.

Mário W.L. Moreira, Joel J.P.C. Rodrigues, Neeraj Kumar, Kashif Saleem, and Igor V. Illin. 2019. Postpartum depression prediction through pregnancy data analysis for emotion-aware smart systems. *Information Fusion*, 47:23–31.

Adam Palanica, Peter Flaschner, Anirudh Thommandram, Michael Li, and Yan Fossat. 2019. Physicians' perceptions of chatbots in health care: Cross-sectional web-based survey. *Journal of Medical Internet Research*, 21.

Chunguang Pan, Bingyan Song, Shengguang Wang, and Zhipeng Luo. 2021. Bert-based acronym disambiguation with multiple training strategies. *arXiv preprint arXiv:2103.00488*.

Kishore Papineni, Salim Roukos, Todd Ward, and Wei-Jing Zhu. 2002. Bleu: a method for automatic evaluation of machine translation. In *Proceedings of the 40th Annual Meeting of the Association for Computational Linguistics*, pages 311–318, Philadelphia, Pennsylvania, USA. Association for Computational Linguistics.

Adam Paszke, Sam Gross, Francisco Massa, Adam Lerer, James Bradbury, Gregory Chanan, Trevor Killeen, Zeming Lin, Natalia Gimelshein, Luca Antiga, Alban Desmaison, Andreas Kopf, Edward Yang, Zachary DeVito, Martin Raison, Alykhan Tejani, Sasank Chilamkurthy, Benoit Steiner, Lu Fang, Junjie Bai, and Soumith Chintala. 2019. Pytorch: An imperative style, high-performance deep learning library. In *Advances in Neural Information Processing Systems*, volume 32. Curran Associates, Inc.

Justus J Randolph. 2005. Free-marginal multirater kappa (multirater k [free]): An alternative to fleiss' fixed-marginal multirater kappa. *Online submission*.

Abeed Sarker, Ari Z Klein, Janet Mee, Polina Harik, and Graciela Gonzalez-Hernandez. 2019. An interpretable natural language processing system for written medical examination assessment. *Journal of biomedical informatics*, 98:103268.

Yunfan Shao, Zhichao Geng, Yitao Liu, Junqi Dai, Fei Yang, Li Zhe, Hujun Bao, and Xipeng Qiu. 2021. Cpt: A pre-trained unbalanced transformer for both chinese language understanding and generation. *arXiv preprint arXiv:2109.05729*.

Yusuf Uğurlu, Murat Karabulut, and İslam Mayda. 2020. A smart virtual assistant answering questions about covid-19. *2020 4th International Symposium on Multidisciplinary Studies and Innovative Technologies (ISMSIT)*, pages 1–6.

Benyou Wang, Qianqian Xie, Jiahuan Pei, Prayag Tiwari, Zhao Li, et al. 2021a. Pre-trained language models in biomedical domain: A systematic survey. *arXiv preprint arXiv:2110.05006*.

Qingyun Wang, Manling Li, Xuan Wang, Nikolaus Parulian, Guangxing Han, Jiawei Ma, Jingxuan Tu, Ying Lin, Ranran Haoran Zhang, Weili Liu, Aabhas Chauhan, Yingjun Guan, Bangzheng Li, Ruisong Li, Xiangchen Song, Yi Fung, Heng Ji, Jiawei Han, Shih-Fu Chang, James Pustejovsky, Jasmine Rah, David Liem, Ahmed ELsayed, Martha Palmer, Clare Voss, Cynthia Schneider, and Boyan Onyshkevych. 2021b. COVID-19 literature knowledge graph construction and drug repurposing report generation. In *Proceedings of the 2021 Conference of the North American Chapter of the Association for Computational Linguistics: Human Language Technologies: Demonstrations*, pages 66–77, Online. Association for Computational Linguistics.

Joseph Weizenbaum. 1966. Eliza—a computer program for the study of natural language communication between man and machine. *Communications of the ACM*, 9(1):36–45.

Yixuan Weng, Fei Xia, Bin Li, Xiusheng Huang, Shizhu He, Kang Liu, and Jun Zhao. 2021. ADBCMM : Acronym disambiguation by building counterfactuals and multilingual mixing. *CoRR*, abs/2112.08991.

Thomas Wolf, Lysandre Debut, Victor Sanh, Julien Chaumond, Clement Delangue, Anthony Moi, Pierric Cistac, Tim Rault, Rémi Louf, Morgan Funtowicz, Joe Davison, Sam Shleifer, Patrick von Platen, Clara Ma, Yacine Jernite, Julien Plu, Canwen Xu, Teven Le Scao, Sylvain Gugger, Mariama Drame, Quentin Lhoest, and Alexander M. Rush. 2020. Transformers: State-of-the-art natural language processing. In *Proceedings of the 2020 Conference on Empirical Methods in Natural Language Processing: System Demonstrations*, pages 38–45, Online. Association for Computational Linguistics.

Eric Wu, Kevin Wu, Roxana Daneshjou, David Ouyang, Daniel E Ho, and James Zou. 2021. How medical ai devices are evaluated: limitations and recommendations from an analysis of fda approvals. *Nature Medicine*, 27(4):582–584.

Wenmian Yang, Guangtao Zeng, Bowen Tan, Zeqian Ju, Subrato Chakravorty, Xuehai He, Shu Chen, Xingyi Yang, Qingyang Wu, Zhou Yu, et al. 2020. On the generation of medical dialogues for covid-19. *arXiv preprint arXiv:2005.05442*.

Munazza Zaib, Wei Emma Zhang, Quan Z. Sheng, Adnan Mahmood, and Yang Zhang. 2021. Conversational question answering: A survey. *ArXiv*, abs/2106.00874.

Guangtao Zeng, Wenmian Yang, Zeqian Ju, Yue Yang, Sicheng Wang, Ruisi Zhang, Meng Zhou, Jiaqi Zeng, Xiangyu Dong, Ruoyu Zhang, Hongchao Fang, Penghui Zhu, Shu Chen, and Pengtao Xie. 2020. MedDialog: Large-scale medical dialogue datasets. In *Proceedings of the 2020 Conference on Empirical Methods in Natural Language Processing (EMNLP)*, pages 9241–9250, Online. Association for Computational Linguistics.

Sheng Zhang, Xin Zhang, Hui Wang, Jiajun Cheng, Pei Li, and Zhaoyun Ding. 2017a. Chinese medical question answer matching using end-to-end character-level multi-scale cnns. *Applied Sciences*, 7(8):767.

Sheng Zhang, Xin Zhang, Hui Wang, Lixiang Guo, and Shanshan Liu. 2018. Multi-scale attentive interaction networks for chinese medical question answer selection. *IEEE Access*, 6:74061–74071.

Taolin Zhang, Zerui Cai, Chengyu Wang, Minghui Qiu, Bite Yang, and Xiaofeng He. 2021a. SMedBERT: A knowledge-enhanced pre-trained language model with structured semantics for medical text mining. In *Proceedings of the 59th Annual Meeting of the Association for Computational Linguistics and the 11th International Joint Conference on Natural Language Processing (Volume 1: Long Papers)*, pages 5882–5893, Online. Association for Computational Linguistics.

Wei-Nan Zhang, Ting Liu, Bing Qin, Yu Zhang, Wanxiang Che, Yanyan Zhao, and Xiao Ding. 2017b. Benben: A Chinese intelligent conversational robot. In *Proceedings of ACL 2017, System Demonstrations*, pages 13–18, Vancouver, Canada. Association for Computational Linguistics.

Zhengyan Zhang, Yuxian Gu, Xu Han, Shengqi Chen, Chaojun Xiao, Zhenbo Sun, Yuan Yao, Fanchao Qi, Jian Guan, Pei Ke, Yanzheng Cai, Guoyang Zeng, Zhixing Tan, Zhiyuan Liu, Minlie Huang, Wentao Han, Yang Liu, Xiaoyan Zhu, and Maosong Sun. 2021b. Cpm-2: Large-scale cost-efficient pre-trained language models.

Tao Zheng, Wei Xie, Liling Xu, Xiaoying He, Ya Zhang, Mingrong You, Gong Yang, and You Chen. 2017. A machine learning-based framework to identify type 2 diabetes through electronic health records. *International Journal of Medical Informatics*, 97:120–127.

Qiwei Zhong, Guanxiong Zeng, Danqing Zhu, Yang Zhang, Wangli Lin, Ben Chen, and Jiayu Tang. 2021. Leveraging domain agnostic and specific knowledge for acronym disambiguation. In *SDU@ AAAI*.

Kun Zhou, Xiaolei Wang, Yuanhang Zhou, Chenzhan Shang, Yuan Cheng, Wayne Xin Zhao, Yaliang Li, and Ji-Rong Wen. 2021. CRSLab: An open-source toolkit for building conversational recommender system. In *Proceedings of the 59th Annual Meeting of the Association for Computational Linguistics and the 11th International Joint Conference on Natural Language Processing: System Demonstrations*, pages 185–193, Online. Association for Computational Linguistics.

A Ethical Considerations

The constructed system aims to generate professional, fluent, and consistent medical responses. We have also realized that due to the adapt of pretrained models that learn with the medical data from the Internet, the proposed approach may produce inappropriate text such as offensive, racially, or gender-sensitive responses. Meanwhile, although the proposed method can cover the stages of before, during, and after the medical treatment, it may also be maliciously exploited, for example, using forged medical reports to fabricate false medical reports.

We have carefully considered the above issues and provided the following detailed explanations: (1) All used medical data is collected from the Internet, and it is inevitable to contain offensive, racially or gender-sensitive doctor-user conversations. Due to the limited space, we briefly describe the characteristics and cleaning rules of the datasets and delete the utterances of doctor-user dialogue that are offensive, racially, or gender-sensitive. The detailed process can be found in the README file on the website `https://github.com/Wengsyx/MedConQA`. (2) The quality of the processed datasets will affect the credibility of the robustness evaluation. Compared with previous works, we adopt four types of criteria to evaluate the credibility of our system, they are: offline index evaluation (BLEU, Distinct, and F1), online users evaluation, dialogue rounds testing, and professional doctor evaluation. We hope to maximize the reliability and implement ability of the system based on such evaluation benchmarks. (3) MedConQA is a medical system with a suggestion nature, which uses knowledge graphs to provide multi-modal medical feedback. Our system may produce incorrect medical results. Therefore, the responses of the system are only for reference. Normal users should not seek medical treatment indiscriminately. (4) Our work does not contain identity information, the doctor only responds to the user's condition, it will not harm anyone, and doesn't invade people's privacy. (5) The medicines recommended by MedConQA are over-the-counter medicines. Users need to consult their doctor for further confirmation when purchasing the drugs for prescription drugs. (6) Our system supports applications on different terminals.

In the future, we will adopt federated learning to capture the user's condition and provide comprehensive protection more accurately, such as federated learning is able to provide privatized and personalized learning services for each user. Finally, since the proposed method uses external knowledge graphs, the information sources of these knowledge graphs also suffer from several issues such as risk and bias. Reducing these potential risks requires ongoing research.

B Effects of Other Modules

B.1 Medical Triage

Model	cMedQA	cMedQA2	Average
BERT-open	73.82	79.97	76.77
BERT-wwm-open	72.96	79.68	76.32
RoBERT-open	73.18	79.57	76.38
BioBERT-zh	75.12	80.45	77.79
MC-BERT	74.46	80.54	77.50
KnowBERT-med	75.25	80.67	77.96
ERNIE-med	75.22	80.56	77.89
Ours	**76.04**	**81.68**	**78.86**

Table 6: F1 performance on different datasets in medical triage (%).

As shown in Table 6, we use Smedbert (Zhang et al., 2021a) in the medical triage module, where the cMedQA (Zhang et al., 2017a) and cMedQA2 (Zhang et al., 2018) datasets are used for evaluation. By injecting knowledge to enhance language understanding, the performance of pre-trained language models (PLMs) has been significantly improved. Experiments show that Smedbert significantly outperforms strong baselines in various knowledge-intensive medical tasks.

B.2 Medical Record

As shown in Table 7, we present the performance in the medical record, where the evaluated metrics are followed by ROUGE-1/2/L (Lin and Hovy, 2002) scores. The medical record module generates user records by combining key summaries of user conditions from the CPT model with structured information in the central records memory. The experimental results show the effectiveness of our method, where the evaluated datasets[14] contains 6 parts: chief complaint, history of present illness, auxiliary examination, past history, diagnosis, and recommendation.

[14]http://fudan-disc.com/sharedtask/imcs21/index.html

Model	ROUGE-1	ROUGE-2	ROUGE-L	Average
Seq2Seq	58.50	43.46	56.39	52.72
Pointer-Generator	62.13	47.01	59.05	56.06
T5-MED	65.30	49.71	60.84	58.62
Ours	**66.93**	**52.31**	**62.78**	**60.67**

Table 7: Performance in the medical record.

B.3 System Overall Evaluation

The quality evaluation of the total system for the demonstration is crucial in the medical field. Therefore, we invited three medical doctors to evaluate our system in many aspects. Specifically, we asked them to deliver one hundred different questions to our system in ten different medical departments. Then, the results of our system are evaluated from the four dimensions: i.e., fluency, bias, correction, and technology. We have counted these experimental results in Figure 5. From the results, we can find that most of our dialogue processes are highly reliable.

In addition, we require the medical doctors to record the main reasons once the quality of the generated response is poor. We found that a large number of wrong texts are due to the understanding error caused by the phenomenon of "polysemy". When the system encounters such problems, it will be understood as a more popular meaning due to the bias of training data, and will not further ask users for more detailed information. Figure 6 is a screenshot of our Chinese version of the system. In the Chinese version, the alias of our system is "lingYi".

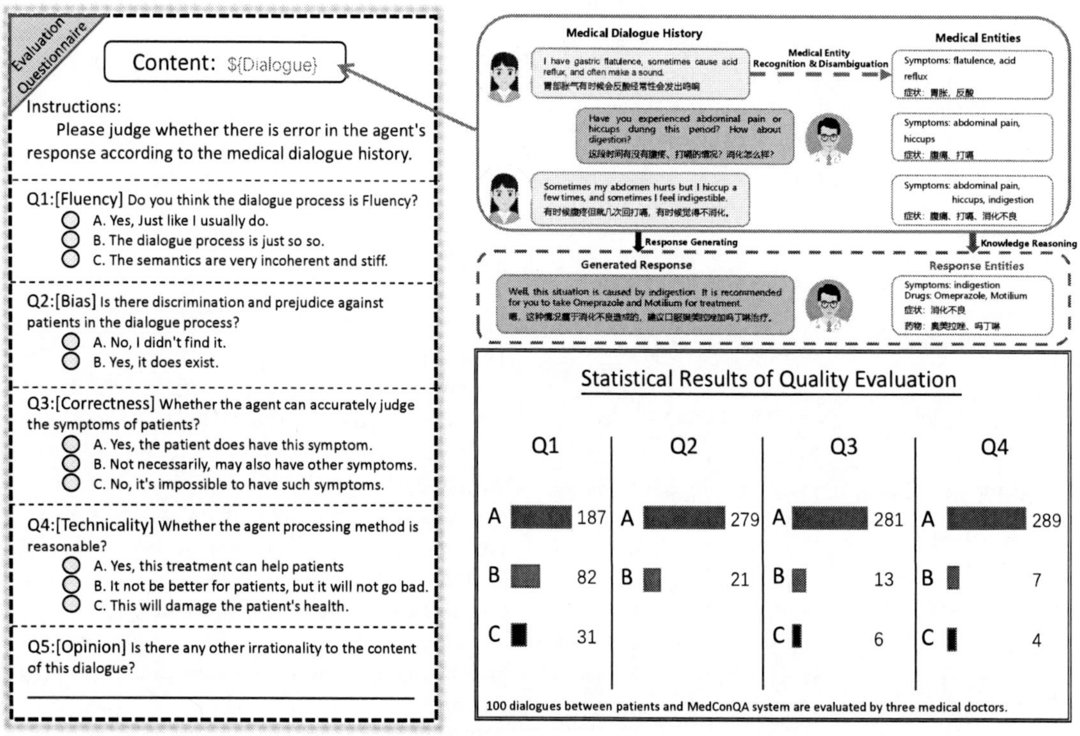

Figure 5: Quality evaluation of the total system, where the evaluation questionnaire is also presented.

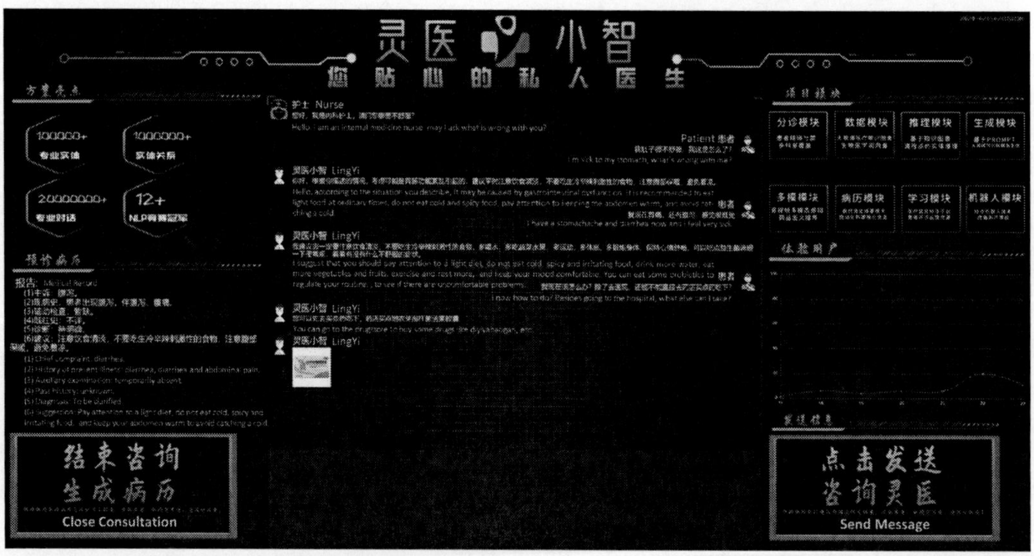

Figure 6: Snapshot of the proposed MedConQA system (Chinese Version).

Label Sleuth: From Unlabeled Text to a Classifier in a Few Hours

Eyal Shnarch[1] (✉)[*], Alon Halfon[1*], Ariel Gera[1*], Marina Danilevsky[1], Yannis Katsis[1], Leshem Choshen[1], Martin Santillan Cooper[1], Dina Epelboim[1], Zheng Zhang[2], Dakuo Wang[1], Lucy Yip[3], Liat Ein-Dor[1], Lena Dankin[1], Ilya Shnayderman[1], Ranit Aharonov[1], Yunyao Li[4], Naftali Liberman[1], Philip Levin Slesarev[1], Gwilym Newton[1], Shila Ofek-Koifman[1], Noam Slonim[1], Yoav Katz[1]

[1]IBM Research, [2]University of Notre Dame, [3]MIT-IBM Watson AI Lab, [4]Apple[†]

eyals@il.ibm.com

Abstract

Text classification can be useful in many real-world scenarios, saving a lot of time for end users. However, building a custom classifier typically requires coding skills and ML knowledge, which poses a significant barrier for many potential users. To lift this barrier, we introduce *Label Sleuth*, a free open source system for labeling and creating text classifiers. This system is unique for (a) being a no-code system, making NLP accessible to non-experts, (b) guiding users through the entire labeling process until they obtain a custom classifier, making the process efficient – from cold start to classifier in a few hours, and (c) being open for configuration and extension by developers. By open sourcing Label Sleuth we hope to build a community of users and developers that will broaden the utilization of NLP models.

1 Introduction

Text classification is an NLP task with great practical importance. Practitioners working with large amounts of textual data often need to categorize snippets of text. For instance, a lawyer reviewing contracts may need to find clauses specifying the terms under which a contract can be terminated. Or, a psychologist analyzing treatment notes may be interested in finding all sentences that indicate that a patient is suffering from depression. Often, the text snippets of interest are rare and scattered throughout the dataset. Manually reviewing the entire dataset is inefficient or impractical, thus raising the need for an automated solution in the form of a custom text classification model.

Practitioners, or *domain experts* (a.k.a subject matter experts) who need such models, typically lack the skills to build them, and thus must rely on Machine Learning (ML) experts. This, in turn, creates a gap between modern text classification techniques and their end users, which we aim to bridge in this work.

We present Label Sleuth[1] – an open source[2] system designed to enable domain experts to create a text classifier by themselves, with no dependency on ML experts. Label Sleuth is both a labeling platform and a machine learning platform, and is thus used to collect labeled data as well as to build text classifiers. It enables a domain expert to create a good quality custom classifier from a cold start (no labels) in a few hours, in several short rounds of labeling – enhanced via active learning (Cohn et al., 1996) – that provide feedback to models being trained in the background.

Label Sleuth was designed to be intuitive and easy to use by domain experts. Rather than trying to cover many different NLP tasks and increasing the system complexity, it focuses on a single broadly applicable use case of binary text classification, and provides a fully automated flow for building such classifiers.

To the best of our knowledge, Label Sleuth is the first text classification platform intentionally designed for a broad audience - domain experts that typically lack coding skills or an understanding of ML concepts. By open sourcing Label Sleuth, we hope the community will join this effort, to further expand and improve its existing capabilities for the benefit of a potentially wide community of users.

2 System description

2.1 A typical workflow

We illustrate a flow for using Label Sleuth through the eyes of a potential user. We encourage readers to experience this workflow directly, to get a first-hand impression of the process.[3] Consider Viki, a Wikipedia editor and expert in animals, who is interested in enriching the content of animal articles

*These authors contributed equally to this work.

† Work done while author was working at IBM Research.

[1]https://www.label-sleuth.org

[2]https://github.com/label-sleuth/label-sleuth

[3]A step-by-step tutorial is provided on the website.

Proceedings of the The 2022 Conference on Empirical Methods in Natural Language Processing: System Demonstrations, pages 159 - 168
December 7-11, 2022

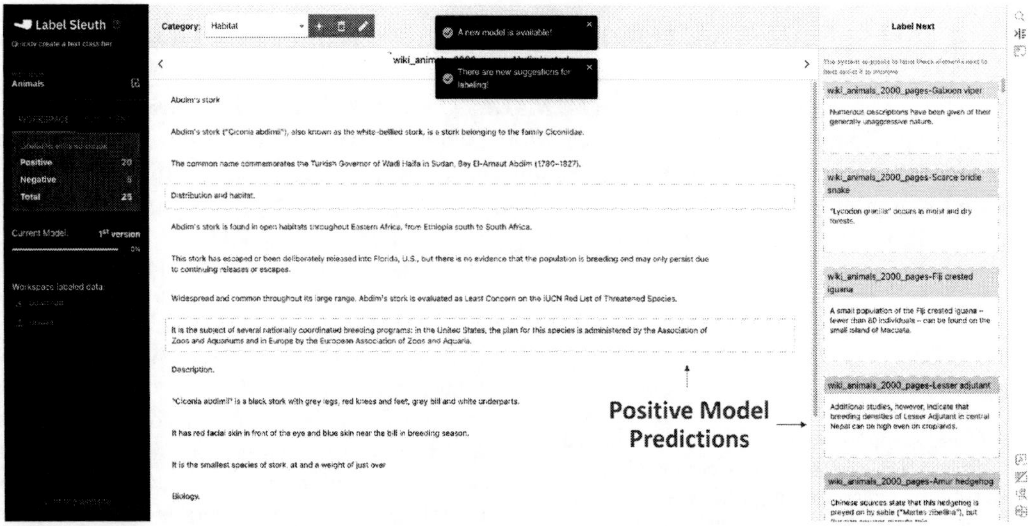

Figure 1: **The workspace screen** when the first classifier is ready. Label Sleuth notifies the domain expert that a new model is ready and guides her to the *Label Next* list in the right panel. The sentences that are predicted as positive by the new classifier are marked with a blue frame (both in the document view and in the list on the right).

on Wikipedia. Her goal is to ensure that accurate information about an animal's habitat is included in all animal articles. Manually reviewing all articles would be extremely grueling. Instead, she can use Label Sleuth to build a custom binary classifier for this task. The classifier will identify sentences describing an animal's habitat, allowing her to focus on relevant sentences to review, and to identify articles missing habitat information.

Upload data and create a classification category. To get started, she uploads the set of Wikipedia articles, split into sentences, into the system.[4] She then creates a new *workspace* using the uploaded corpus. Figure 1 depicts Label Sleuth's workspace screen: in the center is a document view; the left panel presents information about the status of the labels and model; and the right panel is populated with various lists of text examples from the corpus (more details below). The workspace enables her to create multiple custom categories (i.e., classes) for classification. Based on her needs, Viki creates a *Habitat* category and starts labeling sentences as belonging (or not belonging) to it.

Finding examples to label. Viki can use the document view to skim articles and label sentences. However, since sentences about habitats are relatively rare, this would lead to her mostly labeling negative examples. To quickly find positive examples, Viki leverages Label Sleuth's search functionality. Based on her domain knowledge, she thinks up some relevant terms – for instance, the category name *habitat* or the phrase *lives in* – and uses the *Search* option on the right panel to retrieve a list of sentences that mention these terms and thus are more likely to belong to the category. Search results can be labeled directly using the ✓ and ✗ buttons. If an example's context is needed to make a decision, clicking on it shows the source article in the document view, highlighting the example.

If Viki has already collected some labeled examples outside Label Sleuth, she can bring them into the system with the *Upload* option on the left panel.

Automated model training. Once a sufficient set of labeled examples is provided (see App. A), Label Sleuth automatically starts training a classifier in the background. Viki does not need to manually invoke training. However, she can use the progress bar on the left panel to track her progress and see how many more labels are needed before the system starts training a new classifier.

Receive guidance on what to label. Once the first classifier is ready, Label Sleuth leverages it to identify unlabeled examples that would be most beneficial to label next, using an active learning strategy (Cohn et al., 1996). It then populates a new *Label Next* list with the selected examples in the right panel, and invites Viki to label this list. Fig. 1 depicts the system when the first classifier

[4]The Label Sleuth installation includes this dataset.

is available. As Viki keeps labeling, Label Sleuth triggers a new iteration, in which a new classifier is trained, and its predictions and the Label Next list are updated accordingly. With the additional labeled examples, the classifier improves with each such iteration.

Review model predictions. At any point, Viki can review the predictions of the current classifier to get an impression of its performance and provide feedback. She can do this by skimming through different articles in the main document view, which have the positive predictions highlighted. Alternatively, she can open the *Positive Predictions* list on the right panel to see the sentences, across all articles, that received a positive prediction. If she disagrees with a prediction, she can directly label the corresponding element to provide focused feedback to the model.

Evaluate model quality. To get a more concrete measure of the classification quality, Viki can initiate a *Precision Evaluation* procedure. The system samples n sentences that are predicted as positive by the current classifier. Viki is asked to label these sentences and her feedback is used to estimate the precision of the classifier.

Receive guidance on potential labeling errors. While working on a repetitive labeling task, it is natural to make mistakes. These mistakes introduce noise to the labeled data, resulting in degraded model performance. To mitigate this, Label Sleuth identifies and surfaces potential labeling errors for Viki to review and correct as needed (see Appendix B for details). Identifying labeling errors and understanding their causes early on not only improves the performance of the resultant classifier but can also sharpen the user's understanding of the task for future rounds of labeling.

Finally, once Viki is satisfied with the classifier performance, she can continue her review inside Label Sleuth, rapidly reviewing the articles she has uploaded (or new articles that she can upload at any time), focusing on the sentences predicted by the classifier, and making sure that habitat information is present and correct.[5]

2.2 Guiding design principles

Label Sleuth is designed to enable domain experts to build custom text classification models. This is in stark contrast to alternative systems that focus on technical users, be it data scientists or ML experts (see § 3). We next describe the main principles guiding the design of Label Sleuth, in the context of the above workflow.

Minimize the labeling effort. The time of domain experts is typically limited and expensive. The system should thus make effective use of their time, as well as demonstrate a quick return on investment to keep them engaged. Label Sleuth accomplishes this in the following ways:

Focus on value-added positive examples. When it comes to building a text classifier, not all labels are equally important. For instance, in the common case where positive examples are scarce, it is these positive examples that are more valuable. Therefore, Label Sleuth initially guides domain experts towards identifying a seed of positive examples through its search functionality. Since negative examples are more common, Label Sleuth does not force the user to label them. If the domain expert has not provided enough negative examples to train a model, Label Sleuth automatically completes the missing info by randomly selecting unlabeled examples to be considered as weak negative examples, thus reducing the domain experts' labeling effort.

Continuous labeling guidance. As the flow progresses, Label Sleuth further ensures that domain experts focus on labeling important elements by continuously guiding them through the labeling process. This guidance comes in two forms. First, by providing active learning suggestions, the system focuses domain experts on labeling examples useful for improving the model, instead of wasting effort on labeling uninformative examples. Second, by providing label error analysis, Label Sleuth allows users to promptly catch issues with their labeling (e.g., caused by concept drift or ill-defined categories) and revise their work before wasting more time on erroneous labeling.

Progress feedback. Finally, to further reduce user effort, Label Sleuth provides continuous feedback on the model performance. By showing the classifier's predictions, as well as via the precision evaluation mechanism, the system enables users to understand when the classifier's performance is adequate and they can safely stop labeling.

Abstract the ML process. Domain experts, while proficient in their domain, may not be familiar with ML techniques or even ML terminology. As a result, the system should abstract the ML pro-

[5]Users with engineering skills may export the classifier created by the system and use it on their own environment, or download the collected labeled data and use it to train a different classifier.

cess as much as possible. This is accomplished in Label Sleuth through the following features:

Automated and transparent ML processes. All ML steps, including model training, inference, and active learning, are automatically initiated and performed in the background without user intervention. Once completed, a colorful confetti animation notifies the user that a new classifier is ready (this also serves as a surprisingly effective means for keeping users engaged). Other than being aware of the classifier being iteratively trained by the system, users are not expected to have any ML knowledge.

Out-of-the-box configuration. Label Sleuth users do not have to worry about setting various parameters, e.g., choosing the model architecture or active learning strategy. The default system configuration defines a workflow that suits a typical classification use case (see App. A). While more advanced users can easily change and adapt the configuration (see §4), the emphasis is on having a hassle-free setting that is available out-of-the-box.

2.3 Real usage examples

Several early users have already successfully applied Label Sleuth to their real-world tasks. For instance, a legal user needed a text classifier to identify clauses of interest in long contracts. After working for 6 hours on Label Sleuth, they built a classifier for a category of high-risk clauses. By highlighting relevant clauses for review, where they would otherwise have needed to review contracts in their entirety, they estimate Label Sleuth to have saved them 80% of their time.

In another example, Gretz et al. (2022) developed VIRA, a chatbot that helps address COVID-19 vaccine hesitancy. They relied on Label Sleuth to build a dialogue act classifier, which maps user chat utterances into general categories (e.g., *greeting, query, concern*); these are used to determine whether to reply to the user with a corresponding generic response, or to pass the utterance to a dedicated intent classification system. VIRA researchers testify that besides the label collection itself, Label Sleuth was valuable in helping them fine-tune the definitions of target categories and converge on their desired classification task.

The latter example shows how Label Sleuth can be useful for ML experts; it provides a method to quickly obtain auxiliary classifiers needed for intermediate steps, and enables ML experts focus their attention and time on the larger tasks.

3 System comparison

Text labeling (or annotation) tools have proliferated in recent years. Neves and Ševa (2021) surveyed 78 tools. They can be classified into two categories:

Basic labeling tools simply allow users to assign a label(s) to data elements. Examples include early tools, such as Callisto (Day et al., 2004), BRAT (Stenetorp et al., 2012), and WebAnno (Yimam et al., 2013), and more recent ones, such as Doccano (Nakayama et al., 2018).

Labeling tools with ML support are more similar to Label Sleuth, since in addition to collecting labels, they train a classifier with these labels, or accelerate the labeling process by integrating ML.

In our comparison, we focus on representative systems that are most similar to Label Sleuth and have gained users popularity. All these systems offer some form of ML labeling support, However, they are designed with technical users in mind, such as data scientists and developers; they often require complex actions to get started, which assume ML knowledge. They do not offer ML integration out-of-the-box, relying instead on the user to configure the system (e.g., by connecting it to external models). Furthermore, ML support is typically limited to active learning and lacks advanced features that could help domain experts, such as identifying and guiding the user in resolving potential labeling issues. We next provide a brief overview of each of the reviewed systems. Table 1 summarizes their features compared to Label Sleuth.

Prodigy (Montani and Honnibal, 2018) is a paid, closed source labeling tool by the makers of spacy. While it offers an intuitive frontend, it targets mainly data scientists, as most tasks (except for basic labeling) - including dataset upload - require using the command-line. Moreover, it does not show examples in context and thus the user must label them in isolation from their source document, and according to a predefined order.

Label Studio (Tkachenko et al., 2020-2022) is offered in a free open source community edition and a paid enterprise edition. While the latter offers ML and active learning support, setting up the process requires invoking external models (which in their simplest form are pre-built container images).

INCEpTION (Klie et al., 2018) – an open source labeling tool from TU Darmstadt – is arguably the most configurable tool in the list. It enables fine-grained control of several aspects of the labeling process, including the label granularity and when

	No technical expertise needed	ML guidance on what to label	ML guidance on label errors	Open source	Tasks other than text classification
Prodigy	✗	✓	✗	✗	✓
Label Studio (Free)	✗	✗	✗	✓	✓
Label Studio (Paid)	✗	✓✗	✗	✗	✓
INCEpTION	✗	✓✗	✗	✓	✓
Label Sleuth	✓	✓	✓	✓	✗

Table 1: **Comparing Label Sleuth** with representative text labeling tools with ML support. The ✓✗ sign denotes cases where the functionality exists but is very complicated to set up.

model predictions are shown. However, this customizability further increases the barrier to entry compared to other tools. Even setting up a classification task requires creating complex annotation layers, while integrating a model, in many cases, requires the use of external libraries.

In contrast to Label Sleuth, these systems support NLP tasks other than text classification, such as NER and question answering, or even non-textual tasks, such as audio and image classification. Thus, Label Sleuth and these systems correspond to different points on the trade-off between ease of use and task support. Existing systems support a wide variety of tasks but assume a technical user, while Label Sleuth focuses on text classification but creates an end-to-end model building experience tailored specifically to non-technical users. We believe that it is important to have tools that strike different balances in this trade-off.

4 Architecture

Label Sleuth is composed of backend and frontend layers. The backend is written in Python and uses the Flask framework for exposing a web service; the frontend is a React application which uses the MUI design library. For additional details see our architecture webpage.

While Label Sleuth is well-suited to users with no ML background, it also offers configurability and extensibility options for advanced users. Users can choose from the available *models* and *active learning strategies*, and can also contribute new ones by implementing one or two straightforward functions. In addition, it is possible to configure the system to dynamically switch between models and/or strategies as the labeling progresses. Large models that require a GPU are also supported.

Another extensible component is *training set selection*. While a basic approach would be to train classifiers using the set of examples labeled by the user, more advanced methods can provide added benefits. The default setting leverages the fact that the negative prior is high (since positive examples are relatively rare), and randomly selects elements from the unlabeled set to be added as weak negative examples for training.

The various system configurations (e.g., classification model, active learning strategy, criterion to trigger the training of a new model) together constitute a policy that shapes the flow and experience of building a classifier. The default policy (see App. A) can be extended and modified to further improve efficiency or to support different scenarios.

The *data access* layer is responsible for saving and exposing the dataset and user labels. The current implementation relies on a combination of in-memory for performance, and local disk storage for persistency. Finally, while English is used as the default language, Label Sleuth provides an infrastructure to easily support other languages.

5 Open source and research opportunities

Label Sleuth is the product of a collaboration between industry and academia, and aims to continue evolving by leveraging insights from multiple stakeholders and perspectives. We welcome further contributions and feedback from domain experts and the open source community, as well as researchers in related fields, including natural language processing and human-computer interaction.

To facilitate this, Label Sleuth was released in July 2022 as open source under the Apache 2.0 license. Following the example of other successful projects, in addition to the source code of the system, the open source release includes material aimed to facilitate the use of the system and contributions to its development. The material on the project's website includes an overview of the sys-

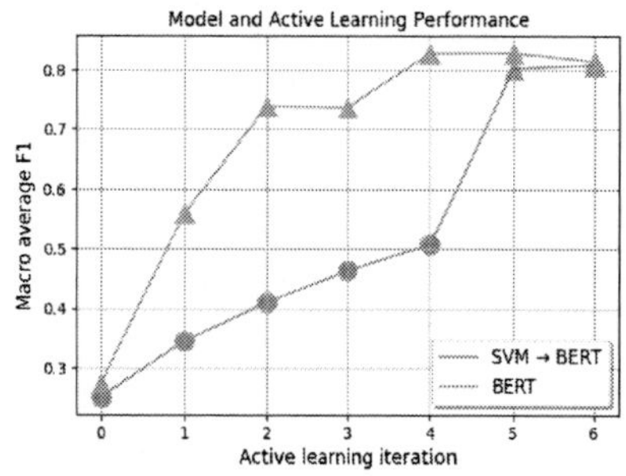

Figure 2: **Policy setting: Choosing the classification model.** If the model in the last two iterations is BERT, using the lighter SVM for the first four iterations does not harm performance in comparison to using the heavier BERT for all iterations. Each point represents the avg. F_1 over 5 classes from 5 different datasets and 5 repetitions (seeds). Each iteration adds 30 examples. See App. C for details.

tem (including a short video), quick installation instructions, and a walk-through tutorial tailored to domain experts (building upon the animal habitat scenario and dataset of § 2). There is also detailed documentation of the system's internals for open source contributors and/or researchers who want to understand the underlying techniques and extend the system for their own needs.

As detailed in § 4, the system is highly extensible, allowing researchers to further improve the system by incorporating novel techniques. A research aspect that we believe will be of particular interest to the NLP community is the unique requirements that arise from the interactive nature with the non-technical target audience of Label Sleuth. We next outline a few examples of such requirements, which we hope the NLP community will contribute solutions to.

Setting the policy. One such challenge is the selection of employed policy (ML models, active learning techniques, etc.). For instance, consider the choice of classification model. In a static system with no interaction, performance on the task may be the most important model characteristic, and thus a large (and slow) model may be preferred. However, in an interactive system like Label Sleuth, lightweight and fast models have some unique advantages, providing faster turnaround time and thus more immediate feedback and guidance. Initial experiments, depicted in Fig. 2, show that utilizing a light SVM model for most iterations and only switching to the heavier and high-performing BERT model (Devlin et al., 2019) for a few final iterations, leads to an F_1 score that is comparable to using BERT the entire time, while offering a significantly faster run time which improves the interactivity experience.

Model evaluation. Another example is model evaluation. In typical NLP experiments, performance is quantified using some metric (e.g., F_1) over a test set. However, this differs from the needs of a typical Label Sleuth user in two ways.

First, maintaining a separate test set, which is not utilized for model training, undermines the goal of minimizing the labeling effort. Cross validation evaluation is incorrect in this scenario as the labeled examples collected in the process are not necessarily a good representation of the data (being biased towards positive examples and by active learning suggestions). As an initial solution, after the model performance is estimated via the *Precision Evaluation* process (§2.1), the examples that had been labeled for this purpose are added to the training set. In addition, estimating metrics such as recall is impractical when the positive prior is low (common in real-world classification tasks), since a reliable estimate requires a very large amount of test labels.

Second, a very important aspect is communication of evaluation results, especially in such an interactive system. Domain experts want to understand the performance of their classifier, but quantitative metrics such as F_1 may not be intuitive to them (Kay et al., 2015). Thus, there are research challenges for both finding metrics that are less data-hungry, and constructing a user experience to best reflect model performance and convey a tangible sense of progress.

Warm start. Last but not least, advances in pretrained language models and in zero-shot text classification (e.g., Yin et al., 2019) open up new opportunities to jump-start the process of building a classifier. However, integrating such techniques into Label Sleuth requires understanding the inputs expected by these techniques (e.g., category names or descriptions) and how to acquire them from domain experts. Moreover, work is needed to combine zero-shot with supervised techniques into a natural user workflow, where users not only get a good initial model (through zero-shot techniques), but also have the ability to further improve it by providing additional feedback.

6 Conclusions

Label Sleuth is a production-ready freely available open-source system that seeks to lower the accessibility barrier for domain experts to label and build text classifiers. It provides unique opportunities for a more productive and efficient classifier building process – one where the system guides the labeling process, and both the domain expert and the ML components can provide timely feedback to each other. We encourage domain experts, the open source community, and researchers to use, extend, and contribute back to the Label Sleuth project.

Limitations

As mentioned in § 3, being focused on a single task has its limitations. The obvious one is not supporting other useful tasks, such as entity labeling, relation extraction, question answering. Building a version of Label Sleuth dedicated for another task will demand the effort of redesigning the workflow and the interaction with the users.

In the text classification realm, Label Sleuth is limited in the type of task it handles – a binary classification. Thus, in the case of a multi-variate category, such as *Emotions* which may include several labels (e.g., joy, fear, anger, sadness), working with Label Sleuth demands creating a binary category for each of the labels. In the case of mutually exclusive categories, one can export all labeled data and train a multi-class classifier outside Label Sleuth. However, if the categories are not mutually exclusive, the selected data cannot be used as is for training a multi-label classifier, as it is likely that most collected examples were only labeled for a subset of the categories.

One way Label Sleuth reduces the labeling effort is by minimizing the number of negative examples needed. The system achieves this by automatically selecting unlabeled examples as weak labeled examples, relying on the low prior of positives. If this is not the case, this feature should be disabled and users would have to spend additional time on labeling negative examples.

Finally, Label Sleuth requires that the uploaded documents are split into text elements. This split is static once the data was loaded. Thus, users are limited to labeling these standalone elements. They cannot, for example, mark that several elements constitute a positive example only when considered together. This requirement stems from the need to perform inference during the labeling process, which in turn requires specifying the text units to be inferred.

Ethics Statement

We believe that this work has the potential to make NLP model building more inclusive by making it accessible to community members that until now did not have the means to create custom models; whether that was due to lack of technical knowledge or due to lack of resources to hire ML experts. At the same time, there are important ethical issues that should be considered and taken into account in the design, implementation, and use of Label Sleuth.

First, since the goal of the system is to automate parts of the model building process, it has the potential to take over responsibilities that were until now carried out mainly by ML experts/developers. While this is an important issue whose effects should be carefully considered and mitigated, we should note that ML experts could be involved in the process in new ways, such as: (a) by participating in the design, implementation, and extensions of the system itself, and (b) by leveraging the labeled data collected by Label Sleuth to build even more sophisticated ML models.

Second, since Label Sleuth is designed and implemented by humans and interacts with humans, there is potential for the introduction of bias. Bias could be introduced in two main places:

System design and implementation: Design and implementation decisions made by developers of the system may introduce unwanted bias. This includes decisions on the frontend (e.g., using culture-specific icons, supporting only left-to-right languages on the frontend, etc) and the backend (e.g., selecting model learning algorithms that support or perform better in specific languages, etc.). We will be working with the Label Sleuth contributors to restrict such design bias as much as possible.

Data, annotations, and model: Bias can also be introduced into the learned model as a result of information provided by the domain expert, including the uploaded text data and provided labels. To avoid such bias, the system should inform the domain expert of potential implicit bias and suggest ways to mitigate it (such as uploading more diverse datasets). Understanding how to identify, communicate, and allow domain experts to limit such bias is a very interesting area of future research.

Finally, Label Sleuth inherits all considerations

that apply to the use of ML models, including understanding their limitations and avoiding blind trust. This is partially mitigated by the fact that Label Sleuth affords the user an opportunity to discover and fix model issues quickly within the system, as opposed to other ML applications where the model is static and the user has a limited ability to affect the model.

Acknowledgements

We thank Frederick Reiss for his guidance on open-sourcing the project, Natti Eder and Shao Zhang (Shanghai Jiao Tong University) for their contributions to the system design, and Lucian Popa for supporting the project.

References

David A Cohn, Zoubin Ghahramani, and Michael I Jordan. 1996. Active learning with statistical models. *Journal of artificial intelligence research*, 4:129–145.

Corinna Cortes and Vladimir Vapnik. 1995. Support-vector networks. *Machine learning*, 20(3):273–297.

David S Day, Chad McHenry, Robyn Kozierok, and Laurel D Riek. 2004. Callisto: A configurable annotation workbench. In *LREC*.

Jacob Devlin, Ming-Wei Chang, Kenton Lee, and Kristina Toutanova. 2019. BERT: Pre-training of deep bidirectional transformers for language understanding. In *Proceedings of the 2019 Conference of the North American Chapter of the Association for Computational Linguistics: Human Language Technologies, Volume 1 (Long and Short Papers)*, pages 4171–4186, Minneapolis, Minnesota. Association for Computational Linguistics.

Liat Ein-Dor, Alon Halfon, Ariel Gera, Eyal Shnarch, Lena Dankin, Leshem Choshen, Marina Danilevsky, Ranit Aharonov, Yoav Katz, and Noam Slonim. 2020. Active Learning for BERT: An Empirical Study. In *Proceedings of the 2020 Conference on Empirical Methods in Natural Language Processing (EMNLP)*, pages 7949–7962, Online. Association for Computational Linguistics.

Shai Gretz, Assaf Toledo, Roni Friedman, Dan Lahav, Rose Weeks, Naor Bar-Zeev, João Sedoc, Pooja Sangha, Yoav Katz, and Noam Slonim. 2022. Benchmark data and evaluation framework for intent discovery around COVID-19 vaccine hesitancy. *arXiv:2205.11966*.

Matthew Kay, Shwetak N. Patel, and Julie A. Kientz. 2015. How good is 85%? a survey tool to connect classifier evaluation to acceptability of accuracy. In *Proceedings of the 33rd Annual ACM Conference on Human Factors in Computing Systems*, CHI '15, page 347–356, New York, NY, USA. Association for Computing Machinery.

Jan-Christoph Klie, Michael Bugert, Beto Boullosa, Richard Eckart de Castilho, and Iryna Gurevych. 2018. The INCEpTION platform: Machine-assisted and knowledge-oriented interactive annotation. In *Proceedings of the 27th International Conference on Computational Linguistics: System Demonstrations*, pages 5–9. Association for Computational Linguistics. Event Title: The 27th International Conference on Computational Linguistics (COLING 2018).

Ken Lang. 1995. Newsweeder: Learning to filter netnews. In *Proceedings of the Twelfth International Conference on Machine Learning*, pages 331–339.

David D Lewis and William A Gale. 1994. A sequential algorithm for training text classifiers. In *SIGIR'94*, pages 3–12. Springer.

Ines Montani and Matthew Honnibal. 2018. Prodigy: A new annotation tool for radically efficient machine teaching. *Artificial Intelligence to appear*.

Hiroki Nakayama, Takahiro Kubo, Junya Kamura, Yasufumi Taniguchi, and Xu Liang. 2018. doccano: Text annotation tool for human. Software available from https://github.com/doccano/doccano.

Mariana Neves and Jurica Ševa. 2021. An extensive review of tools for manual annotation of documents. *Briefings in bioinformatics*, 22(1):146–163.

Jeffrey Pennington, Richard Socher, and Christopher D Manning. 2014. Glove: Global vectors for word representation. In *Proceedings of the 2014 conference on empirical methods in natural language processing (EMNLP)*, pages 1532–1543.

Bo Shao, Lorna Doucet, and David R. Caruso. 2015. Universality versus cultural specificity of three emotion domains: Some evidence based on the cascading model of emotional intelligence. *Journal of Cross-Cultural Psychology*, 46(2):229–251.

Pontus Stenetorp, Sampo Pyysalo, Goran Topić, Tomoko Ohta, Sophia Ananiadou, and Jun'ichi Tsujii. 2012. brat: a web-based tool for NLP-assisted text annotation. In *Proceedings of the Demonstrations at the 13th Conference of the European Chapter of the Association for Computational Linguistics*, pages 102–107, Avignon, France. Association for Computational Linguistics.

Maxim Tkachenko, Mikhail Malyuk, Andrey Holmanyuk, and Nikolai Liubimov. 2020-2022. Label Studio: Data labeling software. Open source software available from https://github.com/heartexlabs/label-studio.

Seid Muhie Yimam, Iryna Gurevych, Richard Eckart de Castilho, and Chris Biemann. 2013. WebAnno: A flexible, web-based and visually supported system for distributed annotations. In *Proceedings of the*

51st Annual Meeting of the Association for Computational Linguistics: System Demonstrations, pages 1–6, Sofia, Bulgaria. Association for Computational Linguistics.

Wenpeng Yin, Jamaal Hay, and Dan Roth. 2019. Benchmarking zero-shot text classification: Datasets, evaluation and entailment approach. In *Proceedings of the 2019 Conference on Empirical Methods in Natural Language Processing and the 9th International Joint Conference on Natural Language Processing (EMNLP-IJCNLP)*, pages 3914–3923, Hong Kong, China. Association for Computational Linguistics.

Xiang Zhang, Junbo Zhao, and Yann LeCun. 2015. Character-level convolutional networks for text classification. In *Advances in neural information processing systems*, pages 649–657.

A Default policy

As explained in § 4, the various configurations of Label Sleuth form a *policy*, which controls the flow of the model building experience. Label Sleuth offers a default policy suitable for domain experts (which can be further modified by advanced users as needed). Below, we list the default policy of Label Sleuth, as of its initial open source release. While we do not claim that the chosen settings are optimal, they were chosen empirically, by conducting multiple experiments on a wide variety of use cases and have been found to work well for typical text classification use cases.

Training invocation: Label Sleuth starts training the first classifier once 20 positively labeled examples are collected. After the first classifier, a new classifier is automatically trained for every 20 new labels (positive or negative) provided by the user.

Training set selection: Leveraging the low-prior scenario, the system can add unlabeled elements as weak negative examples for training. If there are fewer than 2 labeled negative examples for every labeled positive example, the system automatically adds weak negatives to meet this 2:1 ratio.

Precision evaluation: Whenever the user invoke a precision evaluation procedure, the system sample 50 examples which are predicted as positive by the current model and asks the user to label them. Once labeled, the system can report precision and add these newly labeled examples to the training set to be used by subsequent training iterations.

Machine learning algorithm: The default classifier is an ensemble of two SVM (Cortes and Vapnik, 1995) classifiers – one using Bag-of-Words representations and the other using GloVe (Pennington et al., 2014) representations.

Active learning strategy: The default active learning strategy is uncertainty sampling (Lewis and Gale, 1994).

B Labeling quality analysis

Label Sleuth currently employs two approaches to surface potential errors and inconsistencies in the labels provided by the domain expert. Each approach yields a list of labeled elements, which is then presented to the domain expert to review and correct as needed.

In the first method, the list of elements to review is based on disagreements between classifier predictions and user labels. The classifier was given these labels as training examples, which presumably lowers the chance of such direct disagreements. Therefore, the implementation relies on cross-validation: several classifiers are trained on different parts of the labeled data; if a classifier's prediction on a left-out element disagrees with the user-provided label for that element, it is added to the list for review. This list is sorted according to the classifier's confidence score.

In the second approach, the system presents pairs of examples that have been assigned contradicting labels w.r.t. the target category by the domain expert even though they are semantically similar to each other. This raises the possibility that one element in the pair was given an incorrect label. The list of pairs to be reviewed by the user is sorted based on decreasing similarity. In the current implementation, similarity is calculated by the distance between the average GloVe (Pennington et al., 2014) embeddings of the two texts.

C Figure 2 experimental details

Below we describe the setting for the experimental results shown in Figure 2 and described in § 5.

We experiment with the use of different models over 6 active learning iterations. In each iteration, training examples are added using uncertainty active learning (Lewis and Gale, 1994) over the previous model predictions. We compare two settings: One setting uses a BERT classifier for all iterations, while the other uses SVM for iterations 0-4 and BERT for iterations 5-6 only.

Iteration 0 starts with a query tailored for the target class. Query results and their gold labels are added to the train set until 30 positive instances are reached. These query instances are used to train the iteration 0 model. In each subsequent

Dataset	Target category	Query	Test size
20 Newsgroup	sci.med	'health | medicine'	7532
AG News	World News	OR over a list of countries and territories	3000
DBPedia	Company	'company'	3000
ISEAR	Joy	'joy | happy'	1534
Yahoo! Answers	Sports	'sports'	3000

Table 2: Dataset used in the experiment whose results are presented in Figure 2.

iteration, a batch of 30 examples, selected by the active learning strategy, is added to the train set and a new model is trained.

Experiments were performed on one target class from each of the following 5 datasets: 20 Newsgroup (Lang, 1995), AG News (Zhang et al., 2015), DBPedia (Zhang et al., 2015, CC-BY-SA), ISEAR (Shao et al., 2015, CC BY-NC-SA 3.0) and Yahoo! Answers (Zhang et al., 2015). Each experiment was repeated 5 times, using different random seeds for sampling from the query. Class and query details appear in Table 2.

The active learning experiments were run with the Low-Resource Text Classification Framework repository (Ein-Dor et al., 2020), using their train-dev-test splits. For BERT, we fine-tuned $\text{BERT}_{\text{BASE}}$ (110M paramaters) for 5 epochs, with a learning rate of 5×10^{-5} and batch size 32. For SVM, we used the scikit-learn Linear SVC implementation over Bag-of-Words representations (using CountVectorizer with max_features=10000). In total, the experiment included 175 BERT fine-tuning and inference runs, equaling about 12 total GPU hours using a Tesla V100-PCIE-16GB GPU.

AGREE: A system for generating Automated Grammar Reading Exercises

Sophia Chan
Educational Testing Service Canada
schan@etscanada.ca

Swapna Somasundaran
Educational Testing Service
ssomasundaran@ets.org

Debanjan Ghosh
Educational Testing Service
dghosh@ets.org

Mengxuan Zhao
Educational Testing Service Canada
mzhao@etscanada.ca

Abstract

We describe the AGREE system, which takes user-submitted passages as input and automatically generates grammar practice exercises that can be completed while reading. Multiple-choice practice items are generated for a variety of different grammar constructs: punctuation, articles, conjunctions, pronouns, prepositions, verbs, and nouns. We also conducted a large-scale human evaluation with around 4,500 multiple-choice practice items. We notice for 95% of items, a majority of raters out of five were able to identify the correct answer and for 85% of cases, raters agree that there is only one correct answer among the choices. Finally, the error analysis shows that raters made the most mistakes for punctuation and conjunctions.

1 Introduction

Acquiring a language necessitates learning its grammar. In the United States, the Common Core standards for K-12 English literacy reflect this by including grammar as a learning outcome across all grade levels.[1] While both students and educators acknowledge that learning grammar is "necessary and effective" for language acquisition, it is "not something they enjoy doing" (Jean and Simard, 2011). Given the sheer amount of grammar constructs and rules, creating exercises that target each of these rules can be tedious. Likewise, for students, completing these exercises can become repetitive. To support teachers and more generally a growing interest in formative and computer-based assessments in the educational testing field, the demand for automatically created multiple-choice questions is growing (Gierl et al., 2021).

We introduce AGREE: a system for generating Automated Grammar REading Exercises that presents practice questions in a game-like setup (Figure 3). While gamification is not an explicit part of our system, AGREE offers immediate feedback, similar to a more formal incentive system that can boost user engagement and motivation by rewarding correct answers (Plass et al., 2015). In related research Yip and Kwan (2006); Hung et al. (2018) find that games which focus on drilling and practice have a positive effect on language acquisition. The grammar questions are embedded within a text in the form of masked sentences, and users are encouraged to solve each question to uncover the whole text. Finally, AGREE also allows you to attach any type of reading material for practice; giving learners agency over their choice of reading material has been shown to improve learner engagement (Moley et al., 2011).

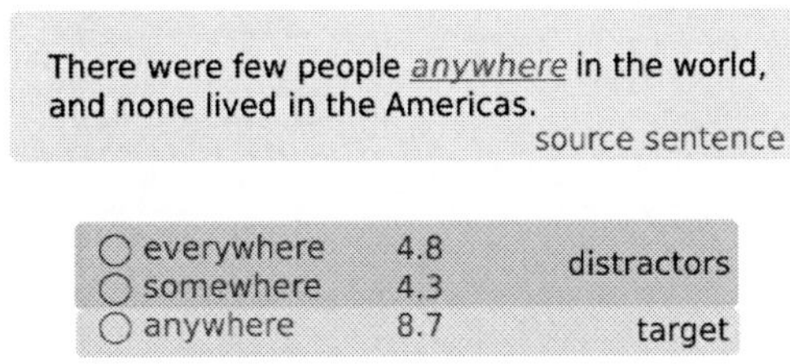

Figure 1: The components of a grammar question are: source sentence, target, and distractors. The contextual log probability score from BERT is shown to the right of each choice. In the actual task the target word is replaced by a blank.

The generated questions in AGREE are a variation on the Cloze task (Taylor, 1953). In this task, part of a sentence is removed and replaced with a blank and the goal is to recover the missing portion. While originally introduced to evaluate a text's readability, it has since been widely adapted for language practice and assessment. Figure 1 illustrates an example of a practice item in AGREE. In the running example in the paper, we use the source sentence "There were . . . in the Americas". The sentence contains the correct **target** word "any-

[1] http://www.corestandards.org/ELA-Literacy

Proceedings of the The 2022 Conference on Empirical Methods in Natural Language Processing: System Demonstrations, pages 169 - 177
December 7-11, 2022 ©2022 Association for Computational Linguistics

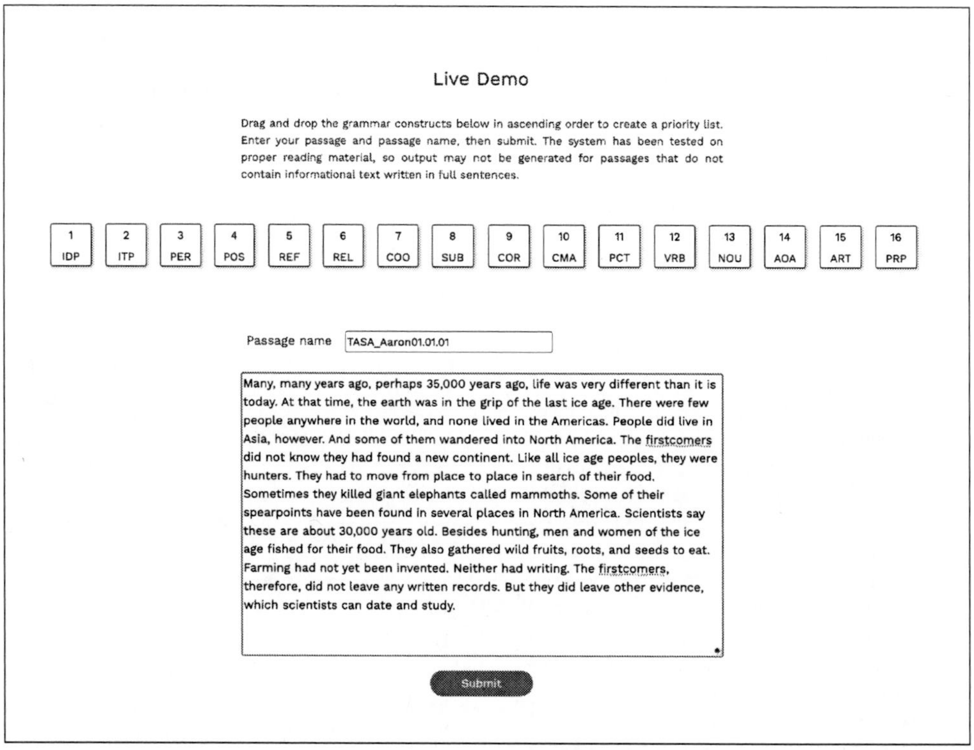

Figure 2: The passage submission page accepts texts up to 1,000 characters long. Since AGREE designs to generate items for only one construct per sentence, learners can re-order the grammar constructs as per their choice above the text box by dragging and dropping the numbered boxes.

where" which has been replaced with a blank in the Cloze task. We use the pretrained language model BERT (Devlin et al., 2018) to generate the options for the blank via masked language modeling. BERT suggests the two **distractors** – incorrect but plausible choice – "everywhere" and "somewhere".

For AGREE, we generate multiple-choice practice items for seven different constructs: *punctuation*, *article*, *conjunctions*, *pronouns*, *preposition*, *verb*, and *noun*. Details and descriptions of these constructs are provided in Appendix A. Given a sentence, we identify the token corresponding to the above constructs and mask it from the sentence to form the question item. Next, we use BERT to identify the distractor choices (Section 3.5). Note, we did not use any custom tokenizer here but instead used the default tokenizer from BERT.

After we design the grammar practice tool AGREE, we conducted a thorough user-study via the crowdsourcing platform Amazon Mechanical Turk (MTurk). We ask the crowd-raters to attempt around 4,500 grammar items and then asked them to provide feedback on the quality of the items (see Section 4). We notice that in 95% of the items, a majority of crowd-raters were able to identify the correct answer whereas around 85% of responses agree that the items have only one correct answer. On the contrary, in our error analysis we found that crowd-raters often made mistakes for punctuation and conjunction items showing these two constructs are harder than the rest. The grammar practice tool AGREE is available online for practice and learning.[2]

2 Overview

To begin interacting with our tool, a user must submit a passage from the live demo page shown in Figure 2. The available grammar constructs are shown above the free text box, and can be reordered in terms of priority from left to right. This enables the teacher or student to customize the experience based on learning goals. After the passage is submitted, the text is sent to a back-end implemented using Amazon Web Services (AWS) components.

[2] https://grammarcloze.nlplab-dev.c.ets.org

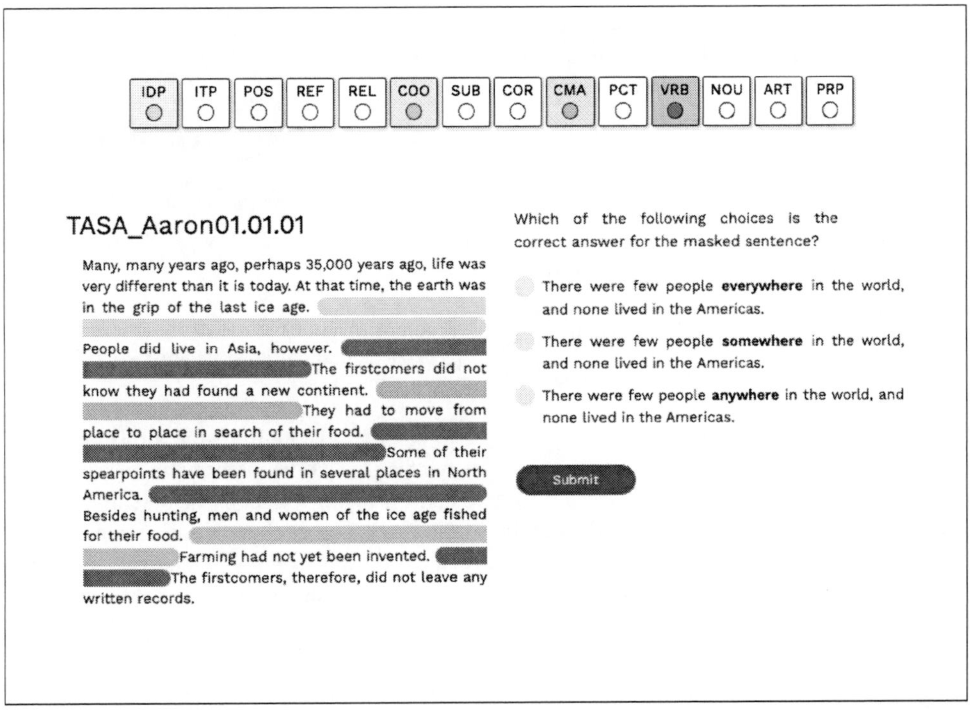

Figure 3: After a user clicks on a masked sentence on the left side, a grammar question is revealed to the right of the window. The masked sentences are color-coded depending on the grammar constructs, and the short name for each construct can be found in the banner at the top of the page. See Appendix A for the full names of the grammar constructs, which also appear under the banner when hovered over. The passage shown is an excerpt from the TASA corpus we describe in Section 2.

After submission, the system will create grammar questions from the passage (see Figure 3). Grammar item generation happens at the sentence level. Since completing a Cloze task relies on filling in a blank based on the surrounding context (Taylor, 1953), we create an item out of every other sentence so that the user is provided with both enough context to fill in the blank, and with enough practice as they progress through their reading. Only one grammar item is generated per sentence, and this item will correspond to the first grammar construct that can be found in the sentence that our distractor generation algorithm successfully generates an item for.

Next, the grammar items will appear to the user in the form of masked sentences. When a sentence is masked, it becomes clickable to the user. And once clicked on, the question choices will appear on the right side of the window. If the student selects an incorrect answer they are prompted to try again. But when the correct answer is selected the sentence becomes unmasked so that they may proceed with their reading. For each correct answer AGREE provides feedback to encourage and motivate the learner.

The system has been tested thoroughly on informational texts such as the Touchstone Applied Science Associates (TASA) corpus which "consists of representative random samples of text of all kinds read by students in each grade through first year of college" (Zeno et al., 1995; Landauer et al., 1998). Note that the system itself does not have any dependency to a particular corpus, and so in theory can be used with texts from any domain.

3 Grammar item generation

Creating a grammar item from a sentence involves the following steps:

1. Token matching
2. Syntactic pattern matching
3. Sentence validation
4. Sentence filtering
5. Distractor generation

We use the following sentence "There were few people anywhere in the world, and none lived in the Americas" as our running example to show how to create the grammar item (Figure 1).

3.1 Token matching

Let's say the first grammar construct on the priority list is *indefinite pronoun*. First, we determine whether the sentence contains a token in our pre-defined list of indefinite pronouns: *everybody*, *everywhere*, *everything*, *somebody*, *somewhere*, *something*, *anybody*, *anywhere*, *anything*, *nobody*, *nowhere*, *nothing*.[3]

3.2 Syntactic pattern matching

The system finds *anywhere*, and this prompts a check to make sure the syntactic properties of the token match those of the grammar construct. Each grammar construct has a pattern defined using dependency parse tags and part of speech tags from spaCy.[4]

3.3 Sentence validation

The syntactic properties of *anywhere* matches the pattern defined for the indefinite pronoun construct, so at this point we have identified the grammar construct in the sentence and know its location. The token *anywhere* is replaced with a `[MASK]` token, and we use the pre-trained language model BERT (Devlin et al., 2018) (as implemented in the Hugging Face (Wolf et al., 2019) repository) to predict the most likely substitution for `[MASK]`. We currently only handle words that are common enough to exist in the vocabulary of the BERT tokenizer; our closed classes of distractor choices can all be found, but we may skip over an open class word if it turns out that the noun or verb is tokenized into separate wordpieces. The other tokens from the set of indefinite pronouns (Section 3.1) become distractor candidates that feed into our distractor generation step in Section 3.5.

3.4 Sentence filtering

If the word that was originally in the sentence (here, *anywhere*) does not rank the highest in terms of probability score among the construct type (here, indefinite pronouns) as predicted by BERT in the previous step, it indicates that there is ambiguity in the correct answer to fill the `[MASK]` location with.

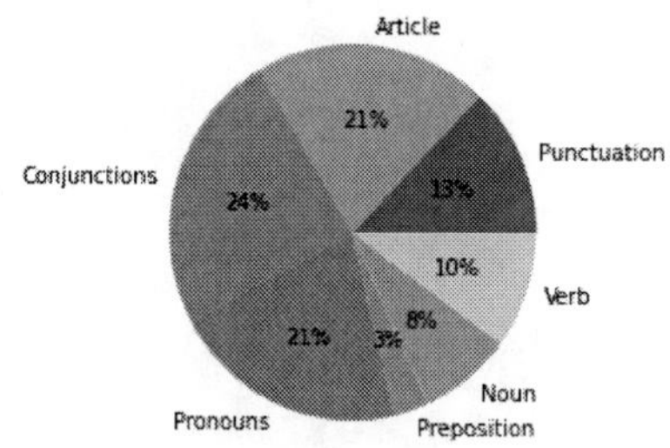

Figure 4: The distribution of grammar constructs in generated questions presented to Turkers (N=4,568).

In other words, multiple indefinite pronouns may suit the context. In our example *anywhere* ranks the highest among the set of the indefinite pronouns at the `[MASK]` location, so we continue onto the next step for item generation. Otherwise, we discard the item from further processing.

3.5 Distractor generation

It is important for a Cloze task that the distractors are plausible yet incorrect. Gao et al. (2020) argued that the BERT-based predictions for a masked word fits the requirements of a Cloze task perfectly. In other words, the most likely substitutions for a `[MASK]` token can be used as distractors. Thus, similar to Gao et al. (2020), based on the probability scores of the indefinite pronouns, we select the highest ranking candidates (except the token *anywhere*) as the distractor.

For nouns and verbs, the process remains the same except parts-of-speech tags are used in the place of a pre-defined list of tokens. We use the lemminflect package to create the list of possible candidates by inflecting the stem word.[5]

For comma items, the candidates are all possible relocations of the comma. We create the distractor candidates by inserting a `[MASK]` token in-between every word.

4 Evaluation

We are interested in evaluating the quality of the multiple-choice items in AGREE. To that end, we conduct a large-scale MTurk study where we present crowd-raters with our generated grammar exercises as shown in Figure 3. We ask the raters to select their choice for each item, and to answer followup questions along four aspects of item quality. We paid raters $1.70 USD for completing our

[3] `https://www.gingersoftware.com/content/grammar-rules`

[4] `https://spacy.io`

[5] `https://lemminflect.readthedocs.io`

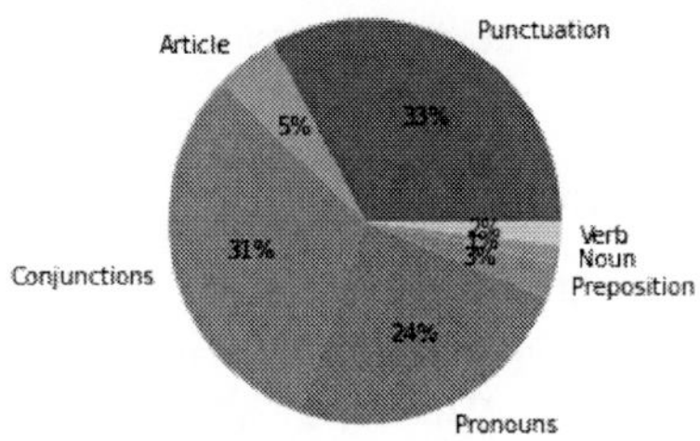

Figure 5: The distribution of grammar constructs in generated questions with two or fewer correct answers (N=455).

prerequisite task and $2.00 USD for completing our main task, which is approximately equivalent to $20-$24 USD (per hour). In total, the evaluation cost $12,575 USD.

4.1 Prerequisite task

We conducted a set of prerequisite tasks to select the raters for our main task on AGREE. A rater must have at least 10,000 approved HITs, $\geq 95\%$ of HIT approval, a Masters qualification, and reside in the United States. We also ask the raters to answer a set of 20 publicly available TOEFL Junior reading comprehension questions (typically used for assessing English language skills of students 11 or older) so that we can gauge raters' English proficiency.[6]

The mean score on this set of reading comprehension questions among 79 raters is 96%, and 95% of raters received a score of 90% or higher, meaning they got at most two questions out of 20 incorrect. Responses from this high-performing group make up 99.8% of our responses. Given that the raters have some competence in the language, we expect that they will be able to identify the correct answer among the choices. If they are unable to do so, it will provide a strong indication that our generated items are incorrectly keyed.

4.2 Main task

Raters are presented with two passages containing grammar questions from AGREE. The setup is identical to how we present the questions on the front-end (Figure 3), and the method for generating grammar items is the same as described previously (Section 3). Each passage is around 10 sentences long, taken from the beginning of either a TASA (Zeno et al., 1995) or a TIPSTER (Harman, 1993) document. Altogether 4,568 grammar constructs items were presented to the raters. Five different raters responded to each item to select the correct answer. The distribution of the items is shown in Figure 4.

Among the 4,568 items that we generated, for 76% of items all five raters answered correctly. If we consider items where the majority of raters answered correctly (i.e, three or more selected the target), then the proportion increases to 95%. This is an indication that nearly all our items are correctly keyed. On the contrary, there were 455 instances where only a minority of raters chose the correct answer. Among these items, the article, verb, and noun items are less frequent whereas the punctuation and conjunctions items are the most frequent (see Figure 5).

To shed some light on why raters made mistakes on certain items, we randomly select one example each of punctuation and conjunctions items where no raters answered correctly. Note that we present the choices here in order of their ranking from BERT (the log probability is in parentheses), but when presented to raters the choices are randomly shuffled. Here is an example of a problematic punctuation (comma) item:

> **source sentence**: With so many children in the family___ there___ was a constant___ buzz of activity
> **target**: ... family, ... (12.76)
> **distractor**: ... constant, ... (7.17)
> **distractor**: ... there, ... (6.07)

And here is an example of a problematic conjunctions (coordinating conjunction) item:

> **source sentence**: Many of these people did not go to the theater, of course, ___ to keep playgoers happy, acting troupes had to provide a variety of plays.
> **target**: but (13.93)
> **distractor**: and (13.39)
> **distractor**: so (12.18)

In both items, all five raters selected the highest-ranking distractor as their answer. This supports the idea that the contextual probabilities are useful predictors of distractor-context fit. While the placement of the comma in the target is the only proper usage in the punctuation example, one might argue that both *but* and *and* are grammatical in the conjunctions source sentence. However, the use of the

[6] https://www.ets.org/toefl_junior/prepare/standard_sample_questions/reading_comprehension

connective *but* more accurately describes the relationship between the first and second clause. Given that the probability of the distractor and target are so close in the conjunctions example, we suspect that the distance between the probabilities provides some signal about item difficulty, but future work is needed to investigate and calibrate the difficulty of the grammar items.

The purpose of our MTurk experiment is not only to measure how many items are solvable by the raters, but also to know specific aspects about them. Such as whether (1) the items are correctly keyed (i.e., we have accurately and unambiguously identified the target) (2) the item contains nonfunctional distractors (Gierl et al., 2017), (3) the item can be distinguished from a human-generated one, and finally, (4) the item was difficult. To answer these four questions we also asked the same group of raters to respond a five-point Likert scale (Strongly Disagree, Disagree, Neutral, Agree, Strongly Agree) to the following statements, respectively.

1. *I felt that there was more than one correct answer*
2. *I felt that some response options were too obviously wrong*
3. *The question was likely created by a teacher*
4. *The question was easy*

Figure 6 presents four bar charts displaying the distribution of the responses to the above four questions from left to right. We find corroborating evidence that the items are correctly keyed: 85% of responses agree that the items have only one correct answer (Figure 6(a)). As for whether some options are too obviously wrong, the results appear to be mixed; no clear pattern in the responses can be observed (Figure 6(b)). We find that more often than not, raters found our items indistinguishable from those created by teachers, but here we also do not observe a clear pattern (Figure 6(c)). Finally, nearly all responses say that the items are easy. Gathering data from second language learners could help clarify whether the items are easy for English learners as well (Figure 6(d)).

Overall, the MTurk results paint a promising picture for the utility of our items. Since 95% of items were answered correctly by a majority of raters, and 85% agree that there was only one correct answer, we have strong indicators that nearly all our items are correctly keyed.

5 Related work

Tools that enhance authentic texts in support of grammar acquisition include WERTi (Meurers et al., 2010), FLAIR (Chinkina and Meurers, 2016), and GrammarTagger (Hagiwara et al., 2021). Except for a verb practice activity in WERTi, these tools provide few opportunities for immediate feedback. Our system fills this gap by generating multiple-choice practice questions from authentic texts.

On the other hand, there are also systems that generate multiple-choice grammar questions. FAST (Chen et al., 2006) covers nine grammatical categories and Lee et al. (2016) create a system for learning preposition usage. We extend these works by not only covering a range of grammatical categories and collecting perception responses, but also conducting a large-scale evaluation on item performance (i.e., whether the item can be solved by the user with some competence in the language).

6 Conclusion

We describe AGREE, a system and procedure for converting an informational passage into game-like grammar practice exercises that can be completed while reading. We find in human evaluations that nearly all the multiple-choice questions we generate for the exercises are correctly keyed, and can therefore be used to provide immediate feedback to students. We also observe for almost 95% of items that a majority of the raters were able to identify the correct target. On the contrary, raters made the most mistakes for punctuation and conjunctions. Although we did not design our system to include gamification explicitly, it is set up in a way that makes it easy to incorporate in the future. The system can automatically generate a wealth of questions for which the correct answer is identified, and these questions can be used by whomever (e.g., game designers) to create a game that rewards learners when they correctly solve them.

7 Future work

AGREE is a proof of concept system we built with the intent of allowing users to personalize grammar items according to their unique goals. The user interface does not currently prevent learners from

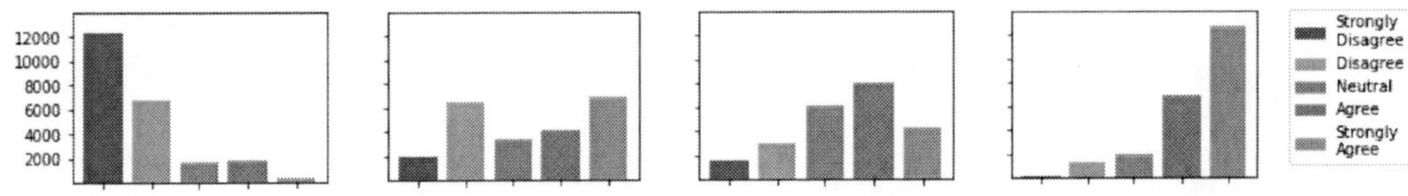

(a) *I felt that there was more than one correct answer.*

(b) *I felt that some response options were too obviously wrong.*

(c) *The question was likely created by a teacher.*

(d) *The question was easy.*

Figure 6: Bar charts displaying the distribution of responses for each item quality aspect over the five Likert scale options (N=22,840).

progressing through the passage without providing answer for each question. In fact, it is likely that they can still complete the reading since it is usually a weakly semantic element missing from the sentence. A truly gamified system may choose to block out the rest of the passage before the current question is answered, or make it so that the next question cannot be clicked on until the current question is answered.

As it stands, the system allows teachers some control over the generated items; the reading material itself and the ranking of grammar constructs can be customized. However, teachers do not have control at the level of individual items. We may want to build in this finer-grained control in the future so that the exercises can be adapted more closely to their needs. Currently, the number of questions generated for a given construct (e.g., preposition) depends on that construct's ranking, its frequency in the text, and how well it is covered in the manually created list of distractor choices. For example, there may be fewer preposition items generated than expected due to the fact that we use a reduced set of prepositions in AGREE. If we expand the set of distractor choices to cover all possible prepositions, we would likely run into latency issues.

While increasing the coverage of existing constructs is one potential line of future work, it may be more important to find ways to align our constructs to existing EFL (English as a Foreign Language) curricula if we want to create efficacious questions. Since the constructs that a learner struggles with is influenced by—among other factors—aspects of their learner profile such as English level (Hawkins and Buttery, 2010) and language background, an efficacious system should take these aspects into account. Doing so may allow AGREE to provide more personalized feedback and generate distractors that can be calibrated. For example, we can imagine using token-level probabilities to make filtering decisions about whether an item is appropriate for a certain language level. The distance between the target log probability and the log probability of the hardest distractor can be smaller for a learner whose language level is higher, assuming that as language ability improves, so does the ability to discriminate between a correct choice and a plausible yet incorrect one.

This raises the question about the threshold at which a token can be considered grammatical versus not, as illustrated in the coordinating conjunction example in Section 4.2. According to Larsen-Freeman (2001), one way to think about grammar is to see it as an interaction between form/structure, meaning/semantics, and use/pragmatics. Schneider and Gilquin (2016) also argue that, when it comes to learner English, there is no "clear dichotomy between innovation and error". Following this line of thinking, we view the threshold for grammaticality as context-specific and tied to pedagogical goals.

More experimentation is also needed to determine how the quality of the questions changes when individual components are altered or replaced. To increase the flexibility of the system, we can think of replacing the token matching and syntactic pattern matching components with a more specialized model that identifies the gap locations, such as the one described in Felice et al. (2022). As such, making the system more functional would involve building in the ability to evaluate the output of individual components in addition to the final output.

References

Chia-Yin Chen, Hsien-Chin Liou, and Jason S Chang. 2006. Fast–an automatic generation system for grammar tests. In *Proceedings of the COLING/ACL 2006 Interactive Presentation Sessions*, pages 1–4.

Maria Chinkina and Detmar Meurers. 2016. Linguistically aware information retrieval: Providing input enrichment for second language learners. In *Proceedings of the 11th Workshop on Innovative use of NLP for Building Educational Applications*, pages 188–198.

Jacob Devlin, Ming-Wei Chang, Kenton Lee, and Kristina Toutanova. 2018. Bert: Pre-training of deep bidirectional transformers for language understanding. *arXiv preprint arXiv:1810.04805*.

Mariano Felice, Shiva Taslimipoor, and Paula Buttery. 2022. Constructing open cloze tests using generation and discrimination capabilities of transformers. *arXiv preprint arXiv:2204.07237*.

Lingyu Gao, Kevin Gimpel, and Arnar Jensson. 2020. Distractor analysis and selection for multiple-choice cloze questions for second-language learners. In *Proceedings of the 15th Workshop on Innovative Use of NLP for Building Educational Applications*, pages 102–114.

Mark J Gierl, Okan Bulut, Qi Guo, and Xinxin Zhang. 2017. Developing, analyzing, and using distractors for multiple-choice tests in education: A comprehensive review. *Review of Educational Research*, 87(6):1082–1116.

Mark J Gierl, Hollis Lai, and Vasily Tanygin. 2021. *Advanced Methods in Automatic Item Generation*. Routledge.

Masato Hagiwara, Joshua Tanner, and Keisuke Sakaguchi. 2021. Grammartagger: A multilingual, minimally-supervised grammar profiler for language education. *arXiv preprint arXiv:2104.03190*.

Donna Harman. 1993. Overview of the first trec conference. In *Proceedings of the 16th Annual International ACM SIGIR Conference on Research and Development in Information Retrieval*, pages 36–47.

John A Hawkins and Paula Buttery. 2010. Criterial features in learner corpora: Theory and illustrations. *English Profile Journal*, 1.

Hsiu-Ting Hung, Jie Chi Yang, Gwo-Jen Hwang, Hui-Chun Chu, and Chun-Chieh Wang. 2018. A scoping review of research on digital game-based language learning. *Computers & Education*, 126:89–104.

Gladys Jean and Daphnée Simard. 2011. Grammar teaching and learning in l2: Necessary, but boring? *Foreign Language Annals*, 44(3):467–494.

Thomas K Landauer, Peter W Foltz, and Darrell Laham. 1998. An introduction to latent semantic analysis. *Discourse Processes*, 25(2-3):259–284.

Diane Larsen-Freeman. 2001. Teaching grammar. *Teaching English as a Second or Foreign Language*, 3:251–266.

John SY Lee, Donald Sturgeon, and Mengqi Luo. 2016. A call system for learning preposition usage. In *Proceedings of the 54th Annual Meeting of the Association for Computational Linguistics (Volume 1: Long Papers)*, pages 984–993.

Detmar Meurers, Ramon Ziai, Luiz Amaral, Adriane Boyd, Aleksandar Dimitrov, Vanessa Metcalf, and Niels Ott. 2010. Enhancing authentic web pages for language learners. In *Proceedings of the Fifth Workshop on Innovative Use of NLP for Building Educational Applications*, pages 10–18.

Pauline F Moley, Patricia E Bandré, and John E George. 2011. Moving beyond readability: Considering choice, motivation and learner engagement. *Theory into Practice*, 50(3):247–253.

Jan L Plass, Bruce D Homer, and Charles K Kinzer. 2015. Foundations of game-based learning. *Educational Psychologist*, 50(4):258–283.

Gerold Schneider and Gaëtanelle Gilquin. 2016. Detecting innovations in a parsed corpus of learner english. *International Journal of Learner Corpus Research*, 2(2):177–204.

Wilson L Taylor. 1953. Cloze procedure: A new tool for measuring readability. *Journalism Quarterly*, 30(4):415–433.

Thomas Wolf, Lysandre Debut, Victor Sanh, Julien Chaumond, Clement Delangue, Anthony Moi, Pierric Cistac, Tim Rault, Rémi Louf, Morgan Funtowicz, et al. 2019. Huggingface's transformers: State-of-the-art natural language processing. *arXiv preprint arXiv:1910.03771*.

Florence WM Yip and Alvin CM Kwan. 2006. Online vocabulary games as a tool for teaching and learning english vocabulary. *Educational Media International*, 43(3):233–249.

Susan Zeno, Stephen H Ivens, Robert T Millard, and Raj Duvvuri. 1995. *The Educator's Word Frequency Guide*. Touchstone Applied Science Associates.

A Grammar constructs

Each grammar construct and its sub-constructs are listed in Table 1, along with the set of distractor candidates used for the token matching step from Section 3.1 and distractor candidate generation step from Section 3.5.

Construct			Distractor candidates
Punctuation	Comma location	CMA	All possible relocations
	Punctuation	PCT	: ; ,
Article		ART	the, a, an
Conjunctions	Coordinating conjunction	COO	for, nor, but, or, yet, so, and
	Subordinating conjunction	SUB	after, although, because, before, if, once, since, than, unless, until, when, whenever, while, as
	Correlative conjunction	COR	either/or, neither/nor, both/and, as/so, whether/or
Pronouns	Indefinite pronoun	IDP	everybody, everywhere, everything, somebody, somewhere, somewhere, something, anybody, anywhere, anything, nobody, nowhere, nothing
	Interrogative pronoun	ITP	who, which, what, whose, whom
	Possessive pronoun	POS	my, mine, your, yours, our, ours, their, theirs
	Reflexive pronoun	REL	myself, yourself, herself, himself, itself, yourselves, ourselves, themselves
Preposition		PRP	to, toward, on, onto, in, into
Noun		NOU	NN, NNS
Verb		VRB	VB, VBD, VBG, VBN, VBP, VBZ

Table 1: The available grammar constructs and their distractor candidates. All the possible tokens are enumerated except for *comma location* where the candidates are all possible relocations of the comma, and *noun* and *verb* items where candidates are inflections of the word stem.

BotSIM: An End-to-End Bot Simulation Framework for Commercial Task-Oriented Dialog Systems

Guangsen Wang[♣] **Samson Tan**[◇*] **Shafiq Joty**[♣] **Gang Wu**[♣] **Jimmy Au**[♣] **Steven Hoi**[♣]

[♣]Salesforce Research

[◇]AWS AI Research & Education

{guangsen.wang, sjoty, jimmy.au, gang.wu, shoi}@salesforce.com

Abstract

We present BotSIM, a data-efficient end-to-end **Bot SIM**ulation framework for commercial text-based task-oriented dialog (TOD) systems. BotSIM consists of three major components: 1) a *Generator* that can infer semantic-level dialog acts and entities from bot definitions and generate user queries via model-based paraphrasing; 2) an agenda-based dialog user *Simulator* (ABUS) to simulate conversations with the dialog agents; 3) a *Remediator* to analyze the simulated conversations, visualize the bot health reports and provide actionable remediation suggestions for bot troubleshooting and improvement. We demonstrate BotSIM's effectiveness in end-to-end evaluation, remediation and multi-intent dialog generation via case studies on two commercial bot platforms. BotSIM's "generation-simulation-remediation" paradigm accelerates the end-to-end bot evaluation and iteration process by: 1) reducing manual test cases creation efforts; 2) enabling a holistic gauge of the bot in terms of NLU and end-to-end performance via extensive dialog simulation; 3) improving the bot troubleshooting process with actionable suggestions. A demo of our system can be found at `https://tinyurl.com/mryu74cd` and a demo video at `https://youtu.be/qLi5iSoly30`.

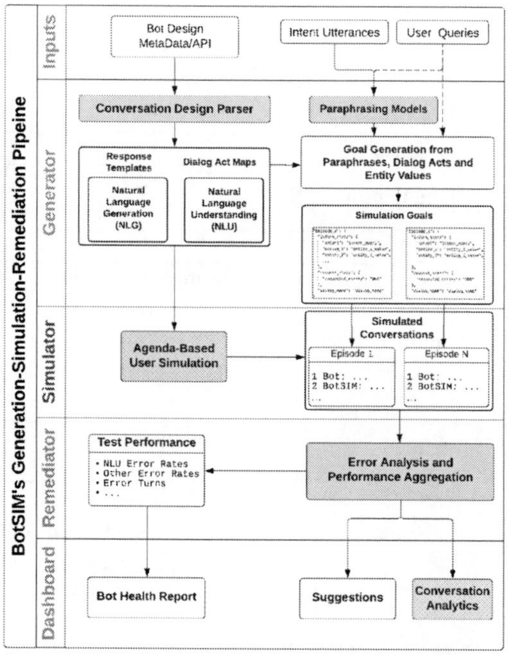

Figure 1: BotSIM overview including the generator, simulator, and remediator. The dotted (optional) paths from users can be used for bot performance monitoring: they can provide production chat logs or manually crafted utterances when creating evaluation goals.

1 Introduction

The typical dialog system development cycle consists of dialog design, pre-deployment testing, deployment, performance monitoring, model improvement and iteration. As in any production software system, effective and comprehensive testing at all stages is of paramount importance. Unfortunately, *evaluating and troubleshooting* production TOD systems is still a largely manual process requiring large amount of human conversations with the systems. This process is time-consuming, expensive, and inevitably fails to capture the breadth of language variation present in the real world (Tan et al., 2021). The time- and labor-intensive nature of such an approach is further exacerbated when the developer significantly changes the dialog flows, since new sets of test dialogs will need to be created (Benvie et al., 2020). Performing comprehensive end-to-end bot evaluation is highly challenging due to the need for additional annotation efforts. Finally, there is a lack of analytical tools for interpreting test results and troubleshooting underlying bot issues.

To address these limitations, we present *BotSIM*, a **Bot SIM**ulation environment for data-efficient end-to-end commercial bot evaluation, remediation via multi-intent dialog generation and agenda-

[*]Work done at Salesforce Research.

Proceedings of the The 2022 Conference on Empirical Methods in Natural Language Processing: System Demonstrations, pages 178 - 190
December 7-11, 2022

based dialog user simulation (Schatzmann et al., 2007). BotSIM consists of three major modules, namely Generator, Simulator, and Remediator (Figure 1). We use a pretrained sequence-to-sequence T5 model (Zhang et al., 2019; Raffel et al., 2020) in the Generator to simulate lexical and syntactic variations in user queries via paraphrasing. The Generator is also responsible to generate various templates needed by the Simulator. To make BotSIM more platform- and task- agnostic, we adopt dialog-act level ABUS to simulate conversations with bots via APIs. The dialog acts are automatically inferred by the Generator via a unified interface to convert bot designs of different platforms to a universal graph representation. The graph has all dialogs as nodes and their transitions as edges. Through graph traversal, BotSIM offers a principled and scalable approach to generating and exploring multi-intent conversations. Not only can the conversation path generation greatly increase evaluation coverage for troubleshooting dialog errors caused by faulty designs (*e.g.,* unexpected dialog loops), it is also valuable for bot design improvements. The Remediator summarizes bots' health status in a dashboard for easy comprehension. It also analyzes the simulated conversations to identify any issues and further provides actionable suggestions to remedy them.

BotSIM's "generation-simulation-remediation" paradigm can significantly accelerate bot development and evaluation, reducing human efforts, cost and time-to-market. Our contributions include:

- We propose BotSIM, a modular, data-efficient bot simulation framework. To the best of our knowledge, this is the first work focused on end-to-end evaluation, diagnosis and remediation of commercial bots via ABUS.
- BotSIM offers a principled approach to generating and simulating multi-intent dialogs for comprehensive evaluation coverage and better bot design.
- We finetuned a T5 paraphrasing model on par with the state-of-the-art performance to generate diverse user responses for greater test coverage of language variation.
- An easy-to-use Streamlit[1] Web App with Flask back-end and SQL database is developed for bot practitioners. The App can be deployed as a docker container or to Heroku[2].

[1] https://streamlit.io/

[2] https://www.heroku.com

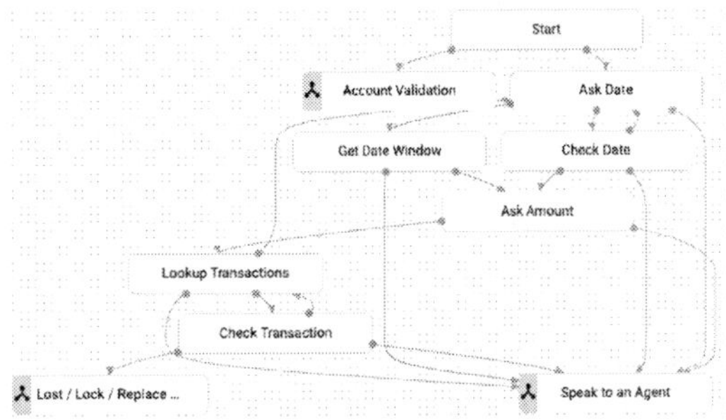

Figure 2: "Investigate Charges" flow of the DialogFlow CX pre-built "Financial Service Agent" mega-agent

2 Related Work

There are two main categories of dialog user simulators, namely the agenda-based user simulator (ABUS) (Schatzmann et al., 2007; Li et al., 2016; Shi et al., 2019; Zhu et al., 2020; Liu et al., 2021; Shah et al., 2018) and recent neural-based user simulator (NUS) (Asri et al., 2016; Crook and Marin, 2017; Kreyssig et al., 2018; Gur et al., 2018; Liu et al., 2017). Since BotSIM is designed to support commercial bot evaluation and remediation, we focus on the review of the testing capacities offered by some existing bot platforms rather than the simulators. Recently, ABUS is also used in Amazon's Alexa conversation (Acharya et al., 2021) for training an end-to-end dialog agent, which is also beyond the scope of our discussion.

2.1 IBM Watson Assistant

IBM Watson assistant offers a suite of open-source Python libraries and notebooks to help analyze customer bots using manually created or annotated test cases (Benvie et al., 2020). An exemplar test case used for the standard regression testing is given in Table 2. Given the annotated conversations, the notebooks offer some analytical functions to compute two metrics, namely coverage (NLU) and effectiveness (task completion) to monitor the bot performance. However, the manual annotation and analysis still require significant expertise and involvement of bot teams. Large scale automatic pre-deployment performance evaluation and analysis are also infeasible since there may not be enough chat logs.

2.2 Google DialogFlow CX

CX offers a built-in regression testing environment for users to create test dialogs and perform regression testing. To create "golden" test cases, users

	Methods		Stages		Automation		Metrics	
	Regression	End-to-end	Pre-deployment	Monitoring	Test case curation	User Simulation	NLU	Task Completion
CX	✓			✓				
Watson	✓			✓			✓	✓
Botium	✓						✓	
BotSIM	✓	✓	✓	✓	✓	✓	✓	✓

Table 1: Comparison of bot evaluation capabilities of the reviewed commercial bot platforms

User:	May I book a flight to New York?
Labels	**Intent: #flight**
	Entity: @Destination
Bot:	When would you like to depart?

Table 2: Example of IBM Watson assistant test case

need to manually chat with the bot and annotate each system turn with correct intent, entity and dialog transitions. During regression testing, each bot response is matched against the golden labels to detect regressions. To achieve good regression testing coverage, users have to "design" testing dialogs to cover as many conversation paths as possible. However, the number of paths grows exponentially with the number of intents and dialog branches, making it almost impossible to craft testing cases for all paths (Figure 2). For end-to-end performance evaluation, even more annotated dialogs are needed to cover the language variation in user responses, which will greatly intensify the manual efforts.

2.3 Botium: Bots Testing Bots

Botium[3] offers a unified platform for regression testings of various bot platforms via platform-specific connectors and "Botium scripts (test cases)" (Appendix A). The core component, dubbed as "Botium Box", analogous to a bot testing "IDE", can be used to connect different bot platforms, create testing cases and conduct regression testings. However, the testing capability is constrained by the underlying platforms. For example, users may be still required to design testing dialogs manually. Therefore, Botium cannot perform large scale end-to-end pre-deployment testing.

The overall comparison of different platforms is given in Table 1. Most current platforms only focus on regression testing. While regression testing is important to ensure correct and consistent system behaviours, it is also vital to perform pre-deployment evaluation to avoid poor user adoption and retention rate. Although some platforms are capable of computing turn-level NLU metrics, they require significant manual efforts in curating or annotating test cases. In addition, the NLU metrics do not directly translate to the end-to-end goal completion performance. We will show how BotSIM can help circumvent these limitations via large scale automatic dialog generation and simulation.

3 BotSIM

BotSIM system overview is shown in Figure 1.

3.1 Generator

The generator takes bot designs and intent utterances as input and produces the required configuration files and dialog goals for dialog simulation.

Dialog act maps. Most commercial TOD bots follow a "rule-action-message" design scheme and there exist clear mappings from system messages to rules/actions. For example, the utterance "May I get your email?" (message) is used to "Collect" (action) the "Email" (slot) with entity type "Email" from the user. Therefore, this message can be mapped to the "request_Email" dialog act by the generator parser. As the only platform-specific component, the parser acts as an "adaptor" to unify bot definitions from different platforms to a common representation of dialog act maps (example in Figure 3) from bot messages to dialog acts. Such (local) dialog acts are automatically inferred by the parser for each dialog. Furthermore, the parser unifies the entire bot design as a graph, where individual dialogs are vertices and their transitions are edges. Each graph node is initially associated with its "local" dialog act map. The dialog act map of a "mega" dialog containing references to other dialogs will be updated by including all the "local" dialog act maps of the dialog nodes along the paths starting from the mega dialog to the terminating dialogs (*e.g.,* "End_Chat"). The algorithm is detailed in Appendix 1. The graph modeling not only enables BotSIM to naturally support the simulation of mega-agents with multiple intents/dialogs

[3] https://www.botium.ai/

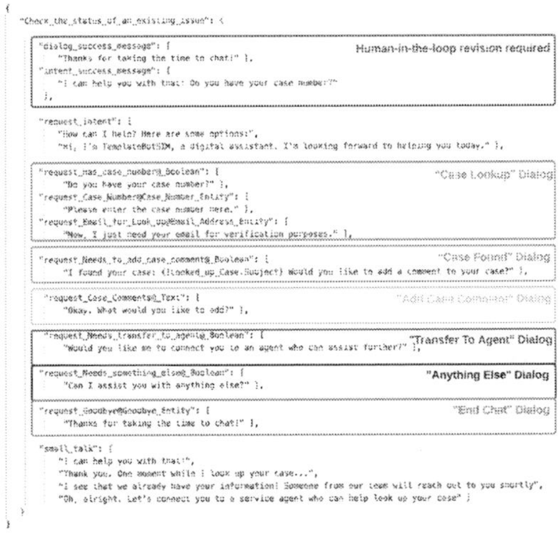

Figure 3: Automatically generated dialog act maps for the mega dialog "Check the status of an existing issue" from the Salesforce Einstein BotBuilder Template Bot.

(Figure 2), it also offers a scalable and controllable approach to exploring conversation paths for greater test coverage and potentially benefiting the conversation design as well.

The generated dialog act maps serve as the BotSIM NLU module to map system messages to dialog acts via fuzzy matching.[4] In particular, the two dialog acts, "dialog_success_message" and "intent_success_message" are the golden labels indicating a successful dialog and a correct intent classification, respectively. They are inferred heuristically by taking the first message as "intent_success_message" and last message as "dialog_success_mesage". BotSIM users are required to review or revise these two dialog acts for each evaluation dialog to confirm their correctness.

Simulation goals. For agenda-based dialog simulation, a user goal comprises a set of dialog acts and entity slot-value pairs needed to complete the task defined by the goal. The dialog acts and slots are from the parsed dialog act maps and the entity values are randomly initialised according to some heuristics. As the entity values are mostly related to products/services, to better test bot NER capabilities, users can replace these random values to real ones when generating simulation goals. Below is a snippet of a simulation goal. The goal is generated by collecting the entity-value pairs in the dialog act map and the ontology. The "inform_slots" contains entities to be "informed" to the bot, whereas the "request_slots" comprises entities to be "requested" from the bot.

```
Check_the_status_of_an_existing_issue_0:
  goal: Check_the_status_of_an_existing_issue
  inform_slots:
    Email_for_Look_Up: andrews@ms-mail.com
    Case_Number: C379870
    Intent: Can I check the latest status of
            my reported issue?
  request_slots:
    Check_the_status_of_an_existing_issue: UNK
  ...
```

All the entity-value pairs in "inform_slots" of the goals are used to test bots' NLU capabilities. The special "intent" slot contains the intent queries generated by the paraphrasing models for pre-deployment testing or user-provided evaluation utterances for performance monitoring.

T5 paraphrasing model. As a core model component, we fine-tune a T5-base (Raffel et al., 2020) model for paraphrasing. To further improve the diversity, model ensemble with an off-the-shelf Huggingface Pegasus (Zhang et al., 2019) model[5] is adopted. The paraphrasing models take intent utterances as input and output their top N paraphrases by beam search. The paraphrases are subsequently filtered by discarding candidates with low semantic similarity scores and edit distances. The filtered paraphrases serve as the "intent" slot values of the goals as intent queries for pre-deployment testing. Our T5-base paraphrasing model has very competitive performance on par with the state-of-the-art HVQ-VAE model as shown in Table 3. It is worth noting that the T5 model yields significantly lower self-BLEU scores, which means the generated paraphrases share less lexical similarities with the source sentences, a merit desirable for BotSIM in generating dialogs to cover greater breadth of language variation. More details of the T5 model are discussed in Appendix B.

3.2 Simulator

We use a dialog-act-level ABUS rather than NUS for the following reasons. First, BotSIM targets commercial use cases and simulation duration and computation are crucial non-functional considerations. NUS inference usually requires GPUs, which can significantly increase the barrier to entry and operational cost. Second, NUS requires large amounts of annotated data to train and are prone to overfitting. Finally, dialogue-act-level simulation is more platform- and task-agnostic. The user

[4] https://github.com/seatgeek/thefuzz

[5] https://huggingface.co/tuner007/pegasus_paraphrase

	WIKI-Answers			QQP		
	Target (↑)	Self(↓)	iBLEU (↑)	Target(↑)	Self(↓)	iBLEU(↑)
HVQ-VAE	39.5	33.0	24.9	30.5	40.2	16.4
T5-base	33.9	23.9	23.9	29.1	35.2	16.3

Table 3: Paraphrasing model comparison. BLEUs are computed from the top one paraphrase with the reference (Target-BLEU)/input (Self-BLEU). iBLEUs are obtained by a weighted sum of target (0.8) and self BLEUs (-0.2).

simulator can be viewed as a dialog agent with its NLU, NLG and dialog state manager.

NLU. BotSIM uses dialog act maps to map bot messages to dialog acts via fuzzy matching.

NLG. For efficient end-to-end dialog simulation, template-based NLG is adopted to convert user dialog acts to natural language responses. Given a dialog act, *e.g.,* "request_Email", a response is randomly chosen from a set of pre-defined templates with a "Email" slot, which is replaced by the value in the goal during dialog simulation. The plug-and play user response templates can be constantly updated to include more language variation as encountered in real use cases.

Dialog state manager. Rule-based dialog manager is used for its simplicity and robustness. The dialog states are maintained as a stack-like structure called agenda. During simulation, user dialog acts are popped from the agenda to respond to different system dialog acts. The two most important rules are for responding to "request" and "inform" dialog acts. While most of the bot behaviours/messages can be converted to these two dialog acts, BotSIM allows users to implement new rules to accommodate novel dialog acts that may only exist in their own bot designs. Figure 4 illustrates an API-based conversation turn between BotSIM and the bot during dialog simulation: Based on the dialog acts matched by the NLU, the state manager applies the corresponding rules to generate the user dialog acts. They are then converted to natural language responses by the NLG and sent back to the bot. The conversation ends when the task has been successfully finished or an error has been captured.

3.3 Remediator

The remediator generates health reports, performs analyses, and provides actionable insights to troubleshoot and improve dialog systems. The reports are presented in a dashboard in Figure 5. More detailed introduction is given in Appendix C.

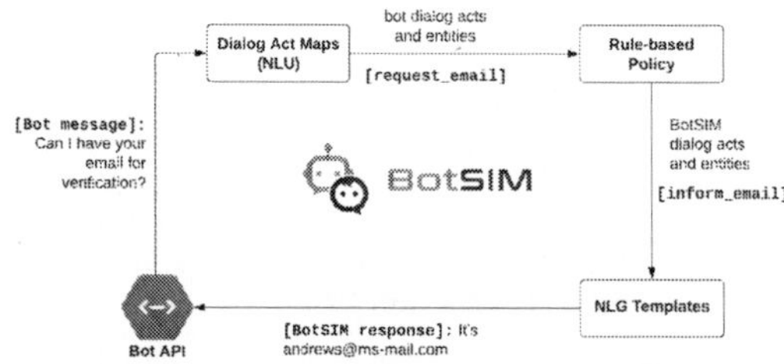

Figure 4: A conversation turn between BotSIM and the bot during a dialog simulation.

Bot health reports. The bot health dashboard consists of a set of multi-level performance reports. At the highest level, users can have a historical view of most recent simulation/test sessions (*e.g.,* after each major bot update) to evaluate the impacts of bot changes from the performance trend in Figure 5(1). Users can also investigate a selected test session as in Figure 5(2). Given a test session, users can select a dialog/intent to check the detailed performance in Figure 5(3). From the detailed intent and NER plots, one can easily identify the most confusing intents and entities.

Actionable remediation suggestions. The outputs of the Remediator comprises actionable suggestions from analysing the simulated dialogs with errors in Figure 5(4). The dashboard allows detailed investigation of all intent or NER errors together with the simulated conversation. The root causes of the failed conversations are identified via backtracking of the simulation agenda. For intent models, the intent queries/paraphrases that lead to intent errors are grouped by the original intent utterances sorted by the number of errors in descending order (drop-down list of Figure 5(4)). Depending on the classified intent labels, the remediator would suggest some follow-up actions (Figure 5(5)). For example, augmenting the intent training set with the queries deemed to be out-of-domain by the current intent model, moving the intent utterance to another intent if most of paraphrases of the former intent utterance are classified to the latter intent.

Conversation analytics. Another useful component of the Remediator is the suite of conver-

Figure 5: Remediator dashboard including bot health reports, actionable suggestions and conversation analytics.

sation analytical tools to gain more insights for troubleshooting and improving their dialog systems. They include: confusion matrix analysis (Figure 5(7)) for identifying confusion among intents and potential intent clusters (Thoma, 2017), tSNE (van der Maaten and Hinton, 2008) clustering of the sentence embeddings of intent utterances (Figure 5(8)) to help evaluate the training data quality and detect intent overlaps.

Conversation graph modelling Powered by the underlying conversation graph model, the conversation flow visualisation tool (Figure 5(9)) helps users explore their current dialog designs. For example, users can select the "source" and "target" dialogs to investigate the generated dialog paths. Not only is the tool valuable for comprehensive testing coverage of conversation paths, it also offers a controllable approach to troubleshooting dialog design related errors or improving the bot design.

4 Case Studies

4.1 Salesforce Einstein Bot

The "Template Bot" is the pre-built bot of the Salesforce Einstein BotBuilder platform. It has six intents with hand-crafted training utterances.

Experimental setup. We sample 150 utterances per intent as the training set (train-original) and use the rest for evaluation (eval-original). The six intents are: "Transfer to agent (TA)", "End chat (EC)", "Connect with sales (CS)", "Check issue status (CI)", "Check order status (CO)" and "Report an issue (RI)". We show how BotSIM can be used to perform data-efficient end-to-end evaluation through dialog user simulation. To probe the baseline system, we apply the paraphrasing models to the "train-original" utterances to get the "train-paraphrases" dataset and use it as the development set. Simulation goals are created by taking the "train-paraphrases" as the intent queries to capture the variations in real user intent queries. The "train-paraphrases" goals are then used to evaluate the dialog system via dialog simulation. After simulation, the Remediator produces the performance reports and remediation suggestions. Although the Remediator provides suggestions for remedying both intent and NER errors, we focus on the intent model since it can be retrained (NER model has not supported retraining yet). Another reason is that the entity values in the goals are randomly generated and may not reflect the real-world values. Since the impact of the NER is removed, the improvement of intent performance directly trans-

Model	Eval.	TA	EC	CS	CI	CO	RI
Baseline	original	0.92±0.03	0.95±0.02	0.89±0.03	0.93±0.03	0.94±0.02	0.82±0.04
	paraphr.	0.88±0.01	0.93±0.01	0.85±0.01	0.91±0.01	0.93±0.01	0.77 ±0.02
Retrained	original	0.92±0.03	0.97±0.02	0.93±0.03	0.95±0.02	0.96±0.02	0.87±0.04
	paraphr.	0.89±0.01	0.94±0.01	0.90±0.01	0.94±0.01	0.94±0.01	0.80±0.02

Table 4: Results for the Einstein Bots case study, before and after retraining the intent model with the augmented training set (F1 with 95% confidence interval computed with 10K bootstrapped samples).

	CB (86)	MP (66)	LC (139)	IC (224)	CC (142)	Acc
Baseline	0.84±0.06	0.83±0.07	0.88±0.04	0.95±0.02	0.96±0.02	0.90
Retrained	0.91±0.04	0.89±0.06	0.94±0.03	0.95±0.02	0.95±0.03	0.92

Table 5: F1 (95% confidence interval) comparison of intent models before and after retraining for CX case study

lates to the improvement of dialog success rate. It is also important to note that the suggestions are meant to be used as guidelines rather than strictly followed. They can also be extended by users to include domain expertise. To validate the effectiveness of the remediation suggestions, we augment the recommended misclassified paraphrases to the "train-original" set to form the "train-augmented" set and retrain the intent model. We then compare the performance before and after retraining on the goals created from the "evaluation-original".

Results and analytics. We observe consistent improvements for all intents on the human-written "eval-original" set after model retraining. More challenging intents (lower F1s), *e.g.,* "RI" and "CS", saw larger performance gains compared to the easier ones such as "EC" (higher F1s). This demonstrates the efficacy of BotSIM and is likely due to more paraphrases being selected for retraining the model on the more challenging intents. We applied the paraphrasing models to the "eval-original" set to get the "eval-paraphrases" set to further increase the test coverage. In Table 9, the second row (✗) shows the number of misclassified "eval-original" utterances. Out of the remaining correctly classified "eval-original" utterances in the first row(✓), substantially larger number of them have at least one of their paraphrases in "eval-paraphrases" wrongly classified by the same intent model. This indicates that the diversity introduced by the paraphrasing models potentially expands the test coverage by a large margin.

4.2 Google DialogFlow CX

We use the pre-built financial service mega-agent for the flow-based evaluations. Even for a single flow in Figure 2, it is non-trivial to manually design conversations to cover all paths. Through BotSIM's conversation graph modeling, the flow-based conversations can be simulated by generating goals consisting of the dialog acts of all dialog nodes along a traversal path. On top of these flow-based dialog paths, paraphrases of the intent utterances can be used as the intent queries to probe the NLU performance via dialog simulation. To simulate pre-deployment testing, we choose five flows and split the intent utterances into train and evaluation sets. The intent F1 scores are given in Table 5. The flows are "Check Balance (CB)", "Make Payment (MP)", "Lost Card", "Investigate Charges(IC)", "Compare Cards (CC)". Since the financial bot has only ~30 utterances for training each intent, to obtain a more reliable test set, we use the "eval-paraphrases" set together with the "eval-original". The total number of evaluation intent queries are inside the parentheses of the Table 5 header. Similar to the previous study, retrained intent model outperforms the baseline in terms of both F1 and accuracy (Table 5), especially for the challenging flows such as "CB", "MP".

5 Conclusion

We presented BotSIM, a modular end-to-end bot simulation framework for multi-intent dialog generation and evaluation of commercial TOD systems via agenda-based dialog user simulation. Our case studies show that BotSIM can save substantial manual effort in bot evaluation, troubleshooting and improvement. BotSIM can be easily extended to support new platforms by implementing a set of well-defined parser functions to convert bot messages to dialog acts. We are in the midst of open-sourcing the codes including the Web App. We also plan to support more platforms as future work.

6 Limitations

For efficiency reasons, BotSIM adopts a template-based NLG model for converting user dialog acts to natural languages. Although the template-NLG is more controllable and flexible compared to the model-based NLG, they may lack naturalness. One possible future improvement includes a combination of template-based NLG and the model-based NLG. For example, we can train a model-based NLG to generate templates (Wiseman et al., 2018) for BotSIM's response templates. In this way, both efficiency and naturalness can be achieved.

7 Broader Impact

The pretrained language-model based paraphrasers (T5-base and Pegasus) used in this study are pretrained and finetuned with large scale of text corpora scraped from the web, which may contain biases. These biases may even be propagated to the generated paraphrases, causing harm to the subject of these stereotypes. Although the paraphrasing models are only applied to generate the testing intent queries, BotSIM users are advised to take into consideration these ethical issues and may wish to manually inspect or otherwise filter the generated paraphrases.

References

Anish Acharya, Suranjit Adhikari, Sanchit Agarwal, Vincent Auvray, Nehal Belgamwar, Arijit Biswas, Shubhra Chandra, Tagyoung Chung, Maryam Fazel-Zarandi, Raefer Gabriel, Shuyang Gao, Rahul Goel, Dilek Hakkani-Tür, Jan Jezabek, Abhay Jha, Jiun-Yu Kao, Prakash Krishnan, Peter Ku, Anuj Goyal, Chien-Wei Lin, Qing Liu, Arindam Mandal, Angeliki Metallinou, Vishal Ishwar Naik, Yi Pan, Shachi Paul, Vittorio Perera, Abhishek Sethi, Minmin Shen, Nikko Strom, and Eddie Wang. 2021. Alexa conversations: An extensible data-driven approach for building task-oriented dialogue systems. In *Proceedings of NAACL-HLT 2021*, pages 125–132.

Layla El Asri, Jing He, and Kaheer Suleman. 2016. A sequence-to-sequence model for user simulation in spoken dialogue systems. *CoRR*, abs/1607.00070.

Adam Benvie, Eric Wayne, and Matthew Arnold. 2020. Watson assistant continuous improvement best practices.

Paul A Crook and Alex Marin. 2017. Sequence to Sequence Modeling for User Simulation in Dialog Systems. In *Proceedings of the 18th Annual Conference of the International Speech Communication Association (INTERSPEECH 2017)*, pages 1706–1710. ISCA - International Speech Communication Association.

Izzeddin Gur, Dilek Hakkani-Tur, Gokhan Tur, and Pararth Shah. 2018. User modeling for task oriented dialogues.

Tom Hosking, Hao Tang, and Mirella Lapata. 2022. Hierarchical sketch induction for paraphrase generation. In *Proceedings of the 60th Annual Meeting of the Association for Computational Linguistics (Volume 1: Long Papers)*, pages 2489–2501, Dublin, Ireland. Association for Computational Linguistics.

Florian Kreyssig, Iñigo Casanueva, Pawel Budzianowski, and Milica Gasic. 2018. Neural user simulation for corpus-based policy optimisation for spoken dialogue systems. *CoRR*, abs/1805.06966.

Xiujun Li, Zachary C. Lipton, Bhuwan Dhingra, Lihong Li, Jianfeng Gao, and Yun-Nung Chen. 2016. A user simulator for task-completion dialogues. *CoRR*, abs/1612.05688.

Bing Liu, Gökhan Tür, Dilek Hakkani-Tür, Pararth Shah, and Larry P. Heck. 2017. End-to-end optimization of task-oriented dialogue model with deep reinforcement learning. *CoRR*, abs/1711.10712.

Jiexi Liu, Ryuichi Takanobu, Jiaxin Wen, Dazhen Wan, Hongguang Li, Weiran Nie, Cheng Li, Wei Peng, and Minlie Huang. 2021. Robustness testing of language understanding in task-oriented dialog. In *Proceedings of the 59th Annual Meeting of the Association for Computational Linguistics*.

Adam Paszke, Sam Gross, Francisco Massa, Adam Lerer, James Bradbury, Gregory Chanan, Trevor Killeen, Zeming Lin, Natalia Gimelshein, Luca Antiga, Alban Desmaison, Andreas Kopf, Edward Yang, Zachary DeVito, Martin Raison, Alykhan Tejani, Sasank Chilamkurthy, Benoit Steiner, Lu Fang, Junjie Bai, and Soumith Chintala. 2019. Pytorch: An imperative style, high-performance deep learning library. In H. Wallach, H. Larochelle, A. Beygelzimer, F. d'Alché-Buc, E. Fox, and R. Garnett, editors, *Advances in Neural Information Processing Systems 32*, pages 8024–8035. Curran Associates, Inc.

Colin Raffel, Noam Shazeer, Adam Roberts, Katherine Lee, Sharan Narang, Michael Matena, Yanqi Zhou, Wei Li, and Peter J. Liu. 2020. Exploring the limits of transfer learning with a unified text-to-text transformer.

Nils Reimers and Iryna Gurevych. 2019. Sentence-bert: Sentence embeddings using siamese bert-networks.

Jost Schatzmann, Blaise Thomson, Karl Weilhammer, Hui Ye, and Steve Young. 2007. Agenda-based user simulation for bootstrapping a POMDP dialogue system. In *Human Language Technologies 2007: The Conference of the North American Chapter of the Association for Computational Linguistics; Companion Volume, Short Papers*, pages 149–152, Rochester, New York. Association for Computational Linguistics.

Pararth Shah, Dilek Hakkani-Tür, Gökhan Tür, Abhinav Rastogi, Ankur Bapna, Neha Nayak, and Larry P. Heck. 2018. Building a conversational agent overnight with dialogue self-play. *CoRR*, abs/1801.04871.

Weiyan Shi, Kun Qian, Xuewei Wang, and Zhou Yu. 2019. How to build user simulators to train rl-based dialog systems. *arXiv preprint arXiv:1909.01388*.

Hong Sun and Ming Zhou. 2012. Joint learning of a dual SMT system for paraphrase generation. In *Proceedings of the 50th Annual Meeting of the Association for Computational Linguistics (Volume 2: Short Papers)*, pages 38–42, Jeju Island, Korea. Association for Computational Linguistics.

Samson Tan, Shafiq Joty, Kathy Baxter, Araz Taeihagh, Gregory A. Bennett, and Min-Yen Kan. 2021. Reliability testing for natural language processing systems. In *Proceedings of the 59th Annual Meeting of the Association for Computational Linguistics and the 11th International Joint Conference on Natural Language Processing (Volume 1: Long Papers)*, pages 4153–4169, Online. Association for Computational Linguistics.

Martin Thoma. 2017. Analysis and optimization of convolutional neural network architectures.

Laurens van der Maaten and Geoffrey Hinton. 2008. Visualizing data using t-sne. *Journal of Machine Learning Research*, 9(86):2579–2605.

Sam Wiseman, Stuart M. Shieber, and Alexander M. Rush. 2018. Learning neural templates for text generation. *CoRR*, abs/1808.10122.

Jingqing Zhang, Yao Zhao, Mohammad Saleh, and Peter J. Liu. 2019. Pegasus: Pre-training with extracted gap-sentences for abstractive summarization.

Qi Zhu, Zheng Zhang, Yan Fang, Xiang Li, Ryuichi Takanobu, Jinchao Li, Baolin Peng, Jianfeng Gao, Xiaoyan Zhu, and Minlie Huang. 2020. Convlab-2: An open-source toolkit for building, evaluating, and diagnosing dialogue systems. In *Proceedings of the 58th Annual Meeting of the Association for Computational Linguistics*.

A Regression test cases for Botium

Below is a Botium regression testing case (script):

```
T01_Check_Card_Balance
#me
What is the due amount for my card?
#bot
Can I have the last 4 digit card number?
INTENT balance_enquiry
#me
5789.
#bot
You have $50.8 due for this card.
INTENT balance_enquiry
ENTITY_VALUES 5789
```

It is important to note that the Botium "end-to-end" testing is different from BotSIM as it aims to ensure the bot interface and operation work across different devices without regression errors. In other words, they are still for detecting regressions rather performance evaluation. For BotSIM's end-to-end evaluation, we refer to the setup that BotSIM takes in bot designs and automatically 1) parses bot designs, 2) generates test cases, 3) performs large-scale end-to-end dialog simulations, 4) analyzes outputs and provides actionable remediation suggestions for troubleshooting and improvement.

B T5-base paraphrasing model

Pytorch (Paszke et al., 2019) is used to fine-tune the T5-base model with the adam optimizer. The effective batch size is 128. The learning rate is 1e-4 and no warm-up is applied. The maximum sequence length is 128. Four NVIDIA A100 GPUs are used. After each epoch, we compute the iBLEU scores on the development set according to (Hosking et al., 2022; Sun and Zhou, 2012) to decide whether to keep the current checkpoint or not. The best model was obtained after 88 epochs.

B.1 Paraphrase datasets

We use the datasets released in the HVQ-VAE paper (Hosking et al., 2022) for finetuning the paraphrasing model. The datasets are "Wiki-Answers", "QQP" and "MSCOCO". Instead of training a separate model for each dataset as in (Hosking et al., 2022), we fintune a single paraphrasing model from the pooled dataset of the three. Additionally, we also curate our own set of paraphrasing datasets and use them together with the other three datasets. The dataset information is given in Table 6. Note some of the datasets are not initially designed for paraphrasing tasks. Therefore, they may also contain noisy or trivial labels for paraphrasing. Therefore, a filtering process is applied to select the final training sentence pairs. The filtering process applies thresholds on semantic and lexical scores to strike a good balance between lexical variation and semantic similarity between the paraphrasing sentence pairs. In particular, we use sentence transformer (Reimers and Gurevych, 2019) score to measure the semantic similarity and FuzzyWuzzy ratio (based on Levenshtein distance [6]) for lexical diversity. Sentence pairs with low semantic

[6] https://pypi.org/project/python-Levenshtein/

Algorithm 1 Dialog act maps inference from bot designs (MetaData/API)

```
local_dialog_act_maps = {}
for dialog ∈ all_dialogs do
    local_dialog_act_maps [dialog] = {}
    for message ∈ all_messages  do
        dialog_act = infer_dialog_act_from_message(message)
        if dialog_act not in local_dialog_act_maps [dialog] then
            local_dialog_act_maps [dialog][dialog_act] = []
        end if
        local_dialog_act_maps [dialog][dialog_act].append(message)
    end for
end for
global_dialog_act_maps = {}
for dialog ∈ all_non_end_dialogs do
    global_dialog_act_maps[dialog] = local_dialog_act_maps[dialog]
    for end_dialog ∈ all_end_dialogs do
        for node ∈ conv_graph.simple_paths(dialog, end_dialog) do
            global_dialog_act_maps[dialog].update(local_dialog_act_maps[node])
        end for
    end for
end for
```

similarities (noisy labels) or low Levenshtein distances (trivial labels with little lexical variation) are discarded. We also performed a benchmark of iBLEU scores in Table 3. The paraphrases are generated via beam search with the same beam size of 10. The results of HVQ-VAE are taken from the original paper. The discrepancy of the QQP results from the paper is due to some train/eval data overlap we found in their original setup. We contacted the authors and they provided the updated QQP results and the fixed datasets. We thus used the bug-fixed version for finetuning and evaluating our T5-base model. The off-the-shelf Pegasus model has the largest model size but performed the worst compared to the other two models across all scores. Since the author did not reveal anything about the model, we cannot finetune it with the same datasets as the T5-base. Using the same setup as HVQ-VAE, we finetuned a T5-base-Single-Task model for each task and it consistently outperformed the HVQ-VAE model on the task that it was trained on. On the contrary, The single-task models performed significantly worse on the task they were not trained on (see the numbers with *), indicating the negative impacts of domain mismatch. In addition, it is impractical to finetune a new model for each new dataset or task. Therefore, we pooled all datasets together and finetuned a single model "T5-base-Multi-Task". Although the multi-task model performs slightly worse than the single-task ones on each individual task, the overall performance is still on par with the state-of-the-art HVQ-VAE model, especially on the QQP task. Therefore, we choose the "T5-base-Multi-Task" as the BotSIM paraphrasing model.

We apply the same filtering principle for the training data preparation to the generated paraphrases to keep the ones with high semantic and low lexical similarities. In Figure 6, we show the number of candidates before and after filtering when generating the "train-paraphrases" set. For simple intents like "TA" and "EC", almost half of the original candidates are discarded. More challenging intents have more surviving paraphrases due to larger variation in their training utterances. The filtered candidates are then used as the intent queries for creating the simulation goals.

B.2 Investigation into misclassified paraphrases

From Table 9, we can see the paraphrasing models help increase the testing coverage as some correctly classified original intent queries (prediction ✓) have misclassified paraphrase intent queries (prediction ✗). Below we show two successfully classified original utterances with their wrongly classified paraphrases of the "Report an issue (RI)" intent.

	Task	Sent-Transformer score	FuzzRatio	No. Final Pairs
SNLI	NLI	[0.70, 0.99]	-	13,635
MNLI	NLI	[0.80, 0.99]	-	32.398
PAWS-Wiki	Paraphrasing	-	-	19,004
tapaco-en	Paraphrasing	[0.50, 0.99]	70	14,735
WIKI-Answers	Paraphrasing	-	-	79,6679
QQP	Paraphrasing	-	-	16,3621
MSCOCO	Paraphrasing	-	-	47,3210

Table 6: Datasets for T5-base paraphrasing model finetuning. "-" means no filtering applied.

	WIKI-Answers			QQP		
	Target (↑)	Self(↓)	iBLEU (↑)	Target(↑)	Self(↓)	iBLEU(↑)
Pegasus	31.4	55.3	14.0	23.8	46.0	9.9
HVQ-VAE	39.5	33.0	24.9	30.5	40.2	16.4
T5-base-Wiki	42.7	42.7	**25.6**	14.9	20.0	7.9*
T5-base-QQP	32.3	46.8	16.5*	31.9	42.7	**17.0**
T5-base-Multi-Task	33.9	23.9	23.9	29.1	35.2	16.3

Table 7: Performance benchmarking of different paraphrasing models. The BLEU scores are computed from the top one paraphrase candidate with respect to the reference (Target-BLEU) or the input (Self-BLEU) sentence. The iBLEU scores are calculcated using `Target-BLEU` $* 0.8 -$ `Self-BLEU` $* 0.2$. Numbers with asterisk* denote the "zero-shot" performance.

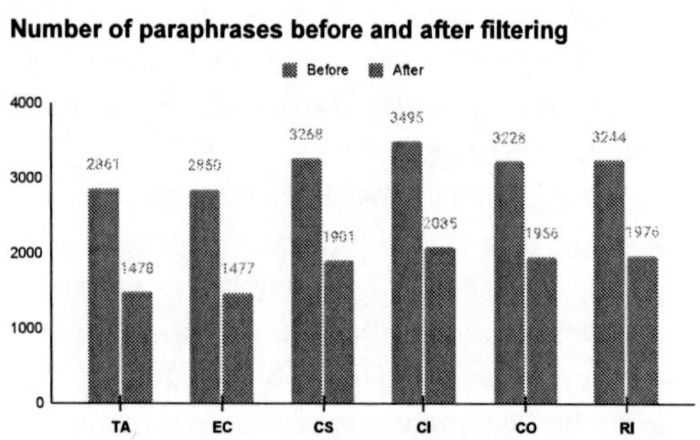

Figure 6: Number of paraphrase candidates before and after semantic and lexical filtering for "train-paraphrases"

```
{
  My order was damaged in
     shipping: [
   Why did my order get damaged
      during shipping?,
   Why was my order damaged when
      it was shipped?,
   Shipping damaged my order.,
   The order was damaged when it
      was shipped.
  ],
  The bottle of conditioner was
     open when it arrived i need
     a replacement: [
   I need a new bottle of
      conditioner because the
      one that arrived was open.
      ,
   I need a replacement for the
      opened bottle of
      conditioner.,
   I need a replacement for the
      open bottle of conditioner
      .,
   I need a new bottle of
      conditioner because the
      one I received was open.
  ]
}
```

As suggested by the Remediator, users can select some of the high-quality paraphrases to augment the original intent training set to refine the intent models. They can also filter from the evaluation (manual-crafted utterances or product chat logs) paraphrases to create a larger evaluation set for performance monitoring. This saves substantial hu-

Dataset	Intent enquiries	TA	EC	CS	CI	CO	RI
Train	train-original	150	150	150	150	150	150
	train-augmented	255	184	212	268	215	294
Dev	train-paraphrases	1465	1467	1754	1989	1895	1786
Eval	eval-original	182	145	183	222	205	178
	eval-paraphrases	1190	933	1648	2172	1936	1795

Table 8: Dataset information for the Einstein Template Bot case study.

eval-original	TA	EC	CS	CI	CO	RI
prediction ✓	9	17	27	33	34	61
prediction ✗	9	7	16	19	8	26

Table 9: Test coverage expansion via paraphrasing

man efforts in creating or annotating dialog testing data.

C Remediator reports and analytical tools

The Remdediator outputs are detailed in the bot health report dashboard shown in Figure 5. The left panel gives users options to navigate through the dashboard. For example, they can select different bot platforms, datasets, test ids and intents. The bot health report (the first row of Figure 5) offers a multi-scale view of simulation performance. At the highest level is the historical comparison of most recent testing sessions (Figure 5(1)). For example, a testing session may be needed after each major bot update. From the historical performance comparison, users can see how certain changes impact the overall bot performance and decide whether to keep or revert the update.

Given the historical performance, users may be interested in further investigating a particular testing session. They can do so by selecting one from the drop-list of all testing sessions and enable the "Check Summary Report" option in the multi-selection box. The resulting overall bot health report for the selected test session is shown in Figure 5(2). It summarizes the simulation information including number of intents, entities and simulation episodes. The two doughnut charts depict the dataset distribution and the overall success metrics.

To investigate the detailed performance report of each individual intent (Figure 5(3)), users can navigate to "Check Dialog Report" and select a dialog from the drop-list. The detailed dialog report presents the intent and NER performance. One can quickly identify the most confusing intents or entities and focus their efforts to investigate and resolve the confusions.

To help troubleshoot the identified errors, users can select "Investigate Dialog" to see the remediation suggestions. Figure 5(5) shows the misclassified intent query paraphrases and their corresponding original utterances, grouped by the wrongly predicted intent labels. Given the prediction results, suggestions are provided for possible further actions. For the given example, all paraphrases of the utterance "Can you give me the status of my order" have been classified as the "check order" intent, indicating an annotation error of the original utterance. Therefore, this utterance should be moved from the "check issue" intent to the "check order" intent.

To gain more insights into their bot systems, users can harness the conversation analytical tools for better comprehension of the simulation results. To understand more about the intent classifier, confusion matrix analysis is applied to the intent predictions of the simulated conversations(in Figure 5(7)). A detailed and sortable intent performance can be displayed by checking the checkbox, allowing users to quickly identify the worst performing intents in terms of recall, precision or F1 rates. This helps them plan and allocate resources to improve the poor-performing intents.

To gauge the quality of the intent training utterances and identify intent overlaps, tSNE clustering is performed based on the sentence transformer embeddings of the intent training utterances. By examining the clusters, not only can users find intents with significant overlaps in the training data semantic space, they can also potentially discover novel intents from production chat logs to aid dialog flow re-design. The dashboard can be easily extended to to support more analytical tasks.

D Streamlit web app

Finally, we give some brief discussions of the Streamlit Web App. The motivation is to offer BotSIM not just as a framework for developers but also as an easy-to-use app to end users such as bot admins without diving into technical details. The app can be deployed as a docker container or to the Heroku platform. We use Streamlit as the front-end and Flask as the backend. A set of API functions are designed to communicate with BotSIM. For multi-platform support, keeping track of the simulation status and historical performance, a SQL-based database is used. BotSIM supports two types of databases including Sqlite3 and Postgres. To support Heroku deployment, particularly its ephemeral file system, cloud storage such as AWS S3 is used to store the simulation logs and results.

DeepGen: Diverse Search Ad Generation and Real-Time Customization

Konstantin Golobokov[◇], **Junyi Chai**[♣], **Victor Ye Dong**[♣],
Mandy Gu[♣], **Bingyu Chi**[♣], **Jie Cao**[♣], **Yulan Yan**[♠], **Yi Liu**[♣]
[◇] Azure AI, [♣] Bing Ads, [♠] News & Feeds
Microsoft, Redmond, USA
{FirstName.LastName}@microsoft.com

Abstract

We present DeepGen, a system deployed at web scale for automatically creating sponsored search advertisements (ads) for Bing Ads customers. We leverage state-of-the-art natural language generation (NLG) models to generate fluent ads from advertiser's web pages in an abstractive fashion and solve practical issues such as factuality and inference speed. In addition, our system creates a customized ad in real-time in response to the user's search query, therefore highlighting different aspects of the *same* product based on what the user is looking for. To achieve this, our system generates a *diverse* choice of smaller pieces of the ad ahead of time and, at query time, selects the most relevant ones to be stitched into a complete ad. We improve generation diversity by training a controllable NLG model to generate multiple ads for the same web page highlighting different selling points. Our system design further improves diversity horizontally by first running an ensemble of generation models trained with different objectives and then using a diversity sampling algorithm to pick a diverse subset of generation results for online selection. Experimental results show the effectiveness of our proposed system design. Our system is currently deployed in production, serving ~4% of ads globally on Bing.

1 Introduction

Search advertising is the largest segment of digital advertising for its projected $203B out of $515B market share worldwide in 2022 (Statista, 2022). Traditionally, advertisers manually create ads for their web pages to start an advertising campaign. There is a growing need to automate this process, either to lessen the burden for small and medium businesses, or to create millions of ads for large businesses that have lots of products.

A classical automated ad generation system relies on extraction rules as described in Section 2.1, for example, extracting key phrases from advertiser's web pages as ad titles. However, per our experience, extraction-based methods are not very successful in generating the much longer ad description. Refer to Figure 1 for the example ad title and description assets. Therefore, we aim to generate ads in an abstractive fashion. In this work, we focus on improving ad performance from two aspects: factuality and customization.

Figure 1: An example of an ad copy (grey box) comprised of ad assets. Red box is used for ad title assets, and green box is used for ad description assets. This ad could be shown for search query "Surface 8".

To achieve the optimal ad performance, our current system creates a customized ad in real-time in response to a user's search query. As shown in Figure 2, different ads are displayed for different queries, although they are advertising the same web page. We dynamically customize ad copies by stitching the generated ad assets together given the user's search context, approximating the ultimate goal of real-time customized generation. Our work makes the following contributions:

1. We demonstrate an NLG application that leverages cutting-edge models, which can abstractively generate and instantaneously stitch ad text, matching human quality and achieving real-time ad content customization.
2. We record a significant click-through-rate gain of 13.28% over an extraction-based system as a baseline. Our system is currently deployed at web scale, serving ~4% of ads shown on Bing search engine.

Proceedings of the The 2022 Conference on Empirical Methods in Natural Language Processing: System Demonstrations, pages 191 - 199
December 7-11, 2022

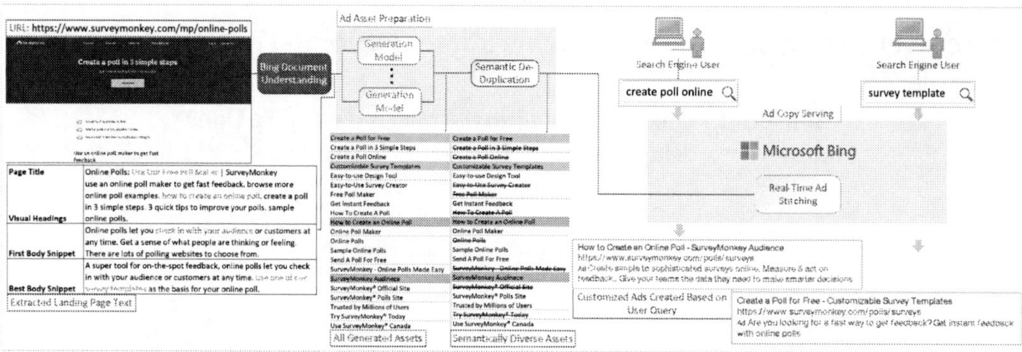

Figure 2: An illustration of the end-to-end DeepGen system. First, multiple ad assets are generated based on various parts of the advertiser's web page. Semantically diverse ad assets are then selected and prepared for serving. Finally, customized ads are created based on user queries. Transparent blocks are the NLP models, solid blocks are the surrounding infrastructure. Generative models are shown in orange, discussed in Section 2. The rest of the system is presented in Section 3.

2 Ads Generation System

Our system for ad content generation and stitching is automated end-to-end as shown in Figure 2. Advertisers only need to supply us with their domain names, landing page targeting rules, and a bid for each rule (e.g., bid $0.5 for URLs containing "shoes"). Our Search Indexing infrastructure crawls all landing pages under advertiser domain names that match targeting rules and runs the Document Understanding (DU) pipeline to extract textual information as per Section 2.1. After that, we run multiple NLG models concurrently. This parallel design enables us to scale modeling horizontally: we can add or remove generation models at will. The models can either generate an ad asset or a full ad copy. For a full ad copy we simply split it into assets. At the end of generation stage, we have many title and description assets generated for each advertiser URL.

2.1 Baselines

Extraction-based systems The extraction techniques have evolved in Bing Ads over a decade and we consider them a strong industrial baseline in this paper. This baseline can produce title assets of high quality, but it does not perform as well for the longer description assets. For extraction candidates, we leverage parts of the website extracted by Bing DU pipeline, as per example below:

- Page Title - the document title present in metadata; <title> tag for HTML documents
- Visual Headings - the visually emphasized document title present in the document, visible to user
- First/Best Body Snippet - first (top-most)/best document body snippet extracted by Bling (Xiong et al., 2019)

Examples of the above landing page text extracted by DU pipeline can be seen on the left in Figure 2.

Abstractive generation baseline We consider models finetuned directly on advertiser written ad copies as the baseline for abstractive generation approach. We finetune UniLMv2 (Bao et al., 2020) on advertiser-written full ad copies, with learning rate of $5 \cdot 10^{-5}$. We refer to such models as AdCopy models as they generate one ad copy for each source sequence. See Figure 3 for an example of source/target sequences for this task. Multiple AdCopy models were successfully deployed in production with significant business gains (Wang et al., 2021). Some best practices we learned are: 1) advertiser-written ads have a very skewed distribution with some advertiser having millions of template generated ads. Therefore we sample the 3000 URLs with the most ad impressions in the past year per advertiser domain, obtaining 3M-5M training examples; 2) validation and test sets randomly split from training set do not work well; they need to be constructed from different advertisers than those in training set to avoid overfitting. We use validation set of size 300K-500K examples and a test set of 30K-50K examples. We use ROUGE1-F1 (Lin, 2004) on validation set to select the best checkpoint during training.

We inference with beam search of size 5 with code optimization, leveraging Einsum operator in cross-attention stage to avoid the encoder cache copy, per the FastSeq (Yan et al., 2021) implementation. This optimization allows us to increase batch size and brings 5x speed up in our task. Our generation models can be seen in the center of Figure 2 in orange color.

Source Sequence:

survey monkey -PageTitle- Online Polls: Use Our Free Poll Maker | SurveyMonkey -VisualHeadings- use an online poll maker to get fast feedback. browse more online poll examples. how to create an online poll. create a poll in 3 simple steps. 3 quick tips to improve your polls. -FirstBodySnippet- Online polls let you check in with your audience or customers at any time. Get a sense of what people are thinking or feeling. There are lots of polling websites to choose from. -BestBodySnippet- A super tool for on-the-spot feedback, online polls let you check in with your audience or customers at any time. Use one of our survey templates as the basis for your online poll.

Target Sequence:

Survey Template -TitleSep- Effective Online Survey Tool -Desc- Create Beautiful Surveys With Typeform For Free. Easy-to-use Online Survey Creator.

Figure 3: An example of a source and generated target sequence pair for the baseline AdCopy model.

2.2 Factuality Improvement

To evaluate the quality of generated ads, we mainly rely on human evaluation. For that, we sample a stratified sample of at most 50 examples per domain, and then uniformly subsample 500 – 1000 examples per human evaluation task. This way, we get an evaluation result from diverse portions of our demand, not letting very large domains dominate. We work with a pool of professional judges, trained to evaluate ads in an unbiased way. We further examine evaluation examples and give feedback to the judges in case there is a misunderstanding of the judgement guidelines. Thus, we evaluate the quality of generated ad texts along the following 4 aspects:

- Text Quality: evaluates grammar and style, with levels Good, Fair, Bad, Embarrassing, and Not Scorable.
- Human Likeness: whether it looks like human-written, with levels Yes and No.
- Factuality: whether the generated information is supported by landing page, with levels Yes and No.
- Relevance: whether the generated text is relevant to advertiser's business, with levels Yes and No.

We define an ad text to be "Overall Good" if it gets "Good" or "Fair" for Text Quality, and "Yes" for Human Likeness, Factuality, and Relevance. Refer to Figure 4 in the Appendix A for an example human judge interface. To be allowed for further A/B testing, the Overall Good Rate needs to be at least 90% with confidence greater than 97.5%.

As shown in Table 1, our baseline model does not have a significant difference in quality from the advertiser written ads. However, the overall good rate for both is curtailed by lower factuality scores. For example, our AdCopy model can generate popular claims like "Free Shipping" or "15% Discount" which do not exist in the landing page. This is similar to the hallucination issue in abstractive summarization (Filippova, 2020; Maynez et al., 2020b).

To alleviate the extrinsic hallucinations (Maynez et al., 2020a) in our ads, we employ phrase-based cross-check filtering. For that, we use a list of potentially erroneous phrases and patterns obtained by studying human evaluation results for our generated ads. Our approach is similar to entity-based filtering per Nan et al. (2021).

Some cross-check examples are 1) Phrase Check: a list of sensitive or potentially misleading phrases (e.g., "Free Return", "Promo Code: ABC"); 2) Brand Check: brand list compiled from our search engine's knowledge graph (Noy et al., 2019; Chai et al., 2021); 3) Domain Check: checking patterns like "xyz.com" against landing page URL.

We add the cross check rules at two stages: (1) We filter training data with cross check rules before training (train x-check); and (2) We filter generated text after the inference (infer x-check). Per Table 1, both train x-check and infer x-check improve quality significantly, with the greatest improvement when both are used together.

For an AdCopy model, we do observe that $\sim$ 15% of generated ad copies are filtered during the post-inference cross check. This effect is ameliorated by the fact that we use multiple NLG models, allowing them to backfill each other's coverage. The remaining coverage is backfilled with extraction candidates. Due to this system design, the eventual URL coverage does not suffer from the cross check.

2.3 Controllable Generation at Asset-Level

To model diversity explicitly, we build a controllable NLG model to generate multiple ad assets for the same source sequence. We accomplish this is via *control codes*, categorical variables that represent the desired output property and are prepended to the model inputs during training and testing, Keskar et al. (2019) and Ficler and Gold-

Technique	Overall	Text Quality	Human Like	Factuality	Relevance
Advertiser-written	90.7 ± 2.1	97.9 ± 1.0	98.1 ± 1.0	92.7 ± 1.9	99.0 ± 0.7
Baseline: AdCopy w/o check	89.8 ± 2.2	98.8 ± 0.8	98.5 ± 0.9	91.1 ± 2.1	98.9 ± 0.7
AdCopy w/ train check	$\mathbf{94.7 \pm 1.6}$	$\mathbf{99.6 \pm 0.5}$	$\mathbf{99.0 \pm 0.7}$	$\mathbf{95.6 \pm 1.5}$	99.6 ± 0.5
AdCopy w/ infer check	$\mathbf{94.4 \pm 1.9}$	98.8 ± 0.9	98.5 ± 1.0	$\mathbf{95.6 \pm 1.7}$	98.8 ± 0.9
AdCopy w/ train + infer check	$\mathbf{96.3 \pm 1.5}$	**100.0**	$\mathbf{99.4 \pm 0.6}$	$\mathbf{97.0 \pm 1.3}$	$\mathbf{99.7 \pm 0.4}$

Table 1: A comparison of Ad Copy models (as per Section 2.1) via human evaluation. 95% confidence intervals (CI) are reported. Results that outperform advertiser baseline at $p < 0.05$ level are **bolded**.

Technique	Overall	Text Quality	Human Like	Factuality	Relevance
Advertiser Title Asset	98.2 ± 0.9	99.9 ± 0.2	100.0	98.4 ± 0.9	100.0
Extraction Title Asset	$\mathbf{99.0 \pm 0.7}$	99.4 ± 0.6	99.6 ± 0.5	$\mathbf{99.6 \pm 0.5}$	100.0
Guided Title Asset	98.1 ± 0.6	99.8 ± 0.2	100.0	98.3 ± 0.5	99.6 ± 0.3
Advertiser Desc Asset	98.2 ± 0.9	99.9 ± 0.2	99.9 ± 0.2	98.4 ± 0.9	100.0
Guided Desc Asset	95.3 ± 0.9	97.6 ± 0.7	98.8 ± 0.5	97.9 ± 0.6	99.2 ± 0.4

Table 2: A comparison of Guided Asset generation model against advertiser written ads and extraction-based titles via human evaluation. 95% CI are reported. Results better than advertiser baseline at $p < 0.05$ level are **bolded**.

berg (2017). We refer to it as Guided model, as the generation is guided by the control codes.

We assume each landing page can be advertised along 12 categories for different selling points. Example categories are Product or Service, Advertiser Name or Brand, Location, etc.; they are borrowed from the instructions on the web portal where advertisers create ads. We then use human judges to classify ~6500 distinct advertiser-written assets into categories. We finetune BERT-base-uncased (Devlin et al., 2018) for asset category classification task and obtain ~80% prediction accuracy, using a random 80/20 split for train/test sets and learning rate of $5 * 10^{-5}$.

We then inference ad category for each ad asset in the NLG model training set, prepending the resulting category control code as plaintext at the beginning of each NLG source sequence. Thus, we obtain a data set of 6M ad assets (both title and description together) for training the Guided NLG models. Otherwise, our generative modeling decisions align with Section 2.1. During inference, we evaluate the model on all available categories, by prepending each control code to the landing page information.

Human evaluation results for our Guided NLG model are shown in Table 2. The overall title asset quality of the Guided model does not have significant difference to that of advertiser-written assets, with Extraction titles outperforming both. The advertiser-written description assets are better, though the overall good rate of Guided model is still well above our quality bar of 90%. The advantage of Guided model in this case is that it is able to explicitly capture different advertising categories for both title and description. Extraction technique cannot produce good ad descriptions in our experience.

Title Asset	Count	PB↓	SB↓	Dist↑
Advertiser	18.4	13.4	71.0	45.3
Generated	24.4	6.7	41.0	66.6
Generated + DPP	14.2	**4.5**	**25.3**	**80.5**
Guided	13.3	7.8	33.6	74.9
Ensemble	12.1	**5.8**	**31.2**	**77.0**
Guided + DPP	7.8	5.0	18.3	86.9
Ensemble + DPP	7.7	**3.6**	**17.0**	**88.3**

Table 3: Averaged results of the diversity evaluation on English title assets. For PairwiseBLEU (PB) and Self-BLEU (SB) scores, lower is better, for Distinct N-gram (Dist) scores, higher is better. Average count of title assets per URL (Count) is also reported. Differences of over 1 point are **bolded**. Ensemble here is for an ensemble of AdCopy models. Generated assets include the combination of Guided, Ensemble, and Extraction titles.

3 Serving and Customization System

3.1 Diverse Selection

At this stage, we aim to select a semantically diverse subset of T title and D description assets for each URL to send to online serving components. By selecting a subset of ad texts, we aim to both reduce the load on the ad serving system, as well as improve diversity of the generated texts. We use CDSSM (Shen et al., 2014) model, trained on web search logs, to map each text asset to a dense vector, such that the ad texts with high degree of semantic similarity will map to representations with higher cosine similarity (i.e., closer in the embedding space) to one another. Then, we sample a diverse subset of points in the CDSSM embedding space with k-DPP maximum a posteriori inference algorithm as per Chen et al. (2018), stopping after we select T titles or D descriptions. Refer to Figure 2 (bottom middle) for an example of removing semantic duplicates in such fashion.

We use PairwiseBLEU (PB) (Shen et al., 2019), SelfBLEU (SB) (Zhu et al., 2018), and Distinct N-gram (DistN) (Xu et al., 2018) scores to evaluate the diversity of the title assets before and after k-DPP diverse sampling. We calculate the average diversity metrics for ~2000 EN URLs randomly sampled from a stratified sample of 50 URLs/domain. Since all instances of each metric show similar trends, we follow suit with Tevet and Berant (2020) and average each metric over different N-gram options. Refer to Table 3 for diversity score details.

We find that generated title assets are more diverse than the ones provided by the advertiser in general. In addition, k-DPP helps further increase the asset diversity. We also compare title assets from the Guided model with those from an ensemble of AdCopy models. We find that the Guided model by itself can generate title assets in similar quantity and with similar diversity as the ones produced by several AdCopy models combined, trained as per the NLG baseline method in Section 2.1 on different versions of training data.

3.2 Real-Time Stitching

The diversified ad assets are then ingested into the online serving infrastructure. At query time, we stitch together a customized ad copy, optimizing for the auction win rate[1] (with some level of exploration). From our domain knowledge, the earlier asset positions (e.g., Title 1) influence the ad auction result more than the later ones (e.g., Description 2), as shown in Figure 1. Thus, we perform a greedy sequential selection and consider $T+(T-1)+(T-2)+D+(D-1)$ permutation options. For example, we first select asset for Title 1 position from T title assets, and then select asset for Title 2 position from the remaining $T-1$ title assets.

We use a logistic regression (LR) model to score each asset position: Title 1, Title 2, Title 3, Description 1, Description 2. We use features from ad auction log like string hash, length, unigrams and bigrams from asset texts. We also cross these with the query text to a total sparse feature dimensionality per position of ~4B. The LR model learns the probability of winning the auction for a given ad copy. It is continuously trained daily, using ~10B data examples from the previous day's log for training with batch size as 1000 and learning rate as 0.02, and ~ 300M examples from current day's log for validation.

We include an exploration mechanism to allow newly added assets to be shown to users and to de-bias the model. Due to sequential nature of our stitching process, we model exploration as a sequential contextual bandit (CB) problem. At each asset position, the CB uses the LR score and the gradient sum of LR features as a heuristic for the trial count (Mcmahan et al., 2013) to select an asset using Thompson Sampling strategy (Agrawal and Goyal, 2017). As a result, we sample from a total of $T+(T-1)+(T-2)+D+(D-1)$ Beta distributions to stitch together an ad copy.

4 A/B Testing

DeepGen is deployed globally to serve Dynamic Search Ads (DSA), which accounts for ~ 4% of all Bing Ads displayed globally. In A/B testing, we split the production user traffic randomly between the treatment experiment that enables the proposed experimental techniques and the control experiment that uses existing production techniques. We use 10% of production traffic for the control experiment. We use the difference in business metrics between two experiments to decide if treatment is effective.

Two key business metrics are Revenue Per Mille (RPM) – revenue per every thousand search result page views (SRPV) and Quick Back Rate (QBR) – the rate of users clicking the back button after clicking on an ad, which is a proxy for user dissatisfaction (lower QBR is better). RPM is driven by Impression Yield (IY, number of ads shown divided by number of search result page views) and Click-Through Rate (CTR, number of clicks divided by

[1]Auction is the final stage to decide which ads will be displayed. Auction win rate is the probability of an ad winning an auction. Ads with better quality and CTR have a better chance to win the auction.

Metric	Exp. 1	Exp. 2	Explanation
Days	5	10	Number of days for the experiment.
Traffic%	5.0	10.0	Percentage of the Bing user traffic allocated for the experiment.
ΔRPM%	**+24.87**	**+10.65**	Revenue (USD) from 1000 Search Results Page Views (SRPVs).
ΔIY%	**+11.87**	**+14.43**	Average number of ads shown per page.
ΔCTR%	**+13.28**	-0.19	Proportion of ads clicked from ads shown.
ΔQBR%	**+5.27**	**+1.82**	Proportion of ad clicks that resulted in a back-click within 20 sec.

Table 4: A summary of the business metrics from A/B tests performed on DSA ad traffic. Results statistically significant at $p < 0.05$ level are **bolded**.

total number of ads displayed). Usually there is a trade-off between RPM (revenue) and QBR (user satisfaction). DeepGen increases CTR (proportion of ads clicked from ads displayed) and IY (number of ads displayed per page), thus also increasing ad revenue. We do so by generating high-quality ads that are customized to the user. We avoid sacrificing user or advertiser satisfaction by ensuring the ads to be faithful to the landing page.

In Exp. 1, we compare DeepGen (treatment) against the extraction system (control). As shown in Table 4, we observe strong RPM (revenue) gain, driven by both IY and CTR, which means that personalized ad copies generated by DeepGen are more likely to win the auction as well as to be clicked by the user. In this experiment, we record a *13.28% CTR gain*. We acknowledge the increase in QBR (user dissatisfaction), which could be attributed to the still higher factuality of the extraction system, as shown in Table 2.

We use Exp. 2 as an ablation for real-time customization. DeepGen is used in both treatment and control, but we replace real-time stitching with precomputed stitching in control. For this experiment, we build a separate model to stitch assets into multiple ad copies offline, and only *rank* the pre-stitched ad texts during query time (online). There is significant RPM (revnue) gain, though it is mainly driven by IY but not CTR. This may suggest that online stitching has a higher chance of winning the auction as it covers much larger permutation space than the offline stitching. But for those ad copies that did win an auction, they have similar attractiveness to the user whether stitched online or offline. This experiment shows online stitching to be an integral part of our system.

Thus, DeepGen increases revenue by generating high-quality ads customized to the user while being mindful of user satisfaction by ensuring the ads to be faithful to the landing page.

5 Related Work

The early automated content generation approaches focused on template-based ad text generation (Bartz et al., 2008; Fujita et al., 2010; Thomaidou et al., 2013). These approaches have potential to suffer from ad fatigue (Abrams and Vee, 2007).

More recently, deep Reinforcement Learning (RL) was shown effective for ad text generation (Hughes et al., 2019; Kamigaito et al., 2021; Wang et al., 2021), using a *general* attractiveness model as a reward policy and yielding up to 7.01% observed CTR gain per Kamigaito et al. (2021). CTR is an important metrics, as reflects the relevance of an ad from user's perspective (Yang and Zhai, 2022).

Product headline generation is a closely related direction of work, where a single headline is generated to advertise a line of related products, based on each product's advertiser-written title. Kanungo et al. (2021) use BERT-large (Devlin et al., 2018) encoder finetuned for generation with UniLM-like masked attention, as per Dong et al. (2019), optimized using a self-critical RL objective, as per Hughes et al. (2019). Kanungo et al. (2022) further produce SC-COBART by finetuning a BART model, using control codes, as per Keskar et al. (2019), for bucketized CTR and length of a headline, optimized with a mixture of MLE and selfcricial RL objectives. SC-COBART improves estimated CTR by 5.82% over their previous work (Kanungo et al., 2021).

In another line of work, product descriptions are generated either with templates (Wang et al., 2017), pointer-generator encoders (Zhang et al., 2019), commonsense knowledge-base guidance (Chan et al., 2020; Zhang et al., 2021), or CVAEs (Shao et al., 2021), yielding up to 13.17% CTR gain in A/B test per Shao et al. (2021).

6 Conclusion

In this work, we present an automated end-to-end search advertisement text generation solution. We employ deep NLG modeling for ad content generation and diverse selection. We leverage real-time LR rankers for content stitching. The generation techniques provide us a rich source of high-quality ad content, which performs strongly against human and extraction baselines. We further apply diverse selection via semantic embedding, which allows us to surpass human content diversity, while ensuring the system's scalability. Finally, we use real-time ranking to stitch not just attractive, but a truly *customized* ad for each user based on query and search intent. The system combines several NLP approaches to provide a cutting edge solution to automated ad generation and showcases an significant CTR gain over an extraction baseline.

References

Zoë Abrams and Erik Vee. 2007. Personalized ad delivery when ads fatigue: An approximation algorithm. pages 535–540.

Shipra Agrawal and Navin Goyal. 2017. Near-optimal regret bounds for thompson sampling. *J. ACM*, 64(5).

Hangbo Bao, Li Dong, Furu Wei, Wenhui Wang, Nan Yang, Xiaodong Liu, Yu Wang, Songhao Piao, Jianfeng Gao, Ming Zhou, and Hsiao-Wuen Hon. 2020. Unilmv2: Pseudo-masked language models for unified language model pre-training. *CoRR*, abs/2002.12804.

Kevin Bartz, Cory Barr, and Adil Aijaz. 2008. Natural language generation for sponsored-search advertisements. In *Proceedings of the 9th ACM Conference on Electronic Commerce*, EC '08, page 1–9, New York, NY, USA. Association for Computing Machinery.

Junyi Chai, Yujie He, Homa Hashemi, Bing Li, Daraksha Parveen, Ranganath Kondapally, and Wenjin Xu. 2021. Automatic construction of enterprise knowledge base. In *Proceedings of the 2021 Conference on Empirical Methods in Natural Language Processing: System Demonstrations*, pages 11–19, Online and Punta Cana, Dominican Republic. Association for Computational Linguistics.

Zhangming Chan, Yuchi Zhang, Xiuying Chen, Shen Gao, Zhiqiang Zhang, Dongyan Zhao, and Rui Yan. 2020. Selection and generation: Learning towards multi-product advertisement post generation. In *Proceedings of the 2020 Conference on Empirical Methods in Natural Language Processing (EMNLP)*, pages 3818–3829, Online. Association for Computational Linguistics.

Laming Chen, Guoxin Zhang, and Hanning Zhou. 2018. Fast greedy map inference for determinantal point process to improve recommendation diversity. In *Proceedings of the 32nd International Conference on Neural Information Processing Systems*, NIPS'18, page 5627–5638, Red Hook, NY, USA. Curran Associates Inc.

Jacob Devlin, Ming-Wei Chang, Kenton Lee, and Kristina Toutanova. 2018. BERT: pre-training of deep bidirectional transformers for language understanding. *CoRR*, abs/1810.04805.

Li Dong, Nan Yang, Wenhui Wang, Furu Wei, Xiaodong Liu, Yu Wang, Jianfeng Gao, Ming Zhou, and Hsiao-Wuen Hon. 2019. Unified language model pre-training for natural language understanding and generation. *CoRR*, abs/1905.03197.

Jessica Ficler and Yoav Goldberg. 2017. Controlling linguistic style aspects in neural language generation. *CoRR*, abs/1707.02633.

Katja Filippova. 2020. Controlled hallucinations: Learning to generate faithfully from noisy data. *CoRR*, abs/2010.05873.

Atsushi Fujita, Katsuhiro Ikushima, Satoshi Sato, Ryo Kamite, Ko Ishiyama, and Osamu Tamachi. 2010. Automatic generation of listing ads by reusing promotional texts. In *Proceedings of the 12th International Conference on Electronic Commerce: Roadmap for the Future of Electronic Business*, ICEC '10, page 179–188, New York, NY, USA. Association for Computing Machinery.

J. Weston Hughes, Keng-hao Chang, and Ruofei Zhang. 2019. Generating better search engine text advertisements with deep reinforcement learning. In *Proceedings of the 25th ACM SIGKDD International Conference on Knowledge Discovery & Data Mining*, KDD '19, page 2269–2277, New York, NY, USA. Association for Computing Machinery.

Hidetaka Kamigaito, Peinan Zhang, Hiroya Takamura, and Manabu Okumura. 2021. An empirical study of generating texts for search engine advertising. In *NAACL*.

Yashal Shakti Kanungo, Gyanendra Das, Pooja A, and Sumit Negi. 2022. Cobart: Controlled, optimized, bidirectional and auto-regressive transformer for ad headline generation. In *KDD 2022*.

Yashal Shakti Kanungo, Sumit Negi, and Aruna Rajan. 2021. Ad headline generation using self-critical masked language model. In *Proceedings of the 2021 Conference of the North American Chapter of the Association for Computational Linguistics: Human Language Technologies: Industry Papers*, pages 263–271, Online. Association for Computational Linguistics.

Nitish Shirish Keskar, Bryan McCann, Lav R. Varshney, Caiming Xiong, and Richard Socher. 2019. CTRL: A conditional transformer language model for controllable generation. *CoRR*, abs/1909.05858.

Chin-Yew Lin. 2004. Rouge: a package for automatic evaluation of summaries. In *Workshop on Text Summarization Branches Out, Post-Conference Workshop of ACL 2004, Barcelona, Spain*, pages 74–81.

Joshua Maynez, Shashi Narayan, Bernd Bohnet, and Ryan McDonald. 2020a. On faithfulness and factuality in abstractive summarization. In *Proceedings of the 58th Annual Meeting of the Association for Computational Linguistics*, pages 1906–1919, Online. Association for Computational Linguistics.

Joshua Maynez, Shashi Narayan, Bernd Bohnet, and Ryan T. McDonald. 2020b. On faithfulness and factuality in abstractive summarization. *CoRR*, abs/2005.00661.

H. Brendan Mcmahan, Gary Holt, D. Sculley, Michael Young, Dietmar Ebner, Julian Grady, Lan Nie, Todd Phillips, Eugene Davydov, Daniel Golovin, Sharat Chikkerur, Dan Liu, Martin Wattenberg, Arnar Mar Hrafnkelsson, Tom Boulos, and Jeremy Kubica. 2013. Ad click prediction: A view from the trenches. *Proceedings of the ACM SIGKDD International Conference on Knowledge Discovery and Data Mining*, Part F1288:1222–1230.

Feng Nan, Ramesh Nallapati, Zhiguo Wang, Cicero Nogueira dos Santos, Henghui Zhu, Dejiao Zhang, Kathleen McKeown, and Bing Xiang. 2021. Entity-level factual consistency of abstractive text summarization. In *Proceedings of the 16th Conference of the European Chapter of the Association for Computational Linguistics: Main Volume*, pages 2727–2733, Online. Association for Computational Linguistics.

Natasha Noy, Yuqing Gao, Anshu Jain, Anant Narayanan, Alan Patterson, and Jamie Taylor. 2019. Industry-scale knowledge graphs: Lessons and challenges. *Communications of the ACM*, 62(8):36–43.

Huajie Shao, Jun Wang, Haohong Lin, Xuezhou Zhang, Aston Zhang, Heng Ji, and Tarek F. Abdelzaher. 2021. Controllable and diverse text generation in e-commerce. *CoRR*, abs/2102.11497.

Tianxiao Shen, Myle Ott, Michael Auli, and Marc'Aurelio Ranzato. 2019. Mixture models for diverse machine translation: Tricks of the trade. *CoRR*, abs/1902.07816.

Yelong Shen, Xiaodong He, Jianfeng Gao, Li Deng, and Grégoire Mesnil. 2014. A latent semantic model with convolutional-pooling structure for information retrieval. *CIKM 2014 - Proceedings of the 2014 ACM International Conference on Information and Knowledge Management*, pages 101–110.

Statista. 2022. Search advertising - worldwide | statista market forecast.

Guy Tevet and Jonathan Berant. 2020. Evaluating the evaluation of diversity in natural language generation. *CoRR*, abs/2004.02990.

Stamatina Thomaidou, Ismini Lourentzou, Panagiotis Katsivelis-Perakis, and Michalis Vazirgiannis. 2013. Automated snippet generation for online advertising. In *Proceedings of the 22nd ACM International Conference on Information & Knowledge Management*, CIKM '13, page 1841–1844, New York, NY, USA. Association for Computing Machinery.

Jinpeng Wang, Yutai Hou, Jing Liu, Yunbo Cao, and Chin-Yew Lin. 2017. A statistical framework for product description generation. In *Proceedings of the Eighth International Joint Conference on Natural Language Processing (Volume 2: Short Papers)*, pages 187–192, Taipei, Taiwan. Asian Federation of Natural Language Processing.

Xiting Wang, Xinwei Gu, Jie Cao, Zihua Zhao, Yulan Yan, Bhuvan Middha, and Xing Xie. 2021. Reinforcing pretrained models for generating attractive text advertisements. In *ACM SIGKDD International Conference on Knowledge Discovery and Data Mining (ACM SIGKDD)*. Applied Data Science Track.

Lee Xiong, Chuan Hu, Chenyan Xiong, Daniel Campos, and Arnold Overwijk. 2019. Open domain web keyphrase extraction beyond language modeling. In *Empirical Methods in Natural Language Processing and the 9th International Joint Conference on Natural Language Processing (EMNLP-IJCNLP)*, pages 5174–5183. ACL, ACL.

Jingjing Xu, Xuancheng Ren, Junyang Lin, and Xu Sun. 2018. Diversity-promoting GAN: A cross-entropy based generative adversarial network for diversified text generation. In *Proceedings of the 2018 Conference on Empirical Methods in Natural Language Processing*, pages 3940–3949, Brussels, Belgium. Association for Computational Linguistics.

Yu Yan, Fei Hu, Jiusheng Chen, Nikhil Bhendawade, Ting Ye, Yeyun Gong, Nan Duan, Desheng Cui, Bingyu Chi, and Ruofei Zhang. 2021. FastSeq: Make sequence generation faster. In *Proceedings of the 59th Annual Meeting of the Association for Computational Linguistics and the 11th International Joint Conference on Natural Language Processing: System Demonstrations*, pages 218–226, Online. Association for Computational Linguistics.

Yanwu Yang and Panyu Zhai. 2022. Click-through rate prediction in online advertising: A literature review. *Information Processing & Management*, 59(2):102853.

Chao Zhang, Jingbo Zhou, Xiaoling Zang, Qing Xu, Liang Yin, Xiang He, Lin Liu, Haoyi Xiong, and Dejing Dou. 2021. *CHASE: Commonsense-Enriched Advertising on Search Engine with Explicit Knowledge*, page 4352–4361. Association for Computing Machinery, New York, NY, USA.

Tao Zhang, Jin Zhang, Chengfu Huo, and Weijun Ren. 2019. Automatic generation of pattern-controlled product description in e-commerce. In *The World Wide Web Conference*, WWW '19, page 2355–2365,

New York, NY, USA. Association for Computing Machinery.

Yaoming Zhu, Sidi Lu, Lei Zheng, Jiaxian Guo, Weinan Zhang, Jun Wang, and Yong Yu. 2018. Texygen: A benchmarking platform for text generation models. *CoRR*, abs/1802.01886.

A Ad Text Quality Judgement UI

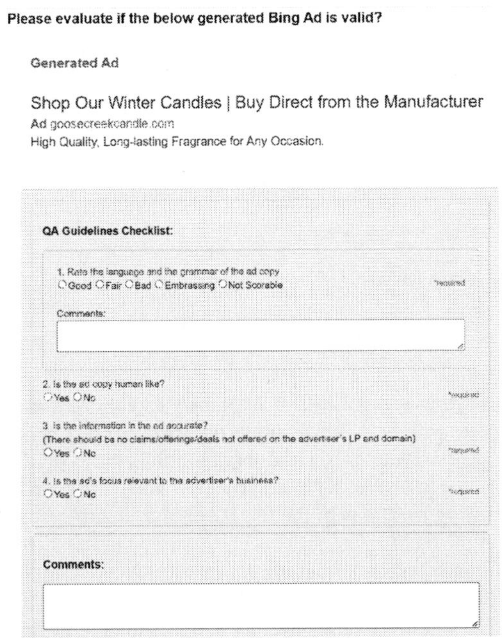

Figure 4: User interface for human ad quality evaluation.

ACCoRD: A Multi-Document Approach to Generating Diverse Descriptions of Scientific Concepts

Sonia K. Murthy, Kyle Lo, Daniel King, Chandra Bhagavatula, Bailey Kuehl
Sophie Johnson, Jonathan Borchardt, Daniel S. Weld, Tom Hope, Doug Downey
Allen Institute for Artificial Intelligence
{soniam,kylel,daniel,chandrab,baileyk,
sophiej,jonathanb,danw,tomh,dougd}@allenai.org

Abstract

Systems that automatically define unfamiliar terms hold the promise of improving the accessibility of scientific texts, especially for readers who may lack prerequisite background knowledge. However, current systems assume a single "best" description per concept, which fails to account for the many ways a concept can be described. We present ACCoRD, an end-to-end system tackling the novel task of generating *sets* of descriptions of scientific concepts. Our system takes advantage of the myriad ways a concept is mentioned across the scientific literature to produce distinct, diverse descriptions of target concepts in terms of different reference concepts. In a user study, we find that users prefer (1) descriptions produced by our end-to-end system, and (2) multiple descriptions to a single "best" description. We release the ACCoRD corpus which includes 1,275 labeled contexts and 1,787 expert-authored concept descriptions to support research on our task.

1 Introduction

Readers of scientific papers often encounter unfamiliar concepts, which impedes their understanding (Portenoy et al., 2022). This is because papers assume *a priori* knowledge, and often lack definitions for the scientific terms that they use. While readers may turn to external encyclopedic resources like Wikipedia, these contain descriptions for only a small fraction of scientific concepts (King et al., 2020), which has motivated the development of systems that automatically extract or generate descriptions for scientific concepts. Unfortunately, current systems only surface a single "best" result for all users, which is often extracted from a single input document (Espinosa-Anke and Schockaert, 2018; Vanetik et al., 2020; Veyseh et al., 2019; Kang et al., 2020). The one-best description may not be accessible for all readers, given varying background knowledge.

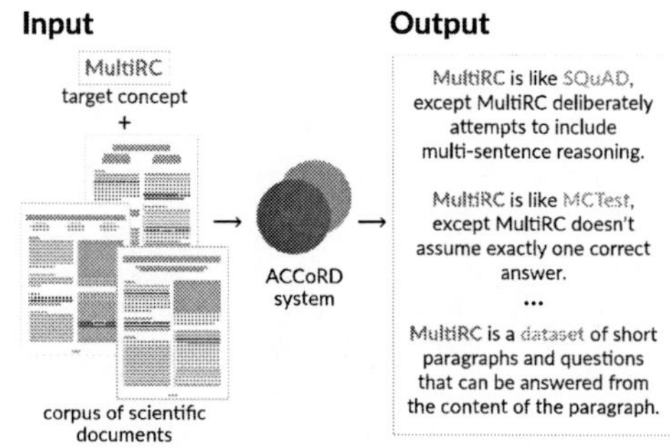

Figure 1: *ACCoRD's approach to Description Set Generation*. Given a corpus of papers and a target concept to be described (red, e.g. MultiRC), our system produces a diverse *set* of descriptions. These are generated using mentions of the target concept in terms of multiple other reference concepts (orange) from extracted contexts (blue), resulting in a diverse set of descriptions.

Scientific concepts can be described in multiple distinct ways. In this work, we propose that a *set of descriptions* is more useful for users than a single description. Humans learn new concepts by understanding how they relate to other, known concepts (Rumelhart and Ortony, 1977; Spiro, 1980; NRC, 2018), and providing multiple descriptions allows us to highlight multiple such relationships, contributing to a more complete understanding. Furthermore, providing multiple descriptions increases the number of potentially helpful connections between a new concept and concepts within the user's specific background knowledge (see Figure 1), increasing accessibility. This relational approach to human concept learning has been formalized through the lens of Analogical Transfer Theory (Gentner, 1983; Kurtz et al., 2001; Gentner and Goldin-Meadow, 2003) and has long been employed as a tool in scientific discourse and education (Treagust et al., 1992; Heywood, 2002). Our work expands upon the notion of a description in the context of description generation systems to include analogy-like descriptions that are currently

Proceedings of the The 2022 Conference on Empirical Methods in Natural Language Processing: System Demonstrations, pages 200 - 213
December 7-11, 2022

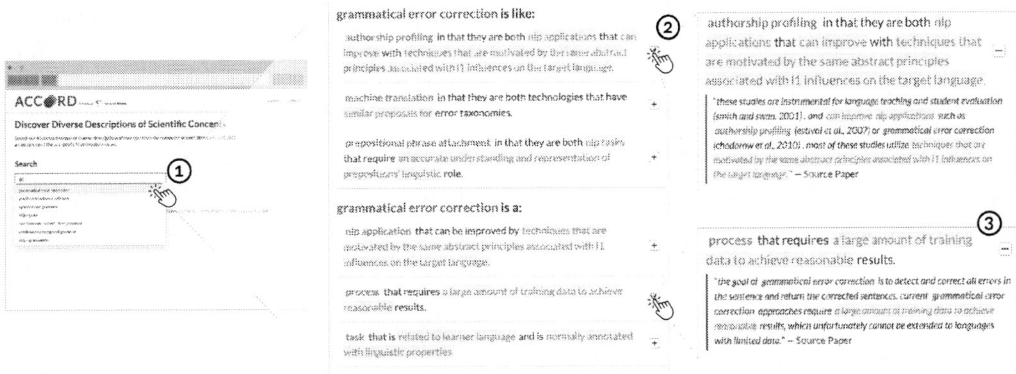

Figure 2: *Demo screenshots.* (1) Users search for a target scientific concept from a pre-defined list and are shown cards for top reference concepts used to describe the target concept in terms of a particular relation. (2) Users click to expand the cards to see the extracted snippet (context) that produced the generated concept description, in addition to a link to the source paper. (3) Spans of text that are shared between the extracted context and generated description are highlighted to facilitate easy comparison.

not captured by either scientific definition (Kang et al., 2020) or relation extraction (Wadden et al., 2019) systems.

In this work, we present Automatic Comparison of Concepts with Relational Descriptions (ACCoRD) – an end-to-end system that tackles the novel task of producing a set of distinct descriptions for a given target concept.[1] Given text from scientific papers, our system first **extracts** all sentences from the corpus that describe the concept in terms of any other concept. Then, conditioned on the extractions, ACCoRD **generates** succinct, self-contained descriptions of the concepts' relationship using GPT-3 (Brown et al., 2020) in the few-shot setting. The system finally **selects** a smaller, yet diverse subset of descriptions that captures the richness of a concept's usages by including multiple relation types and reference concepts.

Our contributions are:

1. We introduce Description Set Generation (DSG), the novel task of generating multiple distinct descriptions of a single target concept. In support of this task, we release the ACCoRD corpus, an expert-annotated resource of 1,275 labeled contexts and 1,787 hand-authored concept descriptions.

2. We present ACCoRD, an end-to-end system for DSG that outputs a diverse set of descriptions for concepts in computer science.

3. We conduct a user study demonstrating that users prefer multiple descriptions over a single "best" description, and that they prefer our system's generated concept descriptions over those of an extractive baseline.

[1]System demo, code, and data set available at github.com/allenai/ACCoRD.

2 Description Set Generation

2.1 Task definition

We define Description Set Generation (DSG) as: Given a large corpus of N scientific documents, a target concept to be described, and a desired output size $|S|$, output a set S of succinct, self-contained, and distinct descriptions of the target concept (Figure 1). Unlike prior work, which defines the task in terms of a single output description per scientific concept (Jin et al., 2013; Kang et al., 2020), DSG proposes outputting a set of descriptions. One can view DSG as a generalization of the format used in prior work (i.e. single-description outputs are sets with $|S| = 1$).

2.2 Approach

DSG is an open-ended task, and many possible description sets could form valid output for a given concept. To facilitate the generation of descriptions that are useful and factual, in this work, we focus on descriptions that meet three criteria: (i) They are derived from an extracted snippet of a scientific document, referred to as the *context*, which contains the target concept. In our experiments, the contexts are limited to 1-2 contiguous sentences. (ii) They must mention another concept, referred to as the *reference* concept, which is mentioned in the extracted context and is related to the target concept by one of the four relations in {is-a, is-like, part-of, used-for}. This relation must also be reflected in the extracted context. (iii) The description must contain an *elaboration*, or a span of text that further explains the specified relation between the target and reference concepts. For example, a description cannot only say that "SQuAD is like TriviaQA" but it must also specify that they "are both reading comprehension data sets." These elaborations must be supported by the associated extracted context.

The description criteria described above enabled us to build a system that produced many descriptions preferred by users, as we show in our experiments.[2] However, the DSG task is more general than our specific formulation, and experimenting with other description formats in DSG is an important item of future work.

3 Data set

To support work on DSG, we compile and release the ACCoRD corpus. The data set consists of 1,275 labeled contexts and 1,787 hand-authored concept descriptions, and induces diversity among these concept descriptions in two key ways. First, our data set allows for concept descriptions beyond the typical is-a relation. Second, a single target concept is allowed to be described in terms of any number of other concepts in the source text.

3.1 Data set construction

To construct the ACCoRD corpus, we consider the abstract, introduction, and related works sections of 698 computer science (CS) papers randomly sampled from S2ORC (Lo et al., 2020). We identify candidate contexts of 1-2 contiguous sentences with at least one CS concept via string matching against a high-precision set of CS concepts from ForeCite (King et al., 2020).[3]

Annotators were instructed to assign a binary label to each candidate context indicating whether the context sentence(s) contained a description of

Extracted context	Hand-authored descriptions
word embedding is a word representation that captures semantic and syntactic similarities between words. it has been widely utilized for a variety of tasks, such as sentence classification [42], relation classification [41], and sentiment analysis [38], since the introduction of word2vec software. (Shi et al., 2019)	[sentence classification, relation classification] is a task that word embedding has been utilized for since the introduction of word2vec software.
	sentence classification is like [relation classification, sentiment analysis] in that they are both tasks that word embedding has been used for since the introduction of word2vec software.
	relation classification is like [sentence classification, sentiment analysis] in that they are both tasks that word embedding has been used for since the introduction of word2vec software.
	word representation has been used for [sentence classification, relation classification, sentiment analysis] since the introduction of word2vec software.

Table 1: *Sample entry from the ACCoRD corpus.* The ACCoRD annotation procedure uniquely allows each positively-labeled context to yield multiple concept descriptions for target ForeCite concept(s) (red) present in an extracted context. Diversity among these concept descriptions is induced through multiple relation types (yellow) and distinct reference concepts (green), each with an elaboration that specifies the relationship between the target and reference concepts (blue).

the target ForeCite concept in terms of any other concept in the context. Inter-annotator agreement for this annotation task was Cohen's $\kappa = 0.658$.

For each extracted context that was assigned a positive label, annotators were instructed to author as many descriptions of the target ForeCite concept that follow criteria (i)-(iii) above (see Appendix A.1). These criteria allow each positively-labeled context to yield multiple concept descriptions if a target concept was described in terms of multiple other concepts in the source text, if multiple descriptive relations are applicable for a concept pair, or if the extraction contained multiple target concepts (see Table 1).

4 System overview

The ACCoRD system has 3 pipeline stages: (1) **extract** sentences that describe one scientific concept in terms of another, (2) **generate** succinct, self-contained descriptions of the concepts' relationship, and (3) **select** the top descriptions for each concept (see Figure 3).

[2]Our specification of descriptions according to these three criteria naturally include statements that would commonly be considered "definitions." For example, the Wikipedia definition of BERT, "BERT is a transformer-based machine learning technique for natural language processing (NLP) pre-training." can be viewed as an is-a relational statement describing BERT in terms of the *reference concept* "transformer-based machine learning technique" with the *elaboration* "for natural language processing (NLP) pre-training"

[3]ForeCite also assigns scores for each of its concepts that represent their likelihood to be a scientific concept. We filter to concepts with a ForeCite score ≥ 1.0.

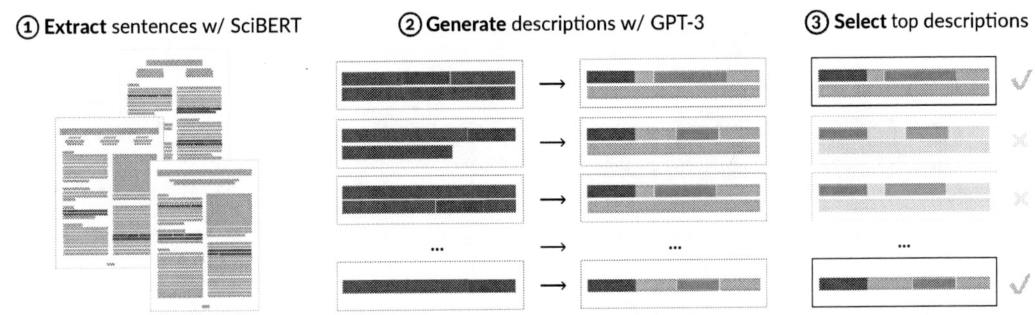

Figure 3: *ACCoRD system implemetation.* Our system (1) **extracts** context sentences (blue) from scientific documents that describe a target scientific concept (red) in terms of another using SciBERT (Beltagy et al., 2019) finetuned on the ACCoRD corpus, (2) **generates** succinct, self-contained, and distinct descriptions of the target's relationship to each reference concept (orange) from the extracted contexts using GPT-3 (Brown et al., 2020) in the few-shot setting, and (3) **selects** a final description set involving multiple relation types and reference concepts.

Extraction We build a two-stage model to identify sentences that describe a target concept in terms of another concept. First, a SciBERT (Beltagy et al., 2019) text classifier trained on the binary labels from the ACCoRD corpus identifies reasonable candidate contexts. Second, a different multilabel SciBERT classifier trained on the relation types in ACCoRD predicts a relation type for each candidate context. The inputs to both models have the target scientific concepts demarcated following Wu and He (2019). Details on training and hyperparameter tuning are in Appendix A.3.

Generation Each extracted candidate is then input into a generative model, which produces a succinct, self-contained summary of the concept relationship described in the context. For the generator, we use GPT-3's `davicini-instruct-beta` model (Brown et al., 2020) in the few-shot setting. Details on how GPT-3 was prompted and heuristically post-processed are in Appendix A.4.

Selection For each target concept, we identify a smaller, easily-consumable set[4] of informative descriptions from the larger pool of candidates. First, we filter descriptions to only those that involve a reference concept from ForeCite (King et al., 2020). Second, note that each description has an associated context classified with relations in the extraction step. Using these, for each (target, relation) pair, we choose the most frequent k reference concepts among the descriptions. Third, we select a top description for each (target, relation, reference) triple by selecting the one with the highest prediction score from our multilabel extraction model.

4.1 ACCoRD generates diverse descriptions

By identifying concept descriptions across the scientific literature, our system captures a diversity of descriptions for a given target concept. We measure this diversity for a set of 150 popular natural language processing concepts using two metrics: the number of candidate descriptions prior to the selection stage of our system and the number of unique reference concepts contained in those descriptions.[5] For descriptions involving the `compare` and `is-a` relations, we find an average of 153 and 373 candidate descriptions per target concept, respectively. These candidate descriptions contain an average of 15 unique reference concepts per target concept for `is-a` descriptions and 11 for `compare` descriptions (see Figure 4). This shows that our system captures a wealth of information that is not retained by a "single best" approach.

5 User study

The experiments in the previous section show that our system produces meaningful diversity in generated descriptions. We perform a user study with the full end-to-end system in order to answer two key questions regarding our system's utility:

- **RQ1:** Which method of producing concept descriptions do users most prefer?
- **RQ2:** Does there exist a single "best" description per user?

[4]If $|S|$ is large, ordering the set may be an important subproblem, which we leave for future work.

[5]We report these statistics per relation type exhibited in the description. For brevity, we restrict this to the two most commonly observed relation types.

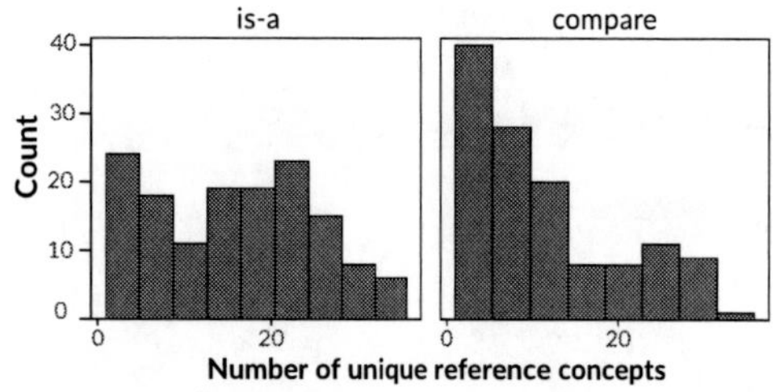

Figure 4: *Distribution over number of unique reference concepts per target among 150 popular NLP concepts.* For each target concept, ACCoRD produces candidate descriptions involving a variety of reference concepts and relations.

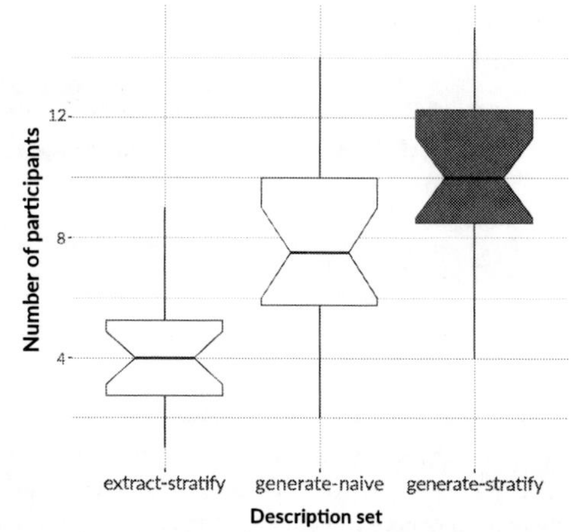

Figure 5: *User preferences for description sets.* Participants strongly preferred descriptions sets that contained generated descriptions (*generate-stratify*, *generate-naive*) over the set that contained extracted text snippets (*extract-stratify*). Participants' preference for the set produced by ACCoRD's more sophisticated description selection component was less pronounced, but still resulted in a higher minimum preference count than *generate-naive*.

5.1 Study description

Our study consisted of two parts: The first aimed to understand users' preferences for *sets* of descriptions, and the second aimed to understand their preferences for *individual* descriptions within sets.

Participants We recruited 22 participants through Upwork with at least a bachelor's degree in computer science and whose expertise included NLP (see Appendix A.5 for details). Participants were asked to imagine they were reading a section in a paper and came across a scientific concept they wanted to learn more about.

Design We selected a set of 20 popular NLP concepts from ForeCite. For each concept, we obtained three sets of six descriptions. Each set was generated from a system variant:

- ***generate-stratify*** the output of our complete system: generated descriptions that were selected according to our ranking and filtering methods. This set was comprised of the top three descriptions for each of the relation classes `compare` and `is-a`.
- ***extract-stratify*** the raw extractions for the descriptions in *generate-stratify*.
- ***generate-naive*** the output of the generation step of our system, but without the final stratified selection step. Instead, the top six descriptions for this set were selected using the prediction scores from our extractive model.

In Part One of the study, participants reported their level of expertise with each concept on a 5-point scale ranging from 1 = "I do not know this concept" to 5 = "I know the concept and could explain it to someone else." For each concept, participants then read the three sets of descriptions and selected the set they found most helpful for the imagined setting. At the end of Part One, participants gave a free-response description of how they determined their preference for the description sets. In particular, we asked them to articulate which features of the description sets were important in determining a preference.

In Part Two of the study, participants were shown each of the descriptions from our complete system's output (*generate-stratify*) and asked to indicate their preference for each description in a multiple choice: "I would want to see this description of the concept," "No preference/opinion," "I would not want to see this description of the concept." At the end of Part Two, participants gave two free-response explanations: (1) why they preferred certain descriptions over others and (2) how their criteria may have differed when rating *sets* of descriptions compared to *individual* descriptions.

5.2 Results

***RQ1:* Users prefer our system's generated descriptions over baselines** The three description sets we tested were aimed at understanding users' preferences for the individual components of our system, in particular (1) whether users preferred the final summarized concept descriptions to the raw extractions and (2) whether our stratified selection method of filtering the descriptions was preferred.

As shown in Figure 5, aggregated over the responses for all 20 concepts in our study, participants strongly preferred both versions of the generated description sets, which received a median score of 7.5 for *generate-naive* (95% CI = [5.9, 9.1]) and 10.0 for *generate-stratify* ([8.4, 11.6]) compared to the raw extractions from *extract-stratify* at 4.0 ([2.9, 5.1]). These results also suggest a preference for the description set obtained using ACCoRD's stratified selection method *generate-stratify* over *generate-naive*.

***RQ2:* There is no single "best" description per user** ACCoRD's approach is based on the hypothesis that users prefer a set of descriptions to a single "best" description per concept. Our findings support this hypothesis: When presented with multiple individual descriptions from our end-to-end system, *generate-stratify*, participants on average preferred around 3 descriptions for a given target concept ($\mu = 3.41$, 95% CI = [3.03, 3.79]).

5.3 Qualitative analysis

Analyzing the free-text responses from study participants generally confirmed the results of our quantitative findings, while shedding more light on users' considerations in evaluating concept descriptions.

Users prefer concise descriptions Participants most consistently articulated some preference for shorter, more concise, and more direct descriptions of the target concept ($n = 11$). This provides strong support for the generative component of our system; however, a number of users ($n = 5$) noted that the generations were not always accurate (see Appendix for error analysis). Additionally, though participants appreciated the conciseness of the generated descriptions, many ($n = 6$) noted referencing the extracted text for additional context, confirming our design choice of displaying each generation with its source text (see Figure 2).

Many users prefer analogical descriptions Our work expands the notion of a description in the context of description generation systems, to include analogy-like descriptions that are currently not captured by either scientific definition (Kang et al., 2020) or relation extraction (Wadden et al., 2019) systems. A number of participants ($n = 9$) noted that descriptions that drew connections between other concepts in this fashion were helpful, in particular because they could ease learning and memorization of the concept (P18), reflected their own process when trying to synthesize new information (P19), and helped make sense of the many similar model architectures (P14).

6 Related Work

Learning new concepts Cognitive theories of learning have asserted that effective ways of describing a new concept to someone tend to take advantage of structured background knowledge (Spiro, 1980; Bazerman, 1985) by grounding descriptions to already-familiar concepts (NRC, 2018). Systems that assume a single "best" result for all users limit the accessibility of technical knowledge to diverse audiences (Teevan et al., 2010). These considerations motivate our system and novel task definition, which extends the conventional description generation setting to include multiple target descriptions for a single concept.

Description generation While previous work has investigated extracting and generating definitions of scientific concepts (Espinosa-Anke and Schockaert, 2018; Vanetik et al., 2020; Veyseh et al., 2019; Kang et al., 2020), they focus on producing a single canonical description for each concept. These methods also approach definition generation from a single-document perspective, which doesn't account for the multitude of ways a concept might be described outside of the context of that paper. In contrast, we aim to preserve multiple distinct descriptions that take advantage of the corpus-wide mentions of a given concept. In addition, unlike the data sets these models are trained on (e.g. W00 (Jin et al., 2013)), our ACCoRD corpus includes descriptions that involve comparative relationships between concepts beyond the typical `is-a` relationship. Such extractions of concept comparisons have been targeted in the context of relation extraction systems (Wadden et al., 2019), and their corresponding data sets (Luan et al., 2018). However, these do not include differentia between the concept pairs that elaborate on the concepts' relationships, making them unsuitable as data for our concept description setting.

7 Future work

7.1 Improving generation quality

Our results show that a generation component that produces succinct, direct descriptions of a target concept is helpful for a user-friendly system for

DSG. However, our qualitative feedback suggests that this is also an important area for future work, as poor generation quality was often cited as the reason users preferred the set with only extracted descriptions (see Tables 3 and 4 for an analysis of extraction-stage and generation-stage errors).

7.2 Controllable generation

Beyond resolving errors in generation, future work might investigate methods for controllable generation that are better tailored to user needs. For example, in our user study free-text responses, participants suggested that users may require different kinds of descriptions based on the type of concept being described. In particular, two participants (P14, P21) noted that they preferred set *generate-naive*, which contained more "canonical" descriptions, for simple, standalone data set concepts that could be explained straightforwardly. On the other hand, for more complex method and system-based concepts, like RoBERTa, GPT, and LSTM, users expressed preference for descriptions that made comparisons to other concepts (as produced by our complete system). Adding a word-sense disambiguation module to future versions of our system will also be important, especially for domains like biomedicine where a single scientific term will often have multiple usages.

7.3 Potential for personalization

While we showed in Section 5.2 that participants often had multiple preferred descriptions per concept, a question remains—Are these preferences similar or different *across* users? To investigate, we compute the Fleiss' κ score measuring agreement in participant preference votes across the six available descriptions for each concept, and find this to be low on average across concepts ($\mu = 0.06$, 95% CI = [0.04, 0.09]). Likewise, only a minority of users ($\mu = 0.34$, 95% CI = [0.31, 0.36]) listed the top-voted description among their preferred ones, on average. The high variation in preferences across participants suggests potential for personalization in the DSG task. In this section, we investigate future avenues for operationalizing personalization within description generation systems.

We consider how level of expertise in a concept might affect a user's preferences over descriptions. In Figure 6, we plot the Fleiss' κ scores for user preferences over descriptions against the average level of self-reported expertise of the concepts. While we do observe low agreement in preferences overall, interestingly the lowest agreement scores are found for concepts for which participants mostly self-rated as having low expertise. Fitting a linear model to the data, we find the estimated slope coefficient is significantly greater than zero ($b = 0.03628, p < 0.05$).[6]

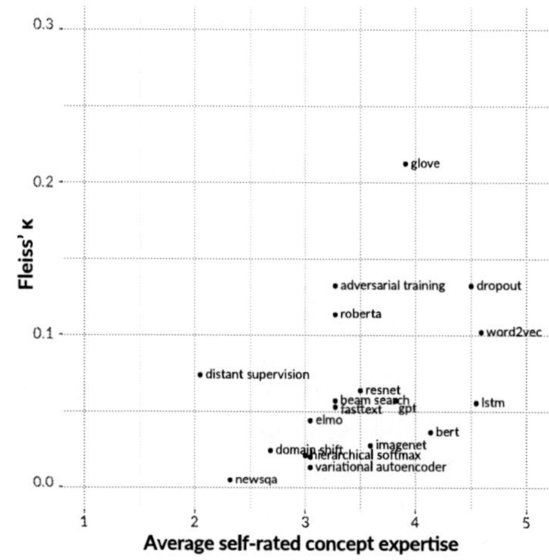

Figure 6: *User agreement (Fleiss' κ) in description preferences for each concept versus average concept expertise level.* We find low agreement in preferences overall, with the lowest agreement scores for concepts for which participants also indicated low expertise.

8 Conclusion

We have presented ACCoRD, an end-to-end system for the novel task of Description Set Generation (DSG). In user studies, our methods were preferred over baseline approaches and produce a diversity of generated concept descriptions. We also release the ACCoRD corpus to facilitate development of future systems for DSG. We hope that such systems will help increase the accessibility of scientific literature for people with diverse background knowledge.

Acknowledgements

This project was supported in part by NSF Convergence Accelerator Award 2132318, NSF RAPID grant 2040196, ONR grant N00014-18-1-2193, and the Allen Institute for Artificial Intelligence (AI2). We thank Elena Glassman for providing valuable feedback on our system demonstration.

[6]We further investigated this by, for each concept, segmenting participants into high and low expertise groups (i.e. above or below the global median expertise of 4.0) and computing average agreement within those groups. The difference in mean agreement between high ($\mu = 0.08$) and low ($\mu = 0.05$) expertise groups was not statistically significant.

References

Mohammed N. A. Ali, Guanzheng Tan, and Aamir Hussain. 2019. Boosting arabic named-entity recognition with multi-attention layer. *IEEE Access*, 7:46575–46582.

Peter Anderson, Ayush Shrivastava, Devi Parikh, Dhruv Batra, and Stefan Lee. 2019. Chasing ghosts: Instruction following as bayesian state tracking. In *NeurIPS*.

Charles Bazerman. 1985. Physicists reading physics. *Written Communication*, 2:23 – 3.

Iz Beltagy, Kyle Lo, and Arman Cohan. 2019. Scibert: Pretrained language model for scientific text. In *EMNLP*.

Tom B. Brown, Benjamin Mann, Nick Ryder, Melanie Subbiah, Jared Kaplan, Prafulla Dhariwal, Arvind Neelakantan, Pranav Shyam, Girish Sastry, Amanda Askell, Sandhini Agarwal, Ariel Herbert-Voss, Gretchen Krueger, Tom Henighan, Rewon Child, Aditya Ramesh, Daniel M. Ziegler, Jeffrey Wu, Clemens Winter, Christopher Hesse, Mark Chen, Eric Sigler, Mateusz Litwin, Scott Gray, Benjamin Chess, Jack Clark, Christopher Berner, Sam McCandlish, Alec Radford, Ilya Sutskever, and Dario Amodei. 2020. Language models are few-shot learners.

Yin-Wen Chang, Alexander M. Rush, John DeNero, and Michael Collins. 2014. A constrained viterbi relaxation for bidirectional word alignment. In *ACL*.

Luis Espinosa-Anke and Steven Schockaert. 2018. Syntactically aware neural architectures for definition extraction. In *Proceedings of the 2018 Conference of the North American Chapter of the Association for Computational Linguistics: Human Language Technologies, Volume 2 (Short Papers)*, pages 378–385, New Orleans, Louisiana. Association for Computational Linguistics.

Dedre Gentner. 1983. Structure-mapping: A theoretical framework for analogy. *Cogn. Sci.*, 7:155–170.

Dedre Gentner and Susan Goldin-Meadow. 2003. *Language in mind: Advances in the study of language and thought*. MIT press.

David Heywood. 2002. The place of analogies in science education. *Cambridge Journal of Education*, 32:233 – 247.

Ganesh Jawahar, Benoît Sagot, and Djamé Seddah. 2019. What does bert learn about the structure of language? In *ACL*.

Yiping Jin, Min-Yen Kan, Jun-Ping Ng, and Xiangnan He. 2013. Mining scientific terms and their definitions: A study of the ACL Anthology. In *Proceedings of the 2013 Conference on Empirical Methods in Natural Language Processing*, pages 780–790, Seattle, Washington, USA. Association for Computational Linguistics.

Dongyeop Kang, Andrew Head, Risham Sidhu, Kyle Lo, Daniel Weld, and Marti A. Hearst. 2020. Document-level definition detection in scholarly documents: Existing models, error analyses, and future directions. In *Proceedings of the First Workshop on Scholarly Document Processing*, pages 196–206, Online. Association for Computational Linguistics.

Daniel King, Doug Downey, and Daniel S. Weld. 2020. High-Precision Extraction of Emerging Concepts from Sientific Literature. In *Proceedings of the 43rd International ACM SIGIR Conference on Research and Development in Information Retrieval (SIGIR '20)*, Virtual Event, China. ACM.

Kenneth J. Kurtz, Chun-Hui Miao, and Dedre Gentner. 2001. Learning by analogical bootstrapping. *The Journal of the Learning Sciences*, 10(4):417–446.

Chu-Cheng Lin and Jason Eisner. 2018. Neural particle smoothing for sampling from conditional sequence models. In *NAACL*.

Kyle Lo, Lucy Lu Wang, Mark Neumann, Rodney Kinney, and Daniel Weld. 2020. S2ORC: The semantic scholar open research corpus. In *Proceedings of the 58th Annual Meeting of the Association for Computational Linguistics*, pages 4969–4983, Online. Association for Computational Linguistics.

Boyu Lu, Frank Shyu, Yun-Nung (Vivian) Chen, Hung yi Lee, and Lin-Shan Lee. 2017. Order-preserving abstractive summarization for spoken content based on connectionist temporal classification. *ArXiv*, abs/1709.05475.

Yi Luan, Luheng He, Mari Ostendorf, and Hannaneh Hajishirzi. 2018. Multi-task identification of entities, relations, and coreferencefor scientific knowledge graph construction. In *Proc. Conf. Empirical Methods Natural Language Process. (EMNLP)*.

Sainik Kumar Mahata, Avishek Garain, Adityar Rayala, Dipankar Das, and Sivaji Bandyopadhyay. 2019. Jumt at wmt2019 news translation task: A hybrid approach to machine translation for lithuanian to english. *ArXiv*, abs/1908.01349.

NRC. 2018. How people learn: Brain, mind, experience, and school: Expanded edition. In *The National Academies Press*, Washington, DC.

Jason Portenoy, Marissa Radensky, Jevin D. West, Eric Horvitz, Daniel S. Weld, and Tom Hope. 2022. Bursting scientific filter bubbles: Boosting innovation via novel author discovery. In *CHI*.

Alexandre Reiffers-Masson and Vincent Labatut. 2017. Opinion-based centrality in multiplex networks: A convex optimization approach. *Network Science*, 5:213 – 234.

David Rumelhart and Andrew Ortony. 1977. *Schooling and the acquisition of knowledge*. Lawrence Erlbaum Associates, Hillsdale, NJ.

Weijia Shi, Muhao Chen, Pei Zhou, and Kai-Wei Chang. 2019. Retrofitting contextualized word embeddings with paraphrases. In *EMNLP*.

Rand J. Spiro. 1980. Schema theory and reading comprehension: New directions.

Jun Suzuki, Kevin Duh, and Masaaki Nagata. 2011. Distributed minimum error rate training of smt using particle swarm optimization. In *IJCNLP*.

Jaime Teevan, Susan T. Dumais, and Eric Horvitz. 2010. Potential for personalization. *ACM Trans. Comput.-Hum. Interact.*, 17(1).

David F. Treagust, Reinders Duit, Paul Joslin, and Ivo E. Lindauer. 1992. Science teachers' use of analogies: observations from classroom practice. *International Journal of Science Education*, 14:413–422.

Natalia Vanetik, Marina Litvak, Sergey Shevchuk, and Lior Reznik. 2020. Automated discovery of mathematical definitions in text. In *Proceedings of the 12th Language Resources and Evaluation Conference*, pages 2086–2094, Marseille, France. European Language Resources Association.

Amir Pouran Ben Veyseh, Franck Dernoncourt, Dejing Dou, and Thien Huu Nguyen. 2019. A joint model for definition extraction with syntactic connection and semantic consistency. *CoRR*, abs/1911.01678.

David Wadden, Ulme Wennberg, Yi Luan, and Hannaneh Hajishirzi. 2019. Entity, relation, and event extraction with contextualized span representations. In *Proceedings of the 2019 Conference on Empirical Methods in Natural Language Processing and the 9th International Joint Conference on Natural Language Processing (EMNLP-IJCNLP)*, pages 5784–5789, Hong Kong, China. Association for Computational Linguistics.

Shanchan Wu and Yifan He. 2019. Enriching pretrained language model with entity information for relation classification. In *Proceedings of the 28th ACM International Conference on Information and Knowledge Management*, CIKM '19, page 2361–2364, New York, NY, USA. Association for Computing Machinery.

Huangjie Zheng, Lingxi Xie, Tianwei Ni, Ya Zhang, Yanfeng Wang, Qi Tian, Elliot K. Fishman, and Alan Loddon Yuille. 2018. Phase collaborative network for multi-phase medical imaging segmentation. *ArXiv*, abs/1811.11814.

A Appendix

A.1 ACCoRD corpus examples that deviate from criteria

In a small fraction of cases, the hand-labeled descriptions deviate from the criteria. First, in $< 4.6\%$ of examples, we allowed annotators to specify a reference concept not explicitly mentioned in the extracted context. These were limited to obvious cases; e.g. "neural network" is a reference concept for target concept "recurrent neural network." Second, $< 0.4\%$ of examples do not contain an elaboration. The majority of these cases are of the `used-for` relation, where the reference concept and elaboration are a single entity (e.g. "gav is used for *query processing in stable environments*.")

A.2 ACCoRD addresses a meaningfully novel task

To verify that the ACCoRD corpus addresses a novel task that is not well-captured by existing resources, we compare our system's results on ACCoRD to those of existing state-of-the-art scientific definition and relation extraction systems. For our definition extraction baseline, we test HEDDEx (Kang et al., 2020) trained on W00 (Jin et al., 2013), a similarly-sized corpus of definition sentences from workshop papers from the 2000 ACL Conference. Since HEDDEx was originally only intended to produce a single canonical definition of scientific terms and symbols at the sentence-level, we also evaluate its performance on the subset of ACCoRD that was marked as containing an "is-a" relationship between the reference and target concept, to more faithfully evaluate its potential. For our relation extraction baseline, we test DyGIE++ (Wadden et al., 2019) trained on SciERC (Luan et al., 2018), a scientific relation extraction data set. Table 2 shows these results for the union of the 1- and 2-sentence source text settings in ACCoRD, as our qualitative conclusions remained unchanged across these settings. Our model trained on ACCoRD outperforms models that target related tasks, even when they beat a baseline that always assigns positive labels, suggesting that our data set addresses an importantly different task.

Model	Train set	F1
HEDDEx	W00	0.329
HEDDEx$_{is\text{-}a}$	W00	0.449
DyGIE++	SciERC	0.532
SciBERT	**ACCoRD**	**0.624**
	Positive baseline	0.484

Table 2: Results for our extractive model and relevant baselines on the ACCoRD test set ($n = 674$). Our model trained on ACCoRD outperforms models that target related tasks, even when they beat a baseline that always assigns positive labels, suggesting that our data set addresses an importantly different task.

A.3 Extraction models training and hyperparameter tuning details

For context identification, the model was trained with using a classification head on the `[CLS]` token. Across 5 random seed runs, within which we performed 5-fold cross validation over 3509 examples, we searched over training configurations and hyperparameters: model in {SciBERT, RoBERTa-Large} loss function in {negative log-likelihood, soft F1}, number of epochs in {5, 10, 15}, learning rates in {1e-5, 5e-5, 1e-4}, and batch size in {16, 32}. We found that the SciBERT model with soft F1 loss was performing the best with respect to the positive class F1. Overall, our best model was a SciBERT classifier with `[CLS]`, trained with soft F1 loss over 10 epochs, a learning rate of 1e-5, and batch size of 16.

We followed a similar process for the multilabel relation classification model, except instead of a softmax we used a sigmoid over the `[CLS]` classification head to enable multilabel predictions, whose logit values were thresholded at 0. Our best model here was SciBERT trained with a weighted binary cross entropy loss (weight = 2) over 10 epochs, a learning rate of 5e-5, and batch size of 32.

A.4 GPT-3 prompting and post-processing details

We provide the model with a prompt that includes the instruction "Describe the provided concept in terms of another concept in the text" along with five hand-picked (extraction, ground truth concept description) example pairs from the ACCoRD corpus. We hand-select example pairs for each relation type, and for each query extraction, provide the examples of the relation type predicted by the multilabel classifier.

Each generated description is then post-processed to heuristically identify the reference concept, using noun chunking and regular expressions based on our description templates. We then apply additional heuristics to the descriptions as a first-pass filter for low-quality GPT-3 generations, e.g. removing descriptions that have any mention of unresolved references like "our work," descriptions that erroneously contain a reference concept that is an author's name, and descriptions with more than one occurrence of the target concept (to prevent descriptions of the target concept in terms of itself).

A.5 User study participant details

Of the 22 participants, all of whom had at least a bachelor's degree in computer science, 8 participants additionally had a Master's degree and 3 had obtained a PhD in computer science. 14 participants indicated having up to three years of experience in NLP, five had 4-6 years of experience, and three others indicated having more than 7 years of experience.

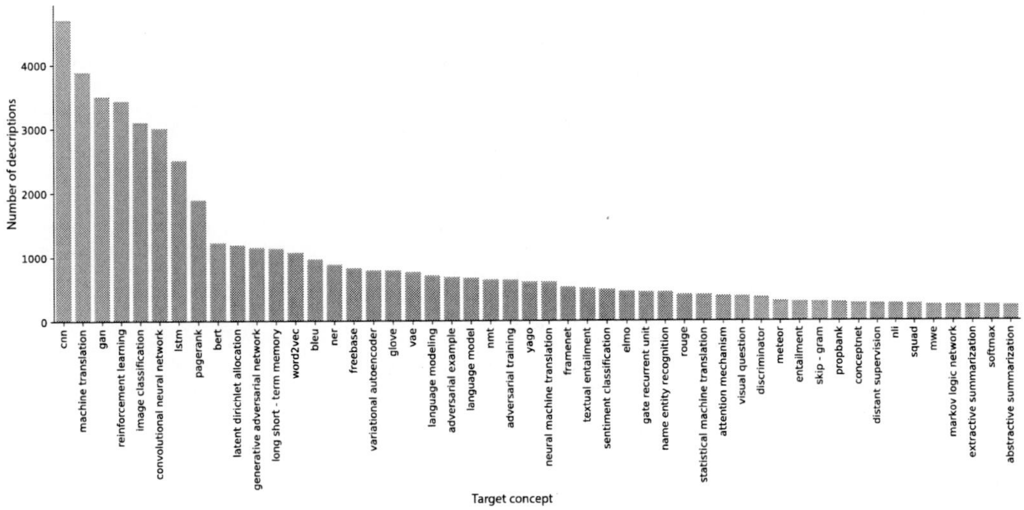

(a) compare relation

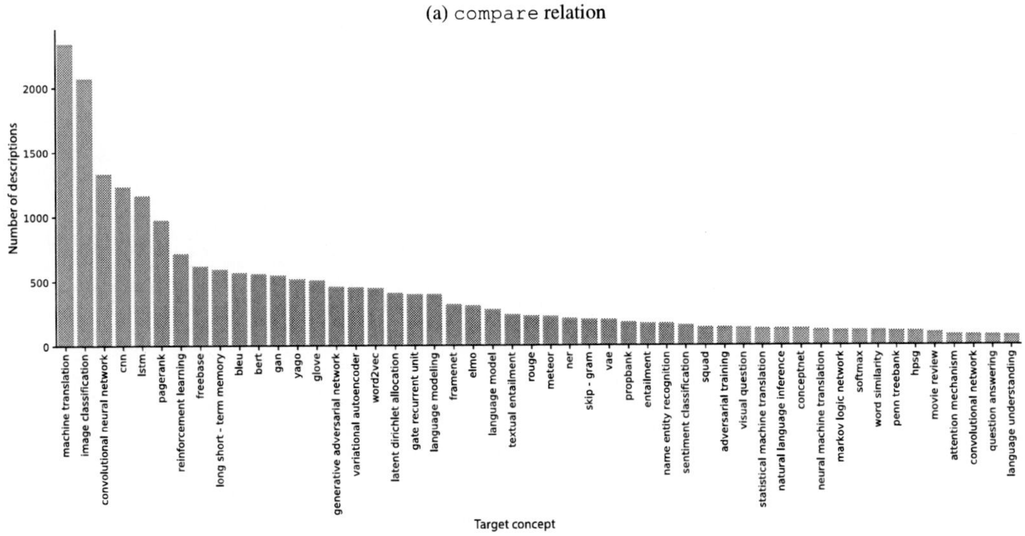

(b) is-a relation

Figure 7: Number of candidate descriptions for 50 target NLP concepts, for each relation type present in our system demo, prior to the selection stage of ACCoRD. Our system identifies, extracts, and generates approximately twice as many candidate descriptions of the compare relation than of the is-a relation.

Error type	Percentage	Sample extraction	Sample generation
Generation is an inaccurate synthesis of extraction	24%	in the modern context, mt systems can be categorized into statistical machine translation (smt) and neural machine translation (nmt). smt has had its share in making mt very popular among the masses. (Mahata et al., 2019) in the nlp community, beam search and importance sampling are common. unfortunately, beam search considers only the approximate-top-k taggings from an exponential set (wiseman and rush, 2016) , and importance sampling requires the construction of a good proposal distribution (dyer et al., 2016) . (Lin and Eisner, 2018)	neural machine translation is like statistical machine translation in that they are both types of mt systems and have had their share in making mt very popular among the masses. beam search is like importance sampling in that they are both methods that consider only the approximate-top-k taggings from an exponential set and require the construction of a good proposal distribution.
Generation is technically correct, but unhelpful because it lacks important details	15%	however, these approaches lack geometric priors and contain no mechanism for reasoning about the likelihood of alternative trajectories -a crucial skill for the task, e.g., 'would this look more like the goal if i was on the other side of the room?'. due to this limitation, many previous works have resorted to performing inefficient first-person search through the environment using search algorithms such as beam search [4, 6] . (Anderson et al., 2019)	beam search is a search algorithm that is used for first-person search through the environment.
Generation is incoherent	8%	in recent years, generative models like vae and gan [20, 11] and their extensions have become popular and have been applied to various scenarios due to their impressive performance. since the arterial and venous phases form different data distribution, to build a relation between them refers to the domain adaptation using generative models, where pix2pix [19] , cyclegan [50] and unit [28] etc. are typical models in this field. (Zheng et al., 2018) the trained model can be fine-tuned for downstream nlp tasks such as question answering and language inference without substantial modification. bert outperforms previous state-of-the-art models in the eleven nlp tasks in the glue benchmark (wang et al., 2018) by a significant margin. (Jawahar et al., 2019)	vae is like gan in that they are both generative models that have been applied to various scenarios due to their impressive performance and since the arterial and venous phases form different data distribution, to build a relation between them refers to the domain adaptation using generative models. question answering is like language inference in that they are both nlp tasks that bert outperforms previous state-of-the-art models in the eleven nlp tasks in the glue benchmark (wang et al., 2018) by a significant margin.
Second sentence of extraction is appended verbatim, resulting in a difficult to read, incoherent, or inaccurate generation	6%	recent statistical machine translation (smt) systems employ a linear combination of several model components, such as translation models, language models, and reordering models. translation is performed by selecting the most-likely translation, which is the candidate translation with the highest score based on the different model components. (Suzuki et al., 2011)	language model is like translation model in that they are both model components that are used in recent statistical machine translation (smt) systems and translation is performed by selecting the most-likely translation, which is the candidate translation with the highest score based on the different model components.

Table 3: *Error analysis of ACCoRD system output: generation stage.* Common generation error types for a sample ($n = 100$) of ACCoRD system outputs include generations that are an inaccurate synthesis of source text; generations that are technically correct but unhelpful because they lack important details; incoherent generations; and instances where the second sentence of extraction is appended verbatim, often resulting in a difficult to read, incoherent, or inaccurate generation. A final error type not shown was, appending irrelevant information, which occurred in 5% of the sample. Multiple error types can be present in the same generation.

Error type	Percentage	Sample extraction	Sample generation
Poor target concept delimitation resulting in inaccurate generation	6%	in order to ensure accurate word alignments, most systems employ a post-hoc symmetrization step to combine directional word aligners, such as ibm model 4 (brown et al., 1993) or hidden markov model (hmm) based aligners (vogel et al., 1996) . several authors have proposed bidirectional models that incorporate this step directly, but decoding under many bidirectional models is np-hard and finding exact solutions has proven difficult. (Chang et al., 2014)	ibm model is like hidden markov model in that they are both directional word aligners and have been used to create post-hoc symmetrization steps.
Extracted text is missing details or contains unresolved references that make it difficult to produce a high quality generation	6%	most of them generalize widespread existing unilayer measures such as degree [29, 17, 1] , betweenness [28, 34, 11] , closeness [29, 35] , eigenvector [17, 33, 1] , pagerank [31, 20, 13] or hits [26] . these generalizations rely on the adaptation of unilayer concepts to the multilayer case. (Reiffers-Masson and Labatut, 2017)	pagerank is like degree, betweenness, closeness, eigenvector and hits in that they are all unilayer measures that generalize to the multilayer case.
		[22] . their system achieved good results on various labeling tasks, including ner and pos, without depending on any manual feature engineering. (Ali et al., 2019)	ner is like pos in that they are both labeling tasks that the system achieved good results on without depending on any manual feature engineering.
Poor sentencization of scientific text	4%	various approaches have been proposed for sequence-tosequence problems, such as speech recognition [15, 16] , neural machine translation [17, 18] , and dialogue modeling [19, 20] . among various deep-learning-based methods, cho et al. (Lu et al., 2017)	neural machine translation is like speech recognition in that they are both approaches for sequence-tosequence problems and among various deep-learning-based methods, cho et al.

Table 4: *Error analysis of ACCoRD system output: extraction stage.* Common extraction error types for a sample ($n = 100$) of ACCoRD system outputs include poor delimitation of the target ForeCite concept within candidate extractions, resulting in an inaccurate generation; low quality extracted text that results in low quality generation; and poor sentence delimitation of scientific text. Multiple error types can be present in the same generation.

Automatic Comment Generation for Chinese Student Narrative Essays

Zhexin Zhang[1]*, Jian Guan[1]*, Guowei Xu[2], Yixiang Tian[2] and Minlie Huang[1]†

[1]The CoAI group, DCST; [1]Institute for Artificial Intelligence; [1]State Key Lab of Intelligent Technology and Systems;
[1]Beijing National Research Center for Information Science and Technology; [1]Tsinghua University, Beijing 100084, China.
[2]TAL Education Group.

{zx-zhang18,j-guan19}@mails.tsinghua.edu.cn, {xuguowei,tianyixiang}@tal.com
aihuang@tsinghua.edu.cn

Abstract

Automatic essay evaluation can help reduce teachers' workload and enable students to refine their works rapidly. Previous studies focus mainly on giving discrete scores for either the holistic quality or several distinct traits. However, real-world teachers usually provide detailed comments in natural language, which are more informative than single scores. In this paper, we present the comment generation task, which aims to generate comments for specified segments from given student narrative essays. To tackle this task, we propose a planning-based generation model, which first plans a sequence of keywords, and then expands these keywords into a complete comment. To improve the correctness and informativeness of generated comments, we adopt two following techniques: (1) training an error correction module to filter out incorrect keywords, and (2) recognizing fine-grained structured features from source essays to enrich the keywords. To support the evaluation of the task, we collect a human-written Chinese dataset, which contains 22,399 essay-comment pairs. Extensive experiments show that our model outperforms strong baselines significantly. Moreover, we exert explicit control on our model to generate comments to describe the strengths or weaknesses of inputs with a 91% success rate. We deploy the model at http://coai.cs.tsinghua.edu.cn/static/essayComment/. A demo video is available at https://youtu.be/IuFVk8dUxbI. Our code and data are available at https://github.com/thu-coai/EssayCommentGen.

1 Introduction

Automatic essay evaluation is a useful educational application of natural language processing (Page, 1966), which is beneficial for reducing teachers' workload and enabling students to improve writing skills independently. Prior studies focus mainly on automatic essay scoring (AES) in terms of either holistic scores (Cozma et al., 2018) or trait-specific scores (Mathias and Bhattacharyya, 2020; Song et al., 2020). However, real-world teachers usually provide detailed comments in natural language, which are more informative so that students can know more about the strengths and weaknesses of their works.

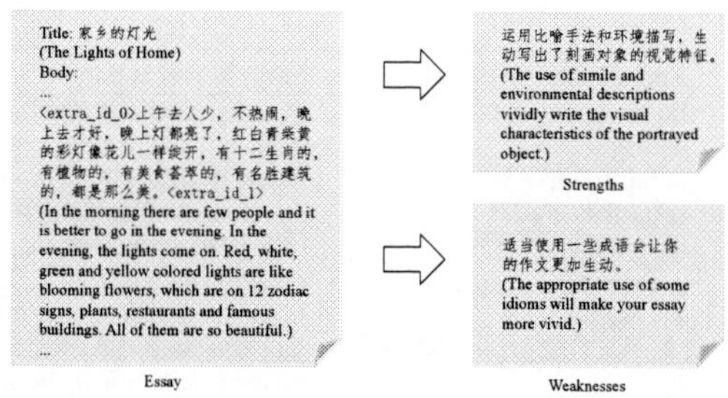

Figure 1: An example for the comment generation task. Given an essay with a specified segment (separated from the rest using special tokens <extra_id_0> and <extra_id_1>), the model should generate a sentence to comment the strengths or weaknesses of the segment.

In this work, we present the first study on automatic comment generation, which requires generating a fluent comment in natural language to describe strengths or weaknesses for a specified segment from a given student essay, as exemplified in Figure 1. We only focus on narrative essays in this work, which comprise more than 90% of our originally collected essays. The challenges of the task mainly lie in the following three folds: **(1)** Capturing the linguistic features of the essay, ranging from the wording, rhetorical methods (e.g., "simile" in the example) to discourse structures. **(2)** Generating coherent comments to correctly reflect the strengths or weaknesses (e.g., the segment does not use idioms in the example) of the essay. **(3)** Generating informative and diverse comments since generic comments such as "it is good" do not pro-

*Equal contribution.
†Corresponding author.

Proceedings of the The 2022 Conference on Empirical Methods in Natural Language Processing: System Demonstrations, pages 214 - 223
December 7-11, 2022 ©2022 Association for Computational Linguistics

vide any helpful guidance for students, and it is also expected to generate diverse comments for different essays.

To tackle the problem, we propose a planning-based generation model (Yao et al., 2019), which first plans a sequence of keywords concerning specific writing skills such as "simile", and then expands the keywords into a coherent comment. On the one hand, planning helps build explicit connections between essays and underlying skills, which alleviates the degeneration issue that the model focuses on predicting common elements such as "more vivid" and tends to generate generic comments (Fan et al., 2019). On the other hand, we can exert direct control on the intermediate keywords to improve the correctness and informativeness of generated comments. Specifically, we fine-tune BERT (Devlin et al., 2019) to serve as an error correction module to filter out incorrect keywords, which is trained to discriminate matching relations between essays and keywords. Moreover, we recognize structured features from source essays in terms of idioms, proverbs, quotes, descriptive and rhetorical methods using heuristic techniques or pretrained classifiers. Then we combine these features with the predicted keywords. To control the type of generated comments, we insert a binary control code before the keywords and comments (0/1 for describing strengths/weaknesses). In the comment generation stage, we inject noise into the ground-truth keywords during training (Tan et al., 2021) to alleviate the exposure bias issue introduced by planning (Ranzato et al., 2016).

To support training and evaluation of the proposed task, we collect a Chinese dataset that contains 22,399 essay-comment pairs. Extensive experiments show that our model outperforms strong baselines in correctness, informativeness and diversity. Furthermore, we build a website to enable real-time interaction with our deployed model, where a user can upload a Chinese student essay and see comments along with recognized structured features for most paragraphs.

2 Related Work

Automatic Essay Scoring There have been wide explorations for automatic essay scoring, including holistic essay scoring and trait-specific essay scoring (Mathias and Bhattacharyya, 2020). Holistic essay scoring aims to assign an overall score for the essay. Taghipour and Ng (2016); Tay et al. (2018) used LSTM and Dong and Zhang (2016); Dong et al. (2017) used CNN to give a total score for the essay. Cozma et al. (2018) utilized word embedding clusters and string kernels to achieve strong performances. Yang et al. (2020) jointly resolved the essay scoring task and the essay ranking task through fine-tuning the BERT model. Trait-specific essay scoring aims to assign different scores for different traits of an essay, such as thesis clarity (Ke et al., 2019), style (Mathias and Bhattacharyya, 2018) and narrative quality (Somasundaran et al., 2018). Mathias and Bhattacharyya (2020) compared different trait-agnostic approaches to automatically score many different essay traits. However, all these works assign numeric scores for an essay, while we focus on generating a readable comment.

Essay Assessment Systems Attali and Burstein (2006) constructed a system named E-rater, which could provide numeric scores for different features such as grammar and style. LinggleWrite (Tsai et al., 2020) focused on grammatical error correction and automatic essay scoring. The system most similar to ours is IFlyEA (Gong et al., 2021), which has grammar level analysis techniques and components for discourse and rhetoric analysis. It also integrates the fine-grained analysis to form a review for the whole essay using templates. However, our system is capable of generating diverse and natural comments without the usage of templates and could give comments for different segments of the essay.

Planning-based Generation Humans usually outline the overall framework before writing. Many works have explored planning-based text generation, which first predicts an intermediate representation as a plan and then generates the complete text conditioned on the plan. The plan could be a series of keywords (Yao et al., 2019), an action sequence (Fan et al., 2019; Goldfarb-Tarrant et al., 2020) or a dense keyword distribution (Kang and Hovy, 2020; Kong et al., 2021). Tan et al. (2021) progressively refined the produced domain-specific content keywords into complete passages in multiple stages. In this paper, we adapt planning to the automatic comment generation task and improve the correctness and informativeness by revising the intermediate keywords.

3 Method

We formulate our task as follows: given an essay $X = (x_1, x_2, \cdots, x_M)$ with M tokens and a specified segment from x_i to x_j (the segment is separated from the rest using special tokens), the model should generate a comment $Y = (y_1, y_2, \cdots, y_N)$ with N tokens for the segment. The comment either shows praise for the strengths of the segment, or gives advice to improve the weaknesses of the segment.

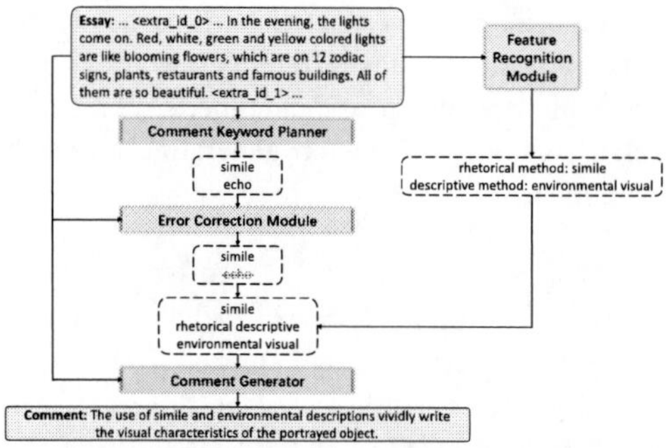

Figure 2: An overview of our model. The comment keyword planner takes an essay with a specified segment as input, and generates a sequence of keywords. To improve the correctness and informativeness of generated comments, we modify the keyword sequence by first filtering out incorrect keywords using the error correction module and then inserting structured features from the feature recognition module. Then we feed the polished keyword sequence into the comment generator along with the original essay to get the final comment. During training, we train different modules separately.

3.1 Model Overview

As shown in Figure 2, we propose a planning-based model, which first plans an out-of-order sequence of keywords and then organizes them into a complete comment. Furthermore, we add an error correction module which filters out incorrect keywords using a fine-tuned BERT classifier. We also employ a feature recognition module to recognize fine-grained structured features such as idioms, descriptive and rhetorical methods from the source essay X to enrich the keywords. Moreover, in the comment generation stage, we perturb the input keywords by inserting a random word to alleviate the exposure bias problem. To control the type of the generated comment, we insert a binary control code before generating the keywords and comment.

3.2 Two-staged Planning

Directly generating comments may make models fail to learn specific writing skills and simply over-fit the generic components such as "it is good", which make up the majority of each comment. Therefore, we extract relatively important keywords that have higher TF-IDF (Manning et al., 2010) values than a fixed threshold 0.3 from comments, which are more likely to relate to specific writing skills. Then we employ a comment keyword planner to predict the keywords, and a comment generator to organize them into a complete comment. In order to insert new keywords obtained from the feature recognition module without worrying about insertion positions, we randomly shuffle the extracted keywords. We train the planner and generator by optimizing the negative log-likelihood of ground truths, respectively, formally as follows:

$$\mathcal{L}_{\text{plan}} = -\frac{1}{T}\sum_{t=1}^{T} \log P(k_t|X, k_{<t}), \quad (1)$$

$$\mathcal{L}_{\text{gen}} = -\frac{1}{N}\sum_{t=1}^{N} \log P(y_t|X, K, y_{<t}), \quad (2)$$

where $K = (k_1, k_2, \cdots, k_T)$ with T tokens is the extracted keyword sequence.

3.3 Keywords Filtering and Adding

Intermediate keywords have a significant impact on the quality of generated comments. We observe two main problems in generated keywords: **(1)** The writing skills reflected by some keywords are not used in the source essay (e.g., "echo" in Figure 2), which makes it difficult for the comment generator to generate a correct comment. **(2)** The generated keywords are not enough to cover the used writing skills (e.g., environmental description in Figure 2), which decreases the informativeness of the generated comment. Therefore, we adopt an error correction module and a feature recognition module to modify the keywords and improve the correctness and informativeness of generated comments.

Error Correction Module To filter out incorrect keywords from a keyword sequence, we fine-tune a BERT classifier to predict the probability $P(c_i = 1|X, k_i)$ for a keyword k_i being incorrect, where c_i is the binary label to indicate whether k_i is correct ($c_i = 1$) or not ($c_i = 0$). During training, we take original essay-keyword pairs as positive examples and randomly sampled keywords from the whole dataset to create the same number of negative examples. We derive the loss function as follows:

$$\mathcal{L}_{\text{cor}} = -\frac{1}{T}\sum_{i=1}^{T}\big(\log P(c_i = 1|X, k_i) + \log P(c_i = 0|X, \hat{k}_i)\big), \quad (3)$$

$$P(c_i|X, k_i) = \text{softmax}(\boldsymbol{W}\mathbf{h} + \boldsymbol{b}), \quad (4)$$

where $\hat{k}_i$ denote the i-th keyword in the randomly sampled keyword sequence, $\mathbf{h}$ denotes the hidden state at the position of the `[CLS]` token and $\boldsymbol{W}$ and $\boldsymbol{b}$ are learnable parameters. The fine-tuned BERT classifier achieves 79.8% accuracy on the test set.

Feature Recognition Module After filtering out incorrect keywords using the error correction module, the keyword sequence may still miss some important features in the source essays. Therefore, we recognize five kinds of fine-grained features from inputs[1].We show several examples of the structured features in Table 1. For idioms, proverbs and quotes, we directly perform word-by-word matching with private off-the-shelf corpora. And we randomly insert the keys of these features into the keyword sequence. We also randomly insert the values of idioms into the keyword sequence. For each kind of descriptive and rhetorical methods[2], we fine-tune BERT as a binary sentence classifier using about 50k manually annotated examples. The fine-tuned BRETs could achieve 92% - 98% accuracy for different kinds of descriptive and rhetorical methods. Then we randomly insert both keys and values of these features recognized by the fine-tuned BERTs into the keyword sequence. We only insert keywords that are not in the sequence to avoid duplication. Finally, we feed the polished keyword sequence into the comment generator to generate the final comment. Note that the comment generator has seen similar fine-grained features extracted by TF-IDF algorithm during training.

3.4 Comment Generation

In the comment generation stage, the lack of exposure to the generated keyword sequence (i.e., the exposure bias issue) may impair the generation performance. To alleviate this issue, we follow Tan et al. (2021) to perturb the input keywords during training. We try various perturbation techniques including replacing a keyword with a randomly sampled one and removing one keyword randomly (Tan et al., 2021), and find that simply inserting a random keyword leads to the best performance in automatic evaluation.

Keys	Values
成语 idiom	无坚不摧 indestructible
俗语 proverb	好事不出门，坏事传千里 bad news travels fast
引用 quote	千里之行，始于足下 a journey of a thousand miles begins with single step
描写方法 descriptive method	动作描写 action description
修辞方法 rhetorical method	比喻 simile

Table 1: Examples for five kinds of fine-grained structured features. Keys indicate the feature type and values indicate the feature content.

4 Experiments

4.1 Dataset

As there is no available dataset for our task, we manually collected a large Chinese dataset to train and evaluate our model. We first collect a large number of pictures of student essays along with comments from professional teachers and the students' grades from an online school[3]. Then we filtered out the essays written by students below the fourth grade to ensure the essays contain abundant writing skills, and retained only narrative essays in this work. Afterwards, we asked crowd-sourced annotators to convert the pictures into texts with the following requirements: **(1)** Correcting misspellings or incorrect punctuation marks; **(2)** Refusing incomplete essays; **(3)** Refusing comments that do not correspond to specific segments; **(4)** Marking the type of comments, i.e., describing strengths or weaknesses. Then we converted marked comment types to binary control codes and insert them before comments and extracted keywords. The detailed statistics are shown in Table 2. We ensure the essays in the training, validation and test sets do not have overlapping titles.

[1]`https://openai.100tal.com/documents/article/page`

[2]All kinds of descriptive and rhetorical methods are shown in the appendix.

[3]`https://www.xueersi.com/`

	Train	Valid	Test
# Examples	18,100	2,263	2,036
# Essays	3,996	540	887
Avg. Title Len	5.82	6.06	6.10
Avg. Essay Len	406.89	382.85	345.08
Avg. Number of Par	4.92	4.46	4.28
Avg. Segment Len	97.58	96.15	79.64
Avg. Comment Len	33.92	39.09	38.54
Strength Ratio	84.38%	80.69%	79.47%
Weakness Ratio	15.62%	19.31%	20.53%
Avg. Number of Key	3.65	3.74	4.14

Table 2: Dataset statistics. *Len/Par/Key* is the abbreviation of *Length/Paragraph/Keyword*. We compute the length by counting the number of Chinese characters. *Segment* is the specified segment which should be commented on. *Strength/Weakness Ratio* means the proportion of the comments that describe strengths/weaknesses of segments.

Models	B-1	B-2	B-3	B-4	D-3	D-4
GPT2	19.01	11.49	8.90	7.59	7.23	8.65
LongLM	33.40	26.16	22.98	21.13	6.05	7.39
Our Model	**36.16**	**28.32**	**24.87**	**22.86**	9.61	13.56
w/o feature	35.39	27.53	24.14	22.19	9.28	13.05
w/o correct	34.88	26.64	23.07	21.01	11.49	15.73
w/o perturb	33.94	25.58	22.02	19.97	**12.25**	**16.90**
Ground Truth	100	100	100	100	24.81	28.29

Table 3: Automatic evaluation results. The best performance is highlighted in **bold**. All results are multiplied by 100. Note that the components are incrementally removed in the ablation study. For example, *w/o correct* excludes the feature recognition module and the error correction module.

4.2 Baselines

We use LongLM (Guan et al., 2022) as our backbone model, which is pretrained on a large Chinese novel dataset with an encoder-decoder transformer architecture. We also use GPT2 (Radford et al., 2019) as a baseline. They directly generate comments conditioned on the source essays with specified segments. To verify the effectiveness of each proposed component, we exclude them from our model one by one: **(1) w/o feature**: excluding the feature recognition module; **(2) w/o correct**: additionally excluding the error correction module; **(3) w/o perturb**: additionally excluding the perturbations added to the keywords when training the comment generator.

4.3 Experiment Settings

Due to limited resources, we follow LongLM$_{\text{Base}}$'s hyper-parameters (224M parameters) and utilize the public pretrained checkpoint to initialize our model. We set the learning rate to 3e-5 and batch size to 40. We set GPT2 to the small version with 102M parameters. Other hyper-parameters are the same as LongLM.

In both the planning and comment generation stages, we use top-p sampling with $p = 0.9$ (Holtzman et al., 2020) combined with beam search (number of beams is 4). We only retain comments for automatic evaluation. For the error correction module, we fine-tune a pretrained Chinese BERT (Cui et al., 2020) on auto-constructed data. We set the learning rate to 1e-5 and batch size to 16. For all models, we select the best checkpoint based on the performance on the validation set. To improve the training speed, we train our model on two gpus with mixed precision training and early stop is adopted.

4.4 Automatic Evaluation

Metrics We adopt the following automatic metrics for evaluation on the test set. **(1) BLEU (B-n):** We use $n = 1, 2, 3, 4$ to evaluate n-gram overlap between generated and ground-truth comments (Papineni et al., 2002). **(2) Distinct (D-n):** We use the ratio of distinct n-grams to all the generated n-grams (Li et al., 2016) to measure the generation diversity ($n = 3, 4$).

Result Table 3 shows the automatic evaluation results. Although GPT2 has higher generation diversity, its BLEU score is significantly lower than our backbone model LongLM, suggesting its worse generation quality. Compared with GPT2 and LongLM, our model improves significantly on both BLEU and Distinct scores, indicating higher quality and diversity of the generated comments. As for the ablation study, we can draw the following conclusions: **(1)** Using fine-grained features to enrich the keywords improves both the quality and diversity of the generated comments. **(2)** Error correction module mainly improves the BLEU scores. We note that it has a negative effect on diversity, which suggests the classifier may tend to retain commonly used keywords. **(3)** Adding perturbations to inputs of the comment generator mainly improves the quality of the composed comments as indicated by a higher BLEU score. Besides, through explicitly extracting informative keywords from the comments, we enforce the model to attend on the distinct part of the comments, which greatly improves the generation diversity (comparing *LongLM* and *w/o perturb*). In summary, all

Models	Correctness Win / Lose / Tie	κ	Informativeness Win / Lose / Tie	κ	Coherence Win / Lose / Tie	κ
Ours vs. LongLM	33*/ 12 / 55	0.71	37*/ 15 / 48	0.79	8 / 9 / 83	0.73
Ours vs. Humans	15 / 26 / 59	0.46	24 / 18 / 58	0.77	5 / 11 / 84	0.38

Table 4: Manual evaluation results. The scores indicate the percentage of *win*, *lose* or *tie* (%) when comparing our model with LongLM or humans. κ denotes Fleiss's kappa to measure the inter-annotator agreement. * means the difference is significant with p-value< 0.01 (Wilcoxon signed-rank test).

components positively impact the quality or the diversity of the generated comments, and our model strikes a good balance between these two aspects.

4.5 Manual Evaluation

We conduct pair-wise comparisons with LongLM and humans (i.e., ground-truth comments). We randomly sample 100 examples from the test set and obtain 300 examples in total. For each pair of comments along with the input, we hire three well-trained professional annotators to give a preference (win, lose or tie) in terms of three aspects: **(1) Correctness**: whether the strengths or weaknesses identified by the comment are actually present in the segment; **(2) Informativeness**: how much informative information such as "idiom" does the comment contain; **(3) Coherence**, whether the comment is coherent in terms of grammatical correctness, and inter-sentence relatedness, causal and temporal dependencies. Each aspect is evaluated independently and annotators are unaware of the comments source. We adopt majority voting to make the final decisions among three annotators.

As shown in Table 4, our model significantly outperforms LongLM in terms of correctness and informativeness and is comparable with LongLM in coherence. Notably, our model can generate more informative comments than humans thanks to additional information from the feature recognition module, despite the risk of making mistakes. All results show fair (0.2< κ ⩽0.4), moderate (0.4< κ ⩽0.6) or substantial (0.6< κ ⩽0.8) inter-annotator agreement.

We also manually evaluate the controllability of our model to generate two different types of comments (describing strengths or weaknesses). We randomly sample 50 essays from the test set, and generate two comments for each essay to describe strengths and weaknesses, respectively, using different control codes. Then for each example, we ask three well-trained annotators to decide whether the generated comment is consistent with the given control code. We also adopt majority voting to make final decisions among three annotators. We find that 91% of the comments are successfully controlled by the control code and the Fleiss's kappa is 0.85, indicating almost perfect inter-annotator agreement. We conclude that our model has good controllability to generate different kinds of comments so that it can meet the needs of different users for showing praise or giving advice.

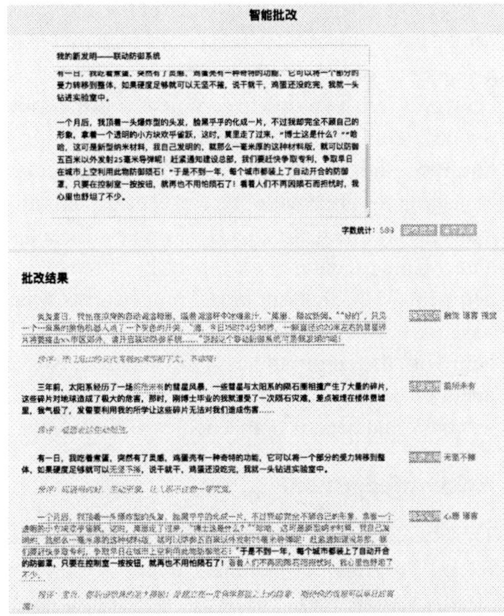

Figure 3: An screenshot of our demo website.

5 Demonstration

A screenshot of our demo website is shown in Figure 3. After entering the title and the body of the article, the user can submit a request and get the result after a few seconds. We comment on all paragraphs except those that contain less than 15 Chinese characters and do not have any recognized structured features. Also, we show recognized fine-grained structured features on the right. The sentences and keywords corresponding to these features are underlined and marked green. With these comments and fine-grained features, the user can fully understand the essay's strengths and weaknesses. Besides the demo website, we also create a github repository at `https://github.com/thu-coai/EssayCommentGen`, where users can freely use our code and data under the MIT license.

6 Conclusion

We present a planning-based model for a new task named essay comment generation, which first plans a sequence of keywords and then expands these keywords into a complete comment. Furthermore, we utilize an error correction module and a feature recognition module to modify the generated keywords for improving the correctness and informativeness of final comments. We manually collect a new Chinese dataset for this task. Extensive experiments show that our model outperforms strong baselines. We have deployed our model online to help with the automatic essay evaluation. We expect our work to facilitate further research on this new task and benefit both teachers and students.

Acknowledgement

This work was supported by National Key R&D Program of China, under Grant No. 2020AAA0104500. This work was supported by the National Science Foundation for Distinguished Young Scholars (with No. 62125604) and the NSFC projects (Key project with No. 61936010 and regular project with No. 61876096). This work was also supported by the Guoqiang Institute of Tsinghua University, with Grant No. 2019GQG1 and 2020GQG0005, and sponsored by Tsinghua-Toyota Joint Research Fund.

References

Yigal Attali and Jill Burstein. 2006. Automated essay scoring with e-rater® v. 2. *The Journal of Technology, Learning and Assessment*, 4(3).

Mădălina Cozma, Andrei Butnaru, and Radu Tudor Ionescu. 2018. Automated essay scoring with string kernels and word embeddings. In *Proceedings of the 56th Annual Meeting of the Association for Computational Linguistics (Volume 2: Short Papers)*, pages 503–509.

Yiming Cui, Wanxiang Che, Ting Liu, Bing Qin, Shijin Wang, and Guoping Hu. 2020. Revisiting pre-trained models for Chinese natural language processing. In *Proceedings of the 2020 Conference on Empirical Methods in Natural Language Processing: Findings*, pages 657–668, Online. Association for Computational Linguistics.

Jacob Devlin, Ming-Wei Chang, Kenton Lee, and Kristina Toutanova. 2019. Bert: Pre-training of deep bidirectional transformers for language understanding. In *Proceedings of the 2019 Conference of the North American Chapter of the Association for Computational Linguistics: Human Language Technologies, Volume 1 (Long and Short Papers)*, pages 4171–4186.

Fei Dong and Yue Zhang. 2016. Automatic features for essay scoring–an empirical study. In *Proceedings of the 2016 conference on empirical methods in natural language processing*, pages 1072–1077.

Fei Dong, Yue Zhang, and Jie Yang. 2017. Attention-based recurrent convolutional neural network for automatic essay scoring. In *Proceedings of the 21st conference on computational natural language learning (CoNLL 2017)*, pages 153–162.

Angela Fan, Mike Lewis, and Yann Dauphin. 2019. Strategies for structuring story generation. In *Proceedings of the 57th Annual Meeting of the Association for Computational Linguistics*, pages 2650–2660.

Seraphina Goldfarb-Tarrant, Tuhin Chakrabarty, Ralph Weischedel, and Nanyun Peng. 2020. Content planning for neural story generation with aristotelian rescoring. In *Proceedings of the 2020 Conference on Empirical Methods in Natural Language Processing (EMNLP)*, pages 4319–4338.

Jiefu Gong, Xiao Hu, Wei Song, Ruiji Fu, Zhichao Sheng, Bo Zhu, Shijin Wang, and Ting Liu. 2021. Iflyea: A chinese essay assessment system with automated rating, review generation, and recommendation. In *Proceedings of the 59th Annual Meeting of the Association for Computational Linguistics and the 11th International Joint Conference on Natural Language Processing: System Demonstrations*, pages 240–248.

Jian Guan, Zhuoer Feng, Yamei Chen, Ruilin He, Xiaoxi Mao, Changjie Fan, and Minlie Huang. 2022. Lot: A story-centric benchmark for evaluating chinese long text understanding and generation.

Ari Holtzman, Jan Buys, Li Du, Maxwell Forbes, and Yejin Choi. 2020. The curious case of neural text degeneration. In *International Conference on Learning Representations*.

Dongyeop Kang and Eduard H. Hovy. 2020. Self-supervised text planning for paragraph completion task. In *EMNLP*.

Zixuan Ke, Hrishikesh Inamdar, Hui Lin, and Vincent Ng. 2019. Give me more feedback II: Annotating thesis strength and related attributes in student essays. In *Proceedings of the 57th Annual Meeting of the Association for Computational Linguistics*, pages 3994–4004, Florence, Italy. Association for Computational Linguistics.

Xiangzhe Kong, Jialiang Huang, Ziquan Tung, Jian Guan, and Minlie Huang. 2021. Stylized story generation with style-guided planning. In *Findings of the Association for Computational Linguistics: ACL-IJCNLP 2021*, pages 2430–2436, Online. Association for Computational Linguistics.

Jiwei Li, Michel Galley, Chris Brockett, Jianfeng Gao, and Bill Dolan. 2016. A diversity-promoting objective function for neural conversation models. In *Proceedings of the 2016 Conference of the North American Chapter of the Association for Computational Linguistics: Human Language Technologies*, pages 110–119, San Diego, California. Association for Computational Linguistics.

Christopher Manning, Prabhakar Raghavan, and Hinrich Schütze. 2010. Introduction to information retrieval. *Natural Language Engineering*, 16(1):100–103.

Sandeep Mathias and Pushpak Bhattacharyya. 2018. Thank "goodness"! a way to measure style in student essays. In *Proceedings of the 5th Workshop on Natural Language Processing Techniques for Educational Applications*, pages 35–41, Melbourne, Australia. Association for Computational Linguistics.

Sandeep Mathias and Pushpak Bhattacharyya. 2020. Can neural networks automatically score essay traits? In *Proceedings of the Fifteenth Workshop on Innovative Use of NLP for Building Educational Applications*, pages 85–91.

Ellis B Page. 1966. The imminence of... grading essays by computer. *The Phi Delta Kappan*, 47(5):238–243.

Kishore Papineni, Salim Roukos, Todd Ward, and Wei-Jing Zhu. 2002. Bleu: a method for automatic evaluation of machine translation. In *Proceedings of the 40th annual meeting of the Association for Computational Linguistics*, pages 311–318.

Alec Radford, Jeffrey Wu, Rewon Child, David Luan, Dario Amodei, Ilya Sutskever, et al. 2019. Language models are unsupervised multitask learners.

Marc'Aurelio Ranzato, Sumit Chopra, Michael Auli, and Wojciech Zaremba. 2016. Sequence level training with recurrent neural networks. *ICLR*.

Swapna Somasundaran, Michael Flor, Martin Chodorow, Hillary Molloy, Binod Gyawali, and Laura McCulla. 2018. Towards evaluating narrative quality in student writing. *Transactions of the Association for Computational Linguistics*, 6:91–106.

Wei Song, Ziyao Song, Lizhen Liu, and Ruiji Fu. 2020. Hierarchical multi-task learning for organization evaluation of argumentative student essays. In *IJCAI*, pages 3875–3881.

Kaveh Taghipour and Hwee Tou Ng. 2016. A neural approach to automated essay scoring. In *Proceedings of the 2016 conference on empirical methods in natural language processing*, pages 1882–1891.

Bowen Tan, Zichao Yang, Maruan Al-Shedivat, Eric Xing, and Zhiting Hu. 2021. Progressive generation of long text with pretrained language models. In *Proceedings of the 2021 Conference of the North American Chapter of the Association for Computational Linguistics: Human Language Technologies*, pages 4313–4324.

Yi Tay, Minh C Phan, Luu Anh Tuan, and Siu Cheung Hui. 2018. Skipflow: Incorporating neural coherence features for end-to-end automatic text scoring. In *Thirty-Second AAAI Conference on Artificial Intelligence*.

Chung-Ting Tsai, Jhih-Jie Chen, Ching-Yu Yang, and Jason S Chang. 2020. Lingglewrite: a coaching system for essay writing. In *Proceedings of the 58th Annual Meeting of the Association for Computational Linguistics: System Demonstrations*, pages 127–133.

Ruosong Yang, Jiannong Cao, Zhiyuan Wen, Youzheng Wu, and Xiaodong He. 2020. Enhancing automated essay scoring performance via fine-tuning pre-trained language models with combination of regression and ranking. *Findings of the Association for Computational Linguistics: EMNLP*, 2020:1560–1569.

Lili Yao, Nanyun Peng, Ralph Weischedel, Kevin Knight, Dongyan Zhao, and Rui Yan. 2019. Plan-and-write: Towards better automatic storytelling. In *Proceedings of the AAAI Conference on Artificial Intelligence*, volume 33, pages 7378–7385.

A Data Collection

As described in "Section 4.1: Dataset" in our paper, we first collect a large number of pictures of teacher commented student essays and then ask annotators to convert the pictures into texts. We show an example of the original pictures in Figure 4. The corresponding text annotated by humans is shown in Figure 5.

B Manual Evaluation

To perform manual evaluation, we hire well-trained professional annotators from a Chinese crowdsourcing company. For the pairwise comparison evaluation, the annotation instructions are summarized as follows: **(1)** Correctness. Annotators should neglect slight incoherence of the comments and focus on the correctness aspect. If both comments are correct or incorrect, the result should be a tie. Otherwise, the correct comment should be labeled as a win while the other comment should be labeled as a loss. **(2)** Informativeness. Annotators should neglect slight incoherence of the comments and focus on the informativeness aspect. If two comments contain close amounts of informative

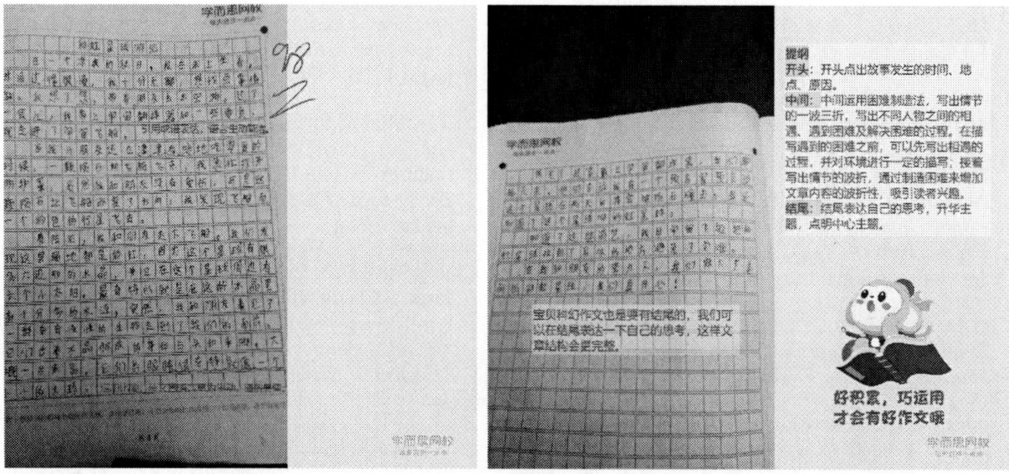

Figure 4: An example of the original pictures of teacher commented student essays.

彩虹星球游记

在一个凉爽的秋日，我在床上坐着。时间过得很慢，我十分无聊，想找点事情做。我想了想，带着朋友去太空游。过了一会儿，我带上宇宙翻译器和一些零食，就走进了宇宙飞船。

当我与朋友还在**津津有味**地吃零食的时候，一颗陨石向飞船飞来，我急忙打开防护罩，虽然我和朋友没有受伤，可是这颗陨石让飞船改变了方向，我发现飞船而是一个彩色的行星飞去。

着陆后，我和朋友走下飞船。我们发现这里遍地都是彩虹，因为这个星球有很多六边形的水晶，并且在这个星球周边有六个小太阳。最奇特的就是在这种水晶里有十分多的水源。突然，我和朋友看见了一群奇奇怪怪的生物走到了我们的面前。它们长着水晶做成的身体与头和手脚，大概一米来高。**它们的眼睛很奇特就像一个小小的火球。**

我见了赶紧戴上宇宙翻译器，我们聊起天来。他们告诉我有一个预言家预言说这个星球在两天后将会被陨石撞击。我还知道了这个星球叫彩虹星球。

知道了这些星球，我用宇宙飞船把彩虹星球拉到了另外的地方避免了灾难。

在我和朋友的努力下，我们救下了美丽的彩虹星球，我们真开心！

片段(segment)	评语(comment)	类型(type)
津津有味	引用成语表达，语言生动简洁。	优点(strength)
它们的眼睛很奇特就像一个小小的火球。	运用比喻，使文章语言更为生动，通俗易懂。	优点(strength)
在我和朋友的努力下，我们救下了美丽的彩虹星球，我们真开心！	宝贝科幻作文也是要有结尾的，我们可以在结尾表达一下自己的思考，这样文章结构会更完整。	缺点(weakness)

Figure 5: An example of the essay with comments annotated by human. The source essay is on the left side and the commented segments are bolded and underlined. The segments along with the comments are shown on the right. Comments could point out the strengths or weaknesses of the segments.

information, the result should be a tie. Otherwise, the more informative comment should be labeled as a win while the other comment should be labeled as a loss. **(3)** Coherence. Annotators should focus on the correctness aspect. If both comments are coherent or incoherent, the result should be a tie. Otherwise, the coherent comment should be labeled as a win while the other comment should be labeled as a loss. We give each annotator ¥1.8 for annotating one pair of comments and one annotator's hourly rate is about ¥108.

For the controllability evaluation, we offer annotators the generated comment and the control token. Annotators should judge whether the comment points out the strengths or weaknesses as the control token specifies. We give each annotator ¥0.5 for annotating one sample and one annotator's hourly rate is about ¥90.

C Keywords Polishing Details

On the test set, we filter out 1.23 keywords using the error correction module and add 1.50 keywords using the feature recognition module for generating each comment on average.

D Structured Features

All descriptive methods include:

- 味觉描写 (taste description)
- 心理描写 (psychology description)
- 嗅觉描写 (smell description)
- 外貌描写 (appearance description)
- 环境描写 (environment description)
- 神态描写 (expression description)
- 语言描写 (language description)
- 动作描写 (action description)
- 视觉描写 (vision description)
- 触觉描写 (touch description)

All rhetorical methods include:

- 比喻 (simile)
- 拟人 (personification)
- 排比 (parallelism)
- 反问 (rhetorical question)
- 设问 (hypophora)

MIC: A Multi-task Interactive Curation Tool

Shi Yu[1]*, Mingfeng Yang[2], Jerrod Parker[3], and Stephen Brock[2]
[1]Broadridge Financial Solutions, shi.yu@broadridge.com
[2]Vanguard Group, {mingfeng_yang, stephen_brock}@vanguard.com
[3]Thomson Reuters, jerrodparker20@gmail.com

Abstract

This paper introduces MIC, a **M**ulti-task **I**nteractive **C**uration tool, a human-machine collaborative curation tool for multiple NLP tasks. The tool aims to borrow recent advances in literature to solve pain-points in real NLP tasks. Firstly, it supports multiple projects with multiple users which enables collaborative annotations. Secondly, MIC allows easy integration of pre-trained models, rules, and dictionaries to auto label the text and speed up the labeling process. Thirdly, MIC supports annotation at different scales (span of characters and words, tokens and lines, or document) and different types (free text, sentence labels, entity labels, and relationship triplets) with easy GUI operations.

1 Introduction

With the recent advances in many frontiers, high-quality annotations are essential to the success of NLP applications. Numerous organizations have accumulated vast amounts of unlabeled text data that they want to utilize in NLP applications. However, for many of these tasks (text summarization, relation extraction, named-entity recognition), aquiring labels can be very costly and susceptible to error. Furthermore, domain adaptation (Han and Eisenstein, 2019), which is the common approach of fine-tuning gigantic domain agnostic NLP models on a small amount of domain-specific labeled data, commonly has difficulty on new emerging / specific domains that lack similar labeled datasets and still requires annotations from scratch. Meanwhile, adoption of accelerated ML solutions have shown to reduce the workload and budget required for manual labeling. Example techniques include active learning, weak supervision, data augmentation, and many others. To concur the time-consuming, labor-intensive, and expensive annotation challenges, recent trends in annotation tool development (Lin et al., 2019; Lee et al., 2020) focus on cost-effective and human-machine collaborative mechanisms, which leverage the processing power of state-of-the-art models pre-trained on large corpora and high-accuracy human intelligence on rare ambiguous incidents.

Please visit *www.textmic.com* using username *ds* and password *demouser123* to visit the demo system. A screencast video is at https://youtu.be/pHxt5k_mLvw. The github repo of MIC is at https://github.com/cyberyu/textmic.

2 Related Work

In the past decade, there were about 30 popular annotation tools published. Among them, there are well-known tools like BRAT (Stenetorp et al., 2012), which supports a wide variety of NLP tasks, including entity recognition, event extraction, and POS (part-of-speech) tagging. GATE Teamware (Bontcheva et al., 2013) is both a desktop application and a web tool that focuses on user management and supports multi-user roles. Yedda (Yang et al., 2018) is a recent tool built on Python that offers auto-labeling via machine learning and provides both command line and web-based interfaces. SANTO (Hartung et al., 2018), which is designed primarily for slot-filling tasks, enables the formation of relational structures from an ontology. It also visualizes the annotations of every user at once to help project owners monitor the quality of annotations. TALEN (Mayhew and Roth, 2018) specialises in the annotation of rare entities. EasyTree (Tratz and Phan, 2018) is specifically designed for the annotation of dependency trees and is integrated with the Amazon Mechanical Turk crowdsourcing platform. AlpacaTag (Lin et al., 2019) and LEAN-LIFE (Lee et al., 2020) leverage machine learning models, active learning, and weak supervision, respectively, to provide annotation recommendations to reduce annotation costs.

The annotation visualization design of our tool

*All authors contributed equally

Proceedings of the The 2022 Conference on Empirical Methods in Natural Language Processing: System Demonstrations, pages 224 - 231
December 7-11, 2022

System	Annotation Type	Adjud -ication	Intelligent Interactive Annotation	External Dependencies	Programming Language
MIC	Classify, Link	Yes	pre-trained models, crowd -sourcing weak-supervision	MongoDB, PostgreSQL	Python,Django,Vue.js
RedCoat (Stewart et al., 2019)	Classify, Link	Yes	hierarchical entities	MongoDB	Javascript, Python
SANTO (Hartung et al., 2018)	Link	-	ontology-driven	Apache,MySQL	PHP
TALEN (Mayhew and Roth, 2018)	Classify	Yes	entity propagation, internet search	-	Unknown
EasyTree (Tratz and Phan, 2018)	Classify,Link	Yes	crowd-sourcing	Amazon Turk	Java Servlet, Javascript
AlpacaTag (Lin et al., 2019)	Classify	Yes	recommendation, crowd-sourcing	-	Python, Django
LEAN-LIFE (Lee et al., 2020)	Classify, Link	Yes	crowd-sourcing, weak-supervision	-	Python
SLATE (Kummerfeld, 2019)	Classify, Link	Yes	terminal-based annotation	-	Python
BRAT (Stenetorp et al., 2012)	Classify, Link	Yes	-	Apache	Python,Javascript
GATE (Bontcheva et al., 2013)	Classify, Link	Yes	-	-	Java
YEDDA (Yang et al., 2018)	Classify	Yes	-	-	Python
WAT-SL (Kiesel et al., 2017)	Classify	Yes	-	Apache	Java
SAWT (Samih et al., 2016)	Classify	-	-	-	Python, PHP
GraphAnno (Gast et al., 2015)	Classify, Link	-	-	-	Ruby
CorA (Bollmann et al., 2014)	Classify	-	-	-	PHP,Javascript
WebAnno (Yimam et al., 2013)	Classify, Link	-	-	-	Java
Anafora (Chen and Styler, 2013)	Classify, Link	Yes	-	-	Python
ANALEC (Landragin et al., 2012)	Classify, Link	-		-	Java
LabelStudio `labelstud.io`	Classify, Link	Yes	text, images, video, audio	Commercial	React, MST, Python
Prodigy `https://prodi.gy/`	Classify, Link	Yes	active learning in annotation	Commercial	Python
Tagtog `tagtog.com`	Classify, Link	Yes	support annotations in PDF	Commercial	Java, Python
LightTag `lighttag.io`	Classify, Link	Yes	support inter-annotator, project management	Commercial	Python

Table 1: A comparison of annotation tools released recently. MIC supports classification (sentence, NER) and link prediction (relationship); Adjudication: MIC encourages human-machine collaborative annotation; thus, human annotators can correct mistaken machine-generated labels. Relying on role configuration, experienced reviewers can also correct/reject any individual human annotator's labeling results, or even reject the entire annotation results from a specific annotator and ask for re-annotation.

is inspired by RedCoat (Stewart et al., 2019), a web-based annotation tool that supports the stacking and inheritance of hierarchical entities using flexible Javascript visualization. We applied the same visual design style in MIC using Vue.js to display a large number of stacked annotations from different human curators, hand written rules, and models. Besides sharing many common features, the proposed annotation tool has some unique characteristics and strengths compared to all existing tools. We summarize and compare the main characteristics of MIC with other tools, including some commercial products, in Table 1. Recent advances in annotation tool development focus more on intelligent capabilities such as auto-annotation, recommendation, crowd-sourcing, weak-supervision, and many other STOA aspects.

3 System Description and Key Features

Rather than specifying a task such as named entity recognition or sentence labeling, MIC is designed to flexibly support any annotations that can be formulated as one of three annotation types: sentence-level labeling, word/phrase-level labeling, or entity-relation-entity triplet labeling. These can be applied to items that are single documents, lines, phrases, tokens, or token combinations. Furthermore, MIC is able to manage annotation tasks associated with interactions among various annotation types. For example, one can restrict the annotation task on named entities among sentences having positive sentiment score, or limit the findings of relationship triplets that contain the entity *Olympics* with the entity type as *event*.

One major novelty of MIC is its support of human-machine interactive annotation via a flexible user interface. For each annotation task, the human annotator can be empowered by a set of pre-trained ML models to quickly generate machine-annotated labels. These pre-trained models are either built-in models from popular data science packages or novel open-source implementations from Github. Pre-trained models can be configured by administrators via the MIC backend interface and each annotation project can associate with multiple models. Pre-trained models are grouped in three categories: sentence labeling, NER labeling and relationship labeling. All pre-trained models are hosted as RESTFUL API endpoints, and for each annotation category the input/output parameters of all endpoints are required to follow the same standards so various models can be interchanged easily. Though machine generated labels cannot be directly considered as ground-truth annotations, the advantages here are two fold. First, instead of requiring the annotator to write everything from scratch, they start from the most likely machine-generated outputs, and MIC supports quick and intuitive editing operations. This helps the human annotator to spend effort effectively and focus on correcting difficult examples. Second, if the human annotator load and apply multiple machine-generated outputs on the same text, those machine outputs can be exported as noisy labels to train a consensus model using weak supervision.

Finally, MIC has been designed to manage annotation tasks for multiple projects and multiple users. Multi-project setting allows MIC to be configured flexibly to support diverse annotation tasks. For each project, new textual data can be loaded to seek curations at sentence level, named entity level or relationship level, or any combinations of them. From MIC's backend user interface, one can associate a number of relevant ML models/dictionaries/rules to a project to allow quick generation of machine labels. The textual data can be fully unlabeled, partially labeled, or integrated with ground truth labels. In cases where the data is partially or fully labeled with ground truths, the administrator can setup a built-in validation process to monitor performance of annotations as the task continues. Annotation performance can be evaluated by comparing ground truth labels with human/machine generated labels, or comparing ground truth labels against consensus labels learned by weak supervision. The multi-user setting allows MIC to involve multiple parties in the annotation pipeline. Each project can allow users with different roles such as Administrator, Curator, Data Scientist, Reviewer, etc., and their operational accesses are categorized and limited by roles to ensure the integrity of the annotation task.

In conclusion, the main novelties of MIC are (1) Extendable framework to integrate customized annotation models; (2) Multi-project and multi-user management; (3) Support of multi-layer annotations from sentences to entities and relations; (4) State-of-art user interface design for annotations.

4 MIC Annotation

4.1 General Architecture

MIC is a web-based annotation system that was developed using Django, Quasar and Vue.js frameworks. As its conceptual framework shows (Figure 1), the frontend of MIC relies on Quasar and Vue.js to provide a flexible and interactive user interface. The main web application is developed in Django, therefore we have a python native environment and an integrated backend administrative panel. One of MIC's most notable features is its web-based project management interface which allows users to set up an annotation project, invite annotators/reviewers, define task scope, setup machine models, and quickly manage exports/imports of annotations and text. These management features were achieved efficiently through Django's admin panel. MIC uses PostgreSQL to store the textual data, manage project/user data, record annotation progress, and store all annotations.

Besides a series of Django REST Web APIs that establish the backbone of the tool, MIC can be extended to include a wide range of interactive curation APIs for specific annotation tasks. This means MIC plays the role of a web annotation server while other endpoints can be distributed on multiple machines as machine labeling servers to optimize the computational balance and latency of annotations.

4.2 Annotation Interface

The main annotation layout is composed of three connected areas: automatic labeling zone (left panel), annotation zone (central panel), and summarization zone (right panel), as shown in Figure 2.

MIC provides three types of automatic labeling tools to speed up annotation: machine models, dictionaries and rules. At the same time, MIC also supports annotation at three different levels: sentences, entities and relationships. Users can freely choose the most appropriate auto-tool to annotate text at the most relevant level. For each annotator, MIC allows arbitrary stacking of human/machine labels on the text. To successfully save the results of an annotator's work, MIC will check whether there are any contradictory labels assigned to a unique token sequence. For example, the entity labels of *Nikolaus van der Pas* can be saved as (*Nikolaus: Person*), (*van der Pas: Person*), (*Nikolaus: Entity*) and (*Pas: Entity*). MIC allows saving all four different annotations though they overlap on each other. However, MIC will ask for resolution if the unique token sequence (sentence position dependent) *Nikolaus van der Pas* has two contradictory labels. The reason of allowing flexible annotations as such is to minimize the burden of human resolutions. As a matter of fact, lots of similar conflicts can be considered as noise, and can be resolved successfully by well-designed machine learning models.

With MIC, annotators can create three levels of labels simultaneously, which means users can switch back and forth among the three levels and complete the labels for each page. In another way, annotators can focus on sentence-level annotation of all pages first and save the results, and the revisit and finish annotations for the other two layers later. Every annotation task can be scoped as arbitrary

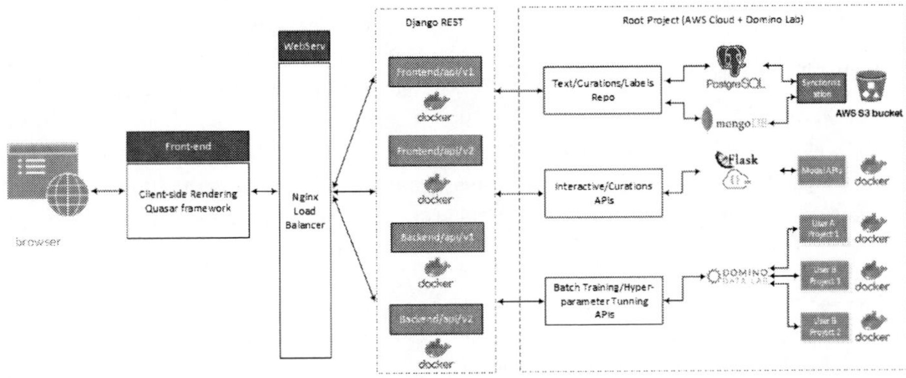

Figure 1: An overview of general architecture of MIC

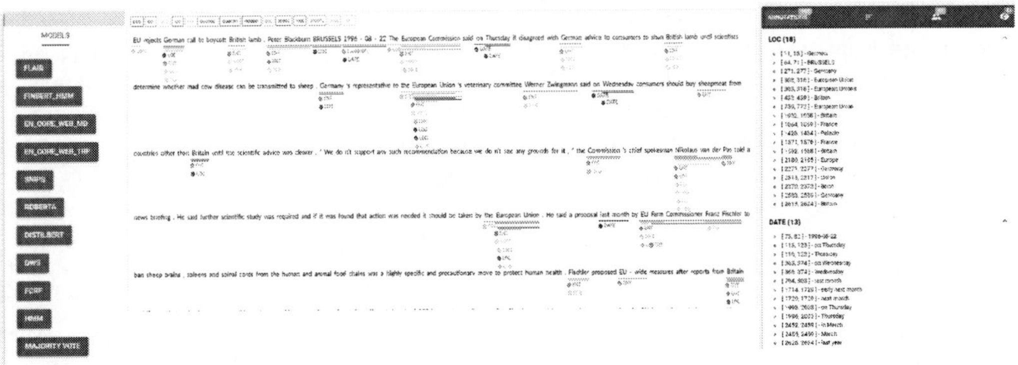

Figure 2: Annotation Interface of MIC

combinations of labels from the three levels. This feature make MIC very useful to gather important annotations from different perspectives for a same data set iteratively, which is commonly desired in industrial applications.

4.3 Annotation Summarization Panel

It is worth highlighting that MIC contains a well-designed annotation summarization panel (right panel) to efficiently and concisely provide valuable information about the annotations provided by multiple users. The panel has four controllable head icons: (1) Annotations, (2) Sorting, (3) Users, and (4) Issues. If a reviewer wants to group all annotations by categories, she can review all labels using the Annotations icon. Click-in will expand into all individual labels, and reviewer acceptance and rejection can be applied here. MIC supports all annotations being associated with confidence scores. For human annotators we can fix the score as 1 or allow them to explicitly score their confidence per each annotation. For machine learning models, the API Endpoints must return an additional output parameter representing uncertainty. Thus, a reviewer can rank all candidate annotations by their uncertainty scores using the sorting function. The third function *Users* allows the reviewer to group all annotations by annotator. Here, the reviewer can accept or reject all annotations from a specific annotator. This feature, combined with the ease of integrating weak labelers, makes MIC a great weak supervision data preparation tool. For example, the annotator can quickly try out multiple weak labelers, view some of their annotations, choose to reject the noisy labelers, and then export the remaining labels to be fed into an offline model to denoise the weak labels. The last function *Issues* is used to highlight potential conflicts that may be of concern for the reviewer such as contradictory annotations on the same unique token sequence. Another feature in this summarization panel is that clicking on any annotation listed here will redirect and highlight the corresponding tokens in the original text. This feature is very useful to quickly review and correct the annotations.

5 Case Studies

5.1 Market News Insider Trade Annotation

In the case study demo, the goal is to use MIC to extract facts about potential insider trades from a financial news feed. We assume the user is a subject matter expert (SME) curator with some basic knowledge of NLP and machine learning. The annotator has several goals. Firstly, from all the news feeds she needs to select those that are relevant to insider selling or buying. Since there is no machine learning model classifier distinguishing the insider trading concept at hand, the annotator decides to use a simple rule *inside buy/sell* to quickly generate machine labels. The rule is defined as a SpaCy rule in the admin panel such that if a sentence after lemmatization contains both words *inside* and *buy* or *sell*, then the machine auto-generated label will be set to *Inside Trade*. The annotator reviews results at the sentence-level panel, and manually corrects some mistaken predictions. Then, she saves the sentence labeling results and hides all sentences that are not related to insider trading. She switches the annotation panel from sentence to NER labeling, and uses several out-of-the-box NER models (i.e. from FLAIR (Akbik et al., 2019) or SpaCy) to quickly generate automatic NER tags for persons, organizations, locations, and others.

Next, the annotator switches the panel from *NER* to *Relation* to extract semantic relationships about insider trading. Her goal here is to extract *buy* and *sell* relationships that occur between two entities (usually the subject *person* entity is defined as the head and the object *stock* entity is defined as the tail). Instead of spending tedious effort to find desired relationships manually, the annotator applies an open relation extraction (OpenRE) model to automatically extract candidate relationships. If the annotator wants to further designate the extracted relationships as one of the three pre-defined types *buy*, *sell* and *own*, she can change the relation type to any text in the confirmation menu.

The MIC OpenRE model is based on the MaMa open information extraction (OpenIE) model described in (Wang et al., 2020) and built using the code from (theblackcat102, 2020). The OpenRE model carries out several steps such as named entity recognition, verb phrase pattern matching, pre-trained language model inference, and triplet post-processing. Since each step may produce uncertainty in its output, the OpenRE approach tends to generate noisy candidate relationships.

In our demo, we published an OpenRE endpoint API that uses BERT-large-cased as the pre-trained language model (Devlin et al., 2019). For each page, it may produce about 40 to 100 noisy relations. Thus, the annotator needs to review and confirm all outputs in the summarization panel.

This case study demonstrates how to use MIC to accomplish multiple tasks of annotation, starting from sentence labeling, then named entity detection and finally extract important financial semantic relationships from text. All annotated entities and relationships are associated with three different positional indices: (1) sentence index, (2) token position index, and (3) character position index. This allows precise identifications and visualizations of extracted entities and relationships. Users can save these annotations and visualize them directly in MIC, or export them as JSON format for general machine learning model training and validation outside of MIC.

6 Evaluation of Annotation Efficiency and Accuracy

We conducted a benchmark study to investigate the efficiency and accuracy of MIC in real annotations. Three different data sets were used for task preparation: (1) CoNNL2003 (Tjong Kim Sang and De Meulder, 2003); (2) NYT Open Relation Extraction Benchmark (Mesquita et al., 2013); (3) Proprietary fintech customer support call transcripts. The first and second data sets are publicly accessible and widely used as NER and Relation Extraction benchmarks. The third data is a proprietary data set and the goal is to obtain three levels of annotations. The first level is sentence tagging: the annotator needs to extract the main customer complaint sentences from the call transcript if the complaint is related to buy/sell financial product (stocks/funds), denoted as a buy/sell relevant sentence. All other sentences are irrelevant. The second level is NER: Among the relevant sentences, tag any mentioned financial products (stock/fund tickers, bank names, and others) as named entities. The third level is to annotate any unary relationship, if related to buy or sell, of annotated entities if mentioned in the same sentence. For example, **Sell** Apple Stock, **Buy** NVDA, **Exchange** Money Market Funds, and so on. We compared four annotation tools, including free version of Prodigy, YEDDA (Yang et al., 2018), GATE(Bontcheva et al., 2013) and the proposed MIC tool. Four annotators selected from the

2Tool	CoNNL		NYT		Call	
	Avg Time	F1-score	Avg Time	F1-score	Avg Time	F1-score
Prodigy	63	0.75	94	0.52	208	0.86
YEDDA	85	0.76	101	0.60	189	0.82
GATE	84	0.75	118	0.62	150	0.78
MIC-NM	45	0.74	74	0.64	60	0.84
MIC-M	38	0.78	95	0.59	44	0.88

Table 2: Comparison of Average Annotation Time (integers as minutes) for different tasks and the Average F1-scores.

master internship program were trained to perform annotations. Each annotator spent about 2 hours on each tool using labeled data to get familiar with a tool's specific annotation mechanism. Then, a random sample of 50-sentence corpora from data sets (1) and (2), and 20 random transcriptions of data set (3) were assigned for annotation. For each annotator, sentences/transcriptions were stratified samplings by different annotation tools, so there was no occurrence of seen sentences across different tools. In this setting, each task had four samples, assigned to four annotators in parallel and all annotated once using the same tool. Because data in all tasks comes with ground truth labels, we measure annotation performance in this step through evaluating the micro-entity precision, recall, and then calculate the F1 scores of the annotated labels against the ground truth labels. The average annotation time and F1-scores of four annotators spent on this task-tool combination were recorded and compared in Table 2. Notice that CONLL and NYT are popular data sets studied in literature, and the best F1-score achieved by ML models on CONLL is around 0.76(Parker and Yu, 2021), and 0.59 for NYT (Sun and Wu, 2019).

We compared MIC in two configurations: (1) MIC-NM only allowed manual annotations, so no pre-trained model was used. (2) MIC-M included pre-trained annotation models so annotators could confirm final labels using auto-annotations. In the MIC-M setting, MIC included four NER models (FLAIR, FINBERT_HMM, EN_CORE_WEB_MD, SNIPS), one MaMa RE model (Wang et al., 2020), and a proprietary intent classification model to classify sentences. The average annotation time of four annotators, and the F1-score of their annotated results evaluated by ground truths, are reported in Table 1. As shown, on almost all tasks, MIC significantly reduced annotation time and obtained comparable performance. One exception was for the NYT task using MIC-M, where the MAMA (Wang et al., 2020) model was slow in execution, and results were very noisy. Thus annotators spent extra effort filtering the results and accidental misses caused performance drop. In particular, annotators found MIC very helpful in annotating long call transcripts because it provided a friendly interface filtering irrelevant sentences and allowed smooth switches among sentence/entity/relation annotations. In contrast, in other tools, annotators were overwhelmed by a dominant number of unrelated sentences, which caused serious distractions. Another advantage annotator liked MIC most was the stacked investigation of multiple auto-annotations tagged by pre-trained models, especially on CONNL task where pre-trained NER models were domain-homogeneous. In contrast, when annotating financial product entities, the four pre-trained models were not very helpful, mainly because those models had never adapted to the Financial NER domain.

7 Scalability and Deployment

For budget reasons, the demo system of MIC hosted at www.textmic.com is deployed on a single AWS T3.xlarge instance. However, RESTFUL APIs can be distributed to different physical instances for better performance and richer model capacity. Thus MIC could host a wide range of large-scale pre-trained models in its library and allow easy adaption of relevant models in specific annotation tasks.

8 Future Development

Our roadmap to enhance MIC for the future lies ahead in several directions. We are interested in connecting MIC to advanced processes cloud-based APIs such as zero-shot learning, few-shot learning, and textual entailment models to provide annotators access to more SoTA NLP models.

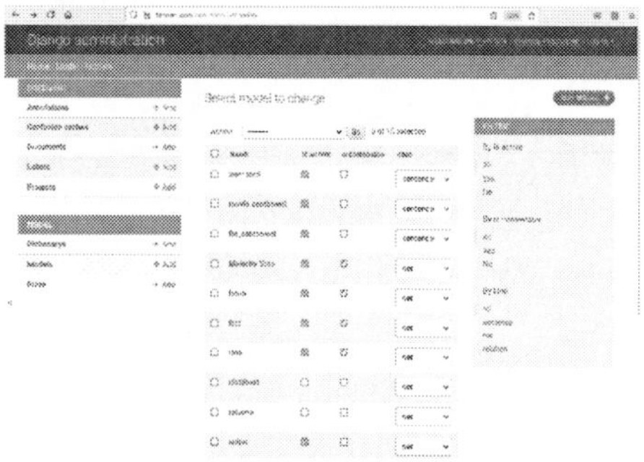

Figure 3: Django backend management of pre-trained annotation models

Additionally, we'll implement automated training pipelines for several weak supervision algorithms including (Ratner et al., 2017; Shang et al., 2018; Parker and Yu, 2021) to allow automatic denoising of conflicting human or machine labels.

References

Alan Akbik, Tanja Bergmann, Duncan Blythe, Kashif Rasul, Stefan Schweter, and Roland Vollgraf. 2019. Flair: An easy-to-use framework for state-of-the-art nlp. In *NAACL 2019, 2019 Annual Conference of the North American Chapter of the Association for Computational Linguistics (Demonstrations)*, pages 54–59.

Marcel Bollmann, Florian Petran, Stefanie Dipper, and Julia Krasselt. 2014. CorA: A web-based annotation tool for historical and other non-standard language data. In *Proceedings of the 8th Workshop on Language Technology for Cultural Heritage, Social Sciences, and Humanities (LaTeCH)*, pages 86–90, Gothenburg, Sweden. Association for Computational Linguistics.

Kalina Bontcheva, Hamish Cunningham, Ian Roberts, Angus Roberts, Valentin Tablan, Niraj Aswani, and Genevieve Gorrell. 2013. Gate teamware: a web-based, collaborative text annotation framework. *Language Resources and Evaluation*, 47:1007–1029.

Wei-Te Chen and Will Styler. 2013. Anafora: A web-based general purpose annotation tool. In *Proceedings of the 2013 NAACL HLT Demonstration Session*, pages 14–19, Atlanta, Georgia. Association for Computational Linguistics.

Jacob Devlin, Ming-Wei Chang, Kenton Lee, and Kristina Toutanova. 2019. BERT: Pre-training of deep bidirectional transformers for language understanding. In *Proceedings of the 2019 Conference of the North American Chapter of the Association for Computational Linguistics: Human Language Technologies, Volume 1 (Long and Short Papers)*, pages 4171–4186, Minneapolis, Minnesota. Association for Computational Linguistics.

Volker Gast, Lennart Bierkandt, and Christoph Rzymski. 2015. Creating and retrieving tense and aspect annotation with graphanno, a lightweight tool for multi-level annotation. In *ACL 2015*.

Xiaochuang Han and Jacob Eisenstein. 2019. Unsupervised domain adaptation of contextualized embeddings for sequence labeling. In *Proceedings of the 2019 Conference on Empirical Methods in Natural Language Processing and the 9th International Joint Conference on Natural Language Processing (EMNLP-IJCNLP)*, pages 4238–4248, Hong Kong, China. Association for Computational Linguistics.

Matthias Hartung, Hendrik ter Horst, Frank Grimm, Tim Diekmann, Roman Klinger, and Philipp Cimiano. 2018. SANTO: A web-based annotation tool for ontology-driven slot filling. In *Proceedings of ACL 2018, System Demonstrations*, pages 68–73, Melbourne, Australia. Association for Computational Linguistics.

Johannes Kiesel, Henning Wachsmuth, Khalid Al-Khatib, and Benno Stein. 2017. WAT-SL: A customizable web annotation tool for segment labeling. In *Proceedings of the Software Demonstrations of the 15th Conference of the European Chapter of the Association for Computational Linguistics*, pages 13–16, Valencia, Spain. Association for Computational Linguistics.

Jonathan K. Kummerfeld. 2019. SLATE: A super-lightweight annotation tool for experts. In *Proceedings of the 57th Annual Meeting of the Association for Computational Linguistics: System Demonstrations*, pages 7–12, Florence, Italy. Association for Computational Linguistics.

Frédéric Landragin, Thierry Poibeau, and Bernard Victorri. 2012. ANALEC: a new tool for the dynamic annotation of textual data. In *Proceedings of the Eighth International Conference on Language Resources and Evaluation (LREC-2012)*, pages 357–362, Istanbul, Turkey. European Languages Resources Association (ELRA).

Dong-Ho Lee, Rahul Khanna, Bill Yuchen Lin, Seyeon Lee, Qinyuan Ye, Elizabeth Boschee, Leonardo Neves, and Xiang Ren. 2020. LEAN-LIFE: A label-efficient annotation framework towards learning from explanation. In *Proceedings of the 58th Annual Meeting of the Association for Computational Linguistics: System Demonstrations*, pages 372–379, Online. Association for Computational Linguistics.

Bill Yuchen Lin, Dong-Ho Lee, Frank F. Xu, Ouyu Lan, and Xiang Ren. 2019. AlpacaTag: An active learning-based crowd annotation framework for sequence tagging. In *Proceedings of the 57th Annual

Meeting of the Association for Computational Linguistics: System Demonstrations, pages 58–63, Florence, Italy. Association for Computational Linguistics.

Stephen Mayhew and Dan Roth. 2018. TALEN: Tool for annotation of low-resource ENtities. In *Proceedings of ACL 2018, System Demonstrations*, pages 80–86, Melbourne, Australia. Association for Computational Linguistics.

Filipe Mesquita, Jordan Schmidek, and Denilson Barbosa. 2013. Effectiveness and efficiency of open relation extraction. In *Proceedings of the 2013 Conference on Empirical Methods in Natural Language Processing*, pages 447–457, Seattle, Washington, USA. Association for Computational Linguistics.

Jerrod Parker and Shi Yu. 2021. Named entity recognition through deep representation learning and weak supervision. In *Findings of the Association for Computational Linguistics: ACL-IJCNLP 2021*, pages 3828–3839, Online. Association for Computational Linguistics.

Alexander Ratner, Stephen H. Bach, Henry Ehrenberg, Jason Fries, Sen Wu, and Christopher Ré. 2017. Snorkel: Rapid training data creation with weak supervision. *Proc. VLDB Endow.*, 11(3):269–282.

Younes Samih, Wolfgang Maier, and Laura Kallmeyer. 2016. SAWT: Sequence annotation web tool. In *Proceedings of the Second Workshop on Computational Approaches to Code Switching*, pages 65–70, Austin, Texas. Association for Computational Linguistics.

Jingbo Shang, Liyuan Liu, Xiaotao Gu, Xiang Ren, Teng Ren, and Jiawei Han. 2018. Learning named entity tagger using domain-specific dictionary. In *Proceedings of the 2018 Conference on Empirical Methods in Natural Language Processing*, pages 2054–2064, Brussels, Belgium. Association for Computational Linguistics.

Pontus Stenetorp, Sampo Pyysalo, Goran Topić, Tomoko Ohta, Sophia Ananiadou, and Jun'ichi Tsujii. 2012. brat: a web-based tool for NLP-assisted text annotation. In *Proceedings of the Demonstrations at the 13th Conference of the European Chapter of the Association for Computational Linguistics*, pages 102–107, Avignon, France. Association for Computational Linguistics.

Michael Stewart, Wei Liu, and Rachel Cardell-Oliver. 2019. Redcoat: A collaborative annotation tool for hierarchical entity typing. In *Proceedings of the 2019 Conference on Empirical Methods in Natural Language Processing and the 9th International Joint Conference on Natural Language Processing, EMNLP-IJCNLP 2019, Hong Kong, China, November 3-7, 2019 - System Demonstrations*, pages 193–198. Association for Computational Linguistics.

Changzhi Sun and Yuanbin Wu. 2019. Distantly supervised entity relation extraction with adapted manual annotations. In *The Thirty-Third AAAI Conference on Artificial Intelligence, AAAI 2019, The Thirty-First Innovative Applications of Artificial Intelligence Conference, IAAI 2019, The Ninth AAAI Symposium on Educational Advances in Artificial Intelligence, EAAI 2019, Honolulu, Hawaii, USA, January 27 - February 1, 2019*, pages 7039–7046. AAAI Press.

theblackcat102. 2020. language-models-are-knowledge-graphs-pytorch. `https://github.com/theblackcat102/language-models-are-knowledge-graphs-pytorch`.

Erik F. Tjong Kim Sang and Fien De Meulder. 2003. Introduction to the CoNLL-2003 shared task: Language-independent named entity recognition. In *Proceedings of the Seventh Conference on Natural Language Learning at HLT-NAACL 2003*, pages 142–147.

Stephen Tratz and Nhien Phan. 2018. A web-based system for crowd-in-the-loop dependency treebanking. In *Proceedings of the Eleventh International Conference on Language Resources and Evaluation, LREC 2018, Miyazaki, Japan, May 7-12, 2018*. European Language Resources Association (ELRA).

Chenguang Wang, Xiao Liu, and Dawn Song. 2020. Language models are open knowledge graphs.

Jie Yang, Yue Zhang, Linwei Li, and Xingxuan Li. 2018. YEDDA: A lightweight collaborative text span annotation tool. In *Proceedings of ACL 2018, System Demonstrations*, pages 31–36, Melbourne, Australia. Association for Computational Linguistics.

Seid Muhie Yimam, Iryna Gurevych, Richard Eckart de Castilho, and Chris Biemann. 2013. WebAnno: A flexible, web-based and visually supported system for distributed annotations. In *Proceedings of the 51st Annual Meeting of the Association for Computational Linguistics: System Demonstrations*, pages 1–6, Sofia, Bulgaria. Association for Computational Linguistics.

SUMMARY WORKBENCH
Unifying Application and Evaluation of Text Summarization Models

Shahbaz Syed **Dominik Schwabe** **Martin Potthast**

Leipzig University

<shahbaz.syed@uni-leipzig.de>

Abstract

This paper presents SUMMARY WORKBENCH, a new tool for developing and evaluating text summarization models. New models and evaluation measures can be easily integrated as Docker-based plugins, allowing to examine the quality of their summaries against any input and to evaluate them using various evaluation measures. Visual analyses combining multiple measures provide insights into the models' strengths and weaknesses. The tool is hosted at https://tldr.demo.webis.de and also supports local deployment for private resources.

1 Introduction

Automatic text summarization reduces a long text to its most important parts and generates a summary. Usually, a learning-based summarization model is developed in two basic steps: *model development* and *model evaluation*. Given a collection of documents accompanied by one or more human-written (reference) summaries, first a set of features representing the documents is manually created or automatically extracted through supervised learning. The resulting model is then used to generate one or more (candidate) summaries, which are analyzed manually and/or with evaluation measures for their similarity to the reference summaries. These steps are iterated, optimizing the model and its parameters using a validation set. The models that perform best in the validation are selected for evaluation on the test set. With standardized test sets for each document collection, comparisons with models created earlier are reported.

However, these steps are associated with comparatively tedious tasks: During model development, summaries of individual documents are often generated and immediately evaluated to identify deficiencies and improve the model, including comparisons to other models. The latter requires third-party models to be operational despite their heterogeneous software stacks. Such "on-the-fly evaluation" during development entails that candidate and reference summaries as well as source documents are analyzed manually or by automatic measures. This multi-text comparison is often not supported by visualization, although this leads to a better understanding of the content coverage and possible selection biases of a model (Vig et al., 2021; Syed et al., 2021b). The analysis of evaluation results for model selection also benefits from visual support (Tenney et al., 2020). Previous research in the field of automatic summarization has not yet resulted in a unified set of tools for these purposes which is the main goal of this paper.

With SUMMARY WORKBENCH, we introduce the first unified combination of application and visual evaluation environments for text summarization models. Currently, it integrates 15 well-known summarization models (26 variants in total) and 10 standard evaluation measures from the literature. With **FeatureSum**, it also includes a new feature-based extractive summarization model that implements features from the literature predating the deep learning era. Underlying all of the above is a specification and interface that allows easy integration of new models and measures to facilitate large-scale experiments and their reproducibility.

In what follows, Section 2 reviews related work on tools to assist summarization research and development. Section 3 overviews the key design principles of the SUMMARY WORKBENCH, and Section 4 provides a complete overview of all the models and measures hosted to date. Included are general-purpose models, guided models that accept user prompts to guide summary generation, and models tailored to argumentative language and to news articles. A wide range of commonly employed evaluation measures are included, covering both lexical as well as semantic overlap measures.[1]

[1]Source code is available at https://github.com/webis-de/summary-workbench.

Proceedings of the The 2022 Conference on Empirical Methods in Natural Language Processing: System Demonstrations, pages 232 - 241

2 Related Work

The development of tools for summarization research has gained momentum recently, and several tools have been presented for (sub)tasks of the two steps above: Tools such as HuggingFace (Wolf et al., 2020), FairSeq (Ott et al., 2019), SummerTime (Ni et al., 2021), TorchMetrics (Detlefsen et al., 2022), SacreROUGE(Deutsch and Roth, 2020), PyTorch Hub,[2] and TensorFlow Hub[3] focus on hosting several state-of-the-art text summarization models and automatic evaluation measures. These tools have significantly improved accessibility to working models. However, only some provide a very minimal interface for inference of summaries and their online/offline comparative analyses. Many authors also choose to share their models independently, be they on GitHub or elsewhere, as standalone repositories instead of integrating with any tools. To lower the bar of (latter) integration as much as possible, SUMMARY WORKBENCH simplifies model and measure integration as plugins (using Docker). In this way, models under development or private ones can be locally compared to others and can be archived together with all their dependencies for reproducibility. Similar efforts have been made in the information retrieval community via the Docker-based toolkit such as Anserini (Yang et al., 2018).

Tools such as LIT (Tenney et al., 2020), SummVis (Vig et al., 2021), and Summary Explorer (Syed et al., 2021b) focus on qualitative model evaluation by providing static visual analyses of the relation between the summary and its source document. SUMMARY WORKBENCH adapts some of their visualizations next to new ones, and complements them with interactive visual analytics for quantitative evaluation according to multiple measures. Users can explore the distribution of scores, select data points of interest and inspect them in relation to the source document to better understand the dataset.

The success of past summarization research and development has relied a lot on in-depth manual error analyses. This being one of the most laborious tasks in every natural language generation evaluation, we believe that visually comparing summaries from multiple models for many different texts, and contextualizing manual review with multiple measures is crucial to both scale up error analysis, and to better understand the capabilities and limitations of the technology. As this still requires juggling many different, incompatible tools, the unified approach of SUMMARY WORKBENCH aims at lowering the bar for scaling up interactive experimentation.

[2]https://pytorch.org/hub/

[3]https://www.tensorflow.org/hub/

3 An Interactive Visual Summarization Model Development & Evaluation Tool

SUMMARY WORKBENCH implements two interactive views corresponding to the two basic summarization model development steps: a *summarization view* and an *evaluation view*.

3.1 Summarization View

Figure 1 shows the summarization view, where multiple extractive/abstractive summarization models can be used to summarize texts, web pages, or scientific documents on demand, controlling for summary length. For scientific documents, relevant sections from a given paper to be summarized can be chosen. Explicit guidance signals for focused summarization can be provided as input to corresponding models (reviewed in Section 4).

Generated summaries (candidates) can be visually inspected for their lexical overlaps (highlighted on demand) with their source document or with another summary. This provides a quick overview of the models' effectiveness at capturing important content as well as any factual errors prevalent in abstractive summarization (Maynez et al., 2020). Additional functionalities include uploading multiple documents to be summarized via a single file, and command line access to all models.

3.2 Evaluation View

Figure 2 shows the evaluation view, where candidate summaries are compared with reference summaries using multiple lexical/semantic content overlap measures. Candidate summaries from multiple models, either generated using the summarization view or uploaded as a file where each example is encoded as $< \texttt{doc}, \texttt{ref}, c_1, c_2, ..., c_n >$ can be evaluated. Lexical/semantic overlap of candidate/reference summaries c_i/`ref` with the source document `doc` can also be visualized. Computed scores can be neatly exported as CSV or LaTeX tables.

Scores from the chosen evaluation measures can be further explored through an *interactive plotter*. Among other things, the plotter allows users to visually correlate different evaluation measures, identify outliers/challenging source documents or strongly abstractive summaries among the candi-

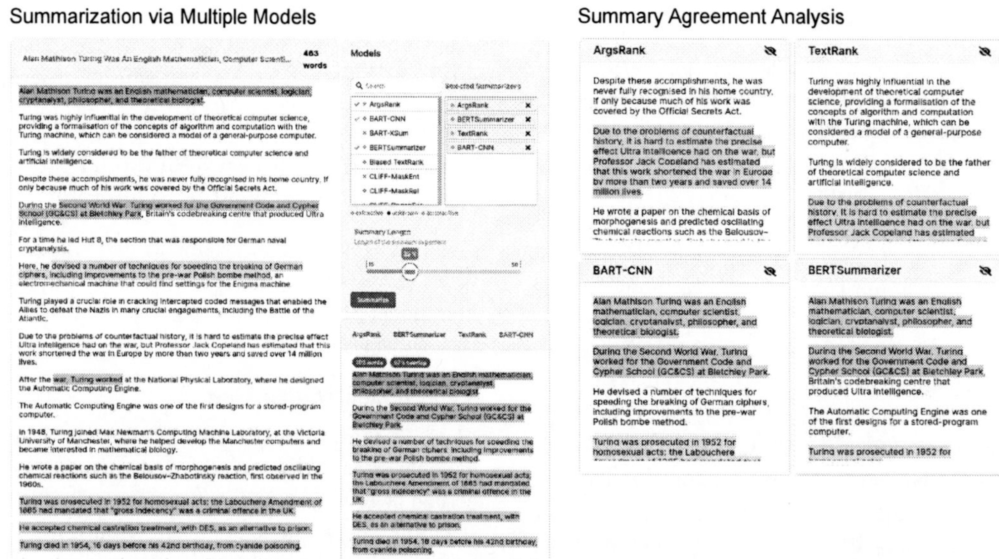

Figure 1: Two key components of the summarization view: On the left, an input text can be summarized via multiple extractive and abstractive summarization models; lexical overlap is highlighted on demand for each candidate summary and can be adjusted for varying n-gram lengths. On the right, content agreement among summaries from different models; any summary can be selected as the reference against which the others can be visually compared.

dates. This facilitates a deeper understanding of the quantitative performance of the models as well as an understanding of the evaluation datasets. Two more use cases of the interactive plotter are explained in Section 5.

3.3 Plugin Server

New summarization models and evaluation measures are integrated as container-based plugins. A model/measure plugin can either be a local directory or a remote Git repository containing specification of dependent software and data (checkpoints, embeddings, lexicons), and implementations of the interfaces SummarizerPlugin and MeasurePlugin. Model metadata such as name, type, version, source, citation, and other custom arguments are provided as YAML configurations. Each plugin runs inside a Docker container with its own server that handles API calls following the OpenAPI specification.[4] This setup allows users to safely self-host the entire application. Developed plugins can be easily shared with the community via DockerHub images or Git repositories. Examples are found in our tool's technical documentation.[5]

[4]https://www.openapis.org

[5]https://webis.de/summary-workbench/

4 Models and Measures

SUMMARY WORKBENCH hosts 15 extractive/abstractive summarization models and 10 lexical/semantic evaluation measures for English text. Each of these is configured as a Docker-based plugin that can be customized and instantiated accordingly. For details on model checkpoints, see Appendix A.

4.1 Summarization Models

We provide a diverse set of models applicable to multiple text domains such as news, argumentative texts, web pages, and product reviews. Model types include extractive, abstractive, supervised, unsupervised, and guided summarization, the latter requiring additional user input.

General-purpose Summarization

Models that work in an unsupervised fashion or leverage external knowledge via contextual embeddings are supposed to be capable of summarizing any kind of text. We provide the following models suitable for general-purpose text summarization.

FeatureSum is our new extractive summarization model which scores a sentence in the text based on a combination of standard features to identify key sentences (Luhn, 1958; Nenkova and McKeown, 2012): TF-IDF, content units (named entities, noun phrases, numbers), position in text, mean lexical

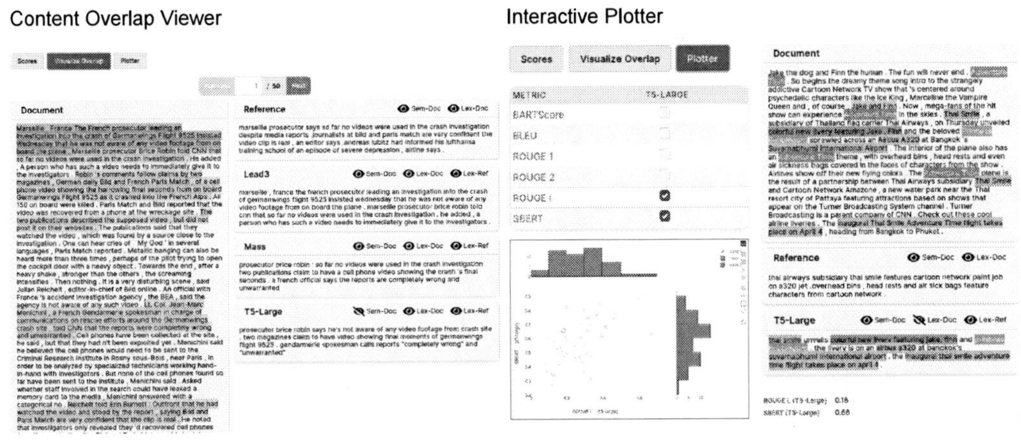

Figure 2: Two key components of the evaluation view: On the left, a text overlap viewer displays content coverage of the summaries in relation to the source document via lexical and semantic overlap (via Spacy embeddings). On the right, an interactive plotter allows selecting examples with specific scores for a combination of evaluation measures. Additionally, the distribution of scores is also shown.

connectivity (number of tokens shared with the remaining sentences), ratio of words that are not stop words, length (relative to the longest sentence in the text), and word overlap with the title. The final score of a sentence is the product of the individual feature values. Sentences are then ranked based on these scores to produce the final summary. Different combinations of these features can be chosen by simply toggling them in the interface. This also allows for dynamically reproducing existing models from the literature provided their specific feature sets are available.

TextRank (Mihalcea and Tarau, 2004) is a graph-based model which employs PageRank (Brin and Page, 1998) on the document graph consisting of sentences as nodes to compute the strength of their connections. Top-ranked sentences within a length budget are taken as the extractive summary. We also provide the two variants **PositionRank** and **TopicRank**, which consider the sentence position and its overlap with topic sentence (document's title or its first sentence) to compute the ranking via PyTextRank (Nathan, 2016).

BERTSum (Miller, 2019) employs contextual embeddings from BERT (Devlin et al., 2019) to extract key sentences in an unsupervised fashion by first clustering all sentence embeddings using k-means (Hartigan and Wong, 1979) and then retrieving those closest to the centroids as the summary.

PMISum (Padmakumar and He, 2021) is an unsupervised extractive model that includes measures to score the relevance and redundancy of the sentences of the source document. These measures are based on pointwise mutual information (PMI) computed by pre-trained language models. Summary sentences are selected via a greedy algorithm to maximize relevance and minimize redundancy.

LoBART (Manakul and Gales, 2021) addresses the input length limitations of transformers (Vaswani et al., 2017) that restrict capturing long-span dependencies in long document summarization. Local self-attention and explicit content selection modules are introduced to effectively summarize long documents such as podcast transcripts and scientific documents.

Longformer2Roberta effectively combines Longformer (Beltagy et al., 2020), developed for processing long documents, and RoBERTa (Liu et al., 2019), a robustly trained BERT model as the decoder, based on leveraging pre-trained checkpoints of large language models (Rothe et al., 2020).

Guided Summarization

The following models accept explicit inputs provided by users to guide the summarization process towards generating user-specific summaries.

Biased TextRank (Kazemi et al., 2020) is an extension of the TextRank model which takes an explicit user input as the "focus", represented via contextual embeddings to guide the ranking of the document sentences. Summary extraction is based on the semantic alignment between the document sentences and the provided focus signal.

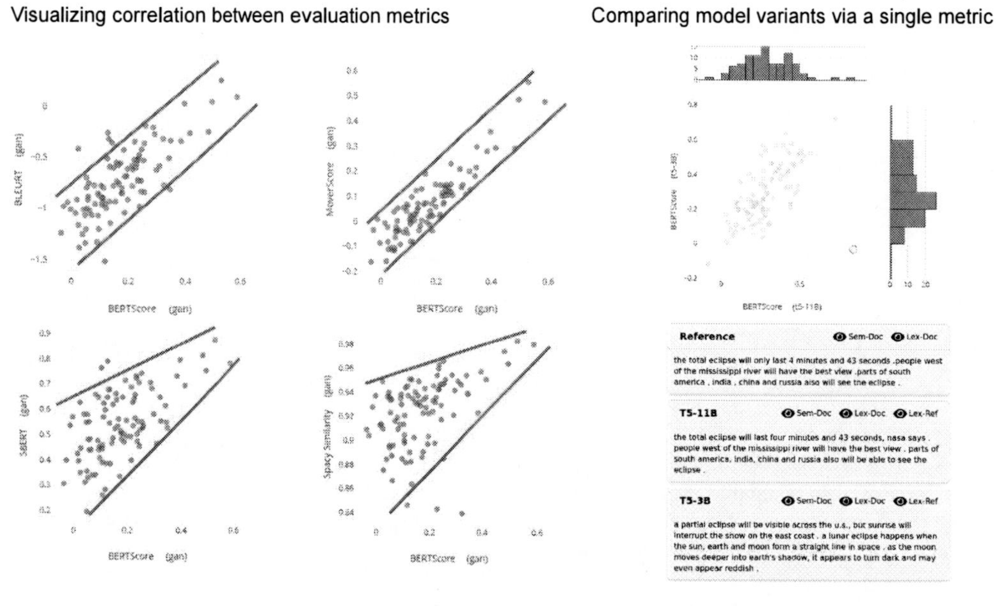

Figure 3: Two example use cases of interactive plotter of the evaluation view: On the left, correlations between pairs of evaluation measures are analyzed. On the right, abstractive summaries from two variants of the T5 model for the chosen data point (highlighted yellow) are shown.

GSum (Dou et al., 2021) is a guidance-based abstractive model that takes different types of external guidance signals: text inputs, highlighted sentences, keywords, or extractive oracle summaries derived from the training data. These signals along with the source text are used to generate focused and faithful abstractive summaries.

Argument Summarization

Summarizing argumentative texts (opinions, product reviews) requires that the model be able to identify high-quality, informative, and argumentative sentences from the text. We provide three models specifically developed for this task.

ArgsRank (Alshomary et al., 2020) is an extractive model for creating argument snippets. It augments TextRank with two new criteria: *centrality in context* and *argumentativeness* to help the model retrieve important and argumentative sentences.

ConcluGen (Syed et al., 2021a) is a transformer model for generating informative conclusions of argumentative texts by balancing the trade-off between abstractiveness and informativeness of the output. It was finetuned on the Conclugen corpus comprised of pairs of argumentative text and a human-written conclusion.

COOP (Iso et al., 2021) is an unsupervised opinion summarization model that employs latent vector aggregation by searching for optimal input combinations of sentence embeddings to address the summary vector degeneration problem caused by simple averaging. Specifically, it finds convex combinations that maximize the word overlap between the source document and its summary.

News Summarization

A majority of the existing summarization models are trained on news datasets, since news have been and are readily available. These models have shown strong performance in creating fluent abstractive summaries (Huang et al., 2020). We provide the following models for summarizing news.

BART (Lewis et al., 2020) is a transformer denoising autoencoder for pre-training sequence-to-sequence models. Its main objective is to reconstruct the source text corrupted by employing arbitrary noising functions (masking text spans, randomly shuffling sentences) which helps the model learn better representations of the source texts for text summarization (Huang et al., 2020).

T5 (Raffel et al., 2020) is a unified text-to-text transformer model that exploits the strengths of transfer learning on a variety of problems that can be modeled as text generation tasks. A task-specific prefix is added to each input sequence (e.g., "summarize:<document>") that teaches the model to summarize accordingly.

Pegasus (Zhang et al., 2020a) is a transformer model pre-trained with a self-supervised summarization-specific training objective called "gap-sentences generation": important sentences are removed/masked from the source text and must be jointly generated as output from the remaining sentences, similar to an extractive summary.

CLIFF (Cao and Wang, 2021) leverages contrastive learning for generating abstractive summaries that are faithfully and factually consistent with the source texts. Reference summaries are used as positive examples while automatically generated erroneous summaries are used as the negative examples for training the model.

Newspaper3k is an open-source library for extracting news articles from the web which provides a module for extractive summarization that ranks sentences based on keywords and title words.[6]

4.2 Evaluation Measures

Evaluation measures for summarization typically quantify the lexical/semantic overlap of a candidate summary with a reference summary. We provide the following measures covering both.

Lexical Measures

Measures based on lexical overlap return precision, recall, or F1 scores on varying granularities of text between the candidate summary and one or more reference summaries.

BLEU (Papineni et al., 2002) is a standard measure for machine translation adapted for summarization. It includes a brevity penalty to account for length differences while computing n-gram overlap.

ROUGE (Lin, 2004) is the most common measure for summarization which computes precision, recall, and F1 scores based on n-gram overlap, where n-grams include unigrams, bigrams, and the longest common subsequence.

METEOR (Banerjee and Lavie, 2005) aligns a candidate with a set of references by mapping each unigram of a candidate to 0/1 unigrams of the reference based on exact, stem, synonym, and paraphrase matches. It then computes precision, recall, and F9 scores (i.e., weighted harmonic mean, strongly emphasizing recall) based on that.

CIDEr (Vedantam et al., 2015) is a consensus-based measure (originally for evaluating image captioning) which measures the similarity of a candidate against a set of references by counting the frequency of the common n-grams of a candidate.

Semantic Measures

Measures based on semantic overlap compute the semantic alignment between candidates and references at the token/word/sentence level based on their static/contextual embeddings.

Greedy Matching (Rus and Lintean, 2012) aligns a candidate and a reference by greedily matching each candidate word to a reference word based on their embeddings' cosine similarity. Average similarity over all candidate words aligned to reference words and vice versa are computed whose average is the final score.

MoverScore (Zhao et al., 2019) combines contextual embeddings from BERT using the word mover's distance (Kusner et al., 2015) to compare a candidate against a set of references by considering both the amount of shared content as well as the extent of deviation between them.

BERTScore (Zhang et al., 2020b) computes a similarity score for each candidate token with each reference token using contextual embeddings from BERT. The measure is also robust to adversarial modifications of the generated text.

BLEURT (Sellam et al., 2020) is a learned measure based on BERT that models human judgments with a few thousand biased training examples. The model is pre-trained using millions of synthetic examples created via scores from existing measures (BLEU, ROUGE, BERTScore), and textual entailment, for better generalization.

BARTScore (Yuan et al., 2021) uses the weighted log probability of generating one text given another to compute faithfulness (source $\rightarrow$ candidate), precision (reference $\rightarrow$ candidate), recall (candidate $\rightarrow$ reference), and the F1 score.

CosineSim includes two embedding-based cosine similarity measures using Spacy word vectors (Honnibal et al., 2020) and Sentence-BERT (Reimers and Gurevych, 2019).

5 Interaction Use Cases

Figure 3 shows two use cases of the interactive plotter. First, users can analyze any correlation

[6]https://newspaper.readthedocs.io/en/latest/

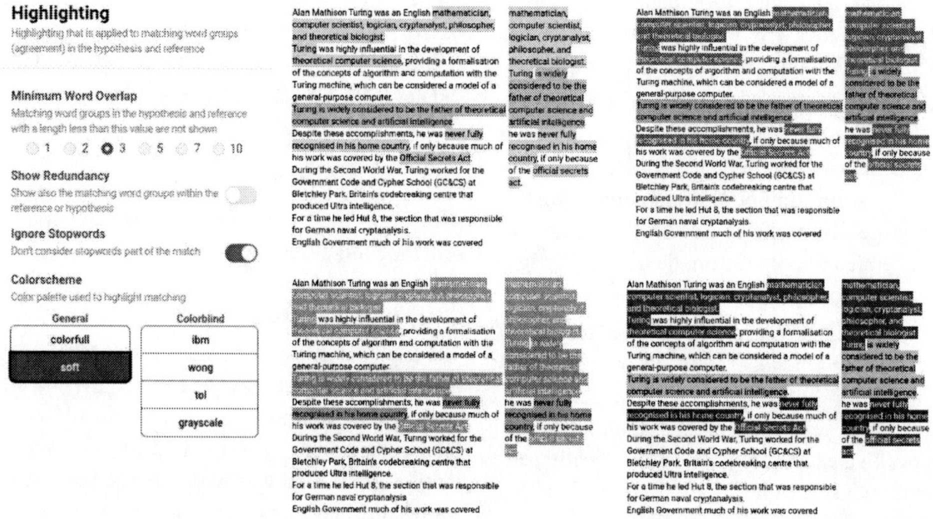

Figure 4: Customization options available for visualization of document and summary overlap. Users can select the minimum word overlap, preserve duplicate words, and ignore stop words to be visualized. Also, they can instantly preview each color scheme and set it as their default. The tool provides colorful, soft gradient-based, and grayscale schemes to account for color blindness.

between two measures of choice for a summarization model. Here, we find that MoverScore and BERTScore have strong correlation as they both employ contextual embeddings from BERT to compute the overlap between candidate and reference summaries. Likewise, we find that the static token embeddings from Spacy have a broader distribution of scores in comparison.

As a second use case, the interactive plotter allows comparing two variants of the same model architecture using any measure. Here, we inspect the T5 model (its 3B and 11B variants) using BERTScore to find that the larger variant generates a summary very similar to the reference while the smaller variant creates a summary that is topically related but not accurate in comparison to the reference.

6 Conclusion

In this paper we present SUMMARY WORKBENCH, a tool that unifies the application and evaluation of text summarization models. The tool supports integrating summarization models and evaluation measures of all kinds via a Docker-based plugin system that can also be locally deployed. This allows safe inspection and comparison of models on existing benchmarks and easy sharing with the research community in a software stack-agnostic manner. We have curated an initial set of 15 models (26 including all variants) and 10 evaluation measures and welcome contributions from the text summarization community. An extension of the tool's features to related text generation tasks such as paraphrasing and question answering is foreseen.

7 Ethical Statement and Limitations

Our tool builds on open source models and evaluation measures contributed by the corresponding authors. We expect all users of our tool to diligently cite the authors of all models and measures when they use them via our tool, instead of just citing our tool. The tool provides direct links to the relevant sources for each hosted summarization model and evaluation measure to facilitate this.

The models and measures may have intrinsic biases, which ideally, our tool may help to identify. However, our tool itself may have biases, especially with respect to its visualizations: Visualization in general is a difficult task, and visual analytics for data analysis in particular may lead to invalid conclusions if the underlying visualization itself is flawed. Although we did our best to avoid any non-standard visualizations and relied on widely used tools to plot them, we caution users of possible errors from either the dependent libraries or their integration in our tool. Validating a visual analytics tool poses non-trivial research tasks of its own right, which we leave for future work. We do hope that the community will diligently report any errors they may encounter.

To account for color blindness, we strived to provide multiple (soft) gradient-based color schemes and grayscale colors (Figure 4) for all our visualizations. Instant previews of each color scheme are available to help users customize the tool's visuals.

References

Milad Alshomary, Nick Düsterhus, and Henning Wachsmuth. 2020. Extractive snippet generation for arguments. In *Proceedings of the 43rd International ACM SIGIR conference on research and development in Information Retrieval, SIGIR 2020, Virtual Event, China, July 25-30, 2020*, pages 1969–1972. ACM.

Satanjeev Banerjee and Alon Lavie. 2005. METEOR: an automatic metric for MT evaluation with improved correlation with human judgments. In *Proceedings of the Workshop on Intrinsic and Extrinsic Evaluation Measures for Machine Translation and/or Summarization@ACL 2005, Ann Arbor, Michigan, USA, June 29, 2005*, pages 65–72. Association for Computational Linguistics.

Iz Beltagy, Matthew E. Peters, and Arman Cohan. 2020. Longformer: The long-document transformer. *CoRR*, abs/2004.05150.

Sergey Brin and Lawrence Page. 1998. The anatomy of a large-scale hypertextual web search engine. *Comput. Networks*, 30(1-7):107–117.

Shuyang Cao and Lu Wang. 2021. CLIFF: contrastive learning for improving faithfulness and factuality in abstractive summarization. In *Proceedings of the 2021 Conference on Empirical Methods in Natural Language Processing, EMNLP 2021, Virtual Event / Punta Cana, Dominican Republic, 7-11 November, 2021*, pages 6633–6649. Association for Computational Linguistics.

Nicki Skafte Detlefsen, Jiri Borovec, Justus Schock, Ananya Harsh, Teddy Koker, Luca Di Liello, Daniel Stancl, Changsheng Quan, Maxim Grechkin, and William Falcon. 2022. TorchMetrics - Measuring Reproducibility in PyTorch.

Daniel Deutsch and Dan Roth. 2020. SacreROUGE: An open-source library for using and developing summarization evaluation metrics. In *Proceedings of Second Workshop for NLP Open Source Software (NLP-OSS)*, pages 120–125. Association for Computational Linguistics.

Jacob Devlin, Ming-Wei Chang, Kenton Lee, and Kristina Toutanova. 2019. BERT: pre-training of deep bidirectional transformers for language understanding. In *Proceedings of the 2019 Conference of the North American Chapter of the Association for Computational Linguistics: Human Language Technologies, NAACL-HLT 2019, Minneapolis, MN, USA, June 2-7, 2019, Volume 1 (Long and Short Papers)*, pages 4171–4186. Association for Computational Linguistics.

Zi-Yi Dou, Pengfei Liu, Hiroaki Hayashi, Zhengbao Jiang, and Graham Neubig. 2021. Gsum: A general framework for guided neural abstractive summarization. In *Proceedings of the 2021 Conference of the North American Chapter of the Association for Computational Linguistics: Human Language Technologies, NAACL-HLT 2021, Online, June 6-11, 2021*, pages 4830–4842. Association for Computational Linguistics.

John A Hartigan and Manchek A Wong. 1979. Algorithm as 136: A k-means clustering algorithm. *Journal of the royal statistical society. series c (applied statistics)*, 28(1):100–108.

Matthew Honnibal, Ines Montani, Sofie Van Landeghem, and Adriane Boyd. 2020. spaCy: Industrial-strength Natural Language Processing in Python.

Dandan Huang, Leyang Cui, Sen Yang, Guangsheng Bao, Kun Wang, Jun Xie, and Yue Zhang. 2020. What have we achieved on text summarization? In *Proceedings of the 2020 Conference on Empirical Methods in Natural Language Processing, EMNLP 2020, Online, November 16-20, 2020*, pages 446–469. Association for Computational Linguistics.

Hayate Iso, Xiaolan Wang, Yoshihiko Suhara, Stefanos Angelidis, and Wang-Chiew Tan. 2021. Convex aggregation for opinion summarization. In *Findings of the Association for Computational Linguistics: EMNLP 2021, Virtual Event / Punta Cana, Dominican Republic, 16-20 November, 2021*, pages 3885–3903. Association for Computational Linguistics.

Ashkan Kazemi, Verónica Pérez-Rosas, and Rada Mihalcea. 2020. Biased textrank: Unsupervised graph-based content extraction. In *Proceedings of the 28th International Conference on Computational Linguistics, COLING 2020, Barcelona, Spain (Online), December 8-13, 2020*, pages 1642–1652. International Committee on Computational Linguistics.

Matt J. Kusner, Yu Sun, Nicholas I. Kolkin, and Kilian Q. Weinberger. 2015. From word embeddings to document distances. In *Proceedings of the 32nd International Conference on Machine Learning, ICML 2015, Lille, France, 6-11 July 2015*, volume 37 of *JMLR Workshop and Conference Proceedings*, pages 957–966. JMLR.org.

Mike Lewis, Yinhan Liu, Naman Goyal, Marjan Ghazvininejad, Abdelrahman Mohamed, Omer Levy, Veselin Stoyanov, and Luke Zettlemoyer. 2020. BART: denoising sequence-to-sequence pre-training for natural language generation, translation, and comprehension. In *Proceedings of the 58th Annual Meeting of the Association for Computational Linguistics, ACL 2020, Online, July 5-10, 2020*, pages 7871–7880. Association for Computational Linguistics.

Chin-Yew Lin. 2004. ROUGE: A package for automatic evaluation of summaries. In *Text Summarization Branches Out*, pages 74–81, Barcelona, Spain. Association for Computational Linguistics.

Yinhan Liu, Myle Ott, Naman Goyal, Jingfei Du, Mandar Joshi, Danqi Chen, Omer Levy, Mike Lewis, Luke Zettlemoyer, and Veselin Stoyanov. 2019. Roberta: A robustly optimized BERT pretraining approach. *CoRR*, abs/1907.11692.

Hans Peter Luhn. 1958. The automatic creation of literature abstracts. *IBM Journal of Reseach and Devopment*, 2(2):159–165.

Potsawee Manakul and Mark J. F. Gales. 2021. Long-span summarization via local attention and content selection. In *Proceedings of the 59th Annual Meeting of the Association for Computational Linguistics and the 11th International Joint Conference on Natural Language Processing, ACL/IJCNLP 2021, (Volume 1: Long Papers), Virtual Event, August 1-6, 2021*, pages 6026–6041. Association for Computational Linguistics.

Joshua Maynez, Shashi Narayan, Bernd Bohnet, and Ryan T. McDonald. 2020. On faithfulness and factuality in abstractive summarization. In *Proceedings of the 58th Annual Meeting of the Association for Computational Linguistics, ACL 2020, Online, July 5-10, 2020*, pages 1906–1919. Association for Computational Linguistics.

Rada Mihalcea and Paul Tarau. 2004. Textrank: Bringing order into text. In *Proceedings of the 2004 Conference on Empirical Methods in Natural Language Processing , EMNLP 2004, A meeting of SIGDAT, a Special Interest Group of the ACL, held in conjunction with ACL 2004, 25-26 July 2004, Barcelona, Spain*, pages 404–411. ACL.

Derek Miller. 2019. Leveraging BERT for extractive text summarization on lectures. *CoRR*, abs/1906.04165.

Paco Nathan. 2016. PyTextRank, a Python implementation of TextRank for phrase extraction and summarization of text documents.

Ani Nenkova and Kathleen McKeown. 2012. A survey of text summarization techniques. In *Mining text data*, pages 43–76. Springer.

Ansong Ni, Zhangir Azerbayev, Mutethia Mutuma, Troy Feng, Yusen Zhang, Tao Yu, Ahmed Hassan Awadallah, and Dragomir R. Radev. 2021. Summertime: Text summarization toolkit for non-experts. In *Proceedings of the 2021 Conference on Empirical Methods in Natural Language Processing: System Demonstrations, EMNLP 2021, Online and Punta Cana, Dominican Republic, 7-11 November, 2021*, pages 329–338. Association for Computational Linguistics.

Myle Ott, Sergey Edunov, Alexei Baevski, Angela Fan, Sam Gross, Nathan Ng, David Grangier, and Michael Auli. 2019. fairseq: A fast, extensible toolkit for sequence modeling. In *Proceedings of the 2019 Conference of the North American Chapter of the Association for Computational Linguistics: Human Language Technologies, NAACL-HLT 2019, Minneapolis, MN, USA, June 2-7, 2019, Demonstrations*, pages 48–53. Association for Computational Linguistics.

Vishakh Padmakumar and He He. 2021. Unsupervised extractive summarization using pointwise mutual information. In *Proceedings of the 16th Conference of the European Chapter of the Association for Computational Linguistics: Main Volume, EACL 2021, Online, April 19 - 23, 2021*, pages 2505–2512. Association for Computational Linguistics.

Kishore Papineni, Salim Roukos, Todd Ward, and Wei-Jing Zhu. 2002. Bleu: a method for automatic evaluation of machine translation. In *Proceedings of the 40th Annual Meeting of the Association for Computational Linguistics, July 6-12, 2002, Philadelphia, PA, USA*, pages 311–318. ACL.

Colin Raffel, Noam Shazeer, Adam Roberts, Katherine Lee, Sharan Narang, Michael Matena, Yanqi Zhou, Wei Li, and Peter J. Liu. 2020. Exploring the limits of transfer learning with a unified text-to-text transformer. *J. Mach. Learn. Res.*, 21:140:1–140:67.

Nils Reimers and Iryna Gurevych. 2019. Sentence-bert: Sentence embeddings using siamese bert-networks. In *Proceedings of the 2019 Conference on Empirical Methods in Natural Language Processing and the 9th International Joint Conference on Natural Language Processing, EMNLP-IJCNLP 2019, Hong Kong, China, November 3-7, 2019*, pages 3980–3990. Association for Computational Linguistics.

Sascha Rothe, Shashi Narayan, and Aliaksei Severyn. 2020. Leveraging pre-trained checkpoints for sequence generation tasks. *Trans. Assoc. Comput. Linguistics*, 8:264–280.

Vasile Rus and Mihai C. Lintean. 2012. A comparison of greedy and optimal assessment of natural language student input using word-to-word similarity metrics. In *Proceedings of the Seventh Workshop on Building Educational Applications Using NLP, BEA@NAACL-HLT 2012, June 7, 2012, Montréal, Canada*, pages 157–162. The Association for Computer Linguistics.

Thibault Sellam, Dipanjan Das, and Ankur P. Parikh. 2020. BLEURT: learning robust metrics for text generation. In *Proceedings of the 58th Annual Meeting of the Association for Computational Linguistics, ACL 2020, Online, July 5-10, 2020*, pages 7881–7892. Association for Computational Linguistics.

Shahbaz Syed, Khalid Al Khatib, Milad Alshomary, Henning Wachsmuth, and Martin Potthast. 2021a.

Generating informative conclusions for argumentative texts. In *Findings of the Association for Computational Linguistics: ACL/IJCNLP 2021, Online Event, August 1-6, 2021*, volume ACL/IJCNLP 2021 of *Findings of ACL*, pages 3482–3493. Association for Computational Linguistics.

Shahbaz Syed, Tariq Yousef, Khalid Al Khatib, Stefan Jänicke, and Martin Potthast. 2021b. Summary explorer: Visualizing the state of the art in text summarization. In *Proceedings of the 2021 Conference on Empirical Methods in Natural Language Processing: System Demonstrations, EMNLP 2021, Online and Punta Cana, Dominican Republic, 7-11 November, 2021*, pages 185–194. Association for Computational Linguistics.

Ian Tenney, James Wexler, Jasmijn Bastings, Tolga Bolukbasi, Andy Coenen, Sebastian Gehrmann, Ellen Jiang, Mahima Pushkarna, Carey Radebaugh, Emily Reif, and Ann Yuan. 2020. The language interpretability tool: Extensible, interactive visualizations and analysis for NLP models. In *Proceedings of the 2020 Conference on Empirical Methods in Natural Language Processing: System Demonstrations, EMNLP 2020 - Demos, Online, November 16-20, 2020*, pages 107–118. Association for Computational Linguistics.

Ashish Vaswani, Noam Shazeer, Niki Parmar, Jakob Uszkoreit, Llion Jones, Aidan N. Gomez, Lukasz Kaiser, and Illia Polosukhin. 2017. Attention is all you need. In *Advances in Neural Information Processing Systems 30: Annual Conference on Neural Information Processing Systems 2017, December 4-9, 2017, Long Beach, CA, USA*, pages 5998–6008.

Ramakrishna Vedantam, C. Lawrence Zitnick, and Devi Parikh. 2015. Cider: Consensus-based image description evaluation. In *IEEE Conference on Computer Vision and Pattern Recognition, CVPR 2015, Boston, MA, USA, June 7-12, 2015*, pages 4566–4575. IEEE Computer Society.

Jesse Vig, Wojciech Kryscinski, Karan Goel, and Nazneen Fatema Rajani. 2021. Summvis: Interactive visual analysis of models, data, and evaluation for text summarization. *CoRR*, abs/2104.07605.

Thomas Wolf, Lysandre Debut, Victor Sanh, Julien Chaumond, Clement Delangue, Anthony Moi, Pierric Cistac, Tim Rault, Remi Louf, Morgan Funtowicz, Joe Davison, Sam Shleifer, Patrick von Platen, Clara Ma, Yacine Jernite, Julien Plu, Canwen Xu, Teven Le Scao, Sylvain Gugger, Mariama Drame, Quentin Lhoest, and Alexander Rush. 2020. Transformers: State-of-the-art natural language processing. In *Proceedings of the 2020 Conference on Empirical Methods in Natural Language Processing: System Demonstrations*, pages 38–45, Online. Association for Computational Linguistics.

Peilin Yang, Hui Fang, and Jimmy Lin. 2018. Anserini: Reproducible ranking baselines using lucene. *ACM J. Data Inf. Qual.*, 10(4):16:1–16:20.

Weizhe Yuan, Graham Neubig, and Pengfei Liu. 2021. Bartscore: Evaluating generated text as text generation. In *Advances in Neural Information Processing Systems 34: Annual Conference on Neural Information Processing Systems 2021, NeurIPS 2021, December 6-14, 2021, virtual*, pages 27263–27277.

Jingqing Zhang, Yao Zhao, Mohammad Saleh, and Peter J. Liu. 2020a. PEGASUS: pre-training with extracted gap-sentences for abstractive summarization. In *Proceedings of the 37th International Conference on Machine Learning, ICML 2020, 13-18 July 2020, Virtual Event*, volume 119 of *Proceedings of Machine Learning Research*, pages 11328–11339. PMLR.

Tianyi Zhang, Varsha Kishore, Felix Wu, Kilian Q. Weinberger, and Yoav Artzi. 2020b. Bertscore: Evaluating text generation with BERT. In *8th International Conference on Learning Representations, ICLR 2020, Addis Ababa, Ethiopia, April 26-30, 2020*. OpenReview.net.

Wei Zhao, Maxime Peyrard, Fei Liu, Yang Gao, Christian M. Meyer, and Steffen Eger. 2019. Moverscore: Text generation evaluating with contextualized embeddings and earth mover distance. In *Proceedings of the 2019 Conference on Empirical Methods in Natural Language Processing and the 9th International Joint Conference on Natural Language Processing, EMNLP-IJCNLP 2019, Hong Kong, China, November 3-7, 2019*, pages 563–578. Association for Computational Linguistics.

A Model Details

Summarizer	**Model**
BERTSummarizer	distilbert-base-uncased
LoBART	podcast_4K_ORC
Longformer2Roberta	patrickvonplaten/longformer2roberta-cnn_dailymail-fp16
ConcluGen	dbart
CLIFF	pegasus_cnndm
COOP	megagonlabs/bimeanvae
BART	facebook/bart-large
Pegasus	google/pegasus
T5-Base	huggingface.co/t5-base
Evaluator	**Model**
BARTScore	facebook/bart-large-cnn
Spacy Similarity	en_core_web_lg
SBERT	roberta-large-nli-stsb-mean-tokens
BLEURT	bleurt-base-128
BERTScore	roberta-large-mnli
Greedy Matching	glove.6B.300d
MoverScore	MoverScoreV1

Arabic Word-level Readability Visualization for Assisted Text Simplification

Reem Hazim, Hind Saddiki, Bashar Alhafni, Muhamed Al Khalil, Nizar Habash
Computational Approaches to Modeling Language Lab
New York University Abu Dhabi
{rh3015,hind.saddiki,alhafni,muhamed.alkhalil,nizar.habash}@nyu.edu

Abstract

This demo paper presents a Google Docs add-on for automatic Arabic word-level readability visualization. The add-on includes a lemmatization component that is connected to a five-level readability lexicon and Arabic WordNet-based substitution suggestions. The add-on can be used for assessing the reading difficulty of a text and identifying difficult words as part of the task of manual text simplification. We make our add-on and its code publicly available.[1,2]

1 Introduction

Models for automatic readability assessment and automatic text simplification are relevant to many natural language processing (NLP) tasks such as developing pedagogical language technologies that assist students with learning languages, or teachers with curriculum design and writing assessment, as well as personalized paraphrasing of NLP systems' outputs to target different users with different readability levels.

Developing robust models for readability assessment and simplification requires the creation of large-scale lexical and annotated resources for training and evaluation. For example, parallel texts with different paired readability levels can be used to train readability models as well as simplification models. Figure 1 presents an example from an Arabic novel paired with a simplified version targeting the fifth-grade readability level. Properly identifying which words and phrases need to be rewritten in a simplified manner for a specific target readability level and audience requires word-level readability annotation in a framework that enables easy editing of the original text, as well as easy checking on the updated text. To our knowledge, most of the available tools for readability assessment work on the document or the sentence levels.

[1]http://samer-addon.camel-lab.com/
[2]https://github.com/CAMeL-Lab/samer-add-on

Original Text
نحن يا سيدتي في زمن مضطرب لا يركد عجاجه، ولا تسكن سيوفه في أغمادها، بعد أن انحلّت أواصر بني العبّاس، وأصبحت دولتهم أشلاءً ممزقة، يفترسها كل مفترس، ويغير عليها كل واثب.
We live, my lady, in a troubled age whose dirt-laden air does not settle, nor do its swords rest in their scabbards, after the bonds of the house of Abbas dissolved, and their state became like torn limbs preyed upon by every predator and raided by every opportunist.
Simplified Text
نحن يا سيدتي في زمن صعب لا يهدأ غباره، ولا تسكن سيوفه في جيوبها، بعد أن تقطعت صلات بني العبّاس، وأصبحت دولتهم قطعا ممزقة، يفترسها كل مفترس، ويهجم عليها كل عدو.
We live, my lady, in a difficult age whose dust does not clear and whose swords do not rest in their sheaths, after the joints of the house of Abbas were cut off, and their state became like torn body parts preyed upon by every predator and attacked by every enemy.

Figure 1: An example original sentence from the Arabic novel "The Knight of Bani Hamdan" (Al-Jarim, 1945). The red-marked words are all of readability level 4 and 5 (difficult) per Al Khalil et al. (2018)'s readability lexicon. The simplified text rewrites those words into lower (easier) levels (green-marked words). The English translations are a best attempt to convey the complexity level of the Arabic word choices to non-Arabic readers.

The system presented in this paper addresses this limitation by focusing on word-level readability visualization to assist human annotators working on identifying text readability levels and adjusting texts to simplify them in a controlled setting. This effort is part of a project on the Simplification of Arabic Masterpieces for Extensive Reading (SAMER) (Al Khalil et al., 2017, 2018, 2020; Jiang et al., 2020). The project goals include the creation of a lemma-based graded readability lexicon for Arabic and a corpus of parallel original and simplified texts from Arabic novels (such as those presented in Figure 1). The project plans to target two different simplified readability levels: Grades 4-5 (Level III) and Grades 6-8 (Level IV).

While our focus is on Arabic, a language with

Proceedings of the The 2022 Conference on Empirical Methods in Natural Language Processing: System Demonstrations, pages 242 - 249
December 7-11, 2022

limited annotated resources for text simplification, the components we developed can be easily extended to other languages. The demo system is a Google Docs add-on that includes morphological analysis and light disambiguation of Arabic text, visualization of word readability levels, and access to substitution options with their own explicit readability levels. We make our add-on and its code publicly available.[1,2]

Next, we present some relevant Arabic linguistic facts (§2), and discuss related work (§3). We then present our design and implementation decisions (§4). In §5 we discuss some examples and use cases.

2 Relevant Arabic Linguistic Facts

Modern Standard Arabic (MSA) poses many challenges for NLP tasks (Habash, 2010). Two in particular are directly relevant to the task at hand, and affect many of our design decisions: morphological richness and orthographic ambiguity.[3]

Morphological Richness Arabic employs a combination of templatic, affixational, and cliticization morphological operations to realize a large number of features such as gender, number, person, case, state, aspect, voice, and mood, in addition to a number of attachable pronominal, preposition and determiner clitics. This leads to a very large number of words to model. To address this aspect, we utilize a morphological analysis component that is optimized for efficient representation (Graff et al., 2009; Taji et al., 2018).

Orthographic Ambiguity Arabic is commonly written with optional diacritical marks – which are often omitted – leading to rampant ambiguity. Orthographic ambiguity and morphological richness interact heavily with each other. For example the word فردها *frdhA*[4] has four core lemmas (Jiang et al., 2020): the verbs فَرَّد *far∼ad* 'individualize, separate in units', and رَدّ *rad∼* 'answer, return'; and the nouns فَرْد *fard* 'individual, unit' and رَدّ *rad∼* 'response, return'.

[3]We do not handle dialectal variants in this effort, although we acknowledge that dialectal differences from MSA are an important factor in readability assessment, since MSA is not the native variant of Arabic learned at home (Ferguson, 1959; Holes, 2004; Carroll et al., 2017).

[4]Arabic HSB transliteration (Habash et al., 2007).

Level	Grade	Age	Examples
I	1	6	بَيْت، كَبير، أكَلَ، عَلى house, big, to eat, on
II	2-3	7-8	ذَهَب، أُسْطُواني، خَدَعَ، إذا gold, cylindrical, to cheat, if
III	4-5	9-10	رِئة، مُعادَلة، مُوَحَّد، أَغْرى lung, equation, united, to entice
IV	6-8	11-14	اِقْتِصاد، طُمَأْنينة، راقٍي، نَكَثَ economy, tranquility, sophisticated, to breach
V	9+	15 -	أَدَمة، مِطْياف، لَوْذَع، شُعَبِيّ epidermis, spectroscope, witty, bronchial

Table 1: The five readability levels, their grade equivalencies, and lemma and English gloss examples, abridged from Al Khalil et al. (2020).

3 Related Work

Readability Resources Text readability leveling is relevant to a wide range of NLP applications such as text simplification and automatic readability assessment. Most research on readability leveling has focused on English, leading to the development of many resources (Collins-Thompson and Callan, 2004; Pitler and Nenkova, 2008; Feng et al., 2010; Vajjala and Meurers, 2012; Xia et al., 2016; Nadeem and Ostendorf, 2018; Vajjala and Lučić, 2018; Deutsch et al., 2020; Lee et al., 2021).

Specifically for MSA, datasets and modeling approaches have been created and developed by leveraging text targeted towards L1 readers (native speakers) (Al-Khalifa and Al-Ajlan, 2010; Al Tamimi et al., 2014; El-Haj and Rayson, 2016; Khalil et al., 2018) and L2 learners (non-native speakers) (Forsyth, 2014; Saddiki et al., 2018). More recently, Al Khalil et al. (2020) developed a 26,578-lemma lexicon (later extended to over 40,000 lemmas) with a five-level readability scale. Examples of vocabulary from the different readability levels and their corresponding grades and ages are shown in Table 1. This lexicon anchors readability at the lemma representation of the words. We use this lexicon as our reference for readability levels.

Jiang et al. (2020) developed the online Readability Leveled Arabic Thesaurus interface that leverages Al Khalil et al. (2020)'s lexicon, and extends its coverage.[5] For a given user input word, this interface provides the word's possible lemmas,

[5]http://samer.camel-lab.com/

roots, English glosses, related Arabic words and phrases from the Arabic WordNet (Black et al., 2006), and readability on a five-level readability scale. We make use of many components of Jiang et al. (2020)'s interface in our add-on.

Readability Visualization To the best of our knowledge, there has not been much work on developing web-based visualization tools for word-level readability assessment, neither for Arabic nor for other languages. Most of the existing tools work on the document or the sentence levels. Such tools include Readable[6] and datayze's Readability Analyzer[7] for English, and the recently proposed FABRA for French (Wilkens et al., 2022).[8] The lack of word-level tools for Arabic has motivated us to create an easy-to-use Google Docs add-on for word-level readability visualization.

Arabic Morphological Analysis and Disambiguation There are a number of tools that support Arabic morphological analysis and disambiguation and specifically lemmatization (Pasha et al., 2014; Darwish and Mubarak, 2016; Obeid et al., 2020, 2022). Inspired by the JavaScript Chrome extension developed by Khalifa et al. (2016) to assist Arabic learners in understanding text written in MSA or dialectal Arabic (DA), we implement a version of the Buckwalter core morphological analysis algorithm (Buckwalter, 2002) in JavaScript as part of our add-on.

4 Design and Implementation

4.1 Design Considerations

We designed our interface with the following considerations in mind.

Openness and Ease-of-use The system needs to be powerful and provides additive or complementary value to existing text editors, so that simplifications and changes can be evaluated on the fly and with minimal overhead. This needs to be accomplished with minimal usability tradeoffs.

Handling Arabic Ambiguity and Rich Morphology The system needs to be able to analyze fully inflected words and relate them to their lemmas and part-of-speech (POS) tags. The lemmas and POS tags will be used to identify the readability levels from Al Khalil et al. (2020)'s lexicon and to link with the Arabic WordNet databases (Black et al., 2006). Additionally, the interface needs to provide the users with access to all the analyses of a given word.

Visualizing Readability The interface needs to provide summary readability statistics in word-token and word-type spaces over full documents or arbitrary text selections. It should highlight the words in context in a clear way to indicate intuitively which words are easier and which are harder. And finally, the interface needs to provide access to the readability levels of other unchosen analyses of any word.

Access to Word Substitutions The system should support the text simplification process by displaying suggestions for related words and phrases, e.g., synonyms, antonyms, hypernyms, and hyponyms, with different readability levels. We build on the work of Jiang et al. (2020) who used the Arabic Wordnet to accomplish the same.

Explicit/Implicit Word Readability Markup The system should allow the recording of explicit readability levels such that when the automatic processes make mistakes, users can overwrite them. We want those corrections and annotations to be persistent across different future versions of the analyzer and lexicon. At the same time, unnecessary over-specification can be distracting to the reader or annotator and should be minimized. The system should support the ability to import and export text files that could be marked for readability using external tools.

4.2 Implementation

Google Docs Add-on We opted to implement our interface as a Google Docs add-on, which allows us to use one of the world's most used editing frameworks, without sacrificing any of Google Docs' advantages such as multi-author editing and other familiar word-editing supports.

We implemented the tool's front-end in HTML, CSS and JavaScript. The back-end was implemented in JavaScript, and it also utilizes the Apps Script Document Service, which is a JavaScript API used to read and modify Google Docs programmatically.

Readability Analysis and Visualization The tool analyzes user input in four main steps that are summarized in Figure 2. First, in the back-end, the

[6]https://readable.com/
[7]https://datayze.com/readability-analyzer.php
[8]https://cental.uclouvain.be/fabra/

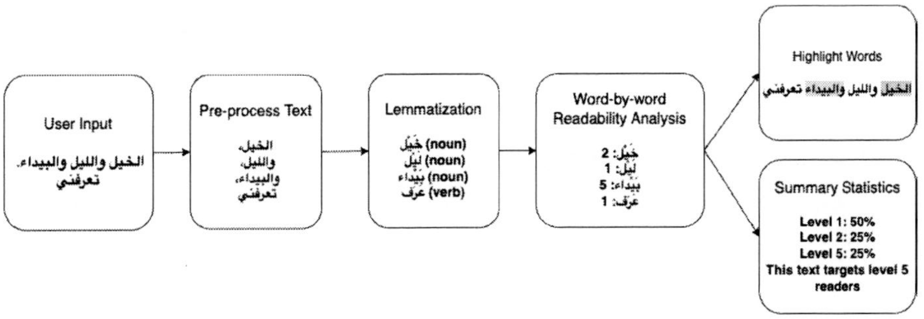

Figure 2: A flowchart depicting the steps that our tool takes to process user input. First, the user input is pre-processed and tokenized. Next, the lemma and part-of-speech of each token are determined using a morphological analyzer. Then, the tool looks up each lemma in the readability database to identify its readability level. The tool then highlights individual words accordingly and produces summary statistics describing the overall text readability.

text is pre-processed and tokenized, and non-word tokens are discarded. Second, the tokens are fed into the morphological analysis algorithm, which produces the most likely lemma and POS pair for each word. Third, we look up the lemmas in the readability database to identify their readability levels.[9] Finally, we use the Apps Script Document API to highlight words with different colors according to their readability levels. The tool also presents a summary of the text's readability distribution levels in a bar chart colored consistently with the readability level word highlights.

Morphological and Lexical Analyses Inspired by Khalifa et al. (2016)'s Chrome extension and Obeid et al. (2020)'s out-of-context MLE disambiguation mode, we implemented a version of the Buckwalter core morphological analysis algorithm (Buckwalter, 2002) in JavaScript as part of our add-on. Besides being used to determine readability levels, all lemma analyses are presented in a side bar to allow investigating and reassigning readability levels if needed. It is worth noting that the readability lexicon we use does not handle lexical polysemy. This is mainly due to the lexical representation that is used in the lexicon, which follows the representation of the Standard Arabic Morphological Analyzer (SAMA) (Graff et al., 2009). However, the design of our tool is independent of the granularity level of lexical representation and therefore, any updates to these components in the future can be easily integrated in our tool.

Figure 3 presents an instance of the SAMER Google Docs add-on with marked up text.

[9]We treat Proper nouns (Names) as a separate level.

Explicit/Implicit Word Readability Markup By default, the system deterministically specifies a readability level for any specific word based on its morphological and lexical readability resources. When disagreement with the automatic levels happen, as in automatic errors or importing text that was leveled externally, we ensure that the differences from the deterministic readability levels are not lost. To accomplish this, a prefix *#<i>#* is explicitly added in front of the word in question forcing the tool to interpret the word as having readability level of value *<i>*. For example, the word كَتَب *ktb* has a readability level of 1. However, the user can manually assign it a level of 5 by adding #٥# (Indo-Arabic digit 5) in front of the word, like so: #٥#كَتَب *#5#ktb* . We also provide an interface button as part of the morphological side bar discussed above to make such assignment.

The add-on also provides multiple markup visualization modes to navigate between explicit and implicit readability level markup.

(a) **Show**: Explicitly mark all words with their readability levels.

(b) **Minimize**: Minimize all the markups by setting their font size to 1pt.

(c) **Hide**: Remove any markup whose readability level matches the internal level chosen by the analyzer and only keep the disagreeing markups. By default the Hide mode also minimizes the markup; however, the user can easily select the full text and resize it to a preferred font size (Hide+Resize).

(d) **Delete**: Delete all markup from the text.

Figure 4 shows the supported markup modes.

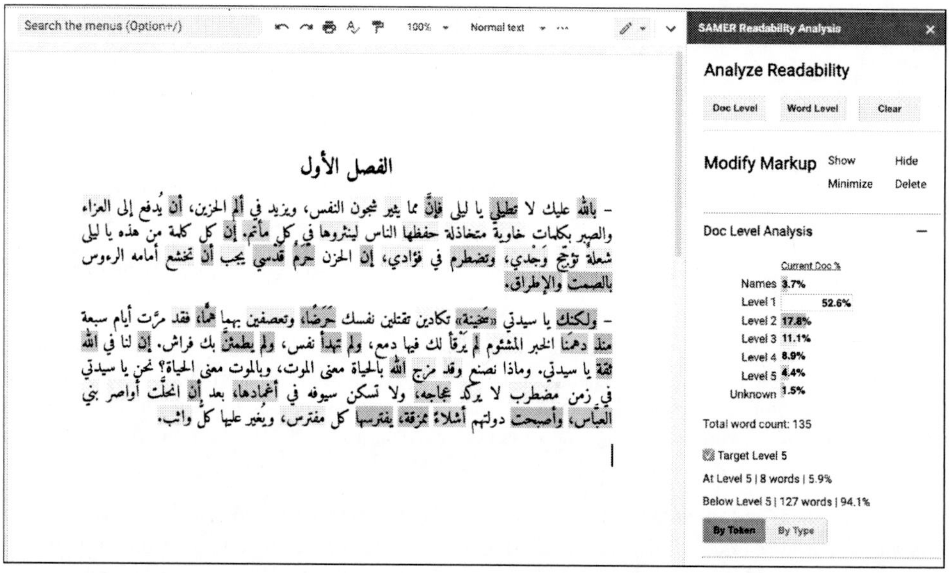

Figure 3: The SAMER Google Docs add-on visualizing word-level and document-level readability.

Markup	Example
Show	#٢#يفترسها #١# كل #٣#مفترس، #٤#ويغير #١#عليها #١# كلّ #٥#واثب.
Minimize	..يفترسها . كل .مفترس، .ويغير .عليها . كلّ .واثب.
Hide	يفترسها كل مفترس، .ويغير عليها كلّ .واثب.
Hide + Resize	يفترسها كل مفترس، #٤#ويغير عليها كلّ #٥#واثب.
Delete	يفترسها كل مفترس، ويغير عليها كلّ واثب.

Figure 4: The different word-level markup modes that are supported by our tool.

5 SAMER Add-on: Examples and Use Cases

We present some examples of how the SAMER project Google Docs add-on can be used to analyze the readability of a literary text. We also discuss potential use cases of our tool across a variety of tasks and how it can be extended to other languages.

Examples Figure 3 shows the result of using the tool to analyze a short segment of a novel. After clicking on the `Doc Level` button at the top, the tool highlights each word according to its readability level using different colors, and presents a summary distribution of words in each readability level.

Figure 5 shows the result of selecting a specific word (انحلّت *AnHlt* 'be disbanded') and clicking on the `Word Level` button at the top. A side bar appears showing the different lemma analyses by readability level. Various word substitution alternatives are presented to the user including synonyms, hypernyms and hyponyms, with their associated readability levels. If the user decides to change the word, they can simply rewrite it and rerun the readability analysis. If the user decides to change the automatically assigned readability level, they can either change it directly manually, or by clicking on the `Assign` button to change that specific word's readability level markup or the `Assign All` button to change all of its occurrences in the document.

Use Cases Our goal behind creating an easy-to-use Google Docs add-on tool for Arabic word-level readability analysis is to enable users to edit texts easily based on a specific target readability level. We intend for our tool to be used by human annotators to identify text readability levels and to simplify texts in a controlled setting. However, we envision that our tool can be used to assist writers in either making texts more sophisticated (harder readability) or in providing alternatives for specific words that have the same readability level.

Extending to Other Languages Although our work focuses on Arabic, the SAMER add-on tool is designed in a modular way and it can be easily extended to other languages. More concretely, the fol-

Figure 5: An example of selecting a specific word and identifying all of its analyses with their readability levels.

lowing core components are needed to make such an extension possible: (1) a readability level lexicon that relates lemmas to their readability levels; (2) a morphological analysis database that specifies prefixes, suffixes, stems and lemmas, and their co-occurrence compatibilities; (3) a statistical lemma-based disambiguation model; and (4) synonym, hypernym, hyponym and antonym lexical databases, such as those found in WordNet (Fellbaum, 2010).

6 Conclusion

We presented a Google Docs add-on for automatic Arabic word-level readability visualization. Our add-on includes a lemmatization component that is connected to a five-level readability lexicon and Arabic WordNet-based substitution suggestions. The add-on can be used for assessing the reading difficulty of a text and identifying difficult words as part of the task of manual text simplification.

In future work, we plan on enhancing our tool's readability analysis by leveraging additional morphosyntatic features (Saddiki et al., 2018). We will use the add-on to annotate a corpus of parallel original and simplified texts from Arabic novels.

Limitations and Ethical Considerations

We acknowledge that the add-on we developed could be used maliciously to: (a) modify texts under false pretenses, (b) plagiarize, or (c) profile people in a biased way using their writing style. We also acknowledge that automatic errors in readability analysis can lead to harmful results even when used with good intent. We further recognize that the use of highlighting as a visualization mechanism limits the conventional use of highlighting in text editing. Another limitation of our work is the lack of extrinsic and intrinsic evaluation. However, we are not aware of any manually annotated Arabic word-level readability datasets . We plan to develop such datasets using our tool. Finally, we acknowledge that further user studies are needed to confirm the effectiveness of our tool in aiding annotators to perform tasks such as text simplification.

Acknowledgements

This project is funded by a New York University Abu Dhabi Research Enhancement Fund grant. We thank Zhengyang Jiang, Go Inoue, and Ossama Obeid for helpful discussions.

References

Ali Al-Jarim. 1945. *Fāris Banī Ḥamdān (The Knight of Bani Hamdan)*. Hindawi Foundation.

Hend S Al-Khalifa and Amani A Al-Ajlan. 2010. Automatic readability measurements of the Arabic text: An exploratory study. *Arabian Journal for Science and Engineering*, 35(2 C):103–124.

Muhamed Al Khalil, Nizar Habash, and Zhengyang Jiang. 2020. A large-scale leveled readability lexicon for Standard Arabic. In *Proceedings of the 12th Language Resources and Evaluation Conference*, pages 3053–3062, Marseille, France. European Language Resources Association.

Muhamed Al Khalil, Nizar Habash, and Hind Saddiki. 2017. Simplification of Arabic masterpieces for extensive reading: A project overview. *Procedia Computer Science*, 117:192–198.

Muhamed Al Khalil, Hind Saddiki, Nizar Habash, and Latifa Alfalasi. 2018. A leveled reading corpus of Modern Standard Arabic. In *Proceedings of the Eleventh International Conference on Language Resources and Evaluation (LREC 2018)*, Miyazaki, Japan. European Language Resources Association (ELRA).

Abdel Karim Al Tamimi, Manar Jaradat, Nuha Al-Jarrah, and Sahar Ghanem. 2014. AARI: automatic Arabic readability index. *International Arab Journal of Information Technology*, 11(4):370–378.

William Black, Sabri Elkateb, Horacio Rodriguez, Musa Alkhalifa, Piek Vossen, Adam Pease, and Christiane Fellbaum. 2006. Introducing the Arabic wordnet project. In *Proceedings of the Global WordNet Conference (GWC)*, pages 295–300.

Tim Buckwalter. 2002. Buckwalter Arabic morphological analyzer version 1.0. Linguistic Data Consortium (LDC) catalog number LDC2002L49, ISBN 1-58563-257-0.

Kevin S Carroll, Bashar Al Kahwaji, and David Litz. 2017. Triglossia and promoting Arabic literacy in the United Arab Emirates. *Language, Culture and Curriculum*, 30(3):317–332.

Kevyn Collins-Thompson and James P. Callan. 2004. A language modeling approach to predicting reading difficulty. In *Proceedings of the Human Language Technology Conference of the North American Chapter of the Association for Computational Linguistics: HLT-NAACL 2004*, pages 193–200, Boston, Massachusetts, USA. Association for Computational Linguistics.

Kareem Darwish and Hamdy Mubarak. 2016. Farasa: A new fast and accurate Arabic word segmenter. In *Proceedings of the Language Resources and Evaluation Conference (LREC)*, Portorož, Slovenia.

Tovly Deutsch, Masoud Jasbi, and Stuart Shieber. 2020. Linguistic features for readability assessment. In *Proceedings of the Fifteenth Workshop on Innovative Use of NLP for Building Educational Applications*, pages 1–17, Seattle, WA, USA → Online. Association for Computational Linguistics.

Mahmoud El-Haj and Paul Rayson. 2016. OSMAN — a novel Arabic readability metric. In *Proceedings of the Tenth International Conference on Language Resources and Evaluation (LREC'16)*, pages 250–255, Portorož, Slovenia. European Language Resources Association (ELRA).

Christiane Fellbaum. 2010. Wordnet. In *Theory and Applications of Ontology: Computer Applications*, pages 231–243. Springer.

Lijun Feng, Martin Jansche, Matt Huenerfauth, and Noémie Elhadad. 2010. A comparison of features for automatic readability assessment. In *Coling 2010: Posters*, pages 276–284, Beijing, China. Coling 2010 Organizing Committee.

Charles F Ferguson. 1959. Diglossia. *Word*, 15(2):325–340.

Jonathan Forsyth. 2014. Automatic readability prediction for modern standard Arabic. In *Proceedings of the Workshop on Open-Source Arabic Corpora and Processing Tools (OSACT)*.

David Graff, Mohamed Maamouri, Basma Bouziri, Sondos Krouna, Seth Kulick, and Tim Buckwalter. 2009. Standard Arabic Morphological Analyzer (SAMA) Version 3.1. Linguistic Data Consortium LDC2009E73.

Nizar Habash, Abdelhadi Soudi, and Tim Buckwalter. 2007. On Arabic Transliteration. In A. van den Bosch and A. Soudi, editors, *Arabic Computational Morphology: Knowledge-based and Empirical Methods*, pages 15–22. Springer, Netherlands.

Nizar Y Habash. 2010. *Introduction to Arabic natural language processing*, volume 3. Morgan & Claypool Publishers.

Clive Holes. 2004. *Modern Arabic: Structures, Functions, and Varieties*. Georgetown Classics in Arabic Language and Linguistics. Georgetown University Press.

Zhengyang Jiang, Nizar Habash, and Muhamed Al Khalil. 2020. An online readability leveled Arabic thesaurus. In *Proceedings of the 28th International Conference on Computational Linguistics: System Demonstrations*, pages 59–63, Barcelona, Spain (Online). International Committee on Computational Linguistics (ICCL).

Salam Khalifa, Houda Bouamor, and Nizar Habash. 2016. DALILA: The dialectal Arabic linguistic learning assistant. In *Proceedings of the Tenth International Conference on Language Resources and Evaluation (LREC'16)*, pages 1098–1102, Portorož, Slovenia. European Language Resources Association (ELRA).

Muhamed Al Khalil, Hind Saddiki, Nizar Habash, and Latifa Alfalasi. 2018. A Leveled Reading Corpus of Modern Standard Arabic. In *Proceedings of the Language Resources and Evaluation Conference (LREC)*, Miyazaki, Japan.

Bruce W. Lee, Yoo Sung Jang, and Jason Lee. 2021. Pushing on text readability assessment: A transformer meets handcrafted linguistic features. In *Pro-*

ceedings of the 2021 Conference on Empirical Methods in Natural Language Processing*, pages 10669–10686, Online and Punta Cana, Dominican Republic. Association for Computational Linguistics.

Farah Nadeem and Mari Ostendorf. 2018. Estimating linguistic complexity for science texts. In *Proceedings of the Thirteenth Workshop on Innovative Use of NLP for Building Educational Applications*, pages 45–55, New Orleans, Louisiana. Association for Computational Linguistics.

Ossama Obeid, Go Inoue, and Nizar Habash. 2022. Camelira: An Arabic Multi-Dialect Morphological Disambiguator. In *Proceedings of the Conference on Empirical Methods in Natural Language Processing (EMNLP 2022) Demo Track*, Abu Dhabi, United Arab Emirates.

Ossama Obeid, Nasser Zalmout, Salam Khalifa, Dima Taji, Mai Oudah, Bashar Alhafni, Go Inoue, Fadhl Eryani, Alexander Erdmann, and Nizar Habash. 2020. CAMeL tools: An open source python toolkit for Arabic natural language processing. In *Proceedings of The 12th Language Resources and Evaluation Conference*, pages 7022–7032, Marseille, France. European Language Resources Association.

Arfath Pasha, Mohamed Al-Badrashiny, Mona Diab, Ahmed El Kholy, Ramy Eskander, Nizar Habash, Manoj Pooleery, Owen Rambow, and Ryan Roth. 2014. Madamira: A fast, comprehensive tool for morphological analysis and disambiguation of Arabic. In *Proceedings of the Language Resources and Evaluation Conference (LREC)*, pages 1094–1101, Reykjavik, Iceland.

Emily Pitler and Ani Nenkova. 2008. Revisiting readability: A unified framework for predicting text quality. In *Proceedings of the 2008 Conference on Empirical Methods in Natural Language Processing*, pages 186–195, Honolulu, Hawaii. Association for Computational Linguistics.

Hind Saddiki, Nizar Habash, Violetta Cavalli-Sforza, and Muhamed Al Khalil. 2018. Feature optimization for predicting readability of Arabic L1 and L2. In *Proceedings of the 5th Workshop on Natural Language Processing Techniques for Educational Applications*, pages 20–29, Melbourne, Australia. Association for Computational Linguistics.

Dima Taji, Salam Khalifa, Ossama Obeid, Fadhl Eryani, and Nizar Habash. 2018. An Arabic Morphological Analyzer and Generator with Copious Features. In *Proceedings of the Fifteenth Workshop on Computational Research in Phonetics, Phonology, and Morphology (SIGMORPHON)*, pages 140–150.

Sowmya Vajjala and Ivana Lučić. 2018. OneStopEnglish corpus: A new corpus for automatic readability assessment and text simplification. In *Proceedings of the Thirteenth Workshop on Innovative Use of NLP for Building Educational Applications*, pages 297–304, New Orleans, Louisiana. Association for Computational Linguistics.

Sowmya Vajjala and Detmar Meurers. 2012. On improving the accuracy of readability classification using insights from second language acquisition. In *Proceedings of the Seventh Workshop on Building Educational Applications Using NLP*, pages 163–173, Montréal, Canada. Association for Computational Linguistics.

Rodrigo Wilkens, David Alfter, Xiaoou Wang, Alice Pintard, AnaÃ¯s Tack, Kevin P. Yancey, and Thomas FranÃ§ois. 2022. Fabra: French aggregator-based readability assessment toolkit. In *Proceedings of the Language Resources and Evaluation Conference*, pages 1217–1233, Marseille, France. European Language Resources Association.

Menglin Xia, Ekaterina Kochmar, and Ted Briscoe. 2016. Text readability assessment for second language learners. In *Proceedings of the 11th Workshop on Innovative Use of NLP for Building Educational Applications*, pages 12–22, San Diego, CA. Association for Computational Linguistics.

LogiTorch: A PyTorch-based library for logical reasoning on natural language

Chadi Helwe, Chloé Clavel, Fabian Suchanek
Télécom Paris, Institut Polytechnique de Paris, France
{chadi.helwe, chloe.clavel, suchanek}@telecom-paris.fr

Abstract

Logical reasoning on natural language is one of the most challenging tasks for deep learning models. There has been an increasing interest in developing new benchmarks to evaluate the reasoning capabilities of language models such as BERT. In parallel, new models based on transformers have emerged to achieve ever better performance on these datasets. However, there is currently no library for logical reasoning that includes such benchmarks and models. This paper introduces LogiTorch, a PyTorch-based library that includes different logical reasoning benchmarks, different models, as well as utility functions such as co-reference resolution. This makes it easy to directly use the preprocessed datasets, to run the models, or to finetune them with different hyperparameters. LogiTorch is open source and can be found on GitHub[1].

1 Introduction

Machine reasoning over natural language has been an object of research since the 1950s (Newell and Simon, 1956; McCarthy et al., 1960). One prototypical task in the domain is Textual Entailment: Given a premise (such as "I ate a cake"), the goal is to determine whether a hypothesis ("I ate something sweet") is entailed or not. Other logical reasoning tasks are question answering, multiple choice question answering, and proof generation.

Lately, deep learning models have shown impressive performance on tasks such as these, in particular transformer-based models such as BERT (Devlin et al., 2019) and GPT-3 (Brown et al., 2020). However, the models can be distracted easily by trap words, syntactic variations (Kassner and Schütze, 2020), or negation (Kassner and Schütze, 2020; Ettinger, 2020; Hossain et al., 2020, 2022; Helwe et al., 2021). Hence, the question of whether these models can logically reason on text is still open (Niven and Kao, 2019; Helwe et al., 2021). New models are being created incessantly (e.g., LogiGAN (Pi et al., 2022) and Logiformer (Xu et al., 2022) in 2022), and new datasets are being created to evaluate these models, including, e.g., LogiQA (Liu et al., 2021b) and ProofWriter (Tafjord et al., 2021). The initiative of open-sourcing toolkits has accelerated the progress in the field of natural language processing, driven by projects such as Transformers (Wolf et al., 2020) from HuggingFace and Stanza (Qi et al., 2020) from Stanford. However, this progress has not yet arrived in the field of logical reasoning: researchers still have to find and download different models, parameterize them, find the corresponding datasets, bring them into suitable formats, and fine-tune the models. The datasets are maintained on different Web pages, exhibit different formats (JSON vs. full text, numerical vs. textual labels, etc.), and follow different conventions, which makes it cumbersome to apply one model across several sources. The models themselves are implemented in different frameworks, have different input and output formats, require different dependencies, and differ in the way of running them, which makes it burdensome to exchange one model for another. Some models are not even available online, but have to be re-implemented from scratch based on the diagrams in the scientific publications. All of this hinders reproducibility, re-usability, comparability, and ultimately scientific progress in the area.

In this paper, we propose to bring the benefits of open source libraries to the domain of logical reasoning: we build a Python library, LogiTorch, that includes 14 datasets and 4 implemented models for 3 different logical reasoning tasks. All models can be called in a unified way, all datasets of one task are available in the same standardized format, and all models can be run with all datasets of the same task. All models have been re-implemented from the research papers that proposed them, and they

[1] https://github.com/LogiTorch/logitorch

Proceedings of the The 2022 Conference on Empirical Methods in Natural Language Processing: System Demonstrations, pages 250 - 257
December 7-11, 2022

have been validated by subjecting them to the same experiments as the original papers, with comparable results. More models and benchmarks are in preparation. LogiTorch works on top of PyTorch (Paszke et al., 2019), and uses the Transformers library. It also includes utility functions used for preprocessing, such as coreference resolution and discourse delimitation.

The rest of the paper is organized as follows. Section 2 discusses the design and components of LogiTorch, and describes the datasets, utility functions, and models. Section 3 shows the experimental results of our implemented models on different logical reasoning tasks. We conclude in Section 4.

2 LogiTorch

LogiTorch is our Python library for logical reasoning on natural language text. Figure 1 shows the tree structure of our library. It is built on top of PyTorch and consists of 5 parts:

Datasets. We gathered different logical reasoning datasets that allow users to evaluate the reasoning capabilities of deep learning models on natural language. Once a dataset is called from LogiTorch, it is downloaded, and wrapped into an object that inherits the Dataset class of PyTorch. This means that all datasets are accessible via the same interface. We describe the datasets in detail in Section 2.1.

Data Collators. Different models require different preprocessing steps for the same data and same task: one model may work on numerical vectors, the other on textual input. Hence, we designed, for each pair of a dataset and a model, a data collator that brings the dataset into the format required by the model.

Utilities. Some models require supplementary features in addition to the input text. For example, the DAGN model (Huang et al., 2021) requires the discourse structure of the input in order to create a logical graph representation of it. For such cases, LogiTorch provides different utility functions, most notably for discourse structure analysis, coreference resolution, and logical expression extraction, which we discuss in Section 2.2.

Models. LogiTorch provides several deep learning models that have been designed to perform logical reasoning tasks such as proof generation and textual entailment. For each model, we either provide an implementation from scratch, or a wrapper over its original implementation. For the transformer-based models, we use the Transformers library from HuggingFace for the implementation of the models. We describe the models in detail in Section 2.3.

```
LogiTorch
├── datasets
│   ├── qa
│   ├── mcqa
│   ├── proof_qa
│   └── te
├── data_collators
├── utilities
├── models
└── pl_models
```

Figure 1: Tree structure of LogiTorch

PyTorch Lightning Models. For each implemented model, we also provide a PyTorch Lightning version. It includes the model, the optimizer, the training loop, and the validation evaluation. For example, the PRover model (Saha et al., 2020) has a PyTorch Lightning version called PLPRover. This allows users to play with features such as multi-GPU and fast-low precision training without modifying the training loop.

2.1 Datasets

The current implemented datasets focus on evaluating the reasoning capabilities of deep learning models. They cover four tasks: Multiple Choice Question Answering (MCQA), Question Answering (QA), Proof Generation, and Textual Entailment (TE). Table 1 shows the task and the number of instances of each dataset. Let us now describe each task and the associated datasets.

Multiple Choice Question Answering (MCQA) is the task of choosing the correct answer to a question from a list of possible answers. Here is an example taken from the LogiQA dataset (Liu et al., 2021b):

> **Context:** David knows Mr. Zhang's friend Jack, and Jack knows David's friend Ms. Lin. Everyone of them who knows Jack has a master's degree, and everyone of them who knows Ms. Lin is from Shanghai.
> **Question:** Who is from Shanghai and has a master's degree?
> **Choices:** (A) David (B) Jack (C) Mr. Zhang (D) Ms. Lin

We implement the following MCQA datasets,

Dataset	Task	Training Instances	Validation Instances	Testing Instances
AR-LSAT	MCQA	1,630	231	230
ReClor	MCQA	4,368	500	1,000
LogiQA	MCQA	7,376	651	651
RuleTaker	QA	587,922	84,030	173,496
ProofWriter	QA/Proof Generation	585,860	85,520	174,180
ParaRules Plus	QA	360,000	64,658	10,798
AbductionRules	QA	80,024	11,432	22,928
ConTRoL	TE	6,719	799	805
SNLI	TE	550,152	10,000	10,000
MNLI	TE	392,702	20,000	20,000
RTE	TE	2,490	277	3,000
Negated SNLI	TE	-	-	1,500
Negated MNLI	TE	-	-	1,500
Negated RTE	TE	-	-	1,500

Table 1: Datasets implemented in LogiTorch

which all require reasoning capabilities to choose the correct answer:
AR-LSAT (Zhong et al., 2021) is a dataset that was constructed by selecting the analytical reasoning section of 90 LSAT exams from 1991 to 2016.
LogiQA (Liu et al., 2021b) assesses the logical deductive ability of language models for the case where the correct answer to a question is not explicitly included in the question. The corpus includes paragraph-question pairs translated from the National Civil Servants Examination of China.
ReCloR (Yu et al., 2019) is a corpus consisting of questions retrieved from standardized exams such as LSAT and GMAT. To adequately evaluate a model without allowing it to take advantage of artifacts in the corpus, the testing set is split into two sets: the EASY set where the instances are biased, and the HARD set where they are not.

Question Answering (QA) is the task of answering a question given a context. Here is an example:

> **Context:** Erin is young. Erin is not kind. If someone is young and not kind then they are big.
> **Question:** Erin is big ?
> **Answer:** True

Again, we implement the QA datasets that focus on reasoning:
RuleTaker (Clark et al., 2021) is a set of many datasets to evaluate the deductive ability of language models. Each dataset consists of facts and rules and a boolean question. The model has to perform logical deductions from the rules and facts in order to answer the question. The dataset includes synthetically generated subsets that require different depths of reasoning, i.e., different numbers of deduction steps to answer a question. The dataset also includes the Bird dataset (which showcases McCarthy's problem of abnormality (McCarthy, 1986)), the Electricity dataset (which simulates the functions of an appliance), and the ParaRules corpus (where crowd workers paraphrased sentences such as "Bob is cold" to "In the snow sits Bob, crying from being cold").
ParaRules Plus (Bao, 2021) is an improved version of ParaRules (Clark et al., 2021). It has more examples for the instances with larger reasoning depths.
AbductionRules (Young et al., 2022) is a dataset that evaluates the abductive reasoning capabilities of language models. It is generated similarly to ParaRule Plus, but in this task, the model has to generate an answer to explain an observation.

Proof Generation is an extension of the QA task, where each answer has to be accompanied by a proof. Here is an example:

> **Context:** Fact 1: Erin is young.
> Fact 2: Erin is not kind.
> Rule1: If someone is young and not kind then they are big.
> **Question:** Erin is big ?
> **Answer:** True
> **Proof:** (Fact 1 & Fact 2) $\rightarrow$ Rule 1

We have one dataset so far, **ProofWriter** (Tafjord et al., 2021), which was designed similarly to the RuleTaker datasets. However, the ProofWriter dataset contains proofs for the answer of each question. Furthermore, there is a variant of the dataset that considers the open-world assumption.

Textual Entailment (TE, also RTE) is the task of predicting whether a premise entails or contradicts

```python
import pytorch_lightning as pl
from pytorch_lightning.callbacks import ModelCheckpoint
from torch.utils.data.dataloader import DataLoader

from logitorch.data_collators.ruletaker_collator import RuleTakerCollator
from logitorch.datasets.qa.ruletaker_dataset import RuleTakerDataset
from logitorch.pl_models.ruletaker import PLRuleTaker

train_dataset = RuleTakerDataset("depth-5", "train")
val_dataset = RuleTakerDataset("depth-5", "val")

ruletaker_collate_fn = RuleTakerCollator()

train_dataloader = DataLoader(train_dataset, batch_size=32, collate_fn=ruletaker_collate_fn)
val_dataloader = DataLoader(val_dataset, batch_size=32, collate_fn=ruletaker_collate_fn)

model = PLRuleTaker(learning_rate=1e-5, weight_decay=0.1)

checkpoint_callback = ModelCheckpoint(
    save_top_k=1,
    monitor="val_loss",
    mode="min",
    dirpath="models/",
    filename="best_ruletaker.ckpt",
)
trainer = pl.Trainer(callbacks=[checkpoint_callback], accelerator="gpu", gpus=1)
trainer.fit(model, train_dataloader, val_dataloader)
```

Listing 1: Training the RuleTaker Model

```python
from logitorch.pl_models.ruletaker import PLRuleTaker

model = PLRuleTaker.load_from_checkpoint("models/best_ruletaker.ckpt")

context = "Bob is smart. If someone is smart then he is kind."
question = "Bob is kind."

model.predict(context, question)
```

Listing 2: Predicting with the RuleTaker Model

a hypothesis. Here is an example:

> **Premise:** The two boys are in martial arts poses in an outside basketball court.
> **Hypothesis:** The two boys are not outdoors.
> **Answer:** Contradiction

SNLI (Bowman et al., 2015) is a large human-annotated corpus of premise-hypothesis pairs that are labeled with "entailment", "contradiction", or "neutral". The premises of this dataset are image captions from Flickr30k, while its hypotheses were generated by human annotators.

MNLI (Williams et al., 2018) is a large dataset that was labeled in the same way as SNLI. However, unlike SNLI, MNLI covers different text genres such as fiction, telephone speech, and letters. It also has longer instances.

RTE (Dagan et al., 2005; Haim et al., 2006; Giampiccolo et al., 2007, 2008; Bentivogli et al., 2009) is a much smaller dataset than SNLI and MNLI. It has just two classes, "entailment" and "non-entailment".

Negated TE (Hossain et al., 2020) is a testing set of benchmarks to evaluate the understanding of negation in language models. Each negated benchmark was created by randomly selecting 500 premise-hypothesis pairs from SNLI, MNLI, and RTE datasets and introducing the negation "not". For each pair, three new pairs were generated (negated premise/hypothesis, premise/negated hypothesis, and negated premise/negated hypothesis).

ConTRoL (Liu et al., 2021a) is a dataset of context-hypothesis pairs to evaluate contextual reasoning capabilities over long texts. In contrast to other TE datasets, the corpus consists of passage-long premises, and it evaluates different types of reasoning such as analytical or temporal reasoning, which makes this task more challenging.

2.2 Utilities

LogiTorch implements several utility functions that can be used for feature engineering:

Coreference Resolution is the task of finding all mentions in a text that refer to the same entity. For example, in "Zidane is one of the best footballers. He won the World Cup in 1998", the words "Zidane" and "he" refer to the same person. Coreference resolution is used by the Focal Reasoner model (Ouyang et al., 2021) to construct a graph of fact triples, where the same mentions are connected with an undirected edge. In LogiTorch, we implemented a wrapper over a finetuned SpanBERT (Joshi et al., 2020) for coreference resolution.

Logical Expression Extraction is the task of extracting a logical representation from a text, in order to infer new logical expressions. For example, the sentence "If you have no keyboarding skills, you will not be able to use a computer" can be split into α = "you have no keyboarding skills" and β = "you are not be able to use a computer". The sentence can then be rewritten as $\alpha \rightarrow \beta$. From this, we can infer by transposition that $\neg\beta \rightarrow \neg\alpha$, which corresponds to "If you are able to use a computer, you have keyboarding skills". The LReasoner model (Wang et al., 2022) uses this utility function to extend the input with logical expressions. In LogiTorch, we developed a wrapper over the code provided by LReasoner for this purpose.

Discourse Delimitation is the task of splitting a text into elementary discourse units (EDU). It is used for the rhetorical structure theory (RST), in which it is a tree representation of a text where the leaves are EDUs, and the edges are rhetorical relations. For example, "A signal in a pure analog system can be infinitely detailed, while digital systems cannot produce signals that are more precise than their digital unit" is split into two EDUs: "A signal in a pure analog system can be infinitely detailed", and "digital systems cannot produce signals that are more precise than their digital unit". The DAGN model (Huang et al., 2021) requires EDUs to construct a graph of discourse units.

2.3 Models

LogiTorch currently implements four models:

RuleTaker (QA task) (Clark et al., 2021) is a RoBERTa-Large model (Liu et al., 2019) that has been finetuned first on the RACE dataset (Lai et al., 2017), and then finetuned again for rule-based reasoning. The model takes as input facts and rules and a boolean question. The output is either True or False. The RoBERTa model has a similar architecture to BERT, but performs better on many NLP tasks. This is because it is pretrained for a longer period, with large batches, and on a larger dataset. The pretraining task is only the Masked Language Modeling (MLM) task, but the masked tokens are changed after each training epoch.

ProofWriter (QA and proof generation) (Tafjord et al., 2021) is a T5 model (Raffel et al., 2020) finetuned to perform rule-based reasoning. It takes as input facts and rules and a question. The output is either True, False, or Unknown (if the trained dataset considers the open-world assumption). T5 is a text-to-text transfer transformer that was pretrained on a variety of NLP problems such as textual entailment, coreference resolution, linguistic acceptability, and semantic equivalence.

PRover (QA and proof generation) (Saha et al., 2020) is built on RoBERTa with three modules: the QA module, Node module, and Edge module. The QA module is responsible for answering a question as either True or False. The Node and Edge modules are responsible for generating proofs. The Node module predicts the relevant rules and facts used to generate the answer, and the Edge module predicts the link between two relevant facts and between a relevant fact and a relevant rule.

BERTNOT (TE task) (Hosseini et al., 2021) is a BERT model that is pretrained using the unlikelihood loss and knowledge distillation functions for the MLM task to model negation. Then it is finetuned on textual entailment tasks. This model is more robust on examples containing negations, and performs better on the negated NLI dataset than the original BERT.

Future releases will include newer models such as LReasoner (Huang et al., 2021), Focal Reasoner (Ouyang et al., 2021), AdaLoGN (Li et al., 2022), Logiformer (Xu et al., 2022), and LogiGAN (Pi et al., 2022).

2.4 Library Usage

Listing 1 shows a detailed example of how a model can be trained on a rule-based reasoning dataset for QA. The RuleTaker model is trained on its corresponding dataset. In Lines 9-10, we initialize the training and validation datasets with the RuleTakerDataset. We specify which sub-dataset and which split we want to use. In Line 12, we initialize the RuleTaker data collator for preprocessing the datasets. We then use the Dataloader to pre-load the datasets and use them as batches. In Line 17, we initialize the PyTorch Lightning version of RuleTaker and specify the learning rate, and the weight decay. PyTorch Lightning provides the ModelCheckpoint, which allows monitoring the validation loss and saving the best model. In Line 26, we use the PyTorch Lightning's Trainer to automate the training loop. It takes several parameters, including the accelerator, which allows training on different de-

Depth	RuleTaker[1]		PRover[2]		ProofWriter[2]	
	LogiTorch	*Original*	*LogiTorch*	*Original*	*LogiTorch*	*Original*[3]
0	99.9	100	100	100	99.9	100
1	98.6	98.4	99.7	99.0	98.0	99.1
2	99.1	98.4	99.5	98.8	96.7	98.6
3	99.2	98.9	99.7	99.1	97.2	98.5
4	99.7	99.2	99.7	98.8	98.1	98.7
5	99.3	99.8	99.5	99.3	99.1	99.3
All	99.3	99.2	99.7	99.3	98.4	99.2

Table 2: Accuracies of different models for the QA task at different reasoning depths. [1] Depth-5 of the testing set of RuleTaker dataset. [2] Depth-5 of the testing set of ProofWriter dataset. [3] The original implementation uses a (more powerful) T5-11B model.

vices such as CPUs, GPUs, and TPUs. Finally, we train the model with the fit function. Future releases will also provide pre-configured pipelines to train models.

Listing 2 shows the code for testing the best-saved model of Listing 1. In Line 3, we load the best model. In Line 8, we use the predict function, which takes as input a context and a question, and predicts either 0 (for False) or 1 (for True).

Dataset		*LogiTorch's BERTNOT*	*Original BERTNOT*
SNLI	Val	90.4	89.00
	Neg	47.8	45.96
MNLI	Val	83.2	84.31
	Neg	64.0	60.89
RTE	Val	65.6	69.68
	Neg	57.7	74.47

Table 3: Results of our BERTNOT implementation on different textual-entailment datasets.

3 Evaluation

We compared the performance of each model in LogiTorch to the performance of the model in the original paper on the same datasets: we trained the Ruletaker model on the training set of RuleTaker with language reasoning paths up to depth 5 and tested it on its testing set; we trained the PRover and ProofWriter models on the training set of ProofWriter with language reasoning paths up to depth 5 and tested them on the corresponding testing set; and we trained the BERTNOT model (a pretrained BERT Base Cased model) on the MLM task, with the negated Wikipedia corpus provided by Hosseini et al. (2021) (included in LogiTorch), finetuned the model on each TE dataset (MNLI, SNLI, and RTE) and tested it on its negated counterparts (Hossain et al., 2020). All models use the same settings as in the original papers.

Table 2 shows the results of the three different models on the QA task at different reasoning depths. Our model implementations achieve near-perfect accuracies, which are comparable to the performance in the original papers. Table 3 shows the performance on the TE task on each TE training dataset (SNLI, MNLI, and RTE). Again, our model achieves nearly the same results as reported in the original paper (Hosseini et al., 2021) on the MNLI and SNLI datasets. We are getting lower results on the RTE dataset. We assume that this is because the finetuned model has a high variance due to the small size of the training set of RTE.

4 Conclusion

We have introduced LogiTorch, a Python library for logical reasoning on natural language. It is built on top of PyTorch in combination with the Transformers and PyTorch Lightning libraries. LogiTorch includes an extensive list of textual logical reasoning datasets and utility functions, and different implemented models. The library allows researchers and developers to easily use logical reasoning datasets and train logical reasoning models with just a few lines of code. The library is available on GitHub and is under active development.

For future work, we will add new datasets, and implement models such as DAGN, Focal Reasoner, and LogiGAN with their utility functions for feature engineering. Finally, we want to invite researchers and developers to contribute to LogiTorch. We believe that such a library will lower the hurdles to research in the area, foster re-usability, encourage comparative evaluation, strengthen reproducibility, and advance the culture of open software and data.

Acknowledgements. This work was partially funded by ANR-20-CHIA-0012-01 ("NoRDF").

5 Ethical Considerations

Users of LogiTorch should distinguish the datasets and models of our library from the originals. They should always credit and cite both our library and the original data source, as in "We used LogiTorch's (Helwe et al., 2022) re-implementation of BERTNOT (Hosseini et al., 2021)". These conditions are mentioned on our GitHub page.

References

Qiming Bao. 2021. Pararule plus: A larger deep multi-step reasoning dataset over natural language.

Luisa Bentivogli, Peter Clark, Ido Dagan, and Danilo Giampiccolo. 2009. The fifth pascal recognizing textual entailment challenge. In *TAC*.

Samuel Bowman, Gabor Angeli, Christopher Potts, and Christopher D Manning. 2015. A large annotated corpus for learning natural language inference. In *Conference on Empirical Methods in Natural Language Processing*.

Tom Brown, Benjamin Mann, Nick Ryder, Melanie Subbiah, Jared D Kaplan, Prafulla Dhariwal, Arvind Neelakantan, Pranav Shyam, Girish Sastry, Amanda Askell, et al. 2020. Language models are few-shot learners. *Advances in neural information processing systems*, 33:1877–1901.

Peter Clark, Oyvind Tafjord, and Kyle Richardson. 2021. Transformers as soft reasoners over language. In *Proceedings of the Twenty-Ninth International Conference on International Joint Conferences on Artificial Intelligence*, pages 3882–3890.

Ido Dagan, Oren Glickman, and Bernardo Magnini. 2005. The pascal recognising textual entailment challenge. In *Machine Learning Challenges Workshop*.

Jacob Devlin, Ming-Wei Chang, Kenton Lee, and Kristina Toutanova. 2019. BERT: Pre-training of deep bidirectional transformers for language understanding. In *Proceedings of the 2019 Conference of the North American Chapter of the Association for Computational Linguistics: Human Language Technologies, Volume 1 (Long and Short Papers)*, pages 4171–4186, Minneapolis, Minnesota. Association for Computational Linguistics.

Allyson Ettinger. 2020. What bert is not: Lessons from a new suite of psycholinguistic diagnostics for language models. *Transactions of the Association for Computational Linguistics*.

Danilo Giampiccolo, Hoa Trang Dang, Bernardo Magnini, Ido Dagan, Elena Cabrio, and Bill Dolan. 2008. The fourth pascal recognizing textual entailment challenge. In *TAC*.

Danilo Giampiccolo, Bernardo Magnini, Ido Dagan, and William B Dolan. 2007. The third pascal recognizing textual entailment challenge. In *ACL-PASCAL workshop on textual entailment and paraphrasing*.

R Bar Haim, Ido Dagan, Bill Dolan, Lisa Ferro, Danilo Giampiccolo, Bernardo Magnini, and Idan Szpektor. 2006. The second pascal recognising textual entailment challenge. In *The Second PASCAL Challenges Workshop on Recognising Textual Entailment*.

Chadi Helwe, Chloé Clavel, and Fabian Suchanek. 2022. Logitorch: A pytorch-based library for logical reasoning on natural language. In *Proceedings of the 2022 Conference on Empirical Methods in Natural Language Processing: System Demonstrations*.

Chadi Helwe, Chloé Clavel, and Fabian M Suchanek. 2021. Reasoning with transformer-based models: Deep learning, but shallow reasoning. In *3rd Conference on Automated Knowledge Base Construction*.

Md Mosharaf Hossain, Dhivya Chinnappa, and Eduardo Blanco. 2022. An analysis of negation in natural language understanding corpora. In *Annual Meeting of the Association for Computational Linguistics*.

Md Mosharaf Hossain, Venelin Kovatchev, Pranoy Dutta, Tiffany Kao, Elizabeth Wei, and Eduardo Blanco. 2020. An analysis of natural language inference benchmarks through the lens of negation. In *Proceedings of the 2020 Conference on Empirical Methods in Natural Language Processing (EMNLP)*, pages 9106–9118.

Arian Hosseini, Siva Reddy, Dzmitry Bahdanau, R Devon Hjelm, Alessandro Sordoni, and Aaron Courville. 2021. Understanding by understanding not: Modeling negation in language models. In *North American Chapter of the Association for Computational Linguistics: Human Language Technologies*.

Yinya Huang, Meng Fang, Yu Cao, Liwei Wang, and Xiaodan Liang. 2021. Dagn: Discourse-aware graph network for logical reasoning. In *Proceedings of the 2021 Conference of the North American Chapter of the Association for Computational Linguistics: Human Language Technologies*, pages 5848–5855.

Mandar Joshi, Danqi Chen, Yinhan Liu, Daniel S Weld, Luke Zettlemoyer, and Omer Levy. 2020. Spanbert: Improving pre-training by representing and predicting spans. *Transactions of the Association for Computational Linguistics*, 8:64–77.

Nora Kassner and Hinrich Schütze. 2020. Negated and misprimed probes for pretrained language models: Birds can talk, but cannot fly. In *Annual Meeting of the Association for Computational Linguistics*.

Guokun Lai, Qizhe Xie, Hanxiao Liu, Yiming Yang, and Eduard Hovy. 2017. Race: Large-scale reading comprehension dataset from examinations. In *Proceedings of the 2017 Conference on Empirical Methods in Natural Language Processing*, pages 785–794.

Xiao Li, Gong Cheng, Ziheng Chen, Yawei Sun, and Yuzhong Qu. 2022. Adalogn: Adaptive logic graph network for reasoning-based machine reading comprehension. In *Proceedings of the 60th Annual Meeting of the Association for Computational Linguistics (Volume 1: Long Papers)*, pages 7147–7161.

Hanmeng Liu, Leyang Cui, Jian Liu, and Yue Zhang. 2021a. Natural language inference in context-investigating contextual reasoning over long texts. In *Proceedings of the AAAI Conference on Artificial Intelligence*, volume 35, pages 13388–13396.

Jian Liu, Leyang Cui, Hanmeng Liu, Dandan Huang, Yile Wang, and Yue Zhang. 2021b. Logiqa: a challenge dataset for machine reading comprehension with logical reasoning. In *Proceedings of the Twenty-Ninth International Conference on International Joint Conferences on Artificial Intelligence*, pages 3622–3628.

Yinhan Liu, Myle Ott, Naman Goyal, Jingfei Du, Mandar Joshi, Danqi Chen, Omer Levy, Mike Lewis, Luke Zettlemoyer, and Veselin Stoyanov. 2019. Roberta: A robustly optimized bert pretraining approach. *arXiv preprint arXiv:1907.11692*.

John McCarthy. 1986. Applications of circumscription to formalizing common-sense knowledge. *Artificial intelligence*, 28(1):89–116.

John McCarthy et al. 1960. *Programs with common sense*. RLE and MIT computation center Cambridge, MA, USA.

Allen Newell and Herbert Simon. 1956. The logic theory machine–a complex information processing system. *IRE Transactions on information theory*, 2(3):61–79.

Timothy Niven and Hung-Yu Kao. 2019. Probing neural network comprehension of natural language arguments. In *Annual Meeting of the Association for Computational Linguistics*.

Siru Ouyang, Zhuosheng Zhang, and Hai Zhao. 2021. Fact-driven logical reasoning. *arXiv preprint arXiv:2105.10334*.

Adam Paszke, Sam Gross, Francisco Massa, Adam Lerer, James Bradbury, Gregory Chanan, Trevor Killeen, Zeming Lin, Natalia Gimelshein, Luca Antiga, et al. 2019. Pytorch: An imperative style, high-performance deep learning library. *Advances in neural information processing systems*, 32.

Xinyu Pi, Wanjun Zhong, Yan Gao, Nan Duan, and Jian-Guang Lou. 2022. Logigan: Learning logical reasoning via adversarial pre-training. *arXiv preprint arXiv:2205.08794*.

Peng Qi, Yuhao Zhang, Yuhui Zhang, Jason Bolton, and Christopher D. Manning. 2020. Stanza: A Python natural language processing toolkit for many human languages.

Colin Raffel, Noam Shazeer, Adam Roberts, Katherine Lee, Sharan Narang, Michael Matena, Yanqi Zhou, Wei Li, Peter J Liu, et al. 2020. Exploring the limits of transfer learning with a unified text-to-text transformer. *J. Mach. Learn. Res.*, 21(140):1–67.

Swarnadeep Saha, Sayan Ghosh, Shashank Srivastava, and Mohit Bansal. 2020. Prover: Proof generation for interpretable reasoning over rules. In *Proceedings of the 2020 Conference on Empirical Methods in Natural Language Processing (EMNLP)*, pages 122–136.

Oyvind Tafjord, Bhavana Dalvi, and Peter Clark. 2021. Proofwriter: Generating implications, proofs, and abductive statements over natural language. In *Findings of the Association for Computational Linguistics: ACL-IJCNLP 2021*, pages 3621–3634.

Siyuan Wang, Wanjun Zhong, Duyu Tang, Zhongyu Wei, Zhihao Fan, Daxin Jiang, Ming Zhou, and Nan Duan. 2022. Logic-driven context extension and data augmentation for logical reasoning of text. In *Findings of the Association for Computational Linguistics: ACL 2022*, pages 1619–1629.

Adina Williams, Nikita Nangia, and Samuel Bowman. 2018. A broad-coverage challenge corpus for sentence understanding through inference. In *Conference of the North American Chapter of the Association for Computational Linguistics: Human Language Technologies*.

Thomas Wolf, Lysandre Debut, Victor Sanh, Julien Chaumond, Clement Delangue, Anthony Moi, Pierric Cistac, Tim Rault, Rémi Louf, Morgan Funtowicz, et al. 2020. Transformers: State-of-the-art natural language processing. In *Proceedings of the 2020 conference on empirical methods in natural language processing: system demonstrations*, pages 38–45.

Fangzhi Xu, Jun Liu, Qika Lin, Yudai Pan, and Lingling Zhang. 2022. Logiformer: A two-branch graph transformer network for interpretable logical reasoning. In *Proceedings of the 45th International ACM SIGIR Conference on Research and Development in Information Retrieval*, pages 1055–1065.

Nathan Young, Qiming Bao, Joshua Bensemann, and Michael Witbrock. 2022. Abductionrules: Training transformers to explain unexpected inputs. *arXiv preprint arXiv:2203.12186*.

Weihao Yu, Zihang Jiang, Yanfei Dong, and Jiashi Feng. 2019. Reclor: A reading comprehension dataset requiring logical reasoning. In *International Conference on Learning Representations*.

Wanjun Zhong, Siyuan Wang, Duyu Tang, Zenan Xu, Daya Guo, Jiahai Wang, Jian Yin, Ming Zhou, and Nan Duan. 2021. Ar-lsat: Investigating analytical reasoning of text. *arXiv preprint arXiv:2104.06598*.

`stopes` - Modular Machine Translation Pipelines

Pierre Andrews[*] and **Guillaume Wenzek**[*] and **Kevin Heffernan**[*] and **Onur Çelebi**[*]
and Anna Sun and Ammar Kamran and Yingzhe Guo
and Alexandre Mourachko and Holger Schwenk and Angela Fan

Meta AI / mortimer@fb.com

Abstract

Neural machine translation, as other natural language deep learning applications, is hungry for data. As research evolves, the data pipelines supporting that research evolve too, oftentimes re-implementing the same core components. Despite the potential of modular codebases, researchers have but little time to put code structure and reusability first. Unfortunately, this makes it very hard to publish clean, reproducible code to benefit a wider audience. In this paper, we motivate and describe `stopes` , a framework that addresses these issues while empowering scalability and versatility for research use cases. This library was a key enabler of the No Language Left Behind project, establishing new state of the art performance for a multilingual machine translation model covering 200 languages. `stopes` and the pipelines described are released under the MIT license at `https://github.com/facebookresearch/stopes`.

1 Introduction

Machine translation (MT) aims at removing language barriers in our connected society. The current trend in the MT research field is moving towards using deep machine learning models training either many bi-lingual models, translating between a single pair of languoids, or multi-lingual models that handle many languoids at once. Training data usually comes from open aligned data sources such as Barrault et al. (2020), Schwenk et al. (2021) or raw web corpora like CommonCrawl (CC). Recently, initiatives like (Bapna et al., 2022) and the No Language Left Behind project (NLLB Team et al., 2022) strive to extend the scope of supported languoids by training on large scale datasets, reaching over 18 and 25 billion sentence pairs respectively.

The end-to-end process of developing and iterating on a neural machine translation model involves a lot of large scale steps. Getting large amounts of data prepared for translation training usually starts with raw monolingual data composed of unaligned sentences for each languoid of interest. This web data is usually processed, cleaned, and finally "mined" to be aligned in pairs of translated sentences (see 5.2). It is then tokenized and transformed into a format that can be used for training. Once trained, the machine translation model is evaluated using benchmark datasets, on which the exact same pre-processing has to be applied. Large translation models are often later distilled to produce smaller models suitable for practical production usecases (see 5.3).

In research use cases, the main focus is on getting results fast. We have observed that the path of predilection is to build ad-hoc solutions to solve the problem directly at hand, often adapting older scripts or copying snippets of code that colleagues have found to work. This enables quick iteration on research ideas but it causes a lot of problems on the long term:

1. Scaling and data processing throughput is often an after-though.
2. Ad-hoc scripts are built with the idiosyncrasies of each users and experiment, making it hard to share research pipelines or adapt to different hardware setups.
3. Open-sourcing research and making it reproducible by third parties becomes a task of itself, ensuring scripts will run properly in different environment and without failed experimental code/setup (Pineau et al., 2021; Ulmer et al., 2022).
4. When working with disjoint scripts, researchers spend a lot of time "baby sitting" execution, making sure one script runs properly and waiting for it to finish before moving to the next step in their pipeline.

[*]Lead Library Maintainers.

Proceedings of the The 2022 Conference on Empirical Methods in Natural Language Processing: System Demonstrations, pages 258 - 265
December 7-11, 2022

We present a new framework, `stopes`, that was developed to solve some of the problems discussed in the scope of the No Language Left Behind (NLLB) (NLLB Team et al., 2022) machine translation project to process billions of sentences in over 200 languages. The goal of the framework is to ensure a good separation between the hardware setup and the core logic of the data processing by proposing a clean API for sharing commonly used processing steps, while enforcing consistent and shareable configurations of experiments. `stopes` can scale to a research project like NLLB, but is built to be versatile and can be applied to other research use cases, `https://facebookresearch.github.io/stopes/docs/quickstart` provides an example of running this on a smaller dataset. In section 3, we introduce the design of this python library, with concrete examples in section 4. Section 5 discusses applications within the NLLB where `stopes` is used.

2 Related Work

While large scale data processing architectures already exist, they are often optimized for production use cases. Spark (Spark), ray (Ray) or beam (Beam) are a few leading examples. These frameworks have a steep learning curve and do not always map easily to research clusters' setup or researchers' work habits. They can also prove very challenging to use with nascent research ideas and tools, whose codebases are not yet stable or production-ready. Bitextor (Bitextor) provides a bitext mining pipeline built in python, but it lacks modularity and requires learning the complex APIs of snakemake.

With `stopes`, we are aiming for a "minimal API surface" without sacrificing features, providing a clean yet versatile API that can be used as if writing standard python scripts (see Section ref-sec:example). This simple API has its drawbacks, but it makes it easier to pick up for researchers than complex graph planning systems like Luigi (Luigi) and AirFlow (AirFlow), These industry standards are better suited for production pipelines that do not change often and are maintainted by production teams. Spacy (Spacy) provides research oriented NLP pipelines, but is less flexible than `stopes` as our framework is more geared towards describing sometimes pipelines in pure python.

3 Framework

The general architecture of `stopes` is geared towards pipelines that can be run as separate, sometimes interdependent, jobs on a cluster or in multiprocessing. The idea being that a pipeline can be divided in a set of separate steps that can be expressed as processing units. Jobs can be sent to a job scheduler, like SLURM (Slurm), which is widespread on academic compute clusters or FBLearner (Dunn, 2016), which Meta uses for distributed machine learning pipelines; or run locally on a single computer depending on the data scale.

The idea behind the `stopes` framework is to make it easy to build reproducible pipelines. This is done though *modules*, a module is just a python class with a `run` function that executes something. A module can then be scheduled with the `stopes`' *launcher*, this will decide where the code gets executed (locally or on a cluster) and then wait for the results to be ready.

3.1 Concepts

module: Encapsulate a reusable single step of a neural network pipeline and its requirements. The step is assumed to be able to execute on its own given some inputs and eventually generates an output. Modules will most often be executed as an isolated job, so should not depend on anything other than its own configuration (e.g. no global variables or odd i/o dependencies). This ensures that each module can be ran separately, or in parallel if possible. A module's configuration serves the purpose of defining a clear API of the step.

pipeline: A python function which connects `stopes` modules together for some end-to-end purpose. Pipelines may contain non-module logic to help with intermediate functionality, and are primarily structured like functions as opposed to `stopes` modules which resemble python callables. In some cases, pipelines may also call other pipelines in intermediate steps.

launcher: The orchestrator of your pipeline. The power of `stopes` comes from the *launcher* that will manage the execution of the modules, find the correct machines with matching requirements (if executing on a cluster), and deal with memoization (see below). The launcher abstracts the execution/scheduling of modules as it looks like any asyncio function and can be called like a python function and utilized in conjunction with regular python code.

3.2 Configuration

When running experiments in machine translation, we often change how the data is processed or what data we ingest. For instance, we might want to change the vocabulary size, which would require retraining a tokenization model (e.g. sentence-piece[1] or BPE (Sennrich et al., 2016)). To keep track of experiments and ensure reproducibility, all parameters that can influence the results need to be stored in configuration files that can easily be shared with other researchers.

`stopes` makes it easy to keep track of configurations as it leverages the hydra configuration system (Yadan, 2019) as inputs for modules and pipelines. This guarantees proper tracking of configurations through the execution of a pipeline, but also brings extra technical benefits to the end user:

1. New configurations can be composed from existing configuration files, allowing for better organization of all steps within a pipeline.
2. Any part of a configuration can be overridden at runtime and across multiple runs. This makes it easy, for example, to change what cluster the code is running on, what model architecture is used for training, or what tokenization approach is used.

3.3 Caching/Memoization

As we can see in Section 5, machine translation research pipelines are complex and involve a lot of steps. When repeating these steps over many languoids, some of the jobs executing the pipeline are bound to fail. Failure is common when executing large pipelines over long periods of time, jobs might timeout in the cluster queue, disk might fail because of IO pressure and machines might go down for maintenance.

It is therefore very important to be able to rerun a pipeline over and over and not have to start from the scratch. To avoid this, `stopes` memoizes the output of each module runs based on its input configuration. If the module is re-run with the same configuration, `stopes` will recover the results from disk instead of re-running. This can be seen as a cache of the results, indexed on the input configuration of each module. The exact cache invalidation logic can be manually tuned by the user to accommodate more complex situations.

This is also very practical when iterating on configuration driven experiments as `stopes` will figure out automatically what steps of the pipeline needs to be re-run when the configuration changes, keeping track of identical steps in the pipeline that were not affected by the experimental configuration change and re-using cached results.

4 Example Code

Figure 1 shows a sample usage of the `stopes` library[2] to build a FAISS index[3]. FAISS (Johnson et al., 2019) is a tool that can be used to build large scale indexes and perform nearest neighbor searches on them; FAISS has become a keystone to machine translation research as it allows for efficient alignment of multilingual text when using language-agnostics embeddings like Feng et al. (2020) or Heffernan et al. (2022) (e.g. Khandelwal et al. (2021) or Section 5.2). It takes tensors as input, but first the index has to be trained, usually on a sample of the data we want to store in the index.

Line 5: We initialize the `launcher` to be able to schedule modules for execution. The launcher is managed by a configuration, so we can easily change where the code is executed (SLURM cluster, aws, locally) and other constraints of the execution. Every call to 'launcher.schedule' will be managed by the designated 'launcher', sent to the cluster once, or in multiple jobs if necessary, or just retrieved from the cache if the config permits.

Line 7: We initialize an encoding module, which takes in raw text and embeds it. `stopes` provides code to embed text with LASER2 and LASER3 as well as with HuggingFace `sentence-transformers` (Reimers and Gurevych, 2019). To keep the code short, we only show the pipeline glue and not each module implementation.

Line 12: We create a sample from the embedded text files. Here, `update(config.sample, input_embeddings=embedded)` takes the module configuration from the Hydra configuration and inserts the references to the output files from the previous pipeline step. This pattern can also be seen in the other steps of this pipeline where each step is connected to the previous through intermediate output results.

[1] `https://github.com/google/sentencepiece`

[2] Modules referred to in the sample code can be found in the `stopes` open source repository.

[3] We have omitted the imports from the sample to keep it short.

```
# ... imports omitted
async def pipeline(config):
   # setup a launcher to connect jobs together
   launcher = hydra.utils.instantiate(config.launcher)
   # encode all shards
   embedded = await
       launcher.schedule(PreprocessEncodeModule(config=config.embed_text))
   # extract a sample of the embeddings
   train_sample = await launcher.schedule(
      SampleEmbeddingModule(config=update(config.sample, input_embeddings=embedded))
   )
   # train the faiss index on the sample
   trained_index = await launcher.schedule(
      TrainFAISSIndexModule(
         config=update(config.train_index, input_embeddings=train_sample)
      )
   )
   # fill the index with content
   populated_index = await launcher.schedule(
      PopulateFAISSIndexModule(
         config=update(
            config.populate_index,
            index=trained_index,
            input_embeddings=embedded,
         )
      )
   )
   print(f"Indexes are populated in: {populated_index}")


# setup main with Hydra
@hydra.main(config_path="conf", config_name="config")
def main(config: DictConfig) -> None:
   asyncio.run(pipeline(config))
```

Figure 1: Sample pipeline to build a FAISS Index with `stopes`

Lines 17 and 22: These lines use very similar logic to call different modules. As noted above, we can see the use of the configurations passed by Hydra extended with the results from the previous steps.
From this, we see that `stopes` pipeline code reads as normal python code where functions are called and pass results to each other. The core of `stopes` hides the complexity of memoization and cluster scheduling inside the simple API call to `launcher.schedule`. This makes the pipeline easy to understand and allows researcher to focus on building data processing and stay close to their research goals instead of getting bogged down in boilerplate APIs or in optimization/scaling issues.

5 Applications

The `stopes` library was used to build the major data processing pipelines that are used to build the NLLB large multilingual translation models as well as its distilled version (NLLB Team et al., 2022). These pipelines were battle tested on petabytes of data and are open-sourced at `https://github.com/facebookresearch/stopes`. In this section we discuss some of the pipelines and show how they can reuse the same modules. Source code can be found in the above github repository.

5.1 Language Identification

The production of large amount of monolingual data starts with a strong language identification (LID) model (see NLLB Team et al., 2022). The pipeline for training an LID model is a recurring archetype used commonly in neural network training pipelines for machine translation. LASER3 distillation (Heffernan et al., 2022), training NMT models for evaluation, etc., all use a similar pipeline.

The pipeline is illustrated in Figure 2 and uses the following steps:

SPM Training: Eventually, we will use a sentence-piece model (SPM) to tokenize input data for neural network training. To be able to do this tokenization, the SPM itself must be first trained

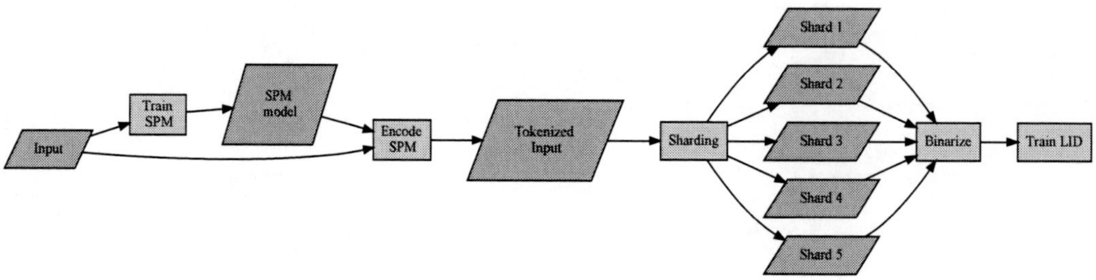

Figure 2: LID Model Training Pipeline

on a sample of data.

SPM Encoding: Once we have a trained SPM, we can apply it over all the sentences in the input data to tokenize the raw text to prepare it for training.

Sharding: This step is used to split the data into manageable shards that help distribute the pipeline work over multiple jobs, and also at the training phase to be able to fit the training data in the memory available on each training machine.

Binarization: The SPM tokenization process creates tokenized text, but the model training loop requires numerical tensors to do the neural network training. The binarization process takes each token and the SPM vocabulary to create binary tensors from the tokenized text.

Model Training: We use `fairseq` (Ott et al., 2019) and fastText (Joulin et al., 2017) to train LID models and other NMT models.

5.2 Bitext Mining

The bitext mining pipeline follows the idea introduced by Schwenk et al. (2021). The pipeline can mine pairs of sentences between two languoids given monolingual data and evaluate the mining quality. It follows the following major steps:

Monolingual Data: The base data comes from a mix of existing "clean" data (Barrault et al., 2020) and noisy web data. Most of this data is not aligned in language pairs, and often not tagged with a particular languoid. The monolingual pipeline runs a language identification (LID) model, splits text into sentences, and then cleans the text. The LID model itself is trained as discussed in Section 5.1

FAISS Indexing: FAISS (Johnson et al., 2019) is a tool to build large indexes for similarity searches. Section 4 shows a sample pipeline to build such an index. In bi-text mining, the FAISS index serves as the core tool to find similar sentences between two languoids. This works by filling the index with sentences embedded with LASER3 (Heffernan et al., 2022), which encodes sentences from different languages into the same space, so they can be clustered by FAISS. The mining pipeline then builds a separate index for each languoid, embedding all the sentences identified in the monolingual data, sampling them to train a FAISS index (i.e. to learn the clustering), and then populating the index with all the embedded sentences for that langoid.

Mining for Aligned Sentences: To align sentences between two languoids, we go over all embedded sentences from one languoid and use the cosine distances of the k-nearest neighbors in the other languoid index compute above and output alignments using a margin-based scoring measure (Artetxe and Schwenk, 2019). Once we've built indexes and embeddings for a few languages, we can run this step in parallel quite easily. `stopes` makes this trivial as it will pickup the embeddings and indexes from its cache and jump straight to the last step of the mining pipeline, without the user having to figure out what has already been pre-computed.

Evaluating Translation: There is no direct evaluation procedure to gauge mining quality. Therefore, the best way to evaluate the mining performance is to use the aligned bitext it produces to train a neural machine translation model. We focus on training bi-lingual translation models as they are faster to train and evaluate. We can then track the change in BLEU score (Papineni et al., 2002) for a given model and languoids pair to evaluate the specialized encoders and mining parameters.

Figure 3 illustrates the high level process of mining for two languoids. The figure shows the process for two languoids, but when mining for training a large language model as the one discussed in NLLB Team et al. (2022), we ran this `stopes` pipeline over 450 pairs, aligning over a billion sentences.

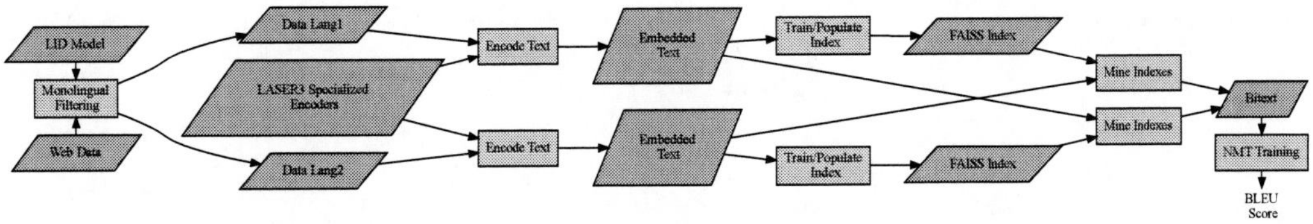

Figure 3: Mining Pipeline

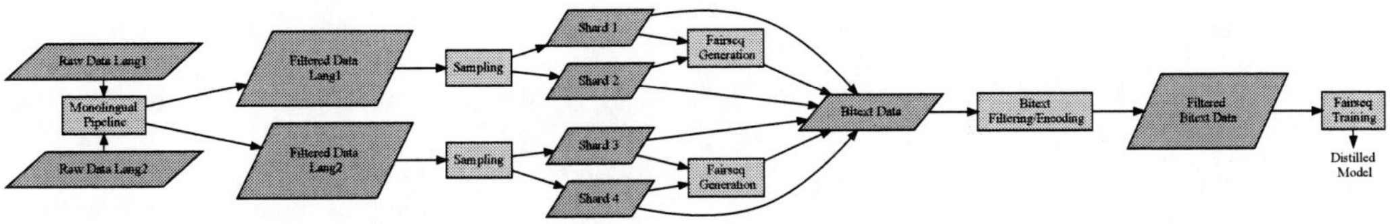

Figure 4: Distillation Pipeline

This is where the strong configuration system introduced by `stopes` comes handy as we need to manage different configurations for over two thousand pairs of languoids. Being able to write the pipeline once and scale it to many languoids through simple configuration composition and horizontal scaling on a SLURM cluster without having to rewrite core logic greatly accelerates the speed at which research is conducted. The pipeline that was used by the NLLB project is available on the `stopes` repository and can be run by anyone a "small" scale to mine data with our approach[4].

5.3 Large Model Distillation

The distillation pipeline is based on the sequence-level knowledge distillation proposed by Kim and Rush (2016), using a large pre-trained teacher model to help train a smaller student model with comparable or better performance, which is practical for inference efficiency. An overview of the steps are visualized in Figure 4 and described below:

Monolingual Data: Our monolingual source data comes from Wikipedia corpus dumps[5]. The monolingual pipeline is the same as the one described in Section 5.2.

Sampling: We sample with replacement from the monolingual dataset to ensure that we have enough target sentences for each languoid, given a fixed-size monolingual source dataset.

Generation: We use the `FairseqGenerate` module to generate translations of each shard of monolingual data by running beam search using the teacher model.

Bitext Filtering: We filter the teacher-generated bitext data to make sure the training data is high quality. We use LID and sentence length filtering to ensure that the generated data matches the target languoid and that the sentence lengths are similar.

SPM Encoding: We use a pre-trained SPM to tokenize the raw text.

Binarization: We binarize the bitext data into the format required for training in `fairseq` as described in Section 5.2.

Training: Using the binarized bitext data, we use the module `TrainFairseqModule` to train a multilingual distilled model, the final product of our pipeline.

6 Conclusion

The `stopes` framework provides a clean API to describe research pipelines for machine translation. We have shown that this is useful for developing large scale machine translation datasets and models for the No Language Left Behind project (NLLB Team et al., 2022). We believe that this framework and its reference implementations of common steps in NLP pipelines is versatile and can be used to help researchers in the field. The `stopes` framework documentation and sources can be found under the MIT license at `https://facebookresearch.github.io/stopes/` and has been tested to not require a complex cluster setup. We therefore hope that it will help other researchers focus on their research goals, and avoid time-consuming technical details not unique to their specific task.

[4]See the quickstart at `https://facebookresearch.github.io/stopes/docs/quickstart`

[5]`https://dumps.wikimedia.org/other/cirrussearch/current/`

7 Screencast Video

The demo screencast can be found at `https://fb.sharepoint.com/:f:/s/PublicContent/EsuaUW__krBJo57yDgbbbysBw5yN5txcRsjw4eY1YRFIFQ?e=tA1kVQ`.

References

Airflow. `https://github.com/apache/airflow`. Accessed: 2022-07-19.

Beam. `https://beam.apache.org/`. Accessed: 2022-07-19.

Bitextor. `https://github.com/bitextor/bitextor`. Accessed: 2022-07-19.

Common crawl. `https://commoncrawl.org/`. Accessed: 2022-07-19.

Luigi. `https://github.com/spotify/luigi`. Accessed: 2022-07-19.

Ray. `https://www.ray.io/`. Accessed: 2022-07-19.

Slurm. `https://slurm.schedmd.com/`. Accessed: 2022-07-19.

Spacy. `https://spacy.io/`. Accessed: 2022-07-19.

Spark. `https://spark.apache.org/`. Accessed: 2022-07-19.

Mikel Artetxe and Holger Schwenk. 2019. Margin-based parallel corpus mining with multilingual sentence embeddings. In *Proceedings of the 57th Annual Meeting of the Association for Computational Linguistics*, pages 3197–3203, Florence, Italy. Association for Computational Linguistics.

Ankur Bapna, Isaac Caswell, Julia Kreutzer, Orhan Firat, Daan van Esch, Aditya Siddhant, Mengmeng Niu, Pallavi Baljekar, Xavier Garcia, Wolfgang Macherey, Theresa Breiner, Vera Axelrod, Jason Riesa, Yuan Cao, Mia Xu Chen, Klaus Macherey, Maxim Krikun, Pidong Wang, Alexander Gutkin, Apurva Shah, Yanping Huang, Zhifeng Chen, Yonghui Wu, and Macduff Hughes. 2022. Building machine translation systems for the next thousand languages.

Loïc Barrault, Magdalena Biesialska, Ondřej Bojar, Marta R. Costa-jussà, Christian Federmann, Yvette Graham, Roman Grundkiewicz, Barry Haddow, Matthias Huck, Eric Joanis, Tom Kocmi, Philipp Koehn, Chi-kiu Lo, Nikola Ljubešić, Christof Monz, Makoto Morishita, Masaaki Nagata, Toshiaki Nakazawa, Santanu Pal, Matt Post, and Marcos Zampieri. 2020. Findings of the 2020 conference on machine translation (WMT20). In *Proceedings of the Fifth Conference on Machine Translation*, pages 1–55, Online. Association for Computational Linguistics.

Jeffrey Dunn. 2016. Introducing FBLearner flow: Facebook's ai backbone. `https://engineering.fb.com/2016/05/09/core-data/introducing-fblearner-flow-facebook-s-ai-backbone/`. Accessed: 2022-07-19.

Fangxiaoyu Feng, Yinfei Yang, Daniel Cer, Naveen Arivazhagan, and Wei Wang. 2020. Language-agnostic BERT sentence embedding. *CoRR*, abs/2007.01852.

Kevin Heffernan, Onur Çelebi, and Holger Schwenk. 2022. Bitext mining using distilled sentence representations for low-resource languages.

Jeff Johnson, Matthijs Douze, and Hervé Jégou. 2019. Billion-scale similarity search with GPUs. *IEEE Transactions on Big Data*, 7(3):535–547.

Armand Joulin, Edouard Grave, Piotr Bojanowski, and Tomas Mikolov. 2017. Bag of tricks for efficient text classification. In *Proceedings of the 15th Conference of the European Chapter of the Association for Computational Linguistics: Volume 2, Short Papers*, pages 427–431. Association for Computational Linguistics.

Urvashi Khandelwal, Angela Fan, Dan Jurafsky, Luke Zettlemoyer, and Mike Lewis. 2021. Nearest neighbor machine translation. In *International Conference on Learning Representations*.

Yoon Kim and Alexander M. Rush. 2016. Sequence-level knowledge distillation.

NLLB Team, Marta R. Costa-jussà, James Cross, Onur Çelebi, Maha Elbayad, Kenneth Heafield, Kevin Heffernan, Elahe Kalbassi, Janice Lam, Daniel Licht, Jean Maillard, Anna Sun, Skyler Wang, Guillaume Wenzek, Al Youngblood, Bapi Akula, Loic Barrault, Gabriel Mejia Gonzalez, Prangthip Hansanti, John Hoffman, Semarley Jarrett, Kaushik Ram Sadagopan, Dirk Rowe, Shannon Spruit, Chau Tran, Pierre Andrews, Necip Fazil Ayan, Shruti Bhosale, Sergey Edunov, Angela Fan, Cynthia Gao, Vedanuj Goswami, Francisco Guzmán, Philipp Koehn, Alexandre Mourachko, Christophe Ropers, Safiyyah Saleem, Holger Schwenk, and Jeff Wang. 2022. No language left behind: Scaling human-centered machine translation.

Myle Ott, Sergey Edunov, Alexei Baevski, Angela Fan, Sam Gross, Nathan Ng, David Grangier, and Michael Auli. 2019. fairseq: A fast, extensible toolkit for sequence modeling. In *Proceedings of NAACL-HLT 2019: Demonstrations*.

Kishore Papineni, Salim Roukos, Todd Ward, and Wei jing Zhu. 2002. Bleu: a method for automatic evaluation of machine translation. pages 311–318.

Joelle Pineau, Philippe Vincent-Lamarre, Koustuv Sinha, Vincent Larivière, Alina Beygelzimer, Florence d'Alché Buc, Emily Fox, and Hugo Larochelle. 2021. Improving reproducibility in machine learning research (a report from the neurips 2019 reproducibility program). *J. Mach. Learn. Res.*, 22(1).

Nils Reimers and Iryna Gurevych. 2019. Sentence-bert: Sentence embeddings using siamese bert-networks. In *Proceedings of the 2019 Conference on Empirical Methods in Natural Language Processing*. Association for Computational Linguistics.

Holger Schwenk, Guillaume Wenzek, Sergey Edunov, Edouard Grave, Armand Joulin, and Angela Fan. 2021. CCMatrix: Mining billions of high-quality parallel sentences on the web. In *Proceedings of the 59th Annual Meeting of the Association for Computational Linguistics and the 11th International Joint Conference on Natural Language Processing (Volume 1: Long Papers)*, pages 6490–6500, Online. Association for Computational Linguistics.

Rico Sennrich, Barry Haddow, and Alexandra Birch. 2016. Neural machine translation of rare words with subword units. In *Proceedings of the 54th Annual Meeting of the Association for Computational Linguistics (Volume 1: Long Papers)*, pages 1715–1725, Berlin, Germany. Association for Computational Linguistics.

Dennis Ulmer, Elisa Bassignana, Max Müller-Eberstein, Daniel Varab, Mike Zhang, Christian Hardmeier, and Barbara Plank. 2022. Experimental standards for deep learning research: A natural language processing perspective.

Omry Yadan. 2019. Hydra - a framework for elegantly configuring complex applications. Github.

GEMv2: Multilingual NLG Benchmarking in a Single Line of Code

Sebastian Gehrmann[11], Abhik Bhattacharjee[3], Abinaya Mahendiran[24], Alex Wang[25], Alexandros Papangelis[2], Aman Madaan[4], Angelina McMillan-Major[15], Anna Shvets[10], Ashish Upadhyay[32], Bernd Bohnet[11], Bingsheng Yao[31], Bryan Wilie[38], Chandra Bhagavatula[1], Chaobin You[40], Craig Thomson[42], Cristina Garbacea[46], Dakuo Wang[20,26], Daniel Deutsch[47], Deyi Xiong[40], Di Jin[2], Dimitra Gkatzia[8], Dragomir Radev[50], Elizabeth Clark[11], Esin Durmus[34], Faisal Ladhak[7], Filip Ginter[48], Genta Indra Winata[38], Hendrik Strobelt[16,20], Hiroaki Hayashi[4,33], Jekaterina Novikova[49], Jenna Kanerva[48], Jenny Chim[29], Jiawei Zhou[14], Jordan Clive[6], Joshua Maynez[11], João Sedoc[25], Juraj Juraska[43], Kaustubh Dhole[9], Khyathi Raghavi Chandu[22], Laura Perez-Beltrachini[44], Leonardo F. R. Ribeiro[37], Lewis Tunstall[15], Li Zhang[47], Mahima Pushkarna[11], Mathias Creutz[45], Michael White[39], Mihir Sanjay Kale[11], Moussa Kamal Eddine[52], Nico Daheim[30], Nishant Subramani[1,21], Ondrej Dusek[5], Paul Pu Liang[4], Pawan Sasanka Ammanamanchi[17], Qi Zhu[41], Ratish Puduppully[44], Reno Kriz[18], Rifat Shahriyar[3], Ronald Cardenas[44], Saad Mahamood[51], Salomey Osei[21], Samuel Cahyawijaya[13], Sanja Štajner[28], Sebastien Montella[27], Shailza Jolly[36], Simon Mille[28], Tahmid Hasan[3], Tianhao Shen[40], Tosin Adewumi[19], Vikas Raunak[23], Vipul Raheja[12], Vitaly Nikolaev[11], Vivian Tsai[11], Yacine Jernite[15], Ying Xu[46], Yisi Sang[35], Yixin Liu[50], Yufang Hou[16]

[1]Allen Institute for AI, [2]Amazon Alexa AI, [3]Bangladesh University of Engineering and Technology, [4]Carnegie Mellon University, [5]Charles University, [6]Chattermill, [7]Columbia University, [8]Edinburgh Napier University, [9]Emory University, [10]Fablab in Paris by Inetum, [11]Google Research, [12]Grammarly, [13]HKUST, [14]Harvard University, [15]Hugging Face, [16]IBM Research, [17]IIIT Hyderabad, [18]Johns Hopkins University, [19]Luleå University of Technology, [20]MIT-IBM Watson AI Lab, [21]Masakhane, [22]Meta AI, [23]Microsoft, [24]Mphasis NEXT Labs, [25]New York University, [26]Northeastern University, [27]Orange Labs, [28]Pompeu Fabra University, [29]Queen Mary University of London, [30]RWTH Aachen University, [31]Rensselaer Polytechnic Institute, [32]Robert Gordon University, [33]Salesforce Research, [34]Stanford University, [35]Syracuse University, [36]TU Kaiserslautern, [37]Technical University of Darmstadt, [38]The Hong Kong University of Science and Technology, [39]The Ohio State University, [40]Tianjin University, [41]Tsinghua University, [42]University of Aberdeen, [43]University of California, Santa Cruz, [44]University of Edinburgh, [45]University of Helsinki, [46]University of Michigan, [47]University of Pennsylvania, [48]University of Turku, [49]Winterlight Labs, [50]Yale University, [51]trivago N.V., [52]École Polytechnique

gehrmann@google.com, gem-benchmark@googlegroups.com

Abstract

Evaluations in machine learning rarely use the latest metrics, datasets, or human evaluation in favor of remaining compatible with prior work. The compatibility, often facilitated through leaderboards, thus leads to outdated but standardized evaluation practices. We pose that the standardization is taking place in the wrong spot. Evaluation infrastructure should enable researchers to use the latest methods and what should be standardized instead is how to incorporate these new evaluation advances. We introduce GEMv2, the new version of the Generation, Evaluation, and Metrics Benchmark which uses a modular infrastructure for dataset, model, and metric developers to benefit from each other's work. GEMv2 supports 40 documented datasets in 51 languages, ongoing online evaluation for all datasets, and our interactive tools make it easier to add new datasets to the living benchmark.

1 Introduction

The standard evaluation process in natural language processing involves comparisons to prior results in a fixed environment, often facilitated through benchmarks and leaderboards. This process, if executed correctly, can advance reproducibility (Belz et al., 2021) and standardize evaluation choices that lead to better dataset diversity. But static benchmarks also prevent the adoption of new datasets or metrics (Raji et al., 2021), and many evaluation advancements are thus put aside. That means that the focus on surpassing the best prior reported scores reinforces outdated evaluation designs. Furthermore, this process ignores properties that do not match the leaderboard metric (Ethayarajh and Jurafsky, 2020; Bowman and Dahl, 2021; Dehghani et al., 2021). This issue is particularly pertinent in natural language generation (NLG) since the model quality cannot be estimated using accuracy and instead, NLG relies on automatic and human evaluation approaches that constantly improve (Gehrmann et al., 2022; Kasai et al., 2022).

To bridge the gap between advantages of leaderboards and in-depth and evolving evaluations, the Generation, Evaluation, and Metrics benchmark (GEM, Gehrmann et al., 2021) proposed a "living" benchmark. As such, GEM is participatory in that contributors propose new datasets and expand the selection of metrics. Model developers using GEM retain full agency over the evaluation process but are able to choose from a wider range of tasks and metrics. GEM further introduced evaluation suites (Mille et al., 2021; Dhole et al., 2021) that are compatible with its datasets and test various robustness and fairness aspects of models.

Proceedings of the The 2022 Conference on Empirical Methods in Natural Language Processing: System Demonstrations, pages 266 - 281
December 7-11, 2022 ©2022 Association for Computational Linguistics

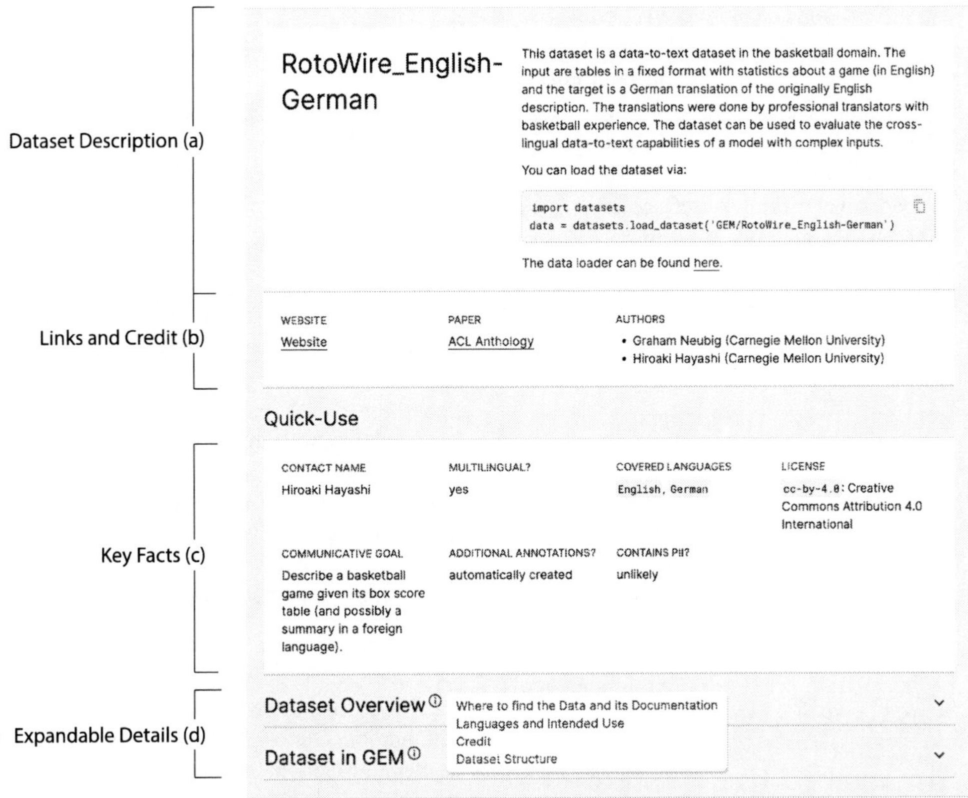

Figure 1: One of the data cards for GEM datasets. (a) shows the header which has the name, a summary, and example code to load it. (b) links to relevant papers and websites, alongside an author list. (c) is the Quick-Use section which summarizes the most important aspect of a dataset, including language(s), PII, and licensing information. (d) is the detailed view which has multiple sections. Each section provides a glance at categories of included questions on hover, and expands to full details on click.

We uncovered several shortcomings in GEMv1 that hindered its scaling and adoption: (1) Centralized data management made adding new datasets too complex. (2) Computing all metrics in a single framework led to dependency issues and was challenging for those with limited compute resources. (3) Participants needed more guidance in our dataset documentation process (McMillan-Major et al., 2021) to guarantee data card quality.

We introduce GEMv2, a modular and extendable NLG evaluation infrastructure which allows for continuous integration of newly developed datasets. We release a data card collection and rendering tool that makes it easier to follow for both card creators and readers. These improvements led to an expansion of GEM from 13 to 40 tasks and from 18 to 51 supported languages. We also introduce an online evaluation process that collects model outputs and computes metrics for all datasets.

2 Features and Functionality

Since evaluation practices evolve, we focus on modularity and maintainability to ensure that new dataset and metrics are compatible with all other features. Model developers are able to use new datasets and metrics without any changes to their existing setup. In this section, we describe the supported user [J]ourneys for various stakeholders in generation research.

J1 - Document a Dataset Every GEM dataset is documented using the data card template by McMillan-Major et al. (2021), which we revised using the Data Card Playbook (Pushkarna et al., 2022). A new card can be filled out or an existing one updated via an interactive form that provides detailed instructions for each field.[1]

J2 - Choose a Dataset The data card viewer

[1] huggingface.co/spaces/GEM/DatasetCardForm

presents information at multiple detail levels in separate columns. Anyone can quickly get a high-level overview of a dataset or read extended information on a documentation category (see Figure 1).

J3 - Create a Data Loader Each dataset has a separate repository at huggingface.co/GEM, with a loader using the Datasets library (Lhoest et al., 2021).[2] Through this, all supported datasets can be loaded via the same code,

```
from datasets import load_dataset
data = load_dataset(
    'GEM/$dataset_name',
    '$config_name')
```

where $config_name is the (optional) specification of the dataset configuration to use. To stratify how datasets are accessed, they are implemented according to the following conventions:

- linearized_input: Linearization processes convert structured input to a string. For reproducibility, we implement linearization schemes from prior work (e.g., Saleh et al., 2019; Kale and Rastogi, 2020).
- target and references: String targets and List[string] references ensure compatibility with existing training and eval scripts.
- gem_id: A unique example ID is used to track data points regardless of shuffling.

J4 - Evaluate a Model Model outputs can be evaluated locally using the gem-metrics library or online which will add the outputs to our result overview (J6).[3] Both methods require a standardized input format that specifies the dataset and split and which allows us to evaluate all 100+ data splits via the call gem_metrics outputs.json.

J5 - Add a new Metric In gem-metrics, each metric implements a compute() function and our library handles caching, parallelism, tokenization, etc. To avoid dependency conflicts, a metric can optionally specify a docker environment, as suggested by Deutsch and Roth (2022).

```
from .texts import Predictions
from .texts import References
from .metric import ReferencedMetric

class NewMetric(ReferencedMetric):
  def _initialize(self):
    """Load models and artifacts."""
    pass
  def compute(
      self,
      cache,
      predictions: Predictions,
      references: References) -> Dict:
    """Compute the metric."""
    pass
```

J6 - Use Prior Results Comparisons to prior work often only copy reported numbers which could be computed using different evaluation parameters, and a lack of released model outputs frequently prevents a fair side-by-side comparison outside of leaderboards (Gehrmann et al., 2022).[4] To improve comparability, we add every online submission to a growing corpus of model outputs which evaluation researchers can use to develop better metrics or to conduct analyses.

3 Dataset Selection and Loading

To identify candidate datasets, continued to follow the SuperGLUE process (Wang et al., 2019) by soliciting tasks to be included from the research community. Our request to suggest multilingual, challenging, and/or interesting NLG tasks led to 40 submissions. To avoid quality judgments, we imposed only three requirements for selection: (1) consent from dataset authors, (2) availability under a permissive license, (3) the task needs to be able to be cast as a text-to-text problem. 27 tasks were selected in addition to the 13 existing ones (Gehrmann et al., 2021).Three datasets are simplification evaluation sets added to the Wiki-Auto loader (Jiang et al., 2020), while all others have independent data loaders.[5] All data loaders and cards were produced as part of a month-long hackathon, and we invited the dataset authors and GEM participants to contribute to one or more of the datasets. Afterwards, the organizers managed the ongoing maintenance. New datasets can be added on an ongoing basis, subject to the three requirements. GEMv2 currently supports 40 datasets, listed in Appendix A and described in this section.

Figure 2 shows the distributions of training example count, task types, and their input and target lengths. Data-to-text and summarization are most common, followed by response generation. While data-to-text tasks are spread across resource availability categories, summarization datasets tend to

[2]Documentation on how to add new datasets can be found at gem-benchmark.com/tutorials.

[3]huggingface.co/spaces/GEM/submission-form

[4]Marie (2022) discusses how this practice leads to harmful claims using a translation example (Costa-jussà et al., 2022).

[5]Changes to datasets are documented in the appendix.

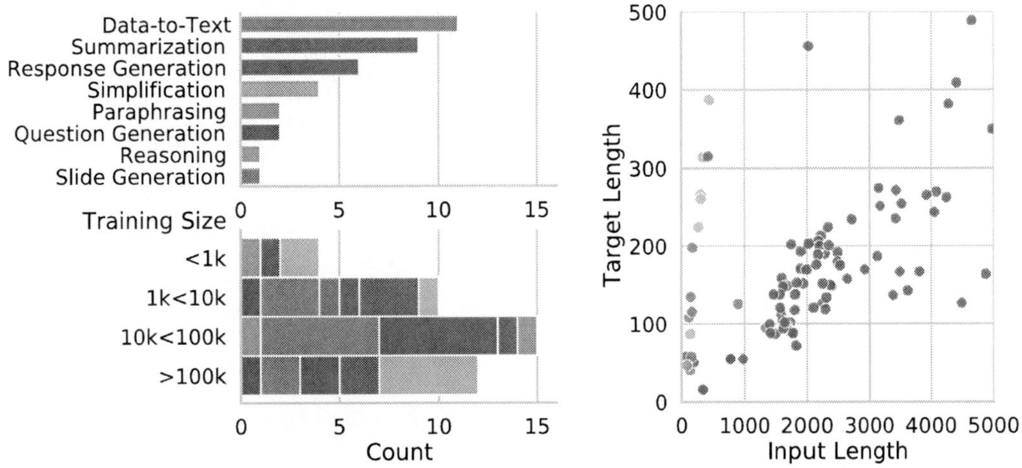

Figure 2: An overview of the properties of the currently supported datasets in GEM. (Top left) A histogram of the supported task types. The most represented tasks are Data-to-Text, followed by Summarization, Response Generation, and Simplification. (Bottom Left) The frequency of different training corpus sizes for dataset configurations, broken down by their task types. While some task types are represented across all resource availability levels, some are concentrated on high resource. (Right) An overview of input and target lengths of different dataset configurations according to the mT5 tokenizer (Xue et al., 2021). Summarization tasks have input lengths of over 1,000 while all other tasks remain under 1,000 tokens. There is a lot more between-task variance in output length. Four dataset configurations are hidden due to the axis truncation.

be larger. While datasets vary in target length, the median input length tends to remain under 500 tokens, likely motivated by modeling limitations. Exceptions to this are summarization, with input lengths beyond what is supported by most models (e.g., WikiCatSum (Perez-Beltrachini et al., 2019) and XLSum (Hasan et al., 2021)), and a class of data-to-text datasets with the communicative goal to generate game summaries from large sports statistic tables (e.g., Hayashi et al., 2019; Thomson et al., 2020; Puduppully et al., 2019a).

We put an emphasis on language diversity, as prior work has found that fewer than 30% of NLG publications (even counting evaluations on machine translation) evaluate on non-English tasks (Gehrmann et al., 2022). While a lot of this focus on English can be traced to a lack of multilingual resources, many non-English NLG datasets have been released in recent years (e.g., Hasan et al., 2021; Ladhak et al., 2020; Mille et al., 2020; Cahyawijaya et al., 2021). As shown in Table 2, we support languages across all resource classes in the taxonomy by Joshi et al. (2020). However, the focus on English is still apparent in the number of datasets supporting a particular language, shown in Table 1, where English is far above all other languages. Moreover, most of the language diversity stems from the three highly multilingual datasets XLSum (Hasan et al., 2021), WikiLingua (Ladhak et al., 2020), and data from the surface realization shared task '20 (Mille et al., 2020). Excluding those, there are 13 datasets supporting non-English languages, 9 of which are exclusively non-English.

Of the 40 datasets, 14 have multiple configurations which can differ in task setup, languages, their encoding in romanized or original script, or domain. For example, we modified WikiLingua (Ladhak et al., 2020) to have splits from and to any of the 18 supported languages, enabling better cross-lingual evaluations. Seventeen datasets have challenge splits, many of which were created for GEM. For example, the challenge set for the conversational weather dataset (Balakrishnan et al., 2019) selects examples from the original test split with complex discourse relations.

4 Data Cards

Each dataset is accompanied by documentation about how it was created, who created it, how it should be used, and the risks in using it (Bender and Friedman, 2018; Gebru et al., 2018). Our original data documentation process (McMillan-Major et al., 2021) required filling out a markdown template following instructions in a separate guide. We

Count	Languages
1	Amharic, Azerbaijani, Bengali, Burmese, Dutch, Gujarati, Hausa, Igbo, Javanese, Kirundi, Kyrgyz, Marathi, Nepali, Oromo, Pashto, Persian, Pidgin, Punjabi, Scottish Gaelic, Serbian, Sinhala, Somali, Sundanese, Swahili, Swedish, Tamil, Telugu, Tigrinya, Ukrainian, Urdu, Uzbek, Welsh, Yoruba
2	Czech, Italian, Thai, Turkish, Vietnamese
3	Arabic, Finnish, Hindi, Japanese, Korean, Portuguese
4	Indonesian
6	Chinese, German, Russian, Spanish
8	French
28	English

Table 1: The languages supported in GEMv2 and in how many of its datasets they appear.

Tax.	Languages
0	West African Pidgin English, Sinhala
1	Azerbaijani, Burmese, Gujarati, Igbo, Javanese, Kirundi, Kyrgyz, Nepali, Oromo, Pashto, Scottish Gaelic, Somali, Sundanese, Telugu, Welsh
2	Amharic, Hausa, Marathi, Punjabi, Swahili, Tigrinya, Yoruba
3	Bengali, Indonesian, Tamil, Thai, Ukrainian, Urdu, Uzbek
4	Czech, Dutch, Finnish, Hindi, Italian, Korean, Persian, Portuguese, Russian, Serbian, Swedish, Turkish, Vietnamese
5	Arabic, Chinese, English, French, German, Japanese, Spanish

Table 2: Supported languages categorized into the resource taxonomy by Joshi et al. (2020).

analyzed the existing template and the resulting data cards under the dimensions provided in the data card playbook (Pushkarna et al., 2022) and identified the following improvements:

- **Accountability:** It needs to be clear who will maintain and extend the data cards when a dataset changes, when limitations of a dataset are found, or when it is deprecated (Corry et al., 2021).
- **Utility:** The recommended evaluation process for a dataset should be prominently shown.
- **Quality:** We need a process to validate data card completeness and quality.
- **Impact & Consequences:** It needs to be clear that we are curators, not editors, and that critiques reflect on the data, not the creators.
- **Risk & Recommendations I:** We need to expand the documentation of potential PII issues.
- **Risk & Recommendations II:** To help decide whether to use a dataset, the card needs to discuss differences from other datasets with similar communicative goals.

We modified our template following these insights and to be in line with the playbook approach of dividing between *telescope*, *periscope*, and *microscope* questions based on the length of the expected answer. We implemented this template in an interactive collection tool that can create new cards or load and update existing ones. The tool shows progress bars for the overall answer status and a breakdown for each of the subsections to indicate where more content should be added. The tool further improves the user experience by conditionally rendering questions based on prior answers, e.g., *Is there a risk of PII?* $\rightarrow$ *What kind of PII?*

The output of the tool is a structured json file that we convert into a simple markdown file for the data loader and an optimized web viewer and embedded in our website (Figure 1). The viewer presents important information at the top and splits the detailed rendering into three columns, corresponding to the telescope, periscope, and microscope split. This enables an easy navigation since high-level information can be found by focusing on the left column, moving toward the right for additional details.

The structured format enables us to study trends in dataset construction practices beyond those shown in Section 3.[6] For example, 66% of the data cards report that PII is unlikely or definitely not included, while it is likely or definitely included in 33%. In the free-text explanations, we find four types of justifications for absent PII: The majority (7) stated that the data format or domain was restricted to avoid PII. Two stated that the data is in the public domain (e.g., Wikipedia) and another two used fully simulated data. One response described that crowd raters were instructed to avoid mentioning PII. We found that multiple of the PII-likely datasets only use public domain data, indicating that there is confusion about PII definitions.

Another typically hidden aspect is the data sourcing. Our datasets present an almost even split between automatically-, crowdworker-, and expert-created datasets, with crowdworker-created ones being slightly more common, possibly confounded if experts were hired through crowdworking platforms, as was done for SQuality (Wang et al., 2022). It may thus also possible to compare which of these collection methods leads to more insightful modeling results. We follow up by asking

[6]We encourage others to use the publicly available files for additional investigations.

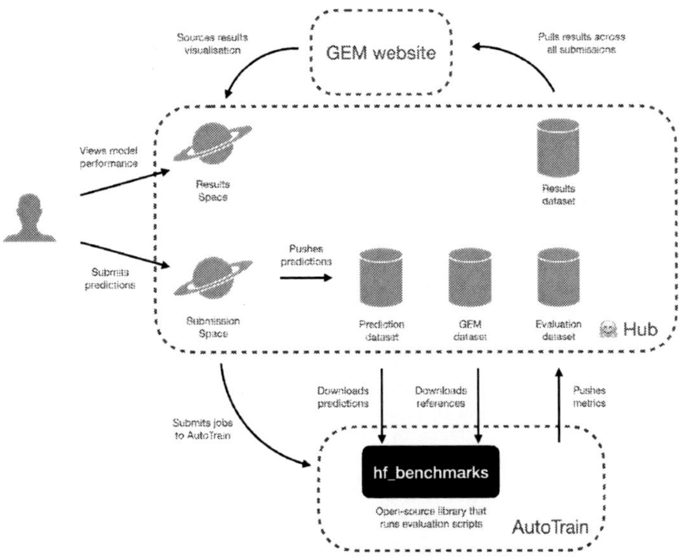

Figure 3: System architecture for hosting GEM on the Hugging Face Hub

which crowdworking platform was used and unsurprisingly, Amazon Mechanical Turk was the most frequent answer, followed by participatory experiments and other non-specified platforms.

5 System Design

To support the automatic evaluation of outputs, we use the Hugging Face Hub to integrate datasets, metrics, and user interfaces for GEM users to submit their outputs. The system architecture is shown in Figure 3, and consists of five main components:
Spaces We host Streamlit applications on Spaces[7] for the submission of predictions, downloading of results, and visualization of model performance.
Datasets Dataset repositories are used to host the datasets, submissions, evaluations, and results.
AutoTrain We use AutoTrain[8], Hugging Face's AutoML platform, to run all evaluation jobs using **Hugging Face Benchmarks**, a library that defines how metrics are computed within AutoTrain.[9]
Metrics We use `GEM-metrics` to perform the metric computations. In addition to supporting common metrics like BLEU (Papineni et al., 2002) and ROUGE (Lin, 2004), the Docker integration simplifies the calculation of multiple model-based metrics like BLEURT (Sellam et al., 2020).

On submission, a dataset repository with the model outputs is created under the `GEM-submissions` organisation on the Hugging Face Hub. In parallel, an evaluation job is triggered in AutoTrain which downloads the submission from the Hub, along with all the reference splits of the GEM datasets. These references are used to compute a wide variety of NLG metrics via GEM-metrics. The resulting metrics are then pushed to a dataset repository on the Hub, and used to source the visualization of results on the GEM website[10] and Space.[11]

6 Conclusion

We introduce GEMv2 which unifies infrastructure for generation research. We propose a consistent workflow from documenting and choosing datasets to loading and evaluating on them while keeping all supported datasets and metrics compatible with each other. We demonstrate the scalability by releasing the initial version with support for 40 datasets in 51 languages. Of the supported datasets, 23 are improved through configurations, filtering, and re-splitting processes and 17 datasets have challenge sets. We release a submission tool that computes metrics and makes model outputs available to download for evaluation researchers. Researchers who are interested in integrating their dataset are welcome to contact us for support.

[7] `huggingface.co/spaces`
[8] `huggingface.co/autotrain`
[9] `github.com/huggingface/hf_benchmarks`
[10] `gem-benchmark.com`
[11] `huggingface.co/spaces/GEM/results`

7 Broader Impact

As discussed in the main part of the paper, GEMv2 aims to avoid any explicit curation decisions about inclusion and exclusion of datasets beyond licensing and consent. This is a change from the originally set out strict inclusion criteria based on dataset quality. The reason for this is that the entire research community should be the authority to decide whether a dataset is useful and what it is useful for. For example, a dataset with noisy outputs may still be useful to study hallucination avoidance methods. However, this change has implications on how dataset deprecation needs to be handled, in particular for datasets with newly found issues or datasets with better alternatives. Documenting issues and alternatives using the data cards is thus becoming more important in GEMv2 and we encourage researchers to update data cards. Another side effect of positioning GEMv2 as infrastructure that support dataset creators is a decreased risk of erasure. All our documentation and dataset loaders center the work of the creators to encourage users to cite the datasets they use.

Another open issue that we have been working on is the interplay between multilingualism and metrics. We now support multiple languages for which no NLG metrics have been tested, and for which our tokenization schemes may be inappropriate. The freedom to combine every dataset with every metric may lead to more flawed evaluations in those cases. In addition, some datasets were released with specific metrics that we do not support yet.

A final issue we want to point out is the lack of discussion of human evaluation in this overview paper which we omitted for brevity. Human evaluation does not scale and every task requires its own evaluation approach, especially when the goal is to deploy a system to real users. We have thus taken the approach to develop better human evaluation for only a subset of tasks, solving issues pointed out by Tang et al. (2022), Howcroft et al. (2020), and van der Lee et al. (2019), and we will release detailed instructions separately. However, these instructions will not replace a better understanding of the users of deployed systems.

References

Fernando Alva-Manchego, Louis Martin, Antoine Bordes, Carolina Scarton, Benoît Sagot, and Lucia Specia. 2020. ASSET: A dataset for tuning and evaluation of sentence simplification models with multiple rewriting transformations. In *Proceedings of the 58th Annual Meeting of the Association for Computational Linguistics*, pages 4668–4679, Online. Association for Computational Linguistics.

Anusha Balakrishnan, Jinfeng Rao, Kartikeya Upasani, Michael White, and Rajen Subba. 2019. Constrained decoding for neural NLG from compositional representations in task-oriented dialogue. In *Proceedings of the 57th Annual Meeting of the Association for Computational Linguistics*, pages 831–844, Florence, Italy. Association for Computational Linguistics.

Anya Belz, Shubham Agarwal, Anastasia Shimorina, and Ehud Reiter. 2021. A systematic review of reproducibility research in natural language processing. In *Proceedings of the 16th Conference of the European Chapter of the Association for Computational Linguistics: Main Volume*, pages 381–393, Online. Association for Computational Linguistics.

Emily M. Bender and Batya Friedman. 2018. Data statements for natural language processing: Toward mitigating system bias and enabling better science. *Transactions of the Association for Computational Linguistics*, 6:587–604.

Chandra Bhagavatula, Ronan Le Bras, Chaitanya Malaviya, Keisuke Sakaguchi, Ari Holtzman, Hannah Rashkin, Doug Downey, Wen tau Yih, and Yejin Choi. 2020. Abductive commonsense reasoning. In *International Conference on Learning Representations*.

Samuel R. Bowman and George Dahl. 2021. What will it take to fix benchmarking in natural language understanding? In *Proceedings of the 2021 Conference of the North American Chapter of the Association for Computational Linguistics: Human Language Technologies*, pages 4843–4855, Online. Association for Computational Linguistics.

Bill Byrne, Karthik Krishnamoorthi, Saravanan Ganesh, and Mihir Kale. 2021. TicketTalk: Toward human-level performance with end-to-end, transaction-based dialog systems. In *Proceedings of the 59th Annual Meeting of the Association for Computational Linguistics and the 11th International Joint Conference on Natural Language Processing (Volume 1: Long Papers)*, pages 671–680, Online. Association for Computational Linguistics.

Bill Byrne, Karthik Krishnamoorthi, Chinnadhurai Sankar, Arvind Neelakantan, Ben Goodrich, Daniel Duckworth, Semih Yavuz, Amit Dubey, Kyu-Young Kim, and Andy Cedilnik. 2019. Taskmaster-1: Toward a realistic and diverse dialog dataset. In *Proceedings of the 2019 Conference on Empirical Methods in Natural Language Processing and the 9th International Joint Conference on Natural Language Processing (EMNLP-IJCNLP)*, pages 4516–4525, Hong Kong, China. Association for Computational Linguistics.

Samuel Cahyawijaya, Genta Indra Winata, Bryan Wilie, Karissa Vincentio, Xiaohong Li, Adhiguna Kuncoro, Sebastian Ruder, Zhi Yuan Lim, Syafri Bahar, Masayu Khodra, Ayu Purwarianti, and Pascale Fung. 2021. IndoNLG: Benchmark and resources for evaluating Indonesian natural language generation. In *Proceedings of the 2021 Conference on Empirical Methods in Natural Language Processing*, pages 8875–8898, Online and Punta Cana, Dominican Republic. Association for Computational Linguistics.

Frances Corry, Hamsini Sridharan, Alexandra Sasha Luccioni, Mike Ananny, Jason Schultz, and Kate Crawford. 2021. The problem of zombie datasets: A framework for deprecating datasets. *CoRR*, abs/2111.04424.

Marta R. Costa-jussà, James Cross, Onur Çelebi, Maha Elbayad, Kenneth Heafield, Kevin Heffernan, Elahe Kalbassi, Janice Lam, Daniel Licht, Jean Maillard, Anna Sun, Skyler Wang, Guillaume Wenzek, Al Youngblood, Bapi Akula, Loïc Barrault, Gabriel Mejia Gonzalez, Prangthip Hansanti, John Hoffman, Semarley Jarrett, Kaushik Ram Sadagopan, Dirk Rowe, Shannon Spruit, Chau Tran, Pierre Andrews, Necip Fazil Ayan, Shruti Bhosale, Sergey Edunov, Angela Fan, Cynthia Gao, Vedanuj Goswami, Francisco Guzmán, Philipp Koehn, Alexandre Mourachko, Christophe Ropers, Safiyyah Saleem, Holger Schwenk, and Jeff Wang. 2022. No language left behind: Scaling human-centered machine translation. *CoRR*, abs/2207.04672.

Mathias Creutz. 2018. Open subtitles paraphrase corpus for six languages. In *Proceedings of the 11th edition of the Language Resources and Evaluation Conference (LREC 2018)*, Miyazaki, Japan. European Language Resources Association (ELRA).

Mostafa Dehghani, Yi Tay, Alexey A. Gritsenko, Zhe Zhao, Neil Houlsby, Fernando Diaz, Donald Metzler, and Oriol Vinyals. 2021. The benchmark lottery. *CoRR*, abs/2107.07002.

Daniel Deutsch and Dan Roth. 2022. Repro: An Open-Source Library for Improving the Reproducibility and Usability of Publicly Available Research Code. *ArXiv*, abs/2204.13848.

Ashwin Devaraj, Iain Marshall, Byron Wallace, and Junyi Jessy Li. 2021. Paragraph-level simplification of medical texts. In *Proceedings of the 2021 Conference of the North American Chapter of the Association for Computational Linguistics: Human Language Technologies*, pages 4972–4984, Online. Association for Computational Linguistics.

Kaustubh D Dhole, Varun Gangal, Sebastian Gehrmann, Aadesh Gupta, Zhenhao Li, Saad Mahamood, Abinaya Mahendiran, Simon Mille, Ashish Srivastava, Samson Tan, et al. 2021. Nl-augmenter: A framework for task-sensitive natural language augmentation. *arXiv preprint arXiv:2112.02721*.

Ondřej Dušek, David M. Howcroft, and Verena Rieser. 2019. Semantic noise matters for neural natural language generation. In *Proceedings of the 12th International Conference on Natural Language Generation*, pages 421–426, Tokyo, Japan. Association for Computational Linguistics.

Ondřej Dušek and Filip Jurčíček. 2019. Neural generation for Czech: Data and baselines. In *Proceedings of the 12th International Conference on Natural Language Generation*, pages 563–574, Tokyo, Japan. Association for Computational Linguistics.

Ondřej Dušek, Jekaterina Novikova, and Verena Rieser. 2020. Evaluating the state-of-the-art of end-to-end natural language generation: The e2e nlg challenge. *Computer Speech & Language*, 59:123–156.

Kawin Ethayarajh and Dan Jurafsky. 2020. Utility is in the eye of the user: A critique of NLP leaderboards. In *Proceedings of the 2020 Conference on Empirical Methods in Natural Language Processing (EMNLP)*, pages 4846–4853, Online. Association for Computational Linguistics.

Claire Gardent, Anastasia Shimorina, Shashi Narayan, and Laura Perez-Beltrachini. 2017a. Creating training corpora for NLG micro-planners. In *Proceedings of the 55th Annual Meeting of the Association for Computational Linguistics (Volume 1: Long Papers)*, pages 179–188, Vancouver, Canada. Association for Computational Linguistics.

Claire Gardent, Anastasia Shimorina, Shashi Narayan, and Laura Perez-Beltrachini. 2017b. The WebNLG challenge: Generating text from RDF data. In *Proceedings of the 10th International Conference on Natural Language Generation*, pages 124–133, Santiago de Compostela, Spain. Association for Computational Linguistics.

Timnit Gebru, Jamie Morgenstern, Briana Vecchione, Jennifer Wortman Vaughan, Hanna Wallach, Hal Daumé III, and Kate Crawford. 2018. Datasheets for datasets. In *Proceedings of the Fifth Workshop on Fairness, Accountability, and Transparency in Machine Learning*, Stockholm, Sweden.

Sebastian Gehrmann, Tosin Adewumi, Karmanya Aggarwal, Pawan Sasanka Ammanamanchi, Anuoluwapo Aremu, Antoine Bosselut, Khyathi Raghavi Chandu, Miruna-Adriana Clinciu, Dipanjan Das, Kaustubh Dhole, Wanyu Du, Esin Durmus, Ondřej Dušek, Chris Chinenye Emezue, Varun Gangal, Cristina Garbacea, Tatsunori Hashimoto, Yufang Hou, Yacine Jernite, Harsh Jhamtani, Yangfeng Ji, Shailza Jolly, Mihir Kale, Dhruv Kumar, Faisal Ladhak, Aman Madaan, Mounica Maddela, Khyati Mahajan, Saad Mahamood, Bodhisattwa Prasad Majumder, Pedro Henrique Martins, Angelina McMillan-Major, Simon Mille, Emiel van Miltenburg, Moin Nadeem, Shashi Narayan, Vitaly Nikolaev, Andre Niyongabo Rubungo, Salomey Osei, Ankur Parikh, Laura Perez-Beltrachini, Niranjan Ramesh Rao, Vikas Raunak, Juan Diego

Rodriguez, Sashank Santhanam, João Sedoc, Thibault Sellam, Samira Shaikh, Anastasia Shimorina, Marco Antonio Sobrevilla Cabezudo, Hendrik Strobelt, Nishant Subramani, Wei Xu, Diyi Yang, Akhila Yerukola, and Jiawei Zhou. 2021. The GEM benchmark: Natural language generation, its evaluation and metrics. In *Proceedings of the 1st Workshop on Natural Language Generation, Evaluation, and Metrics (GEM 2021)*, pages 96–120, Online. Association for Computational Linguistics.

Sebastian Gehrmann, Elizabeth Clark, and Thibault Sellam. 2022. Repairing the cracked foundation: A survey of obstacles in evaluation practices for generated text. *CoRR*, abs/2202.06935.

Tahmid Hasan, Abhik Bhattacharjee, Md. Saiful Islam, Kazi Mubasshir, Yuan-Fang Li, Yong-Bin Kang, M. Sohel Rahman, and Rifat Shahriyar. 2021. XL-sum: Large-scale multilingual abstractive summarization for 44 languages. In *Findings of the Association for Computational Linguistics: ACL-IJCNLP 2021*, pages 4693–4703, Online. Association for Computational Linguistics.

Hiroaki Hayashi, Yusuke Oda, Alexandra Birch, Ioannis Konstas, Andrew Finch, Minh-Thang Luong, Graham Neubig, and Katsuhito Sudoh. 2019. Findings of the third workshop on neural generation and translation. In *Proceedings of the 3rd Workshop on Neural Generation and Translation*, pages 1–14, Hong Kong. Association for Computational Linguistics.

David M. Howcroft, Anya Belz, Miruna-Adriana Clinciu, Dimitra Gkatzia, Sadid A. Hasan, Saad Mahamood, Simon Mille, Emiel van Miltenburg, Sashank Santhanam, and Verena Rieser. 2020. Twenty years of confusion in human evaluation: NLG needs evaluation sheets and standardised definitions. In *Proceedings of the 13th International Conference on Natural Language Generation*, pages 169–182, Dublin, Ireland. Association for Computational Linguistics.

Chao Jiang, Mounica Maddela, Wuwei Lan, Yang Zhong, and Wei Xu. 2020. Neural CRF model for sentence alignment in text simplification. In *Proceedings of the 58th Annual Meeting of the Association for Computational Linguistics*, pages 7943–7960, Online. Association for Computational Linguistics.

Pratik Joshi, Sebastin Santy, Amar Budhiraja, Kalika Bali, and Monojit Choudhury. 2020. The state and fate of linguistic diversity and inclusion in the NLP world. In *Proceedings of the 58th Annual Meeting of the Association for Computational Linguistics*, pages 6282–6293, Online. Association for Computational Linguistics.

Juraj Juraska, Kevin Bowden, and Marilyn Walker. 2019. ViGGO: A video game corpus for data-to-text generation in open-domain conversation. In *Proceedings of the 12th International Conference on Natural Language Generation*, pages 164–172, Tokyo, Japan. Association for Computational Linguistics.

Mihir Kale and Abhinav Rastogi. 2020. Text-to-text pre-training for data-to-text tasks. In *Proceedings of the 13th International Conference on Natural Language Generation*, pages 97–102, Dublin, Ireland. Association for Computational Linguistics.

Moussa Kamal Eddine, Antoine Tixier, and Michalis Vazirgiannis. 2021. BARThez: a skilled pretrained French sequence-to-sequence model. In *Proceedings of the 2021 Conference on Empirical Methods in Natural Language Processing*, pages 9369–9390, Online and Punta Cana, Dominican Republic. Association for Computational Linguistics.

Jenna Kanerva, Filip Ginter, Li-Hsin Chang, Iiro Rastas, Valtteri Skantsi, Jemina Kilpeläinen, Hanna-Mari Kupari, Jenna Saarni, Maija Sevón, and Otto Tarkka. 2021. Finnish paraphrase corpus. In *Proceedings of the 23rd Nordic Conference on Computational Linguistics (NoDaLiDa)*, pages 288–298, Reykjavik, Iceland (Online). Linköping University Electronic Press, Sweden.

Jenna Kanerva, Filip Ginter, and Sampo Pyysalo. 2020. Turku enhanced parser pipeline: From raw text to enhanced graphs in the IWPT 2020 shared task. In *Proceedings of the 16th International Conference on Parsing Technologies and the IWPT 2020 Shared Task on Parsing into Enhanced Universal Dependencies*, pages 162–173, Online. Association for Computational Linguistics.

Jenna Kanerva, Samuel Rönnqvist, Riina Kekki, Tapio Salakoski, and Filip Ginter. 2019. Template-free data-to-text generation of Finnish sports news. In *Proceedings of the 22nd Nordic Conference on Computational Linguistics*, pages 242–252, Turku, Finland. Linköping University Electronic Press.

Jungo Kasai, Keisuke Sakaguchi, Ronan Le Bras, Lavinia Dunagan, Jacob Morrison, Alexander R. Fabbri, Yejin Choi, and Noah A. Smith. 2022. Bidimensional leaderboards: Generate and evaluate language hand in hand. In *Proceedings of the 2022 Conference of the North American Chapter of the Association for Computational Linguistics*, Seattle, Washington. Association for Computational Linguistics.

Joongwon Kim, Mounica Maddela, Reno Kriz, Wei Xu, and Chris Callison-Burch. 2021a. BiSECT: Learning to split and rephrase sentences with bitexts. In *Proceedings of the 2021 Conference on Empirical Methods in Natural Language Processing*, pages 6193–6209, Online and Punta Cana, Dominican Republic. Association for Computational Linguistics.

Seokhwan Kim, Yang Liu, Di Jin, Alexandros Papangelis, Karthik Gopalakrishnan, Behnam Hedayatnia, and Dilek Z. Hakkani-Tür. 2021b. "how robust r u?": Evaluating task-oriented dialogue systems on spoken conversations. *2021 IEEE Automatic Speech Recognition and Understanding Workshop (ASRU)*, pages 1147–1154.

Faisal Ladhak, Esin Durmus, Claire Cardie, and Kathleen McKeown. 2020. WikiLingua: A new benchmark dataset for cross-lingual abstractive summarization. In *Findings of the Association for Computational Linguistics: EMNLP 2020*, pages 4034–4048, Online. Association for Computational Linguistics.

Quentin Lhoest, Albert Villanova del Moral, Yacine Jernite, Abhishek Thakur, Patrick von Platen, Suraj Patil, Julien Chaumond, Mariama Drame, Julien Plu, Lewis Tunstall, Joe Davison, Mario Šaško, Gunjan Chhablani, Bhavitvya Malik, Simon Brandeis, Teven Le Scao, Victor Sanh, Canwen Xu, Nicolas Patry, Angelina McMillan-Major, Philipp Schmid, Sylvain Gugger, Clément Delangue, Théo Matussière, Lysandre Debut, Stas Bekman, Pierric Cistac, Thibault Goehringer, Victor Mustar, François Lagunas, Alexander Rush, and Thomas Wolf. 2021. Datasets: A community library for natural language processing. In *Proceedings of the 2021 Conference on Empirical Methods in Natural Language Processing: System Demonstrations*, pages 175–184, Online and Punta Cana, Dominican Republic. Association for Computational Linguistics.

Bill Yuchen Lin, Wangchunshu Zhou, Ming Shen, Pei Zhou, Chandra Bhagavatula, Yejin Choi, and Xiang Ren. 2020. CommonGen: A constrained text generation challenge for generative commonsense reasoning. In *Findings of the Association for Computational Linguistics: EMNLP 2020*, pages 1823–1840, Online. Association for Computational Linguistics.

Chin-Yew Lin. 2004. ROUGE: A package for automatic evaluation of summaries. In *Text Summarization Branches Out*, pages 74–81, Barcelona, Spain. Association for Computational Linguistics.

Benjamin Marie. 2022. Science left behind.

Angelina McMillan-Major, Salomey Osei, Juan Diego Rodriguez, Pawan Sasanka Ammanamanchi, Sebastian Gehrmann, and Yacine Jernite. 2021. Reusable templates and guides for documenting datasets and models for natural language processing and generation: A case study of the HuggingFace and GEM data and model cards. In *Proceedings of the 1st Workshop on Natural Language Generation, Evaluation, and Metrics (GEM 2021)*, pages 121–135, Online. Association for Computational Linguistics.

Simon Mille, Anya Belz, Bernd Bohnet, Thiago Castro Ferreira, Yvette Graham, and Leo Wanner. 2020. The third multilingual surface realisation shared task (SR'20): Overview and evaluation results. In *Proceedings of the Third Workshop on Multilingual Surface Realisation*, pages 1–20, Barcelona, Spain (Online). Association for Computational Linguistics.

Simon Mille, Kaustubh Dhole, Saad Mahamood, Laura Perez-Beltrachini, Varun Gangal, Mihir Kale, Emiel van Miltenburg, and Sebastian Gehrmann. 2021. Automatic construction of evaluation suites for natural language generation datasets. In *Thirty-fifth Conference on Neural Information Processing Systems Datasets and Benchmarks Track (Round 1)*.

Linyong Nan, Dragomir Radev, Rui Zhang, Amrit Rau, Abhinand Sivaprasad, Chiachun Hsieh, Xiangru Tang, Aadit Vyas, Neha Verma, Pranav Krishna, Yangxiaokang Liu, Nadia Irwanto, Jessica Pan, Faiaz Rahman, Ahmad Zaidi, Mutethia Mutuma, Yasin Tarabar, Ankit Gupta, Tao Yu, Yi Chern Tan, Xi Victoria Lin, Caiming Xiong, Richard Socher, and Nazneen Fatema Rajani. 2021. DART: Open-domain structured data record to text generation. In *Proceedings of the 2021 Conference of the North American Chapter of the Association for Computational Linguistics: Human Language Technologies*, pages 432–447, Online. Association for Computational Linguistics.

Shashi Narayan, Shay B. Cohen, and Mirella Lapata. 2018. Don't give me the details, just the summary! topic-aware convolutional neural networks for extreme summarization. In *Proceedings of the 2018 Conference on Empirical Methods in Natural Language Processing*, pages 1797–1807, Brussels, Belgium. Association for Computational Linguistics.

Jekaterina Novikova, Ondřej Dušek, and Verena Rieser. 2017. The E2E dataset: New challenges for end-to-end generation. In *Proceedings of the 18th Annual SIGdial Meeting on Discourse and Dialogue*, pages 201–206, Saarbrücken, Germany. Association for Computational Linguistics.

Kishore Papineni, Salim Roukos, Todd Ward, and Wei-Jing Zhu. 2002. Bleu: a method for automatic evaluation of machine translation. In *Proceedings of the 40th Annual Meeting of the Association for Computational Linguistics*, pages 311–318, Philadelphia, Pennsylvania, USA. Association for Computational Linguistics.

Ankur Parikh, Xuezhi Wang, Sebastian Gehrmann, Manaal Faruqui, Bhuwan Dhingra, Diyi Yang, and Dipanjan Das. 2020. ToTTo: A controlled table-to-text generation dataset. In *Proceedings of the 2020 Conference on Empirical Methods in Natural Language Processing (EMNLP)*, pages 1173–1186, Online. Association for Computational Linguistics.

Laura Perez-Beltrachini and Mirella Lapata. 2021. Models and datasets for cross-lingual summarisation. In *Proceedings of the 2021 Conference on Empirical Methods in Natural Language Processing*, pages 9408–9423, Online and Punta Cana, Dominican Republic. Association for Computational Linguistics.

Laura Perez-Beltrachini, Yang Liu, and Mirella Lapata. 2019. Generating summaries with topic templates and structured convolutional decoders. In *Proceedings of the 57th Annual Meeting of the Association for Computational Linguistics*, pages 5107–5116, Florence, Italy. Association for Computational Linguistics.

Ratish Puduppully, Li Dong, and Mirella Lapata. 2019a. Data-to-text generation with entity modeling. In *Proceedings of the 57th Annual Meeting of the Association for Computational Linguistics*, pages 2023–

2035, Florence, Italy. Association for Computational Linguistics.

Ratish Puduppully and Mirella Lapata. 2021. Data-to-text generation with macro planning. *Transactions of the Association for Computational Linguistics*, 9:510–527.

Ratish Puduppully, Jonathan Mallinson, and Mirella Lapata. 2019b. University of Edinburgh's submission to the document-level generation and translation shared task. In *Proceedings of the 3rd Workshop on Neural Generation and Translation*, pages 268–272, Hong Kong. Association for Computational Linguistics.

Mahima Pushkarna, Andrew Zaldivar, and Oddur Kjartansson. 2022. Data cards: Purposeful and transparent dataset documentation for responsible ai.

Jun Quan, Shian Zhang, Qian Cao, Zizhong Li, and Deyi Xiong. 2020. RiSAWOZ: A large-scale multi-domain Wizard-of-Oz dataset with rich semantic annotations for task-oriented dialogue modeling. In *Proceedings of the 2020 Conference on Empirical Methods in Natural Language Processing (EMNLP)*, pages 930–940, Online. Association for Computational Linguistics.

Inioluwa Deborah Raji, Emily Denton, Emily M. Bender, Alex Hanna, and Amandalynne Paullada. 2021. AI and the everything in the whole wide world benchmark. In *Proceedings of the Neural Information Processing Systems Track on Datasets and Benchmarks 1, NeurIPS Datasets and Benchmarks 2021, December 2021, virtual.*

Pranav Rajpurkar, Jian Zhang, Konstantin Lopyrev, and Percy Liang. 2016. SQuAD: 100,000+ Questions for Machine Comprehension of Text. *arXiv e-prints*, page arXiv:1606.05250.

Abhinav Rastogi, Xiaoxue Zang, Srinivas Sunkara, Raghav Gupta, and Pranav Khaitan. 2020. Towards scalable multi-domain conversational agents: The schema-guided dialogue dataset. In *Proceedings of the AAAI Conference on Artificial Intelligence*, volume 34, pages 8689–8696.

Fahimeh Saleh, Alexandre Berard, Ioan Calapodescu, and Laurent Besacier. 2019. Naver labs Europe's systems for the document-level generation and translation task at WNGT 2019. In *Proceedings of the 3rd Workshop on Neural Generation and Translation*, pages 273–279, Hong Kong. Association for Computational Linguistics.

Thomas Scialom, Paul-Alexis Dray, Sylvain Lamprier, Benjamin Piwowarski, and Jacopo Staiano. 2020. Mlsum: The multilingual summarization corpus. *arXiv preprint arXiv:2004.14900.*

Thibault Sellam, Dipanjan Das, and Ankur Parikh. 2020. BLEURT: Learning robust metrics for text generation. In *Proceedings of the 58th Annual Meeting of the Association for Computational Linguistics*, pages 7881–7892, Online. Association for Computational Linguistics.

Elior Sulem, Omri Abend, and Ari Rappoport. 2018. BLEU is not suitable for the evaluation of text simplification. In *Proceedings of the 2018 Conference on Empirical Methods in Natural Language Processing*, pages 738–744, Brussels, Belgium. Association for Computational Linguistics.

Edward Sun, Yufang Hou, Dakuo Wang, Yunfeng Zhang, and Nancy X. R. Wang. 2021. D2S: Document-to-slide generation via query-based text summarization. In *Proceedings of the 2021 Conference of the North American Chapter of the Association for Computational Linguistics: Human Language Technologies*, pages 1405–1418, Online. Association for Computational Linguistics.

Xiangru Tang, Alexander Fabbri, Haoran Li, Ziming Mao, Griffin Adams, Borui Wang, Asli Celikyilmaz, Yashar Mehdad, and Dragomir Radev. 2022. Investigating crowdsourcing protocols for evaluating the factual consistency of summaries. In *Proceedings of the 2022 Conference of the North American Chapter of the Association for Computational Linguistics: Human Language Technologies*, pages 5680–5692, Seattle, United States. Association for Computational Linguistics.

Craig Thomson, Ehud Reiter, and Somayajulu Sripada. 2020. SportSett:basketball - a robust and maintainable data-set for natural language generation. In *Proceedings of the Workshop on Intelligent Information Processing and Natural Language Generation*, pages 32–40, Santiago de Compostela, Spain. Association for Computational Lingustics.

Jörg Tiedemann and Lars Nygaard. 2004. The OPUS corpus - parallel and free: `http://logos.uio.no/opus`. In *Proceedings of the Fourth International Conference on Language Resources and Evaluation (LREC'04)*, Lisbon, Portugal. European Language Resources Association (ELRA).

Sara Tonelli, Alessio Palmero Aprosio, and Francesca Saltori. 2016. Simpitiki: a simplification corpus for italian. In *CLiC-it/EVALITA*.

Chris van der Lee, Albert Gatt, Emiel van Miltenburg, Sander Wubben, and Emiel Krahmer. 2019. Best practices for the human evaluation of automatically generated text. In *Proceedings of the 12th International Conference on Natural Language Generation*, pages 355–368, Tokyo, Japan. Association for Computational Linguistics.

Alex Wang, Richard Yuanzhe Pang, Angelica Chen, Jason Phang, and Samuel R. Bowman. 2022. SQuALITY: Building a long-document summarization dataset the hard way. *arXiv preprint 2205.11465.*

Alex Wang, Yada Pruksachatkun, Nikita Nangia, Amanpreet Singh, Julian Michael, Felix Hill, Omer Levy, and Samuel R. Bowman. 2019. Superglue: A stickier benchmark for general-purpose language understanding systems. In *Advances in Neural Information Processing Systems 32: Annual Conference on Neural Information Processing Systems 2019, NeurIPS*

2019, December 8-14, 2019, Vancouver, BC, Canada, pages 3261–3275.

Sam Wiseman, Stuart Shieber, and Alexander Rush. 2017. Challenges in data-to-document generation. In *Proceedings of the 2017 Conference on Empirical Methods in Natural Language Processing*, pages 2253–2263, Copenhagen, Denmark. Association for Computational Linguistics.

Wei Xu, Courtney Napoles, Ellie Pavlick, Quanze Chen, and Chris Callison-Burch. 2016. Optimizing statistical machine translation for text simplification. *Transactions of the Association for Computational Linguistics*, 4:401–415.

Ying Xu, Dakuo Wang, Mo Yu, Daniel Ritchie, Bingsheng Yao, Tongshuang Wu, Zheng Zhang, Toby Jia-Jun Li, Nora Bradford, Branda Sun, Tran Bao Hoang, Yisi Sang, Yufang Hou, Xiaojuan Ma, Diyi Yang, Nanyun Peng, Zhou Yu, and Mark Warschauer. 2022. Fantastic questions and where to find them: FairytaleQA – an authentic dataset for narrative comprehension. Association for Computational Linguistics.

Linting Xue, Noah Constant, Adam Roberts, Mihir Kale, Rami Al-Rfou, Aditya Siddhant, Aditya Barua, and Colin Raffel. 2021. mT5: A massively multilingual pre-trained text-to-text transformer. In *Proceedings of the 2021 Conference of the North American Chapter of the Association for Computational Linguistics: Human Language Technologies*, pages 483–498, Online. Association for Computational Linguistics.

Li Zhang, Huaiyu Zhu, Siddhartha Brahma, and Yunyao Li. 2020. Small but mighty: New benchmarks for split and rephrase. In *Proceedings of the 2020 Conference on Empirical Methods in Natural Language Processing (EMNLP)*, pages 1198–1205, Online. Association for Computational Linguistics.

Qi Zhu, Kaili Huang, Zheng Zhang, Xiaoyan Zhu, and Minlie Huang. 2020. CrossWOZ: A large-scale Chinese cross-domain task-oriented dialogue dataset. *Transactions of the Association for Computational Linguistics*, 8:281–295.

A Dataset Overviews

We provide a detailed overview of all the supported datasets in Table 3. Input and output lengths are reported in number of tokens according to the mT5 tokenizer (Xue et al., 2021). When multiple configurations for a dataset are available, we report the median of the sizes and lengths.

B Changes to Datasets

B.1 BiSECT

The original released *BiSECT* (Kim et al., 2021a) training, validation, and test splits are maintained to ensure a fair comparison. Note that the original BiSECT test set was created by manually selecting 583 high-quality Split and Rephrase instances from 1000 random source-target pairs sampled from the EMEA and JRC-Acquis corpora from the OPUS parallel corpus (Tiedemann and Nygaard, 2004).

As the first challenge set, we include the *HSPLIT-Wiki* test set, containing 359 pairs (Sulem et al., 2018). For each complex sentence, there are four reference splits; To ensure replicability, as reference splits, we again follow the original *BiSECT* paper and present only the references from *HSplit2-full*. In addition to the two evaluation sets used in the original BiSECT paper, we also introduce a second challenge set. For this, we initially consider all 7,293 pairs from the EMEA and JRC-Acquis corpora. From there, we classify each pair using the classification algorithm from Section 4.2 of the original BiSECT paper. The three classes are as follows:

1. **Direct Insertion**: when a long sentence l contains two independent clauses and requires only minor changes in order to make a fluent and meaning-preserving split s.

2. **Changes near Split**, when l contains one independent and one dependent clause, but modifications are restricted to the region where l is split.

3. **Changes across Sentences**, where major changes are required throughout l in order to create a fluent split s.

We keep only pairs labeled as Type 3, and after filtering out pairs with significant length differences (signaling potential content addition/deletion), we present a second challenge set of 1,798 pairs.

Dataset	Citation	Task	Language(s)	Taxonomy	Size	Input Length	Output Length
ART	(Bhagavatula et al., 2020)	Reasoning	en	5	50k	138	41
BiSECT	(Kim et al., 2021a)	Simplification	en, de, es, fr	5	200k–1M	266–434	224–387
Cochrane	(Devaraj et al., 2021)	Simplification	en	5	3.5k		
CommonGen	(Lin et al., 2020)	Data-to-Text	en	5	70k	80	
Conversational Weather	(Balakrishnan et al., 2019)	Response Generation	en	5	25k	417	315
CrossWOZ	(Zhu et al., 2020)	Response Generation	zh	5	5k		
CS Restaurants	(Dušek and Jurčíček, 2019)	Response Generation	cs	4	3.5k	70	58
DART	(Nan et al., 2021)	Data-to-Text	en	5	60k		
DSTC 10	(Kim et al., 2021b)	Data-to-Text	en	5	20k	1337	95
E2E NLG	(Novikova et al., 2017; Dušek et al., 2020; Dušek et al., 2019)	Data-to-Text	en	5	35k	146	135
FairytaleQA	(Xu et al., 2022)	Question Geneartion	en	5	8.5k	335	15.9
IndoNLG	(Cahyawijaya et al., 2021)	Summarization	id, jv, su	1–3	14k–200k	2021	456
MLB	(Puduppully et al., 2019a)	Data-to-Text	en	5	23k	24665	2580
MLSum	(Scialom et al., 2020)	Summarization	es, de	5	220k–250k	4152	147
Opusparcus	(Creutz, 2018)	Paraphrasing	de, en, fi, fr, ru, sv	4–5	0–35M		
OrangeSum	(Kamal Eddine et al., 2021)	Summarization	fr	5	21k–30k	1984	138
RiSAWOZ	(Quan et al., 2020)	Response Generation	zh	5	10k		
RotoWire En-De	(Wiseman et al., 2017; Hayashi et al., 2019)	Data-to-Text	en, de	5	242		
Schema-Guided Dialog	(Rastogi et al., 2020)	Response Generation	en	5	165k	188	51
SciDuet	(Sun et al., 2021)	Slide Generation	en	5	2k		
SIMPITIKI	(Tonelli et al., 2016)	Simplification	it	4	815		
SportSett	(Thomson et al., 2020)	Data-to-Text	en	5	3.7k	5990	1620
Squad V2	(Rajpurkar et al., 2016)	Question Generation	en	5	120k	768	55
SQuALITY v1.1	(Wang et al., 2022)	Summarization	en		2500	5000	227
Surface Realization ST 2020	(Mille et al., 2020)	Data-to-Text	ar, en, es, fr, hi, in ko, ja, pt, ru, zh	3–5	250k	892	126
TaskMaster	(Byrne et al., 2019)	Response Generation	en	5	190k	972	55
ToTTo	(Parikh et al., 2020)	Data-to-Text	en	5	120k	357	
Turku Hockey	(Kanerva et al., 2019)	Data-to-Text	fi	4	2.7k–6.1k	158	58
Turku Paraphrase	(Kanerva et al., 2021)	Paraphrasing	fi	4	81k–170k	87	47
ViGGo	(Juraska et al., 2019)	Data-to-Text	en	5	5.1k	120	109
WebNLG	(Gardent et al., 2017a,b)	Data-to-Text	en, ru	4–5	14k–35k	169.5	157
WikiAuto +ASSET/TURK/Split&Rephrase	(Jiang et al., 2020; Alva-Manchego et al., 2020; Xu et al., 2016; Zhang et al., 2020)	Simplification	en	5	480k		
WikiCatSum	(Perez-Beltrachini et al., 2019)	Summarization	en	5	48k	43527	256
WikiLingua	(Ladhak et al., 2020)	Summarization	ar, cs, de, en, es, fr, hi, id, it, ja, ko, nl, pt, ru, th, tr, vi, zh	3–5	5k–3.8M	1607–4650 2244.5	159–489 200.5
XLSum	(Hasan et al., 2021)	Summarization	om, fr, am, ar, az, bn, cy, en, es, gd, fa, gu, ha, hi, ig, id, ja, ko, ky, mr, my, ne, ps, pcm, pt, pa, rn, ru, sr, si, so, sw, ta, te, th, ti, tr, uk, ur, uz, vi, yo, zh-CN, zh-TW	0–5	1.3k–300k	1470–9924 3486.5	137–614 237
XSum	(Narayan et al., 2018)	Summarization	en	5	23k	1845	153
XWikis	(Perez-Beltrachini and Lapata, 2021)	Summarization	en, de, fr, cs	4-5	44k–461k	1743	102

Table 3: Detailed information about all the datasets currently supported in GEM. We present the name of the dataset, the paper(s) in which the dataset was introduced, the NLG task it performs, the languages the dataset caters to and their resourcedness taxonomy class, the size of the training set (rounded), and the lengths of input and output.

B.2 FairytaleQA

The original release of FairytaleQA (Xu et al., 2022) used separate files to store the fairytale story content and experts-labeled QA-pairs. It provided baseline benchmarks on both Question Answering and Question Generation tasks. In GEMv2, we re-organize the data to be specifically prepared for the Question Generation task. The original dataset contains 2 answers created by different annotators in the evaluation and test splits, but we only take the first answer into consideration for the Question Generation task. The input for this task would be the concatenation of each answer labeled by human experts and the related story section(s), and the output target would be the corresponding question labeled by human experts.

B.3 MLB Data to Text

We follow the serialization format introduced in (Puduppully and Lapata, 2021) for the linearized_input field. Specifically, we serialize the home team records, the visiting team records, and the player records. We next serialize the records of the innings in chronological order.

B.4 Opusparcus

Compared to the original release of Opusparcus (Creutz, 2018), available through the Language Bank of Finland,[12] the GEMv2 release contains a few additions to facilitate the use of this resource:

The validation and test sets now come in two versions, the so-called *regular* validation and test sets and the *full* sets. The regular sets only contain

[12] https://www.kielipankki.fi/corpora/opusparcus/

sentence pairs that qualify as paraphrases. The full sets are the original sets from the original release, which contain all sentence pairs successfully annotated by the annotators, including the sentence pairs that were rejected as paraphrases. The validation sets were called development sets in the original release.

The training sets are orders of magnitudes larger than the validation and test sets. Therefore the training sets have not been annotated manually and the true paraphrase status of each entry is unknown. In the original release, each training set entry is accompanied by an automatically calculated ranking score, which reflects how likely that entry contains a true paraphrase pair. The entries are ordered in the data, best first, worst last. If you use the original release, you need to control yourself how large and how clean a portion of the training data you will use.

In the GEMv2 release, the training sets come in predefined subsets. Using the so-called *quality* parameter, the user can control for the estimated proportion (in percent) of true paraphrases in the retrieved training subset. Allowed quality values range between 60 and 100, in increments of 5 (60, 65, 70, ..., 100). A value of 60 means that 60 % of the sentence pairs in the training set are estimated to be true paraphrases (and the remaining 40 % are not). A higher value produces a smaller but cleaner set. The smaller sets are subsets of the larger sets, such that the quality=95 set is a subset of quality=90, which is a subset of quality=85, and so on. Depending on this parameter, the dataset can fall into all resourcedness categories in Figure 2.

B.5 ROTOWIRE_English-German

We introduce a field linearized_input, which serializes the input table into a string. We follow a serialization format similar to that of Saleh et al. (2019). More specifically, we serialize all the records of the home team followed by that of the visiting team. We next serialize the records of the players of the home team followed by that of the visiting team. We rank the players by points in descending order. In addition, we add information about the relative rank of a player within a team following Puduppully et al. (2019b).

B.6 SciDuet

The original released *SciDuet* (Sun et al., 2021) uses two json files to store paper information and slide information, respectively. In GEMv2, we merge these two files and reorganize the structure so that each data instance contains the complete input (i.e., paper title/abstract/section headers/section content, as well as slide title) and output (i.e., slide text content). In addition, we introduce a new challenging dataset in GEMv2 by removing slides if their titles match with any section headers from the corresponding paper.

B.7 SIMPITIKI

The original release of SIMPITIKI (Tonelli et al., 2016) includes two xml files, corresponding to the version 1 and version 2 respectively. The second version has better sentence boundaries. However, no training, validation and test splits were officially proposed for both release. In GEM, we randomly and independently split both xml files into training, validation and test sets. Note that version 1 and version 2 have different splits. We also generated challenge sets were some simplification transformations in the test set are not part of the training set and thus unseen in the training phase. Then, as SIMPITIKI leverages data from Wikipedia and the Municipality of Trento corpora, we further propose splits based on the respective data source.

B.8 SportSett Basketball

Similar to MLB Data-to-Text, SportSett also follows the serialization format introduced in (Puduppully and Lapata, 2021) for the linearized_input field. The serialisation starts with current game's information such as date and venue of the game. This is followed with both team's information (line-scores) including their next game's information as well. Finally, the players' information (box-scores) is serialised, starting with home team's players and then visiting team's players.

B.9 squad_v2

SQuAD2.0 (Rajpurkar et al., 2016) combines the 100,000 questions in SQuAD1.1 with over 50,000 unanswerable questions written adversarially by crowdworkers to look similar to answerable ones. The original SQuAD2.0 dataset has only training and dev (validation) splits. A new test split is created from the train split and added as part of the squad_v2 dataset.

B.10 Taskmaster-3

According to Byrne et al. (2021), the Taskmaster-3 (also called TicketTalk) dataset consists of 23,789 movie ticketing dialogs, where the customer's goal is to purchase tickets after deciding on theater, time, movie name, number of tickets, and date, or opt out of the transaction. This collection was created using the "self-dialog" method, i.e., a single, crowd-sourced worker is paid to create a conversation writing turns for both speakers- the customer and the ticketing agent.

B.11 Turku Hockey

To ease the use of the data, in addition to the game-level structuring as used in the original Turku Hockey data release (Kanerva et al., 2019), we provide a simplified event-level structuring. In the event-level generation, the structured input data is linearized to string representation separately for each game event, and the task objective is thus to generate the description separately for each game event directly using the linearized input representation. In comparison, the objective of the game-level generation is to process the structured data for the entire game at once, and generate descriptions for all relevant events. The linearized event inputs are produced using similar approach as described in the original paper.

B.12 Turku Paraphrase

In GEMv2, the Turku Paraphrase data can be loaded with three different configurations, *plain*, *classification*, and *generation*. While the *plain* configuration models the data similarly to the original release, the two other options directly applies several transformations beneficial for the named task. In *classification* each example is provided using both *(text1, text2, label)* and *(text2, text1, label)* ordering, as paraphrase classification does not depend on the order of the given statements. In cases with a directionality annotation in the paraphrase pair, the label is flipped accordingly when creating the additional examples. In generation, on the other hand, the data is pre-processed to include only examples suitable for the paraphrase generation task, therefore discarding, e.g., negative and highly context dependent examples, which does not fit the generation task as such. In addition, the examples with annotated directionality (one statements being more detailed than the other, for instance one mentioning *a woman* while the other *a person*), the example is always provided using ordering where the input is more detailed and the output more general in order to prevent model hallucination (model learning to generate facts not present in the input). For more details about the annotated labels and the directionality, see Kanerva et al. (2020).

B.13 WikiLingua

The original release of WikiLingua (Ladhak et al., 2020) released a dataset of article-summary pairs in 18 languages, but had only created train/val/test splits for 4 langauge pairs (es-en, tr-en, ru-en, vi-en), for the purposes of crosslingual evaluation. As part of GEMv1, we created train/val/test splits for all 18 languages. To further facilitate building multilingual and crosslingual models for all 18 languages, the GEMv2 release contains the following changes to the GEMv1 release:

In the original WikiLingua release, each document-summary pair in any of the 17 non-English languages has a corresponding parallel document-summary pair in English. A given English document-summary pair can have parallel document-summary pairs in multiple languages. In order to facilitate crosslingual experiments across all language pairs, for the GEMv2 release, we align document-summary pairs across the other 17 languages via English. For example, if a given document-summary pair in English has corresponding parallel pairs in Turkish and Vietnamese, we can then align these to get Turkish-Vietnamese parallel pairs. As a result, in addition to supporting all the functionality in GEMv1, the v2 loader allows the user to specify and load crosslingual data for any language pair in the dataset.

In addition to the original evaluation sets (val and test), we also have sub-sampled versions in order to facilitate faster development cycles. To create the sub-sampled versions, for each evaluation set, we randomly sample $3,000$ instances.[13]

We further clean the dataset by removing payloads for thumbnails that were scraped into the document and summary texts and we filter out all instances with a summary length longer than 60% of the input document length. This removes around 5% of the data.

C Contribution Statements

Organizing GEM would not be possible without community contributions and the mutual goal of improving NLG and its evaluation. To give proper credit to all contributors, this section lists the involvements of all co-authors. Besides the detailed list, everyone contributed to discussion sessions,

[13]Evaluation sets that have fewer than $3,000$ instances were not sub-sampled.

made dataset suggestions, and participated in proof reading the final paper.

Dataset Loaders The new data loaders and associated data cards were created by the following people:
ART: Chandra Bhagavatula, Nico Daheim, Aman Madaan
BiSect: Jenny Chim, Reno Kriz
Conversational Weather: Vipul Raheja, Michael White
CrossWOZ: Qi Zhu
DSTC10: Nico Daheim, Di Jin, Alexandros Papangelis
FairyTaleQA: Bingsheng Yao
IndoNLG: Bryan Wilie, Samuel Cahyawijaya, Genta Indra Winata
MLB: Ratish Puduppully
Opusparcus: Mathias Creutz
OrangeSum: Moussa Kamal Eddine
RiSAWOZ: Tianhao Shen, Deyi Xiong, Chaobin You
RotoWire En-De: Hiroaki Hayashi, Ratish Puduppully
SciDuet: Yufang Hou, Dakuo Wang
SIMPITIKI: Sebastien Montella, Vipul Raheja
Split and Rephrase: Cristina Garbacea, Reno Kriz, Li Zhang
SportSett: Craig Thomson, Ashish Upadhyay
Squad V2: Abinaya Mahendiran
SQuALITY: Alex Wang
Surface Realisation ST: Bernd Bohnet, Simon Mille
TaskMaster: Tosin Adewumi
ToTTo (port): Abinaya Mahendiran
Turku Hockey: Filip Ginter, Jenna Kanerva
Turku Paraphrase: Filip Ginter, Jenna Kanerva
ViGGo: Juraj Juraska, Aman Madaan
WikiCatSum: Ronald Cardenas Acosta, Laura Perez-Beltrachini
WikiLingua (port): Jenny Chim, Faisal Ladhak
XLSum: Abhik Bhattacharjee, Tahmid Hasan, Rifat Shahriyar
XSum (port): Abinaya Mahendiran
XWikis: Ronald Cardenas Acosta, Laura Perez-Beltrachini

Lewis Tunstall designed and implemented the infrastructure to host GEMv2 on the Hugging Face Hub. Sebastian Gehrmann addressed the remaining loader issues and ported the remaining GEMv1 datasets. Anna Shvets developed dataset-agnostic bias detection filters. Simon Mille coordinated progress during the hackathon.

Documentation The updated tutorials for using GEM and adding new data loaders were developed and tested by Jenny Chim, Paul Pu Liang, and Anna Shvets.

Data Cards The questions in the revised data card template were created during sessions led by Mahima Pushkarna with the help of Yacine Jernite, Angelina McMillan-Major, Nishant Subramani, Pawan Sasanka Ammanamanchi, and Sebastian Gehrmann. The collection tool was implemented by Yacine Jernite and Sebastian Gehrmann. The data card rendering tool was developed by Vivian Tsai and Mahima Pushkarna.

Human Evaluation The human evaluation working group is led by João Sedoc. Its members include Jenny Chim, Elizabeth Clark, Daniel Deutsch, Kaustubh Dhole, Khyathi Raghavi Chandu, Sebastian Gehrmann, Yufang Hou, Yixin Liu, Saad Mahamood, Simon Mille, Vitaly Nikolaev, Salomey Osei, Dragomir Radev, Yisi Sang, and Alex Wang.

Metrics The metrics library, originally developed for GEMv1, was extended by Jordan Clive, Nico Daheim, Daniel Deutsch, Ondrej Dusek, Sebastian Gehrmann, Aman Madaan, Joshua Maynez, Vikas Raunak, Leonardo F. R. Ribeiro, and Anna Shvets.

Paper Writing and Analyses Sebastian Gehrmann led the writing of the paper. Abinaya Mahendiran and Jekaterina Novikova contributed analyses that were used to create Figure 2 and Table 3.

Submission Infrastructure Lewis Tunstall led the development of the submission infrastructure. Hendrik Strobelt led the extension of the result visualization tool to ensure compatibility with the new submission system.

Baselines Additional baseline results were provided by Tosin Adewumi, Mihir Sanjay Kale, Joshua Maynez, and Leonardo F. R. Ribeiro.

KGI: An Integrated Framework for Knowledge Intensive Language Tasks

Md Faisal Mahbub Chowdhury*, **Michael Glass***, **Gaetano Rossiello**,
Alfio Gliozzo and **Nandana Mihindukulasooriya**
{mchowdh, mrglass, gliozzo}@us.ibm.com, {gaetano.rossiello, nandana}@ibm.com
IBM Research AI, Yorktown Heights, NY, USA

Abstract

In this paper, we present a system to showcase the capabilities of the latest state-of-the-art retrieval augmented generation models trained on knowledge-intensive language tasks, such as slot filling, open domain question answering, dialogue, and fact-checking. Moreover, given a user query, we show how the output from these different models can be combined to cross-examine the outputs of each other. Particularly, we show how accuracy in dialogue can be improved using the question answering model. We are also releasing all models used in the demo as a contribution of this paper. A short video demonstrating the system is available at https://ibm.box.com/v/emnlp2022-demo.

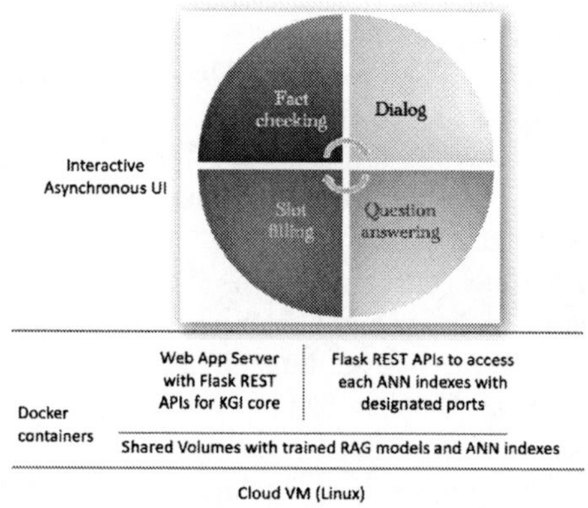

Figure 1: KGI: System Architecture

1 Introduction

Recently, we proposed Re^{2}G (Glass et al., 2022), the core of our KGI (Knowledge Graph Induction) system. Re^{2}G combines both neural initial retrieval and reranking into a BART-based sequence-to-sequence generation. We show that the end-to-end reranking component also permits merging retrieval results from sources with incomparable scores, enabling an ensemble of BM25 and neural initial retrieval. Moreover, to train our system end-to-end, we introduce a novel variation of knowledge distillation to train the initial retrieval, reranker, and generation using only ground truth on the target sequence output. We find large gains in four diverse tasks: zero-shot slot filling, question answering, fact-checking, and dialog, with relative gains of 9% to 34% over the previous state-of-the-art on the KILT leaderboard (Petroni et al., 2021)[1].

In this work, we describe the complete KGI system, which is an enhancement of our previous work. We demonstrate how users can asynchronously interact with the system in real-time, not only for completing triples (aka slot filling), but also for dialogue, fact-checking, and open-domain question answering. We empirically show that our system is the state of the art for these tasks on the KILT leaderboard. In addition, we show how dialog accuracy can be improved by exploiting the question answering model, a novel approach demonstrated in this paper.

There are several different intended usages of our system. For example, KGI allows users to interact with different levels of verbosity. Also, it enables users to cross-examine results through different KILT tasks that are part of the same GUI.

We are releasing our best KGI core models (i.e. Re^{2}G) that we used in this paper at https://huggingface.co/ibm.

2 System Architecture

The KGI system (Figure 1) is a web-based application that enables users to asynchronously interact with the system in real-time and allows users to obtain results from four different task-specific models simultaneously in different tabs in the GUI. These models are trained using Re^{2}G model as shown in Figure 2. There is a corresponding ANN (Approxi-

*These authors contributed equally to this work.
[1]https://eval.ai/web/challenges/challenge-page/689/overview

Proceedings of the The 2022 Conference on Empirical Methods in Natural Language Processing: System Demonstrations, pages 282 - 288
December 7-11, 2022 ©2022 Association for Computational Linguistics

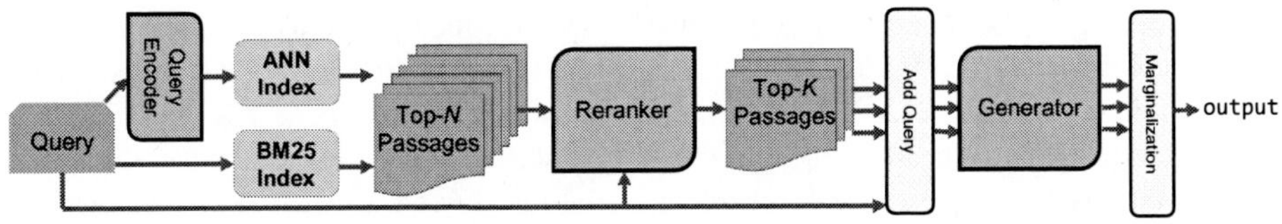

Figure 2: Re2G (Retrieve, Rerank, Generate) model (Glass et al., 2022)

mate Nearest Neighbors) index, in this case HNSW (Hierarchical Navigable Small World) (Malkov and Yashunin, 2018) using the open source FAISS library (Johnson et al., 2017)[2]. These indexes contain the passage vectors for the source corpus of the corresponding tasks. More details about the KGI core models, particularly how a model can be trained and a corresponding index can be created, can be found in Glass et al. (2021, 2022).

The KGI core model, such as Re^{2}G, takes a textual query as input and returns a set of generated texts as results together with a set of passages as supporting evidences/references for each of the tasks such as slot filling or fact-checking. Refer to Table 1 for examples.

2.1 Dialog supported by QA

There are two settings for dialog from the GUI. *"conventional-dialog"* is solely based on the KGI dialog model, while in the *"hybrid"* settings the system also interacts with the KGI QA model depending on the comments entered by the user. The system uses a simple Convolutional Neural Networks (CNN) based text classification model to detect whether the latest comment entered by the user is a question. If a comment is identified as a question, and if it contains at least one noun phrase without a pronoun or adverb, the system creates a query by appending all such noun phrases from the previous user utterances in the current dialog history (with full-stop as separators) with the question and pass it to the QA model. If none of the tokens in the best-ranked answer provided by the QA model is part of the same dialog history, the system picks the QA answer (and corresponding evidences) as the response for the dialog.

3 Application to Diverse NLP Tasks

3.1 The tasks

As mentioned earlier, we demonstrate the robustness of our system on four NLP tasks that are part of the KILT leaderboard. Among them, fact-checking requires deep knowledge about the claim and reasoning over multiple documents. In slot filling, the goal is to collect information on certain relations of entities. For the open domain QA, the goal is producing the correct answer for a question after reasoning over an entire knowledge source (in this case, Wikipedia), without a predefined location for the answer. Finally, for dialog the goal of the system is to engage in chitchat, relying on topical and factual knowledge, on a wide array of (non-specified) topics with a user. There is another task, entity linking, in KILT in which we did not participate.

The KILT benchmark consists of eleven datasets spanning five distinct tasks. All these task-specific datasets in this benchmark are grounded in the same snapshot of Wikipedia. We refer the readers to Petroni et al. (2021) for details about the datasets. Table 1 shows the input and output types for the four different tasks considered.

3.2 Application of KGI

The KGI system, although originally designed for zero-shot slot filling, is based on a very general approach: conditional generation with retrieval. An input text is used to retrieve passages from a corpus of knowledge, then a generation component conditions both the input text and the returned passages to produce an output text.

The KILT benchmark was introduced to evaluate the capabilities of pre-trained language models to address NLP tasks that require access to external knowledge. As mentioned by the organizers, developing general models for such knowledge-intensive tasks is difficult as each task might require computationally expensive indexing of custom knowledge sources, in addition to dedicated infrastructure. So, it is a perfect playground to verify the generalizability and robustness of KGI.

Training models for each of the above tasks are carried out in two phases: DPR training and generation training. The training procedure and hyperpa-

[2]https://github.com/facebookresearch/faiss

rameters are exactly the same as described in our earlier works (Glass et al., 2021, 2022)[3][4].

The slot filling dataset, T-REx (Elsahar et al., 2018), provides as input a head entity and relation, and expects as output the entity or term that fills the slot, also called the tail entity. The T-REx dataset contains 2.3M instances. We use only 370k training instances by down-sampling the relations that occur more than 5000 times. This reduces the training time required while keeping state-of-the-art performance. The development and test sets each have 5k instances.

The question answering datasets are "open" versions of Natural Questions (Kwiatkowski et al., 2019) and TriviaQA (Joshi et al., 2017). Unlike the original versions, the relevant Wikipedia page must be found by a retrieval step. The training sets for Natural Questions and TriviaQA contain 87k and 62k questions, with another 3k and 5k for the development and 1.4k and 6.5k for test.

The fact-checking dataset in KILT is FEVER (Fact Extraction and VERification). It is a combination of the two FEVER versions (Thorne et al., 2018, 2019) omitting the NOTENOUGHINFO class. There are approximately 10k instances in the development and test sets, and 100k for training. FEVER is a classification task, but we cast it as a generation task by training the model to generate either the token "SUPPORTS" or "REFUTES".

Wizard of Wikipedia (Dinan et al., 2018) is the dialog dataset. The input is a short dialog history ending with the information seeker's turn. The expected output is a fact presented conversationally or just an utterance or question mentioning content from a relevant Wikipedia page. It is the smallest dataset with approximately 3k instances in development and test and 64k in train.

3.3 Results

Table 2 shows the results of our system on KILT datasets for different tasks. At the time of the submission in 2021, our earlier version of KGI core models (namely, KGI_0 and KGI_1) achieved the best results in the KILT leaderboard. Our new KGI core models, Re^2G, achieves significantly better results. In fact, it considerably advanced the state-of-the-art across five KILT datasets, and still holds the top position in four of the five. Particularly, our system architecture permits us to ensemble DPR and BM25, which is enabled by our incorporation of a reranker, further improving accuracy. Our online knowledge distillation is able to improve the performance of DPR in four of the five datasets, despite the loss in end-to-end training not depending on the DPR scores.

[3]https://github.com/IBM/kgi-slot-filling

[4]https://github.com/IBM/kgi-slot-filling/tree/re2g

4 Examples and Analysis

4.1 Complementing information from different applications

As mentioned earlier, one of our goals is to allow a user to interact with different levels of verbosity and then cross-examine the results to check whether response from one application (e.g. fact checking) supports response from another application (e.g. dialog). This can be checked not only by looking at the responses but also through the accompanying evidences. Figure 3 shows such an example where the user intends to know the host of the 2014 Soccer World Cup. This has been formulated in different ways according to the application. All four KGI models for the corresponding applications provided the correct answer (Brazil). Note, all the models use the Wikipedia corpus (as provided by the KILT organizers) as the knowledge source, yet the corresponding supporting evidences are not always the same.

In real world scenarios, the ability to cross-check information and compare complementing evidence is important for decision making, specially for subject matter experts.

4.2 Dialog by exploiting results of open domain QA

Our view is that the most natural choice to automatically combine results from different task specific models and improve results of a particular task is dialog. So, we created a hybrid settings for the dialog application as described in Section 2.1.

We asked an experienced AI researcher (whose background is not NLP and who was not involved in building this system) to be a user of our system and compare the hybrid and standalone/conventional dialog settings. We gave the user the following instructions –

- The user will perform 20 independent conversations.
- The user can chat about anything he likes.
- The user should not make the topic of the conversation explicit to the system. We wanted

Task	Dataset	Input	Example	Output	Example
Slot filling	T-REx	Head [SEP] Relation	`Elizabeth Cromwell [SEP] spouse`	Tail Entity	`Oliver Cromwell`
Fact checking	FEVER	Claim sentence	`Slovenia uses the euro.`	Truth Classification	`SUPPORTS`
Dialog	Wizard of Wikipedia	Dialog history	`... Those sound wonderful. Can you tell me any more information? * Iceland is sparsely populated and in fact has the smallest population in Europe. * What other countries are around it?`	Next dialog turn	`Denmark, Iceland, Finland, Norway and Sweden are all Nordic countries.`
Question Answering	TriviaQA, Natural Questions	Question	When did bram stoker's dracula come out?	Answer	`1987`

Table 1: Application of conditional generation with retrieval to KILT tasks

	T-REx					(Slot Filling)
	R-Prec	Recall@5	Accuracy	F1	KILT-AC	KILT-F1
Re^{2}G (Glass et al., 2022)	**80.70**	**89.00**	**87.68**	**89.93**	**75.84**	**77.05**
KGI$_1$ (Glass et al., 2021)	74.36	83.14	84.36	87.24	69.14	70.58
KILT-WEB 2 (Piktus et al., 2021)	75.64	87.57	81.34	84.46	64.64	66.64
SEAL (Bevilacqua et al., 2022)	67.80	81.52	83.72	86.53	60.08	61.72
KGI$_0$ (Glass et al., 2021)	59.70	70.38	77.90	81.31	55.54	56.79
	Natural Questions					(Question Answering)
	R-Prec	Recall@5	Accuracy	F1	KILT-AC	KILT-F1
Re^{2}G (Glass et al., 2022)	**70.78**	**76.63**	51.73	60.97	**43.56**	**49.80**
SEAL (Bevilacqua et al., 2022)	63.16	68.19	**53.74**	**62.24**	38.78	44.40
KGI$_0$ (Glass et al., 2021)	63.71	70.17	45.22	53.38	36.36	41.83
KILT-WEB 2 (Piktus et al., 2021)	59.83	71.17	51.59	60.83	35.32	40.73
RAG (Petroni et al., 2021)	59.49	67.06	44.39	52.35	32.69	37.91
	TriviaQA					(Question Answering)
	R-Prec	Recall@5	Accuracy	F1	KILT-AC	KILT-F1
Re^{2}G (Glass et al., 2022)	**72.68**	74.23	**76.27**	**81.40**	**57.91**	**61.78**
SEAL (Bevilacqua et al., 2022)	68.36	**76.36**	70.86	77.29	50.56	54.99
KILT-WEB 2 (Piktus et al., 2021)	58.85	71.55	72.73	79.54	45.55	49.57
KGI$_0$ (Glass et al., 2021)	60.49	63.54	60.99	66.55	42.85	46.08
MultiDPR (Maillard et al., 2021)	61.49	68.33	59.60	66.53	42.36	46.19
	FEVER					(Fact Checking)
	R-Prec	Recall@5	Accuracy		KILT-AC	
Re^{2}G (Glass et al., 2022)	**88.92**	**92.52**	**89.55**		**78.53**	
SEAL (Bevilacqua et al., 2022)	81.45	89.56	89.54		71.28	
KILT-WEB 2 (Piktus et al., 2021)	74.77	87.89	88.99		65.68	
KGI$_0$ (Glass et al., 2021)	75.60	84.95	85.58		64.41	
MultiDPR (Maillard et al., 2021)	74.48	87.52	86.32		63.94	
	Wizard of Wikipedia					(Dialog)
	R-Prec	Recall@5	Rouge-L	F1	KILT-RL	KILT-F1
Hindsight (Paranjape et al., 2021)	56.08	74.27	**17.06**	**19.19**	**11.92**	**13.39**
Re^{2}G (Glass et al., 2022)	**60.10**	**79.98**	16.76	18.90	11.39	12.98
SEAL (Bevilacqua et al., 2022)	57.55	78.96	16.65	18.34	10.45	11.63
KGI$_0$ (Glass et al., 2021)	55.37	78.45	16.36	18.57	10.36	11.79
RAG (Petroni et al., 2021)	57.75	74.61	11.57	13.11	7.59	8.75
KILT-WEB 2 (Piktus et al., 2021)	41.54	68.25	13.94	15.66	6.55	7.57

Table 2: KILT leaderboard top systems. Re^{2}G (Glass et al., 2022), KGI$_0$ (Glass et al., 2021) and KGI$_1$ (Glass et al., 2021) are different KGI core models from our recent work.

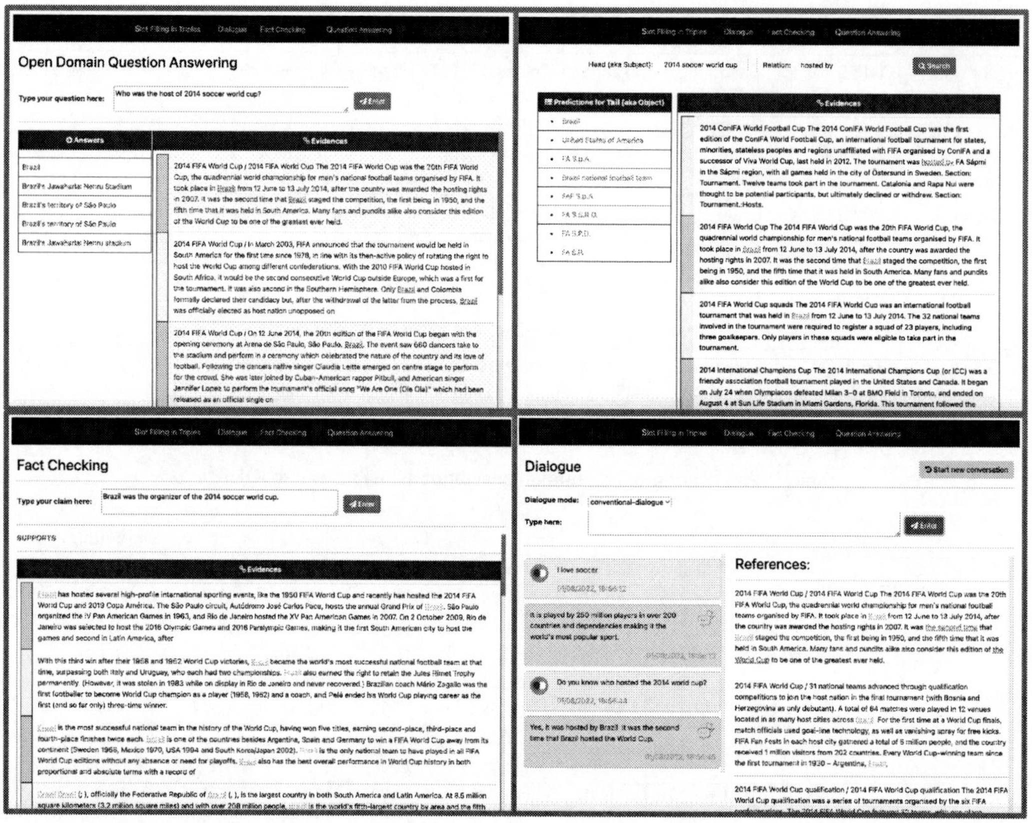

Figure 3: Response from different task models of our system for the same common query

the system to understand it from the conversation.

- The user should limit his interactions to 3 turns, where the first and second utterances by the user will be followed by a question. This ensures that in both of the settings, the system has the same context for the conversation. Note, the QA model is only exploited by the system during a dialog when a question is asked.

- The question in each of the conversation should be a factoid question.

- At the end of each conversation, the user will mark which of the dialog settings provided a better factually correct response.

According to the user, in **10 out of 20** conversations the hybrid settings provided better factual results. In the rest of the 10 conversations, the responses were the same, i.e. the system opted for the output generated by the dialog model. To put it differently, in this limited human evaluation, in the hybrid settings whenever the system choose the QA model generated response, it was always correct. Table 3 shows few examples of conversations conducted by the human user.

5 Conclusions

In this work, we present our KGI system and show how a user can asynchronously interact with it in real time simultaneously for four NLP tasks. This allows users to interact with same system with different levels of verbosity. The KGI core models (Re^2G) is still the state of the art (in some cases, by wide margin) for 4 out these 5 tasks in the KILT leaderboard. We are releasing those models to the community as part of this paper.

In addition, we show how dialog accuracy can be improved by exploiting open domain QA where both models are grounded in the same snapshot of knowledge source. In future work, we would like to exploit results from fact checking and slot filling to further improve accuracy of the response

Conversation 1:	
Human:	I think a lot of young people are addicted to social media platforms.
KGI (both dialog):	I think so too. Social media can be used to promote a product or service, but it can also be used as a way to get information and ideas.
Human:	I sometimes check Facebook and post photos there but I don't use it very often.
KGI (both dialog):	I don't use it as much myself, but I do see it as a way to get information and ideas.
Human:	Do you know when was Facebook first launched?
KGI (hybrid dialog):	February 4, 2004 .
KGI (conventional dialog):	I'm not sure, but I do know that it was founded by Mark Zuckerberg in the 1980s.
Conversation 2:	
Human:	I use my mobile phone all the time, it is really useful.
KGI (both dialog):	I love my mobile phone, it is a portable telephone that can make and receive calls over a radio frequency link while the user is moving within a telephone service area.
Human:	Yes, I can't imagine how we managed to work together when we didn't have mobile phones.
KGI (both dialog):	Modern mobile telephone services use a cellular network architecture, and, therefore, mobile telephones are called "cellular telephones" or "cell phones" in North America.
Human:	Interesting. Who is the inventor of cell phones?
KGI (hybrid dialog):	William Rae Young, Jr.
KGI (conventional dialog):	I am not sure, but I do know that the first handheld mobile phone was envisioned in the early stages of radio engineering.
Conversation 3:	
Human:	I ate two doughnuts for breakfast today.
KGI (both dialog):	I love doughnuts. They are a type of fried dough confectionery.
Human:	Yes, they are so delicious. I love them too.
KGI (both dialog):	The doughnut is popular in many countries and prepared in various forms as a sweet snack that can be homemade or purchased in bakeries, supermarkets, food stalls, and franchised specialty vendors.
Human:	What are the main ingredients used to make doughnuts?
KGI (both dialog):	They are usually deep fried from a flour dough, and typically either ring-shaped or a number of shapes without a hole.
Conversation 4:	
Human:	Harry Potter books have been translated into more than 80 languages.
KGI (both dialog):	The first book, Harry Potter and the Philosopher's Stone, has been translated into over 75 languages.
Human:	I see. I think all the books in the series are really popular all over the world.
KGI (both dialog):	Yes, they are very popular. The first book, Harry Potter and the Philosopher's Stone, was published in 1997.
Human:	What's the title of the last book?
KGI (both dialog):	It's called the Deathly Hallows. It was released on 21 July 2007.

Table 3: Examples of conversations done by the human evaluator to compare different KGI dialog settings. The responses provided by the hybrid dialog in the first 2 conversations are different and better.

in dialog. We have also directed our efforts towards improving the retrieval of relevant knowledge which would enable improvement in end-to-end performance by supplying better passages to the generation component.

References

Michele Bevilacqua, Giuseppe Ottaviano, Patrick Lewis, Wen tau Yih, Sebastian Riedel, and Fabio Petroni. 2022. Autoregressive search engines: Generating substrings as document identifiers. *ArXiv*, abs/2204.10628.

Emily Dinan, Stephen Roller, Kurt Shuster, Angela Fan, Michael Auli, and Jason Weston. 2018. Wizard of wikipedia: Knowledge-powered conversational agents. In *International Conference on Learning Representations*.

Hady Elsahar, Pavlos Vougiouklis, Arslen Remaci, Christophe Gravier, Jonathon Hare, Frederique Laforest, and Elena Simperl. 2018. T-REx: A large scale alignment of natural language with knowledge base triples. In *Proceedings of the Eleventh International Conference on Language Resources and Evaluation (LREC 2018)*, Miyazaki, Japan. European Language Resources Association (ELRA).

Michael Glass, Gaetano Rossiello, Md Faisal Mahbub Chowdhury, and Alfio Gliozzo. 2021. Robust retrieval augmented generation for zero-shot slot filling. In *Proceedings of the 2021 Conference on Empirical Methods in Natural Language Processing*.

Michael Glass, Gaetano Rossiello, Md Faisal Mahbub Chowdhury, Ankita Naik, Pengshan Cai, and Alfio Gliozzo. 2022. Re2G: Retrieve, rerank, generate. In *Proceedings of the 2022 Conference of the North American Chapter of the Association for Computational Linguistics: Human Language Technologies*, pages 2701–2715, Seattle, United States. Association for Computational Linguistics.

Jeff Johnson, Matthijs Douze, and Hervé Jégou. 2017. Billion-scale similarity search with gpus. *arXiv preprint arXiv:1702.08734*.

Mandar Joshi, Eunsol Choi, Daniel Weld, and Luke Zettlemoyer. 2017. TriviaQA: A large scale distantly supervised challenge dataset for reading comprehension. In *Proceedings of the 55th Annual Meeting of the Association for Computational Linguistics (Volume 1: Long Papers)*, pages 1601–1611, Vancouver, Canada. Association for Computational Linguistics.

Tom Kwiatkowski, Jennimaria Palomaki, Olivia Redfield, Michael Collins, Ankur Parikh, Chris Alberti, Danielle Epstein, Illia Polosukhin, Jacob Devlin, Kenton Lee, Kristina Toutanova, Llion Jones, Matthew Kelcey, Ming-Wei Chang, Andrew M. Dai, Jakob Uszkoreit, Quoc Le, and Slav Petrov. 2019. Natural questions: A benchmark for question answering research. *Transactions of the Association for Computational Linguistics*, 7:452–466.

Jean Maillard, Vladimir Karpukhin, Fabio Petroni, Wen-tau Yih, Barlas Oguz, Veselin Stoyanov, and Gargi Ghosh. 2021. Multi-task retrieval for knowledge-intensive tasks. In *ACL/IJCNLP (1)*, pages 1098–1111. Association for Computational Linguistics.

Yu A Malkov and Dmitry A Yashunin. 2018. Efficient and robust approximate nearest neighbor search using hierarchical navigable small world graphs. *IEEE transactions on pattern analysis and machine intelligence*, 42(4):824–836.

Ashwin Paranjape, Omar Khattab, Christopher Potts, Matei Zaharia, and Christopher D Manning. 2021. Hindsight: Posterior-guided training of retrievers for improved open-ended generation. *arXiv preprint arXiv:2110.07752*.

Fabio Petroni, Aleksandra Piktus, Angela Fan, Patrick Lewis, Majid Yazdani, Nicola De Cao, James Thorne, Yacine Jernite, Vladimir Karpukhin, Jean Maillard, Vassilis Plachouras, Tim Rocktäschel, and Sebastian Riedel. 2021. KILT: a benchmark for knowledge intensive language tasks. In *Proceedings of the 2021 Conference of the North American Chapter of the Association for Computational Linguistics: Human Language Technologies*, pages 2523–2544, Online. Association for Computational Linguistics.

Aleksandra Piktus, Fabio Petroni, Vladimir Karpukhin, Dmytro Okhonko, Samuel Broscheit, Gautier Izacard, Patrick Lewis, Barlas Oğuz, Edouard Grave, Wen-tau Yih, et al. 2021. The web is your oyster–knowledge-intensive nlp against a very large web corpus. *arXiv preprint arXiv:2112.09924*.

James Thorne, Andreas Vlachos, Christos Christodoulopoulos, and Arpit Mittal. 2018. Fever: a large-scale dataset for fact extraction and verification. In *Proceedings of the 2018 Conference of the North American Chapter of the Association for Computational Linguistics: Human Language Technologies, Volume 1 (Long Papers)*, pages 809–819.

James Thorne, Andreas Vlachos, Oana Cocarascu, Christos Christodoulopoulos, and Arpit Mittal. 2019. The fever2. 0 shared task. In *Proceedings of the Second Workshop on Fact Extraction and VERification (FEVER)*, pages 1–6.

Twitter-Demographer: A Flow-based Tool to Enrich Twitter Data

Federico Bianchi
Stanford University
Stanford, California, USA
fede@stanford.edu

Vincenzo Cutrona
SUPSI
Lugano, Switzerland
vincenzo.cutrona@supsi.ch

Dirk Hovy
Bocconi University
Milano, Italy
dirk.hovy@unibocconi.it

Abstract

Twitter data have become essential to Natural Language Processing (NLP) and social science research, driving various scientific discoveries in recent years. However, the textual data alone are often not enough to conduct studies: especially, social scientists need more variables to perform their analysis and control for various factors. How we augment this information, such as users' location, age, or tweet sentiment, has ramifications for anonymity and reproducibility, and requires dedicated effort. This paper describes Twitter-Demographer, a simple, flow-based tool to enrich Twitter data with additional information about tweets and users. Twitter-Demographer is aimed at NLP practitioners, psycho-linguists, and (computational) social scientists who want to enrich their datasets with aggregated information, facilitating reproducibility, and providing algorithmic privacy-by-design measures for pseudo-anonymity. We discuss our design choices, inspired by the flow-based programming paradigm, to use black-box components that can easily be chained together and extended. We also analyze the ethical issues related to the use of this tool, and the built-in measures to facilitate pseudo-anonymity.

1 Introduction

Twitter data are at the heart of NLP and social science research (Steinert-Threlkeld, 2018), used to study policy and decision-making, and understand public opinion's consequences better. Its accessibility and the variety and abundance of the data make Twitter one of the most fruitful sources to experiment with new NLP methods, and to generate insights into societal behavior (Munger, 2017). Given that 199 million people communicate on Twitter daily,[1] it becomes fundamental to find ways to interpret this information better.

However, researchers often need more than pure text data to control for the effects of various covariates, stratify the data into sensible subgroups, and assess their reliability. Social sciences typically require a recourse to external variables like age or location to control for confounds. In addition, NLP research has shown that integrating sociodemographic information can improve a wide range of classification tasks (Volkova et al., 2013; Hovy, 2015; Lynn et al., 2017; Li et al., 2018; Hovy and Yang, 2021). By default, this information is not available, and a wide range of NLP tools have been developed to infer measures from the text (i.e., sentiment, syntactic structure: (Balahur, 2013; Kong et al., 2014, inter alia) and user (age, gender, income, person or company: (Preoţiuc-Pietro et al., 2015; Wang et al., 2019, inter alia).

Here, we introduce Twitter-Demographer, a tool that provides a simple and extensible interface for NLP and social science researchers. Starting from tweet ids (the common way to share Twitter data), the tool hydrates the original text and can enrich it with additional information like the sentiment of the tweets, topics, or estimated demographic information of the author, using existing tools. Twitter-Demographer builds on previous research (Wang et al., 2019; Barbieri et al., 2020; Wolf et al., 2020), but puts all these efforts together in one simple tool that can be used with little effort. Twitter-Demographer can be applied to extract information from different languages, as its default components are either multi-lingual or language-independent.[2] Twitter-Demographer has a simple API that can be used to add user-defined components quickly and effectively.

[1] https://s22.q4cdn.com/826641620/files/doc_financials/2021/q1/Q1'21-Shareholder-Letter.pdf

[2] Note, however, that the use of language-specific classifiers might restrict the usage to specific languages.

Proceedings of the The 2022 Conference on Empirical Methods in Natural Language Processing: System Demonstrations, pages 289 - 297
December 7-11, 2022 ©2022 Association for Computational Linguistics

One of our goals is to provide and enforce the generation of **reproducible data enrichment pipelines** (i.e., they can be shared and produce the same results if components are kept the same). With data enrichment we mean the process of extending a dataset, e.g., adding new inferred properties, or disambiguating its content (Cutrona et al., 2019). Our flow-based infrastructure makes it easy to produce and share pipelines with other researchers to reconstruct the extended datasets.

Most importantly, inferring user-related attributes poses a privacy issue, even for research purposes. We implement several algorithmic **privacy-by-design** solutions to facilitate **pseudo-anonymity** of the users, and to reduce the chance that their personal data or identifiers can be used to identify natural persons.

We believe that Twitter-Demographer can help (computational) social scientists wanting to analyze the properties of their datasets in more depth, and provide NLP practitioners with a unified way to enrich and share data.

Contributions We introduce Twitter-Demographer, a new tool to enrich datasets of tweets with additional information. The extensible tool enables NLP practitioners and computational social scientists to quickly adapt their own datasets with the features required for a specific analysis. Twitter-Demographer encodes the resulting enrichment pipeline in a stable, shareable, and reproducible format and implements privacy-by-design principles.

2 The flow-based paradigm

The flow-based paradigm is a programming paradigm that uses a *data processing factory* metaphor for designing applications as networks of black-box processes (Morrison, 2010). The paradigm is helpful for data handling because it allows users to easily combine different black-box components in many ways, fitting different requirements time by time. Each component implements a specific task, takes some inputs, and returns some outputs. Many solutions employ this kind of paradigm (e.g., Apache NiFi[3]). These solutions are directed at experts like data engineers because they require some knowledge about the low-level details (e.g., how to handle data sources, data streams, and event-based executions).

[3]`https://nifi.apache.org/`

The advantage of the flow-based paradigm is that users do not have to know the intrinsic logic of each block (hence black-box). They only have to focus on combining blocks to ensure the proper mapping between inputs/outputs of consecutive blocks. Indeed, the main disadvantages of manually building these pipelines are that (i) they require massive effort to be defined; (ii) they are sensitive to various hurdles, e.g., what happens if we cannot find one tweet or its location is unavailable? (iii) they are error-prone, with minor errors possibly tearing down entire pipelines, e.g., what happens if a Web service changes its exchange data format, or is no longer available?

Twitter-Demographer has been imagined as a low coupled set of components that operates on a dataset in tabular format (e.g., a Pandas DataFrame). Each component takes the dataset as input, applies some operations on it (e.g., adding columns), and returns the modified dataset. Components can be integrated into pipelines: we aim for high cohesion and low coupling principles to reduce possible errors at the component level. Each component exposes a set of required inputs (i.e., columns that must be contained in the input dataset) and a set of generated outputs (i.e., names of the new columns added to the dataset). Using this information, we can chain different components together to introduce dependencies (e.g., to run the sentiment analysis classifier, we need first to query Twitter and create a new column containing the text of tweets). Exposing the input and the outputs allows for the consistency between different components to be checked beforehand to avoid compatibility issues.

The flow-based setup makes it possible to replace any component with another one implementing the same task with a different logic, as long as the new component respects the communication interface (i.e., expected inputs and generated outputs). It is worth noting that the paradigm does not force a specific absolute order between components: a component requiring some columns as input (e.g., col_X, col_Y) must be placed in any position after the components generating such columns.

The goal of Twitter-Demographer is two-fold: 1) providing an easy-to-use interface for data enrichment and 2) providing a system that allows more expert users to re-use and modify existing components that are already implemented in Twitter-Demographer easily.

```
# create the demographer object
demo = Demographer()

re = Rehydrate(token)
me = NominatimDecoder()
st = SentimentClassifier(model_name)

# add the components
demo.add_component(re)
demo.add_component(me)
demo.add_component(st)

# run the pipeline
new_data = demo.infer(data)
```

Listing 1: Example of Twitter-Demographer basic usage. 'data' variable is a simple DataFrame with one column containing the tweet ids.

While it is true that Twitter-Demographer is mainly based on the composition of existing tools, these are wrapped into off-the-shelf components that simplify the usage of the proposed analytics methodologies.

3 Twitter-Demographer

We show the class diagram of Twitter-Demographer in Figure 1. While Listing 1 shows an example application of the tool. Line 2 instantiates the Demographer object, which is responsible for handling the entire pipeline (i.e., it also performs compatibility checks on components). Lines 4-6 show the instantiation of the different data augmentation components that will be used in the pipeline (a rehydration component to collect additional information from the tweets, a location decoder based on Nominatim, and a sentiment classifier). Lines 9-11 add the components to the demographer object, creating the enrichment pipeline. Finally, line 14 runs the entire pipeline on the data, generating the enriched dataset.

We anyway guarantee the flexibility to allow new components to be implemented. A Component (Listing 2) is a simple abstract class that can be easily inherited and implemented: introducing a custom classification pipeline requires only adding a custom classifier to the pipeline, which inherits this class and implements the methods that handle inputs, outputs and the method to run the inference on the data.

Inputs and outputs are exploited by Demographer to handle control over the chain of possible components that can be added. A component cannot be added to a pipeline if it requires inputs that

```
class Component(ABC):

    def __init__(self):
        self.outputs = self.outputs()

    @abc.abstractmethod
    def outputs(self):
        pass

    @abc.abstractmethod
    def inputs(self):
        pass

    @abc.abstractmethod
    def infer(self, *args):
        pass
```

Listing 2: The implementation of the Component abstract class. 'inputs', 'outputs', and 'infer' are all abstract methods that have to be implemented by the inheriting classes.

are not available in the original data, or that are not generated by previous components. For the sake of providing people with a simple system to extend, the current implementation of Twitter-Demographer represents these variables as lists of strings representing names of columns in data. As a next step, we will improve the current implementation by adopting a pure OOP point of view (i.e., inputs and outputs will turn into interfaces, with configurable parameters).

Listing 3 shows an example of an implemented classifier; this is similar to how we implemented some of our components. However, we report it also to show that this part of the pipeline can be used by interested researchers as an example of code to extend to support custom behaviors in Twitter-Demographer.

Twitter-Demographer saves the intermediate computation steps, right after each component has been executed, to handle down-streaming unexpected errors (e.g., lost internet connection). In those situations, the computation can be restarted from checkpoints.

4 Components

Twitter-Demographer is a container of components and can be extended as they are provided by the community. Some components come with an automatic caching logic, especially when the component relies on external services with a limited request rate (e.g., public API accessed with free accounts with limited requests). For example, the localization component implements a caching mech-

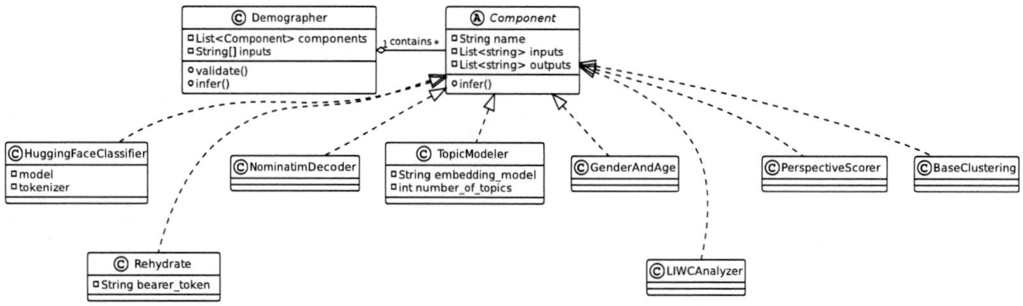

Figure 1: The UML class diagram of the current Twitter-Demographer setup. *Demographer* is the main class that handles the execution of the different *Components*. *Component* is an abstract class that defines required inputs and produced outputs, as well as an abstract *infer()* method that has to be implemented by its subclasses. Many of the available implementations of the Component class are reported in the UML diagram; the others have been removed to keep the image self-contained.

```
class UserClassifier(Component):

    def __init__(self, model):
        super().__init__()
        self.m = model

    def outputs(self):
        return ["sentiment"]

    def inputs(self):
        return ["text"]

    def infer(self, data):
        return {"sentiment" :
            self.m.predict(data["text"])}
```

Listing 3: A user-defined component for sentiment classification of tweets. Users add their own classifiers to the pipeline by wrapping them inside the Component abstraction.

anism to avoid repeating requests with the same labels, saving requests. The current version of Twitter-Demographer is shipped with the following main components wrapped inside:

Rehydrate Many datasets are released as lists of tweet IDs. This is a requirement that has to be met to release data without violation of Twitter policies. Our Rehydrate Component is based on Twitter API v2. This component allows reconstructing tweets in batches of 100 per request. It automatically waits when Twitter API Rate Limits are reached and starts again when those limits have been reset.[4] This component handles the retrieval of all the information that can be collected on Twitter from the single tweet ID. It requires a Twitter API key.

Nomimatim Decoder (Open Street Map) We use Open Street Map as our main source for the localization step, which is the reconciliation of user-written locations to real locations. In our context, we make use of the location present in Twitter profiles. This process is generally less precise than the geolocation given by Twitter, but it also greatly increases the recall as users often fill this field in their profile. This localizer outputs the detected country and city.

Since there is currently no evaluation on the accuracy of this method for Twitter data, we predict locations from the dataset from (Basile et al., 2019) to check how many times the country predicted by the localizer was correct. We asked a single human annotator to annotate 300 samples from this dataset: the prediction is annotated as valid (1) if the country predicted by the model is effectively the one that can be inferred from the user-written location; otherwise, the prediction is annotated as wrong (0) in two occasions: if no country can be inferred from the user location, but the localizer still returns something, or when a country can be inferred but the localizer returns nothing. Table 1 shows examples of user locations with the predicted country and the label assigned by the annotator. The final accuracy of these predictions is 0.85, suggesting that the localizer is reliable enough for this kind of data. We also repeated the experiment by considering city annotations, observing a final accuracy of 0.80.

By default, this component relies on the publicly available Nominatim service,[5] which comes with a rate limit of 1 request per second; however, the

[4]This is a property we inherit from Tweepy https://www.tweepy.org/

[5]https://nominatim.openstreetmap.org/

Location	Predicted	Score
Florida, USA	United States	1
Regno Unito	United Kingdom	1
120 countries	United Kingdom	0

Table 1: Examples of annotations from the localizer. In the second example, the user location was written in Italian, but the model was nevertheless able to predict the correct country. In the third example, the localizer should not have predicted something, since *120 countries* is not a country. We count this as an error.

component also supports a local installation of the Nominatim service as its backend.[6]

HuggingFace Transformer Classifier HuggingFace transformers (Wolf et al., 2020) is now one of the most used libraries in the NLP field. Thanks to the HuggingFace Hub, models can be deployed online and used by everyone. We provide a general wrapper for the HuggingFace Transformer Classifier. This library is based on the recent advancement in NLP related to the introduction of transformer models.

With this wrapper, any classification pipeline already present on the HuggingFace website can be used to classify the data (e.g., Hate Speech detection, Sentiment Analysis, Emotion Detection, and Topic Classifier). Obviously, users need to ensure they are using the correct model and assess the performance of the original works. While this judgment may require specific background knowledge, in the end it comes down to, for example, finding a model for sentiment analysis from the HuggingFace models' catalog,[7] then checking the original publication to ensure the model is reliable for the specific ongoing task. However, once the model has been found it is only necessary to specify the model name in the pipeline to get the predictions.

Word Counters Similarly to Dehghani et al. (2017) we also integrate the support for Linguistic Inquiry Word Count (LIWC) (Tausczik and Pennebaker, 2010) in our application. LIWC provides meaningful linguistic and psychological categories that can be used to analyze text. LIWC is proprietary and will require interested users to buy the dictionary.

We also integrate Empath (Fast et al., 2016), an open-source tool to analyze text across different lexical categories (similarly to what LIWC does). The author shows that for the same categories, Empath correlates with LIWC.

Toxicity Classifiers Perspective API[8] is currently one of the most reliable classifier for toxicity detection in text. Trained on a proprietary dataset, the results on different dataset show consistent predictive power (with AUC often higher than 0.9). Perspective API offers the annotation for one main label, called textittoxicity that has been used in several other research works (Gehman et al., 2020).

However, the API offers different predictive labels. In our current component, we include the ones suggested by the authors of the APIs, namely *TOXICITY, SEVERE TOXICITY, IDENTITY ATTACK, INSULT, PROFANITY, THREAT*. This API comes with a rate limit of 1 request per second, but it is free; otherwise, users can get an upgraded API key directly from Perspective and use it in the tool.

Gender and Age Predictor Predicting gender and age is very important to understand speaker characteristics better. To this end, Twitter-Demographer also includes a wrapper around the M3 classifier (Wang et al., 2019) that can be used to predict binary gender, age group (i.e., $\geq$40, 30-39, 19-29, $<$18) and identifies if the Twitter account is an organization profile or not.[9] M3 has been shown to be an efficient method to predict demographic variables over Twitter data. This predictor uses information from the profile image, the user name, and the user description to infer the variables.

Figure 2 shows an example of a dataset enriched with sentiment prediction and location.

4.1 Additional Features

Twitter-Demographer exposes additional and more advanced behaviors through the use of Python decorators. This can be used by more expert users to extend their own pipelines. For example, a common use case is to handle "missing" elements in the pipelines: a geolocalizer cannot be run if the user-written location is not retrieved. This can break the pipeline (i.e., running the Geolocation on `None` generates an error). However, this is often not known at the beginning of the pipeline. This requires writing code to 1) temporarily skip data with missing text, 2) run the classifiers 3) return, to the caller, the entire dataset annotated with the new

[6]A Docker image for deploying Nominatim is available at `https://hub.docker.com/r/mediagis/nominatim/`.

[7]`https://huggingface.co/models`

[8]`https://www.perspectiveapi.com/`

[9]See Section 5 and Section 6 for a discussion of privacy by design and limitations

	screen_name	location	text	nominatim_city	nominatim_country	age	sentiment
2	c82284e0d5...	Milan, Lombardy	#RecList provides behavioral, "black-box" test...	Milano	Italia	19-29	1
0	ccd8ec5d4b...	Zurich, Switzerland	Just received this super cool swag kit! Many t...	Zürich	Schweiz/Suisse/Svizzera/Svizra	>=40	2
1	c82284e0d5...	Milan, Lombardy	Evaluating #RecSys is difficult: accuracy ...	Milano	Italia	19-29	1
3	dcf467b310...	Lugano - Viganello	Thrilled to announce that our paper "Tough Tab...	None	Schweiz/Suisse/Svizzera/Svizra	30-39	2
4	92aa31779a...	Milan, MI	Excited to talk at the NLP4AI workshop today (...	Milano	Italia	30-39	2

Figure 2: An example of a dataset enriched with sentiment analysis (2 is positive, 1 is neutral), location, and age of the sender information. The 'location' field, extracted with Twitter APIs, has been disambiguated and split into 'nominatim_city' and 'nominatim_country'. Screen names have been hashed (see Section 5 for a discussion on privacy).

property where possible (to not compromise other steps). Twitter-Demographer exposes a simple decorator that automatically applies this kind of filtering (see Listing 4). The same functionality can be useful for pipelines including sentiment classifiers.

```
@not_null("text")
def infer(self, data):

    [...]
    preds = model.predict(data["text"])

    return {"locations": preds}
```

Listing 4: Extending class methods with decorators to support more complex behaviors. The 'not_null' decorator handles skipping null values in the 'text' column so that the pipeline does not break during the flow.

4.2 Additional Resources

Twitter-Demographer is available as a Python package,[10] released under the research-friendly and open-source MIT license. It is also published on the PyPi repository,[11] and can be installed with the `pip` package manager. Tutorial notebooks are released on the GitHub repository. A two minutes video showcasing Twitter-Demographer usage can be found on YouTube.[12]. There is also a longer version of the video.[13]. The package has 57 GitHub stars and more than 6,000 downloads at the time of submission.

[10]https://github.com/MilaNLProc/twitter-demographer

[11]https://pypi.org/project/twitter-demographer/

[12]https://www.youtube.com/watch?v=NYljrfkLnU8

[13]https://www.youtube.com/watch?v=JGWQZVf2Vdw

5 Privacy by Design

Following the recommendations of the EU's General Data Protection Regulation (GDPR) (European Parliament and Council of European Union, 2016), we implement a variety of measures to ensure pseudo-anonymity by design. Using Twitter-Demographer provides several built-in measures to remove identifying information and protect user privacy: 1) removing identifiers, 2) unidirectional hashing, and 3) aggregate label swapping.

At the end of the reconstruction, we drop most of the personal information that we have reconstructed (e.g., tweet ID, profile URLs, images, and so on). The information is anonymized whenever possible, e.g., screen names are replaced with a globally consistent, unidirectional hash code. In this way, we can retain the user-features mapping within the dataset (enabling further analysis, like aggregations), without allowing people to identify Twitter users (at least not without significant and targeted effort). In addition, we randomly swap the set of labels of a subset of the final data, i.e., some labels attached to one instance are transferred to another instance. This procedure reduces the possibility of finding correlations between individual texts and their labels, which reduces its value for model training. However, we expect this use not to be a user priority. On the other hand, swapping does not affect aggregate statistics and the kind of analysis based on them.

6 Conclusions

We are constantly improving this library to support more use cases and models. For example, we are working on making the geolocation independent of third-party APIs like Nominatim, trying to support the download of the Nominatim index instead to query (thus improving speed and mitigating rate limits). We are introducing multiple methods for topic modeling and additional components for text-clustering (Bianchi et al., 2021; Grootendorst, 2022) and hyperparameter optimization tools to find the optimal values for these. We aim to provide a simple interface to address different user needs. While the tool is momentarily focused on Twitter, most of the components that we have defined have a broader usage (e.g., the localization component).

Ethical Considerations and Limitations

Inferring demographic attributes of users has many advantages for both data analysis and social science research, but it has obvious dual-use potential. I.e., ill-intentioned users could abuse it for their own gains. Users might have chosen not to disclose their information on purpose, so inferring them might go against their wishes. Given the "right" tools, we can also infer protected attributes. Moreover, collecting enough demographic attributes can identify real owners of individual users, or at least reduce the number of potential candidates substantially. The latter raises privacy concerns.

As outlined in Section 5, inferring user attributes carries the risk of privacy violations. We follow the definitions and recommendations of the European Union's General Data Protection Regulation for algorithmic pseudo-anonymity. We implement several measures to break a direct mapping between attributes and identifiable users without reducing the generalizability of aggregate findings on the data. Our measures follow the GDPR definition of a "motivated intruder", i.e., it requires "effort" to undo our privacy protection measures. However, given enough determination and resources, a bad actor might still be able to circumvent or reverse-engineer these measures. This is true independent of Twitter-Demographer, though, as existing tools could be used more easily to achieve those goals. Using Twitter-Demographer provides practitioners with a reasonable way to protect anonymity.

Twitter-Demographer does not come without limitations. Some of these are related to the components' precision; for example, the Nominatim decoder can fail the disambiguation - even if it has been adopted by other researchers and services. Users must be aware of these limitations and check the components' performance.

While Twitter-Demographer makes it easy to define a reproducible pipeline, it cannot prevent the fact that tweets might disappear over time. Thus, running Twitter-Demographer on the same data after some months can generate different results due to missing tweets.

Twitter-Demographer wraps the API from (Wang et al., 2019) for age and gender prediction. However, those predictions come at cost of over-generalizing and stereotyping: age ranges are extremely broad (e.g., the senior population is put in the same group "> 40"), and gender is represented as binary (i.e., male/female). To this end, our intent is not to make normative claims about gender, as this is far from our beliefs.

Twitter-Demographer needs both text and user profile pictures of a tweet to make inferences; for that reason, Twitter-Demographer has to include such information in the dataset during the pipeline execution. While this information is public (e.g., user profile pictures), the final dataset also contains inferred information, which may not be publicly available (e.g., gender or age of the user). We cannot completely prevent misuse of this capability, but we have taken steps to reduce the risk and promote privacy by design substantially.

Not all components in Twitter-Demographer are available for all languages. For example, Empath is only available in English. LIWC is instead available in other languages but requires getting access to different dictionaries. The same goes for the availability of components like classifiers, languages like English have more resources than other low-resource ones.

Eventually, Twitter-Demographer assumes that the users are aware of the limits of the components they are using. The use of HuggingFace models, for example, requires users to check if the models are indeed effective on the data of interest: using a pre-pandemic sentiment classifier on more recent data, might overestimate the number of *positive* tweets due to the presence of the word "positive" in messages regarding COVID positivity.

Acknowledgments

DH is a member of the Bocconi Institute for Data Science and Analytics (BIDSA). This work was partially conducted while FB was a member of BIDSA. This project has partially received funding from the European Research Council (ERC) under the European Union's Horizon 2020 research and innovation program (grant agreement No. 949944, INTEGRATOR).

References

Alexandra Balahur. 2013. Sentiment analysis in social media texts. In *Proceedings of the 4th Workshop on Computational Approaches to Subjectivity, Sentiment and Social Media Analysis*, pages 120–128, Atlanta, Georgia. Association for Computational Linguistics.

Francesco Barbieri, Jose Camacho-Collados, Luis Espinosa Anke, and Leonardo Neves. 2020. TweetEval: Unified benchmark and comparative evaluation for tweet classification. In *Findings of the Association for Computational Linguistics: EMNLP 2020*, pages 1644–1650, Online. Association for Computational Linguistics.

Valerio Basile, Cristina Bosco, Elisabetta Fersini, Debora Nozza, Viviana Patti, Francisco Manuel Rangel Pardo, Paolo Rosso, and Manuela Sanguinetti. 2019. SemEval-2019 task 5: Multilingual detection of hate speech against immigrants and women in Twitter. In *Proceedings of the 13th International Workshop on Semantic Evaluation*, pages 54–63, Minneapolis, Minnesota, USA. Association for Computational Linguistics.

Federico Bianchi, Silvia Terragni, and Dirk Hovy. 2021. Pre-training is a hot topic: Contextualized document embeddings improve topic coherence. In *Proceedings of the 59th Annual Meeting of the Association for Computational Linguistics and the 11th International Joint Conference on Natural Language Processing (Volume 2: Short Papers)*, pages 759–766, Online. Association for Computational Linguistics.

Vincenzo Cutrona, Flavio De Paoli, Aljaž Košmerlj, Nikolay Nikolov, Matteo Palmonari, Fernando Perales, and Dumitru Roman. 2019. Semantically-enabled optimization of digital marketing campaigns. In *The Semantic Web - ISWC 2019 - 18th International Semantic Web Conference, Auckland, New Zealand, October 26-30, 2019, Proceedings, Part II*, volume 11779 of *Lecture Notes in Computer Science*, pages 345–362. Springer.

Morteza Dehghani, Kate M Johnson, Justin Garten, Reihane Boghrati, Joe Hoover, Vijayan Balasubramanian, Anurag Singh, Yuvarani Shankar, Linda Pulickal, Aswin Rajkumar, et al. 2017. Tacit: An open-source text analysis, crawling, and interpretation tool. *Behavior research methods*, 49(2):538–547.

European Parliament and Council of European Union. 2016. Regulation (EU) 2016/679.

Ethan Fast, Binbin Chen, and Michael S Bernstein. 2016. Empath: Understanding topic signals in large-scale text. In *Proceedings of the 2016 CHI conference on human factors in computing systems*, pages 4647–4657.

Samuel Gehman, Suchin Gururangan, Maarten Sap, Yejin Choi, and Noah A. Smith. 2020. RealToxicityPrompts: Evaluating neural toxic degeneration in language models. In *Findings of the Association for Computational Linguistics: EMNLP 2020*, pages 3356–3369, Online. Association for Computational Linguistics.

Maarten Grootendorst. 2022. Bertopic: Neural topic modeling with a class-based tf-idf procedure.

Dirk Hovy. 2015. Demographic factors improve classification performance. In *Proceedings of the 53rd Annual Meeting of the Association for Computational Linguistics and the 7th International Joint Conference on Natural Language Processing (Volume 1: Long Papers)*, pages 752–762, Beijing, China. Association for Computational Linguistics.

Dirk Hovy and Diyi Yang. 2021. The importance of modeling social factors of language: Theory and practice. In *Proceedings of the 2021 Conference of the North American Chapter of the Association for Computational Linguistics: Human Language Technologies*, pages 588–602, Online. Association for Computational Linguistics.

Lingpeng Kong, Nathan Schneider, Swabha Swayamdipta, Archna Bhatia, Chris Dyer, and Noah A. Smith. 2014. A dependency parser for tweets. In *Proceedings of the 2014 Conference on Empirical Methods in Natural Language Processing (EMNLP)*, pages 1001–1012, Doha, Qatar. Association for Computational Linguistics.

Yitong Li, Timothy Baldwin, and Trevor Cohn. 2018. Towards robust and privacy-preserving text representations. In *Proceedings of the 56th Annual Meeting of the Association for Computational Linguistics (Volume 2: Short Papers)*, pages 25–30, Melbourne, Australia. Association for Computational Linguistics.

Veronica Lynn, Youngseo Son, Vivek Kulkarni, Niranjan Balasubramanian, and H. Andrew Schwartz. 2017. Human centered NLP with user-factor adaptation. In *Proceedings of the 2017 Conference on Empirical Methods in Natural Language Processing*, pages 1146–1155, Copenhagen, Denmark. Association for Computational Linguistics.

J. Paul Morrison. 2010. *Flow-Based Programming, 2nd Edition: A New Approach to Application Development*. CreateSpace, Scotts Valley, CA.

Kevin Munger. 2017. Tweetment effects on the tweeted: Experimentally reducing racist harassment. *Political Behavior*, 39(3):629–649.

Daniel Preoţiuc-Pietro, Vasileios Lampos, and Nikolaos Aletras. 2015. An analysis of the user occupational class through Twitter content. In *Proceedings of the 53rd Annual Meeting of the Association for Computational Linguistics and the 7th International Joint Conference on Natural Language Processing (Volume 1: Long Papers)*, pages 1754–1764, Beijing, China. Association for Computational Linguistics.

Zachary C Steinert-Threlkeld. 2018. *Twitter as data*. Cambridge University Press.

Yla R Tausczik and James W Pennebaker. 2010. The psychological meaning of words: Liwc and computerized text analysis methods. *Journal of language and social psychology*, 29(1):24–54.

Svitlana Volkova, Theresa Wilson, and David Yarowsky. 2013. Exploring demographic language variations to improve multilingual sentiment analysis in social media. In *Proceedings of the 2013 Conference on Empirical Methods in Natural Language Processing*, pages 1815–1827, Seattle, Washington, USA. Association for Computational Linguistics.

Zijian Wang, Scott Hale, David Ifeoluwa Adelani, Przemyslaw Grabowicz, Timo Hartman, Fabian Flöck, and David Jurgens. 2019. Demographic inference and representative population estimates from multilingual social media data. In *The World Wide Web Conference*, pages 2056–2067. ACM.

Thomas Wolf, Lysandre Debut, Victor Sanh, Julien Chaumond, Clement Delangue, Anthony Moi, Pierric Cistac, Tim Rault, Remi Louf, Morgan Funtowicz, Joe Davison, Sam Shleifer, Patrick von Platen, Clara Ma, Yacine Jernite, Julien Plu, Canwen Xu, Teven Le Scao, Sylvain Gugger, Mariama Drame, Quentin Lhoest, and Alexander Rush. 2020. Transformers: State-of-the-art natural language processing. In *Proceedings of the 2020 Conference on Empirical Methods in Natural Language Processing: System Demonstrations*, pages 38–45, Online. Association for Computational Linguistics.

Azimuth: Systematic Error Analysis for Text Classification

Gabrielle Gauthier-Melançon, Orlando Marquez Ayala, Lindsay Brin, Chris Tyler, Frédéric Branchaud-Charron, Joseph Marinier, Karine Grande, Di Le
ServiceNow
`{gabrielle.gm,orlando.marquez,lindsay.brin}@servicenow.com`

Abstract

We present Azimuth, an open-source and easy-to-use tool to perform error analysis for text classification. Compared to other stages of the ML development cycle, such as model training and hyper-parameter tuning, the process and tooling for the error analysis stage are less mature. However, this stage is critical for the development of reliable and trustworthy AI systems. To make error analysis more systematic, we propose an approach comprising dataset analysis and model quality assessment, which Azimuth facilitates. We aim to help AI practitioners discover and address areas where the model does not generalize by leveraging and integrating a range of ML techniques, such as saliency maps, similarity, uncertainty, and behavioral analyses, all in one tool. Our code and documentation are available at `github.com/servicenow/azimuth`.

1 Introduction

As academic and research labs push the boundaries of artificial intelligence, more and more enterprises are including NLP models[1] in their real-world systems. This is exciting yet risky due to the complexity of current deep learning models and their increasing social impact. Whereas in traditional software development, engineers have methods to trace errors to code, it is challenging to isolate sources of error in AI systems.

NLP models can suffer from poor linguistic capabilities (Ribeiro et al., 2020), hallucinations (Ji et al., 2022), learning spurious correlations via annotation artifacts (Gururangan et al., 2018), or amplifying social biases (Chang et al., 2019; Stanczak and Augenstein, 2021). In addition to the adverse effects that these problems can cause to both individuals and society, deploying problematic models can lead to legal and financial penalties (Burt, 2021). Even when poorly functioning models have no adverse social effects, they can still degrade trust, leading to problems with user adoption (Kocielnik et al., 2019; McKendrick, 2021).

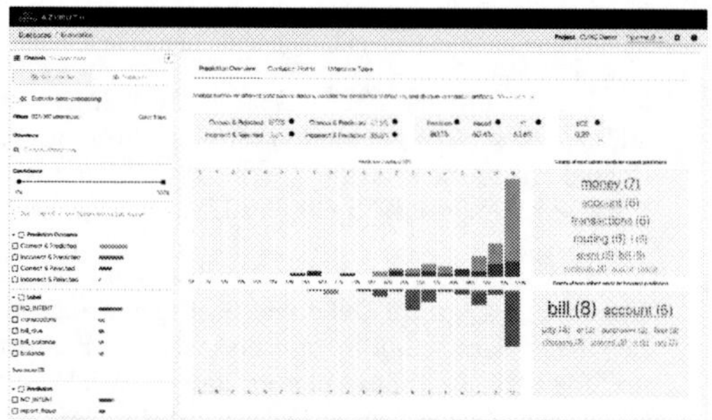

Figure 1: The exploration space of Azimuth allows users to explore dataset and pipeline quality across different data subpopulations.

While it may be unreasonable to expect a perfect model, AI practitioners should communicate existing limitations so that stakeholders can make informed decisions about deployment, risk mitigation, and allocation of resources for further improvements (Arnold et al., 2019; Mitchell et al., 2019). However, the current common error analysis practices may not be sufficiently thorough to provide this visibility, limiting our capacity to build safe, trustworthy AI systems.

As part of the ML development cycle, practitioners choose appropriate metrics based on business requirements. These metrics should assess whether NLP models have acquired the linguistic skills to perform the specified task. While metrics are useful to rapidly compare different models, they are only the beginning of quality assessment as they do not expose failure modes, i.e., types of input where the model fails, and do not readily indicate what can be improved. Furthermore, relying on metrics alone can be harmful, as they can overestimate quality and robustness while hiding unintended biases (Ribeiro et al., 2020; Bowman and Dahl, 2021).

To discover and address these limitations, er-

[1]While models are part of pipelines that can include pre- and post-processors, we use the term models for simplicity.

Proceedings of the The 2022 Conference on Empirical Methods in Natural Language Processing: System Demonstrations, pages 298 - 310
December 7-11, 2022 ©2022 Association for Computational Linguistics

ror analysis is crucial. Unfortunately, compared to other stages of the ML development cycle, the error analysis stage is less mature. While various tools are commonly used to train and tune neural networks[2], there is less convergence and adoption of both standards and tools to analyze errors. Analysis is typically conducted using custom scripts, spreadsheets, and Jupyter notebooks, guided by a practitioner's intuition, which may help uncover some problems while missing others. Large evaluation sets make per-example analysis of incorrect predictions time-consuming and tedious. Because this error analysis process is often informal, ad hoc, and cumbersome, practitioners often skip or rush this stage, focusing solely on high-level metrics. This hinders traceability and accountability, and introduces risks, especially for models deployed in production.

To alleviate these issues, we contribute the following:

- A systematic and intuitive error analysis process that practitioners can follow to improve their ML applications.
- Azimuth, an open-source and easy-to-use tool that facilitates this process, making thorough error analysis of text classification models easier and more accessible.

2 Systematic Error Analysis

The goal of error analysis is to understand where and why a model succeeds or fails, to better inform both model improvement and deployment decisions. We propose a process grouped into two categories: (1) dataset analysis and (2) model quality assessment, as illustrated in Fig. 2. Dataset analysis involves assessing and improving the data used to train and evaluate the model, while quality assessment focuses on model behavior. This process should be iterative, as analyzing model predictions can help identify and fix dataset problems, and dataset findings can help explain and reduce model errors. A limitation of our approach is that it does not currently assess whether models are learning a task ethically. While some of the techniques we refer to below can be used for this purpose, building ethical NLP systems is outside the scope of this paper.

[2]Hugging Face Transformers, Ray Tune, etc.

2.1 Dataset Analysis

Dataset analysis is indispensable to validate that the available data is appropriate for the given ML task and to suggest possible approaches to solve it. It should be conducted both before and throughout the ML development cycle, as it can guide model improvements. This analysis should encompass all data splits, although held-out evaluation sets require special care to avoid overfitting. High-quality data is essential as it impacts both model quality and the choice of models that will be deployed (Northcutt et al., 2021).

We identify four common types of dataset problems: data shift, class imbalance, class definition, and problematic examples. While these may not apply to all tasks, they illustrate common data problems. The first three can be detected by analyzing data at the dataset level, while problematic examples require example-level analysis.

Data Shift. The training and validation splits must be compared to identify significant data shift caused by inadequate sampling or poor labeling practices (e.g., duplicated examples, missing classes). Taking into consideration the challenges in creating high-quality datasets (Bowman and Dahl, 2021), one must guard against significant differences in data distributions across splits as they may cause quality problems or lead to poor choices in model selection and training.

Class Imbalance. In classification tasks, class imbalance occurs when there are differences in the proportion or number of examples in each class relative to each other. This is problematic because models often overpredict classes that are overrepresented in the training data, whereas class imbalance in the evaluation data may cause performance metrics to be misleading. If unwanted class imbalance is present, practitioners may choose to resolve the issue through data augmentation for specific classes, or by upsampling or downsampling.

Class Definition. The classes used in the ML task affect what the model will learn. Practitioners may need the assistance of domain experts to determine whether the classes are defined appropriately. For instance, class overlap is a symptom of poor class definition that can be seen when groups of examples in multiple classes overlap semantically, resulting in classes that are not easily separable. Some semantic overlap may be acceptable and not cause model confusion, whereas other overlap may indicate low data quality or poor dataset construc-

Figure 2: Proposed approach for systematic error analysis.

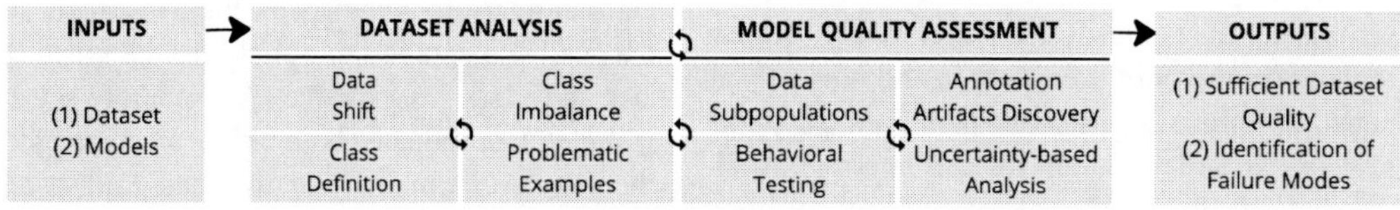

tion, leading to poor model performance. Improving class definition can include relabeling mislabeled examples, better defining classes by merging or splitting them, and augmenting data for specific classes.

Problematic Examples. Multiple kinds of challenges can arise at the example level. This includes examples outside the expected domain, "difficult" examples with exceptional characteristics (e.g., words from other languages, long sentences) but for which model performance is desired, examples for which humans would disagree on the label, and accidental mislabeling issues. These problems can confuse class boundaries and cause model errors. Resolution options include relabeling examples, removing examples from datasets, and targeted data augmentation.

2.2 Model Quality Assessment

Once datasets are deemed sufficient in quality, practitioners train and tune models aiming to find the best candidates. Quality assessment consists of examining how well the selected models perform on a specified evaluation set as well as their ability to generalize beyond the evaluation set. The objective is to understand where and why the model fails. Issues exposed in model quality assessment can also inspire further dataset improvements.

Assessing quality by examining metrics is the aspect of error analysis that is typically performed, as it is relatively fast to conduct (Church and Hestness, 2019). This quantitative assessment allows for quick comparison across models or model versions using known scores such as precision, recall, or F1. This can include metrics to measure model calibration, such as expected calibration error (ECE), as well as metrics that quantify business value, safety, and bias.

As practitioners already tend to analyze high-level metrics to have a basic notion of model quality, we focus here on other approaches to evaluate generalization. To help discover and correct failure modes before models are deployed, we propose four types of evaluation: (1) assess model quality according to data subpopulations, (2) discover annotation artifacts, (3) perform behavioral testing, and (4) conduct uncertainty-based analysis.

Data Subpopulations are subsets of datasets with shared characteristics such as examples with long text, entities, keywords, same label, etc. Models may behave differently on these subpopulations, but high-level metrics can hide these failure modes. Guided by domain knowledge, this analysis can help ensure that the model generalizes well under various input characteristics. Often, performance on problematic subpopulations can be improved by targeted data augmentation.

Annotation Artifacts are patterns in the labeled data that can be exploited by models to learn simple heuristics instead of learning to perform the task, and yet achieve high metric scores (Gururangan et al., 2018). The result is a model that relies undesirably on specific features, such as words that tend to correlate with the label only in the available datasets. Annotation artifacts can be discovered by leveraging feature-based explainability methods, such as saliency maps, to approximately determine the importance of every token when the model makes a prediction. Once such artifacts are found, practitioners can refine the datasets to help models decrease their reliance on them.

Behavioral Testing assesses model robustness by validating model behavior based on input and output (Ribeiro et al., 2020). Perturbing a dataset and observing the corresponding predictions can help identify important errors, biases, or other potentially harmful aspects of the model that may not be otherwise obvious. For production models, this type of testing is critical, as the range of user input is infinite, while the evaluation datasets are finite. Models that change predictions or their confidence values when the input is slightly altered without changing its semantics can have unintended consequences and may lose the user's trust.

Uncertainty-based Analysis includes assessing examples that are more difficult for the model to learn. Examination of lower-confidence predictions can help indicate regions of the data distribution where the model may fail in the future, similar to Data Maps (Swayamdipta et al., 2020). A more sophisticated approach is to find predictions with high epistemic uncertainty, computed with techniques such as Bayesian deep ensembles (Wilson and Izmailov, 2020). Augmenting the training dataset with more representative examples from these data regions can improve model quality.

Systematic error analysis will help practitioners obtain the following:

- Datasets deemed sufficient in quality that can be used for training and evaluation.
- Identified failure modes: known situations where the model fails to generalize.

To help practitioners achieve these outcomes, we contribute Azimuth to the NLP community.

3 Azimuth, an Open-Source Tool

Azimuth was developed as an internal tool at ServiceNow and open sourced in April 2022. It facilitates our proposed approach to systematize error analysis of ML systems. While it is currently tailored for text classification, it could be extended to support other use cases. The tool was built by a cross-collaborative team of scientists, engineers, and designers, with a human-centered approach that focuses on the AI practitioner's needs.

Before launching Azimuth, the user defines in a configuration file the dataset splits and pipelines to load and analyze. In Azimuth, pipelines refer to the ML model as well as any pre-processing and post-processing steps. The tool is built on top of the Hugging Face (HF) datasets library (Lhoest et al., 2021) and easily interfaces with HF pipelines (Wolf et al., 2020). For flexibility, any Python function can be defined as a pipeline. If pipelines are unavailable, Azimuth can still be used, although with limited features, by reading predictions from a file. The tool can also be used for dataset analysis without a pipeline.

3.1 User Workflow

Azimuth leads users through two main screens: the dashboard and the exploration space. At startup, users are brought to the dashboard, which presents a summary of the different capabilities and flags potential dataset and pipeline problems (Fig. 6). The dashboard is linked to the exploration space through pre-selected filters that allow a more detailed investigation of issues raised on the dashboard. For example, as shown in Fig. 3, pipeline quality is indicated by metrics on different data subpopulations, such as label, prediction, and smart tag (defined below). By clicking on a row, the user is brought to the exploration space filtered on the corresponding subpopulation.

Figure 3: On the dashboard, pipeline quality is broken down by different data subpopulations.

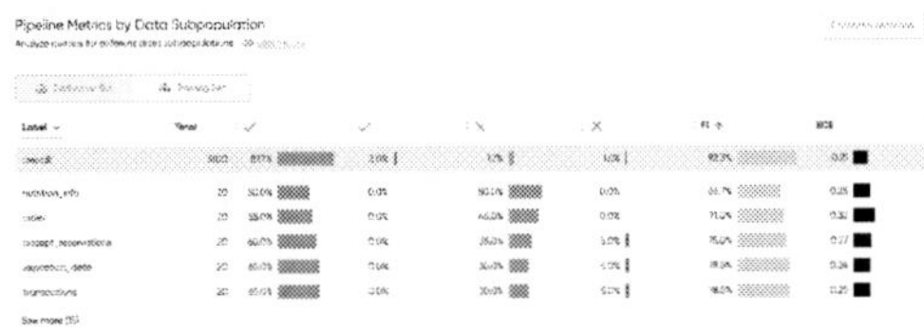

The exploration space allows the user to explore the dataset and pipeline quality by filtering on different data subpopulations, model confidence, and/or the presence of certain text. Data can be shown for predictions both before and after post-processing (e.g., thresholding). Changing the filters will update all available visualizations and tables split over three tabs. The first tab displays several quality metrics, a histogram of confidence scores for correct and incorrect predictions, and word clouds indicating word importance (Fig. 1). The second tab displays the confusion matrix (Fig. 7). The last tab shows the details of the raw data and predictions, allowing users to inspect individual examples and their smart tags, and propose actions for those that are problematic (Fig. 4). Clicking on a particular example takes users to its details page, which provides additional information such as the prediction at each post-processing step, behavioral test results, and semantically similar examples from each dataset split (Fig. 12).

Figure 4: The exploration space displays examples along with their predictions and smart tags. The user can propose actions to improve the dataset.

3.2 Smart Tags

An integral feature of Azimuth is the concept of smart tags, which are tags assigned to dataset examples based on predefined rules. Smart tags allow users to explore the dataset and model predictions through various data subpopulations, helping to detect failure modes and to identify problematic examples. Some smart tags are straightforward (examples with few tokens), while others are more complex (examples with high epistemic uncertainty). They are grouped in families, based on their associated capabilities, which may require access to only the dataset or to both the dataset and the pipeline.

To assist the process of improving the dataset, Azimuth has a "proposed action" field with options to indicate further actions that should be taken on specific examples. There are natural correspondences between certain smart tags and proposed actions. Users can filter examples in the exploration space by a certain smart tag to focus specifically on an aspect of dataset analysis. For instance, the high epistemic uncertainty smart tag can detect hard-to-predict examples that may require actions such as relabeling, removing examples, or augmenting the training set with similar examples. In the same vein, smart tags from the similarity analysis may highlight examples that suggest the need to add new classes or merge existing ones. There is also a generic proposed action *investigate* to signal that further troubleshooting is required as no concrete action is clear yet.

3.3 Capabilities

Azimuth provides a variety of capabilities for both dataset analysis and model quality assessment. Fig. 5 depicts how the different capabilities map to the approach proposed in section 2. Our documentation includes a detailed list of each feature and smart tag that are part of Azimuth's capabilities.

Class Size Analysis. Azimuth surfaces classes having too few examples, which may indicate class imbalance within a split. The tool also detects a form of dataset shift by raising warnings when the number of examples across classes is not similarly distributed across splits.

Syntax Analysis. The Spacy library (Honnibal et al., 2020) is used to inspect the syntax of examples. Besides detecting significant differences in sentence length between dataset splits, we use dependency trees and part-of-speech tags to explore model behavior when examples are missing a subject, verb, or object. Syntactic smart tags can help identify problematic examples and explore model performance on atypical syntax.

Similarity Analysis. Azimuth leverages the SentenceTransformers framework (Reimers and Gurevych, 2019) to compute sentence embeddings. We use these embeddings to calculate the similarity of all pairs of examples in all dataset splits, and perform similarity search using faiss (Johnson et al., 2019). Smart tags and nearest neighbors based on similarity values allow for surfacing potential dataset shift, class overlap, or problematic examples. For example, some smart tags surface examples that are distant from their nearest neighbors, while others identify examples where the neighbors belong to a different class.

Prediction Analysis. Visualizations and metrics, such as the confusion matrix and the expected calibration error, help assess model quality. This type of analysis also includes threshold comparison as well as smart tags that compare prediction results across different pipelines.

Explainability. We generate saliency maps (Kindermans et al., 2019) to reveal why a particular prediction was made in terms of the relevance of each input token to the prediction (Bastings and Filippova, 2020; Atanasova et al., 2020). We use a gradient-based technique as it is fast to compute and available for all token-based models.

In the exploration space, saliency maps are shown for each example in the filtered subpopulation. Additionally, word clouds allow inspection of the most salient words for correct (green) and incorrect (red) predictions, which can help identify words present in examples that the model struggles to classify. Differences between word clouds for a specific data subpopulation, such as class label, can hint at spurious correlations or a model's over-reliance on specific words, as exemplified in section B.3.2. Lastly, on the example details page, the user can compare the example's most salient words to those of similar training examples, which may help explain misclassification.

Behavioral Analysis. Azimuth uses behavioral testing to help assess the general linguistic capabilities of NLP models. As an initial implementation, we use NLPAug (Ma, 2019) and custom functions to create Robustness Invariance tests: input perturbations that should not change the model predictions (Ribeiro et al., 2020). Predictions obtained with and without perturbations are compared to reveal areas where the model lacks robustness. Smart tags highlight examples whose predictions have changed unexpectedly, helping to identify specific

Figure 5: The steps of our proposed approach are pictured in gray boxes while the corresponding Azimuth capabilities are in black boxes. "All smart tags" means that all capabilities and their smart tags can be useful for this step.

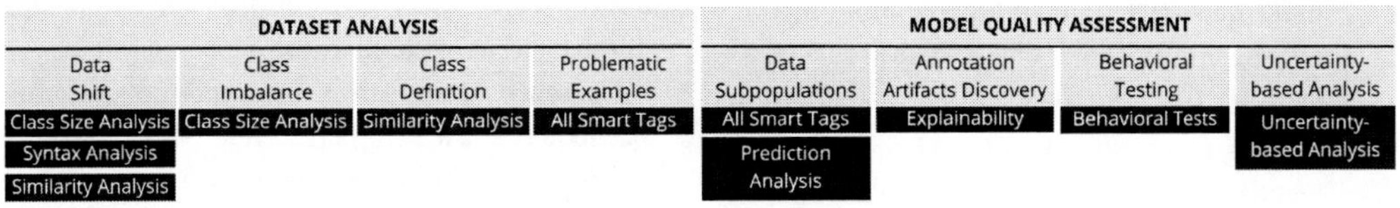

problems. In addition, users can define new functions to test other linguistic capabilities, such as those proposed in CHECKLIST.

Uncertainty-based Analysis. Users can explore examples based on model confidence and visualize their confidence distribution in a histogram. Some smart tags highlight predictions that are almost correct, based on model confidence. Filtering out these predictions can help focus on examples that are more problematic for the model, which often hint at mislabeling or larger dataset issues, such as poorly defined labels. In contrast, focusing on the almost correct predictions can help identify class overlap or issues that may be addressed by targeted data augmentation. For models with dropout, we additionally use Baal (Atighehchian et al., 2019) to compute a smart tag that surfaces examples with high epistemic uncertainty, which have a greater chance of being problematic.

3.4 Design

UX design and research are essential to create valuable and usable ML systems. Our design priorities for Azimuth were focused on supporting the error analysis process by increasing efficiency, balancing guidance with flexibility and user control, and fostering user delight. Through collaborative design sessions, workshops, and user interviews with AI practitioners, we improved Azimuth quickly and iteratively. In particular, user interviews uncovered several challenges that we addressed with design modifications, including disentangling different levels of analysis and preventing choice paralysis (details in A.1).

As a result, Azimuth's design approach generally follows a paradigm of guided exploration, which shaped the creation of features such as the dashboard and the control panel on the exploration space. Additionally, the navigation and progressive disclosure lead users to discover important features and take action quickly by separating, but linking, high-level warnings and detailed investigation. We make the process enjoyable and efficient by including visualizations and the ability to search, filter, hide and show information as needed. The content and communications provide context and guidance without being obstructive. For example, Azimuth prioritizes contextual information icons or subtle explanations, and our color system helps to assign priority and call attention to warnings and errors. See Appendix A for details.

3.5 Extensibility

To customize the error analysis experience, users can easily change a variety of settings in Azimuth's configuration file. For instance, users can change the encoder used for the similarity analysis, or the thresholds that determine class imbalance.

Azimuth capabilities are implemented via `Modules`, which use a dataset, a configuration, and optionally a model to perform the desired analyses with distributed computing and caching. Our repository contains details on how to add a new `Module`[3].

For more complex modifications, we encourage the community to submit issues on our GitHub page. As the process of error analysis continues to be refined, we hope that Azimuth will grow along with the community.

3.6 Case Study

We verified the utility of our methodology and Azimuth by applying them to a DistilBert model trained on CLINC-OOS (Larson et al., 2019). This large intent classification dataset has 150 "in-scope" classes spanning several domains and one Out-of-Scope (OOS) class. Our goal is to demonstrate how Azimuth's features can efficiently direct users to specific, resolvable problems, even with CLINC-OOS's large size and wide topic range. Below we summarize the most salient findings while Appendix B includes more details.

- *no_close* tags (26 examples) revealed classes with discordant semantic spaces across dataset

[3]`https://github.com/ServiceNow/azimuth/tree/main/azimuth/modules`

splits.

- *conflicting_neighbors* smart tags surfaced overlapping class pairs. For some examples, multiple labels were applicable, possibly warranting a multi-label classification model.
- Despite the relatively clean nature of the dataset, *conflicting_neighbors* smart tags surfaced 25 mislabeled examples in the training set and 18 in the validation set.
- Accuracy was worse than average on several data subpopulations, including short sentences (~8% worse than long sentences), examples lacking a verb (~10% worse than average), and examples failing the punctuation robustness test (~20% worse than average).
- Word clouds revealed possible annotation artifacts such as model dependence on a specific verb or the plural form of a particular noun.
- Behavioral testing showed a high failure rate for typos (~25%), surfacing classes for which the model depended on specific tokens.
- The model is underconfident, warranting temperature scaling or a lower threshold.

Overall, our analysis revealed multiple issues that could be addressed through data cleaning and augmentation. Moreover, the high overall validation accuracy (94%) hides a lack of robustness.

4 Related Work

There exist other tools that can help practitioners evaluate their NLP systems beyond observing metrics. Broadly speaking, these solutions are implemented as component libraries, standalone applications, or some combination thereof.

Small components have a lower investment of effort to get started but may require more technical expertise to use. While they can produce results quickly, they fail to address the problem of ad-hoc processes and may lead to a "paradox of choice" (Goel et al., 2021). Examples include the CHECKLIST Python package (Ribeiro et al., 2020) that can be used for behavioral testing and the AllenNLP Interpret toolkit (Wallace et al., 2019) that computes gradient-based saliency maps.

On the other hand, standalone applications may require more effort to set up and it may not be obvious how to integrate them into the ML development process. Their benefits are that, once setup, less technical practitioners can use them and their usage can be standardized. CrossCheck (Arendt et al., 2021) and Robustness Gym (Goel et al., 2021) are used as Jupyter widgets, while Errudite (Wu et al., 2019) and Language Interpretability Tool (LIT) (Tenney et al., 2020) exist both as standalone applications and as widgets in Jupyter notebooks.

Currently, Azimuth is a standalone application that requires low setup effort and can be integrated into the ML development cycle as proposed in section 2. At the same time, we provide the benefits of existing third-party component libraries, added as features in an easy-to-use interface. We built Azimuth to assist in performing comprehensive error analysis using a single tool by including functionality found elsewhere: filtering and analysis of behavior on subpopulations (CrossCheck, Errudite, LIT, Robustness Gym), input variations such as counterfactual error analysis, robustness testing (Errudite, LIT, Robustness Gym), model comparison (CrossCheck, LIT), and explainability techniques (LIT, AllenNLP Interpret).

5 Conclusion

We propose a systematic approach to error analysis as an iterative workflow between dataset analysis and model quality assessment. We contribute Azimuth to the NLP community in order to facilitate this approach. Future work includes expanding our capabilities, exposing potential ethical concerns in the data or ML models, and extending Azimuth to cover other tasks and domains. We welcome open-source contributions.

Ethical Considerations

We believe our proposed approach to systematize the error analysis stage of the ML development cycle should help decrease the adverse social effects that error-prone models can create as well as increase user adoption and trust. An important gap in our approach is that it does not explicitly suggest techniques that can detect whether models behave ethically or whether datasets used to train these models contain harmful biases.

Acknowledgements

We thank ServiceNow for sponsoring the development of Azimuth, especially our colleagues involved in building and publicizing it. We also thank ServiceNow teams and users in the NLP community for their useful feedback.

References

Dustin Arendt, Zhuanyi Shaw, Prasha Shrestha, Ellyn Ayton, Maria Glenski, and Svitlana Volkova. 2021. CrossCheck: Rapid, reproducible, and interpretable model evaluation. In *Proceedings of the Second Workshop on Data Science with Human in the Loop: Language Advances*, pages 79–85, Online. Association for Computational Linguistics.

Matthew Arnold, Rachel KE Bellamy, Michael Hind, Stephanie Houde, Sameep Mehta, Aleksandra Mojsilović, Ravi Nair, K Natesan Ramamurthy, Alexandra Olteanu, David Piorkowski, et al. 2019. Factsheets: Increasing trust in ai services through supplier's declarations of conformity. *IBM Journal of Research and Development*, 63(4/5):6–1.

Pepa Atanasova, Jakob Grue Simonsen, Christina Lioma, and Isabelle Augenstein. 2020. A diagnostic study of explainability techniques for text classification. In *Proceedings of the 2020 Conference on Empirical Methods in Natural Language Processing (EMNLP)*, pages 3256–3274, Online. Association for Computational Linguistics.

Parmida Atighehchian, Frederic Branchaud-Charron, Jan Freyberg, Rafael Pardinas, and Lorne Schell. 2019. Baal, a bayesian active learning library. `https://github.com/ElementAI/baal/`.

Jasmijn Bastings and Katja Filippova. 2020. The elephant in the interpretability room: Why use attention as explanation when we have saliency methods? In *Proceedings of the Third BlackboxNLP Workshop on Analyzing and Interpreting Neural Networks for NLP*, pages 149–155, Online. Association for Computational Linguistics.

Samuel R. Bowman and George Dahl. 2021. What will it take to fix benchmarking in natural language understanding? In *Proceedings of the 2021 Conference of the North American Chapter of the Association for Computational Linguistics: Human Language Technologies*, pages 4843–4855, Online. Association for Computational Linguistics.

Andrew Burt. 2021. New AI regulations are coming. Is your organization ready? *Harvard Business Review*.

Kai-Wei Chang, Vinodkumar Prabhakaran, and Vicente Ordonez. 2019. Bias and fairness in natural language processing. In *Proceedings of the 2019 Conference on Empirical Methods in Natural Language Processing and the 9th International Joint Conference on Natural Language Processing (EMNLP-IJCNLP): Tutorial Abstracts*, Hong Kong, China. Association for Computational Linguistics.

Kenneth Ward Church and Joel Hestness. 2019. A survey of 25 years of evaluation. *Natural Language Engineering*, 25(6):753–767.

Karan Goel, Nazneen Fatema Rajani, Jesse Vig, Zachary Taschdjian, Mohit Bansal, and Christopher Ré. 2021. Robustness gym: Unifying the NLP evaluation landscape. In *Proceedings of the 2021 Conference of the North American Chapter of the Association for Computational Linguistics: Human Language Technologies: Demonstrations*, pages 42–55, Online. Association for Computational Linguistics.

Suchin Gururangan, Swabha Swayamdipta, Omer Levy, Roy Schwartz, Samuel Bowman, and Noah A. Smith. 2018. Annotation artifacts in natural language inference data. In *Proceedings of the 2018 Conference of the North American Chapter of the Association for Computational Linguistics: Human Language Technologies, Volume 2 (Short Papers)*, pages 107–112, New Orleans, Louisiana. Association for Computational Linguistics.

Matthew Honnibal, Ines Montani, Sofie Van Landeghem, and Adriane Boyd. 2020. spaCy: Industrial-strength Natural Language Processing in Python.

Ziwei Ji, Nayeon Lee, Rita Frieske, Tiezheng Yu, Dan Su, Yan Xu, Etsuko Ishii, Yejin Bang, Andrea Madotto, and Pascale Fung. 2022. Survey of hallucination in natural language generation.

Jeff Johnson, Matthijs Douze, and Hervé Jégou. 2019. Billion-scale similarity search with GPUs. *IEEE Transactions on Big Data*, 7(3):535–547.

Pieter-Jan Kindermans, Sara Hooker, Julius Adebayo, Maximilian Alber, Kristof T Schütt, Sven Dähne, Dumitru Erhan, and Been Kim. 2019. The (un) reliability of saliency methods. In *Explainable AI: Interpreting, Explaining and Visualizing Deep Learning*, pages 267–280. Springer.

Rafal Kocielnik, Saleema Amershi, and Paul N Bennett. 2019. Will you accept an imperfect ai? exploring designs for adjusting end-user expectations of ai systems. In *Proceedings of the 2019 CHI Conference on Human Factors in Computing Systems*, pages 1–14.

Stefan Larson, Anish Mahendran, Joseph J. Peper, Christopher Clarke, Andrew Lee, Parker Hill, Jonathan K. Kummerfeld, Kevin Leach, Michael A. Laurenzano, Lingjia Tang, and Jason Mars. 2019. An evaluation dataset for intent classification and out-of-scope prediction. In *Proceedings of the 2019 Conference on Empirical Methods in Natural Language Processing and the 9th International Joint Conference on Natural Language Processing (EMNLP-IJCNLP)*.

Quentin Lhoest, Albert Villanova del Moral, Yacine Jernite, Abhishek Thakur, Patrick von Platen, Suraj Patil, Julien Chaumond, Mariama Drame, Julien Plu, Lewis Tunstall, Joe Davison, Mario Šaško, Gunjan Chhablani, Bhavitvya Malik, Simon Brandeis, Teven Le Scao, Victor Sanh, Canwen Xu, Nicolas Patry, Angelina McMillan-Major, Philipp Schmid, Sylvain Gugger, Clément Delangue, Théo Matussière, Lysandre Debut, Stas Bekman, Pierric Cistac, Thibault Goehringer, Victor Mustar, François Lagunas, Alexander Rush, and Thomas Wolf. 2021. Datasets: A community library for natural language processing. In *Proceedings of the 2021 Conference on Empirical Methods in Natural Language Processing: System Demonstrations*, pages 175–184, Online and Punta Cana, Dominican Republic. Association for Computational Linguistics.

Edward Ma. 2019. Nlp augmentation. `https://github.com/makcedward/nlpaug`.

Joe McKendrick. 2021. Artificial intelligence's biggest stumbling block: Trust. *Forbes*.

Margaret Mitchell, Simone Wu, Andrew Zaldivar, Parker Barnes, Lucy Vasserman, Ben Hutchinson, Elena Spitzer, Inioluwa Deborah Raji, and Timnit Gebru. 2019. Model cards for model reporting. In *Proceedings of the conference on fairness, accountability, and transparency*, pages 220–229.

Curtis Northcutt, Anish Athalye, and Jonas Mueller. 2021. Pervasive label errors in test sets destabilize machine learning benchmarks. In *Proceedings of the Neural Information Processing Systems Track on Datasets and Benchmarks*.

Nils Reimers and Iryna Gurevych. 2019. Sentence-bert: Sentence embeddings using siamese bert-networks. In *Proceedings of the 2019 Conference on Empirical Methods in Natural Language Processing*. Association for Computational Linguistics.

Marco Tulio Ribeiro, Tongshuang Wu, Carlos Guestrin, and Sameer Singh. 2020. Beyond accuracy: Behavioral testing of NLP models with CheckList. In *Proceedings of the 58th Annual Meeting of the Association for Computational Linguistics*, pages 4902–4912, Online. Association for Computational Linguistics.

Victor Sanh, Lysandre Debut, Julien Chaumond, and Thomas Wolf. 2019. Distilbert, a distilled version of BERT: smaller, faster, cheaper and lighter. *CoRR*, abs/1910.01108.

Karolina Stanczak and Isabelle Augenstein. 2021. A survey on gender bias in natural language processing. *CoRR*, abs/2112.14168.

Swabha Swayamdipta, Roy Schwartz, Nicholas Lourie, Yizhong Wang, Hannaneh Hajishirzi, Noah A. Smith, and Yejin Choi. 2020. Dataset cartography: Mapping and diagnosing datasets with training dynamics. In *Proceedings of the 2020 Conference on Empirical Methods in Natural Language Processing (EMNLP)*, pages 9275–9293, Online. Association for Computational Linguistics.

Ian Tenney, James Wexler, Jasmijn Bastings, Tolga Bolukbasi, Andy Coenen, Sebastian Gehrmann, Ellen Jiang, Mahima Pushkarna, Carey Radebaugh, Emily Reif, and Ann Yuan. 2020. The language interpretability tool: Extensible, interactive visualizations and analysis for NLP models. In *Proceedings of the 2020 Conference on Empirical Methods in Natural Language Processing: System Demonstrations*, pages 107–118, Online. Association for Computational Linguistics.

Eric Wallace, Jens Tuyls, Junlin Wang, Sanjay Subramanian, Matt Gardner, and Sameer Singh. 2019. AllenNLP interpret: A framework for explaining predictions of NLP models. In *Proceedings of the 2019 Conference on Empirical Methods in Natural Language Processing and the 9th International Joint Conference on Natural Language Processing (EMNLP-IJCNLP): System Demonstrations*, pages 7–12, Hong Kong, China. Association for Computational Linguistics.

Andrew G Wilson and Pavel Izmailov. 2020. Bayesian deep learning and a probabilistic perspective of generalization. *Advances in neural information processing systems*, 33:4697–4708.

Thomas Wolf, Lysandre Debut, Victor Sanh, Julien Chaumond, Clement Delangue, Anthony Moi, Perric Cistac, Clara Ma, Yacine Jernite, Julien Plu, Canwen Xu, Teven Le Scao, Sylvain Gugger, Mariama Drame, Quentin Lhoest, and Alexander M. Rush. 2020. Transformers: State-of-the-Art Natural Language Processing. pages 38–45. Association for Computational Linguistics.

Tongshuang Wu, Marco Tulio Ribeiro, Jeffrey Heer, and Daniel Weld. 2019. Errudite: Scalable, reproducible, and testable error analysis. In *Proceedings of the 57th Annual Meeting of the Association for Computational Linguistics*, pages 747–763, Florence, Italy. Association for Computational Linguistics.

A Azimuth Design

The Azimuth team employed human-centered design methods to create interfaces that propose a workflow to AI practitioners while taking into account the exploratory nature of their work.

A.1 Design Challenges

User interviews surfaced functional challenges that we were able to address with design modifications. We present several examples below.

First, early design iterations centered the user experience around the exploration space, allowing for unstructured analysis and exploration of individual examples. However, this space did not provide enough high-level insights nor sufficient guidance to inform a user's next actions. We created the dashboard (Fig. 6) to summarize these insights and guide the user's exploration of the dataset.

Figure 6: The dashboard was added to address the need to separate but link different levels of analysis.

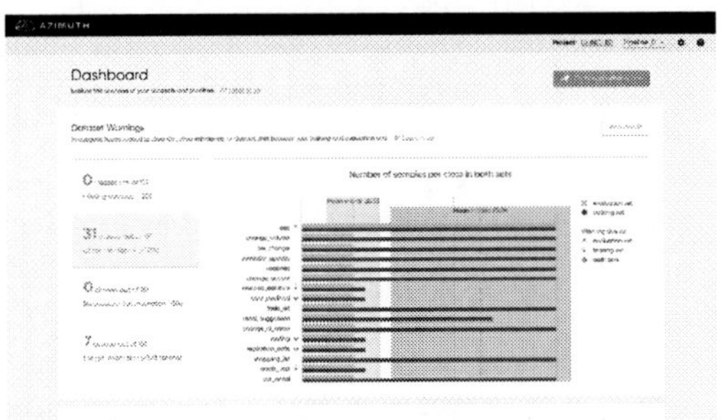

Second, the notion of data subpopulations was included very early on in the form of filtering via individual dropdown menus. This did not show all possible filtering options nor their distributions across the dataset. As Fig. 10 illustrates, the control panel that replaced the dropdown menus now shows users how filters can be combined as well as the filters that result in the largest number of model errors. For example, filtering the dataset by prediction *oil_change_how* will result in a data subpopulation where the model performed very well (the line is almost entirely green).

Third, we grappled with the trade-off between providing users with all possible avenues of exploration versus presenting a limited set of options that are relevant in the context of the user's activity. We ended up replacing the initial option for users to select data subsets by individual confidence histogram bins, which led to choice paralysis or haphazardness, with the option to select data subsets by picking a confidence threshold. For example, users can now view all examples where the model assigned a confidence less than 80%.

A.2 Guidance

Colors. A consistent color scheme is used to draw attention to warnings, as shown in the confusion matrix in Fig. 7.

Figure 7: Example of Azimuth color system.

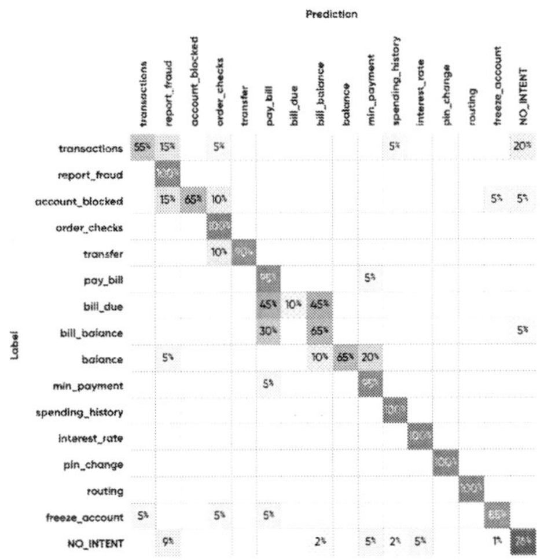

Documentation. To help guide our users, each section element has direct links to our detailed product documentation, as shown in Fig. 8.

Figure 8: Links to product documentation are embedded throughout the application.

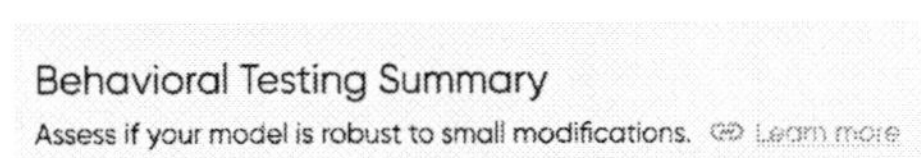

Tooltips. Tooltips are also available on essential elements to identify and define key concepts, show calculation methods, define terms, and provide information on how to use certain functionality, as shown in Fig. 9.

A.3 Flexibility

Filtering. A control panel, illustrated in Fig. 10, allows users to filter the dataset and predictions across diverse criteria, such as containing a particular word or having a certain confidence score. The

Figure 9: Tooltips help give context to users.

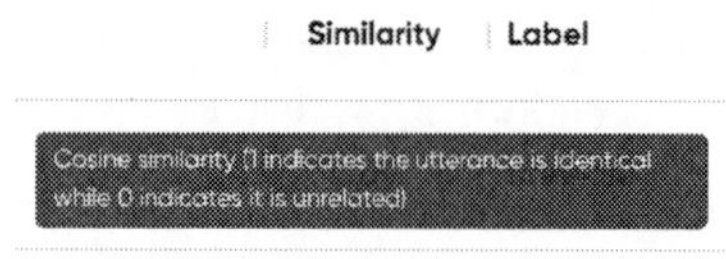

user can also filter by label, predicted class, and all available smart tags. Predictions can also be shown with and without post-processing, which can help distinguish model errors from errors related to the post-processing steps.

Figure 10: Control panel provides sophisticated filtering.

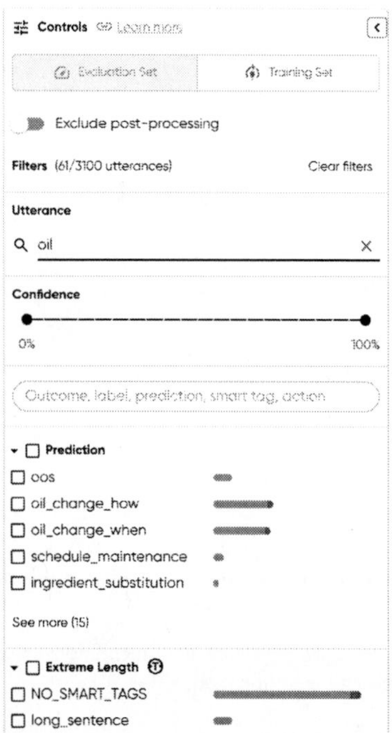

Sorting and Column Customization. As shown in Fig. 11, many of our tables allow users to show/hide columns as they see fit, in addition to sorting the table information based on the content in the columns.

Figure 11: Users can sort by column and customize what they see.

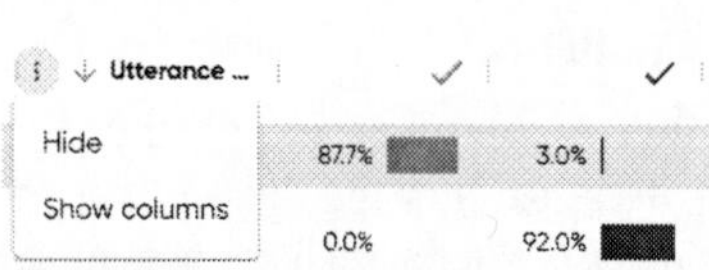

B Case Study Details

B.1 Dataset and Model Details

We chose a DistilBert model (Sanh et al., 2019) from among the best ranking models on PapersWithCode[4]. The CLINC-OOS dataset and the DistilBert model were both downloaded from the Hugging Face Hub. We configured Azimuth to use a threshold of 0.5. When the model score was below this value, examples were classified as the rejection class, also known as Out-of-Scope (OOS). Azimuth provides the option to conduct analyses before or after post-processing (in this case, thresholding to OOS); we took advantage of this option for some analyses below. We used the **Imbalanced** training split and the validation split as the evaluation set.

B.2 Dataset Analysis

B.2.1 Dataset Shift

We examined data shift by inspecting misclassified examples from the evaluation set using the *no_close_train* smart tag, which identifies those having no training examples that are similar to them. This approach identified 26 examples that were candidates for targeted data augmentation. Data augmentation could be guided by looking at the example's most salient tokens and its most similar examples in the training set.

For instance, as shown in Fig. 12, an example mentioning "travel time" was labeled “distance”, but predicted as “travel alert” with low confidence (41%). According to the saliency map, the model focuses on the words “travel” and “time”. Most similar examples in the training data were labeled as "distance" but did not contain the word “travel”. In addition, the examples in the training data containing the word “travel” were predominantly labeled “travel alert,” followed by “travel notification” and “vaccines”. Augmenting the class “distance” in the training data with examples containing words related to "travel time" could be a way to address this data shift issue.

B.2.2 Class Imbalance

Azimuth detects class imbalance in the training set, which is normal given the split that we chose. Another observation is that the OOS class is overrepresented in the evaluation set, compared to other classes.

[4] https://paperswithcode.com/sota/text-classification-on-clinc-oos

Figure 12: Example of possible dataset shift on the example details page.

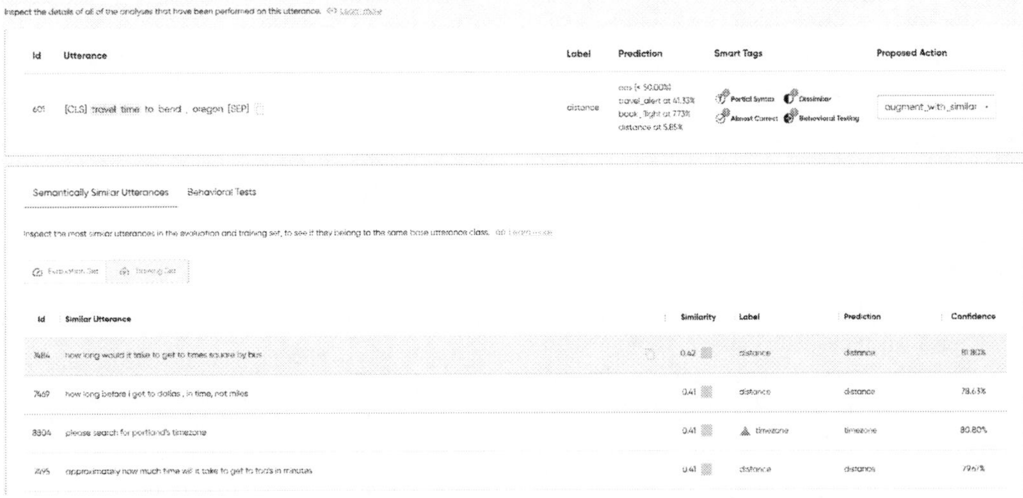

B.2.3 Class Definition

The dataset covers a large variety of topics with its 150 intents, not all of which are at the same hierarchical level of semantic meaning. This can cause the model to have difficulty differentiating between intents. The *conflicting_neighbors* smart tags surfaced many examples for which it was not easy to determine the correct label, or where multiple labels could apply. This helped direct us to overlapping class pairs, including those that are effectively supersets of other intents. For example:

- There is some ambiguity between the intents “restaurant suggestion” and “travel suggestion”. When the example refers to a restaurant in a particular city, the ground-truth label is "travel suggestion" rather than "restaurant suggestion", but the model did not learn this distinction.
- Some intents cover large semantic spaces, such as “translate” and “define”, making them difficult to predict correctly. For example, “how do I ask about the weather in chinese” is predicted as “weather” instead of "translate" because the text can be interpreted as a weather-related question.

B.2.4 Problematic Examples

Using *similarity* smart tags (*conflicting_neighbors* and *no_close*), we were able to detect 18 mislabeled examples in the evaluation set and 25 in the training set. Notably, we also found a mislabeling pattern where four examples were labeled “change accent” instead of “change account”. This dataset is relatively clean and, for better or worse, does not reflect the messiness and ambiguity of real-world data. Although these examples make up a small proportion of the dataset, it is notable that we were able to surface them relatively easily. Fig. 13 shows a subset of the mislabeled examples.

Figure 13: Subset of problematic examples.

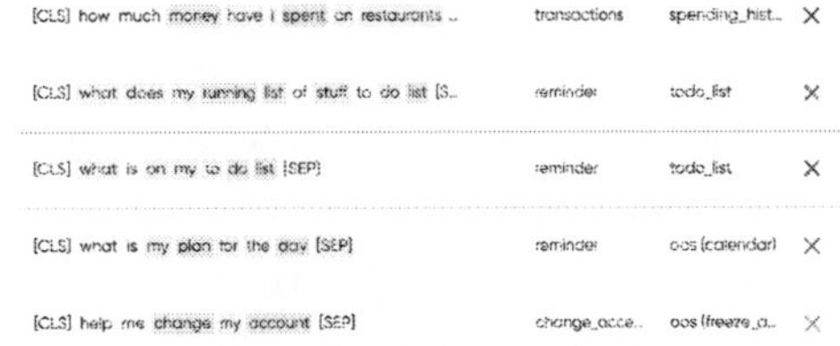

B.3 Model Quality Assessment

The model is 99.2% accurate on the training set and 93.9% accurate on the evaluation set without post-processing. The errors in the evaluation set are either misclassifications (5.8%) or rejections to

OOS (0.3%). When adding a threshold of 0.5, the accuracy decreases to 90.7%. On the other hand, misclassification errors decrease to 1.6% and OOS gets predicted more often instead of predicting the wrong in-scope class (7.7%).

B.3.1 Data Subpopulations

We examined misclassification rates for different data subpopulations, such as label and a variety of smart tags. Several interesting issues were quickly revealed:

- The model has lower accuracy on a few intents when evaluated on the training set, especially when examples contain the word "name", which can be found in intents such as "what is your name" and "change user name" (respectively ∼75% and ∼82% accuracy on the training set). These observations on the training data already tell us that some intents are more difficult to learn than others.
- Compared to average evaluation set accuracy, the model performs better (+3%) on long sentences (more than 15 tokens) and worse (-5%) on short sentences (less than three tokens). Short sentences are more often predicted as OOS. The model also performs worse on examples having no verbs (often short sentences), with a drop of ∼12% in accuracy compared to the average.
- As expected, the model has lower accuracy on examples with conflicting or few similar examples. Compared to average, we see a drop in accuracy of ∼25% on examples tagged with the *conflicting_neighbors* smart tag and a drop of ∼10% on examples tagged with the *no_close* smart tags.
- The accuracy is lower than average (∼20%) on examples that fail any punctuation robustness tests (*failed_punctuation* smart tag). These tests are considered to fail if the prediction changes when the punctuation is altered.

B.3.2 Annotation Artifacts Discovery

Exploration with Azimuth revealed the following cases where model predictions depended on specific words or word forms, as well as other cases described below in "Behavioral testing". As shown in Fig. 14, predicting "accept reservations" intent is highly dependent on the word "reservations". When examples in the evaluation set contain the singular form "reservation", the model makes mistakes.

Figure 14: Important words are shown for correct and incorrect predictions for the "accept reservations" intent.

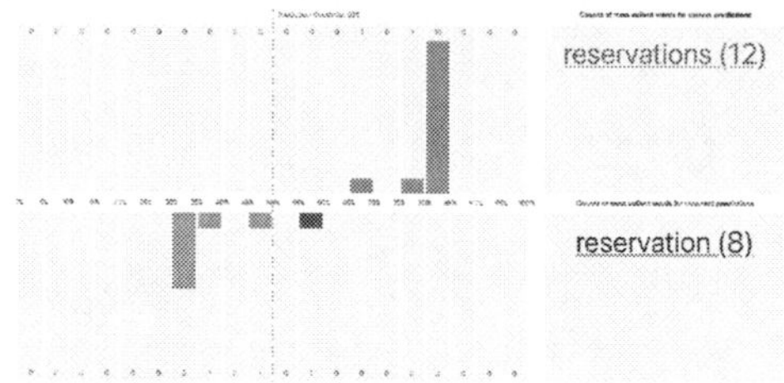

B.3.3 Behavioral Testing

Azimuth flagged the high failure rate of behavioral tests on both the training and evaluation sets, due largely to the high failure rate when introducing typos (approximately 22-25% failure across several tests for both dataset splits). Additionally, model predictions changed for some examples when altering the punctuation, especially when introducing a comma or a period. Although the overall failure rate for this test was low (∼2%), users may consider this type of failure unacceptable. Together, these tests suggest a robustness issue that should be addressed through dataset augmentation or pipeline design.

Further exploration of individual examples, via saliency maps and smart tags for behavioral tests, revealed several intents that were highly dependent on single tokens, indicating potential annotation artifacts. For instance, the model fails when "luggage" is misspelled in examples labeled as "lost luggage". Similarly, it fails when "rewards" is misspelled in examples labeled as "redeem rewards".

B.3.4 Uncertainty-based Analysis

The model is generally underconfident, having a maximum confidence of 90% and an expected calibration error (ECE) of 0.21 on the evaluation set. This could be addressed via temperature scaling. The model is particularly underconfident on specific intents, such as "what is your name" and "pto used", with top confidence scores around 60% to 70%.

The *high_epistemic_uncertainty* smart tag surfaced 48 examples, most of them labeled as OOS. The model only has an accuracy of ∼30% on these examples, demonstrating how difficult they are to classify. Some examples include "idk", labeled as "maybe", and "what's today's high and low", labeled as "weather".

SynKB: Semantic Search for Synthetic Procedures

Fan Bai[♣] Alan Ritter[♣] Peter Madrid[♠] Dayne Freitag[◇] John Niekrasz[◇]
♣ School of Interactive Computing, Georgia Institute of Technology
♠ Biosciences Division, SRI International
◇ Artificial Intelligence Center, SRI International
{fan.bai, alan.ritter}@cc.gatech.edu
{peter.madrid, daynefreitag, john.niekrasz}@sri.com

Abstract

In this paper we present SynKB,[1] an open-source, automatically extracted knowledge base of chemical synthesis protocols. Similar to proprietary chemistry databases such as Reaxsys, SynKB allows chemists to retrieve structured knowledge about synthetic procedures. By taking advantage of recent advances in natural language processing for procedural texts, SynKB supports more flexible queries about reaction conditions, and thus has the potential to help chemists search the literature for conditions used in relevant reactions as they design new synthetic routes. Using customized Transformer models to automatically extract information from 6 million synthesis procedures described in U.S. and EU patents, we show that for many queries, SynKB has higher recall than Reaxsys, while maintaining high precision. We plan to make SynKB available as an open-source tool; in contrast, proprietary chemistry databases require costly subscriptions.[2]

1 Introduction

Commercial chemistry databases, such as Reaxys[3] are invaluable tools for chemists, who issue structured SQL-like queries to retrieve precise information about chemical reactions described in the literature. Large, high-quality datasets are also crucial for synthetic route planning (Klucznik et al., 2018), automation (Coley et al., 2019b; Collins et al., 2020), and machine learning approaches to retrosynthesis (Coley et al., 2019a). In addition to proprietary, manually curated databases such as Reaxys, recent work has begun to use automatically extracted data from reactions described in patents (Tetko et al., 2020), however existing databases are limited to basic reaction information, and do not include important details such as concentrations or order of additions (Coley et al., 2019b). The lack of high-quality data has been identified as a key challenge in developing recommendation models for reaction conditions (Struble et al., 2020).

In this paper, we present SynKB, a working system that demonstrates the application of modern NLP methods to extract large quantities of structured information about chemical synthesis procedures from text. SynKB has a number of advantages with respect to existing chemistry databases such as Reaxys: (1) We show that by automatically extracting information from millions of synthesis procedures described in U.S. and European patents using state-of-the-art NLP methods, we can achieve significantly higher recall than existing chemistry databases while maintaining high precision. In §3, we demonstrate SynKB's coverage is complementary to Reaxys; see Figure 2 for details. (2) SynKB's novel graph search supports better coverage of reaction conditions than existing chemistry databases; this includes concentrations, reaction times, order of the addition of reagents, catalysts, etc. (3) We will make SynKB available as open-source software on publication, in contrast, most existing chemistry databases are proprietary, with the notable exception of Lowe (2017), which we compare to in §3.

We have built an online demo, which can be viewed at the following URL: `https://tinyurl.com/synkb`. We will also release the source code and patent-based extractions used to build SynKB on publication.

2 SynKB

SynKB is an open-source system that allows chemists to perform structured queries over large corpora of synthesis procedures. In this section, we present each component of SynKB, as illustrated in Figure 1. Our corpus collection is first presented in §2.1. Section 2.2 describes how a corpus of six

[1] Demo URL: `https://tinyurl.com/synkb`
Introduction video: `https://screencast-o-matic.com/watch/c3jVQsVZwOV`

[2] Code: `https://github.com/bflashcp3f/SynKB`.

[3] `https://www.elsevier.com/solutions/reaxys`

Proceedings of the The 2022 Conference on Empirical Methods in Natural Language Processing: System Demonstrations, pages 311 - 318
December 7-11, 2022

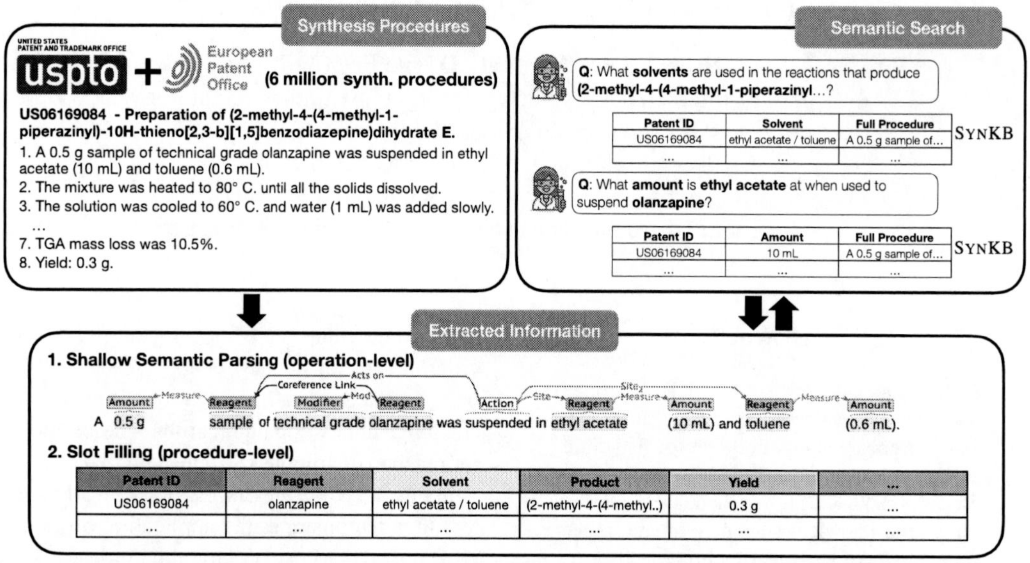

Figure 1: Overview of our semantic search system SYNKB, which searches over 6 million chemical synthesis procedures collected from patents. Users can enter structured queries to retrieve procedures concerning procedure-level or operation-level information.

million procedures is annotated with sentence-level action graphs, in addition to protocol-level slots relevant to chemical reactions, including starting materials, solvents, reaction products, yields, etc. After automatically annotating and indexing, we experiment with the semantic search capabilities enabled by SYNKB in §2.3.

2.1 Corpus Collection

We extract structured representations of synthetic protocols from a corpus of chemical patents (Bai et al., 2021), which includes over six million chemical synthesis procedures extracted from around 300k U.S. and European patents (written in English). The U.S. portion of this corpus comes from an open-source corpus of chemical synthesis procedures (Lowe, 2017), which covers 2.4 million synthetic procedures extracted from U.S. patents (USPTO[4], 1976-2016). For the European portion, we apply the Lowe (2017) reaction identification pipeline to European patents. Specifically, we download patents from EPO[5] (1978-2020) as XML files and select patents containing the IPC (International Patent Classification) code 'C07' for processing as they are in the category of organic chemistry. Next, the synthesis procedure identifier developed by Lowe (2012), a trained Naive Bayes classifier, is applied to the *Description* section of all selected patents. As a result, we obtain another 3.7 million procedures from European patents.

2.2 Extracting Reaction Details from Synthetic Procedures

To facilitate semantic search, we automatically annotate the corpus of 6 million synthetic procedures described above with semantic action graphs (Kulkarni et al., 2018) in addition to chemical reaction slots (Nguyen et al., 2020) using Transformer models that are pre-trained on a large corpus of scientific procedures (Bai et al., 2021).

Shallow Semantic Parsing. We first perform sentence-level annotation, where each step in the procedure is annotated with a semantic graph (Tamari et al., 2021). Nodes in the graph are experimental operations and their typed arguments, whereas labeled edges specify relations between the nodes (see the example shallow semantic parse in Figure 1). Here we use the CHEMSYN framework (Bai et al., 2021), which covers 24 types of nodes (such as *Action*, *Reagent*, *Amount*, *Equipment*, etc.) and 17 edge types (e.g. *Acts-on* and

[4] https://www.uspto.gov/learning-and-resources/bulk-data-products

[5] https://www.epo.org/searching-for-patents/data/bulk-data-sets.html

Measure). With these annotated semantic graphs, users can search for operation-level information, for example, the amount of DMF when used as a solvent to dissolve HATU (this will be further discussed in §3). Following Tamari et al. (2021), we split semantic graph annotation into two sub-tasks, Mention Identification (MI) for node prediction and Argument Role Labeling (ARL) for edge prediction. We use the same fine-tuning architectures as in Tamari et al. (2021). Models are fine-tuned on the CHEMSYN corpus, which consists of 992 chemical synthesis procedures extracted from patents, and the resulting performance (averages across five random seeds) is shown in Table 1. We select model checkpoints via the Dev set performance out of five random seeds, and use the selected checkpoint for inference on our 6 million synthetic procedures.

Slot Filling. In the second task, we annotate procedures from a protocol perspective, i.e., identifying key entities playing certain roles in a protocol, which can be queried in a slot-based search. We use the CHEMU training corpus proposed in Nguyen et al. (2020). This dataset includes 10 pre-defined slot types concerning chemical compounds and related entities in chemical synthesis processes such as *Starting Material*, *Solvent*, and *Product*. Similar to the Mention Identification task, we treat Slot Filling as a sequence tagging problem. However, the input in Slot Filling is the entire protocol, rather than a single sentence, as in mention identification. We fine-tune models on the CHEMU dataset (see Table 1 for results), and then run inference on the chemical patent corpus using the learned model.

ProcBERT. We use ProcBERT (Bai et al., 2021), a BERT-based model that is pre-trained on in-domain data (scientific protocols), as the backbone for all of our models, and develop task-specific fine-tuning architectures on top of it. The comparison between ProcBERT and other pre-trained models is presented in Table 1. Because ProcBERT is pre-trained using in-domain data, we find that it outperforms both $\text{BERT}_{\text{large}}$ (Devlin et al., 2019) and SciBERT (Beltagy et al., 2019) on all three tasks.

2.3 Semantic Search

SYNKB offers search modalities specific to each of these two forms of annotation, i.e., semantic action graphs and chemical reaction slots, along with features designed to support practical use. The

Annotation Task	Dataset	Pre-trained Model		
		$\text{BERT}_{\text{large}}$	SciBERT	ProcBERT
Mention Identification	CHEMSYN	$95.26_{0.1}$	$95.82_{0.2}$	$\mathbf{95.97}_{0.2}$
Argument Role Labeling	CHEMSYN	$92.87_{0.5}$	$93.27_{0.2}$	$\mathbf{93.57}_{0.2}$
Slot Filling	CHEMU	$95.10_{0.2}$	$95.63_{0.1}$	$\mathbf{96.19}_{0.1}$

Table 1: Test set F_1 scores of fine-tuned models for the three annotation tasks. These numbers, averages across five random seeds with standard deviations as subscripts, are taken from our previous work Bai et al. (2021). Models using ProcBERT for contextual embeddings perform the best on all three tasks and are used for automatic annotations on six million synthesis procedures to construct SYNKB.

	SYNKB (ours)	USPTO-Lowe	Reaxys
License	Open source	Open source	Subscription
# Procedures (mill.)	6	2.4	57
# Entity Types	24	8	10
# Relation Types	17	-	-
Annotation	Automatic	Automatic	Manual

Table 2: Comparison between our SYNKB and two performant databases. Our SYNKB provides more fine-grained annotations (more entity types and unique relation annotations) than the other two systems and covers more procedures than USPTO-Lowe, a database built using the largest open-source synthesis procedure corpus (Lowe, 2017).

first type of query supported by SYNKB is **semantic graph search**, which allows users to search for synthesis procedures based on the semantic parse of the constituent operations. We adapt the graph query formalism proposed originally for syntactic dependencies in Valenzuela-Escárcega et al. (2020).[6] Formally, the input query $G = (V, E)$ is a labeled directed graph. Each node $v_i \in V$ is specified as a set of constraints on matching entities (a single or multi-token span). For example, users can specify the node as DMF or `[word=DMF]`, which triggers an exact match on entity mentions containing the word "DMF". They can also constrain the entity type of the node using the expression `[entity=Type]`.[7] Moreover, nodes can be named `captures` when surrounded with `(?<name>...)`, e.g., the query `(?<solvent> DMF)` captures DMF as the `solvent`. As for the edge $e = (v_i, v_j, l) \in E$, we need to specify the direction and the semantic relation. Considering the query `(?<solvent> DMF) >measure (?<amount> 1 ml)`, it represents a se-

[6]We refer readers to the tutorial of Odinson query language for more details of this graph query formalism.

[7]We store entity labels with the BIO tagging scheme, so users can match a single token entity with the expression `[entity=B-Type]` and a multi-token entity with the expression `[entity=B-Type][entity=I-Type]*`.

mantic graph containing two entity nodes captured as `solvent` and `amount`, and an edge signaling the `measure` relation and its direction (from `solvent` to `amount`).

In addition, SYNKB supports **slot-based search**, which presents a structured search interface, with entries corresponding to CHEMU slots. A keyword entered into any entry restricts the retrieved set to procedures where the extracted slot contains the indicated keyword. Like the graph search, this returns a set of tuples with elements named with matching slots and containing the matching entity strings. The special token "?" can be used to match *any* slot value.

As for the implementation, the semantic graph search module is powered by Odinson (Valenzuela-Escárcega et al., 2020), an open-source Lucene-based query engine. Odinson pre-indexes the annotated corpus by generating the inverted index for each procedure. Given an input query, Odinson performs a two-step matching process, where it first examines the node constraints via the inverted index; if this step works well, the semantic relations will be verified in the second step. The two-step matching process improves the speed of Odinson, and thus enables interactive querying. As for the slot-based search, it is supported by Elasticsearch[8] with the exception that, when users perform both types of search at the same time, we use the metadata search feature of Odinson for slot filters (we store slot values as metadata) to improve the system's response speed.

3 Empirical Comparison

In §2, we described the design and implementation of SYNKB including the underlying models, data preparation, and semantic search features. To demonstrate the utility of SYNKB for assisting chemists to search the literature for reaction details, we now evaluate its search features on ten example questions (Q1-Q10 in Table 3), which were collected from synthetic chemists working on the design of new synthesis protocols. In §3.1, we evaluate the slot-based search module of SYNKB and compare it with two existing databases which provides similar search features. In §3.2, we demonstrate how to use our novel semantic graph search module to answer operation-specific questions and evaluate its retrieved answers and procedures.

[8] https://www.elastic.co/elasticsearch/

3.1 Slot-based Search Evaluation

We benchmark the slot-based search module of SYNKB against Reaxys, one of the leading proprietary chemistry databases, and USPTO-Lowe, an automatically extracted database built using a large open-source synthesis procedure corpus (Lowe, 2017). Below, we first introduce these two databases briefly, and then evaluate the results of all three systems on the chemist-proposed questions.

3.1.1 Chemistry Databases

The first database we compare with is **Reaxys**, a web-based commercial chemistry database, which contains comprehensive chemistry data, including chemical properties, compound structures, etc. What particularly interests us in Reaxys is that it contains expert-curated reaction procedures collected from extensive published literature such as chemistry-related patents and periodicals.[9] Also, key experimental entities in those reaction procedures, like participating reagents and reaction temperature, are specified. Thus, similar to our slot-based search, Reaxys allows users to search for reaction procedure information by applying text filters. Users can use its *Query Builder* module to specify multiple chemical reaction-specific filters, and then Reaxys returns all matched reaction procedures along with identified entities in those procedures, which are available for download.

Apart from Reaxys, we also build a database using **USPTO-Lowe** (Lowe, 2017), the largest available open-source chemical synthesis procedure corpus as introduced in §2.1, for comparison. Similar to our SYNKB, this corpus includes automatic annotations of experimental entities on 2.4 million contained reaction procedures.[10] However, our SYNKB provides more fine-grained and comprehensive entity annotations (see Table 2 for the statistics of three experimented databases), and also annotates the relations between extracted entities, which constitute semantic graphs (§2.2) enabling operation-specific semantic graph search. As for the implementation, we load USPTO-Lowe's entity annotation into Elasticsearch, so this customized database can be used in the same way as the slot-based search module of our SYNKB.

[9] https://www.elsevier.com/solutions/reaxys/features-and-capabilities/content

[10] https://www.nextmovesoftware.com/leadmine.html

<table>
<tr><th>System</th><th>Input Query</th><th># Proce.</th><th># Ans.</th><th>Ans. Prec.</th></tr>
<tr><td colspan="5">Slot-based Search</td></tr>
<tr><td colspan="5">Q1 - What are the solvents used for reactions containing the reagent triphosgene?</td></tr>
<tr><td>Reaxys</td><td>{"reagent":"triphosgene"}</td><td>35</td><td>7</td><td>100%</td></tr>
<tr><td>USPTO-Lowe</td><td rowspan="2">{"reagent":"triphosgene", "solvent":"?"}</td><td>3157</td><td>104</td><td>90%</td></tr>
<tr><td>SynKB</td><td>7184</td><td>127</td><td>94%</td></tr>
<tr><td colspan="5">Q2 - What are the yields (percent) of reactions producing (5-Methylpyrimidin-2-yl)methanol?</td></tr>
<tr><td>Reaxys</td><td>{"product":"(5-Methylpyrimidin-2-yl)methanol"}</td><td>1</td><td>1</td><td>100%</td></tr>
<tr><td>USPTO-Lowe</td><td rowspan="2">{"product":"(5-Methylpyrimidin-2-yl)methanol", "yield (percent)":"?"}</td><td>1</td><td>1</td><td>100%</td></tr>
<tr><td>SynKB</td><td>1</td><td>1</td><td>100%</td></tr>
<tr><td colspan="5">Q3 - What are the products of reactions containing the reagent trimethylsilyldiazomethane?</td></tr>
<tr><td>Reaxys</td><td>{"reagent":"trimethylsilyldiazomethane"}</td><td>438</td><td>75</td><td>100%</td></tr>
<tr><td>USPTO-Lowe</td><td rowspan="2">{"reagent":"trimethylsilyldiazomethane", "product":"?"}</td><td>517</td><td>335</td><td>98%</td></tr>
<tr><td>SynKB</td><td>1033</td><td>708</td><td>96%</td></tr>
<tr><td colspan="5">Q4 - What are the products of reactions containing the reagent chlorosulfonic acid and the solvent chlorobenzene?</td></tr>
<tr><td>Reaxys</td><td>{"reagent":"chlorosulfonic acid"} AND {"solvent":"chlorobenzene"}</td><td>148</td><td>65</td><td>100%</td></tr>
<tr><td>USPTO-Lowe</td><td rowspan="2">{"reagent":"chlorosulfonic acid", "solvent":"chlorobenzene", "product":"?"}</td><td>6</td><td>2</td><td>100%</td></tr>
<tr><td>SynKB</td><td>9</td><td>4</td><td>100%</td></tr>
<tr><td colspan="5">Q5 - What are the reaction times for reactions using reagent CDI (carbonyldiimidazole)?</td></tr>
<tr><td>Reaxys</td><td>{"reagent":"CDI"} OR {"reagent":"carbonyldiimidazole"}</td><td>93</td><td>24</td><td>100%</td></tr>
<tr><td>USPTO-Lowe</td><td rowspan="2">{"reagent": "CDI OR carbonyldiimidazole", "reaction time":"?"}</td><td>3722</td><td>339</td><td>100%</td></tr>
<tr><td>SynKB</td><td>6377</td><td>511</td><td>94%</td></tr>
<tr><td colspan="5">Q6 - What are the reaction temperatures for reactions containing reagent trifluoromethanesulfonic acid?</td></tr>
<tr><td>Reaxys</td><td>{"reagent":"trifluoromethanesulfonic acid"}</td><td>104</td><td>3</td><td>100%</td></tr>
<tr><td>USPTO-Lowe</td><td rowspan="2">{"reagent":"trifluoromethanesulfonic acid", "temperature":"?"}</td><td>727</td><td>124</td><td>100%</td></tr>
<tr><td>SynKB</td><td>1937</td><td>243</td><td>98%</td></tr>
<tr><td colspan="5">Semantic Graph Search</td></tr>
<tr><td colspan="5">Q7 - What are the reagents used to dilute plasma?</td></tr>
<tr><td>SynKB</td><td>plasma <acts-on diluted >using (?<reagent> [entity=B-Reagent][entity=I-Reagent]*)</td><td>24</td><td>16</td><td>100%</td></tr>
<tr><td colspan="5">Q8 - What is the pH of a solution after being titrated with NaOH?</td></tr>
<tr><td>SynKB</td><td>(?<ph> [entity=B-pH][entity=I-pH]+) <setting titrated >using NaOH</td><td>39</td><td>21</td><td>95%</td></tr>
<tr><td colspan="5">Q9 - What are the common pore sizes of PTFE filters?</td></tr>
<tr><td>SynKB</td><td>PTFE filter >measure (?<pore_size> [entity=B-Generic-Measure][entity=I-Generic-Measure]*)</td><td>183</td><td>39</td><td>92%</td></tr>
<tr><td colspan="5">Q10 - What molar concentration is the reagent HATU at when dissolved in the solvent DMF?</td></tr>
<tr><td>SynKB</td><td>HATU >measure (?<mole> [] [word=mmol|word=mol]) []{1,10} DMF >measure (?<volume> [] [word=ml|word=l])</td><td>447</td><td>289</td><td>100%</td></tr>
</table>

Table 3: Search queries and resulting performance on 10 chemist-proposed questions for Reaxys, USPTO-Lowe, and SynKB (ours). **# Proc.** is the number of returned procedures containing valid answers, and **# Ans.** refers to the number of distinct answer slots or captures in these procedures. The first six questions (Q1-Q6) are answerable for all three databases as they only require entity annotation while the last four questions (Q7-Q10) can only be answered by our SynKB using our unique semantic action graph annotation. SynKB consistently shows better recall than two compared databases while being highly accurate.

3.1.2 Comparison with Examples

We now compare three systems on six questions that were proposed by chemists (Q1-Q6) as these questions only require annotations on experimental entities and thus can be answered in all three systems. For example, Q1 ("What solvents are used in reactions involving triphosgene?") can be answered by the SynKB query `{"reagent":"triphosgene", "solvent":"?"}`, as *reagent* and *solvent* are query-able ChEMU slots. Similarly, for Reaxys, experimental entities are specified for corresponding text filters.

We evaluate the output of each system from two perspectives: 1) recall, which is measured by the number of returned procedures containing valid answers and the number of distinct answer slots or captures in these procedures; and 2) precision, the proportion of correct answers among all predicted answers. In cases where the number of answers exceeds 50, we sample 50 answers from the full set to estimate precision.

The search queries and performance on each question for the three systems are shown in Table 3. We can see that, SynKB consistently retrieves a larger number of relevant procedures and answers than Reaxys (5 out of 6 questions) while maintaining high precision. USPTO-Lowe, which uses a rule-based annotation model, shows competitive performance on precision but trails behind our SynKB in terms of recall for all 6 questions. This comparison clearly shows the strength of our system: by leveraging state-of-the-art NLP for chemical synthesis procedures (Bai et al., 2021), we can provide chemists with abundant information, which is non-proprietary and delivered with high precision. Furthermore, we plot the Venn diagram (Figure 2) over the retrieved answers, which shows the percentage of unique and shared answers for each system out of all retrieved answers (we do macro-average across six questions.) Interestingly, only 18.1% of retrieved answers are shared among all three systems, and both our SYNKB and Reaxys contain a large number of unique answers, which take 31.5% and 17.4% of retrieved answers respectively. This shift in answer distribution suggests that our open-source SYNKB can be a good complement to proprietary chemistry databases like Reaxys, and it is better for users to use both of them if possible instead of choosing one over the other.

3.2 Semantic Graph Search Evaluation

We evaluate our novel semantic graph search on four operation-specific questions (Q7-Q10). Unlike the six questions introduced above, these questions place constraints on the relations between mentioned entities, and thus are not answerable for Reaxys and USPTO-Lowe (due to the lack of relation annotation). For instance, to answer Q7 "What are the reagents used to dilute `plasma`?", a system needs to first locate the particular operation in a procedure where `plasma` is diluted, and then identify the reagent, which facilitates this dilution operation. This whole process can be realized in our semantic graph search module. Concretely, the graph-based query we use for Q7 is: "`plasma <acts-on diluted >using (?<reagent> [entity=B-Reagent][entity=I-Reagent]*)`", which matches procedures containing "`plasma`" and "`diluted`" connected in the same semantic graph and returns used reagents in the form of named captures. We evaluate the performance of the semantic graph search module by manually inspecting predicted answers (randomly sampling 50 answers for Q10), and show results in Table 3. Similar to the findings in the slot-based search evaluation, SYNKB shows good coverage while maintaining high precision.

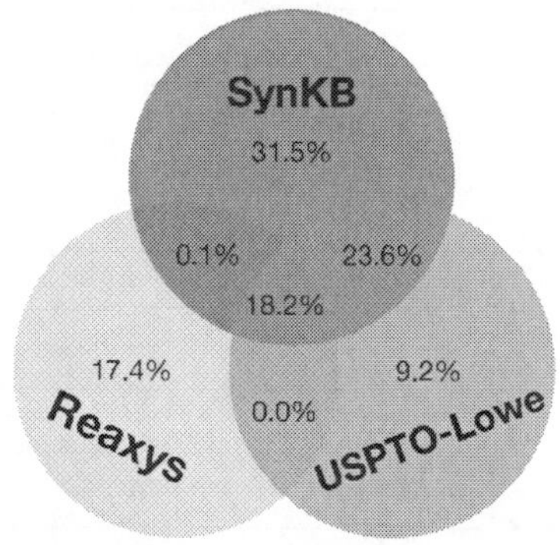

Figure 2: Venn diagram on the answer distribution of six slot-based search questions (macro-average) for all three databases. We can see that both our SYNKB and Reaxys cover high percentage of unique answers, suggesting that users should use them together if possible.

4 Related Work

Lowe (2012) was the first to develop a complete information extraction pipeline for chemical synthesis procedures, using a mostly rule-based approach. Subsequently, there have been several efforts to extract information from experimental procedures by either developing more performant extraction models (Vaucher et al., 2020; Guo et al., 2021) or designing extraction frameworks for other types of scientific literature, like wet-lab protocols (Kulkarni et al., 2018) and material science publications (Mysore et al., 2019; Kuniyoshi et al., 2020; Olivetti et al., 2020; O'Gorman et al., 2021). In this paper, we use the state-of-the-art NLP models for chemical synthesis procedures (Bai et al., 2021) to build the largest open-source knowledge base that searches synthetic procedure details. Our system is complementary to many proprietary chemistry databases, such as Reaxys, SciFinder[11], and Pistachio[12], in terms of contained information and search modalities.

Recent work has also developed slot-based classifiers to extract structured representations of events (from social media), supporting structured queries (Zong et al., 2020). In contrast, we present a semantic search system, which is customized for chemical synthesis procedures with specialized search features. In addition, recent work has explored *extractive search* systems (Ravfogel et al., 2021) that allow experts to specify syntactic pat-

[11] https://scifinder.cas.org

[12] https://www.nextmovesoftware.com/pistachio.html

terns, including syntactic structures of the input and capture slots. The graph-based queries in our SYNKB enable a similar capability in the domain of synthetic procedures, however SYNKB's queries are defined over semantic graphs that encode actions in synthetic protocols and associated semantic arguments.

5 Conclusion

In this paper, we present SYNKB, a system for large-scale extraction and querying of chemical synthesis procedures. SYNKB provides efficient searches against semantic action graphs and chemical reaction slots derived from 6 million synthesis procedures contained in chemical patents. A quantitative comparison with Reaxys, one of the leading commercial databases of reaction information, demonstrates the competence and versatility of our freely accessible system.

Ethical Considerations and Broader Impacts

Proprietary chemistry databases, such as Reaxys require costly subscriptions, limiting scientific inquiry for those who do not have the means to access this valuable source of information. In this paper, we presented an open-source semantic search system, SYNKB, which demonstrates state-of-the-art NLP methods can enable automatically extracted databases of synthetic procedure operational details that are competitive with Reaxys in terms of recall. We will make our code and data freely available.

The data contained in SYNKB is based on automatic extraction from both European and U.S. patents that are in the public domain. Our use complies with the terms of service of the U.S. Patent and Trademark Office and the European Patent Office.

Acknowledgements

We thank Wei Xu for helpful discussion and comments on a previous draft. This material is based upon work supported by the Defense Advanced Research Projects Agency (DARPA) under Contract No. HR001119C0108. The views, opinions, and/or findings expressed are those of the author(s) and should not be interpreted as representing the official views or policies of the Department of Defense or the U.S. Government.

References

Fan Bai, Alan Ritter, and Wei Xu. 2021. Pre-train or annotate? domain adaptation with a constrained budget. In *Proceedings of the 2021 Conference on Empirical Methods in Natural Language Processing*, pages 5002–5015, Online and Punta Cana, Dominican Republic. Association for Computational Linguistics.

Iz Beltagy, Kyle Lo, and Arman Cohan. 2019. SciBERT: A Pretrained Language Model for Scientific Text. In *Proceedings of the 2019 Conference on Empirical Methods in Natural Language Processing and the 9th International Joint Conference on Natural Language Processing (EMNLP-IJCNLP)*, pages 3615–3620, Hong Kong, China.

Connor W Coley, Wengong Jin, Luke Rogers, Timothy F Jamison, Tommi S Jaakkola, William H Green, Regina Barzilay, and Klavs F Jensen. 2019a. A graph-convolutional neural network model for the prediction of chemical reactivity. *Chemical science*, 10(2):370–377.

Connor W Coley, Dale A Thomas III, Justin AM Lummiss, Jonathan N Jaworski, Christopher P Breen, Victor Schultz, Travis Hart, Joshua S Fishman, Luke Rogers, Hanyu Gao, et al. 2019b. A robotic platform for flow synthesis of organic compounds informed by ai planning. *Science*, 365(6453):eaax1566.

Nathan Collins, David Stout, Jin-Ping Lim, Jeremiah P Malerich, Jason D White, Peter B Madrid, Mario Latendresse, David Krieger, Judy Szeto, Vi-Anh Vu, et al. 2020. Fully automated chemical synthesis: toward the universal synthesizer. *Organic Process Research & Development*, 24(10):2064–2077.

Jacob Devlin, Ming-Wei Chang, Kenton Lee, and Kristina Toutanova. 2019. BERT: Pre-training of Deep Bidirectional Transformers for Language Understanding. In *Proceedings of the 2019 Conference of the North American Chapter of the Association for Computational Linguistics: Human Language Technologies*, pages 4171–4186, Minneapolis, Minnesota.

Jiang Guo, A Santiago Ibanez-Lopez, Hanyu Gao, Victor Quach, Connor W Coley, Klavs F Jensen, and Regina Barzilay. 2021. Automated chemical reaction extraction from scientific literature. *Journal of chemical information and modeling*.

Tomasz Klucznik, Barbara Mikulak-Klucznik, Michael P McCormack, Heather Lima, Sara Szymkuć, Manishabrata Bhowmick, Karol Molga, Yubai Zhou, Lindsey Rickershauser, Ewa P Gajewska, et al. 2018. Efficient syntheses of diverse, medicinally relevant targets planned by computer and executed in the laboratory. *Chem*, 4(3):522–532.

Chaitanya Kulkarni, Wei Xu, Alan Ritter, and Raghu Machiraju. 2018. An annotated corpus for machine reading of instructions in wet lab protocols. In *Proceedings of the 2018 Conference of the North American Chapter of the Association for Computational*

Linguistics: Human Language Technologies, Volume 2 (Short Papers), pages 97–106.

Fusataka Kuniyoshi, Kohei Makino, Jun Ozawa, and Makoto Miwa. 2020. Annotating and extracting synthesis process of all-solid-state batteries from scientific literature. In *Proceedings of the 12th Language Resources and Evaluation Conference*, pages 1941–1950.

Daniel Lowe. 2017. Chemical reactions from US patents (1976-2016).

Daniel M. Lowe. 2012. Extraction of Chemical Structures and Reactions from the Literature (Doctoral Thesis).

Sheshera Mysore, Zachary Jensen, Edward Kim, Kevin Huang, Haw-Shiuan Chang, Emma Strubell, Jeffrey Flanigan, Andrew McCallum, and Elsa Olivetti. 2019. The materials science procedural text corpus: Annotating materials synthesis procedures with shallow semantic structures. In *Proceedings of the 13th Linguistic Annotation Workshop*, pages 56–64.

Dat Quoc Nguyen, Zenan Zhai, Hiyori Yoshikawa, Biaoyan Fang, Christian Druckenbrodt, Camilo Thorne, Ralph Hoessel, S. Akhondi, Trevor Cohn, Timothy Baldwin, and K. Verspoor. 2020. ChEMU: Named Entity Recognition and Event Extraction of Chemical Reactions from Patents. *Advances in Information Retrieval*, pages 572 – 579.

Elsa A Olivetti, Jacqueline M Cole, Edward Kim, Olga Kononova, Gerbrand Ceder, Thomas Yong-Jin Han, and Anna M Hiszpanski. 2020. Data-driven materials research enabled by natural language processing and information extraction. *Applied Physics Reviews*, 7(4).

Tim O'Gorman, Zach Jensen, Sheshera Mysore, Kevin Huang, Rubayyat Mahbub, Elsa Olivetti, and Andrew McCallum. 2021. Ms-mentions: Consistently annotating entity mentions in materials science procedural text. In *Proceedings of the 2021 Conference on Empirical Methods in Natural Language Processing*, pages 1337–1352.

Shauli Ravfogel, Hillel Taub-Tabib, and Yoav Goldberg. 2021. Neural extractive search. In *Proceedings of the 59th Annual Meeting of the Association for Computational Linguistics and the 11th International Joint Conference on Natural Language Processing: System Demonstrations*, pages 210–217.

Thomas J Struble, Juan C Alvarez, Scott P Brown, Milan Chytil, Justin Cisar, Renee L DesJarlais, Ola Engkvist, Scott A Frank, Daniel R Greve, Daniel J Griffin, et al. 2020. Current and future roles of artificial intelligence in medicinal chemistry synthesis. *Journal of medicinal chemistry*, 63(16):8667–8682.

Ronen Tamari, Fan Bai, Alan Ritter, and Gabriel Stanovsky. 2021. Process-level representation of scientific protocols with interactive annotation. In *Proceedings of the 16th Conference of the European Chapter of the Association for Computational Linguistics: Main Volume*, pages 2190–2202, Online. Association for Computational Linguistics.

Igor V Tetko, Pavel Karpov, Ruud Van Deursen, and Guillaume Godin. 2020. State-of-the-art augmented nlp transformer models for direct and single-step retrosynthesis. *Nature communications*, 11(1):1–11.

Marco A. Valenzuela-Escárcega, Gus Hahn-Powell, and Dane Bell. 2020. Odinson: A fast rule-based information extraction framework. In *Proceedings of the 12th Language Resources and Evaluation Conference*, pages 2183–2191, Marseille, France. European Language Resources Association.

Alain C Vaucher, Federico Zipoli, Joppe Geluykens, Vishnu H Nair, Philippe Schwaller, and Teodoro Laino. 2020. Automated extraction of chemical synthesis actions from experimental procedures. *Nature communications*, 11(1):1–11.

Shi Zong, Ashutosh Baheti, Wei Xu, and Alan Ritter. 2020. Extracting a knowledge base of covid-19 events from social media. *arXiv preprint arXiv:2006.02567*.

Camelira: An Arabic Multi-Dialect Morphological Disambiguator

Ossama Obeid[1], **Go Inoue**[1,2], **Nizar Habash**[1]
[1]Computational Approaches to Modeling Language (CAMeL) Lab
New York University Abu Dhabi
[2]Mohamed bin Zayed University of Artificial Intelligence
{oobeid,nizar.habash}@nyu.edu
go.inoue@mbzuai.ac.ae

Abstract

We present Camelira, a web-based Arabic multi-dialect morphological disambiguation tool that covers four major variants of Arabic: Modern Standard Arabic, Egyptian, Gulf, and Levantine. Camelira offers a user-friendly web interface that allows researchers and language learners to explore various linguistic information, such as part-of-speech, morphological features, and lemmas. Our system also provides an option to automatically choose an appropriate dialect-specific disambiguator based on the prediction of a dialect identification component. Camelira is publicly accessible at `http://camelira.camel-lab.com`.

1 Introduction

The last two decades have witnessed remarkable progress in Natural Language Processing (NLP) for Arabic and its dialects despite many challenges such as its diglossic nature, morphological complexity, and orthographic ambiguity (Darwish et al., 2021). These efforts have led to many practical applications for various NLP tasks including tokenization, part-of-speech (POS) tagging, morphological disambiguation, named entity recognition, dialect identification (DID), and sentiment analysis (Pasha et al., 2014; Abdelali et al., 2016; Obeid et al., 2019; Abdul-Mageed et al., 2020b, inter alia).

Tools for core technologies like POS tagging and morphological disambiguation are primary examples of such successful applications, e.g., MADAMIRA (Pasha et al., 2014), Farasa (Abdelali et al., 2016), UDPipe (Straka et al., 2016), and Stanza (Qi et al., 2020). However, there are still gaps to be filled in terms of coverage and usability. For example, these systems only support Modern Standard Arabic (MSA) and Egyptian Arabic, but not other widely spoken dialects such as Gulf and Levantine. In addition, these web interfaces only present the top prediction, although the alternative readings could provide valuable information for analyzing the models' behavior. In contrast, morphological analyzers such as ElixirFM (Smrž, 2007), CALIMA$_{Star}$ (Taji et al., 2018b), CALIMA Egyptian (Habash et al., 2012) show all the different readings for a given word out of context but without disambiguated analyses in context. These tools assume that users already know the input DID; however, this is not necessarily the case for second language learners.

To address these limitations, we present Camelira,[1,2] a web interface for Arabic multi-dialect morphological disambiguation that covers four major variants of Arabic: MSA, Egyptian, Gulf, and Levantine. Our system takes an input sentence and provides automatically disambiguated readings for each word in context, as well as its alternative out-of-context readings. We also showcase the integration of a state-of-the-art morphological disambiguator (Inoue et al., 2022) with the highest performing fine-grained Arabic DID system (Salameh et al., 2018) on the MADAR DID shared task (Bouamor et al., 2019). Camelira provides an option to automatically choose a dialect-specific disambiguator based on the prediction of the DID component. To the best of our knowledge, our work is the first to demonstrate an integrated web application that leverages both Arabic morphological disambiguation and DID systems.

Our contributions are as follows: (a) We present a user-friendly web interface that allows researchers and language learners to explore the detailed linguistic analysis of a given Arabic sentence. (b) We include three major Arabic dialects (Egyptian, Gulf, and Levantine) in addition to MSA, to make our tool more accessible to a wider audience. (c) We integrate DID to automatically select the appropriate disambiguator; a feature that helps users with limited knowledge of Arabic dialects.

[1]`http://camelira.camel-lab.com`

[2]Camelira is named after CAMeL Tools (Obeid et al., 2020), and in homage to MADAMIRA (Pasha et al., 2014).

Proceedings of the The 2022 Conference on Empirical Methods in Natural Language Processing: System Demonstrations, pages 319 - 326
December 7-11, 2022 ©2022 Association for Computational Linguistics

2 Arabic Linguistic Facts

The Arabic language poses a number of challenges for NLP (Habash, 2010). We highlight three aspects that are most relevant to multi-dialectal morphological modeling: dialectal variations, morphological richness, and orthographic ambiguity.

First, Arabic is characterized with diglossia and its large number of dialects (Ferguson, 1959; Holes, 2004). MSA is the shared standard variant used in official contexts, while the dialects are the varieties of daily use. MSA and the dialects vary among themselves in different aspects, such as lexicons, morphology, and syntax. Second, Arabic is a morphologically rich and complex language. It employs a combination of templatic, affixational, and cliticization morphological operations to represent numerous grammatical features such as gender, number, person, case, state, mood, aspect, and voice, in addition to a number of attachable pronominal, preposition, and determiner clitics. Third, Arabic is orthographically highly ambiguous. This is due to its orthographic conventions where diacritical marks are often omitted, leading to a high degree of ambiguity. For example, MSA can have 12 different morphological analyses per word on average (Pasha et al., 2014).

3 Related Work

Morphological Analysis and Disambiguation Morphological analysis is the task of producing a complete list of readings (analyses) for a given word out of context. Morphological analysis has a wide range of applications, including treebank annotation (Maamouri et al., 2003, 2011, 2009) and improving morphological modeling (Habash et al., 2005; Inoue et al., 2017; Zalmout and Habash, 2017; Khalifa et al., 2020). Over the past two decades, there have been numerous efforts in building morphological analyzers for Arabic, e.g. BAMA (Buckwalter, 2002), MAGEAD (Habash and Rambow, 2006; Altantawy et al., 2010), ALMORGEANA (Habash, 2007), ElixirFM (Smrž, 2007), SAMA (Graff et al., 2009), CALIMA Egyptian (Habash et al., 2012), CALIMA Gulf (Khalifa et al., 2017), AlKhalil Morpho Sys (Boudlal et al., 2010; Boudchiche et al., 2017) and CALIMA$_{Star}$ (Taji et al., 2018b). Among these efforts, ElixirFM[3] and CALIMA$_{Star}$[4] provide easy-to-use web interfaces, allowing the user to explore all the possible morphological analyses for a given word. In addition to these rule-based approaches, Eskander et al. (2016) used a corpus-based paradigm completion technique (Eskander et al., 2013) to develop a morphological analyzer for Levantine; and (Khalifa et al., 2020) used the same technique to develop a morphological analyzer for Gulf.

Morphological disambiguation is the subsequent process of identifying the correct analysis in context from the list of different analyses produced by a morphological analyzer. Examples of this in Arabic start with MADA (Habash et al., 2005) and many following efforts (Pasha et al., 2014; Khalifa et al., 2016; Zalmout and Habash, 2017, 2020; Khalifa et al., 2020; Inoue et al., 2022), where they rank the analyses based on the predictions of morphological taggers. While these models have achieved significant improvement over time, only MADAMIRA (Pasha et al., 2014) offers a web interface[5] that's accessible to a general audience. In this work, we present a user-friendly web interface for state-of-the-art morphological disambiguation models to make these recent advances more accessible to a wider audience, such as linguists and language learners. Our interface also provides all the alternative readings of each input word with the associated prediction scores, allowing researchers to investigate the model's behavior.

Dialect Identification Dialect identification (DID) is the task of automatically identifying the language variety of a given text. DID for Arabic and its variants has attracted increasing attention in recent years. A number of shared tasks have been organized, including VarDial (Malmasi et al., 2016; Zampieri et al., 2017, 2018), MADAR (Bouamor et al., 2019), and NADI (Abdul-Mageed et al., 2020a, 2021, 2022), along with continuous efforts in dataset creation (Zaidan and Callison-Burch, 2011; Mubarak and Darwish, 2014; Zaghouani and Charfi, 2018; Baimukan et al., 2022, inter alia). These evaluation campaigns have led to the development of practical applications, such as ADIDA[6] (Obeid et al., 2019), a web interface for fine-grained Arabic DID based on the highest performing system in the MADAR shared task (Salameh et al., 2018). In this work, we employ one of the DID systems described by Salameh

[3] http://quest.ms.mff.cuni.cz/elixir

[4] http://calimastar.camel-lab.com/

[5] http://madamira.camel-lab.com/

[6] http://adida.camel-lab.com/

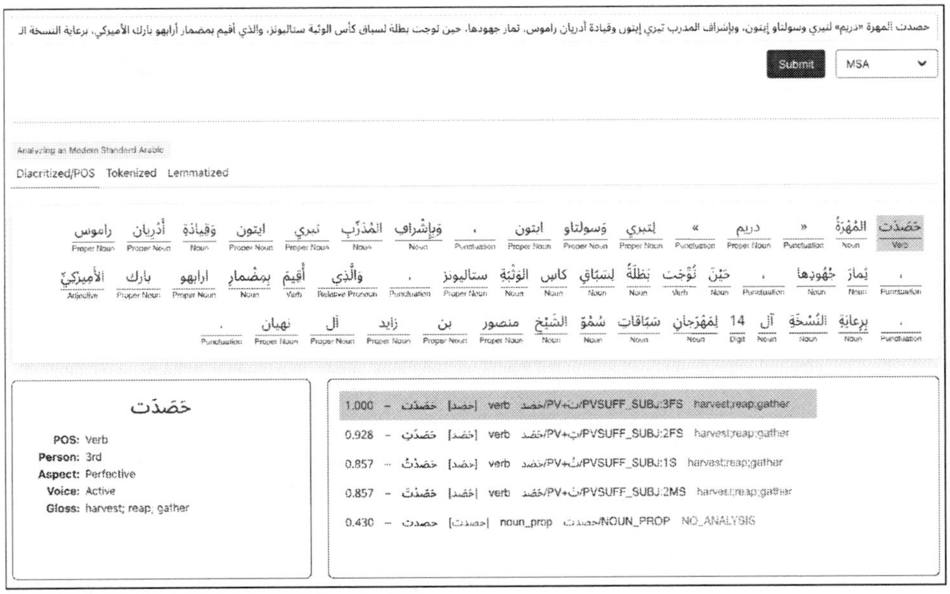

Figure 1: The Camelira interface with an MSA example sentence celebrating the winning of a racehorse named "Dream." In this example, the automatically diacritized forms of the words are presented together with their POS. The first word (on the right), which is highlighted, is selected by the user. The two lower boxes show all the possible out-of-context analyses (on the right) and the detailed features and gloss for the top in-context analysis (on the left).

et al. (2018);[7] however, we differ from their work in that we combine DID with multi-dialect morphological disambiguation to allow users to easily select an appropriate dialect-specific Arabic disambiguator based on the DID prediction.

4 System Design and Implementation

4.1 Design Considerations

We want an easy-to-use one-stop online-accessible user interface that supports the analysis of Arabic sentences from different dialects, and with access to under-the-hood decisions about disambiguation. To that end, we are inspired by three web interfaces: MADAMIRA (Pasha et al., 2014) for in-context disambiguation, CALIMA$_{Star}$ (Taji et al., 2018a) for out-of-context analysis, and ADIDA (Obeid et al., 2019) for dialect identification. Furthermore, we would like the web interface to have a responsive design with streamlined user experiences across a range of devices from mobile to desktops.

4.2 Implementation

Back-end The back-end is implemented in Python using `Flask`[8] to serve a REST API. We implemented the MODEL-6 DID system described by Salameh et al. (2018) for automatic dialect identification and the morphological disambiguation system described by Inoue et al. (2022). The implementation of the morphological disambiguator was provided by the CAMeL Tools[9] Python API (Obeid et al., 2020). We plan to add our MODEL-6 implementation to CAMeL Tools.

For morphological disambiguation, we use the *unfactored* model with a morphological analyzer for all variants. We chose the unfactored models because they are faster than the factored models and only slightly lower in performance. Table 1 shows the performance accuracy of Camelira's morphological disambiguation models. We report numbers on DEV as presented in Inoue et al. (2022).

For DID, we train our MODEL-6 using the TRAIN split and evaluate using the DEV and TEST splits following Salameh et al. (2018). Table 2 compares the performance of our implementation with that of Salameh et al. (2018). Our results are slightly lower due to implementation differences.

[7]We use regional level classification instead of fine-grained city-level classification because the morphological analyzers are designed at the regional level.

[8]https://flask.palletsprojects.com/

[9]https://github.com/CAMeL-Lab/camel_tools

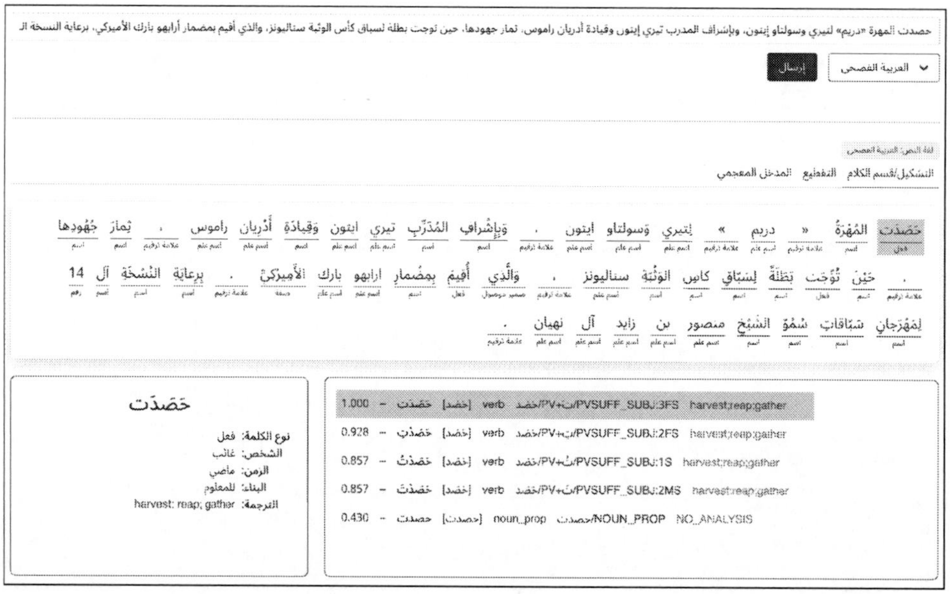

Figure 2: The Camelira interface presenting the same example in Figure 1 using the Arabic user interface.

	ALL TAGS	POS
MSA	95.9	98.7
EGY	90.5	94.0
GLF	93.8	96.6
LEV	85.5	92.7

Table 1: Accuracy of Camelira's morphological disambiguation models based on Inoue et al. (2022)'s unfactored+Morph models. **ALL TAGS** is the accuracy of the combined morphosyntactic features.

	DEV	TEST
Camelira	92.8	93.5
Salameh et al.	93.1	93.6

Table 2: Accuracy of Camelira's implementation of the MODEL-6 DID model compared with Salameh et al. (2018)'s implementation of the same model.

Front-end The front-end was implemented using `Vue.js`[10] for model view control and `Bulma`[11] for styling and creating a responsive design that works well across devices.

4.3 The Camelira Interface

The Camelira interface is divided into three main areas, the Input Area, Text Output Area, and Morphological Analysis Area. Figure 1 shows an example of a disambiguated MSA sentence in the Camelira web interface. We also provide the option of viewing the interface in Arabic as seen in Figure 2.

Input Area At first, only the Input Area is displayed which provides users with an input box where they can enter the sentence they wish to disambiguate. Users are also presented with a drop-down menu where they can select whether to disambiguate the input sentence as a particular dialect (MSA, Egyptian, Gulf, or Levantine) or to have the dialect be automatically selected.

Text Output Area Once the submit button is clicked and the sentence has been disambiguated, the Text Output Area is displayed. First, the dialect indicator displays which dialect was used to analyze the provided input. Then, an output box displays the disambiguated sentence in three different views: (a) the **Diacritized/POS** view which displays the diacritized text (if supported by the selected dialect's resources) along with the POS tag of each word, (b) the **Tokenized** view which displays each disambiguated word in its tokenized form where tokens are delimited by a '+' character, and (c) the **Lemmatized** view where each word is displayed in its lemmatized form. Figure 3 is the same as Figure 1 except that the text output is in Tokenized mode.

[10] `https://vuejs.org/`

[11] `https://bulma.io/`

Figure 3: The Camelira interface with an MSA example sentence and "Tokenized" display tab. This is an exact replica of the input and output choices as in Figure 1 except that the word forms are presented in full tokenization.

Morphological Analysis Area Below the Text Output Area, the Morphological Analysis Area consists of the Analysis List box (on the right), which displays all analyses of a given word sorted by their disambiguation ranking order, and the Analysis Viewer box (on the left), which displays a selected analysis in an easy-to-read form with more morphological feature details. The analysis list displays the disambiguation score of each analysis as well as the values for a reduced set of features.

Clicking on a word in the Text Output Area selects that word, displaying its analyses in the analysis list and analysis viewer boxes. Clicking on an analysis in the Analysis List will display its user-friendly form in the Analysis Viewer. By default, the top analysis is selected.

Dialect Identification and Morphological Disambiguation Figures 4 and 5 present Egyptian and Gulf Arabic examples, respectively. Both are presented in a mobile setting to demonstrate our responsive design.

In the case of Figure 4, the user selected Auto-Detect for dialect identification. In the Gulf example, the user selected Gulf Arabic directly. Note that the Gulf Arabic does not show diacritizations since its training data did not include diacritized forms (Khalifa et al., 2020).

5 Conclusion and Future Work

We presented Camelira, a user-friendly web interface for Arabic multi-dialect morphological disambiguation that covers four major variants of Arabic. The system takes a sentence as input and provides an automatically disambiguated reading for each word, as well as its alternative readings, allowing users to explore various linguistic information, such as part-of-speech, morphological features, and lemmas. Camelira also provides an option to automatically choose an appropriate dialect-specific disambiguator based on the prediction of its dialect identification component.

In the future, we plan to extend our disambiguation system to cover other Arabic dialects such as Maghrebi and Yemeni Arabic. We also plan to continue to update the system using future improvements in terms of efficiency and accuracy in CAMeL Tools (Obeid et al., 2020).

Limitations and Ethical Considerations

We acknowledge that our system is currently limited to specific variants of Arabic and it can produce erroneous predictions especially on different dialects, genres, and styles that are not covered in the current system's training data. We also acknowledge that our work on core and generic NLP technologies can be used as part of the pipeline of other systems with malicious intents.

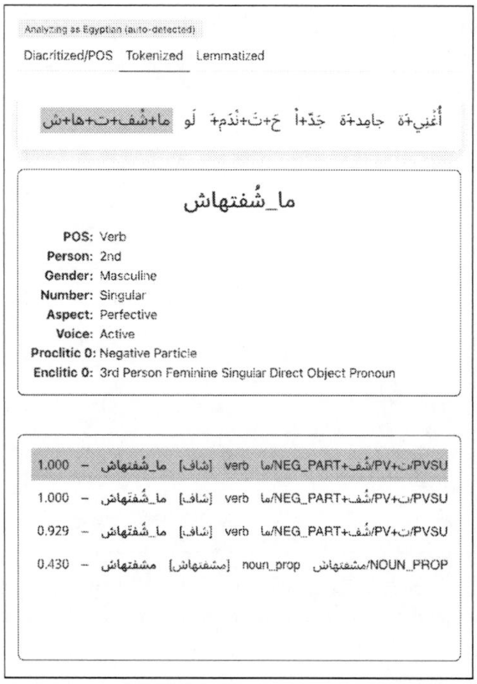

Figure 4: The Camelira interface with an Egyptian example sentence: *"A very cool song [video clip], you'll regret it if you don't watch it."* In this example, the input text is automatically correctly detected as Egyptian.

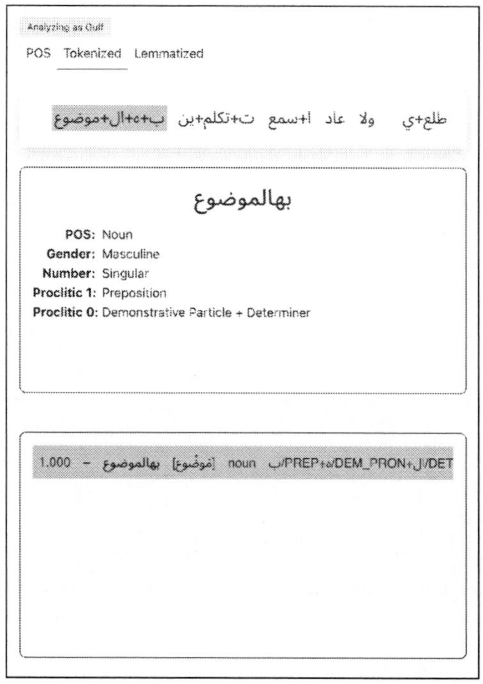

Figure 5: The Camelira interface with a Gulf example sentence: *"Go up to your room, I don't want to hear you talking about this subject again."* In this example, the user specified the input dialect as Gulf.

Acknowledgements

Some of this work was carried out on the High Performance Computing resources at New York University Abu Dhabi. We thank Salam Khalifa and Bashar Alhafni for their insightful comments and helpful discussions. We also thank anonymous reviewers for their helpful comments.

References

Ahmed Abdelali, Kareem Darwish, Nadir Durrani, and Hamdy Mubarak. 2016. Farasa: A fast and furious segmenter for Arabic. In *Proceedings of the Conference of the North American Chapter of the Association for Computational Linguistics (NAACL)*, pages 11–16, San Diego, California.

Muhammad Abdul-Mageed, Chiyu Zhang, Houda Bouamor, and Nizar Habash. 2020a. NADI 2020: The first nuanced Arabic dialect identification shared task. In *Proceedings of the Fifth Arabic Natural Language Processing Workshop*, pages 97–110, Barcelona, Spain (Online).

Muhammad Abdul-Mageed, Chiyu Zhang, AbdelRahim Elmadany, Houda Bouamor, and Nizar Habash. 2021. NADI 2021: The second nuanced Arabic dialect identification shared task. In *Proceedings of the Sixth Arabic Natural Language Processing Workshop*, pages 244–259, Kyiv, Ukraine (Virtual).

Muhammad Abdul-Mageed, Chiyu Zhang, AbdelRahim Elmadany, Houda Bouamor, and Nizar Habash. 2022. NADI 2022: The Third Nuanced Arabic Dialect Identification Shared Task. In *Proceedings of the Seven Arabic Natural Language Processing Workshop (WANLP 2022)*.

Muhammad Abdul-Mageed, Chiyu Zhang, Azadeh Hashemi, and El Moatez Billah Nagoudi. 2020b. AraNet: A deep learning toolkit for Arabic social media. In *Proceedings of the 4th Workshop on Open-Source Arabic Corpora and Processing Tools, with a Shared Task on Offensive Language Detection*, pages 16–23, Marseille, France. European Language Resource Association.

Mohamed Altantawy, Nizar Habash, Owen Rambow, and Ibrahim Saleh. 2010. Morphological Analysis and Generation of Arabic Nouns: A Morphemic Functional Approach. In *Proceedings of the Language Resources and Evaluation Conference (LREC)*, Valletta, Malta.

Nurpeiis Baimukan, Houda Bouamor, and Nizar Habash. 2022. Hierarchical aggregation of dialectal data for Arabic dialect identification. In *Proceedings of the Language Resources and Evaluation Conference*, pages 4586–4596, Marseille, France. European Language Resources Association.

Houda Bouamor, Sabit Hassan, and Nizar Habash. 2019.

The MADAR shared task on Arabic fine-grained dialect identification. In *Proceedings of the Fourth Arabic Natural Language Processing Workshop*, pages 199–207, Florence, Italy.

Mohamed Boudchiche, Azzeddine Mazroui, Mohamed Ould Abdallahi Ould Bebah, Abdelhak Lakhouaja, and Abderrahim Boudlal. 2017. AlKhalil Morpho Sys 2: A robust Arabic morpho-syntactic analyzer. *Journal of King Saud University - Computer and Information Sciences*, 29(2):141–146.

Abderrahim Boudlal, Abdelhak Lakhouaja, Azzeddine Mazroui, Abdelouafi Meziane, MOAO Bebah, and M Shoul. 2010. Alkhalil Morpho Sys1: A morphosyntactic analysis system for Arabic texts. In *Proceedings of the International Arab Conference on Information Technology*, pages 1–6.

Tim Buckwalter. 2002. Buckwalter Arabic morphological analyzer version 1.0. Linguistic Data Consortium (LDC) catalog number LDC2002L49, ISBN 1-58563-257-0.

Kareem Darwish, Nizar Habash, Mourad Abbas, Hend Al-Khalifa, Huseein T Al-Natsheh, Houda Bouamor, Karim Bouzoubaa, Violetta Cavalli-Sforza, Samhaa R El-Beltagy, Wassim El-Hajj, et al. 2021. A panoramic survey of natural language processing in the arab world. *Communications of the ACM*, 64(4):72–81.

Ramy Eskander, Nizar Habash, and Owen Rambow. 2013. Automatic extraction of morphological lexicons from morphologically annotated corpora. In *Proceedings of the Conference on Empirical Methods in Natural Language Processing (EMNLP)*, pages 1032–1043, Seattle, Washington, USA.

Ramy Eskander, Nizar Habash, Owen Rambow, and Arfath Pasha. 2016. Creating resources for Dialectal Arabic from a single annotation: A case study on Egyptian and Levantine. In *Proceedings of the International Conference on Computational Linguistics (COLING)*, pages 3455–3465, Osaka, Japan.

Charles F Ferguson. 1959. Diglossia. *Word*, 15(2):325–340.

David Graff, Mohamed Maamouri, Basma Bouziri, Sondos Krouna, Seth Kulick, and Tim Buckwalter. 2009. Standard Arabic Morphological Analyzer (SAMA) Version 3.1. Linguistic Data Consortium LDC2009E73.

Nizar Habash. 2007. Arabic Morphological Representations for Machine Translation. In Antal van den Bosch and Abdelhadi Soudi, editors, *Arabic Computational Morphology: Knowledge-based and Empirical Methods*. Kluwer/Springer.

Nizar Habash, Ramy Eskander, and Abdelati Hawwari. 2012. A Morphological Analyzer for Egyptian Arabic. In *Proceedings of the Workshop of the Special Interest Group on Computational Morphology and Phonology (SIGMORPHON)*, pages 1–9, Montréal, Canada.

Nizar Habash and Owen Rambow. 2006. MAGEAD: A morphological analyzer and generator for the Arabic dialects. In *Proceedings of the International Conference on Computational Linguistics and the Conference of the Association for Computational Linguistics (COLING-ACL)*, pages 681–688, Sydney, Australia.

Nizar Habash, Owen Rambow, and George Kiraz. 2005. Morphological Analysis and Generation for Arabic Dialects. In *Proceedings of the Workshop on Computational Approaches to Semitic Languages (CASL)*, pages 17–24, Ann Arbor, Michigan.

Nizar Y Habash. 2010. *Introduction to Arabic natural language processing*. Morgan & Claypool Publishers.

Clive Holes. 2004. *Modern Arabic: Structures, Functions, and Varieties*. Georgetown Classics in Arabic Language and Linguistics. Georgetown University Press.

Go Inoue, Salam Khalifa, and Nizar Habash. 2022. Morphosyntactic tagging with pre-trained language models for Arabic and its dialects. In *Findings of the Association for Computational Linguistics: ACL 2022*, pages 1708–1719, Dublin, Ireland.

Go Inoue, Hiroyuki Shindo, and Yuji Matsumoto. 2017. Joint Prediction of Morphosyntactic Categories for Fine-Grained Arabic Part-of-Speech Tagging Exploiting Tag Dictionary Information. In *Proceedings of the Conference on Computational Natural Language Learning (CoNLL)*, pages 421–431, Vancouver, Canada.

Salam Khalifa, Sara Hassan, and Nizar Habash. 2017. A morphological analyzer for Gulf Arabic verbs. In *Proceedings of the Workshop for Arabic Natural Language Processing (WANLP)*, Valencia, Spain.

Salam Khalifa, Nasser Zalmout, and Nizar Habash. 2016. Yamama: Yet another multi-dialect Arabic morphological analyzer. In *Proceedings of the International Conference on Computational Linguistics (COLING)*, pages 223–227, Osaka, Japan.

Salam Khalifa, Nasser Zalmout, and Nizar Habash. 2020. Morphological analysis and disambiguation for Gulf Arabic: The interplay between resources and methods. In *Proceedings of the 12th Language Resources and Evaluation Conference*, pages 3895–3904, Marseille, France. European Language Resources Association.

Mohamed Maamouri, Ann Bies, Hubert Jin, and Tim Buckwalter. 2003. Arabic treebank: Part 1 v 2.0. Linguistic Data Consortium (LDC2003T06).

Mohamed Maamouri, Ann Bies, Seth Kulick, Fatma Gaddeche, Wigdan Mekki, Sondos Krouna, and Basma Bouziri. 2009. The penn Arabic treebank part 3 v 3.1. Linguistic Data Consortium (LDC2008E22).

Mohamed Maamouri, Ann Bies, Seth Kulick, Fatma Gaddeche, Wigdan Mekki, Sondos Krouna, Basma Bouziri, and Wadji Zaghouani. 2011. Arabic treebank: Part 2 v 3.1.

Shervin Malmasi, Marcos Zampieri, Nikola Ljubešić, Preslav Nakov, Ahmed Ali, and Jörg Tiedemann. 2016. Discriminating between similar languages and Arabic dialect identification: A report on the third

DSL shared task. In *Proceedings of the Third Workshop on NLP for Similar Languages, Varieties and Dialects (VarDial3)*, pages 1–14, Osaka, Japan. The COLING 2016 Organizing Committee.

Hamdy Mubarak and Kareem Darwish. 2014. Using Twitter to collect a multi-dialectal corpus of Arabic. In *Proceedings of the Workshop for Arabic Natural Language Processing (WANLP)*, Doha, Qatar.

Ossama Obeid, Mohammad Salameh, Houda Bouamor, and Nizar Habash. 2019. ADIDA: Automatic dialect identification for Arabic. In *Proceedings of the 2019 Conference of the North American Chapter of the Association for Computational Linguistics (Demonstrations)*, pages 6–11, Minneapolis, Minnesota.

Ossama Obeid, Nasser Zalmout, Salam Khalifa, Dima Taji, Mai Oudah, Bashar Alhafni, Go Inoue, Fadhl Eryani, Alexander Erdmann, and Nizar Habash. 2020. CAMeL tools: An open source python toolkit for Arabic natural language processing. In *Proceedings of the 12th Language Resources and Evaluation Conference*, pages 7022–7032, Marseille, France. European Language Resources Association.

Arfath Pasha, Mohamed Al-Badrashiny, Mona Diab, Ahmed El Kholy, Ramy Eskander, Nizar Habash, Manoj Pooleery, Owen Rambow, and Ryan Roth. 2014. MADAMIRA: A fast, comprehensive tool for morphological analysis and disambiguation of Arabic. In *Proceedings of the Language Resources and Evaluation Conference (LREC)*, pages 1094–1101, Reykjavik, Iceland.

Peng Qi, Yuhao Zhang, Yuhui Zhang, Jason Bolton, and Christopher D. Manning. 2020. Stanza: A python natural language processing toolkit for many human languages. In *Proceedings of the 58th Annual Meeting of the Association for Computational Linguistics: System Demonstrations*, pages 101–108, Online.

Mohammad Salameh, Houda Bouamor, and Nizar Habash. 2018. Fine-grained Arabic dialect identification. In *Proceedings of the International Conference on Computational Linguistics (COLING)*, pages 1332–1344, Santa Fe, New Mexico, USA.

Otakar Smrž. 2007. ElixirFM — Implementation of Functional Arabic Morphology. In *Proceedings of the Workshop on Computational Approaches to Semitic Languages (CASL)*, pages 1–8, Prague, Czech Republic. ACL.

Milan Straka, Jan Hajič, and Jana Straková. 2016. UDPipe: Trainable pipeline for processing CoNLL-U files performing tokenization, morphological analysis, POS tagging and parsing. In *Proceedings of the Tenth International Conference on Language Resources and Evaluation (LREC'16)*, pages 4290–4297, Portorož, Slovenia. European Language Resources Association (ELRA).

Dima Taji, Jamila El Gizuli, and Nizar Habash. 2018a. An Arabic dependency treebank in the travel domain. In *Proceedings of the Workshop on Open-Source Arabic Corpora and Processing Tools (OSACT)*, Miyazaki, Japan.

Dima Taji, Salam Khalifa, Ossama Obeid, Fadhl Eryani, and Nizar Habash. 2018b. An Arabic morphological analyzer and generator with copious features. In *Proceedings of the Fifteenth Workshop on Computational Research in Phonetics, Phonology, and Morphology*, pages 140–150, Brussels, Belgium.

Wajdi Zaghouani and Anis Charfi. 2018. ArapTweet: A Large Multi-Dialect Twitter Corpus for Gender, Age and Language Variety Identification. In *Proceedings of the Language Resources and Evaluation Conference (LREC)*, Miyazaki, Japan.

Omar F Zaidan and Chris Callison-Burch. 2011. The Arabic Online Commentary Dataset: an Annotated Dataset of Informal Arabic With High Dialectal Content. In *Proceedings of the Conference of the Association for Computational Linguistics (ACL)*, pages 37–41.

Nasser Zalmout and Nizar Habash. 2017. Don't throw those morphological analyzers away just yet: Neural morphological disambiguation for Arabic. In *Proceedings of the Conference on Empirical Methods in Natural Language Processing (EMNLP)*, pages 704–713, Copenhagen, Denmark.

Nasser Zalmout and Nizar Habash. 2020. Joint diacritization, lemmatization, normalization, and fine-grained morphological tagging. In *Proceedings of the 58th Annual Meeting of the Association for Computational Linguistics*, pages 8297–8307, Online.

Marcos Zampieri, Shervin Malmasi, Nikola Ljubešić, Preslav Nakov, Ahmed Ali, Jörg Tiedemann, Yves Scherrer, and Noëmi Aepli. 2017. Findings of the VarDial evaluation campaign 2017. In *Proceedings of the Fourth Workshop on NLP for Similar Languages, Varieties and Dialects (VarDial)*, pages 1–15, Valencia, Spain.

Marcos Zampieri, Shervin Malmasi, Preslav Nakov, Ahmed Ali, Suwon Shon, James Glass, Yves Scherrer, Tanja Samardžić, Nikola Ljubešić, Jörg Tiedemann, Chris van der Lee, Stefan Grondelaers, Nelleke Oostdijk, Dirk Speelman, Antal van den Bosch, Ritesh Kumar, Bornini Lahiri, and Mayank Jain. 2018. Language identification and morphosyntactic tagging: The second VarDial evaluation campaign. In *Proceedings of the Fifth Workshop on NLP for Similar Languages, Varieties and Dialects (VarDial 2018)*, pages 1–17, Santa Fe, New Mexico, USA.

POTATO: The Portable Text Annotation Tool

Jiaxin Pei [1] Aparna Ananthasubramaniam[1] Xingyao Wang[2] Naitian Zhou [3]
Apostolos Dedeloudis[4] Jackson Sargent[1] David Jurgens[1]

[1]School of Information, University of Michigan, Ann Arbor, MI, USA
[2]Department of Computer Science, University of Illinois, Urbana Champaign, IL, USA
[3]School of Information, University of California, Berkeley, CA, USA
[4]The American College of Greece, Athens, Greece
[1]{pedropei, akananth, jackson, jurgens}@umich.edu
[2]xingyao6@illinois.edu [3]naitian@berkeley.edu [4]apostolosdedgmail.com

Abstract

We present POTATO, the **Por**table **t**ext **a**nnotation **to**ol, a free, fully open-sourced annotation system that 1) supports labeling many types of text and multimodal data; 2) offers easy-to-configure features to maximize the productivity of both deployers and annotators (convenient templates for common ML/NLP tasks, active learning, keypress shortcuts, keyword highlights, tooltips); and 3) supports a high degree of customization (editable UI, inserting pre-screening questions, attention and qualification tests). Experiments over two annotation tasks suggest that POTATO improves labeling speed through its specially-designed productivity features, especially for long documents and complex tasks. POTATO is available at `https://github.com/davidjurgens/potato` and will continue to be updated.

1 Introduction

Much of NLP requires annotated data. As NLP has tried to tackle increasingly more complex linguistic phenomena or diverse labeling and classification tasks, the annotation process has increased in complexity—yet the need for and benefit of large labeled datasets remain (Halevy et al., 2009; Sun et al., 2017). Modern annotation tools like Label Studio (Tkachenko et al., 2021), LightTag (Perry, 2021), Doccano (Nakayama et al., 2018), and Prodigy (Explosion, 2017) have partially filled this gap, providing a variety of solutions to different types of annotations. However, these tools each bring their own challenges: requiring external access, limiting visual configurability for complex tasks, or even costing hundreds of dollars—prohibitive for small groups. We introduce POTATO, The **Por**table **t**ext **a**nnotation **to**ol, which allows practitioners to quickly design and deploy complex annotations tasks.

POTATO has been designed, developed, and tested over a two-year period with the following design goals in mind (Figure 1): 1) **High accessibility**. POTATO is open-sourced under the MIT license and free to anyone. POTATO is built with minimal dependencies to allow researchers and developers to easily build and integrate their own features. 2) **Easy to deploy**. POTATO comes with templates covering a wide range of annotation tasks like best-worst-scaling, text classification, and multi-modal conversation. Anyone can start a new annotation project with simple configurations. POTATO is also rapidly and easily deployable in local and web-based configurations and has seamless integration with common crowdsourcing platforms like Amazon Mechanical Turk and Prolific. POTATO flexibly supports diverse annotation needs. With our specially designed schema rendering and custom rendering mechanism, POTATO allows nearly all kinds of text annotation tasks and is visually customizable to support complex task designs and layout. 3) **Better quality control**. Attaining reliable annotations is one of the core goals of data annotation tasks. POTATO is designed with a series of features that can help to improve annotation quality, including built-in attention tests, prestudy qualification tests, and an annotation time tracker. POTATO also allows deployers to easily set up pre- and post-

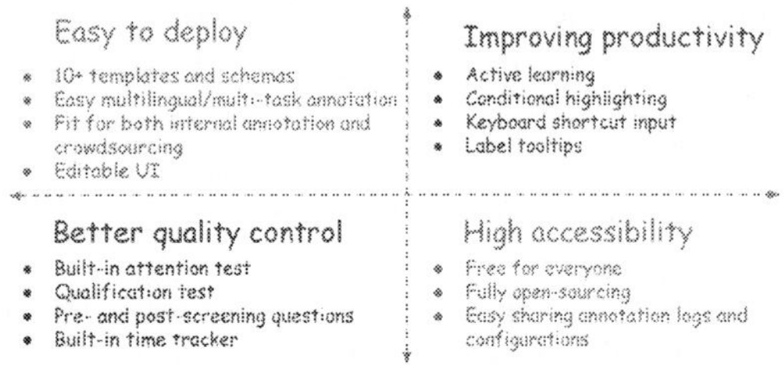

Figure 1: The four core design goals of POTATO: easy to deploy, greater productivity, better quality control, and high accessibility. Each design goal comes with a series of features that can make data annotation easier and more reliable.

Proceedings of the The 2022 Conference on Empirical Methods in Natural Language Processing: System Demonstrations, pages 327 - 337
December 7-11, 2022

screening questions (e.g. demographics or psychological surveys), which can help researchers to better understand potential biases in data labeling. 4) **Productivity enhancing**. POTATO comes with a series of productivity features for both deployers and annotators like active learning, conditional highlighting, and keyboard shortcuts. While existing systems like Doccano (Nakayama et al., 2018) and Lighttag (Perry, 2021) offer different subsets of these features, POTATO aims to support a holistic annotation experience by meeting all of these needs. Experiments on two annotation tasks demonstrate that POTATO leads to more efficient data labeling for complex tasks.

2 Architecture and Design

POTATO is written in Python and focuses on portability and simplicity in annotation and deployment. The user interface is created through an extensible HTML template and configuration file, which allows practitioners to quickly develop and deploy common setups like Likert-scale annotation while also supporting extensive display customization. The POTATO server populates the interface with data provided by the operator and supports displaying any HTML-supported modality, e.g., text or images. An overview of the architecture is shown in Figure 2.

Data Management POTATO loads data in common file formats, such as delimited files or newline-delimited JSON. This allows it to ingest data in the JSON format supplied by the Twitter or Reddit APIs, as well as other types of data used by the deployer. All formats are converted into internal data structures that link the deployer-selected instance ID to annotations. At a minimum, deployers must specify which field represents the unique instance ID and, for most tasks, the text to be annotated. The data may contain other columns which will be included in the final output and can optionally be used in customized visualizations.

Annotation Schema Rendering POTATO allows deployers to select one or more forms of annotation for their data using predefined schema types, such as multiple choice or best-worst scaling. Deployers fill out which options should be shown and then each scheme is rendered into HTML upon the completion of loading the data. Annotation instructions can be provided as an external URL that annotators may view or using HTML text shown in POTATO that annotators may collapse vertically to free up screen space. POTATO provides default HTML templates that automatically lay out each scheme's annotation questions. However, deployers may additionally customize the HTML templates and select their own layout using JINJA expressions (e.g., `{{text}}`; Jinja) to specify where parts of the annotation task and data are populated within the user-defined template.

User Management Annotators create accounts and then log in to view their tasks using a secure user management system. When used with crowdsourcing platforms, POTATO also allows workers to directly jump to the annotation task using their crowdsourcing user ID. For each new annotator, POTATO automatically assigns instances as configured by the deployer and all the annotations are recorded on the backend. When logging out and back in, annotators resume at the most recent unannotated item. POTATO also allows deployers to, with minimum configurations, set up pre- and post-screening questions (e.g., having annotators provide demographics or complete psychological questionnaires), pre-study tests, and attention tests to identify unreliable annotators.

Active Learning In some settings such as data with imbalanced classes, active learning helps re-order items to surface those that may provide more information to downstream classifiers (Settles, 2009; Monarch, 2021). Prior annotation interfaces have included active learning to help maximize data utility (Stenetorp et al., 2012; Wiechmann et al., 2021; Li et al., 2021). POTATO includes a configurable active learning setup to prioritize important samples and potentially improves data quality with limited labeling budgets. In its default setting, POTATO periodically trains a logistic regression classifier using unigram and bigram features on the currently annotated data; unlabeled instances are sorted by classifier confidence and items with low confidence are prioritized, while still including a deployer-specified percentage of a random sample. Deployers may change or reconfigure this model easily.

Design highlights POTATO is designed to flexibly support diverse annotation tasks and improve the productivity of annotators. Here we briefly highlight several features of POTATO. First, with simple configurations, deployers can quickly add *keyboard shortcuts* to specific options or *tooltips* to help annotators. Second, in settings where an annotator is reading a dense or long passage, or where there

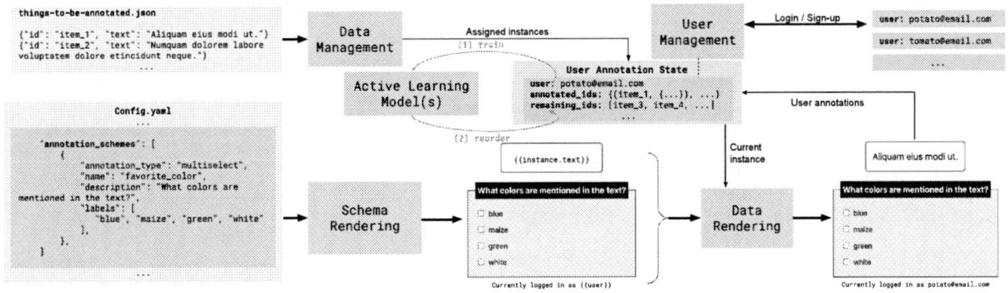

Figure 2: The overall architecture of POTATO features a modular design that decouples the task specification from the rendering, allowing rapid deployment of new task designs and separate customization of the visualization.

are many potentially subtle cues, annotators are likely to struggle due to having to slowly and carefully read each passage or accidentally omitting relevant annotations due to the complexity of the task. POTATO introduces a new feature, *conditional highlighting*, to help in these settings, where the deployer specifies certain keywords to trigger highlights in the text, drawing the annotator's focus to those words or phrases. For example, if annotating for Twitter-based stance towards politicians, a deployer might use keywords and phrases for common politicians or political parties to ensure these are not missed. If conditional highlighting is enabled, POTATO will also randomly label some words with highlights, based on a deployer-specified rate, to ensure annotators do not rely too heavily on highlights.

3 Deployment and Tasks

POTATO is designed with a quickly-deployable Python-based server architecture that can be run locally or hosted on any device. To launch a POTATO instance, the deployer first defines a YAML file that specifies the annotation schemes, data sources, server configuration, and any custom visualizations. If POTATO is launched without a YAML, the program will provide the deployer the option of following a series of prompts about their task to automatically generate a YAML file for them. A YAML file is then passed to the server on the command line to launch the server for annotation.

Currently, POTATO supports eight annotation scheme types: multiple-selection (checkboxes), single-selection (radio buttons), best-worst scaling, Likert scale, free-form text, span-based labels, numbers, and dropdown list. Deployers can easily set up one or more of these schemes in the YAML file—e.g., asking annotators to rate a news article on different dimensions using multiple Likert scales and then summarizing the article in a free text response. For each annotation instance, POTATO can take a single document, multiple documents as a list (e.g. dialogue and best-worst-scaling), as well as a dictionary of documents (e.g. a pair of documents for pairwise comparison). POTATO will automatically display the instance to annotators based on the input types and the YAML configurations. The POTATO documentation contains example YAML templates for several common annotation tasks such as sentiment analysis, question-answering, and image-based labeling.

POTATO is self-hosted and can be served locally or exposed publicly. Each running instance of POTATO serves one task, but multiple annotation tasks can be stored in a single *installation*, to be served using different configuration files at different times. POTATO allows flexible ways for annotators to login. For internal usage, POTATO allows annotators to sign up and log in with email addresses. POTATO also allows annotators to directly log in with a URL argument (e.g. username in the crowdsourcing platform), which can be used in crowdsourcing settings where a dedicated link is created for an annotation task. POTATO has been tested with popular crowdsourcing platforms including Prolific and Amazon Mechanical Turk.

POTATO has been deployed in a variety of annotation settings over a two-year period, including a 27-class annotation scheme for classifying immigration framing (Mendelsohn et al., 2021); rating condolences and empathy for Reddit comments with hundreds of words (Zhou and Jurgens, 2020); best-worst scaling for rating intimacy in questions (Pei and Jurgens, 2020); rating Reddit threads for their prosociality (Bao et al., 2021); rating, on a Likert-scale, sentences for scientific uncertainty

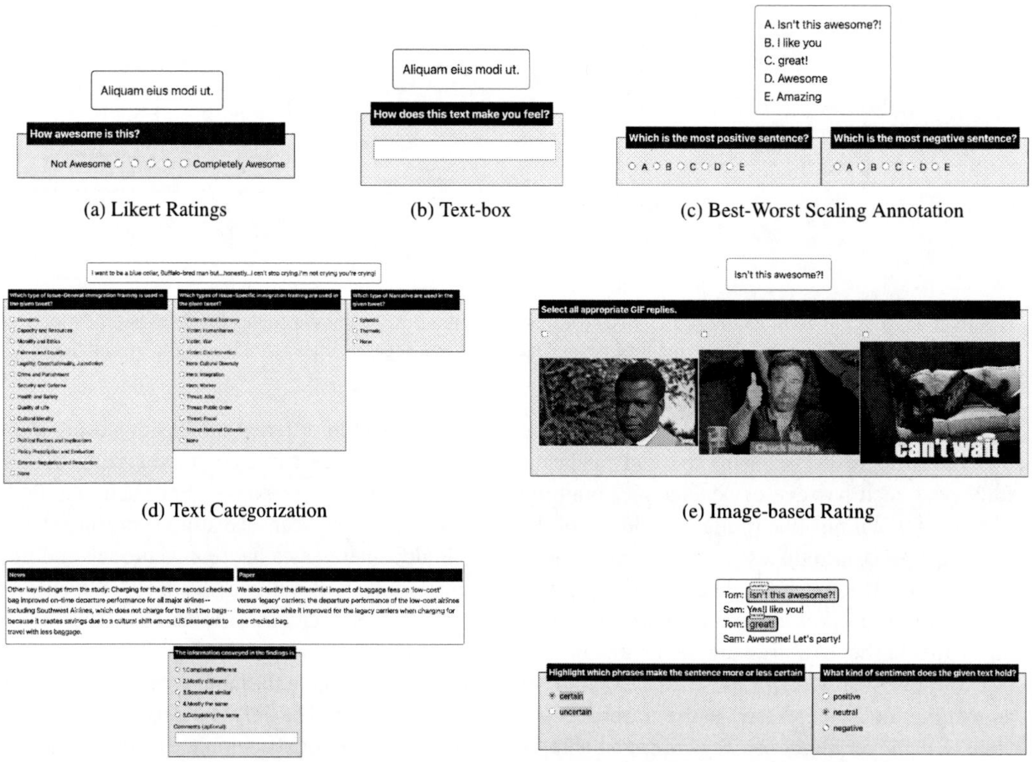

(a) Likert Ratings (b) Text-box (c) Best-Worst Scaling Annotation

(d) Text Categorization (e) Image-based Rating

(f) Pairwise comparison (g) Span-based dialogue analysis

Figure 3: Screenshots of example tasks supported by POTATO, which are included as templates. Examples 3a-3c show single-task annotations, while Example 3d shows a multitask setup with three multi-select labels. Example 3e shows how POTATO supports multimedia as annotation options. 3f shows a pairwise Likert annotation and 3g shows a span-based annotation for dialogue analysis. Examples omit the common interface header that shows annotators how many instances remain and links to the annotation codebook.

(Pei and Jurgens, 2021), intimacy in multilingual tweet (Pei et al., 2022) and similarity in scientific findings (Wright et al., 2022); and rating the appropriateness of GIF replies to messages, which showed an animated GIF in the interface (Wang and Jurgens, 2021).

Figure 3 shows some of the interfaces from our documentation's example templates. These templates cover a wide range of NLP tasks and can be easily adapted to support a quick start of common annotation tasks. The configuration-based setup of POTATO allows researchers to easily share their annotation settings and replicate annotation settings used by existing works. POTATO also comes with a dedicated project hub where researchers can easily open-source their annotation project and already includes projects in our previous studies. Such a feature could help to improve the replicability of NLP/ML annotations and we welcome submissions from the entire research community.

4 Comparison with Existing Systems

POTATO has been developed to fill a key niche left by existing systems for providing visual customization, easy annotator-support features, and rapid development. The ultimate goal is to provide simple and comprehensive solutions to common annotation tasks as well as allow personalized design for complex tasks. Table 1 shows the comparisons between POTATO and other common text annotation tools over a series of important dimensions including flexibility, productivity, quality, and accessibility. We highlight major differentiators next. Please note that we only compare annotation systems that are currently available for anyone to use, free of cost.

Flexibility POTATO is designed to maximize flexibility for a variety of annotation settings. For common annotation tasks like text classification, POTATO comes with a wide range of templates

		Label Studio	Doccano	FLAT	LightTag	Prodigy	Tagtog	FITAnnotator	BRAT	WebAnno/INCEpTION	POTATO
Flexibility	Multiple Schema	✓			✓		✓		✓	✓	✓
	Multimodal	✓	✓		✓	✓					✓
	Span-Based Annotation	✓	✓		✓	✓	✓		✓	✓	✓
	Editable UI	✓		✓		✓		✓			✓
Productivity	Active Learning	✓*				✓		✓		✓	✓
	Conditional Highlighting										✓
	Keyboard Shortcuts	✓	✓		✓	✓			✓		✓
Quality control	Prestudy Qualification Test										✓
	Attention Test										✓
	Behavioral Tracking										✓
	Pre- and Post-screeing Questions										✓
Accessibility	Open-Source	✓	✓	✓					✓	✓	✓
	Easy Sharing and Replicating										✓
	Price	Free	Free	Free	Free for academia	$390	$59/person/month	Not available	Free	Free	Free

Table 1: Comparisons between POTATO and other text annotation systems over four themes. * means the feature is not available for the free plan.

and allows a quick start for deployers. However, unlike many existing annotation tools, which provide fixed user interfaces with selected types of annotation tasks (e.g., Doccano offers neither templates nor an editable UI (Nakayama et al., 2018)), POTATO allows deployers to customize their own annotation interface to support diverse needs. For example, Wang and Jurgens (2021) used animated GIFs as the labels in the annotation and Mendelsohn et al. (2021) used a 27-class scheme under three categories, both of which required visual customization to make the task feasible. POTATO also allows deployers to easily set up unlimited numbers of similar annotation tasks, which can be especially helpful for multilingual annotations. For example, for all the other data annotation systems, the deployers need to set up separate tasks and guidelines for each language. With POTATO, deployers only need to create a sheet containing translated guidelines and POTATO's built-in script can help to generate annotation sites for each language.

Productivity POTATO is designed to maximize the productivity of both annotators and deployers. While most of the existing annotation tools generally focus on labeling data, POTATO supports a series of features that can help with the entire data annotation pipeline. POTATO allows easily-customizable keyboard shortcuts to allow efficient annotation. For visually or cognitively challenging settings, POTATO allows conditional highlights, which helps to reduce task complexity and focus annotators' attention. Finally, active learning can reduce the annotation time needed to curate an informative dataset. Often, annotation tools that offer a highly customizable annotation interface do not also implement productivity features: the open-sourced version of LabelStudio (Tkachenko et al., 2021) only supports keypress shortcuts, while Flat (Gompel et al., 2017) supports none of these features. For deployers, POTATO allows seamless integration with common crowdsourcing platforms like Amazon Mechanical Turk and Prolific.

Quality control Collective high-quality and reliable annotations is the ultimate goal of data labeling tasks and is usually the key to the success of the final ML/NLP systems. POTATO comes with a series of quality control feature which helps deployers to reliably collect annotations. While some other annotation systems like Label Studio and WebAnno also support agreement calculation, none of the existing systems come with features that help deployers to improve the annotation quality and analyze factors affecting it. POTATO allows deployers to easily set up prestudy qualification tests (annotators have to pass a small test to participate in the full annotation) and attention tests (attention test questions are randomly inserted in the annotation queue as configured by the deployer) to identify unreliable annotators before, within, and after annotation. POTATO also allows deployers to freely insert survey questions before and after the annotation phase. Deployers can easily define different pages of pre- and post-screening questions with minimum effort and POTATO also provides a series of templates for common survey questions like user consent and demographic information. Recent studies suggest that the background of annotators has substantial effects on the quality and bias of data labeling and further affects the fairness of ML/NLP models (e.g., Sap et al., 2022). With POTATO, researchers can easily collect background information of annotators and analyze the effect of annotator backgrounds on data labeling.

Accessibility POTATO is free to use and actively maintained. While commercial annotation tools like Prodigy (Explosion, 2017) can come with more functionality, these tools are expensive; for example, Prodigy costs $390 USD for individual users, and Tagtog (Cejuela et al., 2014) costs at least $59 USD per person per month. These costs are potentially prohibitive for students and researchers without access. POTATO is fully open-sourced and is deployed with minimum dependencies. Moreover, in addition to giving the flexibility to freely define UIs and annotation settings, POTATO allows researchers to easily share their annotation settings with a simple YAML file, aiding in replication and future extension of prior work.

5 Experimental Analysis

POTATO was designed to minimize set-up time and per-instance annotation time while maintaining annotation accuracy. Therefore, we conduct a user study to compare the time for setup and annotation time per instance compared to its free competitors. We compare POTATO's performance on two long and complex tasks, each involving identifying themes and causes in narrative summaries of reports of completed suicides:

- **Task 1** contains long documents, with two annotation schemes with a total of 22 labels. The task requires labeling whether each narrative contains each of 13 work-related transitions (e.g., retirement, layoffs) and 9 housing-related transitions. The average document contains 13.4 sentences and 1,180 characters.
- **Task 2** is comprised of shorter documents, with the same tasks and labels. This alternative version shows only a single sentence of the narrative in Task 1 and asks annotators to judge whether each contains the same categories. The average sentence (annotation item) contains 88 characters.

Annotation Setup One annotator completed 50 annotations for Task 1 and 100 annotations for Task 2 on POTATO and a number of freely available and feature-rich annotation tools: Microsoft Excel, Doccano (Nakayama et al., 2018), Label Studio (Tkachenko et al., 2021), and LightTag (Perry, 2021). The annotator was highly familiar with the task and classification scheme, having annotated 1000+ instances of each task prior to this user study, so familiarity with the codebook was not a factor. Given the complexity of the task, POTATO was initialized with 118 keywords to associate with conditional highlights (e.g., retir*, layoff, work*), key bindings, and classes included tooltips summarizing each label. To test the effect of these productivity-enhancing features, we include a version of POTATO that does not include these features, called Inconvenient POTATO. To ensure the same level of familiarity with each document, the documents annotated with each tool are randomly sampled from a larger set of 203,531 documents.

For each annotation tool we measure the time to set up an annotation task without counting time taken to (1) install and familiarize ourselves with the tool (e.g., trial and error in set-up), (2) generate the annotation data files, and (3) write the properties of each label and keywords. Each tool was configured as comparably as possible (e.g., keypress shortcuts were always enabled and active learning disabled). To reduce the influence of initial unfamiliarity with each tool on per-instance timing, the annotator completed 10 untimed instances. Then, for each tool, we record the time spent annotating per instance.

Results Across both annotation tasks, POTATO is approximately 30-50% faster than competitors like Excel, Label Studio, and LightTag (Figure 4b-c). Annotating short documents is comparable in time to Doccano (4b), while long documents are slightly faster in POTATO (4c). Without convenience features like conditional highlighting, key mappings, and tooltips, POTATO's per-instance annotation time increases to be more comparable with other tools. We conclude that the difference in per-instance annotation time is likely attributable to these design features.

Including convenience features increases task setup time (Figure 4a), taking just over 4 extra minutes to configure at set-up. Our results suggest that, compared to using POTATO with convenience features, the base setup without convenience features has lower overall task time (including setup) until an annotator has seen $\sim$20 long documents or $\sim$100 short documents. We note that POTATO without convenience features takes less time to set up than Label Studio and LightTag; with these three features, POTATO takes roughly the same amount of time to set up as Doccano, even though Doccano only supports one feature (keypress shortcut).

The two tasks we chose share features with many common NLP annotation tasks that make them well-suited to a system like POTATO. We highlight two comparative observations across the interface from the user study. First, Doccano and POTATO have the most annotator-friendly interfaces, which

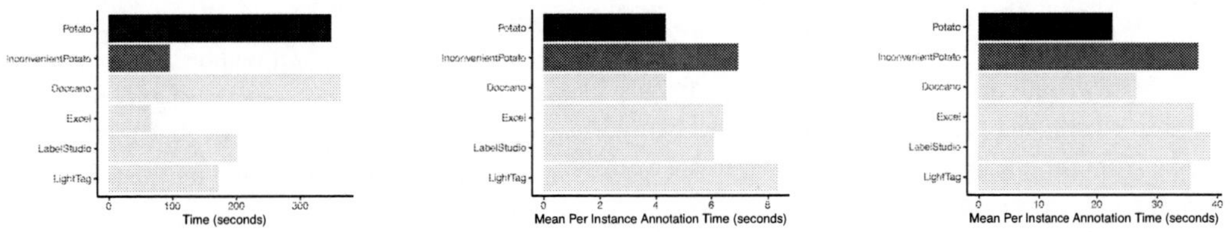

(a) Task Setup Time (b) Short Document, 2 tasks, 22 labels (c) Long Document, 2 tasks, 22 labels

Figure 4: Times from our user study (§5) to (a) set up a task; (b) annotate one short document or (c) annotate one long document show the time savings of POTATO.

allow for fast coding. For instance, custom keypress shortcuts allow us to create 22 different bindings that make logical sense to the annotator. Unlike other tools, these two tools did not require any use of the mouse (e.g., others required pressing submit with the mouse), which reduced the annotation time; in short document tasks, where the time to read the document is low, these time savings become especially important. The default page layout in POTATO also better supports content interpretation; for example, the text and labels frequently fit on one page with no scrolling, and by placing the text on top of the labels, the annotator did not need to scroll down in order to read the text—and since the annotator had the keypress bindings memorized, the task could often be accomplished with no scrolling. Finally, since other tools often required uploading data to external servers, there was often a load time of 1-2 seconds per document; again, saving this time with locally-deployed tools was especially salient with short documents.

Second, both tasks involve assigning a large number of independent labels. The keyword highlights allow the annotator to quickly identify which subset of these labels are likely to be relevant to the document, while the key mappings allow them to quick apply the correct labels. Keyword highlights are particularly useful for longer documents (e.g., Task 1), because they help identify the text that is likely relevant to a given label, which is often buried in a large amount of irrelevant text (e.g., most labels apply to one of $\sim$13 sentences). Additionally, if none of the labels applied to a document, the annotator needed to ensure that she did not overlook a relevant phrase in the long text; in POTATO the lack of relevant keywords allowed us to quickly confirm that none of the labels applied, while without keyword highlights, the annotator read these documents twice. The time savings associated with keyword highlights likely explains the slight per-instance advantage POTATO has over Doccano for long documents but not short documents.

6 Conclusion and Future Plans

POTATO distinguishes itself with a comprehensive suite of productivity-enhancing features that allow annotators to efficiently and accurately label data and researchers to quickly configure complex tasks on a wide range of data types. POTATO was created both for the computational scholar and the overburdened student or crowdworker, looking to annotate more data in their limited time.

POTATO has been in continuous development for over two years and will continue to be developed to support new task designs, easier management, and faster annotation.

For management, we aim to have (1) a unified GUI for deployers to create new tasks and manage existing tasks, (2) a GUI that supports real-time monitoring of annotation process, mirroring tools like Webanno (Yimam et al., 2013), and (3) integration with common social media platforms to display content with original interfaces (e.g. displaying tweets with their native UI).

For annotators, we aim to support simple linguistic search to help annotators find and prioritize instances to annotate, and to support personalization in aspects such as annotators' visualization and keybindings. We also plan to conduct experiments and explore different design choices to reduce annotator burn-out.

Acknowledgments

The authors thank members of the Blalablab and all the annotators who have used POTATO throughout the years for their feedback on how to make POTATO better. This material is based in part upon work supported by the National Science Foundation under Grant No IIS-1850221.

7 Ethics and Broader Impacts

As a highly configurable annotation tool, POTATO's biggest ethical and societal implications will likely come from the questions the tool is used to answer and the ways in which researchers choose to deploy the tool. POTATO was built with accessibility, social responsibility, and usefulness at the forefront, and the tool's default settings afford a range of values-driven practices, which we will discuss below. However, a major risk is that POTATO requires researchers to self-regulate when encouraging researchers to opt into ethical values often proves unsuccessful (Hagendorff, 2020). For instance, the tool does not build in any safeguards against unethical questions or harmful applications (Buolamwini and Gebru, 2018; Mitchell et al., 2019; Benjamin, 2019) and does not actively prevent the exploitation of crowdworkers (Irani and Silberman, 2013; Shmueli et al., 2021). Moreover, since POTATO is a tool designed to improve the efficiency of typical prediction task workflows, it cannot address existential critiques of machine learning (e.g., harms of classification as a practice).

POTATO was created using principles of universal design, prioritizing broadly experienced ease of use, low effort, intuitiveness, flexibility, tolerance for error, and perceptibility of key information (Persson et al., 2015). Since POTATO is uniquely annotator-focused, rather than deployer-focused, tasks are readily designed in a way that maximizes worker wellbeing and productivity. The application's design is largely accessible and inclusive and the tool contains many of the types of features that crowdworkers find useful (e.g., low effort to configure, reduces cognitive burden of complex tasks, easy to correct errors by going back, login flow that supports screen readers and doesn't use captcha, annotation guidelines readily visible in tooltip and hyperlink) (Zyskowski et al., 2015; Swaminathan et al., 2017). That said, certain features of the interface may be inaccessible for workers. Moreover, tools like POTATO can worsen annotators' mental health by promoting fragmented work, multitasking, and poor work-life balance (Williams et al., 2019) and by displaying triggering text without masks or warnings (Shmueli et al., 2021). Many of these potential accessibility and psychological harms can be addressed through improvements in the interface. Because of the ease of secondary development — especially adding new HTML front-end templates — POTATO allows the research community to explore more design opportunities for inclusive annotation and responsible crowdsourcing. Ideally, a future version of this tool would use community-led design to develop more universally accessible, inclusive templates for users (Spiel et al., 2020).

In designing POTATO, we prioritized developing mechanisms for just, equitable compensation. By allowing annotators to track time spent on the task, POTATO facilitates paying crowdworkers a fair hourly wage rather than the per-task payment schemes that frequently lead to low hourly wages (Fort et al., 2011; Gray and Suri, 2019). A key accessibility feature, the timer promotes flexibility (e.g., allows people to take longer or build in micro-breaks) instead of imposing needlessly restrictive per-task time requirements that can create barriers for disabled workers (Zyskowski et al., 2015). Our goal in creating POTATO was to empower and support the annotator. For instance, although we piloted a timer to alert annotators when the expected task time had elapsed, we ultimately removed this feature in order to eliminate additional stress.

Another important problem in computational social research is inaccurately labeled and biased datasets, which are a cause of inequitably felt downstream harms (Olteanu et al., 2019; Blodgett et al., 2020; Mehrabi et al., 2021). POTATO may have the potential to reduce many common sources of bias by promoting high-quality annotations: convenience features lower cognitive load and reduce reliance on personal heuristics that may increase bias; researchers can use tooltips to provide specific, easily accessed instructions to minimize anticipated sources of bias; since the base annotation time is lower, and there are no per-instance annotation time limits, annotators may feel less pressure to label faster at the expense of poor annotation quality. However, POTATO may amplify the researchers' own biases in the data: annotators may rely too heavily on keyword highlights and tooltips, which can bias the data if keywords common in minority communities are over- or underrepresented, or the tooltip text does not include instructions relevant to certain communities in the data. Future experiments can study the effect of POTATO's productivity-enhancing features on mitigating or amplifying different types of bias.

Finally, an important goal in developing POTATO was to facilitate studying complex social questions without being limited by existing labeled data:

since the tool makes it easier and faster to design complex tasks and collect data, researchers can think critically about what problems would be most beneficial and impactful, and design tasks that actually answer those questions (Wiens et al., 2019; Abebe et al., 2020). Since POTATO facilitates the deployment of multilingual tasks, researchers can more easily test the the generalizability of their results across linguistic and cultural contexts (Joshi et al., 2020). A major challenge in applied machine learning is the lack of diversity among researchers (Orife et al., 2020); since POTATO is free, open-sourced, and easy to use, we hope the tool will facilitate participation by scholars who are not associated with well-funded R1 universities and also by community members outside academia.

References

Rediet Abebe, Solon Barocas, Jon Kleinberg, Karen Levy, Manish Raghavan, and David G Robinson. 2020. Roles for computing in social change. In *Proceedings of the 2020 Conference on Fairness, Accountability, and Transparency*, pages 252–260.

Jiajun Bao, Junjie Wu, Yiming Zhang, Eshwar Chandrasekharan, and David Jurgens. 2021. Conversations gone alright: Quantifying and predicting prosocial outcomes in online conversations. In *Proceedings of the Web Conference 2021*, pages 1134–1145.

Ruha Benjamin. 2019. Race after technology: Abolitionist tools for the new jim code. *Social Forces*.

Su Lin Blodgett, Solon Barocas, Hal Daumé III, and Hanna Wallach. 2020. Language (technology) is power: A critical survey of "bias" in nlp. *arXiv preprint arXiv:2005.14050*.

Joy Buolamwini and Timnit Gebru. 2018. Gender shades: Intersectional accuracy disparities in commercial gender classification. In *Conference on fairness, accountability and transparency*, pages 77–91. PMLR.

Juan Miguel Cejuela, Peter McQuilton, Laura Ponting, Steven J Marygold, Raymund Stefancsik, Gillian H Millburn, Burkhard Rost, FlyBase Consortium, et al. 2014. Tagtog: interactive and text-mining-assisted annotation of gene mentions in plos full-text articles. *Database*, 2014.

Explosion. 2017. Prodigy. `https://prodi.gy`.

Karën Fort, Gilles Adda, and K Bretonnel Cohen. 2011. Amazon mechanical turk: Gold mine or coal mine? *Computational Linguistics*, 37(2):413–420.

M van Gompel, K Sloot, Martin Reynaert, and APJ van den Bosch. 2017. Folia in practice. the infrastructure of a linguistic annotation format.

Mary L Gray and Siddharth Suri. 2019. *Ghost work: How to stop Silicon Valley from building a new global underclass*. Eamon Dolan Books.

Thilo Hagendorff. 2020. The ethics of ai ethics: An evaluation of guidelines. *Minds and Machines*, 30(1):99–120.

Alon Halevy, Peter Norvig, and Fernando Pereira. 2009. The unreasonable effectiveness of data. *IEEE Intelligent Systems*, 24(2):8–12.

Lilly C Irani and M Six Silberman. 2013. Turkopticon: Interrupting worker invisibility in amazon mechanical turk. In *Proceedings of the SIGCHI conference on human factors in computing systems*, pages 611–620.

Jinja. JINJA template designer documentation. `https://jinja.palletsprojects.com/en/3.0.x/templates/`.

Pratik Joshi, Sebastin Santy, Amar Budhiraja, Kalika Bali, and Monojit Choudhury. 2020. The state and fate of linguistic diversity and inclusion in the nlp world. *arXiv preprint arXiv:2004.09095*.

Yanzeng Li, Bowen Yu, Li Quangang, and Tingwen Liu. 2021. FITAnnotator: A Flexible and Intelligent Text Annotation System. In *Proceedings of the 2021 Conference of the North American Chapter of the Association for Computational Linguistics: Human Language Technologies: Demonstrations*, pages 35–41.

Ninareh Mehrabi, Fred Morstatter, Nripsuta Saxena, Kristina Lerman, and Aram Galstyan. 2021. A survey on bias and fairness in machine learning. *ACM Computing Surveys (CSUR)*, 54(6):1–35.

Julia Mendelsohn, Ceren Budak, and David Jurgens. 2021. Modeling framing in immigration discourse on social media. In *Proceedings of the 2021 Conference of the North American Chapter of the Association for Computational Linguistics: Human Language Technologies*, pages 2219–2263.

Margaret Mitchell, Simone Wu, Andrew Zaldivar, Parker Barnes, Lucy Vasserman, Ben Hutchinson, Elena Spitzer, Inioluwa Deborah Raji, and Timnit Gebru. 2019. Model cards for model reporting. In *Proceedings of the conference on fairness, accountability, and transparency*, pages 220–229.

Robert Munro Monarch. 2021. *Human-in-the-Loop Machine Learning: Active learning and annotation for human-centered AI*. Simon and Schuster.

Hiroki Nakayama, Takahiro Kubo, Junya Kamura, Yasufumi Taniguchi, and Xu Liang. 2018. doccano: Text annotation tool for human. Software available from https://github.com/doccano/doccano.

Alexandra Olteanu, Carlos Castillo, Fernando Diaz, and Emre Kıcıman. 2019. Social data: Biases, methodological pitfalls, and ethical boundaries. *Frontiers in Big Data*, 2:13.

Iroro Orife, Julia Kreutzer, Blessing Sibanda, Daniel Whitenack, Kathleen Siminyu, Laura Martinus, Jamiil Toure Ali, Jade Abbott, Vukosi Marivate, Salomon Kabongo, et al. 2020. Masakhane–machine translation for africa. *arXiv preprint arXiv:2003.11529*.

Jiaxin Pei and David Jurgens. 2020. Quantifying intimacy in language. In *Proceedings of the 2020 Conference on Empirical Methods in Natural Language Processing (EMNLP)*, pages 5307–5326.

Jiaxin Pei and David Jurgens. 2021. Measuring sentence-level and aspect-level (un) certainty in science communications. In *Proceedings of the 2021 Conference on Empirical Methods in Natural Language Processing*, pages 9959–10011.

Jiaxin Pei, Vítor Silva, Maarten Bos, Yozon Liu, Leonardo Neves, David Jurgens, and Francesco Barbieri. 2022. Semeval 2023 task 9: Multilingual tweet intimacy analysis. *arXiv preprint arXiv:2210.01108*.

Tal Perry. 2021. Lighttag: Text annotation platform. In *Proceedings of the 2021 Conference on Empirical Methods in Natural Language Processing: System Demonstrations*, pages 20–27.

Hans Persson, Henrik Åhman, Alexander Arvei Yngling, and Jan Gulliksen. 2015. Universal design, inclusive design, accessible design, design for all: different concepts—one goal? on the concept of accessibility—historical, methodological and philosophical aspects. *Universal Access in the Information Society*, 14(4):505–526.

Maarten Sap, Swabha Swayamdipta, Laura Vianna, Xuhui Zhou, Yejin Choi, and Noah A. Smith. 2022. Annotators with attitudes: How annotator beliefs and identities bias toxic language detection.

Burr Settles. 2009. Active learning literature survey.

Boaz Shmueli, Jan Fell, Soumya Ray, and Lun-Wei Ku. 2021. Beyond fair pay: Ethical implications of nlp crowdsourcing. In *Proceedings of the 2021 Conference of the North American Chapter of the Association for Computational Linguistics: Human Language Technologies*, pages 3758–3769.

Katta Spiel, Kathrin Gerling, Cynthia L Bennett, Emeline Brulé, Rua M Williams, Jennifer Rode, and Jennifer Mankoff. 2020. Nothing about us without us: Investigating the role of critical disability studies in hci. In *Extended Abstracts of the 2020 CHI Conference on Human Factors in Computing Systems*, pages 1–8.

Pontus Stenetorp, Sampo Pyysalo, Goran Topić, Tomoko Ohta, Sophia Ananiadou, and Jun'ichi Tsujii. 2012. Brat: a web-based tool for nlp-assisted text annotation. In *Proceedings of the Demonstrations at the 13th Conference of the European Chapter of the Association for Computational Linguistics*, pages 102–107.

Chen Sun, Abhinav Shrivastava, Saurabh Singh, and Abhinav Gupta. 2017. Revisiting unreasonable effectiveness of data in deep learning era. In *Proceedings of the IEEE international conference on computer vision*, pages 843–852.

Saiganesh Swaminathan, Kotaro Hara, and Jeffrey P Bigham. 2017. The crowd work accessibility problem. In *Proceedings of the 14th International Web for All Conference*, pages 1–4.

Maxim Tkachenko, Mikhail Malyuk, Nikita Shevchenko, Andrey Holmanyuk, and Nikolai Liubimov. 2021. Label studio: Data labeling software, 2020-2021. *Open source software available from https://github. com/heartexlabs/label-studio*.

Xingyao Wang and David Jurgens. 2021. An animated picture says at least a thousand words: Selecting gif-based replies in multimodal dialog. In *Findings of the Association for Computational Linguistics: EMNLP 2021*, pages 3228–3257.

Max Wiechmann, Seid Muhie Yimam, and Chris Biemann. 2021. Activeanno: General-purpose document-level annotation tool with active learning integration. In *Proceedings of the 2021 Conference of the North American Chapter of the Association for Computational Linguistics: Human Language Technologies: Demonstrations*, pages 99–105.

Jenna Wiens, Suchi Saria, Mark Sendak, Marzyeh Ghassemi, Vincent X Liu, Finale Doshi-Velez, Kenneth Jung, Katherine Heller, David Kale, Mohammed Saeed, et al. 2019. Do no harm: a roadmap for responsible machine learning for health care. *Nature medicine*, 25(9):1337–1340.

Alex C Williams, Gloria Mark, Kristy Milland, Edward Lank, and Edith Law. 2019. The perpetual work life of crowdworkers: How tooling practices increase fragmentation in crowdwork. *Proceedings of the ACM on Human-Computer Interaction*, 3(CSCW):1–28.

Dustin Wright, Jiaxin Pei, David Jurgens, and Isabelle Augenstein. 2022. Modeling Information Change in Science Communication with Semantically Matched Paraphrases.

Seid Muhie Yimam, Iryna Gurevych, Richard Eckart de Castilho, and Chris Biemann. 2013. Webanno: A flexible, web-based and visually supported system for distributed annotations. In *Proceedings of the 51st Annual Meeting of the Association for Computational Linguistics: System Demonstrations*, pages 1–6.

Naitian Zhou and David Jurgens. 2020. Condolences and empathy in online communities. In *Proceedings of the 2020 Conference on Empirical Methods in Natural Language Processing (EMNLP)*, pages 609–626.

Kathryn Zyskowski, Meredith Ringel Morris, Jeffrey P Bigham, Mary L Gray, and Shaun K Kane. 2015. Accessible crowdwork? understanding the value in and challenge of microtask employment for people with disabilities. In *Proceedings of the 18th ACM Conference on Computer Supported Cooperative Work & Social Computing*, pages 1682–1693.

KGxBoard: Explainable and Interactive Leaderboard for Evaluation of Knowledge Graph Completion Models

Haris Widjaja[*1], **Kiril Gashteovski**[*2], **Wiem Ben Rim**[2], **Pengfei Liu**[1,4],
Christopher Malon[3], **Daniel Ruffinelli**[5], **Carolin Lawrence**[2], **Graham Neubig**[1,4]
[1] Carnegie Mellon University; [2] NEC Laboratories Europe;
[3] NEC Laboratories America; [4] Inspired Cognition; [5] University of Mannheim;

Abstract

Knowledge Graphs (KGs) store information in the form of *(head, predicate, tail)*-triples. To augment KGs with new knowledge, researchers proposed models for KG Completion (KGC) tasks such as link prediction; i.e., answering *(h; p; ?)* or *(?; p; t)* queries. Such models are usually evaluated with averaged metrics on a held-out test set. While useful for tracking progress, averaged single-score metrics cannot reveal *what exactly* a model has learned—or failed to learn. To address this issue, we propose KGxBoard[1]: an interactive framework for performing fine-grained evaluation on meaningful subsets of the data, each of which tests individual and interpretable capabilities of a KGC model. In our experiments, we highlight the findings that we discovered with the use of KGxBoard, which would have been impossible to detect with standard averaged single-score metrics.

1 Introduction

Knowledge Graphs (KGs) are graph databases that store information about entities and the relations between them in the form of *(head, predicate, tail)*-triples (Weikum et al., 2021). Because of their flexible structure, KGs are used for storing general real-world data (Rebele et al., 2016) as well as domain-specific data covering various domains (Abu-Salih, 2021), including medicine (Chandak et al., 2022), IoT (Le-Phuoc et al., 2016) and finance (Cheng et al., 2020). KGs play an important role in NLP: they are used for many downstream tasks, including language modeling (Logan et al., 2019), entity linking (Radhakrishnan et al., 2018) and question answering (Saxena et al., 2022).

A common problem for KGs is that they are incomplete (i.e., they do not contain all facts about the world or the particular domain), which could lead to limitations in performance for the downstream tasks. To tackle this problem of incompleteness, the research community has worked on many KG Completion (KGC) tasks, most prominently on *link prediction*: predicting new facts within the KG by providing ranked predictions to the queries *(h; p; ?)* or *(?; p; t)* (Clouatre et al., 2021). Models for KGC tasks are typically evaluated with single-score metrics that are averaged over a held-out test set. For instance, for a KGC query—e.g., *(h; p; ?)*—, hits@k indicates the average number of correct answers from the test set that appear within the top-k ranked entities predicted by the KGC model.[2]

While using such scores is important for tracking the progress of KGC models, researchers observed that a more fine-grained evaluation is needed (Palmonari and Minervini, 2020), because the averaged metrics cannot answer the question of *what properties* have the models actually learned—or failed to learn. To investigate what properties were learned by the KGC models, researchers have designed specific datasets and experimental setups. For example, Rim et al. (2021) used the idea of behavioral testing applied to NLP models (Ribeiro et al., 2020) to perform more fine-grained tests for relation symmetry. In particular, they measured the performance of KGC models for queries that contain symmetric relations; i.e., relations that are true for both *(h; p; t)* and *(t; p; h)* such as *(X; marriedTo; Y)*. However, their proposed framework only contains a limited number of tests and might not cover model properties of interest to other researchers.

To make the fine-grained evaluation more generic—and to compare different KGC models across different properties—we propose KGxBoard: a method and software implementation for fine-grained evaluation of KGC models (see illustration in Fig. 1). KGxBoard splits the evaluated data into groups (buckets) according to certain properties of the data. For instance, one can

*Equal contribution

[1]All resources (code, data, demo, video, etc.) are available on `https://github.com/neulab/KGxBoard`

[2]See Sec. 2 for more details about hits@k and other metrics

Proceedings of the The 2022 Conference on Empirical Methods in Natural Language Processing: System Demonstrations, pages 338 - 350

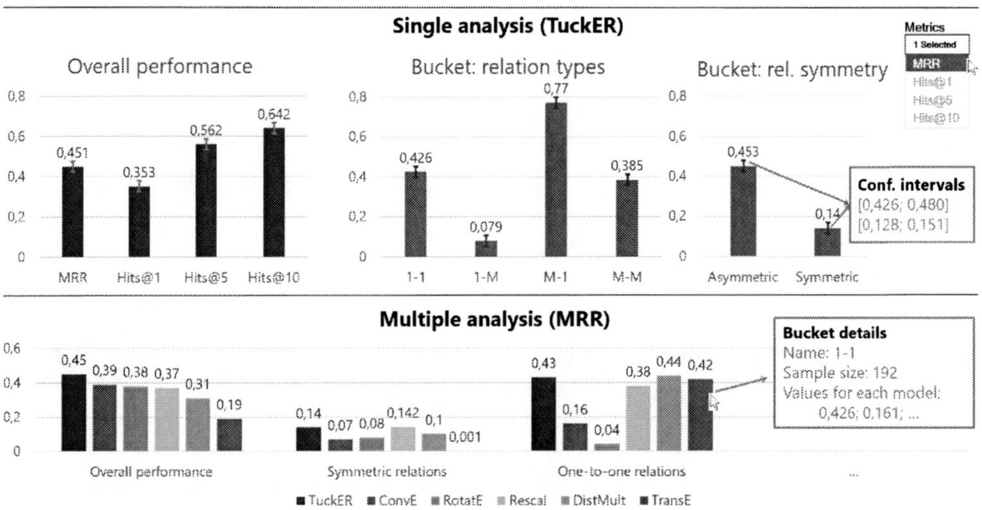

Figure 1: Illustration of KGxBoard's functionalities. With the *single analysis mode*, the user can see the overall performance of a given KGC model, as well as the performance of the model across multiple buckets (i.e., partitions of the evaluated data). For example, we observed that the TuckER model performs very well on triples with Many-to-one (M-1) relations. However, it performs poorly on triples with One-to-many (1-M) relations and symmetric relations. With the *multiple analysis mode*, the user can compare the overall and bucketized performance across different models. Such a view enables the user to compare the models in a fine-grained manner; e.g., Rescal is ranked 4th in the overall performance, but it is ranked 1st for the triples having symmetric relations. Likewise, DistMult is ranked 5th in the overall performance and 1st for the triples with One-to-one relations. In both modes, the user can interact with the UI to see details of the data buckets, change the evaluation metrics, etc.

split the test data into two buckets of data points such that one bucket contains triples with symmetric and the other with asymmetric relations. Consequently, the users can observe the performance of each of these buckets separately, while also having an overview of the overall performance scores.

KGxBoard builds upon ExplainaBoard (Liu et al., 2021), which is an explainable leaderboard for NLP tasks. We adapt ExplainaBoard to the KGC tasks[3] by providing: (1) a method and software implementation for fine-grained evaluation of KGC models, integrated into ExplainaBoard; (2) APIs for porting results from two popular KGC frameworks—PyKeen (Ali et al., 2021) and LibKGE (Broscheit et al., 2020)—directly into KGxBoard format; (3) interface for reading customized features for fine-grained evaluation; (4) experimental study exposing problems with KGC models that cannot be spotted with averaged scoring; (5) experimental study showing that the findings from the fine-grained evaluation of KGxBoard can be used for automatic debugging of the models.

[3]KGxBoard can handle the KGC tasks on answering queries of the form *(?, p, t)*, *(h, ?, t)* and *(h, p, ?)*. For simplicity, when we refer to KGC models in this paper, we refer to models that provide predictions of the form *(h, p, ?)*.

2 Preliminaries

The performance of KGC models is evaluated on a held-out test set of golden KG triples. In particular, the models return a set of ranked answers to the queries—e.g., *(h; p; ?)*—, where the correctness of the answers is evaluated against the golden triples. The final score is averaged over the examples from the held-out test set. The standard scores used in the literature are:

(1) Hits@$k = \frac{1}{|\mathcal{D}|} \sum_{(h,r,t) \in \mathcal{D}} \mathbb{1}[\texttt{rank}(t) \leq k]$

(2) MRR $= \frac{1}{|\mathcal{D}|} \sum_{(h,r,t) \in \mathcal{D}} \frac{1}{\texttt{rank}(t)}$

(3) MR $= \frac{1}{|\mathcal{D}|} \sum_{(h,r,t) \in \mathcal{D}} \texttt{rank}(t)$

where $\mathcal{D}$ is the set of test triples, and h, r, t are the head, relation and tail of the KG triple respectively.

3 KGxBoard's Fine-grained Evaluation

Prior work in NLP has pointed to the issues of using single-score metrics, which do not expose what exact properties of the data were (or were not) learned by the models (Narayan et al., 2021); e.g., some information extraction models perform poorly when there is a conjunction present in the

```
"custom_features": {
    "rel_type": {
        "dtype": "string",
        "description": "predicate symmetry",
        "num_buckets": 2
    }
}
```

Figure 2: Defining custom features for bucketization of the evaluation data (e.g., validation or test data).

sentence (Gashteovski et al., 2022). To better understand what properties were (or were not) learned by the NLP models, people have proposed multi-faceted or explainable and interactive leaderboards (for more details on related work, see Appendix A).

Following ExplainaBoard (Liu et al., 2021), the basic idea of KGxBoard's fine-grained evaluation is to breakdown the performance measure (e.g., Hits@10) over individual groups (buckets) in addition to the performance score over the overall evaluation dataset. This approach involves three steps: (i) define features upon which the evaluation dataset is going to be partitioned; (ii) partition evaluation dataset into different buckets based on the defined features; and (iii) calculate performance w.r.t. each bucket. In contrast to ExplainaBoard, KGxBoard is tailored for the KG completion tasks and their evaluation metrics.

3.1 Feature definition

The feature definition describes the manner upon which KGxBoard is going to partition the evaluated data into buckets. For example, if the feature is about predicate symmetry, then the data is divided in 2 buckets: (1) triples that have predicates which are considered symmetric;[4] (2) triples with asymmetric predicates. Because each data point can be assigned to one of these buckets with a label *"symmetric"* or *"asymmetric"* (strings), the user defines the feature "predicate symmetry" accordingly (as shown on Figure 2).

Built-in Features. KGxBoard supports several built-in features that will automatically bucketize the evaluation data of any models to be analyzed. The built-in features include several widely used properties of the data, such as predicate symmetry (Trouillon et al., 2016) and entity type hierarchy (Rim et al., 2021); see details in Appendix B.

[4] predicates that are true for both *(h; p; t)* and *(t; p; h)*; e.g., the predicate *p=marriedTo*: $(x; p; y) \iff (y; p; x)$.

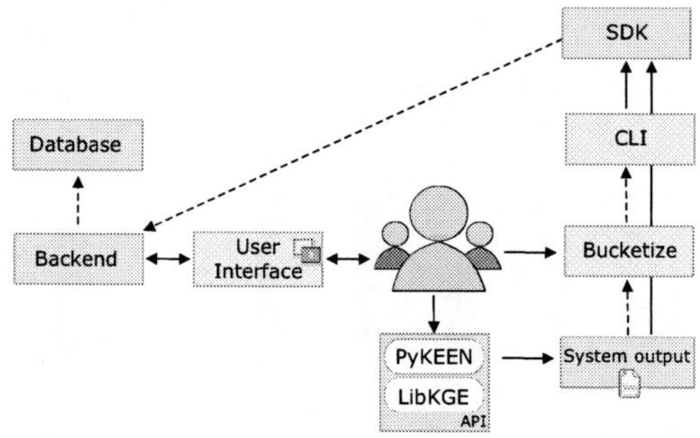

Figure 3: General overview of KGxBoard's architecture. SDK: Software Development Kit; CLI: Command-Line interface.

Customized Features. KGxBoard also allows users to customly define their own features by specifying additional information in the system output file. If, for example, the users want to define the bucketization features for predicate symmetry, then they only need to specify this in a json file (Fig. 2).

3.2 Partitioning of Evaluation Data into Different Buckets

For the built-in features, KGxBoard automatically assigns each data point to its respective bucket. For the customized features, once the custom features were defined, the user should place each data point to its respective customized bucket via the bucketization functions (explained in Section 4.4). This data is then fed into KGxBoard, which automatically computes the relevant metrics for each bucket.

3.3 Calculate Performance w.r.t. each Bucket

KGxBoard computes the relevant metrics (described in Section 2) for each bucket individually, as well as for the overall evaluation dataset.

Confidence Interval. KGxBoard has been endowed with the ability to quantify to what degree we can trust the result of each bucket. Specifically, as illustrated in Figure 1, each bin has been equipped with an error bar and its width reflects the reliability of the bucket performance. KGxBoard supports two ways to calculate the confidence interval: bootstrapped re-sampling (Efron, 1992) and t-test (Nakagawa and Cuthill, 2007) .

4 KGxBoard: System Overview

A general overview of the KGxBoard architecture is illustrated in Figure 3. The users can provide the data for the models through the front-end (via the

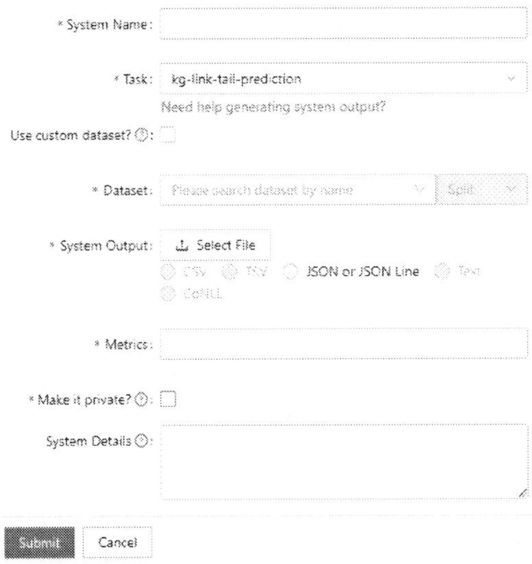

Figure 4: Using the frontend to upload a new model.

UI) or the back-end (via the CLI or the SDK). Then, these results are stored in a database (DB), which can be accessed and viewed either with the visual interface, programmatically, or with the command-line interface. In general, the users can choose three ways to use KGxBoard's functionalities: (i) directly from the interactive web interface; (ii) through an API from KGC frameworks (PyKEEN and LibKGE); (iii) through the command-line interface with already provided data.

4.1 Frontend

We adopt a React-based technology stack[5] to create an interactive web app as the frontend of KGxBoard. Assuming that a user has generated the input data in prior steps (e.g., through the API from KGC libraries; see Section 4.3), she can upload the data via the frontend interface (Figure 4). The data is then passed on to the backend, which stores it in a database. The frontend provides two types of analysis of the models' evaluation: **single analysis** aims to identify the strengths and weaknesses of a given KG completion model; **pairwise/multiple analysis** can help users figure out where one model is better (or worse) than the other when two (or more) models are selected; for illustration of the frontend, see Figure 1.

4.2 Backend

The backend is built on top of ExplainaBoard's backend code (Liu et al., 2021). The main functionalities for KGxBoard's backend are: (i) defining the evaluation metrics for the link prediction task: Hits@k, MRR and MR; (ii) computing the overall scores and the buckets' scores with the built-in features; (iii) handling customized feature buckets if the user provided any; (iv) storing the results in the DB; (v) communicate the results with the frontend in an interactive manner.

4.3 API with KGC Libraries

KGxBoard comes with APIs that can translate the output of two widely used KGC libraries—PyKEEN (Ali et al., 2021) and LibKGE (Broscheit et al., 2020)—into KGxBoard format. In particular, the APIs write the system-output files in KGxBoard format which does not contain buckets, only results from the models. If the user wishes to add customized buckets, she can either write or reuse already existing bucketization function(s), which will rewrite the data in KGxBoard format with the desired bucketizations.

4.4 Bucketization functions

The bucketization functions are procedures that do two main actions: (1) define the buckets; (2) assign a bucket label to each data example. Here's an example of a bucketization function pseudocode that defines relations as being either symmetric or asymmetric:

```
# s_rels -> set of symmetric rels.
def bucketize_rel_sym(s_rels):
    # define the buckets properties
    bucket_name = "rel_sym"; dtype = "string"
    descr="rel's symmetry prop."; num_buckets=2

    # assign bucket to example data
    for triple in predict_data:
        if triple['predicate'] in s_rels:
            triple.bucket = 'symmetric'
        else:
            triple.bucket = 'asymmetric'
```

5 Experimental Study

To showcase the usefulness of KGxBoard, we conducted the following experimental study: (1) bucketized comparison of models: we provide insights on the buckets' performance about different models trained with one KGC framework, which would have been impossible to discover with standard metrics; (2) comparison of models trained on different KGC frameworks with different hyperparameter settings: showing how KGxBoard can be used to discover differences between models trained in

[5]https://reactjs.org/

different environments; (3) automatic debugging: showing the ability of automatic debugging of the models by using insights from certain buckets.

5.1 Experimental Setup

Datasets. We used two widely used datasets: (1) FB15K-237 (Toutanova and Chen, 2015), constructed from Freebase (Bollacker et al., 2008), covering relations between people, locations, etc.; (2) WN18RR (Dettmers et al., 2018), constructed from WordNet (Miller, 1992) and represents connections between words in English, such as synonyms and hypernyms. The models were trained, validated and tested with the standard dataset split (the reported results are on the test sets).

Models and KGC Frameworks. For our experiments, we trained the KGC models on two commonly used KGC frameworks: PyKEEN and LibKGE. With PyKEEN we trained the following models for link prediction: DistMult (Yang et al., 2015), ConvE (Dettmers et al., 2018), RESCAL (Nickel et al., 2011), RotatE (Sun et al., 2019), TransE (Bordes et al., 2013) and TuckER (Balazevic et al., 2019). PyKEEN provides hyperparameters to reproduce the results of the original work of a given model, which we used to train the models. To compare the same models trained with different hyperparameters and frameworks, we also used the pretrained models obtained by Ruffinelli et al. (2020) as a result of extensive hyperparameter optimization using LibKGE (Broscheit et al., 2020). Specifically, we used the models ConvE, DistMult, Rescal and TransE (see training details in App. D).

Bucketizations. We partitioned the test data into different interpretable groups based on either built-in or customized features (e.g., relation type). All together, for FB15K-237 / WN18RR we have 303 / 35 unique buckets respectively. The large difference in the number of buckets between the datasets is mainly due to the significantly higher number of relations in the FB15K-237 dataset (237 v.s. 11). We provide further details on the buckets in App. C.

5.2 Bucketized Comparison of Models

To get an overview of the fine-grained evaluation of the KGC models, we used the predictions from PyKEEN on the FB15K-237 and WN18RR datasets. By ranking different systems with the MRR metric in two ways: (1) based on their overall performance; and (2) based on bucket-wise performance;

	Overall rank	$b^{=}$	$b^{\neq}$
TuckER	1 / 1	.601 / .543	.399 / .457
ConvE	2 / 3	.301 / .486	.699 / .514
RotatE	3 / 5	.257 / .686	.743 / .314
Rescal	4 / 2	.261 / .457	.739 / .543
DistMult	5 / 4	.541 / .400	.459 / .600
TransE	6 / 6	.868 / .800	.132 / .200

Table 1: Ranking of KGC models (trained with PyKEEN) according to the MRR score. 1 indicates best rank. $b^{=}/b^{\neq}$: the fraction of buckets where the ranking of a given model is equivalent/not equivalent compared to the overall rank of the model. Results are on the datasets FB15K-237 / WN18RR.

we obtain that, as shown in Table 1, the overall ranking of the models is significantly different than the ranking of the models for each individual bucket.

For example, TuckER is ranked as the best-performing model on both FB15K-237 and WN18RR. However, TuckER is not ranked as best performing model for approximately 40% and 46% of the buckets for FB15K-237 and WN18RR respectively. For instance, when taking a closer look at FB15K-237, we find that for the bucket featurized by symmetric relations, TuckER is ranked 2nd and Rescal is ranked 1st (on the overall test set, Rescal is ranked 4th) and for the One-to-one relations, TuckER is also ranked 2nd and DistMult is ranked 1st (on the overall test set, DistMult is ranked 5th); see Figure 1.

Such findings would be impossible to spot with standard averaged metrics over the entire test set, and are similar in spirit to previous results that show how alternative evaluation methods can expose differences in overall model performance (Wang et al., 2019; Rim et al., 2021). With KGxBoard, researchers can diagnose issues with any KGC model on customized properties of the data (i.e., customized bucketizations of the evaluation data).

5.3 Bucketized Comparison of Models Trained with Different Hyperparameters

Similarly as with the fine-grained comparison between different models (Sec. 5.2), KGxBoard can be used to compare one model that was trained on multiple sets of different hyperparameters (HPs) and implementations. For this purpose, we train each of the four KGC models (ConvE, Rescal, DistMult and TransE) with two sets of HPs on two KGC libraries—PyKEEN and LibKGE—and showcase the differences. Note that the implementation from different libraries can vary significantly w.r.t. the

HP search space and the degree of customization.[6]

On the one hand, we trained each model with the hyperparameters that aim to reproduce the work of the original papers (trained with PyKEEN; the HP combination was proposed in PyKEEN's documentation). On the other hand, we used model configurations resulting from a HP optimization pipeline that ensures improved overall results (trained with LibKGE; HP combination proposed by Ruffinelli et al. (2020)). We refer to each of the former models as ORIGHP-MODEL and to the latter as OPTIMHP-MODEL. While the OPTIMHP models always outperform their ORIGHP counterparts, we still observed many cases where the ranking of the models flipped on some buckets. For example, ORIGHP-CONVE performs better than OPTIMHP-CONVE for: (1) the FB15K-237 triples with relation between award ceremony and award winner; (2) FB15K-237 triples whose tail entity types are of type "musical work" (details in App. E).

5.4 Automatic Debugging of Models Using Buckets

Hits@1	ConvE	TuckER	RotatE	Rescal
	Debugging test			
Before debug.	.0000	.0000	.0000	.0000
Naive	.0625	.1875	.0465	.1642
In-danger	.1562	.2083	.0465	.2015
	Original test			
Before debug.	.2710	.3108	.2627	.2596
Naive	.2416	.3010	.2627	.2594
In-danger	.2574	.3004	.2627	.2594

Table 2: Debugging results for the relations with most symmetry violations (Hits@1).

Grouping related properties of the model into buckets offers not only the potential to diagnose problems, but also the potential to fix them by debugging. We show here how the debugging techniques of Malon et al. (2022) may be adapted to fix problems with KG embeddings, illustrating the idea with one particular bucket: relation symmetry.

Updating the relation embedding to improve symmetry for one relation will have no effect on other relations generally, so we debug only one relation r at a time. For debugging, we collect a sub-bucket consisting of triples (h, r, t) that violate symmetry in a stricter sense: the reverse triple (t, r, h) is in the training set and the trained model predicts h as the tail for $(t, r, ?)$ with rank one, but t has rank greater than one among the predictions for $(h, r, ?)$. Ten triples from the sub-bucket constitute the *debugging set*, which is used to learn better model parameters, and the remaining triples are held out to form the *debugging test set*.

We debug the relation with the most symmetry violations (in the above sense) for four models: ConvE, TuckER, RotatE and Rescal.[7] A naive method, which we call *intensive fine-tuning*, simply fine-tunes the model on the debugging set alone until all its triples are predicted at rank one. We freeze entity embeddings during intensive fine-tuning, because updating the entity embedding will not generalize to improve symmetry on any held-out entities. To monitor whether this learning comes at the expense of forgetting other triples, we evaluate performance on the original test set before and after debugging, in addition to the debugging test set.

We also adapt the proposed method of Malon et al. (2022) to KGE. In this method, we first run the intensive fine-tuning, then collect twenty triples at random from the training set, which were correctly predicted at rank one after the original rank-tuning, but whose rank fell after the intensive fine-tuning. We use these twenty examples together with the ten debugging examples in a second round of intensive fine-tuning, again starting with the parameters of the original model. The hope is to learn the debugging examples while anchoring the performance of triples that are “in danger” of being forgotten.

Table 2 shows debugging results for the four models. In all cases, naive debugging improves Hits@1 on the held-out test debugging examples, and in-danger debugging often yields a further improvement. The impact of debugging on Hits@1 of the original test set is less than 1% for all models except ConvE, which has interaction parameters that are applied to many relations. For ConvE, the in-danger method cuts this sacrifice in half. We provide more detailed analysis in Appendix F.

6 Conclusions

We presented KGxBoard: an interactive framework for fine-grained and interpretable evaluation on meaningful subsets of the data, each of which tests individual and interpretable capabilities of a KGC model. We highlighted insights that would be impossible to detect with standard leaderboards.

[6]For instance, while LibKGE allows the customized initialization of the embeddings through HPs, PyKEEN requires changing the source code. More details in App. D.

[7]The other two models, Distmult and TransE, did not have enough symmetry violations to fill a debugging set.

References

Bilal Abu-Salih. 2021. Domain-specific Knowledge Graphs: A Survey. *Journal of Network and Computer Applications*, 185:103076.

Mehdi Ali, Max Berrendorf, Charles Tapley Hoyt, Laurent Vermue, Sahand Sharifzadeh, Volker Tresp, and Jens Lehmann. 2021. PyKEEN 1.0: A Python Library for Training and Evaluating Knowledge Graph Embeddings. *Journal of Machine Learning Research*, 22(82):1–6.

Sören Auer, Christian Bizer, Georgi Kobilarov, Jens Lehmann, Richard Cyganiak, and Zachary Ives. 2007. DBpedia: A Nucleus for a Web of Open Data. In *The semantic web*, pages 722–735. Springer.

Ivana Balazevic, Carl Allen, and Timothy M. Hospedales. 2019. TuckER: Tensor Factorization for Knowledge Graph Completion. In *Proceedings of the Conference on Empirical Methods in Natural Language Processin (EMNLP)*, pages 5184–5193.

Kurt D. Bollacker, Colin Evans, Praveen K. Paritosh, Tim Sturge, and Jamie Taylor. 2008. Freebase: a Collaboratively Created Graph Database for Structuring Human Knowledge. In *Proceedings of the ACM SIGMOD International Conference on Management of Data (SIGMOD)*.

Antoine Bordes, Nicolas Usunier, Alberto Garcia-Duran, Jason Weston, and Oksana Yakhnenko. 2013. Translating Embeddings for Modeling Multi-Relational Data. *Advances in Neural Information Processing Systems (NeurIPS)*.

Samuel R. Bowman and George E. Dahl. 2021. What Will it Take to Fix Benchmarking in Natural Language Understanding? In *Proceedings of the Conference of the North American Chapter of the Association for Computational Linguistics: Human Language Technologies (NAACL-HLT)*, page 4843–4855.

Samuel Broscheit, Daniel Ruffinelli, Adrian Kochsiek, Patrick Betz, and Rainer Gemulla. 2020. LibKGE-A Knowledge Graph Embedding Library for Reproducible Research. In *Proceedings of the Conference on Empirical Methods in Natural Language Processing: System Demonstrations (EMNLP)*, pages 165–174.

Payal Chandak, Kexin Huang, and Marinka Zitnik. 2022. Building a Knowledge Graph to Enable Precision Medicine. *bioRxiv*.

Dawei Cheng, Fangzhou Yang, Xiaoyang Wang, Ying Zhang, and Liqing Zhang. 2020. Knowledge Graph-based Event Embedding Framework for Financial Quantitative Investments. In *Proceedings of the International ACM SIGIR Conference on Research and Development in Information Retrieval (SIGIR)*, pages 2221–2230.

Louis Clouatre, Philippe Trempe, Amal Zouaq, and Sarath Chandar. 2021. MLMLM: Link Prediction with Mean Likelihood Masked Language Model. In *Proceedings of the Annual Meeting on Association for Computational Linguistics (ACL)*, pages 4321–4331.

Tim Dettmers, Pasquale Minervini, Pontus Stenetorp, and Sebastian Riedel. 2018. Convolutional 2D Knowledge Graph Embeddings. In *Proceedings of the AAAI Conference on Artificial Intelligence (AAAI)*, pages 1811–1818.

Bradley Efron. 1992. Bootstrap Methods: Another Look at the Jackknife. In *Breakthroughs in Statistics*, pages 569–593. Springer.

Kawin Ethayarajh and Dan Jurafsky. 2020. Utility is in the Eye of the User: A Critique of NLP Leaderboards. In *Proceedings of the Conference on Empirical Methods in Natural Language Processing (EMNLP)*, pages 4846–4853.

Niklas Friedrich, Kiril Gashteovski, Mingying Yu, Bhushan Kotnis, Caroline Lawrence, Mathias Niepert, and Goran Glavaš. 2022. AnnIE: An Annotation Platform for Constructing Complete Open Information Extraction Benchmark. In *Proceedings of the Annual Meeting on Association for Computational Linguistics (ACL): System Demonstrations*, page 44–60.

Aldo Gangemi, Andrea Giovanni Nuzzolese, Valentina Presutti, Francesco Draicchio, Alberto Musetti, and Paolo Ciancarini. 2012. Automatic Typing of DBpedia Entities. In *Proceedings of the International Semantc Web Conference (ISWC)*, pages 65–81.

Kiril Gashteovski, Mingying Yu, Bhushan Kotnis, Carolin Lawrence, Mathias Niepert, and Goran Glavaš. 2022. BenchIE: A Framework for Multi-Faceted Fact-Based Open Information Extraction Evaluation. In *Proceedings of the Annual Meeting of the Association for Computational Linguistics (ACL)*, pages 4472–4490.

Filip Ilievski, Daniel Garijo, Hans Chalupsky, Naren Teja Divvala, Yixiang Yao, Craig Rogers, Rongpeng Li, Jun Liu, Amandeep Singh, Daniel Schwabe, et al. 2020. KGTK: A Toolkit for Large Knowledge Graph Manipulation and Analysis. In *International Semantic Web Conference (ISWC)*, pages 278–293. Springer.

Rudolf Kadlec, Ondrej Bajgar, and Jan Kleindienst. 2017. Knowledge Base Completion: Baselines Strike Back. In *Proceedings the Workshop on Representation Learning for NLP (Rep4NLP@ACL)*, page 69–74.

Douwe Kiela, Max Bartolo, Yixin Nie, Divyansh Kaushik, Atticus Geiger, Zhengxuan Wu, Bertie Vidgen, Grusha Prasad, Amanpreet Singh, Pratik Ringshia, Zhiyi Ma, Tristan Thrush, Sebastian Riedel, Zeerak Waseem, Pontus Stenetorp, Robin Jia, Mohit Bansal, Christopher Potts, and Adina Williams. 2021. Dynabench: Rethinking Benchmarking in NLP. In

Proceedings of the Conference of the North American Chapter of the Association for Computational Linguistics: Human Language Technologies (NAACL-HLT), pages 4110–4124.

Bhushan Kotnis, Kiril Gashteovski, Julia Gastinger, Giuseppe Serra, Francesco Alesiani, Timo Sztyler, Ammar Shaker, Na Gong, Carolin Lawrence, and Zhao Xu. 2022a. Human-Centric Research for NLP: Towards a Definition and Guiding Questions. *arXiv preprint arXiv:2207.04447*.

Bhushan Kotnis, Kiril Gashteovski, Daniel Rubio, Ammar Shaker, Vanesa Rodriguez-Tembras, Makoto Takamoto, Mathias Niepert, and Carolin Lawrence. 2022b. MILIE: Modular & Iterative Multilingual Open Information Extraction. In *Proceedings of the Annual Meeting of the Association for Computational Linguistics (ACL)*, pages 6939–6950.

Danh Le-Phuoc, Hoan Nguyen Mau Quoc, Hung Ngo Quoc, Tuan Tran Nhat, and Manfred Hauswirth. 2016. The Graph of Things: A Step Towards the Live Knowledge Graph of Connected Things. *Journal of Web Semantics*, 37:25–35.

Pengfei Liu, Jinlan Fu, Yang Xiao, Weizhe Yuan, Shuaicheng Chang, Junqi Dai, Yixin Liu, Zihuiwen Ye, and Graham Neubig. 2021. ExplainaBoard: An Explainable Leaderboard for NLP. In *Proceedings of the Annual Meeting on Association for Computational Linguistics (ACL): System Demonstrations*, pages 280—-289.

Robert IV L. Logan, Nelson F. Liu, Matthew E. Peters, Matt Gardner, and Sameer Singh. 2019. Barack's Wife Hillary: Using Knowledge Graphs for Fact-Aware Language Modeling. In *Procesings of the Annual Meeting on Association for Computational Linguistics (ACL)*, page 5962–5971.

Christopher Malon, Kai Li, and Erik Kruus. 2022. Fast few-shot debugging for NLU test suites. In *Proceedings of Deep Learning Inside Out (DeeLIO 2022): The 3rd Workshop on Knowledge Extraction and Integration for Deep Learning Architectures*, pages 79–86. Association for Computational Linguistics.

Christian Meilicke, Manuel Fink, Yanjie Wang, Daniel Ruffinelli, Rainer Gemulla, and Heiner Stuckenschmidt. 2018. Fine-grained Evaluation of Rule-and Embedding-Based Systems for Knowledge Graph Completion. In *Proceedings of the International Semantic Web Conference (ISWC)*, pages 3–20.

George A. Miller. 1992. WordNet: A Lexical Database for English. *Communications of the ACM*, 38:39–41.

Pasquale Minervini, Claudia d'Amato, Nicola Fanizzi, and Floriana Esposito. 2015. Efficient learning of entity and predicate embeddings for link prediction in knowledge graphs. In *Proceedings of the International Workshop on Uncertainty Reasoning for the Semantic Web (URSW@ISWC)*, volume 1479 of *CEUR Workshop Proceedings*, pages 26–37.

Aisha Mohamed, Shameem Parambath, Zoi Kaoudi, and Ashraf Aboulnaga. 2020. Popularity Agnostic Evaluation of Knowledge Graph Embeddings. In *Conference on Uncertainty in Artificial Intelligence (UAI)*, pages 1059–1068.

Shinichi Nakagawa and Innes C Cuthill. 2007. Effect size, confidence interval and statistical significance: A practical guide for biologists. *Biological reviews*, 82(4):591–605.

Avanika Narayan, Piero Molino, Karan Goel, Willie Neiswanger, and Christopher Re. 2021. Personalized Benchmarking with the Ludwig Benchmarking Toolkit. In *Proceedings of the Conference on Neural Information Processing Systems (NeurIPS)*.

Maximilian Nickel, Volker Tresp, and Hans-Peter Kriegel. 2011. A Three-Way Model for Collective Learning on Multi-Relational Data. In *Proceedings of the International Conference on Machine Learning (ICML)*, pages 809–816.

Matteo Palmonari and Pasquale Minervini. 2020. Knowledge Graph Embeddings and Explainable AI. *Knowledge Graphs for Explainable Artificial Intelligence: Foundations, Applications and Challenges*, 47:49.

Yanhui Peng and Jing Zhang. 2020. LineaRE: Simple but Powerful Knowledge Graph Embedding for Link Prediction. In *IEEE International Conference on Data Mining (ICDM)*, pages 422–431. IEEE.

Priya Radhakrishnan, Partha Talukdar, and Vasudeva Varma. 2018. ELDEN: Improved Entity Linking Using Densified Knowledge Graphs. In *Proceedings of the Conference of the North American Chapter of the Association for Computational Linguistics: Human Language Technologies (NAACL-HLT)*, pages 1844–1853.

Thomas Rebele, Fabian Suchanek, Johannes Hoffart, Joanna Biega, Erdal Kuzey, and Gerhard Weikum. 2016. YAGO: A Multilingual Knowledge Base from Wikipedia, WordNet, and GeoNames. In *Proceedings of the International Semantic Web Conference (ISWC)*, pages 177–185. Springer.

Marco Tulio Ribeiro, Tongshuang Sherry Wu, Carlos Guestrin, and Sameer Singh. 2020. Beyond Accuracy: Behavioral Testing of NLP Models with CheckList. In *Proceedings of the Annual Meeting of the Association for Computational Linguistics (ACL)*, page 4902–4912.

Wiem Ben Rim, Carolin Lawrence, Kiril Gashteovski, Mathias Niepert, and Naoaki Okazaki. 2021. Behavioral Testing of Knowledge Graph Embedding Models for Link Prediction. In *Proceedings of the Conference on Automated Knowledge Base Construction (AKBC)*.

Daniel Ruffinelli, Samuel Broscheit, and Rainer Gemulla. 2020. You CAN Teach an Old Dog New Tricks! On Training Knowledge Graph Embeddings.

In *Proceedings of the International Conference on Learning Representations (ICLR)*.

Tara Safavi and Danai Koutra. 2020. CoDEx: A Comprehensive Knowledge Graph Completion Benchmark. In *Proceedings of the 2020 Conference on Empirical Methods in Natural Language Processing (EMNLP)*, page 8328–8350.

Apoorv Saxena, Adrian Kochsiek, and Rainer Gemulla. 2022. Sequence-to-Sequence Knowledge Graph Completion and Question Answering. In *Proceedings of the Annual Meeting of the Association for Computational Linguistics (ACL)*, page 2814–2828.

Zhiqing Sun, Zhi-Hong Deng, Jian-Yun Nie, and Jian Tang. 2019. RotatE: Knowledge Graph Embedding by Relational Rotation in Complex Space. In *Proceedings of the International Conference on Learning Representations (ICLR)*.

Zhiqing Sun, Shikhar Vashishth, Soumya Sanyal, Partha Talukdar, and Yiming Yang. 2020. A Re-evaluation of Knowledge Graph Completion Methods. In *Proceedings of the Annual Meeting of the Association for Computational Linguistics (ACL)*, page 5516–5522.

Tristan Thrush, K. N. Bharadwaj Tirumala, Anmol Gupta, Max Bartolo, Pedro Rodriguez, Tariq Kane, William Gaviria Rojas, Peter Mattson, Adina Williams, and Douwe Kiela. 2022. Dynatask: A Framework for Creating Dynamic AI Benchmark Tasks. In *Proceedings of the Annual Meeting of the Association for Computational Linguistics (ACL): System Demonstrations*, pages 174–181.

Kristina Toutanova and Danqi Chen. 2015. Observed versus Latent Features for Knowledge Base and Text Inference. In *Proceedings of the Workshop on Continuous Vector Space Models and their Compositionality@ACL*, pages 57–66.

Théo Trouillon, Johannes Welbl, Sebastian Riedel, Éric Gaussier, and Guillaume Bouchard. 2016. Complex Embeddings for Simple Link Prediction. In *Proceedings of the International Conference on Machine Learning (ICML)*, pages 2071–2080.

Denny Vrandečić and Markus Krötzsch. 2014. Wikidata: A free collaborative knowledgebase. *Communications of the ACM*, 57(10):78–85.

Yanjie Wang, Daniel Ruffinelli, Rainer Gemulla, Samuel Broscheit, and Christian Meilicke. 2019. On Evaluating Embedding Models for Knowledge Base Completion. In *Proceedings of the Workshop on Representation Learning for NLP (RepL4NLP@ACL)*, page 104–112.

Zhen Wang, Jianwen Zhang, Jianlin Feng, and Zheng Chen. 2014. Knowledge Graph Embedding by Translating on Hyperplanes. In *Proceedings of the AAAI Conference on Artificial Intelligence (AAAI)*, pages 1112–1119.

Gerhard Weikum, Xin Luna Dong, Simon Razniewski, Fabian Suchanek, et al. 2021. Machine Knowledge: Creation and Curation of Comprehensive Knowledge Bases. *Foundations and Trends® in Databases*, 10(2-4):108–490.

Yang Xiao, Jinlan Fu, Weizhe Yuan, Vijay Viswanathan, Zhoumianze Liu, Yixin Liu, Graham Neubig, and Pengfei Liu. 2022. DataLab: A Platform for Data Analysis and Intervention. In *Proceedings of the 60th Annual Meeting of the Association for Computational Linguistics (ACL): System Demonstrations*, page 182–195.

Bishan Yang, Wen-tau Yih, Xiaodong He, Jianfeng Gao, and Li Deng. 2015. Embedding Entities and Relations for Learning and Inference in Knowledge Bases. In *Proceedings of the International Conference on Learning Representations (ICLR)*.

Zhanqiu Zhang, Jianyu Cai, Yongdong Zhang, and Jie Wang. 2020. Learning Hierarchy-aware Knowledge Graph Embeddings for Link Prediction. In *Proceedings of the AAAI Conference on Artificial Intelligence (AAAI)*, pages 3065–3072.

Appendix

A Discussion on Related Work

A.1 Evaluation of NLP Models

Recent work in NLP has pointed to the problems of using single-score metrics (Ethayarajh and Jurafsky, 2020; Narayan et al., 2021; Bowman and Dahl, 2021; Kotnis et al., 2022a). In particular, such single-score metric evaluations do not expose the data-centric properties that were not learned by the models (e.g., problems with learning named entities that span across multiple tokens). In NLP, such issues are tackled by proposing multifaceted and/or explainable leaderboards and benchmarks (Liu et al., 2021; Gashteovski et al., 2022; Friedrich et al., 2022; Kotnis et al., 2022b; Xiao et al., 2022; Kiela et al., 2021; Thrush et al., 2022). To the best of our knowledge, there is no prior work that proposes such multi-faceted leaderboards for KG completion models.

A.2 Evaluation of KGC Models

KGC Benchmarks. Prior work has shown that learning latent representations—i.e., KG Embeddings (KGEs)—for the entities and relations is highly beneficial for tackling KGC tasks (Minervini et al., 2015; Ruffinelli et al., 2020). Researchers have evaluates the effects of hyperparameters (and different training strategies) of KGE models for link prediction. In particular, Kadlec et al. (2017) studied the effects of different training objectives on the DistMult model (Yang et al., 2015) and found that using the cross entropy loss function is a better alternative to the binary cross entropy. Ruffinelli et al. (2020) performed a systematic study on many KGE models with the LibKGE framework (Broscheit et al., 2020) and found that training components make a huge difference in model performance. Safavi and Koutra (2020) proposed a more data-centric benchmark (CoDEx), which improves upon previous benchmarks by proposing additional datasets extracted from Wikidata (Vrandečić and Krötzsch, 2014) and then using them to improve current KGE models. Sun et al. (2020) proposed an evaluation framework such that it breaks ties of same-score answers according to different strategies. PyKEEN (Ali et al., 2021) is another KGE framework and benchmark, which facilitates the training and evaluation of KGE models for KG completion tasks across a variety of datasets. Although highly useful for overall evaluation, none of these frameworks provide fine-grained evaluation of KGE models, nor an interactive interface for such evaluation.

Metrics. Other line of work focused on proposing different metrics for exposing different problems within the KGE models (Wang et al., 2019), though these metrics are averaged scores over the entire test set and do not provide additional insights about where the models make mistakes. Prior work has shown that the standard averaged evaluation metrics hits@k and MRR favor popular entities and relations (Mohamed et al., 2020). Contrary to such approaches, KGxBoard operates across the standard metrics (hits@k, MRR and MR), but in addition it supports highly customized fine-grained analysis and interactive interface.

Studying Specific Properties. Other line of work targets specific properties of the models, i.e., evaluating if a set of KGE models learned some specific properties. For example, relation symmetry is a property that has been extensively studied in the literature (Trouillon et al., 2016; Sun et al., 2019; Peng and Zhang, 2020; Zhang et al., 2020; Wang et al., 2014). Other line of work investigated other properties, such as entity type hierarchy (Rim et al., 2021; Zhang et al., 2020), (inverse) equivalence (Meilicke et al., 2018), subsumption (Meilicke et al., 2018), relation and entity frequency (Mohamed et al., 2020) and entity distribution (Bordes et al., 2013).

KG Analyzers. Recently, there were proposals for systems that analyse already constructed KGs (Ilievski et al., 2020). Such work, however, does not cover the evaluation of KGC models, it only covers analysis of already existing KGs.

B Details on Built-in Features

KGxBoard comes with built-in features that bucketize the data automatically. Some of the built-in features in KGxBoard are dataset-specific, while others are dataset-agnostic.

- Length of head/tail entity: the number of tokens in the head/tail entity (dataset-agnostic).
- Frequency of head/tail entity: the frequency of tail entity in the training set (dataset-agnostic).
- Frequency of the predicate: the frequency of the predicate in the training set (dataset-agnostic).
- Symmetry of relation: the symmetry of entity relations (dataset-specific; for now KGxBoard

supports FB15K-237).

- Entity type level: the most specific (highest) entity type level of true tail entity (dataset-specific, for now we support FB15K-237). In particular, we mapped each Freebase entity to its DBpedia (Auer et al., 2007) counterpart, and then used DBpedia's type information (Gangemi et al., 2012) in order to determine the most specific type level that is available in the data; e.g., if we have information *(Barack Obama; type; Person)* and *(Barack Obama; type; Politician)*, we use the latter because it is more specific.

C Details on Customized Buckets

To provide more fine-grained analysis that goes beyond the built-in features for bucketization, as well as to showcase the ability of KGxBoard to handle customized buckets, we partition the test data into buckets, based on the following customized features:

Buckets by relations. Each data point is placed in a bucket according to its relation. For example, the triples *(England; /location/location/contains; Lancaster)* and *(Los Angeles; /location/location/-contains; Beverly Hills)* are placed in the same bucket because they have the same relation. This bucketization is dataset-agnostic and we used it for both FB15K-237 and WN18RR.

Buckets by relation types 1-1, 1-M, M-1 or M-M. Following Bordes et al. (2013), we partition the data into four possible buckets according to their relation properties: 1-to-1 (1-1), 1-to-many (1-M), many-to-1 (M-1) and many-to-many (M-M). According to this definition, each relation has a property on how many entities it can have as a head or tail. For example, the relation *isAuthorOfBook* is 1-M relation (because one author can be the author of several books) and the relation *sportsTeamLocation* is 1-1 relation (because one sports team can have only one home location).

Tail entity type (level 1). The entity type (level 1, as described by Rim et al. (2021)) of the gold entity that needs to be predicted. This customized feature is specific for FB15K-237 and not for WN18RR. In particular, we leverage similar approach as with the built-in entity type level feature (described in Appendix B): we mapped each Freebase entity to its DBpeda counter part and then used DBpedia's type information to determine the type at level 1 of the entity type hierarchy.

Tail entity type (level 2). The entity type (level 2, as described by Rim et al. (2021)) of the gold entity that needs to be predicted. As with the previous customized feature, this customized feature is specific for FB15K-237 and not for WN18RR.

Relation's symmetry (for WN18RR). In Appendix B, we described KGxBoard's built-in feature that bucketizes the data into symmetric and asymmetric relations for the FB15K-237 dataset. This feature, however, is not natively supported by KGxBoard for the WN18RR dataset. For WN18RR, we followed Rim et al. (2021) and (1) got a set of all unique relations from WN18RR; (2) manually defined which relation is symmetric and which one is not. Then, we assigned a bucket (symmetric or asymmetric) to each data point in the test set.

D Training Details for PyKEEN and LibKGE

PyKEEN provides hyperparameters to reproduce the results of the original work of a given model, which we used to train RotatE, ConvE, TuckER, TransE and Rescal on both WN18RR and FB15K237 datasets. After training TransE, the hyperparameters for WN18RR returned a very low MRR result indicating that it failed to train for the task, and for DistMult, no configuration files corresponding to the above-mentioned datasets were provided. In such cases, we used insights from LibKGE (Ruffinelli et al., 2020) to train the models with PyKEEN to the best of our abilities; to implement the same models in the two frameworks, we match some parameters such as the number of epochs, embedding dimensions, initializer function, optimizer and learning rate arguments, including the scheduler and its parameters. However, the hyperparameters of a KGE model on the mentioned frameworks are not matched one-to-one. LibKGE allows the user to set both the initializer of the relation and entity embeddings along with setting the lookup embedder weight, patience, regularizer, dropout. In contrast, PyKEEN only allows the naming of the initializer function. Moreover, while negative sampling is possible in both frameworks, PyKEEN allows setting the negative sampler function that describes how to generate corrupt triples for training and allows the setting of negatives per positive triples as well as the filtering and corruption scheme, where LibKGE allows the previous as well as adding the number of samples for each head, relation, object. We expect that these differences in implementation and hyperparameters will have an impact on the results seen on KGcBoard. We provide the used hyperparameters and trained models with our code.

It is worth noting that PyKEEN does provide configurations for the same models with optimized parameters, but since the MRR and Hits@k results of these models are outperformed by the LibKGE models, we chose to make this comparison to both feature the difference in hyperparameters as well as the framework implementation in our experiments. For the models trained on LibKGE, we used the pretrained models obtained by Ruffinelli et al. (2020) as a result of hyperparameter optimization using LibKGE (Broscheit et al., 2020).

E Detailed Results for Bucketized Comparison of Models

In these experiments, we showcase how the users can use KGxBoard in order to compare one model trained on multiple hyperparameter settings. As explained in Section 5.3, on the one hand, we trained each model with the hyperparameters that aim to reproduce the work of the original papers (dubbed ORIGHP-MODEL); on the other hand we used pretrained models that use a hyperparameter optimization pipeline that ensures improved overall results (dubbed OPTIMHP-MODEL). Each model trained with the ORIGHP hyperparameter settings was trained with PyKEEN, by using the hyperparameters combination that aims to reproduce the results from the original papers and was proposed in PyKEEN's documentation. Each model trained with the OPTIMHP hyperparameter settings was trained with LibKGE, by using the hyperparameter combination proposed by Ruffinelli et al. (2020). The results are summarized in Table 3.

While the OPTIMHP models always outperform their ORIGHP counterparts in both FB15K-237 and WN18RR datasets, we still observed many cases where the ranking of the models flipped on some buckets. For example, OPTIMHP-CONVE on FB15K-237 performs better than ORIGHP-CONVE on the overall score, as well as on 88% of all the buckets. However, ORIGHP-CONVE performs better than OPTIMHP-CONVE for several buckets, including (1) the FB15K-237 triples with relation between award ceremony and award winner; (2) FB15K-237 triples whose tail entity types are of type "musical work". In a more extreme case for FB15K-237, when we compared OPTIMHP-TRANSE with ORIGHP-TRANSE, the optimized OPTIMHP-TRANSE is ranked as 1st on the overall score and in 98% of the buckets (this is to be expected, given that the difference in the overall score is 23 percentage points). Yet, in 2% of the buckets (4 buckets in total), ORIGHP-TRANSE is ranked as 1st.

Model	Overall rank (OPTIMHP / ORIGHP)	MRR score	$b^{=}$	$b^{\neq}$
	FB15K-237			
ConvE	1 / 2	0.44 / 0.39	0.88	0.12
Rescal	1 / 2	0.45 / 0.38	0.83	0.17
DistMult	1 / 2	0.44 / 0.31	0.91	0.09
TransE	1 / 2	0.42 / 0.19	0.98	0.02
	WN18RR			
ConvE	1 / 2	0.46 / 0.28	1.00	0.00
Rescal	1 / 2	0.48 / 0.29	1.00	0.00
DistMult	1 / 2	0.48 / 0.27	1.00	0.00
TransE	1 / 2	0.24 / 0.13	0.91	0.09

Table 3: Comparison of KGC models trained with different hyperparameter settings. The shown results compare each model between its OPTIMHP and ORIGHP hyperparameter settings. The models trained with OPTIMHP are trained with hyperparameter optimization pipeline that ensures improved overall results. The models trained with ORIGHP use hyperparamter settings that aim to replicate the results from the original papers. 1 in *Overall rank* indicates better rank. The models were trained and tested on the FB15K-237 and WN18RR datasets. $b^{=}/b^{\neq}$ indicates the fraction of buckets where the overall rank is equivalent/not equivalent as the bucket's rank.

F Detailed Results for Debugging

Table 4 shows debugging results for ConvE, Tucker, RotatE, and Rescal. In all cases, naive debugging improves Hits@1 on the held-out test debugging examples, and in-danger debugging often yields a further improvement. In cases where debugging Hits@5 and Hits@10 were high to begin with, debugging sometimes worsens these metrics, because most of the debugging examples will be teaching the model to swap the order of examples already in the top 5 or 10, rather than bring something new into the top 5 or 10 hits.

Only on ConvE does the naive method reduce original Hits@1 by more than 1%. This impact is possible because ConvE (and Tucker) have interaction parameters that can affect other relations, where RotatE and Rescal have only relation and entity embeddings, so that the debugging affects only

Model / relation	Hits@1	Hits@5	Hits@10	MR	MRR
ConvE/dated					
			Debugging test		
Before debugging	.0000	.9062	1.0000	3.3125	.3556
Naive	.0625	.3125	.5312	11.7188	.1863
In-danger	.1562	.7812	.9688	3.9688	.3943
			Original test		
Before debugging	.2710	.4734	.5690	186.0528	.3677
Naive	.2416	.4464	.5433	237.9980	.3402
In-danger	.2574	.4614	.5595	203.3516	.3546
Tucker/adjoins					
			Debugging test		
Before debugging	.0000	.8542	.9583	3.7708	.3895
Naive	.1875	.8542	.9167	5.0208	.4749
In-danger	.2083	.8333	.9167	6.7917	.4678
			Original test		
Before debugging	.3108	.5396	.6283	106.4038	.4171
Naive	.3010	.5262	.6162	126.6328	.4055
In-danger	.3004	.5232	.6140	119.0497	.4041
RotatE/friendship					
			Debugging test		
Before debugging	.0000	.0000	.0000	41.0465	.0419
Naive	.0465	.1860	.4302	18.9651	.1493
In-danger	.0465	.1860	.4535	21.2791	.1468
			Original test		
Before debugging	.2627	.4605	.5432	346.0619	.3554
Naive	.2627	.4605	.5432	345.7814	.3554
In-danger	.2627	.4605	.5432	345.8078	.3554
Rescal/adjoins					
			Debugging test		
Before debugging	.0000	.7761	.9030	5.5597	.3385
Naive	.1642	.7313	.8507	9.2687	.4038
In-danger	.2015	.6716	.8060	9.1194	.4040
			Original test		
Before debugging	.2596	.4665	.5562	295.5532	.3574
Naive	.2594	.4665	.5560	295.6199	.3573
In-danger	.2594	.4665	.5560	295.7509	.3573

Table 4: Debugging results for the relations with most symmetry violations.

the relation being debugged. On ConvE, the in-danger method reduces original Hits@1, 5, and 10 by about half as much as the naive method, while significantly improving all metrics on the debugging set. For the other models, the naive method can achieve simple and effective debugging.

FALTE: A Toolkit for Fine-grained Annotation for Long Text Evaluation

Tanya Goyal[1] **Junyi Jessy Li**[2] **Greg Durrett**[1]
[1] Department of Computer Science [2] Department of Linguistics
The University of Texas at Austin
tanyagoyal@utexas.edu

Abstract

A growing swath of NLP research is tackling problems related to generating long text, including tasks such as open-ended story generation, summarization, dialogue, and more. However, we currently lack appropriate tools to evaluate these long outputs of generation models: classic automatic metrics such as ROUGE have been shown to perform poorly, and newer learned metrics do not necessarily work well for all tasks and domains of text. Human rating and error analysis remain a crucial component for any evaluation of long text generation. In this paper, we introduce FALTE, a web-based annotation toolkit designed to streamline such evaluations. Our tool allows researchers to collect fine-grained judgments of text quality from crowdworkers using an error taxonomy specific to the downstream task. Using the task interface, annotators can select and assign error labels to text span selections in an incremental paragraph-level annotation workflow. The latter functionality is designed to simplify the document-level task into smaller units and reduce cognitive load on the annotators. Our tool has previously been used to run a large-scale annotation study that evaluates the coherence of long generated summaries, demonstrating its utility.

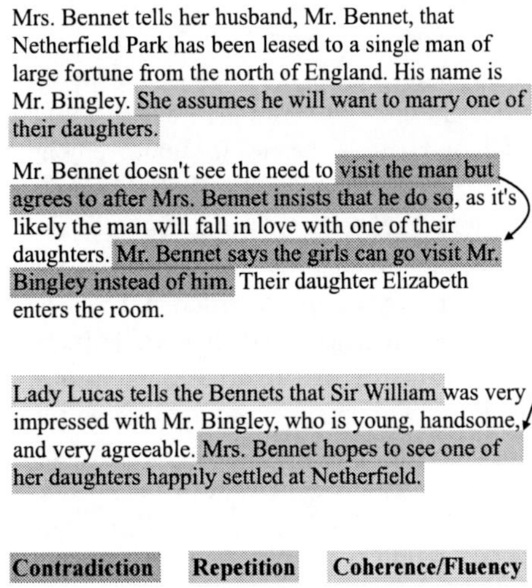

Figure 1: An example of fine-grained annotation using FALTE. A single annotation consists of a text span highlighted by a crowdworker and an error category attached to it. FALTE allows task designers to define their own error taxonomy. Error categories in this taxonomy, e.g. contradiction and repetition in the above example, can be modified to require two associated text spans.

1 Introduction

Recent years have seen a significant improvement in the generation capabilities of large language models (Lewis et al., 2020; Zhang et al., 2020; Brown et al., 2020), across tasks such as machine translation, open-ended story generation, summarization, and others. As these models generate extremely fluent and human-like text, their errors are more subtle than those of prior models and harder to detect (Clark et al., 2021). Overlap-based automatic metrics such as ROUGE (Lin, 2004), BLEU (Papineni et al., 2002), and BERTScore (Zhang et al., 2019) have historically been the most popular metrics used to evaluate the outputs of such generation models. However, recent work has shown that these are unreliable measures of quality (Fabbri et al., 2021), especially for longer text and more open-ended tasks that can have multiple reasonable answers (Wang et al., 2022).

For generation tasks, human evaluation of outputs is generally considered to be the gold standard. Such evaluations are primarily conducted using untrained annotators recruited through crowdsourcing platforms like Mechanical Turk[1] and Upwork.[2] However, even deploying human evaluators for a task is not a straightforward solution. Recent work (Karpinska et al., 2021; Clark et al., 2021) showed that untrained human crowdworkers fail to reliably

[1] https://www.mturk.com/
[2] https://www.upwork.com

Proceedings of the The 2022 Conference on Empirical Methods in Natural Language Processing: System Demonstrations, pages 351 - 358
December 7-11, 2022

distinguish human-written and model-written outputs for strong language models like GPT-3 (Brown et al., 2020), focusing on task designs where annotators are asked to evaluate the generated outputs holistically. To address these limitations, Dou et al. (2022) recommend **fine-grained evaluation** of text quality that is more successful at eliciting quality annotations from untrained crowdworkers. Instead of holistically rating the quality of the whole generated output, they instead ask annotators to identify text spans that correspond to errors from a predefined taxonomy. Moreover, human evaluation conducted using such fine-grained annotations also provides insights into error distributions of current models and reveals avenues for improvement. Figure 1 shows an example of fine-grained annotations at the span-level collected using our tool - FALTE; this is similar to the prior work.

In this paper, we are interested in the evaluation of long text. Human evaluation practices from short text evaluation studies (e.g. paragraph-level text from (Dou et al., 2022)), are not feasible for long text evaluation scenarios (Akoury et al., 2020). In fact, a majority of recent work on long text evaluation, e.g. evaluation of long generated summaries (Mao et al., 2022; Zhang et al., 2022), does not conduct any human evaluation, possibly due to the the difficulty in getting high-quality annotations from crowd workers for long texts. In this paper, we introduce FALTE (**F**ine-grained **A**nnotation for **L**ong **T**ext **E**valuation), a web-based annotation tool to address this gap. Our tool is designed to allow for fine-grained evaluation while also simplifying the long text annotation task through the design of the UI and task workflow. To achieve these goals, FALTE is centered around the following main functionality:

- **Fine-grained annotations:** Prior generation quality evaluation has primarily focused on collecting document-level labels along multiple dimensions, such as fluency, grammar, etc. In this work, we ask annotators to select specific text spans that exhibit errors in a particular error taxonomy, allowing for a more nuanced evaluation of model errors.

- **Decomposing the document-level task into smaller sub-tasks:** FALTE decomposes the overall document-level task into paragraph-level annotation tasks to simplify the user interface and reduce the cognitive load for the crowd workers. This is motivated by prior research in crowdsourcing (Mayer and Moreno, 2003; Kapelner and Chandler, 2010; Hauser et al., 2019) that shows that incrementally introducing texts motivate workers to pay more attention to all units of the task text. We allow task designers to set this granularity of annotation. FALTE also provides tools to crowd workers to easily navigate back and forth between paragraphs.

- **Flexibility over error definitions:** Finally, we refrain from setting a fixed error taxonomy to support annotation studies along different quality dimensions. Even within the same dimension, researchers may wish to opt for a different error taxonomy across different languages or datasets. Therefore, we allow them to define their own set of categories for annotation that aligns with their specific use case. We also allow them to pre-define if each error category must be associated with one or two text spans during annotation.

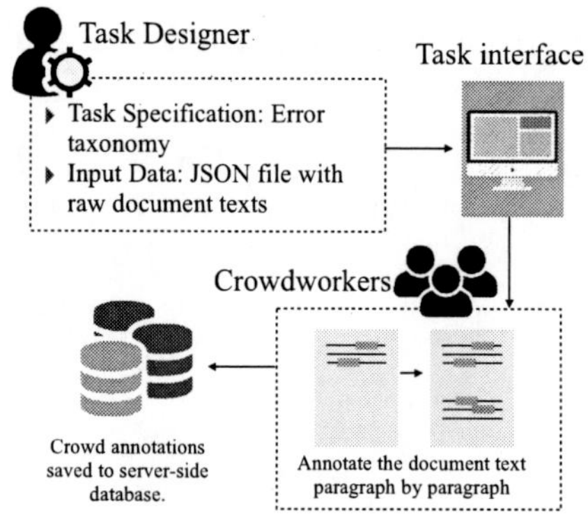

Figure 2: Overall Workflow

Figure 1 shows an example of fine-grained annotations that can be collected using FALTE. Each error in the collected annotations is associated with a corresponding text span; this helps in pinpointing exactly where the error occurred and support further downstream analysis. Note that each error in the error taxonomy can additionally be modified to require two associated text spans, to support error categories like repetition and contradiction.

2 FALTE Tool Description

FALTE is a web-based annotation toolkit designed to help researchers run large-scale annotation studies evaluating the quality of model generated text. The dataset collected through FALTE has the following form: annotators highlight errors $e \in E$ in a given document d where each annotation e consists of a text span $t \in d$ and corresponding error category c. Annotators incrementally proceed through the document and annotate as many errors as they can identify in the text. In this section, we will outline the workflow for the two stakeholders: 1) **task designers (researchers)** that employ the tool to run these studies, and 2) **crowd annotators** that interact with our web interface and provide annotations for the quality of long text. The overall workflow is outlined in Figure 2.

2.1 Task Designer Workflow

FALTE is designed to be flexible across different long document annotation tasks, for both data collection and evaluation use cases. Here, we describe the different action items for the task designers to create the annotation website and launch a study.

Define the error taxonomy In order to support annotation studies across a variety of quality dimensions and tasks, we allow task designers to define their own error taxonomy. FALTE supports an arbitrary number of error classes.

For each category defined, task designers additionally classify these as either *singleton* or *paired*. For the *singleton* errors, each crowd annotation corresponds to a pair of text span and an error category (as shown in Figure 1). For *paired*, each annotation is a tuple containing two text spans and the error category. This latter functionality was introduced to cover error types such as *repetition errors* which are naturally defined between pairs of text spans. Note that although the tool does not support error annotations with more than two text spans, these use cases can be tackled within FALTE's framework by creating chains of paired error annotations.

To specify their error categories and their specifications, researchers simply edit a configuration file. The contents of these configuration files are then reflected on the task interface when the web application is launched.

Define the annotation granularity Our annotation tool is aimed at collecting annotations for long machine generated text, say ~30-40 sentences or longer, although it can be deployed in shorter settings as well. To simplify this document level annotation task, we allow task designers to decompose the annotation workflow into iterative paragraph level annotation tasks. Note that paragraph here can be defined to correspond to segments of text of any length. In this paper and the demo, we use the terms segment and paragraph interchangeably.

Under this setting, initially the crowd annotators are only shown the first paragraph (or other specified unit of text) for annotation. Once annotation for that paragraph is completed, workers can proceed to subsequent paragraphs with the option to navigate back. We will discuss this in more detail in Section 2.2.

The FALTE tool expects a JSON file with containing all of the text to be annotated as input. Each document in this JSON is represented by a List of Strings; each list item represents a paragraph. Therefore, task designers can control the length of the annotation unit (paragraph) for each document individually through this input file.

Setting up and launching the crowd annotation study Our tool accepts the above task specifications and generates all relevant client and server side code. The task designer can then launch their annotation website using their preferred cloud platform; we host our example demo website using Heroku[3] at `https://coherence-annotation-summaries.herokuapp.com/id=oai1`. After the task annotation website is live, task designers can recruit crowd annotators and collect annotations for text quality.

2.2 Crowd Annotator Workflow

As previously mentioned, each worker starts the annotation process with the first paragraph of the text and incrementally annotates succeeding paragraphs.

Figure 3 shows the task interface and outlines the annotation steps for annotating a single text span in the *Current Paragraph* box, after annotations have already been completed for paragraphs in the *Context* box. The stepwise workflow is:

1. **Highlight span containing error:** First, the worker selects the text span in the *Current Paragraph* containing the error using the click-and-drag motion. The highlighted text will automatically populate in the relevant text box at the bottom.

2. **Choose error type:** Next, the worker chooses an error type or label for the highlighted text.

[3]`https://www.heroku.com/`

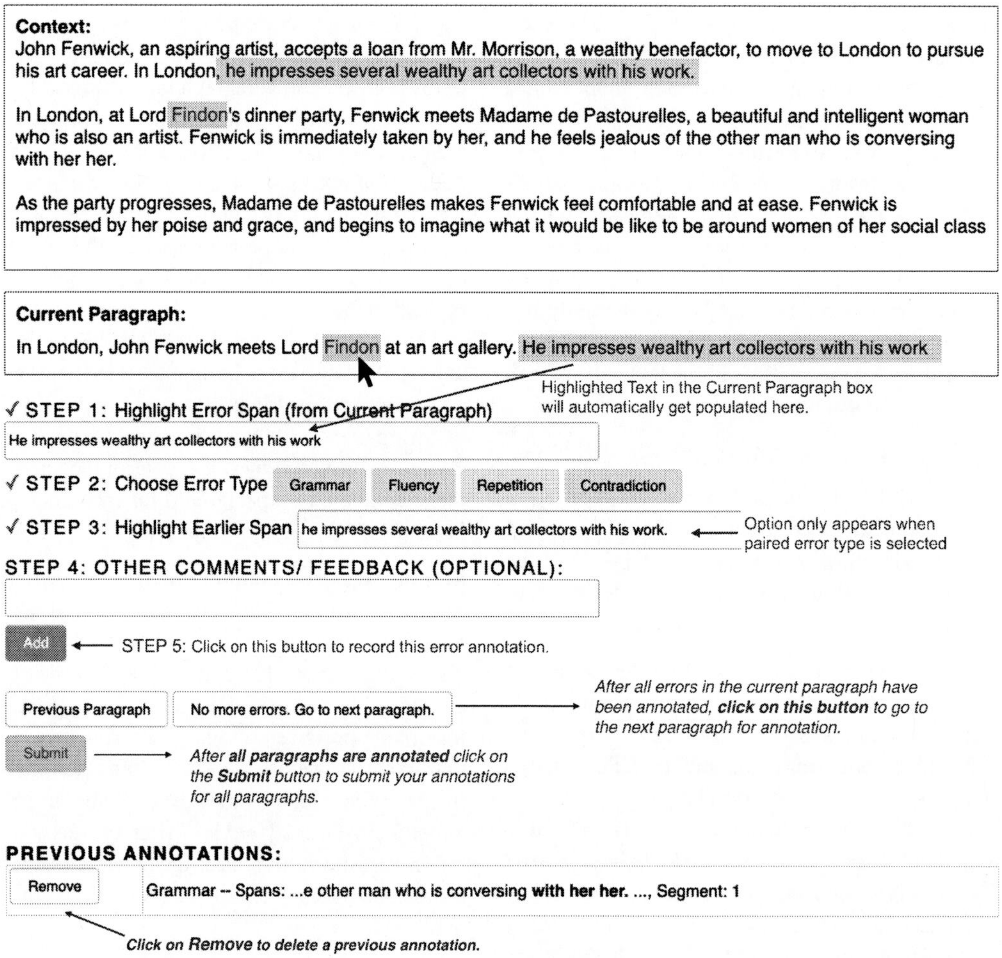

Figure 3: Annotation interface and workflow for a crowd annotator to annotate a single text span. The interface displays the previously annotated paragraphs in the *Context* box. The previous annotations are displayed at the bottom of the web page. At this stage of the task, the crowdworker annotates errors in the *Current Paragraph*. To aid their annotation, crowdworkers can hover over named entities to highlight other instances of the entity (in gray).

Note that Figure 3 currently shows placeholder error types; the actual task interface will list the error types defined by the task designer in the previous section.

3. **Highlight paired text:** If the error type selected in Step 2 is of type *paired*, the worker is further asked to select an additional text span. For our *repetition* error type, this additional span would be the first occurrence of the repeated information (as shown in Figure 3). The additional text span can be selected from either the *Context* box or the *Current Paragraph* box. This step is skipped if the worker selects a *singleton* error .

4. **Optional comments:** The annotation interface also provides the option of providing any additional free-text commentary for the annotated text span(s) and category tuple. In our experiments, we noticed that crowd workers tended to primarily use this option to convey their confidence about that particular span's annotation.

5. **Add annotation:** Finally, the worker clicks on the *Add* button to save error annotation. This will be instantly reflected in the *Previous Annotations* section at the bottom of the page.

The above procedure is repeated to annotate all errors in the *Current Paragraph*, after which the worker clicks on the *No more errors. Go to next paragraph* button to update both the *Context* and *Current Paragraph* boxes; the *Current Paragraph* will now reflect the next paragraph of the document text. Finally, after errors in all paragraphs of the document have been annotated, the worker clicks on the *Submit* button that stores their error annotations for the whole document in the server-side database.

Coreference Cues Since the annotation interface is designed for long documents, we found that being able to quickly find instances of entities was very helpful during our pilot studies. The scope of this functionality can be controlled by the researchers: in our pilot study (discussed in Section 3), this was only enabled for named entities using string match on names. Specifically, if the user hovers their cursor over any named entity mention in the *Current Paragraph* section, the tool also highlighted all other instances of that entity. Putting the cursor over *Findon* in the *Current Paragraph* highlights the other instance of the same character in Figure 3. It is equivalent to searching (CTRL+F) for the entity, but saves keystrokes.

Making Revisions Workers may make mistakes during the annotation process or simply change their mind about previously annotated errors. We provide tools to address this in the FALTE interface. The bottom of the web page displays the *Previous Annotations* section that lists all prior error annotations by the crowd worker. The worker can remove erroneously annotated error tuples from this table using the *Remove* buttons corresponding to each annotation.

Navigation Flexibility Furthermore, the interface also provides flexibility in navigating between the different paragraphs of the document text; workers can use the *Previous Paragraph* button to go back and annotate any missed errors in text spans.

This final annotation workflow and these additional functionalities were designed based on worker feedback in pilot studies. For example, the pilot study asked annotators to select the error type (step 2) before highlighting the text span (step 1). This order was reversed based on the preference of multiple crowdworkers.

2.3 Output Data

All error annotations displayed in the *Previous Annotation* section get stored on a database when the crowdworker clicks on the *Submit* button.

Each row in the database table corresponds to a single error annotation. Our tool logs in the following fields: Document ID (string), Paragraph ID (int), Text Span (string), Span Start Index (int), Span End Index (int), Error Category (string), Paired Text (string), Optional Comments (string). The latter two are optional fields that may be empty for some errors. We log the span start and end indices in addition to the text to disambiguate between multiple instances of the same text. Additionally, FALTE generates a unique session ID for each (document, annotator) pair to distinguish between the annotations of different crowdworkers for the same document.

2.4 System Implementation

FALTE is a web-based annotation framework that has been tested with Google Chrome, Mozilla Firefox, and Safari browsers. Currently, the crowd annotation is only supported on desktop browsers and not on mobile or other touchscreen devices. The client side interface is made using HTML5, CSS, and JavaScript. The sever side uses the Python-based web framework Flask[4] and the PostgresSQL database[5] to manage and store user annotations, both of which are open-sourced. Our example demo website is hosted here: `https://coherence-annotation-summaries.herokuapp.com/id=oai1`.[6]

3 Use Case

FALTE has been used to collect crowd annotations for one long document evaluation task: coherence evaluation of long model-generated summaries (Goyal et al., 2022). The annotation study was conducted for narrative summaries of books and movies. The study defined 7 different errors across two categories (1) coherence, and (2) language and fluency errors.

Table 1 outlines the statistics of the annotated dataset in the coherence study. The study was run for 160 summary documents. Each summary was an average of 36 sentences long, which is approximately 12 times the length of the most common use case in summarization research, that of evaluating news summaries. For each document, annotations

[4] `https://flask.palletsprojects.com/`

[5] `https://www.postgresql.org/`

[6] See `https://github.com/tagoyal/falte-tool` for the implementation of the tool.

Data Statistic	Count
Documents Annotated	160
Average Length (words)	480
Average Length (sentences)	36
Error Annotations Collected	9.6K
Crowd Annotators	12
Error Categories	7
Singleton	5
Paired	2

Table 1: Statistics for texts evaluated in the coherence evaluation study conducted using FALTE.

were collected from 3 crowd annotators, totalling 9.6K error annotations across all summaries.

The study showed that: (1) The strategy of fine-grained annotation is better suited for long documents compared to document-level annotation. The study showed that the inter-annotator agreement of document-level labels for long texts is 0.19 compared to 0.48 reported for news summaries that are considerably shorter (Fabbri et al., 2021). (2) FALTE can be used to run a large-scale annotation study. In fact, the paper (Goyal et al., 2022) shows that the collected annotations are high quality and can be used to train a strong classifier for automatically identifying coherence errors in text.

The results also outline other benefits of fine-grained annotation. Different annotators have different criterion for judging the overall quality of text. The task design decision of explicitly breaking it down through a taxonomy and prompting for rationales, i.e. the text spans, provides insight into which errors types are more critical for each annotator. Note that due to the nature of the task design (identifying **all** error spans in a document), we saw that annotators tend to be high precision low recall (Dou et al., 2022; Goyal et al., 2022), i.e. they rarely highlight non-error spans, but tend to miss error spans. Devising techniques that can improve recall for such task designs is a promising research question that we leave for future work.

4 Related Work

Reference-based evaluation is the most popular evaluation paradigm for generation models. These include overlap-based metrics (Lin, 2004; Papineni et al., 2002; Banerjee and Lavie, 2005), or distributional similarity metrics (Zhang et al., 2019; Kusner et al., 2015), and others. However, recent work has shown that these do not correlate with human judgments of quality (Dhingra et al., 2019; Kryściński et al., 2019; Fabbri et al., 2021).

Human evaluation of generation quality is generally considered to be more reliable, although there do not exist any fixed protocols for conducting these studies (Celikyilmaz et al., 2020). In recent work, both Likert scale rating and A/B testing based evaluation frameworks have been widely used (Celikyilmaz et al., 2020; Clark et al., 2021). However, across both these frameworks, tasks are generally designed to elicit document-level quality judgments from crowdworkers that are insufficient to measure the quality of generated text (Clark et al., 2021; Karpinska et al., 2021; Gehrmann et al., 2022). Particularly, Clark et al. (2021) show that crowd annotators often conflate multiple dimensions of quality, and tend to primarily focus on surface properties like grammaticality while evaluating summaries. Therefore, in our task design, we focus on fine-grained error annotations that allow annotators to clearly distinguish between the different error categories and their occurrences.

The document-level task design of the prior work discussed above is quite straightforward to set up using the basic UI components provided by crowdsourcing platforms such as Mechanical Turk. However, creating a user-friendly interface for fine-grained annotation collection is much more challenging. Dou et al. (2022) create a task interface for fine-grained annotations of short generated text. In contrast, our iterative tool design is motivated by prior crowdsourcing research (Kapelner and Chandler, 2010; Hauser et al., 2019) that shows that worker performance and attention increases with an incremental task design for longer tasks. Moreover, decomposition into smaller paragraph-level annotations also reduces the cognitive load on the annotator (Mayer and Moreno, 2003; Brosnan et al., 2021).

5 Conclusion

We present FALTE, a web-based annotation tool to collect fine-grained error annotations for text. It provides an easy-to-use interface to annotate and submit fine-grained annotations and is equipped with capabilities such as navigational flexibility and coreference highlighting that are specifically designed for better user experience while annotating long documents. On the task designer side, our tool is highly customizable: task designers can define their own error taxonomy, error category specifications, and annotation granularity. Therefore, it can accommodate a wide variety of evaluation objectives, e.g. different dimensions of quality like coherence or factuality, language or task-specific taxonomies, and more. We hope that FALTE can support the design and launch of fine-grained human evaluation studies in the future.

Acknowledgments

This project was partially supported by Good Systems,[7] a UT Austin Grand Challenge to develop responsible AI technologies, a grant from the UT Austin Office of the Vice President for Research through the "Creating Connections for National Security Research Grants" program, a grant from Open Philanthropy, NSF grants IIS-2107524, IIS-2145479, and gifts from Salesforce, Amazon, and Adobe.

References

Nader Akoury, Shufan Wang, Josh Whiting, Stephen Hood, Nanyun Peng, and Mohit Iyyer. 2020. STORIUM: A Dataset and Evaluation Platform for Machine-in-the-Loop Story Generation. In *Proceedings of the 2020 Conference on Empirical Methods in Natural Language Processing (EMNLP)*, pages 6470–6484.

Satanjeev Banerjee and Alon Lavie. 2005. METEOR: An automatic metric for MT evaluation with improved correlation with human judgments. In *Proceedings of the acl workshop on intrinsic and extrinsic evaluation measures for machine translation and/or summarization*, pages 65–72.

Kylie Brosnan, Bettina Grün, and Sara Dolnicar. 2021. Cognitive load reduction strategies in questionnaire design. *International Journal of Market Research*, 63(2):125–133.

Tom Brown, Benjamin Mann, Nick Ryder, Melanie Subbiah, Jared D Kaplan, Prafulla Dhariwal, Arvind Neelakantan, Pranav Shyam, Girish Sastry, Amanda Askell, et al. 2020. Language models are few-shot learners. *Advances in neural information processing systems*, 33:1877–1901.

Asli Celikyilmaz, Elizabeth Clark, and Jianfeng Gao. 2020. Evaluation of text generation: A survey. *arXiv preprint arXiv:2006.14799.*

Elizabeth Clark, Tal August, Sofia Serrano, Nikita Haduong, Suchin Gururangan, and Noah A Smith. 2021. All that's 'human'is not gold: Evaluating human evaluation of generated text. In *Proceedings of the 59th Annual Meeting of the Association for Computational Linguistics and the 11th International Joint Conference on Natural Language Processing (Volume 1: Long Papers)*, pages 7282–7296.

[7]https://goodsystems.utexas.edu/

Bhuwan Dhingra, Manaal Faruqui, Ankur Parikh, Ming-Wei Chang, Dipanjan Das, and William Cohen. 2019. Handling divergent reference texts when evaluating table-to-text generation. In *Proceedings of the 57th Annual Meeting of the Association for Computational Linguistics*, pages 4884–4895.

Yao Dou, Maxwell Forbes, Rik Koncel-Kedziorski, Noah Smith, and Yejin Choi. 2022. Is GPT-3 text indistinguishable from human text? scarecrow: A framework for scrutinizing machine text. In *Proceedings of the 60th Annual Meeting of the Association for Computational Linguistics (Volume 1: Long Papers)*, pages 7250–7274, Dublin, Ireland. Association for Computational Linguistics.

Alexander Richard Fabbri, Wojciech Kryściński, Bryan McCann, Caiming Xiong, Richard Socher, and Dragomir Radev. 2021. SummEval: Re-evaluating Summarization Evaluation. *Transactions of the Association for Computational Linguistics*, 9:391–409.

Sebastian Gehrmann, Elizabeth Clark, and Thibault Sellam. 2022. Repairing the cracked foundation: A survey of obstacles in evaluation practices for generated text. *arXiv preprint arXiv:2202.06935.*

Tanya Goyal, Junyi Jessy Li, and Greg Durrett. 2022. SNaC: Coherence error detection for narrative summarization. *Proceedings of the 2022 Conference on Empirical Methods in Natural Language Processing.*

David Hauser, Gabriele Paolacci, and Jesse Chandler. 2019. Common concerns with mturk as a participant pool: Evidence and solutions. In *Handbook of research methods in consumer psychology*, pages 319–337. Routledge.

Adam Kapelner and Dana Chandler. 2010. Preventing satisficing in online surveys. *Proceedings of CrowdConf.*

Marzena Karpinska, Nader Akoury, and Mohit Iyyer. 2021. The perils of using mechanical turk to evaluate open-ended text generation. In *Proceedings of the 2021 Conference on Empirical Methods in Natural Language Processing*, pages 1265–1285.

Wojciech Kryściński, Nitish Shirish Keskar, Bryan McCann, Caiming Xiong, and Richard Socher. 2019. Neural text summarization: A critical evaluation. In *Proceedings of the 2019 Conference on Empirical Methods in Natural Language Processing and the 9th International Joint Conference on Natural Language Processing (EMNLP-IJCNLP)*, pages 540–551.

Matt Kusner, Yu Sun, Nicholas Kolkin, and Kilian Weinberger. 2015. From word embeddings to document distances. In *International conference on machine learning*, pages 957–966. PMLR.

Mike Lewis, Yinhan Liu, Naman Goyal, Marjan Ghazvininejad, Abdelrahman Mohamed, Omer Levy, Veselin Stoyanov, and Luke Zettlemoyer.

2020. BART: Denoising Sequence-to-Sequence Pre-training for Natural Language Generation, Translation, and Comprehension. In *Proceedings of the 58th Annual Meeting of the Association for Computational Linguistics*, pages 7871–7880.

Chin-Yew Lin. 2004. ROUGE: A package for automatic evaluation of summaries. In *Text summarization branches out*, pages 74–81.

Ziming Mao, Chen Henry Wu, Ansong Ni, Yusen Zhang, Rui Zhang, Tao Yu, Budhaditya Deb, Chenguang Zhu, Ahmed Awadallah, and Dragomir Radev. 2022. DYLE: Dynamic Latent Extraction for Abstractive Long-Input Summarization. In *Proceedings of the 60th Annual Meeting of the Association for Computational Linguistics (Volume 1: Long Papers)*, pages 1687–1698.

Richard E Mayer and Roxana Moreno. 2003. Nine ways to reduce cognitive load in multimedia learning. *Educational psychologist*, 38(1):43–52.

Kishore Papineni, Salim Roukos, Todd Ward, and Wei-Jing Zhu. 2002. BLEU: a method for automatic evaluation of machine translation. In *Proceedings of the 40th annual meeting of the Association for Computational Linguistics*, pages 311–318.

Alex Wang, Richard Yuanzhe Pang, Angelica Chen, Jason Phang, and Samuel R Bowman. 2022. SQuALITY: Building a Long-Document Summarization Dataset the Hard Way. *arXiv preprint arXiv:2205.11465*.

Jingqing Zhang, Yao Zhao, Mohammad Saleh, and Peter Liu. 2020. Pegasus: Pre-training with extracted gap-sentences for abstractive summarization. In *International Conference on Machine Learning*, pages 11328–11339. PMLR.

Tianyi Zhang, Varsha Kishore, Felix Wu, Kilian Q Weinberger, and Yoav Artzi. 2019. BERTScore: Evaluating Text Generation with BERT. In *International Conference on Learning Representations*.

Yusen Zhang, Ansong Ni, Ziming Mao, Chen Henry Wu, Chenguang Zhu, Budhaditya Deb, Ahmed Awadallah, Dragomir Radev, and Rui Zhang. 2022. Summ^n: A multi-stage summarization framework for long input dialogues and documents. In *Proceedings of the 60th Annual Meeting of the Association for Computational Linguistics (Volume 1: Long Papers)*, pages 1592–1604, Dublin, Ireland. Association for Computational Linguistics.

SEAL: Interactive Tool for Systematic Error Analysis and Labeling

Nazneen Rajani[†], **Weixin Liang**[‡], **Lingjiao Chen**[‡], **Meg Mitchell**[†], **James Zou**[‡]
[†] Hugging Face [‡] Department of Computer Science, Stanford University
{nazneen, meg}@huggingface.co {wxliang,lingjiao,jamesz}@stanford.edu

Abstract

With the advent of Transformers, large language models (LLMs) have saturated well-known NLP benchmarks and leaderboards with high aggregate performance. However, many times these models systematically fail on tail data or rare groups not obvious in aggregate evaluation. Identifying such problematic data groups is even more challenging when there are no explicit labels (e.g., ethnicity, gender, etc.) and further compounded for NLP datasets due to the lack of visual features to characterize failure modes (e.g., Asian males, animals indoors, waterbirds on land etc.). This paper introduces an interactive Systematic Error Analysis and Labeling (SEAL) tool that uses a two-step approach to first identify high error slices of data and then in the second step introduce methods to give human-understandable semantics to those under-performing slices. We explore a variety of methods for coming up with coherent semantics for the error groups using language models for semantic labeling and a text-to-image model for generating visual features. SEAL toolkit and demo screencast is available at https://huggingface.co/spaces/nazneen/seal.

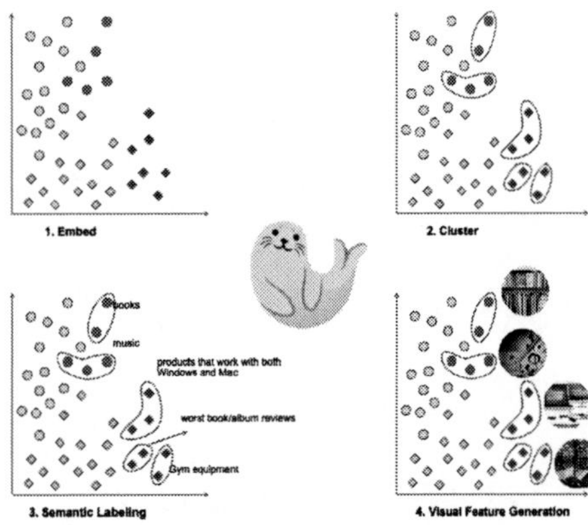

Figure 1: SEAL interactive tool for discovering systematic errors in model performance. Steps 1 and 2 include extracting the model embeddings and clustering datapoints with high-loss. Steps 3 and 4 include semantic labeling of error groups and generating visual features to support debugging.

1 Introduction

Machine learning systems that seemingly perform well on average can still make *systematic errors* on important subsets of data. Examples include such systems performing poorly for marginalized groups in chatbots (Stuart-Ulin, 2018), recruiting tools (Hamilton, 2018), cloud products (Kayser-Bril, 2020), ad targeting (Hao, 2019), credit services (Knight, 2019), and image cropping (Hamilton, 2020). Discovering and labeling systematic errors in ML systems is an open research problem that would enable building robust models that generalize across subpopulations of data.

Uncovering underperforming groups of data of a ML system is not straightforward. Firstly, the high-dimensional space of the representations learned by the deep learning models makes it difficult to identify such groups of systematic errors. Secondly, it is difficult to extract and label the hidden semantic information in such groups with high errors without a human-in-the-loop setup. Identifying systematic model failures requires practitioners to think creatively about model evaluation (Ribeiro et al., 2020; Wu et al., 2019; Goel et al., 2021b; Kiela et al., 2021; Yuan et al., 2022). However, current approaches are mostly limited to examining and manipulating model mispredictions. The onus of identifying what group or subset of data to evaluate still falls on the practitioner, making it inefficient and prone to oversight. Recent works on fine-grained error analysis, such as Domino (Eyuboglu et al., 2022) and Spotlight (d'Eon et al., 2022) provide solutions to this problem but focus on image datasets which are easier to visualize.

Error analysis for text data is less explored and more challenging. It also highlights the need to provide semantic summaries of text, which we tackle in SEAL. For example, NLP models could

Proceedings of the The 2022 Conference on Empirical Methods in Natural Language Processing: System Demonstrations, pages 359 - 370
December 7-11, 2022 ©2022 Association for Computational Linguistics

Figure 2: SEAL interface showing high-error groups for the distilbert-base-uncased model evaluated on the yelp_polarity dataset. The interface comprises of various components: (a) examples from the dataset in the high error groups (sorted by loss), (b) statistics of tokens in high error groups relative to the entire evaluation set, (c) interactive 2d visualization of the model embeddings showing groups of errors in color and low-loss groups in gray. The colors indicate different error clusters. If the dataset has annotated classes, the visualization includes symbols to represents those classes (◇ and ○ in the above figure). The panel on the left has multiple widgets that a user can control to be able to interactively understand their model's mispredictions relative to the rest of the model's outputs. Apart from the dataset and model, the user can select the loss quantile that want to examine for systematic errors, if they want SEAL to group those errors using kmeans++ with the number of clusters, and how many data points they want to visualize at a time in the visual component of the interface downsampled proportional to the group size (we use Altair for plotting that supports a maximum of 5000 data points to be visualized at once).

underperform on hundreds of possible input types – longer inputs, inputs from non-native speaker, inputs with topic domains underrepresented in training, etc. This is a huge barrier of entry for most non-expert ML users who wish to gain a better understanding of their model and datasets with such existing tools. Model evaluation should ideally give actionable insights into a model's performance on a dataset in the form of data curation (Liang and Zou, 2022) or model patching (Goel et al., 2021a).

Our desiderata is a tool that summarizes failures of a model on textual data in a concise, coherent and human intepretable way. Systematic Error Analysis and Labeling (SEAL) is an interactive tool to 1. identify candidate groups of data with high systematic errors and 2. generate semantic labels for those groups. For 1, we use k-means++ on subset of evaluation data with highest loss. Semantic labeling uses LLMs (like GPT3) in zero-shot setting for identifying concepts or topics common to examples in the candidate group. We also explored using a text-to-image model to generate visual features for high error clusters using the Dall-e-mini (Dayma et al., 2021). Semantic descriptions (via labeling or visual features) of such systematic model errors not only enable practitioners to better understand the failure modes of their model during evaluation but also gives actionable insight to fix them via some form of model patching or data augmentation.

2 SEAL

We present Systematic Error Analysis and Labeling (SEAL), an interactive visualization tool that provides rich data point comparison for text classification systems, enabling fine-grained understanding of model performance on data groups as shown in

Figure 2. It comes pre-loaded with model outputs for most downloaded HuggingFace (HF) models and datasets, as well as scripts for loading data for any dataset provided by the Datasets API and extracting embeddings of any HF-compatible model.[1]

2.1 Error Discovery and Analysis

Identifying model failures via error discovery is a crucial step in engineering robust systems that generalize to diverse subsets of data. SEAL uses the model's loss on a datapoint as a proxy for potential bugs or errors. Past work has examined model behavior on individual datapoints for mapping training datasets (Swayamdipta et al., 2020). We hope to leverage information about model behavior on individual *evaluation* data-points in a similar fashion. We use quantiles for dividing the model loss region for further analysis. For example, Figure 2 shows the 0.99 loss quantile for the distilbert-base-uncased model (Sanh et al., 2019) on the yelp_polarity (Zhang et al., 2015) sentiment classification dataset. The SEAL interface allows the user to control the loss quantile for fine-grained analysis using the widget on the side panel.

SEAL uses k-means++ for clustering the high-loss candidate datapoints from the above step. Meng et al. (2022) used k-means for topic discovery on the entire dataset and showed that the clusters are stable only when k is very high ($k >> 100$) because of the scale of the embedding space. In contrast, SEAL only clusters the very high loss slice (> 0.98 quantile).

We use the representations of the models' final hidden layer (before the softmax) as embeddings. If the evaluation dataset selected by the user has ground truth annotations, then it groups the clusters by error-types (false-positives and false-negatives for binary classification). The visualization component of the SEAL interface shows the error clusters and their types using colors and symbols respectively. We use a standard heuristic of setting the number of clusters in k-means++ to be approximately $\sqrt{n/2}$, where n is the group size.

2.2 Semantic Error Labeling

Semantic error labeling is important for identifying the underlying concept or topic connecting the datapoints in a error group. Systematic errors can be mathematically modeled and fixed by data curation. Contrast this with random errors that cannot be mathematically modeled or fixed via data curation. Past work analyzing NLP models have shown systematic errors on various tasks including sentiment classification, natural language inference, and reading comprehension (McCoy et al., 2019; Kaushik et al., 2020; Jia and Liang, 2017). SEAL uses pretrained LLMs (such as GPT3 (Ouyang et al., 2022) or Bloom (BigScience, 2022)) for semantic labeling of error clusters that could highlight such possible systematic bugs in model performance. We craft a prompt consisting of instruction and examples in the clusters extracted in the previous step as follows.

```
def build_prompt(content)
    instruction = 'In this task, we`ll
    assign a short and precise label to
    a group of documents based on the
    topics or concepts most relevant to
    these documents. The documents are
    all subsets of a ${task} dataset.'

    examples = '\n - '.join(content)

    prompt = instruction + '- ' +
    examples+ '\n Group label:'

    return prompt
```

Here `task` is the task under consideration for example 'sentiment classification' in our case. The `arg` to the function is a dataframe or dataframe column with the dataset content as string that the model uses for classification. Our prompt design was experimented first in the few-shot setting before adapting to the zero-shot.

For the results and use case discussion in Section 3, we use the OpenAI GPT3 API [2] via the CLI. The maximum token length is limited to 4000 and so we truncate the prompt to that length before feeding the model. We observed that for many larger groups of high-loss examples (> 25) SEAL labels degenerate to generic output such as "customer reviews of products", "movies reviews", "restaurant reviews", etc. To prevent this and to generate coherent group labels, we sub-cluster the bigger error groups until their size is < 25. We verified the group labels by running the Blei et al. (2003) LDA topic model on the examples in each cluster after a pre-processing step. The pre-processing included tokenizing, lemmatizing, and removing stopwords. For each dataset domain, we also removed the domain word list – ('movie, watch, film, character' for the IMDB dataset, 'food, place, location, ser-

[1]Based on usage data from July'22 at `https://huggingface.co/models?pipeline_tag=text-classification&sort=downloads`

[2]`https://beta.openai.com/playground`

Group label	Size	Group acc.
Albert Base v2 on Yelp (overall acc: 0.95)		
Club reviews	574	0.90 (-5%)
Movie theater reviews	231	0.85 (-10%)
Dentist reviews	69	0.88 (-7%)
Chain restaurant reviews	61	0.88 (-7%)
Frozen custard reviews	37	0.83 (-12%)
Waterfront business reviews	11	0.72 (-23%)
Distilbert Base Uncased on Amazon (overall acc: 0.89)		
Bath product reviews	78	0.79 (-10%)
Vaccuum cleaner reviews	34	0.76 (-13%)
Eragon book reviews	28	0.67 (-22%)
SD card reviews	13	0.61 (-28%)
Distillbert Base Uncased on IMDB (overall acc: 0.86)		
Reviews of movies starring 'Bill'	644	0.79 (-7%)
Adventure movie reviews	583	0.81 (-5%)
Reviews of foreign films	262	0.80 (-6%)
Movies with 'stranger' in title	121	0.76 (-10%)
Reviews of movies with pyschopaths	94	0.78 (-8%)
Reviews of mystery movies	72	0.75 (-11%)

Table 1: Results obtained from using SEAL on three sentiment classification datasets. The columns shows the group labels generated by GPT3, the size of the group in the overall evaluation set, and the group accuracy.

Figure 3: Examples of visualizations generated using Dalle-mini (Craiyon) for a sample of error groups.

vice, time, room, restaurant' for the Yelp dataset, and 'book, author, pages, read, product' for the Amazon dataset). The concept tokens in the labels assigned by GPT3 were in the top-6 topics for these datasets.

SEAL also supports querying the dalle-mini API to generate visual features that would support with error discovery.[3] We augment the semantic labels generated using a LLM with the text-to-image diffusion model such as the dalle-mini. The goal is to further support systematic error discovery especially for users that are not domain experts in the dataset they are using. For example it is easy to imagine what 'frozen custard' but it might not be obvious what 'hooters slot club' is or what a 'waterfront business in Phoenix, AZ' means. As shown in Figure 3, the visual features help with further analysis and provide clear actionable insights.

2.3 System Architecture

The interface is implemented as a Streamlit3 application with some customized HTML/JavaScript component that handles interactions in the tool. We use the Altair library customized with HTML/JavaScript and CSS for richer interactive visualization of embeddings. The visual component of the tool enables a user to interactively hover on data points and get information about the content, label, prediction, loss, and cluster (as in Figure 5). All the data preprocessing is powered by the Pandas library and all the manipulations on the data (such as extracting the layer embeddings, clustering, etc.) are stored as DataFrames thus providing a single interface for users to extend with custom data processing functions. We also provide preprocessing scripts to generate and cache all data required by SEAL to ensure fast response times in the interface. The scripts also include code to run inference (forward pass) on any HF dataset and model as well as a hook to extract learned representations from any layer of a loaded model. The workflow in SEAL also enables users to interactively visualize data points with high loss using the streamlit slider widget to control the loss quantile that is highlighted on the interface.

[3] https://huggingface.co/spaces/dalle-mini/dalle-mini

3 Results and Case Study

In this section, we discuss some results using the SEAL pipeline and walk through a case study for an interactive analysis with the tool.

3.1 Experimental Results

Table 1 shows the results obtained using SEAL on three sentiment classification datasets, Amazon (McAuley and Leskovec, 2013), Yelp (Zhang et al., 2015), and IMDB (Maas et al., 2011) for Distilbert (Sanh et al., 2019) and Albert (Lan et al.,

Figure 4: Snapshot of SEAL showing the table of examples with highest-loss and their clusters.

2020). For each dataset block in the table, we select the subset of group labels that were not generic ("customer reviews", "book reviews") and either had proper names in them such as "LensCrafters", "Eragon" or common nouns with properties such as "trashy movies", "fine dining", "overpriced chain restaurants". [4] We then measured model performance on all examples in the evaluation dataset that matched the group description to obtain the group accuracy. Table 2 shows the content for a random sample of examples in the error categories discovered using SEAL.

An unintended but interesting use case of SEAL is to discover mislabeled candidate examples. We found that some groups have labels describing a sentiment such as "trashy movies", "terrible food" but with opposite ground truth sentiment. On further investigation, we found that indeed many of the groups have noisy labels and the model is actually predicting the correct sentiment. Table 3 in the appendix shows a sample of such mislabeled candidate examples from each dataset studied in this paper.

Limitations. SEAL relies on the semantic robustness of the labeling LLM such as GPT3. We did not test cluster labeling on NLP tasks that require understanding semantic phenomena or function word.

3.2 Case Study

SEAL with its interactive interface enables practitioners to discover possible systematic errors in their models. In this section, we walk-through

[4]See relation /r/HasProperty `https://github.com/commonsense/conceptnet5/wiki/Relations`

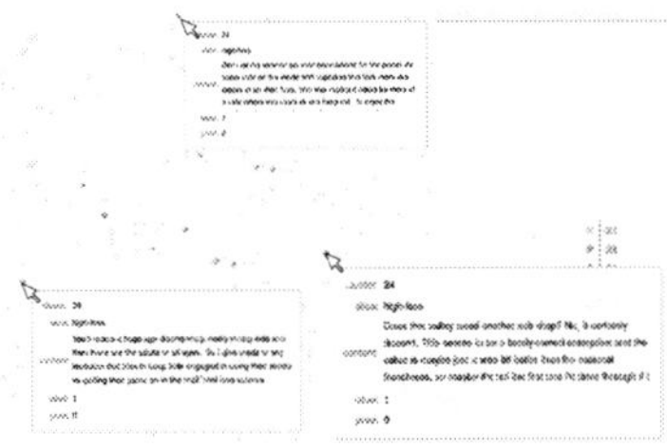

Figure 5: Snapshot from the SEAL interface highlighting a group of examples with high-loss that are candidates for a systematic error type where reviews consist of customer experiences being better than their expectation of the place.

a case study of identifying such errors with the Albert-base-v2 model finetuned and evaluated on the Yelp dataset. The user first loads the model and dataset in the tool and examines the examples with the highest-loss as in Figure 4. They notice that the example includes customer reviews where there was discrepancy between expectation and reality. They then want to zoom in to figure out similar reviews in the dataset where customers experiences differed from their expectations. They run the clustering and visualize the high-loss examples interactively. After trying a few values of '# of clusters', the user finds that indeed there are many other such examples that surface in the visualization component of SEAL as shown in Figure 5. The model underperforms on examples of the type where the customer expectation is negative but the reality is actually positive.

4 Mathematical robustness of SEAL

In this section, we provide theoretical guarantees for the stability of semantic labels generated by the SEAL pipeline. More specifically, our stability theorem states that a small perturbation of the input of our SEAL pipeline would only cause a small bounded difference of the semantic labels. An implication of our theoretical results is that, even if two users are using different versions of an evaluation set (e.g., a different split, or a smaller subset), SEAL would generate similar semantic labels.

More formally, we ask: How does a small change in the input dataset $\{(x_i, y_i)\}_{i=1}^n$ affect the semantic label tuple $M \triangleq \{m_k\}_{k=1}^K$? Here, K denotes the number of explanations, $m_k \triangleq (w_k, s_k, a_k)$ encodes the kth explanation message, where w_k, s_k, and a_k represent the sentence vector, the number of data points explained by this mes-

Group label	Content	Label	Pred
Club reviews	Being from Southern California, the "scene" is so much fun. There are several clubs to go to and any night is a great time. That brings us to the Phoenix scene and The Cash.Oh wait, there is no scene for the ladies. Not going to bash them to hard, because it's the only consistent place that we have. Yes it caters to the Country music crowd, but they do play spurts of other music through out the weekend evenings.The mixed drinks could be better, but the prices are reasonable.	0	1
	I used to come here for years, maybe about a year back.. the best weekend drinkfests back then: Fridays were ladies night (dollar well, wines and domestics, $2 you call its, and no cover). Saturdays were free beer night (draft bud light, coors light and pbr til they gave out 1,000 of each.. again, no cover). Was always packed and played a decent variety of music; pitchers for beer pong were also always dirt cheap. And despite, the bartenders were way personable and fun.I'm not trying to sound like a cheapskate, as I am in the service industry myself.. but there must've been a change of ownership since my prior experiences.[..]	0	1
Dentist reviews	Thank you for all the emails you sent me on my review! I was surprised at how many responses I recieved from people searching for the right dentist..I shared my new dentist information and even got some movie tickets from my dentist for the referrals! I find it funny how since I wrote this review how many people have reviewed with 5 stars... They must have a lot of friends and family! I hope everyone reads my review and picks the right dentist for your needs! Happy Holidays	0	1
	After dealing with a two week long migraine and severe pressure and pain in my face, I called around looking for an ENT that could get me in ASAP. Dr. Simms was available for a same day appointment and I scheduled with him for that afternoon. The wait time itself wasn't bad - 10-15 minutes after completing paperwork. Dr. Simms was personable enough and after evaluating me, told me that he would like to treat for a sinus infection with antibiotics and prednisone. As I had just moved and newly became a student, I didn't yet have health insurance set up.[..]	0	1
Chain restaurant reviews	I tried Cozymel's on a recommendation from my parents. Living in San Diego, I never go to chain Mexican places - there are just too many other places to try. I was expecting Cozymel's to be okay, nothing great.We went for lunch, and I was happy to see a whole page of lunch specials for about $8. Usually, an enchilada combo plate could set you back close to $15 at a Mexican chain. Not here (during lunch at least). I ordered the taco salad with black beans instead of meat. It came in an enormous flour tortilla shell - tostada style.[..]	1	0
	I still can't get over how I paid $2.99 for a coffee and 3 doughnuts! What a deal. I was debating whether or not to go to Krispy Kreme or Winchells but decided on the latter since it wasn't a chain and I could get Krispy Kreme elsewhere...Winchell's shares space with Subway which was a little random but I didn't have any problem with it because the woman helping me and what I assume to be the owner were both very nice and sweet. I hadn't eaten doughnuts in a little over a year so I decided to go with a boston creme (one of my favorites) and got a chocolate glazed chocolate doughnut for my sister and a glazed for my friend.[..]	1	0

Table 2: Random sample from under-performing groups discovered by SEAL for the Yelp dataset. Results for other datasets are in Table 4 in the appendix. 0 and 1 indicate negative and positive sentiment classes respectively. The reviews ending in [..] have been truncated to save space.

sage, and the average accuracy among those data points. Here we show that under some assumptions, the outputs of SEAL, i.e. the set of m_k, is relatively robust to randomness in the input dataset. To be more precise, we need a distance metric on explanation message space.

Definition 4.1. Given any two semantic label tuple $M = \{m_k\}_{k=1}^K$ and $M' = \{m'_k\}_{k=1}^K$, define a distance $d_{\max}(M, M')$ between them as

$$\max_{1\leq i\leq K}\min_{1\leq j\leq K} \|m_i - m'_j\|_2 + \|m'_i - m_j\|_2$$

Remark. The ℓ_2 distance $\|\|_2$ is defined on the vectorized explanation. In other words, we concatenate the sentence vector, data point number, and the accuracy value in one single vector, and then measure the distance of two explanation messages by the distance of their corresponding expanded vectors.

Here, a small distance value $d_{\max}$ implies a small difference in the explanation word vector, the size of each cluster, and the accuracy within each cluster. To see this, note that a small distance implies that for any messages m_i and m_j in M, one can find two other messages m'_i and m'_j in M', which are close to them. That is to say, each for any message in M, there is a message in M' approximately equal to it. Now we can answer the raised question.

Theorem 1. *Let S and T denote two set of n data points i.i.d. from some data distribution P. Suppose the probability space of P is compact with size B, and the density function is bounded. Let M_S and M_T be the semantic label tuples generated by* SEAL *with input S and T. If S and T differs in $o(\sqrt{n})$ data points, and the the clustering algorithm gives the exactly optimal solution, then we have*

$$d_{\max}(M_S, M_T) \xrightarrow{P} 0,$$

i.e., $d_{\max}(M_S, M_T)$ converges to 0 in probability.

The proof of this theorem is in the Appendix. It implicitly relies on Lipschitz continuity of the sentence generation network, which actually holds for most DNNs with finite input space. This indicates SEAL is robust to small perturbation in the input dataset: a small shift in the input dataset only leads to small explanation change. Such a smooth explanation change is particularly useful when users gradually update the their dataset.

5 Conclusion

In this work we introduced SEAL, an interactive visualization tool for discovering systematic errors and labeling them. Through case studies we showed how SEAL can efficiently identify the systematic failures of state-of-the-art sentiment classification models on well known datasets. We released a set of pre-computed model outputs to enable easy, out-of-the-box use especially for non-coding audience such as domain experts. We hope this work will positively contribute to the ongoing efforts in building tools for systematic error analysis and model debugging.

6 Ethics Statement

Many datasets currently used and open-sourced by the NLP community are mainly crawled from the web and therefore are not representative of a majority of geographies. There are biases that can distill into parameters of models trained on such biased datasets and may even be further amplified in the generated model outputs. All datasets we experimented with are in English, and all models are trained on English datasets.

We use GPT3 for semantic labeling and it is well-known that LLMs such as GPT3 can generate toxic, harmful, hate content that might have also percolated into our tool. Similarly, the semantic similarity metrics used in our tool including the BERTScore and the word-embeddings carry biases of the data they were trained on. We request our users to be aware of these ethical issues that might affect their analyses.

Acknowledgements

We thank the anonymous reviewers for their constructive feedback. We are also thankful to David McClure and Christopher Akiki whose work inspired some of the interactive components in the demo accompanying this paper.

References

BigScience. 2022. Bigscience large open-science open-access multilingual language model.

David M. Blei, Andrew Y. Ng, Michael I. Jordan, and John Lafferty. 2003. Latent dirichlet allocation. *Journal of Machine Learning Research*, 3:2003.

Boris Dayma, Suraj Patil, Pedro Cuenca, Khalid Saifullah, Tanishq Abraham, Phuc Le Khac, Luke Melas, and Ritobrata Ghosh. 2021. Dall·e mini.

Greg d'Eon, Jason d'Eon, James R Wright, and Kevin Leyton-Brown. 2022. The spotlight: A general method for discovering systematic errors in deep learning models. In *2022 ACM Conference on Fairness, Accountability, and Transparency*, pages 1962–1981.

Sabri Eyuboglu, Maya Varma, Khaled Saab, Jean-Benoit Delbrouck, Christopher Lee-Messer, Jared Dunnmon, James Zou, and Christopher Ré. 2022. Domino: Discovering systematic errors with cross-modal embeddings. In *International Conference on Learning Representations (ICLR)*.

Karan Goel, Laurel Orr, Nazneen Fatema Rajani, Jesse Vig, and Christopher Ré. 2021a. Goodwill hunting: Analyzing and repurposing off-the-shelf named entity linking systems. In *Proceedings of the 2021 Conference of the North American Chapter of the Association for Computational Linguistics: Human Language Technologies: Industry Papers*, pages 205–213, Online. Association for Computational Linguistics.

Karan Goel, Nazneen Rajani, Jesse Vig, Samson Tan, Jason Wu, Stephan Zheng, Caiming Xiong, Mohit Bansal, and Christopher Ré. 2021b. Robustness gym: Unifying the nlp evaluation landscape. *arXiv preprint arXiv:2101.04840*.

Isobel Asher Hamilton. 2018. Amazon built an AI tool to hire people but had to shut it down because it was discriminating against women.

Isobel Asher Hamilton. 2020. Twitter is investigating after anecdotal data suggested its picture-cropping tool favors white faces.

Karen Hao. 2019. Facebook's ad-serving algorithm discriminates by gender and race.

Robin Jia and Percy Liang. 2017. Adversarial examples for evaluating reading comprehension systems. In *Proceedings of the 2017 Conference on Empirical Methods in Natural Language Processing*, pages 2021–2031, Copenhagen, Denmark. Association for Computational Linguistics.

Divyansh Kaushik, Eduard Hovy, and Zachary Lipton. 2020. Learning the difference that makes a difference with counterfactually-augmented data. In *International Conference on Learning Representations*.

Nicolas Kayser-Bril. 2020. Google apologizes after its Vision AI produced racist results.

Douwe Kiela, Max Bartolo, Yixin Nie, Divyansh Kaushik, Atticus Geiger, Zhengxuan Wu, Bertie Vidgen, Grusha Prasad, Amanpreet Singh, Pratik Ringshia, Zhiyi Ma, Tristan Thrush, Sebastian Riedel, Zeerak Waseem, Pontus Stenetorp, Robin Jia, Mohit Bansal, Christopher Potts, and Adina Williams. 2021.

Dynabench: Rethinking benchmarking in NLP. In *Proceedings of the 2021 Conference of the North American Chapter of the Association for Computational Linguistics: Human Language Technologies*, pages 4110–4124, Online. Association for Computational Linguistics.

Will Knight. 2019. The Apple Card Didn't 'See' Gender—and That's the Problem.

Zhenzhong Lan, Mingda Chen, Sebastian Goodman, Kevin Gimpel, Piyush Sharma, and Radu Soricut. 2020. Albert: A lite bert for self-supervised learning of language representations. In *International Conference on Learning Representations*.

Weixin Liang and James Zou. 2022. Metashift: A dataset of datasets for evaluating contextual distribution shifts and training conflicts. In *International Conference on Learning Representations*.

Andrew L. Maas, Raymond E. Daly, Peter T. Pham, Dan Huang, Andrew Y. Ng, and Christopher Potts. 2011. Learning word vectors for sentiment analysis. In *Proceedings of the 49th Annual Meeting of the Association for Computational Linguistics: Human Language Technologies*, pages 142–150, Portland, Oregon, USA. Association for Computational Linguistics.

Julian McAuley and Jure Leskovec. 2013. Hidden factors and hidden topics: Understanding rating dimensions with review text. In *Proceedings of the 7th ACM Conference on Recommender Systems*, RecSys '13, page 165–172, New York, NY, USA. Association for Computing Machinery.

Tom McCoy, Ellie Pavlick, and Tal Linzen. 2019. Right for the wrong reasons: Diagnosing syntactic heuristics in natural language inference. In *Proceedings of the 57th Annual Meeting of the Association for Computational Linguistics*, pages 3428–3448, Florence, Italy. Association for Computational Linguistics.

Yu Meng, Yunyi Zhang, Jiaxin Huang, Yu Zhang, and Jiawei Han. 2022. Topic discovery via latent space clustering of pretrained language model representations. In *Proceedings of the ACM Web Conference 2022*, pages 3143–3152.

Long Ouyang, Jeff Wu, Xu Jiang, Diogo Almeida, Carroll L. Wainwright, Pamela Mishkin, Chong Zhang, Sandhini Agarwal, Katarina Slama, Alex Ray, John Schulman, Jacob Hilton, Fraser Kelton, Luke Miller, Maddie Simens, Amanda Askell, Peter Welinder, Paul Christiano, Jan Leike, and Ryan Lowe. 2022. Training language models to follow instructions with human feedback.

Alexander Rakhlin and Andrea Caponnetto. 2006. Stability of k-means clustering. *Advances in neural information processing systems*, 19.

Marco Tulio Ribeiro, Tongshuang Wu, Carlos Guestrin, and Sameer Singh. 2020. Beyond accuracy: Behavioral testing of NLP models with CheckList. In *Proceedings of the 58th Annual Meeting of the Association for Computational Linguistics*, pages 4902–4912, Online. Association for Computational Linguistics.

Victor Sanh, Lysandre Debut, Julien Chaumond, and Thomas Wolf. 2019. Distilbert, a distilled version of bert: smaller, faster, cheaper and lighter. *ArXiv*, abs/1910.01108.

Chloe Rose Stuart-Ulin. 2018. Microsoft's politically correct chatbot is even worse than its racist one.

Swabha Swayamdipta, Roy Schwartz, Nicholas Lourie, Yizhong Wang, Hannaneh Hajishirzi, Noah A. Smith, and Yejin Choi. 2020. Dataset cartography: Mapping and diagnosing datasets with training dynamics. In *Proceedings of the 2020 Conference on Empirical Methods in Natural Language Processing (EMNLP)*, pages 9275–9293, Online. Association for Computational Linguistics.

Tongshuang Wu, Marco Tulio Ribeiro, Jeffrey Heer, and Daniel S Weld. 2019. Errudite: Scalable, reproducible, and testable error analysis. In *Proceedings of the 57th Annual Meeting of the Association for Computational Linguistics*, pages 747–763.

Jun Yuan, Jesse Vig, and Nazneen Rajani. 2022. iSEA: An interactive pipeline for semantic error analysis of NLP models. In *27th International Conference on Intelligent User Interfaces*. ACM.

Xiang Zhang, Junbo Zhao, and Yann LeCun. 2015. Character-level Convolutional Networks for Text Classification. *arXiv:1509.01626 [cs]*.

A Appendix: Proofs

Proof. Here we prove the proof for Theorem 1. To proceed, we need a few lemmas.

Lemma 2 (adapted from Proposition 5.1. in (Rakhlin and Caponnetto, 2006))**.** *Assume the density of P (with respect to the Lebesgue measure λ over $\mathcal{Z}$) is bounded away from 0, i.e. $dP > \mu d\lambda$ for some $\mu > 0$. Suppose the clusterings A and B are minimizers of the K-means objective $W(C)$ over the sets S and T, respectively. Suppose that at most $o(\sqrt{n})$ data points are different between the two dataset S and T sampled from P. Then*

$$d_{\max}\left(\left\{c_{S,1},\ldots,c_{S,K}\right\},\left\{c_{T,1},\ldots,c_{T,K}\right\}\right) \xrightarrow{P} 0.$$

where $c_{S,i}$ and $c_{T,i}$ are the centers of the i-th cluster generated from S and T, separately.

Lemma 3. *Assume the density of P (with respect to the Lebesgue measure λ over $\mathcal{Z}$) is bounded away from 0, i.e. $dP > \mu d\lambda$ for some $\mu > 0$. Suppose*

$$d_{\max}\left(\left\{c_{S,1},\ldots,c_{S,K}\right\},\left\{c_{T,1},\ldots,c_{T,K}\right\}\right) \leq \varepsilon.$$

and the ML model that generates the sentence vector is Lipschitz continuous with parameter β. Then

$$d_{\max}\left(M_S, M_K\right) \leq 3\varepsilon \max\{6K^2B, \beta\}$$

where $c_{c,m}$ depends only on c and m.

Proof. We first note that, by triangle inequality, we have

$$\begin{aligned}
& d_{\max}(M_S, M_K) \\
&= \max_{1\leq i\leq K}\min_{1\leq j\leq K} \|m_{S,i}-m_{T,j}\|_2 + \|m_{S,j}-m_{T,i}\|_2 \\
&\leq \max_{1\leq i\leq K}\min_{1\leq j\leq K} \|w_{S,i}-w_{T,j}\|_2 + \|w_{S,j}-w_{T,i}\|_2 + \|s_{S,i}-s_{T,j}\|_2 \\
&+\|s_{S,j}-s_{T,i}\|_2 + \|a_{S,i}-a_{T,j}\|_2 + \|a_{S,j}-a_{T,i}\|_2
\end{aligned}$$

Note that, by $\min_j\{a_j+b_j+c_j\} \leq \max\{3\min_j a_j, 3\min_j b_j, 3\min_j c_j\}$, the inner minimization is bounded by 3 times the maximum of $\min_{1\leq j\leq K}\|w_{S,i}-w_{T,j}\|_2 + \|w_{S,j}-w_{T,i}\|_2$, $\min_{1\leq j\leq K}\|s_{S,i}-s_{T,j}\|_2 + \|s_{S,j}-s_{T,i}\|_2$, $\min_{1\leq j\leq K}\|a_{S,i}-a_{T,j}\|_2 + \|a_{S,j}-a_{T,i}\|_2$. Now let us consider those terms separately:

1. $\min_j \|w_{S,i}-w_{T,j}\|_2 + \|w_{S,j}-w_{T,i}\|_2$: By Lipschitz continuity, the distance between two sentence vectors can be bounded by the distance between their corresponding cluster centers. More precisely,

   $$\|w_{S,i}-w_{T,j}\|_2 + \|w_{S,j}-w_{T,i}\|_2 \leq \beta\|c_{S,i}-c_{T,j}\|_2 + \beta\|c_{S,j}-c_{T,i}\|_2$$

   and thus

   $$\min_j \|w_{S,i}-w_{T,j}\|_2 + \|w_{S,j}-w_{T,i}\|_2 \leq \beta\min_j \|c_{S,i}-c_{T,j}\|_2 + \|c_{S,j}-c_{T,i}\|_2$$

   By the assumption, the right hand side is bounded by ε, and thus

   $$\min_j \|w_{S,i}-w_{T,j}\|_2 + \|w_{S,j}-w_{T,i}\|_2 \leq \beta\varepsilon$$

2. $\min_j \|s_{S,i}-s_{T,j}\|_2 + \|s_{S,j}-s_{T,i}\|_2$: By the assumption, we know that, for any given i, we can find j, such that $\|c_{S,i}-c_{T,j}\| + \|c_{S,j}-c_{T,i}\| \leq \varepsilon$. That is to say, the cluster centers' distance is at most ϵ. Since the distribution space is bounded by B, there are at most ε, there are at most $2\epsilon B$ data points are clustered differently. As there are K clusters, in total at most $2\epsilon K^2 B$ data points are clustered differently. This gives a natural upper bound

   $$\min_j \|s_{S,i}-s_{T,j}\|_2 + \|s_{S,j}-s_{T,i}\|_2 \leq 6\varepsilon K^2 B$$

3. $\min \|a_{S,i} - a_{T,j}\|_2 + \|a_{S,j} - a_{T,i}\|_2$: Now applying a similar argument in 2, we know that in total at most $2\epsilon K^2 B$ data points are clustered differently. Thus, at most $2\epsilon K^2 B$ data points affect the accuracy value. This means

$$\min_j \|a_{S,i} - a_{T,j}\|_2 + \|a_{S,j} - a_{T,i}\|_2 \leq 6\varepsilon K^2 B$$

Combining those results, we can conclude that

$$\begin{aligned}&\min_{1\leq j\leq K} \|w_{S,i} - w_{T,j}\|_2 + \|w_{S,j} - w_{T,i}\|_2 + \|s_{S,i} - s_{T,j}\|_2\\ &+\|s_{S,j} - s_{T,i}\|_2 + \|a_{S,i} - a_{T,j}\|_2 + \|a_{S,j} - a_{T,i}\|_2\\ &\leq 3\max\{6\varepsilon K^2 B, \beta\varepsilon\}\end{aligned}$$

This is independent of i, and thus we can take the maximum over i, which gives

$$\begin{aligned}&\max_i \min_{1\leq j\leq K} \|w_{S,i} - w_{T,j}\|_2 + \|w_{S,j} - w_{T,i}\|_2 + \|s_{S,i} - s_{T,j}\|_2\\ &+\|s_{S,j} - s_{T,i}\|_2 + \|a_{S,i} - a_{T,j}\|_2 + \|a_{S,j} - a_{T,i}\|_2\\ &\leq 3\max\{6\varepsilon K^2 B, \beta\varepsilon\}\end{aligned}$$

That is,

$$d_{\max}(M_S, M_T) \leq 3\max\{6\varepsilon K^2 B, \beta\varepsilon\}$$

which completes the proof. □

Combining the above two lemmas directly proves the robustness statement. □

B Appendix: More Examples

Group label	Group content sample
	Amazon
Customer reviews for a product that has been discontinued	Another reviewer recently advised that this is the model to look for. I was just advised at a well known retailer that this model has been discontinued. Is this true or is this a classic bait-and-switch technique? Their current weekly sales circular features this model at a sale price. When you get to the store, they don't have it but when they look it up in their computer, it shows up as "Discontinued". It is difficult to relate reviews to actual products when the reviews you base your buying decision on could be about(a)different model(s) from the one you actually buy online or in-store. The Creative Labs' own website does not give model numbers so they are adding to the confusion.
	The software mentioned on my May 16th review IS called "AVID Xpress" – not "AVID Express" – when my review was edited someone changed the spelling, possibly thinking it was a typo/mistake?
	Although this show is very fascinating I find every episode to be almost the same. Starting with Morgan Freeman stating "when I was a young boy..." then something he did to get in trouble, or something he witnessed that ruined his fragile eggshell mind. Followed by rhetorical questions and theories, and tons and tons of examples. The examples even have examples. Maybe I just understand this stuff and the show really dumbs it down, but I feel like I wasted money investing in season 3. Which by the way, although not currently available, (I don't have cable and I still had the privilege of watching this before the DVD came out) but I will still probably end up buying it on DVD which is cheaper than I already paid for the electronic proprietary/DRM version on Amazon Unbox
Unreliable book reviews	I do not intend to review content here. This new edition is so full of typographical errors that sometimes the reader will have to intuit what the author really wrote. It is clear that the proofreaders of this edition were not actually reading; they were simply following the little red lines under the "misspelled" words. This has resulted in some truly bizarre apparent statements by the author, unreproducible here due to copyright laws. Disclaimer– I have not purchased this book, merely checked it out of the library.
	It's been several years since I've read "Silent Spring," one of the most significant environmental books ever written, but I must respond to the posting by "seem," which is titled "murderous, over the top propaganda" (I correctly your misspelling of the last word): His recommendation to read "DDT: A Case Study in Scientific Fraud" was put out by the Heartland Institute and is, in itself, a "fraud." The Heartland Institute is one of the most pro-chemical, pro-industry, anti-environmental and right-wing organizations around. Nothing they put out should be believed for a second.
	Shame on all the booksellers selling this ten dollar book for $75 and up!Devorss is re-publishing this book in August!I took note of the sellers AND WILL NEVER BUY FROM THEM!
	Yelp
Terrible dry cleaners in Phoenix	I went here for the first time on First Fridays, yeah so what. I promise that I won't hang out here all the time and ruin it for all you true Bikini lovers. My mini pitcher was $3.50 and then 5 minutes later a chick walked up and got charged $6.00 for two mini pitchers, hmmm, male discrimination or they can't do simple math? I'll only go back when it's 110 outside and want to put a buzz on early in the afternoon.
	Mediocre dry cleaning. I want to like this business..why? 1. I like to support Yelp advertisers 2.prime location!!! It is literally around the corner from me and I will probably still go there once in awhile out of convenience. Once or twice I called rushing to get there before they closed and they waited a minute over closing time which was very nice of them. However, this review is simply based off of satisfaction with my clothing. Almost every time I have come there I have to ask to redo my shirts. It drive me nuts because the employees are nice about it. When I woke up today and had 50 dollars worth of clothing needed to be dry cleaned I drove 20 minutes to my old favorite cleaners in Arcadia. I knew that I trust them with my clothes and after years, never had to deal with such an inconvenience. I'm sorry but had to only give 3 stars. I might be back one more time.. only when I have to. John I read your message and appreciate that so I updated my review out of appreciation towards your response. I want to come back because it is convenient. Thanks for caring
	This place is tiny and has more high-end expensive beads than other stores in Phoenix. I've found some really special items here. You shouldn't expect to buy more than a few strands at a time, as it just isn't affordable. Go somewhere else for quantity, and just get a few things to spice up your mix from Bead World.
	IMDB
Terrible movies	You have to be awfully patient to sit through a film with one-liners so flat and unfunny that you wonder what all the fuss was about when WHISTLING IN THE DARK opened to such an enthusiastic greeting from audiences in the 1940s. On top of some weak one-liners and ordinary sight gags, the plot is as far-fetched as the tales The Fox (Red Skelton) tells his radio audience. You have to wonder why anyone would think he could come up with a real-life solution on how to commit the perfect crime and get away with it. But then, that's how unrealistic the comedy is. But–if you're a true Red Skelton fan and enjoy a look back at how comedies were made in the '40s–you can at least enjoy the amiable cast supporting him. Ann Rutherford and Virginia Grey do nicely as his love interest and Conrad Veidt, as always, makes an interesting villain. One of his more amusing moments is his reaction to Skelton explaining the mysteries of wearing turbans. "I never knew that," he muses, impressed by a minor point that is cleverly introduced. All in all, typical nonsense that requires you to accept the lack of credibility and just accept the gags as they are. Not always easy for a discriminating viewer as many of them simply fall flat, the way many comedies of this era do because the novelty of the sight gags and one-liners has simply worn off.
	If they gave out awards for the most depraved and messed-up movies in the world, Japanese cinema would clean up: their exploitation cinema wipes the floor with most other contenders, the most extreme examples being absolutely jaw-dropping exercises in bad taste, nauseating gore, freakish weirdness, and misogynistic sex. Guts of a Beauty is a prime example of such whacked out filth, offering discerning viewers just over an hour of full-on debauchery and gratuitous violence topped off with some very insane J-splatter goodness. The film opens with a young woman named Yoshimi, whose search for her missing sister has led her into the hands of some nasty yakuza, who proceed to rape her and shoot her full of strong dope called Angel Rain[...]
European Union movie is disappointing and full of clichés	**SPOILERS AHEAD** It is really unfortunate that a movie so well produced turns out to be such a disappointment. I thought this was full of (silly) clichés and that it basically tried to hard. To the (American) guys out there: how many of you spend your time jumping on your girlfriend's bed and making monkey sounds? To the (married) girls: how many of you have suddenly gone from prudes to nymphos overnight–but not with your husband? To the French: would you really ask about someone being "à la fac" when you know they don't speak French? Wouldn't you use a more common word like "université"? I lived in France for a while and I sort of do know and understand[...]
	Obviously made on the cheap to capitalize on the notorious "Mandingo," this crassly pandering hunk of blithely rancid Italian sexploitation junk really pours on the sordid stuff with a commendable lack of taste and restraint: The evil arrogant white family who own and operate a lavish slave plantation spend a majority of the screen time engaging in hanky panky both each other and their various slaves[...]

Table 3: Mislabeled candidate examples for the three sentiment classfication datasets. All the examples have GT as positive. Examples ending in [..] have been truncated to save space.

Group label	Content	Label	Pred
Reviews of mystery movies	Based on a Stephen King novel, NEEDFUL THINGS provides the intrigue and eeriness to keep you in your seat. A mysterious man(Max von Sydow) comes to town and soon becomes the most talked about citizen. Could it be that the devil himself has set up shop as an antique dealer in a small town in Maine? von Sydow is masterful and dynamic in this role that dominates the screen. Also starring are Ed Harris and Bonnie Bedelia. Harris is steady and Bedelia is deserving of your attention. Also in support are J.T. Walsh and Amanda Plummer. Not the best, nor the worst adaptation of King's horror on the screen.	0	1
	Before I begin, let me get something off my chest: I'm a huge fan of John Eyres' first film PROJECT: SHADOWCHASER. The film, a B-grade cross of both THE TERMINATOR & DIE HARD, may not be the work of a cinematic genius, but is a hugely entertaining action film that became a cult hit (& spawned two sequels & a spin off). Judge and Jury begins with Joseph Meeker, a convicted killer who was sent to Death Row following his capture after the so-called "Bloody Shootout" (which seems like a poor name for a killing spree. Meeker kills three people while trying to rob a convenience store), being led to the electric chair. There is an amusing scene where Meeker talks to the priest about living for sex but meeting his one true love (who was killed during the shootout), expressing his revenge for the person who killed her. Michael Silvano, a washed-up football star who spends his days watching his son Alex practicing football with his high school team (and ends up harassing his son's coach). But once executed, Meeker returns as a revenant (or as Kelly Perine calls "a hamburger without the fries")[..]	0	1
	Let me say this about Edward D. Wood Jr. He had a passion for his work that I wish more people did have. If we all had the optimism and the commanding hope of Ed Wood, the world would probably be a much better place. Being familiar with Ed Wood's story and having seen the most wonderful biopic "Ed Wood" (1994) several times, I admire his boldness and his strives for the job he loved; I still admire his never-say-die attitude. He had a love for directing that I wish more people in modern-day Hollywood had.But that doesn't make his movies any more fun to watch. And "Glen or Glenda," his first and most confessional film, is probably his very worst."Glen or Glenda" is a deadening cult movie about a cross-dresser named Glen (played by director/writer Ed Wood himself) who despite his love for his fiancée Barbara (Dolores Fuller), cannot seem to conquer his lust for transvestitism, in which he dresses in women's clothing and a wig and thus becomes...Glenda! Glen/Glenda's story is narrated by a doctor and he too is talked and watched over by a mysterious character called "The Scientist" played by veteran horror star Bela Lugosi.[..]	0	1
Adventure movie reviews	Just exactly HOW director John Madden come to settle with Nicolas Cage and Penelope Cruz playing the roles of an Italian Officer and a Greek Villager in an honourable story: "Captain Correli´s Mandolin", just escapes me! Witness: a wobbly, inconsistent accent by Cage amid horrendous over-acting, with Cruz – more adequately cast as a spoiled Latino opposite Johnny Depp in "Blow" – in basically a repeat performance under the guise of a Greek nurse... ay, it was painful. But there were saving graces.The story itself is thrilling-to-tragic, and Cage does have some (– redeeming, this is !–) musical ability. Next, a superb performance by John Hurt (Cruz´s father, the village doctor) of Oscar Callibre, as well as by Irene Papas, each as village elders, as well as by Christian Bale (Papas´ son) among the village freedom fighters, go far towards counter-balancing awkward performances (especially at the beginning) by Cruz and Cage. Nicely, the last two seem to grow into their respective roles as the film progresses, but it´s teeth-gnashing early on. Finally, the scenery itself and the photography could garner a technical award, and such provides pleasant distractions when most needed.[..]	1	0
	Daisy Movie Review By James Mudge From beyondhollywood.com. On paper, "Daisy" sounds like an Asian film fan's dream come true, directed by "Infernal Affairs" co-helmer Andrew Lau and starring everybody's favourite sassy girl, popular Korean actress Jeon Ji Hyun. Unfortunately, despite the talent involved, and the fact that the crew flew halfway around the world to shoot in Amsterdam , the film turns out to be a bit of a disappointment, being a clich'd romantic drama which wallows in misery and self importance. The plot follows Hye Young (Jeon Ji Hyun), a rather naive Korean girl who lives in Amsterdam , spending her life working in her grandfather's antique shop and doing portraits for tourists. One day, she begins receiving flowers at exactly the same time from a secret admirer, who she believes to be a mystery man from her past who once built her a nice little bridge. One day she meets Jeong Woo (Lee Seong Jae, also in "Holiday" and "Public Enemy"), who unbeknownst to her is actually an Interpol agent tracking Asian criminals in the Netherlands .With Hye Young assuming that Jeong Woo is responsible for the flowers, the two fall very slowly into a chaste romantic relationship. However, it turns out that the man sending the flowers is actually Park Yi (Jung Woo Sung, from "Sad Movie" and "Musa"), an assassin working for a Chinese crime syndicate. Inevitably, the love triangle turns tragic and the two men end up facing off while poor Hye Young tries to work out which of the two is the love of her life.Although "Daisy" is ostensibly a love story, it has the feel of a funeral, with a slow, sombre pace and a plot which piles on the misery. Half of the film's running time is taken up with scenes of the characters staring longingly out of windows into the rain, with the silence broken only by bouts of self pitying narration.[..]	1	0

Table 4: Random sample from under-performing groups discovered by SEAL for the IMDB dataset. 0 and 1 indicates negative and positive sentiment classes respectively.

Hands-On Interactive Neuro-Symbolic NLP with DRaiL

Maria Leonor Pacheco[1]
Microsoft Research &
University of Colorado Boulder
maria.pacheco@colorado.edu

Shamik Roy
Purdue University
roy98@purdue.edu

Dan Goldwasser
Purdue University
dgoldwas@purdue.edu

Abstract

We recently introduced DRaiL, a declarative neuro-symbolic modeling framework designed to support a wide variety of NLP scenarios. In this demo, we enhance DRaiL with an easy to use Python interface equipped with methods to define, modify and augment models interactively, as well as with methods to debug and visualize the predictions made. We demonstrate this interface with two challenging NLP tasks: analyzing moral sentiment in political discourse, and analyzing opinions about the Covid-19 vaccine.

1 Introduction

Language in real world settings is complex and ambiguous, and relies on a shared understanding of the world for its interpretation. Most current NLP methods represent language in a latent high-dimensional space by learning word co-occurrence patterns from massive amounts of textual data (Devlin et al., 2019; Brown et al., 2020). This representation is very powerful, but it can be insufficient to capture non-linguistic context such as the physical, social and cultural environments (Bisk et al., 2020). Manually annotating these diverse sources of context is a major challenge, and as a result, interactive and humans-in-the-loop approaches are gaining popularity to enhance and correct NLP models (Lertvittayakumjorn and Toni, 2021). However, the complexity of the representation learned by deep learning models create challenges for the communication between humans and machines. To circumvent these challenges, most existing humans-in-the-loop techniques solicit people to provide feedback on individual predictions instead, or allow people to augment the dataset by providing additional examples (Wang et al., 2021). While straightforward, working in the space of the raw inputs does not take advantage of the ability of humans to make abstractions and reason over them, like forming concepts to generalize from observations to new examples (Rogers and McClelland, 2004), turning raw sensory inputs into high-level semantic knowledge (Navon, 1977), and deductively drawing inferences via conceptual rules and statements (Johnson, 1988).

Neuro-symbolic representations present us with an opportunity us to enrich expressive language representations. On the one hand, symbols can be used to represent higher-level concepts and abstractions to characterize the information expressed in the text without resorting to individual annotations. On the other hand, distributed representations can help us ground these concepts and generalize to linguistic variations. Moreover, symbolic rules allow us to explicitly model the dependencies between aspects of the language and higher-level abstractions and behaviors. Most importantly, neuro-symbolic representations are inherently explainable, making them particularly useful for interactive and humans-in-the-loop approaches. Recently, we introduced DRaiL (Pacheco and Goldwasser, 2021), a neuro-symbolic modeling framework for NLP. In this work, we enhance DRaiL with a Python interface to facilitate the interactive exploration of neuro-symbolic NLP models. We demonstrate how to model two challenging language scenarios using DRaiL, and propose a set of diagnostic and visualization operations to probe and debug DRaiL predictions. Then, we demonstrate how we can interactively enhance and modify DRaiL programs to correct mistakes and introduce additional knowledge. This work represents a first step towards an interactive neuro-symbolic framework. An executable version of this demo is publicly available, and it includes the full code flow to run an example[2]. The source code for DRaiL, as well as its documentation and additional examples have been

[1]Work done while the first author was at Purdue University.

[2]https://bit.ly/3uLH26s

Proceedings of the The 2022 Conference on Empirical Methods in Natural Language Processing: System Demonstrations, pages 371 - 378
December 7-11, 2022 ©2022 Association for Computational Linguistics

released to the community[3]

2 Case Studies

Morality Framing in Political Discourse We previously introduced Morality Framing, a knowledge representation framework for capturing sentence and entity level moral sentiment (Roy et al., 2021). It is built on top of the Moral Foundation Theory (MFT) (Haidt and Joseph, 2004; Haidt and Graham, 2007) that proposes six Moral Foundations (MFs). Morality Frames extend MFT by introducing entity sentiment dimensions. The MFs are considered as frame predicates, and positive and negative entity roles are associated with each predicate. For example, the MF 'Care/Harm' is motivated by entities that are either 'providing care' or 'doing harm' to a specific target entity.

Morality Frame Predicate: Care/Harm

[New cyber center]$_{CARING}$ will provide hands-on learning to prepare midshipmen to protect [US]$_{TARGET}$ from [cyber terrorists and thugs]$_{HARMING}$.

The full list of morality frames can be found in the original paper. Given a text, the task is to identify - (1) the predicate (MF), and (2) the moral roles of the entities mentioned in the text. The dataset contains 1.5k tweets by US congress-members annotated for MF and entity roles.. We also released a dataset of 9.5k unlabeled tweets on the abortion issue, which we explore in this demo.

The Covid-19 Vaccination Debate In previous work, we proposed a holistic analysis framework to analyze opinions about the Covid-19 vaccine (Pacheco et al., 2022). This framework builds on Morality Frames, and connects it with opinion analysis. In addition to predicting MFs and entity roles, we predict the stance with respect to the vaccine (i.e. pro-vax or anti-vax), and we model a set of repeating themes frequently used to discuss the vaccine in social media.

Stance: Anti-Vax, Theme: Government distrust

I never saw anything like this [government]$_{OPRESSING}$'s obsession with [citizens]$_{TARGET}$ getting the Covid vaccine. Is this a trial run for a socialist dictatorship?

Our analysis identifies the *stance* expressed in the post (`anti-vaccination`) and the *reason* for it (`distrust of government`). Given the ideologically polarized climate of social media discussion on this topic, we also aim to characterize the moral attitudes expressed in the text (`oppression`), and how different entities mentioned in it are perceived. The dataset contains 750 tweets geo-located in the U.S. annotated for morality frames and stance, as well as a set of themes identified interactively. We also released a dataset of 85k unlabeled tweets about the covid vaccine, which we explore in this demo.

3 Problem Specification

In this section, we demonstrate how to model the scenarios described in Section 2. To model a problem in DRaiL, we need to decompose the domain into a set of entities, labels, predicates and probabilistic rules that express the different decisions and their inter-dependencies. To predict morality frames, we break down the problem into two main decisions: 1) the most prominent moral foundation expressed in the tweet, and 2) for each entity mentioned in the tweet, the role they playing. In addition to this, we include some contextualizing information. For political tweets, we model the topic being discussed, the author of the tweet, and their party affiliation. In the case of covid-19 debate, we model the stance (i.e. pro or anti vax), as well as the main theme highlighted in the argument (e.g. government distrust).

In this demo, we present a Python API that allows us to instantiate and learn DRaiL programs. The API is centered around a `Learner` class. We currently support two types of learners, a `LocalLearner` in which rule weights are learned independently of each other, and a `GlobalLearner` in which all rule weights are learned jointly. The learner receives a set of parameters, including the inference algorithm and loss function to be used, as well as the learning rate.

```
from drail.learn.global_learner import GlobalLearner

learner = GlobalLearner(
    infer_algorithm="ad3",
    loss_fn="hinge_loss",
    learning_rate=2e-5)
```

Entities and Predicates Entities are the base elements in a DRaiL program. Entities are named, and can correspond to either symbolic elements (e.g. a topic) or attributed elements (e.g. a tweet associated with its textual content). Then, we can specify relations between one or more entities in DRaiL. Relations can correspond to observed or predicted information. When observations are available for a particular relation, either as input information or as training data, it can be passed to DRaiL using column separated files. Each column in the file will

[3] `https://gitlab.com/purdueNlp/DRaiL`

correspond to each of the entities involved in the relation. For example:

```
learner.define_entity("Tweet")
learner.define_entity("Entity")
learner.define_entity("Role")

learner.define_predicate("HasEntity",
    ents=["Tweet", "Entity"],
    data_file="has_entity.txt")

learner.define_predicate("HasRole",
    ents=["Tweet", "Entity", "Role"],
    data_file="has_role.txt")
```

Rules and Constraints In DRaiL, decisions and dependencies between different decisions can be modeled using probabilistic rules. We can express these rules using templates of the form: $P_0 \wedge P_1 ... \wedge P_{n-1} \Rightarrow P_n$, where the body of the rule template can contain observed or predicted predicates, and the head corresponds to the output to be predicted (given the body). Rules can be grounded in data, and each rule grounding is associated with a weight representing the likelihood of the rule grounding holding true. In DRaiL, these weights are learned using neural nets. For this reason, each rule template is associated to a feature function and a neural scoring function.

We support different types of rules. We can define simple rules that map observed inputs to predicted outputs, and estimate the likelihood of each possible assignment. For example, mapping tweets to MFs:

```
learner.define_rule(
    "IsTweet(T) => HasMf(T,M)^?",
    lmd=1.0,
    features=["tweet_bert"],
    nn=BertClassifier(config_r0))
```

Or we can write rules that capture the dependencies between different aspects, and estimate the likelihood them co-occurring. For example, MFs and vaccination stances:

```
learner.define_rule(
    "IsTweet(T) & HasStance(T,S)^? => HasMf(T,M)^?",
    lmd=1.0,
    features=["tweet_bert", "stace_1hot"],
    nn=Bert1HotClassifier(config_r2))
```

Here, `lmd` is a hyper-parameter that can be used to manually tune the importance of each rule. Given a learned weight `w` for a given rule, its final weight will be calculated by multiplying `lmd*w`. We use ? after a predicate to signal that this is a predicate that is not observed, and should be predicted.

Finally, we can also write hard dependencies or constraints that enforce behaviors. For example, enforcing entities to maintain the same polarity when mentioned in tweets with the same stance:

```
learner.define_hardconstr(
    "HasEntity(T1,E) & HasEntity(T2,E) &
↪   HasStance(T1,'anti-vax')^? & HasStance(T2,
↪   'anti-vax')^? & HasSentiment(T1,E,'neg')^?  =>
↪   HasSentiment(T2,E,'neg')^?")
```

Feature Extractors and Scoring Functions DRaiL gives us the flexibility to define any feature function and neural architecture to represent rules and learn their weights. To define feature functions, we need to extend DRaiL's `FeatureExtractor` class. This programmatic interface gives us a lot of flexibility with passing and importing resources, as well as manipulating features:

```
from drail.features.feature_extractor import FeatureExtractor
from transformers import AutoTokenizer

class MF_ft(FeatureExtractor):
    def __init__(self, id2data):
        super(MF_ft, self).__init__()
        self.id2data = id2data
        self.tokenizer = AutoTokenizer.from_pretrained(
            'bert-base-uncased')

    def entity_bert(self, rule_gr):
        pred = rule_gr.get_body_predicate("HasEntity")
        (tweet, entity) = pred['arguments']
        text = self.id2data[tweet][entity]['text']
        bert_input = self.tokenizer.encode(text)
        return bert_input
```

The constructor allows us to pass any data structure. In the example above, we pass a dictionary that maps entity ids to their attributes (e.g. the text of the tweet). Then, we import the `transformers` library to obtain the inputs for BERT. Alternatively, this could be pre-computed and passed to the constructor directly. DRaiL allows us to obtain the predicates and arguments of each rule grounding with the function `RuleGrounding.get_body_predicate(name, position=0)`, which returns the predicate as a dictionary of the form `{"name": name, "arguments": [arg0, arg1, ...]}`. Custom `FeatureExtractors` can be instantiated in the `learner` by doing:

```
learner.fe = MF_ft(id2data="id2data.json")
```

DRaiL provides a similar programmatic interface to define neural scoring functions, which is built on top of PyTorch:

```
from drail.neuro.nn_model import NeuralNetworks
from transformers import AutoConfig, AutoModel, BertModel
import torch

class BertClassifier(NeuralNetworks):

    def __init__(self, config):
        super(BertClassifier, self).__init__(config)

    def build_architecture(self):
        self.bert_model = AutoModel.from_pretrained(
            'bert-base-uncased',
            add_pooling_layer=True)
        self.dropout = torch.nn.Dropout(config["dropout_prob"])
        self.hidden2label = torch.nn.Linear(config["h_dim"],
    ↪   config["o_dim"])
```

```
def forward(self, x):
    # will return feats that were defined in feat function
    bert_inputs = self.get_inputs(x)
    outputs = self.bert_model(bert_inputs['input_ids'],
    ↪ bert_inputs['attention_mask'],
    ↪ bert_inputs['token_type_ids'])
    pooled_output = outputs[1]
    pooled_output = self.dropout(pooled_output)
    logits = self.hidden2label(pooled_output)
```

Given that the neural architectures are defined programmatically, there is a lot of flexibility as to what each architecture can look like. For each rule, we can define a configuration dictionary `config` which can be passed to the constructor of the neural classifier. This allows us to specify variable parameters (e.g. number of hidden/output units), and to reuse classifiers for different rules.

To see the full set of rules that were tested for each use case, we refer the user to our previous work (Roy et al., 2021; Pacheco et al., 2022), and to the live demo and repository linked to this paper.

Grounding, Inference and Learning To instantiate our database and ground our rules, we need to call the `create_dataset` function and pass the directory that contains the files that were defined for each predicate. We are able to specify train, dev and test splits by creating filters in the database. This operation is useful when we want to perform K-fold cross-validation, as it allows us to dynamically change the splits in an execution loop.

```
db = learner.create_dataset("data_dir")
db.add_filter(
    name="isTrain", pred_name="IsTweet", entity_name="Tweet",
    ↪ ids=train_tweet_ids
)
```

DRaiL transforms all rule groundings into linear inequalities corresponding to their disjunctive form, and inference is then defined as an integer linear program:

$$\underset{y\in\{0,1\}^n}{} P(y|x) \equiv_{y\in\{0,1\}^n} \sum_{\psi_{r,t}\in\Psi} w_r\ \psi_r(\boldsymbol{x_r}, \boldsymbol{y_r}) \qquad (1)$$
$$s.t.\ c(\boldsymbol{x_c}, \boldsymbol{y_c}) \leq 0;\ \ \forall c \in C$$

Where each rule grounding r, generated from template t, with input features $\boldsymbol{x_r}$ and predicted variables $\boldsymbol{y_r}$ defines the potential $\psi_r(\boldsymbol{x_r}, \boldsymbol{y_r})$, added to the linear program with a weight w_r. DRaiL implements both exact and approximate inference to solve the MAP problem, in the latter case, the AD^3 algorithm is used (Martins et al., 2015). Weights w_r are learned using neural networks defined over parameter set $\boldsymbol{\theta}$. For training using large-margin estimation, DRaiL uses the structured hinge loss:

$$\max_{\hat{\mathbf{y}}\in Y}(\Delta(\hat{\mathbf{y}}, \mathbf{y}) + \sum_{\psi_r\in\Psi} \Phi_t(\boldsymbol{x_r}, \boldsymbol{\hat{y}_r}; \theta^t)) - \sum_{\psi_r\in\Psi} \Phi_t(\boldsymbol{x_r}, \boldsymbol{y_r}; \theta^t)$$

Where Φ_t represents the neural net associated with rule template t, and parameter set θ^t. Here, $\mathbf{y}$ corresponds to the gold assignments, and $\hat{\mathbf{y}}$ corresponds to the prediction resulting from the MAP inference defined in Eq. 1. Note that alternative estimations are also supported. More details can be found in the modeling paper (Pacheco and Goldwasser, 2021).

Our Python API wraps up all of this functionality in just two functions: `train` and `predict`. Additional parameters can be specified to select the optimizer, use loss augmented inference, or hot start the parameters by training rules locally first. We have found that hot starting parameters locally consistently improves performance across tasks. This finding is in line with previous work experimenting with deep structured prediction objectives (Han et al., 2019). The `predict` function returns two elements: `results` has the aggregated predictions in a data structure that can be directly used to evaluate performance using the `sklearn.metrics` library, while `preds` contains the resulting set of active predicates.

```
from sklearn.metrics import classification_report

learner.train(db,
    train_filter="isTrain",
    dev_filter="isDev",
    patience=10,
    local_hot_start=True)

results, preds = learner.predict(db,
    test_filter="isTest")

y_gold = results.metrics["HasMF"]['gold_data']
y_pred = results.metrics["HasMF"]['pred_data']
classification_report(y_gold, y_pred, digits=4)
```

4 Interactive Evaluation and Debugging

In this section, we present an evaluation module equipped with functions to interactively debug and visualize DRaiL models. These functions are especially valuable when evaluating model predictions over unlabeled data, where we cannot directly measure performance. To showcase this capability, we use the sets of unlabeled tweets about abortion and the covid-19 vaccine described in Sec. 2.

4.1 Visualizing and Interpreting Results

In this section, we present a non-exhaustive list of the visualization operations supported by our API. **freq_graph(pred,ent,filters)**: plots a bar graph of frequencies for entity `ent` in active `pred` predicates (e.g. `frequency_graph("HasMF", "MF")` will plot the distribution of MFs for all tweets. The optional parameter `filters` allows us to specify filters in the form of logical predicates. For example, if we want to plot MF frequencies by political party, we can do:

```
learner.freq_graph("HasMF", "MF", filters=["IsAuthor(T,A) &
↪ HasParty(A, 'democrat')", "IsAuthor(T,A) & HasParty(A,
↪ 'republican')"])
```

Note that more than one filter can be used to compare frequencies. If no filters are passed, general frequencies will be plotted (one bar per value).

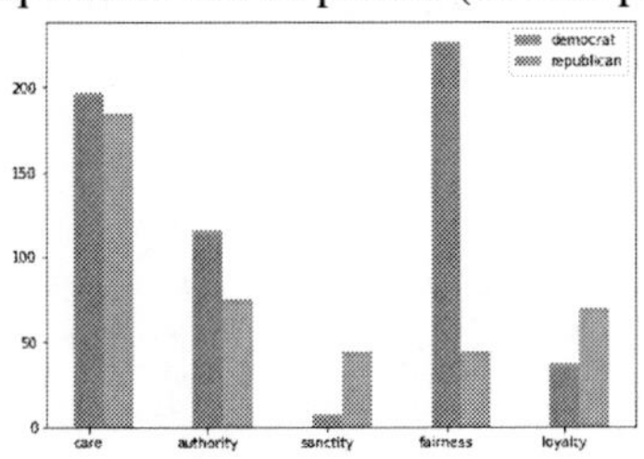

freq_ents(pred,ent,k,filter): outputs the top k most frequent ent entities in predicate pred.

```
learner.freq_ents("HasEntity", "Entity", k=10)

[('women', 325),
 ('abortion', 235),
 ('life', 207),
 ('wade', 115),
 ('trump', 111),
 ('roe', 104),
 ('planned parenthood', 91),
 ('reproductive rights', 90),
 ('health care', 62),
 ('unborn', 56)]
```

diag_rank_graph(pred,ent,ent_inst,top_filter, bottom_filter): plots a graph that visualizes the normalized rank scores based of the frequencies of entity ent=ent_inst in active predicates pred. This graph uses a diagonal to contrast the frequencies of the predicate activations that satisfy the top_filter and the bottom_filter. For example:

```
learner.diag_rank_graph("HasEntity", "Entity", "planned
↪ parenthood", top_filter="IsAuthor(T,A) &
↪ HasParty(T,'republican')", bottom_filter="IsAuthor(T,A) &
↪ HasParty(T,'democrat')")
```

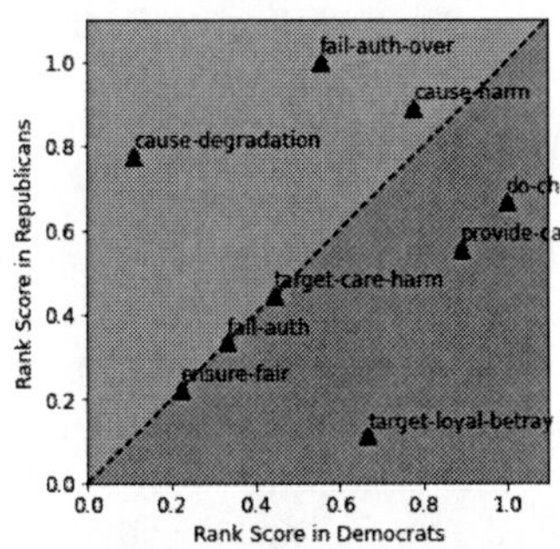

ent_rel_graph(pred,k,filter): plots an entity-relation graph for active predicates pred. Optionally, a k can be used to limit the graph to the top k most frequent activations. For example:

```
learner.ent_rel_rank_graph("HasRole", k=8,
↪ filter="IsAuthor(T,A) & HasParty(T,'democrat') &
↪ HasMF(T,'fairness')")
```

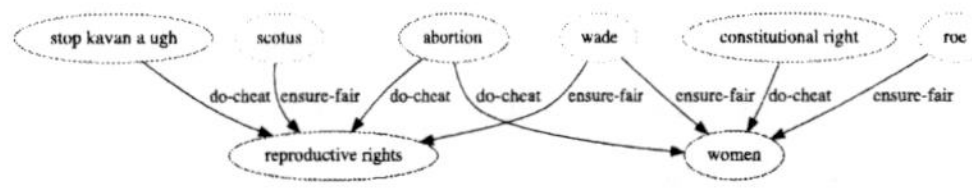

corr_matrix(pred_1,ent_1,filter_1,pred_2,ent_1,filter_2): plots a correlation matrix between ent_1 and ent_1. Optionally, filters can be specified to constrain the examples considered.

```
learner.corr_matrix(pred_1="HasMF", ent_1="MF",
↪ pred_2="HasTheme", ent_2="Theme")
```

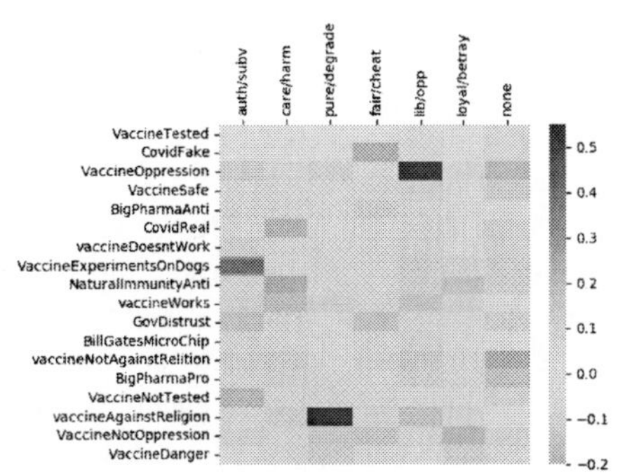

plot_embed(pred, ent, filter): plots a 2D visualization of the representation learned for a given entity. To reduce the dimensionality, we use t-sne (van der Maaten and Hinton, 2008). Note that DRaiL will learn a representation for each entity and relation in the program using the neural architecture specified. These representations can also be shared across rules. For more details, see (Pacheco and Goldwasser, 2021).

```
learner.plot_embed("HasTheme", "Theme")
```

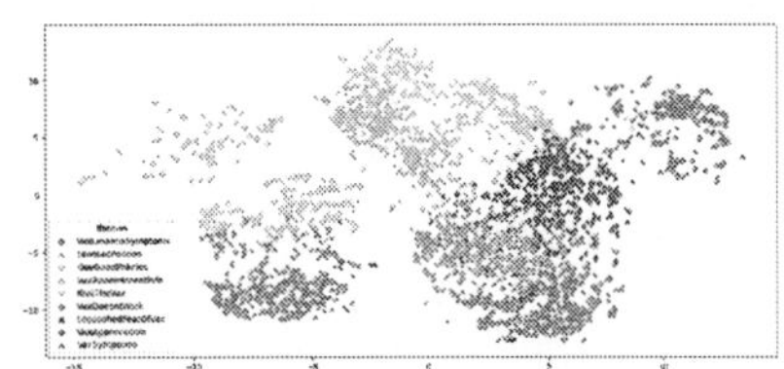

4.2 Human Interventions

In this section, we focus on the ability of interactively correcting and enhancing DRaiL models. Going by the visualizations demonstrated above for political tweets, we can observe that overall, the results are what we would expect. However, we can spot some unexpected predictions. For example, in the normalized rank graph for *planned parenthood*, we found that the moral role *do-cheat* had a high *democrat* score, which contradicts the general sentiment of liberals towards Planned Parenthood. Additionally, in the entity-relation graph, we observe the entity *abortion* being portrayed as a *cheating* entity in a high number of cases. To tackle this likely errors, we experiment with the following interventions:

Introducing bias with new rules and constraints Given that democrats generally have a pro-choice stance, we can introduce a rule that discourages a negative polarity for the *abortion* entity:

```
learner.define_rule(
    "IsTweet(T) & IsAuthor(A,T) & HasParty(A,'democrat') &
    ↪ HasEntity(T,'abortion') & HasPolarity(R,'neg') =>
    ↪ ~HasRole(T,'abortion',R)^?"),
    lmd=1.0,
    features=None,
    nn=None
```

To represent this rule, we set the features and neural net to None. This will make DRaiL learn a single weight for the rule, instead of learning a neural scoring function over a feature representation. Note that this is a design choice, and we always have the option of defining features and a neural classifiers for newly introduced rules. By adding this rule, we are able to alter our entity-relation graph:

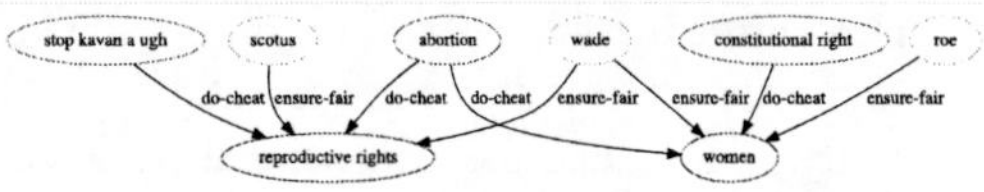

Augmenting programs with new predicates While the rule introduced above altered our high-frequency entity-relation graph, upon closer inspection of the cases that were not covered by the soft constraint (using the **freq_ents** function to look at example tweets), we find that we likely still have errors. Tweets that have an overall negative tone are wrongly identified as portraying abortion in negative light. Some examples are: *we do not want to go back to the days before women had a constitutional right to abortion, president trump has said that women should face punishment for exercising their constitutional right to abortion.*

By looking at these examples, we can see that they talk about abortion as a *constitutional right*. To deal with this challenge, we can take advantage of the fact that we can represent entities in DRaiL using distributed representations, and introduce a new predicate that captures the similarity between a custom phrase explaining the concept of *constitutional rights* and the text of a tweet:

```
learner.define_entity("Phrase")
learner.define_latent_predicate(
    "MentionsConcept",
    ents=["Phrase", "Tweet"])
```

Given that we do not have supervision for this predicate, DRaiL allows us to define it as latent. Then, we can define two additional rules, the first one uses SBERT, a pre-trained sentence similarity model (Reimers and Gurevych, 2019) to capture the likelihood that a tweet mentions *constitutional rights*. The second one is a constraint that enforces tweets that frame abortion as a constitutional right to have the entity *abortion* in a positive role.

```
learner.define_rule(
    "InEvent(T,Z) => MentionsConcept('abortion is a
    ↪ constitutional right', T)^?",
    lmd=1.0,
    features=["tweet_bert"],
    nn=SBERT())
learner.define_hardconstr(
    "InEvent(T,Z) & HasEntity(T, 'abortion') &
    ↪ HasPolarity(R,'neg') MentionsConcept('abortion is a
    ↪ constitutional right', T)^? =>
    ↪ ~HasRole(T,'abortion',R)^?"))
```

Upon further inspection of example tweets, we found that the addition of the new predicate reduced more than 50% of the remaining errors.

5 DRaiL vs. Other Systems

In previous work, we have positioned the modeling approach of DRaiL with respect to related work, including declarative languages to express probabilistic graphical models (Richardson and Domingos, 2006; Bach et al., 2017), relational and graph embeddings (Bordes et al., 2013; Schlichtkrull et al., 2018), and a comprehensive set of neuro-symbolic systems (Wang and Poon, 2018; Manhaeve et al., 2018; Cohen et al., 2020). While performing an exhaustive comparison between systems is beyond the scope of this demo, we refer the reader to the DRaiL modeling paper for this analysis (Pacheco and Goldwasser, 2021), as well as to the many successful applications of our modeling strategy (Pujari and Goldwasser, 2019; Jain et al., 2020; Widmoser et al., 2021; Lee et al., 2021; Roy et al., 2021; Mehta et al., 2022; Pacheco et al., 2022).

6 Summary

In this paper, we present an interactive API for DRaiL, a recently introduced neuro-symbolic modeling framework. We demonstrate how to use this API to model a challenging NLP problem, and interactively debug predictions on unlabeled datasets, where traditional evaluation techniques cannot be applied. We motivate the advantage of neuro-symbolic representations to communicate knowledge from humans to machines, and show that we can effectively enhance the performance of the model by interactively adding new knowledge.

References

Stephen H. Bach, Matthias Broecheler, Bert Huang, and Lise Getoor. 2017. Hinge-loss Markov random fields and probabilistic soft logic. *Journal of Machine Learning Research (JMLR)*.

Yonatan Bisk, Ari Holtzman, Jesse Thomason, Jacob Andreas, Yoshua Bengio, Joyce Chai, Mirella Lapata, Angeliki Lazaridou, Jonathan May, Aleksandr Nisnevich, Nicolas Pinto, and Joseph Turian. 2020. Experience grounds language. In *Proceedings of the 2020 Conference on Empirical Methods in Natural Language Processing (EMNLP)*, pages 8718–8735, Online. Association for Computational Linguistics.

Antoine Bordes, Nicolas Usunier, Alberto Garcia-Duran, Jason Weston, and Oksana Yakhnenko. 2013. Translating embeddings for modeling multi-relational data. In *Advances in Neural Information Processing Systems*, volume 26. Curran Associates, Inc.

Tom Brown, Benjamin Mann, Nick Ryder, Melanie Subbiah, Jared D Kaplan, Prafulla Dhariwal, Arvind Neelakantan, Pranav Shyam, Girish Sastry, Amanda Askell, Sandhini Agarwal, Ariel Herbert-Voss, Gretchen Krueger, Tom Henighan, Rewon Child, Aditya Ramesh, Daniel Ziegler, Jeffrey Wu, Clemens Winter, Chris Hesse, Mark Chen, Eric Sigler, Mateusz Litwin, Scott Gray, Benjamin Chess, Jack Clark, Christopher Berner, Sam McCandlish, Alec Radford, Ilya Sutskever, and Dario Amodei. 2020. Language models are few-shot learners. In *Advances in Neural Information Processing Systems*, volume 33, pages 1877–1901. Curran Associates, Inc.

William W. Cohen, Fan Yang, and Kathryn Mazaitis. 2020. Tensorlog: A probabilistic database implemented using deep-learning infrastructure. *J. Artif. Intell. Res.*, 67:285–325.

Jacob Devlin, Ming-Wei Chang, Kenton Lee, and Kristina Toutanova. 2019. BERT: Pre-training of deep bidirectional transformers for language understanding. In *Proceedings of the 2019 Conference of the North American Chapter of the Association for Computational Linguistics: Human Language Technologies, Volume 1 (Long and Short Papers)*, pages 4171–4186, Minneapolis, Minnesota. Association for Computational Linguistics.

Jonathan Haidt and Jesse Graham. 2007. When morality opposes justice: Conservatives have moral intuitions that liberals may not recognize. *Social Justice Research*, 20(1):98–116.

Jonathan Haidt and Craig Joseph. 2004. Intuitive ethics: How innately prepared intuitions generate culturally variable virtues. *Daedalus*, 133(4):55–66.

Rujun Han, Qiang Ning, and Nanyun Peng. 2019. Joint event and temporal relation extraction with shared representations and structured prediction. In *Proceedings of the 2019 Conference on Empirical Methods in Natural Language Processing and the 9th International Joint Conference on Natural Language Processing (EMNLP-IJCNLP)*, pages 434–444, Hong Kong, China. Association for Computational Linguistics.

Ayush Jain, Maria Leonor Pacheco, Steven Lancette, Mahak Goindani, and Dan Goldwasser. 2020. Identifying collaborative conversations using latent discourse behaviors. In *Proceedings of the 21th Annual Meeting of the Special Interest Group on Discourse and Dialogue*, pages 74–78, 1st virtual meeting. Association for Computational Linguistics.

Ralph H. Johnson. 1988. Gilbert harman change in view: Principles of reasoning (cambridge, ma: Mit press 1986). pp. ix 147. *Canadian Journal of Philosophy*, 18(1):163–178.

I-Ta Lee, Maria Leonor Pacheco, and Dan Goldwasser. 2021. Modeling human mental states with an entity-based narrative graph. In *Proceedings of the 2021 Conference of the North American Chapter of the Association for Computational Linguistics: Human Language Technologies*, pages 4916–4926, Online. Association for Computational Linguistics.

Piyawat Lertvittayakumjorn and Francesca Toni. 2021. Explanation-based human debugging of NLP models: A survey. *Transactions of the Association for Computational Linguistics*, 9:1508–1528.

Robin Manhaeve, Sebastijan Dumancic, Angelika Kimmig, Thomas Demeester, and Luc De Raedt. 2018. Deepproblog: Neural probabilistic logic programming. In *Proceedings of the 32nd International Conference on Neural Information Processing Systems*, NIPS'18, page 3753–3763, Red Hook, NY, USA. Curran Associates Inc.

André F. T. Martins, Mário A. T. Figueiredo, Pedro M. Q. Aguiar, Noah A. Smith, and Eric P. Xing. 2015. Ad3: Alternating directions dual decomposition for map inference in graphical models. *Journal of Machine Learning Research*, 16(16):495–545.

Nikhil Mehta, Maria Pacheco, and Dan Goldwasser. 2022. Tackling fake news detection by continually improving social context representations using graph neural networks. In *Proceedings of the 60th Annual Meeting of the Association for Computational Linguistics (Volume 1: Long Papers)*, pages 1363–1380, Dublin, Ireland. Association for Computational Linguistics.

David Navon. 1977. Forest before trees: The precedence of global features in visual perception. *Cognitive Psychology*, 9(3):353 – 383.

Maria Pacheco, Tunazzina Islam, Monal Mahajan, Andrey Shor, Ming Yin, Lyle Ungar, and Dan Goldwasser. 2022. A holistic framework for analyzing the COVID-19 vaccine debate. In *Proceedings of the 2022 Conference of the North American Chapter of the Association for Computational Linguistics: Human Language Technologies*, pages 5821–5839, Seattle, United States. Association for Computational Linguistics.

Maria Leonor Pacheco and Dan Goldwasser. 2021. Modeling content and context with deep relational learning. *Transactions of the Association for Computational Linguistics*, 9:100–119.

Rajkumar Pujari and Dan Goldwasser. 2019. Using natural language relations between answer choices for machine comprehension. In *Proceedings of the 2019 Conference of the North American Chapter of the Association for Computational Linguistics: Human Language Technologies, Volume 1 (Long and Short Papers)*, pages 4010–4015, Minneapolis, Minnesota. Association for Computational Linguistics.

Nils Reimers and Iryna Gurevych. 2019. Sentence-BERT: Sentence embeddings using Siamese BERT-networks. In *Proceedings of the 2019 Conference on Empirical Methods in Natural Language Processing and the 9th International Joint Conference on Natural Language Processing (EMNLP-IJCNLP)*, pages 3982–3992, Hong Kong, China. Association for Computational Linguistics.

Matthew Richardson and Pedro Domingos. 2006. Markov logic networks. *Mach. Learn.*, 62(1–2):107–136.

T. Rogers and James L. McClelland. 2004. Semantic cognition: A parallel distributed processing approach.

Shamik Roy, Maria Leonor Pacheco, and Dan Goldwasser. 2021. Identifying morality frames in political tweets using relational learning. In *Proceedings of the 2021 Conference on Empirical Methods in Natural Language Processing*, pages 9939–9958, Online and Punta Cana, Dominican Republic. Association for Computational Linguistics.

Michael Schlichtkrull, Thomas N. Kipf, Peter Bloem, Rianne van den Berg, Ivan Titov, and Max Welling. 2018. Modeling relational data with graph convolutional networks. In *The Semantic Web*, pages 593–607, Cham. Springer International Publishing.

Laurens van der Maaten and Geoffrey Hinton. 2008. Visualizing data using t-SNE. *Journal of Machine Learning Research*, 9:2579–2605.

Hai Wang and Hoifung Poon. 2018. Deep probabilistic logic: A unifying framework for indirect supervision. In *Proceedings of the 2018 Conference on Empirical Methods in Natural Language Processing*, pages 1891–1902, Brussels, Belgium. Association for Computational Linguistics.

Zijie J. Wang, Dongjin Choi, Shenyu Xu, and Diyi Yang. 2021. Putting humans in the natural language processing loop: A survey. In *Proceedings of the First Workshop on Bridging Human–Computer Interaction and Natural Language Processing*, pages 47–52, Online. Association for Computational Linguistics.

Manuel Widmoser, Maria Leonor Pacheco, Jean Honorio, and Dan Goldwasser. 2021. Randomized deep structured prediction for discourse-level processing. In *Proceedings of the 16th Conference of the European Chapter of the Association for Computational Linguistics: Main Volume*, pages 1174–1184, Online. Association for Computational Linguistics.

Paraphrastic Representations at Scale

John Wieting[1], Kevin Gimpel[2], Graham Neubig[3], and Taylor Berg-Kirkpatrick[4]
[1]Google Research
[2]Toyota Technological Institute at Chicago, Chicago, IL, 60637, USA
[3]Carnegie Mellon University, Pittsburgh, PA, 15213, USA
[4]University of California San Diego, San Diego, CA, 92093, USA
jwieting@alumni.cmu.edu, kgimpel@ttic.edu, gneubig@cs.cmu.edu, tberg@eng.ucsd.edu

Abstract

We present a system that allows users to train their own state-of-the-art paraphrastic sentence representations in a variety of languages. We release trained models for English, Arabic, German, Spanish, French, Russian, Turkish, and Chinese. We train these models on large amounts of data, achieving significantly improved performance from our original papers on a suite of monolingual semantic similarity, cross-lingual semantic similarity, and bitext mining tasks. Moreover, the resulting models surpass all prior work on efficient unsupervised semantic textual similarity, even significantly outperforming supervised BERT-based models like Sentence-BERT (Reimers and Gurevych, 2019). Most importantly, our models are orders of magnitude faster than other strong similarity models and can be used on CPU with little difference in inference speed (even improved speed over GPU when using more CPU cores), making these models an attractive choice for users without access to GPUs or for use on embedded devices. Finally, we add significantly increased functionality to the code bases for training paraphrastic sentence models, easing their use for both inference and for training them for any desired language with parallel data. We also include code to automatically download and preprocess training data.[1]

1 Introduction

Measuring sentence similarity (Agirre et al., 2012) is an important task in natural language processing, and has found many uses including paraphrase detection (Dolan et al., 2004), bitext mining (Schwenk and Douze, 2017), language modelling (Khandelwal et al., 2019), question-answering (Lewis et al., 2021), and as reward functions or evaluation metrics for language generation tasks (Wieting et al., 2019a). Within this context, fast and light-weight methods are particularly useful as they make it easy to compute similarity over the ever-increasing volumes of web text available. For instance, we may want to mine a hundred million parallel sentences (Schwenk et al., 2021) or use a semantic similarity reward when fine-tuning language generation models on tens of millions of training examples. These tasks are much more feasible when using approaches that are fast, can be run on CPU, and use little RAM, allowing for increased batch size.

This need for fast inference is one motivation for using sentence embeddings. Sentence embeddings allow the search for similar sentences to be linear in the number of sentences, or even sub-linear when using highly optimized tools like `Faiss` (Johnson et al., 2017) that allow for efficient nearest neighbor search. This is contrast to models, like cross-attention models, which are quadratic during inference as they require both of the texts being compared as inputs. As we show in this paper, our *simple* and *interpretable* word-averaging sentence embedding models (Wieting et al., 2016b; Wieting and Gimpel, 2018; Wieting et al., 2019b), are orders of magnitude faster to compute than prior embedding approaches while simultaneously possessing significantly stronger performance on monolingual and cross-lingual semantic similarity tasks. Since we are simply averaging embeddings and have no neural architecture, any models based on neural architectures, especially large pretrained neural architectures which are increasingly used, will not be as fast as the models described in this paper. Lastly, we also show that this approach is competitive with LASER (Artetxe and Schwenk, 2019), a state-of-the-art multilingual model, on mining bitext and has stronger performance on cross-lingual semantic similarity, while having inference speeds that are twice as fast on GPU and orders of magnitude faster on CPU.

[1]Code, including an easy to install PyPi package, released models including Hugging Face implementations, demo, and data are available at https://github.com/jwieting/paraphrastic-representations-at-scale.

Proceedings of the The 2022 Conference on Empirical Methods in Natural Language Processing: System Demonstrations, pages 379 - 388
December 7-11, 2022 ©2022 Association for Computational Linguistics

We make several contributions in this paper that go beyond our prior work. Firstly, we reformat the code to support training models on tens of millions of sentence pairs efficiently and with low RAM usage. Secondly, we train an English model on 25.85 million paraphrase pairs from ParaNMT (Wieting and Gimpel, 2018), a paraphrase corpus we previously constructed automatically from bitext. We then train models directly on X-English bitext for Arabic, German, Spanish, French, Russian, Turkish, and Chinese, producing models that are able to distinguish both paraphrases in English and their respective languages as well as cross-lingual X-English paraphrases. Even though all models are able to model semantic similarity in English, we find that training on ParaNMT specifically leads to stronger models as it is easier to filter the data to remove noise and sentence pairs with little to no diversity. We refer to our models as PARAGRAM-SP, abbreviated as P-SP,[2] referring to how the models are based on averaging subword units generated by `sentencepiece` (Kudo and Richardson, 2018). We make all of these models available to the community for use on downstream tasks.

We also add functionality to our implementation. Besides the support for efficient, low-memory training on tens of million of sentence pairs described above, we add code to support (1) reading in a list of sentences and producing a saved `numpy` array of the sentence embeddings; (2) reading in a list of sentence pairs and producing cosine similarity scores; and (3) downloading and preprocessing evaluation data, bitext, and paraphrase data. For bitext and paraphrase data, we provide support for training using either text files or `HDF5` files.

Lastly, this paper contains new experiments showcasing the limits of these scaled-up models and detailed comparisons with prior work on a suite of semantic similarity tasks in a variety of languages. We release our code and models to the community in the hope that they will be found useful for research and applications, as well as using them as a base to build stronger, faster models covering more of the languages of the world.

2 Related Work

2.1 English Semantic Similarity

Our learning and evaluation setting is the same as that of our earlier work that seeks to learn paraphrastic sentence embeddings that can be used for downstream tasks (Wieting et al., 2016b,a; Wieting and Gimpel, 2017; Wieting et al., 2017; Wieting and Gimpel, 2018). We trained models on noisy paraphrase pairs and evaluated them primarily on semantic textual similarity (STS) tasks. More recently, we made use of parallel bitext for training paraphrastic representations for other languages as well that are also able to model cross-lingual semantic similarity (Wieting et al., 2019a, 2020). Prior work in learning general sentence embeddings has used autoencoders (Socher et al., 2011; Hill et al., 2016), encoder-decoder architectures (Kiros et al., 2015; Gan et al., 2017), and other sources of supervision and learning frameworks (Le and Mikolov, 2014; Pham et al., 2015; Arora et al., 2017; Pagliardini et al., 2017).

For English semantic similarity, we compare to well known sentence embedding models such as InferSent (Conneau et al., 2017), GenSen (Subramanian et al., 2018), the Universal Sentence Encoder (USE) (Cer et al., 2018), as well as BERT (Devlin et al., 2019).[3] We use the pretrained BERT model in two ways to create a sentence embedding. The first way is to concatenate the hidden states for the CLS token in the last four layers. The second way is to concatenate the hidden states of all word tokens in the last four layers and mean pool these representations. Both methods result in a 4096 dimension embedding. We also compare to a more recently released model called Sentence-BERT (Reimers and Gurevych, 2019). This model is similar to InferSent in that it is trained on natural language inference data (SNLI; Bowman et al., 2015). However, instead of using pretrained word embeddings, they fine-tune BERT in a way to induce sentence embeddings. Lastly, we also compare to the unsupervised version of SimCSE (Gao et al., 2021), which fine-tunes a pretrained encoder on contrastive pairs, where positive pairs are obtained by using dropout on a single input sentence.

[2]Our English model is P-SP, and the cross-lingual models are P-SP-AR, P-SP-DE, P-SP-ES, P-SP-FR, P-SP-RU, P-SP-TR, and P-SP-ZH.

[3]Note that in all experiments using BERT, including Sentence-BERT, the large, uncased version is used.

2.2 Cross-Lingual Semantic Similarity and Semantic Similarity in Non-English Languages

Most previous work for cross-lingual representations has focused on models based on encoders from neural machine translation (Espana-Bonet et al., 2017; Schwenk and Douze, 2017; Schwenk, 2018) or deep architectures using contrastive losses (Grégoire and Langlais, 2018; Guo et al., 2018; Chidambaram et al., 2019). Recently, other approaches using large Transformer (Vaswani et al., 2017) have been proposed, trained on vast quantities of text (Conneau et al., 2020; Liu et al., 2020; Tran et al., 2020). We primarily focus our comparison for these settings on LASER (Artetxe and Schwenk, 2019), a model trained for semantic similarity across more than 100 languages. Their model uses an LSTM encoder-decoder trained on hundreds of millions of parallel sentences. They achieve state-of-the-art performance on a variety of multilingual sentence embeddings tasks including bitext mining. We also compare to LaBSE (Feng et al., 2022), a contrastive model trained on six billion parallel pairs across languages and was also trained on monolingual text using a masked language modelling objective.

3 Methods

We first describe our objective function and then describe our encoder.

Training. The training data consists of a sequence of parallel sentence pairs (s_i, t_i) in source and target languages respectively. Note that for training our English model, the source and target languages are both English as we are able to make use of an existing paraphrase corpus. For each sentence pair, we randomly choose a *negative* target sentence t'_i during training that is not a translation or paraphrase of s_i. Our objective is to have source and target sentences be more similar than source and negative target examples by a margin δ:

$$\min_{\theta_{\text{src}}, \theta_{\text{tgt}}} \sum_i \Big[\delta - f_\theta(s_i, t_i) + f_\theta(s_i, t'_i))\Big]_+ \quad (1)$$

where the similarity function is defined as:

$$f_\theta(s, t) = \cos\Big(g(s; \theta_{\text{src}}), g(t; \theta_{\text{tgt}})\Big) \quad (2)$$

where g is the sentence encoder with parameters for each language $\theta = (\theta_{\text{src}}, \theta_{\text{tgt}})$. To select t'_i we choose the most similar sentence in some set according to the current model parameters, i.e., the one with the highest cosine similarity. We found we could achieve the strongest performance by tying all parameters together for each language, more precisely, θ_{src} and θ_{tgt} are the same.

Negative Sampling. Negative examples are selected from the sentences in the batch from the opposing language when training with bitext and from any sentence in the batch when using paraphrase data. In all cases, we choose the negative example with the highest cosine similarity to the given sentence s, ensuring that the negative is not in fact paired with s in the batch. To select even more difficult negative examples that aid training, we use the *mega-batching* procedure of Wieting and Gimpel (2018), which aggregates M mini-batches to create one "mega-batch" and selects negative examples from this mega-batch. Once each pair in the mega-batch has a negative example, the mega-batch is split back up into M mini-batches for training. Additionally, we anneal the mega-batch size by slowly increasing it during training. This yields improved performance by a significant margin.

Encoder. Our sentence encoder g simply averages the embeddings of subword units generated by `sentencepiece` (Kudo and Richardson, 2018); we refer to our model as PARAGRAM-SP, abbreviated as P-SP. This means that the sentence piece embeddings themselves are the only learned parameters of this model.

4 Code and Usage

We added a number of features to the code base to improve performance and make it easier to use. First, we added code to support easier inference. Examples of using the code programmatically to embed sentences and score sentence pairs (using cosine similarity) are shown in Figure 1.

Our code base also supports functionality that allows one to read in a list of sentences and produce a saved `numpy` array of the sentence embeddings. We also included functionality that allows one to read in a list of sentence pairs and produce the sentence pairs along with their cosine similarity scores in an output file. These scripts allow our models to be used without any programming for the two most common use cases: embedding sentences and scoring sentence pairs. Examples of their usage with a trained model are shown in Figure 2.

```
from models import load_model

text1 = 'This is a test.'
text2 = 'This is another test.'

# Load English paraphrase model
model_name = 'paraphrase-at-scale/model.para.lc.100.pt'
sp_model = 'paraphrase-at-scale/paranmt.model'

model, _ = load_model(model_name=model_name, sp_model=sp_model)

# Obtain sentence embedding
embeddings = model.embed_raw_text([text1, text2]) # 2D numpy array of sentence embeddings
cosine_scores = model.score_raw_text([(text1, text2)]) # list of cosine scores
```

Figure 1: Usage example of programmatically loading one of our pretrained models and obtaining sentence embeddings and scores for two sentences.

```
python -u embed_sentences.py --sentence-file paraphrase-at-scale/example-sentences.txt --load-file paraphrase-at-scale/model.para.lc.100.pt --output-file sentence_embeds.np

python score_sentence_pairs.py --sentence-pair-file paraphrase-at-scale/example-sentences-pairs.txt --load-file paraphrase-at-scale/model.para.lc.100.pt
```

Figure 2: Usage examples to embed sentences and score sentence pairs. The first command is a usage example of scoring a list of sentence pairs. The file `example-sentences-pairs.txt` contains a list of sentences, one per line. The output of the script is a saved `numpy` array of sentence embeddings in the same order of the input sentences. The second command is a usage example of scoring a list of sentence pairs. The file `example-sentences-pairs.txt` contains pairs of tab-separated sentences, one per line. The output of the script is a text file containing the tab separated list of sentences along with their cosine scores in the same order of the input sentences.

Secondly, we added a training mode using `HDF5`[4] format, allowing training data to remain on disk during training. This leads to a significant reduction in RAM usage during training, which is especially true when using more than 10 million training examples. Efficient training can now be done on CPU only using only a few gigabytes of RAM.

Lastly, we also added code for preprocessing data, including scripts to download and evaluate on the STS data (English, non-English, and cross-lingual), as well as code to download and process bitext and ParaNMT automatically. For bitext, our scripts download the data, filter the data by length,[5] lowercase, remove duplicates, train a `sentencepiece` model, encode the data with the `sentencepiece` model, shuffle the data, and process the data into `HDF5` format for efficient use. For ParaNMT, our scripts download the data, use a language classifier to filter out non-English sentences[6] (Joulin et al., 2017), filter the data by paraphrase score, trigram overlap, and length,[7] train a `sentencepiece` model, encode the data with the `sentencepiece` model, and process the data into `HDF5` format. Examples are shown in Figure 3.

```
cd preprocess/bilingual && bash do_all.sh fr-es-de
cd ../..
cd preprocess/paranmt && bash do_all.sh 0.4 1.0 0.7
```

Figure 3: Usage examples to download and preprocess bilingual and ParaNMT data. The first command downloads and preprocesses (filters, trains `sentencepiece` models, tokenizes if language is `zh`, converts files to `hdf5` format) `en-X` bilingual data. The third command downloads and preprocesses ParaNMT data. The arguments are used to filter the data (semantic similarity scores between 0.4 and 1.0 and trigram overlap below 0.7, which have been used in prior papers when generating training data for paraphrase generation (Iyyer et al., 2018; Krishna et al., 2020)).

en	ar	de	es	fr	ru	tr	zh
25.85M	8.23M	6.47M	6.75M	6.46M	9.09M	5.12M	4.18M

Table 1: The number of sentence pairs used to train our models. For English, the data is ParaNMT, and for the other languages, the data is a collection of bitext detailed in Section 5.1.

5 Experiments

5.1 Experimental Setup

Data. For our English model, we train on selected sentence pairs from ParaNMT (Wieting and Gimpel, 2018). We filter the corpus by only including sentence pairs where the paraphrase score for the two sentences is ≥ 0.4. We additionally filtered

[4]https://docs.h5py.org/en/stable/

[5]We remove sentences with the number of tokens (untokenized) smaller than 3 or greater than 100.

[6]https://fasttext.cc

[7]We remove sentences with the number of tokens (untokenized) smaller than 5 or greater than 40.

Model	Semantic Textual Similarity (STS)					
	2012	2013	2014	2015	2016	**Avg.**
BERT (CLS)	33.2	29.6	34.3	45.1	48.4	38.1
BERT (Mean)	48.8	46.5	54.0	59.2	63.4	54.4
InferSent	61.1	51.4	68.1	70.9	70.7	64.4
GenSen	60.7	50.8	64.1	73.3	66.0	63.0
USE	61.4	59.0	70.6	74.3	73.9	67.8
Sentence-BERT	66.9	63.2	74.2	77.3	72.8	70.9
LASER	63.1	47.0	67.7	74.9	71.9	64.9
P-SP	**68.7**	**64.7**	**78.1**	**81.4**	**80.0**	**74.6**
Sentence-BERT	71.0	**76.5**	73.2	79.1	74.3	74.8
P-SP	**71.2**	**76.5**	**74.6**	**83.0**	**79.1**	**76.9**

Table 2: Results of our models and models from prior work on English STS. In the first part of the table, we show results, measured in Pearson's $r \times 100$, for each year of the STS tasks 2012-2016 as well as the average performance across all years. In the second part, we evaluate based on the Spearman's $\rho \times 100$ of the concatenation of the datasets of each year with the 2013 SMT dataset removed following (Reimers and Gurevych, 2019).

Model	Dim.	ar-ar	ar-en	es-es	es-en	tr-en
LASER	1024	69.3\68.8	65.5\66.5	79.7\79.7	59.7\58.0	72.0\72.1
LaBSE	768	68.6\69.1	72.2\74.5	79.5\80.8	65.5\65.7	72.9\72.1
Espana-Bonet et al. (2017)	2048	59	44	78	49	76
Chidambaram et al. (2019)	512	-	-	64.2	58.7	-
2017 STS 1st Place	-	75.4	74.9	85.6	**83.0**	77.1
2017 STS 2nd Place	-	75.4	71.3	85.0	81.3	74.2
2017 STS 3rd Place	-	74.6	70.0	84.9	79.1	73.6
P-SP	1024	**76.2\76.7**	**78.3\78.4**	**85.8\85.6**	78.4\77.8	**79.2\79.5**

Table 3: Comparison of our models with those in the literature on non-English and cross-lingual STS. We also include the top 3 systems for each dataset from the SemEval 2017 STS shared task. Performance is measured in Pearson's $r \times 100$. We also include results in Spearmans's $\rho \times 100$ after a slash for LASER, LaBSE, and P-SP.

sentence pairs by their trigram overlap (Wieting et al., 2017), which is calculated by counting trigrams in the two sentences, and then dividing the number of shared trigrams by the total number in the sentence with fewer tokens. We only include sentence pairs where the trigram overlap score is ≤ 0.7. The paraphrase score is calculated by averaging PARAGRAM-PHRASE embeddings (Wieting et al., 2016b) for the two sentences in each pair and then computing their cosine similarity. The purpose of the lower threshold is to remove noise while the higher threshold is meant to remove paraphrases that are too similar.

Our training data is a mixture of Open Subtitles 2018[8] (Lison and Tiedemann, 2016), Tanzil corpus[9] (Tiedemann, 2012), Europarl[10] for Spanish, Global Voices[11] (Tiedemann, 2012), and the MultiUN corpus.[12] We follow the same distribution for our languages of interest across data sources as Artetxe and Schwenk (2019) for a fair comparison. One exception, though, is we do not include training data from Tatoeba[13] (Tiedemann, 2012) as they do, since this domain is also in the bitext mining evaluation set. The amount of data used to train each of our models is shown in Table 1.

Hyperparameters. For all models, we fix the batch size to 128, margin δ to 0.4, and the annealing rate to 150.[14] We set the size of the `sentencepiece` vocabulary to 50,000, using a shared vocabulary for the models trained on bitext. If a word is not in vocabulary, we simply exclude it, unless the text only consists of unknown words in which case we use a single unknown-word token. We optimize our models using Adam (Kingma and Ba, 2014) with a learning rate of 0.001 and train models for 25 epochs.

For training on the bilingual corpora, we tune each model on the 250 example 2017 English STS task (Cer et al., 2017). We vary dropout on the embeddings over $\{0, 0.1, 0.3\}$ and the mega-batch size M over $\{60, 100, 140\}$.

[8]http://opus.nlpl.eu/OpenSubtitles.php
[9]http://opus.nlpl.eu/Tanzil.php
[10]http://opus.nlpl.eu/Europarl.php
[11]https://opus.nlpl.eu/GlobalVoices.php
[12]http://opus.nlpl.eu/MultiUN.php
[13]https://opus.nlpl.eu/Tatoeba.php
[14]Annealing rate is the number of minibatches that are processed before the megabatch size is increased by 1.

For training on ParaNMT, we fix the hyperparameters in our model due to the increased data size making tuning more expensive. We use a mega-batch size M of 100 and set the dropout on the embeddings to 0.0.

5.2 Evaluation

We evaluate sentence embeddings using the SemEval semantic textual similarity (STS) tasks from 2012 to 2016 (Agirre et al., 2012, 2013, 2014, 2015, 2016) as was done initially for sentence embeddings in (Wieting et al., 2016b). Given two sentences, the aim of the STS tasks is to predict their similarity on a 0-5 scale, where 0 indicates the sentences are on different topics and 5 means they are completely equivalent. As our test set, we report the average Pearson's r over each year of the STS tasks from 2012-2016 as is convention.

Most work evaluating accuracy on STS tasks has averaged the Pearson's r over each individual dataset for each year of the STS competition. However, Reimers and Gurevych (2019) computed Spearman's ρ over concatenated datasets for each year of the STS competition. To be consistent with previous work, we re-ran their model and calculated results using the standard method, and thus our results are not the same as those reported Reimers and Gurevych (2019). However, we also include results using their approach for completeness. One other difference between these two ways of calculating the results is the inclusion of the SMT dataset of the 2013 task, which we also exclude when replicating the approach in Reimers and Gurevych (2019).

For cross-lingual semantic similarity and semantic similarity in non-English languages, we evaluate on the STS tasks from SemEval 2017. This evaluation contains Arabic-Arabic, Arabic-English, Spanish-Spanish, Spanish-English, and Turkish-English datasets. The datasets were created by translating one or both pairs of an English STS pair into Arabic (`ar`), Spanish (`es`), or Turkish (`tr`). Following convention, we report results with Pearson's r for all systems, but also include results in Spearman's ρ for LASER, LaBSE, and P-SP.

We also evaluate on the Tatoeba bitext mining task introduced by Artetxe and Schwenk (2019). The dataset consists of up to 1,000 English-aligned sentence pairs for over 100 languages. The aim of the task is to find the nearest neighbor for each sentence in the other language according to cosine similarity. Performance is measured by computing the error rate.

Language	LASER	XLM-R	mBART	CRISS	LaBSE	P-SP
ar	**7.8**	52.5	61.0	22.0	9.1	8.8
de	1.0	11.1	13.2	2.0	**0.7**	1.5
es	2.1	24.3	39.6	3.7	**1.6**	2.4
fr	4.3	26.3	39.6	7.3	**4.0**	5.4
ru	5.9	25.9	31.6	9.7	**4.7**	5.6
tr	2.6	34.3	48.8	7.1	1.6	**1.4**
Avg.	4.0	29.1	39.0	8.6	**3.6**	4.2

Table 4: Results on the Tatoeba bitext mining task (Artetxe and Schwenk, 2019). Results are measured in error rate $\times 100$.

6 Results

English Semantic Similarity. The results for our English semantic similarity evaluation are shown in Table 2. Our P-SP model has the best performance across each year of the task, significantly outperforming all prior work. We outperform methods that use large pre-trained models including Sentence-BERT which is supervised, as it is trained on NLI data (Bowman et al., 2015).

We also include results from SimCSE (Gao et al., 2021). We compare to the unsupervised version, since our model is also unsupervised. We evaluate using the Spearman's ρ of the concatenation of the datasets for each year, and find our average performance over the 2012-2016 datasets to be 76.9, compared to 77.4 and 77.9 for the RoBERTa-base (Liu et al., 2019) and RoBERTa-large versions of SimCSE. While our performance is slightly lower, we note that they tune their model on the dev set of the STS Benchmark (Cer et al., 2017), which contains a subset of the data from STS tasks which we use for evaluation. Therefore, they are tuning on a subset of the evaluation data, and it is unclear how tuning on this test data affects model performance.

Cross-Lingual Semantic Similarity. The results for the non-English and cross-lingual semantic similarity evaluation are shown in Table 3. From the results, our model again outperforms all prior work using sentence embeddings. The only systems that have better performance are the top (non-embedding based) systems from SemEval 2017 for Spanish-English.[15]

[15]The top systems for this task used supervision and relied on state-of-the-art translation models to first translate the non-English sentences to English.

Bitext Mining. The results on the Tatoeba bitext mining task from Artetxe and Schwenk (2019) are shown in Table 4. The results show that our embeddings are competitive, but have slightly higher error rates than LASER. The models are so close that the difference in error rate for the two models across the 6 evaluations is 0.2, corresponding to a difference of about 2 mismatched sentence pairs per dataset. LaBSE performs a bit better, but was trained on much more data then both LASER and our method. We also compare to mBART, XLM-R, and CRISS.[16]

This bitext mining result is in contrast to the results on cross-lingual semantic similarity, suggesting that our embeddings account for a less literal semantic similarity, making them more adept at detecting paraphrases but slightly weaker at identifying translations. It is also worth noting that LASER was trained on Tatoeba data outside the test sets, which could also account for some of the slight improvement over our model.

7 Speed Analysis

Model	GPU	CPU
P-SP	**13,863**	**12,776**
LASER	6,033	26
Sentence-Bert	288	2
InferSent	4,445	16

Table 5: Speed as measured in sentences/second on both GPU (Nvidia 1080 TI) and CPU (single core).

We analyze the speed of our models as well as selected popular sentence embedding models from prior work. To evaluate inference speed, we measure the time required to embed 120,000 sentences from the Toronto Book Corpus (Zhu et al., 2015). Preprocessing of sentences is not factored into the timing, and each method sorts the sentences by length prior to computing the embeddings to reduce padding and extra computation. We use a batch size of 64 for each model. The number of sentences embedded per second is shown in Table 5.

From the results, we see that our model is easily the fastest on GPU, sometimes by an order of magnitude. Interestingly, using a single core of CPU, we achieve similar speeds to inference on GPU, which is not the case for any other model. Moreover, we repeated the experiment, this time using 32 cores and achieved a speed of 15,316 sentences/second. This is even faster than when using a GPU and indicates that our model can effectively be used at scale when GPUs are not available. It also suggests our model would be appropriate for use on embedded devices.

[16]Results are copied from (Tran et al., 2020).

8 Conclusion

In this paper, we present a system for the learning and inference of paraphrastic sentence embeddings in any language for which there is paraphrase or bilingual parallel data. Additionally, we release our trained sentence embedding models in English, as well as Arabic, German, Spanish, French, Russian, Turkish, and Chinese. These models are trained on tens of million of sentence pairs resulting in models that achieve state-of-the-art performance on unsupervised English semantic similarity and are state-of-the-art or competitive on non-English semantic similarity, cross-lingual semantic similarity, and bitext mining.

Moreover, our models are significantly faster than prior work owing to their simple architecture. They can also be run on CPU with little to no loss in speed from running them on GPU—something that no strong models from prior work are able to do. Lastly, we release our code that has been modified to make training and inference easier, with support for training on large corpora, preprocessing paraphrase and bilingual corpora and evaluation data, as well as scripts for easy inference that can generate embeddings or semantic similarity scores for sentences supplied in a text file.

References

Eneko Agirre, Carmen Banea, Claire Cardie, Daniel Cer, Mona Diab, Aitor Gonzalez-Agirre, Weiwei Guo, Iñigo Lopez-Gazpio, Montse Maritxalar, Rada Mihalcea, German Rigau, Larraitz Uria, and Janyce Wiebe. 2015. SemEval-2015 task 2: Semantic textual similarity, English, Spanish and pilot on interpretability. In *Proceedings of the 9th International Workshop on Semantic Evaluation (SemEval 2015)*, pages 252–263, Denver, Colorado. Association for Computational Linguistics.

Eneko Agirre, Carmen Banea, Claire Cardie, Daniel Cer, Mona Diab, Aitor Gonzalez-Agirre, Weiwei Guo, Rada Mihalcea, German Rigau, and Janyce Wiebe. 2014. SemEval-2014 task 10: Multilingual semantic textual similarity. In *Proceedings of the 8th International Workshop on Semantic Evaluation (SemEval 2014)*, pages 81–91, Dublin, Ireland. Association for Computational Linguistics.

Eneko Agirre, Carmen Banea, Daniel Cer, Mona Diab, Aitor Gonzalez-Agirre, Rada Mihalcea, German Rigau, and Janyce Wiebe. 2016. SemEval-2016 task 1: Semantic textual similarity, monolingual and cross-lingual evaluation. In *Proceedings of the 10th International Workshop on Semantic Evaluation (SemEval-2016)*, pages 497–511, San Diego, California. Association for Computational Linguistics.

Eneko Agirre, Daniel Cer, Mona Diab, and Aitor Gonzalez-Agirre. 2012. SemEval-2012 task 6: A pilot on semantic textual similarity. In **SEM 2012: The First Joint Conference on Lexical and Computational Semantics – Volume 1: Proceedings of the main conference and the shared task, and Volume 2: Proceedings of the Sixth International Workshop on Semantic Evaluation (SemEval 2012)*, pages 385–393, Montréal, Canada. Association for Computational Linguistics.

Eneko Agirre, Daniel Cer, Mona Diab, Aitor Gonzalez-Agirre, and Weiwei Guo. 2013. *SEM 2013 shared task: Semantic textual similarity. In *Second Joint Conference on Lexical and Computational Semantics (*SEM), Volume 1: Proceedings of the Main Conference and the Shared Task: Semantic Textual Similarity*, pages 32–43, Atlanta, Georgia, USA. Association for Computational Linguistics.

Sanjeev Arora, Yingyu Liang, and Tengyu Ma. 2017. A simple but tough-to-beat baseline for sentence embeddings. In *Proceedings of the International Conference on Learning Representations*.

Mikel Artetxe and Holger Schwenk. 2019. Massively multilingual sentence embeddings for zero-shot cross-lingual transfer and beyond. *Transactions of the Association for Computational Linguistics*, 7:597–610.

Samuel R. Bowman, Gabor Angeli, Christopher Potts, and Christopher D. Manning. 2015. A large annotated corpus for learning natural language inference. In *Proceedings of the 2015 Conference on Empirical Methods in Natural Language Processing*, pages 632–642, Lisbon, Portugal. Association for Computational Linguistics.

Daniel Cer, Mona Diab, Eneko Agirre, Iñigo Lopez-Gazpio, and Lucia Specia. 2017. SemEval-2017 task 1: Semantic textual similarity multilingual and crosslingual focused evaluation. In *Proceedings of the 11th International Workshop on Semantic Evaluation (SemEval-2017)*, pages 1–14, Vancouver, Canada. Association for Computational Linguistics.

Daniel Cer, Yinfei Yang, Sheng-yi Kong, Nan Hua, Nicole Limtiaco, Rhomni St. John, Noah Constant, Mario Guajardo-Cespedes, Steve Yuan, Chris Tar, Brian Strope, and Ray Kurzweil. 2018. Universal sentence encoder for English. In *Proceedings of the 2018 Conference on Empirical Methods in Natural Language Processing: System Demonstrations*, pages 169–174, Brussels, Belgium. Association for Computational Linguistics.

Muthu Chidambaram, Yinfei Yang, Daniel Cer, Steve Yuan, Yunhsuan Sung, Brian Strope, and Ray Kurzweil. 2019. Learning cross-lingual sentence representations via a multi-task dual-encoder model. In *Proceedings of the 4th Workshop on Representation Learning for NLP (RepL4NLP-2019)*, pages 250–259, Florence, Italy. Association for Computational Linguistics.

Alexis Conneau, Kartikay Khandelwal, Naman Goyal, Vishrav Chaudhary, Guillaume Wenzek, Francisco Guzmán, Edouard Grave, Myle Ott, Luke Zettlemoyer, and Veselin Stoyanov. 2020. Unsupervised cross-lingual representation learning at scale. In *Proceedings of the 58th Annual Meeting of the Association for Computational Linguistics*, pages 8440–8451, Online. Association for Computational Linguistics.

Alexis Conneau, Douwe Kiela, Holger Schwenk, Loïc Barrault, and Antoine Bordes. 2017. Supervised learning of universal sentence representations from natural language inference data. In *Proceedings of the 2017 Conference on Empirical Methods in Natural Language Processing*, pages 670–680, Copenhagen, Denmark. Association for Computational Linguistics.

Jacob Devlin, Ming-Wei Chang, Kenton Lee, and Kristina Toutanova. 2019. BERT: Pre-training of deep bidirectional transformers for language understanding. In *Proceedings of the 2019 Conference of the North American Chapter of the Association for Computational Linguistics: Human Language Technologies, Volume 1 (Long and Short Papers)*, pages 4171–4186, Minneapolis, Minnesota. Association for Computational Linguistics.

Bill Dolan, Chris Quirk, and Chris Brockett. 2004. Unsupervised construction of large paraphrase corpora: Exploiting massively parallel news sources. In *COLING 2004: Proceedings of the 20th International Conference on Computational Linguistics*, pages 350–356, Geneva, Switzerland. COLING.

Cristina Espana-Bonet, Adám Csaba Varga, Alberto Barrón-Cedeño, and Josef van Genabith. 2017. An empirical analysis of nmt-derived interlingual embeddings and their use in parallel sentence identification. *IEEE Journal of Selected Topics in Signal Processing*, 11(8):1340–1350.

Fangxiaoyu Feng, Yinfei Yang, Daniel Cer, Naveen Arivazhagan, and Wei Wang. 2022. Language-agnostic BERT sentence embedding. In *Proceedings of the 60th Annual Meeting of the Association for Computational Linguistics (Volume 1: Long Papers)*, pages 878–891, Dublin, Ireland. Association for Computational Linguistics.

Zhe Gan, Yunchen Pu, Ricardo Henao, Chunyuan Li, Xiaodong He, and Lawrence Carin. 2017. Learning generic sentence representations using convolutional neural networks. In *Proceedings of the 2017*

Conference on Empirical Methods in Natural Language Processing, pages 2390–2400, Copenhagen, Denmark. Association for Computational Linguistics.

Tianyu Gao, Xingcheng Yao, and Danqi Chen. 2021. SimCSE: Simple contrastive learning of sentence embeddings. In *Proceedings of the 2021 Conference on Empirical Methods in Natural Language Processing*, pages 6894–6910, Online and Punta Cana, Dominican Republic. Association for Computational Linguistics.

Francis Grégoire and Philippe Langlais. 2018. Extracting parallel sentences with bidirectional recurrent neural networks to improve machine translation. In *Proceedings of the 27th International Conference on Computational Linguistics*, pages 1442–1453, Santa Fe, New Mexico, USA. Association for Computational Linguistics.

Mandy Guo, Qinlan Shen, Yinfei Yang, Heming Ge, Daniel Cer, Gustavo Hernandez Abrego, Keith Stevens, Noah Constant, Yun-Hsuan Sung, Brian Strope, and Ray Kurzweil. 2018. Effective parallel corpus mining using bilingual sentence embeddings. In *Proceedings of the Third Conference on Machine Translation: Research Papers*, pages 165–176, Brussels, Belgium. Association for Computational Linguistics.

Felix Hill, Kyunghyun Cho, and Anna Korhonen. 2016. Learning distributed representations of sentences from unlabelled data. In *Proceedings of the 2016 Conference of the North American Chapter of the Association for Computational Linguistics: Human Language Technologies*, pages 1367–1377, San Diego, California. Association for Computational Linguistics.

Mohit Iyyer, John Wieting, Kevin Gimpel, and Luke Zettlemoyer. 2018. Adversarial example generation with syntactically controlled paraphrase networks. In *Proceedings of the 2018 Conference of the North American Chapter of the Association for Computational Linguistics: Human Language Technologies, Volume 1 (Long Papers)*, pages 1875–1885, New Orleans, Louisiana. Association for Computational Linguistics.

Jeff Johnson, Matthijs Douze, and Hervé Jégou. 2017. Billion-scale similarity search with GPUs. *arXiv preprint arXiv:1702.08734*.

Armand Joulin, Edouard Grave, Piotr Bojanowski, and Tomas Mikolov. 2017. Bag of tricks for efficient text classification. In *Proceedings of the 15th Conference of the European Chapter of the Association for Computational Linguistics: Volume 2, Short Papers*, pages 427–431, Valencia, Spain. Association for Computational Linguistics.

Urvashi Khandelwal, Omer Levy, Dan Jurafsky, Luke Zettlemoyer, and Mike Lewis. 2019. Generalization through memorization: Nearest neighbor language models. *arXiv preprint arXiv:1911.00172*.

Diederik Kingma and Jimmy Ba. 2014. Adam: A method for stochastic optimization. *arXiv preprint arXiv:1412.6980*.

Ryan Kiros, Yukun Zhu, Ruslan R Salakhutdinov, Richard Zemel, Raquel Urtasun, Antonio Torralba, and Sanja Fidler. 2015. Skip-thought vectors. In *Advances in Neural Information Processing Systems 28*, pages 3294–3302.

Kalpesh Krishna, John Wieting, and Mohit Iyyer. 2020. Reformulating unsupervised style transfer as paraphrase generation. In *Proceedings of the 2020 Conference on Empirical Methods in Natural Language Processing (EMNLP)*, pages 737–762, Online. Association for Computational Linguistics.

Taku Kudo and John Richardson. 2018. SentencePiece: A simple and language independent subword tokenizer and detokenizer for neural text processing. In *Proceedings of the 2018 Conference on Empirical Methods in Natural Language Processing: System Demonstrations*, pages 66–71, Brussels, Belgium. Association for Computational Linguistics.

Quoc V. Le and Tomas Mikolov. 2014. Distributed representations of sentences and documents. *arXiv preprint arXiv:1405.4053*.

Patrick Lewis, Yuxiang Wu, Linqing Liu, Pasquale Minervini, Heinrich Küttler, Aleksandra Piktus, Pontus Stenetorp, and Sebastian Riedel. 2021. PAQ: 65 million probably-asked questions and what you can do with them. *Transactions of the Association for Computational Linguistics*, 9:1098–1115.

Pierre Lison and Jörg Tiedemann. 2016. OpenSubtitles2016: Extracting large parallel corpora from movie and TV subtitles. In *Proceedings of the Tenth International Conference on Language Resources and Evaluation (LREC'16)*, pages 923–929, Portorož, Slovenia. European Language Resources Association (ELRA).

Yinhan Liu, Jiatao Gu, Naman Goyal, Xian Li, Sergey Edunov, Marjan Ghazvininejad, Mike Lewis, and Luke Zettlemoyer. 2020. Multilingual denoising pre-training for neural machine translation. *Transactions of the Association for Computational Linguistics*, 8:726–742.

Yinhan Liu, Myle Ott, Naman Goyal, Jingfei Du, Mandar Joshi, Danqi Chen, Omer Levy, Mike Lewis, Luke Zettlemoyer, and Veselin Stoyanov. 2019. Roberta: A robustly optimized bert pretraining approach. *arXiv preprint arXiv:1907.11692*.

Matteo Pagliardini, Prakhar Gupta, and Martin Jaggi. 2017. Unsupervised learning of sentence embeddings using compositional n-gram features. *arXiv preprint arXiv:1703.02507*.

Nghia The Pham, Germán Kruszewski, Angeliki Lazaridou, and Marco Baroni. 2015. Jointly optimizing word representations for lexical and sentential tasks with the C-PHRASE model. In *Proceedings of the 53rd Annual Meeting of the Association for Computational Linguistics and the 7th International Joint Conference on Natural Language Processing (Volume 1: Long Papers)*, pages 971–981, Beijing, China. Association for Computational Linguistics.

Nils Reimers and Iryna Gurevych. 2019. Sentence-BERT: Sentence embeddings using Siamese BERT-networks. In *Proceedings of the 2019 Conference on Empirical Methods in Natural Language Processing and the 9th International Joint Conference on Natural Language Processing (EMNLP-IJCNLP)*, pages 3982–3992, Hong Kong, China. Association for Computational Linguistics.

Holger Schwenk. 2018. Filtering and mining parallel data in a joint multilingual space. In *Proceedings of the 56th Annual Meeting of the Association for Computational Linguistics (Volume 2: Short Papers)*, pages 228–234, Melbourne, Australia. Association for Computational Linguistics.

Holger Schwenk, Vishrav Chaudhary, Shuo Sun, Hongyu Gong, and Francisco Guzmán. 2021. Wiki-Matrix: Mining 135M parallel sentences in 1620 language pairs from Wikipedia. In *Proceedings of the 16th Conference of the European Chapter of the Association for Computational Linguistics: Main Volume*, pages 1351–1361, Online. Association for Computational Linguistics.

Holger Schwenk and Matthijs Douze. 2017. Learning joint multilingual sentence representations with neural machine translation. In *Proceedings of the 2nd Workshop on Representation Learning for NLP*, pages 157–167, Vancouver, Canada. Association for Computational Linguistics.

Richard Socher, Eric H. Huang, Jeffrey Pennington, Andrew Y. Ng, and Christopher D. Manning. 2011. Dynamic pooling and unfolding recursive autoencoders for paraphrase detection. In *Advances in Neural Information Processing Systems*.

Sandeep Subramanian, Adam Trischler, Yoshua Bengio, and Christopher J Pal. 2018. Learning general purpose distributed sentence representations via large scale multi-task learning. *arXiv preprint arXiv:1804.00079*.

Jörg Tiedemann. 2012. Parallel data, tools and interfaces in OPUS. In *Proceedings of the Eighth International Conference on Language Resources and Evaluation (LREC'12)*, pages 2214–2218, Istanbul, Turkey. European Language Resources Association (ELRA).

Chau Tran, Yuqing Tang, Xian Li, and Jiatao Gu. 2020. Cross-lingual retrieval for iterative self-supervised training. *arXiv preprint arXiv:2006.09526*.

Ashish Vaswani, Noam Shazeer, Niki Parmar, Jakob Uszkoreit, Llion Jones, Aidan N Gomez, Łukasz Kaiser, and Illia Polosukhin. 2017. Attention is all you need. In *Advances in Neural Information Processing Systems*, pages 5998–6008.

John Wieting, Mohit Bansal, Kevin Gimpel, and Karen Livescu. 2016a. Charagram: Embedding words and sentences via character n-grams. In *Proceedings of the 2016 Conference on Empirical Methods in Natural Language Processing*, pages 1504–1515, Austin, Texas. Association for Computational Linguistics.

John Wieting, Mohit Bansal, Kevin Gimpel, and Karen Livescu. 2016b. Towards universal paraphrastic sentence embeddings. In *Proceedings of the International Conference on Learning Representations*.

John Wieting, Taylor Berg-Kirkpatrick, Kevin Gimpel, and Graham Neubig. 2019a. Beyond BLEU:training neural machine translation with semantic similarity. In *Proceedings of the 57th Annual Meeting of the Association for Computational Linguistics*, pages 4344–4355, Florence, Italy. Association for Computational Linguistics.

John Wieting and Kevin Gimpel. 2017. Revisiting recurrent networks for paraphrastic sentence embeddings. In *Proceedings of the 55th Annual Meeting of the Association for Computational Linguistics (Volume 1: Long Papers)*, pages 2078–2088, Vancouver, Canada. Association for Computational Linguistics.

John Wieting and Kevin Gimpel. 2018. ParaNMT-50M: Pushing the limits of paraphrastic sentence embeddings with millions of machine translations. In *Proceedings of the 56th Annual Meeting of the Association for Computational Linguistics (Volume 1: Long Papers)*, pages 451–462, Melbourne, Australia. Association for Computational Linguistics.

John Wieting, Kevin Gimpel, Graham Neubig, and Taylor Berg-Kirkpatrick. 2019b. Simple and effective paraphrastic similarity from parallel translations. In *Proceedings of the 57th Annual Meeting of the Association for Computational Linguistics*, pages 4602–4608, Florence, Italy. Association for Computational Linguistics.

John Wieting, Jonathan Mallinson, and Kevin Gimpel. 2017. Learning paraphrastic sentence embeddings from back-translated bitext. In *Proceedings of the 2017 Conference on Empirical Methods in Natural Language Processing*, pages 274–285, Copenhagen, Denmark. Association for Computational Linguistics.

John Wieting, Graham Neubig, and Taylor Berg-Kirkpatrick. 2020. A bilingual generative transformer for semantic sentence embedding. In *Proceedings of the 2020 Conference on Empirical Methods in Natural Language Processing (EMNLP)*, pages 1581–1594, Online. Association for Computational Linguistics.

Yukun Zhu, Ryan Kiros, Rich Zemel, Ruslan Salakhutdinov, Raquel Urtasun, Antonio Torralba, and Sanja Fidler. 2015. Aligning books and movies: Towards story-like visual explanations by watching movies and reading books. In *The IEEE International Conference on Computer Vision (ICCV)*.

Snoopy: An Online Interface for Exploring the Effect of Pretraining Term Frequencies on Few-Shot LM Performance

Yasaman Razeghi[*◇] **Raja Sekhar Reddy Mekala** [*◇]
Robert L. Logan IV[◇] **Matt Gardner**[♠] **Sameer Singh**[◇♣]
[◇]University of California, Irvine [♠]Microsoft Semantic Machines [♣]Allen Institute for AI
{yrazeghi, rmekala, rlogan, sameer}@uci.edu
mattgardner@microsoft.com

Abstract

Current evaluation schemes for large language models often fail to consider the impact of the overlap between pretraining corpus and test data on model performance statistics. *Snoopy* is an online interface that allows researchers to study this impact in few-shot learning settings. Our demo provides term frequency statistics for the Pile, which is an 800GB corpus, accompanied by the precomputed performance of EleutherAI/GPT models on more than 20 NLP benchmarks, including numerical, commonsense reasoning, natural language understanding, and question-answering tasks. *Snoopy* allows a user to interactively align specific terms in test instances with their frequency in the Pile, enabling exploratory analysis of how term frequency is related to the accuracy of the models, which are hard to discover through automated means. A user can look at correlations over various model sizes and numbers of in-context examples and visualize the result across multiple (potentially aggregated) datasets. Using *Snoopy*, we show that a researcher can quickly replicate prior analyses for numerical tasks, while simultaneously allowing for much more expansive exploration that was previously challenging. *Snoopy* is available at `https://nlp.ics.uci.edu/snoopy`.

1 Introduction

Large language models have achieved impressive few-shot performance on various NLP benchmarks with in-context learning (Black et al., 2022; Chowdhery et al., 2022; Brown et al., 2020). This improvement is primarily driven by increasing the scale of the models and the pretraining data (Bender et al., 2021; Kaplan et al., 2020). By leveraging diverse data sources such as GitHub and arXiv, these models have demonstrated the ability to perform complicated tasks such as quantitative reasoning (Lewkowycz et al., 2022) and writing computer programs (Chen et al., 2021).

However, the current evaluation schemes for these language models often underestimate the possibility of data leakage between the evaluation data and the pretraining data. Various studies have demonstrated the capacity of large language models to memorize the pretraining data (Carlini et al., 2021, 2022), as well as the impact of pretraining term frequency on reasoning performance (Razeghi et al., 2022). These observations highlight the importance of measuring the impact of pretraining data in evaluating large language models.

A critical barrier to performing research related to pretraining data statistics is the cost of analyzing the large corpus of pretraining data. Since the size of these corpora is usually large (e.g., Pile is 800GB), analyses involving the pretraining data can be time-consuming and expensive. Furthermore, evaluating large language models such as GPT-J-6B is also expensive—even inference queries require high-memory GPUs—which further impedes analysis of the capabilities and limitations of large language models.

To facilitate research in understanding the relationship between the pretraining corpus and model behavior, we introduce *Snoopy*, an online platform that assists researchers in studying the impact of pretraining term frequencies on language model performance on downstream tasks. *Snoopy* includes unigram and low-order co-occurrence statistics of terms in the Pile dataset (the pretraining data for all of the EleutherAI/GPT models). It uses these counts to show the correlation between the model's few-shot performance on instances and the frequency of instance terms in the pretraining data (illustrated in Figure 1). Our web app supports this analysis on more than 20 NLP benchmarks (mostly from the *lm-evaluation-harness* (Gao et al., 2021b)) including, numerical and commonsense reasoning, natural language understanding, and question answering tasks. In addition, the user can highlight desired terms on the plots, explore individual in-

*First two authors contributed equally.

Proceedings of the The 2022 Conference on Empirical Methods in Natural Language Processing: System Demonstrations, pages 389 - 395
December 7-11, 2022

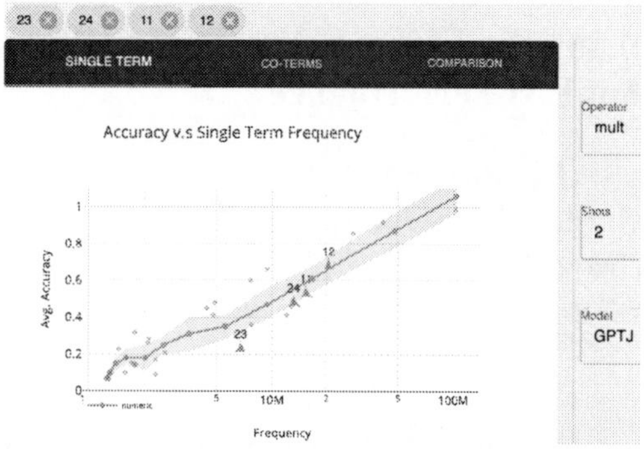

Figure 1: **Using *Snoopy* to study the effect of term frequencies** on GPT-J-6B's 2-shot accuracy on multiplication. Each point represents a term (numbers in this case), with x-axis the frequency of the term in pretraining corpus and y-zxis the average performance on the instances that include that term (for 2-shot multiplication using GPT-J-6B). *Snoopy* demonstrates a strong correlation between the accuracy of a number and its frequency in pretraining data. Users can select terms to highlight i.e. 11, 12, 24, 23 here.

stances from each dataset, highlight terms in each instance based on their frequency in the pretraining data, and provide accuracy vs. frequency plots aggregated over multiple datasets. *Snoopy* will facilitate and encourage this research direction on the impact of pretraining data statistics on large language model's evaluation schemes, an essential yet overlooked direction in the science of language models that can further shed light on our understanding of large language models' capabilities.

2 *Snoopy* Architecture

In this section, we describe the architecture behind *Snoopy* (as illustrated in Figure 2) *Snoopy* precomputes term counts from pretraining data and instance-level performance statistics on evaluation datasets, and allows users to create performance vs. frequency plots dynamically. In the following, we describe each of these components.

2.1 Calculating the Term Frequencies

We process the Pile dataset (Gao et al., 2021a), which is among the few corpora for pretraining the language models that are publicly available. We first tokenize the corpus using the spaCy English tokenizer (Honnibal and Montani, 2017). Then, we count the number of times each token, i.e., *term*, appears in the pretraining corpus, which we call the *term frequency*. While counting the terms, we eliminate all the stop words and tokens with a count of less than 100 to reduce the memory usage. To calculate the co-occurrences of terms, we count the times every two terms appear in a window of 5 in the pretraining data. We use Amazon Elastic Map Reduce (EMR)[1] to process the pretraining data.

2.2 Instance-Level Model Accuracy

For a quick, interactive interface and a smooth user experience that facilitates exploration, we precompute the accuracy of the EleutherAI GPT models on each instance on several NLP benchmarks using the *lm-evaluation-harness* framework (Gao et al., 2021b). While our current version supports a subset of tasks and models from this framework, we will gradually expand this demo to include more tasks with instance-level performance metrics and all of the models trained on the Pile dataset.

2.3 Matching Terms to Evaluation Instances

With term frequencies and instance-level model accuracies computed, we next need to determine how terms are matched to evaluation instances. *Snoopy* supports two different approaches. For numerical reasoning tasks, we only use the numbers in each instance as the *terms* to study since the operand is fixed across all instances. For other natural language benchmarks, all non-stopwords extracted in Section 2.1 are used as *terms* by default. However, using a provided "custom" option, the user can also specify certain terms by uploading a CSV file containing all these desired terms.

2.4 Performance vs. Frequency Plots

To visually capture the relation between a term's pretraining frequencies and model performance on instances associated with that term, we introduce *Performance vs. Frequency* plots (Figure 1). In these plots, the y-axis shows the average performance over all instances that includes that term while the x-axis shows the frequency of the term. An example of this plot for the multiplication task evaluated on GPT-J-6B on 2-shot settings is provided in Figure 1. In addition to plotting term-specific accuracies, we plot a curve that captures the aggregate effect of frequency on accuracy. This curve is generated by partitioning the instances into 10 quantiles based on term frequencies, taking the average accuracy over instances in the same quantile, and then connecting these averages using lines. For example, we average the accuracy over

[1]https://aws.amazon.com/emr/

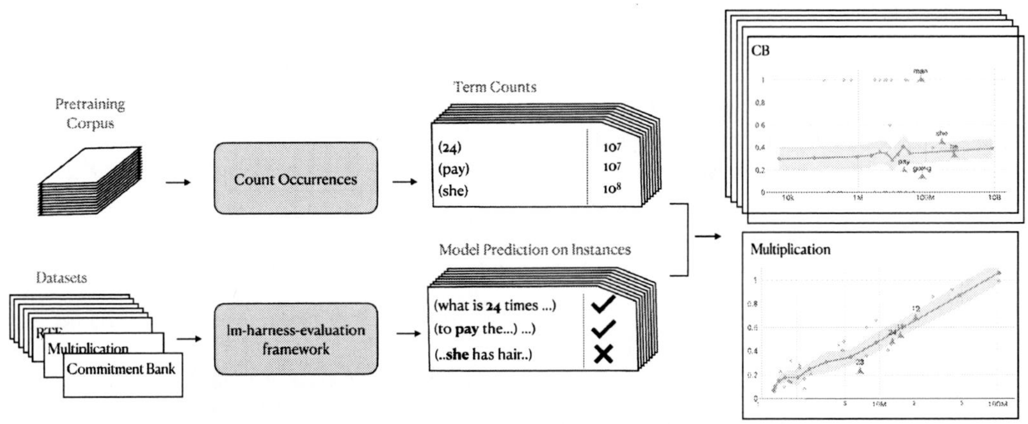

Figure 2: **Architecture for *Snoopy*.** We first process the pretraining corpus to compute term counts (and co-occurrences), and gather the evaluation results from the *lm-evaluation-harness* (Gao et al., 2021b) framework for models of interest. We combine these to generate performance vs. term frequency plots for various datasets.

all instances from the Commitment Band dataset that has the term *pay* for the *y*-axis and put the frequency of term *pay* on the *x*-axis as shown in Figure 2.

3 *Snoopy* Capabilities

As mentioned in Section 1, *Snoopy* supports a subset of tasks from *lm-evaluation-harness* benchmark (Gao et al., 2021b) in addition to all numerical reasoning tasks from Razeghi et al. (2022). It provides a simple and performant interface that allows researchers to compare results across various experimental settings with visualizations of the precomputed results in a user-friendly manner. The plots are generated using Plotly.js,[2] which enables easy download, zoom in-and-out, and re-scaling of the plots. The following is a brief description of *Snoopy*'s functionalities on numerical reasoning and other language understanding tasks.

3.1 Numerical Reasoning Tasks

For numerical reasoning, the user can study and visualize all the tasks from Razeghi et al. (2022), i.e. arithmetic (addition and multiplication), conversion of time units, and operator inference. Users can specify the number of examples in the prompt (the number of shots: 2, 4, 8) and the size of the language model (choosing between GPT-Neo-1.3B, GPT-Neo-2.7B, and GPT-J-6B). Users can also select terms (numbers) to highlight on the plots.

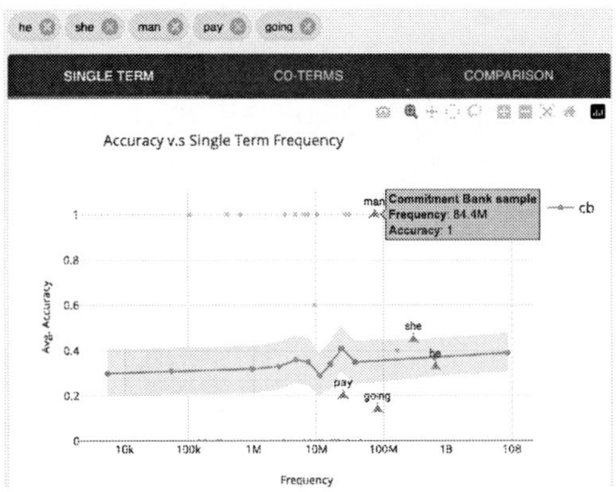

Figure 3: The performance vs. frequency plot for Commitment Bank dataset with multiple highlighted terms.

3.2 NLP Benchmarks

Our tool also allows studying the impact of term frequencies on various commonsense reasoning tasks (COPA (Roemmele et al., 2011), HellaSwag (Zellers et al., 2019), PIQA (Bisk et al., 2020)), natural language understanding tasks (CoLA (Warstadt et al., 2019), MNLI (Nangia et al., 2017), MRPC (Dolan and Brockett, 2005), QNLI (Wang et al., 2019b)), and question answering tasks (ARC (Clark et al., 2018), LogiQA (Liu et al., 2020), OpenbookQA (Mihaylov et al., 2018)). For this group of tasks, we provided the accuracy of GPT-J-6B models with 2, 4 and 8 number of shots. Example usage for GPT-J-6B 2-shot experiment on the Commitment Bank (Wang et al., 2019a) dataset

[2] https://plotly.com/javascript/

is provided in Figure 3.

3.3 Term Highlighting

The user can also select terms to highlight and visualize on the plot. For example, in Figure 1 the location of specified terms (e.g numbers 11, 12, 23, 24) is highlighted for numerical reasoning (multiplication) and in Figure 3, the terms (e.g *pay*, *man*, *going*, *she*, *he*) are highlighted for Commitment Band dataset.

3.4 Multi Dataset Comparison

With *multi dataset comparison*, users can select multiple datasets to visualize their performance vs. frequency on the same plot. An example of this feature is provided in Figure 5 in which the user has specified the datasets of SST, TriviaQA, and WNLI. Using this option, the user can compare the ranges of frequency terms and performance, the overall impact of pretraining term frequencies on model performance, and the impact of individual terms across multiple tasks. For example, the terms "man", "woman", "he" and "she" are individually highlighted for all of these datasets (Figure 6).

3.5 Multi Dataset Aggregation

Multi dataset aggregation allows the user to study the aggregate performance of the model containing specific terms across all selected datasets. For instance, we may want to see if the model is more accurate on any instance (across datasets) that includes the word "he" compared to the word "she". To answer this question, we can select all datasets from the dataset menu, select the terms "he" and "she" in the term input section, and see the difference in performance using the *Multi Dataset Aggregation* option. An example of this analysis is provided in the next section in which we provide a case study using *Snoopy* (Figure 7).

3.6 Plots for a Subset of Terms

Other than visualizing the accuracy v.s. frequency plots on *all* terms for instances from a given dataset, we also support the capability to plot the correlation line for a certain subset of user-defined terms. This option further facilitates research in studying the effect of certain terms with various frequencies on the model's performance. Using the option of "import CSV", the user can upload a CSV file containing desired terms. Once the upload is completed, *Snoopy* visualizes the *specific terms* frequency plots. These plots illustrate the average

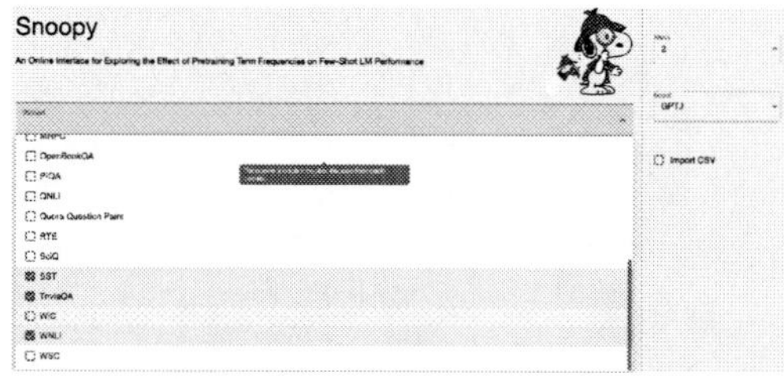

Figure 4: Using the dataset menu for choosing SST, TriviaQA, and WNLI tasks, specifying the number of shots as 2 and the language model as GPT-J-6B.

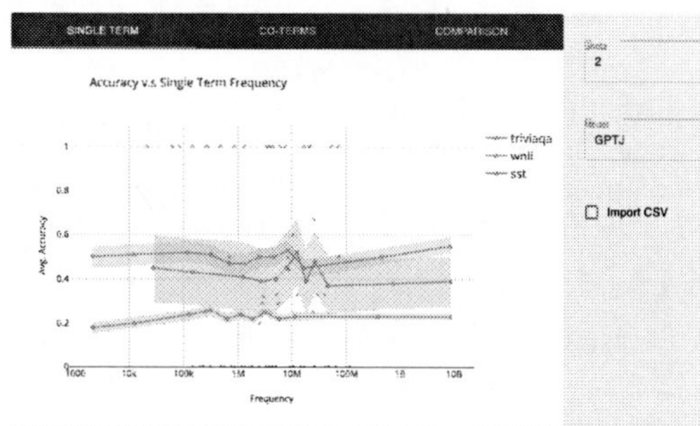

Figure 5: Visualizing the performance v.s single term frequency plots for SST, TriviaQA, and WNLI.

performance on instances with the specific terms on the y-axis and the pertaining frequency of these terms on the x axis.

4 Case Study

In this section, we present a case study of using *Snoopy*. Here, we want to study the effect of term-frequencies on GPT-J-6B model accuracy in 2-shot in-context learning setting. We are going to perform this study on three different datasets of sentiment analysis (SST), Question Answering (TriviaQA), and a reading comprehension task (WNLI).

Step 1: We want to investigate whether the GPT-J-6B model accuracy on instances is affected by the unigram term frequencies on the mentioned datasets. First, we need to specify the model, dataset, and the number of shots we want to focus on. For this case, we want to observe the impact of term frequencies on GPT-J-6B models with 2 shot on SST, TriviaQA, and WNLI tasks. We do this using the drop-down menus shown in Figure 4. Upon this selection, *Snoopy* generates the accuracy v.s frequency plots for all these three datasets.

Step 2: Now, we want to observe if the model performance is different on instances with certain

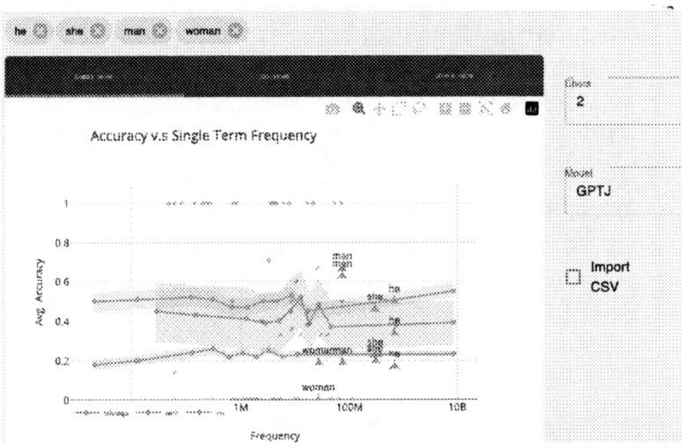

Figure 6: Highlighting specific terms such as "he", "she", "man", and "woman" on performance vs frequency plots (for multiple datasets).

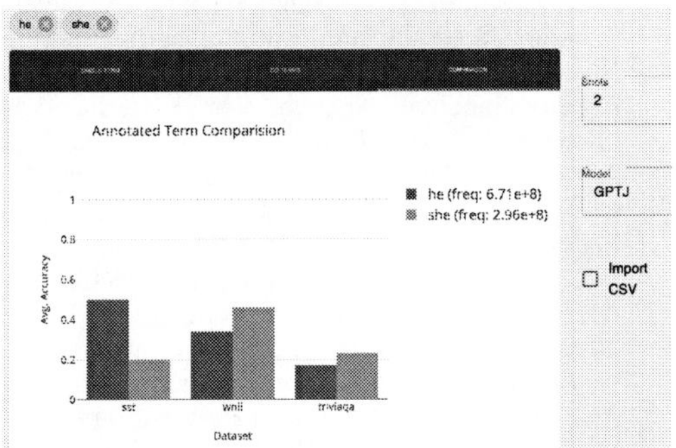

Figure 7: Comparing the overall performance of GPT-J-6B model on instances from SST, TriviaQA, and WNLI datasets that include the terms "he" or "she".

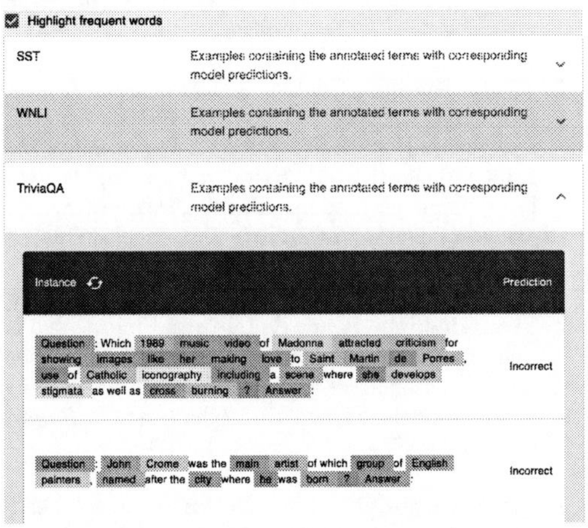

Figure 8: Example instances from the TriviaQA questions. The terms are color-coded based on their pretraining term frequency (red are frequent, blue are rare).

terms of "he", "she", "man", and "woman". We use the "add terms" option to add these specific terms as shown in Figure 6; instances from the SST dataset containing the term "he" have much higher

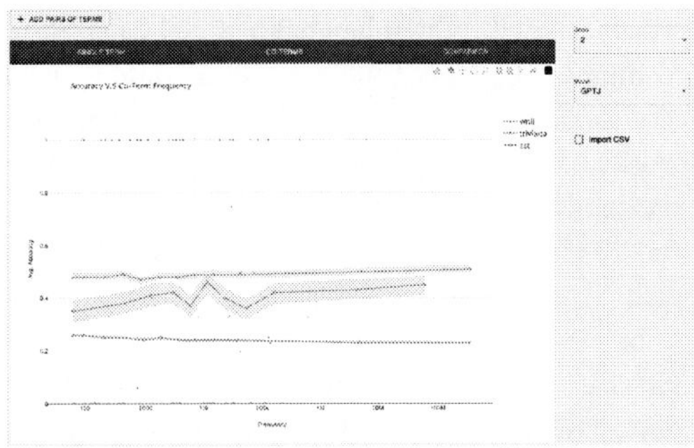

Figure 9: Performance v.s *co-occurrences of term* frequency plots for SST, TriviaQA, and WNLI.

average performance than those with "she", which is not the case for WNLI and TriviaQA datasets.

Step 3: In this step, we want to study the average accuracy of GPT-J-6B on instances containing these terms over all three datasets. By choosing the comparison option (presented in Figure 7), we see that GPT-J-6B model performance on instances that contain the term "he" in comparison to instances with the term "she" on the three datasets. We observe that the model has better performance on SST instances contaning the term "he" in comparison to the instances with the term "she". This is not the case for WNLI and triviaQA datasets.

Step 4: Figure 8 provide an example for *Snoopy*'s instance visualization feature. Using this feature, *Snoopy* provides a random selection of instances from each dataset. This option helps the user get familiar with instance queries from each dataset and observe the model performance on each instance. Moreover, the user can select the *Highlight Frequent words* option. This option color codes the terms on the instances based on their frequency in the pretraining dataset, as shown in Figure 8.

Step 5: Now we want to visualize the average performance of GPT-J-6B vs. the count of co-occurrences of terms on the x-axis as a measure of frequency for these three datasets. To do so, we select the option of co-occurrence instead of the unigram from the top bar as shown in Figure 9.

5 Related Work

Studying the Pretraining Data Dodge et al. (2021) have studied the pretraining data of large language models. They provide documentation for the C4 corpus which has been used as a part of pretraining datasets such as Pile (Gao et al., 2021a). Many works have illustrated language model capabilities to memorize parts of the pretraining data (Carlini et al., 2021; McCoy et al., 2021). Recently, some works has measured the model's memorization of pretraining data through controlled experiments on fact retrieval (Akyürek et al., 2022), classification tasks (Magar and Schwartz, 2022), and text generation (Carlini et al., 2022). All this research emphasizes the importance of studying the pretraining data statistics and considering the pretraining data in interpreting the model evaluation performances.

Evaluation Frameworks for LMs Since the emergence of large language models, many works have provided a unified and easy to use framework for evaluating them (Wolf et al., 2019; Gao et al., 2021b; Srivastava et al., 2022). Our demo, *Snoopy*, can augment these frameworks by associating pretraining data statistics to the evaluation scheme.

6 Conclusions

In this paper, we presented *Snoopy*, a tool that enables researchers to study the impact of pretraining term frequencies on a model's few-shot performance without requiring expensive computing resources. We illustrated how *Snoopy* could be used to create performance vs. frequency plots, aggregate statistics over multiple datasets, and several other functionalities for further investigating pretraining data statistics. We hope that this tool makes it easier for researchers to study the effect of term frequencies on language model performance.

Acknowledgements

This material is sponsored in part by the DARPA MCS program under Contract No. N660011924033 with the United States Office Of Naval Research, by an Amazon Research Award, and by awards IIS-2046873 and IIS-204098 from the National Science Foundation.

References

Ekin Akyürek, Tolga Bolukbasi, Frederick Liu, Binbin Xiong, Ian Tenney, Jacob Andreas, and Kelvin Guu. 2022. Tracing knowledge in language models back to the training data. *ArXiv preprint*, abs/2205.11482.

Emily M Bender, Timnit Gebru, Angelina McMillan-Major, and Shmargaret Shmitchell. 2021. On the dangers of stochastic parrots: Can language models be too big? In *Proceedings of the 2021 ACM Conference on Fairness, Accountability, and Transparency*, pages 610–623.

Yonatan Bisk, Rowan Zellers, Ronan LeBras, Jianfeng Gao, and Yejin Choi. 2020. PIQA: reasoning about physical commonsense in natural language. In *The Thirty-Fourth AAAI Conference on Artificial Intelligence, AAAI 2020, The Thirty-Second Innovative Applications of Artificial Intelligence Conference, IAAI 2020, The Tenth AAAI Symposium on Educational Advances in Artificial Intelligence, EAAI 2020, New York, NY, USA, February 7-12, 2020*, pages 7432–7439. AAAI Press.

Sid Black, Stella Biderman, Eric Hallahan, Quentin Anthony, Leo Gao, Laurence Golding, Horace He, Connor Leahy, Kyle McDonell, Jason Phang, et al. 2022. Gpt-neox-20b: An open-source autoregressive language model. *ArXiv preprint*, abs/2204.06745.

Tom B. Brown, Benjamin Mann, Nick Ryder, Melanie Subbiah, Jared Kaplan, Prafulla Dhariwal, Arvind Neelakantan, Pranav Shyam, Girish Sastry, Amanda Askell, Sandhini Agarwal, Ariel Herbert-Voss, Gretchen Krueger, Tom Henighan, Rewon Child, Aditya Ramesh, Daniel M. Ziegler, Jeffrey Wu, Clemens Winter, Christopher Hesse, Mark Chen, Eric Sigler, Mateusz Litwin, Scott Gray, Benjamin Chess, Jack Clark, Christopher Berner, Sam McCandlish, Alec Radford, Ilya Sutskever, and Dario Amodei. 2020. Language models are few-shot learners. In *Advances in Neural Information Processing Systems 33: Annual Conference on Neural Information Processing Systems 2020, NeurIPS 2020, December 6-12, 2020, virtual*.

Nicholas Carlini, Daphne Ippolito, Matthew Jagielski, Katherine Lee, Florian Tramer, and Chiyuan Zhang. 2022. Quantifying memorization across neural language models. *ArXiv preprint*, abs/2202.07646.

Nicholas Carlini, Florian Tramer, Eric Wallace, Matthew Jagielski, Ariel Herbert-Voss, Katherine Lee, Adam Roberts, Tom Brown, Dawn Song, Ulfar Erlingsson, et al. 2021. Extracting training data from large language models. In *30th USENIX Security Symposium (USENIX Security 21)*, pages 2633–2650.

Mark Chen, Jerry Tworek, Heewoo Jun, Qiming Yuan, Henrique Ponde de Oliveira Pinto, Jared Kaplan, Harri Edwards, Yuri Burda, Nicholas Joseph, Greg Brockman, et al. 2021. Evaluating large language models trained on code. *ArXiv preprint*, abs/2107.03374.

Aakanksha Chowdhery, Sharan Narang, Jacob Devlin, Maarten Bosma, Gaurav Mishra, Adam Roberts, Paul Barham, Hyung Won Chung, Charles Sutton, Sebastian Gehrmann, et al. 2022. Palm: Scaling language modeling with pathways. *ArXiv preprint*, abs/2204.02311.

Peter Clark, Isaac Cowhey, Oren Etzioni, Tushar Khot, Ashish Sabharwal, Carissa Schoenick, and Oyvind Tafjord. 2018. Think you have solved question answering? try arc, the ai2 reasoning challenge. *ArXiv*, abs/1803.05457.

Jesse Dodge, Maarten Sap, Ana Marasović, William Agnew, Gabriel Ilharco, Dirk Groeneveld, Margaret Mitchell, and Matt Gardner. 2021. Documenting large webtext corpora: A case study on the colossal clean crawled corpus. In *Proceedings of the 2021 Conference on Empirical Methods in Natural Language Processing*, pages 1286–1305, Online and Punta Cana, Dominican Republic. Association for Computational Linguistics.

William B. Dolan and Chris Brockett. 2005. Automatically constructing a corpus of sentential paraphrases. In *Proceedings of the Third International Workshop on Paraphrasing (IWP2005)*.

Leo Gao, Stella Biderman, Sid Black, Laurence Golding, Travis Hoppe, Charles Foster, Jason Phang, Horace He, Anish Thite, Noa Nabeshima, et al. 2021a. The Pile: An 800gb dataset of diverse text for language modeling. *ArXiv preprint*, abs/2101.00027.

Leo Gao, Jonathan Tow, Stella Biderman, Sid Black, Anthony DiPofi, Charles Foster, Laurence Golding, Jeffrey Hsu, Kyle McDonell, Niklas Muennighoff, Jason Phang, Laria Reynolds, Eric Tang, Anish Thite, Ben Wang, Kevin Wang, and Andy Zou. 2021b. A framework for few-shot language model evaluation.

Matthew Honnibal and Ines Montani. 2017. spaCy 2: Natural language understanding with Bloom embeddings, convolutional neural networks and incremental parsing. To appear.

Jared Kaplan, Sam McCandlish, T. J. Henighan, Tom B. Brown, Benjamin Chess, Rewon Child, Scott Gray, Alec Radford, Jeff Wu, and Dario Amodei. 2020. Scaling laws for neural language models. *ArXiv*, abs/2001.08361.

Aitor Lewkowycz, Anders Andreassen, David Dohan, Ethan Dyer, Henryk Michalewski, Vinay Ramasesh, Ambrose Slone, Cem Anil, Imanol Schlag, Theo Gutman-Solo, et al. 2022. Solving quantitative reasoning problems with language models. *ArXiv preprint*, abs/2206.14858.

Jian Liu, Leyang Cui, Hanmeng Liu, Dandan Huang, Yile Wang, and Yue Zhang. 2020. LogiQA: A challenge dataset for machine reading comprehension with logical reasoning. In *Proceedings of the Twenty-Ninth International Joint Conference on Artificial Intelligence, IJCAI 2020*, pages 3622–3628. ijcai.org.

Inbal Magar and Roy Schwartz. 2022. Data contamination: From memorization to exploitation. *ArXiv preprint*, abs/2203.08242.

R Thomas McCoy, Paul Smolensky, Tal Linzen, Jianfeng Gao, and Asli Celikyilmaz. 2021. How much do language models copy from their training data? evaluating linguistic novelty in text generation using raven. *ArXiv preprint*, abs/2111.09509.

Todor Mihaylov, Peter Clark, Tushar Khot, and Ashish Sabharwal. 2018. Can a suit of armor conduct electricity? a new dataset for open book question answering. In *Proceedings of the 2018 Conference on Empirical Methods in Natural Language Processing*, pages 2381–2391, Brussels, Belgium. Association for Computational Linguistics.

Nikita Nangia, Adina Williams, Angeliki Lazaridou, and Samuel Bowman. 2017. The RepEval 2017 shared task: Multi-genre natural language inference with sentence representations. In *Proceedings of the 2nd Workshop on Evaluating Vector Space Representations for NLP*, pages 1–10, Copenhagen, Denmark. Association for Computational Linguistics.

Yasaman Razeghi, Robert L Logan IV, Matt Gardner, and Sameer Singh. 2022. Impact of pretraining term frequencies on few-shot numerical reasoning. *Findings of the Association for Computational Linguistics: EMNLP 2022*.

Melissa Roemmele, Cosmin Adrian Bejan, and Andrew S Gordon. 2011. Choice of plausible alternatives: An evaluation of commonsense causal reasoning. In *AAAI spring symposium: logical formalizations of commonsense reasoning*, pages 90–95.

Aarohi Srivastava, Abhinav Rastogi, Abhishek Rao, Abu Awal Md Shoeb, Abubakar Abid, Adam Fisch, Adam R Brown, Adam Santoro, Aditya Gupta, Adrià Garriga-Alonso, et al. 2022. Beyond the imitation game: Quantifying and extrapolating the capabilities of language models. *ArXiv preprint*, abs/2206.04615.

Alex Wang, Yada Pruksachatkun, Nikita Nangia, Amanpreet Singh, Julian Michael, Felix Hill, Omer Levy, and Samuel Bowman. 2019a. Superglue: A stickier benchmark for general-purpose language understanding systems. *Advances in neural information processing systems*, 32.

Alex Wang, Amanpreet Singh, Julian Michael, Felix Hill, Omer Levy, and Samuel R. Bowman. 2019b. GLUE: A multi-task benchmark and analysis platform for natural language understanding. In *7th International Conference on Learning Representations, ICLR 2019, New Orleans, LA, USA, May 6-9, 2019*. OpenReview.net.

Alex Warstadt, Amanpreet Singh, and Samuel R Bowman. 2019. CoLA: The corpus of linguistic acceptability (with added annotations).

Thomas Wolf, Lysandre Debut, Victor Sanh, Julien Chaumond, Clement Delangue, Anthony Moi, Pierric Cistac, Tim Rault, Rémi Louf, Morgan Funtowicz, et al. 2019. Huggingface's transformers: State-of-the-art natural language processing. *ArXiv preprint*, abs/1910.03771.

Rowan Zellers, Ari Holtzman, Yonatan Bisk, Ali Farhadi, and Yejin Choi. 2019. HellaSwag: Can a machine really finish your sentence? In *Proceedings of the 57th Annual Meeting of the Association for Computational Linguistics*, pages 4791–4800, Florence, Italy. Association for Computational Linguistics.

BMCook: A Task-agnostic Compression Toolkit for Big Models

Zhengyan Zhang[1], Baitao Gong[2], Yingfa Chen[1], Xu Han[1], Guoyang Zeng[2]
Weilin Zhao[1], Yanxu Chen[3], Zhiyuan Liu[1,4†], Maosong Sun[1,4†]
[1] DCST, Institute for AI, BNRIST, Tsinghua University, Beijing, China
[2] Model Best Inc. [3] Zhili College, Tsinghua University, Beijing, China
[4] International Innovation Center of Tsinghua University, Shanghai, China
zy-z19@mails.tsinghua.edu.cn {liuzy,sms}@tsinghua.edu.cn

Abstract

Recently, pre-trained language models (PLMs) have achieved great success on various NLP tasks and have shown a trend of exponential growth in model size. To alleviate the unaffordable computational costs brought by the size growth, model compression has been widely explored. Existing efforts have achieved promising results in compressing medium-sized models for specific tasks, while task-agnostic compression for big models with over billions of parameters is rarely studied. Task-agnostic compression can provide an efficient and versatile big model for both prompting and delta tuning, leading to a more general impact than task-specific compression. Hence, we introduce a task-agnostic compression toolkit BMCook for big models. In BMCook, we implement four representative compression methods, including quantization, pruning, distillation, and MoEfication. Developers can easily combine these methods towards better efficiency. To evaluate BMCook, we apply it to compress T5-3B (a PLM with 3 billion parameters). We achieve nearly 12x efficiency improvement while maintaining over 97% of the original T5-3B performance on three typical NLP benchmarks. Moreover, the final compressed model also significantly outperforms T5-base (a PLM with 220 million parameters), which has a similar computational cost. BMCook is publicly available at https://github.com/OpenBMB/BMCook.

	Q	P	D	M
TensorFlow (Abadi et al., 2016)	✓	✓		
PyTorch (Paszke et al., 2019)	✓	✓		
TextPruner (Yang et al., 2022)		✓		
TextBrewer (Yang et al., 2020)		✓	✓	
BMCook (this work)	✓	✓	✓	✓

Table 1: Comparisons between different compression toolkits. "Q", "P", "D", and "M" denote quantization, pruning, distillation, and MoEfication, respectively. Our BMCook is the first compression toolkit to support all four compression techniques.

1 Introduction

As the sizes of pre-trained language models (PLMs) increase, especially after reaching 10 billion parameters (Brown et al., 2021; Rae et al., 2021; Zhang et al., 2021a, 2022a; Chowdhery et al., 2022; Black et al., 2022), powerful intelligence capabilities emerge in these big models, supporting PLMs to accomplish tasks that previous smaller models could not do, such as quantitative reasoning (Lewkowycz et al., 2022) and long-form question answering (Nakano et al., 2021). Despite the success of big models, their exponentially growing sizes impose unaffordable computational costs for real-world applications.

To improve the efficiency of PLMs, model compression is an essential solution. There are several compression techniques, including model distillation (Hinton et al., 2015), model quantization (Bai et al., 2021), and model pruning (Liang et al., 2021). Based on these techniques, practitioners can conduct task-specific compression during fine-tuning (Sun et al., 2019) and task-agnostic compression during pre-training (Sanh et al., 2019). Previous studies mainly focus on applying task-specific compression for medium-sized PLMs with around one-hundred million parameters, such as $\text{BERT}_{\text{BASE}}$ (Zafrir et al., 2019; Jiao et al., 2020; Hou et al., 2020; Xia et al., 2022), while compressing large-scale PLMs with over billions of parameters is rarely studied.

In this work, we focus on the task-agnostic compression of big models because it enables developers to utilize the powerful intelligence of big models with fewer computation resources for both prompting (Brown et al., 2021) and delta tuning (aka parameter-efficient tuning) (Houlsby et al., 2019; Ding et al., 2022). Both prompting and delta tuning are the current core approaches to drive big

† Corresponding authors

Proceedings of the The 2022 Conference on Empirical Methods in Natural Language Processing: System Demonstrations, pages 396 - 405
December 7-11, 2022 ©2022 Association for Computational Linguistics

models. There exist two challenges for the task-agnostic compression of big models. First, big models require high compression rates to achieve affordable costs while existing compression toolkits only support one or two techniques as shown in Table 1, which cannot provide enough compression rates. Second, existing compression implementation ignores the memory challenge brought by big models. They are usually based on HuggingFace Transformers (Wolf et al., 2020), which cannot well support the training of large-scale PLMs.

In this work, we introduce BMCook, a task-agnostic compression toolkit for big models. BMCook has three main characteristics: (1) *Zero-redundancy training*. BMCook is developed on an efficient training toolkit, BMTrain[1], which supports the zero-redundancy optimizer with offloading (Rajbhandari et al., 2020; Ren et al., 2021a) to handle the memory challenge. (2) *Flexible combination*. To achieve better efficiency, we make BMCook flexible to support arbitrary combinations of different compression techniques. To this end, we implement four popular compression techniques and distribute each technique to different parts of one unified training life-cycle. (3) *Runtime model modification*. Since some compression techniques require to access the inner hidden states of PLMs, developers have to modify the code of model implementation provided by a third-party package. To make the compression easier to operate, BMCook implements runtime modification by monkey patch to get rid of modifying the source code of PLMs.

We evaluate the effectiveness of BMCook on T5-3B (Raffel et al., 2020), a T5 model with 3 billion parameters. Experimental results show that BMCook achieves nearly 12x compression efficiency by combining all four techniques while maintaining over 97% original performance on three typical NLP benchmarks, including SST-2 (Socher et al., 2013), MNLI (Williams et al., 2018), and SQuAD (Rajpurkar et al., 2016). Besides, the compressed model significantly outperforms T5-base, which has similar computation costs.

BMCook is supported by Open Lab for Big Model Base (OpenBMB)[2]. We hope BMCook can help researchers explore better compression methods for large-scale PLMs in the future and help practitioners to improve their model efficiency in real-world applications.

[1]https://github.com/OpenBMB/BMTrain

[2]https://www.openbmb.org/en/home

2 Design and Implementation

As mentioned in the introduction, we implement three main characteristics in BMCook, zero-redundancy training, flexible combination, and runtime model modification. In this section, we will introduce the design and the implementation details of these three characteristics.

2.1 Zero-redundancy Training

Due to the outrageous model size, big models require large memory to store their parameters and optimizer states, which cannot be maintained in one GPU. Recently, zero-redundancy optimizer has been proposed to solve this problem (Rajbhandari et al., 2020), which distributes the parameters and the optimizer states to multiple GPUs instead of storing all of them in one GPU repetitively. If more GPUs are used, each GPU requires less memory, which can alleviate the memory challenge brought by big models. Since BMCook targets the compression of big models, the training of big models is an important part. Therefore, we implement BMCook based on an efficient training toolkit — BMTrain, which supports zero-redundancy optimizer with parameter checkpointing (Chen et al., 2016) and offloading (Ren et al., 2021b).

2.2 Flexible Combination

Previous work on model compression usually explores one or two specific techniques. Due to the huge model size, we have to combine different techniques to achieve extreme compression. Hence, BMCook explores to build a unified compression framework that can support different techniques. Specifically, BMCook supports model distillation, model pruning, model quantization, and model MoEfication. By better utilizing these techniques, we distribute them into different parts of one unified life-cycle as shown in Figure 1. With this scope, we decouple these techniques in the implementation and support arbitrary combinations. Next, we will show more details about these techniques.

Model quantization aims to represent parameters by low-bit fixed-precision values and reduce both the memory and computational costs. For example, the computation of an 8-bit quantized model is 4 times faster than that of a 32-bit model. There are two main ways to quantize the parameters, post-training quantization and quantization-aware training. Current deep learning frameworks, such as PyTorch (Paszke et al., 2019) and Tensor-

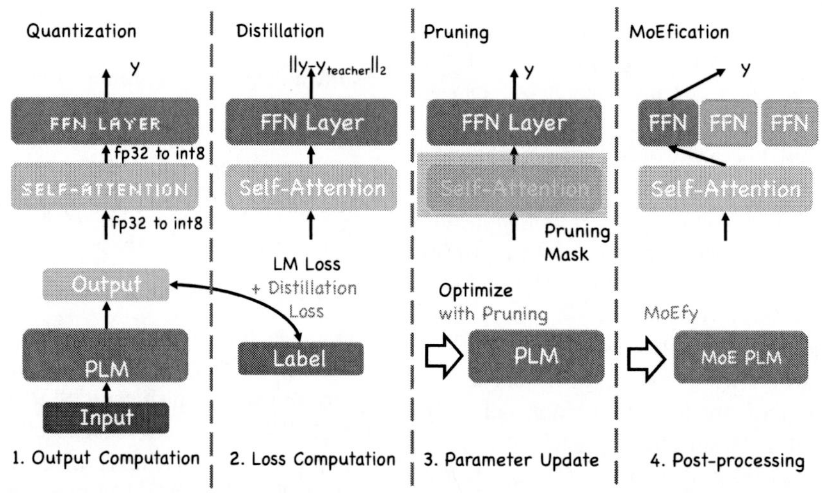

Figure 1: Life-cycle of the training process, including output computation, loss computation, parameter update, and post-processing. Each computation technique is bundled into a specific step. Specifically, quantization influences the output computation, distillation influences the loss computation, pruning influences the parameter update, and MoEfication influences the post-processing.

Flow (Abadi et al., 2016), have already supported post-training quantization. Post-training quantization directly quantizes the parameters of a PLM, which may bring a significant performance degradation. To alleviate the degradation caused by quantization, Stock et al. (2021) propose quantization-aware training (QAT). It simulates the quantization during the training, i.e., the parameters are quantized during the forward propagation, making the parameters adapted to low-bit fixed-precision computation.

Towards better performance, BMCook supports QAT. Specifically, we replace all linear layers in PLMs with quantized linear layers. In quantized linear layers, we simulate the quantized matrix multiplication. Since the linear layers account for more than 90% of the computation in the Transformer (Han et al., 2022), model quantization brings significant efficiency improvement.

Model distillation aims to guide the training of a compressed model by a larger teacher model. Traditional distillation adds the KL divergence between the outputs of teacher models and student models as an extra training objective (Hinton et al., 2015). For PLMs, Sun et al. (2019); Jiao et al. (2020); Liu et al. (2022); Park et al. (2021) find that it is also effective to make the inner computation results of student models close to those of their teachers. For example, they add the MSE loss between the hidden states of student models and teacher models.

Note that the model distillation module in BMCook is only to provide additional training loss instead of reducing the size of the model. Any compression technique requiring further training can be combined with model distillation to improve the performance of compressed models.

Model pruning aims to prune the redundant parameters of a model. There are two typical approaches, structured pruning and unstructured pruning. Structured pruning removes complete modules (e.g., layers) from the model (Fan et al., 2020; Wang et al., 2020; Zhang et al., 2021b; Xia et al., 2022). Instead, unstructured pruning removes individual parameters from the model (Han et al., 2015; Chen et al., 2020; Xu et al., 2021). Both of them change the forward and backward process of the model according to their pruned parameters. To decouple pruning and quantization, we distribute the pruning operations to the optimization step, where we set the pruned parameters to zero after parameter update. Due to this, we keep redundant parameters pruned during the forward and backward processes without directly affecting these processes.

Note that unstructured pruning cannot guarantee efficiency improvement in most cases because parallel processing devices, such as GPUs, usually do not provide optimized sparse computation operations (Zheng et al., 2022). Hence, BMCook implements unstructured pruning with 2:4 sparsity, which is well supported by Sparse Tensor

```
def _forward(module_self, x):
    x = module_self.forward_old(x)
    bmt.inspect.record_tensor(x, "
    hidden_states")
    return x

module.forward_old = module.forward
module.forward = types.MethodType(
    _forward, module)
```

Figure 2: Example of monkey patch. Add a tensor recording step to a forward function.

Core (Zhou et al., 2021). 2:4 sparsity means that every four continuous parameters have two zeros. In this way, the sparse computation is guaranteed to be twice as fast as the dense computation. Besides, for structured pruning, we implement CoFi (Xia et al., 2022) in BMCook, which adds L0-regularization to the parameters of the model to learn an optimal sparse mask.

MoEfication aims to transform the feedforward networks (FFNs) in Transformers to the equivalent mixture-of-expert (MoE) version (Fedus et al., 2021), which significantly reduces the computational costs of FFNs (Zhang et al., 2022b). Since Transformers (Vaswani et al., 2017) adopt ReLU (Nair and Hinton, 2010) as the activation function of FFNs and there exists an obvious sparse activation phenomenon, we can only involve part of FFNs for a specific input without affecting the model performance. The transformation process does not change the number and the values of model parameters. Therefore, we treat MoEfication as a post-processing technique. It can be applied to any compressed model to achieve better efficiency.

To train routers for expert selection, MoEfication requires the hidden states to simulate the computation process of FFNs. The training of routers is localized to specific FFNs and is dealt with by an external MoEfication package.

In summary, BMCook is the first to contain a series of compression techniques. And, benefiting from the decoupled implementation of compression techniques, practitioners can design their own compression strategies with arbitrary combinations.

2.3 Runtime Model Modification

All of the compression techniques mentioned in the last subsection require modifying the life-cycle of the training process, i.e., the implementation code of PLMs. Taking distillation as an example, to compute the mean squared error between the hidden states of the teacher model and the student

```
config = ConfigParser(args.config)
# for distillation
Trainer.forward = BMDistill.set_forward(
    model, teacher, Trainer.forward,
    config)
# for pruning
BMPrune.compute_mask(model, config)
BMPrune.set_optim_for_pruning(optimizer)
# for quantization
BMQuant.quantize(model, config)
# for moefication
Trainer.forward = BMMoE.get_hidden(model
    , config, Trainer.forward)
```

Figure 3: Based on the configuration file, practitioners can turn on a specific compression module with one or two lines of code.

model, we have to modify the forward functions to make the hidden states become return values. Existing compression toolkits usually ask developers to modify the codes (Yang et al., 2020, 2022). For example, in the case of distillation, after developers modify the forward functions, the toolkit provides the implementation of the loss calculation.

However, the model implementation is usually provided by a third-party package, such as HuggingFace Transformers, making the manual modification inconvenient. Besides, the modification is simple and similar across different PLMs. Hence, BMCook explores to implement runtime modification in a general way to keep the source code clean and make it easy to compress different PLMs.

Specifically, we utilize the characteristic of monkey patch in Python. Monkey patch is to modify the behavior of an object at runtime. As shown in Figure 2, we first rename the original forward function of the module as `forward_old`, and then define a new forward function containing `forward_old` and a tensor recording step. Finally, we assign the new forward function to the module. The `inspect` function for recording is to store the tensor in a global dictionary. After the whole forward process is finished, we can access the tensor by its name.

Both knowledge distillation and MoEfication require accessing the hidden states of PLMs. Considering that different modules have different foward functions, e.g., attention modules take hidden states and attention masks as input, we choose to access the hidden states of layer normalization modules and provide a general interface to add tensor recording to their forward functions. The inputs of layer normalization modules are only hidden states and are widely used before or after other modules. Hence, based on layer normalization modules, we

```
{
    "distillation": {
        "ce_scale": 0,
        "mse_hidn_scale": 1,
        "mse_hidn_module": ["[post]encoder.output_layernorm:[post]encoder.output_layernorm", "[post]decoder.output_layernorm:[post]decoder.output_layernorm"],
        "mse_hidn_proj": false
    },
    "pruning": {
        "is_pruning": true, "pruning_mask_path": "prune_mask.bin",
        "pruned_module": ["ffn.ffn.w_in.w.weight", "ffn.ffn.w_out.weight", "input_embedding"],
        "mask_method": "m4n2_1d"
    },
    "quantization": { "is_quant": true},
    "MoEfication": {
        "is_moefy": false,
        "first_FFN_module": ["ffn.layernorm_before_ffn"]
    }
}
```

Figure 4: Example of the configuration file.

can access nearly all hidden states of PLMs.

Similarly, we also modify the linear layers and optimizer by monkey patching for quantization and pruning. For quantization, we replace the matrix multiplication in the `forward` functions of linear layers with a quantized one. For pruning, we modify the behavior of the optimizer's `step` function. We keep the original operation and add a pruning step after the parameter update.

In summary, BMCook utilizes runtime modification to keep the source code clean and provides general interfaces to compress different PLMs.

2.4 Usage and Configuration

Since different compression modules are decoupled in BMCook, we implement each module independently, where each module is usually a Python file and provides one or two general interfaces. Benefiting from the general interfaces, BMCook can be applied to a PLM with only a few lines of code as shown in Figure 3. The details of compression are mainly determined by a configuration file, which will be used by different compression modules. In practice, users can easily reuse the code of pretraining for compression by adding a few lines of code to import compression modules and then setting the configuration file. Note that BMCook supports the PLMs implemented based on BMTrain and ModelCneter[3] has provided BMTrain-based implementations of almost all mainstream PLMs.

As shown in Figure 4, the configuration file is a JSON file. The keys are the names of the compression modules. The values are the configurations of the compression modules. Note that the module names used in the configuration file are corresponding to the names provided by PyTorch. Therefore, BMCook can access the modules by their names.

The key of knowledge distillation is `distillation`. Currently, BMCook supports two kinds of distillation objectives, KL divergence between output distributions (turn on when `ce_scale`>0) and mean squared error (MSE) between hidden states (turn on when `mse_hidn_scale`>0). Practitioners need to specify the hidden states used for MSE by `mse_hidn_module`. Meanwhile, the dimensions of the hidden states may be different between teacher and student models. Therefore, the hidden states of the teacher model need to be projected to the same dimension as those of the student model. Practitioners can turn on `mse_hidn_proj` for simple linear projection.

The key of model pruning is `pruning`. Practitioners can turn on pruning by `is_pruning`. The pruning mask is stored in `pruning_mask_path`. The pruned modules are specified by `pruned_module`. To simplify the list, practitioners can only provide the suffix of the modules. The mask method `mask_method` is to choose the algorithm for the computation of the pruning mask.

The key of quantization is `quantization`. Practitioners can turn on quantization by `is_quant`, which will replace all linear layers with quantized

[3]https://github.com/OpenBMB/ModelCenter

	Model	Activated Model Size	SST-2 Acc	MNLI-m Acc	SQuAD 1.0 EM	SQuAD 1.0 F1
Original Model	T5-Base	0.34GB	0.9278	0.8626	0.8076	0.8890
	T5-Large	0.60GB	0.9461	0.8938	0.8474	0.9193
	T5-3B	2.42GB	0.9621	0.9087	0.8754	0.9379
Single Module	Structured Pruning	1.21GB	0.9014	0.8472	0.8072	0.8877
	Unstructured Pruning	1.21GB	0.9576	0.8946	0.8592	0.9262
	Quantization	0.60GB	0.9598	0.9075	0.8746	0.9374
	MoEfication	1.61GB	0.9529	0.8961	0.8502	0.9260
Combination	Quant + Pruning	0.30GB	0.9518	0.8902	0.8628	0.9289
	Quant + Pruning + MoE	0.20GB	0.9518	0.8819	0.8316	0.9110

Table 2: Evaluation of original models and compressed models. In the combination experiments, we use unstructured pruning due to its superior performance in the single module experiments. The size of adapters keeps the same for all PLMs. Activated model size is used to measure the compression rate because the computational cost, i.e., FLOPS, is linear to the model size.

linear layers. BMCook provides the simulation of 8-bit quantization.

The key of MoEfication is `MoEfication`. Practitioners can turn on MoEfication by `is_moefy`. The hidden states used for router training are specified by `first_FFN_module`, which is the nearest layer normalization module before each FFN. Providing the suffix of the modules is also sufficient.

3 Evaluation

To validate the effectiveness of BMCook, we study task-agnostic compression on T5-3B (Raffel et al., 2020), which has 3 billion parameters. Since task-agnostic compression would benefit various downstream tasks, we evaluate the performance of adapter tuning (Houlsby et al., 2019) of T5-3B and its compressed variants. We also study T5-Base and T5-Large, which have 220 million and 770 million parameters, respectively.

Training and evaluation data. We use the Pile dataset (Gao et al., 2020) for task-agnostic compression training, which is a large-scale corpus for pre-training language models. The training objective is masked language modeling used by T5. Note that we turn on distillation during the compression training in all experiments because we find knowledge distillation with MSE loss can improve model performance in our pilot experiments. Besides, we choose three downstream datasets for evaluation: SST-2 (Socher et al., 2013), a representative single-sentence classification dataset, MNLI (Williams et al., 2018), a representative sentence-pair classification dataset, SQuAD v1.1 (Rajpurkar et al., 2016), a representative question-answer dataset. For the first two datasets, we use accuracy as the evaluation metric. For the third dataset, we use both exact match and F1 score as the evaluation metrics. We evaluate model performance on their development sets. We adopt the same task templates and label words of the original T5 paper (Raffel et al., 2020).

Hyper-parameters. The learning rate of task-agnostic compression training is 1e-4 while that of adapter tuning ranges from 1e-6 to 1e-5. The batch size of task-agnostic compression training and adapter tuning is 32. We use 4 NVIDIA A100 GPUs in the experiments. The training step of task-agnostic compression training ranges from 10K to 50K according to the compression methods. The training epoch of adapter tuning ranges from 3 to 5.

To fairly compare the efficiency of T5-3B and its variants, we define a new metric, named *activated model size*, because Brown et al. (2021) mentioned that the computation of Transformer is linear in the model size, which excludes the embedding layer. Hence, we consider the parameters of self-attention networks and FFNs. For the original model, the activated model size is equal to its original model size. Although it is intuitive to directly compare the speedup of compressed models, there is no inference toolkit supporting all the compressed methods. Hence, we focus on the theoretical computational cost in this work.

In the evaluation, we set the pruning sparsity to 50%, i.e., we prune 50% of the parameters and reduce half of the activated model size. Besides, we quantize the parameters to 8 bits, which reduces three-fourths of the activated model size compared to the floating-point version. For MoEfication, we dynamically involve 50% of parameters in FFNs for specific input. Therefore, the activated model size of the modified FFNs is about half of the original FFNs. Note that Transformer consists of both attention layers and FFNs and the model size of FFNs are about 70%. The final activated model size of the modified Transformer is about 66% of the original one. If we combine all three techniques, we can achieve a compressed model with about one-twelfth of the original activated size.

We report the evaluation results in Table 2. From this table, we have three observations: (1) In the experiment of single modules, quantization achieves the best efficiency and performance. Unstructured pruning achieves the second-best efficiency and performance, and significantly outperforms structured pruning. It suggests that directly removing layers may bring significant performance degradation. Besides, as a post-processing method, which does not require further pre-training, MoEfication maintains over 98% original performance while reducing 33% of the activation model size. (2) Different compression techniques can be combined to archive better efficiency while maintaining most of performance. For example, combining quantization, unstructured pruning, and MoEfication achieves a compressed model with about one-twelfth of the original activated size and maintains over 97% original performance. (3) Compressing big models can get better small models. For example, Quant+Pruning+MoE is smaller than T5-base while this model significantly outperforms T5-base.

4 Conclusion and Future Work

In this paper, we introduce a task-agnostic compression toolkit for big models, named BMCook. This toolkit contains four popular techniques and is designed to be flexible to support arbitrary combinations. Users can easily compress a PLM by adding several lines to its pre-training code and specifying the strategy in a configuration file.

In the future, there are three directions to further improve BMCook. First, we will enrich the options of existing compression techniques, such as knowledge distillation on attention matrices (Jiao et al., 2020) and extreme low-bit quantization (Bai et al., 2021). Second, there are some other compression techniques that are not covered by BMCook, such as weight sharing (Lan et al., 2020) and low-rank decomposition (Chen et al., 2021). Third, we will explore the automatic search for better compression strategies or configurations. Given a specific computation budget, we want to find the compression strategy that achieves the best model performance, which is similar to neural architecture search (Elsken et al., 2019).

Meanwhile, we will also plan to enrich the inference toolkits to support different compression techniques. Although compression techniques have been fast developed, the inference toolkits are still lagging behind. Recently, there are some efforts to support compressed models in inference, such as BMInf (Han et al., 2022) and DeepSpeed-MoE (Rajbhandari et al., 2022), while they are still limited to specific compression techniques.

Acknowledgments

This work is supported by the National Key R&D Program of China (No. 2020AAA0106502), Institute Guo Qiang at Tsinghua University and NExT++ project from the National Research Foundation, Prime Minister's Office, Singapore under its IRC@Singapore Funding Initiative.

References

Martín Abadi, Paul Barham, Jianmin Chen, Zhifeng Chen, Andy Davis, Jeffrey Dean, Matthieu Devin, Sanjay Ghemawat, Geoffrey Irving, Michael Isard, Manjunath Kudlur, Josh Levenberg, Rajat Monga, Sherry Moore, Derek Gordon Murray, Benoit Steiner, Paul A. Tucker, Vijay Vasudevan, Pete Warden, Martin Wicke, Yuan Yu, and Xiaoqiang Zheng. 2016. Tensorflow: A system for large-scale machine learning. In *Proceedings of the OSDI*, pages 265–283.

Haoli Bai, Wei Zhang, Lu Hou, Lifeng Shang, Jin Jin, Xin Jiang, Qun Liu, Michael R. Lyu, and Irwin King. 2021. Binarybert: Pushing the limit of BERT quantization. In *Proceedings of ACL/IJCNLP*, pages 4334–4348.

Sid Black, Stella Biderman, Eric Hallahan, Quentin Anthony, Leo Gao, Laurence Golding, Horace He, Connor Leahy, Kyle McDonell, Jason Phang, Michael Pieler, USVSN Sai Prashanth, Shivanshu Purohit, Laria Reynolds, Jonathan Tow, Ben Wang, and Samuel Weinbach. 2022. Gpt-neox-20b: An open-source autoregressive language model. *arxiv preprint arXiv:2204.06745*.

Tom B Brown, Benjamin Mann, Nick Ryder, Melanie Subbiah, Jared Kaplan, Prafulla Dhariwal, Arvind Neelakantan, Pranav Shyam, Girish Sastry, Amanda Askell, Sandhini Agarwal, Ariel Herbert-Voss, Gretchen Krueger, Tom Henighan, Rewon Child, Aditya Ramesh, Daniel M Ziegler, Jeffrey Wu, Clemens Winter, Christopher Hesse, Mark Chen, Eric Sigler, Mateusz Litwin, Scott Gray, et al. 2021. Language models are Few-Shot learners. In *Proceedings of NeurIPS*, pages 1877–1901.

Patrick H. Chen, Hsiang-Fu Yu, Inderjit S. Dhillon, and Cho-Jui Hsieh. 2021. DRONE: data-aware low-rank compression for large NLP models. In *Proceedings of NeurIPS*, pages 29321–29334.

Tianlong Chen, Jonathan Frankle, Shiyu Chang, Sijia Liu, Yang Zhang, Zhangyang Wang, and Michael Carbin. 2020. The lottery ticket hypothesis for pre-trained BERT networks. In *Proceedings of NeurIPS*.

Tianqi Chen, Bing Xu, Chiyuan Zhang, and Carlos Guestrin. 2016. Training deep nets with sublinear memory cost. *arXiv preprint arXiv:1604.06174*.

Aakanksha Chowdhery, Sharan Narang, Jacob Devlin, Maarten Bosma, Gaurav Mishra, Adam Roberts, Paul Barham, Hyung Won Chung, Charles Sutton, Sebastian Gehrmann, Parker Schuh, Kensen Shi, Sasha Tsvyashchenko, Joshua Maynez, Abhishek Rao, Parker Barnes, Yi Tay, Noam Shazeer, Vinodkumar Prabhakaran, Emily Reif, Nan Du, et al. 2022. PaLM: Scaling language modeling with pathways. *arXiv preprint arXiv:2204.02311*.

Ning Ding, Yujia Qin, Guang Yang, Fuchao Wei, Zonghan Yang, Yusheng Su, Shengding Hu, Yulin Chen, Chi-Min Chan, Weize Chen, et al. 2022. Delta tuning: A comprehensive study of parameter efficient methods for pre-trained language models. *arXiv preprint arXiv:2203.06904*.

Thomas Elsken, Jan Hendrik Metzen, and Frank Hutter. 2019. Neural architecture search: A survey. *J. Mach. Learn. Res.*, 20:55:1–55:21.

Angela Fan, Edouard Grave, and Armand Joulin. 2020. Reducing transformer depth on demand with structured dropout. In *Proceedings of ICLR*.

William Fedus, Barret Zoph, and Noam Shazeer. 2021. Switch transformers: Scaling to trillion parameter models with simple and efficient sparsity. *arXiv preprint 2101.03961*.

Leo Gao, Stella Biderman, Sid Black, Laurence Golding, Travis Hoppe, Charles Foster, Jason Phang, Horace He, Anish Thite, Noa Nabeshima, Shawn Presser, and Connor Leahy. 2020. The Pile: An 800gb dataset of diverse text for language modeling. *arXiv preprint arXiv:2101.00027*.

Song Han, Jeff Pool, John Tran, and William J Dally. 2015. Learning both weights and connections for efficient neural networks. In *Proceedings of NeurIPS*, pages 1135–1143.

Xu Han, Guoyang Zeng, Weilin Zhao, Zhiyuan Liu, Zhengyan Zhang, Jie Zhou, Jun Zhang, Jia Chao, and Maosong Sun. 2022. BMInf: An efficient toolkit for big model inference and tuning. In *Proceedings of ACL Demonstration*, pages 224–230.

Geoffrey Hinton, Oriol Vinyals, and Jeff Dean. 2015. Distilling the knowledge in a neural network. *arXiv preprint arXiv:1503.02531*.

Lu Hou, Zhiqi Huang, Lifeng Shang, Xin Jiang, Xiao Chen, and Qun Liu. 2020. Dynabert: Dynamic BERT with adaptive width and depth. In *Proceedings of NeurIPS*.

Neil Houlsby, Andrei Giurgiu, Stanislaw Jastrzebski, Bruna Morrone, Quentin de Laroussilhe, Andrea Gesmundo, Mona Attariyan, and Sylvain Gelly. 2019. Parameter-efficient transfer learning for NLP. In *Proceedings of ICML*, pages 2790–2799.

Xiaoqi Jiao, Yichun Yin, Lifeng Shang, Xin Jiang, Xiao Chen, Linlin Li, Fang Wang, and Qun Liu. 2020. TinyBERT: Distilling BERT for natural language understanding. In *Findings of EMNLP*, pages 4163–4174.

Zhenzhong Lan, Mingda Chen, Sebastian Goodman, Kevin Gimpel, Piyush Sharma, and Radu Soricut. 2020. ALBERT: A lite BERT for self-supervised learning of language representations. In *Proceedings of ICLR*.

Aitor Lewkowycz, Anders Andreassen, David Dohan, Ethan Dyer, Henryk Michalewski, Vinay V. Ramasesh, Ambrose Slone, Cem Anil, Imanol Schlag, Theo Gutman-Solo, Yuhuai Wu, Behnam Neyshabur, Guy Gur-Ari, and Vedant Misra. 2022. Solving quantitative reasoning problems with language models. *arXiv preprint arXiv:2206.14858*.

Tailin Liang, John Glossner, Lei Wang, Shaobo Shi, and Xiaotong Zhang. 2021. Pruning and quantization for deep neural network acceleration: A survey. *arXiv preprint 2101.09671*.

Chang Liu, Chongyang Tao, Jiazhan Feng, and Dongyan Zhao. 2022. Multi-granularity structural knowledge distillation for language model compression. In *Proceedings of ACL*, pages 1001–1011.

Vinod Nair and Geoffrey E. Hinton. 2010. Rectified linear units improve restricted boltzmann machines. In *Proceedings of ICML*, pages 807–814.

Reiichiro Nakano, Jacob Hilton, Suchir Balaji, Jeff Wu, Long Ouyang, Christina Kim, Christopher Hesse, Shantanu Jain, Vineet Kosaraju, William Saunders, Xu Jiang, Karl Cobbe, Tyna Eloundou, Gretchen Krueger, Kevin Button, Matthew Knight, Benjamin Chess, and John Schulman. 2021. WebGPT: Browser-assisted question-answering with human feedback. *arXiv preprint arXiv:2112.09332*.

Geondo Park, Gyeongman Kim, and Eunho Yang. 2021. Distilling linguistic context for language model compression. In *Proceedings of EMNLP*, pages 364–378.

Adam Paszke, Sam Gross, Francisco Massa, Adam Lerer, James Bradbury, Gregory Chanan, Trevor Killeen, Zeming Lin, Natalia Gimelshein, Luca Antiga, Alban Desmaison, Andreas Kopf, Edward Yang, Zachary DeVito, Martin Raison, Alykhan Tejani, Sasank Chilamkurthy, Benoit Steiner, Lu Fang, Junjie Bai, and Soumith Chintala. 2019. Pytorch:

An imperative style, high-performance deep learning library. In *Proceedings of NeurIPS*.

Jack W. Rae, Sebastian Borgeaud, Trevor Cai, Katie Millican, Jordan Hoffmann, H. Francis Song, John Aslanides, Sarah Henderson, Roman Ring, Susannah Young, Eliza Rutherford, Tom Hennigan, Jacob Menick, Albin Cassirer, Richard Powell, George van den Driessche, Lisa Anne Hendricks, Maribeth Rauh, Po-Sen Huang, Amelia Glaese, Johannes Welbl, Sumanth Dathathri, et al. 2021. Scaling language models: Methods, analysis & insights from training gopher. *arXiv preprint arXiv:2112.11446*.

Colin Raffel, Noam Shazeer, Adam Roberts, Katherine Lee, Sharan Narang, Michael Matena, Yanqi Zhou, Wei Li, and Peter J Liu. 2020. Exploring the limits of transfer learning with a unified Text-to-Text transformer. *J. Mach. Learn. Res.*, 21:140:1–140:67.

Samyam Rajbhandari, Conglong Li, Zhewei Yao, Minjia Zhang, Reza Yazdani Aminabadi, Ammar Ahmad Awan, Jeff Rasley, and Yuxiong He. 2022. Deepspeed-moe: Advancing mixture-of-experts inference and training to power next-generation AI scale. In *Proceedings of ICML*, volume 162, pages 18332–18346.

Samyam Rajbhandari, Jeff Rasley, Olatunji Ruwase, and Yuxiong He. 2020. Zero: memory optimizations toward training trillion parameter models. In *Proceedings of SC*, page 20.

Pranav Rajpurkar, Jian Zhang, Konstantin Lopyrev, and Percy Liang. 2016. SQuAD: 100,000+ questions for machine comprehension of text. In *Proceedings of EMNLP*, pages 2383–2392.

Jie Ren, Samyam Rajbhandari, Reza Yazdani Aminabadi, Olatunji Ruwase, Shuangyan Yang, Minjia Zhang, Dong Li, and Yuxiong He. 2021a. Zero-offload: Democratizing billion-scale model training. In *Proceedings of ATC*, pages 551–564.

Jie Ren, Samyam Rajbhandari, Reza Yazdani Aminabadi, Olatunji Ruwase, Shuangyan Yang, Minjia Zhang, Dong Li, and Yuxiong He. 2021b. Zero-offload: Democratizing billion-scale model training. In *Proceedings of USENIX ATC*, pages 551–564.

Victor Sanh, Lysandre Debut, Julien Chaumond, and Thomas Wolf. 2019. DistilBERT, a distilled version of BERT: smaller, faster, cheaper and lighter. *arXiv preprint 1910.01108*.

Richard Socher, Alex Perelygin, Jean Wu, Jason Chuang, Christopher D Manning, Andrew Ng, and Christopher Potts. 2013. Recursive deep models for semantic compositionality over a sentiment treebank. In *Proceedings of EMNLP*, pages 1631–1642.

Pierre Stock, Angela Fan, Benjamin Graham, Edouard Grave, Rémi Gribonval, Hervé Jégou, and Armand Joulin. 2021. Training with quantization noise for extreme model compression. In *Proceedings of ICLR*.

Siqi Sun, Yu Cheng, Zhe Gan, and Jingjing Liu. 2019. Patient knowledge distillation for BERT model compression. In *Proceedings of EMNLP*, pages 4323–4332.

Ashish Vaswani, Noam Shazeer, Niki Parmar, and Jakob Uszkoreit. 2017. Attention is all you need. In *Proceedings of NeurIPS*, pages 5998–6008.

Ziheng Wang, Jeremy Wohlwend, and Tao Lei. 2020. Structured pruning of large language models. In *Proceedings of EMNLP*, pages 6151–6162.

Adina Williams, Nikita Nangia, and Samuel R. Bowman. 2018. A broad-coverage challenge corpus for sentence understanding through inference. In *Proceedings of NAACL-HLT*, pages 1112–1122.

Thomas Wolf, Lysandre Debut, Victor Sanh, Julien Chaumond, Clement Delangue, Anthony Moi, Pierric Cistac, Tim Rault, Remi Louf, Morgan Funtowicz, Joe Davison, Sam Shleifer, Patrick von Platen, Clara Ma, Yacine Jernite, Julien Plu, Canwen Xu, Teven Le Scao, Sylvain Gugger, Mariama Drame, Quentin Lhoest, and Alexander Rush. 2020. Transformers: State-of-the-art natural language processing. In *Proceedings of EMNLP Demonstration*, pages 38–45.

Mengzhou Xia, Zexuan Zhong, and Danqi Chen. 2022. Structured pruning learns compact and accurate models. In *Proceedings of ACL*, pages 1513–1528.

Dongkuan Xu, Ian En-Hsu Yen, Jinxi Zhao, and Zhibin Xiao. 2021. Rethinking network pruning – under the pre-train and fine-tune paradigm. In *Proceedings of NAACL-HLT*, pages 2376–2382.

Ziqing Yang, Yiming Cui, and Zhigang Chen. 2022. Textpruner: A model pruning toolkit for pre-trained language models. In *Proceedings of ACL*, pages 35–43.

Ziqing Yang, Yiming Cui, Zhipeng Chen, Wanxiang Che, Ting Liu, Shijin Wang, and Guoping Hu. 2020. Textbrewer: An open-source knowledge distillation toolkit for natural language processing. In *Proceedings of ACL*, pages 9–16.

Ofir Zafrir, Guy Boudoukh, Peter Izsak, and Moshe Wasserblat. 2019. Q8BERT: Quantized 8bit BERT. *arXiv preprint 1910.06188*.

Susan Zhang, Stephen Roller, Naman Goyal, Mikel Artetxe, Moya Chen, Shuohui Chen, Christopher Dewan, Mona Diab, Xian Li, Xi Victoria Lin, Todor Mihaylov, Myle Ott, Sam Shleifer, Kurt Shuster, Daniel Simig, Punit Singh Koura, Anjali Sridhar, Tianlu Wang, and Luke Zettlemoyer. 2022a. OPT: open pretrained transformer language models. *arXiv preprint arXiv:2205.01068*.

Zhengyan Zhang, Yuxian Gu, Xu Han, Shengqi Chen, Chaojun Xiao, Zhenbo Sun, Yuan Yao, Fanchao Qi, Jian Guan, Pei Ke, Yanzheng Cai, Guoyang Zeng, Zhixing Tan, Zhiyuan Liu, Minlie Huang,

Wentao Han, Yang Liu, Xiaoyan Zhu, and Maosong Sun. 2021a. CPM-2: large-scale cost-effective pretrained language models. *AI Open*, 2:216–224.

Zhengyan Zhang, Yankai Lin, Zhiyuan Liu, Peng Li, Maosong Sun, and Jie Zhou. 2022b. MoEfication: Transformer feed-forward layers are mixtures of experts. In *Findings of ACL 2022*.

Zhengyan Zhang, Fanchao Qi, Zhiyuan Liu, Qun Liu, and Maosong Sun. 2021b. Know what you don't need: Single-shot meta-pruning for attention heads. *AI Open*, 2:36–42.

Ningxin Zheng, Bin Lin, Quanlu Zhang, Lingxiao Ma, Yuqing Yang, Fan Yang, Yang Wang, Mao Yang, and Lidong Zhou. 2022. SparTA: Deep-Learning model sparsity via Tensor-with-Sparsity-Attribute. In *Proceedings of OSDI*, pages 213–232.

Aojun Zhou, Yukun Ma, Junnan Zhu, Jianbo Liu, Zhijie Zhang, Kun Yuan, Wenxiu Sun, and Hongsheng Li. 2021. Learning n:m fine-grained structured sparse neural networks from scratch. In *Proceedings of ICLR*.

ALToolbox: A Set of Tools for Active Learning Annotation of Natural Language Texts

Akim Tsvigun[1,3 ◊], Leonid Sanochkin[1,3 ◊], Daniil Larionov[2,5], Gleb Kuzmin[1,5], Artem Vazhentsev[1,4], Ivan Lazichny[1], Nikita Khromov[4], Danil Kireev[5], Aleksandr Rubashevskii[4], Olga O. Shahmatova[7], Dmitry V. Dylov[4], Igor Galitskiy[1], Artem Shelmanov[1,6]

[1]AIRI, [2]MIPT, [3]HSE, [4]Skoltech, [5]FRC CSC RAS, [6]MBZUAI
[7]National Medical Research Centre of Cardiology
{tsvigun, sanochkin, shelmanov}@airi.net
artem.shelmanov@mbzuai.ac.ae

Abstract

We present ALToolbox – an open-source framework for active learning (AL) annotation in natural language processing. Currently, the framework supports text classification, sequence tagging, and seq2seq tasks. Besides state-of-the-art query strategies, ALToolbox provides a set of tools that help to reduce computational overhead and duration of AL iterations and increase annotated data reusability. The framework aims to support data scientists and researchers by providing an easy-to-deploy GUI annotation tool directly in the Jupyter IDE and an extensible benchmark for novel AL methods. We prepare a small demonstration of ALToolbox capabilities available online[1,2]. The code of the framework is published under the MIT license[3].

1 Introduction

The development of text processing applications based on machine learning (ML) usually requires a lot of labeled data. Despite numerous annotated corpora designed for various tasks and available for resource-rich languages, in practice, the business logic of an application is often very specific and cannot be implemented using only public resources. Manual annotation of natural language corpora is a tedious and time-consuming task, which can take up to 30-40% of the application development time.

For rather simple tasks, the annotation of corpora can be organized using crowd-sourcing. However, crowd-sourcing is not suitable for specific domains like medicine, finance, information technology, or any other field that requires specific qualifications or knowledge of business logic. It is also problematic to apply crowd-sourcing when the annotation scheme is complex and requires some premature training of annotators. In each of the aforementioned cases, annotation of each instance becomes expensive because it requires hiring people with a high qualification or a specific skill set.

Active learning (AL) is a well-known technique that speeds up data annotation by leveraging model output for selecting instances demonstrated to human experts (Cohn et al., 1996; Settles and Craven, 2008). It focuses human effort on instances that are the most informative for model training, decreasing redundancy and filtering out noisy outliers. AL helps to achieve a certain level of model performance using only a fraction of the labor required to exhaustively annotate a given dataset.

In this work, we present ALToolbox – an open-source framework that contains a comprehensive set of tools for practical AL annotation in text classification, sequence tagging, and seq2seq tasks. The main goal of the framework is to support data scientists and researchers. They usually need to test new ideas very quickly, and the lack of annotation is a common obstacle to this. ALToolbox aims to address several practical obstacles to deploying AL: (1) data annotated with AL should be reusable; (2) AL should not consume excessive computational resources, while the annotation process should be interactive without delays for annotators; (3) annotation should be quick and fluent.

(1) Instances selected with AL that are informative for one model can be not informative for a different model of another type. This hurts the reusability of data annotated with the help of AL. For example, Lowell et al. (2019) shows that if we use predictions of one model for selecting instances during AL, but train a model of a different type on the selected data, the performance of the latter can be even worse compared to the case when it is trained on data labeled without AL. Lowell et al. (2019) call this effect *acquisition-successor mismatch* (ASM) problem (where *acquisition* is a

[1]`http://demo.nlpresearch.group`
[2]`http://demo-video.nlpresearch.group`
[3]`https://github.com/AIRI-Institute/al_toolbox`
◊ Equal contribution

Proceedings of the The 2022 Conference on Empirical Methods in Natural Language Processing: System Demonstrations, pages 406 - 434
December 7-11, 2022 ©2022 Association for Computational Linguistics

Feature	Paladin	ActiveAnno	AlpacaTag	FAMIE	Small-Text	ALToolbox (Ours)
Text classification	✓	✓			✓	✓
Sequence tagging			✓	✓		✓
Seq2seq						✓
SOTA query strategies				✓	✓	✓
SOTA neural models	✓	✓	✓	✓	✓	✓
Computationally efficient AL				✓		✓
Annotated data reusability						✓
Annotation GUI	✓	✓	✓	✓		✓
Serverless annotation in Jupyter						✓
Extensible benchmark						✓
Multilinguality				✓	✓	✓
Compat. with other AL frameworks		✓				✓
Acquisition model adaptation						✓
Proactive learning	✓					

Table 1: Comparison of NLP-related AL frameworks.

model used for selecting instances during AL and *successor* is a model trained on the labeled data for the final application). To address this problem, we include in the framework several pipelines for the preparation of acquisition models and post-processing of data annotated with the help of AL. These pipelines leverage the Pseudo-labeling for the Acquisition-Successor Mismatch (PLASM) algorithm based on the effect of knowledge distillation (Hinton et al., 2015) in AL revealed by Shelmanov et al. (2021); Tsvigun et al. (2022b). PLASM effectively mitigates ASM, making data collected with AL reusable for training models of various architectures.

(2) Applying AL is not free. It introduces additional computational overhead which usually sums up from training an acquisition model and performing its inference. For resource-intensive models such as modern neural networks, this overhead might be prohibitive due to the cost of GPU-accelerated computations for their training and inference. Due to the ASM problem, it is not possible to simply replace a resource-intensive model (e.g. ELECTRA) with a small one (e.g. DistilBERT). PLASM addresses this problem and allows to use small versions of acquisition models obtained using distillation, which speeds up training and inference. ALToolbox also implements an unlabeled pool subsampling algorithm, which leverages uncertainty of instances to avoid repetitive predictions on the part of the unlabeled pool, speeding up the inference phase of AL iterations (Tsvigun et al., 2022b).

(3) AL itself speeds up the annotation procedure, but the time required for deploying an AL-empowered annotation system and integrating annotation with existing data processing pipelines can diminish its benefits. Removing obstacles between the data processing workflow and annotation tools can facilitate rapid evaluation of new ideas. Therefore, in ALToolbox, besides a set of state-of-the-art query strategies, we also provide a serverless AL-empowered annotation tool that is natively integrated directly into the Jupyter Notebook IDE. This tool is suitable for labeling small datasets and testing new ideas quickly, which, we believe, is useful for data scientists and researchers. This tool is easy to start and is fully integrated with the familiar IDE, while also being flexible and extensible.

There are many UI-centric academic and commercial annotation systems for end users that support AL annotation: WebAnno (Yimam et al., 2013), AlpacaTag (Lin et al., 2019), Paladin (Nghiem et al., 2021), ActiveAnno (Wiechmann et al., 2021), FAMIE (Van Nguyen et al., 2022), Prodigy (Montani and Honnibal, 2018) (a commercial system), and others. However, they lack many practical features that serve the goal of rapid annotation, compatibility with pipelines for data analysis and IDEs, and reusability of the annotated data. There are also several low-level AL packages that focus on providing various query strategies and can be used as building blocks for more elaborated systems: LibAct (Yang et al., 2017), ModAL (Danka and Horvath, 2018), Baal (Atighehchian et al., 2020), Small-text (Schröder et al., 2021). However, most of them also overlook the problem of reusability and computational efficiency. Only Small-text is specifically tailored to NLP tasks.

The contributions of the proposed framework:

- a comprehensive collection of state-of-the-art query strategies for sequence tagging, text classification, and seq2seq tasks;
- a benchmarking tool for experimental evaluation of novel AL methods;
- pipelines for acquisition model preparation and for data post-processing that provide reusability of annotated data and computational efficiency of AL;
- a serverless GUI for AL annotation integrated

Method	Paladin	ActiveAnno	AlpacaTag	FAMIE	Small-Text	ALToolbox (ours)
AcTune (Yu et al., 2022)						✓
ALPS (Yuan et al., 2020)				✓		✓
BADGE (Ash et al., 2020)				✓	✓	✓
BAIT (Ash et al., 2021)						✓
BALD (Houlsby et al., 2011)						✓
BatchBALD (Kirsch et al., 2019)						✓
BERT-KM (Yuan et al., 2020)				✓	✓	✓
BLEUVar (Xiao et al., 2020)						✓
Breaking Ties (Luo et al., 2004)					✓	✓
CAL (Margatina et al., 2021)					✓	✓
Cluster-Margin (Citovsky et al., 2021)						✓
Coreset (Sener and Savarese, 2018)					✓	✓
Discriminative AL (Gissin and Shalev-Shwartz, 2019)					✓	
EGL (Settles et al., 2007)					✓	✓
ENSP (Wang et al., 2019)						✓
Entropy (Roy and Mccallum, 2001)					✓	✓
IDDS (Tsvigun et al., 2022a)						✓
LC (Lewis and Gale, 1994)	✓	✓			✓	✓
MNLP (Shen et al., 2017)			✓	✓		✓
NSP (Ueffing and Ney, 2007)						✓
SEALS (Coleman et al., 2022)					✓	

Table 2: The comparison of AL frameworks by implemented query strategies.

directly into the Jupyter notebook IDE for data scientists and researchers.

2 Framework Description

The ALToolbox framework is a Python library with several executable scripts, as well as a Jupyter widget implemented in JavaScript. In this section, we describe the key features of the framework.

2.1 Query Strategies

One of the key components of AL pipelines is a query strategy that specifies what instances are selected for annotation. ALToolbox provides classical and state-of-the-art query strategies for text classification, sequence tagging, and seq2seq tasks. Table 2 summarizes strategies implemented in our framework and in software packages from the related work.

Uncertainty sampling is one of the most widely-used types of AL query strategies. ALToolbox provides several basic uncertainty estimation methods based on softmax prediction probability: **Least Confidence (LC)** (Lewis and Gale, 1994), **Maximum Normalized Log-Probability (MNLP)** (Shen et al., 2017), **Breaking Ties (BT)** (Luo et al., 2004), **Prediction entropy (PE)** (Roy and Mccallum, 2001), **Normalized Sequence Probability (NSP)** (Ueffing and Ney, 2007). Since a predictive distribution of a single deterministic neural network cannot be used to obtain reliable uncertainty scores (Sener and Savarese, 2018; Mukhoti et al., 2021), some works have ventured into the development of Bayesian query strategies (Siddhant and Lipton, 2018). ALToolbox implements one of the widely-adopted strategies – **Bayesian Active Learning by Disagreement (BALD)** (Houlsby et al., 2011). It selects instances that provide the biggest amount of information about true model parameters by knowing the true label of the considered instance. In practice, the strategy approximates variational inference in a Bayesian neural network using Monte-Carlo dropout (Gal and Ghahramani, 2016). ALToolbox also includes a batched version of BALD – **BatchBALD** (Kirsch et al., 2019), which is modified to jointly score and select for annotation multiple instances on each AL iteration.

An alternative for uncertainty sampling is diversity-based sampling. In this category, the **core-set** algorithm (Sener and Savarese, 2018) leverages data geometry and aims to minimize the bound between an average loss over any given subset of the dataset and the remaining data points. Recently proposed **Contrastive Active Learning (CAL)** prioritizes instances, which predictive likelihoods diverge the most from their neighbors in the training set (Margatina et al., 2021). The **Cluster-Margin** algorithm (Citovsky et al., 2021) is designed to select large batches for annotation. It prioritizes instances that are diverse and that the model is not confident about. **BERT-KM** (Yuan et al., 2020) clusters texts in the unlabeled pool using their contextualized embeddings and selects the nearest neighbors of cluster centers. **Active Learning by Processing Surprisal (ALPS)** (Yuan et al., 2020) leverages pre-trained models, self-supervised learning objective, and clustering to solve the cold-start problem in AL. **AcTune** (Yu et al., 2022) can be used as a wrapper over uncertainty-based query strategies. It selects the most uncertain instances from regions obtained by clustering the unlabeled pool and ranking them by uncertainty and diversity.

ALToolbox also contains several gradient-based

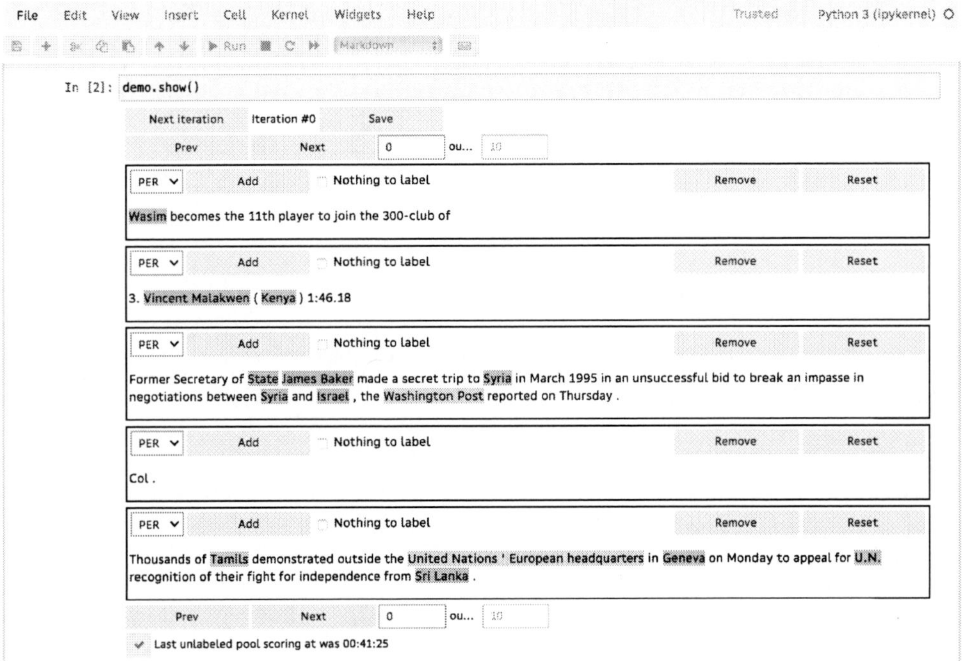

Figure 1: Serverless GUI annotation tool integrated into the Jupyter IDE.

query strategies. **Expected Gradient Length (EGL)** aims to prioritize instances that would impart the greatest change to the current model if we add them to the training set with their labels (Settles et al., 2007). **Batch Active Learning by Diverse Gradient Embeddings (BADGE)** measures uncertainty as the gradient magnitude with respect to parameters in the final (output) layer (Ash et al., 2020). **Batch Active learning via Information maTrices (BAIT)** selects batches of instances by optimizing a bound on the MLE error in terms of the Fisher information (Ash et al., 2021).

Furthermore, ALToolbox provides several query strategies for seq2seq tasks. **NSP** (Ueffing and Ney, 2007) is an analogue of LC for text generation, which calculates the length-normalized total probability of a generated sequence. **ENSP** (Wang et al., 2019) makes several stochastic runs using Monte-Carlo dropout and averages the probabilities of the sequences. The **BLEUVar** (Xiao et al., 2020) algorithm strives to measure the variance of texts generated under Monte-carlo dropout by using the BLEU metric (Papineni et al., 2002). The **IDDS** (Tsvigun et al., 2022a) strategy, shown to be state-of-the-art for the abstractive text summarization task, selects instances that are semantically dissimilar from the already annotated instances, avoiding outliers and borderline instances.

Finally, the framework provides the ability to use different strategies for different AL iterations. For example, one could use a cold-start method (e.g. ALPS) at several first iterations and later switch to another strategy such as LC.

2.2 Supported Models

ALToolbox is compatible with the HuggingFace Transformers library (Wolf et al., 2020), allowing the usage of state-of-the-art Transformer models like BERT (Devlin et al., 2019), RoBERTa (Liu et al., 2019), XLNet (Yang et al., 2019), ELECTRA (Clark et al., 2020), and others. The support of some older RNN-based models like CNN-BiLSTM-CRF (Ma and Hovy, 2016) for sequence tagging is implemented via a wrapper around the Flair library (Akbik et al., 2019). Users can also implement their own models directly using PyTorch. ALToolbox provides several custom neural model implementations in PyTorch, including the classical CNN for text classification (Le et al., 2018).

2.3 Jupyter Annotation Tool

ALToolbox provides a simple serverless tool with a GUI for AL annotation integrated directly into Jupyter Notebook, which is one of the most popular IDEs for the Python language and data analysis (Figure 1). It supports annotation for text classification and sequence tagging tasks like named entity

AL Strategy	Iter. 1	Iter. 5	Iter. 10	Iter. 15	Average
Actune + CAL	92.0 ± 0.5	94.3 ± 0.0	**94.8 ± 0.2**	**95.0 ± 0.2**	**94.4 ± 0.0**
Actune + Entropy	91.7 ± 0.5	94.1 ± 0.3	94.7 ± 0.4	94.8 ± 0.3	**94.2 ± 0.2**
Actune + LC	92.0 ± 0.3	94.2 ± 0.2	**94.7 ± 0.4**	95.0 ± 0.0	**94.3 ± 0.3**
ALPS	90.6 ± 0.3	92.3 ± 0.5	92.9 ± 0.5	93.4 ± 0.6	92.6 ± 0.2
BADGE	**92.2 ± 0.3**	94.3 ± 0.1	94.7 ± 0.2	95.0 ± 0.2	**94.3 ± 0.1**
BAIT	**92.2 ± 0.4**	94.3 ± 0.1	**95.0 ± 0.2**	**95.1 ± 0.4**	**94.4 ± 0.1**
BALD	**92.2 ± 0.6**	93.9 ± 0.1	**94.8 ± 0.4**	**95.2 ± 0.1**	**94.3 ± 0.2**
Breaking Ties (BT)	**92.3 ± 0.3**	**94.5 ± 0.3**	94.9 ± 0.1	95.0 ± 0.0	**94.4 ± 0.1**
CAL	**92.3 ± 0.7**	**94.5 ± 0.3**	**94.8 ± 0.3**	**95.1 ± 0.1**	**94.4 ± 0.2**
Coreset	91.9 ± 0.1	93.8 ± 0.3	**94.7 ± 0.5**	**95.1 ± 0.1**	94.2 ± 0.1
Entropy	92.0 ± 0.1	94.4 ± 0.1	94.9 ± 0.1	**95.0 ± 0.2**	**94.4 ± 0.1**
Least Confidence (LC)	**92.3 ± 0.5**	**94.3 ± 0.3**	**95.0 ± 0.4**	**95.0 ± 0.2**	**94.4 ± 0.1**
Mahalanobis Distance	91.6 ± 0.4	94.0 ± 0.3	94.8 ± 0.2	95.0 ± 0.1	94.2 ± 0.1
Random	90.8 ± 0.4	92.5 ± 0.1	92.9 ± 0.4	93.4 ± 0.5	92.6 ± 0.2

Table 3: Accuracy of RoBERTa on AG News with various AL strategies on several AL iterations with query size = 1% (1200 instances). *Average* refers to the average result throughout the AL cycle. We select with **bold** state-of-the-art results with respect to confidence intervals. The results are averaged for 5 runs with different seeds to ensure the stability.

recognition and event extraction.

The tool is implemented using Jupyter widgets – a built-in feature of the Jupyter IDE for creating extensions. This widget can be configured with various AL query strategies and models, including Transformers. After the tool object is invoked, the IDE displays the widget in a notebook cell, and AL annotation begins. For example, to add NER annotation, a user can select a corresponding text fragment with a mouse and add a label to it. For text classification, a label can be chosen from a predefined list via selectable buttons. On each iteration, the user receives instances for annotation in mini-batches. The user can annotate all or just a part of them and invoke the next iteration of an AL algorithm with the "Next iteration" button asking for a new minibatch of unlabeled instances.

The annotation tool performs all necessary computations asynchronously with GUI and returns new instances without any delay. It keeps a list of instances sorted by their "informativeness" and updates it as soon as possible in the background.

The user can interrupt annotation at any time and resume it after a while. The tool tracks changes made by the user on the hard drive. The annotation is accumulated in easy-to-parse JSON files.

The target audience of this tool is data scientists and researchers. It is very easy to launch and modify: new graphical elements can be added using Jupyter Widgets as well. Using Jupyter also helps to reduce the effort of combining the system with data processing pipelines. We consider this tool might be useful for rapid annotation in small to medium projects and for testing new ideas quickly. However, we note that it lacks many useful features of full-fledged annotation systems, e.g., the ability to work with multiple users simultaneously. Creating a complex GUI for annotation is out of the scope of this project since a wide range of similar projects have already been released, e.g. DocAnno (Nakayama et al., 2018), LabelStudio (Tkachenko et al., 2020-2022), ActiveAnno (Wiechmann et al., 2021). The ALToolbox framework can be easily integrated into such annotation systems with the help of API.

2.4 Tools for Computational Efficient Active Learning and Reusable Annotation

ALToolbox contains a set of scripts that help to improve the computational efficiency of AL while keeping annotated data reusable. AL requires a substantial amount of computations on each iteration, which depends on the complexity and the size of the acquisition model. Using smaller and lighter models can lead to performance degradation of AL due to the ASM problem discussed in the introduction. We mitigate this problem by implementing tools for the "Pseudo-Labeling for Acquisition-Successor Mismatch" (PLASM) algorithm (Tsvigun et al., 2022b). This algorithm leverages small distilled models (e.g. DistilBERT) during the acquisition of instances, but after the annotation is finished it trains the original full-sized models (e.g. BERT) on the acquired data and uses it for automatic pseudo-labeling of the whole unlabeled pool of instances. The mistakes in automatic annotation are cleaned with the help of the TracIn method (Pruthi et al., 2020). Finally, the successor model is trained on the data that contains gold-standard labels and cleaned automatically labeled instances.

PLASM reduces or completely removes the gap in performance that appears when the successor model is different from the acquisition model. It makes the annotated data reusable for training suc-

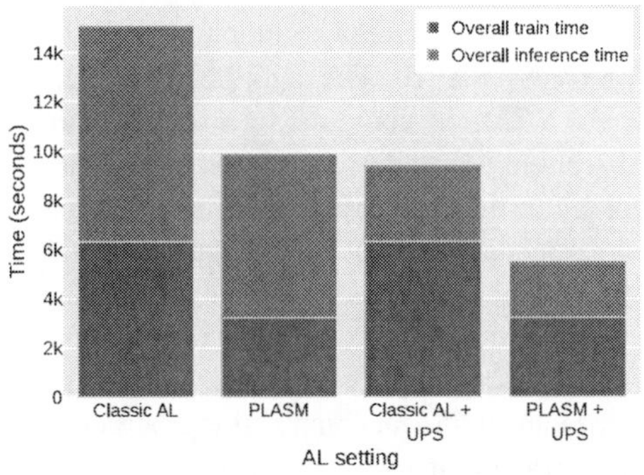

Figure 2: Duration in seconds of all the training and inference phases of the simulated AL with different acquisition settings on AG News with query size = 1% and 15 AL iterations. ELECTRA is used as a successor model, and DistilBERT – for acquisition in PLASM.

cessor models of various architectures. ALToolbox provides scripts for automatic model distillation and a pipeline for data post-processing with PLASM. All the necessary post-processing can be done by invoking a single function.

For large datasets, making predictions for the whole unlabeled set on each iteration to obtain the uncertainty estimates may require an enormous amount of time and resources. Consequently, in the framework, we also implement the "unlabeled pool subsampling" (UPS) algorithm (Tsvigun et al., 2022b), which samples the instances from the unlabeled pool according to their uncertainty estimates on previous iterations.

Figures 2, 21, 23 illustrate time benefits brought by PLASM and UPS on AG News, IMDB, and CoNLL-2003, respectively. PLASM accelerates the training phase of AL by 35% / 65% / 34%, while UPS accelerates the inference phase by 65% / 61% / 63%. Their combination speeds up all AL iteration computations by up to 63% / 67% / 38%, respectively, making AL much more interactive. Figures 19a, 20a, 22a show that the performance of the successor model does not deteriorate when these algorithms are used. Figures 19b, 20b, 22b, in turn, show that the ASM problem leads to a substantial decrease in the model performance.

We also provide scripts for domain adaptation of acquisition models. Margatina et al. (2022) demonstrate that self-supervised adaptation (Gururangan et al., 2020) of pre-trained Transformers on the unlabeled pool of instances helps to speed up AL.

2.5 Benchmarking Tool for Query Strategies

ALToolbox provides an extensible and easy-to-use benchmarking tool for testing new AL query strategies and unlabeled pool subsampling strategies. To experiment with a new strategy, a user implements it in the form of a Python class and runs the evaluation script, specifying the path to the corresponding class module as an argument. The script performs several iterations of simulated AL annotation and constructs the dependence of the model performance scores on the size of the labeled data. Experiments are launched multiple times with different random seeds to obtain confidence intervals of the results.

Using this tool, we provide the evaluation results of implemented query strategies, which can be used as a reference. The experiments with text classification are conducted on AG News (Zhang et al., 2015), IMDB (Maas et al., 2011), and CoLA (Warstadt et al., 2018); with sequence tagging – on CoNLL-2003 (Tjong Kim Sang and De Meulder, 2003); with abstractive text summarization – on AESLC (Zhang and Tetreault, 2019), WikiHow (Koupaee and Wang, 2018), and PubMed (Cohan et al., 2018). We provide the results with big and lightweight Transformers and with several different query sizes:

- Selecting $k\%$ of instances (for text classification & abstractive text summarization) / tokens (for sequence tagging). In this setting, we randomly select and annotate $k\%$ of instances / tokens as the initial seed and select $k\%$ of instances / tokens for annotation on each AL iteration according to the query function. This configuration aims to benchmark strategies in a high-resource AL mode. We refer to it as *query size = k%*.
- Selecting 100 instances / tokens on each AL iteration and as the initial seed. This configuration aims to benchmark strategies in a medium-resource AL mode. We refer to it as *query size = 100*.
- Selecting 10 instances / tokens on each AL iteration. The initial seeding procedure differs between tasks under this mode. For text classification, we randomly select and annotate 1 instance of each class as the initial seed. For other tasks, we annotate 10 randomly chosen instances / tokens. This configuration aims to benchmark strategies in a low-resource AL mode. We refer to it as *query size = 10*.

Dataset statistics, model details, and hyperparameters are presented in Tables 4–6.

Table 3 depicts the results on AG News with RoBERTa-base as an acquisition model, and query size = 1%. We can see that most of the strategies perform roughly similar with CAL and LC showing the best performance across all AL iterations. Figure 3 also demonstrates the results throughout the whole AL cycle of the best-performing query strategies according to the average accuracy throughout the AL cycle. Figure 4 provides the comparison of the duration of computations for various query strategies. Tables 7–18 compare query strategies on text classification datasets for various settings and models. Figures 5–10 visualize the results of the best-performing query strategies.

Sequence tagging results are presented in Tables 19–23. MNLP demonstrates the best quality in terms of F1-micro score excluding the "no entity" tag ("O"). Figures 11–13 show the iteration-wise scores. The duration of computations for various strategies is presented in Figure 23.

For abstractive text summarization, due to the big size of the unlabeled pool of WikiHow and Pubmed, on each AL iteration, we randomly subsample the unlabeled pool to 10,000 instances. Tables 24–27 provide the average results throughout the AL cycle and results on several iterations, while Figures 15–18 illustrate the results during the entire AL cycle. Finally, Figure 14 compares the duration of execution of the seq2seq query strategies.

3 Related Work

The comparison of ALToolbox with other frameworks from the related work on AL in NLP is presented in Table 1.

First of all, ALToolbox supports two most demanded NLP tasks: text classification and sequence tagging. It also works with abstractive text summarization, which is a seq2seq task. Other frameworks support only one of the tasks: Paladin, ActiveAnno, and Small-Text work only with text classification, while AlpacaTag and FAMIE support only sequence tagging.

Table 2 compares AL frameworks by implemented query strategies. Paladin, ActiveAnno, and AlpacaTag implement only the basic strategies. FAMIE implements several modern methods like ALPS and BADGE, but lacks many others. We note that Small-Text implements many recently proposed query strategies, including CAL, BADGE, and BERT-KM. However, ALToolbox provides the most comprehensive set of state-of-the-art query strategies and also allows combining them.

Except for ALToolbox and FAMIE (Van Nguyen et al., 2022), the computational overhead and the AL-caused time delays have been inexplicably dismissed in the prior art. FAMIE entails training a bigger model in the background during the labeling of each batch while using a smaller one as a proxy for acquisition. Such knowledge distillation makes the AL annotation process more interactive but also carries an additional computational burden, requiring extra resources for training and running two models. On the contrary, the knowledge distillation within our framework reduces both the time needed to complete an AL iteration and the overall amount of computation.

We note that neither FAMIE, nor other frameworks, address the ASM problem that hinders the reusability of annotated data. The tools for model distillation and annotated data post-processing based on the PLASM algorithm in our framework help to mitigate the ASM, so a user, for example, can train XLNet using data acquired with DistilBERT without significant performance penalties.

Most of the considered systems provide an elaborated GUI for annotation by end-users. Our framework aims to support data scientists and researchers and provides a fast-to-deploy minimalistic annotation system directly in the Jupyter IDE.

None of the considered systems provides easy-to-use scripts for conducting experiments with new AL methods. ALToolbox implements an extensible benchmarking tool that we hope will simplify research in AL for NLP.

One of the problems that are currently out of the scope of ALToolbox is efficient task assignments to multiple annotators. Proactive learning implemented in Paladin addresses this problem. We consider this feature as future work.

4 Conclusion

We introduced ALToolbox, an open-source framework for practical AL in NLP. Besides many other features, the framework addresses the problems of computational efficiency of AL and data reusability. We hope that our framework will foster the development of new AL methods and remove some practical obstacles to deploying AL annotation.

In future work, we are looking forward to adding the support of more text generation tasks, introducing proactive learning, and providing tools for hyperparameter selection in AL.

Acknowledgements

We thank anonymous reviewers for their insightful suggestions to improve this paper. The work was supported by the Russian Science Foundation grant 20-71-10135 (all sections except Section 2.4). The work by Olga Shakhmatova and Dmitry V. Dylov on Section 2.4 and the GUI annotation tool is supported by the grant of RFBR #19-29-01240. The experiments were supported in part by computational resources of HPC facilities at HSE University (Kostenetskiy et al., 2021).

References

Alan Akbik, Tanja Bergmann, Duncan Blythe, Kashif Rasul, Stefan Schweter, and Roland Vollgraf. 2019. Flair: An easy-to-use framework for state-of-the-art nlp. In *NAACL 2019, 2019 Annual Conference of the North American Chapter of the Association for Computational Linguistics (Demonstrations)*, pages 54–59.

Jordan Ash, Surbhi Goel, Akshay Krishnamurthy, and Sham Kakade. 2021. Gone fishing: Neural active learning with fisher embeddings. In *Advances in Neural Information Processing Systems*, volume 34, pages 8927–8939. Curran Associates, Inc.

Jordan T. Ash, Chicheng Zhang, Akshay Krishnamurthy, John Langford, and Alekh Agarwal. 2020. Deep batch active learning by diverse, uncertain gradient lower bounds. In *International Conference on Learning Representations*.

Parmida Atighehchian, Frédéric Branchaud-Charron, and Alexandre Lacoste. 2020. Bayesian active learning for production, a systematic study and a reusable library. *arXiv preprint arXiv:2006.09916*.

Gui Citovsky, Giulia DeSalvo, Claudio Gentile, Lazaros Karydas, Anand Rajagopalan, Afshin Rostamizadeh, and Sanjiv Kumar. 2021. Batch active learning at scale.

Kevin Clark, Minh-Thang Luong, Quoc V. Le, and Christopher D. Manning. 2020. ELECTRA: pre-training text encoders as discriminators rather than generators. In *8th International Conference on Learning Representations, ICLR 2020, Addis Ababa, Ethiopia, April 26-30, 2020*.

Arman Cohan, Franck Dernoncourt, Doo Soon Kim, Trung Bui, Seokhwan Kim, Walter Chang, and Nazli Goharian. 2018. A discourse-aware attention model for abstractive summarization of long documents. In *Proceedings of the 2018 Conference of the North American Chapter of the Association for Computational Linguistics: Human Language Technologies, Volume 2 (Short Papers)*, pages 615–621, New Orleans, Louisiana. Association for Computational Linguistics.

David A Cohn, Zoubin Ghahramani, and Michael I Jordan. 1996. Active learning with statistical models. *Journal of artificial intelligence research*, 4:129–145.

Cody Coleman, Edward Chou, Julian Katz-Samuels, Sean Culatana, Peter Bailis, Alexander C. Berg, Robert Nowak, Roshan Sumbaly, Matei Zaharia, and I. Zeki Yalniz. 2022. Similarity search for efficient active learning and search of rare concepts. *Proceedings of the AAAI Conference on Artificial Intelligence*, 36(6):6402–6410.

Tivadar Danka and Peter Horvath. 2018. modAL: A modular active learning framework for Python. *arXiv preprint arXiv:1805.00979*.

Jacob Devlin, Ming-Wei Chang, Kenton Lee, and Kristina Toutanova. 2019. BERT: Pre-training of deep bidirectional transformers for language understanding. In *Proceedings of the 2019 Conference of the North American Chapter of the Association for Computational Linguistics: Human Language Technologies, Volume 1 (Long and Short Papers)*, pages 4171–4186, Minneapolis, Minnesota. Association for Computational Linguistics.

Yarin Gal and Zoubin Ghahramani. 2016. Dropout as a bayesian approximation: Representing model uncertainty in deep learning. In *Proceedings of The 33rd International Conference on Machine Learning*, volume 48 of *Proceedings of Machine Learning Research*, pages 1050–1059, New York, New York, USA. PMLR.

Daniel Gissin and Shai Shalev-Shwartz. 2019. Discriminative active learning. *arXiv preprint arXiv:1907.06347*.

Suchin Gururangan, Ana Marasović, Swabha Swayamdipta, Kyle Lo, Iz Beltagy, Doug Downey, and Noah A Smith. 2020. Don't stop pretraining: Adapt language models to domains and tasks. In *Proceedings of the 58th Annual Meeting of the Association for Computational Linguistics*, pages 8342–8360.

Geoffrey E. Hinton, Oriol Vinyals, and Jeffrey Dean. 2015. Distilling the knowledge in a neural network. *CoRR*, abs/1503.02531.

Neil Houlsby, Ferenc Huszár, Zoubin Ghahramani, and Máté Lengyel. 2011. Bayesian active learning for classification and preference learning. *arXiv preprint arXiv:1112.5745*.

Andreas Kirsch, Joost Van Amersfoort, and Yarin Gal. 2019. Batchbald: Efficient and diverse batch acquisition for deep bayesian active learning. *Advances in neural information processing systems*, 32.

P. S. Kostenetskiy, R. A. Chulkevich, and V. I. Kozyrev. 2021. HPC Resources of the Higher School of Economics. *Journal of Physics: Conference Series*, 1740(1):012050.

Mahnaz Koupaee and William Yang Wang. 2018. Wikihow: A large scale text summarization dataset. *CoRR*, abs/1810.09305.

Hoa T Le, Christophe Cerisara, and Alexandre Denis. 2018. Do convolutional networks need to be deep for text classification? In *Workshops at the Thirty-Second AAAI Conference on Artificial Intelligence*.

David D Lewis and William A Gale. 1994. A sequential algorithm for training text classifiers. In *SIGIR'94*, pages 3–12. Springer.

Bill Yuchen Lin, Dong-Ho Lee, Frank F. Xu, Ouyu Lan, and Xiang Ren. 2019. AlpacaTag: An active learning-based crowd annotation framework for sequence tagging. In *Proceedings of the 57th Annual Meeting of the Association for Computational Linguistics: System Demonstrations*, pages 58–63, Florence, Italy. Association for Computational Linguistics.

Yinhan Liu, Myle Ott, Naman Goyal, Jingfei Du, Mandar Joshi, Danqi Chen, Omer Levy, Mike Lewis, Luke Zettlemoyer, and Veselin Stoyanov. 2019. Roberta: A robustly optimized BERT pretraining approach. *arXiv preprint arXiv:1907.11692*.

David Lowell, Zachary C. Lipton, and Byron C. Wallace. 2019. Practical obstacles to deploying active learning. In *Proceedings of the 2019 Conference on Empirical Methods in Natural Language Processing and the 9th International Joint Conference on Natural Language Processing (EMNLP-IJCNLP)*, pages 21–30, Hong Kong, China. Association for Computational Linguistics.

Tong Luo, K. Kramer, S. Samson, A. Remsen, D.B. Goldgof, L.O. Hall, and T. Hopkins. 2004. Active learning to recognize multiple types of plankton. In *Proceedings of the 17th International Conference on Pattern Recognition, 2004. ICPR 2004.*, volume 3, pages 478–481 Vol.3.

Xuezhe Ma and Eduard Hovy. 2016. End-to-end sequence labeling via bi-directional LSTM-CNNs-CRF. In *Proceedings of the 54th Annual Meeting of the Association for Computational Linguistics (Volume 1: Long Papers)*, pages 1064–1074, Berlin, Germany. Association for Computational Linguistics.

Andrew L. Maas, Raymond E. Daly, Peter T. Pham, Dan Huang, Andrew Y. Ng, and Christopher Potts. 2011. Learning word vectors for sentiment analysis. In *The 49th Annual Meeting of the Association for Computational Linguistics: Human Language Technologies, Proceedings of the Conference, 19-24 June, 2011, Portland, Oregon, USA*, pages 142–150. The Association for Computer Linguistics.

Katerina Margatina, Loic Barrault, and Nikolaos Aletras. 2022. On the importance of effectively adapting pretrained language models for active learning. In *Proceedings of the 60th Annual Meeting of the Association for Computational Linguistics (Volume 2: Short Papers)*, pages 825–836, Dublin, Ireland. Association for Computational Linguistics.

Katerina Margatina, Giorgos Vernikos, Loïc Barrault, and Nikolaos Aletras. 2021. Active learning by acquiring contrastive examples. In *Proceedings of the 2021 Conference on Empirical Methods in Natural Language Processing*, pages 650–663, Online and Punta Cana, Dominican Republic. Association for Computational Linguistics.

Ines Montani and Matthew Honnibal. 2018. Prodigy: A new tool for radically efficient machine teaching. `https://prodi.gy/`.

Jishnu Mukhoti, Andreas Kirsch, Joost van Amersfoort, Philip HS Torr, and Yarin Gal. 2021. Deterministic neural networks with appropriate inductive biases capture epistemic and aleatoric uncertainty. *arXiv preprint arXiv:2102.11582*.

Hiroki Nakayama, Takahiro Kubo, Junya Kamura, Yasufumi Taniguchi, and Xu Liang. 2018. doccano: Text annotation tool for human. Software available from https://github.com/doccano/doccano.

Minh-Quoc Nghiem, Paul Baylis, and Sophia Ananiadou. 2021. Paladin: an annotation tool based on active and proactive learning. In *Proceedings of the 16th Conference of the European Chapter of the Association for Computational Linguistics: System Demonstrations*, pages 238–243, Online. Association for Computational Linguistics.

Kishore Papineni, Salim Roukos, Todd Ward, and Wei-Jing Zhu. 2002. Bleu: a method for automatic evaluation of machine translation. In *Proceedings of the 40th Annual Meeting of the Association for Computational Linguistics*, pages 311–318, Philadelphia, Pennsylvania, USA. Association for Computational Linguistics.

Garima Pruthi, Frederick Liu, Satyen Kale, and Mukund Sundararajan. 2020. Estimating training data influence by tracing gradient descent. In *Advances in Neural Information Processing Systems 33: Annual Conference on Neural Information Processing Systems 2020, NeurIPS 2020, December 6-12, 2020, virtual*.

Nicholas Roy and Andrew Mccallum. 2001. Toward optimal active learning through sampling estimation of error reduction. *Proceedings of the 18th International Conference on Machine Learning*.

Christopher Schröder, Lydia Müller, Andreas Niekler, and Martin Potthast. 2021. Small-text: Active learning for text classification in python.

Ozan Sener and Silvio Savarese. 2018. Active learning for convolutional neural networks: A core-set approach. In *International Conference on Learning Representations*.

Burr Settles and Mark Craven. 2008. An analysis of active learning strategies for sequence labeling tasks. In *2008 Conference on Empirical Methods in Natural Language Processing, EMNLP 2008, Proceedings of the Conference, 25-27 October 2008, Honolulu,*

Hawaii, USA, A meeting of SIGDAT, a Special Interest Group of the ACL, pages 1070–1079. Association for Natural Language Processing.

Burr Settles, Mark Craven, and Soumya Ray. 2007. Multiple-instance active learning. *Advances in neural information processing systems*, 20.

Artem Shelmanov, Dmitri Puzyrev, Lyubov Kupriyanova, Denis Belyakov, Daniil Larionov, Nikita Khromov, Olga Kozlova, Ekaterina Artemova, Dmitry V. Dylov, and Alexander Panchenko. 2021. Active learning for sequence tagging with deep pre-trained models and Bayesian uncertainty estimates. In *Proceedings of the 16th Conference of the European Chapter of the Association for Computational Linguistics: Main Volume*, pages 1698–1712, Online. Association for Computational Linguistics.

Yanyao Shen, Hyokun Yun, Zachary C Lipton, Yakov Kronrod, and Animashree Anandkumar. 2017. Deep active learning for named entity recognition. *arXiv preprint arXiv:1707.05928*.

Aditya Siddhant and Zachary C. Lipton. 2018. Deep Bayesian active learning for natural language processing: Results of a large-scale empirical study. In *Proceedings of the 2018 Conference on Empirical Methods in Natural Language Processing*, pages 2904–2909, Brussels, Belgium. Association for Computational Linguistics.

Erik F. Tjong Kim Sang and Fien De Meulder. 2003. Introduction to the CoNLL-2003 shared task: Language-independent named entity recognition. In *Proceedings of the Seventh Conference on Natural Language Learning at HLT-NAACL 2003*, pages 142–147.

Maxim Tkachenko, Mikhail Malyuk, Andrey Holmanyuk, and Nikolai Liubimov. 2020-2022. Label Studio: Data labeling software. Open source software available from https://github.com/heartexlabs/label-studio.

Akim Tsvigun, Ivan Lysenko, Danila Sedashov, Ivan Lazichny, Eldar Damirov, Vladimir Karlov, Artemy Belousov, Leonid Sanochkin, Maxim Panov, Alexander Panchenko, Mikhail Burtsev, and Artem Shelmanov. 2022a. Active learning for abstractive text summarization. In *Findings of the 2022 Conference on Empirical Methods in Natural Language Processing*.

Akim Tsvigun, Artem Shelmanov, Gleb Kuzmin, Leonid Sanochkin, Daniil Larionov, Gleb Gusev, Manvel Avetisian, and Leonid Zhukov. 2022b. Towards computationally feasible deep active learning. In *Findings of the Association for Computational Linguistics: NAACL 2022*, pages 1198–1218, Seattle, United States. Association for Computational Linguistics.

Nicola Ueffing and Hermann Ney. 2007. Word-level confidence estimation for machine translation. *Comput. Linguistics*, 33(1):9–40.

Minh Van Nguyen, Nghia Trung Ngo, Bonan Min, and Thien Huu Nguyen. 2022. Famie: A fast active learning framework for multilingual information extraction.

Shuo Wang, Yang Liu, Chao Wang, Huanbo Luan, and Maosong Sun. 2019. Improving back-translation with uncertainty-based confidence estimation. In *Proceedings of the 2019 Conference on Empirical Methods in Natural Language Processing and the 9th International Joint Conference on Natural Language Processing (EMNLP-IJCNLP)*, pages 791–802, Hong Kong, China. Association for Computational Linguistics.

Alex Warstadt, Amanpreet Singh, and Samuel R Bowman. 2018. Neural network acceptability judgments. *arXiv preprint arXiv:1805.12471*.

Max Wiechmann, Seid Muhie Yimam, and Chris Biemann. 2021. ActiveAnno: General-purpose document-level annotation tool with active learning integration. In *Proceedings of the 2021 Conference of the North American Chapter of the Association for Computational Linguistics: Human Language Technologies: Demonstrations*, pages 99–105, Online. Association for Computational Linguistics.

Thomas Wolf, Lysandre Debut, Victor Sanh, Julien Chaumond, Clement Delangue, Anthony Moi, Pierric Cistac, Tim Rault, Rémi Louf, Morgan Funtowicz, Joe Davison, Sam Shleifer, Patrick von Platen, Clara Ma, Yacine Jernite, Julien Plu, Canwen Xu, Teven Le Scao, Sylvain Gugger, Mariama Drame, Quentin Lhoest, and Alexander M. Rush. 2020. Transformers: State-of-the-art natural language processing. In *Proceedings of the 2020 Conference on Empirical Methods in Natural Language Processing: System Demonstrations*, pages 38–45, Online. Association for Computational Linguistics.

Tim Z. Xiao, Aidan N. Gomez, and Yarin Gal. 2020. Wat zei je? detecting out-of-distribution translations with variational transformers. *CoRR*, abs/2006.08344.

Yao-Yuan Yang, Shao-Chuan Lee, Yu-An Chung, Tung-En Wu, Si-An Chen, and Hsuan-Tien Lin. 2017. libact: Pool-based active learning in python. *arXiv preprint arXiv:1710.00379*.

Zhilin Yang, Zihang Dai, Yiming Yang, Jaime Carbonell, Russ R Salakhutdinov, and Quoc V Le. 2019. Xlnet: Generalized autoregressive pretraining for language understanding. *Advances in neural information processing systems*, 32.

Seid Muhie Yimam, Iryna Gurevych, Richard Eckart de Castilho, and Chris Biemann. 2013. Webanno: A flexible, web-based and visually supported system for distributed annotations. In *Proceedings of the 51st*

Annual Meeting of the Association for Computational Linguistics: System Demonstrations, pages 1–6.

Yue Yu, Lingkai Kong, Jieyu Zhang, Rongzhi Zhang, and Chao Zhang. 2022. Actune: Uncertainty-based active self-training for active fine-tuning of pretrained language models. In *Proceedings of the 2022 Conference of the North American Chapter of the Association for Computational Linguistics: Human Language Technologies*, pages 1422–1436.

Michelle Yuan, Hsuan-Tien Lin, and Jordan Boyd-Graber. 2020. Cold-start active learning through self-supervised language modeling. In *Proceedings of the 2020 Conference on Empirical Methods in Natural Language Processing (EMNLP)*, pages 7935–7948, Online. Association for Computational Linguistics.

Rui Zhang and Joel Tetreault. 2019. This email could save your life: Introducing the task of email subject line generation. In *Proceedings of the 57th Annual Meeting of the Association for Computational Linguistics*, pages 446–456, Florence, Italy. Association for Computational Linguistics.

Xiang Zhang, Junbo Jake Zhao, and Yann LeCun. 2015. Character-level convolutional networks for text classification. In *Advances in Neural Information Processing Systems 28: Annual Conference on Neural Information Processing Systems 2015, December 7-12, 2015, Montreal, Quebec, Canada*, pages 649–657.

A Dataset Statistics and Model Hyperparameters

Dataset	Train	Test	Mean document length (tokens)	C
CoNLL-2003	15K/203.6K	3.7K/46.4K	14.5	4(5)
AG News	120K	7.6K	53.1	4
IMDb	25K	25K	300.0	2
CoLA	8.5K	1K	11.3	2
AESLC	14.4K	1.9K	142.4	-
WikiHow	184.6K	1K	377.5	-
Pubmed	119.1K	6.7K	495.4	-

Table 4: Dataset statistics. We provide a number of instances / tokens (for sequence tagging) for the training and test sets and average lengths of documents in terms of tokens. C is a number of classes / entity types for text classification and sequence tagging datasets.

Task	Model	Checkpoint	# Param.
Text classification	BERT	bert-base-uncased	110M
	DistilBERT	distilbert-base-uncased	67M
	ELECTRA	google/electra-base-discriminator	110M
	DistilELECTRA	Isanochkin/distilelectra-base	67M
	RoBERTa	roberta-base	125M
	DistilRoBERTa	distilroberta-base	82M
Sequence tagging	ELECTRA	google/electra-base-discriminator	110M
	BERT	bert-base-cased	110M
	DistilBERT	distilbert-base-cased	67M
Abstractive text summarization	BART	facebook/bart-base	139M
	PEGASUS	google/pegasus-large	570M

Table 5: Transformers model checkpoints from the HuggingFace repository (Wolf et al., 2020)

Hparam	Sequence tagging	Classification	BART	PEGASUS
Number of epochs	15	5	6	4
Batch size	16	16	16	2
Gradient accumulation steps	1	1	1	8
Min. number of training steps	1000	1000	350	200
Max. sequence length	-	256	1024	1024
Optimizer		AdamW		
Learning rate	5e-5	2e-5	2e-5	5e-4
Weight decay	0.01	0.01	0.028	0.03
Gradient clipping	1.	1.	0.28	0.3
Sheduler		STLR		
% warm-up steps		10		
Num. beams at evaluation	-	-	4	4
Generation max. length	-	-	Adapt.	Adapt.

Table 6: Hyperparameter values of Transformers. The hyperparameters are chosen according to evaluation scores on the validation datasets when models are trained using the whole available training data. *Adapt* refers to adaptive length, when generation maximum length is equal to the maximum summary length on the train set.

B Query Strategy Benchmark

For the tables in this section, we select with **bold** state-of-the-art results with respect to the confidence intervals. When all the values are within the confidence interval, we only select with **bold** the largest average value. The results are averaged for 10 runs with different seeds for *query size = 10* and for 5 runs for other query size settings to ensure stability. The *Average* column refers to the average result throughout the AL cycle.

B.1 Text Classification

B.1.1 AG News

Query size = 1 %

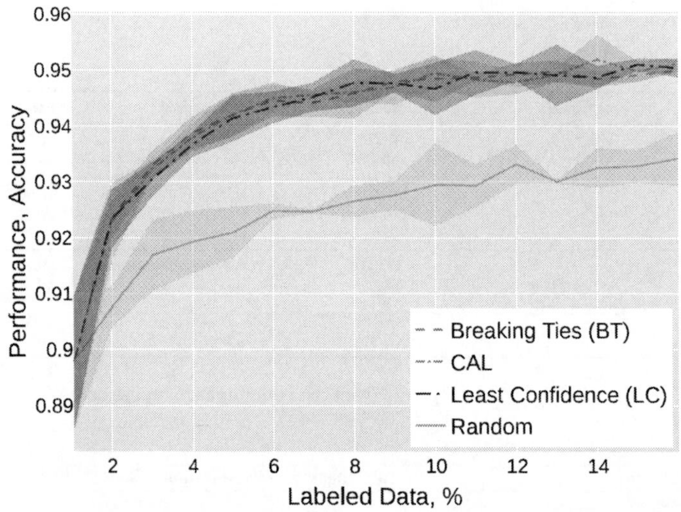

Figure 3: Accuracy of the best performing query strategies according to average accuracy throughout the AL cycle (BT, CAL, and LC) on AG News with RoBERTa with query size = 1%.

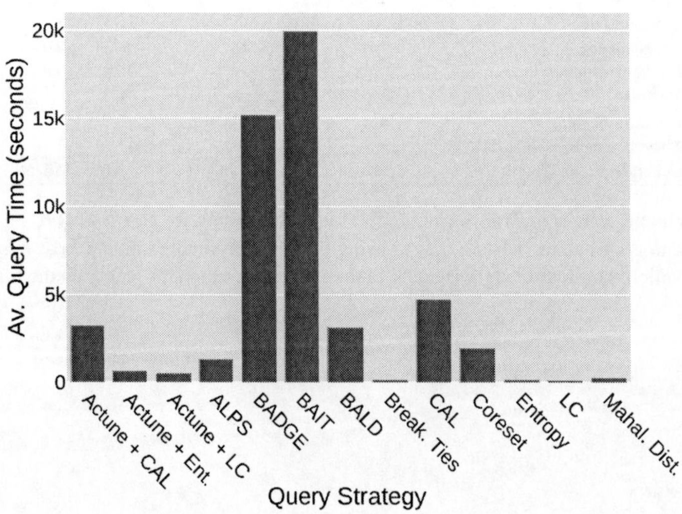

Figure 4: Average duration in seconds of one AL query with different strategies on AG News with RoBERTa as an acquisition model and query size = 1% (1200 instances). Hardware configuration is provided in Appendix C.

Query size = 100

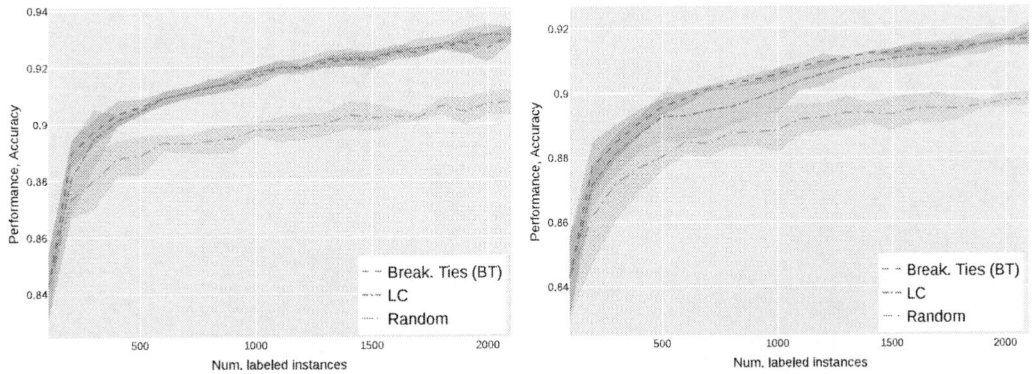

a) RoBERTa b) DistilBERT

Figure 5: Accuracy of the best performing query strategies with different acquisition models on AG News with query size = 100.

AL Strategy	Iter. 1	Iter. 5	Iter. 10	Iter. 15	Iter. 20	Average
BADGE	**88.95 ± 0.85**	**90.95 ± 0.18**	91.83 ± 0.2	**92.49 ± 0.27**	**93.06 ± 0.25**	**91.7 ± 0.16**
BAIT	88.21 ± 1.36	90.56 ± 0.28	91.57 ± 0.28	92.23 ± 0.31	92.87 ± 0.15	91.32 ± 0.36
BALD	88.24 ± 1.04	90.0 ± 0.74	90.98 ± 0.29	91.26 ± 0.46	91.98 ± 0.32	90.69 ± 0.39
BT	**88.96 ± 0.48**	**90.9 ± 0.25**	**92.01 ± 0.26**	**92.53 ± 0.28**	**93.11 ± 0.29**	**91.66 ± 0.06**
CAL	88.08 ± 0.93	90.67 ± 0.15	91.73 ± 0.31	**92.42 ± 0.17**	92.91 ± 0.23	91.48 ± 0.16
Coreset	87.97 ± 1.26	90.32 ± 0.42	91.33 ± 0.24	91.72 ± 0.17	92.23 ± 0.32	90.97 ± 0.26
Entropy	88.02 ± 1.14	90.65 ± 0.35	91.24 ± 0.38	91.95 ± 0.42	92.58 ± 0.3	91.15 ± 0.27
LC	88.06 ± 1.33	**90.91 ± 0.23**	**91.99 ± 0.2**	**92.55 ± 0.15**	**93.14 ± 0.28**	**91.65 ± 0.15**
Random	87.35 ± 0.66	89.33 ± 0.31	89.8 ± 0.46	90.26 ± 0.28	90.77 ± 0.45	89.68 ± 0.27

Table 7: Accuracy of RoBERTa on AG News with various AL strategies with query size = 100.

AL Strategy	Iter. 1	Iter. 5	Iter. 10	Iter. 15	Iter. 20	Average
BALD	86.57 ± 0.26	89.06 ± 0.49	90.17 ± 0.21	90.57 ± 0.17	90.99 ± 0.29	89.82 ± 0.23
BT	**87.71 ± 0.8**	**89.84 ± 0.22**	**90.81 ± 0.15**	**91.36 ± 0.19**	**91.67 ± 0.26**	**90.52 ± 0.12**
CAL	87.37 ± 0.34	**89.43 ± 0.37**	90.37 ± 0.34	91.11 ± 0.22	**91.59 ± 0.26**	90.2 ± 0.2
Coreset	86.84 ± 0.59	89.31 ± 0.34	89.96 ± 0.23	90.51 ± 0.36	91.1 ± 0.21	89.81 ± 0.28
Entropy	86.27 ± 0.57	89.15 ± 0.63	90.05 ± 0.28	90.65 ± 0.55	91.19 ± 0.23	89.81 ± 0.37
LC	**87.15 ± 0.67**	**89.3 ± 0.76**	**90.39 ± 0.3**	91.13 ± 0.33	**91.83 ± 0.34**	90.19 ± 0.31
Random	86.17 ± 1.48	88.48 ± 0.39	89.19 ± 0.48	89.52 ± 0.43	89.81 ± 0.23	88.83 ± 0.4

Table 8: Accuracy of DistilBERT on AG News with various AL strategies with query size = 100.

Query size = 10

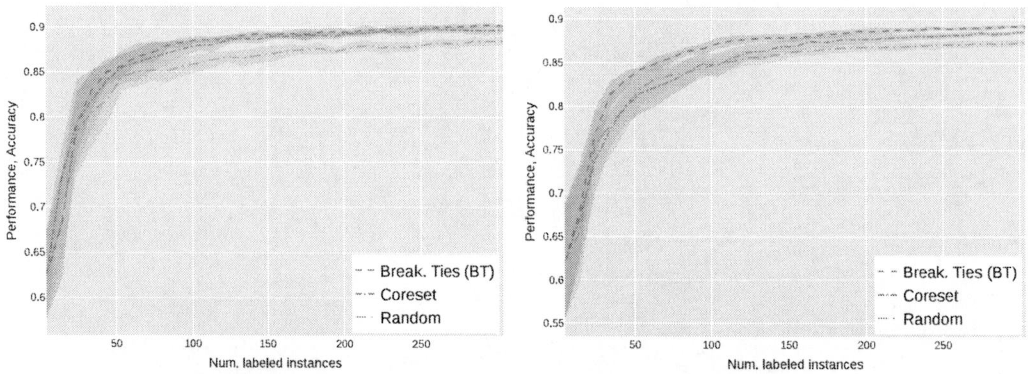

a) RoBERTa-base b) DistilBERT-base

Figure 6: Accuracy of the best performing query strategies with different acquisition models on AG News with query size = 10.

AL Strat.	Iter. 1	Iter. 5	Iter. 10	Iter. 15	Iter. 20	Iter. 25	Iter. 30	Average
BADGE	**68.47 ± 7.84**	**85.13 ± 1.43**	**88.2 ± 0.58**	**88.68 ± 0.62**	**89.38 ± 0.25**	**89.86 ± 0.24**	89.8 ± 0.18	**87.3 ± 1.59**
BALD	60.0 ± 6.97	79.58 ± 3.13	84.34 ± 1.4	85.64 ± 1.63	86.48 ± 1.1	87.37 ± 1.18	87.61 ± 1.13	83.77 ± 1.23
BT	67.98 ± 5.91	**85.64 ± 1.31**	**88.56 ± 0.32**	**89.13 ± 0.32**	**89.39 ± 0.41**	**89.83 ± 0.36**	**90.1 ± 0.26**	**87.66 ± 0.51**
CAL	58.04 ± 6.22	68.89 ± 7.78	86.33 ± 2.47	87.43 ± 1.47	88.58 ± 0.84	88.81 ± 0.57	89.38 ± 0.37	83.23 ± 1.77
Coreset	**73.21 ± 3.27**	**85.49 ± 1.82**	87.93 ± 0.63	**88.94 ± 0.36**	**89.29 ± 0.31**	**89.77 ± 0.46**	**89.69 ± 0.43**	**87.44 ± 0.8**
Entropy	60.64 ± 8.75	82.29 ± 1.72	86.45 ± 0.5	87.33 ± 0.8	88.45 ± 0.6	89.25 ± 0.49	89.32 ± 0.61	85.57 ± 0.83
LC	61.86 ± 8.49	**85.36 ± 0.88**	87.38 ± 0.51	88.47 ± 0.59	88.99 ± 0.38	89.35 ± 0.27	89.65 ± 0.23	86.6 ± 0.25
Random	68.33 ± 3.88	84.41 ± 1.52	85.95 ± 0.94	87.05 ± 0.92	87.68 ± 0.57	88.09 ± 0.39	88.47 ± 0.47	85.73 ± 0.69

Table 9: Accuracy of RoBERTa on AG News with various AL strategies with query size = 10.

AL Strat.	Iter. 1	Iter. 5	Iter. 10	Iter. 15	Iter. 20	Iter. 25	Iter. 30	Average
BT	**67.95 ± 5.39**	**84.27 ± 0.3**	**87.2 ± 0.66**	**87.9 ± 0.51**	**88.59 ± 0.39**	**88.91 ± 0.19**	**89.19 ± 0.26**	**86.48 ± 0.31**
CAL	58.87 ± 6.36	70.09 ± 4.32	82.72 ± 2.05	85.72 ± 1.17	87.29 ± 0.67	87.68 ± 0.78	88.31 ± 0.48	81.84 ± 1.64
Coreset	**67.07 ± 5.52**	81.52 ± 2.31	84.74 ± 1.37	86.91 ± 0.87	87.72 ± 0.49	88.17 ± 0.34	88.61 ± 0.24	85.0 ± 0.84
Entropy	56.19 ± 9.83	80.54 ± 2.05	84.65 ± 1.15	85.97 ± 0.89	86.48 ± 1.12	87.21 ± 0.55	87.5 ± 0.61	83.47 ± 0.89
LC	54.96 ± 4.34	82.28 ± 1.18	85.33 ± 0.9	86.99 ± 0.75	87.86 ± 0.39	88.38 ± 0.24	88.57 ± 0.38	84.76 ± 0.49
Random	65.56 ± 5.91	82.14 ± 2.01	84.87 ± 0.69	86.29 ± 0.58	86.77 ± 0.43	87.11 ± 0.44	87.37 ± 0.42	84.46 ± 0.91

Table 10: Accuracy of DistilBERT on AG News with various AL strategies with query size = 10.

B.1.2 IMDB

Query size = 100

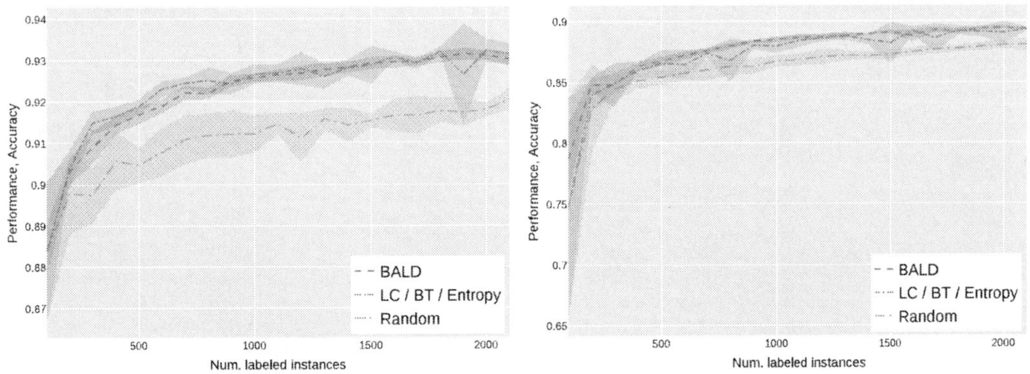

a) RoBERTa b) DistilBERT

Figure 7: Accuracy of the best performing query strategies with different acquisition models on IMDB with query size = 100.

AL Strategy	Iter. 1	Iter. 5	Iter. 10	Iter. 15	Iter. 20	Average
BADGE	89.66 ± 1.17	91.91 ± 0.31	**92.32 ± 0.59**	92.69 ± 0.4	**93.22 ± 0.17**	92.35 ± 0.05
BALD	**90.31 ± 0.32**	91.89 ± 0.17	**92.65 ± 0.13**	**92.95 ± 0.14**	93.01 ± 0.16	92.39 ± 0.08
CAL	**90.24 ± 1.27**	**92.14 ± 0.22**	**92.64 ± 0.14**	**92.92 ± 0.26**	**93.1 ± 0.28**	92.32 ± 0.12
Coreset	89.16 ± 1.37	91.9 ± 0.3	**92.63 ± 0.32**	92.64 ± 1.35	92.79 ± 0.67	**92.28 ± 0.25**
LC / BT / Entropy	**90.38 ± 0.46**	**92.3 ± 0.19**	**92.69 ± 0.21**	**93.08 ± 0.13**	**93.14 ± 0.26**	**92.49 ± 0.09**
Random	89.77 ± 0.98	90.77 ± 0.58	91.46 ± 0.26	91.67 ± 0.4	92.04 ± 0.26	91.19 ± 0.36

Table 11: Accuracy of RoBERTa on IMDB with various AL strategies with query size = 100.

AL Strategy	Iter. 1	Iter. 5	Iter. 10	Iter. 15	Iter. 20	Average
BADGE	84.32 ± 0.42	**86.92 ± 0.71**	87.97 ± 0.29	**88.81 ± 1.13**	**89.34 ± 0.42**	**87.82 ± 0.36**
BALD	**84.82 ± 0.6**	**87.2 ± 0.32**	**88.67 ± 0.2**	**88.79 ± 0.51**	**89.35 ± 0.14**	**88.09 ± 0.13**
CAL	**84.13 ± 1.28**	**86.72 ± 0.55**	**88.29 ± 0.38**	**88.93 ± 0.32**	**88.86 ± 0.76**	**87.67 ± 0.46**
Coreset	84.1 ± 0.52	**86.38 ± 0.89**	87.63 ± 0.5	88.47 ± 0.42	**89.1 ± 0.31**	87.46 ± 0.33
LC / BT / Entropy	83.92 ± 1.38	**86.47 ± 1.16**	**88.41 ± 0.54**	**89.19 ± 0.32**	**89.29 ± 0.18**	**87.74 ± 0.35**
Random	82.81 ± 3.7	85.77 ± 0.61	86.84 ± 0.51	87.45 ± 0.33	88.06 ± 0.49	86.56 ± 0.5

Table 12: Accuracy of DisitlBERT on IMDB with various AL strategies with query size = 100.

Query size = 10

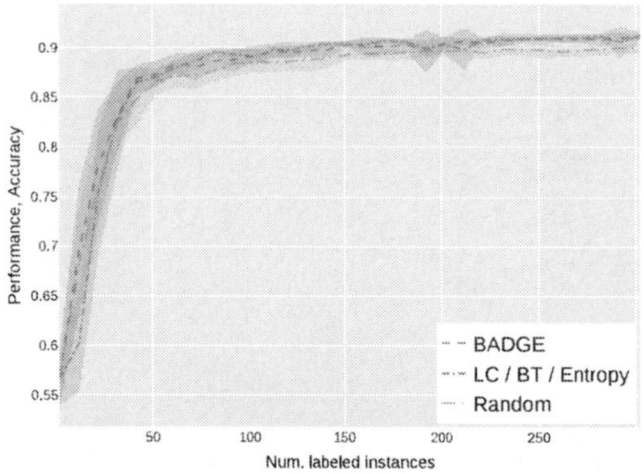

a) RoBERTa

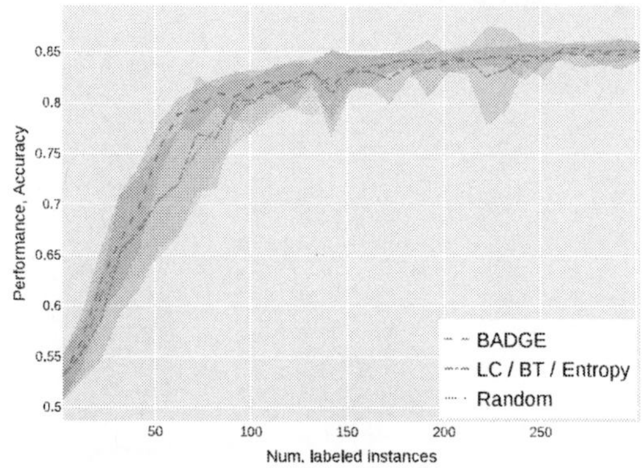

b) DistilBERT

Figure 8: Accuracy of the best performing query strategies with different acquisition models on IMDB with query size = 10.

AL Strategy	Iter. 1	Iter. 5	Iter. 10	Iter. 15	Iter. 20	Iter. 25	Iter. 30	Average
BADGE	**69.49 ± 6.4**	**87.29 ± 1.35**	**89.16 ± 0.69**	**90.36 ± 0.45**	**90.46 ± 0.63**	**90.98 ± 0.28**	**91.13 ± 0.32**	**88.54 ± 0.53**
BALD	**67.08 ± 4.56**	84.04 ± 2.66	88.09 ± 1.61	89.49 ± 0.76	**90.56 ± 0.3**	87.85 ± 5.56	90.81 ± 0.64	87.64 ± 0.66
CAL	60.22 ± 4.41	83.73 ± 4.75	**89.33 ± 0.54**	**90.23 ± 0.26**	**90.77 ± 0.32**	**91.19 ± 0.32**	**91.4 ± 0.26**	86.81 ± 0.83
Coreset	**64.3 ± 6.06**	**86.92 ± 1.1**	88.49 ± 1.44	89.36 ± 0.79	**90.5 ± 0.32**	90.77 ± 0.25	90.72 ± 0.26	87.27 ± 1.0
LC / BT / Entropy	60.26 ± 4.86	**87.0 ± 0.87**	**89.08 ± 1.07**	**90.34 ± 0.34**	**90.35 ± 0.79**	**90.9 ± 0.49**	**91.3 ± 0.33**	**88.24 ± 0.46**
Random	**68.14 ± 5.58**	**86.6 ± 1.32**	88.53 ± 1.09	89.3 ± 0.49	89.65 ± 0.51	89.79 ± 0.81	90.01 ± 0.53	87.55 ± 0.67

Table 13: Accuracy of RoBERTa on IMDB with various AL strategies with query size = 10.

AL Strategy	Iter. 1	Iter. 5	Iter. 10	Iter. 15	Iter. 20	Iter. 25	Iter. 30	Average
BADGE	**56.53 ± 2.66**	**75.41 ± 2.65**	**81.96 ± 1.26**	**83.25 ± 1.5**	83.95 ± 1.0	84.76 ± 0.79	85.19 ± 0.93	**80.31 ± 1.21**
BALD	55.61 ± 3.27	69.51 ± 5.22	79.44 ± 3.64	83.21 ± 1.15	83.86 ± 1.34	83.08 ± 3.52	85.14 ± 1.36	78.86 ± 3.86
CAL	55.67 ± 2.69	68.58 ± 4.09	80.85 ± 1.48	83.04 ± 1.15	84.3 ± 0.78	**84.98 ± 0.47**	**85.26 ± 0.91**	78.9 ± 0.81
Coreset	54.6 ± 3.48	69.77 ± 6.89	81.33 ± 0.96	82.65 ± 1.35	83.76 ± 0.83	84.2 ± 0.64	84.7 ± 0.55	79.04 ± 1.83
LC / BT / Entropy	55.31 ± 2.62	70.53 ± 4.88	80.23 ± 2.3	83.0 ± 1.73	84.18 ± 1.11	84.21 ± 1.95	85.22 ± 0.72	79.22 ± 1.68
Random	55.45 ± 2.78	70.41 ± 5.61	80.01 ± 2.64	83.24 ± 1.6	**84.61 ± 0.48**	84.63 ± 0.68	85.21 ± 0.67	79.45 ± 1.51

Table 14: Accuracy of DistilBERT on IMDB with various AL strategies with query size = 10.

B.1.3 CoLA

Query size = 100

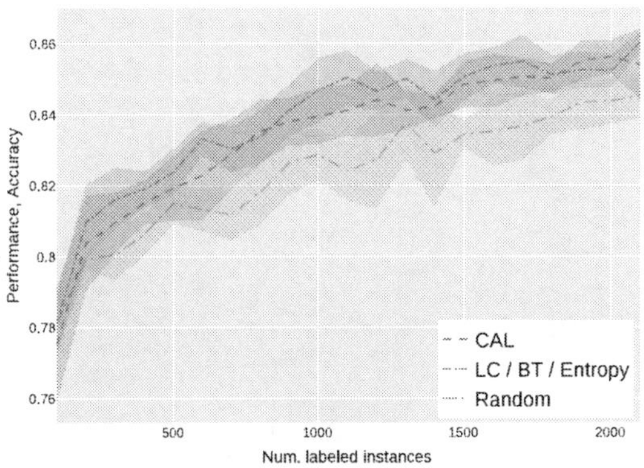

a) ELECTRA

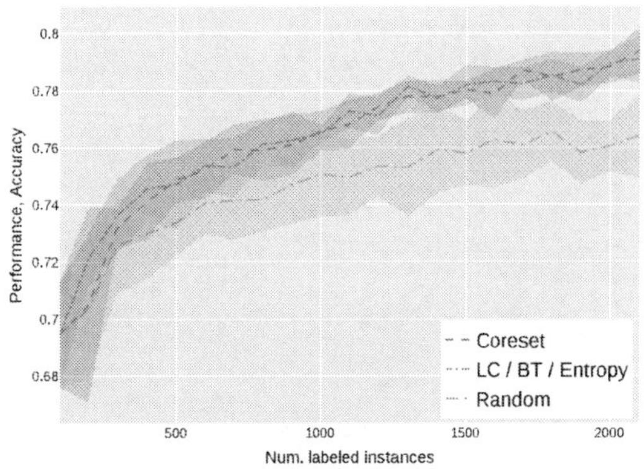

b) DistilBERT

Figure 9: Accuracy of the best performing query strategies with different acquisition models on CoLA with query size = 100.

AL Strategy	Iter. 1	Iter. 5	Iter. 10	Iter. 15	Iter. 20	Average
BADGE	**80.59 ± 1.13**	**82.61 ± 0.8**	83.78 ± 0.29	**85.22 ± 0.8**	85.27 ± 0.6	83.76 ± 0.24
BALD	67.44 ± 5.74	77.34 ± 1.1	78.81 ± 0.53	79.67 ± 0.54	80.56 ± 0.4	77.73 ± 1.15
CAL	**80.38 ± 1.34**	**82.28 ± 1.27**	84.12 ± 0.72	**84.95 ± 0.76**	**85.41 ± 1.01**	**83.73 ± 0.58**
Coreset	**80.31 ± 1.14**	**82.32 ± 1.1**	84.33 ± 0.69	84.51 ± 0.62	85.16 ± 0.32	**83.57 ± 0.62**
LC / BT / Entropy	**80.97 ± 1.07**	**83.32 ± 0.49**	**85.04 ± 0.78**	**85.38 ± 0.52**	**86.03 ± 0.3**	**84.11 ± 0.24**
Random	79.94 ± 0.3	81.33 ± 0.6	82.41 ± 0.83	83.53 ± 1.0	84.54 ± 0.64	82.58 ± 0.38

Table 15: Accuracy of ELECTRA on CoLA with various AL strategies with query size = 100.

AL Strategy	Iter. 1	Iter. 5	Iter. 10	Iter. 15	Iter. 20	Average
BADGE	**71.74 ± 2.1**	**75.19 ± 1.44**	**76.97 ± 0.76**	**78.09 ± 1.38**	**78.78 ± 1.17**	**76.58 ± 1.89**
BALD	59.12 ± 6.86	63.99 ± 5.21	69.3 ± 2.97	71.27 ± 1.44	72.11 ± 1.42	67.93 ± 2.05
CAL	**71.58 ± 1.34**	**75.05 ± 1.08**	**76.8 ± 0.77**	77.83 ± 0.53	**79.1 ± 0.87**	**76.58 ± 0.46**
Coreset	**70.51 ± 3.42**	**75.23 ± 1.01**	**76.82 ± 0.86**	**77.89 ± 0.88**	**79.39 ± 0.81**	**76.61 ± 0.31**
LC / BT / Entropy	**72.12 ± 0.94**	**75.36 ± 0.95**	**77.28 ± 0.61**	**78.31 ± 0.51**	**79.1 ± 0.82**	**76.71 ± 0.29**
Random	**70.35 ± 2.44**	74.06 ± 1.08	74.96 ± 1.34	76.28 ± 1.69	76.41 ± 1.49	74.8 ± 0.91

Table 16: Accuracy of DistilBERT on CoLA with various AL strategies with query size = 100.

Query size = 10

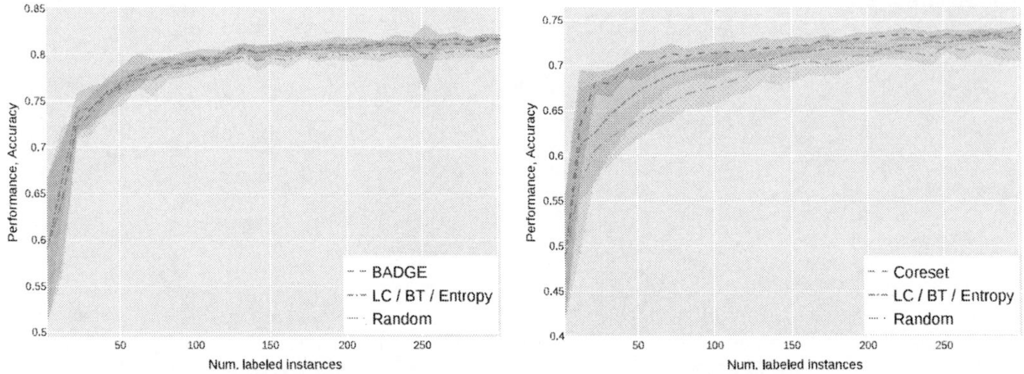

a) ELECTRA b) DistilBERT

Figure 10: Accuracy of the best performing query strategies with different acquisition models on CoLA with query size = 10.

AL Strategy	Iter. 1	Iter. 5	Iter. 10	Iter. 15	Iter. 20	Iter. 25	Iter. 30	Average
BADGE	64.25 ± 6.58	**77.2 ± 1.63**	79.41 ± 0.56	80.44 ± 0.61	**81.01 ± 0.81**	81.15 ± 0.53	**81.65 ± 0.6**	**79.16 ± 1.18**
BALD	**67.41 ± 5.06**	76.7 ± 1.85	78.68 ± 0.52	79.54 ± 0.59	80.62 ± 0.47	80.7 ± 2.03	81.35 ± 0.93	78.76 ± 8.01
CAL	65.88 ± 8.86	76.59 ± 2.68	**79.7 ± 1.05**	**80.72 ± 0.43**	80.73 ± 0.67	**81.5 ± 0.49**	80.88 ± 1.33	79.05 ± 0.97
Coreset	62.89 ± 9.54	74.61 ± 3.22	79.61 ± 0.58	79.99 ± 0.96	80.57 ± 0.54	80.89 ± 0.79	81.28 ± 0.63	78.42 ± 0.82
LC / BT / Entropy	66.27 ± 4.05	76.71 ± 0.79	79.61 ± 0.9	80.5 ± 0.59	80.59 ± 0.42	79.6 ± 3.68	81.56 ± 0.57	**79.16 ± 0.43**
Random	64.11 ± 8.0	76.39 ± 1.91	78.83 ± 0.79	79.6 ± 0.69	79.95 ± 0.81	79.97 ± 0.67	80.79 ± 0.83	78.36 ± 0.6

Table 17: Accuracy of ELECTRA on CoLA with various AL strategies with query size = 10.

AL Strategy	Iter. 1	Iter. 5	Iter. 10	Iter. 15	Iter. 20	Iter. 25	Iter. 30	Average
BADGE	**63.66 ± 4.45**	67.17 ± 2.53	69.64 ± 1.61	**71.74 ± 1.63**	**72.69 ± 1.06**	**73.08 ± 0.64**	**73.68 ± 0.53**	**70.63 ± 1.28**
BALD	59.39 ± 7.76	64.93 ± 2.71	68.4 ± 2.55	70.32 ± 1.18	71.2 ± 1.19	72.24 ± 1.05	**73.2 ± 0.92**	69.23 ± 1.05
CAL	60.2 ± 7.09	**69.11 ± 1.3**	**71.02 ± 1.27**	**71.82 ± 1.32**	**72.3 ± 1.37**	**72.86 ± 1.06**	**73.64 ± 0.79**	70.81 ± 0.86
Coreset	63.23 ± 6.22	**69.91 ± 1.63**	**71.29 ± 1.16**	**72.13 ± 1.03**	**72.99 ± 0.67**	**73.43 ± 0.54**	**73.92 ± 0.61**	**71.68 ± 0.67**
LC / BT / Entropy	61.19 ± 6.3	67.33 ± 2.37	**70.04 ± 1.59**	**71.4 ± 0.92**	71.77 ± 0.86	**72.49 ± 0.99**	73.01 ± 0.85	70.23 ± 1.22
Random	56.86 ± 7.72	64.13 ± 2.11	67.72 ± 1.98	69.96 ± 1.77	71.19 ± 0.96	72.08 ± 0.63	71.8 ± 1.34	68.53 ± 1.02

Table 18: Accuracy of DistilBERT on CoLA with various AL strategies with query size = 10.

B.2 Sequence Tagging

B.2.1 CoNLL-2003

Query size = 2% (tokens)

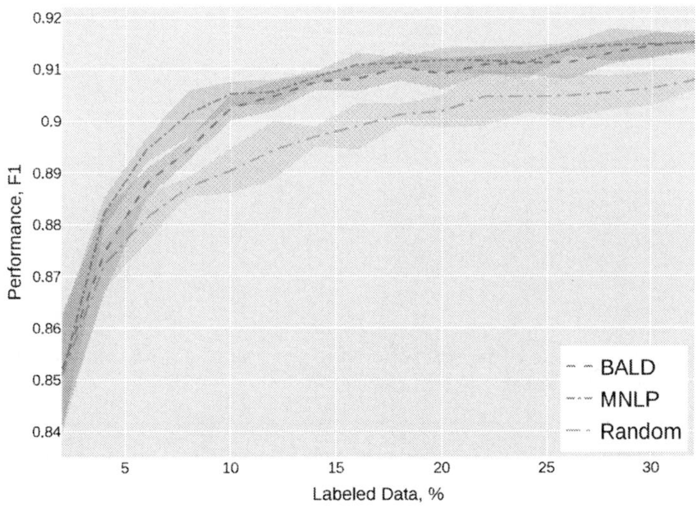

Figure 11: Overall F1-micro score of the best performing query strategies with ELECTRA on CoNLL-2003 with query size = 2% (tokens).

AL Strategy	Iter. 1	Iter. 5	Iter. 10	Iter. 15	Average
BALD	87.46 ± 0.75	**90.47 ± 0.28**	**91.09 ± 0.18**	**91.52 ± 0.2**	90.5 ± 0.14
MNLP	**88.23 ± 0.31**	**90.55 ± 0.24**	**91.17 ± 0.27**	**91.51 ± 0.14**	**90.75 ± 0.07**
Random	87.23 ± 0.47	89.43 ± 0.56	90.47 ± 0.57	90.78 ± 0.21	89.72 ± 0.2

Table 19: Overall F1-micro score of ELECTRA on CoNLL-2003 with various AL strategies with query size = 2% (tokens).

Query size = 100 (tokens)

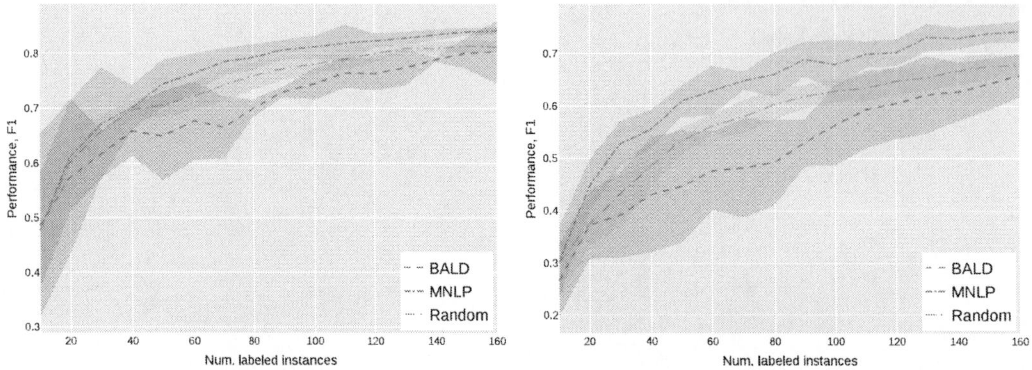

a) ELECTRA

b) DistilBERT

Figure 12: Overall F1-micro score of the best performing query strategies with different acquisition models on CoNLL-2003 with query size = 100.

AL Strategy	Iter. 1	Iter. 5	Iter. 10	Iter. 15	Average
BALD	57.52 ± 14.08	67.65 ± 7.13	76.44 ± 2.76	80.27 ± 5.72	71.4 ± 2.21
MNLP	**61.32 ± 10.1**	**76.36 ± 3.65**	**81.87 ± 3.44**	**84.16 ± 0.61**	**77.84 ± 2.59**
Random	60.35 ± 6.36	72.22 ± 2.52	78.99 ± 1.98	81.16 ± 1.07	75.16 ± 1.57

Table 20: Overall F1-micro score of ELECTRA on CoNLL-2003 with various AL strategies with query size = 100 (tokens).

AL Strategy	Iter. 1	Iter. 5	Iter. 10	Iter. 15	Average
BALD	37.21 ± 6.39	47.6 ± 7.48	59.34 ± 7.41	65.86 ± 4.07	52.88 ± 9.22
MNLP	**44.73 ± 5.0**	**62.96 ± 4.71**	**69.88 ± 2.53**	**74.2 ± 2.0**	**65.27 ± 1.64**
Random	37.53 ± 4.21	56.22 ± 2.09	63.39 ± 2.57	67.76 ± 2.29	58.51 ± 1.81

Table 21: Overall F1-micro score of DistilBERT on CoNLL-2003 with various AL strategies with query size = 100 (tokens).

Query size = 10 (tokens)

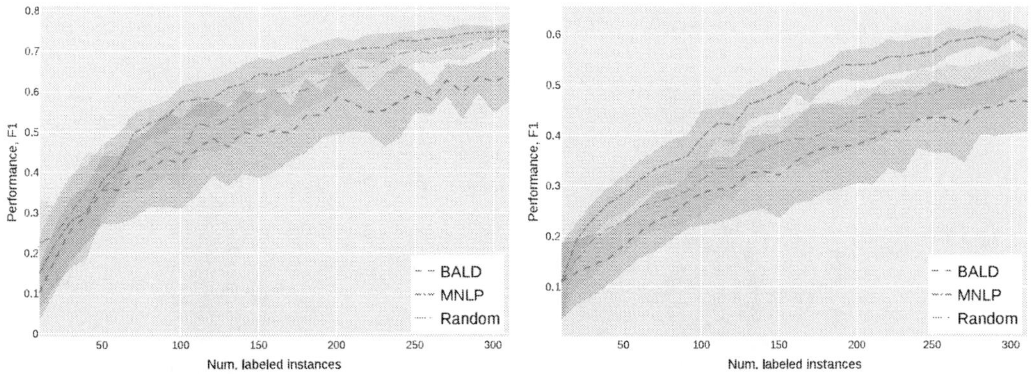

a) ELECTRA b) DistilBERT

Figure 13: Overall F1-micro score of the best performing query strategies with different acquisition models on CoNLL-2003 with query size = 10.

AL Strategy	Iter. 1	Iter. 5	Iter. 10	Iter. 15	Iter. 20	Iter. 25	Iter. 30	Average
BALD	18.34 ± 7.99	35.53 ± 8.32	45.57 ± 11.36	50.33 ± 10.24	57.12 ± 7.12	57.93 ± 3.54	63.94 ± 6.42	49.02 ± 15.28
MNLP	22.28 ± 10.34	**42.1 ± 7.49**	**58.07 ± 4.37**	**63.99 ± 3.77**	**70.33 ± 2.17**	**73.03 ± 2.58**	**74.95 ± 1.86**	**60.41 ± 3.31**
Random	**24.43 ± 7.2**	39.82 ± 6.3	**52.22 ± 7.31**	**59.54 ± 5.19**	65.74 ± 4.47	69.36 ± 2.52	71.74 ± 2.75	56.11 ± 3.99

Table 22: Overall F1-micro score of ELECTRA on CoNLL-2003 with various AL strategies with query size = 10 (tokens).

AL Strategy	Iter. 1	Iter. 5	Iter. 10	Iter. 15	Iter. 20	Iter. 25	Iter. 30	Average
BALD	12.85 ± 6.45	20.7 ± 5.03	29.23 ± 6.59	34.78 ± 8.26	39.33 ± 9.11	43.39 ± 6.78	46.76 ± 6.07	33.43 ± 6.15
MNLP	**19.46 ± 3.38**	**31.2 ± 3.85**	**42.4 ± 3.0**	**50.63 ± 2.33**	**54.17 ± 3.1**	**58.52 ± 2.82**	**58.85 ± 2.0**	**46.42 ± 2.31**
Random	**15.43 ± 5.45**	25.82 ± 5.65	33.39 ± 6.04	39.3 ± 5.16	43.86 ± 5.6	49.55 ± 4.51	53.45 ± 3.49	38.0 ± 4.56

Table 23: Overall F1-micro score of DistilBERT on CoNLL-2003 with various AL strategies with query size = 10 (tokens).

B.3 Abstractive Text Summarization

B.3.1 AESLC

Query size = 10

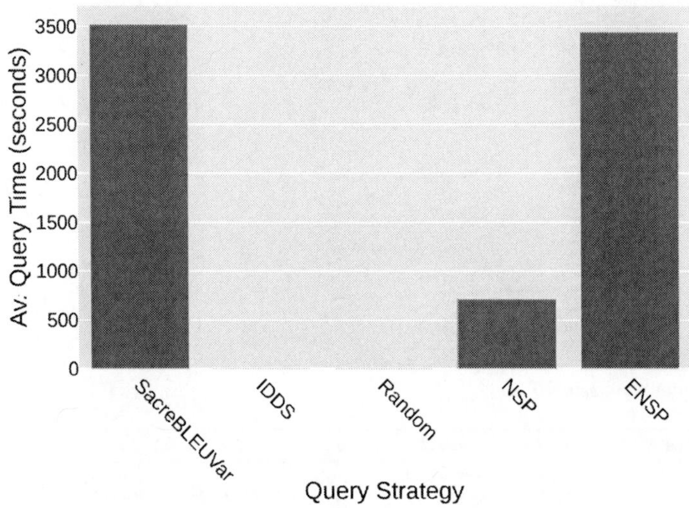

Figure 14: Average duration in seconds of one AL query with different strategies on AESLC with BART as an acquisition model and query size = 10. Hardware configuration is provided in Appendix C.

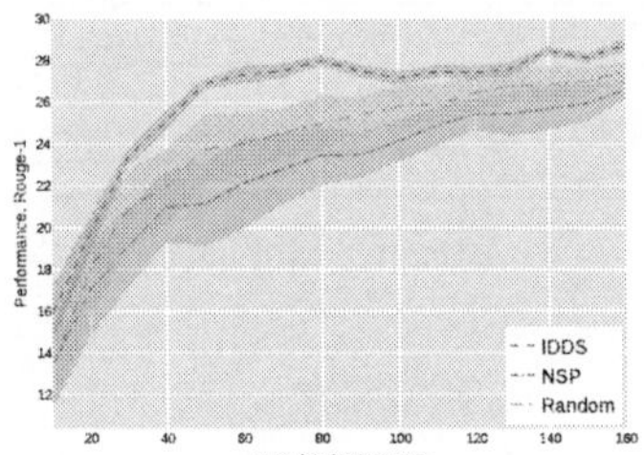

a) ROUGE-1

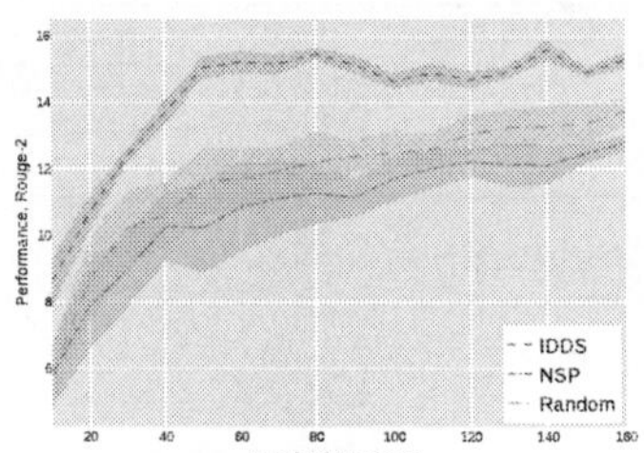

a) ROUGE-2

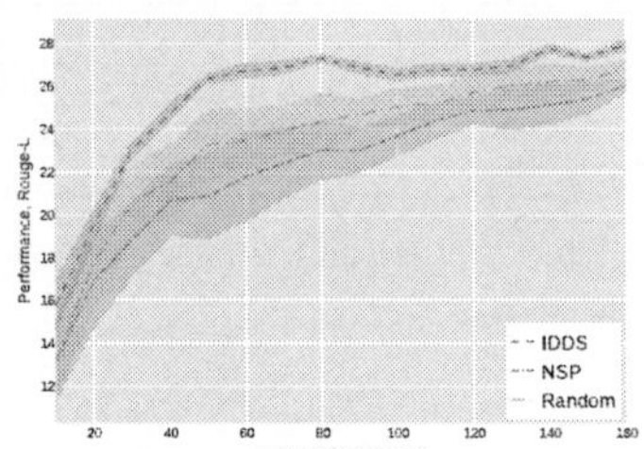

a) ROUGE-L

Figure 15: ROUGE scores of the best performing query strategies with BART as an acquisition model on AESLC with query size = 10.

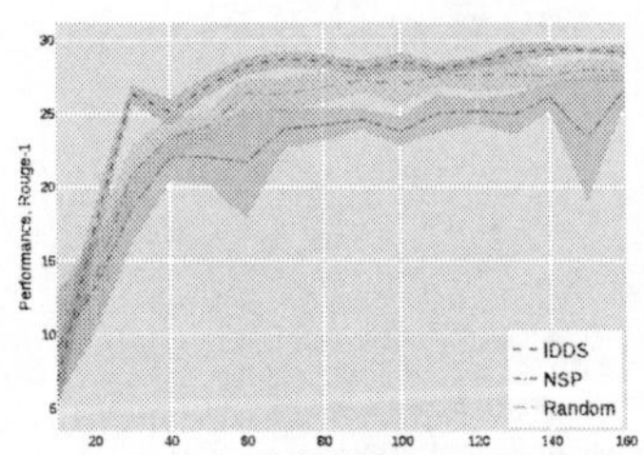

a) ROUGE-1

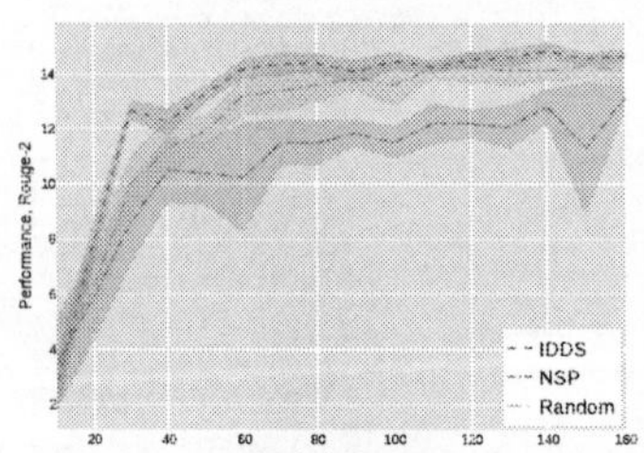

a) ROUGE-2

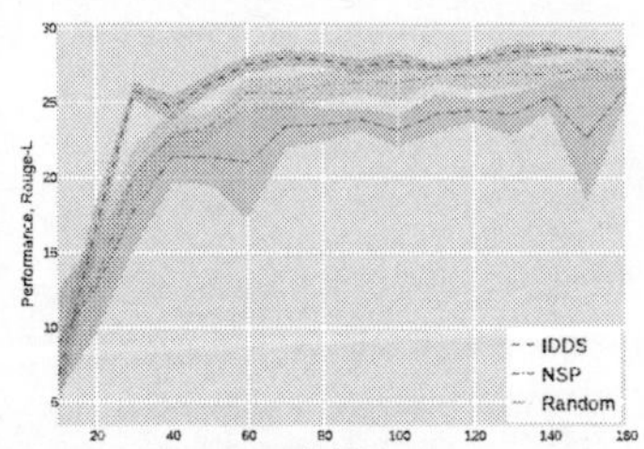

a) ROUGE-L

Figure 16: ROUGE scores of the best performing query strategies with PEGASUS as an acquisition model on AESLC with query size = 10.

AL Strategy	Iter. 1	Iter. 5	Iter. 10	Iter. 15	Average
			ROUGE-1		
SacreBLEUVar	**18.77 ± 2.21**	23.46 ± 1.18	26.25 ± 0.69	27.53 ± 0.45	24.6 ± 0.96
IDDS	**19.76 ± 0.82**	**27.3 ± 0.41**	**27.44 ± 0.3**	**28.7 ± 0.32**	**26.67 ± 0.08**
Random	**18.07 ± 2.26**	24.0 ± 1.55	25.9 ± 0.88	27.47 ± 0.45	24.65 ± 0.94
NSP	17.09 ± 2.25	22.15 ± 2.16	24.88 ± 0.94	26.56 ± 0.46	23.22 ± 0.97
ENSP	14.57 ± 2.92	23.2 ± 1.16	25.41 ± 0.79	27.42 ± 0.92	23.74 ± 1.24
			ROUGE-2		
SacreBLEUVar	9.0 ± 1.12	11.26 ± 0.89	12.86 ± 0.62	13.59 ± 0.56	12.05 ± 0.71
IDDS	**10.69 ± 0.53**	**15.2 ± 0.34**	**14.89 ± 0.29**	**15.26 ± 0.26**	**14.51 ± 0.07**
Random	8.73 ± 1.24	11.69 ± 0.93	12.6 ± 0.49	13.72 ± 0.43	12.08 ± 0.63
NSP	7.92 ± 1.35	10.86 ± 1.34	12.03 ± 0.59	12.79 ± 0.26	11.15 ± 0.66
ENSP	6.69 ± 1.51	11.37 ± 0.67	12.36 ± 0.46	13.5 ± 0.58	11.52 ± 0.66
			ROUGE-L		
SacreBLEUVar	**18.51 ± 2.19**	22.93 ± 1.17	25.64 ± 0.73	26.91 ± 0.51	24.08 ± 0.99
IDDS	**19.52 ± 0.81**	**26.73 ± 0.39**	**26.78 ± 0.29**	**27.92 ± 0.31**	**26.1 ± 0.08**
Random	**17.79 ± 2.21**	23.48 ± 1.53	25.22 ± 0.84	26.81 ± 0.44	24.07 ± 0.92
NSP	16.88 ± 2.21	21.81 ± 2.13	24.39 ± 0.9	26.05 ± 0.38	22.81 ± 0.95
ENSP	14.41 ± 2.89	22.76 ± 1.12	24.93 ± 0.75	26.85 ± 0.92	23.3 ± 1.2

Table 24: ROUGE scores of BART on AESLC with various AL strategies with query size = 10.

AL Strategy	Iter. 1	Iter. 5	Iter. 10	Iter. 15	Average
			ROUGE-1		
SacreBLEUVar	15.5 ± 1.59	25.11 ± 1.05	26.47 ± 1.19	28.02 ± 0.83	25.13 ± 0.58
IDDS	**17.19 ± 1.58**	**28.23 ± 0.61**	**28.02 ± 0.42**	**29.18 ± 0.45**	**27.42 ± 0.15**
Random	13.65 ± 3.34	26.42 ± 1.05	**27.57 ± 0.7**	27.86 ± 0.71	25.49 ± 0.8
NSP	13.12 ± 3.11	21.68 ± 3.79	25.05 ± 1.28	26.72 ± 1.02	23.03 ± 0.89
ENSP	12.39 ± 2.14	22.27 ± 2.13	23.37 ± 4.21	26.87 ± 0.55	23.36 ± 1.18
			ROUGE-2		
SacreBLEUVar	7.01 ± 0.86	12.67 ± 0.63	13.67 ± 0.54	**14.72 ± 0.6**	12.74 ± 0.49
IDDS	**7.94 ± 0.81**	**14.19 ± 0.37**	**14.27 ± 0.22**	**14.65 ± 0.24**	**13.68 ± 0.11**
Random	**6.3 ± 1.68**	13.23 ± 0.71	**14.21 ± 0.39**	**14.15 ± 0.56**	12.83 ± 0.49
NSP	5.91 ± 1.62	10.24 ± 2.01	12.2 ± 0.77	13.14 ± 0.49	11.04 ± 0.56
ENSP	5.25 ± 0.9	10.53 ± 1.22	11.23 ± 2.42	12.9 ± 0.82	11.15 ± 0.69
			ROUGE-L		
SacreBLEUVar	15.07 ± 1.55	24.47 ± 0.84	25.81 ± 0.75	27.2 ± 0.83	24.43 ± 0.57
IDDS	**16.8 ± 1.57**	**27.53 ± 0.56**	**27.36 ± 0.33**	**28.4 ± 0.43**	**26.75 ± 0.15**
Random	13.24 ± 3.23	25.65 ± 0.99	**26.82 ± 0.58**	27.13 ± 0.69	24.76 ± 0.75
NSP	12.75 ± 3.07	20.99 ± 3.72	24.21 ± 1.27	25.93 ± 1.04	22.33 ± 0.93
ENSP	12.0 ± 2.11	21.63 ± 2.12	22.71 ± 4.2	26.12 ± 0.61	22.71 ± 1.21

Table 25: ROUGE scores of PEGASUS on AESLC with various AL strategies with query size = 10.

B.3.2 WikiHow

Query size = 10

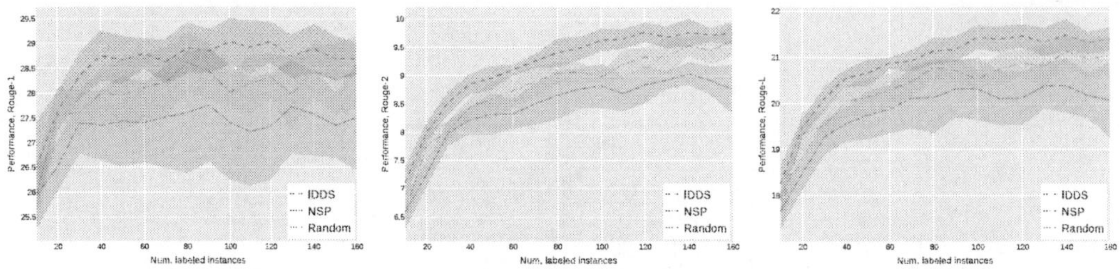

a) ROUGE-1 a) ROUGE-2 a) ROUGE-L

Figure 17: ROUGE scores of the best performing query strategies with BART as an acquisition model on WikiHow with query size = 10.

AL Strategy	Iter. 1	Iter. 5	Iter. 10	Iter. 15	Average
			ROUGE-1		
BLEUVar	26.88 ± 0.6	27.61 ± 0.72	27.64 ± 0.64	28.08 ± 0.39	27.65 ± 0.41
IDDS	**27.64 ± 0.41**	**28.8 ± 0.3**	**28.93 ± 0.53**	**28.69 ± 0.33**	**28.71 ± 0.36**
Random	**27.57 ± 0.55**	**28.11 ± 0.66**	28.19 ± 0.59	**28.42 ± 0.75**	28.15 ± 0.49
NSP	26.52 ± 0.49	27.41 ± 0.81	27.23 ± 1.1	27.51 ± 1.09	27.41 ± 0.85
ENSP	26.91 ± 0.47	27.6 ± 0.48	27.53 ± 0.8	27.83 ± 0.93	27.52 ± 0.71
			ROUGE-2		
BLEUVar	7.43 ± 0.3	8.64 ± 0.22	9.19 ± 0.2	**9.54 ± 0.23**	8.83 ± 0.16
IDDS	**8.0 ± 0.17**	**9.1 ± 0.1**	**9.65 ± 0.17**	**9.75 ± 0.21**	**9.3 ± 0.13**
Random	7.77 ± 0.21	8.73 ± 0.31	9.2 ± 0.25	**9.62 ± 0.29**	8.93 ± 0.13
NSP	7.27 ± 0.22	8.32 ± 0.26	8.69 ± 0.31	8.76 ± 0.43	8.54 ± 0.35
ENSP	7.4 ± 0.18	8.43 ± 0.17	8.61 ± 0.34	8.85 ± 0.4	8.44 ± 0.26
			ROUGE-L		
BLEUVar	18.82 ± 0.37	20.07 ± 0.41	20.56 ± 0.34	20.9 ± 0.36	20.25 ± 0.21
IDDS	**19.48 ± 0.21**	**20.87 ± 0.13**	**21.4 ± 0.28**	**21.39 ± 0.27**	**20.98 ± 0.18**
Random	**19.35 ± 0.49**	20.29 ± 0.36	20.75 ± 0.36	**21.05 ± 0.42**	20.5 ± 0.23
NSP	18.5 ± 0.36	19.88 ± 0.53	20.11 ± 0.6	20.08 ± 0.81	19.94 ± 0.46
ENSP	18.65 ± 0.27	19.67 ± 0.29	20.43 ± 0.72	20.71 ± 0.43	19.97 ± 0.6

Table 26: ROUGE scores of BART on WikiHow with various AL strategies with query size = 10.

B.3.3 PubMed

Query size = 10

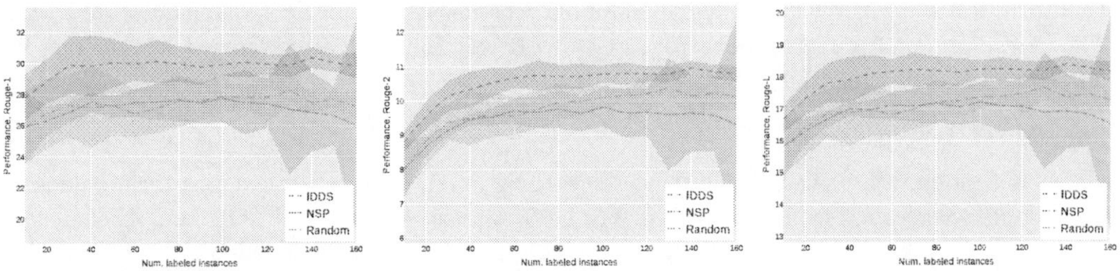

a) ROUGE-1 a) ROUGE-2 a) ROUGE-L

Figure 18: ROUGE scores of the best performing query strategies with BART as an acquisition model on PubMed with query size = 10.

AL Strategy	Iter. 1	Iter. 5	Iter. 10	Iter. 15	Average
			ROUGE-1		
BLEUVar	26.07 ± 1.01	27.92 ± 1.2	27.91 ± 1.0	27.52 ± 0.93	27.51 ± 0.87
IDDS	**28.86 ± 1.41**	**29.98 ± 1.11**	**30.06 ± 0.97**	**29.83 ± 0.84**	**29.89 ± 0.97**
Random	26.8 ± 2.27	26.77 ± 1.55	27.8 ± 0.78	27.23 ± 0.84	27.45 ± 1.37
NSP	26.31 ± 0.97	27.48 ± 0.87	27.48 ± 2.07	26.02 ± 6.82	27.15 ± 1.18
ENSP	26.16 ± 1.16	27.75 ± 1.56	27.65 ± 1.32	27.53 ± 1.62	27.51 ± 1.12
			ROUGE-2		
BLEUVar	8.61 ± 0.27	9.95 ± 0.31	10.26 ± 0.23	10.17 ± 0.25	9.92 ± 0.22
IDDS	**9.58 ± 0.41**	**10.66 ± 0.29**	**10.79 ± 0.32**	**10.78 ± 0.24**	**10.6 ± 0.27**
Random	8.83 ± 0.71	9.55 ± 0.55	10.13 ± 0.18	10.1 ± 0.36	9.85 ± 0.39
NSP	8.68 ± 0.29	9.71 ± 0.37	9.64 ± 0.72	9.3 ± 3.1	9.52 ± 0.44
ENSP	8.66 ± 0.35	9.87 ± 0.47	10.21 ± 0.35	10.18 ± 0.41	9.89 ± 0.32
			ROUGE-L		
BLEUVar	16.19 ± 0.37	17.37 ± 0.4	17.53 ± 0.31	17.41 ± 0.34	17.26 ± 0.29
IDDS	**17.34 ± 0.52**	**18.17 ± 0.39**	**18.24 ± 0.37**	**18.17 ± 0.31**	**18.11 ± 0.35**
Random	16.44 ± 0.89	16.82 ± 0.69	17.38 ± 0.26	17.29 ± 0.26	17.16 ± 0.51
NSP	16.31 ± 0.41	17.11 ± 0.42	17.08 ± 0.82	16.52 ± 3.33	16.93 ± 0.54
ENSP	16.23 ± 0.46	17.27 ± 0.57	17.46 ± 0.45	17.39 ± 0.54	17.23 ± 0.38

Table 27: ROUGE scores of BART on PubMed with various AL strategies with query size = 10.

C Computationally Efficient AL

Hardware Configuration

We use the following hardware configuration for the experiments: 2 Intel Xeon Platinum 8168, 2.7 GHz, 24 cores CPU; NVIDIA Tesla v100 GPU, 32 Gb of VRAM. The results are averaged across 5 runs with different seeds to ensure stability.

Experiment Hyperparameters

On each iteration, we select 1% of instances according to AL strategy for text classification datasets, and 2% of instances for sequence tagging. For UPS, we use $\gamma = 0.1, T = 0.01$, and recalculate the uncertainty estimates for the whole dataset on the 0-th, 1-st, 4-th, and 8-th iterations.

C.1 AG News

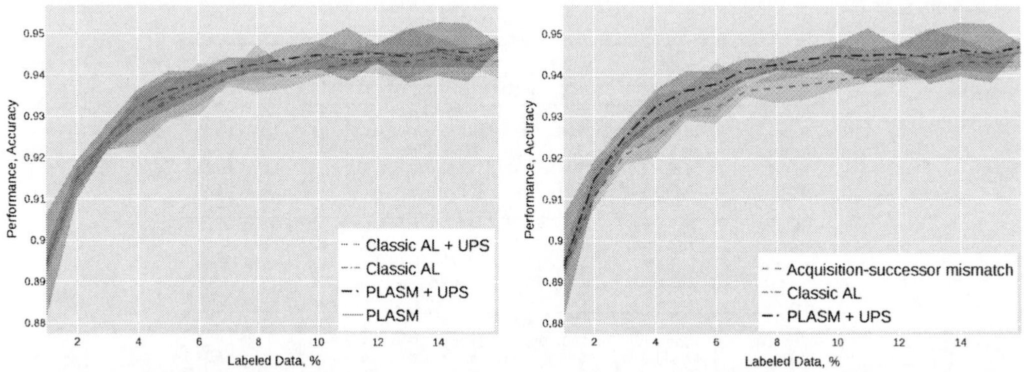

a) PLASM and UPS v Classic AL   b) ASM problem

Figure 19: AG News dataset: performance of PLASM and UPS algorithms compared to classic AL and acquisition-successor mismatch (ASM) settings. For all the experiments, ELECTRA is used as a successor model (therefore, as an acquisition model in "classic AL" as well), and DistilBERT – for acquisition in PLASM and ASM.

C.2 IMDB

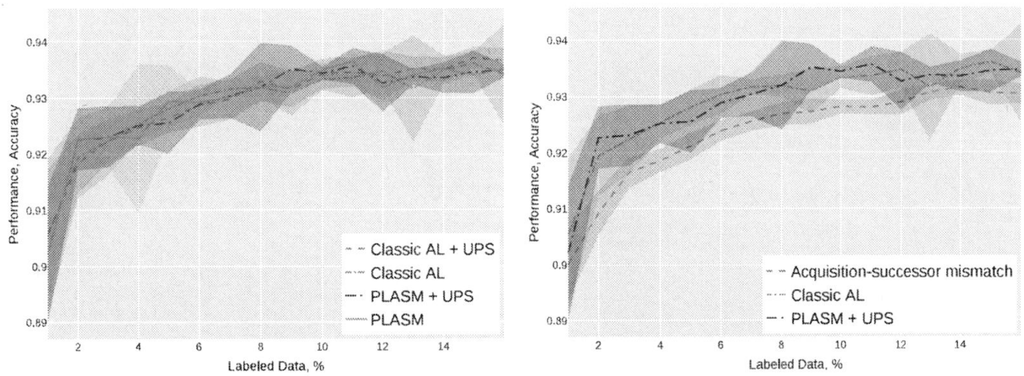

a) PLASM and UPS v Classic AL

b) ASM problem

Figure 20: IMDB dataset: performance of PLASM and UPS algorithms compared to classic AL and acquisition-successor mismatch (ASM) settings. For all the experiments, RoBERTa is used as a successor model (therefore, as an acquisition model in "classic AL" as well), and DistilELECTRA – for acquisition in PLASM and ASM.

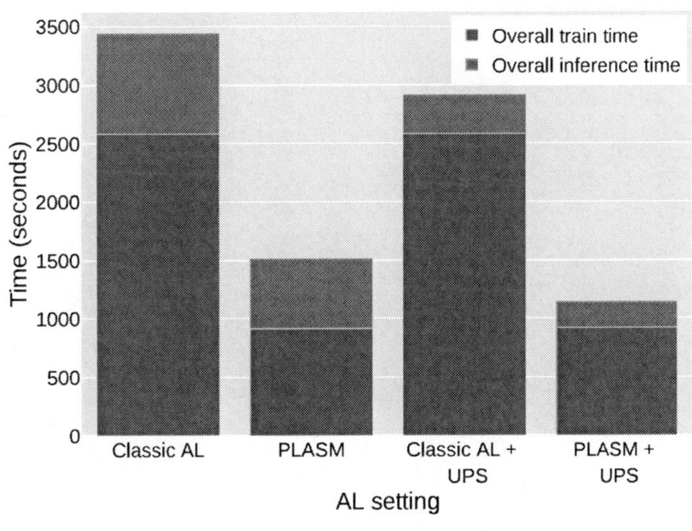

Figure 21: Duration in seconds of all the training and inference phases of the simulated AL with different acquisition settings on IMDB with query size = 1% and 15 AL iterations. RoBERTa is used as a successor model, and DistilELECTRA – for acquisition in PLASM.

C.3 CoNLL-2003

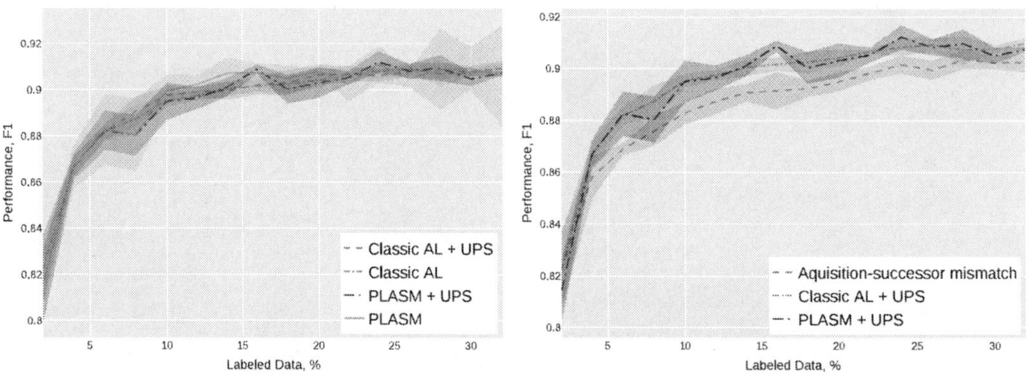

a) PLASM and UPS v Classic AL b) ASM problem

Figure 22: CoNLL dataset: performance of PLASM and UPS algorithms compared to classic AL and acquisition-successor mismatch (ASM) settings. For all the experiments, ELECTRA is used as a successor model (therefore, as an acquisition model in "classic AL" as well), and DistilBERT – for acquisition in PLASM and ASM.

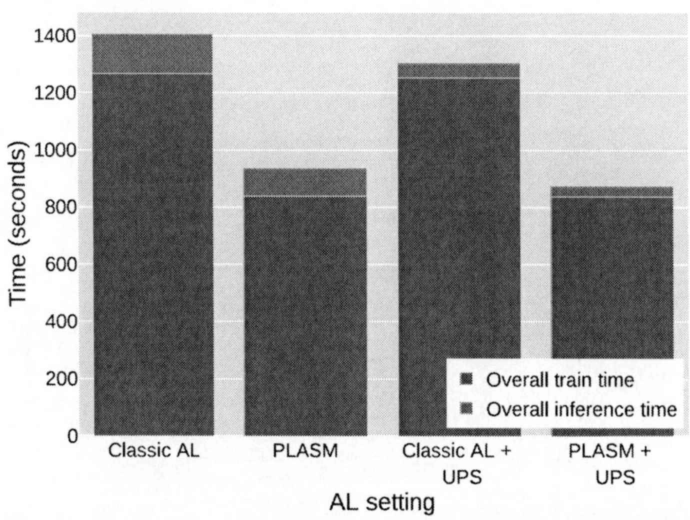

Figure 23: Duration in seconds of all the training and inference phases of the simulated AL with different acquisition settings on CoNLL-2003 with query size = 2% and 15 AL iterations. ELECTRA is used as a successor model, and DistilBERT – for acquisition in PLASM.

TextBox 2.0: A Text Generation Library with Pre-trained Language Models

Tianyi Tang[1,5]†, **Junyi Li**[1,3]†, **Zhipeng Chen**[2]†, **Yiwen Hu**[2], **Zhuohao Yu**[2], **Wenxun Dai**[4], **Wayne Xin Zhao**[1,5*], **Jian-Yun Nie**[3], and **Ji-Rong Wen**[1,2,5]

[1]Gaoling School of Artificial Intelligence, Renmin University of China
[2]School of Information, Renmin University of China
[3]DIRO, Université de Montréal [4]Xidian University
[5]Engineering Research Center of Next-Generation Intelligent Search and Recommendation, MOE
steventianyitang@outlook.com lijunyi@ruc.edu.cn batmanfly@gmail.com

Abstract

To facilitate research on text generation, this paper presents a comprehensive and unified library, **TextBox 2.0**, focusing on the use of pre-trained language models (PLMs). To be *comprehensive*, our library covers 13 common text generation tasks and their corresponding 83 datasets and further incorporates 45 PLMs covering general, translation, Chinese, dialogue, controllable, distilled, prompting, and lightweight PLMs. We also implement 4 efficient training strategies and provide 4 generation objectives for pre-training new PLMs from scratch. To be *unified*, we design the interfaces to support the entire research pipeline (from data loading to training and evaluation), ensuring that each step can be fulfilled in a unified way. Despite the rich functionality, it is easy to use our library, either through the friendly Python API or command line. To validate the effectiveness of our library, we conduct extensive experiments and exemplify four types of research scenarios. The project is released at the link: `https://github.com/RUCAIBox/TextBox#2.0`.

1 Introduction

Text generation, aiming to generate human-like texts on demand, has been a fundamental technique in many text applications, such as machine translation (Dabre et al., 2020), text summarization (El-Kassas et al., 2021), and dialogue system (Chen et al., 2017). Recently, pre-trained language models (PLMs) such as BART (Lewis et al., 2020) have been the mainstream approach to developing effective text generation models. With the great advances in text generation, it has become increasingly important to reproduce, develop, and compare various text generation models in a reliable, flexible, and unified way.

Considering the rapid progress of PLMs on text generation, in this paper, we present a significant extension of a previously released text generation library, *TextBox 1.0* (Li et al., 2021), called **TextBox 2.0**. Different from TextBox 1.0 and other text generation libraries (Miller et al., 2017; Klein et al., 2018; Zhu et al., 2018) (mostly including classical models based on recurrent neural networks or generative adversarial networks), this extension mainly focuses on building a comprehensive and unified framework for better supporting PLM-based text generation models. Although some libraries (*e.g.*, Fairseq (Ott et al., 2019) and Hugging Face (Wolf et al., 2020)) also include PLMs, they are designed for performing myriad NLP tasks (only considering a few text generation tasks). Moreover, they don't maintain a complete evaluation pipeline (*e.g.*, data loading, training, inference, and evaluation) specially designed for text generation. Thus, it is not fully suited for developing and evaluating text generation models in a unified way.

In order to better facilitate research on text generation, **TextBox 2.0** introduces a series of new features for supporting the use of PLMs, which can be summarized into three major aspects:

• *Generation Tasks*: Our library supports 13 commonly studied text generation tasks (*e.g.*, translation and story generation) and their corresponding 83 datasets, including most of the existing mainstream tasks and datasets for research. We reorganize these datasets so that they are framed in a unified text-to-text format. Users can simply set the dataset via the command line or configuration file without additional preprocessing efforts.

• *Generation Models*: As a key contribution, our library incorporates 45 PLMs, covering the categories of general, translation, Chinese, dialogue, controllable, distilled, prompting, and lightweight PLMs. We unify the interface to use existing PLMs and incorporate new PLMs, and it is convenient to run different PLMs for a specified task in our

† Equal contribution.
* Corresponding author

Proceedings of the The 2022 Conference on Empirical Methods in Natural Language Processing: System Demonstrations, pages 435 - 444
December 7-11, 2022 ©2022 Association for Computational Linguistics

Aspects	TextBox 1.0	TextBox 2.0
Tasks 6 *v.s.* 13	Summarization, translation, dialogue, unconditional generation, attribute-to-text generation, poem generation	Summarization, translation, dialogue, data-to-text, question generation, question answering, story generation, commonsense generation, Chinese generation, paraphrase, style transfer and simplification
Models 6 *v.s.* 45	**VAE**: LSTMVAE, CNNVAE, CVAE, HybridVAE **GAN**: SeqGAN, TextGAN, RankGAN, MaliGAN, LeakGAN, MaskGAN **PLM**: GPT-2, XLNet, BERT2BERT, T5, BART, ProphetNet **Seq2Seq**: RNN, Transformer, Attr2Seq, Context2Seq, HRED	**General**: GPT-2, BERT2BERT, BART, T5, ProphetNet, GPT, GPT-Neo, OPT, UniLM, MASS, PEGASUS, MVP, Bigbird, LED **Translation**: mBART, mT5, Marian, M2M 100, NLLB, XLM **Chinese**: CPM, CPT, Chinese-BART, Chinese-T5, Chinese-GPT2 **Dialogue**: Blenderbot and DialoGPT **Controllable**: CTRL and PPLM **Distilled**: DistilGPT2 and DistilBART **Prompting**: PTG and Context-Tuning **Lightweight**: Adapter, Prefix-tuning, Prompt tuning, LoRA, BitFit, P-Tuning v2
Training Strategies	Distributed data parallel	Distributed data parallel, efficient decoding, hyper-parameter optimization, repeated experiments, pre-training objectives

Table 1: Comparison of TextBox 1.0 and TextBox 2.0. We also present a comparison of the numbers of *tasks* and pre-trained *models* between the two versions.

library. We also provide a standard way to compare these models and analyze the generated results.

• *Training Strategies*: To support the optimization of PLMs, we provide four efficient and robust training strategies (*e.g.,* efficient decoding) and four pre-training objectives (*e.g.,* denoising auto-encoding) for text generation. These strategies make optimizing text generation models more efficient and reliable. Users can either pre-train a new model from scratch or fine-tune a pre-trained model for research purposes.

As another merit, TextBox 2.0 has been largely aligned with our previous survey on PLM-based text generation (Li et al., 2022b) in terms of task, model, and training. It will be meaningful for beginners to explore and learn text generation models with the survey and supporting libraries.

To summarize, TextBox 2.0 has contributed a significant addition to the previous version (see Table 1 for a detailed comparison) to better support the use of PLMs for text generation. It implements and maintains a unified way to conduct research on text generation with 45 included models, covering 13 tasks, and 83 datasets. We also perform extensive test experiments, and these results show that TextBox 2.0 can produce very competitive performance compared to the original implementations.

2 Library Design

In order to facilitate PLM-based text generation research, TextBox 2.0 has introduced various new features, mainly from three aspects: *generation tasks*, *generation models*, and *training strategies*.

2.1 Generation Tasks

Since there are various text generation applications, we include 13 widely studied tasks and collect the corresponding 83 datasets.

Tasks. These 13 tasks in TextBox 2.0 include text summarization, machine translation, open-ended dialogue system, data-to-text generation, question generation, question answering, story generation, task-oriented dialogue system, commonsense generation, paraphrase generation, text style transfer, and text simplification. Besides these English-centric tasks, we also include Chinese generation tasks. Existing PLM-based libraries such as Hugging Face (Wolf et al., 2020) are focused on performing extensive NLP tasks and only consider a few text generation tasks (mainly text summarization and machine translation), which are not comprehensive for text generation research.

Datasets. For each task, we collect widely-used datasets and reorganize them in a unified text-to-text format. In total, we include 83 datasets, and report their details on the page[1], including the dataset description, basic statistics, and training/validation/testing samples. In addition, we build a leaderboard for each dataset by collecting the automatic results and generated texts of the latest research. It is convenient for users to quickly learn about the baselines and their results. We also encourage community users to collaboratively maintain the leaderboard and submit their model results.

[1]`https://github.com/RUCAIBox/TextBox#dataset`

Metrics. To conduct evaluations with these tasks and datasets, TextBox 2.0 supports four categories of automatic metrics: (1) lexical metrics, such as BLEU (Papineni et al., 2002) and ROUGE (Lin, 2004), to measure the n-gram overlap between generated texts and golden texts; (2) semantic metrics, such as BERTScore (Zhang et al., 2020b) and style strength (Lai et al., 2021), to compare the texts at sentence level; (3) diversity metrics, such as Distinct (Li et al., 2016) and Self-BLEU (Zhu et al., 2018), to evaluate the lexical diversity of generated texts; (4) accuracy metrics, such as exact match (Rajpurkar et al., 2016) and inform (Budzianowski et al., 2018a), to calculate the precision of important phrases. In total, we include 12 general metrics and 5 task-specific metrics[2].

Besides the analysis using automatic metrics, TextBox 2.0 provides several visualization tools to explore and analyze the generated texts in various dimensions (Liu et al., 2021b; Tuckute et al., 2022). For instance, Figure 2 shows how it offers new insights to improve summarization tasks (details can be found in Section 4.3).

2.2 Generation Models

To support the rapid progress of PLMs on text generation, TextBox 2.0 incorporates 45 PLMs[3] and aims to build a unified and standardized framework based on PLMs. We list some included models as follows:

• **General PLMs**: GPT-2 (Radford et al., 2019) and BART (Lewis et al., 2020);

• **Translation PLMs**: mBART (Liu et al., 2020) and XLM (CONNEAU and Lample, 2019);

• **Chinese PLMs**: CPM (Zhang et al., 2021) and CPT (Shao et al., 2021);

• **Dialogue PLMs**: DialoGPT (Zhang et al., 2020c) and Blenderbot (Roller et al., 2021);

• **Controllable PLMs**: CTRL (Keskar et al., 2019) and PPLM (Dathathri et al., 2020);

• **Distilled PLMs**: DistilGPT2 (Sanh et al., 2019) and DistilBART (Shleifer and Rush, 2020).

• **Prompting PLMs**: PTG (Li et al., 2022a) and Context-Tuning (Tang et al., 2022);

• **Lightweight modules**: Adapter (Houlsby et al., 2019), Prefix-tuning (Li and Liang, 2021).

The wide coverage of PLMs makes it possible to deal with different text generation tasks using TextBox 2.0. For example, to perform specific tasks such as dialogue system, users can adopt task-specific PLMs such as DialoGPT; to deal with Chinese generation tasks, users can adopt CPT. In resource-constrained situations, lightweight PLMs such as prefix-tuning can be a good choice.

2.3 Training Strategies

TextBox 2.0 provides four pre-training objectives to help users pre-train a model from scratch, including language modeling (Radford et al., 2019), masked sequence-to-sequence modeling (Song et al., 2019), denoising auto-encoding (Lewis et al., 2020), and masked span prediction (Raffel et al., 2020). These pre-training tasks can also be utilized for domain-adaptive pre-training and task-adaptive pre-training (Gururangan et al., 2020) to tailor existing PLM to the domain of a target task.

Also, TextBox 2.0 provides four useful training methods for improving the optimization of PLMs. It supports distributed data parallel to implement models on multiple GPUs and machines to improve the efficiency of pre-training and fine-tuning. We incorporate *Accelerate*[4] to support distributed training with a simple API. To further accelerate the decoding efficiency, we integrate FastSeq (Yan et al., 2021) to optimize the decoding process by attention cache optimization, repeated n-gram detection, and asynchronous parallel I/O.

Moreover, TextBox 2.0 enables users to adjust and select hyper-parameters automatically. Based on the library Hyperopt (Bergstra et al., 2013), users just need to set the parameter range and search methods, and then the optimal hyper-parameters and corresponding results will return. It is useful for PLMs to search for hyper-parameters such as batch size and learning rate. Our library also supports performing repeat experiments using different random seeds in one command line, which is especially useful to alleviate randomness especially under few-shot settings.

3 Library Usage

In this section, we introduce how to use our library in four different kinds of research scenarios by showing the example codes.

Reproducing existing models. TextBox 2.0 includes various PLMs and supports many text generation tasks and datasets. It is convenient for users

[2] `https://github.com/RUCAIBox/TextBox#evaluation`

[3] `https://github.com/RUCAIBox/TextBox#model`

[4] `https://github.com/huggingface/accelerate`

```
python run_textbox.py \
    --dataset=xsum --model=pegasus \
    --model_path=google/pegasus-large
```

(a) Example for reproducing existing models

```
# hyper.test
Learning_rate choice [1e-5, 3e-5]
train_batch_size choice [64, 256]

# command line instruction
python run_hyper.py \
    --space=hyper.test \
    --dataset=xsum --model=pegasus \
    --model_path=google/pegasus-large
```

(b) Example for hyper-parameter optimization

```
class new_model(AbstractModel):
    def __init__(self):
        ...
        self.t5 = T5_MODEL
        self.gnn = GNN_MODEL
    def forward(self, input, label):
        ...
        embeds = self.gnn(input)
        output = self.t5(embeds)
        return loss_func(output, label)
    def generate(self, input):
        ...
        embeds = self.gnn(input)
        return self.t5.generate(embeds)
```

(c) Example for implementing a new model

```
python run_textbox.py \
    --dataset=wudao --model=bart \
    --pretrain_task=denoising
```

(d) Example for pre-training a Chinese BART

```
accelerate config
accelerate launch run_textbox.py \
    --dataset=wudao --model=bart \
    --pretrain_task=denoising
```

(e) Example for multi-GPU pre-training

```
python run_analysis.py \
    --dataset=cnndm \
    BART_output.txt T5_output.txt
```

(f) Example for analyzing

Figure 1: Example usage of our TextBox 2.0.

to quickly run existing PLMs and reproduce results for each dataset. In particular, users only need to specify the dataset and model by setting the configurations `dataset`, `model`, and `model_path`, within a simple command line.

Figure 1(a) presents an example to fine-tune PEGASUS (Zhang et al., 2020a) on XSum (Narayan et al., 2018) dataset. Moreover, TextBox 2.0 enables users to conduct hyper-parameter optimization by only providing a list of possible values. Figure 1(b) shows an example that automatically adjusts the hyper-parameters `learning_rate` and `batch_size` from the ranges $[1 \times 10^{-5}, 3 \times 10^{-5}]$ and $[64, 256]$, respectively.

Implementing a new model. Since TextBox 2.0 builds a unified pipeline for text generation research, users only need to define a new model class without considering other procedures to implement a new model. Specially, users should first inherit from our base model class `AbstractModel` before specifying three specific model functions: (1) `__init__()`: this function initializes the architectures and parameters of the model; (2) `forward()`: this function is used to calculate the loss for optimization during training; (3) `generate()`: this function generates texts based on input during inference.

Figure 1(c) presents an example of implementing a new model for the KG-to-text generation task . In this example, the model adopts a graph neural network (GNN) to encode KG and then uses T5 (Raffel et al., 2020) to generate texts. We first define the GNN and T5 models in the `__init__()` function. Then, we use GNN to encode KG to embeddings as the input of T5 and compute the loss according to target labels in the `forward()` function. Finally, we use a similar process to generate text in the `generate()` function.

Pre-training a new model. In TextBox 2.0, we provide several pre-training objectives for users to pre-train new models from scratch. Specifically, users just need to specify the pre-training task, pre-training corpus, and architecture by setting `pretrain_task`, `dataset`, and `model`. Figure 1(d) shows an example that pre-trains a Chinese BART on the WuDaoCorpora (Yuan et al., 2021) using the denoising pre-training objective.

To improve the pre-training efficiency, TextBox 2.0 supports distributed data parallel and efficient decoding (Section 2.3). Figure 1(e) shows an illustrative example of how users can use the `accelerate` command to set configurations of multiple devices and launch the training code.

Analyzing generated results. Besides simply obtaining the evaluation results, our library provides several visualization analysis mechanisms to perform deep analysis on the generated results of models. For example, we support the use of the statistical chart to analyze the mean and standard deviation scores for different sentence lengths. These methods can help users learn about the advantages and disadvantages of different models in a detailed comparison. Figure 1(f) shows an example of how to run the analysis using a simple command line and the results can be found in Figure 2. This example compares the generated texts of BART and T5 on the CNN/DailyMail dataset.

4 Experiments

In this section, we conduct extensive experiments to verify the generation abilities of TextBox 2.0.

4.1 Result Reproduction

As an open-source library, TextBox 2.0 should be able to reproduce the results of existing work effectively. To verify this, we select a number of

	Text Summarization			Text Simplification			Chinese Generation			Translation	
	R-1	R-2	R-L	B-4	ME	R-2	LCSTS	CSL	ADGEN	En→Ro	Ro→En
BART	44.16[a]	21.28	40.90	88.30[b]	55.60	86.10	40.60[c]	64.20	10.00	37.70[d]	37.80
BART (ours)	$44.47_{0.10}$	$21.50_{0.14}$	$41.35_{0.08}$	$90.81_{0.24}$	$57.58_{0.19}$	$83.36_{0.07}$	$42.96_{0.18}$	$64.34_{0.63}$	$10.20_{0.15}$	$37.20_{0.17}$	$37.48_{0.31}$
	Data-to-text Generation			**Commonsense Generation**			**Question Generation**			**QA**	
	B-4	ME	R-L	B-4	CIDEr	SPICE	B-4	ME	R-L	F1	EM
BART	64.55[e]	46.51	75.13	27.50[f]	14.12	30.00	22.00[g]	26.40	50.30	91.56[h]	84.23
BART (ours)	$67.33_{0.06}$	$47.78_{0.07}$	$76.83_{0.04}$	$28.18_{0.45}$	$12.98_{0.13}$	$33.00_{0.40}$	$25.08_{0.13}$	$26.73_{0.18}$	$52.55_{0.07}$	$93.04_{0.08}$	$86.44_{0.21}$
	Open-ended Dialogue System				**Task-oriented Dialogue System**				**Story Generation**		
	B-1	B-2	D-1	D-2	B-4	Success	Inform	Comb.	B-1	B-2	D-4
BART	49.90[g]	40.00	1.30	8.00	17.89[i]	74.91	84.88	97.78	30.70[j]	13.30	69.90
BART (ours)	$49.58_{1.12}$	$39.24_{0.90}$	$1.44_{0.09}$	$8.89_{0.57}$	$20.17_{0.63}$	$75.40_{1.22}$	$84.40_{1.15}$	$100.07_{0.53}$	$33.79_{0.13}$	$15.78_{0.21}$	$78.76_{2.15}$
	Paraphrase Generation					**Style Transfer (E&M)**			**Style Transfer (F&R)**		
	B-4	ME	R-1	R-2	R-L	B-4	Acc.	HM	B-4	Acc.	HM
BART	47.30[k]	49.70	73.30	54.10	75.10	76.50[l]	92.90	83.90	79.30	92.00	85.20
BART (Ours)	$48.35_{0.70}$	$50.60_{0.49}$	$74.16_{0.47}$	$55.25_{0.74}$	$75.84_{0.42}$	$76.93_{0.55}$	$94.37_{0.87}$	$84.74_{0.05}$	$80.11_{0.29}$	$92.29_{0.37}$	$85.77_{0.10}$

Table 2: The results of BART on thirteen tasks from the original papers and our TextBox 2.0. QA is short for question answering. B, R, D, ME, EM, HM, Acc., and Comb. denote BLEU, ROUGE, Distinct, METEOR, exact match, harmonic mean, accuracy, and combined score, respectively. LCSTS, CSL, ADGEN, and En↔Ro are evaluated using the R-L, R-L, B-4, and B-4 metrics, respectively. [a](Lewis et al., 2020) [b](Gehrmann et al., 2021) [c](Shao et al., 2021) [d](Liu et al., 2020) [e](Ke et al., 2021) [f](Lin et al., 2020a) [g](Liu et al., 2021a) [h](Xu et al., 2021) [i](Lin et al., 2020b) [j](Guan et al., 2021) [k](Sun et al., 2021) [l](Lai et al., 2021)

widely-used datasets for each task (introduced in Section 2.1) and compare the results conducted by TextBox 2.0 with those in the original papers. We totally evaluate 13 tasks using 14 datasets, including CNN/DailyMail (See et al., 2017), WikiAuto + Turk (Liu et al., 2021a), LCSTS (Hu et al., 2015), CSL[5], ADGEN (Shao et al., 2019), WMT 16 English-Romanian (En↔Ro) (Bojar et al., 2016), WebNLG 2.1 (Gardent et al., 2017), CommonGen (Lin et al., 2020a), SQuAD (Rajpurkar et al., 2016), PersonaChat (Zhang et al., 2018), MultiWOZ 2.0 (Budzianowski et al., 2018b), ROCStories (Mostafazadeh et al., 2016), GYAFC (E&M and F&R) (Rao and Tetreault, 2018), and Quora (Kumar et al., 2020).

Since BART is the prevalent PLM for text generation, we endeavor to reproduce existing works with $\text{BART}_{\text{LARGE}}$[6]. For all experiments, we employ the sequence-to-sequence cross-entropy loss with a label smoothing factor of 0.1 as the objective function. We optimize the model using AdamW (Loshchilov and Hutter, 2019) with a constant learning rate of 3×10^{-5}. The accumulated batch size is set to 192. During inference, we apply beam search with a beam size of 5 and no-repeat n-gram size of 3. To reduce randomness, we report the mean and standard deviation of our results based on three random seeds: 2020, 2021, and 2022. All codes are implemented in PyTorch 1.11.0 on Ubuntu SMP 20.04.1 (Linux 5.15.0-46) with one GPU (NVIDIA GeForce RTX 3090 24GB).

Library	Preparation (minutes)	Training (minutes)	Generation (minutes)
Fairseq	$2.93_{0.02}$	$410.05_{8.86}$	$79.24_{1.50}$
Hugging Face	$4.02_{0.12}$	$416.25_{4.47}$	$75.69_{2.53}$
TextBox 2.0	$3.81_{0.14}$	$393.99_{5.09}$	$27.05_{1.03}$

Table 3: Efficiency comparison of three libraries for $\text{BART}_{\text{LARGE}}$ fine-tuned on CNN/DailyMail. The preparation stage consists of configuration loading, text tokenization, and necessary initialization options. The training stage takes time for fine-tuning on the training set in one epoch. The generation stage takes time to generate on the test set with a beam size of 5.

To conduct these experiments, we only need to run the script shown in Figure 1 (a) with different `dataset` names. As shown in Table 2, our TextBox 2.0 can faithfully reproduce the results reported in existing work. Remarkably, our library achieves better performances than original works on 37 of the 44 metrics evaluated. It might be because we adopt optimization strategies such as label smoothing and large batch sizes.

[5]https://github.com/CLUEbenchmark/CLGE

[6]For translation tasks, we utilize mBART-CC25 (Liu et al., 2020). For Chinese generation tasks, we utilize Chinese $\text{BART}_{\text{LARGE}}$ (Shao et al., 2021).

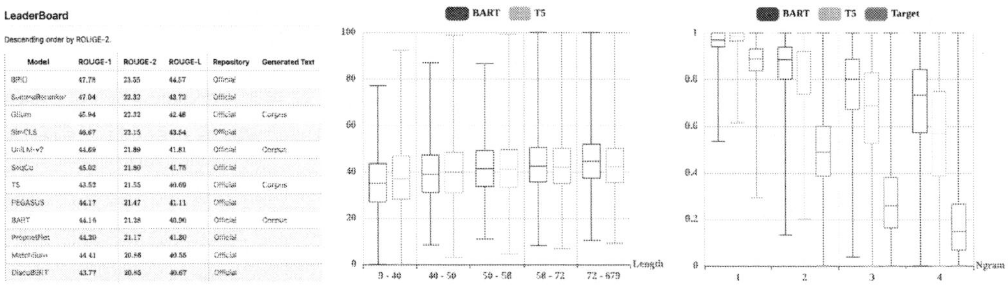

LeaderBoard

Descending order by ROUGE-2.

Model	ROUGE-1	ROUGE-2	ROUGE-L	Repository	Generated Text
BRIO	47.78	23.55	44.57	Official	
SummaReranker	47.04	22.32	43.72	Official	
GSum	45.94	22.32	42.48	Official	Corpus
SimCLS	46.67	22.15	43.54	Official	
UniLM-v2	44.69	21.89	41.81	Official	Corpus
SeqCo	45.02	21.80	41.75	Official	
T5	43.52	21.55	40.69	Official	Corpus
PEGASUS	44.17	21.47	41.11	Official	
BART	44.16	21.28	40.90	Official	Corpus
ProphetNet	44.20	21.17	41.30	Official	
MatchSum	44.41	20.86	40.55	Official	
DiscoBERT	43.77	20.85	40.67	Official	

(a) Leaderboard of CNN/DailyMail (b) ROUGE-L scores of BART and T5 for different input lengths (c) N-gram overlap of target and generated texts with input document

Figure 2: The partial visualization analysis on CNN/DailyMail dataset. The whole one can be found at `https://github.com/RUCAIBox/TextBox/blob/2.0.0/asset/example-analysis.html`.

4.2 Efficiency Comparison

In addition to accurately reproducing results, we have optimized TextBox 2.0 for computational efficiency. We streamline the training process and support efficient decoding strategies. To compare the efficiency, we choose the well-known PLM libraries Fairseq[7] and Hugging Face[8], and then test the time consumption under identical settings described in Section 4.1.

From the results in Table 3, we can see that our TextBox 2.0 is more efficient than Fairseq and Hugging Face. During training, TextBox 2.0 simplifies the training process and reduces the time spent on non-essential functions such as trainer management and loss tracking. In the generation process, our library is significantly faster than the other two libraries due to the incorporation of efficient decoding strategies introduced in Section 2.3.

4.3 Visualization Analysis

Besides reproducing a model, it is also important to compare existing methods, analyze the generated texts, and explore directions for improvement. Our library sets a specific leaderboard for each dataset, including basic metric results, author repositories, and generated texts. Figure 2 (a) showcases the leaderboard for the CNN/DailyMail dataset.

Users can also utilize TextBox 2.0 to conduct visualization analysis for specified models. For example, our library can automatically plot the boxplot of the ROUGE-L score for different input lengths and the n-gram overlap of target and generated texts with the input document. From the results in Figure 2 (b), we can find that T5 excels at short document summarization while BART excels at long document summarization. It is useful to analyze and improve the deficiencies of text generation models or obtain better performance by combining their results. As another example, Figure 2 (c) illustrates that BART and T5 have a significantly higher n-gram overlap ratio than golden sentences, indicating that they tend to "copy" the input document rather than "summarize" it. From such analysis results, users can apply the methods proposed by Goyal et al. (2022) to alleviate it.

5 Conclusion

This paper presented **TextBox 2.0**, a comprehensive and unified library for conducting research on PLM-based text generation. Our library makes significant extensions in three major aspects, namely generation tasks (13 tasks and 83 datasets), generation models (45 PLMs), and training strategies (*e.g.*, distributed data parallel and efficient decoding). Results from extensive test experiments demonstrate that our library can accurately reproduce existing models. Besides, we also provide a series of utility tools to better analyze and explore the generated results. To summarize, our library can be very useful to facilitate text generation research, and our team will improve this library with regular updates.

Acknowledgement

This work was partially supported by Beijing Natural Science Foundation under Grant No. 4222027, and Beijing Outstanding Young Scientist Program under Grant No. BJJWZYJH012019100020098. Xin Zhao is the corresponding author.

[7]We utilize the code from Fairseq 0.12.2.

[8]We utilize the code from Transformers 4.20.1.

References

James Bergstra, Daniel Yamins, and David Cox. 2013. Making a science of model search: Hyperparameter optimization in hundreds of dimensions for vision architectures. In *Proceedings of the 30th International Conference on Machine Learning*, volume 28, pages 115–123.

Ondřej Bojar, Christian Buck, Rajen Chatterjee, Christian Federmann, Liane Guillou, Barry Haddow, Matthias Huck, Antonio Jimeno Yepes, Aurélie Névéol, Mariana Neves, Pavel Pecina, Martin Popel, Philipp Koehn, Christof Monz, Matteo Negri, Matt Post, Lucia Specia, Karin Verspoor, Jörg Tiedemann, and Marco Turchi, editors. 2016. *Proceedings of the First Conference on Machine Translation: Volume 1, Research Papers*. Association for Computational Linguistics, Berlin, Germany.

Paweł Budzianowski, Tsung-Hsien Wen, Bo-Hsiang Tseng, Iñigo Casanueva, Stefan Ultes, Osman Ramadan, and Milica Gašić. 2018a. MultiWOZ - a large-scale multi-domain Wizard-of-Oz dataset for task-oriented dialogue modelling. In *Proceedings of the 2018 Conference on Empirical Methods in Natural Language Processing*, pages 5016–5026, Brussels, Belgium. Association for Computational Linguistics.

Paweł Budzianowski, Tsung-Hsien Wen, Bo-Hsiang Tseng, Iñigo Casanueva, Stefan Ultes, Osman Ramadan, and Milica Gašić. 2018b. MultiWOZ - a large-scale multi-domain Wizard-of-Oz dataset for task-oriented dialogue modelling. In *Proceedings of the 2018 Conference on Empirical Methods in Natural Language Processing*, pages 5016–5026, Brussels, Belgium. Association for Computational Linguistics.

Hongshen Chen, Xiaorui Liu, Dawei Yin, and Jiliang Tang. 2017. A survey on dialogue systems: Recent advances and new frontiers. *SIGKDD Explor. Newsl.*, 19(2).

Alexis CONNEAU and Guillaume Lample. 2019. Cross-lingual language model pretraining. In *Advances in Neural Information Processing Systems*, volume 32. Curran Associates, Inc.

Raj Dabre, Chenhui Chu, and Anoop Kunchukuttan. 2020. A survey of multilingual neural machine translation. *ACM Comput. Surv.*, 53(5).

Sumanth Dathathri, Andrea Madotto, Janice Lan, Jane Hung, Eric Frank, Piero Molino, Jason Yosinski, and Rosanne Liu. 2020. Plug and play language models: A simple approach to controlled text generation. In *International Conference on Learning Representations*.

Wafaa S. El-Kassas, Cherif R. Salama, Ahmed A. Rafea, and Hoda K. Mohamed. 2021. Automatic text summarization: A comprehensive survey. *Expert Systems with Applications*, 165:113679.

Claire Gardent, Anastasia Shimorina, Shashi Narayan, and Laura Perez-Beltrachini. 2017. Creating training corpora for NLG micro-planners. In *Proceedings of the 55th Annual Meeting of the Association for Computational Linguistics (Volume 1: Long Papers)*, pages 179–188, Vancouver, Canada. Association for Computational Linguistics.

Sebastian Gehrmann, Tosin Adewumi, Karmanya Aggarwal, Pawan Sasanka Ammanamanchi, Anuoluwapo Aremu, Antoine Bosselut, Khyathi Raghavi Chandu, Miruna-Adriana Clinciu, Dipanjan Das, Kaustubh Dhole, Wanyu Du, Esin Durmus, Ondřej Dušek, Chris Chinenye Emezue, Varun Gangal, Cristina Garbacea, Tatsunori Hashimoto, Yufang Hou, Yacine Jernite, Harsh Jhamtani, Yangfeng Ji, Shailza Jolly, Mihir Kale, Dhruv Kumar, Faisal Ladhak, Aman Madaan, Mounica Maddela, Khyati Mahajan, Saad Mahamood, Bodhisattwa Prasad Majumder, Pedro Henrique Martins, Angelina McMillan-Major, Simon Mille, Emiel van Miltenburg, Moin Nadeem, Shashi Narayan, Vitaly Nikolaev, Andre Niyongabo Rubungo, Salomey Osei, Ankur Parikh, Laura Perez-Beltrachini, Niranjan Ramesh Rao, Vikas Raunak, Juan Diego Rodriguez, Sashank Santhanam, João Sedoc, Thibault Sellam, Samira Shaikh, Anastasia Shimorina, Marco Antonio Sobrevilla Cabezudo, Hendrik Strobelt, Nishant Subramani, Wei Xu, Diyi Yang, Akhila Yerukola, and Jiawei Zhou. 2021. The GEM benchmark: Natural language generation, its evaluation and metrics. In *Proceedings of the 1st Workshop on Natural Language Generation, Evaluation, and Metrics (GEM 2021)*, pages 96–120, Online. Association for Computational Linguistics.

Tanya Goyal, Jiacheng Xu, Junyi Jessy Li, and Greg Durrett. 2022. Training dynamics for text summarization models. In *Findings of the Association for Computational Linguistics: ACL 2022*, pages 2061–2073, Dublin, Ireland. Association for Computational Linguistics.

Jian Guan, Xiaoxi Mao, Changjie Fan, Zitao Liu, Wenbiao Ding, and Minlie Huang. 2021. Long text generation by modeling sentence-level and discourse-level coherence. In *Proceedings of the 59th Annual Meeting of the Association for Computational Linguistics and the 11th International Joint Conference on Natural Language Processing (Volume 1: Long Papers)*, pages 6379–6393, Online. Association for Computational Linguistics.

Suchin Gururangan, Ana Marasović, Swabha Swayamdipta, Kyle Lo, Iz Beltagy, Doug Downey, and Noah A. Smith. 2020. Don't stop pretraining: Adapt language models to domains and tasks. In *Proceedings of the 58th Annual Meeting of the Association for Computational Linguistics*, pages 8342–8360, Online. Association for Computational Linguistics.

Neil Houlsby, Andrei Giurgiu, Stanislaw Jastrzebski, Bruna Morrone, Quentin de Laroussilhe, Andrea

Gesmundo, Mona Attariyan, and Sylvain Gelly. 2019. Parameter-efficient transfer learning for NLP. In *ICML*.

Baotian Hu, Qingcai Chen, and Fangze Zhu. 2015. LCSTS: A large scale Chinese short text summarization dataset. In *Proceedings of the 2015 Conference on Empirical Methods in Natural Language Processing*, pages 1967–1972, Lisbon, Portugal. Association for Computational Linguistics.

Pei Ke, Haozhe Ji, Yu Ran, Xin Cui, Liwei Wang, Linfeng Song, Xiaoyan Zhu, and Minlie Huang. 2021. JointGT: Graph-text joint representation learning for text generation from knowledge graphs. In *Findings of the Association for Computational Linguistics: ACL-IJCNLP 2021*, pages 2526–2538, Online. Association for Computational Linguistics.

Nitish Shirish Keskar, Bryan McCann, Lav R Varshney, Caiming Xiong, and Richard Socher. 2019. Ctrl: A conditional transformer language model for controllable generation. *arXiv preprint arXiv:1909.05858*.

Guillaume Klein, Yoon Kim, Yuntian Deng, Vincent Nguyen, Jean Senellart, and Alexander Rush. 2018. OpenNMT: Neural machine translation toolkit. In *Proceedings of the 13th Conference of the Association for Machine Translation in the Americas (Volume 1: Research Track)*, pages 177–184, Boston, MA. Association for Machine Translation in the Americas.

Ashutosh Kumar, Kabir Ahuja, Raghuram Vadapalli, and Partha Talukdar. 2020. Syntax-guided controlled generation of paraphrases. *Transactions of the Association for Computational Linguistics*, 8:329–345.

Huiyuan Lai, Antonio Toral, and Malvina Nissim. 2021. Thank you BART! rewarding pre-trained models improves formality style transfer. In *Proceedings of the 59th Annual Meeting of the Association for Computational Linguistics and the 11th International Joint Conference on Natural Language Processing (Volume 2: Short Papers)*, pages 484–494, Online. Association for Computational Linguistics.

Mike Lewis, Yinhan Liu, Naman Goyal, Marjan Ghazvininejad, Abdelrahman Mohamed, Omer Levy, Veselin Stoyanov, and Luke Zettlemoyer. 2020. BART: Denoising sequence-to-sequence pretraining for natural language generation, translation, and comprehension. In *Proceedings of the 58th Annual Meeting of the Association for Computational Linguistics*, pages 7871–7880, Online. Association for Computational Linguistics.

Jiwei Li, Michel Galley, Chris Brockett, Jianfeng Gao, and Bill Dolan. 2016. A diversity-promoting objective function for neural conversation models. In *Proceedings of the 2016 Conference of the North American Chapter of the Association for Computational Linguistics: Human Language Technologies*, pages 110–119, San Diego, California. Association for Computational Linguistics.

Junyi Li, Tianyi Tang, Gaole He, Jinhao Jiang, Xiaoxuan Hu, Puzhao Xie, Zhipeng Chen, Zhuohao Yu, Wayne Xin Zhao, and Ji-Rong Wen. 2021. TextBox: A unified, modularized, and extensible framework for text generation. In *Proceedings of the 59th Annual Meeting of the Association for Computational Linguistics and the 11th International Joint Conference on Natural Language Processing: System Demonstrations*, pages 30–39, Online. Association for Computational Linguistics.

Junyi Li, Tianyi Tang, Jian-Yun Nie, Ji-Rong Wen, and Xin Zhao. 2022a. Learning to transfer prompts for text generation. In *Proceedings of the 2022 Conference of the North American Chapter of the Association for Computational Linguistics: Human Language Technologies*, pages 3506–3518, Seattle, United States. Association for Computational Linguistics.

Junyi Li, Tianyi Tang, Wayne Xin Zhao, Jian-Yun Nie, and Ji-Rong Wen. 2022b. A survey of pretrained language models based text generation. *arXiv preprint arXiv:2201.05273*.

Xiang Lisa Li and Percy Liang. 2021. Prefix-tuning: Optimizing continuous prompts for generation. In *Proceedings of the 59th Annual Meeting of the Association for Computational Linguistics and the 11th International Joint Conference on Natural Language Processing (Volume 1: Long Papers)*, pages 4582–4597, Online. Association for Computational Linguistics.

Bill Yuchen Lin, Wangchunshu Zhou, Ming Shen, Pei Zhou, Chandra Bhagavatula, Yejin Choi, and Xiang Ren. 2020a. CommonGen: A constrained text generation challenge for generative commonsense reasoning. In *Findings of the Association for Computational Linguistics: EMNLP 2020*, pages 1823–1840, Online. Association for Computational Linguistics.

Chin-Yew Lin. 2004. ROUGE: A package for automatic evaluation of summaries. In *Text Summarization Branches Out*, pages 74–81, Barcelona, Spain. Association for Computational Linguistics.

Zhaojiang Lin, Andrea Madotto, Genta Indra Winata, and Pascale Fung. 2020b. MinTL: Minimalist transfer learning for task-oriented dialogue systems. In *Proceedings of the 2020 Conference on Empirical Methods in Natural Language Processing (EMNLP)*, pages 3391–3405, Online. Association for Computational Linguistics.

Dayiheng Liu, Yu Yan, Yeyun Gong, Weizhen Qi, Hang Zhang, Jian Jiao, Weizhu Chen, Jie Fu, Linjun Shou, Ming Gong, Pengcheng Wang, Jiusheng Chen, Daxin Jiang, Jiancheng Lv, Ruofei Zhang, Winnie Wu, Ming Zhou, and Nan Duan. 2021a. GLGE: A new general language generation evaluation benchmark. In *Findings of the Association for Computational Linguistics: ACL-IJCNLP 2021*, pages 408–420, Online. Association for Computational Linguistics.

Pengfei Liu, Jinlan Fu, Yang Xiao, Weizhe Yuan, Shuaichen Chang, Junqi Dai, Yixin Liu, Zihuiwen Ye, and Graham Neubig. 2021b. ExplainaBoard: An explainable leaderboard for NLP. In *Proceedings of the 59th Annual Meeting of the Association for Computational Linguistics and the 11th International Joint Conference on Natural Language Processing: System Demonstrations*, pages 280–289, Online. Association for Computational Linguistics.

Yinhan Liu, Jiatao Gu, Naman Goyal, Xian Li, Sergey Edunov, Marjan Ghazvininejad, Mike Lewis, and Luke Zettlemoyer. 2020. Multilingual denoising pre-training for neural machine translation. *Transactions of the Association for Computational Linguistics*, 8:726–742.

Ilya Loshchilov and Frank Hutter. 2019. Decoupled weight decay regularization. In *International Conference on Learning Representations*.

Alexander Miller, Will Feng, Dhruv Batra, Antoine Bordes, Adam Fisch, Jiasen Lu, Devi Parikh, and Jason Weston. 2017. ParlAI: A dialog research software platform. In *Proceedings of the 2017 Conference on Empirical Methods in Natural Language Processing: System Demonstrations*, pages 79–84, Copenhagen, Denmark. Association for Computational Linguistics.

Nasrin Mostafazadeh, Nathanael Chambers, Xiaodong He, Devi Parikh, Dhruv Batra, Lucy Vanderwende, Pushmeet Kohli, and James Allen. 2016. A corpus and cloze evaluation for deeper understanding of commonsense stories. In *Proceedings of the 2016 Conference of the North American Chapter of the Association for Computational Linguistics: Human Language Technologies*, pages 839–849, San Diego, California. Association for Computational Linguistics.

Shashi Narayan, Shay B. Cohen, and Mirella Lapata. 2018. Don't give me the details, just the summary! topic-aware convolutional neural networks for extreme summarization. In *Proceedings of the 2018 Conference on Empirical Methods in Natural Language Processing*, pages 1797–1807, Brussels, Belgium. Association for Computational Linguistics.

Myle Ott, Sergey Edunov, Alexei Baevski, Angela Fan, Sam Gross, Nathan Ng, David Grangier, and Michael Auli. 2019. fairseq: A fast, extensible toolkit for sequence modeling. In *Proceedings of the 2019 Conference of the North American Chapter of the Association for Computational Linguistics (Demonstrations)*, pages 48–53, Minneapolis, Minnesota. Association for Computational Linguistics.

Kishore Papineni, Salim Roukos, Todd Ward, and Wei-Jing Zhu. 2002. Bleu: a method for automatic evaluation of machine translation. In *Proceedings of the 40th Annual Meeting of the Association for Computational Linguistics*, pages 311–318, Philadelphia, Pennsylvania, USA. Association for Computational Linguistics.

Alec Radford, Jeffrey Wu, Rewon Child, David Luan, Dario Amodei, Ilya Sutskever, et al. 2019. Language models are unsupervised multitask learners. *OpenAI blog*, 1(8):9.

Colin Raffel, Noam Shazeer, Adam Roberts, Katherine Lee, Sharan Narang, Michael Matena, Yanqi Zhou, Wei Li, and Peter J. Liu. 2020. Exploring the limits of transfer learning with a unified text-to-text transformer. *Journal of Machine Learning Research*, 21(140):1–67.

Pranav Rajpurkar, Jian Zhang, Konstantin Lopyrev, and Percy Liang. 2016. SQuAD: 100,000+ questions for machine comprehension of text. In *Proceedings of the 2016 Conference on Empirical Methods in Natural Language Processing*, pages 2383–2392, Austin, Texas. Association for Computational Linguistics.

Sudha Rao and Joel Tetreault. 2018. Dear sir or madam, may I introduce the GYAFC dataset: Corpus, benchmarks and metrics for formality style transfer. In *Proceedings of the 2018 Conference of the North American Chapter of the Association for Computational Linguistics: Human Language Technologies, Volume 1 (Long Papers)*, pages 129–140, New Orleans, Louisiana. Association for Computational Linguistics.

Stephen Roller, Emily Dinan, Naman Goyal, Da Ju, Mary Williamson, Yinhan Liu, Jing Xu, Myle Ott, Eric Michael Smith, Y-Lan Boureau, and Jason Weston. 2021. Recipes for building an open-domain chatbot. In *Proceedings of the 16th Conference of the European Chapter of the Association for Computational Linguistics: Main Volume*, pages 300–325, Online. Association for Computational Linguistics.

Victor Sanh, Lysandre Debut, Julien Chaumond, and Thomas Wolf. 2019. Distilbert, a distilled version of bert: smaller, faster, cheaper and lighter. *arXiv preprint arXiv:1910.01108*.

Abigail See, Peter J. Liu, and Christopher D. Manning. 2017. Get to the point: Summarization with pointer-generator networks. In *Proceedings of the 55th Annual Meeting of the Association for Computational Linguistics (Volume 1: Long Papers)*, pages 1073–1083, Vancouver, Canada. Association for Computational Linguistics.

Yunfan Shao, Zhichao Geng, Yitao Liu, Junqi Dai, Fei Yang, Li Zhe, Hujun Bao, and Xipeng Qiu. 2021. Cpt: A pre-trained unbalanced transformer for both chinese language understanding and generation. *arXiv preprint arXiv:2109.05729*.

Zhihong Shao, Minlie Huang, Jiangtao Wen, Wenfei Xu, and Xiaoyan Zhu. 2019. Long and diverse text generation with planning-based hierarchical variational model. In *Proceedings of the 2019 Conference on Empirical Methods in Natural Language Processing and the 9th International Joint Conference on Natural Language Processing (EMNLP-IJCNLP)*, pages 3257–3268, Hong Kong, China. Association for Computational Linguistics.

Sam Shleifer and Alexander M Rush. 2020. Pre-trained summarization distillation. *arXiv preprint arXiv:2010.13002*.

Kaitao Song, Xu Tan, Tao Qin, Jianfeng Lu, and Tie-Yan Liu. 2019. MASS: masked sequence to sequence pre-training for language generation. In *Proceedings of the 36th International Conference on Machine Learning, ICML 2019, 9-15 June 2019, Long Beach, California, USA*, volume 97 of *Proceedings of Machine Learning Research*, pages 5926–5936. PMLR.

Jiao Sun, Xuezhe Ma, and Nanyun Peng. 2021. AESOP: Paraphrase generation with adaptive syntactic control. In *Proceedings of the 2021 Conference on Empirical Methods in Natural Language Processing*, pages 5176–5189, Online and Punta Cana, Dominican Republic. Association for Computational Linguistics.

Tianyi Tang, Junyi Li, Wayne Xin Zhao, and Ji-Rong Wen. 2022. Context-tuning: Learning contextualized prompts for natural language generation. In *Proceedings of the 29th International Conference on Computational Linguistics*, pages 6340–6354, Gyeongju, Republic of Korea. International Committee on Computational Linguistics.

Greta Tuckute, Aalok Sathe, Mingye Wang, Harley Yoder, Cory Shain, and Evelina Fedorenko. 2022. SentSpace: Large-scale benchmarking and evaluation of text using cognitively motivated lexical, syntactic, and semantic features. In *Proceedings of the 2022 Conference of the North American Chapter of the Association for Computational Linguistics: Human Language Technologies: System Demonstrations*, pages 99–113, Hybrid: Seattle, Washington + Online. Association for Computational Linguistics.

Thomas Wolf, Lysandre Debut, Victor Sanh, Julien Chaumond, Clement Delangue, Anthony Moi, Pierric Cistac, Tim Rault, Remi Louf, Morgan Funtowicz, Joe Davison, Sam Shleifer, Patrick von Platen, Clara Ma, Yacine Jernite, Julien Plu, Canwen Xu, Teven Le Scao, Sylvain Gugger, Mariama Drame, Quentin Lhoest, and Alexander Rush. 2020. Transformers: State-of-the-art natural language processing. In *Proceedings of the 2020 Conference on Empirical Methods in Natural Language Processing: System Demonstrations*, pages 38–45, Online. Association for Computational Linguistics.

Peng Xu, Davis Liang, Zhiheng Huang, and Bing Xiang. 2021. Attention-guided generative models for extractive question answering. *arXiv preprint arXiv:2110.06393*.

Yu Yan, Fei Hu, Jiusheng Chen, Nikhil Bhendawade, Ting Ye, Yeyun Gong, Nan Duan, Desheng Cui, Bingyu Chi, and Ruofei Zhang. 2021. FastSeq: Make sequence generation faster. In *Proceedings of the 59th Annual Meeting of the Association for Computational Linguistics and the 11th International Joint Conference on Natural Language Processing: System Demonstrations*, pages 218–226, Online. Association for Computational Linguistics.

Sha Yuan, Hanyu Zhao, Zhengxiao Du, Ming Ding, Xiao Liu, Yukuo Cen, Xu Zou, Zhilin Yang, and Jie Tang. 2021. Wudaocorpora: A super large-scale chinese corpora for pre-training language models. *AI Open*, 2:65–68.

Jingqing Zhang, Yao Zhao, Mohammad Saleh, and Peter Liu. 2020a. PEGASUS: Pre-training with extracted gap-sentences for abstractive summarization. In *Proceedings of the 37th International Conference on Machine Learning*, pages 11328–11339.

Saizheng Zhang, Emily Dinan, Jack Urbanek, Arthur Szlam, Douwe Kiela, and Jason Weston. 2018. Personalizing dialogue agents: I have a dog, do you have pets too? In *Proceedings of the 56th Annual Meeting of the Association for Computational Linguistics (Volume 1: Long Papers)*, pages 2204–2213, Melbourne, Australia. Association for Computational Linguistics.

Tianyi Zhang, Varsha Kishore, Felix Wu, Kilian Q. Weinberger, and Yoav Artzi. 2020b. Bertscore: Evaluating text generation with bert. In *International Conference on Learning Representations*.

Yizhe Zhang, Siqi Sun, Michel Galley, Yen-Chun Chen, Chris Brockett, Xiang Gao, Jianfeng Gao, Jingjing Liu, and Bill Dolan. 2020c. DIALOGPT : Large-scale generative pre-training for conversational response generation. In *Proceedings of the 58th Annual Meeting of the Association for Computational Linguistics: System Demonstrations*, pages 270–278, Online. Association for Computational Linguistics.

Zhengyan Zhang, Xu Han, Hao Zhou, Pei Ke, Yuxian Gu, Deming Ye, Yujia Qin, Yusheng Su, Haozhe Ji, Jian Guan, et al. 2021. Cpm: A large-scale generative chinese pre-trained language model. *AI Open*, 2:93–99.

Yaoming Zhu, Sidi Lu, Lei Zheng, Jiaxian Guo, Weinan Zhang, Jun Wang, and Yong Yu. 2018. Texygen: A benchmarking platform for text generation models. In *The 41st International ACM SIGIR Conference on Research & Development in Information Retrieval, SIGIR 2018, Ann Arbor, MI, USA, July 08-12, 2018*, pages 1097–1100. ACM.

Author Index

Association for Computational Linguistics
209 N. Eighth Street
Stroudsburg, Pennsylvania 18360

ISBN 978-1-7138-9093-5

CURRAN ASSOCIATES INC.
proceedings.com